Commercial and Consumer Transactions
Cases, Text and Materials

Third Edition
by Jacob S. Ziegel, Benjamin Geva and R.C.C. Cuming

Volume III
Secured Transactions in Personal Property, Suretyships and Insolvency

by

Jacob S. Ziegel
Professor of Law Emeritus
Faculty of Law
University of Toronto

and

R.C.C. Cuming
Professor of Law
College of Law
University of Saskatchewan

1995
EMOND MONTGOMERY PUBLICATIONS LIMITED
TORONTO, CANADA

Printed in Canada

Produced by WordsWorth Communications of Toronto, Canada.

Canadian Cataloguing in Publication Data

Ziegel, Jacob S.
    Commercial and consumer transactions

3rd ed.
Contents: v. I. Sales transactions. — v. II. Negotiable instruments and banking. — v. III. Secured transactions in personal property, suretyships and insolvency.
ISBN 0-920722-71-7 (set)   ISBN 0-920722-68-7 (v. I)
ISBN 0-920722-69-5 (v. II)   ISBN 0-920722-70-9 (v. III)

I. Commercial law – Canada – Cases. I. Geva, Benjamin, 1946-   .
II. Cuming, Ronald C.C. III. Title.

KE919.Z54 1995   346.71'07   C95-931760-0
KF888.Z54 1995

To our students,
past and present

Preface to the Casebook

As readers will have noticed, our Casebook on Commercial and Consumer Transactions has been divided into three volumes: volume I on sales transactions; volume II on negotiable instruments and banking; and volume III on secured transactions, suretyships and insolvency law.

There were two reasons for this change. The first was that Professor Geva needed more space for his part on negotiable instruments and banking, and that it had been decided to add several new chapters to volume III dealing with the principles of suretyships and insolvency law. The resulting expansion in size would have made a single volume unwieldy, especially since students studying commercial and consumer transactions would require only a small part of the materials at any one time.

The second and more important reason was that law schools have different courses on commercial and consumer law. Some only have a basic survey course, but most have broken down the area into one or more courses on sales, negotiable instruments and banking, and secured transactions and insolvency law. Given this pattern, it made sense to divide the casebook into several volumes to reflect this diversity so that students would not be required to buy more than they needed. At the same time, our publisher has assured us that the prices will be kept as reasonable as possible so as to encourage students to acquire all three volumes.

We have been very gratified by the friendly reception accorded the earlier editions of our casebook and hope that the new edition and its new format will continue to serve the needs of students and teachers.

Consumer law has not fared well over the past decade and the prospects for the foreseeable future are not much better. Given these circumstances, the sceptic may wonder why the title of the casebook gives equal weight to consumer law and commercial law and why so much space is given in the sales volume to consumer issues. Our reply is that consumer law has lost neither its relevance nor its importance and that the demotion of the subject from governmental agendas is dictated more by preoccupation with higher priorities than by any permanent ideological shifts.

As before, we have accumulated many debts—to Paul Emond, our publisher, who has strongly encouraged and supported this enterprise with tact, wisdom and infinite patience; to Paula Pike and her able staff at WordsWorth Communications, who have worked diligently and with good cheer in the face of many pressures; and to our various student assistants whose contributions are acknowledged separately in the preface to each volume. Finally, we are grateful to the deans of our respective law schools for finding the funds necessary to cover our modest expenses in the face of growing financial constraints, and to the law librarians at our schools who, as before, have been most helpful in helping us to locate materials.

June 1995   J.S.Z.
                                                       B.G.
                                                       R.C.C.C.

Preface to Volume III

This volume of the *Commercial and Consumer Transactions* casebook differs in important respects from what used to be Part III of earlier editions of the casebook. The most important changes are these.

A new Part II has been added on general principles of Canadian insolvency law comprising seven chapters (chapters 12 to 19). The part was added at the suggestion of University of Toronto law students who felt that a course on secured transactions was very incomplete without some understanding of how secured creditors' rights are treated when the debtor becomes bankrupt or reorganization proceedings are initiated on the debtor's insolvency. This in turn requires an exposure to the other principal elements of Canadian insolvency law since the position of secured creditors cannot be viewed in isolation.

Apart from Part II, new chapters have been added on liens arising by statute or operation of law and priority conflicts with consensually created security interests (chapter 8), and on contracts of suretyship (chapter 11). We added chapter 8 because of its intrinsic importance and the extraordinarily complex and Byzantine state of the case law, both where the debtor has been made bankrupt and where he remains solvent. Chapter 11 owes its addition to the simple fact that contracts of suretyships are merely another form of security and are as common as, if not more common than, property-based security interests.

Apart from these major changes, all the other chapters have been revised in the light of new case law developments and the fact that personal property security legislation is now in force in all the four Western provinces and in Ontario, New Brunswick, and the Yukon Territory. We have been told that Nova Scotia may also adopt such an Act before the end of 1995. Quebec incorporated substantial elements of an Article 9 regime as part of the new Civil Code that came into effect at the beginning of 1994. However, we have not attempted to include any Quebec materials in this volume.

The overall result of these changes and revisions is that volume III is about twice as long as Part III of the previous edition of the casebook. This does not of course mean that instructors should expect to be able, or would wish, to cover so much ground even in a four-hour one-semester course. Each instructor will wish to make his or her own selections in the light of the instructor's needs and related course offerings in the law school. Our own view is that volume III contains enough material for two three-hour-a-week courses or one four-hour course on secured transactions and suretyships and a two-hour course on insolvency law.

Readers are entitled to know who did what between us. Chapter 1 is a product of our joint efforts. Prof. Cuming assumed exclusive responsibility for chapters 2, 4, 10, and 11. Prof. Ziegel was responsible for all the other chapters.

We have accumulated many debts in the course of trying to produce this volume with almost obscene haste: to Paul Emond, our publisher, for his unflagging support; to Paula Pike of WordsWorth Communications and her two magnificent assistants, Cindy Gold and Jim Lyons, for racing against almost impossible odds to produce a respectable text in time for the fall 1994 school term; and to Desmond Harty of Emond Montgomery for looking after the copyright permissions and other essential matters. Another critically important linchpin was Michelle Cooke, a third year University of Toronto law student, who served as Prof. Ziegel's research assistant in the summer of 1995. She discharged her many responsibilities with admirable speed, tact, and conscientiousness and, no less important, with consistent good humour and a winning smile.

Having said all this, we are also bound to add that we alone are responsible for the errors of commission and omission that will no doubt be found in abundance. We should be glad to have them brought to our attention.

August 15, 1995   J.S.Z.
                                                                         R.C.C.C.

Acknowledgments

A book of this nature borrows heavily from other published material. We have attempted to request permission from, and to acknowledge in the text, all sources of such material. We wish to make specific references here to the authors, publishers, journals, and institutions that have generously given permission to reproduce in this text works already in print. If we have inadvertently overlooked an acknowledgment or failed to secure a permission, we offer our sincere apologies and undertake to rectify the omission in the next edition.

Butterworths Canada Ltd. John Varley, "Receivership: The Contest Between Secured and General Creditors" from Springman and Gertner (eds.) Debtor-Creditor Law: Practice and Doctrine (1985).

Carswells. Diane Saxe, "Lender's Liability for Provincial Environmental Protection Requirements—Recent Developments" (1992), 14 *Canadian Bankruptcy Report* (3d) 197.

Canadian Business Law Journal. J.S. Ziegel, "Perfection by Registration, Instruments, Securities, Documents of Title, and the Personal Property Security Act 1989" (1989), 15 *CBLJ* 242.

Harvard Law Review. P.F. Coogan, "The New UCC Article 9" (1972-73), 86 *Harv. L Rev.* 477.

Harvard University Press. Thomas H. Jackson, *The Logic and Limits on Bankruptcy Law* (1986).

Law Society of Upper Canada. J.S. Ziegel, "Recent and Prospective Developments in the Personal Property Security Area and the Recommendations of the Ontario Advisory Committee," Special Lectures of the Law Society of Upper Canada, 1985.

Little, Brown and Company. Grant Gilmore, *Security Interests in Personal Property*, volume II.

R.G. Marantz. Memorandum by R.G. Marantz on the Future of the CCAA, February 15, 1994.

Missouri Law Review. G.L. Blackburn, "Mortgages to Secure Future Advances" (1956), 21 *Mo. L Rev.* 209.

Revenue Canada and B.J. Skulski. "The Deemed Trust and Enhanced Garnishment Provisions of the *Excise Tax Act* and Their Application in Relation to the *Bankruptcy and Insolvency Act.*" Unpublished paper prepared in 1993 by Mr. Skulski for use by the Preferences and Priorities Working Group of BIAC.

Yale Law Journal. Jackson and Kronman, "Secured Financing and Priorities Among Creditors" (1979), 88 *Yale LJ* 1143.

Yale Law School. Schwartz, "Security Interests and Bankruptcy Priorities: A Review of Current Theories" (1981), 10 *Journal of Legal Studies* 1.

Ziegel and Garton. Statistical Profile of Creditors in Bankruptcy, April 1989.

We also express our warm appreciation to the following agencies and companies for permission to reproduce copies of forms and documents in the casebook:

American Express Canada Inc.
Canadian Imperial Bank of Commerce
Ford Motor Company of Canada Ltd.
John Deere Ltd.
Ontario Department of Transportation and Highways
Ontario Motor Vehicle Arbitration Plan
Toronto-Dominion Bank

Short Table of Contents

Part I
Secured Transactions in Personal Property and Suretyships

Part II
Principles of Canadian Insolvency Law

Table of Contents

Part I
Secured Transactions in Personal Property and Suretyships

Chapter Three   Validity and Enforceability, Attachment and Perfection of the Security Interest 71

Chapter Six   The Purchase-Money Security Interest Priority ... 223

Chapter Seven   Fixtures, Accessions, Commingled Goods and Subordination Agreements 259

Part II
Principles of Canadian Insolvency Law

Chapter Twelve   Historical Introduction, Statistics and Modern Objectives

Chapter Thirteen   Initiation of Bankruptcy Proceedings

Chapter Nineteen   II Reorganization Under Part III, Division 1 of the BIA   821

Appendix   Forms of Agreement in Secured Transactions   853

Table of Cases

(Page numbers in bold face type indicate that the text of the case or a significant extract therefrom is reproduced in this volume.)

Table of Abbreviations

A. REFERENCE TEXTS AND FREQUENTLY CITED TREATISES, REPORTS AND OTHER MATERIALS

B.C. PPS REPORT

Law Reform Commission of British Columbia, Report on Debtor-Creditor Relationships (Project No. 2) Part V—Personal Property Security, LRC 23 (1975)

BAIRD AND JACKSON

D.G. Baird and T.H. Jackson, Cases, Problems and Materials on Bankruptcy, 2nd ed. (1990) (1994 Supplement)

CATZMAN

F.M. Catzman et al., Personal Property Security Law in Ontario (1976)

COLTER REPORT

See Report of the Advisory Committee on Bankruptcy and Insolvency

CUMING AND WOOD

R.C.C. Cuming and R.J. Wood, Alberta Personal Property Security Handbook, 2nd ed. (1993)

CUMING AND WOOD

R.C.C. Cuming and R.J. Wood, British Columbia Personal Property Security Handbook, 2nd ed. (1993)

CUMING AND WOOD

R.C.C. Cuming and R.J. Wood, Saskatchewan and Manitoba Personal Property Security Acts Handbook (1994)

FLETCHER

Ian F. Fletcher, The Law of Insolvency, Sweet & Maxwell (1990)

GILMORE

G. Gilmore, Security Interests in Personal Property (1965, 2 vols.)

GOODE

R.M. Goode, Commercial Law (1982)

GOODE	R.M. Goode, Legal Problems of Credit and Security, 2nd ed. (1988)
GOODE AND ZIEGEL	R.M. Goode and J.S. Ziegel, Hire-Purchase Law and Conditional Sale: A Comparative Study (1965)
HOULDEN AND MORAWETZ	Houlden and Morawetz, The Annotated Bankruptcy and Insolvency Act 1995 (1995)
JACKSON	T.H. Jackson, The Logic and Limits of Bankruptcy Law (1986)
McLAREN	R.M. McLaren, Secured Transactions in Personal Property in Canada, 2nd ed. (1992) (Looseleaf, 4 vols.)
REPORT OF (FEDERAL) ADVISORY COMMITTEE	Report of the (Federal) Advisory Committee on Bankruptcy and Insolvency ("Colter Report") (Ottawa, 1986)
REPORT OF ONTARIO ADVISORY COMMITTEE	Ontario, Ministry of Consumer and Commercial Relations, Report of the Advisory Committee on the Personal Property Security Act (1985)
SUPPLEMENTARY REPORT	Ontario, Ministry of Consumer and Commercial Relations, Supplementary Report of the Advisory Committee the Personal Property Security Act (1986)
TASSÉ REPORT	Canada, Study Committee on Bankruptcy and Insolvency Legislation, Report of the Study Committee on Bankruptcy and Insolvency Legislation (Ottawa, 1970)
WHITE AND SUMMERS	J.J. White and R.S. Summers, Handbook of the Law under the Uniform Commercial Code, 3rd ed. (1988)
ZIEGEL	J.S. Ziegel (ed.), Current Developments in International and Comparative Corporate Insolvency Law, Clarendon Press, Oxford (1994)
ZIEGEL AND DENNOMÉ	J.S. Ziegel and David L. Denomme, The Ontario Personal Property Security Act: Commentary and Analysis (1994)

B. FREQUENTLY CITED STATUTES

APA   Assignment and Preferences Act, RSO 1990, c. A.33

APPSA   Alberta, Personal Property Security Act, SA 1988,
                            c. P-4.05, as am.

Article 9   Article 9 of Uniform Commercial Code[1]

BANK ACT   Bank Act, SC 1991, c. 46

BCPPSA   British Columbia, Personal Property Security Act, SBC
                            1989, C.36, as am., and Regs.

BIA   Bankruptcy and Insolvency Act, RSC 1985, c. B-3, as
                            am. 1992, c. 27

CCAA   Companies' Creditors Arrangement Act, RSC 1985,
                            c. C.36

CCQ   Civil Code of Québec, SQ 1991, c. 64, as am.
                            (proclaimed January 1, 1994)

CPA   Consumer Protection Act, RSO 1990, c. C.31

FCA   Fraudulent Conveyances Act, RSO 1990, c. F.29

LTA   Ontario, Landlord and Tenant Act, RSO 1990, c. L.7

MPPSA   Manitoba, Personal Property Security Act, RSM 1987,
                            c. P.35, as am. 1992, to be replaced by Personal
                            Property Security and Consequential Amendments Act,
                            SM 1993, c. 14 (not yet proclaimed)

NBPPSA   New Brunswick Personal Property Security Act, SNB
                            1993, P..7.1, as am.

OPPSA   Ontario, Personal Property Security Act, RSO 1990,
                            c. P.10, as am.

RSLA   Repair and Storage Liens Act, RSO 1990, c. R.25,
                            as am.

---

[1] References are to the 1991 Official Text unless otherwise indicated.

SGA   Sale of Goods Act, RSO 1990, c. S.1, as am.

SPPSA   Saskatchewan Personal Property Security Act, SS
                                 1979-80, c. P-6.1, replaced by Personal Property
                                 Security Act 1993, SS 1993, c. P-6.2

UCC   Uniform Commercial Code[2]

UPPSA   Uniform Personal Property Security Act 1982[3]

---

[2] References are to the 1991 Official Text unless otherwise indicated.

[3] The Uniform Act was drafted by a joint committee of the Canadian Bar Association and the Uniform Law
   Conference of Canada and was adopted by these bodies in 1982.

Selected Bibliography on Insolvency Law

A. TEXTBOOKS AND MONOGRAPHS: CANADA

T.G. Anderson, *Proprietary and Quasi-proprietary Rights Arising upon Insolvency*, University of Toronto (1981).

D.G. Baird and T.H. Jackson, *Cases, Problems and Materials on Bankruptcy*, 2nd ed. (1990).

F. Bennett, *Receiverships*, 2nd ed., Carswell (1995).

F. Bennett, *Bennett on Bankruptcy*, 3rd ed., CCH Canada (1993).

Canadian Bar Association—Ontario (CBAO), *Business Law: Commercial Insolvency* (1983).

_____ , *Impact of Insolvency on Business Relationships* (1987).

_____ , *Is Bankruptcy Merely "Back to Business"?* (1983).

_____ , *Mega International Insolvencies: Are They "Bailouts", Rescues, or Merely Financial Footwork?* (1983).

_____ , *Priorities: Who Gets What After the Fall?* (1984).

_____ , *Staying Alive: Proposals and Reorganizations*, (1984).

Duncan and Honsberger, *Bankruptcy in Canada*, 3rd ed., Canadian Legal Authors Ltd. (1961).

Faculty of Law, McGill University, *Meredith Memorial Lectures, Bankruptcy: Present Problems and Future Perspectives*, McGill University (1986).

J.D. Honsberger, *Debt Restructuring: Principles and Practice* (looseleaf), Canada Law Book (1990)

Houlden and Morawetz, *Bankruptcy and Insolvency Law of Canada*, 3rd ed., Carswell (1992).

Houlden and Morawetz, *The Annotated Bankruptcy and Insolvency Act 1994* (1994).

J.S. Ziegel (ed.), *Current Developments in International and Comparative Corporate Insolvency Law*, Clarendon Press, Oxford (1994).

B.   TEXTBOOKS AND MONOGRAPHS: ENGLAND AND AUSTRALIA

M. Crystal & Brinsley Nicholson, *A Handbook on Bankruptcy and Deeds of Arrangement Law and Practice*, London (1978).

Ian F. Fletcher, *The Law of Insolvency*, Sweet & Maxwell (1990).

R.M. Goode, *Proprietary Rights and Insolvency in Sales Transactions*, Sweet & Maxwell, 2nd ed. (1989).

W.W. Kerr, *Kerr on the Law and Practice as to the Receivers*, 17th ed., Sweet & Maxwell (1989).

G. Lightman, *The Law of Receivers of Companies*, Sweet & Maxwell (1986).

D. Milman, *Corporate Insolvency: Law and Practice*, Sweet & Maxwell (1987).

J. O'Donovan, *Company Receivers and Managers*, The Law Book Company Limited (1981).

H.A.P. Picarda, *The Law Relating to Receivers and Managers*, Butterworths, 2nd ed. (1993).

P. Totty, *Corporate Insolvency*, McGraw-Hill (1982).

C. TEXTBOOKS AND MONOGRAPHS: U.S.

American Enterprise Institute for Public Policy Reform, *Bankruptcy Reform* (1978).

P. Blumberg, *The Law of Corporate Groups: Problems in Bankruptcy Reorganization of Parent and Subsidiary Corporations*, Little Brown (1985).

W.M. Collier, *Collier Bankruptcy Manual*, Matthew Bender (looseleaf) (1979).

D.R. Cowans, *Bankruptcy Law and Practice*, West Publishing (1989).

T.H. Jackson, *The Logic and Limits of Bankruptcy Law*, Harvard University Press (1986).

L. Kruger and Quittner, *Bankruptcy Practice and Procedure*, Practising Law Institute (1985).

L. Kruger and Quittner, *Current Developments in Bankruptcy and Reorganization, 1986*, Practicing Law Institute (1986).

M.S. Lurey, *Lending Transactions and the Bankruptcy Code, 1987*, Practicing Law Institute (1987).

A.L. Paskay, *Handbook for Trustees and Receivers in Bankruptcy*, Bender (1978).

E. Warren, J. Westbrook and T.A. Sullivan, *As We Forgive our Debtors: Bankruptcy and Consumer Credit in America*, Oxford University Press (1989).

D. REPORTS

Brighton and Connidis, *Consumer Bankrupts in Canada*, Policy Research, Analysis and Liaison Directorate, Policy Coordination Bureau, Consumer and Corporate Affairs Canada (1982).

D.J.M. Brown, *Final Report of the Commission of Inquiry into Wage Protection in Insolvency Situations* (1985).

Law Reform Commission of British Columbia, *Fraudulent Conveyances and Preferences, Working Paper No. 53* (1986).

Report of the Advisory Committee on Bankruptcy and Insolvency: Proposed Bankruptcy Act Amendments ("Colter Report"), Ministry of Supply and Services Canada (1986).

Report of the Study Committee on Bankruptcy and Insolvency Legislation in Canada 1970 (Tassé Report), Ministry of Supply and Services Canada (1970).

Report of the Review Committee on Insolvency Law and Practice, Cmnd. 8558 (1982).

PART I

Secured Transactions in Personal Property and Suretyships

CHAPTER ONE

Security Devices and the Personal Property Security Act

EVOLUTION OF CANADIAN PERSONAL PROPERTY SECURITY LAW

Introduction

In volumes I and II of this casebook there have been many references to the role of credit in commercial transactions and the various ways in which creditors seek to protect themselves against the consequences of non-payment and other forms of default by debtors. These topics must now be pursued more systematically. The particular focus of this volume is the law regulating security interests in personal property. Security interests in land are only peripherally addressed.

"Credit" is not a term of art and it is used in different senses in different branches of the law. For the purposes of this volume we use it to mean the agreed deferred payment of a debt. It therefore embraces loans of money and the supply of goods and services on a deferred payment basis, regardless of the length of the period of credit.

Credit plays a role even in very simple societies. Not surprisingly, however, its importance grows apace with the industrial and economic development of a country. This is because a country's capital needs expand enormously as it seeks to widen its industrial base and to increase its production of goods and services. At the other end of the spectrum, consumers need credit facilities to enable them to acquire the goods and services produced by the new technology. This is especially true if the cost of the goods and services exceeds consumers' current income. As an industry's capital needs are satisfied, it generates surplus funds which can then be made available to those who are capital seekers, whether within or outside the country. The role of financial intermediaries is to provide efficient means for the reinvestment of such funds.

A measure of the current importance of credit in Canada can be gleaned from the following figures.

Credit Held by Major Grantors*

(annual averages for 1993, in millions)

Consumer Credit (not including residential mortgages)

Chartered Banks:	$ 67,716	(66% of market)
Credit Unions:	$ 13,393	(13.1% of market)
Finance Companies and other institutions:	$ 10,066	(9.9% of market)
Trust Companies:	$ 7,352	(7.3% of market)

Short Term Business Credit

Chartered Banks:	$115,362	(57.8% of market)
Finance Companies:	$ 8,040	(4% of market)
Others:	$ 20,140	(10.1% of market)

Consumer Credit

There has been phenomenal growth of consumer credit use in Canada since the end of the Second World War. Until comparatively recently, the buying of consumer goods or services on credit was disparaged because, unlike commercial credit, it was regarded as an unproductive use of money. The change in attitude began to take place in the last quarter of the 19th century with the appearance of mass produced durable household and leisure time goods—ice boxes, sewing machines, pianos, bicycles, etc. Most consumers could not afford to pay for such goods immediately, yet without a broad consumer base, manufacturers could not market the goods economically. Manufacturers and retailers bridged the gap by making the goods available on instalment sale (that is, conditional sale) or, in the United Kingdom, hire-purchase terms. Consumer credit was given a tremendous boost with the advent of the motor vehicle age. Even well-heeled consumers could not afford to pay cash for their cars. At the same time, the early auto manufacturers could not, or did not wish to, tie up the large amounts of capital needed to sell the automobiles on credit. A new type of financial intermediary, the sales finance company, which specialized in this type of consumer credit, came to the rescue. See further E.R.A. Seligman, *The Economics of Installment Selling* (2 vols., 1927); Plummer and Young, *Sales Finance Companies and Their Credit Practices* (1940); Federal Reserve System, *Consumer Installment Credit: Part I* (2 vols., 1957).

In Canada, the chartered banks did not become heavily involved in the extension of consumer credit until the decennial revision of the Bank Act in 1967. The Act greatly encouraged their participation, first, by repealing the 6% ceiling on permissible interest rates on bank loans and, second, by allowing the banks to take consumer goods as security for consumer loans. Since 1967, the banks have penetrated the market so successfully that, at the present time, they hold about two-thirds of the total volume of consumer credit. The introduction of credit cards in the late 1960s strengthened their hold still further.

---

* Source: Bank of Canada Review, Statistical Supplement, March 1995, Table E2.

Different Types of Credit Terms

Financial economists usually distinguish between short-term, medium-term and long-term credit. Short-term credit is credit for a period of up to one year; medium-term credit covers one to five years; and long-term credit represents any duration longer than five years. (These periods of course are not written in stone and have no legal significance.)

The most familiar and oldest type of short-term credit is provided by suppliers of goods and services. Typically, depending on the trade custom, the buyer is given 10, 30 or 60 days to pay the account without an *explicit* interest charge and generally without being required to put up security. Revolving lines of credit made available by banks to commercial customers are usually negotiated on a yearly basis. They are an important source of short-term working capital for many businesses and are often secured by a security interest on inventory and/or an assignment of receivables in favour of the bank.

Medium-term credit, both for commercial and consumer purposes, is often used to enable the debtor to acquire new capital items such as equipment, machinery, vehicles for business or professional use, and automobiles, large household appliances and entertainment units for consumer use. Frequently, the goods being acquired will serve as security (collateral).

Long-term credit serves some of the same purposes as medium-term credit except that typically the goods being acquired (for example, an aircraft or a printing press) are considerably more expensive and the terms of repayment longer. Long-term credit may be a source of permanent or semi-permanent additions to the borrower's capital (and will be treated as such on the borrower's balance sheet), as where a loan is not repayable for 20 years or more. The security required by the lender may be the same as for a medium-term loan. Frequently, however, given the higher degree of risk, the lender will demand a security interest in all of the debtor's assets.

The Role and Evolution of Chattel Security Devices

There are many reasons why a modern creditor will find it desirable, if not essential, to take security to secure payment or performance of the debtor's obligations. Some of the most important reasons are the following: (1) There is a risk that the debtor may go bankrupt. A recession sharply increases the risk of non-payment for both commercial and consumer debts.* An unsecured creditor can expect to receive only a small dividend (on average five cents on the dollar) from the realization of the bankrupt's assets, and frequently will receive nothing at all. Even where a secured creditor's recovery is limited to the value of the collateral, if the secured creditor is first in line, realization of 60 to 70% of the claim is quite common, and may be higher. (2) Even if the debtor does not become insolvent, having to sue the debtor to recover the amount owing and to levy execution on the debtor's property is time consuming and expensive. A secured creditor, on the other hand, is free in many of the provinces, and generally under federal law, to seize the collateral and dispose

---

* In 1993, there were 12,527 business bankruptcies in Canada with total liabilities of over $5 billion dollars and $3.5 billion dollars in estimated deficiencies. There were 54,456 consumer bankruptcies with total liabilities of over $3 billion dollars and $1.5 billion dollars in estimated deficiencies.

of it without needing prior judicial authorization. (3) If the creditor does not take security, there is always the danger that a subsequent creditor will demand it and, thereby, acquire priority in the event of non-payment of both debts. Again, the debtor may be tempted to sell some of its assets to generate cash. Obviously this will reduce the volume and value of assets available for distribution among the debtor's creditors. Finally, (4) a secured creditor is often given power in the security agreement to monitor the debtor's affairs and such monitoring is more effective with the benefit of security than without it. The secured creditor can also threaten to seize the collateral if the debtor fails to make payment or otherwise fails to meet its obligations under the security agreement.

The existence of these advantages does not mean that every creditor seeks to, or can, obtain security. Whether or not the creditor does so will depend on such factors as the strength of its bargaining position, the size of the debt, and the period of repayment.

Early History of Chattel Security Law

Chattel Mortgages

The pledge was the earliest security device. The chattel mortgage, the oldest of the *non-possessory* security devices and the counterpart of the land mortgage, apparently did not make its appearance until the 17th century. Even then it remained under a cloud until well into the 19th century. This was because, from Lord Coke's day onwards, a sale of goods (a chattel mortgage was frequently referred to as a "conditional" bill of sale) without transfer of possession to the buyer was regarded as presumptively or conclusively fraudulent *vis-à-vis* the seller's creditors. See *Twyne's Case* (1601), 76 ER 809, and *cf. Cookson v. Swire* (1884), 9 AC 653, at 664. However, it was not necessary in Canada, as it was in the United States, for legislation to validate chattel mortgages, and when such statutes began to be adopted, from the mid-19th century onwards, it was done for the protection of third parties and not to enhance the mortgagee's status.

Nevertheless, the chattel mortgage served an increasingly important economic function. While there are no statistics showing how widely chattel mortgages were used during the colonial period, there is clear evidence that they played an important role in financing arrangements. The enactment in 1849 by the Legislative Assembly of the Province of Canada of legislation requiring public filing of chattel mortgages indicates that the use of this type of financing device was sufficiently common to arouse the concerns of unsecured creditors and persons buying or taking mortgages on goods in the hands of mortgagors. The use of chattel mortgages was not confined to commercial credit contracts. An examination of reported cases reveals that, as early as the 1850s, chattel mortgages were commonly taken on household furnishings, farm livestock and crops to secure what would now be categorized as personal or farm loans. Frequently, chattel mortgages were used to provide security against liability incurred by mortgagees as sureties of mortgagors' obligations or as endorsers or accommodation parties on instruments drawn by mortgagors.

Even before the use of equitable mortgages on after-acquired property had been sanctioned by the courts, chattel mortgages played a role in business financial arrangements to secure credit obtained by primary producers, small manufacturers and retailers. The collateral given covered both fixed assets and stock-in-trade. During the last half of the 19th century, chattel mortgage legislation was frequently amended to encompass the increasing variety of situations in which chattel mortgages were being used as security devices. By 1897, the Ontario Bills of Sale and Chattel Mortgage Act, RSO 1897, c. 148, contained specific provisions dealing with mortgages to secure future advances for the purpose of enabling the borrower to carry on business. By the turn of the century all common law provinces and the Northwest Territories had enacted chattel mortgage legislation and had established accompanying registry systems.

The decision of the House of Lords in *Holroyd v. Marshall* (1862), 10 HLC 191, enormously increased the usefulness of the chattel mortgage. Generally speaking, at common law there cannot be an effective mortgage of future goods without a further confirmation of the transfer of title after the goods have come into existence and the mortgagor has acquired title to them. In *Holroyd v. Marshall*, as subsequently explained in *Tailby v. Official Receiver* (1888), 13 AC 523, the House of Lords held that a mortgage of after-acquired property is valid in equity without the need for any further confirmatory act and that the mortgagor's conscience will be bound and the mortgage will attach as soon as the mortgagor acquires title or other interest in the chattel.

There were other developments in the 19th century that firmly laid the basis for the modern law of chattel security, of which the following were the most important:

Section 427 Bank Act Security*

Pre-confederation legislation of 1861 authorized banks to make advances against the security of bills of lading and warehouse receipts. These provisions were retained in the successive Bank Acts adopted by Parliament after Confederation and are still in force today, albeit in a much modified form.†

The warehouse receipts provisions led to abuses since they were not confined to warehousekeepers acting as bailees of the goods of others. As a result the provisions were materially amended in 1890 and the s. 427 security was partially divorced from its documentary pledge lineage. A mandatory registration requirement was added in 1923. The scope of s. 427 was progressively enlarged in the decennial revisions of the Bank Act. Today it covers security interests in goods (generally inventory but not invariably so) given by retailers, wholesalers, manufacturers, farmers, fishers, and those handling mining and forestry products. Security interests given by consumers are still excluded. Apart from these limitations, ss. 427-429 of the present Bank Act, SC 1991, c. 46, do not constitute a complete code even with respect to the goods and persons to which and to whom they do apply. The provisions are badly dated and often difficult to understand. Of equal concern is the fact that they do not mesh with the concepts and principles underlying the provincial personal property security Acts.

---

* In earlier versions of the Bank Act, the section had a different number.

† The federal Parliament has constitutional responsibility for the regulation of banks and banking. Constitution Act, 1867, s. 91(15). This also gives it the power to regulate security interests taken by banks. *Tennant v. Union Bank of Can.*, [1894] AC 3 (PC) and *Bank of Montreal v. Hall* (1990), 65 DLR (4th) 361 (SCC).

Fixed and Floating Charges

Fixed and floating charges were an English innovation of the late 19th century based on the concepts established by the House of Lords in *Holroyd v. Marshall* (1862), 10 HLC 191. These concepts quickly found a hospitable home in Canada. The two distinctive features of this security device are, first, that it is purely equitable in character and, second, that its "floating" component does not fasten or attach to any specific assets of the debtor until the charge has "crystallized." Crystallization is an event which usually occurs on the debtor ceasing to carry on business or when a receiver is privately appointed by the secured party or is appointed by a court at the secured party's request. See further, *infra*, chapter 2.

Initially the fixed and floating charge was primarily used, in conjunction with the issue of debentures, as a long-term financing device. [A "debenture" is merely a document acknowledging an indebtedness (from the Latin word *debeo*, "I owe") and setting forth the terms of payment of the debt and other terms agreed upon between the parties.]

In the United Kingdom and other Commonwealth countries (but no longer in Canada), debentures are also frequently used to secure short-term advances. The charge may cover all of the debtor's assets, present and future (an "all asset" debenture), or it may be limited to a particular class of collateral (e.g., receivables).

Conditional Sale Agreements

Conditional sale contracts were being used in common law jurisdictions, as early as the 1860s and 1870s, as financing devices for the acquisition of high cost consumer goods and business assets (both inventory and equipment). However, if the number of reported cases is a reliable guide it is clear that, at least until the turn of the century, conditional sales contracts played a minor role as a method of financing the acquisition of goods relative to chattel mortgages. The first provincial legislature to address the problem of third party deception endemic to conditional sales of goods was that of Nova Scotia, which enacted legislation in 1882. By the turn of the century all common law jurisdictions had enacted legislation dealing with conditional sale contracts. The use of conditional sale contracts grew rapidly after the turn of the century. Conditional sale contracts became one of the primary security devices used in instalment purchases of automobiles and agricultural equipment. Provincial legislation was refined to deal with matters such as fixtures and registration requirements where goods subject to conditional sales contracts executed in other jurisdictions were brought into the jurisdiction.

Assignment of Book Debts (Accounts Receivable Financing)

Receivables are an attractive form of collateral because of their liquid character. Security assignments of book debts first made their appearance in bank loan agreements in the late 19th century, and they continue to be widely used by banks to this day, sometimes alone and sometimes in conjunction with a security interest in inventory. At common law, receivables as collateral have both advantages and disadvantages. The advantages are that the documentary formalities are simple and that in *Tailby v. Official Receiver* (1888), 13 AC 523, the House of Lords extended the doctrine in *Holroyd v. Marshall* to a security assignment of future book debts. The disadvantages arose out of the rule in *Dearle v. Hall* (1823), 3 Russ. 1. This rule provides that where there are competing assignments of a debt, priority goes to the assignee who gives first notice to the account debtor. This is a very inconvenient rule since in "non-notification" forms of receivables financing, notice of the assignment is usually not given by the secured party until there is default by the assignor. The rule in *Dearle v. Hall* was held to apply even though the secured party had registered the assignment in compliance with provincial registration requirements under the Assignment of Book Debts Act.

The single most important factor inducing provinces to establish registration provisions for general assignment of accounts was the enactment of the federal Bankruptcy Act in 1919 under which a general assignment of existing or future book debts by a person engaged in trade or business was void against the assignor's trustee in bankruptcy unless the assignment was registered in compliance with a provincial statute that provided for the registration of assignments.

A form of receivables financing that has long been popular in the United States and has also gained a small foothold in Canada is known as factoring. Unlike its 19th century ancestor, the modern factoring company no longer acts as an agent for the sale of goods. Instead, it often buys the receivables outright and proceeds to collect them direct from the account debtors. Hence this form of assignment is usually referred to as "notification" financing.

Summary of Pre-PPSA Position

In the light of the preceding description, it will be seen that, before the adoption of the personal property security Acts, the Canadian law of chattel security was very complex. There was no general concept of a security interest. Instead, there were a multiplicity of security devices, each with its own distinctive set of rules and registration requirements. Some of the devices were of common law origins, some were purely equitable in character, and at least one (the s. 427 Bank Act security device) derived its validity from statute. Many of the substantive rules were not appropriate to post-war conditions and the registration requirements were often technical and difficult to comply with. As noted later in this Introduction, the personal property security Acts were designed to eliminate these shortcomings.

Article 9 of the American Uniform Commercial Code

American chattel security law in the pre-Article 9 period suffered from the same shortcomings as its Canadian counterpart and from a good many more. In general, American state law was not as generous to secured creditors as Canadian law. In particular, many states imposed significant restrictions on the validity of "after-acquired" property clauses or did not recognize them at all. The doctrine in *Benedict v. Ratner* (1925), 268 US 353, held that an accounts receivable financer (and by inference an inventory financer as well) could not enforce its security interest against the debtor's creditors unless the secured party also carefully policed the debtor's collection of receivables and required the debtor to account for them. American common law never adopted the English style fixed and floating charge. The Uniform Trust Receipts Act, adopted in 1933 by the National Conference of Commissioners on Uniform State Law (NCCUSL), was designed to facilitate inventory financing in domestic transactions but the Act itself was highly technical and difficult to interpret.

In 1942 the NCCUSL launched its ambitious Uniform Commercial Code project in conjunction with the American Law Institute. The revision and integration of the uniform laws on chattel security comprised an important part of this effort. Professor Grant Gilmore of the Yale Law School and Professor Allison Dunham of the University of Chicago Law School were appointed Joint Reporters of what became Article 9 of the Code. After attempting to deal separately with different forms of secured financing they independently reached the conclusion that this was unnecessary and that all forms of financing and the different types of security devices could be accommodated in a single Article of the Code on Secured Transactions.

The first version of the Code was completed in 1951. A revised *Official Text* appeared in 1962. A further revision, adopted in 1972, incorporated important changes recommended by the Article 9 Review Committee. Smaller changes, conformably to those made in Article 8, were added in 1978 to take account of certificateless securities. In 1987, the Code's sponsors added a new Article to the Code, Article 2A—Leases, which is concerned with personal property leases. At the same time, the definition of "security interest" in UCC 1-201(37) was completely recast. The current edition of the Code is known as the *1991 Official Text*. Most Articles of the Code, including Article 9, have been or are currently being revised. The Code is in force in all of the American common law states and in the District of Columbia. Louisiana, a civil law jurisdiction, has adopted many parts of the Code, including Article 9. It is generally agreed that it was the innovative character of Article 9, and its sympathetic approach to secured transactions, that led many state bars and commercial lawyers to support the enactment of the Code in their state.

Article 9 Comes to Canada

In 1959, the then Attorney General of Ontario invited a committee of the Canadian Bar Association to review the provincial registration statutes and to make recommendations for their improvement. The committee's attention was drawn to Article 9. It liked what it saw and endorsed the Article 9 approach. The committee then set about to prepare an Ontario version of Article 9. The task was completed in 1963 and, after various reviews, the Personal Property Security Act was enacted by the Ontario legislature in 1967. However, only that part of the Act involving the establishment of a central registry came into effect on royal assent to the Bill. The rest of the Act, the major part, was not proclaimed until 1976.

The Ontario initiative was followed with interest in the other provinces. In 1964 the Canadian Bar Association established a special committee to determine whether or not it was feasible to adapt the then proposed Ontario Act so that it could be a model for similar legislation in other provinces. The committee decided to prepare a model Personal Property Security Act that would serve as the basis for reform of personal property security law throughout the country. The committee published the Uniform Personal Property Security Act in 1969. This was adopted by the Canadian Bar Association in 1970 and provided the pattern for the 1973 Manitoba Act.

While the 1969 Uniform Act adopted most features of the 1967 Ontario Act, it differed in some important respects. Thereafter, the committee monitored the operation of the Ontario Act and developments in the United States. The very substantial revisions of

Article 9 of the Uniform Commercial Code that were made in 1972 and the weaknesses in the Ontario Act and the 1969 Uniform Act induced the committee to prepare a second draft of the Uniform Act. In the meantime the Saskatchewan Law Reform Commission published a report in 1971 proposing a Personal Property Security Act for Saskatchewan based in part on the Uniform Act, but containing a number of significant new features. The Saskatchewan Legislature responded by enacting a Personal Property Security Act in 1980. The Model Uniform Personal Property Security Act (MUPPSA), adopted by the Canadian Bar Association and the Uniform Law Conference in 1982, replicated many of the features of the Saskatchewan Act.

When it became clear in 1984, with the release of the Report of the Minister's Advisory Committee on the Personal Property Security Act that Ontario would not adopt the 1982 Uniform Personal Property Security Act as a model for further reform of personal property security legislation in that province, the Western Canada Personal Property Security Act Committee was formed. The goal of the committee was to develop a model for adoption by jurisdictions in Western Canada. This model ultimately provided the basis for the British Columbia, Alberta and Northwest Territories Acts and the new Saskatchewan and Manitoba Acts. In 1991, the Western Canada Personal Property Security Act Committee was reconstituted as the Canadian Conference on Personal Property Security Law (CCPPSL).

In the autumn of 1988, the Alberta Legislature enacted a Personal Property Security Act and in the early summer of 1989 the British Columbia Personal Property Security Act was passed. Minor housekeeping amendments were made to both of these Acts before they came into force in 1990. In 1993 new Acts were adopted in Manitoba and Saskatchewan and PPS legislation, based on the Western Canada model, was enacted in New Brunswick and the Northwest Territories. As of January 1995, only the New Brunswick and Saskatchewan Acts were in force.

The Ontario position has not remained static. In 1976 the Minister of Consumer and Commercial Relations established an Advisory Committee on the PPSA to prepare a revised Act in the light of the 1972 amendments to Article 9 and the work of the MUPPSA committee. The Advisory committee reported in June 1984 with an accompanying draft revised Act. See *Report of the Minister's Advisory Committee on the Personal Property Security Act* (Toronto, June 1984). The committee issued a *Supplementary Report* in January 1986 incorporating changes in the draft Act and responding to the many briefs received by it on its original report. The new legislation, the Personal Property Security Act, 1989, was enacted in March 1989 and came into force in October 1989. The new Act closely follows the recommendations of the Advisory Committee except in one important respect. The Ontario government did not follow the Committee's recommendation that leases of goods for a year or more and commercial consignment agreements be included in the scope provisions of the Act, whether or not the lease or consignment agreement was a true security agreement.

Most interesting from a comparative point of view is the fact that the new Quebec Civil Code (the relevant provisions of which came into force on January 1, 1994) provides for a regime for security interests in movable property that has many features in common with personal property security Acts in other provinces.

It may be said that Canada is now well launched into the second generation of personal property security legislation. Nevertheless, the national scene is far from harmonious.

Instead, Canada has the dubious distinction of possessing *four* different chattel security regimes—the common law rules and registration statutes in Newfoundland, Nova Scotia and Prince Edward Island; the CCPPSL model PPSA in five provinces and the Northwest Territories; the non-model Acts in Ontario and the Yukon; the civil law system in Quebec; and the Section 427 Bank Act regime for security interests taken by federally regulated banks. Even more disturbing is the fact that there are substantial differences between the CCPPSL model and the Ontario Act, mostly on points of detail but sometimes on points of substance.

BIBLIOGRAPHICAL NOTE

The following monographs and looseleaf publications have been published on Canadian personal property security law:

Cuming and Wood, *Alberta Personal Property Security Handbook*, 2nd ed., (Carswell, 1993)

Cuming and Wood, *British Columbia Personal Property Security Handbook,* 2nd ed., (Carswell, 1993)

Cuming and Wood, *Saskatchewan and Manitoba Personal Property Security Handbook* (Carswell, 1994)

McLaren, *Secured Transactions in Personal Property in Canada* (Carswell, 1992), 4 vols., looseleaf

Ziegel and Denomme, *The Ontario Personal Property Security Act* (Canada Law Book Co., 1994)

The following reports recommending personal property security legislation have been published by law reform agencies or committees:

New Brunswick Reform Branch, Department of Justice, *The Proposed New Brunswick Personal Property Security Act,* 1991; Ontario Ministry of Consumer and Commercial Relations, *Report of the Minister's Advisory Committee on the Personal Property Security Act,* 1984, and the *Supplementary Report of the Minister's Advisory Committee on the Personal Property Security Act,* 1986; Law Reform Commission of Saskatchewan, *Tentative Proposals for a Saskatchewan Personal Property Act,* 1976, and *Proposals for a Saskatchewan Personal Property Security Act,* 1977; *Tentative Proposals for a New Saskatchewan Personal Property Act,*1990; *Proposals for a New Saskatchewan Personal Property Security Act,* 1992; British Columbia Law Reform Commission, *Report on Debtor-Creditor Relationships, Project No. 2,* 1975; British Columbia Ministry of Consumer and Corporate Affairs, *A Proposed Personal Property Security Act,* 1978; and Canadian Bar Association, Committee on a Uniform Personal Property Security Act, *Draft Uniform Personal Property Security Act,* 1969.

The following is a selection of overview articles on Canadian personal property security law:

R.C.C. Cuming, "Second Generation Personal Property Security Legislation in Canada" (1981-82), 46 *Sask. L Rev.* 5.

Law Society of Upper Canada and Canadian Bar Association, *The Personal Property Security Act: Setting New Sails*, papers presented at a conference in Toronto on May 25, 1989.

Symposium, "Chattel Security: Order Out of Chaos" (1964), 7 *Can. Bar J* 278.

Jacob S. Ziegel, "The Draft Ontario Personal Property Security Act" (1966), 44 *Can. Bar Rev.* 104.

_____ (together with R.C.C. Cuming), "The Modernization of Canadian Personal Property Security Law" (1981), 31 *UTLJ* 249.

_____ , "The New Provincial Chattel Security Regimes" (1991), 70 *Can. Bar Rev.* 681.

The literature on Article 9 is vast. The three leading texts are Gilmore, *Security Interests in Personal Property* (Little, Brown & Co., 1965), 2 vols.; Clark, *The Law of Secured Transactions under the Uniform Commercial Code* (Warren Gorham Lamont, 1993), (looseleaf); Coogan, Hogan, Vagts and McDonnell, *Secured Transactions Under the Uniform Commercial Code* (M. Bender, 1980), 4 vols, (looseleaf). *Gilmore* is treated as the "bible" of United States secured transactions law although its discussion of the Code case law is now substantially dated. Clark's book is directed to practitioners and is less analytical than the other two. *Coogan* is a collection of law journal articles dealing with a wide range of issues that arise under Article 9. A much shorter but very readable overview of Article 9 appears in White and Summers, *Uniform Commercial Code*, 3rd ed., chapters 22-26 (1988). A comprehensive collection of Code case law is published by the Uniform Commercial Code Reporting Service (UCC Rep. Serv.).

CURRENT PERSONAL PROPERTY SECURITY ACTS

Currently, there are six jurisdictions in Canada which have Personal Property Security Acts: Alberta, SA 1988, c. P-4.05, as amended 1990, c. 31; 1991, c. 21; 1992, c. 21, s. 34(1); British Columbia, SBC 1989, c. 36, as amended 1990, c. 11, c. 25, and c. 53, s. 12; 1991, c. 13; 1992, c. 48; 1993, c. 28, s. 16; Manitoba, SM 1973, c. P35 and SM 1993, c. 14 (not in force); New Brunswick, SNB 1993, c. P-7.1, as amended 1994, c. 22; Northwest Territories, SNWT 1994, c. 8 (not in force); Ontario, RSO 1990, c. P.10, as amended 1993, c. 13, s. 2; Saskatchewan, SS 1993, c. P-6.2; Yukon, RSY 1986, c. 130, as amended 1988, c. 17, s. 9; 1991, c. 11, s. 202. While all of the Acts have the same basic structures and concepts, there are some important differences among them. The most significant differences are between the Ontario Act on the one hand and the Acts based on the CCPPSL model (Alta., BC, Man., NWT, NB, and Sask.) on the other. Some of the differences reflect policy choices; however, most result from different drafting styles.

Table of Concordance

The following table provides a concordance for the sections of the provincial Personal Property Security Acts. Note that the table includes the former and the current Ontario and Saskatchewan Acts, the existing and new, unproclaimed Manitoba Act, and the new unproclaimed Northwest Territories Act.

Alta.	BC	Man. (old)	Man. (new)	NB	NWT	Ont. (old)	Ont. (new)	Sask. (old)	Sask. (new)	Yukon
1(1)	1(1)	1	1	1	1	1	1	2	2(1)	1
1(2)	1(2)	N/A	2(1)	2(1)	1(2)	N/A	N/A	N/A	2(2)	N/A
1(5)	1(4)	N/A	2(2)	2(2)	1(4)	N/A	N/A	N/A	2(3)	N/A
1(6)	1(5)	N/A	2(3)	2(3)	1(5)	N/A	N/A	N/A	2(4)	N/A
2	N/A	72	71	2(6)	4	3	3	74	3(3)	71
N/A	N/A	N/A	2(4)	2(4)	1(6)	N/A	N/A	N/A	3(5)	N/A
N/A	N/A	N/A	N/A	2(5)	N/A	N/A	N/A	N/A	N/A	N/A
3(1)	2(1)	2	3(1)	3(1)	2(1)	2	2	3	3(1)	2
3(2)	3	2	3(2)	3(2)	2(2)	2	2	3	3(2)	2
4	4	3	4	4	4	3	4	4	4	3
5	5	6-8	5	5	5	6-8	5	5	5	4
6	6	6	6	6	6	6	6	6	6	5
7	7	5	7	7	7	5	7	7	7	6
8	8	N/A	8	8	8	8	8	8	8	7
9	9	9	9	9	9	9	9	9	9(1)	63(2)
10	10	10	10	10	10	10	11(1)	10	10	8
11	11	11	11	11	11	11	10	11	11	9, 10
12	12	12	12	12	12	12	11	12	12	11
13	13	13, 14	13	13	13	13	13	12	13	12
14	14	15	14	14	14	15	13	14	14	13
15	15	17	15	15	15	17	15	15	15	14
16	16	18	16	16	16	18	16	16	16	15
17	17	19	17	17	17	19	17	17	17	16
18	18	20	18	18	18	20	18	18	18	17
19	19	21	19	19	19	21	19	19	19	18
20	20	22	20	20	20	22	20	20	20	19
21	21	N/A	21	21	21	N/A	N/A	N/A	21	N/A
22	22	22(3)	22	22	22	22(3)	20(3)	21	22	20
23	23	23	23	23	23	23	21	23	23	21
24	24	24	24	24	24	24	22	24	24	22
25	25	25	25	25	25	25	23	25	25	23
26	26	26(2), 26(3)	26	26	26	26	24(2), 24(3)	26(2), 26(3)	26	25(2), 25(3)
27	27	28	27	27	27	28	26	27	27	27
28	28	27	28	28	28	27	25	28	28	26
29	29	29	29	29	29	29	27	29	29	28
30	30	30	30	30	30	30(1)	28	30	30	29
31	31	31	31	31	31	30(2), 30(3), 31	28(3)-28(8)	31	31	30
32	32	32	32	32	32	32	31	32	32	31
33	33	33	33	33	33	33	39	33	33	32

(Continued ...)

Alta.	BC	Man. (old)	Man. (new)	NB	NWT	Ont. (old)	Ont. (new)	Sask. (old)	Sask. (new)	Yukon
34	34	34	34	34	34	34	32-33	34	34	33
35	35	35	35	35	35	35	30	35	35	34
36	36	36	36	36	36	36	34	36	36	35
37	37	N/A	37	37	37	N/A	N/A	N/A	37	N/A
38	38	37	38	38	38	37	35	37	38	36
39	39	38	39	39	39	38	37	38	39	37
40	40	39	40(1)	40	40	39	38	39	40(1)	38
41	41	40	41	41	41	40	40	40	41	39
42	42	41-43	42	42	42	41-43	41-42	41-42	42	40-41
43	43	46-48, 4	43	43	43	46-47	45-46	44, 46, 66	43	42, 64(2)
44	44	51, 52(1)	44	44	44	47, 50, 52	49, 51, 52	46, 48	44	46, 48
45	45	49, 52(2)	45	45	45	48, 50	47, 50	45, 47	45	44, 47
46	46(2)	N/A	46(2)	46	46	68	71	48(3)	46(2)	50(1)
47	47	53(7)	47	47	47	53	46(5)	51	47	52(3)
48	48	44	48	48	48	44	43	43	48	41
49	49	53	49	49	49	54	54	54	49	43
50	50	55	50	50	50	55	56	50	50	50
51	51	50	51	51	51	49	48	49	51	45
52	52, 54(4)	45	52	52	52	45	44	53	52	51
53	53	N/A	53	53	53	44(7)	44(7)	53(4), 53(5)	53	51(4), 51(5)
52	54(1), 54(2)	N/A	54	54	54	45	44	52	54	51
55	55	57	55	55	55	56	58, 59(6)-(7)	55	55	53
56	56(1)-56(3)	57	56	56	56	56	59	56	56	53
57	57	58	57	57	57	57	61	57	57	55
58	58	59	58	58	58	57	62	58	58	56
59	59	60	59	59	59	59	63	59	59	57
61	60	61	60	60	60	60	64	60	60	58
62	61	62	61	61	61	61	65	61	61	59
63	62	63	62	62	62	62	66	62	62	60
64	63	64(1)	63	63	63	63	67	63	63	61
65	64(1), 65, 66	57(3)	64	64	64	N/A	60	56	64	54
66	68	N/A	65	65	65	72	72	64(1), 64(5)	65(1)-65(4)	62(1), 63(1)

(Continued ...)

Alta.	BC	Man. (old)	Man. (new)	NB	NWT	Ont. (old)	Ont. (new)	Sask. (old)	Sask. (new)	Yukon
67	69	64(2)	65	66	65	63	67(2), 67(3)	64(2)-64(4)	65(5)-65(10)	62(2)-62(4)
68	70	N/A	66(1), 67	67	66	N/A	67(1)(c)	N/A	66(1)	N/A
69	71	65	66(2)	68	66	64	70	65	66(2)	66
70	72	N/A	68	69	68	68	68	67	68	65
72	73	66	69	70	69	69	73	69	69	70
73	76	70	72	71	71	N/A	N/A	70	71	N/A
71	77	71	N/A	72	70	70	74	73	70	67
75	78	67	73	73	72	66	77	72	73	69
71	78	71	74	74	73	70	74	73	74	67

The following materials introduce the basic concepts and structures of the current personal property security legislation. The materials focus primarily on the Ontario Act, but there are also frequent references to the Acts based on the CCPPSL model and to the 1991 Official Text of Article 9 of the Uniform Commercial Code.

LEGISLATIVE OBJECTIVES

Before focusing on the detailed features of the Personal Property Security Act, it is important to consider the legislative objectives underlying it. The Act contains an elaborate and detailed system for the regulation of personal property security transactions. It is not just a consolidation of prior law. Not only does it employ new concepts and legislative approaches, but, in addition, embedded in its provisions are important policy choices that affect credit grantors, credit users, unsecured creditors and buyers dealing with credit users. The full implications of these concepts, approaches and policy choices and the significance of the differences in approach and choices among the Acts are becoming progressively clearer as experience is gained by their practical operation.

A comparison of the Personal Property Security Act with the personal property security law it replaced highlights several of its most important features: structural integration, conceptual unity, comprehensiveness, legal predictability, accommodation of modern business financing techniques, and detailed regulation of default rights and remedies.

Structural Integration

The Act prescribes a single system of law in place of the disparate and sometimes conflicting structures of common law, equity and statutory law relating to security agreements existing prior to its enactment (and still existing in provinces that do not have personal property security Acts). The initial failure to include in the 1967 Ontario Act mortgages, charges and assignments governed by the Corporation Securities Registration Act, an exclusion not copied in other jurisdictions, stood out as an important and troublesome departure from the goal of structural integration. This deficiency was addressed in the 1989 Ontario Act. While the Act does not completely pre-empt common law and equitable principles, it leaves little scope for the continued recognition of differences between the traditional types of security agreements such as conditional sales contracts, equitable chattel mortgages, legal chattel mortgages, assignment of choses in action and floating charges.

Conceptual Unity

Structural integration was made possible by the legislative recognition of a single generic concept as the central feature of all security agreements providing for an interest in property to secure performance of an obligation.

At common law and equity, the primary mechanisms for securing obligations involved the security transfer of title (legal or equitable) in the obligor's personal property in favour of the secured party, the retention of title by the seller where the obligation arose out of the sale of property, or the creation of equitable charges and special property interests. The fact that different types of interests were involved dictated that differences would exist among the various types of security devices with respect to both *inter partes* and priority rights. It also prevented the consistent and rational development of personal property security law.

Neither form nor locus of title to collateral plays a significant role as a determinant of the application of the PPSA or the rules applicable to a particular transaction. So long as it creates or provides for an interest in personal property to secure payment or performance of an obligation, a transaction falls within the scope of the Act (see OPPSA ss. 1(1) "security agreement" and "security interest," and 2). The Act does draw distinctions between types of transactions, but not on the basis of form or locus of title. Purely functional considerations provide justification for differential treatment. For example, security agreements providing for purchase money security interests (OPPSA ss. 1(1) "purchase-money security interest," 20(3), 33) or security interests in chattel paper (OPPSA ss. 1(1) "chattel paper," 28(3)) are given, for public policy and commercial reasons, a special priority status if prescribed conditions are met.

Comprehensiveness

The PPSA is not a code of law in the sense that it is totally self-contained. Nevertheless, it is much more complete than anything existing prior to its enactment. The statutory personal property security law that the Act replaced focused primarily on forcing public disclosure of the existence of security interests. Loss of priority to other persons claiming interests in the collateral was the consequence of non-compliance with public disclosure requirements. Apart from this, priority issues were left to be resolved by common law and equity principles.

The PPSA deals with a wide range of matters involving personal property security transactions, including the form of a security agreement (OPPSA ss. 9(2)-(3), 11(2), 12-17, 59); the creation of a security interest (OPPSA ss. 11-13); perfection of the security interest and registration rules (OPPSA ss. 22-46, 41-57); a complete set of rules to determine priorities among competing interests (OPPSA ss. 27-37); the rights and remedies of the secured party in the event of the debtor's default (OPPSA ss. 58-66); and choice of law rules governing the validity and perfection of foreign security interests (OPPSA ss. 5-8).

Legal Predictability

The ability to predict accurately the relative priority position a credit grantor will occupy in the event it is required to rely on a security interest is often an important consideration in the initial decision to grant credit. The lack of a single, integrated system of priority rules which characterized prior law meant that a decision whether or not to grant credit often had to be made in the context of considerable legal uncertainty about the outcome of a priority dispute involving other claims to the collateral. The much more complete priority system of the PPSA not only ensures greater consistency in court decisions dealing with priority disputes, but also facilitates more accurate assessment of the legal risks involved in granting credit.

Accommodation of Modern Business Financing

While equity facilitated business financing through its recognition of equitable interests in after-acquired property, much more was required to bring the law abreast of the needs of modern business financing. The PPSA was designed to do this. The Act permits parties to a security agreement a large measure of freedom to tailor their agreement to fit their particular circumstances (OPPSA s. 9). A security interest can be taken in a revolving line of inventory (OPPSA s. 12). A line of credit can be secured without fear of loss of priority to intervening interests (OPPSA ss. 13, 30(4)). Special priority rules are included to deal with the distinctive features of the purchase and sale of chattel paper (OPPSA s. 28(3)). Perhaps the most important feature of the Act in this context is the flexibility supplied by the notice filing registration system (OPPSA ss. 45-46, 18).

Regulation of Default Rights and Remedies

Under prior law the relative rights of the secured party and the debtor in the event of default by the debtor depended upon the type of security agreement involved and the terms of the agreement. Proceeding from the premise that all security agreements are designed to accomplish the same end and that borrowers usually have little bargaining power, the PPSA prescribes a detailed system for the regulation of default rights and remedies which is designed to provide consistency and fairness in the enforcement of security interests (OPPSA ss. 58-66).

The Acts based on the CCPPSL model contain provisions dealing with several important aspects of receiverships. See, for example, BCPPSA, ss. 64-66. The OPPSA does little more than recognize the use of receiverships and to provide for general judicial supervision of the conduct of receivers (OPPSA, s. 60).

NOTE

A modern and efficient legal system designed to facilitate the granting of security interests will necessarily affect the parties to a security agreement and, at least in the event of insolvency of the debtor, other creditors of the debtor. It can be argued that the PPSA provides so much flexibility and freedom to the parties that debtors often end up in a captive position. Having given a security interest in all or most of their personal property to one secured party, they are powerless to obtain secured credit from other sources when it is needed. While this was a concern under prior law as well, it is thought by some to be much more of a problem under the Act. Keep this issue in mind when considering the priority structure of the Act. Note particularly the exception to the first to register priority rule (OPPSA s. 30(1)) providing for purchase-money security interests (OPPSA s. 33).

The effect of a security agreement on the rights of unsecured creditors of the debtor involve important social and economic considerations. Over the past decade, interest in the economic analysis of law has generated an inconclusive debate in the United States on the economic efficiency and other justifications for secured debt. The debate was initiated by Prof. Alan Schwartz, now a faculty member at the Yale Law School.

Alan Schwartz
"Security Interests and Bankruptcy Priorities: A Review of Current Theories"
(1981), 10 *J Legal Studies* 1 (all footnotes omitted)

In recent years, finance economists have begun to study several practices that the law traditionally regulates. Examples include attempted explanations of the variety of debt and equity instruments that firms issue, the nature of bond covenants, the functions that trade credit serves and the likely actions of creditors when their debtor becomes insolvent. These studies are illuminating and provocative, but represent only the beginning of coherent explanations of the phenomena. Also, the normative implications of this relatively incomplete understanding have been unexplored. Lawyers assume these financial practices to be well understood and, consequently, have erected regulatory structures that presuppose the truth of what now seem preliminary or questionable positivist theories. This paper explores a particular financial practice—the issuance of debt secured by personal property—and a regulatory scheme relevant to this practice—the setting of distributional priorities when an insolvent firm is liquidated. My principal purpose is to illuminate the unresolved problems in this field and to illustrate the relevance of the achievements and unaccomplished tasks of modern finance to areas of business law that have developed largely independently of this discipline.

If an insolvent debtor's business is liquidated, its secured creditors may take property subject to their liens before any other creditors are paid. Congress has also created six classes of "priority" creditors, the most important of which are expenses of administration (first priority), wage and employee-benefit claims up to limited amounts (third and fourth priority) and taxes (sixth priority). Each priority class is paid in full, to the extent available assets exist, before the next class is paid. Finally, "general" creditors, those without security interests or priority status, receive payment if payment is possible. As this priority list suggests, secured creditors do much better than general creditors in bankruptcy liquidations.

The principal justification for a distribution scheme that seemingly advantages the sophisticated and relatively affluent, who often take security, at the expense of the relatively poor and unsophisticated, who often do not, is that the institution of secured debt is efficient. Lawyers commonly make this claim in a slightly different form, asserting that the ability of firms to give security increases the amount of credit available to the firms, but the implicit premise is that the gains to firms and secured creditors from additional credit exceed the costs that security may occasionally impose on priority and general creditors. This efficiency justification has prevailed; the accepted wisdom holds that the current bankruptcy priority list is normatively desirable.

This paper reviews the accepted wisdom. Part I briefly discusses the factual context and the law of personal property security. Part II explores the efficiency justification for the Bankruptcy Act's favorable treatment of personal property secured debt. It argues that this justification is weak because efficiency explanations for why firms issue secured debt either predict wrongly when it will and when it will not be sold, fail to account for the use of security rather than other contractual devices that apparently accomplish the same ends, or fail to show that security reduces net social costs. Part III next considers distributional explanations for the practice of firms to issue secured debt. It is shown that firms sometimes have incentives to issue secured debt to redistribute wealth from particular unsecured creditors to themselves, but that distributional explanations for the existence of secured debt are also ultimately unsatisfying. Finally, Part IV initially asks what should be done if the efficiency justification for current law is rejected. This stance implies that the most appropriate reform would be to elevate the priority status in bankruptcy liquidations of creditors thought deserving of help. Part IV, however, also shows that the normative theories relevant to the question of which bankruptcy priority list is preferable are sufficiently primitive to make questionable any such case for radically altering present law.

This essay's principal conclusion, therefore, is that scholars and decision makers should no longer regard as settled the question which bankruptcy priority list is normatively preferable. Much more work must be done to make compelling the efficiency defense of current law, yet normative justifications for altering this law are also poorly developed.

I. *The Factual Context and the Law*

A. *The Factual Context*

Firms issue debt on short and long-term bases. Short-term debt usually is payable within a year, whereas long-term debt may be outstanding for thirty or more years. Debt of two kinds is issued because firms often have cyclical financing needs. If firms issued only long-term debt to finance long-term and current needs, they would thus be paying interest for short-term financing in periods when no short-term financing was necessary. To avoid this waste, firms finance long-term needs, such as for capital assets or realty, with long-term debt and short-term needs, such as for inventory and raw materials, with short-term or current debt.

To be used as collateral for long-term debt, personal property must have sufficient longevity to make a satisfactory lien possible. Much personal property fails to satisfy this requirement. Thus long-term debt is commonly secured with real estate and unusually long-lived industrial capital such as railroad-rolling stock. Short-term debt is usually secured with inventory, accounts receivable, equipment with a relatively short life, and negotiable instruments or instruments of credit. This paper's concern with security interests in personal property thus requires it to focus primarily on short-term debt. The security interests that sometimes accompany short-term debt are regulated by the Uniform Commercial Code.

B. *The Law*

Although secured parties always have come first in bankruptcy liquidations, the law was traditionally believed to have struck a rough balance between the interests of secured and unsecured creditors. This was largely because security, especially personal property security, was costly to take, state law having established difficult requirements for creating and giving public notice of security interests. Consequently, it was inconvenient for creditors to put a lien on all of a debtor's assets; a "cushion of free assets" was sometimes available to satisfy at least a portion of the claims of those creditors thought least able to protect themselves—employees, tenants, small-trade creditors. The Uniform Commercial Code, which was adopted in the middle 1960s, upset this supposed balance. The principal object and chief success of article 9 of the code was significantly to reduce the costs accompanying the issuance of debt secured by personal property. As a result, secured creditors are allegedly taking more and broader security interests than previously.

Article 9 reduces the costs of becoming secured primarily by relaxing legal requirements for creating liens. An agreement to give a security interest ordinarily must be written, but the writing need contain only language of grant and a description of the collateral. The description, moreover, must only "reasonably identify what is described." The code also reduces the cost of giving public notice of the existence of a security interest. The secured party must file in a public record office a "financing statement," but this document only has to identify and give the addresses of the secured party and debtor and again "reasonably" describe the collateral.

Significantly, article 9 also reduces the costs of taking security interests in "after-acquired property." A creditor who lends on the basis of inventory or accounts receivable is lending on a wasting asset because the inventory or accounts existing when the loan was made will soon disappear. Pre-code law sometimes required a secured party to give public notice of its interest in each new item of collateral as the debtor received it, a costly requirement with such rapid turnover items as inventory and accounts. The code, however, allows a financing statement to be effective notice of a creditor's interest in collateral existing when the credit was extended and in "after-acquired" collateral. Further, the new Bankruptcy Act, settling a dispute that existed under prior law, makes security interests in after-acquired property commonly enforceable in bankruptcy if the property is inventory or accounts. Most security interests in after-acquired property are in collateral of this kind. In addition, article 9 makes a financing statement effective for five years from the date of filing. Thus, if a particular debt is fully paid, the creditor commonly can make another loan without giving a second public notice or obtaining a new security agreement. These provisions of the code and the Bankruptcy Act rest on the premise that secured debt increases welfare, and they implement this premise by making secured debt much less costly to buy. Further, because secured creditors come first in bankruptcy liquidations, the code reforms significantly advantage secured at the expense of unsecured debt.

II. *Efficiency Explanations of Short-Term Secured Debt*

A. *The Problem*

Firms issue and creditors buy secured debt when the private gains from doing so exceed the costs. An efficiency explanation of secured debt must show when this is so and also that the social gains from security exceed the social costs. The conventional efficiency story is that high risk firms prefer issuing security because it enables them to borrow, and creditors prefer buying it because it enables them to make loans they otherwise would refuse. Security has these properties because it reduces the risks of creditors in the event of default, largely by allowing the secured party to take the property subject to its security interest and sell it to reduce or eliminate the debt. As we have seen, the power to seize and sell often survives the debtor's bankruptcy.

This conventional story seems unpersuasive if creditors (i) can learn of and react to the existence of security; (ii) can calculate risks of default reasonably precisely; (iii) are risk-neutral; and (iv) have homogeneous expectations respecting default probabilities. To see why this is so, it is helpful to consider more precisely just how secured financing reduces a creditor's risks. A lender that extends credit on an unsecured basis looks not only to the debtor's earning capacity for repayment but also to the debtor's assets. When a creditor becomes secured, however, certain (or all) assets of the debtor are set aside to help insure that this creditor is paid; in consequence, its chance of collecting its debt are much increased. And when these assets are removed from the general pool, the chance that the debtor's unsecured creditors will collect their debts correspondingly decreases. If all creditors are informed, the secured creditor will charge a lower interest rate because it is secured, whereas the unsecured creditors will charge higher interest rates because the pool of assets available to satisfy their claims has shrunk. The debtor's total interest bill is thus unaffected by the existence of security. Since the issuance of secured debt is itself costly, however, the debtor would be worse off with security than without it. Firms would never sell secured debt.

[Prof. Schwartz proceeds to discuss other efficiency explanations for secured credit—monitoring costs, debt as a signal, staggering of debt, and risk aversion—and finds them equally unpersuasive. He then discusses distributional explanations in the following extract and concludes with a discussion of the normative implications of his analysis.]

IV. *Normative Implications and a Research Agenda*

Parts II and III of this paper argue that no convincing explanation for the issuance of short-term secured debt exists; it is not known with assurance whether security is efficient, as some explanations of its existence assert, or inefficient, as the signalling and distributional explanations suggest is possible. With the record in this state, it may seem appropriate for a decision maker to pursue whatever normative views respecting bankruptcy liquidations he happens to hold. In particular, since Congress has already selected a set of creditors for special treatment, the priority of these creditors perhaps should be raised above that of secured parties, on the ground that a good case for subordinating them has yet to be made. Such an action, or others actuated by similar motives, would now be premature because satisfactory normative reasons for altering current law are also hard to find. In consequence, this part first explores the implications of law reform that follow from a rejection of the efficiency justification for the current bankruptcy priority list. It next illustrates the difficulties that make significant law reform unwise at present and concludes with a brief summary of the important unresolved positive and normative issues respecting bankruptcy liquidations.

A. *Possible Reforms*

Suppose that the assumption of creditor knowledge and ability to react to security is partially false, that some creditors are disadvantaged by firm failures they can neither foresee nor avoid. Two reforms are then implied: to prohibit security or make it much more difficult to take, or to elevate the priority status in bankruptcy liquidations of particular creditor groups. The former reform is unwise. Secured debt has not been shown to be inefficient; the signalling and distributional explanations indicate only that inefficiency is conceivable. Thus significantly reducing the opportunity to take security seems precipitate. Further, creditors and firms are likely to want a good deal of security even at higher cost levels, as they did before the code. Reducing the costs to many parties of doing what they would do anyway thus will produce some gains. Finally, any harm that secured debt generates will fall heaviest on particular unsecured creditors. The freedom of firms and secured creditors is maximized if these commercial parties are unregulated but those disadvantaged by security are helped directly. All these reasons suggest that the cost-reducing innovations of article 9 should be preserved even if the assumption of creditor knowledge is sometimes false.

The appropriate response to creditor ignorance is to elevate the priority status of those creditors thought deserving of help. At present, secured parties are paid in full, to the extent of their security interests, before *any* other creditors are paid. Any effort at law reform should alter this priority list: consumers, employees, small-trade creditors, tort claimants, or any others whom Congress wants to favor should be paid first, either in full or up to statutorily created levels. Such a reform would increase the costs of secured debt. Secured creditors would be able to realize less on default, and greater uncertainty would attend the use of security since secured creditors would have difficulty predicting the extent to which they may later be subordinated. Nevertheless, revising priorities is preferable to increasing the costs of secured debt in other ways. Priority revision helps directly those thought deserving of help and gives firms and secured creditors more freedom in arranging their affairs.

B. *Issues to Be Resolved Before Revising the Priority List*

That distributional or other normative objectives should be pursued more vigorously in bankruptcy contexts fails to follow from a showing that security conceivably is inefficient. An affirmative law reform case must be made because pursuit of any such case is expensive. The case for revising priorities seems strongest when particular creditors are unaware of or cannot react to security. In this circumstance, firms and sophisticated creditors use secured debt with the possible intention and certain effect of redistributing wealth to themselves and from creditors who would prevent these redistributions were they informed. Notions of corrective justice imply a remedy for the disadvantaged creditors in this circumstance. A theory of corrective justice provides that a plaintiff cannot prevail against a defendant unless the defendant has wrongfully harmed some interest of the plaintiff. Such a theory must therefore identify which interests "belong to" or are "owned" by the plaintiff as well as what actions "wrongfully" harm these interests. Corrective justice theorists give content to the concepts of interest and wrongs by reference both to moral theories and to widely shared moral sentiments. In issues of bankruptcy priority, most moral entities protected interests in property. When wealth is redistributed from inept or uninformed creditors, their interests prima facie have been invaded. Further, the moral sentiments of ordinary persons might consider the invasion to be wrongful, for it reflects the disadvantaging of the weak by the strong. Thus corrective justice could require unsophisticated or ignorant creditors to have a remedy against the firms and secured creditors that harmed them.

The case for corrective justice does not seem compelling because ordinary persons probably would not regard security as wrongful in the same sense that fraud or theft is, particularly since secured parties and firms sometimes may fail to realize that they are inflicting harm on other creditors. Also, the harm done often seems relatively slight. A decision maker deciding whether to recognize a right on corrective justice grounds is entitled to consider the consequences that recognition would entail. If security were shown to be efficient in the Kaldor-Hicks sense, this efficiency would count against a corrective justice right to a revised priority list, because pursuit of this right would raise the costs and thus reduce the gains from security. But a persuasive showing of efficiency has not been made and in its absence a decision maker could justifiably pursue the plausible corrective justice case for revising bankruptcy priorities.

Before acting on this case, however, the factual accuracy of its premises must be shown, not asserted. This is a difficult task. Plausibly establishing the incompetence of contracting parties, such as the employees and consumers at issue here, is hard to do. The incompetence of employees is especially problematic when, as often happens, the employees are organized in unions. Further, it is not enough to show that *some* of these parties are uninformed, because markets can work well in the face of substantial numbers of uninformed persons. The informed employees and consumers in some cases may police the market sufficiently to ensure that wages and prices accurately reflect the existence of security. Thus the seemingly plausible corrective justice case for revising bankruptcy priorities is in fact premature because the circumstances in which it would apply have yet to be established.

When this case is inapplicable, a persuasive normative argument for revising bankruptcy priorities seem hard to find. Consider "small-trade" creditors, who supposedly are among the class disadvantaged by current law. These creditors must now be assumed able to anticipate bankruptcy and learn of security, for such creditors would otherwise be injured by security in the way the corrective justice case supposes. But if these assumptions were true, the small-trade creditors would be compensated for bearing the risk of a low priority status in bankruptcy because the cost of this risk would be an element of the market price that their buyers must pay. The trade creditors would seem to need no help from the state in this circumstance. Further, if bankruptcy priorities were revised, the costs to banks and finance companies of extending credit would be raised, with the result that these entities might make fewer loans. This outcome would disadvantage the employees and shareholders of the banks and finance companies. On the information that now exists, it is difficult to say that these persons are less "deserving" than the persons who own or work for the small-trade creditors. No normative ground for revising bankruptcy priorities thus seems apparent except the corrective justice case.

C. *Issues That Deserve Study*

The normative desirability of any bankruptcy priority list cannot be convincingly established on the basis of current knowledge. The conventional view that article 9 of the Uniform Commercial Code and the Bankruptcy Act strike a desirable balance between the interests of secured and unsecured creditors thus is seriously deficient. Before accepting it or any other conclusion, research should be done on the following issues: (i) Can explanations of the existence of secured debt be developed that are testable and account for much of the observed data? (ii) The observed data is largely the product of casual empiricism. Would rigorous empirical work confirm theories that now seem questionable or indicate possibilities of new theories? (iii) When do the factual premises of the corrective justice case hold? (iv) Apart from this case, can a coherent normative argument for revising the bankruptcy priority list be made?

Conclusion

Present bankruptcy law provides that secured parties are to be paid first and in full before any other creditors of an insolvent debtor are paid at all. The principal justification for this priority list is that short-term secured debt is efficient and thus its purchase should be as convenient as possible. This justification has not been proved; no plausible showing that secured debt actually increases welfare exists. Further, firms in some circumstances may issue such debt to redistribute wealth to themselves from just those persons to whom standard distributional rationales would accord special treatment. If, in light of these conclusions, different normative concerns should be pursued in bankruptcy liquidations, the appropriate method for doing so is to elevate the priority status of those thought to require more favorable treatment. But these conclusions do not themselves support such a course. That the efficiency justification for present law is problematic means only that other concerns should become relevant, not paramount. Attention should now focus on whether the efficiency justification can be made persuasive and whether attractive normative cases for particular bankruptcy priority lists can be made out. Inquiries for this sort, it may be remarked, probably are appropriate in related contexts as well because positivist explanations of several other legally relevant financial practices also seem relatively undeveloped.

NOTES AND QUESTIONS

1) Prof. Schwartz's challenge has been taken up by subsequent lawyer economists who have argued that secured credit can be justified on efficiency grounds. See, *inter alia*, White, "Efficiency Justification for Personal Property Security" (1984), 37 *Vand. L Rev.*, 473; Buckley, "The Bankruptcy Priority Puzzle" (1986), 72 *Virg. L Rev.* 1393; Scott, "A Relational Theory of Secured Financing" (1986), 86 *Col. L Rev.* 901; and Shupack,

"Solving the Puzzle of Secured Transactions" (1989), 41 *Rutg. L Rev.* 1067. For a recent contrary critique see Lynn M. LoPucki, "The Unsecured Creditor's Bargain" (1994), 80 *Va. L Rev.* 1887.

2) Practising lawyers, particularly those acting for secured creditors, have so far shown little interest in such theoretical speculations. To the extent that they feel called upon to justify secured debt at all, they do so on very pragmatic and "common sense" grounds. A good example is the following extract from a chapter written by a Toronto practitioner.

John Varley
"Receivership: The Contest Between Secured and General Creditors"
Debtor-Creditor Law: Practice and Doctrine, 1985
(Springman and Gertner, ed.), 424, at 434-35

The business justification would appear to be that secured lenders are those who, normally, are providing the basic capital and operating funds that enable the corporation to buy its assets—to build or buy its plant, equipment, and machinery, to purchase its inventory and raw materials, and to spread the gap between its receivables and its payables. He who pays for it should get first crack at it as a source of repayment. Moreover, secured financing would be permanent or at least medium-term support, which is kept current by interest payments, but as to which principal repayments are gradual or incidental. To induce that longer-term lending, some assurance must be given that ultimate repayment is likely—that there is a source from which repayment can be (more or less) guaranteed. Thus, specific security is taken—both as protection if enforced liquidation becomes required, but also to provide for reporting requirements, financial tests, stipulated ratios, events of default, and the like, which might provide an early warning system which, if heeded, could make actual enforcement unnecessary. Reminding the customer of ultimate enforcement rights sometimes, in my experience, does wonders for a banker seeking more updated financial statements, inside management information, and some role in planning business reorganizations. Full security is also effective, as Professor Goode notes, in restraining "a trigger-happy unsecured creditor seeking to steal a march on his less aggressive brethren" when what the company needs is a moratorium to reorganize, and imposes "a useful discipline" on the debtor company. (See, Goode, "Is the Law Too Favourable to Secured Creditors?" (1983-84), 8 *CBLJ* 53 at 56.) Thus, there are quite a number of commercially justifiable functions performed by the existing regime of secured creditor rights, quite apart from the need for eventual liquidation potential. In fact, if one questioned a banker, he would likely reply that it is bad banking practice to lend in reliance on realization recovery potentials, since "any security should be regarded as a last line of defence to fall back upon in exceptional circumstances only. (See Milnes Holden, *The Law and Practice of Banking* (6th ed., 1980), vol. 1, paras. 1-3.) Nonetheless, no banker can ignore the crucial need for realization protection when insolvency occurs.

Unsecured credit is of a different quality. Although each situation will have its own variations, unsecured debt is most likely to be short-term (thirty, sixty, or ninety days) trade credit or float credit (between employee deductions and forwarding of those deductions to Revenue Canada, deposits on future deliveries, etc.). The creditor does not expect to make a permanent contribution to the company's balance sheet and has no obligation to refrain from pressing for payment immediately after his terms of trade have been exceeded. The entire relationship may be quite ephemeral. Suppliers might prefer to be in a long-term contractual relationship with their customers, but in fact the purchasing company is free to vary its sources, and buys goods, or services, from innumerable different sources, subject to franchise and similar tied arrangements and to the breadth of any particular supply market. Formalization of a relationship in the manner appropriate with its bankers is, by and large, impractical and inefficient for trade credit. If the relationship does become long-term, or of large magnitude, then security becomes appropriate for trade creditors as well.

3) Is the line between long-term credit and short-term trade credit or floating credit as easily drawn as Mr. Varley implies? Where do employees, landlords and public utilities fit in? Do these creditors not have long-term relationships with the debtor? Do they not contribute in a very important way to the "company's (debtor's) balance sheet." Can they been seen as providing credit on a 30, 60 or 90 day basis? Can they terminate relationships with the debtors as easily as an *ad hoc* supplier of services or small value goods?

4) Does Mr. Varley's contention that "[h]e who pays for it should get first crack at it as a source of repayment" justify the now very common use by banks of security agreements providing for a security interest in all of the debtor's present and future-acquired personal property? In any event, the author's explanation does not accommodate the fact that there may be several credit grantors who provide long-term credit support to a business. Does his approach not suggest some type of pro-rating of the debtor's assets held as collateral if there is not enough to pay all secured creditors?

5) Long-term lenders are not the only inventory financers. All secured inventory suppliers are given a special priority under the PPSA if they satisfy the statutory requirements. See OPPSA ss. 1(1) "purchase-money security interest," 31, 32, 33(1). Do the creditors falling within these sections also fall into the category of long-term credit grantors?

6) The evidence does not justify the conclusion that lenders holding broadly based security interests use the power thereby acquired to protect the debtor against trigger-happy creditors who proceed against the debtor "when what is needed is a moratorium to reorganize." Indeed, the Supreme Court of Canada has enunciated a doctrine, the so-called rule in *Lister v. Dunlop* [1982] 1 SCR 726, to control trigger-happy banks and other lenders holding such security interests. (This rule is examined in detail in a later chapter.)

7) A legal argument favouring the traditional approach to the recognition of security interests is that the principle of freedom of contract dictates that a potential creditor should be free to bargain for a preference over other creditors, and that a prospective debtor should be free to confer by contract a preference on a creditor so long as the debtor obtains value and a "fraudulent preference" is not involved. See generally, Goode, "Is the Law Too Favourable to Secured Creditors?" (1983-84), 8 *CBLJ* 53. If, as is the case, the legal system requires adequate disclosure of a security interest, there can be no objection. A lender is under no obligation to supply credit. If credit is provided, the creditor is free to make contractual arrangements that reflect the additional risk assumed by advancing unsecured or subordinate credit. However, do all unsecured creditors have the choice to deal or not to deal with a debtor or the bargaining power to obtain a premium that reflects the added risk they undertake? Consider the position of a judgment creditor for damages resulting from tortious conduct of the debtor or the position of employees of the debtor.

8) A corollary of the freedom to contract rule is that the first creditor to obtain an executed security agreement should have first priority. Accordingly (it may be argued), the

rule precludes any special priority rules based on a public policy choice of one type of credit grantor over the other.

9) The traditional view of the relationship between secured and unsecured creditors is not universally accepted. Consider the following:

The Bank Act
SC 1991, c. 46, s. 427

Section 427 ...

(7) Notwithstanding subsection (2) and notwithstanding that a notice of intention by a person giving security on property under this section has been registered pursuant to this section, where, under the *Bankruptcy Act*, a receiving order is made against, or an assignment is made by, that person,

(a) claims for wages, salaries or other remuneration owing in respect of the period of three months next preceding the making of such order or assignment, to employees of the person employed in connection with the business or farm in respect of which the property covered by the security was held or acquired by the person, and

(b) claims of a grower or producer of products of agriculture for money owing by a manufacturer to the grower or producer for such products that were grown or produced by the grower or producer on land owned or leased by the grower or producer and that were delivered to the manufacturer during the period of six months next preceding the making of such order or assignment to the extent of the lesser of

(i) the total amount of the claims of the grower or producer therefor, and

(ii) the amount determined by multiplying by one thousand one hundred dollars the most recent annual average Index Number of Farm Prices of Agricultural Products for Canada published by Statistics Canada at the time the receiving order or claim is made,

have priority to the rights of the bank in a security given to the bank under this section, in the order in which they are mentioned herein, and if the bank takes possession or in any way disposes of the property covered by the security, the bank is liable for such claims to the extent of the net amount realized on the disposition of such property, after deducting the cost of realization, and the bank is subrogated in and to all the rights of the claimants to the extent of the amounts paid to them by the bank.

For an example of the same approach used in the context of provincial personal property security legislation, see the Labour Standards Act, RSS 1978, c. L-1, s. 56, which gives priority to unpaid wages over "every interest, lien, charge, encumbrance, mortgage, assignment, including an assignment of book debts, debenture or other security, whether perfected within the meaning of The Personal Property Security Act or not, made or given, accepted or issued before or after the wages accrued due ... ." The deemed security interest for wages, however, does not have priority over a purchase-money security interest taken prior to the time the wages became accruing due.

Note on Consumer Protection

The PPSA contains a few provisions that recognize the imbalance in bargaining power that often exists between parties to a secured credit transaction. Part V, which regulates rights and remedies in the event of default by a debtor, leaves little room for freedom of contract.

While the parties may include clauses in their agreements dealing with the consequences of default, for the most part such clauses are ineffective. (See OPPSA s. 59(5).) However, apart from a few provisions (OPPSA ss. 12(2)(b), 45(2), 51(5) and 65(1) and 66(2)), the Act leaves consumer protection to other legislation. In cases of conflict between the Act and the Consumer Protection Act (CPA), the latter prevails (OPPSA s. 73). There are instances of conflict between the OPPSA and the CPA. Compare the following: Consumer Protection Act, RSO 1990, c. C.31, s. 22, and OPPSA ss. 9 and 13(1); Consumer Protection Act s. 23 and OPPSA ss. 61(1) and 65(1).

THE STRUCTURE OF THE ONTARIO ACT

Structure and Terminology

The OPPSA is divided into seven parts preceded by a definition section (s. 1):

Part I (ss. 2-8) "Application and Conflict of Laws," deals with the scope of the Act and conflict of laws rules.

Part II (ss. 9-18) "Validity of Security Agreements and Rights of Parties," deals with the creation of the security interest.

Part III (ss. 19-40) "Perfection and Priorities," deals with the steps required to make a security interest effective against a third party and with the priority rules among competing security interests or between a security interest and a third party.

Part IV (ss. 41-57) "Registration," provides for a province-wide unified system for the registration of financing statements.

Part V (ss. 58-66) "Default Rights and Remedies," sets out the secured party's rights and remedies on the debtor's default.

Part VI (ss. 67-74) "Miscellaneous," deals with judicial supervision of the exercise of rights and remedies given by the Act, compensation for non-compliance with statutory requirements, service of notices, what constitutes knowledge, interface with other statutes, and regulation-making powers.

Part VII (ss. 75-86) "Application, Transition, Amendments, Repeals, Commencement" deals with the transition from prior registry statutes, an amendment to the Execution Act relating to the seizure of security interests and the repeal of Acts replaced by the new Act.

The PPSA introduces into the legal lexicon of personal property security law a few new terms (for example, OPPSA, "attach," s. 11, "perfected," s. 19) that are undefined. It gives statutory definition to other terms which had been in general use in secured financing arrangements but which had no legal meaning [for example, OPPSA, s. 1(1) "chattel paper," "proceeds," "purchase-money security interest," and "security interest." Other commonly used terms (for example, OPPSA, s. 1(1) "consumer goods," "debtor," "equipment," and "inventory") have been converted into legal terms of art].

Since the PPSA was designed to implement a highly integrated, structurally complete system of law for the regulation of personal property security transactions, a proper understanding of it requires careful attention to the meanings ascribed by the Act to the key words used in its provisions.

The Personal Property Registry

A central feature of the OPPSA is protection of third parties who may deal with a debtor in the mistaken belief that personal property in the possession or control of such a debtor is unencumbered by security interests. One, and by far the most important, of the measures prescribed by the Act for this purpose is to require public disclosure of the existence or potential existence of security interests as a prerequisite to recognition of the priority of these interests over competitive claims to the property in which the interests are held. This approach is not new; the province of Canada established a registry for chattel mortgages taken in Upper Canada as far back as 1849. However, the system prescribed by the PPSA for public disclosure of security interests is modern and, compared with the systems it displaced, efficient but necessarily complex. The details of its structure and the rules which must be met by secured parties seeking perfection of their interests by registration are set out in Part IV (OPPSA ss. 41-57) of the Act and in the Regulations under the OPPSA (RRO 1990, Reg. 912). See also BC Reg. 279/90, as amended; Alta. Reg. 234/90, as amended; Man. Regs. 268/85 and 323/87R. The regulations for the New Brunswick and Saskatchewan Acts were not available at the date of publication.

Classification of Collateral

(All references are to the OPPSA.)

With several minor exceptions (see ss. 4(1)(c), 4(1)(d), 4(1)(e)), the OPPSA encompasses security interests in all types of personal property [collateral—s. 1(1)]. However, different rules apply to different types of collateral. Note the relevance of collateral type in the context of the following:

- Conflicts of laws (see ss. 5(1), 5(2)).
- Consumer protection (see ss. 12(2)(b), 45(2), 51(5) and 65(1) and 66(2)).
- Perfection by possession (see s. 22).
- Perfection by registration (see s. 23 and Regs. 3(1), 3(7)-(13)).
- Temporary perfection (see s. 24).
- Special priority rules (see, for example, ss. 28, 33, 34 and 35).
- Default rights and remedies (see ss. 61 and 62(b)).

Special attention should be directed to the ways in which the Act deals with goods collateral. (See chart, *infra*.) Note that the classification of goods as consumer goods, inventory or equipment does not depend upon any essential characteristic of the goods involved but upon the use being made of the goods at the relevant time by the debtor in possession. Accordingly, a truck would be "consumer goods" if used by the debtor for personal, family or household purposes; "inventory" if held by the debtor for sale or lease; or "equipment" if it is being used by the debtor as other than "consumer goods" or "equipment." Note too that under the OPPSA regulations goods may be described on a financing statement (and, therefore, in the computerized record of the registry) according to the use being made of the goods by the debtor. See Regulation 3(1)(f). Under the Acts based on the CCPPSL model, with the exception of inventory, goods must be described specifically or generically. See, e.g., BC Reg. s. 13. The significance of this difference is addressed in a later chapter.

Classification of Collateral

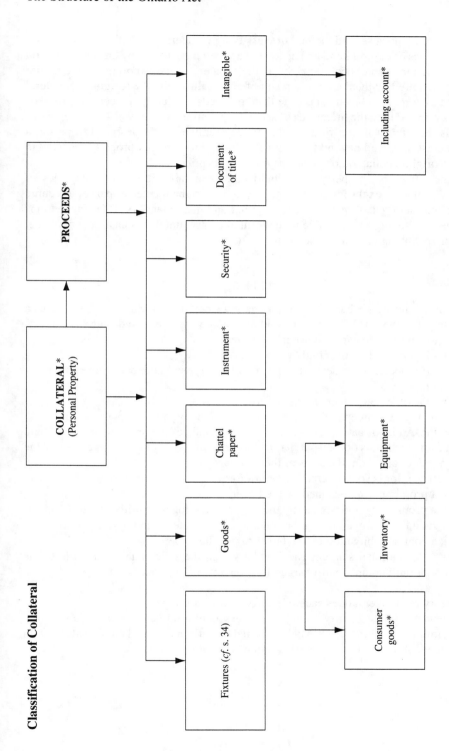

Note: The terms marked with an asterisk (*) are defined in section 1 of the OPPSA.

The PPSA adopts a second method of classifying collateral—a method based not on the characteristics of the collateral and not on the use being made of it by the debtor, but on the way in which the debtor acquires rights in the collateral. Personal property or a fixture in any form acquired by the debtor as a result of any dealing with the (original) collateral is described as "proceeds" in s. 1(1). Note that "proceeds" includes proceeds of proceeds (sometimes referred to in the literature as "second generation proceeds"). This category of collateral is the subject matter of a special priority regime (s. 25) designed to permit a security interest to extend beyond the original collateral to personal property received in place of the original collateral or in part payment of its price.

In some situations, property that would otherwise fall within two categories of collateral is limited by exclusion to one category. An instrument taken as part of a secured instalment contract ("chattel paper" s. 1(1)) is not an "instrument" (s. 1(1)) for the purposes of the Act. Again, an intangible in the form of an account that is an aspect of chattel paper is not an "intangible" or an "account" (s. 1(1)).

PROBLEMS

1) A car dealer uses a bank loan to purchase a stock of new cars. The bank takes a security interest in the cars. The cars are sold on secured credit by the dealer as follows:

     a) to a businessperson for use in a business;

     b) to an individual for family purposes;

     c) to a doctor for use partly for family purposes and partly in his or her profession;

     d) to another car dealer for the purpose of resale;

     e) to a rental company for the purpose of renting out to customers.

What is the PPSA classification (i) of the cars in the hands of the original car dealer; and (ii) of each car in the hands of each purchaser? Describe the types of proceeds collateral the car dealer might obtain from the sales of the new cars.

2) A refrigerator is sold on credit in return for:

     a) a promissory note signed by the buyer;

     b) a promissory note signed by the buyer, taken together with a security agreement signed by the buyer giving the seller a security interest in the refrigerator;

     c) a contract obligation by the buyer to pay the price;

     d) a "conditional sale contract" under which the seller retains full title to the refrigerator until complete discharge of the buyer's obligation;

     e) cash.

What category of collateral does each of the five items fall into?

3) A lender takes a security interest in the assets of a farmer including dairy cows, beef cattle, milking machinery, grain held to be fed to cattle, and grain held for sale to grain buyers. Categorize the collateral for registration and priority purposes.

CHAPTER TWO

The Scope of the Act

INTRODUCTION

The scope of the PPSA is stated in very broad and imprecise terms. Essentially, OPPSA s. 2 states that the Act applies to every transaction that "creates" an interest in personal property or a fixture that secures payment or performance of an obligation. A closer look at s. 2 reveals some important, albeit essentially negative, information concerning the types of transactions falling within the regulatory regime of the Act. It is clear that the form of a transaction is not a relevant factor. Accordingly, the fact that a transaction is in the form of a lease in which the parties are described as lessor and lessee and the payment obligations of the lessee are described as rental payments, is not determinative. Nor, according to s. 2, is the locus of title a factor. One of the traditional common law tests that distinguishes a secured sale transaction from a hiring contract is whether or not title is transferred from one party to the other; if no title passes, a contract of bailment, not of sale, is involved. See *Helby v. Matthews*, [1895] AC 471, reproduced in volume I of this casebook, chapter 2. However, this test is now irrelevant in determining whether or not a transaction is a security agreement. The rejection of title as a characterization factor means that a debtor can create a security interest in personal property without transferring a "title" to the secured party. If the secured party does not get "title" what is the nature of the interest acquired by it?

The broad, general description of the scope of the Act contained in OPPSA s. 2 has been, and will continue to be, a source of difficulty, at least on the periphery. Some of these problems are explored in the following pages.

What Is "Personal Property"?—The Ontario Production Licence Imbroglio

Re Foster
(1992), 89 DLR (4th) 555 (Gen. Div.)

D. LANE J: Frederick L. Foster obtained a standard taxi-cab owner's licence from the City of Mississauga. The original date of issue was November 2, 1987. Under the by-laws of Mississauga such a licence is not transferable in the first three years after issue except by petition to city council. Foster was evidently in financial difficulties because he obtained money against this licence from no fewer than four persons in 1988 and 1989, before making an assignment in bankruptcy on October 22, 1990, just 11 days before the licence would have become transferable as of right. Each of the four persons filed documentation on this motion evidencing the terms on which he dealt with Foster.

• • •

Question 1

Is the licence property for the purposes of the PPSA?

Any agreement which creates a security interest over personal property falls within the ambit of the PPSA and, if not validly perfected under that Act, is subordinate to the interest of a trustee in bankruptcy, so that the security holder is in the position of an ordinary creditor: see s. 20(1)(b) PPSA. Is the cab owner's licence personal property within the meaning of the PPSA and thus capable of registration under that Act? There is no hard and fast rule as to the nature of a business or professional licence. It appears that the characterization of such a licence depends on the extent to which the licence holder can be said to have been granted a vested right on the one hand; or a privilege wholly dependent on the discretion of the issuing Ministry or regulatory body on the other hand. No case law dealing specifically with whether interests in taxi owners' licences are registrable under the PPSA was cited to me.

The question of whether a licence to carry on the business of tobacco-growing was property for the purposes of the PPSA was addressed by the Court of Appeal in *National Trust Co. v. Bouckhuyt* (1987), 43 DLR (4th) 543, 38 BLR 77, 61 OR (2d) 640. Under the *Farm Products Marketing Act*, RSO 1980, c. 158, tobacco farming was regulated by means of assigning individual growers a "basic production quota" (BPQ). The system is fully described in the trial judgment at 39 DLR (4th) 60 at pp. 83-4, 7 PPSAC 113, 59 OR (2d) 556.

The BPQ did not entitle the holder to grow tobacco. Rather it was a fixed allotment which entitled the holder to apply annually to the board for a licence to produce an annual production quota which was a percentage of the BPQ. The only right conferred was this right to apply. The evidence was that there was a market for BPQ's but they could not be directly transferred from seller to buyer. Instead seller and buyer jointly applied to the board to cancel the seller's BPQ and allot it to the buyer. The trial judge (pp. 85-6) was of the view that the existence of a commercial market, plus what he saw as a power in the court to compel the board to act to comply with the joint application, combined to create a species of intangible personal property which was subject to the PPSA. The Court of Appeal disagreed, holding that the right conferred was too transitory and ephemeral to be considered property. Cory JA, for the court, concluded, at pp. 550-2:

The regulations do indeed control each and every aspect of the production, sale and marketing of tobacco in Ontario. For example, the regulations provide for the licensing of all persons who are engaged in the producing or marketing of tobacco. As well, no one can produce or market tobacco without such a licence. The regulations provide for the fixing and allotting by the Tobacco Board of quotas for the marketing of tobacco. The Tobacco Board can refuse to fix or allot to any person such a quota and may cancel or reduce or refuse to increase a quota. No one can market tobacco in excess of the quota which has been allotted. The board regulations go so far as to provide for the seizure, removal or destruction of tobacco which has been produced in violation of the regulations to the BPQ. In sum, the control exercised by the Tobacco Board is absolute and complete.

It is true that the BPQ may be leased and, in a rather peculiar form, it may be transferred and pledged. This is accomplished by the board first cancelling the BPQ and then reissuing it to the purchaser. This same formula is utilized for the leasing from year to year of a quota. However, what is of paramount significance is that all transactions pertaining to the BPQ are made subject to the approval of the board and are subject to the unfettered discretion of the board.

There may well be a market for BPQs among licensed producers of tobacco. However, the BPQ, and its allotment, reduction and cancellation are at the complete discretion of the Tobacco Board. The very essence of the authorizing legislation and the regulations passed pursuant to it is the control of every aspect of the industry. That control is, as it must be, based upon the control of the quotas themselves. The Act and regulations are such that a tobacco crop cannot even be produced in the absence of a licence and a quota (BPQ). In fact, it is apparent from the Act and regulations that to grow tobacco without such licence or quota would be illegal. The BPQ is thus no more than the manifestation of permission to do that which is otherwise prohibited by statute and regulation; the BPQ represents the granting of a privilege. It is by its nature subject to such discretionary control and is so transitory and ephemeral in its nature that it cannot, in my view, be considered to be property.

The notion of "property" imports the right to exclude others from the enjoyment of, interference with or appropriation of a specific legal right. This is distinct from a revocable licence, which simply enables a person to do lawfully what he could not otherwise do ...

• • •

Although the BPQ might be sold in a limited market, the mere fact that it could be exchanged, sold, pledged or leased does not in itself make it property.

Bouckhuyt was referred to (albeit in *obiter*) by Anderson J in *209991 Ontario Ltd. v. Canadian Imperial Bank of Commerce* (1988), 39 BLR 44, 24 CPC (2d) 248, 8 PPSAC 135 (Ont. HCJ). That case dealt with the issue of whether a security interest could be created over a nursing home licence through a mortgage instrument. At p. 54:

I have already said that it is not strictly necessary that I decide this issue. However, I think similar reasoning is applicable to the nursing home licence. Under s. 3 of the *Nursing Home Act*, RSO 1980, c. 320, no one may operate a nursing home without a licence, the granting and renewal of which is subject to the discretion of the Director appointed by the Minister of Health. Although it is not an "unfettered" discretion as in *Bouckhuyt*, the Director has a wide discretion in deciding whether a licence should issue and whether a licence should be revoked or renewed. Thus, the nursing home licence can also be characterized as a privilege, granted at the discretion of the Board, to do that which is otherwise prohibited.

His Lordship also emphasized in the judgment the fact that the nursing home licence was not transferable.

In the context of real property assessment, the Ontario Court of Appeal ruled that licences issued under the *Nursing Home Act* were not personal property in *Re Restfulcare Inc. and Regional Assessment Commissioner* (1986), 25 DLR (4th) 477 at pp. 479-80, 53 OR (2d) 673. The decision was largely based on the facts that the licence was not transferable, had *per se* no market value and was in effect attached to the premises for which it was issued. Hence the value of the licence was not to be deducted from the value of the enterprise to arrive at the value of the land alone.

The reasoning in *Bouckhuyt* was discussed by another panel of the Ontario Court of Appeal in *Canadian Imperial Bank of Commerce v. Hallahan* (1990), 69 DLR (4th) 449, 48 BLR 113, 1 PPSAC (2d) 58; leave to appeal to SCC refused 74 DLR (4th) viii, 49 BLR 320*n*, 46 OAC 237*n*. The court ruled that the transfer of an assigned milk quota could not be considered a fraudulent conveyance under the *Fraudulent Conveyances Act*. The parties agreed that essentially the criteria for determining what constitutes "property" under the PPSA were identical to those under the *Fraudulent Conveyances Act*. At pp. 451-2 of the judgment:

We were asked to overrule *National Trust v. Bouckhuyt* but we are not disposed to do so. That decision is a recent one and was reached after careful consideration of the relevant authorities and statutes. It could not be described as rendered *per incuriam*.

It occurs to us, however, that it would be useful to have *Bouckhuyt* reconsidered. It seems to us that the court placed too much emphasis on traditional definitions of personal property and did not give enough consideration to the realities of commercial transactions within the regulatory framework of a modern farm products marketing scheme. *Bouckhuyt* may well be correct in its result in that the issue was whether the transfer to National Trust created an interest which the Board was bound to recognize. The Board could never recognize that interest because National Trust was not a producer. In the case at bar there is no question that the inter-family transfer was valid on its face and was routinely approved by the Board. The issue was whether that transfer amounted to a fraudulent conveyance. If the reasoning in *Bouckhuyt* as to what constitutes personal property had been more narrowly focused, it might have permitted a finding that the transfer of quota from Hallahan to Lazy Meadows was in law a fraudulent preference within the meaning of the two statutes for the protection of creditors.

•   •   •

What this case law reveals is a tension between the commercial reality that licences, like any commodity in restricted supply, have a value and may be traded, and the legal impact of the legislator's desire to maintain, in varying degrees, control over the industry in question. Where the control is absolute and unfettered, no property interest exists even though there is a market: *Bouckhuyt*; *Sanders*; where there is a market and a practical, historical assurance of renewal, the licensee has a right akin to a chose in action, and hence property: *Johnson*; *Ackerman*. It is obvious from all the cases that the regulatory framework is a decisive factor.

The governing Ontario authorities are *Bouckhuyt* and *Hallahan*. The essence of *Bouckhuyt*, what Cory JA called "of paramount significance," is the fact that all transactions pertaining to the BPQ were subject to the unfettered discretion of the board. It was this feature that rendered the BPQ too transitory and ephemeral to be considered to be property. This is a theme that runs through many of the cases and is, I think, central to the issue I have before me. The essence of *Hallahan* is the need to have regard to "... the realities of commercial transactions within the regulatory framework ..." [at pp. 451-2], as well as to the considerations enunciated in *Bouckhuyt*. The present question therefore is whether the degree of discretion exercisable by the Mississauga City Council in connection with the renewal, leasing or transfer of taxi-cab owners' licences is so great that notwithstanding the commercial reality that they are traded, such licences are nevertheless too ephemeral and transitory to be regarded as property. I do not include the discretion exercised in issuing the licence in the first place in this analysis because that does not affect the permanence or lack of permanence of the licence once granted.

I turn therefore to an analysis of the city's bylaws.

The regulations concerning taxi owners' licences are set out in By-law 142-89: s. 9 provides the licensing prerequisites for a taxicab owner. These include possession of a driver's licence; a valid motor vehicle permit; vehicle insurance, and vehicle safety approval.

Section 14 of the by-law sets out the terms for licence issuance or renewal:

· · ·

Schedule 6 to the by-law deals with procedure on transfer of taxi-cab owners' licences. It requires that the owner provide a copy of the contract of sale; return the licence being transferred, and file a form with the city.

Upon the death of a taxi-cab owner licensee, s. 68 provides that the licence becomes an asset of the estate of the deceased owner which may hold it for up to a year and dispose of it to a person qualified to hold it.

A number of aspects of this by-law are of importance. First, it specifically contemplates transfer including leases and sub-leases, and after the first three years imposes no restriction on transfer other than the personal suitability of the proposed transferee and the satisfactory inspection of the vehicle. Second, it creates a *prima facie* entitlement to renewal (s. 18). Third, council's discretion in revoking or suspending a licence is not unfettered, but is, by s. 22, confined to the grounds specified in s. 18. Fourth, there is an appeal procedure entitling the licensee to a hearing by the appeal committee of council under the rules laid down in the *Statutory Powers Procedure Act,* RSO 1980, c. 484, if it is proposed not to renew the licence. Fifth, the licence is expressly recognized as an asset of the estate of a deceased owner. These are not the characteristics of a "transitory and ephemeral" privilege.

One of the grounds for refusal of renewal is that it would be contrary to the public interest to renew. It was argued that this meant the discretion of council was in fact unfettered despite the apparent restrictions on it. I do not agree. At least since *Roncarelli v. Duplessis* (1959), 16 DLR (2d) 689, [1959] SCR 121, it has been recognized that issuers of licences for the carrying on of business must act in good faith for the legitimate purposes of the regulatory framework. In my opinion, the characteristics of this licence in its regulatory setting are those of property. It is transferable after the three-year waiting period. There is a *prima facie* right to renewal protected by a right to a hearing and a stated list of criteria. The licence becomes an asset of the estate of a deceased owner. Moving out of the regulatory setting and into the world of commerce, there is clearly a market for these licences. The degree of control exercised by the city is vastly different from the control exercised by the Tobacco Board in *Bouckhuyt, supra.* In my view, this taxi cab owner's licence is intangible personal property and dealings with it are therefore subject to the PPSA.

· · ·

[The final disposition of the case depended on a number of additional factors.]

NOTES AND QUESTIONS

1) If the test for determining what is and what is not "personal property" is the amount of control a regulatory body exercises, how do you identify the point at which the control is such as to preclude the licence from being treated as personal property (collateral). Should the test be anything more than whether or not someone is prepared to take a security interest in the right?

2) The reasoning in *Bouckhuyt* has been widely criticized both on practical and conceptual grounds. See, for example, Ziegel and Denomme, *op. cit.*, §1.30.1. It was rejected by Matheson J of the Saskatchewan Court of Queen's Bench in *Saskatoon Auction Mart Ltd. v. Finesse Holsteins* [1993] 1 WWR 265. The court concluded that a milk "quota" is "personal property" that can be collateral under a security agreement. See also, Mercier, "Commentary—Saskatoon Auction Mart: Milk Quotas and Finally Some Commercial Reality" (1993), 22 *CBLJ* 466. SPPSA s. 2(w) defines "intangible" to include a "licence" and s. 2(z) defines "licence" to mean "a right, whether or not exclusive, to manufacture, produce, sell, transport or otherwise deal with personal property or to provide services, that is transferrable by the grantee with or without restriction or the consent of the grantor." What is the relevance (if any) of the transferability of the right? Note that in *Phenix (Trustee of) v. Bank of Nova Scotia* (1989), 9 PPSAC 95, the Saskatchewan Court of Appeal held that a security interest cannot be taken in a RRSP because of the prohibition on assignment of RRSP interest in s. 146 of the Income Tax Act.

3) Which of the following are "personal property" that can be subject to a security interest: copyright owned by the debtor; a debtor's rights as lessee under an equipment lease; a debt owing to the debtor; a medical practitioner's patient records (see *Josephine V. Wilson Family Trust v. Swartz* (1994), 16 OR (3d) 268 (Gen. Div.); and *Re Axelrod* (1994), 20 OR (3d) 189 (CA))? As to whether or not a deposit-taking organization (e.g., bank) can take a security interest in a debt it owes to a customer (i.e., a credit in a deposit account), see *In re Charge Card Services Ltd.*[1986] 3 All ER 289.* The SPPSA s. 9(4) provides that "an account debtor as defined in clause 41(1)(a) may take a security interest in the account or chattel paper under which the account debtor is obligated."

The Essentials of a Security Agreement

Guntel v. Kocian
[1985] 6 WWR 458 (Man. QB)

[Fay Kocian, at the urging of Bryan Ward, borrowed money from the Bank of Nova Scotia and purchased a truck. Kocian gave a security interest in the truck to the Bank. Kocian then transferred her interest in the truck to Ward who executed the following document:

I Bryan Ward owe Fay Kocian $7,699.99 plus the interest of the Bank of Nova Scotia for 1979 GMC truck SETCS249B517824

Bryan Ward (signed)
(Exhibit 22)

---

* The difficulty is said to arise because a person cannot be a secured party and a debtor in respect of the same collateral. See further, Ziegel and Denomme, *op. cit.*, §§1.30.2, 25.4.8.3.

Kocian registered a financing statement. Ward sold the truck to Guntel on the same day as Kocian's financing statement was registered. When Ward failed to pay her, Kocian seized the truck from Guntel.

One of the issues before the Manitoba Queen's Bench Court was whether or not Kocian had a security interest in the truck.]

DUREAULT J: ... The question then is, did Ward in signing Ex. 22 above effectively create a valid non-possessory security interest in the truck in favour of Kocian?

A close examination of Ex. 22 shows that the debtor Ward acknowledges a debt to Kocian in the amount of $7,699 plus the interest of Scotia for the truck. The truck itself is clearly identified by the year, make and serial number. Can this be nothing more than a simple I.O.U., or can it be fairly construed as creating a valid security interest, i.e., an interest that secures payment or performance of an obligation?

In Catzman on Personal Property Security Law in Ontario (1976), the learned authors, in considering the scope of the Ontario Personal Property Security Act, make the following comments in their introductory chapter (at 1 and 2):

The Act applies to all transactions that are intended to create a security interest in personal property and fixtures ...

The chief consequence of its enactment will be emancipation from the constricted moulds into which security devices must fit under existing law to obtain legal sanction.

And finally, at 3:

On the other hand, it [the Act] does embrace transactions where the parties intend that the personal property serve as security, even though the intent is not reflected in the form, such as a consignment and a hire-purchase. *It is the substance of the transaction and not its form that determines* the applicability of the Act. (The italics are mine.)

It is well recognized that the Manitoba Act was modelled closely on the Ontario legislation.

I do not think there can be the slightest doubt that Kocian intended to secure her interest in the truck as a condition to the transfer of ownership to Ward. Ward had agreed that he would assume and perform Kocian's obligation to Scotia, an obligation she necessarily incurred in order to purchase the vehicle. If it was intended as a simple I.O.U., why then the reference to the Scotia debt followed by the words "for 1979 GMC truck SETCS249B517842"? Nor do I feel that, looking at this document, any reasonable person would fail to recognize it as giving Kocian some special right in that truck. I accept Kocian's evidence that it was intended to secure the performance by Ward of his obligation to make all payments that Kocian herself had undertaken in respect of the Scotia loan.

Ex. 22 is an agreement signed by the debtor Ward containing an accurate description of the truck offered as collateral. While conceding that it is not a draughtsman's model, still giving it a broad interpretation, as I feel I must, I conclude that it meets all of the statutory requirements of a valid security agreement. It did provide Kocian with a security interest in the vehicle described therein securing Ward's performance of the obligation which he had undertaken. Though imperfect in form that is the substance of the agreement. Otherwise, the reference therein to "the Bank of Nova Scotia" would be meaningless.

When Ward defaulted, Kocian became entitled to exercise the remedies provided for under Pt. V of the Act. And again see Catzman, above, at the bottom of 47, where the innovative impact of Pt. II of the Ontario Act is described in the following words:

The provisions of this Part clearly set forth and exemplify one of the cornerstones of this Act, namely, that the parties should be as free and unregulated as possible in the making of the agreement between them. The device used to create the security interest can be as simple or as complicated as they feel the transaction warrants and as a consequence, the parties are not forced to wrestle the transaction into a specified mould or form in order to register it in the proper system as was the case prior to this Act, but can make the documentation suit the circumstances of the transaction contemplated.

At 54, the same authors set out an over-simplified example of a valid security agreement in these terms:

"I, John Jones, 3450 Any Street, Toronto, Ontario, grant a security interest in my office safe to William Smith, 245 Such Street, Toronto, Ontario, Executed June 15, 1967. John Jones (signature)."

If simplicity is a fault then Ex. 22 is guilty of it. But that characterization does not, in my view, affect its intrinsic validity as a security agreement, and I so hold.

Action dismissed;
judgment for plaintiff by counterclaim.

QUESTIONS

1) Is there any essential difference between the example of a simple, valid security agreement as set out in Catzman, *Personal Property Security Law* (cited by the Court) and Exhibit 22?

2) The Court concluded that Kocian intended to secure her interest in the truck "as a condition to the transfer of ownership to Ward." Was this evidenced in the written document signed by Ward? Can there be a valid security agreement without written evidence of the creation of a security interest? See OPPSA s. 11(2)(a).

3) Does a sale of goods on "C.O.D." terms create a security interest? See *Joseph Group of Companies Inc. v. Pickles Tents & Awnings Ltd.* (1981), 127 DLR (3d) 176 (Man. CA). See also s. 81.1 of the Bankruptcy and Insolvency Act RSC 1985, c. B-3 as am. SC 1992, c. 27.

Security Leases

Common Law Position: The Legal Obligation Test

When instalment credit agreements first became popular in England in the late 19th century, sellers were confronted with the obstacle presented by s. 9 of the Factors Act, 1889, subsequently reproduced almost verbatim in s. 25(2) of the Sale of Goods Act, 1893. Section 9 provides that where a buyer having bought or agreed to buy goods obtains, with the seller's consent, possession of the goods, the delivery by the buyer of the goods under any sale, pledge or other disposition thereof to any person, receiving the goods in good faith and without notice of the seller's lien or other right in respect of the goods, has the same effect as if the person making the delivery were a mercantile agent in possession of the goods with the owner's consent. For the difficult case law on this provision, see volume I of this casebook, chapter 10. The effect of s. 9 (and of SGA s. 25(2)) was to seriously jeopardize the seller's security of title under a conditional sale agreement. This was shown by the Court of Appeal's decision in *Lee v. Butler*, [1893] 2 QB 318.

In order to overcome this difficulty English traders engaging in instalment sales introduced what came to be known as "hire-purchase agreements." Under such an agreement the goods were "hired" by the prospective buyer and the agreement provided that if the hirer made an agreed number of periodical payments (which were usually equal to the cash purchase price together with an implicit credit charge) the hirer would either become the owner of the goods or would have the option of becoming so on making a nominal payment. However, the hirer was not obliged to retain the goods for the full hiring period and she was entitled to terminate the agreement at any time, subject to making good any arrears in rentals.

This type of hire-purchase agreement was tested before the House of Lords in *Helby v. Matthews*, [1895] AC 471, reproduced in volume I of this casebook, chapter 2. The law lords, reversing the Court of Appeal, held that it was not a sale agreement (and therefore not governed by s. 9) because the hirer was under no obligation to buy the chattel since she was entitled to terminate the hiring agreement at any time before the agreement matured into a sale. Counsel argued that since the monthly payments were larger than they would be under a simple hiring agreement, the agreement should be treated as a contract of sale. Lord Hershell rejected the argument on the ground that an expectation was not the same as an "obligation" to buy and the definition of contract of sale in the SGA speaks of the buyer's agreement to buy, not merely an option or opportunity to do so. In short, the House of Lords adopted a "legal obligation" test in determining the existence of a conditional sale agreement. This is very different from the "substance" test of a security agreement adopted in s. 2 of the OPPSA and the other provincial Acts.

Substance Test under the PPSA Legislation

Even before the enactment of Article 9, American courts had adopted a substance test for the characterization of equipment leases, so that the reaffirmation of the substance test in UCC 1-201(37), which defines "security interest," came as no surprise. The original definition contained some guidelines for the treatment of leases, but these proved to be unhelpful and generated a lot of litigation. For a good discussion of the American case law, see Clark, *The Law of Secured Transactions under the Uniform Commercial Code*, rev. ed. (1993), pp. 1-32 to 1-52. As a result, the definition was completely recast in 1987. The revised definition is reproduced below.

Section 2 of the original OPPSA made it clear that the Act applied to leases "intended as security" but provided no further guidance. The intention language is omitted in the current section but it is still left up to the courts to determine on a case-by-case basis whether a lease is in substance a security lease. Not surprisingly, the question has generated much difference of opinion. The cases reproduced below provide a sampling of the abundant case law. See further Cuming, "True Leases and Security Leases under

Canadian Personal Property Security Acts" (1982), 7 *CBLJ* 251 and Ziegel & Denomme, *op. cit.*, pp. 49-55. The characterization issue has lost much of its importance in the other provincial Acts because their scope sections expressly include a lease for a year or more, whether or not the lease otherwise amounts to a security lease. See further, *infra*, p. 63.

Standard Finance Corp. v. Coopers & Lybrand
[1984] 4 WWR 543 (Man. QB)

MORSE J: In this action, the plaintiff seeks a declaration that it is the owner of a certain model NP80 photocopier machine.

The bankrupt Econ was interested in acquiring a photocopier machine. To this end, it negotiated with National Typewriter & Office Equipment, the Manitoba distributor of Canon photocopiers. National Typewriter is in the business of marketing office equipment products, including the sale and servicing of photocopier machines. National Typewriter and Econ negotiated an agreement (Ex. 1) under which Econ agreed to lease the photo-copier from Standard Leasing, a division of the plaintiff corporation. Under the terms of this lease, Econ was required to make regular monthly instalment payments of $171.83, together with provincial sales tax, for a period of 65 months, at the end of which time Econ was to have the right to purchase the photocopier for 10 per cent of its original cost. The cost of the machine was the manufacturer's suggested list price of $7,235. The monthly payments were sufficient to allow the plaintiff to recover the purchase price of the machine together with interest.

National Typewriter had an established relationship with the plaintiff. It knew the plaintiff's interest rates, time periods, and the buy-out or purchase options offered by the plaintiff. Based on this information, National Typewriter was able to prepare the form of lease in this case. All the plaintiff did was to investigate the credit worthiness of Econ, and, when the credit was approved and the necessary documents were received, to pay National Typewriter the cost of the machine in the amount of $7,235. The evidence on examination for discovery of Mr. Thiessen, the president of the plaintiff, was:

Q. Do you know who in the plaintiff's company negotiated this lease with Econ Consulting Ltd.? A. Well, this is handled by National Typewriter. When we approve the credit, then we buy the paper from them … .

Q. The document itself—who would have prepared it? A. The document was prepared by National Typewriter, and was given to us in blank, which we approved and signed.

Q. All right. What documents would you receive from National Typewriter to approve? A. Our total lease agreement. First of all, what they had to do, they would give us a credit application from these people.

Q. Yes— A. Which, if we approved it, they take our lease document down there, have it signed by the customer—also have them sign an acceptance slip that he has received the leased equipment in good condition and it is on his premises. He signs that document, which I thought we had here … .

Q. I see. Then what happens? A. They would then forward to us the complete lease agreement, along with their invoice, and along with a cheque covering the agreed two initial payments, which we would then process and pay them their funds.

Although the plaintiff had a number of photocopier machines on hand which presumably could have been leased or sold, the plaintiff would not have bought the photocopier machine unless there had been a person who intended to lease it. On examination for discovery, Mr. Thiessen expressed the matter in this way:

Q. Would the purchase of equipment and lease thereafter by your company on a direct basis be basically through subdivisions of the same corporation?   A. Well, let's not get confused. We are not buying it for inventory. If we bought it—we wouldn't have bought it unless we had a lease for it, because there would be no point to it.

Q. So you don't buy anything really for inventory?   A. No.

Q. You have an end lease in mind when you buy equipment?   A. Yes, sure.—that is the business we are in.

Mr. Ragoux, the president of Econ, gave evidence, but he had little recollection of this particular transaction. His evidence, basically, was that Econ intended to keep the machine at the end of the term of the lease and that all he knew was that there was some type of arrangement by which Econ was to acquire the machine some day.

The plaintiff's leasing business is in connection with trucks and what Mr. Thiessen referred to as "mobilizing equipment." However, the plaintiff has no showroom, and its offices are located in the sixth floor of a Winnipeg office building. While the plaintiff may have photocopiers on hand, I am not persuaded that it is in the business of leasing such machines except as a means of financing the purchase of them.

The essential issue to be decided in this case is whether the lease in question is a true lease or whether it is a lease intended as security. If the latter, it was, by virtue of the provisions of the Manitoba Personal Property Security Act, 1973 (Man.), c. 5 (also CCSM, c. P35) ("the Act"), required to be registered, and, this not having been done, the interest of the plaintiff would be subordinate to the interest of the defendant trustee in bankruptcy.

Section 2(a)(ii) of the Act provides:

2 ... this Act applies

(a) to every transaction without regard to its form and without regard to the person who has title to the collateral that in substance creates a security interest including, without limiting the foregoing, ...

(ii) an assignment, lease or consignment intended as security.

Security interest is defined by s. 1(aa) to mean:

(aa) "security interest" means

(i) an interest in goods, fixtures, documents of title, instruments, securities, chattel papers or intangibles that secures payment or performance of an obligation, and ...

• • •

In the present case, the role of the plaintiff, in my view, was to act as the means by which National Typewriter was enabled to sell the photocopier in question. The effect of the transaction was to enable National Typewriter to sell the machine and Econ to acquire possession and use of it without having to pay the full amount of the purchase price at the time of acquisition. As well, Econ was enabled to acquire title to the equipment at the end of the term of the lease. The plaintiff was to recover the cost of the machine together with interest. My impression of the evidence is that the parties did not, in fact, regard this transaction as a true lease but as a means of financing the purchase of the photocopier. The plaintiff was not, I think, interested in retaining title to the machine at the end of the term of the lease because it had no facilities for leasing such a machine to others.

An analysis of the lease agreement in this case indicates that it is similar to the lease which was considered in *Speedrack*. In particular, the lease (Ex. 1) contains an acceleration clause which, under its terms, purports to permit the plaintiff lessor, on default, to recover as liquidated damages all amounts due or to become due under the lease. As was pointed out in the article by Cuming, "True Leases and Security Leases under Canadian Personal Property Security Acts" (1983), 7 *CBLJ* 251, at 279:

> However, while the relationship between the lessor and a defaulting lessee may be one of creditor and debtor, an acceleration clause should, at least in some cases, be viewed as foreign to the lessor-lessee relationship. Unlike a defaulting buyer or borrower, a lessee is generally not obligated under the rules of damages to pay a specific predetermined sum to the lessor. The lessor may well be entitled to damages for breach of contract, but there is no certainty that those damages will be assessed as the equivalent of all rental payments owing under the lease with or without deduction of an amount realized from the sale of the leased chattels by the lessor.

Reference was made in the article to the decision of the Manitoba Court of Appeal in *Can. Accept. Corp. Ltd. v. Regent Park Butcher Shop Ltd.* (1969), 67 WWR 297, 13 CBR (NS) 8, 3 DLR (3d) 304 (Man. CA), and to the remarks of Dickson JA at 310 (DLR):

> We do not suggest that all acceleration clauses are in the nature of a penalty and unenforceable. On the contrary, in a mortgage given to secure the due payment by instalments of a sum due, a provision making the total sum due enforceable on any default is not to be considered a penalty: ... The same holds true with respect to instalments of purchase price payable under a sale agreement. Here, however, we are not dealing with a mortgage nor with a sale agreement. We are dealing with a lease, and in our opinion a provision accelerating the due date of rental payments on default is as foreign to a lease of chattels as to a lease of land.

The principal contention of the plaintiff in this case was that the amount required to be paid by Econ to purchase the equipment bore a reasonable resemblance to its fair market value and that the lease, therefore, was, in fact, a true lease. The plaintiff relied on what was stated by Henry J in *Re Ont. Equipment* at 651 as follows:

•   •   •

The evidence in the present case showed, as I have indicated, that Econ was required to pay to the plaintiff the purchase price of the equipment together with interest over the term of the lease. The option to purchase for 10 per cent of the cost of the machine was stated in evidence to be the "norm" in the leasing industry so far as a 65-month lease is concerned. It is a standard percentage used by finance companies in similar situations. It is an amount which Revenue Canada is prepared to accept for income tax purposes, and I incline to the view that it is probably used by finance companies not because it necessarily represents the fair market value but because it is acceptable to Revenue Canada. The plaintiff's evidence was that 10 per cent of the purchase price actually represents the fair market value of the equipment at the end of the lease but that the 10 per cent figure was determined without regard to the condition of the equipment.

In my opinion, the parties could not realistically have considered that 10 per cent of the purchase price would necessarily be the fair market value of the equipment at the end of the term of the lease. I think the condition of the equipment must have a bearing on its fair market value at any given time. In my view, therefore, the fact that the purchase price option may have approximated the fair market value of the property at the end of the term of the lease is not determinative of the issue in this case. Obviously, it is a significant factor, but, by itself, it cannot be conclusive, particularly where, as here, the figure is chosen as an arbitrary percentage of the purchase price without regard to the actual condition of the equipment. Indeed, in *Re Ont. Equipment*, Henry J, after referring to the *Crown Cartridge* case, supra, went on to say (at 651) that "The crucial issue in every case is the intention of the parties and this depends upon the facts of the case." On the facts of this particular case, I am persuaded that the intention of the parties was that the lease was to be security within the meaning of the Act and that it was intended, although, of course, not required, that Econ would, at the end of the term of the lease, acquire title to the equipment.

Action dismissed.

Adelaide Capital Corp v. Integrated Transportation Finance
(1994), 111 DLR (4th) 493 (Ont. Gen. Div.)

R.A. BLAIR J: The four leases entered into between Greyvest and ITFI have all the indicia of lease agreements. They are for fixed terms, at "rental" payments set out in a schedule to the lease. Each lease contains "purchase options" at various stages of the lease term. In three of the four leases, the option to purchase at the end of the term is at fair market value; in the first lease, the lessee is entitled to return the 50 trailers which are the subject of the transaction to the lessor. In all cases, the options to purchase are for more than nominal amounts. In addition, title to the trailers is stated to remain with the lessor, the right to take capital cost allowances is reserved to the lessor, improvements to the leased trailers accrue to the benefit of the lessor, and there is no obligation on the part of the lessee to make any payments at the end of the lease.

In spite of the foregoing, however, I am satisfied that in substance the transactions between Greyvest and ITFI were in the nature of financing arrangements, in which the leases—as "lease-like" as they are—were intended, as well as operating in the fashion of leases, to secure the repayment of the monies advanced by Greyvest to ITFI respecting the acquisition of the trailers and to secure the performance of ITFI's obligations in connection therewith.

• • •

Much emphasis is placed by counsel, as a result of this passage, on the purchase options contained in the Greyvest leases, and on whether or not the option prices resemble fair market value or are merely nominal, and on whether title ultimately passes to the lessee. These are important and relevant considerations, to be sure. However, in my view, too much focus can be placed on them, and too much energy expended in finely honed exercises designed to determine whether property ultimately passes or whether the option price is sufficiently substantial. The test is not whether the document in question is a lease or a conditional sale agreement. The test is whether the transaction, as a whole, in substance creates a security interest, and, in the context of a lease instrument, whether the lease is one "that secures payment or performance of an obligation."

In this case, I conclude that what Greyvest and ITFI negotiated was, in the language of *Re Speedrack, supra,* "a loan or advance on security," rather than "a standard lease of property, *not by way of security.*" The leases are caught by the PPSA.

I reach this conclusion on the basis of the following.

Greyvest is in the business of financing transactions. It facilitates the acquisition of machines, vehicles and equipment by advancing funds, without holding any significant inventory, itself, for sale or lease. Transactions are not entered into until they have been approved by Greyvest's "Investment" Committee and a "term sheet" or "lease proposal" has been accepted and signed.

While the lease as ultimately signed may differ somewhat, in detail, from the lease proposal that was its precursor, the lease proposal documents, the lease payment schedules, and the *viva voce* evidence of Mr. Micallef and Mr. McCleary themselves, make it plain that the rental payments are driven by cost-of-money considerations more than anything else. "Yield" is the by-word.

Consideration is given, through the use of sophisticated, albeit standard, computerized calculations, to such concepts as "the apparent rate of the transaction"—what Mr. McCleary called "the pure money on money rate of return"—and the "self sheltered yield" of the transaction, which I understand to be the yield over and above the "apparent rate," after taking into account capital cost allowance and other income tax considerations. Rental payments, according to the lease proposals, are "based upon current funding costs," and the lease documents contain what is referred to as a "refix" provision, i.e., a provision whereby, after the 60th month of the term—five-year money—"the rental rate shall be refixed at a rate that results in a rental based on the Lessor's then current cost of funds and *which reflects a yield* to the Lessor identical to that generated by the first sixty (60) rentals" (emphasis added).

The trailers in question here were obtained for the specific purpose of a leasing agreement between ITFI and an already arranged end user. Indeed, the purchase of the units, generally speaking, *follows* the execution of the lease, according to Mr. Micallef on his cross-examination. A credit check is done on the ultimate end user of the trailers before the transaction is approved by Greyvest's Investment Committee, and, as part of the overall transaction, Greyvest takes an assignment of the lease between ITFI and the end user. All costs relating to the trailers, including the obligation to insure against risks, are the responsibility of ITFI.

Finally, Greyvest's conduct towards the transaction itself reflects the financing nature of the transaction. I have already described the manner in which the rental payments were arrived at. Internally, the leases were recorded on Greyvest's books as "direct finance leases," rather than as "operating leases," and were treated as such. While registration under the PPSA does not create a presumption that the PPSA applies to the transaction, Greyvest treated the registrations as if it did, in seeking and obtaining waivers and postponements from other secured creditors when it was considering what Mr. Micallef referred to—significantly, I think—as "a *refinancing of* lease 308700-01 (Day & Ross)."

Mr. Micallef described this latter development as follows, in para. 4 of his affidavit sworn September 23, 1993:

4. In early 1992 we had been approached by ITFI *to do a refinancing* of lease 308700-01 (Day & Ross). As a condition of a new agreement, waivers had to be obtained from all parties then having registrations affecting ITFI acknowledging that they did not claim any interest in any of the *equipment financed by Greyvest.* (Emphasis added.)

Lease 308700-01 is the document reflecting the first transaction between Greyvest and ITFI, in December 1986, involving 50 trailers. All other secured creditors except NAT provided waivers. NAT refused to do so. The "refinancing" did not proceed as a result.

All of this, it seems to me, is clear evidence that Greyvest considered and treated the transactions between it and ITFI, in *substance,* as financing transactions, and intended them to be such. Greyvest advanced monies to ITFI to enable ITFI to acquire trailers as inventory to lease to end-users. The leases between Greyvest and ITFI were mechanisms to ensure and secure the repayment of those monies, together with a profitable rate of return. In circumstances such as this, there is nothing anomalous in a lease having all of the trappings of a true lease and at the same time operating to secure the payment or performance of an obligation: PPSA, s. 2(a)(ii).

Transactions such as this should be caught by the PPSA, in my view. They typically involve the advancing of funds by a financing institution to facilitate the acquisition of a large number of vehicles or pieces of equipment. This type of personal property, again typically, is not infrequently the object of security interest claims by other creditors advancing credit to the business operation in question. If the financing markets are to achieve the kind of stability and predictability, in terms of priority, which the PPSA envisages, creditors who are truly in the business of financing transactions should be required to indicate the collateral over which they are claiming a security interest, and not leave matters to guesswork as to whether they have truly leased the property to the debtor/lessee or not.

I conclude, therefore, that the four leases in question between Greyvest and ITFI must be perfected by registration in order to preserve Greyvest's priority over the claims of other secured creditors.

Re Ontario Equipment (1976) Ltd.
(1981), 33 OR (2d) 648 (Ont. SC Bankruptcy)

HENRY J (orally): The issue in this application by the trustee is whether a lease of a truck for a term of three years, at the end of which the lessee was entitled to buy the truck, is a lease intended as security under s. 2 of the *Personal Property Security Act*, RSO 1970, c. 344, as amended [now RSO 1980, c. 375], and as such must be registered under that Act to protect the lessor's interest against the trustee in bankruptcy of the lessee.

The application of the *Personal Property Security Act* to a lease is found in s. 2, which reads, in part, as follows:

2. Subject to subsection 1 of section 3, this Act applies,

    (a) to every transaction without regard to its form and without regard to the person who has title to the collateral that in substance creates a security interest, including, without limiting the foregoing,

        (ii) an assignment, lease or consignment intended as security ...

If the lease is intended as security it must be perfected by registration under the Act otherwise it is subordinate to the interest of the trustee in bankruptcy. The trustee seeks an order declaring that the lease here in question is a security interest requiring perfection under the *Personal Property Security Act* and declaring that the security interest is unperfected and subordinate to the interest of the trustee.

The lessor, Toronto Motor Car Leasing, is a division of Sorenson Chrysler Plymouth Inc., an automobile dealer which both sells automobiles and leases them to customers. The lessor provided two main types of lease agreements called an open end lease and a closed end lease. The distinction between the two was explained by Gary Peacock, the general manager of Toronto Motor Car Leasing, in his affidavit as follows:

4. The quotation was on the basis of an Open End lease whereby the Lessee agreed to purchase the leased vehicle at the agreed upon price in order to avoid the possibility of the payment of an excess mileage charge at the end of the lease. The excess mileage charge is a charge pursuant to the terms of a Closed End lease and is a factor in consideration of the market value of the vehicle on re-sale by the Lessor. Under normal circumstances a reasonable number of kilometers at the expiration of a three year lease is 80,000 kilometers.

Under the open end lease here in issue, the dealer lessor acquired a small truck for lease to its customer, the bankrupt herein, and in September, 1980, leased it for a term of three years to the bankrupt. By the terms of the lease, the lessee is responsible for most of the obligations of ownership including insurance, maintenance, repairs and licensing. At the end of the term the lessor is obliged to sell the vehicle at a price determined by the market and is entitled to recover $2,500 for itself. If the price is insufficient to provide $2,500, the lessee must make good the deficiency; if the price exceeds $2,500, the lessee is entitled to the excess. The customer, the lessee, has the option of buying the vehicle at the best price offered to the lessor—in effect, the right of first refusal at a price determined by the market.

The *rationale* of this arrangement is explained by Mr. Peacock in his affidavit as follows:

6. Pursuant to the terms of the Lease Agreement, the Lessee arranges liability, collision and comprehensive insurance coverage for the motor vehicle rather than the lessor. The reasoning for these insurance arrangements is to avoid the inequality of a Fleet Policy carried by the Lessor and enables a Lessee, with a good driving record to obtain more favourable premiums. However in the instant case, the Lessee had a Fleet Policy and advised the Lessor of the addition to the said Policy of the leased vehicle. Attached hereto and marked as exhibit "C" to this my Affidavit is a true copy of the confirmation received from the insurance agency of the Lessee with respect to insurance coverage.

7. Toronto Motor Car Leasing maintains an inventory of vehicles for the purpose of leasing, however was required to purchase the motor vehicle in question as the required vehicle was not in its inventory. Attached hereto and marked as exhibit "D" to this my Affidavit is a true copy of the

sales agreement with Sorenson Chrysler Plymouth Inc. in the total amount of $7,525.00. Toronto Motor Car Leasing purchases its vehicles whether or not Chrysler products from various automobile dealers dependent upon price and availability.

8. The monthly payment of $239.00 exclusive of Provincial Sales Tax is calculated based on the estimated depreciation of the vehicle and interest carrying costs to Toronto Motor Car Leasing which at the time was 13.25 per cent per annum. The estimated value of the vehicle at Lease end was $1,895.00. Attached hereto and marked as exhibit "E" to this my Affidavit is a true copy of the Vehicle Cost and Rate Worksheet prepared by me in preparation of the Lease Agreement.

9. It was my intention at all times and that of Toronto Motor Car Leasing to enter into a Lease Agreement both in form and in substance. The Open End Lease in the instant case provides the Lessor with its reasonable profit at Lease end and simultaneously was intended to provide the Lessee with a basis to control the ultimate costs of the Lease by removing the excess mileage factor and in its place substituting the maximum liability amount.

The lessee, Ontario Equipment (1976) Limited, is in bankruptcy by virtue of a receiving order made February 13, 1981. The trustee takes the position that the lease is akin to a conditional sale agreement whereby the property remains in the vendor until the purchase price is paid in full, a transaction which must be registered under the *Personal Property Security Act* to protect the vendor against the claims of creditors, including a trustee in bankruptcy. The trustee submits that the transaction is in reality one of purchase and sale on the security of the lease which has not been registered under the *Personal Property Security Act*, and hence the interest of the lessor as owner of the vehicle is subordinate to that of the trustee.

It is of the essence of a lease intended as security within the meaning of the *Personal Property Security Act* that the property in the subject of the lease is to pass ultimately to the lessee, who is obliged to pay the lessor what might be reasonably regarded as the purchase price with interest and carrying charges over the life of the lease. In such a case the transaction is not unlike a conditional sale agreement or hire purchase agreement.

What I consider to be a practical definition of the distinction between a true lease and a lease by way of security was adopted in *Re Crown Cartridge Corp., Debtor* (1962), 220 F. Supp. 914, by Croake DJ from the decision of Referee Asa S. Herzog:

The test in determining whether an agreement is a true lease or a conditional sale is whether the option to purchase at the end of the lease term is for a substantial sum or a nominal amount. ... If the purchase price bears a resemblance to the fair market price of the property, then the rental payments were in fact designated to be in compensation for the use of the property and the option is recognized as a real one. On the other hand, where the price of the option to purchase is substantially less than the fair market value of the leased equipment, the lease will be construed as a mere cover for an agreement of conditional sale.

The critical issue in every case is the intention of the parties and this depends upon the facts of the case. In *Re Speedtrack Ltd.* (1980), 1 PPSAC 109, 33 CBR (N.S.) 209, 11 BLR 220, for example, the facts led to the conclusion that the lease was a security for the financing of the ultimate purchase of the subject-matter, and the failure to register a financing statement left the security interest unperfected and subordinate to the interest of the trustee in bankruptcy.

Each case must stand on its own facts. In the case at bar the terms of the lease assure to the lessor recapture of its cost plus a profit with the guarantee that it will recoup $2,500 on the final sale at market price. As I interpret the lease agreement, the lessee is not obliged to take title at the end of the term. I am aware that Mr. Peacock in his affidavit says that under the open end lease "the lessee agreed to purchase the leased vehicle at the agreed upon price." That, however, is not my interpretation of the agreement; clearly the lessee has an option. It may elect to purchase or not. It cannot be said that the final transaction is such that no reasonable lessee would refuse to purchase the vehicle, which would be some evidence that the intention of the parties was that the transaction from the beginning was in reality an agreement of purchase and sale. The prospect of the lessee reaping a profit on final liquidation of the vehicle is not conclusive of this intention. It is quite consistent with the lessor holding out an incentive to the lessee to maintain the value of the asset during the term of the lease by proper maintenance, repair and careful use.

Parties must be free to contract as they see fit without restraint except as clearly imposed by law. It is only if on a reasonable view of the agreed arrangements the lessor has financed the purchase of the vehicle under the guise of a lease which is in reality a security instrument, that the Act requires registration to protect the interest of the lessor owner against creditors.

In the present case I am not persuaded that the lease is anything more than a straightforward leasing arrangement which recovers for the lessor, as owner, over the effective life of the vehicle, his cost, together with a reasonable profit. The lessor is entitled to do that. There is no additional evidence, as there was in *Re Speedtrack Ltd.*, supra, to lead to the conclusion that the true nature of the transaction was a sale of the asset financed on the security of the lease.

Application dismissed.

UCC 1-201(37)

(37) "Security interest" means an interest in personal property or fixtures which secures payment or performance of an obligation. ...

Whether a transaction creates a lease or security interest is determined by the facts of each case; however, a transaction creates a security interest if the consideration the lessee is to pay the lessor for the right to possession and use of the goods is an obligation for the term of the lease not subject to termination by the lessee, and

(a) the original term of the lease is equal to or greater than the remaining economic life of the goods,

(b) the lessee is bound to renew the lease for the remaining economic life of the goods or is bound to become the owner of the goods,

(c) the lessee has an option to renew the lease for the remaining economic life of the goods for no additional consideration or nominal additional consideration upon compliance with the lease agreement, or

(d) the lessee has an option to become the owner of the goods for no additional consideration or nominal additional consideration upon compliance with the lease agreement.

A transaction does not create a security interest merely because it provides that

(a) the present value of the consideration the lessee is obligated to pay the lessor for the right to possession and use of the goods is substantially equal to or is greater than the fair market value of the goods at the time the lease is entered into,

(b) the lessee assumes risk of loss of the goods, or agrees to pay taxes, insurance, filing, recording, or registration fees, or service or maintenance costs with respect to the goods,

(c) the lessee has an option to renew the lease or to become the owner of the goods,

(d) the lessee has an option to renew the lease for a fixed rent that is equal to or greater than the reasonably predictable fair market rent for the use of the goods for the term of the renewal at the time the option is to be performed, or

(e) the lessee has an option to become the owner of the goods for a fixed price that is equal to or greater than the reasonably predictable fair market value of the goods at the time the option is to be performed.

For purposes of this subsection (37):

(x) Additional consideration is not nominal if (i) when the option to renew the lease is granted to the lessee the rent is stated to be the fair market rent for the use of the goods for the term of the renewal determined at the time the option is to be performed, or (ii) when the option to become the owner of the goods is granted to the lessee the price is stated to be the fair market value of the goods determined at the time the option is to be performed. Additional consideration is nominal if it is less than the lessee's reasonably predictable cost of performing under the lease agreement if the option is not exercised;

(y) "Reasonably predictable" and "remaining economic life of the goods" are to be determined with reference to the facts and circumstances at the time the transaction is entered into; and

(z) "Present value" means the amount as of a date certain of one or more sums payable in the future, discounted to the date certain. The discount is determined by the interest rate specified by the parties if the rate is not manifestly unreasonably at the time the transaction is entered into; otherwise, the discount is determined by a commercially reasonable rate that takes into account the facts and circumstances of each case at the time the transaction was entered into.

NOTES AND QUESTIONS

1) In *Standard Finance*, counsel for the plaintiff thought it was important to establish that the amount payable by the lessee to exercise the purchase option was equivalent to the market price of the equipment at the date when the option could have been exercised. What relevance does this have to the characterization of the lease as a true lease or security lease? Why did the court reject it as not relevant in this case?

2) The court seems to have felt that other factors were important evidence of the intention of the parties. Consider each of the following and assess its relevance to the issue:

- The monthly payments were sufficient to allow Standard Finance to recover the purchase price of the machine together with interest.
- National Typewriter filled in the form contract and "negotiated" its terms with Econ Consulting.
- Standard Finance would not have purchased the copier if Econ Consulting had not agreed to lease it.
- Standard Finance had no showroom and no facilities to handle the equipment at the end of the lease.

3) In *Adelaide Capital Corp.*, *supra*, Blair J appears to have gone much farther than the court in *Standard Finance* and the Ontario courts in earlier cases, and to have assimilated all financial leases with security leases, at least for perfection purposes. What is the basis of Blair J's approach: (i) the indistinguishability of security leases and financial leases; or (ii) the importance of providing protection (through registration) to third parties? If it is the latter, can it be justified, given the decision of the Ontario Legislature not to require the registration of "true leases." See discussion, *infra*, under the heading "An Expanded Scope—Deemed Security Interests."

4) So-called "open-end leases," such as the lease used in *Ontario Equipment (1976) Ltd.*, *supra*, continue to be a source of difficulties for the courts. For other examples, see *Re W. Altmann & Sons Ltd.* (1993), 17 CBR (3d) 141 (Ont. Gen. Div.); and compare *Misener Financial Corp. v. General Home Systems Ltd.* (1985), 27 BLR 247 (Ont. SC); and *Re Cronin Fire Equipment Ltd.* (1993), 14 OR (3d) 269 (Gen. Div.). Should the lessee's contingent liability for an additional payment at the end of the lease be assimilated to a debtor's liability for a deficiency following the debtor's default and repossession and sale of the collateral by the secured party? See OPPSA, s. 64(3). Should it depend on whether the lessee is also entitled to a retrospective reduction in the lease payments (the equivalent of a surplus on resale of the collateral under OPPSA, s. 64(1) because the residual value of the vehicle is more than the parties had anticipated at the inception of the lease)?

5) Much of the interest in "leasing" as a financing device has been induced by taxation laws. Often "lessees" are companies that do not have a great deal of taxable income, but need to acquire new equipment for which an accelerated capital cost allowance can be claimed. Leases have been used as vehicles to trade this capital cost allowance for a reduced finance charge. Under a leasing arrangement (generally referred to as a "financial lease") the financer buys the equipment from the supplier and "leases" it to the "lessee" at a credit cost to the "lessee" below what it would pay if it borrowed the purchase price of the equipment. As to the test applied by Revenue Canada to determine whether a true lease or security lease is involved, see Department of National Revenue, Taxation, *Interpretation Bulletin* IT-233R, February 11, 1983.

Consignment Agreements

A parallel, but commercially less significant, problem of characterization arises in the context of consignments. A true consignment arrangement exists where a supplier furnishes supplies to a trader on the understanding that the trader will not be liable to pay for the goods unless she opts to buy the goods. The trader will be deemed to exercise the option by reselling the goods. See SGA, s. 19, r. 4, and volume I of this casebook, chapter

2. If the trader cannot find a buyer for the goods she will be entitled to return them. Such an arrangement, very common in the 19th century, is a cheap form of inventory financing for traders and is still found in some sectors (for example, oriental carpets).

The characterization issue arises where the traditional terms are changed and the trader is in some fashion obligated to pay for the goods. If she is, then the agreement is probably only a disguised conditional sale agreement. See *Re Stephanian's Persian Carpets Limited* (1979), 34 CBR (NS) 35 (Ont. SC); *Re Toyerama Ltd.* (1980), 34 CBR (NS) 153 (Ont. SC); *Re Revere Electric Inc.* (1994), 13 OR (3d) 637 (Gen. Div.); and *cf. Seven Limers Coal & Fertilizer Co. Inc. v. Hewitt* (1985), 52 OR (2d) 1 (Ont. CA). For a detailed discussion of consignment agreements under the PPS legislation and the UCC, see Colburn, "Consignment Sales and the Personal Property Security Act" (1981-82), 6 *CBLJ* 40.

Other Contentious Situations

Which of the following transactions create security interests:

- A loan agreement in which the borrower undertakes not to encumber some or all of his assets until the indebtedness is paid (generally described as a "negative covenant").
- A subordination agreement under which a party (the senior creditor) agrees to postpone its rights against the debtor until the claim of the other party (the junior creditor) is satisfied. See OPPSA ss. 38 and 50, and *infra*, chapter 7. In some subordination agreements, the senior creditor merely waives or postpones its rights in favour of the junior creditor; in others, the senior creditor surrenders rights to the junior creditor which are taken by the latter to secure payment of the obligation of the common debtor.
- A contractual right of distress contained in a real property lease.
- A contractual right given by A to B under which B is entitled to set off any obligations owing by A to B against the obligation of B to A.

Security Interests and Trusts

Re Berman
(1979), 79 OR (2d) 390

HOULDEN JA: This is an appeal from an order of Steele J, which directed the appellant, Astra Trust Company, to pay the proceeds of a mortgage retirement savings plan to the respondent, the trustee in bankruptcy of Dr. Barry Berman. The facts are simple and not in dispute.

In February, 1977, Dr. Berman obtained a loan of $5,500 from Astra. He invested the moneys in a mortgage retirement savings plan which was registered under s. 146 of the *Income Tax Act*, 1970-71-72 (Can.), c. 63. Astra was the trustee of the plan. To secure Astra for the loan, Dr. Berman executed a letter of direction which authorized Astra to first apply the proceeds of any redemption of the plan against the indebtedness of Dr. Berman. Astra did not register a financing statement pursuant to the *Personal Property Security Act*, RSO 1970, c. 344. On August 15, 1978, Dr. Berman made an assignment in bankruptcy.

The trustee in bankruptcy applied to Steele J, for an order declaring that the trustee was entitled to the proceeds of the redemption of the plan. Steele J, granted the order on the ground that the *Personal Property Security Act* applied to the transaction, and Astra not having complied with that Act, the trustee was entitled to the proceeds. With respect, we think that the learned Judge erred in finding that the *Personal Property Security Act* applied to the facts of this case.

In our opinion, the law that applies to this situation is correctly stated in the *Restatement of the Law of Trusts*, 2nd ed., s. 250, at 632:

If the beneficiary incurs a liability to the trustee individually and agrees that the trustee may discharge the liability out of the trust estate, the trustee is entitled to a charge on the interest of the beneficiary in the trust estate, and may deduct the amount of the liability from or set it off against what it would otherwise be his duty under the trust to pay to the beneficiary.

See also Scott, *The Law of Trusts*, 3rd ed. (1967) s. 250, at 2175-6. The right of Dr. Berman to redeem the plan and to receive the proceeds of the redemption, which right has vested in his trustee in bankruptcy, gave Dr. Berman a beneficial interest in the trust that was created when the plan was set up. Astra did not, therefore, have to rely upon the letter of direction. It had a charge on the proceeds of the registered retirement savings plan for the money that it had advanced to Dr. Berman. As the *Restatement* points out, the agreement that the trustee may discharge the liability out of the trust estate need not be expressed in words: the trustee has the right to discharge the liability out of the trust estate. The *Personal Property Security Act* has, therefore, no application to this case.

In the recent decision of *Re Papdopoulos* (1978), 93 DLR (3d) 621, [1979] 2 WWR 203, 29 CBR (NS) 295, Anderson J, of the British Columbia Supreme Court arrived at a similar result in an almost identical fact situation. The reasoning of Anderson J, is, however, somewhat different from the reasoning of this Court.

The appeal will be allowed, the judgment below set aside, and in its place there will be a declaration that the appellant is entitled to deduct from the proceeds of the registered retirement savings plan, the money owing to it; the balance, if any, shall be remitted to the trustee in bankruptcy.

Appeal allowed.

NOTES AND QUESTIONS

1) In *MacMahon v. Canada Permanent Trust Company* [1980] 2 WWR 438 (the appeal from the decision of *Re Papdopoulos* referred to by Mr. Justice Houlden), the British Columbia Court of Appeal concluded that Mr. Justice Houlden was wrong in law in his conclusion that as a trustee Astra was entitled to be reimbursed out of the proceeds of the registered retirement savings plan. The Court also noted that a trustee generally does not have a right to set off obligations owing by him to a beneficiary in his capacity as trustee against debts owing to him by the beneficiary. If the British Columbia Court of Appeal is correct, then Astra's right to be repaid could be found only in the letter of direction. Mr. Justice Steele in the lower court concluded that this letter constituted a security agreement with the result that the PPSA applies.

2) In *Berman*, the Court recognized the legal relationship between Berman and Astra Trust Co. as that of beneficiary and trustee with the result that trust law protected Astra. But, has the Court not avoided the central issue: why should one system of law (i.e., trust law) be chosen over another (that is, PPSA)? What if a trust arrangement is used by the parties to do precisely what a security agreement would otherwise do: e.g., A, who owes money to B, declares himself trustee of his property in favour of B. Under pre-PPSA law this type of trust clause was recognized by the courts as creating a trust effective at least in bankruptcy. See, for example, *Flintoft v. Royal Bank* [1964] SCR 631; *Ford Tractor & Equipment Sales of Canada Ltd. v. Trustee of Estate of Otto Grundman Implements Ltd.* (1970), 72 WWR 1 (Man. CA). Professor D. Waters, Canada's preeminent trust expert, sees nothing technically objectionable about finding a trust in such a situation. See "Trusts in the Setting of Business, Commerce and Bankruptcy" (1983), 21 *Alta. L Rev.* 395, at 419-20, 426, 427, but see *contra* Ziegel and Denomme, *op. cit.*, § 2.2.6. The Acts based on the CCPPSL model provide that the PPSA includes "a trust" in the list of specified transactions that fall within the scope of the Act. See, for example, BCPPSA s. 2(1)(b). Was it necessary to state this? In *Re Hounsome* (1991), 4 CBR (3d) 32 (Ont. SC), Rosenberg J refused to recognize that a trust could be used to circumvent the registration requirements of the OPPSA and defeat a trustee in bankruptcy. He said:

> From my analysis of the cases it appears that where the funds are never the property of the assignor, then the trust arrangement does not require a registration of a statement under the *Personal Property Security Act*. However, in cases where the receivable or property is that of the assignor at the time of making the assignment, then the assignment must be registered by filing a financing statement under the *Personal Property Security Act*.

• • •

> In addition the statutory provisions are designed to protect the public so that they can regulate their affairs knowing what security interests are held. If the creating of [the] trust agreement of this kind could avoid the necessity of filing under the *Personal Property Security Act*, then the proposed creditor could not act prudently with knowledge of the true state of affairs of the debtor.

As to the use of the tracing rules of equity to earmark proceeds, see chapter 9, *infra*.

3) Trust language has long been common in documentary pledge agreements where the documents of title are entrusted to the pledgee so that he can obtain the release of the underlying goods from the vessel or warehouse, dispose of them and hand over the proceeds to the pledgor to satisfy the pledgor's claim. The document of entrustment is frequently referred to as a "trust receipt." See, for example, *In re David Allester Limited*, [1922] 2 Ch. 211. However, see now OPPSA ss. 2(a)(i) and 24. The trust receipt concept was subsequently adapted by American lawyers for domestic inventory financing purposes, as a means of avoiding the badly dated and unsuitable chattel mortgage legislation, and led to the adoption of the Uniform Trust Receipts Act in 1933. The Act was repealed in the Code states when they adopted the Uniform Commercial Code. See further, Ziegel, "The Legal Problems of Wholesale Financing of Durable Goods in Canada" (1963), 41 *Can. Bar Rev.* 54, at 70-72.

Section 427 Bank Act Security

Bank of Nova Scotia v. International Harvester Credit Corp.
(1990), 73 DLR (4th) 385 (Ont. CA)

McKINLAY JA: The appellant, International Harvester Credit Corporation of Canada Limited ("I.H.C.C."), now known as Navistar Financial Corporation of Canada Inc., is assignee of the rights of a vendor of farm equipment under two conditional sales contracts. It appeals the judgement of the learned trial judge, reported in 36 DLR (4th) 278, 58 OR (2d) 493, 7 PPSAC 1, which declared its interest in the equipment to be subsequent in priority to the interest of the respondent bank under its security taken pursuant to s. 178 (now s. 427) of the *Bank Act*, SC 1980-81-82-83, c. 40 (Part I, s. 2).

In 1981 financing statements were registered by I.H.C.C. pursuant to the provisions of the *Personal Property Security Act*, RSO 1980, c. 375 ("PPSA"), for the purpose of perfecting its security interest in the equipment. The financing statements named the debtor as "Richard Howe."

Subsequent to these registrations, the Bank of Nova Scotia registered with the Bank of Canada a notice of intention from Mr. Howe to give the bank security pursuant to s. 178 of the *Bank Act*. Some two years later he did in fact give security over all farm equipment of which "the undersigned [Howe] is now or may hereafter become the owner." The bank also registered a financing statement pursuant to the provisions of the PPSA, describing the collateral as "all farm machinery and the proceeds thereof," and naming the debtor as "Richard Howe."

The full name of the debtor is Richard Glen Howe. It is conceded by both parties that pursuant to the provisions of the PPSA and the regulations thereunder at the time of these registrations and at the time of trial, as interpreted by this court in *Re Gibbons* (1984), 8 DLR (4th) 316, 45 OR (2d) 664, 51 CBR (NS) 235 (CA), a security interest remained unperfected where the middle initial of the debtor (if he had one) was not included in the debtor's name on the financing statement.

On June 8, 1984, approximately one year after filing its original financing statement, the bank registered a financing change statement naming the debtor as "Richard G. Howe." The decision of the learned trial judge that this registration did not result in the perfection of the bank's security appropriately is not appealed.

On June 15, 1984, solicitors for the bank obtained an order ex parte, under s. 64 of the PPSA extending the time for registration of a financing statement and pursuant thereto, registered a financing statement on June 21, 1984, naming the debtor as "Richard G. Howe."

Following default by Mr. Howe, the bank obtained a default judgment against him on October 16, 1984, in the amount of $163,335.38.

On November 20, 1984, I.H.C.C. repossessed the machinery pursuant to the provisions of the conditional sales contracts between it and Mr. Howe. It then notified the bank of its intention to sell the machinery if Mr. Howe's indebtedness to it was not satisfied by December 7, 1984. Although the bank notified I.H.C.C. of its claim to priority, I.H.C.C. sold the equipment and applied the proceeds against Mr. Howe's indebtedness to it.

Many issues apparently argued before the trial judge were not addressed before us.

· · ·

The numerous problems resulting from inconsistencies between the provisions of the PPSA and the *Bank Act* have been the subject of a number of learned treatises, but the subject of very little in the way of judicial interpretation. Of the cases which have addressed the problems, most were decided prior to the enactment of modern personal property security legislation, and dealt primarily with questions of title to the property involved, and the possible invalidity of conditional sales contracts and chattel mortgages resulting from non-registration pursuant to the relevant provincial statutes. Title to collateral is, for most purposes, irrelevant under the PPSA, and priority, rather than possible invalidity, is now the major issue: see s. 2(a).

The conflict between these two Acts should be looked at in the light of the history of bank lending against personalty. Prior to 1967, the *Bank Act* prohibited the lending against personalty. Prior to 1967, the *Bank Act* prohibited the lending of money on the security of "goods, wares and merchandise" except by way of security pursuant to ss. 87 and 88—the predecessors of ss. 177 and 178 of the present Act—(see SC 1953-54, c. 48, s. 75(2)(d), and see SC 1966-67, c. 87, ss. 75(1)(c) and (3)). One of the results of this broadening of the bank's security taking powers has been the practice of many banks of taking security pursuant to the provisions of s. 178 of the *Bank Act*, and, in addition, taking security in the form of a general security agreement covering all of the assets of the same debtor and registering a financing statement under PPSA with respect thereto. That was not done in this case, but rather, the bank purported to treat the s. 178 security itself as a "security interest" within the terms of the PPSA.

The procedure followed by the bank in this case raises the following series of questions:

(i) Does the s. 178 security of a chartered bank fall within the definition of "security interest" in s. 1(y) of the PPSA, and, if so, is the giving of s. 178 security a transaction to which the PPSA applies?

(ii) What interest does the bank take from its debtor under the provisions of the *Bank Act* and of the s. 178 security document?

(iii) If the PPSA applies to s. 178 security, can the bank attain, as a result of prior registration of a financing statement under the PPSA, an interest in the collateral which neither the *Bank Act* nor the security document may have given it?

There can be no doubt that by virtue of taking s. 178 security a bank obtains "an interest in goods ... that secures payment or performance of an obligation"—a "security interest" within the meaning of s. 1(y). Whether or not the transaction is one to which the PPSA applies is governed by s. 2(a), which reads:

2. Subject to subsection 3(1), this Act applies,
    (a) to every transaction without regard to its form and without regard to the person who has title to the collateral that in substance creates a security interest ...

The relevant portion of s. 3(1) reads:

3(1) This Act does not apply,
    (a) to a lien given by statute or rule of law ...

Section 178(2)(d) of the *Bank Act* (which is quoted under question (ii) below) vests in the bank "a first and preferential lien and claim" upon the property which is the subject of the s. 178 security. That lien being "given by statute" to the bank falls within the exception in s. 3(1) of the PPSA, and consequently that Act does not apply to it. However, s. 178 in addition thereto vests in the bank "the same rights and powers in respect of the property as if the bank had acquired a warehouse receipt or bill of lading in which the property was described." Thus, the PPSA applies to rights vested in the bank pursuant to that provision.

(ii) What interest does the bank take from its debtor under the provisions of the *Bank Act* and of the s. 178 security document?

In an attempt to answer this question, it is necessary to consider the following provisions of the *Bank Act*:

[Sections 178(1)(c); 178(2)(a), (b), (d); 179(1), (2), (7), (9)]

The security in this case was given in a form "to ... like effect" to that set out in Sch. VI of the Act (see s. 178(1)). The relevant portions of the security document read:

... the undersigned hereby assigns to the Bank as security for the payment of the said loan or advance or renewals thereof or substitutions therefor and interest on such loan or advance and on any such renewals and substitutions, the property hereinafter described of which the undersigned is now or may hereafter become the owner, to wit—all farm machinery that is now or may hereafter be in the place or places hereinafter designated, to wit—Lots 3 and 4 Concession 1 and Lot 2 Concession 2, Harris Township, District of Temiskaming ...
This security is given under section 178 of the Bank Act.

(Emphasis added.)

It should be noted that, pursuant to the security document and pursuant to s. 178(2)(a) and (b), the debtor must, when the security is given or before it is released, be the "owner" of the property described therein before any of the statutorily given rights vest in the bank. Nowhere in the Act is the word "owner" defined, but for the purposes of this case it is sufficient to say that a conditional purchaser is an "owner" within the meaning of s. 178(2)(a) and (b): *Royal Bank v. Hodges*, [1930] 1 DLR 397, [1929] 3 WWR 605, 42 BCR 44 (CA); *Mutchenbacker v. Dominion Bank* (1911), 21 Man. R. 320, 18 WLR 19 (CA); *Grouse Mountain Resorts Ltd. v. Bank of Montreal* (1960), 25 DLR (2d) 371 (BCSC).

• • •

Section 178(2)(d) vests in the bank "a first and preferential lien" for the debt secured plus interest, and also "the same rights and powers ... as if the bank had acquired a warehouse receipt or bill of lading in which the property was described." The provisions of s. 179(1) and (2) expand and elaborate upon the priority rights of a bank holding s. 178 security. Section 179(1) gives the bank priority over all subsequently acquired rights in the property. That portion of s. 179(1) is inapplicable to the facts of this case, since the rights of I.H.C.C. pre-dated the taking of the bank's security. However, that section also gives the bank priority over "the claim of any unpaid vendor." In the *Rogerson* case, Arnup JA made no reference to s. 179(1) (then s. 89(1)). Houlden JA simply stated at p. 682: "In my opinion, the word 'vendor' should not be interpreted to include a person who sells goods to a purchaser pursuant to a conditional sales contract."

• • •

The holder of s. 178 security, by virtue of that provision, gets only the right and title to the equipment that the owner of the equipment had. Therefore, the conditional purchaser being an owner, the bank gets priority under s. 179(1) over the claim of a conditional vendor only to the extent of the right and title of its customers—the conditional purchaser—which in the *Rogerson* case could have been no more than a right of possession until payment of the purchase price, none of which had been paid.

According to the majority's reasoning in that case, it appears that if a conditional purchaser had paid some of the purchase price, the bank's priority over the vendor's rights would be limited to the rights provided the conditional purchaser by the conditional sales contract.

(iii) If the PPSA applies to s. 178 security, can the bank attain, as a result of prior registration of a financing statement under the Act, an interest in the collateral which neither the *Bank Act* nor the security document may have given it?

One of the frequently stated objectives of the PPSA was to do away with the concept of title which permeated the numerous and confusing statutory and common law interests which vendors and other financers of personal property could obtain. As stated above, s. 2 of the Act provides that the Act applies to "every transaction without regard to its form and without regard to the person who has title to the collateral that in substance creates a security interest … ."

I have no doubt that the PPSA can apply to security taken pursuant to s. 178 of the *Bank Act* where the bank elects to utilize the provisions of the Act. In so stating, I wish to lodge the caveat that no consideration has been given in these reasons of the complications that would arise should there be a competition between a s. 178 security which has not been registered under the PPSA and other security interests in the same collateral which are so registered.

The learned trial judge appears to have assumed that once it was established that s. 178 security constituted a security interest under the PPSA and was registered under that Act, it was entitled to the collateral in priority to the holder of an unperfected security interest in the same collateral. That conclusion arises as a result of the application of the general priority rule set out in s. 35(1)(a) of the Act. Section 35(1)(a) states:

35(1) If no other provision of this Act is applicable, priority between security interests in the same collateral shall be determined,

(a) by the order of registration …

Section 9 of the Act reads:

9. Except as otherwise provided by this or any other Act, a security agreement is effective according to its terms between the parties to it and against third parties.

The provisions of s. 35 in no way give to a secured party anything that has not been given to that party by the security document itself. Consequently, the provisions of s. 9

apply and the security agreement remains effective according to its terms between the parties and against third parties. In this case, neither the provisions of the *Bank Act* which provide for the security nor the provisions of the security document itself give to the bank anything other than the interest which Howe had in the equipment. Of course, most documents which would come within the definition of "security agreement" under the PPSA would not be so limited in their terms.

Consequently, I am of the view that the bank's prior registration under the PPSA does not, on the facts of this case, give it any right in the equipment, or in the proceeds from its sale, other than the rights that its customer might have had.

HOULDEN JA: While I agree with McKinlay JA's proposed disposition of the appeal, I would like to set out briefly my own reasons for arriving at that conclusion.

I agree with McKinlay JA that s. 64 of the Personal Property Security Act, RSO 1980, c. 375 ("PPSA"), is of no assistance to I.H.C.C. The "rights" protected by s. 64 are rights which have been acquired under the PPSA prior to the order permitting late registration. The only right which I.H.C.C. had prior to the perfection of the respondent's security interest was that of the holder of an unperfected security interest. Any prejudice suffered by I.H.C.C. was caused, not by the late registration, but by I.H.C.C.'s failure to perfect its security interest.

Counsel for I.H.C.C. conceded that the agreement creating the s. 178 security was a "security agreement" and gave rise to a "security interest" as those terms are defined in the PPSA. However, he submitted that the provisions of the *Bank Act*, SC 1980-81-82-83, c. 40 (Part I, s. 2), for registration and validation of a s. 178 security interest were incompatible with the provisions of the PPSA and, hence, "security interest" under the PPSA would be nugatory, and I.H.C.C., on the basis of this court's decision in *Rogerson Lumber Co. Ltd. v. Four Seasons Chalet Ltd.* (1980), 113 DLR (3d) 671, 29 OR (2d) 193, 12 BLR 93 (CA), would have priority over the bank.

In support of his submission that the provisions of the *Bank Act* were incompatible with the provisions of the PPSA, counsel for I.H.C.C. relied on the following differences in the two statutes:

(a) To have a valid security under s. 178 as against other creditors, a bank must comply with the registration requirements of the *Bank Act*. To have a valid security interest under the PPSA as against other creditors, a creditor must perfect its security interest in accordance with the PPSA; this can be accomplished by registration of a financing statement or by taking possession of the collateral.

If the definition of "security interest" under the PPSA is interpreted so as to include a security interest under s. 178 of the *Bank Act*, then it would include a s. 178 security interest which was not registered in accordance with the *Bank Act*. Such a security interest would be unenforceable under the *Bank Act* but could be perfected under the PPSA by taking possession of the collateral. Counsel for I.H.C.C. contended that it was not the intention of the legislature in enacting the PPSA to create a process whereby an otherwise unenforceable security interest created by federal statute would become enforceable by operation of provincial law.

With respect, I do not agree. Under the PPSA, a security interest in certain defined collateral may be perfected by possession. If the bank's s. 178 security interest creates a security interest in collateral coming within those defined categories, I see no reason why the bank should not be able to perfect its security interest by taking possession of the collateral, even though the bank has failed to comply with the registration provisions of the *Bank Act*. The security interest of the bank would be invalid under the *Bank Act*, so that the bank would be unable to claim the benefit of the priority provisions of that statute; but it would be perfected under the PPSA, and the bank, like any other holder of a security interest, could claim the benefit of the priority provision of that statute.

(b) The priority rules under the two statutes are different. If a bank is permitted to take advantage of both statutes, it can claim, counsel for I.H.C.C. submitted, the benefit of the priority rules under the *Bank Act* as well as the benefit of the priority rules under the PPSA. While this is undoubtedly true, I do not believe that this is a valid reason for holding that "security interest" under the PPSA is not intended to include a security interest created by s. 178 of the *Bank Act*. If a bank has validly perfected its security interest under both statutes, the bank should be able, in my opinion, to claim the benefit of the priority rules of both statutes.

(c) The enforcement procedures under the two Acts are different. If a bank is permitted to register under both Acts, it could, counsel for I.H.C.C. contended, rely on the perfection of its interest under the PPSA to achieve priority, but utilize the enforcement procedure of the *Bank Act* in realizing its security. This is not the problem that arises in this case, and I, therefore, prefer to express no opinion on it. Suffice it to say, that the existence of this difficulty—if there is a difficulty—is no reason, in my opinion, to interpret "security interest" in the PPSA as not including a security interest created by s. 178 of the *Bank Act*.

There may be, as Cuming and Wood point out in their article "Compatibility of Federal and Provincial Personal Property Security Law" (1986), 65 *Can. Bar Rev.* 267 at p. 284-6, difficulties in permitting a s. 178 security interest to be registered under the PPSA. If there are such difficulties, then the solution is legislative action, not judicial stretching of the plain words of the PPSA.

• • •

Watt J, like McKinlay JA, held that the respondent's security interest under s. 178 of the *Bank Act* could be registered under the PPSA [36 DLR (4th) 278, 58 OR (2d) 493, 35 BLR 299]. Having done so, he turned his attention to the question of priorities, and after reviewing the matter, he found that the bank's perfected security interest had priority over the unperfected security interest of I.H.C.C. I agree with McKinlay JA that he erred in so finding. If the security agreement which gives rise to the bank's security interest were not given pursuant to s. 178 of the *Bank Act*, Watt J would be clearly right. If, for example, instead of s. 178 security, the bank had taken a general security agreement covering all the farm machinery of Howe and had properly perfected its security interest under the PPSA, the bank would have had priority over the unperfected security interest of I.H.C.C. But the bank's security agreement was given pursuant to s. 178 of the *Bank Act*, and it is essential, therefore, to turn to that statute to see what rights are given to the bank by its security agreement:

• • •

GRANGE JA: I have no doubt that the bank intended and tried to get priority over the I.H.C.C. collateral but to succeed in that endeavour it would have had to use a document which purports to give it security on the whole and not just one which on its face and under the *Bank Act*, SC 1980-81-82-83, c. 49 (Part I, s. 2), gave it security only on the borrower's interest in the whole.

• • •

Appeal allowed.

NOTES AND QUESTIONS

1) The Ontario Court of Appeal in *International Harvester Credit Corp.* appears, either in the ratio of the case or in *dicta,* to have addressed five vexing features of the overlap between the PPSA and s. 427 Bank Act regimes. Each of these is addressed in the following notes.

2) *Question 1*: Is a s. 427 security a "security interest" within the scope of the PPSA? The court had no difficulty in answering this in the affirmative notwithstanding its own decision in *Rogerson Lumber Co. v. Four Seasons Chalet Ltd.* (1980), 29 OR (2d) 193 in which Arnup JA stated at 199 that "[t]he PPSA confers no rights or priority on the Bank ... The only relevance of the PPSA is whether it prejudicially affects the plaintiff's interest."

3) *Question 2*: Do the priority rules of the PPSA apply where a s. 427 security interest is in competition with a provincial security interest? This was the main issue before the court, but the answer to it was predicated on the court's affirmative reply to Question 1.

4) *Question 3*: Can banks holding s. 427 security opt in and out of the regulatory regime of the PPSA? McKinlay JA stated that the PPSA would apply to a s. 427 security "where the bank elects to utilize the provisions of the Act." Do you see a logical inconsistency in this approach? Is there anything in the PPSA that allows a secured party to opt in or out of the system? Does mere failure to register a financing statement relating to a security interest take the security interest out of the scope of the Act?

5) *Question 4*: Can a bank rely on PPSA priority rules to give it a better priority than it has under s. 427 of the Bank Act? See Houlden JA, *supra*. Implicit in Mr. Justice Houlden's opinion is the conclusion that a bank can use the PPSA as a mechanism for avoiding the consequences of non-compliance with s. 427 of the Bank Act. It is revealing to apply his conclusion in the context of situations other than the one he apparently had in mind.

Assume that Bank A takes a s. 427 security but fails to register as required by the Bank Act, and that Bank B acquires a subsequent s. 427 security, which is properly registered as required by s. 427(4). Can A acquire priority over B simply by registering a financing statement in the Personal Property Registry and asserting priority under the PPSA on the basis that Bank A has a perfected (PPSA) security interest and that Bank B has an unperfected security interest? Assume that Bank A does comply with the registration requirements of s. 427(4). Can it circumvent s. 427(7)(a) (which gives priority to unpaid employees of a bankrupt debtor of Bank A), by basing its claim to priority on the PPSA, which gives no similar preferential treatment to unpaid employees? To accept that the answer to these questions is yes is to accept that a bank can invoke its position under the

PPSA as a method of frustrating the public policies clearly spelled out in the Bank Act. Even if one concluded that it is constitutional for a provincial legislature to facilitate circumvention of the Bank Act in this way, is there any good reason why it should be seen as having intended this result?

6) *Question 5*: Can a bank hold simultaneously a s. 427 security and PPSA security interest in the same collateral to secure the same debt? See the judgment of Grange JA. Does it follow from this that a bank can have the best of both systems—can it choose the priority rule or enforcement measure from each of the systems that is most advantageous to it under the circumstances?

7) The problems raised by the overlap of the two systems have been extensively discussed in the academic literature. See Ziegel, "Interaction of Personal Property Security Legislation and Security Interests Under the Bank Act" (1986-87), 12 *CBLJ* 73; Cuming and Wood, "Compatibility of Federal and Provincial Personal Property Security Law" (1986), 65 *Can. Bar Rev.* 267, at 284, 301; Cuming, "The Relationship Between Personal Property Security Acts and Section 178 of the Bank Act: Federal Paramountcy and Provincial Legislative Policy" (1988), 14 *CBLJ* 315; Cuming, "PPSA—Section 178 Bank Act Overlap: No Closer to Solutions" (1991), 18 *CBLJ* 135; and Ziegel, "The Interaction of Section 178 Security Interests and Provincial PPSA Security Interests: Once More into the Black Hole" (1991), 6 *BFLR* 343.

8) The Acts based on the CCPPSL model all contain a provision specifically excluding from their scope "a security agreement governed by an Act of the Parliament of Canada that deals with rights of parties to the agreement or the rights of third parties affected by a security interest created by agreement, including ... any agreement governed by Part V, Division B, of the Bank Act (Canada)" (see, for example, BCPPSA, s. 4(b)). In addition, s. 9(2) of the SPPSA provides that "[a] security interest in collateral is void to the extent that it secures payment or performance of an obligation that is also secured by a security interest in the same collateral arising pursuant to an agreement, whenever executed, to which any of sections 425 to 436 of the *Bank Act* (Canada) applies."

AN EXPANDED SCOPE: DEEMED SECURITY INTERESTS

Report of The Minister's Advisory Committee on the
Personal Property Security Act
June 1984 (Ontario)

Clause 2(a) of the present [Ontario] Act provides that the Act applies to a lease or consignment intended as security. The Committee recommends that the scope of the Act be extended to all leases for a term of more than one year and to consignments that do not secure payment or performance of an obligation. See the definitions of "lease for a term of more than one year" and "consignment" in ss. 1(5) and (17) and the related commentaries. The Act will continue to apply to leases for a term of less than one year that secure payment or performance of an obligation. A similar provision is included in the Uniform and Saskatchewan Acts. The rationale for this amendment is that leases and consignments are similar to security agreements in that they put a person, who is not the owner of property, in possession and thus create a potential for the deception of innocent third parties who deal with the lessee or consignee in the belief that no one else has a claim or interest in the property. It is often difficult to distinguish between the true consignment and lease and a lease and consignment that secures payment or performance of an obligation.

NOTES

1) For reasons, based partly on industry opposition and partly on Ministry concerns, the lease recommendations of the Ontario Minister's Advisory Committee were not accepted by the Ontario government. See Ziegel, "Commentary: Protecting the Integrity of the Ontario Personal Property Security Act" (1987-88), 13 *CBLJ* 359, 362-64. As the Ontario report indicates, "leases for a term of more than one year" and "commercial consignments" have been subject to the conflict of laws, registration and priority requirements of the Saskatchewan Act since its implementation in 1981. The Saskatchewan position has found favour in all other jurisdictions that have accepted the CCPPSL model. See, for example, BCPPSA, s. 1, definition of "commercial consignment" and "lease for a term of more than one year" and s. 3.

2) The issue as to whether or not true leases should be brought within the registration and priority regimes of a PPSA has been hotly debated in the academic literature. See generally, Mooney, "The Mystery and Myth of Ostensible Ownership and Article 9 Filing: A Critique of Proposals to Extend Filing Requirements to Leases" (1988), 39 *Ala. L Rev.* 683; Filing Requirements for Personal Property Leases: A Comment and Response to Professor Ziegel" (1990), 16 *CBLJ* 419. Professor Mooney is a strong opponent of registration requirements for leases in the United States. In "Should Canada Adopt an Article 2A Type Law on Personal Property Leasing?" (1990), 16 *CBLJ* 369, Professor Ziegel answers in detail Professor Mooney's principal objections to registration. In a study of the practices of lawyers who work in the areas of secured financing in Ontario, it was found that 70.4% of respondents to a questionnaire supported the inclusion of long-term leases within the scope of the registration, priorities and conflict of laws provisions of the OPPSA. The survey also revealed that 54.9% of respondents always and an additional 28.7% often registered financing statements relating to chattel leases in the Ontario Personal Property Registry. See Ziegel and Denomme, "How Ontario Lawyers View the Personal Property Security Act: An Empirical Survey" (1992), 20 *CBLJ* 90, at 102-4.

3) It should be noted that the decision to exclude non-security leases and commercial consignments from the scope of the OPPSA was not induced by a desire to preserve the conceptual purity of the Act since the Act applies to an absolute assignment of an account or chattel paper.

EXCLUSIONS FROM THE SCOPE OF THE ACT

Commercial Credit Corp. Ltd. v. Harry Shields Ltd.
(1981), 32 OR 703 (Ont. CA)

The judgment of the Court was delivered orally by

WEATHERSTON JA: This appeal raises a question as to the priority between a chattel mortgagee (the appellant) and a landlord who distrained for arrears of rent (the respondent). The chattel mortgage was properly registered in accordance with the provisions of the *Personal Property Security Act*, RSO 1970, c. 344. The landlord on its part had distrained properly for arrears of rent some time after the chattel mortgagee had sent a notice claiming possession of the secured property for default in payment.

Section 3(1)(a) of the *Personal Property Security Act* exempts from the application of that Act "a lien given by statute or rule of law." A distress is the right of a landlord to take and hold possession until rent is paid, plus the statutory right to sell the distrained goods. We agree with the trial Judge that a distress, when made, confers on the landlord a lien within the meaning of s. 3(1)(a) of the *Personal Property Security Act* notwithstanding that it has other legal incidents. The effect of this is twofold. First of all the landlord's rights after making of a distress need not be registered in accordance with the *Personal Property Security Act*; and secondly, s. 68 has no application to the case. Section 68 provides that:

> 68. ... where there is conflict between a provision of this Act and a provision of any general or special Act ... the provision of this Act prevails.

At common law a landlord could levy a distress on all goods found on the demised premises. That right is limited by s. 31(2) of the *Landlord and Tenant Act*, RSO 1970, c. 236, to the tenant's goods unless "title is derived ... by way of mortgage." So here the appellant's title having been derived by way of mortgage, the appellant does not have the benefit of s. 31(2) and the landlord therefore has priority as found by the trial Judge.

Appeal dismissed.

NOTES AND QUESTIONS

1) For a more recent decision discussing the distinction between a lien and a right to distrain see *Leavere v. Port Colbourne (City)* (1995), 22 OR (3d) 44 (Ont. CA), reproduced *infra*, chapter 8. In *Commercial Credit Corp.*, Weatherstone JA's judgment suggests it would have made a difference if the landlord's right to distrain were not treated as a lien upon its execution. Is the conclusion justified? Is there anything in s. 4 of the OPPSA to support it? Would the conflict between the consensual security interest and the non-consensual right not still have to be resolved by non-OPPSA principles?

2) Several provinces, including Saskatchewan, Alberta and British Columbia have amended their landlord and tenant law to provide specific priority rules for dealing with conflicting claims of distraining landlords and secured parties holding security interests in tenants' personal property. See, for example, The Landlord and Tenant Act, RSS 1978, c. L-6, s. 25. Regrettably, Ontario has not so far updated its landlord and tenant legislation.

3) There is a wide range of liens created by statute and rules of law, and the statutory liens continue to expand at an impressive and (from the secured parties' points of view) alarming rate. Most of the provincial PPS Acts do not purport to apply to these liens, although they all contain a priority rule dealing with artisan's liens. See, for example, OPPSA s. 31. The OPPSA stands alone, however, to the extent that it contains a more general (and controversial) priority rule governing the priority between an *unperfected* security interest and a lien created by statute or arising at common law. See OPPSA ss. 4(1)(a) and 20(1)(a)(i) and, *infra*, chapter 5.

The provisions do not address the most important question in this context: what are the respective priority positions of a lien holder and a secured party with a *perfected* security interest? The issue has attracted a very large, complex and expanding volume of litigation. The answer depends in part on the terms of the statute creating the lien and in part on whether the question arises before or after the debtor's bankruptcy. See further, *infra*, chapter 8 (pre-bankruptcy position) and chapter 17 (post-bankruptcy position).

3) Section 4(1)(d) of the OPPSA excludes from the scope of the Act "a transaction under the Pawnbrokers Act." What justification is there for this exclusion? A pawn transaction (pledge) is a security agreement with ancient and respectable lineage. The Acts based on the CCPPSL model apply to pledge transactions, but exclude them from the enforcement (seizure and sale) provisions. Which approach is more consistent with the policies underlying the PPSA?

Re Urman
(1984), 3 DLR (4th) 631 (Ont. CA)

WEATHERSTON JA: A receiving order was made against Nathan N. Urman on August 13, 1980. He was a mortgage broker whose principal business seems to have been the purchase and sale of mortgages. Sometimes he sold mortgages outright, in which case he would simply assign them to the purchasers. We are concerned in this appeal with the priorities in respect of two mortgage transactions that were somewhat more complicated.

Urman financed his transactions by means of a revolving line of credit with the Canadian Imperial Bank of Commerce. The bank had as security a general assignment of book debts, dated April 21, 1976, and duly registered under the *Personal Property Security Act*, RSO 1980, c. 375, the material parts of which were as follows:

FOR VALUABLE CONSIDERATION the undersigned Nathan N. Urman of 161 Kenwood Avenue, Toronto, Ontario hereby assign(s) and transfer(s) all debts, accounts, claims, moneys and choses in action which now are or which may at any time hereafter be due or owing to or owned by the undersigned, and also all securities, bills, notes and other documents now held or owned or which may be hereafter taken, held or owned by the undersigned or anyone on behalf of the undersigned in respect of the said debts, accounts, claims, moneys and choses in action or any part thereof, and also all books and papers recording, evidencing or relating to said debts, accounts, moneys and choses in action or any part thereof (all of the foregoing being herein called the "assigned premises") to CANADIAN IMPERIAL BANK OF COMMERCE (herein called the "Bank") as a general and continuing collateral security for payment of all existing and future indebtedness and liability of the undersigned to the Bank wheresoever and howsoever incurred and any ultimate unpaid balance thereof, and as a first and prior claim upon the assigned premises.

• • •

5. All moneys collected or received by the undersigned in respect of the assigned premises shall be received as trustee for the Bank and shall be forthwith paid over to the Bank.

At all material times the bank was aware that Urman, in the ordinary course of his business, was acquiring mortgages for the most part for resale and the revolving line of credit was provided for this purpose. Repayment was expected to be from the sale of mortgages, payments on the mortgages and profits on the sale of mortgages.

By a document dated April 24, 1979, entitled "Assignment of Mortgage as Security," Urman assigned to Kreindel Investments Limited two second mortgages as security for a loan by Kreindel to Urman of $65,000. In form, the document was an absolute assignment of the mortgage debts, and a conveyance of the mortgaged lands, but it contained the following proviso:

Provided that if the Assignor shall pay to the Assignee the sum of $65,000 together with interest thereon at the rate of 11% per annum ... then the Assignee shall, at the request and cost of the Assignor, reassign the said Mortgage to the Assignor giving trustee covenants only.

This assignment was registered in the registry office but no financing statement was registered under the *Personal Property Security Act*. On April 24, 1979, Kreindel gave notice to the mortgagors of its assignment, requiring them to make payments to Urman until notified of default by Urman. In July, 1980, Kreindel notified them of Urman's default and required mortgage payments to be made to their solicitors. The bank notified the mortgagors of its assignment of book debts on August 29, 1980.

The other mortgage transaction with which we are concerned involved a second mortgage for $160,000 from Phyllis Eckhardt to Nathan N. Urman dated March 1, 1978. The principal sum secured by the mortgage was advanced by Urman on March 1, 1978. At various times between May 9, 1978 and April 30, 1979, clients of Urman paid him sums of money to participate in the mortgage loan. In each case Urman signed a "Trust Agreement," the terms of which I shall set out later.

No financing statement was registered under the *Personal Property Security Act* in respect of these Trust Agreements. Urman continued to collect the mortgage payments, depositing them in a trust account at the bank, and, from time to time, forwarding to the trust claimants "T 5" statements of investment income in respect of payments made by him to them for their respective shares of mortgage payments. The bank gave the mortgagor notice of its assignment on August 29, 1980.

On a motion for advice to determine the respective interests and priorities of the bank, the trustee in bankruptcy and of Kreindel and the trust claimants, Steele J held that the bank had waived its rights under its assignment of book debts, and that the Kreindel assignment and the Trust Agreements created security interests within the meaning of the *Personal Property Security Act* which, since no financing statement was registered, were unperfected and so subordinate to the interest of the trustee in bankruptcy [128 DLR (3d) 33, 1 PPSAC 340, 38 CBR (NS) 261].

Steele J was of the opinion that because a mortgage is personal property, the *Personal Property Security Act* applied both to the assignment of a mortgage and to a debt secured by a real property mortgage. The effect of his ruling is that anyone acquiring an interest in a real property mortgage would be required to search under the *Personal Property Security Act* as well as under the *Registry Act*, RSO 1980, c. 445, or the *Land Titles Act*, RSO 1980, c. 230.

By s. 2 of the *Personal Property Security Act*, it is provided that the Act applies:

(a) to every transaction without regard to its form and without regard to the person who has title to the collateral that in substance creates a security interest, including, without limiting the foregoing,

(i) a chattel mortgage, conditional sale, equipment trust, floating charge, pledge, trust deed or trust receipt, and

(ii) an assignment, lease or consignment intended as security; and

(b) to every assignment of book debts not intended as security, but not to an assignment for the general benefit or creditors to which the *Assignments and Preferences Act* applies.

Section 1 has the following definitions:

(y) "security interest" means an interest in goods, other than building materials that have been affixed to the realty, fixtures, documents of title, instruments, securities, chattel papers or intangibles that secures payment or performance of an obligation, and includes an interest arising from an assignment of book debts;

• • •

(m) "intangible" means all personal property, including choses in action, that is not goods, chattel paper, documents of title, instruments or securities;

A mortgage, by which a mortgagor mortgages his land to secure a debt, creates an interest in land. It does not create a "security interest" as defined by the Act, and so the Act does not apply to it. But mortgages are said to have a dual character, and the right of the mortgagee to receive the mortgage money is treated in equity as personal property and is therefore an "intangible." An interest in an intangible that secures payment or performance of an obligation is a "security interest." However, an absolute assignment of a mortgage does not secure payment or performance of an obligation and does not create a "security interest." It absolutely transfers the mortgagee's interest in the mortgage; it does not create an interest in the right to receive the mortgage money (an intangible) that secures payment or performance of an obligation. So the Act does not apply to the absolute assignment of a mortgage.

Here, the Kreindel assignment was not absolute. The mortgages were assigned as security for the mortgagee's own debt. The mortgagee's right to receive the mortgage moneys was an intangible that secured payment or performance of an obligation, and so, on its literal wording, the Act can be said to apply to this assignment.

But the dual character of real estate mortgages has not been universally applied. By a rule established as long ago as 1804, a mortgage debt is not to be separated from the land on which it is secured for the purpose of determining priority between competing assignees. In *Taylor v. London & County Banking Co.; London & County Banking Co. v. Nixon*, [1901] 2 Ch. 231, Stirling LJ said, at 254-55:

Although a mortgage debt is a chose in action, yet, where the subject of the security is land, the mortgagee is treated as having "an interest in land," and priorities are governed by the rules applicable to interests in land, and not by the rules which apply to interests in personalty. The reason is thus stated by Sir William Grant in *Jones v. Gibbons* [(1804), 9 Ves. Jun. 407 at 410-1, 32 ER 659]: "A mortgage consists partly of the estate in the land, partly of the debt. So far as it conveys the estate, the assignment" that is, of the mortgage "is absolute and complete the moment it is made according to the forms of law. Undoubtedly it is not necessary to give notice to the mortgagor, that the mortgage has been assigned, in order to make it valid and effectual. The estate being absolute at law, the debtor has no means of redeeming it but by paying the money. Therefore he, who has the estate, has in effect the debt; as the estate can never be taken from him except by payment of the debt."

Jones v. Gibbons, referred to by Stirling LJ, is remarkably similar to the present case. A West Indies merchant was in financial difficulties, and an arrangement was made with his creditors whereby he assigned to trustees several securities for debts due to him, including mortgage debts, as security for his own debts. He remained in possession of the assets, and the assignments of mortgages were not registered. Later, he became bankrupt, and a contest arose between the trustees for the creditors on the one hand, and the assignees in bankruptcy on the other hand, who attacked the earlier assignment as being fraudulent and void against the general creditors. The attack was resisted as to the mortgage debts. Sir William Grant MR held that the other debts and chattels covered by the assignment to trustees, since they remained in the possession, order and disposition of the bankrupt at the time of the bankruptcy, passed to the assignees in bankruptcy. Then came the passage in his judgment as to the mortgage debts that was quoted by Stirling LJ. He held that they passed by the assignment of the mortgages to the trustees for the first creditors, and the general creditors were not entitled to any account of them [at 411]:

With regard to the objection, that these deeds were not registered, the Registry Acts have no effect as between those claiming by conveyance and the assignees of the bankrupt, who made the conveyance. It was never held bad, because not registered; the object being purely for the protection of subsequent purchasers.

These two cases are sufficient authority to hold that the Kreindel assignment, although in effect a mortgage of a mortgage, is to be treated as an interest in land and not in an intangible, and, accordingly, the Act did not apply to it. Kreindel is entitled to priority over the trustee in bankruptcy to the extent of its security interest in the mortgages.

After Steele J had given judgment on the motion before him, the Legislature enacted s. 3(1)(e) by the *Personal Property Security Amendment Act (No. 2)*, 1981 (Ont.), c. 58, s. 1, by which it was provided that the Act does not apply

(e) to the creation or assignment of an interest in real property, including a mortgage, charge or lease of real property ...

This enactment must now be taken as merely a declaration of the existing law.

• • •

Appeal allowed.

NOTES AND QUESTIONS

1) Section 4(1)(e), by negative inference, brings within the scope of the OPPSA the assignment of a right to payment under a mortgage, charge or lease where the assignment does not convey or transfer the assignor's interest in real property. See also, ss. 36(1) and 54(1)(b). Are these sections to be taken as a legislative reversal of the legal conclusion of the Court of Appeal that a mortgage debt cannot be separated from the land on which it is secured for the purposes of determining priority between competing assignees? Note that these provisions were enacted before the Court of Appeal's decision. Professor Geva, also writing before the Court of Appeal decision, concluded:

Read alone, new s. 3(1)(e)(ii) [now s.4(1)(e)] seems to raise the possibility of a split priority between a debt and the right to a real estate mortgage securing it. Yet, read in conjunction with new section 36a(2) [now s.36(2)], new s. 3(1)(e)(ii) makes more sense. The combined effect of the two provisions is that the registration of a specific assignment in the proper land registry office will put the assignee ahead of a secured party who subsequently registered his PPSA security interest in the land registry office under new section 54(1)(b). The assignee's priority will be with respect to the land as well as to the debt.

What is the position of a security interest in a right to payment under a real estate mortgage to which the PPSA will apply under Bill 163, vis-à-vis the interest of an assignee of a specific real estate mortgage, where the latter registered the mortgage assignment *after* a notice of the security interest had been registered in the proper land registry office? The negative implication from new section 36a(2) is that priority is given to the security interest in the right to payment governed by the PPSA. But does this priority extend to the real estate mortgage securing the right to payment? A positive answer is suggested if one recalls that the mortgage follows the debt. Nonetheless, is not this rule explicitly rejected by proposed section 3(1)(e)(ii)? Does this mean a split priority? Does this mean that real estate law determines priority? I do not know.

See Geva, "Security Interests on Secured Obligations" (1982), 60 *CBR* 151, at 170-71, and *cf.* Ziegel (1981-82), 6 *CBLJ* 107, at 118-26.

2) For the most part, the Western Acts exclude from their scope real property interests or rights to payment that arise in connection with a real property interest. Consequently, assignments of mortgage payments or rentals are excluded. See, for example, BCPPSA ss. 4(f) and 4(g).

CHAPTER THREE

Validity and Enforceability, Attachment and Perfection of the Security Interest

This chapter deals with the following questions. *First*, to what extent are the parties free to design their own security agreement and how far is the agreement binding on third parties? *Second*, what evidentiary requirement must the security agreement satisfy? *Third*, when does the security interest "attach" against the collateral and, finally, what must the secured party do in order to obtain the maximum degree of protection available under the Act with respect to the collateral against the competing claims of third parties. Section 9(1) of the OPPSA deals with the first question, ss. 11(2)(a) and 9(2) with the second. "Attachment," as used in the PPS Acts, is a term of art and is described in s. 11(2) of the OPPSA. To attain maximum possible safety a security interest must be "perfected." This too is a term of art and its ingredients are prescribed in s. 19.

VALIDITY OF THE SECURITY AGREEMENT

Section 9(1) of the OPPSA is identical with s. 9 of the old Act and provides that "Except as otherwise provided by this or any other Act, a security agreement is effective according to its terms between the parties to it and against third parties." The section is of great conceptual significance. It embraces the principle of freedom of contract for security agreements. Its importance is greater for American law than for Anglo-Canadian law since, as we saw in chapter 1, for more than a century Anglo-Canadian law has generally been very accommodating to chattel security agreements.

Section 9(1) seems so far to have generated no important case law. Nevertheless, it raises some difficult interpretational issues. The parties' contractual freedom is limited by contrary provisions in "this or any other Act." The PPSA restrictions appear throughout the Act and are of two principal kinds. First, there are those that apply to all security interests and agreements. These include the requirements for the attachment and perfection of a security interest and the rules in Part V of the Act governing the enforcement of the security interest. Second, there is a group of limitations applicable only to consumer transactions or consumer goods. See, e.g., OPPSA, ss. 12(2)(b), 14(2), 45(2), 57, 65(1), 66(2), 73. These are largely based on comparable provisions in Article 9. There have been intermittent discussions about whether they should be deleted and re-enacted in consumer protection legislation. In Ontario, at any rate, they are likely to stay in the Act for the time being—their number has actually been increased in the new Act.

What is the rationale for retaining the restrictions on security agreements in *non*-PPSA Acts? Does it not dilute the PPSA aim to present a comprehensive statement of the modern Law? Catzman et al., at 50, claim that:

> The reference to other Acts in the first phrase of s. 9 is for all intents and purposes superfluous because s. 68 [s. 73 in new Act] of the Act deals with the effect of this Act vis-à-vis the provisions of other Acts and lays down the rule that with the exception of The Consumer Protection Act, the provisions of The Personal Property Security Act prevail over the provisions of any other general or special Act in the event of a conflict.

Is this correct? Does s. 73 override s. 9?

What of common law restrictions on the validity of security agreements? They too fall into two groups. First, there are the restrictions common to all contracts, e.g., capacity, requirements of consideration, effects of misrepresentations and stipulations contrary to public policy, etc. Presumably these continue to apply. UCC 1-103 expressly so provides for all Code transactions. The new Ontario Act, s. 72, contains a similar provision, as does UPPSA 1982, s. 63.

The second group of common law restrictions are those particular to security agreements, e.g., clogs on the equity of redemption. Is there an equally valid argument for their intention or does it depend on whether the restriction conflicts with a specific provision or the general philosophy of the PPSA?

"STATUTE OF FRAUDS" REQUIREMENTS: SECTION 11(2)(a)

Atlas Industries v. Federal Business Development Bank: S.K.T.N. Farm and Truck Equipment Ltd. (debtor)
(1983), 3 PPSAC 39 (Sask. QB)

NOBLE J: The applicant is a manufacturer and as a result of four orders received from the debtor dated July 29, August 11, 16 and 20 all in 1982, manufactured and delivered certain equipment parts to the debtor. All of the equipment parts so ordered were delivered to the debtor as they were manufactured and delivery was completed prior to October 25, 1982. On that date the applicant became aware that the "bank" had decided to realize on the security it had on the assets of the debtor by way of a registered debenture, by appointing a receiver to take control of the debtor's business. On October 27, 1982 the applicant delivered four invoices to the bank's receiver recovering the goods described in the four work orders already mentioned. On each invoice the applicant stamped the following words:

> Title to property described on this invoice retained by vendor until payment in full. Vendor has right of repossession on default. Power to forceably retake. This is a security agreement.

The bank, under date of February 9, 1981 had acquired a debenture to secure a loan of $150,000 from the debtor. The debenture was duly registered pursuant to the Corporation Securities Registration Act, RSS 1978, c. C-39 [subsequently repealed 1979-80, c. 18, s. 2] on February 26, 1981. Without going into detail, the said debenture represented a floating debenture which forms a charge, *inter alia*, "on all chattels now owned or hereafter acquired by the Company (debtor) ... ."

The applicant now seeks, pursuant to the Personal Property Security Act, SS 1979-80, c. P-6.1, an order firstly that it has a security interest in the equipment parts sold to the debtor by virtue of the work orders and the invoices; and secondly, that such security interest takes priority over the bank's debenture and is enforceable.

The first issue is whether or not the debtor's work orders, when combined with the applicant's invoices, represent a security agreement as defined by the Act. Section 2(mm) of the Act defines security agreement as "... an agreement that creates or provides for a security interest, and includes a document evidencing a security agreement when the context permits." The applicant argues that the work orders taken together with the invoices can be read together to fall within the definition of a security agreement. The work orders are a request to supply certain equipment parts which the applicant agrees were ordered for resale by the debtor. They contain a signature of someone who was apparently authorized to place such orders. The chattels were, as indicated, delivered as they became available with the invoices being issued later on October 26, 1982. As I understand the applicant's argument, notwithstanding that the debtor was unaware of the applicant's intention to reserve title to the goods until the invoices were delivered, the documents taken together represent a security agreement based on the terms of the invoices in particular. In my opinion it is clear that the applicant attempted to create a security agreement after it became apparent that the bank was about to swallow up the equipment parts as part of the inventory of the debtor covered by the debenture security. The fact is that it was open to the applicant to search the Personal Property Registry even before it delivered the goods to the debtor, and had it done so, would no doubt have discovered the bank's security on all chattels including those "hereafter acquired." It might then have insisted on cash or made a separate arrangement for payment which would circumvent the floating charge of the bank. It is, in my opinion, a little late to claim a security interest after the fact and in circumstances which make it clear the buyer of the goods was not aware of the terms of the transaction at the time the goods were delivered. So I am drawn to the conclusion that the documents evidencing the transaction between the applicant and the debtor do not represent a security agreement as defined by the statute. In my opinion, the sale by the applicant to the debtor was on the basis of goods and chattels delivered pursuant to an order on an open account. On this basis alone the applicant's motion fails.

However, even if I am wrong in this conclusion, the applicant fails because the documents of the sale (i.e., the work orders and the invoices) do not comply with s. 10 of the statute and are not therefore enforceable as against a third party:

10.—(1) No security interest is enforceable against a third party unless:
    (a) the collateral is in the possession of the secured party; or
    (b) the debtor has signed a security agreement that contains a description of the collateral which enables the type or kind of collateral taken under the security agreement to be distin-

guished from types or kinds of collateral which are not collateral under the security agreement, and, in the case of a security interest taken in all of the debtor's present and after-acquired property, a statement indicating that a security interest has been taken in all of the debtor's present and after-acquired property is sufficient.

The flaw in the documents, even if one could find them to be a security agreement, is that they are not signed by the debtor. It is true that a signature appears on each of the four work orders, but there is no evidence as to whether that person was in fact authorized to sign on behalf of the debtor company. Even if one assumes that the signature on each work order is an authorization which binds the debtor, it cannot be said to be a signature as contemplated by s. 10(1)(b) of the Act. As counsel for the bank argued, a purchase order is delivered without conditions and in this instance was delivered to the debtor in the ordinary course of business so that the debtor could acquire the equipment parts for its inventory. While the signature authorizes the delivery of the goods, it would be absurd to suggest that it was intended to authorize delivery upon any terms the applicant chose to impose as to price, security or payment. Thus, if there is to be an agreement that the applicant shall retain title to the goods once they were delivered, that condition should be imposed before the transaction is finalized, and in any event it cannot be said that the signature on the work order somehow authorized the unknown condition in advance. So I am inclined to agree that even if it could be successfully argued that the applicant had a "security agreement" and thereby acquired a security interest in the equipment parts, it is not enforceable as against the bank's security in any event. In this regard *Pickles Tents & Awnings Ltd. v. Joseph Group of Cos.*, [1981] 6 WWR 300, 10 Man. R. (2d) 19, 2 PPSAC 1, 127 DLR (3d) 176 (CA) and the case of *Roynat Inc. v. United Rescue Services Ltd.*, [1982] 3 WWR 512, 2 PPSAC 49 (Man. CA) in McLaren's *Secured Transactions in Personal Property in Canada*, seem to support the bank's position.

Application dismissed.

Re Ayerst and Ayerst
(1984), 4 PPSAC 81 (Ont. CA)

CATZMAN J: Two motions—one brought by the trustee in bankruptcy and one by Gail Clark—are before the Court. At the outset, I expressed my concern to counsel for both parties regarding the hearing of these motions on the basis of the material filed rather than on the basis of evidence viva voce upon the trial of an issue, particularly in view of the relief sought in Gail Clark's notice of motion. In discussions with the Court and with each other, counsel urged that the motions should proceed and for that purpose they made the following concessions:

(1) Gail Clark acknowledged that her position on her motion was that s. 4 of the Personal Property Security Act, RSO 1980, c. 375 [s. 9(2) in the new Act], affords her the opportunity of asking the Court to find that the omission of a description of chattels in the chattel mortgage does not invalidate the claim to a security interest in the said chattels, and she withdrew the claim made in her notice of motion for amendment of the chattel mortgage;

(2) The trustee conceded that it was mutually intended by the chattel mortgagor and the chattel mortgagee that a schedule marked as "A" in the same form as that forming part of the agreement of purchase and sale and the bill of sale between the parties, which schedule would also include reference to the inventory referred to in the bill of sale between the parties, would be prepared and form part of the chattel mortgage and that, by mutual error, such a schedule was not prepared and did not form part of the chattel mortgage.

Despite Mr. Gringorten's strong submission as to the limitations of the scope of the curative provisions of s. 4 of the Personal Property Security Act, it is my view that the provisions of that section apply in the circumstances of the present case, and that the material filed, coupled with the acknowledged mutual intention and mutual error to which I have referred, establish, within the meaning of s. 4, an omission or error in a document to which the Act applies. Counsel for the trustee did not assert that, if s. 4 were otherwise applicable, it did not apply in the present case because some person whose interests are affected by the document was actually misled.

My decision in *Re 471283 Ont. Ltd. (No. 1)* (1982), 2 PPSAC 83, 42 CBR (NS) 206 (Ont. SC), on which Mr. Gringorten relied, is distinguishable from the present case. Although it does not appear with sufficient clarity from the oral reasons for judgment which I delivered, there was no evidence in that case, as there is in this, of any error or omission in the preparation or completion of the chattel mortgage there in question. The question there decided was whether the language of the document, without more, created a security interest in collateral in favour of the chattel mortgagee.

There will be a declaration that the chattel mortgage in question in this case is not invalidated nor its effect destroyed by reason of the absence of the schedule referred to, and an order that the trustee deliver to Gail Clark the proceeds of sale presently held by it. In the circumstances, this is not a case for costs, save and except for the usual order for payment of the trustee's costs out of the estate.

May 15, 1982. The following was endorsed upon the Appeal Book by

MacKINNON ACJO: There was an inadequate description of the collateral covered by the chattel mortgage. However, it is agreed that the omission of the detailed description of the goods and chattels covered by the mortgage was omitted through mutual error. It is also acknowledged that no one whose interests have been affected has been actually misled by the omission or error.

Accordingly, in our view this is a case in which s. 4 of the Personal Property Security Act, RSO 1980, c. 375, can be prayed in aid. The plain intent of the legislation, and remedial thrust of s. 4, which should be given a large and liberal interpretation, is to avoid, in appropriate cases, the hardship which resulted from the highly technical and mechanical interpretations and applications of sections of previous legislation on the subject. There is no legislative reason why the respondent here should suffer the loss of her moneys honestly owed.

Appeal dismissed.

NOTES

1) Section 10 of the old Ontario Act corresponded to the 1962 version of UCC 9-203. The Article 9 Review Committee thought it anomalous that a security interest could attach [under the UCC 9-204(1)] when the security interest itself was unenforceable under 9-203. The 1972 Official Text therefore incorporated old 9-203 into new 9-203(1)(a) detailing the requirements of attachment. See also, SPPSA, s. 12(1). The new Ontario Act, s. 11(2)(a), follows suit.

2) The previous Canadian registration Acts did not contain separate writing requirements for the enforceability of chattel security agreements. Instead, they typically provided that the security agreement was "void" against third parties unless the agreement was in writing and the original agreement or a copy thereof was registered in a public office as prescribed in the Act. The PPS legislation, following Article 9, severs the writing requirements from the registration requirements because under the new legislation only a financing statement, not the agreement itself, is required to be registered. See, e.g., OPPSA, s. 45(1). (Under Art. 9, UCC 9-402(1), a copy of the security agreement may be filed to satisfy the filing requirements; this is not possible under the OPPSA or the other provincial Acts.)

3) What is the rationale of s. 11(2)(a)? Why is possession of the collateral by the secured party an acceptable alternative to a written security agreement?

4) Do you agree with the reasoning in *Re Ayerst and Ayerst*? Section 9(2) of the OPPSA (old s. 4) is copied from earlier registration statutes where the section was intended to protect the secured party against non-compliance with registration requirements that had not prejudiced a third party. Given the new role of s. 11(2)(a), does it make sense to retain the reliance test? Will a trustee in bankruptcy ever be able to show that he has been prejudiced by non-compliance with the writing requirements? The Ontario Advisory Committee (*Supplementary Report*, at 63, paras. 2-3), recommended the deletion of s. 4 and the insertion of a new curative provision in Part IV of the Act limited to errors, etc., in a financing statement or financing change statement. The committee reasoned that in view of the different contexts in which writing or notice requirements appear in the Act it was not realistic to apply a uniform curative test. The committee also noted that several of the provisions in the new Act, like the old Act, contain their own test as to the consequences of an error. See new Act, ss. 18(5) and (10), 67(2), and *cf.* s. 72.

5) So far as the description requirements in s. 11(2)(a) [old s. 10] are concerned, it has been observed that:

The section requires the debtor to have signed a security agreement that contains a "description" of the collateral. "Description" is not defined nor does s. 10 itself indicate what will be deemed a sufficient description. The pre-PPSA registration Acts usually required "such sufficient and full description of the goods and chattels that the same may be thereby readily and easily known and distinguished." Will the courts imply a similar requirement under s. 10 or will any description, however broad and unhelpful, be deemed sufficient? UCC 9-110 provides that, for the purposes of Article 9, any description of personal property or real estate is sufficient, whether or not it is specific, if it reasonably identifies what is described. The accompanying Comment explains that this test is designed to do the job assigned to a description while rejecting the fastidious and overly exacting demands of earlier chattel mortgage jurisprudence. Until such time as s. 10 is amended, one must hope the Ontario courts will follow the same intermediate route even in the absence of a UCC 9-110 type guide-line.

(Ziegel, "The Quickening Pace of Jurisprudence ..." (1980), 4 *CBLJ* 54, at 92-93.)

In order to clarify the position, the new Act provides in s. 11(2)(a) that the security agreement must contain a description of the collateral "sufficient to enable it to be identified." Will a description in a security agreement that covers "all of the debtor's present and after-acquired property wherever located" satisfy the new test? *Cf. McCall v. Wolfe* (1885), 13 SCR 130, and *Hovey v. Whiting* (1886), 14 SCR 515, both decisions rendered under pre-PPSA registration legislation.

ATTACHMENT OF THE SECURITY INTEREST

"Attachment" is a key concept in the Act since a security interest cannot be perfected unless it has first attached to the collateral. See s. 19. According to s. 11(2),

11.—(2) A security interest, including a security interest in the nature of a floating charge, attaches when,
    (a) the secured party or a person on behalf of the secured party other than the debtor or the debtor's agent obtains possession of the collateral or when the debtor signs a security agreement that contains a description of the collateral sufficient to enable it to be identified;
    (b) value is given; and
    (c) the debtor has rights in the collateral,
unless the parties have agreed to postpone the time for attachment, in which case the security interest attaches at the agreed time.

These provisions should be compared with the much leaner language of old s. 12(1):

12.—(1) A security interest attaches when,
    (a) the parties intend it to attach;
    (b) value is given; and
    (c) the debtor has rights in the collateral.

The reason for the important changes is explained in the following materials.

Time of Attachment and the Floating Charge

Ordinarily the security agreement itself will make it clear when the parties intend the security interest to attach. However, without further clarification this may not be sufficient with respect to English style floating charges. This is because of the special meaning which the English courts gave to attachment in turn of the century cases and their perception of the role of a floating charge. Typically the floating charge covered all of the debtor's circulating assets. It was clear to the courts that the parties meant the debtor to be able to carry on his business as before unless a winding up order was made or a receiver was appointed. The difficulties that the courts faced were how to reconcile the debtor's freedom to deal with the collateral with the traditional concept of a fixed charge. Earlier 19th century common law courts, when confronted with chattel mortgages on a debtor's inventory, resolved the conflict by finding that the debtor had *an implied licence* to dispose of the inventory in the ordinary course of his business. See, e.g., *Dedrick v. Ashdown* (1888), 15 SCR 227, and Ziegel (1963), 41 *Can. Bar Rev.* 54, at 76-78. With the introduction of secured debentures covering all of the debtor's assets, the courts swept aside the implied licence theory and adopted a new concept of the floating charge. See Pennington, "The Genesis of the Floating Charge" (1960), 23 *Mod. L Rev.* 630, at 644 *et seq.*

The courts, however, have had difficulty nailing down the precise characteristics of the floating charge. Three frequently cited descriptions are the following:

1) Lord Macnaghten in *Governments Stocks & Other Securities Investment Co. v. Manila Ry. Co.*, [1897] AC 81, at 86:

A floating security is an equitable charge on the assets for the time being of a going concern. It attaches to the subject charged in the varying condition in which it happens to be from time to time. It is of the essence of such a charge that it remains dormant until the undertaking charged ceases to be a going concern, or until the person in whose favour the charge is created intervenes. His right to intervene may of course be suspended by agreement. But if there is no agreement for suspension, he may exercise his right whenever he pleases after default.

2) Buckley LJ in *Evans v. Rival Granite Quarries, Ltd.*, [1910] 2 KB 979, at 999 (CA):

A floating security is not a future security; it is a present security, which presently affects all the assets of the company expressed to be included in it. On the other hand, it is not a specific security; the holder cannot affirm that the assets are specifically mortgaged to him. The assets are mortgaged in such a way that the mortgagor can deal with them without the concurrence of the mortgagee. A floating security is not a specific mortgage of the assets, plus a licence to the mortgagor to dispose of them in the course of his business, but is a floating mortgage applying to every item comprised in the security, but not specifically affecting any item until some event occurs or some act on the part of the mortgagee is done which causes it to crystallize into a fixed security. This crystallization may be brought about in various ways. A receiver may be appointed, or the company may go into liquidation and a liquidator be appointed, or any event may happen which is defined as bringing to an end the licence to the company to carry on business.

3) Romer LJ in *In Re Yorkshire Woolcombers Association Ltd.* [1903] 2 Ch. 284, at 295:

I certainly do not intend to attempt to give an exact definition of the term 'floating charge' nor am I prepared to say that there will not be a floating charge within the meaning of the Act, which does not contain all the three characteristics that I am about to mention, but I certainly think that if a charge has the three characteristics that I am about to mention it is a floating charge. (1) If it is a charge on a class of assets of a company present and future. (2) If that class is one which in the ordinary course of the business of the company would be changing from time to time; and (3) If you find that by the charge it is contemplated that, until some future step is taken by or on behalf of those interested in the charge, the company may carry on its business in the ordinary way so far as concerns the particular class of assets I am dealing with.

In *Re Bond Worth Ltd.* [1979] 3 All ER 919, Slade J held that, to establish the existence of a floating charge, it is not necessary for the fund to be open-ended. If the three characteristics identified in Romer J's judgment (as qualified in *Re Bond Worth*) are satisfied in a case then, in equity, a floating charge will be deemed to exist regardless of how the parties choose to describe it. This proposition has long been established in England and was reaffirmed, for Canada, in the BC Court of Appeal's important judgment in *B.C. v. Federal Business Development Bank*, [1988] 1 WWR 1.* If the secured party wants to obtain a fixed charge over floating assets then it must exercise strict control over the proceeds of disposition of the collateral either by requiring the debtor to pay the proceeds into a trust account or by remitting them to the secured party or other designated non-debtor related person: see *Siebe Gorman & Co. Ltd. v. Barclays Bank plc*, [1979] 2 Ll. Rep. 142; R.M. Goode, *Legal Problems of Credit and Security*, 2nd ed., p.49 (1988).

In equity, the distinction between a fixed and floating charge is fundamental. A fixed charge is binding upon the debtor and third parties, subject to the doctrine of purchase for value without notice which applies to all equitable interests. A floating charge, on the other hand, (i) entitles the debtor to continue to carry on business as before, subject only to such negative covenants as are contained in the agreement, to deal with the floating charge collateral and to retain the proceeds from its disposition; (ii) entitles the debtor to create further security interests over the same collateral ranking *pari passu*, and even in priority to, with the first floating charge, unless otherwise provided in the agreement. Even if the agreement prohibits it (as it almost invariably does), a subsequent secured party will not be bound by such restrictions unless it actually knows of them or is deemed to know of them. (However, under the English Companies Act registration of notice of the floating charge is not sufficient to bind a third party unless the notice also specifies the restrictions); and (iii) entitles third parties to seize the collateral by operation of law, free of the floating charge, to satisfy their claims. These incidents make the floating charge a very vulnerable security interest. To reduce the vulnerability the courts introduced the concept of crystal-lization of the floating charge, on the happening of which the floating charge is converted into a fixed charge. Crystallization can occur by operation of law (as where the debtor voluntarily ceases to carry on business or becomes bankrupt) or pursuant to the terms of the agreement. A typical agreement contains many crystallizing event provisions. There is considerable doubt whether crystallization can happen automatically under the terms of the agreement without formal notice to the debtor and whether some overt action by the secured party to alert third parties of the change in the debtor's position is not essential. *Cf.* Goode, *op. cit.*, pp. 59-75.

The hybrid nature of the English floating charge has given rise to much debate about its precise juristic character, and equally to much difference of opinion among judges about the practical consequences. The English courts were guided by two principal considerations in embracing the floating charge. The first was to reconcile the creation of the charge with the debtor's freedom to carry on business as before. The second was to preserve a cushion of free assets to satisfy the claims of unsecured creditors. It seems clear that equity was not successful in the second goal. In the great majority of cases, where the

---

* Lambert JA wrote a strong dissenting judgment arguing that the Supreme Court's decision in *Dedrick v. Ashdown*, *supra*, and the explicit provisions in s. 427 of the Bank Act demonstrated that Canadian law did recognize the availability of a fixed security interest in revolving assets even if there was no policing by the secured party of the proceeds of disposition. The majority's rejection of the proposition was no doubt influenced by policy considerations.

debtor is in financial difficulties the floating charge will crystallize before unsecured creditors have an opportunity to enforce their claims. See e.g., *Access Advertising Management Inc v. Servex Computers Inc.*, *infra* this section.

Position under the OPPSA

There is no doubt that the old Act applied to floating charges: s. 2(a)(i) expressly so provided, as does s. 2(a)(i) of the new Act. What the old Act failed to make clear was when the security interest in a floating charge type agreement was deemed to attach for the purposes of old s. 12(1)(a). The Ontario Court of Appeal had an opportunity to resolve the issue in *Re Huxley Catering Limited* (1982), 2 PPSAC 22, but gave a very ambiguous answer. See Ziegel (1985), 10 *CBLJ* 131, at 151-52. As a result the drafters of the revised Ontario Act deemed it desirable to clarify the position in new s.11(2). A similar provision appears in the Western Provinces' Acts and in s.11(1) of the Uniform Act 1982. The following cases illustrate the courts' reactions to these provisions:

Access Advertising Management Inc. v. Servex Computers Inc.
(1994), 15 OR (3d) 635 (Ont. Gen. Div.)

SAUNDERS J: This is a motion under rule 60.08(16) of the Rules of Civil Procedure for an order setting aside a notice of garnishment and declaring that the funds held in court to the credit of this matter be paid to the moving party. The issue is whether funds collected under a notice of garnishment are subject to the interest of the moving party under a security agreement.

The background facts are as follows:

1. By agreement in writing executed on April 6, 1992 (the "guarantee agreement") Everex Systems (Canada) Inc. ("Everex-Canada") guaranteed the indebtedness, liabilities and obligations of Everex Systems, Inc. ("Everex-US") to the CIT Group/Credit Finance, Inc. ("CIT").

2. In support of the guarantee, Everex-Canada executed an agreement (the "security agreement") with CIT on April 6, 1992 whereby, as continuing security for its obligations under the guarantee agreement, Everex-Canada created a security interest in all its present and after-acquired personal property "together with … all deposit accounts."

3. A financial statement with respect to the security interest created by the security agreement was registered on April 14, 1992 pursuant to the Personal Property Security Act, RSO 1990, c. P.10 (the "PPSA").

4. On January 4, 1993, Everex-US filed a voluntary petition pursuant to c. 11 of the United States Bankruptcy Code. Everex-US as borrower and CIT as lender had entered into an agreement executed on June 4, 1991 (the "loan agreement"). Under the loan agreement any petition or any application for relief under the bankruptcy laws of the United States is an event of default. Under the guarantee agreement, upon the occurrence of any default under the loan agreement, the obligations under the guarantee agreement become immediately due and payable. Also under the security agreement, the security constituted thereunder becomes enforceable at the option of CIT upon the occurrence of any event of default under the loan agreement.

5. On January 5, 1993, the solicitors for CIT wrote to Everex-Canada advising of the default, terminating the right of Everex-Canada to receive proceeds and directing Everex-Canada that all such property was to be received by it in trust for CIT pursuant to the terms of the security agreement.

6. On January 6, 1993, CIT sent to Everex-Canada, described as an insolvent person, a notice of intention to enforce the security under the security agreement pursuant to s. 244(1) of the Bankruptcy and Insolvency Act, RSC 1985, c. B-3 (the "BIA"), as amended.

7. On January 7, 1993, Price Waterhouse Limited was appointed interim receiver by order of this court on an application under s. 47 of the BIA.

8. On January 12, 1993, the creditor, Access Advertising Management Inc. ("Access"), obtained judgment against Everex-Canada in the amount of $54,437.35. On January 14 Access issued a notice of garnishment against the Bank of Nova Scotia (the "Bank"). The notice was served on the Bank on the same day. On January 15 the Bank debited the account of Everex-Canada by the amount of the judgment and remitted the funds to the sheriff. The funds were subsequently paid into court to the credit of this matter pursuant to court order.

9. On January 17, 1993, CIT appointed Price Waterhouse Limited as receiver pursuant to the terms of the security agreement.

Price Waterhouse Limited claims the money in court on the basis that CIT had a perfected security interest on the moneys in the account at the Bank which interest had priority over the notice of garnishment. Access submits that the floating charge of CIT did not crystallize until Price Waterhouse Limited was appointed receiver on January 17, 1993, and that by that time the moneys had been removed from the account and were beyond the reach of the receiver: see *Royal Bank of Canada v. Mohawk Moving & Storage Ltd.* (1985), 49 OR (2d) 734, 16 DLR (4th) 434 (HCJ).

Section 19 of the PPSA provides: ...

And s. 11(2) of the PPSA provides: ...

There is agreement that the security interest of CIT is in the nature of a floating charge. The collateral described in the security agreement includes "all deposit accounts." That description in my opinion is sufficient to identify the funds in the account of Everex-Canada at the Bank. Property subject to a floating charge changes from time to time. Assets are acquired and disposed of between the time the charge is given and the time it is discharged or converted into a specific charge. In such circumstances, collateral can only be described in general terms. For example, a floating charge on the inventory of a dealer in appliances could not describe the collateral by serial number or even by make or model. It is sufficient if the property in question (here a deposit account at a bank) falls within the general description of collateral in the security agreement: see McLaren, *Secured Transactions in Personal Property in Canada*, 2nd ed. (1992), pp. 2-8 and 2-29.

It was argued that because the security was a floating charge there was an agreement to postpone attachment until crystallization.

The security agreement provides otherwise. The charge on deposit accounts is described as a floating charge. The security agreement provides that the security interests created by it attach to the collateral when Everex-Canada has rights in the collateral. CIT and Everex-Canada in the agreement acknowledge that the security interests created pursuant to it have not been postponed.

A security agreement was signed, value was given and Everex-Canada had rights in the deposit accounts at the Bank. When all those three events occurred the security interest in the collateral in issue attached. The security interest was perfected by registration of the financing statement. The possibility that attachment did not occur until crystallization does not have to be dealt with. As indicated subsequently I consider the time of crystallization to be a crucial matter for determination. The security interest attached at the latest upon crystallization of the charge. As registration had already been done, the charge was also perfected no later than the time of crystallization.

The effect of perfection was that the floating charge was not subordinate to the interest of Access who assumed control of the funds on deposit through the garnishment (see PPSA s. 20(1)(a)(ii)). It did not follow that CIT by attaining perfection acquired priority over the garnishment by Access. To acquire priority the floating charge must have become specific. There must have been crystallization: *Royal Bank of Canada v. Mohawk*, *supra*; and *Re Standard-Modern Technologies Corp.* (1992), 6 OR (3d) 161, 87 DLR (4th) 442 (CA).

The critical issue, therefore, is the determination of when the charge crystallized. There is no dispute that there was crystallization on January 17, 1993 when the receiver was appointed. The issue is whether crystallization occurred at an earlier date. If crystallization occurred before the funds left the hands of the Bank, the claim of Price Waterhouse Limited prevails over the claim of Access. On the other hand, if crystallization occurred after that time the claim of Access prevails.

Part XI of the BIA dealing with secured creditors and receivers came into force on November 30, 1992 (SC 1992, c. 27). Where the debtor is an "insolvent person" (as defined in s. 2) a secured creditor who intends to enforce a security on all or substantially all of the property of the debtor must give the debtor notice of that intention in the prescribed form and manner (s. 244(1)). Subsection 244(2) provides that the creditor shall not enforce the security until the expiry of 10 days after sending the notice unless the insolvent person consents to an earlier enforcement. In order to protect the property covered by its security where a notice has been sent, an interim receiver may be appointed with wide powers to take such action as the court considers advisable (s. 47). The powers that may be given to an interim receiver under s. 47 are broader than those that may be given to such a receiver after the filing of a petition for a receiving order (see s. 46).

• • •

It would appear to be settled that a default rendering a security in the form of a floating charge enforceable at the option of the chargee does not of itself cause the charge to crystallize. There must be some intervention by the chargee to enforce the security: *Evans v. Rival Granite Quarries*, [1910] 2 KB 979, 79 LJKB 970 (CA); *R. v. Consolidated Churchill Copper Corp.* (1978), 30 CBR (NS) 27, 90 DLR (3d) 357 (BCSC); and *Bayhold Financial Corp. v. Community Hotel Co. (Receiver of)* (1991), 86 DLR (4th) 127, 10 CBR (3d) 159 *sub nom. Bayhold Financial Corp. v. Clarkson Co.* (CA). Crystallization may be brought about in various ways. An appointment of a receiver crystallizes a charge. A demand for payment of the money secured does not: *Evans, supra*.

There has been some uncertainty as to when a floating charge crystallizes. It has been the position of some that an event which involved no action by the chargee could nevertheless crystallize a charge. As indicated, it now appears settled that there must be some intervention by the chargee. The question is to determine how much intervention is required.

There are sound policy reasons for requiring some intervention. If no intervention were required, a chargee in an event of default could do nothing and allow the chargor to continue carrying on business. If in the course of that business a claim arose such as a garnishment, the chargee could rely on crystallization resulting from the earlier default to establish priority.

There are equally sound policy reasons for protecting a chargee who is entitled to enforce his security and has determined to do so but is prevented from taking immediate action. Under the BIA, if the chargor is insolvent, the chargee must give notice of his intention and wait 10 days. If he is uncertain about the insolvency, it would still be prudent to follow the BIA procedure.

In my opinion the sending of the notice pursuant to s. 244(1) of the BIA was sufficient intervention to crystallize the charge. It was not necessary to actually enforce the security by appointing a receiver in order to effect crystallization and, as I have said, that could not be done until the 10-day period had expired. To hold otherwise would mean that secured creditors with a floating charge security would be exposed during the 10-day period to subsequent claims which would have priority over their security. Secured creditors should not be so prejudiced because of the requirements of the BIA.

The BIA would have no application if Everex-Canada was not an insolvent person within the meaning of that statute. Nevertheless, if such were the case, the notice effectively communicated the intention of CIT to enforce its security. The sending of the notice was sufficient intervention to effect crystallization. Whether or not Everex-Canada was insolvent made no difference.

The charge crystallized on January 6, 1993 when the notice pursuant to s. 244(1) of the BIA was sent. The security had attached and was perfected. The charge had priority over the subsequent garnishment of Access.

There will be an order setting aside the notice of garnishment issued to the Bank and a declaration that Price Waterhouse Limited as receiver of Everex-Canada has priority over Access to the funds in court to the credit of this matter.

• • •

Order accordingly.

National Bank of Canada v. Grinnell Corp. of Canada
(1993), 5 PPSAC (2d) (Ont. Div. Ct.)

O'DRISCOLL J: This appeal involves a dispute between the bank, as holder of a general security agreement from Moore, and Grinnell, one of Moore's judgment creditors, which issued a notice of garnishment.

Borkovich J held the garnishment had priority over the general security agreement.

On October 27, 1987, the bank obtained a general security agreement from Moore. It registered that agreement as required under the Personal Property Security Act on October 30, 1987. That agreement granted a security interest in Moore's inventory, accounts receivable, equipment, intangibles, leasehold, real and immovable property and any proceeds therefrom.

Grinnell, an unpaid creditor of Moore, obtained a judgment against Moore, and, on August 2, 1991, issued a notice of garnishment and served it on Simcoe Erie in an attempt to satisfy its judgment. Grinnell learned that Simcoe Erie was holding $22,333 in respect of a claim for theft of some of Moore's inventory.

Simcoe Erie paid that amount to the sheriff of the Region of Hamilton-Wentworth, where it remains.

The bank then brought this application for determination of the rights to that money.

We conclude Borkovich J erred in his interpretation of the PPSA. In our view, the security agreement attached and was perfected prior to the garnishment proceedings of August 1991.

The definition of "proceeds" in s. 1(1) of the PPSA, together with ss. 11(2) and 25 of the Act, extended the bank's security interest to the insurance proceeds of Moore's inventory.

Section 11(2) makes specific reference to a floating charge attaching upon occurrence of three events:

(a) the signing of a security agreement containing a description of the collateral sufficient to identify it;

(b) value is given;

(c) the debtor has rights in the collateral.

Here all these requirements were met and there was no agreement to postpone attachment.

The appeal is allowed, the order of Borkovich J is set aside, and an order to go that the appellant has priority over the claim of the respondent with respect to the funds and an order directing the sheriff for the Regional Municipality of Hamilton-Wentworth to pay the money out to the bank with any accrued interest.

Appeal allowed.

Royal Bank of Canada v. G.M. Homes Inc.
(1984), 4 PPSAC 116 (Sask. CA)

[This case involved a priority conflict between the Royal Bank, which held a secured debenture given by the debtor, and claims advances by Revenue Canada and the Departments of Labour and Supply and Services of the Saskatchewan Government. The Bank's debenture covered all of the debtor's present and after-acquired property. The government departments each claimed a statutory lien against the debtor's property for monies owing to them by the debtor. In the course of his judgment for the court, Vancise JA dealt as follows with the status of the Bank's security interest under the SPPSA (at 124):]

VANCISE JA: The bank submits that its security interest was perfected in accordance with s. 19 of the Personal Property Security Act and therefore has priority over any claim by Revenue Canada, notwithstanding the provisions of ss. 24 and 71 of the respective Acts. Under s. 19, a security interest is perfected when it has attached and when all steps required for perfection have been taken regardless of the order of occurrence. In [January] of 1982, G.M. Homes granted a security agreement by way of debenture to the bank. On December 22, 1981, the bank had previously registered a financing statement which stated that a security interest had been taken in all of G.M. Homes present and after-acquired property as contemplated by subs. 10(b) of the said Act. Under s. 12 of the Act, attachment occurs when value is given, and the debtor has rights in the collateral and, except for certain purposes, it becomes capable of enforcement under subs. 10(b) unless the parties indicate it is to attach at a later time. The requirements for perfection under subs. 19(b) were therefore completed. It was submitted that the security interest was a floating charge and did not attach to the assets of G.M. Homes until the security was crystallized. The fact that the security interest was a floating charge was submitted as evidence of the parties' intention to have the security interest attach at a later time.

The purpose of the Personal Property Security Act is to create a complete commercial code which provides a system of priorities for security interests in personal property in consensual transactions when security interests are granted. The Act specifically sets out when a security interest attaches to collateral. The use by the parties of a floating charge in a consensual transaction does not, in my opinion, raise a presumption that the parties intended the security interest to attach to the collateral at a later time. This form of security alone is not, without more, evidence of the intention of the parties that the security interest would not attach to the collateral at the time of execution. The Act, in my opinion, contemplates that for attachment to occur at a time other than on the execution of the security agreement, there must be a contrary intention contained in the agreement itself. Not only was there no contrary intention in this case, the parties expressly stated that:

[G.M. Homes] shall not be at liberty to, and shall not, create or suffer to be created or incurred any security interest, mortgage, encumbrance, hypothec, lien or charge of any kind upon the mortgaged premises or any part thereof ranking or purporting to rank in priority to or pari passu with this debenture and the said security interest and the said fixed and specific charges created hereby, or to sell, assign, transfer or otherwise dispose of the mortgaged premises or any part thereof without the consent in writing of the Holder first had and received; provided that, with the exception of the lands set forth and described in said Schedule "A," the Company may sell the mortgaged premises in the ordinary course of business of the Company as at present conducted:

The security interest therefore attached at the time of execution and not [at] a later date.

NOTES

1) *Access Advertising* and *National Bank* were decided within a short period of each other and it is astonishing that neither decision makes reference to the other. (What does this tell us about the effectiveness of decisional reporting in Ontario or do judges and the members of the bar feel so overwhelmed by the volume of cases that they cannot keep up with them? *National Bank* apparently is only reported in the PPSAC series.) It seems equally surprising that O'Driscoll J showed so little hesitation in accepting the clear

language of s. 11(2) whereas Saunders J, a very experienced commercial law judge, showed obvious reluctance to abandon old floating charge concepts. *Access Advertising* is critiqued by Ziegel in (1994), 23 *CBLJ* 470. Prof. Ziegel notes, among other things, that the two earlier cases relied on by Saunders J—*Royal Bank v. Mohawk Moving & Storage Ltd.* and *Re Standard-Modern Technologies Corp.*—either do not support him or can be distinguished on their facts.

2) The effect of s. 2 of the Ontario Act, coupled with s. 11(2), is to restore the early 19th century concept of a security interest in inventory and accounts receivable as a fixed interest with an implied licence to the debtor to continue to carry on business. The legal consequences of this reversion are examined in later chapters and especially in chapter 8. For a general overview, see Ziegel in *LSUC Special Lectures 1985*, 1, at 11-17, reproduced in chapter 9. The position however remains fluid. Recent lower court decisions in Saskatchewan and Alberta have given a surprising (and unintended) degree of elasticity to the meaning of an implied licence in giving priority to Crown liens for unpaid taxes over a prior perfected consensual security interest. Similar results have been reached in Ontario and elsewhere in construing the provisions of the PPS legislation as well as s. 427 of the Bank Act. These important developments are discussed, *infra*, in chapter 8.

The Meaning of "Value"

"Value" was defined in s. 1 of the old Act as "any consideration sufficient to support a simple contract." Does this include past value, as where a security interest is given to secure an existing debt or liability, or will it depend on the circumstances? *Cf.* Catzman *et al.*, at 31-32. The definition of value in UCC 1-201(44), which applies throughout the Code, expressly includes a binding commitment to extend credit and deems value to have been given where security is given for, or in partial or total satisfaction of, a pre-existing claim. The definition of value in s. 1 of the new Ontario Act has been amended to include an antecedent debt or liability.

PROBLEM

D has made a pledge under seal to make annual contributions to her alma mater. To secure payment of the pledge she has given a security interest in a block of shares which she owns. Has "value" been given?

"Rights in the Collateral"

Kinetics Technology International Corp. v. Fourth National Bank of Tulsa
(1983), 705 F.2d 396 (CCA 10)

SEYMOUR Circuit Judge: Kinetics Technology International Corporation (KTI) brought this diversity action seeking damages for an alleged conversion of goods by Fourth National Bank of Tulsa (the Bank). The Bank admits taking possession of the goods from the custody of a third party, Oklahoma Heat Transfer Corporation (OHT), but claims a right to the goods arising under the Oklahoma version of the Uniform Commercial Code (hereinafter UCC or Code), Okla. Stat. tit. 12A, §1-101 to 11-107 (1981). For the reasons set out below, we affirm in part and reverse in part.

OHT, now defunct, was a manufacturer specializing in constructing heat exchangers to specifications supplied by its customers. On May 25, 1977, the Bank issued OHT a line of credit for $600,000, taking a security interest in OHT's inventory. On June 1, the Bank filed a financing statement covering, *inter alia*, "[a]ll inventory now or hereafter owned by the Debtor." Rec., vol. I, at 37.

KTI is a company that designs and supplies process furnaces for the refinery and petrochemical industry. On August 18, 1977, it entered into a contract with OHT under which OHT was to build eight furnace economizers to KTI's specifications, in part from materials supplied by KTI, and in part from materials supplied by OHT. KTI was to ship to OHT certain specially designed and manufactured goods consisting of finned tubes, castings, fittings, and anchors (hereinafter referred to as the KTI Goods). OHT was to build eight box units (hereinafter referred to as the Box Units) from materials out of OHT's inventory, and then install the KTI Goods into the Box Units, resulting in eight completed furnace economizers. KTI agreed to make progress payments to OHT at various stages in the process. The purchase order form, supplied by KTI, provided that title to goods delivered to OHT by KTI would remain in KTI. Title to goods acquired by OHT from other sources for use in the KTI contract would pass to KTI upon the first progress (or other) payment made by KTI to OHT. KTI did not file under the UCC.

KTI procured the goods specified in the contract (the KTI Goods), and had them delivered to OHT. Delivery was complete by January 25, 1978. OHT began work on the contract. During this time, OHT's financial situation deteriorated, and it became necessary to seek additional financing from the Bank. The Bank agreed to make additional loans (separate from the line of credit), secured in part by specified accounts receivable of OHT. A loan was made to OHT on January 10, 1978, secured by the progress payments specified in the KTI-OHT contract. The Bank instructed KTI to make the first two progress payments directly to the Bank.

OHT's work on the contract reached the point at which OHT was entitled to the first two progress payments, a total of $42,600. Both payments, which KTI made on January 10 and January 19, 1978, were received by the Bank. OHT began work on the Box Units, but prior to their completion OHT management determined that the business' financial state could not support continued operation. On January 27, OHT shut down, and on January 30, OHT's management delivered the plant keys to the Bank. At that time, the Bank took possession and control of the plant where OHT's inventory, the Box Units, and the KTI Goods were located.

KTI demanded the surrender of the Box Units and the KTI Goods, but the Bank refused on the strength of its security interest in OHT's inventory, offering instead to sell the Box Units and the KTI Goods to KTI. Consequently, KTI filed this suit for conversion. A prolonged series of negotiations culminated in KTI's purchase of the Box Units and the KTI Goods on March 20, 1978. KTI reserved the right to litigate all issues. After a trial to the bench, the court found that KTI was entitled both to the KTI Goods and to the Box Units, and awarded damages in the amount of $156,272.30 plus interest. Although we reach a similar result, we do so by a different route.

The Bank's argument for reversal is based on its status as a holder of a perfected security interest on OHT's inventory. The Bank asserts that both the KTI Goods and the Box Units were inventory collateral in OHT's hands, to which the Bank was entitled when OHT defaulted on the line of credit. The Bank contends that KTI's interest in the Box Units and in the KTI Goods amounted only to an unperfected security interest over which the Bank's perfected security interest had priority. KTI argues that the Bank's security interest was ineffective as to the goods at issue because, under the contract, KTI retained title and ownership rights in the KTI Goods and acquired title and ownership rights in the Box Units when it made the progress payments. The Bank asserts alternatively that even if the trial court was correct on the issue of liability, it erroneously computed the amount of damages.

I.   Bank Security Interest in the KTI Goods

The Bank's claim to the KTI Goods is based on its perfected security interest in OHT's inventory. The Bank argues that when KTI had the KTI Goods delivered to OHT and OHT began work on the contract, the goods became inventory for the purposes of the Bank's security interest. The Bank insists that KTI's rights in the KTI Goods at most amounted to a retained, unperfected security interest. KTI bases its claim on its ownership of the goods as evidenced by the title retention clause in the contract, arguing that OHT was in the position of a bailee. Thus, KTI asserts, the goods were never part of OHT's inventory, and therefore never became subject to the Bank's security interest.

The trial court examined the transaction between KTI and OHT to determine whether a "sale" by KTI to OHT had occurred when the KTI Goods were delivered to OHT. Finding none, it concluded that "Article Two has no application, and §2-401(1) cannot operate to convert KTI's retention of title into a security interest under Article Nine." Rec., vol. I, at 252. The court held additionally that, as a matter of law, "OHT has never had any interest in KTI's Goods other than that of a bailee." *Id.*, at 253. The court concluded that KTI was entitled to possession of the KTI Goods notwithstanding the Bank's security interest.

In order for the Bank's security interest to include the KTI Goods and be enforceable, it must have attached to the goods. Tit. 12A, §9-203(1). A security interest attaches to collateral when (1) the debtor (here OHT) has signed a security agreement describing the collateral, (2) value has been given, and (3) the debtor has "rights in the collateral." *Id.* The first two requirements are met in this case. The issue here is whether OHT had sufficient rights in the collateral to meet the third requirement. The parties' disagreement is centered on whether OHT was a mere bailee of the KTI Goods, or instead had a greater property interest in them.

The phrase "rights in the collateral" is not defined in the UCC. The Code clearly does not require that a debtor have full ownership rights. See, *e.g.*, tit. 12A, §9-112. The Seventh Circuit has said that the requirement of "rights in the collateral" illustrates the general principal that "one cannot encumber another man's property in the absence of consent, estoppel, or some other special rule." *In re Pubs, Inc.*, 618 F.2d 432, at 436 (7th Cir. 1980) (quoting *First National Bank & Trust Co. v. McElmurray*, 120 Ga. App. 134, at 138, 169 SE 2d 720, at 724 (1969)).

In *Amfac Mortgage Corp. v. Arizona Mall*, 127 Ariz. 70, 618 P.2d 240 (Ct. App. 1980), the debtor Mall had contracted with a third party for the construction of a shopping mall. The contract specified that the contractor would obtain the needed materials, and that title to the materials would pass to the Mall upon satisfaction of various conditions, including payment. Amfac loaned money to the Mall, taking a security interest in all materials to be incorporated in the Mall. The contractor acquired the materials and had them delivered, but prior to their incorporation and before any payments were made by the Mall to the contractor, the enterprise folded. Amfac brought an action to recover the unincorporated steel. The court, in deciding whether the Mall had had sufficient rights in the steel for Amfac's security interest to attach, stated that a debtor acquires sufficient rights when the debtor obtains possession of collateral pursuant to an agreement with the seller or manufacturer. Possession with contingent rights of ownership was held to be sufficient with or without payment on the contract. See *Evans Products Co. v. Jorgensen*, 245 Or. 362, 421 P.2d 978, at 981 (1966) (en banc).

In *Manger v. Davis*, 619 P.2d 687 (Utah 1980), a consignment case, the Utah Supreme Court found that a debtor's "rights" in collateral must be in the nature of authority to subject the property to a security interest, and looked to the law of agency to resolve the issue. *Id.*, at 690. In *Connecticut Bank & Trust Co. v. Schindelman (In re Bosson)*, 432 F. Supp. 1013 (D. Conn. 1977), the court found that under prevailing case law a debtor had sufficient rights when the debtor acquired possession of collateral pursuant to a sales contract or like agreement. The court looked to principles of law external to the Code to find if such "rights" existed. *Id.*, at 1018.

Thus, it is clear that for a security interest to attach, a debtor must have some degree of control or authority over collateral placed in the debtor's possession. The Oklahoma Supreme Court, in a case factually similar to the case before us, has said that the requisite authority exists "where a debtor gains possession of collateral pursuant to an agreement endowing him with any interest other than naked possession." *Morton Booth Co. v. Tiara Furniture, Inc.*, 564 P.2d 210, at 214 (Okl. 1977). But see *Chrysler Corp. v. Adamatic, Inc.*, 59 Wis. 2d 219, 208 NW 2d 97, at 104 (1973) (bailee's possessory interest for limited purpose of repair not sufficient "rights in the collateral"). The *Morton Booth* definition strongly supports the Article Nine purpose of promoting certainty in commercial loan transactions. See UCC, §9-101, Official Comment. Otherwise, if a debtor received collateral from a third party under an agreement giving the debtor authority to exercise any outward indicia or manifestations of ownership or control, a would-be creditor could easily be misled into making a loan under an ineffective security agreement. For example, in *Morton Booth*, the debtor, Tiara, contracted to build gun cabinets from materials supplied primarily by Morton Booth, and then sell the completed products to Morton Booth. Tiara, a furniture manufacturer, subsequently sought and received financing from the Small Business Association, giving the participating banks a security interest in Tiara's present and after-acquired inventory, which apparently consisted of the same types of materials that were supplied it by Morton Booth. See 564 P.2d, at 211. Had the court found that Tiara lacked sufficient "rights" in the Morton Booth-supplied collateral for the banks' security interest to attach, the bank's claim to the goods upon Tiara's default would have been defeated by the sort of hidden-title subterfuge the Code was intended to prevent.

This reason for the *Morton Booth* result is supported by another feature of Article Nine. In this context, buyers such as Morton Booth and KTI finance a debtor's operation by supplying materials rather than money with which to buy materials. Such a buyer-lender could easily protect itself from after-acquired property creditors of its contractor by filing an Article Nine purchase money security interest in the goods supplied by it to the contractor, as well as those purchased or otherwise identified in the contract by the contractor. See tit. 12A, §§9-107, -312(3). Requiring buyers such as KTI to take this additional step—done easily and at minimal cost—thoroughly advances the Code policy of providing notice and certainty to inventory lenders.

In accordance with *Morton Booth Co.*, we conclude contrary to the district court that the Bank's perfected security interest in OHT's collateral attached to the KTI Goods.

• • •

[The Court went on to find, however, that since the debtor's business consisted of custom fabricating steel pursuant to contractual terms with its customers, the sale from OHT to KTI was in the ordinary course of OHT's business and as such was authorized by the bank's security agreement. KTI therefore took the goods free of the bank's security interest.]

Affirmed in part, reversed in part and remanded.

NOTES

1) Curiously, the Official Comment to UCC 9-203 (1990 edition) casts no light on the intended meaning of the requirement in UCC 9-203(1)(c) that the debtor "has rights in the collateral." Grant Gilmore, *Security Interests*, vol. I, at 353, acknowledges that Article 9 does not specify the quantum of rights which a debtor must have in collateral to support a security interest in it but he suggests that something less than full legal title will do. Do you agree? What is the reason for the requirement that the debtor must have rights in the collateral?

2) Was the court in *KTI v. Fourth National Bank* correct in holding that so long as the debtor has *some* rights in the collateral a security interest given by the debtor will bind the owner of the collateral? Do UCC 9-203(1) or the comparable provisions in the PPS Acts support this interpretation? Was the court influenced in its ruling on this point by the fact that the materials supplied by KTI appeared to form part of OHT's inventory, thus misleading a potential lender to OHT? Does this mean that every customer that orders goods to its specifications and supplies part of the components is at risk so long as the components are in the debtor's possession? The PPS Acts, like UCC 9-203(1), all require the debtor to have "rights" in the collateral. Does this preclude the invocation of estoppel principles or of statutory provisions such as SGA 25(1) and (2) and s. 2 of the Factors Act?

3) What do you make of the following observation by White and Summers, 3rd ed., at 990:

One final caveat: There is good reason to believe that judges do not often mechanically apply the phrase "rights in the collateral." Nor do they mechanically determine when those rights arise. Rather, equities between competing claimants may be fought out in the name of this phrase. And the time when a court determines that the debtor acquired rights in the collateral may not only depend on such equities, but also on the nature of the competing parties and the kind of law involved.

Interests in After-Acquired Property

Section 12(1) of the OPPSA expressly recognizes (subject to some modest exceptions to be discussed hereafter) the validity of a security agreement that covers after-acquired as well as present property of the debtor. This is consistent with the prior law. It is important, however, to have some understanding of the route by which 19th century equity courts reached this conclusion and the limitations that were attached to it. The following cases tell the essential story:

A.P. Holroyd v. J.G. Marshall
(1861-62), 11 ER 999, 10 HLC 191

[T was the owner of machinery in a mill. It was purchased by H but not removed and T continued in possession of it. T executed a deed in favour of H, which was registered. The deed declared that the machinery was H's property, that T desired to repurchase it but had not the money to do so, and that therefore it was conveyed to B to transfer to T when T should pay the money. If he failed to do so, the property was to be held absolutely for H. In effect the transaction amounted to a chattel mortgage in H's favour to secure T's debt and it was so treated in the court below and on appeal.

The deed contained a covenant by T to insure the machinery, and another covenant that all the machinery which, during the continuance of the deed should be placed in the mill in addition to, or substitution for, the original machinery, should be subject to the same trusts. T sold some of the original machinery, purchased new machinery, and sent H accounts of these sales and purchases. However, nothing was done by or on behalf of H to take possession of the newly purchased machinery. On April 2, 1860, H served T with notice of a demand for payment of the £5000 owing under the deed. An execution against T was afterwards put in by a creditor:

The issue in the action was whether H had a sufficient equitable interest in the after-acquired machinery to entitle him to prevail over the execution creditor's claim. In the court below Campbell LC, reversing Stuart VC, held he did not. He said in part (11 ER, at 1000):

... I am of opinion that, notwithstanding the equitable title of the Plaintiffs to this property, as they had not perfected their title to it by any intervening act before possession taken under the execution, the judgment creditor is to be preferred. Till possession taken by the Plaintiffs, they had only *jus ad rem*, the property remained in the judgment debtor, and the machinery was part of his goods and chattels liable to be taken under the *fieri facias*.

The House of Lords unanimously reversed.]

THE LORD CHANCELLOR (LORD WESTBURY), after stating the facts of the case, continued: My Lords, the question is, whether as to the machinery added and substituted since the date of the mortgage the title of the mortgagees, or that of the judgment creditor, ought to prevail. It is admitted that the judgment creditor has no title as to the machinery originally comprised in the bill of sale; but it is contended that the mortgagees had no specific estate or interest in the future machinery. It is also admitted that if the mortgagees had an equitable estate in the added machinery, the same could not be taken in execution by the judgment creditor.

The question may be easily decided by the application of a few elementary principles long settled in Courts of Equity. In equity it is not necessary for the alienation of property that there should be a formal deed of conveyance. A contract for valuable consideration, by which it is agreed to make a present transfer of property, passes at once the beneficial interest, provided the contract is one of which a Court of Equity will decree specific performance. In the language of Lord Hardwicke, the vendor becomes a trustee for the vendee; subject, of course, to the contract being one to be specifically performed. And this is true, not only of contracts relating to real estate, but also of contracts relating to personal property, provided that the latter are such as a Court of Equity would direct to be specifically performed.

A contract for the sale of goods, as, for example, of five hundred chests of tea, is not a contract which would be specifically performed, because it does not relate to any chests of tea in particular; but a contract to sell five hundred chests of the particular kind of tea which is now in my warehouse in Gloucester, is a contract relating to specific property, and which would be specifically performed. The buyer may maintain a suit in equity for the delivery of a specific chattel when it is the subject of a contract, and for an injunction (if necessary) to restrain the seller from delivering it to any other person.

The effect in equity of a mere contract as amounting to an alienation, may be illustrated by the law relating to the revocation of wills. If the owner of an estate devises it by will, and afterwards contracts to sell it to a purchaser, but dies before the contract is performed, the will is revoked as to the beneficial or equitable interest in the estate, for the contract converted the testator into a trustee for the purchaser; and, in like manner, if the purchaser dies intestate before performance of the contract, the equitable estate descends to his heir at law, who may require the personal representative to pay the purchase money. But all this depends on the contract being such as a Court of Equity would decree to be specifically performed.

There can be no doubt, therefore, that if the mortgage deed in the present case had contained nothing but the contract which is involved in the aforesaid covenant of Taylor, the mortgagor, such contract would have amounted to a valid assignment in equity of the whole of the machinery and chattels in question, supposing such machinery and effects to have been in existence and upon the mill at the time of the execution of the deed.

But it is alleged that this is not the effect of the contract, because it relates to machinery not existing at the time, but to be acquired and fixed and placed in the mill at a future time. It is quite true that a deed which professes to convey property which is not in existence at the time is as a conveyance void at law, simply because there is nothing to convey. So in equity a contract which engages to transfer property, which is not in existence, cannot operate as an immediate alienation merely because there is nothing to transfer.

But if a vendor or mortgagor agrees to sell or mortgage property, real or personal, of which he is not possessed at the time, and he receives the consideration for the contract, and afterwards becomes possessed of property answering the description in the contract, there is no doubt that a Court of Equity would compel him to perform the contract, and that the contract would, in equity, transfer the beneficial interest to the mortgagee or purchaser immediately on the property being acquired. This, of course, assumes that the supposed contract is one of that class of which a Court of Equity would decree the specific performance. If it be so, then immediately on the acquisition of the property described the vendor or mortgagor would hold it in trust for the purchaser or mortgagee, according to the terms of the contract. For if a contract be in other respects good and fit to be performed, and the consideration has been received, incapacity to perform it at the time of its execution will be no answer when the means of doing so are afterwards obtained.

Apply these familiar principles to the present case; it follows that immediately on the new machinery and effects being fixed or placed in the mill, they became subject to the operation of the contract, and passed in equity to the mortgagees, to whom Taylor was bound to make a legal conveyance, and from whom he, in the meantime, was a trustee of the property in question.

There is another criterion to prove that the mortgagee acquired an estate or interest in the added machinery as soon as it was brought into the mill. If afterwards the mortgagor had attempted to remove any part of such machinery, except for the purpose of substitution, the mortgagee would have been entitled to an injunction to restrain such removal, and that because of his estate in the specific property. The result is, that the title of the Appellants is to be preferred to that of the judgment creditor.

Some use was made at the bar and in the Court below of the language attributed to Mr. Baron Parke in the case of *Mogg v. Baker* (3 M. and Wels. 198). That learned Judge appears to have given, not his own opinion, but what he understood would have been the decision of a Court of Equity upon the case. He is represented as speaking upon the authority of one of the Judges of the Court of Chancery. Any communication so made was of course extra-judicial, and there is much danger in making communications of such a nature the ground of judicial decision; but I entirely concur in what appears to have been the principle intended to be stated; for Mr. Baron Parke, speaking of the agreement in the case, says, "It would cover no specific furniture, and would confer no right in equity." I have already explained, that a contract relating to goods, but not to any specific goods, would not be the subject of a decree for specific performance, and that a contract that could not be specifically performed would not avail to transfer any estate or interest.

If, therefore, the contract in *Mogg v. Baker* related to no specific furniture, it is true that it would not, *at the time of its execution*, confer any right in equity; but it is equally true that it would attach on furniture answering the contract when acquired, provided the contract remained in force at the time of such acquisition.

Whether a correct construction was put upon the agreement in *Mogg v. Baker* [3 M. & W. 198] is a different question, and which it is needless to consider, as I am only desirous of showing that the proposition stated by the learned Judge is quite consistent with the principles on which this case ought to be decided.

I therefore advise your Lordships to reverse the order of Lord Chancellor Campbell, and direct the petition of re-hearing presented to him to be dismissed, with costs.

[Concurring judgments were delivered by Lord Wensleydale and Lord Chelmsford.]

Edward Tailby v. The Official Receiver
(1888), 13 AC 523

LORD MACNAGHTEN: My Lords, I venture to think that this case is free from difficulty when the facts are understood.

Izon was a packing-case manufacturer. In 1879 he compounded with his creditors. At Izon's request, Tyrrell signed promissory notes for the last instalment of the composition, taking from Izon a bill of sale as a counter-security.

The bill of sale is dated the 13th of May 1879. It assigns to Tyrrell by way of mortgage, among other property, all the stock-in-trade and effects which during the continuance of the security might be on the mortgagor's then premises, or at any other place at which during the continuance of the security he might carry on business, and also (to quote the words of the deed) "all the book debts due and owing, or which may during the continuance of this security become due and owing to the said mortgagor." Then there is a power of attorney in the most ample terms; a proviso that if the mortgagor on demand fails to pay the amount due, the mortgagee may take possession and sell the property in mortgage; and a proviso that until default the mortgagor may use and enjoy all the mortgaged premises; and lastly, there is a covenant for further assurance. Another bill of sale was given in 1880, but I need not refer to it; it was admitted at the bar that it had no bearing on the question before your Lordships.

I pause for a moment to point out the nature and effect of the security created by the bill of sale in 1879. It belongs to a class of securities of which perhaps the most familiar example is to be found in the debentures of trading companies. It is a floating security reaching over all the trade assets of the mortgagor for the time being, and intended to fasten upon and bind the assets in existence at the time when the mortgagee intervenes. In other words, the mortgagor makes himself trustee of his business for the purpose of the security. But the trust is to remain dormant until the mortgagee calls it into operation.

The business in the immediate contemplation of the parties was, of course, the business in existence at the date when the bill of sale was given. But the assignment is not limited to that; it extends to any business which the mortgagor may carry on during the continuance of the security. That was an obvious, and, if not forbidden by law, a proper precaution. A tradesman who has been unfortunate in his business is perhaps as likely to try a change as one who has been uniformly successful. The draftsman I think would have shewn more simplicity than skill if he had left it in the power of the mortgagor to imperil or defeat the security by altering his business, or by transferring his capital to some other enterprise.

In reliance on the arrangements I have described, Tyrrell paid a large sum to Izon's creditors. But he seems to have been content with his security; and Izon continued to trade without any interference on his part, and apparently without any alteration in the character of the business. In 1885 the executors of Tyrrell, who was then dead, thought fit to call in the money due to his estate. They demanded payment. They took possession of the mortgaged premises, so far as it was practicable to do so, and they sold the book debts.

Among the book debts which were sold was one which had recently become due from Messrs. Wilson Brothers & Co. The purchaser at once gave notice to them. The next thing that happened was that Izon became bankrupt. After that Messrs. Wilson Brothers & Co. paid the purchaser.

The Court of Appeal has held unanimously that the official receiver is entitled to recover the money from the purchaser. Your Lordships have now to determine whether that decision is right.

The question is not complicated by any circumstances other than those I have mentioned. The transaction between Izon and Tyrrell is not impeached as fraudulent under the Act of Elizabeth, or on any other ground. Nor is it necessary to consider the provisions of the Bills of Sale Acts. Choses in action are expressly declared not to be personal chattels within the meaning of those Acts.

The grounds on which my noble and learned friend opposite has founded his opinion were not discussed at the bar, nor is there, I think, sufficient evidence before your Lordships to enable your Lordships to act on them.

The claim of the purchaser was rested on well-known principles. It has long been settled that future property, possibilities and expectancies are assignable in equity for value. The mode or form of assignment is absolutely immaterial provided the intention of the parties is clear. To effectuate the intention an assignment for value, in terms present and immediate, has always been regarded in equity as a contract binding on the conscience of the assignor and so binding the subject-matter of the contract when it comes into existence, if it is of such a nature and so described as to be capable of being ascertained and identified.

The position of the purchaser was assailed on one point, and one point only. It was not disputed that Tyrrell gave valuable consideration for the bill of sale, or that Tyrrell's executors were within their rights in selling whatever was comprised in the security. It was not denied that the debt purchased was a book debt which became due and owing to Izon during the continuance of the security, nor was any question raised as to the sufficiency of the notice which the purchaser gave to Messrs. Wilson Brothers & Co. The contention of the learned counsel for the respondent was this: They asserted as a proposition of law that an assignment of future book debts not limited to any specified business is too vague to have any effect. Starting from that proposition they asked your Lordships to come to the conclusion that the assignment of book debts in the present case was void from the beginning as including in its terms book debts which could not be made the subject of valid assignment. I do not stop to consider whether that is a necessary or legitimate conclusion. It is a startling result certainly, and I shall have a word to say about it by-and-by. At present I am merely inquiring whether the original proposition is sound. In the leading judgment in the Court of Appeal it is said that the doctrine which covers the proposition is well established, because "in every one of the cases in point that were cited its existence has been assumed." The principle of the doctrine, however, is not stated; the doctrine itself is not defined; the cases which are supposed to be in point are not reviewed or even named.

[Lord MacNaghten found the proposition was not supported by authority, and continued:]

So much for authority. What foundation is there for the doctrine apart from authority? The learned counsel for the respondent did not pretend to be wiser than the Court of Appeal. They, too, neither defined the doctrine the aid of which they invoked, nor stated any principle on which it could be supposed to rest. They contented themselves with endeavouring to maintain the proposition that an assignment by a trader of future book debts not confined to a specified business is too vague to be effectual. Why should this be so? If future book debts be assigned, the subject-matter of assignment is capable of being identified as and when the book debts come into existence, whether the description be restricted to a particular business or not. Indeed the restriction may render the task of identification all the more difficult. An energetic tradesman naturally develops and extends his business. One business runs into another, and the line of demarcation is often indistinct and undefined. The linendraper of today in the course of a few years may come to be the proprietor of an establishment providing everything that man wants, or woman either, from the cradle to the grave. In such a case I can easily conceive that difficult questions might arise if the book debts assigned were limited to a particular business.

It was admitted by the learned counsel for the respondent, that a trader may assign his future book debts in a specified business. Why should the line be drawn there? Between men of full age and competent understanding ought there to be any limit to the freedom of contract but that imposed by positive law or dictated by considerations of morality or public policy? The limit proposed is purely arbitrary, and I think meaningless and unreasonable. The rule laid down by the Court of Appeal would not help to identify or ascertain the subject-matter of the contract in any case. It might have the opposite effect. It would be no benefit to the assignor's general creditors. It might prevent a man from raising money on the credit of his expectations in his existing business—on that which is admitted to be capable of assignment—in consequence of the obvious risk that some alteration in the character of the business might impair or defeat the security.

Under these circumstances I think your Lordships will come to the conclusion that the proposition on which the respondent relies as the foundation of his case cannot be supported on principle, and that the authorities on which it was supposed to rest may be traced to a decision of the Court of Exchequer which itself is founded on an erroneous view of the principles recognised in this House in *Holroyd v. Marshall*.

[Lord MacNaghten then went on to discuss Lord Westbury's judgment in *Holroyd v. Marshall* (*supra*) and dispelled the false impression it had generated that the enforceability of a security interest in future property depended on principles of specific performance. He concluded:]

The truth is that cases of equitable assignment or specific lien, where the consideration has passed, depend on the real meaning of the agreement between the parties. The difficulty, generally speaking, is to ascertain the true scope and effect of the agreement. When that is ascertained you have only to apply the principle that equity considers that done which ought to be done if that principle is applicable under the circumstances of the case. The doctrines relating to specific performance do not, I think, afford a test or a measure of the rights created. ...

Appeal allowed.

[Concurring judgments were delivered by the Lord Chancellor and Lords Watson and Fitzgerald.]

Joseph v. Lyons
(1884), 15 QBD 280 (CA)

[Manning, a jeweller and gold and silversmith, agreed to purchase the plaintiff's business. On February 3, 1881, he executed a conditional bill of sale (i.e., chattel mortgage) in the plaintiff's favour to secure the purchase price of the business. The bill of sale covered all the stock in trade and all other chattels, present and future, belonging to the shop, dwelling and premises containing the business, whether in addition to, or in substitution for, the original chattels on the premises.

Manning pledged goods to a third party while an earlier bill of sale in the plaintiff's favour was still in force. The plaintiff seized the chattels covered by that bill of sale on October 24, 1883. They then discovered that Manning had pledged chattels with the defendant on September 17, 1883, to secure an advance for £70. The chattels in question had all been acquired by M. after the execution of the bill of sale of 1881.

The defendant was a pawnbroker and he had accepted the pledges in the ordinary course of his business. He was not aware of the bill of sale at the time of the pledge. Huddleston, B. gave judgment for the plaintiff.]

COTTON LJ: The plaintiff sues for goods which, he alleges, have been converted or detained from him by the defendant. The bill of sale to the plaintiff purports to assign the after-acquired stock-in-trade. The first question is whether the plaintiff has acquired any property in that stock-in-trade. In *Holroyd v. Marshall* [10 HLC 101] it was held, with some doubt on the part of some of the Law Lords, that when future-acquired property is assigned, pursuant to a contract capable of specific performance, that property, when it has been sufficiently ear-marked and identified, may pass to the assignee and become his property; it may be that there was not a valid assignment at law, but where there was a valuable consideration, the assignment might be valid in equity. The law stood in this position before the Supreme Court of Judicature Acts, 1873, 1875. It has been argued before us that the difference between legal and equitable interests has been swept away by those statutes. But it was not intended by the legislature, and it has not been said, that legal and equitable rights should be treated as identical, but that the Courts should administer both legal and equitable principles. I think that the clause enacting that the rules of equity shall prevail (Supreme Court of Judicature Act, 1873, s. 25, sub-s. 11) shews that it was not intended to sweep away altogether the principles of the common law. And it was not intended that a conveyance void at common law should, after the passing of those statutes, become valid as a conveyance at common law. I repeat what I said in *Clements v. Matthews*. [11 QBD 808, at 814] I think that this bill of sale, although it was a deed, gave no legal title. Then reliance was placed upon a contract that the after-acquired property should belong to the plaintiff: it was the rule at common law that the property in future-acquired goods should not pass, except, perhaps, where there was a contract that the property in them should pass: that rule still remains in force; and it follows that the legal title remains as it stood at law; only an interest in equity passed to the plaintiff. Then the defendant had the legal title: he had no notice of the equitable title existing in the plaintiff: at least nothing has been proved shewing that he had notice: here the defendant was a pawnbroker, and he was not bound to search the register of bills of sale: he was not bound to inquire as to goods pledged with him in the course of his business. Of course, if he had been informed of the existence of the bill of sale, he would have been bound to search the register in order to inform himself of its contents; but I think that the doctrine as to constructive notice has gone too far, and I shall not extend it. The appeal is successful, and must be allowed. ...

Judgment for defendant.

[Concurring judgments were delivered by Brett MR and Lindley LJ.]

NOTES

1) As shown by *Holroyd v. Marshall* and *Tailby v. Official Receiver*, the Courts of Equity in the last century appear to have experienced no difficulty in accepting a mortgage on after-acquired property regardless of whether that property consisted of machinery and equipment used in the debtor's business or represented inventory or future receivables. What accounts for this ready willingness? Were the courts unaware of the practical consequences of their acquiescence or did the decisions reflect the dominant utilitarian philosophy of the time. What is the underlying philosophy of s. 12(1) of the OPPSA? Could inventory and accounts receivable financing be carried on successfully without the recognition of AAP clauses?

2) The pre-Code American law of AAP clauses had a far more chequered history. The courts were much more hostile to the stock-in-trade mortgage and, later, to receivables financing than they were to the role of the after-acquired property interest in industrial financing. See Gilmore, *Security Interests*, vol. I, at 38-39; Cohen and Gerber, "The After-Acquired Property Clause" (1939), 87 *U Pa. L Rev.* 635; and Skilton, "The Law of Mortgages on Merchandise" (1963), *Wis. L Rev.* 359. As Gilmore notes (at 39), this disparate treatment had a decisive effect in pre-Code days on financing patterns and led to a divorce between the financing on the security of the fixed or long-term assets of an enterprise and the financing on the security of short-term or liquid assets.

3) *Joseph v. Lyons, supra,* a leading pre-PPSA decision, stands for two propositions: (a) that the interest in after-acquired property is only an equitable interest which can be defeated by a *bona fide* purchaser or pledgee for value of the legal interest; and (b) third parties are not deemed to have constructive notice of the contents of a registered bill of sale containing an AAP clause. Do these doctrines apply to the PPS Acts? Section 53(1)(a) of the old Ontario Act provided that registration of a financing statement constituted notice of the security interest to which it related to all persons claiming an interest in the collateral. The provision is omitted in the new Act. The Advisory Committee felt it was redundant, even misleading, because competing claims to the same collateral ordinarily turn on whether the security interest has been properly perfected and not on doctrines of constructive notice. The rule that the doctrine of constructive notice does not apply to registered security agreements was more or less faithfully followed in Canada until it was rejected by the Saskatchewan Court of Appeal in *Kozak v. Ford Motor Credit Co. of Can. Ltd.* (1971), 18 DLR (3d) 735. The New Brunswick Court of Appeal refused to follow this lead in

GMAC of Can. Ltd. v. Hubbard (1978), 87 DLR (3d) 39, but it won the support of the Ontario Court of Appeal in *Acmetrack Ltd. v. BCN* (1984), 12 DLR (4th) 428. See further, Ziegel, "Registration Statutes and the Doctrine of Constructive Notice" (1985), 63 *Can. Bar Rev.* 630. SPPSA s. 51 states that registration does not constitute constructive notice or knowledge of the contents of registered documents to third parties, but this may create difficulties in conflicts between PPSA security interests and security interests governed by non-PPS legislation.

After-Acquired Property Clauses (AAP) in Agricultural and Consumer Transactions

Section 12(2)(a) of the OPPSA is based on UCC 9-204(4)(a) [1962 text], which in turn was inspired by one-year limitations on AAP clauses in crop mortgages common in pre-Code American state law. See Gilmore, *Security Interests*, vol. II, §32.4, at 864. AAP clauses do not appear to have caused comparable problems in Canadian crop mortgages—why, we do not know, though the well established role of Canadian banks in providing current crop financing under s. 427 of the Bank Act may have something to do with it.

Section 12(2)(b) of the OPPSA is also of Code origin—in this case UCC 9-204(4)(b) [1962 text]. Gilmore explains that the Code provision is "one of the vestiges of the original plan, later abandoned, to include in Article 9 a full-scale treatment of the problems of consumer finance" (*Security Interests*, vol. I, §11.6, at 357). He also notes that existing state retail instalment sales Acts frequently contain more extensive prohibitions on "add-on" clauses than those in 9-204(4)(b).

Why are AAP clauses objectionable in consumer security agreements? Is it because of concern that an unscrupulous lender will tie up all the debtor's household goods? If this is the basis of the objection, would it not be better to prohibit altogether mortgages on household goods? See, e.g., the Exemptions Act, RSS 1978, c. E-14, ss. 2, 5. Should a distinction be drawn between a purchase money security interest in consumer goods and other security interests?

Note that s. 12(2)(b) only applies to consumer goods, not to other types of collateral. Presumably a consumer is free to pledge his future rights under an RRSP, a trust or a will. Is the distinction justified? What of a wage assignment? In most provinces it is expressly outlawed under separate legislation, except for assignments in favour of a credit union or similar cooperative. See, e.g., Wages Act, RSO 1990, c. W.1, s. 7(2). Wages, however, do not include the fees earned by a self-employed professional: *Re Kryspin* (1983), 40 OR (2d) 424.

Future Advances

It has long been common for security agreements securing a line of credit to cover both present and future advances by the secured party. Such agreements are valid at common law. See *Hopkinson v. Rolt* (1861), 9 HLC 514. However, they raise difficult questions of priority when the debtor grants a second security interest between the creation of the first security interest and the making of further advances by the first secured party. These questions are discussed in chapter 5 of this volume.

PERFECTION OF THE SECURITY INTEREST

Introduction

According to s. 19 of the OPPSA, "a security interest is perfected when, (a) it has attached; and (b) all steps required for perfection under any provision of this Act have been completed." Like its source, UCC 9-303(1), the definition is circular since perfection is defined partly in terms of itself. This unfortunate result has come about because perfection is used in two senses in this Act: first, in terms of the *procedural steps* required to give public notice of an existing or future security interest (usually by registering a financial statement or by the secured party taking possession of the collateral), and, second, to describe the *status* of a security interest that has attached under s. 11(1) and that meets the procedural requirements. The double meaning has not so far given rise to reported difficulties and it is usually fairly straightforward to determine whether a section refers to perfection in the first sense or the second. Thus, in ss. 20, 28, 34-35 it is used in the status sense whereas in such sections as 21-24, 30 and 45 it is used in the procedural sense.

The Act recognizes three types of perfection: (a) perfection by possession; (b) perfection by registration; and (c) temporary perfection.

Perfection by possession is regulated in OPPSA s. 22. As will be seen, only tangible things, including specific documentary expression of rights, *viz.* chattel paper, instruments, securities, letters of credit and advices of credits and negotiable documents of title can be perfected by possession. (Most of the aforegoing terms are defined in s. 1.) The reason of course is obvious.

Perfection by registration. OPPSA s. 23 provides that "Registration perfects a security interest in any type of collateral." The same provision appears in UPPSA 1982 and in the Saskatchewan, Alberta, and British Columbia Acts. Section 23 marks an important departure from old s. 25(1), which only permitted perfection by registration for security interests in goods and intangibles but not in documentary intangibles (i.e., instruments, securities, letters of credit, and advices of credit). The exclusions were based on UCC 9-304(1) and American forms of secured financing. However, it appeared to the Uniform Act Committee that the exclusions were unwarranted since Canadian practice has long been for a fixed and floating charge to include all of a debtor's assets of whatever character so that, in case of default, the receiver will be able to continue to operate the enterprise or to dispose of it as a going concern. In the US, too, suggestions have been made to make registration the predominant if not exclusive means of perfecting a security interest. See P.F. Coogan, "Article 9—An Agenda for the Next Decade": (1978), 87 *Yale LJ* 1012, and D.M. Phillips, "Flawed Perfection: From Possession to Filing Under Article 9" (1979), 59 *Bo. Univ. L* 1 and 209. Is it practicable to make registration the exclusive means of perfection?

Where more than one method of perfection is permissible the secured party is free to switch from one method to the other without interrupting the continuity of perfection: see OPPSA s. 21.

Temporary perfection exists when a security interest is protected even though no financing statement has been registered and the secured party is not in possession of the collateral. OPPSA s. 24 enumerates two such cases. However, the Act recognizes a number of other situations where the secured party is given a grace period within which to perfect an as yet unperfected security interest or to reperfect a security interest which has or may become unperfected by reason of a change of circumstances. See, e.g., ss. 20(3), 25(4), 48(2) and (3), and 6(2), 6(5), and 7(2). The reason for these derogations from the normal rules is that it is not always practicable or possible for the secured party to perfect his security interest immediately, and in the case of very short term security interests (those covered in s. 24) it is unreasonable to require him to do so.

Perfection by Possession

Re Raymond Darzinskas
(1981), 34 OR (2d) 782 (Ont. SC)

STEELE J: The Trustee brings this application to declare that the security interest of Joel Morgenstern, as evidenced by a chattel mortgage dated January 24, 1979, is subordinate in interest to that of the Trustee in Bankruptcy. Council agree that the financing statement, registered under the Personal Property Security Act, RSO 1980, c. 375 (the PPSA), was improperly registered and therefore the sole issue before the Court is whether the security of Morgenstern was perfected by possession.

The property in question is a heavy piece of manufacturing equipment. There is no evidence that it was attached to the real property. It was located within the building and was connected with heavy electrical wiring for its use. It was not a fixture.

By reason of a default under the security, Morgenstern instructed a bailiff to seize the equipment which was done on July 28, 1981, in the presence of both the bailiff and Morgenstern. The lien warrant was served on the landlord of the premises occupied by the bankrupt. The bankrupt himself was not present at the time. Because of the size of the equipment, it was not removed from the premises, nor were any operative parts of the equipment removed therefrom. On or about August 4, 1981, the bailiff re-attended at the premises and requested that the bankrupt bring the chattel mortgage into good standing but no money was forthcoming.

An affidavit filed by the Trustee upon information received from the bankrupt is to the effect that because the equipment was not removed or placed in a non-working condition the bankrupt was permitted to use the equipment in the ordinary course of business. However, the affidavit does not say that the bankrupt in fact used the equipment. It merely states that as a result of promises of payment Morgenstern permitted the bankrupt to use the equipment some time in late July 1981. Morgenstern's affidavit is much clearer. Apart from confirming the seizure by the bailiff and the re-attendance by the bailiff, he states that on or about August 12, 1981, he was approached by the bankrupt who advised him that he was arranging finances to pay off the chattel mortgage which money would be available within a few days, and that in view of those circumstances he, Morgenstern, consented to the bankrupt using the equipment. When no refinancing was arranged, Morgenstern proceeded to file the petition for a receiving order which was dated August 17, 1981.

Based on the above evidence, I find that the bailiff in fact seized the property on July 28, 1981, and that the bankrupt did not use the equipment thereafter until August 12, 1981, when he was given permission so to do by Morgenstern. In *Johnson v. Pickering*, [1907] 2 KB 437, at 443-44, it was stated as follows:

Now it is clear that a sheriff may seize goods and chattels without actually laying his hands upon them; it is sufficient if he enters upon land on which the goods and chattels are and announces his present intention of seizing all the goods and chattels upon that land: *Gladstone v. Padwick* (1871), LR 6 Ex. 203.

I am therefore satisfied that the bailiff seized the goods in question, notwithstanding the fact that the bankrupt was not present. I particularly find this in view of the uncontradicted affidavit of Morgenstern that at a later date the bankrupt approached him requesting permission to use the goods.

The question is, is this seizure an effective possession under the provision of s. 24 of the PPSA.

Section 24 provides as follows [see now OPPSA s. 22]:

24. Except as provided in section 26, possession of the collateral by the secured party, or on his behalf by a person other than the debtor or the debtor's agent, perfects a security interest in,

   (a) chattel paper;

   (b) goods;

   (c) instruments;

   (d) securities;

   (e) letters of credit and advices of credit; or

   (f) negotiable documents of title,

but subject to section 23, only during its actual holding as collateral.

I am of the opinion that the intention of the Act is to provide notice to persons dealing with the property or with the owner thereof that the secured party claims an interest in the goods. This can be effected by constructive notice, by registration or by actual notice by possession. In the present case Morgenstern had constructive possession by reason of his seizure but he did not have actual possession. He left the equipment in full working order on the premises. Section 58 of the Personal Property Security Act provides for the right to take possession or where there has been perfected registration to render the equipment unusable without removal upon default. I am of the opinion that s. 24 of the Act requires actual physical possession to be taken and the goods held by the secured party to perfect his security interest in order to give notice to all persons dealing therewith. This possession is required even more where the security interest was not perfected by registration. No such physical possession was taken in the present case and therefore Morgenstern's possession was not perfected. Therefore, his interest is subordinate to the interest of the Trustee by virtue of s. 22 of the PPSA.

Declaration in favour of trustee.

Sperry Inc. v. Canadian Imperial Bank of Commerce
(1985), 4 PPSAC 314 (Ont. CA)

The judgment of the Court was delivered by MORDEN JA: The defendants, Canadian Imperial Bank of Commerce and Thorne Riddell Inc., appeal from a judgment of Montgomery J [reported at 40 OR (2d) 54, 2 PPSAC 225, 44 CBR (NS) 69, 141 DLR (3d)

119] declaring that the plaintiff, Sperry Inc. (Sperry) "is entitled as against the defendants to title and delivery of the goods covered by its Dealer Security Agreement free from any claims by either of the defendants." The appeal involves the resolution of the competing claims of Sperry and the bank to farm equipment sold by Sperry to a dealer. There is also a cross-appeal respecting expenses incurred by Sperry in maintaining a letter of credit filed with the Court.

The basic facts, apart from the relevant terms of the competing security documents, are set forth in the trial judgment which, as indicated, is reported and, accordingly, I shall not repeat them in detail. The following outline is sufficient to deal with the issues on which this appeal turns.

W.J. Allinson Farm Equipment & Supplies Limited [Allinson] was a dealer in farm equipment and supplies in Kingston. On August 27, 1976 it entered into a dealer security agreement with Sperry. The material provisions of this document read as follows:

1. It is anticipated that Company [Sperry] in its continuing sole discretion, from time to time may sell its goods on credit to Dealer [Allinson] and purchase Lien Notes and Conditional Sales Contracts from Dealer. Dealer agrees to pay Company for such credit sales of Company goods in the manner and at the times prescribed in the Terms of Sale or Terms of Sale Schedules published from time to time by Company and in effect at the time of sale.

2. In order to induce Company to make such sales, and to purchase such Lien Notes and Conditional Sales Contracts, *Dealer hereby grants to Company a security interest under the Personal Property Security Act in the collateral described in Paragraph 3 below to secure all present and future obligations* and liabilities of Dealer to Company, including but not limited to contingent liabilities and future advances made for taxes, levies and repairs to or maintenance of the collateral (all of which obligations and liabilities together are herein called the "indebtedness").

3. The word collateral, as used in this Agreement, shall mean: (a) Dealer's entire inventory now owned or hereafter acquired by Dealer from Company comprising new and used agricultural equipment, industrial equipment, other machinery, equipment and supplies, repair parts therefor, twine and wire; (b) all replacements, attachments and additions thereto; and (c) all proceeds thereof.

• • •

5. *Dealer represents and warrants that: (a) at the time Company's security interest attaches with respect to any collateral, the Dealer shall be the owner of said collateral* with good rights to sell, transfer, assign or pledge the same, free from any lien, security interest, encumbrances or other right, title or interest, other than that of Company; ... [The italics are mine.]

On September 9, 1977 Allinson entered into a general security agreement with the bank. The terms of the agreement which are relevant to the issues on this appeal are as follows:

1. As a general and continuing collateral security for payment of all existing and future indebtedness and liability of the undersigned [Allinson]to Canadian Imperial Bank of Commerce (the "Bank") wheresoever and howsoever incurred and any ultimate unpaid balance thereof, *the undersigned hereby charges in favour of and grants to the Bank a security interest in the undertaking of the undersigned and all property of the kinds hereinafter described of which the undersigned is now or may hereafter become the owner* and which, insofar as the same consists

of tangible property, is now or may hereafter be in the place or places designated in paragraph 14 hereof; and the undersigned agrees with the Bank as hereinafter set out.

2. In this agreement

• • •

"Collateral" means and includes all of the above mentioned undertaking and property whether now owned or hereafter acquired, and whether tangible or otherwise;

• • •

3. *Description of Property*

01. *Inventory* All goods now or hereafter forming part of the inventory of the undersigned including, without limiting the generality of the foregoing, the following: goods held for sale or lease; ...

• • •

4. *Ownership of Collateral*

The undersigned represents and warrants that, except for the security interest created hereby and except for purchase money obligations, the undersigned is, or with respect to Collateral acquired after the date hereof will be, the owner of the Collateral free from any mortgage, lien, charge, security interest or encumbrance. "Purchase money obligations" means any mortgage, lien or other encumbrance upon property assumed or given back as part of the purchase price of such property, or arising by operation of law or any extension or renewal or replacement thereof upon the same property, if the principal amount of the indebtedness secured thereby is not increased.

• • •

9. *Default*

01. Upon default by the undersigned in payment of all or any part of the indebtedness or liability of the undersigned to the Bank or in the performance or observance of any of the provisions hereof (in this agreement called "default") the Bank may appoint in writing any person to be a receiver (which term shall include a receiver and manager) of the Collateral, including any rents and profits thereof, and may remove any receiver and appoint another in his stead, and such receiver so appointed shall have power to take possession of the Collateral and to carry on or concur in carrying on the business of the undersigned, and to sell or concur in selling the Collateral or any part thereof. *Any such receiver shall for all purposes be deemed to be the agent of the undersigned.* The Bank may from time to time fix the remuneration of such receiver. All moneys from time to time received by such receiver shall be paid by him first in discharge of all rents, taxes, rates, insurance premiums and outgoings affecting the Collateral, secondly in payment of his remuneration as receiver, thirdly in keeping in good standing all liens and charges on the Collateral prior to the security constituted by this agreement, and fourthly in or toward payment of such parts of the indebtedness and liability of the undersigned to the Bank as to the Bank seems best, and any residue of such moneys so received shall be paid to the undersigned. The Bank in appointing or refraining from appointing such receiver shall not incur any liability to the receiver, the undersigned or otherwise.

• • •

18. *General*

... The security interest created or provided for by this agreement is intended to attach when this agreement is signed by the undersigned and delivered to the Bank. ... [The italics are mine.]

Initially, the security interests secured by each of these agreements were duly perfected by registration under the Personal Property Security Act, RSO 1970, c. 344, as amended (the Act). For reasons that are not material to this appeal both of these perfections lapsed, that of the bank early in 1979 and that of Sperry in September 1979.

On or about the 14th day of March 1980 the bank appointed Thorne Riddell Inc. to act as receiver and manager of Allison's business. Thorne Riddell took immediate possession of Allison's premises and of all of its property, equipment and undertaking, including the inventory supplied by Sperry which is in issue in this appeal. On or about March 14, 1980 Sperry learned that the bank had appointed a receiver and manager and within a few days, apparently on or before March 17, 1980, its representative attended at the Allinson premises. They were not permitted to remove the inventory in dispute. They valued it at $246,256.64. On March 17, 1980 Thorne Riddell wrote to Sperry as follows:

This is to confirm that a representative of your firm has counted the Sperry New Holland equipment on the premises of W.J. Allinson (Equipment) Limited on March 17, 1980.

We further confirm that the above equipment will not be sold or removed from the premises by us until the security agreements are reviewed by the lawyers appointed by the Canadian Imperial Bank of Commerce.

The evidence on behalf of the bank and the receiver was that the receiver "elected to run the business on a day to day basis until Friday, March 21, 1980." There is no evidence that the security agreements were "reviewed." The next dealing with the Sperry equipment appears to be its delivery to Sperry under the court order to which I shall refer shortly.

On March 25, 1980 Sperry filed a renewal of its financing statement with a view to perfecting its security interest in the inventory.

In May 1980 Sperry commenced this action against the bank and Thorne Riddell asserting its rights under the dealer security agreement and claimed "[a] declaration that as against both defendants the plaintiff is entitled to title and delivery of the goods covered by its Dealer Security Agreement free from any claims by both defendants." As indicated above, the trial Judge granted judgment in favour of Sperry in these terms.

Very soon after the action was commenced, Master Garfield made an order, on consent, in a motion brought by Sperry that upon the delivery by Sperry to the accountant of the Court of a letter of credit in a specified form the bank was to deliver to Sperry the inventory in dispute. The bank and Thorne Riddell counterclaimed against Sperry for the value of the goods returned. In this appeal they seek what is said to be the sum owing to the bank as of the time of trial ($220,798.04) with interest at 15 per cent per annum from then to date.

Sperry cross-appealed for an order that the costs of maintaining the letter of credit (said to be some $8,000 at the time of the trial) be awarded to it. The trial Judge had refused to make such an order.

At the trial the two basic issues were: (1) did the bank have a security interest in the inventory covered by the dealer security agreement between Sperry and Allinson? and (2), if it did, which party's claim was entitled to priority? The learned trial Judge resolved the first issue against the bank and this was sufficient for Sperry's claim to succeed. He went on to express the opinion that if he were wrong with respect to the scope of the bank's security interest and the case were to be determined on the basis of who had priority then he would have decided in favour of the bank on the basis that its possession of the inventory on March 20, 1980 was a perfection of its interest under s. 24 [now s. 22] of the Act. I shall in due course refer to the trial Judge's reasons relating to the date March 20, 1980. ...

[Morden JA found that the trial judge had erred on the first issue, and continued:]

The next issue is—which party has priority? The relevant provision is s. 35(1) of the Act [now s. 30], which provides:

35.—(1) If no other provision of this Act is applicable, priority between security interests in the same collateral shall be determined.

(a) by the order of registration, if the security interests have been perfected by registration;

(b) by the order of perfection, unless the security interests have been perfected by registration; or

(c) by the order of attachment under subsection 12(1), if no security interest has been perfected.

The bank relies on s. 35(1)(b) to support its claim for priority on the basis of its perfection by possession under s. 24 of the Act. Sperry relies on s. 35(1)(c) on the basis of the earlier attachment of its security interest.

As indicated earlier in these reasons the trial Judge was of the view that if the case were to be determined on the basis of which party had priority he would have decided in favour of the bank on the basis that its possession of the inventory on and after March 20, 1980 (I think he meant March 21) was a perfection of its interest under s. 24 of the Act. The trial Judge was concerned with the effect of the provision in para. 9 of the bank's general security agreement that the receiver "shall for all purposes be deemed to be the agent of [Allinson]." He quoted the following passage from the judgment of Houlden JA for this Court in *Peat Marwick Ltd. v. Consumers' Gas Co.* (1980), 29 OR (2d) 336, 1 PPSAC 149, 11 BLR 114, 35 CBR (NS) 1, 113 DLR (3d) 754, at 344 [29 OR (2d)]:

It seems to me that the receiver and manager in a situation, like the present, is wearing two hats. When wearing one hat, he is the agent of the debtor company; when wearing the other, the agent of the debenture holder. In occupying the premises of the debtor and in carrying on the business, the receiver and manager acts as the agent of the debtor company. In realizing the security of the debenture holder, notwithstanding the language of the debenture, he acts as the agent of the debenture holder, and thus is able to confer title on a purchaser free of encumbrance.

The trial Judge then said [2 PPSAC, at 235]:

Thorne Riddell acted as agent for Allinson from the time it took possession on March 14, 1980 until March 20, 1980. On March 20, a decision was made to realize on the security and liquidate the assets. At that point the receiver was acting as agent of the Bank notwithstanding the wording of the security agreement.

• • •

If I had not found there was no attachment under s. 21 because of the failure of the Bank to comply with s. 12, possession by the Bank's agent would have given the Bank priority of perfection of its general security agreement.

It is helpful at this point to set out the relevant parts of s. 24:

24. Except as provided in section 26, possession of the collateral by the secured party, or on his behalf by a person other than the debtor or the debtor's agent, perfects a security interest in,

• • •

(b) goods;

• • •

but subject to section 23, only during its actual holding as collateral.

The bank initially submitted that the trial Judge was correct in concluding that perfection took place on March 20 but, when the query was raised whether a mere decision to realize on the security could amount to perfection and, in any event, whether there was any evidence respecting a decision to realize on the Sperry inventory, the bank submitted that it had perfected on March 14.

Several issues arise with respect to the bank's claim to have perfected its security interest by possession but it is not necessary to deal with all of them. I do not need to deal with Sperry's contention that "repossession" of collateral on default cannot amount to possession for the purpose of s. 24. There is a helpful discussion of this issue in J.A. Carfagnini, *Statutory Requirements for Perfection by Possession under the Ontario Personal Property Security Act* (1982), 7 *CBLJ* 234. The requirement in s. 24 that perfection by possession is "only during its actual holding as collateral" would have to be addressed. However, it need not be in this case because I think it turns on more basic considerations.

In my view the bank never perfected its security interest in the Sperry-supplied inventory in contention. The bank seeks to minimize the effect of the agency provision in its general security agreement. It submits that the taking of possession of Allinson's assets was an act taken by the receiver as agent for the bank and was the initial act of realization.

The apparent logic of the first part of the bank's submission ignores the effect of the agency provision in the general security agreement under which Thorne Riddell was appointed. This term bound not only the parties to the agreement but was "effective ... against third parties" (Act, s. 9). The possession required by s. 24 of the Act should be unequivocal. Expressly, it cannot be by the debtor's agent (s. 24). I have difficulty seeing how the receiver's possession could be to a person informed of the basic facts that "reasonable, clear and actual possession" of the creditor which satisfies one of the main objects of perfection—to inform outsiders: see Catzman, F.M., *Personal Property Security Law in Ontario* (1976), at 121. The bank is really seeking the best of both worlds and in this respect the following words of Houlden JA in *Peat Marwick* are apposite [29 OR (2d), at 346]:

If the bank chooses to provide in its debenture that the receiver and manager shall be deemed to be the agent of the debtor company, then it must not only take the benefits, but it must also accept detriments which flow from such a provision.

I turn now to the trial Judge's opinion that the bank took possession of the inventory on March 20 when "a decision was made to realize on the security and liquidate the assets." The trial Judge in this passage was adverting to the passage in the judgment in *Peat Marwick* which I have just quoted. With respect, I think the trial Judge applied the analysis in *Peat Marwick* beyond its proper scope. It is only "in realizing" that the receiver acts as the creditor's agent—to give commercial efficacy to the security agreement, i.e., so that title may be conferred on the purchaser free of encumbrance. The mere decision to realize falls short of realizing on the security.

In any event, I think the evidence does not support a conclusion in favour of either the realization or a decision to realize on Sperry's inventory. I have earlier quoted Thorne Riddell's letter of March 17, 1980 to Sperry. It clearly indicated that as of that date no decision had been made to realize on the Sperry inventory and there is nothing of sufficient weight in the subsequent evidence to deflect the inference that this position continued to the commencement of the action. Further, it may be noted that if the bank or receiver had decided to sell the Sperry inventory it did not manifest this decision in the form of a notice to Sperry under s. 59(5) of the Act.

Appeal dismissed.

NOTES

1) In *Re Darzinskas* Steele J notes the contrasting provisions in ss. 24 and 58(b) of the Act [now ss. 22 and 62(b)] but without deciding whether a secured party's taking possession of the collateral on the debtor's default also satisfies the perfection requirements in s. 24. The point was also left open by Morden JA in *Sperry v. CIBC*. In his "Comment" in (1982-83), 7 *CBLJ* 234, J.A. Carfagnini argues that the perfection requirements in s. 24 should not be satisfied. He relies heavily on the requirement in the concluding lines of s. 24 that possession perfects a security interest "only during its actual holding as collateral." (Section 22 of the new Act has changed this slightly to read, "but only while it is actually held as collateral," but no change in substance was intended.) He reasons that collateral that is seized on default is possessed for purposes of realization and not to be held as collateral. Do you find this reasoning persuasive? It appealed to Nobleton J in *Deloitte, Haskins & Sells Ltd. v. Folden* (1986), 6 PPSAC 102 (Sask.), but it was rejected, at least implicitly, in *Re Charron* (1984), 4 PPSAC 228 (Ont.), *Re Olmstead* (1984), 4 PPSAC 220 (Ont.), and in *Sifton Credit Union Ltd. v. Barber* (1986), 6 PPSAC 9 (Man.). In all these cases seizure of the collateral on the debtor's default was held to perfect the security interest by possession.

The Ontario Advisory Committee was also not persuaded by Carfagnini's distinction, but thought the position should be clarified. Accordingly, s. 22 of the new Act speaks of "possession or repossession" of the collateral by the secured party as perfecting a security interest in the described collateral.

2) However, this amendment does not resolve the question of the meaning of "but only while it is actually held as collateral." This qualifier does not appear in UCC 9-305 and American courts have held that it does not matter in which capacity the secured party

holds the collateral so long as he is lawfully in possession of it. See, e.g., *Raleigh Industries of America Inc. v. Tassone* (1977), 141 Cal. Rep. 641, and *In re Chapman* (1968), 5 UCCR 649 (Ref. Bkcy WD Mich.). Do you find these rulings objectionable? Should the concluding words in s. 22 be deleted? Catzman et al., at 121, suggests their purpose is to establish the time of perfection where the secured party held the collateral in an earlier capacity before the security agreement was concluded, for example, goods held by a bailee. Is this persuasive? Is s. 22 concerned with the *time* of perfection?

PROBLEM

SP, a truck dealer, has sold a truck to D on a conditional sale basis. D returns the truck to SP for a check-up under the manufacturer's warranty. While the truck is in the dealer's possession D becomes bankrupt. Does SP have a perfected security interest by possession under the Ontario Act?

NOTES

1) Note carefully the provisions in s. 26 with respect to perfection by possession where the goods are in the hands of a bailee. For the distinction between a negotiable and non-negotiable warehouse receipt see, e.g., Warehouse Receipts Act, RSO 1990, c. W.3, ss. 19-24. See also *supra*, volume I of this casebook, chapter 8. None of the provinces has adopted comprehensive legislation on documents of title comparable to Article 7 of the UCC.

2) *Field Warehousing*. Perfection by possession is sometimes used in the United States in connection with an inventory type of financing referred to as "field warehousing." Part of the debtor's business premises is cordoned off into a locked area under the exclusive control of an agent of the secured party and appropriate notices are posted around the area. The agent issues warehouse receipts (a type of "document of title" as defined in s. 1(i)) to the secured creditor for goods supplied to the debtor and placed in the area (called a "field warehouse"). The secured party advances money to the debtor against the warehouse receipts. Since the secured party holds the warehouse receipts the debtor cannot deal with the goods without his consent. Besides providing a method of perfection, field warehousing thus also provides an effective means of protecting the inventory financer against unauthorized dealings with the collateral. Field warehousing has occasionally been used in Canada. For early examples, see *Banque Nationale v. Royer* (1910), 20 Que. KB 351, and *In re Wedlock Ltd.*, [1926] 2 DLR 263 (PEI), discussing whether possession by an employee of the debtor, to whom part of the premises were leased, is not the debtor's possession for the purposes of s. 86 of the old Bank Act (now s. 435 of SC 1991, c. 46). As to field warehousing in general, see D.M. Friedman, "Field Warehousing" (1942), 42 *Colum. L Rev.* 991. See also *Bostian v. Park National Bank of Kansas City* (1955), 226 F.2d 753 (8th Cir.), and in particular its discussion as to whether access to the field warehouse by the debtor destroys the exclusiveness of the secured party's possession and the perfection of his security interest.

Re M.C. United Masonry Ltd.; Peat Marwick Ltd. v. Goldfarb
(1983), 44 CBR (NS) 174, 142 DLR (3d) 470 (Ont. CA)

The judgment of the court was delivered by HOULDEN JA: This is an appeal from an order of Steele J dated 29th December 1981 [*Re M.C. United Masonry Ltd.* (1981), 40 CBR (NS) 106, 16 BLR 176], declaring that a security agreement given by M.C. United Masonry Limited to Stanley Goldfarb in trust is null and void [*sic*] as against Peat Marwick Limited, the trustee in bankruptcy of M.C. United. The issue in the appeal is whether Goldfarb, as a result of receiving the security agreement together with possession of certain shares in Palm Hill Investments Limited, acquired a perfected security interest in the shares, having priority over the interest of the trustee in the collateral. The security agreement was not registered in accordance with the Personal Property Security Act (the "PPSA"), RSO 1970, c. 344 (now RSO 1980, c. 375), and the appellant's claim to priority rests, therefore, on perfection by possession.

The appellant Goldfarb acts in these proceedings as trustee for the firm, Goldfarb, Shulman, Wilner & Co. ("GSW"), chartered accountants. GSW were the general accountants for M.C. United and companies associated with it. The companies formed part of what was known as the Bianchini-Scodeller Group. In July 1978 the companies in the group being serviced by GSW owed GSW some $100,000 for accounting and consulting services. GSW was unwilling to provide any further services unless arrangements were made for payment of its outstanding accounts.

During July and August 1978 negotiations took place between GSW and Aurelio Bianchini and Amodeo Scodeller, the principals of the Bianchini-Scodeller Group, regarding the payment of GSW's account. Mr. Bianchini and Mr. Scodeller agreed that if GSW would not seek immediate payment of its outstanding fees, and if GSW would continue to provide its services to the companies in the group, then M.C. United would guarantee payment of the outstanding fees and the future fees of GSW. M.C. United was the owner of a 50 per cent interest in Palm Hill Investments Limited. As security for its guarantee, it was agreed that M.C. United would give GSW a pledge of its Palm Hill shares.

The principals of the Bianchini-Scodeller Group prepared an agreement dated 1st September 1978 ("the security agreement"). This was presented to GSW in final executed form without any member of the firm, or any solicitor on its behalf, having participated in the drafting of it. Although the parties to the agreement are shown as M.C. United and Stanley Goldfarb, in trust, the agreement was only executed by M.C. United. The agreement is badly drafted, some of the clauses being almost unintelligible.

The agreement commences with three recitals which state that Goldfarb has performed accounting, auditing (in actual fact GSW did not perform auditing services), and consulting services for M.C. United and companies that M.C. United had business dealings with from time to time. M.C. United acknowledged that there was $100,000 owing to Goldfarb at the date of the agreement. There was no listing of the companies or the amounts owed by them, but Goldfarb testified that the parties understood what companies were meant to be covered by the agreement. M.C. United further acknowledged that because it had business dealings with the various companies, the services of Goldfarb were of material advantage to it and it, therefore, guaranteed payment of the unpaid fees and any future fees for services performed by Goldfarb for the companies. Finally, the recitals stated that M.C. United had agreed to secure its guarantee by the collateral security set forth in the agreement. There are four operative clauses in the agreement that are, I believe, relevant to this appeal. They are cls. 1, 2, 3 and 6 which provide:

1. The recitals contained herein are true and are confirmed and acknowledged in all their respects.

2. As security for its guarantee for the repayment of the said fees and any future fees as aforesaid M.C. *hereby assigns* to Goldfarb all its shareholdings in Palm Hill Investments Limited ("Palm Hill") as general and continuing collateral security for the fulfillment of its said guarantee.

3. Immediately upon default by M.C. unde [*sic*] its said guarantee, Goldfarb may enforce the said security [*sic*] and from time to time sell at public or private sale or otherwide [*sic*] realize upon the said shares for such price in money or other consideration and upon such terms and cinditions [*sic*] as Goldfarb deems best, the whole without advertisement or notice to the under-signed or others ... .

16. This shall be a continuing agreement and shall have effect whenever and so often as the guarantee exists. (The italics are mine.)

From these clauses I think it is manifest that Goldfarb's interest in the shares was intended to take effect immediately. I can find nothing in the agreement to indicate that the parties intended it to become effective at some future date, or that its effect was conditional on the happening of some future event. Goldfarb's rights were stated to be enforceable on default, not on registration of the transfer on the books of Palm Hill followed by default.

Steele J was of the opinion that the agreement "clearly contemplated that the shares would be transferred on the books of Palm Hill": see *Re M.C. United Masonry Ltd., supra*, at 181 BLR. With respect, I have difficulty in deriving this intention from the provisions of the agreement. However, even if Steele J is right, I do not think that such an intention would detract from the fact that the agreement plainly envisages that the security interest of GSW was to come into effect immediately on the execution of the agreement by M.C. United.

The agreement was only signed by one officer of M.C. United under the company seal. Steele J found that the agreement was validly executed, and this finding was not challenged on the argument of the appeal.

M.C. United's interest in Palm Hill was represented by three share certificates: a certificate for 48 common shares in the name of M.C. United; a certificate for one common share in the name of Judith Shiff; and a certificate for one common share in the name of Aurelio Bianchini. The respondent admits that M.C. United had the right to pledge the shares of Palm Hill as security for indebtedness.

Upon receiving the executed security agreement, Goldfarb took possession of the three share certificates which had been endorsed by the holders. At no time before the petition in bankruptcy was filed against M.C. United did Goldfarb ever relinquish posses-sion of the certificates.

The other 50 issued common shares of Palm Hill were owned by Ismor Investments Limited, a company controlled by Morris Wagner. The letters patent of Palm Hill re-stricted transfers of shares by requiring the express sanction of the board of directors to the transfer, such sanction to be signified by a resolution passed by the board. The share certificates on their face stated that they were "transferable only on the books of the Company (subject to the restrictions imposed by the letters patent of the Company) by the holder hereof in person or by duly authorized attorney upon surrender of this Certificate properly endorsed."

After receiving the Palm Hill shares, Goldfarb, in the fall of 1978, approached the solicitor for Palm Hill concerning the registration of the transfer but was told that Mr. Wagner only wanted to be a partner of Mr. Bianchini. Although Mr. Goldfarb made persistent efforts during 1979 to have Mr. Wagner approve the transfer, he was unsuccessful in obtaining the approval.

GSW, in reliance upon the security agreement and the pledge of shares, took no steps to collect its outstanding accounts and continued to provide services to the Bianchini-Scodeller Group. As a result, at the date of bankruptcy, the amount owing to GSW had increased to $204,000.

On 18th April 1980 a petition in bankruptcy was filed against M.C. United. On 2nd May 1980 the solicitor for GSW informed the solicitor for Palm Hill that he would apply for the appointment of a receiver if the shares were not transferred immediately. Following this conversation, the board of directors of Palm Hill, by resolution dated 6th May 1980, signified its sanction to the transfer. On 9th May 1980 a receiving order was made against M.C. United. Goldfarb did not surrender his old share certificates for new certificates until after the date of the receiving order, and he did not surrender his old certificates until he had first received the new certificates.

As I see it, the outcome of this appeal turns on the answers to three questions: (1) Did the appellant's security interest attach when the agreement of 1st September 1978 was executed by M.C. United, and the agreement and the shares were delivered to the appellant? (2) Was the security interest perfected? and (3) Was the guarantee contained in the security agreement unenforceable by reason of s. 4 [am. 1978, c. 2, s. 88] of the Statute of Frauds, RSO 1970, c. 444 (now RSO 1980, c. 481)? I shall deal with each of these questions beginning with the first question:

(1) *Did the appellant's security interest attach when the agreement of 1st September 1978 was executed by M.C. United, and the agreement and the shares were delivered to the appellant?*

A "security agreement" is an agreement that creates or provides for a security interest: s. 1(x) of the PPSA. A "security interest" includes an interest in securities that secures payment or performance of an obligation: s. 1(y) of the PPSA. "Securities" is defined by s. 1(w) of the PPSA as meaning, among other things, shares issued by a corporation. Subsection (w) makes no distinction between shares in a corporation that offers its securities to the public, and shares in a corporation, such as Palm Hill, that does not offer its securities to the public: see the Business Corporations Act, RSO 1980, c. 54, s. 1(8); nor does it restrict the term "shares" to shares which are free of transfer restrictions.

By s. 90(1) of the Business Corporations Act, Goldfarb could not compel Palm Hill to register the transfer until the restrictions on transfer had been complied with. However, if shares in a corporation are transferred without complying with restrictions on transfer, the transferee acquires an equitable interest in the shares: *Harrold v. Plenty*, [1901] 2 Ch. 314, 17 TLR 545; *Hawks v. McArthur*, [1951] 1 TLR 308, [1951] 1 All ER 22. Although the PPSA makes no distinction between legal and equitable interests, Goldfarb, when he received the security agreement and the pledge of the shares, received, in my opinion, an "interest" in the shares sufficient to constitute a "security interest" for the purposes of

s. 1(y) of the PPSA. I can find nothing in the Business Corporations Act which prohibits this result. Indeed, it seems to me that ss. 75, 77(2)(a), 78, 80 and 83(1)(a) of that Act are consonant with it.

Subsection (1) of s. 12 of the PPSA [now s. 11(1)] deals with the time when a security interest attaches. It provides:

12.—(1) A security interest attaches when,
    (a) the parties intend it to attach;
    (b) value is given; and
    (c) the debtor has rights in the collateral.

There is no doubt, and this is conceded by the respondent, that the requirements of cls. (b) and (c) were met in this case. Steele J was of the opinion, however, that the requirements of cl. (a) had not been met. He was of the view that the security interest was not intended to attach until the shares were validly transferred on the books of Palm Hill, and that this not having occurred prior to bankruptcy, the security interest had not attached. In this connection, he said (at 182):

A security interest attaches under the Personal Property Security Act when the parties intend it to attach. The parties' intention, as evidenced in the agreement, was that attachment was to take place when the shares were transferred on the books of Palm Hill and the respondent was recognized by Palm Hill as a shareholder therein. This was not accomplished prior to bankruptcy and I find that the security interest did not attach prior to bankruptcy.

Fortunately, there is no problem in this case of credibility. The evidence for the respondent in support of the motion to declare the appellant's security agreement null and void (*sic*) consisted of the affidavit of a manager of the respondent who had knowledge of the bankrupt estate. The appellant filed two affidavits in reply: the affidavit of Stanley Goldfarb, and the affidavit of Jonathan Arlen Levin, the solicitor for GSW. Only Mr. Goldfarb was cross-examined on his affidavit. No oral evidence was called before Steele J, and there was no material filed to contradict the evidence of Mr. Goldfarb. Consequently, we are in as good a position as Steele J to determine the matter of intention.

As stated previously, it is my opinion that the security interest was intended to take effect immediately upon the execution of the agreement of 1st September 1978 and the delivery of the agreement and the shares. There was some $100,000 owing to GSW, and GSW was obligating itself to provide substantial future services to companies in the Bianchini-Scodeller Group. I can see no conceivable reason why Goldfarb would want to postpone attachment of the security interest until the shares were transferred on the books of Palm Hill. With respect, I think that Steele J erred in finding that the appellant's security interest had not attached. In my opinion, the security interest attached when the agreement of 1st September 1978 was executed, and the agreement and the Palm Hill shares were delivered to Goldfarb.

(2) *Was the security interest perfected?*

For a security interest in collateral to be valid against a trustee in bankruptcy, it must be perfected: s. 22(1)(a)(iii) of the PPSA. On this point Steele J said (at 182-83):

Alternatively, even if the interest did attach under the provisions of s. 12 of the Personal Property Security Act, I find that there was no possession of the collateral by the secured party as contemplated by s. 24. There was physical possession of pieces of paper known as share certificates of Palm Hill still registered in the name of M.C. United and properly endorsed in favour of the respondent. These were not negotiable securities. However, what the respondent is claiming as his security is the actual ownership of shares of Palm Hill, namely a one-half interest in that company. Prior to bankruptcy, there never was any effective ownership of such shares that he could exercise as a shareholder of Palm Hill, and therefore there was no possession of a proper share in Palm Hill. Even if the respondent did not have actual notice of the prohibition of the transfer of shares without consent, the share certificates on their face drew the matter to his attention and he is deemed to have constructive notice of such requirements because the letters patent are a public document.

Section 21 of the PPSA provides that a security interest is perfected when (a) it has attached, and (b) all steps for perfection under the Act have been completed, regardless of the order of occurrence. In this case, if perfection occurred, it occurred by possession. Section 24 sets out the steps required for perfection by possession. The relevant portion of the section for this appeal is the following:

24. Except as provided in section 26, possession of the collateral by the secured party, or on his behalf by a person other than the debtor or the debtor's agent, perfects a security interest in. ...
    (d) securities; ...
but subject to section 23, only during its actual holding as collateral.

"Securities," as has been pointed out, is defined by s. 1(w) to include shares issued by a corporation. There is nothing in s. 24 or s. 1(w) which requires that the shares be negotiable or that they be in such a form that the secured party could exercise effective ownership of them. The PPSA applies to transactions creating security interests "without regard to the person who has title to the collateral": s. 2 of the PPSA.

For perfection by possession, s. 24 requires that the secured party have possession by "actual holding as collateral." "Collateral" is defined by s. 1(d) to mean property that is subject to a security interest and, as has been noted, "security interest" is defined by s. 1(y) to mean, among other things, an interest in "securities" that secures payment or perform- ance of an obligation. Here, Goldfarb obtained actual physical possession of the Palm Hill shares as security for payment or performance of the obligations undertaken by M.C. United in the agreement of 1st September 1978. In my opinion, that possession was sufficient to perfect Goldfarb's security interest under s. 24.

Mr. Langley submitted that, if perfection by possession could be achieved by mere physical possession of restricted transfer shares, then the secured party would gain the benefit of the remedies in s. 59 of the PPSA. He contended that s. 59(8) was irreconcilably inconsistent with the non-assignable nature of such shares. Section 59(8) reads as follows:

(8) Where collateral is disposed of in accordance with this section, the disposition discharges the security interest of the secured party making the disposition and, if such disposition is made to a *bona fide* purchaser for value, discharges also any subordinate security interest and termi- nates the debtor's in the collateral.

Mr. Langley argued that, if s. 59(8) was applied literally, the interest of the registered owner of the shares would be terminated, and this is clearly contrary to well-established principles of common law. While it is difficult to apply s. 59(8) to a disposition by a secured creditor of restricted transfer shares, I believe that the best that can be done with it is to say that, although the debtor's interest in the shares is terminated by the disposition, s. 59(8) in no way affects the company, and the company is not obligated to consent to a transfer until the restrictions have been complied with. I appreciate that, if this is the correct interpretation of s. 59(8), then the PPSA has changed the law as stated by the House of Lords in *Hunter v. Hunter*, [1936] AC 222. However, we are not concerned in this appeal with a disposition under s. 59, and it is therefore unnecessary to express any firm opinion on this issue.

Since Goldfarb's security interest was perfected, it has priority over the interest of the respondent, the trustee in bankruptcy of M.C. United, in the shares: *Re Bellini Mfg. & Importing Ltd.* (1981), 32 OR (2d) 684, 37 CBR (NS) 209, 14 BLR 63, 122 DLR (3d) 472 (CA).

• • •

Application dismissed.

NOTES

The trial court's decision in *Re M.C. United Masonry* is discussed in Ziegel, "Comment" (1982), 6 *CBLJ* 378. The effect of the Court of Appeal's decision is to enable a secured party to obtain a perfected security interest in shares of a closely held corporation even though the shares have not been transferred on the corporation's share register and even if the directors have not given their consent to the transfer. The result is consistent with the intentions of the Article 9 draftpersons and, seemingly, with the definition of "certificated security" in UCC 8-102. The new federal and provincial Business Corporations Acts have adopted provisions similar to those in Article 8 governing the negotiability of investment securities. See, e.g., Business Corporations Act, RSO 1990, c. B.16, Pt. VI. However, the fact that a secured party has a perfected security interest in a closely held corporation does not relieve him from having to comply with the corporation's by-laws if he wants to dispose of and transfer the shares to another party.

Perfection and Conflict of Laws Issues

It is common for goods to be ordered on conditional sale terms from a seller in one province for delivery in another. It is equally common for goods subject to a security interest, especially motor vehicles, to be taken by the debtor into another jurisdiction without notifying the secured party of the removal. In these types of cases, Canadian courts have had to determine from about the beginning of the century onwards which law governs the original secured transaction and to what extent the registration requirements of the *lex fori* apply to goods brought into the province from another jurisdiction. The courts held that (1) the original *lex situs* of the goods determines whether the security interest was validly created and perfected and that (2), as a matter of statutory construction, the registration Acts were not meant to apply to security interests in chattels created outside the province. See, *inter alia, Ross v. Henderson* (1909), 11 WLR 656 (Man.); *McGregor v. Kerr* (1896), 29 NSR 45, and Ziegel, "Conditional Sales and the Conflict of Laws" (1967),

45 *Can. Bar Rev.* 284. The second result was regarded as unsatisfactory since it meant that registration records were incomplete and unscrupulous debtors could dispose of the collateral by concealing the extra-provincial security interest. The conditional sales Acts were therefore amended to provide that the foreign seller had to register the conditional sale agreement after he became aware of the removal of the goods into the forum. For a typical provision, see the former New Brunswick Conditional Sales Act, s. 5, discussed in *GMAC v. Hubbard* (1978), 87 DLR (3d) 39, volume I of this casebook, chapter 10.

The conflict of laws provisions in OPPSA ss. 5-8 are based on (but not identical with) the changes adopted in the 1972 revision of Article 9. Similar provisions appear in most of the western provincial Acts. The new provisions are more comprehensive than the rules appearing in ss. 5-8 of the old Ontario Act. The principal features of the new rules are as follows. Section 5(1) prescribes which law governs the validity, perfection, and effect of perfection of a security interest in goods and a possessory security interest in other types of collateral, and continues the long-established *lex situs* rule. Section 5(2) determines the status in Ontario of goods brought into the province while subject to a security interest created under the first *lex situs*. Section 5(5) is particular to Ontario and continues a provision in the old Conditional Sales Act involving goods sold by a Quebec seller and subject to an unpaid seller's right of revendication under the Quebec civil code. See Falconbridge, *Conflict of Laws*, 2nd ed. (1984), chapter 19. Section 6 incorporates an important exception to the *lex situs* rule where the parties to a security agreement understand at the time the security interest attaches that the goods will be kept in another jurisdiction and the goods are removed to that other jurisdiction within 30 days after the security interest attaches. What is the rationale of s. 6?

Section 7 deals with the choice of law rule governing the creation and perfection of a security interest in collateral other than goods, and a possessory interest in documentary intangibles. (Note carefully that s. 7(1)(a)(ii) also applies to non-consumer mobile goods, i.e., goods that are normally kept in more than one jurisdiction.) These types of collateral are governed by the law of the debtor's location at the time the security interest attaches. Section 7(4) indicates how that location is to be determined. If the debtor changes its location then the security interest must be reperfected: s. 7(2). Finally, s. 8 determines the law governing the enforcement of a security interest and distinguishes between the procedural and substantive aspects of the secured party's enforcement rights.

The cases that follow illustrate, very incompletely, some of the policy and construc-tional issues raised by these provisions.

Re Adair; Re General Motors Acceptance Corporation
(1985), 4 PPSAC 262 (Ont. CA)

GOODMAN JA: ... This is an appeal by Ward Mallette Inc., trustee in bankruptcy (the trustee) from an order [reported at 48 CBR (NS) 214] pronounced on October 11, 1983 by the presiding Judge in bankruptcy on an application by General Motors Acceptance Corporation (GMAC) for an order declaring that GMAC has a security interest in a 1982 Chevrolet van in accordance with a security agreement made between the bankrupt and GMAC in priority to the trustee in bankruptcy of Alice Marie Adair (Adair).

The undisputed facts which gave rise to these proceedings are as follows. Adair purchased the Chevrolet van and financed its purchase under a conditional sales agreement which was executed in Florida on September 8, 1982. This agreement was assigned to GMAC which duly perfected its security interest in the van in accordance with the law of the State of Florida at a time prior to the date upon which the van was brought into Ontario by Adair, *viz.* April 21, 1983.

The van remained in Ontario on and after that date.

On May 26, 1983, Adair made a voluntary assignment in bankruptcy and the trustee herein was appointed as the trustee in bankruptcy of her estate. At that time at least two creditors of her estate had no knowledge of any security interest of GMAC in the van.

On May 31, 1983, notices in the prescribed form were mailed by the trustee to all known creditors of the estate of Adair including GMAC in Jacksonville, Florida. The parties agree that pursuant to the Rules of Practice and the Bankruptcy Rules, GMAC is deemed to have received the notice on the fourth day following that on which it was mailed, *viz.* June 4, 1983.

On June 15, 1983, GMAC filed a proof of claim with the trustee claiming the van pursuant to the terms of its conditional sales agreement. On June 17, 1983, the trustee mailed to GMAC a notice of disallowance of claim as a secured creditor on the basis of "No evidence of registration under the Personal Property Security Act," and accepted the claim as that of an unsecured creditor for the amount claimed.

On June 28, 1983, GMAC filed a financing statement with respect to the van pursuant to the provisions of the Personal Property Security Act, RSO 1980, c. 375 (PPSA).

The parties have agreed that the van had a value of $8,000 net of costs of disposition. On consent the van, at some time after October 15, 1983, has been exported by GMAC and the sum of $8,000 has been deposited in the name of the solicitors for GMAC in an interest bearing account with Guaranty Trust of Canada pending disposition of this appeal and the determination of entitlement.

On these facts the learned Judge in bankruptcy made an order with short reasons as follows [at 214]:

Order to go declaring that General Motors Acceptance Corporation has priority to the trustee with respect to the van in question. This order is based upon a consideration of *Re Johnson* (1979), 30 CBR (NS) 210 (Ont. SC), and a consideration of *Trans-Can. Credit Corp. v. Bachand* (1980), 1 PPSAC 185 (Ont. CA). This latter decision did not involve bankruptcy. I am also relying on the provisions of s. 7(1) of the Personal Property Security Act, RSO 1980, c. 375, together with ss. 22(1)(a)(iii) and 22(2) of that Act. The applicant and trustee are entitled to their costs forthwith after taxation thereof.

The parties are in agreement that for the purpose of the determination of the issue in this appeal, regard must be had in particular to the provisions of s. 7 and s. 22 of the PPSA. The relevant portions of those sections are as follows:

7.—(1) Subject to section 5, a security interest in collateral already perfected under the law of the jurisdiction in which the collateral was when the security interest attached and before being brought into Ontario continues perfected in Ontario for sixty days and also thereafter if within the sixty-day period it is perfected in Ontario.

(2) Notwithstanding subsection (1), where the secured party receives notice within the sixty-day period mentioned therein that the collateral has been brought into Ontario, his security interest in the collateral ceases to be perfected in Ontario unless he registers a financing statement in the prescribed form within fifteen days from the date that he receives such notice or upon the expiration of the sixty-day period, whichever is earlier.

(3) A security interest that has ceased to be perfected in Ontario due to the expiration of the sixty-day period may thereafter be perfected in Ontario, but such perfection takes effect from the time of its perfection in Ontario.

• • •

22.—(1) Except as provided in subsection (3), an unperfected security interest is subordinate to,

    (a) the interest of a person,

        (i) who is entitled to a priority under this or any other Act, or

        (ii) who, without knowledge of the security interest and before it is perfected, assumes control of the collateral through legal process, or

        (iii) who represents the creditors of the debtor as assignee for the benefit of creditors, trustee in bankruptcy or receiver; and ...

(2) The rights of a person under subclause (1)(a)(iii) in respect of the collateral are referable to the date from which his status has effect and arise without regard to the personal knowledge of the representative if any represented creditor was, on the relevant date, without knowledge of the unperfected security interest.

There is no doubt that if GMAC had perfected its security interest in Ontario within the 60-day period mentioned in s. 7(1) or within the 15-day period mentioned in s. 7(2), whichever expired the earlier, it would have had a security interest in the van in priority to the interest of the trustee. The parties are agreed that the 60-day period referred to in s. 7(1) expired on June 21, 1983 and the 15-day period referred to in s. 7(2) expired on June 19, 1983. It is common ground that GMAC did not register a financing statement in prescribed form within 15 days from the date it received notice that its collateral had been brought into Ontario nor did it perfect its security interest in the collateral (the van) within the 60-day period after it was brought into Ontario.

It was the submission of GMAC that the failure to perfect its security interest within the appropriate time period specified in s. 7 did not affect the priority of its security interest over the claim of the trustee. GMAC claimed that its security interest continued perfected in Ontario for the 60-day period, if s. 7(1) were applicable or for the 15-day period following notice, if s. 7(2) were applicable. It then submitted that under s. 22(1)(a)(iii) and s. 22(2) the rights of the trustee were fixed as of the date of its appointment, *viz.*, May 16, 1983, and that on that date GMAC's security interest having continued to be perfected in Ontario, it was entitled to priority over the interest acquired by the trustee.

It appears that the learned Judge in bankruptcy accepted this reasoning. There is some support for this viewpoint from the academic realm and in the United States courts. Professor Jacob S. Ziegel in an article published in 4 *CBLJ* 54 (1979-80), commenting on the trial decision of His Honour Judge Staniszewski in *Bachand v. Trans-Can. Credit Corp.* May 2, 1979 [now reported 1 PPSAC 41, at 83 (Ont. Co. Ct.)] said:

The question the court should have asked itself in the present case was whether the lapse of the 60-day period without reperfecting by Trans Canada *retroactively* invalidated Trans Canada's security interest and cured plaintiff's defective title.

A literal reading of PPSA, s. 7(1) leads to the conclusion that the secured party has an unqualified perfected security interest during the 60-day period. American case law decided under the pre-1972 version of UCC [Uniform Commercial Code] 9-103(3) supports this reading as does an important line of cases decided under the analogous (but not identical) provisions of the prior provincial Conditional Sales and Chattel Mortgages Acts. The Article 9 Review Committee criticized the American jurisprudence for failing to consider the effect of the subsequent lapse of the security interest. In any event, UCC 9-103 was amended in 1972 to make it clear that if the foreign security interest is not reperfected in the jurisdiction to which the collateral was removed before the expiration of the period of perfection in the foreign jurisdiction or within four months [60 days under PPSA, s. 7(1)] after the collateral is brought into the forum, whichever occurs first, it is thereafter deemed to have been unperfected "as against a person who became a purchaser after removal." Such an amendment should also be considered in Ontario to prevent the anomalies that may otherwise arise.

The facts in the *Bachand* case, *supra*, are very similar to the facts in the present case except that the contest in *Bachand* was between an assignee of a conditional sales agreement and a subsequent purchaser, whereas the contest in the present case is between an assignee of a conditional sales agreement and a trustee in bankruptcy.

The facts in *Bachand* were that on February 26, 1976, L. Company in New Brunswick sold a motor vehicle on conditional sales terms to one M. The agreement was assigned to T.C.C. Corp. and registered in New Brunswick. On May 20, 1976, T.C.C. Corp. learned that the vehicle was located in Alberta and registered the agreement in that province. On August 13, 1976, the vehicle was registered by M. in Ontario. The registration permit for the vehicle was then transferred to the H. & J. Auto Centre who resold the vehicle to the plaintiff on September 3, 1976. T.C.C. Corp. registered a financing statement in Ontario on October 27, 1976 (more than 60 days after the vehicle was brought into Ontario). On December 13, 1976, bailiffs acting on T.C.C. Corp.'s instructions, seized the vehicle while it was in the plaintiff's possession. The issue before the Court was whether the plaintiff had obtained a good title when he purchased the vehicle. Judge Staniszewski upheld the plaintiff's claim and found that the 60-day registration on October 27 was "inoperative and null and void."

Professor Ziegel in his article said at 82-83 in commenting on this conclusion:

The soundness of the decision is open to serious question. In the first place, the learned Judge was mistaken in holding that Trans Canada's registration was a nullity. PPSA, s. 7(3) provides that a security interest that has ceased to be perfected in Ontario because of the expiration of the 60-day period may thereafter be perfected in Ontario but that such perfection only operates from the time of perfection in Ontario. This provision is quite inconsistent with the notion that a foreign security interest becomes "null and void" if it is not reperfected within 60 days. In fact, the Act throughout consciously eschews use of the terminology of nullity because of its misleading character; "unperfected" is the Act's characterization of a security interest that has not been perfected and the effect of an unperfected security interest is to "subordinate" the security interest to the interest described in PPSA, s. 22.

In the second place, the learned trial judge overlooked the effect of s. 7(2) conferring a perfected status on the New Brunswick security interest for a 60-day period. That period had not expired on September 3rd when the plaintiff purchased the vehicle from H. & J. Auto Centre. Prima facie, therefore, it was the plaintiff who had committed the act of conversion.

Professor Ziegel then posed the question which I have quoted above. Professor Ziegel's article was written prior to the time this Court heard an appeal by the defendant from the decision of Judge Staniszewski.

The judgment in that appeal is reported as *Trans Can. Credit Corp. v. Bachand* (1980), 30 OR (2d) 405, 1 PPSAC 185, 12 BLR 247, 117 DLR (3d) 653 (Ont. CA). On that appeal the appellant took the position that the perfection mentioned in s. 7(1) was absolute and although the holder of the security interest did nothing thereafter, if an innocent purchaser buys the goods during that 60-day period, the transaction is liable to be vitiated at any time thereafter; if he still has possession of the goods innocently purchased they can be seized, or, in any event he will be liable for their money value if he has disposed of them. The appellant relied on a decision of the New Jersey Supreme Court in *First Nat. Bank of Bay Shore v. Stamper*, 3 UCC Reporting Service 949, 225 A.2d 162 (Sup. Ct. NJ 1966), which followed a decision of the New York Supreme Court, Appellate Division in *Churchill Motors Inc. v. A.C. Lohman Inc.*, 16 AD 2d 560, 229 NY 2d 570 (App. Div. 1962). In the latter case it was held that the four-month period provided in the Uniform Commercial Code for recording a conditional sales contract in a state to which property has been removed is not a grace period for filing, but is an absolute period of protection of vendor's security interest designed to give him time to locate the property. At 577 Justice Halpern said:

Under the provisions of the Uniform Commercial Code, the conditional vendor's interest continued to be perfected interest for four months. At the end of the period, it ceased to be a perfected interest and became an unperfected one but there is no provision which forfeits the four month period of protection because of failure to file prior to its expiration.

The provisions of the UCC at the time of these decisions was similar in nature to those contained in s. 7(1) of the PPSA except that the period of protection was four months instead of 60 days. In *Trans Can. v. Bachand* this Court refused to follow the American line of cases. MacKinnon ACJO said at 408 [30 OR (2d)]:

I can only say that I am not persuaded by the reasoning in that case and note that it is subject to some editorial criticism in the report.

The appellant was given 60 days within which to locate the property covered by its security interest and perfect that interest in Ontario. If he perfects it within the 60-day period it continues to be perfected after the expiration of that period. But, if he fails to perfect it within the 60-day period but perfects it thereafter then under s. 7(3) "such perfection takes effect from the time of its perfection within Ontario." It clearly does not relate back to the day when the collateral is brought into Ontario. To hold that the 60-day perfection is absolute without need for any subsequent action by the security holder could lead to obvious injustice to innocent parties. They would never be secure.

The appeal was accordingly dismissed. As previously mentioned the facts in *Trans Can. v. Bachand* are similar to those in the present case except that the grace period involved in the present case is the 15-day period allowed under s. 7(2) rather than the 60-day period allowed under s. 7(1) which does not affect the principle enunciated and except for the further fact that the present case involves a trustee in bankruptcy rather than a subsequent purchaser.

The appellant trustee in the present case relies on the decision of this Court in *Trans Can. v. Bachand*. GMAC, on the other hand, submits that the rationale in *Trans Can. v. Bachand* was that bona fide purchasers within the 60-day period should be protected from being dispossessed by a previously unknown secured party after the 60-day period has expired and that that is not a consideration in a bankruptcy case. In my view the submission of GMAC cannot prevail. In *Trans Can. v. Bachand* and in the present case financing statements were filed in Ontario after the expiration of the appropriate period of grace. The effect of the decision in *Trans Can. v. Bachand* was to treat a conditional sales agreement, properly perfected as a security interest in a foreign jurisdiction but not perfected in Ontario during the 60-day period after the collateral was brought into Ontario, as an unperfected security interest until the date of filing of the financing statement and accordingly the holder of the agreement had an unperfected security interest which was subordinated to the interest of a subsequent purchaser pursuant to the provisions of s. 22(1)(a)(i). Such subsequent purchaser acquired such priority as of the date of his purchase of the collateral.

In my view the principle enunciated in the *Trans Can.* case is that a security interest in collateral perfected under the law of jurisdiction in which the collateral was when the security interest attached and before being brought into Ontario becomes an unperfected security interest as of the date upon which the collateral is brought into Ontario if the person who owns such security interest fails to perfect it in Ontario within the times limited by s. 7(1) and (2), whichever is applicable, and it remains an unperfected security interest unless and until it is perfected as provided by s. 7(3). In my view this principle applies regardless of the manner in which the claimant, who claims an interest in priority to that of the unperfected security interest, has obtained his interest. The only question that remains to be decided in such a case is whether the claimant has obtained priority over the other contending party's security interest under the provisions of the PPSA.

It is of some interest to note that Minister of Consumer and Commercial Relations Advisory Committee on the Personal Property Security Act, presented to the Minister in April, 1984, a draft Personal Property Security Act. It is provided in s. 5(2) of that draft Act, which pertains to goods which have been brought into Ontario from another jurisdiction, as follows:

5.—(2) A security interest in goods perfected under the law of the jurisdiction in which the goods are situated at the time the security interest attaches but before the goods are brought into Ontario continues perfected in Ontario if it is perfected in Ontario,

(a) within sixty days after the goods are brought into Ontario;

(b) within fifteen days after the day the secured party receives notice that the goods are brought into Ontario; or

(c) … whichever is the earliest. …

This proposed sub-section is a revised version of s. 7(1) and (2) of the present Act and is in accord with the decision of the Court in *Trans Can. v. Bachand*.

In the present case, following this Court's decision in *Trans Can. v. Bachand*, the security interest of GMAC must be deemed to have been unperfected until June 28, 1983. The interest of the trustee was acquired therein on May 26, 1983 as provided by s. 22(2) of the PPSA. Accordingly, by virtue of the provisions of s. 22(1)(a)(iii), the unperfected security interest of GMAC in the van is subordinate to the interest of the trustee therein.

The appeal is therefore allowed, the order of the learned Judge in bankruptcy is set aside, and an order will go declaring that the security interest of GMAC in the 1982 Chevrolet van evidenced by a conditional sales contract dated September 8, 1982 is subordinate to the interest of the trustee therein. The trustee shall have its costs of this appeal and of the application in Bankruptcy Court.

Appeal allowed.

NOTES

1) Why do the Ontario provisions distinguish between a security interest perfected under the first *lex situs* and a security interest not so perfected? Is it to assist a third party in Ontario to make a registry search in the first jurisdiction? How often would she know that the goods have come from another state or province? How does s. 7 allocate the risks of loss arising from the debtor's wrongdoing between the foreign secured party and the third party in Ontario? Is the 60 days' grace period (it is 4 months in UCC 9-103(1)(d)(i), 1978 Official Text) too generous to the secured party? Should he be at risk at all before he knows that the goods have been brought into the forum?

2) The Code's conflict of laws provisions were substantially revised in the 1972 edition of Article 9. Many—but not all—of the changes were adopted in the Uniform Act and have in turn influenced the provisions in the revised OPPSA. See Ziegel and Cuming (1981), 31 *UTLJ* 231, at 256-60; Ontario, *Report of the Advisory Committee*, at 29-32; and *Ontario Supplementary Report, 1986*, at 13-15. New s. 5(2), as submitted in the *Supplementary Report*, reads:

(2) A security interest in goods perfected under the law of the jurisdiction in which the goods are situated at the time the security interest attaches but before the goods are brought into Ontario continues perfected in Ontario if a financing statement is registered in Ontario before the goods are brought in or if it is perfected in Ontario,

(a) within sixty days after the goods are brought in;

(b) within fifteen days after the day the secured party receives notice that the goods have been brought in; or

(c) before the date that perfection ceases under the law of the jurisdiction in which the goods were situated at the time the security interest attached,

whichever is earliest, but the security interest is subordinate to the interest of a buyer or lessee of those goods who acquires the goods from the debtor as consumer goods in good faith and without knowledge of the security interest and before the security interest is perfected in Ontario.

How does it compare with existing s. 7? Does it affirm the result in *Re Adair*? What is the reason for the special treatment of consumer goods? See *Ontario Supplementary Report, 1986*, Commentary, at 14-15. The Saskatchewan Act does not confine the protection of s. 5(2) to situations in which the goods are consumer goods in the hands of the debtor and are acquired as consumer goods from the debtor. See SPPSA s. 5(2). Is this a fair allocation of risks?

Re Claude A. Bedard
(1983), 46 CBR (NS) 172 (Ont. SC)

SMITH J: This application is by the trustee for an order that the security interest claimed by the Banque Nationale du Canada in a 1982 Buick Serial No. 1G4AW69YOCH436461 is subordinate to the interest of the trustee.

The parties are completely *ad idem* on the facts. The assignment in bankruptcy was made on 10th September 1982. The bank filed a secured claim based upon a conditional sales contract acquired by the bank when it supplied the purchase moneys for the purchase by the bankrupt of the said automobile on 16th May 1982.

The security attached in the province of Quebec on the date of purchase. The parties agree however that there is no statutory framework for an act of registration or perfection in Quebec as there is under the Personal Property Security Act, RSO 1980, c. 375, in Ontario. The partial statement of facts, to which the parties agreed in writing and filed with the court, also states that the conditional sales contract between the two parties is binding against third parties in Quebec.

On the basis of the foregoing, the bank invites the court to conclude that the security interest was perfected in Quebec so as to enable it to take advantage of the conflict of laws provisions embodied in s. 7 of the Personal Property Security Act. They read as follows:

7.—(1) Subject to section 5, a security interest in collateral already perfected under the law of the jurisdiction in which the collateral was when the security interest attached and before being brought into Ontario continues perfected in Ontario for sixty days and also thereafter if within the sixty-day period it is perfected in Ontario ... .

(3) A security interest that has ceased to be perfected in Ontario due to the expiration of the sixty-day period may thereafter be perfected in Ontario, but such perfection takes effect from the time of its perfection in Ontario.

The collateral was brought into Ontario on 17th May 1982. The financing statement was registered by the bank on 20th July 1982, namely, 65 days after the security interest attached and 64 days after the vehicle was brought to Ontario.

Subject to the provisions of s. 7(2), to which I will turn in a moment, and leaving aside any question that may arise under s. 6, the bank is seeking a pronouncement by this court on the question of whether perfection of the security interest in the province of Quebec had occurred in the circumstances recited above on the theory that the bank in Quebec had acquired the greatest bundle of rights possible. I am prepared to accept that the principle of comity suggests, and the Act implies, that a functional equivalence will suffice. I need not pass upon the question however, nor would I be inclined to do so in the appropriate case, in the absence of additional expert evidence as to the state of the law of Quebec regarding protection of third parties.

The point is academic, for I am of the view that s. 7(2) disposes of the issue in this case. It reads:

(2) Notwithstanding subsection (1), where the secured party receives notice within the sixty-day period mentioned therein that the collateral has been brought into Ontario, his security interest in the collateral ceases to be perfected in Ontario unless he registers a financing statement in the prescribed form within fifteen days from the date that he receives such notice or upon the expiration of the sixty-day period, whichever is earlier.

The secured party knew that the car was for personal use and that the residence of the debtor was Ontario. It thereby *received notice* in the sense which must be ascribed to those words of *acquiring* notice. The interest accordingly ceased to be perfected after the expiration of 15 days and by virtue of s. 22 of the said Act it became subordinated to the interest of the trustee.

Application granted.

NOTE

As will be noted, Smith J did not find it necessary to decide whether a conditional sale concluded in Quebec is deemed to be a perfected security interest in Ontario. The Advisory Committee thought the position should be clarified. Section 8(2) of the Act provides:

(2) For the purposes of this Part, a security interest shall be deemed to be perfected under the law of a jurisdiction if the secured party has complied with the law of the jurisdiction with respect to the creation and continuance of a security interest that is enforceable against the debtor and third parties.

Is the result too favourable to foreign secured parties? What is the meaning of "that is enforceable against the debtor and third parties"? Does it mean enforceable in all cases or is it sufficient if the security interest would be enforceable in the particular circumstances before the court?

CHAPTER FOUR

The Registration System

INTRODUCTION

Public disclosure of security interests through registration has long been a feature of personal property security law in common law jurisdictions in Canada. The Legislature of the Assembly of the Province of Canada enacted legislation in 1849 requiring public registration of chattel mortgages as a condition of their enforceability against subsequent interests acquired in mortgaged property from mortgagors. By the turn of the century, all common law jurisdictions required chattel mortgages to be registered, and all but Manitoba extended registration requirements to conditional sales contracts. The enactment of a Bankruptcy Act in 1919 forced provinces to enact registration requirements for general assignment of book debts by providing that a general assignment of book debts was void as against the trustee in bankruptcy unless registered in a provincial registry.

A few jurisdictions included in companies' legislation provisions for the registration of secured corporate bonds, debentures, floating charges, and other corporate securities. Much of the early legislation of this kind was patterned on s. 14 of the English Companies Act of 1900. In 1932 the Uniform Law Conference of Canada put forward the Uniform Corporation Securities Registration Act which, shortly thereafter, was adopted in several provinces, including Ontario. Starting in 1922, the Uniform Law Conference of Canada, a semi-official organization established in 1918 by the Canadian Bar Association to encourage uniformity of provincial law, adopted a series of uniform acts in the area of personal property security law. These acts dealt primarily with registration of security agreements and, while not implemented in all jurisdictions, have been influential in shaping chattel security legislation in several common law provinces.

The enactment of Personal Property Security Acts resulted in the repeal of separate registry statutes dealing with chattel mortgages, conditional sales contracts, assignment of book debts, and corporate securities. Three, and in many cases, four separate, antiquated and disparate systems were replaced by a single modern system applicable to all types of security interests. However, not all of the PPSA registry systems are identical. Refinement of registration systems accompanied refinement of substantive personal property security law. While the various provincial systems are coming closer together, largely as a result of the efforts of the Canadian Conference on Personal Property Security Law (CCPPSL), it is not yet possible to assume that the compliance requirements of one system are identical with those of others. The differences among the systems are a product of a number of factors, including policy choices. For example, the New Brunswick system is entirely electronic while all other systems permit the use of "hard copy" financing statements or financing change statements as alternatives to electronic financing statements or financing change statements. Collateral description requirements in financing statements and financing change statements are very different under the Acts based on the CCPPSL model from those of the Ontario Act. In particular, the requirements for specific collateral identification by serial number are much broader under the CCPPSL Acts.*

In this chapter, the basic features of a central, computerized notice registration system are briefly examined. The primary focus is on the Ontario Personal Property Registry. Significant features of other systems, based on the CCPPSL model, that differ from the Ontario system are noted.

THE BASIC STRUCTURE OF THE SYSTEM

The Context

A starting point in understanding the role of registry law is an appreciation of the principle of law and logic that a person cannot give another person a greater interest in property than the transferor herself has (*nemo dat quod non habet* or *nemo dat qui non habet*). While there are many common law and statutory exceptions to the principle, it remains a part of the bedrock of the property law of common law jurisdictions. The significance of the principle becomes apparent in the context of registration law when it is rigorously applied in situations where non-possessory security interests are involved. The debtor retains possession or control of the personal property subject to the security interest, but the secured party has *in rem* rights (the security interest) in that property. In many situations, possession or control, while not necessarily good evidence of ownership, may be the best evidence that is available. A third party to whom the debtor offers to give unencumbered ownership, and who is unaware of the existence of the security interest in the property and does not have the facilities to discover its existence, is forced to rely on appearances or to decline the offer. If the third party assumes the risk and purchases or takes a security interest in the property, the third party will lose the investment or, at the very least, be required to discharge the security interest, thereby paying much more for the property than she had intended. There are various exceptions to the *nemo dat* rule, some of them of great practical importance, but they only apply in a limited number of circumstances.

Since our society encourages commercial activity, there is a need to reduce the risk to which good faith purchasers and other creditors are exposed as a result of unqualified application of the *nemo dat* principle. Registration plays this role.

Another public policy was discernible in earlier registration law. Legislators looked to registration as a method of precluding fraud in the form of sham transactions in which debtors colluded with third parties with a view to shielding debtors' assets from the reach of creditors by arranging to have third parties claim a prior, undisclosed security interest in the event of the debtor's creditors seeking to attach the assets. Consider the possible impact of this policy on the minds of the designers of the PPSA registry system.

---

* The practical significance of these differences is explored later in this chapter.

The need for an efficient personal property registry is directly proportional to the extent to which the law facilitates the use of non-possessory secured financing devices and the extent to which lenders and credit grantors rely on these devices when granting credit. Because of the high volume of modern secured business and consumer financing, registries play a very important role in regulating competing claims to personal property. Unlike their counterparts in the United States, the Canadian provinces never adopted certificate of title systems for motor vehicles. Under the U.S. systems, a security interest in a motor vehicle is recorded on the paper title to the motor vehicle. A third party intending to acquire an interest in the motor vehicle can be apprised of the security interest simply by examining the title to it. The lack of certificate of title systems in Canada meant that security interests in motor vehicles had to be registered in public registries. The volume of such registrations along with increased volumes of registrations relating to security interests in other kinds of personal property soon reached the point where city and county based manual systems became completely inadequate. The demand for alternative approaches reached its zenith about the same time that computer technology became available, and this technology was applied to the problem. The result has been that Canadian registries are the most advanced of their kind in the world.

Statutory registration requirements have been called into question on the grounds that the benefits they produce do not offset the problems associated with them. It is argued that credit grantors no longer rely on the fact of possession or control of assets by the debtor as proof of ownership of those assets. It is also pointed out that, when determining whether or not to extend credit, a banker does not rely on public records, but rather looks to financial statements or to private credit information organizations when assessing the creditworthiness of a potential borrower.* This line of argument has not convinced legislators and designers of secured financing systems. There are good reasons for this. The argument assumes that debtors can be forced to keep accurate records and that the accounting records will disclose encumbered assets. It entirely misses the point where consumer and small business financing is involved. Reliable financial statements may not be available. Third parties want to be able to determine from a reliable source whether or not a particular asset is subject to a security interest.

Intrinsic to any registration system for secured financing transactions is the need to make the fact, and to some extent the details, of private legal relationships available to anyone prepared to pay the required search fee and conduct a search of the registry. This was particularly so when under pre-PPSA legislation document filing was required to effect registration. While measures can be taken to minimize this problem, it cannot be eliminated. By definition, the purpose of a registry is to give public notice of the existence or potential existence of *in rem* interests in property of an identified debtor. The benefits gained from the imposition of registration requirements must be balanced against the importance of allowing parties to keep their commercial dealings confidential.

---

* See generally, Gilmore, *Security in Personal Property*, vol. I, at 463-64 (1965).

Characteristics of a Modern Personal Property Security Registry

Structural Unity of Substantive Personal Property Security Law

As has been noted in chapter 1, prior to the enactment of the Personal Property Security Acts secured financing was carried out through a range of different types of financing devices including chattel mortgages, conditional sales contracts, assignments of accounts and corporation securities. Because of the way in which these devices developed, each came equipped with its own registry. Frequently the technical requirements of one registry were not the same as another. This unsatisfactory state of affairs ended when secured financing law was completely reconfigured in the PPSAs so as to eliminate the traditional security devices and to consolidate all regulation of secured financing in a single regime. The benefits of this transformation were very significant. All registrations were made subject to substantially the same requirements. A single search would disclose all charges against the name of the debtor or against a specified item of property.

Notice Registration

Prior to enactment of the PPSAs, most registry statutes required that the secured party file a copy of the security agreement with the registry. Searches entailed actual examination of filed agreements or requests for registrar's certificates indicating that no agreements had been filed. One of the most significant problems associated with this approach was the need to store vast numbers of written security agreements. It is not unusual to encounter a security agreement that is 100 or more pages in length! This problem was addressed by requiring secured parties to "renew" the registration periodically. Under this approach, a registration was effective for a specified period of time (usually three or five years), after which it lapsed unless renewed. The assumption underlying the approach was that many security agreements would have a duration of less than the original registration period. Consequently, at the end of that period, the registry could safely discard the registered agreement and dispose of obsolete registered documents. Secured parties whose agreements extended beyond the initial registration period would be obliged to renew the registrations.*

The PPSAs introduced notice registration as a substitute for document filing. (See OPPSA s. 45.)† This entails registration of a simple notice (called a "financing statement") containing basic information but not the complete security agreement between the parties. (See OPPSA s. 46(1)-(2) and RRO 1990, Reg. 912, ss. 2-3.)

There are many other important advantages associated with notice registration. It provides a greater measure of confidentiality of business information than is permitted by document filing. The secured party need not release the details of a security agreement with respect to which a financing statement has been registered except upon demand by the

---

* This approach continues to be used in many American states under Article 9 of the Uniform Commercial Code even though only financing statements and not complete security agreements are filed. See UCC § 9-403(2).

† See also Bank Act, SC 1991, c. 46, s. 427(4).

debtor or other person specifically authorized to make the demand (OPPSA s. 18). Unless the cooperation of the debtor or of someone else authorized to make the demand is obtained, competitors of the secured party do not have access to these details. Important features of the PPSA are facilitated by notice registration. Modern financing arrangements require the flexibility that a PPSA system provides. A single financing statement can relate to one or more than one security agreement. Indeed, it is possible that a properly drawn financing statement can meet registration requirements for many security agreements between the same parties entered into over a period of several years. (See OPPSA s. 45(4), and see the discussion of this issue in the context of *Adelaide Capital Corp. v. Integrated Transportation Finance Inc.* (1994), 16 OR (3d) 414 (Gen. Div.), *infra.*) A financing statement can be registered before a security agreement is executed between the parties. (See OPPSA s. 45(3).)*

Notice registration works extremely well in the context of a computerized registry like those in operation in several provinces. Under these systems, a financing statement is a computer screen (referred to under some Acts as an electronic financing statement) provided to the secured party by the registry software. (See, e.g., BC Reg. 279/90, s. 1 (definition of "electronic financing statement"), and Ontario Electronic Registration Act, SO 1991, c. 44.) The person registering the financing statement simply enters the basic information required by the regulations, which is then transmitted to the registry data base. What is stored in the data base of the registry is the text entered on the financing statement.

Length of Registration

Computerization eliminates any need to limit the length of registrations in order to clean out great volumes of paper security agreements or financing statements. Text data are stored, not hard copy documents. Consequently, it is possible to allow the secured party to choose the duration of a registration to parallel the duration of the security agreement with the debtor or the potential duration of the relationship the secured party expects to have with the debtor. Under most systems, it is possible for the registering party to select the duration of a registration. He can choose any period of years between 1 and 25; he may also choose infinite registration. (See RRO 1990, Reg. 912, ss. 3(1)(b), 3(3) and 3(6).)

User Access Through Computer Terminals

Several of the personal property registries are accessible both for registering financing statements and searching for registrations through remote computer terminals (simple PC equipment and a modem) which can be located in a remote government office (court house or county office), in the office of a financing institution or any business premises. See OPPSA ss. 1(1) "financing statement," 46(1)-(2) and 74(g.1) as amended by the Electronic Registration Act (Ministry of Consumer and Commercial Relations Statutes), SO 1991, c. 44, amending the definition of "financing statement." The Acts based on the CCPPSL model were originally drafted with remote access in mind. The use of electronic financing statements and electronic financing change statements is dealt with in detail in regulations

---

* Pre-agreement registration is not permitted in Ontario where the collateral is consumer goods.

made under these Acts. Registrations and searches can be effected by remote computer access from any place in the world where long distance telephone communication to the registries is available. However, users of remote communication facilities must make prior arrangements for payment of registration and search fees. Casual users of the system can go to regional government offices and obtain direct access to the registry upon payment of the applicable fees.

Some of the registries provides for "bulk" electronic delivery of financing statements to the registry through the delivery of magnetic media containing electronic financing statements.

Verification Statements

When a registration is effected in a personal property registry, the computer automatically prints out a verification statement containing the information that has been entered into the data base of the registry relating to that registration. This is immediately sent to the registering party. In most systems, a verification statement has two principal functions. It provides a fail-safe measure permitting a registering party to determine whether or not the information contained in the data base of the registry relating to its registration is accurate. Errors on the part of the registering party can be immediately identified and corrected. In addition it is part of a scheme to encourage early discharge of unnecessary registrations. As to the effect of a verification statement on the obligations of the registry, see *Re Clinton's Flowers & Gifts Ltd.*, *infra*. The verification statement has a second page that contains the registered information. When a secured party wishes to discharge a registration, all it needs to do is to send the discharge verification form to the registry. No clerical costs are incurred in preparing the discharge and no fee for discharge of the registration is charged by the registry.

Expanded Use of Personal Property Registries

The personal property registries are also made available for the registration of *in rem* interests other than security interests. See, e.g,. Repair and Storage Liens Act, RSO 1990, c. R.25. Other provincial registries are used for the registration of a wide variety of interests ranging from buyers' interests when the goods are left in the possession of sellers (see, e.g., Sale of Goods Act, RSS 1978, c. S-11, s. 26(1.1)), to statutory liens arising from unpaid parking tickets (see The Summary Conviction Act, CCSM c. S230 as amended SM 1993, c. 2 adding ss. 23.1-23.4).

Other Features

Other features of the Canadian personal property registries are addressed in the following materials.

What Constitutes Registration?

Bank of Nova Scotia v. Clinton's Flowers & Gifts Ltd.
(1994), 108 DLR (4th) 448 (Ont. CA)

GALLIGAN JA: The appellant appeals from the order of Registrar Browne whereby he declared that the security interest of the bank in the inventory, equipment and accounts receivable of the bankrupt, Clinton's Flowers & Gifts Ltd. ("Clinton's"), is subordinate in interest to that of the respondent, who is the bankrupt's trustee in bankruptcy.

The facts are not in dispute. On September 20, 1990, Clinton's executed security agreements charging, among other things, its inventory, equipment and accounts receivable to the bank. The bank prepared a financing statement for registration pursuant to the *Personal Property Security Act*, RSO 1990, c. P.10 (the "PPSA"). It is common ground that the financing statement was properly prepared in accordance with the prescribed regulations and without any errors or omissions. Clinton's correct name was used. The bank contends that it registered its financing statement on September 25, 1990.

On June 5, 1991, Clinton's made an assignment in bankruptcy. The respondent was appointed trustee of its estate. The appellant filed proof of claim in the bankruptcy, as a secured creditor claiming an entitlement to Clinton's inventory, equipment and accounts receivable by virtue of its security agreements. The trustee investigated the validity of the claim by searching in the registration system established under the PPSA, using the bankrupt's correct name: Clinton's Flowers & Gifts Ltd. The result of the search was a "no match." Further investigation showed that someone in the registration system made an error when recording the information from the bank's financing statement into the PPSA information storage and retrieval system. It was later determined that instead of recording the name of the debtor correctly, as it was set out in the financing statement, the name Clinton Flowers & Gifts Ltd. was recorded in the registration system.

It is the contention of the respondent that the appellant's financing statement was not properly registered and was therefore unperfected. It contended that its interest in the inventory, equipment and accounts receivable takes priority over the unperfected security interest of the appellant, because of the provisions of s. 20(1)(b) of the PPSA. That provision reads as follows:

> 20(1) Except as provided in subsection (3), until perfected, a security interest,

• • •

>   (b) in collateral is not effective against a person who represents the creditors of the debtor, including an assignee for the benefit of creditors and a trustee in bankruptcy.

This contention found favour with Registrar Browne [2 PPSAC (2d) 139].

In my view, because of the provisions of s. 23 of the PPSA, the issue is a very narrow one. That section provides as follows:

> 23. Registration perfects a security interest in any type of collateral.

If the bank's financing statement was registered before the bankruptcy then s. 20(1) would not apply to it. The issue, therefore, is did the bank register its security interest before the bankruptcy, i.e., before June 5, 1991.

The financing statement was correct in every aspect including the debtor's correct name. On September 25, 1990, the bank took the financing statement to the appropriate registry office. It was accepted and the registrar assigned the time 90 09 25 08 33 as the time the registration period began.

The issue is determined by s. 51(3) of the PPSA. The provision is as follows:

51(3) The registration period for a financing statement begins with the time assigned to its registration by the registrar. ...

It is inescapable that a registration period cannot begin until there is a completed registration. Since the registration period began on September 25, 1990, at 8:33 a.m., registration must have been completed on September 25, 1990, at 8:33 a.m.

There is a further piece of evidence which confirms that the registration was completed on September 25, 1990. The documents which are found as ex. D to the affidavit of Norene Cooper and as ex. A to the affidavit of Helen Fernandes, are copies of a copy of the appellant's financing statement, which was provided by the registrar pursuant to the provisions of s. 43(4) of the PPSA. That section reads as follows:

43(4) Upon the request of any person and upon payment of the prescribed fee, the registrar shall furnish the person with a certified copy of a registered financing statement ...

That document contains the following certification by the registrar: "Certified to be a true copy *as registered under the Personal Property Security Act*." (Emphasis added.)

The copy shows that the financing statement contained the debtor's correct name and that it was registered on September 25, 1990, at 8:33 a.m. There can, therefore, be no doubt in this case that the registration was completed on September 25, 1990. Because of the provisions of s. 23 of the PPSA, the appellant's security interest was perfected on that date, which was prior to the debtor's bankruptcy. Therefore, the provisions of s. 20(1)(b) PPSA are inapplicable and do not give the respondent priority over the appellant.

It is unfortunate when an error of this kind occurs. Nevertheless, it was not the bank's error. It was an error made by a member of the registrar's personnel. Regrettable as the error was, it cannot affect the validity of the appellant's properly registered security interest.

A not dissimilar situation occurred in *Atkinson v. Canadian Imperial Bank of Commerce*, [1988] 4 WWR 267, 68 Sask. R 265 (QB), which involved a question of priorities pursuant to the *Banks and Banking Law Revision Act*, SC 1980-81-82-83, c. 40. In that case the bank correctly registered a notice of intention with the Bank of Canada. Incorrect information was given in response to a search. It was argued that the search result was misleading and rendered the registration of the bank's security interest invalid. In his reasons for judgment, Gerein J said, at p. 271:

As I see it, there was no error in the preparation and registration of the notice of intention. Rather, the error was subsequent thereto in the search result and that does not bear upon the validity of the registration.

In my view a very similar situation exists here. An error made by the registrar in recording a properly registered document cannot invalidate the registration.

It is my opinion that the appellant's financing statement was properly registered pursuant to the provisions of the PPSA and that its security interest was, therefore, perfected before the debtor's bankruptcy.

• • •

I would allow the appeal and set aside the order of Registrar Browne. In its place I would make an order declaring that the security interest of the appellant in and to the inventory, equipment and accounts receivable of the bankrupt is effective as against the respondent.

Appeal allowed.

NOTES AND QUESTIONS

1) A system that is a central feature of a regime of priority rules affecting very significant commercial rights must be reliable. A necessary consequence of the decision in *Clinton's Flowers* is that financing statements will be deemed to be registered, but may not be searchable. What negative consequences flow from this conclusion? Consider OPPSA s. 44, esp. ss. 44(4), 44(6) and 44(18-21). What is the position of a secured party who tenders a financing statement that, due to an error on the part of the registry, is not registered? Compare SPPSA s. 52 (which is representative in this respect of Acts based on the CCPPSL model).

2) In *Royal Bank of Canada v. Dawson Motors (Guelph) Ltd.* (1981), 1 PPSAC 359 (Ont. Co. Ct.), the Bank took a security interest in an automobile owned by Woods. The Bank's financing statement was registered on August 16, at 8:47 a.m. However, on August 15, Woods sold the automobile to Dawson Motors without disclosing the Bank's security interest in it. On August 16, before paying Woods, Dawson conducted a telephone search at the Registry. The Bank's security interest was not disclosed because a search of the registry on the morning of August 16 disclosed only registrations up to and including August 15. The only way Dawson could have taken free of the Bank's security interest was to establish that it had priority under the former OPPSA s. 22(1)(b). According to the court, it failed to do this. This decision dramatizes a basic issue associated with the design of any registry system: should a financing statement only be deemed to be registered when it is searchable? The problems associated with the lack of coincidence of registration and searchability will be encountered in the context of the Ontario "regional" registry structure.

There are 49 branch registry offices located throughout the province that "feed" the central registry in Toronto. All branch offices have equal standing with respect to the effectiveness of registrations. Under OPPSA s. 51(3), a financing statement is deemed registered from the time assigned by a registrar, whether located in Toronto or in a branch registry. Accordingly, it may be registered before it is searchable since there may well be a time lapse between the time assigned by a branch registrar and the time the registration is entered into the registry data base. Certificates issued under OPPSA s. 43 state a "file currency date," which is the last date on which registrations received by the Registry have been entered into the data base.

Assume you are acting for a lender who intends to take a security interest in a customer's collateral. What measures would you take to ensure that your client has first priority? Assume you are acting for a buyer of goods. Would the precautionary measures you take differ from those you would take if your client were a lender? The problems that may arise in the context of this type of system are examined by Professor Cuming in "Modernization of Personal Property Security Registries: Some Old Problems Solved and Some New Ones Created" (1983-84), 48 *Sask. L Rev.* 189, at 192-94. The registry systems of Alberta, Saskatchewan and New Brunswick adopt a "what-you-see-is-what-you-get" approach. In other words, unless searchable, a registration does not exist. This approach is greatly facilitated in systems that give registering parties remote, direct access to the registry data base.

3) As to what must be established to succeed in a claim against the Ontario Assurance Fund under OPPSA s. 44(4), see *Re Royal Bank* (1994), 5 PPSAC (2d) 158 (Adjudicator).

4) One of the peculiarities of the OPPSA, not found in the other Acts, is the special treatment of security interests in consumer goods. See OPPSA s. 45(2) (which precludes effective registration of a security interest in consumer goods before the security agreement is signed by the debtor); s. 45(3) (which requires a separate registration for each security interest in consumer goods); and 51(5) (which limits the effectiveness of a registration relating to a security interest in consumer goods to a maximum of five years). See also RRO 1990, Reg. 912, s. 3(1)(i) and (j). What are the policy reasons behind these special rules? Are the problems associated with compliance worth the benefits they produce?

5) The Acts based on the CCPPSL model contain no provisions equivalent to OPPSA s. 45(2), 45(3), 51(5) or 54(2). They address the perceived problems of abuse of consumer interests in the form of pre-agreement, unauthorized registration or refusal to discharge a registration when it is not supported by an extant security interest through a system that, in some respects, is very similar to OPPSA ss. 46(6), 56 and 57. (The following statutory references are to the SPPSA.)

The secured party is required to deliver a copy of a financing statement or verification statement to the person named as debtor in a registration (s. 43(12)). Where a registration relates exclusively to a security interest in consumer goods and the obligations associated with the security interest are performed, the secured party is required to register a financing change statement discharging the registration. However, a discharge of the financing statement is not required if the registration automatically lapses within one month of the date the obligations are performed (s. 50(2)). A secured party who fails without reasonable excuse to meet this requirement is liable for deemed damages under s. 65(6). Section 50(3) sets out the circumstances in which a debtor (whether or not a consumer) is entitled to demand that the registration be discharged or amended. In particular, a demand can be made and enforced where (i) a pre-agreement registration has been effected under s. 43(4) but no agreement has been concluded between the "secured party" and the "debtor"; (ii) a security agreement has been discharged but the secured party has maintained a registration relating to it; (iii) the collateral description in the registration is broader than is warranted by the terms of the security agreement between the parties; or (iv) the registration does not distinguish between original collateral and proceeds. A secured party who fails, without reasonable excuse, to comply with a demand under s. 50(3) is liable to the debtor (or the person disclosed as debtor in the registration) for deemed damages under s. 65(4). This remedy is available to both consumer debtors and business debtors. Section 50(5) permits a person making a demand to enforce compliance unless a court order is obtained by the secured party. This is accomplished by providing proof to the registrar that the demand was made and that the 15-day period for compliance has passed together with a financing change statement providing for the discharge or amendment of the registration, as the case may be, which the registrar must accept and register.

6) Assume that at the date a financing statement was registered the debtor held the collateral as equipment but shortly thereafter began using it as consumer goods. The financing statement provided for a registration period of 15 years. Does the registration become invalid as soon as the use of the collateral changes from equipment to consumer goods? See *Royal Bank v. Wheaton Pontiac Buick Cadillac GMC Ltd.* (1990), 88 Sask. R 151 (QB). The problem is directly addressed in the Acts based on the CCPPSL model. For example, SPPSA s. 2(3) provides that, "[u]nless otherwise provided in the Act, the determination of whether goods are consumer goods, inventory or equipment is to be made at the time when the security interest in the goods attaches."

Errors or Omissions in a Financing Statement

Re Lambert
(1994), 20 OR (3d) 108 (CA)

DOHERTY JA:

I. *The Issue*

When will an error in the contents of a financing statement render the statement invalid and the security interest it represents unperfected as against third parties? The answer depends on the reach of s. 46(4) of the *Personal Property Security Act*, RSO 1990, c. P.10 ("PPSA"), which reads:

46(4) A financing statement or financing change statement is not invalidated nor is its effect impaired by reason only of an error or omission therein or in its execution or registration unless a reasonable person is likely to be misled materially by the error or omission.

II. *The Facts*

Mr. Lambert purchased a motor vehicle under the terms of a conditional sales contract. The vendor sold the contract to the appellant (GMAC). GMAC registered its security interest in the vehicle by filing a financing statement as provided in the PPSA. The financing statement referred to the debtor as Gilles J. Lambert. This was the name used by Mr. Lambert when he signed the conditional sales contract and was also the name used to identify the owner of the vehicle in the records of the Ministry of Transportation and Communication. Unfortunately, it is not Mr. Lambert's proper name. His name, as shown on his birth certificate, is Joseph Phillipe Gilles Lambert. The financing statement correctly identified Mr. Lambert's date of birth and correctly set out the Vehicle Identification Number (the VIN).

Subsequent to the registration, Mr. Lambert made an assignment in bankruptcy and his trustee took possession of the motor vehicle. GMAC filed a proof of claim contending that it was a secured creditor with a security interest in the motor vehicle. At some point subsequent to the assignment in bankruptcy, the trustee acquired a copy of the GMAC financing statement. It identified the vehicle as "consumer goods."

The trustee caused its solicitor to inquire into the claim of GMAC. To do so, she turned to the computerized registration system established under the PPSA. That system made three inquiries available. A searcher could conduct an individual specific debtor name inquiry (a specific debtor inquiry), an individual non-specific debtor name inquiry (a non-specific debtor inquiry) and a vehicle number inquiry (a VIN search). To conduct the specific debtor inquiry, a searcher must enter into the computer the debtor's first name, middle initial, last name and date of birth. This search retrieves only financing statements in which the debtor's first name, middle initial, last name and date of birth as set out in the financing statement exactly match the data entered by the searcher. The non-specific inquiry requires the searcher to enter the debtor's first and last name. It reveals all financing statements where the debtor is described by that first and last name regardless of the middle initial, if any, or the date of birth shown in the financing statement. A VIN search is made by entering the VIN only and retrieves all financing statements in which the collateral is described by the same VIN entered by the searcher regardless of the name of the debtor.* The VIN search is available only where the collateral is a motor vehicle. The VIN must be recorded in the financing statement where the motor vehicle is classified as consumer goods. Where the motor vehicle is not so classified, the VIN may be included in the financing statement.

The trustee's solicitor, relying on the name on Lambert's birth certificate, made individual specific inquiries using the names Joseph P. Lambert and Joseph G. Lambert and Lambert's birth date. She also made an individual non-specific search using the name Joseph Lambert. None of these searches revealed the financing statement filed by GMAC since it referred to the debtor as Gilles J. Lambert. The solicitor did not conduct a VIN search, although the trustee had access to that number. A VIN search would have revealed the GMAC financing statement.

The trustee moved for a declaration that the GMAC security interest was not perfected and was, therefore, not effective against the trustee in bankruptcy. The trustee submitted that the errors in the recording of the debtor's name in the financing statement were fatal to the perfection of that interest as against the trustee. GMAC maintained that the errors were cured by s. 46(4) of the PPSA since the trustee should have performed a VIN search and had he done so, he would not have been misled by the errors in the debtor's name. Farley J found in favour of the trustee. His reasons are now reported at (1991), 2 PPSAC (2d) 160, 11 CBR (3d) 165 (Gen. Div.).

III. *Analysis*

But for s. 46(4), there would be little difficulty applying the terms of the PPSA to this fact situation.

Section 19(b) of the PPSA provides that a security interest is perfected when all steps required for perfection under the PPSA have been completed. Section 23 of the PPSA

---

* The searcher may also request additional registrations containing similar VIN numbers: *Personal Property Act Enquiry Guide*: Ministry of Consumer and Commercial Relations (1993) at 70-71.

declares that registration perfects the security interest in all types of collateral. Perfection by registration requires the registering of a financing statement (s. 45). The financing statement must be in the prescribed form (s. 46(2)). The prescribed form is set out in O. Reg. 372/89 (now RRO 1990, Reg. 912). Section 16 of that regulation provides:

16(1) The name of a debtor who is a natural person shall be set out in the financing statement to show the first given name, followed by the initial of the second given name, if any, followed by the surname.

Sections 3(7), (8) and (9) of the same regulation are also relevant:

3(7) If the collateral includes a motor vehicle and the motor vehicle is classified as consumer goods, the motor vehicle shall be described on line 11 or 12 on the financing statement or in the appropriate place on a motor vehicle schedule.

(8) If the collateral includes a motor vehicle and the motor vehicle is not classified as consumer goods, the motor vehicle may be described on line 11 or 12 on the financing statement or in the appropriate place on a motor vehicle schedule.

(9) The description of the motor vehicle on line 11 or 12 or on a motor vehicle schedule shall include the vehicle identification number, the last two digits of the model year, if any, the model, if any, and the make or the name of the manufacturer.

GMAC's financing statement complied with the relevant parts of s. 3 of the regulation, but did not comply with s. 16 in that it incorrectly stated both Lambert's first name and his middle initial. Accordingly, GMAC's financing statement was not in the prescribed form and but for the possible effect of s. 46(4) of the PPSA, GMAC's security interest in the vehicle was not perfected.

Section 20(1)(b) of the PPSA declares that an unperfected security interest in any collateral is not effective against a trustee in bankruptcy. Again, setting aside s. 46(4) of the PPSA, it would follow that since GMAC's security interest was not registered in accordance with the Act and hence not perfected, it was ineffective as against the trustee in bankruptcy. But for s. 46(4) of the PPSA, the trustee was entitled to the declaration made by Farley J.

Does s. 46(4) of the PPSA alter this result? Two features of s. 46(4) are non-controversial. First, it is potentially applicable to any error in a financing statement: *Re Weber* (1990), 78 CBR (NS) 224 (Ont. SC) at p. 227. Secondly, an error in a financing statement does not *per se* invalidate that statement or impair the security interest claimed by the statement. The validity of the financing statement is unaffected by the error unless the party seeking to invalidate the financing statement demonstrates that "a reasonable person is likely to be misled materially by the error."

Interpreting s. 46(4) becomes more difficult once one ventures beyond these two propositions. Some trial courts in this province have approached s. 46(4) by looking to the effect of the error in the financing statement on the party challenging the security. Cases taking that view include: *Fritz v. Ford Credit Canada Ltd.* (1992), 15 CBR (3d) 311 (Ont. Gen. Div.) at p. 314; *Prenor Rust Co. of Canada v. 652729 Ontario Ltd.* (1992), 4 PPSAC (2d) 139 (Ont. Gen. Div.) at pp. 141-42; *Canamsucco Road House Food Co. v. Lngas Ltd.* (1991), 2 PPSAC (2d) 203 (Ont. Gen. Div.) at p. 208; *General Motors Acceptance Corp. of Canada v. Stetsko* (1992), 8 OR (3d) 537 (Gen. Div.) at pp. 541-42; *Re Rose* (1993), 16 OR (3d) 360, 23 CBR (3d) 58 (Gen. Div.).

In *Fritz, supra*, the debtor's name had been incorrectly spelled on the financing statement, but the VIN was accurately recorded. The trustee performed only a specific debtor inquiry. That inquiry did not retrieve the financing statement. A VIN search would have located the financing statement. The trustee had been told by the debtor that the automobile in question was pledged to the creditor. Chadwick J found that the mistake in the debtor's name constituted an error in the financing statement. He then turned to s. 46(4) of the PPSA. In holding that the creditor had a valid security interest, Chadwick J said at p. 314:

The "reasonable person" that is referred to in considering subs. 46(4) is not an imaginary person but the person who is challenging the validity of the security agreement. In this case, the trustee in bankruptcy had actual notice of the interests of Ford Credit Canada Limited at the time of the assignment in bankruptcy. He was informed by the bankrupt that the 1989 Ford Tempo was fully secured by Ford Canada Limited. The name search under the PPSA by the trustee was only for the purpose of determining whether there were any errors in the registration of the documentation and not for the purpose of a *bona fide* purchaser.

It is obvious from the facts in this case that the trustee was not materially misled as a result of the incorrect registration.

In *Stetsko, supra*, a creditor placed the wrong birth date of the debtor in the financing statement. The trustee was told by the debtor of the creditor's secured interest in the automobile, but he conducted only a specific debtor inquiry. That inquiry did not retrieve the creditor's financing statement because of the error in the birth date. In holding that the creditor's interest remained perfected as against the trustee Maloney J referred, with approval, to the analysis of s. 46(4) found in *Canamsucco*, and said at p. 542:

[I]n trying to determine whether the "reasonable person" is likely to be misled one can only look to: (1) who that person is, (2) what knowledge he may have had, and (3) how he may be affected by it.

On this view of s. 46(4), the error in the financing statement is of no consequence if the party challenging the statement had knowledge of the security interest, or if that party acting reasonably, given its knowledge, could have located the financing statement using the various searches available under the PPSA. This approach has some attraction, especially in cases where the trustee in bankruptcy is seeking to take advantage of an error in the financing statement. In those cases, the trustee appears more as an opportunist pouncing on a windfall than as a vulnerable prospective creditor or purchaser seeking the protection of reliable registration system: Ziegel, "The New Provincial Chattel Security Law Regimes" (1991), 70 *Can. Bar Rev.* 681 at pp. 715-16. The subjective approach may be said to do "justice" in cases involving the trustee in bankruptcy in that it denies the trustee the windfall.

I cannot, however, agree with this interpretation of s. 46(4). By using the reasonable person standard, the legislature intended that the test provided in s. 46(4) should be an objective one. To limit the inquiry to the effect of the error on the party challenging the security is to impose a personal or subjective test peculiar to that party. Furthermore, this interpretation substitutes a test based on actual prejudice for the reasonable person standard set out in the section. As written, s. 46(4) does not require evidence that the error actually misled any person.

The language of s. 46(4) may be usefully compared to that found in s. 9(2) of the PPSA:

9(2) A security agreement is not unenforceable against a third party by reason only of a defect, irregularity, omission or error therein or in the execution thereof unless the third party is actually misled by the defect, irregularity, omission or error.

Section 9(2) expressly declares that a security agreement is not unenforceable by virtue of an error in that agreement unless "the third party is actually misled by the ... error." The language of s. 46(4) which specifically targets financing statements stands in marked contrast to the subjective language of s. 9(2). The approach taken in *Fritz, supra, Stetsko, supra,* and similar cases is appropriate to the language of s. 9(2), but not to the very different language found in s. 46(4).

• • •

Support for the conclusion that the reasonable person referred to in s. 46(4) cannot be equated with a person in the position of the party seeking to invalidate the financing statements is found in *Kelln (Trustee of) v. Strasbourg Credit Union Ltd.* (1992), 89 DLR (4th) 427, 9 CBR (3d) 144 (Sask. CA). Section 66(1) of the *Personal Property Security Act,* SS 1979-80, c. P-6.1, provides:

66(1) The validity or effectiveness of a document to which this Act applies is not affected by reason of a defect, irregularity, omission or error therein or in the execution or registration thereof unless the defect, irregularity, omission or error is seriously misleading.

This section applies to financing statements registered under the Saskatchewan Act. If anything, the language of s. 66(1), which does not contain any specific reference to the reasonable person, is more susceptible to the subjective actual prejudice approach than in s. 46(4) of the PPSA. Despite that arguable ambiguity, the Saskatchewan Court of Appeal unanimously held that s. 66(1) sets out a purely objective test. The court specifically rejected trial decisions in Saskatchewan which had considered the effect of the error from the vantage point of the party challenging the validity of the financing statement. Bayda CJS at p. 430, speaking only for himself, held that the application of the curative proviso was to be determined by asking:

... whether a reasonable person using the registration and search systems put in place by the Act is apt by reason of the omission and the circumstances surrounding it to end up believing that something important is so when in fact it is not so.

Vancise JA at p. 442, writing for himself and Wakeling JA, adopted the question posed by Professor Cumming as the appropriate approach:

Would the defect, irregularity, omission or error be seriously misleading to any reasonable person within the class of person for whose benefit registration or other methods of perfection are required.

Professor Ziegel and Mr. Denomme in their recent text, *The Ontario Personal Property Security Act: Commentary and Analysis* (1994), also favour the objective approach to s. 46(4). After a comparison of the present section and its predecessor, they write at pp. 361-62:

As noted, s. 46(4) implements an objective test—would "a reasonable person" be "misled materially" by the error or omission? If the question is answered "yes," it matters not whether the party attacking the erroneous statement, or indeed anyone else, was actually misled. The reason for the use of such a test is to maintain the integrity of the registration system and to avoid costly litigation; registrants must have such a test in mind and attempt always to complete registrations so that no reasonable person could be so misled. If they fail to do so, it will not matter that, fortuitously, no one can be found who actually reviewed and relied upon the erroneous portion of the statement. This will provide an incentive to registrants to ensure that registrations are correct and complete and will result in a more reliable and useful system.

A continuing problem in the jurisprudence in this area is the tendency to render fact-specific decisions which, while seeming to be more fair in the particular case, introduce uncertainties which serve to weaken the structure and purpose of the registration system. There is an understandable reluctance to deprive secured parties of perfected security interest for what seem like minor and technical errors in financing statements or financing change statements. This has led some courts to seek to do justice as between a registrant and a party challenging the registration by finding that the challenger has not been prejudiced by the error. It bears repeating that the plain words of s. 46(4) require an objective enquiry into whether "a reasonable person is likely to be misled materially" by the defect in question.

Later, after a consideration of *Kelln*, *supra*, and the conflicting authority in Ontario, the authors conclude at pp. 364-65:

With respect to registration errors, the initial question posed by the statute is "would a reasonable person have been misled materially by this error?" The answer to this question cannot depend on the facts of a particular case—to allow it to do so leads to random results. The registration process, insofar as it is under the control of the registrant, should be very carefully monitored for errors because it is not possible to predict, at the date of registration, who may later access the information or for what purpose. Therefore, to the extent an onus should be placed on anyone it should be placed on the registrant in order to preserve the reliability of the registration system.

Without adopting the ultimate conclusions reached in *Kelln* and the supporting Ontario authorities, or all of the reasons put forward by Ziegel and Denomme in support of their position, I do agree that s. 46(4) sets out an objective test. The inquiry dictated by s. 46(4) cannot focus on a particular party, but must look to the broader class of persons who may have cause to use the search facilities of the registration system. In looking to that broader class of persons, one must determine, not the existence of actual prejudice, but the probability of some member of that class of persons being materially misled by the error. As s. 46(4) lays down an objective test, a party challenging the security on the basis of errors in the financing statement need not demonstrate actual prejudice to that party or anyone else. The trustee in bankruptcy may rely on an error in a financing statement to invalidate a secured interest claimed in that statement if the trustee or other third party can show that the error in the financing statement was likely to materially mislead a reasonable person.

My conclusion that s. 46(4) creates an objective test which requires an assessment of the error's impact on those persons who might use the search facilities of the registration system does not resolve this appeal. It remains to provide a concrete formulation of that test.

I begin with the purpose of s. 46(4). The section is designed to preserve the integrity of the registration system provided by the PPSA. That system has two constituencies: those who register financing statements; and those who search the system for prior registrations. The integrity of the overall system must address the interests of both groups. Section 46(4) seeks to maintain the system's integrity by distributing the impact of errors, no matter how unavoidable, made in financing statements between the two groups. An interpretation of s. 46(4) which is too forgiving of such errors places too much of the burden on prospective creditors and purchasers (searchers). An interpretation which is too unforgiving of those errors places too much of the burden on creditors (registrants). In either event, the integrity of the registration system suffers. Section 46(4) should be interpreted, to the extent that its language permits, so as to assign the burden of the error system in a manner which best promotes the overall integrity of the system.

I turn next to the context in which s. 46(4) exists. Its reach and limitations can be understood only in the framework of the registration system established under the PPSA and the purposes for which that system is used.

•   •   •

In my view, the "reasonable person" in s. 46(4) is a person using the search facilities of the registration system for their intended purpose, that is, to find out whether personal property to be purchased or taken as collateral is subject to prior registered encumbrances. To assess the potential effect of an error in a financing statement one must assume that the property which is the subject of the flawed financing statement is the property targeted by the inquiry made by the prospective purchaser or lender. In this case, therefore, the question becomes—would a potential purchaser of the motor-vehicle referred to in the financing statement, or a person considering taking that motor vehicle as security, be materially misled by the error in a previously registered financing statement? This articulation of the test accords with the purpose of the inquiry function of the system, and gives meaning to the requirement that the error be "likely to mislead materially." Unless the effect of the error is addressed in the context of a potential purchase or loan involving the property specified in the financing statement, I am unable to see how an error in that financing statement could be "likely to materially mislead" a prospective purchaser or lender.

In so describing the purpose of the search function of the system, I am not unaware that it has other uses in the commercial world. Some potential creditors may do a PPSA search as part of their inquiry into the credit worthiness of a potential borrower. Those creditors will not be interested in the status of any particular property, but will be looking for any information that may assist in assessing the potential borrower's overall debt situation and credit worthiness. In describing the reasonable person for the purposes of s. 46(4), I would distinguish between a use to which the PPSA system can be put and the purpose for which the system exists. The system was not designed as a credit inquiry service, although it can provide information which will assist in determining credit worthiness. That same incidental use exists with respect to information stored in various other data banks established for a myriad of other purposes.

The preservation of the integrity of the PPSA registration system requires that those who use the system for its intended purpose be protected from errors made by other users where those errors are likely to mislead materially. In my view, the same protection should not be extended to those who put the system to some different use which while commercially beneficial is not the purpose for the system. In my view, the reasonable person in s. 46(4) is not the person using the search facility as part of a general inquiry into a prospective borrower's credit worthiness.

The "reasonable person" using the inquiry function of the registration system for the purpose described above must also be regarded as a person who is familiar with the search facilities provided by the system. That is not to say that the standard is that of the most sophisticated and skilled user. The standard must be that of a reasonably competent user of the system: *Re Millman* (1994), 17 OR (3d) 653, 24 CBR (3d) 190 (Gen. Div.). That reasonable user would be aware of the various searches available in the system and the product produced by each. Furthermore, the reasonable user must be taken to know that potential security interests in motor vehicles may be retrieved through two discrete searches of the system, one using the name of the debtor and the other the motor vehicle's VIN.

Having identified the reasonable person in s. 46(4) as a potential purchaser or lender seeking to locate prior encumbrances on the targeted property, and as a reasonably competent user of the search function of the registration system, I turn now to the information which that reasonable person could be expected to have when making his or her inquiry. No one suggests that the reasonable person would not be able to get the name and birth date of the vendor or borrower through the relevant records. Clearly, he or she would be able to obtain that information.

The reasonable person, as a potential purchaser or lender would not, however, necessarily have access to the names and birth dates of prior owners of the motor vehicle. These prior owners may have encumbered the vehicle. Financing statements giving notice of those encumbrances will be registered under the name of the prior owner and perhaps under the VIN.

In my opinion, the potential purchaser or lender acting reasonably would also obtain the VIN of the motor vehicle. He or she would be in a position to require access to the motor vehicle as a condition of the purchase or loan. Access to the motor vehicle means access to the VIN since it is found on a plate attached to the vehicle's dashboard. Furthermore, a reasonably prudent purchaser or lender familiar with the registration system would appreciate that the VIN could be used to search for prior encumbrances on the vehicle, particularly those registered against prior owners of the vehicle whose identity was unknown to the potential purchaser or lender. Fixed with this knowledge, the reasonable person would realize the importance of the VIN, and would take advantage of his or her position as a purchaser or lender to require access to the VIN.

Would the reasonable person, having access to the seller or borrower's name (and birth date) and the VIN of the motor vehicle, use both sources of information to conduct two searches of the registration system? With respect to the contrary view, I have no doubt that a reasonable person in possession of the information needed to conduct the two searches would in fact conduct both searches. The reasonable person would want to know about any prior encumbrances registered against the motor vehicle and would take all reasonable steps to locate notice of any prior encumbrance in the system. As a reasonable user of the registration system, he or she would know that prior encumbrances for motor vehicles could be registered under the debtor's name, the VIN, or both. A name search might not locate all prior encumbrances. A VIN search might not locate all prior encumbrances if the motor vehicle was not classified as consumer goods for the purposes of a prior transaction. By performing the two searches, the reasonable user would increase the probability of recovering all prior encumbrances. The added protection would come at minimal cost. Any reasonable user would spend the few dollars required for the added information and comfort provided by two independent searches of the registration system.

Those who have held that the reasonable person in s. 46(4) would conduct only a specific debtor name search have emphasized the importance to the registration system of using the debtor's correct name in the financing statement. For example, Donnelly J in *Re Ghilzon* (1993), 21 CBR (30) 71 (Ont. Gen. Div.). "The integrity of the registration system is name-dependent." No doubt this observation is accurate with regard to personal property other than motor vehicles. But where motor vehicles are involved, the integrity of the registration system does not depend only on accurately recording the debtor's name in the financing statement. Indeed, the VIN search function exists specifically because a name-dependent system for motor vehicles would be inadequate and would leave potential purchasers and lenders vulnerable to encumbrances placed on the motor vehicle by prior owners of the motor vehicle. In the case of motor vehicles, the registration system is not name-dependent. Rather, it provides for identification of prior registrations by the combined access to the system afforded by name and VIN searches.

An approach to s. 46(4) which excludes errors in the debtor's name from those which are curable by s. 46(4) harks back to the language of the former curative proviso (s. 47(5)) which declared that only clerical errors or errors in immaterial or non-essential parts of the financing statement were curable under that provision: *Re Weber, supra*, at pp. 228-29. The debtor's name is clearly a material and essential part of the financing statement: *Re Bellini Manufacturing & Importing Ltd.* (1981), 32 OR (2d) 684 at pp. 692-93, 37 CBR (NS) 209 (CA). The present curative proviso does not, however, fix on the part of the financing statement in which the error occurred, but instead looks to the effect of the error on the reasonable person. The present provision may cure any error no matter where it occurs in the financing statement, if that error is not likely to mislead materially a reasonable person. An error may occur in a material part of the financing statement, but may not, in light of additional information, found in the same financing statement and available to the reasonable person, materially mislead that person. Case law under the prior provision identifying the materiality of the debtor's name to the financing statement does not assist in deciding whether the reasonable person referred to in the current section would conduct more than a specific debtor search.

Proponents of the single-search approach also rely on the absence of any requirement in the PPSA that more than one search be done. *Re Weber, supra*, at p. 228. The PPSA does not require that any search be done. A search for prior registered interests is triggered by self-interest, not by any statutory obligation. The nature of the search to be expected from a reasonable person reflects the extent to which a reasonable person would go to protect his or her interests. The absence of any statutory provision requiring one or more searches is of no consequence.

In summary, the reasonable person in s. 46(4) has the following attributes:

- He or she is a reasonably prudent prospective purchaser or lender who looks to the registration system of the PPSA to provide notice of any prior registered claims against the property he or she is proposing to buy or take as collateral for a loan.

- He or she is conversant with the search facilities provided by the registration system and is a reasonably competent user of those facilities.
- Where the property to be bought or taken as collateral is a motor vehicle, the reasonable person will obtain the name and birth date of the seller/borrower as well as the VIN of the motor vehicle.
- Where the property is a motor vehicle, the reasonable person will conduct both a specific debtor name search and a VIN search.

Bearing this reasonable person in mind I move to the final question. Is that reasonable person "likely to be misled materially" by a financing statement which contained an error in the debtor's name, but accurately set out the VIN? The purpose for which the reasonable person uses the search function of the registration system provides the key to determining when it can be said that the reasonable person would be materially misled by an error in a financing statement. The reasonable person uses the system to find prior registered secured interests in the property in question. If the error in the financing statement results in the reasonable person not retrieving that financing statement from the system, then the reasonable person will probably be misled materially. If despite the error, the reasonable person as defined above will still retrieve the flawed financing statement from the system, then the error in the financing statement is not likely to mislead materially.

A reasonable person would not likely be misled materially by an error in a financing statement relating to the debtor's name if that same financing statement accurately set out the VIN. That financing statement would come to the attention of the reasonable person through a VIN search despite the error in the name. The reasonable person would, therefore, be put on notice of the security interest referred to in the financing statement and could proceed accordingly. This conclusion accords with that reached in *Ford Credit Canada Ltd. v. Percival Mercury Sales Ltd. (No. 1)*, [1986] 6 WWR 569, 50 Sask. R 268 (CA).

The result would be very different if the financing statement incorrectly set out the debtor's name and did not contain the VIN, as could be the case if the motor vehicle had not been classified as consumer goods for the purposes of the transaction giving rise to the financing statement. In that situation, the error in the debtor's name would be fatal since the reasonable person conducting both a specific debtor search and a VIN search could not locate the financing statement. That is, however, not this case. This financing statement did include the VIN, and the impact of the error in the debtor's name must be assessed in that light. It supports the purpose behind the registration system to hold that a creditor who includes information in the financing statement which potentially permits a subsequent searcher to locate the financing statement through two independent means is in a better position than a creditor who chooses to limit itself to the bare essentials required by the regulations.

My conclusion would also be different if the VIN was improperly recorded in the financing statement and the debtor's name was accurately set out. In that situation, a reasonable person could well be materially misled by the error in the financing statement. Consider this example. P agrees to purchase a car from V. The car had been previously owned by X who pledged it to Y. Y registered a financing statement correctly identifying X as the debtor, but incorrectly setting out the VIN of the motor vehicle. P, proceeding as I have held a reasonable purchaser would, conducts a specific debtor search in the name of

V (his vendor) and a VIN search using the proper VIN. The two searches conducted by P would not reveal Y's financing statement, because of the error made by Y with respect to the VIN. This error would, therefore, probably materially mislead P since it would leave him unaware of Y's claim to a prior security interest in the motor vehicle. My conclusion that an error in the VIN even when coupled with a correct identification of the debtor would not be curable under s. 46(4) is consistent with the result in *Kelln, supra*.

Further reference to *Kelln* is necessary. In that case, the VIN was improperly recorded in the relevant financing statement, but the debtor's name was accurately recorded. The court held that the error could not be cured by the Saskatchewan equivalent of s. 46(4) of the PPSA. As indicated above, I agree with that result. Vancise JA went on to hold that an error in the debtor's name where the VIN was properly recorded would be equally fatal. In doing so, he appears to have rejected the same court's holding in *Ford Credit Canada Ltd., supra*. Vancise JA and I part company at this point.

Vancise JA observes at p. 443 that an error in a financing statement is not curable if that error would result in "the failure to properly register or retrieve the information from the register concerning the collateral." I agree with this comment, except I would limit the concern to the proper retrieval of the information.

Vancise JA goes on at pp. 443-44 to hold:

> Thus the conclusion is that the failure to include both of the mandatory registration-search criteria where it is required will result in the registration being seriously misleading and render the security interest unperfected.
>
> As noted, the reason for such objective interpretation is to provide a consistent approach to the registration and perfection of security interests.
>
> The failure to include the debtor's name on a financing statement where there is already a serial number which correctly describes the collateral should render the security interest unperfected. In other words, when there is a requirement for both criteria the failure to include one is seriously misleading and the failure to comply renders the registration invalid. If one or both of the mandatory registration-search criteria contain errors which do not prevent the proper identification or retrieval of the financing statement, the error is not seriously misleading and the security interest should be perfected.

This analysis proceeds on the basis that only a single search need be performed by the prospective purchaser or lender. Consequently, an error in either the name or the VIN which prevented a person conducting either, but not both of those searches from locating the financing statement would be materially misleading.

I reach a different result than Vancise JA because, for the reasons I have already set out, I proceed on the premise that the prospective purchaser or lender would have access to both the seller/borrower's name and the VIN, and would conduct both searches. An error in a financing statement would probably be materially misleading only if the error caused the financing statement to escape the net cast by the combined reach of both searches.

Vancise JA quite properly supports his approach on the basis of the certainty and predictability it achieves. My approach borrows from his, save for the different assessment of the searches a reasonable person would conduct, and achieves the same consistency and predictability. In my estimation, it also more effectively preserves the integrity of the registration system by more fairly balancing the interests of secured creditors and prospective purchasers and lenders. A creditor's secured interest should not fail as against third parties by virtue of an error in the financing statement, if that error would not preclude retrieval of the financing statement by a prospective purchaser or lender taking reasonable steps to protect his or her interest and making reasonable use of the search facilities provided by the registration system.

I would hold that the trustee has not established that the error in the GMAC financing statement would probably have misled materially a reasonable person. The financing statement is therefore not invalidated and GMAC's security interest in the motor vehicle is perfected.

Appeal allowed.

NOTES AND QUESTIONS

1) For an excellent comment on *Lambert* see R.A. Wood (1995), 24 *CBLJ* 444. The *Lambert* decision addresses several important issues that have arisen in the context of a modern, computerized personal property security registry system. At the same time, it exacerbates the difference between the Ontario registry system and its counterparts in most other jurisdictions in Canada.

2) An understanding of these issues begins with some technical information as to how search results are obtained from a PPS registry. In this respect, the Ontario system is quite different from systems in other provinces. There are four types of searches under the Ontario system: an individual specific search; an individual non-specific search, a business debtor search and a V (vehicle) I (identification) N (number) search. See OPPSA s. 43(1). An individual specific search using the correct given name, middle initial, surname and birth date will not reveal registrations in which any one of these items is incorrectly recorded. In other words, exact matches are required if the registration is to be revealed. An individual non-specific search is provided for enquirers who are unsure or unaware of some of the details of the debtor's name or birth date. Generally speaking, Ontario courts have taken the position that the disclosure of a registration in a non-specific search does not save it from invalidity if it would not be disclosed using the appropriate information in an individual specific search. In other words, the individual non-specific search facility is for the benefit of searchers and not secured parties who happen to make a mistake in recording the name and birth date of the debtor. See, e.g., *Re Weber* (1990), 73 OR (2d) 238 (SC); *Re Haasen* (1992), 92 DLR (4th) 204 (Ont. Gen. Div.) Is there anything in *Re Lambert* that calls this conclusion into question?

A VIN search or a business debtor search will disclose exact matches and other registrations based on a business name or VIN which are, in the opinion of the registrar, similar to the one used in the search. See OPPSA s. 43(3). There appears to be no discussion in the post-1990 case law as to whether or not an error in recording a business debtor name or a VIN can be treated as not invalidating the registration since the registration would have been disclosed in the additional information supplied by the registrar. Academic opinion favours treating these registrations in the same way as individual debtor name registrations. See Ziegel and Denomme, *op. cit.*, pp. 366 and 370-71.

3) The court in *Re Lambert* removed prior doubt as to whether or not OPPSA s. 46(4) provides for an objective or subjective test. In this respect, the OPPSA now parallels the Acts based on the CCPPSL model which have codified the *Kelln* decision. See, e.g., SPPSA s. 43(6) and (8). However, the test plays a much less important role under the OPPSA if, as appears to be the case, disclosure of a defective registration in a non-specific debtor name search or additional registration information supplied by the registrar plays no role in the determination as to whether or not an error in the name of the debtor or in the VIN is likely to materially mislead a reasonable person.

4) *Fritz v. Ford Credit Canada Ltd.* (1992), 15 CBR (3d) 311 (Ont. Gen. Div.) and *General Motors Corporation v. Stetsko* (1992), 8 OR (3d) 537 (Gen. Div.) (both referred to with disapproval in *Re Lambert*) are representative of a significant number of decisions, not only in Ontario but as well in courts of Alberta, British Columbia and Saskatchewan, in which judges refused to subordinate defectively registered security interests to debtors' trustees in bankruptcy. Indeed, Doherty JA in *Re Lambert* noted that a trustee who attacks a registration on the grounds of non-compliance with registration requirements "appears more as an opportunist pouncing on a windfall than as a vulnerable prospective creditor or purchaser seeking the protection of [a] reliable registration system." The objective test prescribed in *Re Lambert,* and by specific provisions of the Acts based on the CCPPSL model, closes only one avenue available to judges who object to the clear legislative policy contained in OPPSA s. 20(1)(b) and equivalent provisions in other PPSAs. Others are available.

5) Recent decisions of Alberta, British Columbia and Saskatchewan trial courts have raised an important issue in the context of the operation of the registries of these provinces. This issue is whether or not a registration is "seriously misleading" (the test used in the Acts based on the CCPPSL model) simply because the registration would not be disclosed as a close similar match when the searching party uses the correct legal name of the debtor as the search criterion. (Another issue associated with disclosures in search results is addressed in *Case Power & Equipment v. Price Waterhouse Ltd.* (1994), 118 DLR (4th) 63 (Alta. CA), *infra.*) This issue has arisen in cases where the name appearing on the registration (the registration criterion) was not the legal name of the debtor appearing on his or her birth certificate, but a name that the debtor used on another document such as a driver's licence. A search using the legal name of the debtor does not reveal the registration as an inexact match.

In several of these decisions, the courts concluded that the registration was not seriously misleading merely because it was not revealed using the legal name of the debtor as the search criterion. Two different approaches were used to justify this conclusion. One approach was to conclude that the relevant regulations did not require the secured party to use the name of the debtor as it appears on his or her birth certificate. The regulations are interpreted as allowing the use of a name appearing on other documents such as a driver's licence, credit card or the business documents of an incorporated debtor. See, e.g., *Re Fraser* (1994), 25 CBR (3d) 58 (BCSC). Another approach is to ignore the regulations when determining what is required as property identification of the debtor in a registration. See *Re Paquette*, [1994] 6 WWR 113 (application for reconsideration refused 19 Alta. LR (3d) 142 (QB)). See *Re Baisley & Richer Air Freight Inc.* (1994), 93 BCLR (2d) 372 (SC). Do you see any difficulties with these approaches?

6) The question often arises as to what is the debtor's name, or, more accurately, what source should the registering party use when determining the name of the debtor. In *Re Haasen* (1992), 92 DLR (4th) 204 (Ont. Gen. Div.) at 210, Farley J concluded that the "correct" name of a debtor is the name found on his or her birth certificate. Killeen J in *CIBC v. Melnitzer* (1994), 6 PPSAC 5 (Ont. Gen. Div.) stated at pp. 42-43:

The PPSA is somewhat vague on the subject of the correct name of a debtor for registration purposes. Section 46(4) says this about errors in general:

(4) A financing statement or financing change statement is not invalidated nor is its effect impaired by reason only of an error or omission therein or in its execution or registration unless a reasonable person is likely to be misled materially by the error or omission.

On the other hand, s. 16(l) of O. Reg. 372/89 [now RRO 1990, Reg. 912], passed under the PPSA, specifies this:

16.(1) The name of a debtor who is a natural person shall be set out in the financing statement to show the first given name, followed by the initial of the second given name, if any, followed by the surname.

One might have thought that the *Change of Name Act*, RSO 1990, c. C.7 might be helpful on the question of correct names but it, too, seems wanting in some respects. Section 2 of this Act, reads, in part, this way:

2.(1) For all purposes of Ontario law,

(a) a person whose birth is registered in Ontario is entitled to be recognized by the name appearing on the person's birth certificate or change of name certificate, unless clause (c) applies;

(b) a person whose birth is not registered in Ontario is entitled to be recognized by,

(i) the name appearing on the person's change of name certificate, if the person's name has been changed under this Act or a predecessor of it, or

(ii) in all other cases, the name recognized in law in the last place with which the person had a real and substantial connection before residing in Ontario

It might be said that s. 2(l)(a) above provides a useful guide for persons born in Ontario by saying that the name on the Ontario birth certificate is recognized for "all purposes of Ontario law." However, for a person like Melnitzer, born out of Ontario, one is directed to the law of the last place with which the person had a real and substantial connection. This rule is of no real assistance because I have no evidence before me as to Melnitzer's legally recognized name in Quebec, where he resided for many years before coming to Ontario in young adulthood.

Mr. Grace argued, relying on *Re Takhtalian* (1982), 2 PPSAC 90 (Ont. HC), that, for foreign-born citizens, it should be sufficient to use the name of the debtor on his Canadian citizenship certificate.

While, perhaps, a respectable argument can be made for the position that, in the case of foreign-born persons, their original birth-certificate name should be used, I think, on balance, that it is practical and rational to opt for the name on a Canadian citizenship certificate, if one exists. The entire subject of correct names on a registration should probably be revisited by the legislature to staunch the flow of cases into the courts: see such cases as *Re Weber* (1990), 73 OR (2d) 238, 1 PPSAC (2d) 36 (Bktcy.); *Re Lambert* (1991), 2 PPSAC (2d) 160 (Ont. Bktcy.) and *Re Haasen* (1992), 8 OR (3d) 489, 3 PPSAC (2d) 250 (Bktcy.).

7) The central ruling in the *Re Lambert* decision was that the debtor's name and the VIN are not cumulative registration-search criteria: the VIN is adequate by itself. The Acts based on the CCPPSL model specifically provide that in order for a registration to be valid, *both* the debtor's name and the serial number of the collateral (where serial number goods are involved) must be recorded in the registration in a manner that is not seriously misleading. Assess the merits and deficiencies in each approach. As to the significance of an error in one or both of the two registration-search criteria, see *Case Power & Equipment v. Price Waterhouse Ltd.* (1994), 118 DLR (4th) 63 (Alta. CA), *infra*.

8) The Acts based on the CCPPSL model provide for a much broader range of collateral which must be specifically described (by serial number) on a financing statement, and serial number identification of collateral is much more important to these systems than it is under the OPPSA. (See OPPSA ss. 23, 25(5), 28(5) and RRO 1990, Reg. 912, s. 1 "motor vehicle" and ss. 3(7) and (9).) For example, under s. 1 of the BC Personal Property Security Reg. 279/90 as amended, "serial numbered goods" are consumer goods or equipment in the form of motor vehicles (very broadly defined to include combines, tractors and self-propelled road construction and maintenance equipment), mobile homes, boats, trailers and aircraft. As to the significance of serial number registration, see also BCPPSA ss. 30(6)-(7), 35(4) and 43(7). Note that it is not necessary to include the serial number of equipment on a financing statement in order to have priority over the debtor's trustee in bankruptcy or execution creditors.

9) No doubt, the *Re Lambert* approach results in the OPPSA being more forgiving than the Acts based on the CCPPSL model when errors are made in recording the debtor's name. Indeed, a logical extension of the decision is that the debtor's name need not be recorded at all on the financing statement.

10) Doherty JA concluded that a reasonable person who obtains a search result from the registry would know of the necessity to request a search of both the debtor's name and the VIN. While by itself this is a doubtful assumption, the requirements of s. 11.1 of the Highway Traffic Act RSO 1990, c. H.8, and s. 43.1 of the OPPSA (added by SO 1993, c. 13, s.1) will substantially reduce the chances that a buyer of a motor vehicle will only rely on the debtor's name as a search criterion since, in most cases, the buyer will receive a "used vehicle information package" which contains a registry search based on the VIN of the vehicle being purchased. However, dealers registered under the Motor Vehicle Dealers Act are exempt from the requirement to deliver an information package to a buyer. See O. Reg. (Highway Traffic Act) 601/93, s. 2(10). Does this represent a major area of exposure for legally unsophisticated buyers of motor vehicles?

11) Doherty JA left one important question unanswered. He set out a scenario in which X gives a security interest in his car to Y. Y correctly registers a financing statement against X's name but incorrectly describes the VIN. X sells the car to V, who offers it for sale to P. Doherty JA concludes that the registration would be invalid with respect to P since a search using V's name and the VIN would not reveal the registration. However, he does not state what would happen if V had purchased the vehicle from X without knowledge of Y's security interest and on the basis of a VIN search. Is the registration valid because V could have discovered it by using the debtor's name as the search criterion? According to Doherty JA, debtor name and VIN are not alternatives when P, a remote party, is a purchaser. Are they alternatives where an immediate party (V) is claiming priority?

If they are, how would the Ontario Court of Appeal address the following situation? Assume the scenario above, but add another party, Y1, who takes a properly perfected security interest in the car after Y took her security interest but before the sale of the vehicle to V. Assume, again, the resale of the car to P. Y1 does not have priority over Y because X's name was correctly recorded in Y's registration. However, Y1 does have priority over P because Y1's security interest was properly registered. P has priority over Y because Y failed to include the VIN in her registration. In summary, the following priority picture emerges: Y has priority over Y1, Y1 has priority over P but P has priority over Y1. Who gets the car? For a brief discussion of solutions for circular priority problems, see, *infra*, this chapter, note 7 following *Heidelberg Canada Graphic Equipment Ltd. v. Arthur Andersen Inc.*

12) Some problems exist in the context of the special rules contained in OPPSA s. 28(5). After reading the *Adelaide* case, *infra*, and the notes following it dealing with categories of goods collateral, consider the following scenario. SP takes and perfects a security interest in a car held by Debtor as "equipment." However, SP elects not to include the VIN of the vehicle in the registration. Debtor sells the car to Used Car Dealer and discloses SP's security interest. Used Car Dealer sells the car to Buyer, fraudulently representing that it is free from encumbrances. Buyer obtains a registry search using the car's VIN as the search criterion, but, of course, finds no indication of SP's security interest. Debtor defaults and SP seeks to enforce its security interest in the car in the hands of Buyer. What is Buyer's priority position under OPPSA s. 28(5) in relation to SP? Would Buyer be in a better position if she had bought the car out of the ordinary course of Used Car Dealer's business? Would she be in a better position if the goods had been consumer goods? What policy justification is there for drawing a distinction in this context between sales of consumer goods and equipment and sales in or out of the ordinary course of business of Used Car Dealer? Note that s. 28(2) protects lessees but s. 28(5) does not. What is the justification for this difference in treatment?

Case Power & Equipment v. Price Waterhouse Ltd.
(1994), 118 DLR (4th) 637 (Alta. CA)

CÔTÉ JA:

A. *Introduction*

The issue here is priorities where there are errors in registering encumbrances against chattels. In effect this is a contest about two secured creditors with claims against the same chattels of the same debtor. (The respondent is the receiver of the debtor company.)

B. *Facts*

Four different pieces of earth-moving equipment are in issue. Each of the competing creditors made more than one registration. Some of the facts are common to two or more, but some differ. A simplified list of events in date order follows:

June 8, 1990	Appellant's assignor registers notice of its conditional sales contract over the Volvo loader under wrong debtor name, but correct serial number.
November 27, 1990	Appellant's assignor registers notice of its conditional sales contract over the Case Dozer and Case Rammer under wrong debtor name. It gives wrong serial number for dozer, but correct serial number for rammer.
June 28, 1991	Appellant's assignor registers notice of its security agreement over Case Excavator under wrong debtor name, but correct serial number.
December 2, 1991	First Calgary registers notice of a general security agreement with the debtor under correct debtor name, but with no serial numbers and no specific descriptions of individual items encumbered.
January 8, 1992	Appellant files amending registrations for three items (all but the excavator) correcting the debtor name.
March 2, 1992	First Calgary amends its registrations to give the correct serial numbers and specific descriptions of the Volvo Loader, the Case Dozer, and the Case Excavator.

In the meantime, the debtor company had gone into receivership, and then bankruptcy. For each piece of machinery, one or the other of these two creditors has priority; the issue is which one.

Counsel for the respondent conceded freely in oral argument that each item is a motor vehicle and is equipment, and none is consumer goods. Therefore, the *Personal Property Security Act*, SA 1988, c. P-4.05, defines each item as "serial number goods," with consequences discussed below.

C. *Statutory test for priority*

At common law and in equity, priority flowed from an inter-action of several elements: when one acquired rights, whether they were legal or equitable, and who had notice of them. Alberta's *Conditional Sales Act*, RSA 1980, c. C-21, and *Bills of Sale Act*, RSA 1980, c. B-5, invalidated some such rights vis-à-vis certain classes of people, but otherwise left in place the rules for priority. Under those Acts, registration merely prevented such invalidation, i.e., left in place the equitable or common law rights. And of course it created a registration which people sometimes found, and so they sometimes got notice.

But those statutes were replaced by the *Personal Property Security Act*. It does legislate priorities, using a very different scheme. It says that priority between competing secured creditors depends on order of registration: s. 35(1). There are a number of statutory exceptions to that, most irrelevant in this suit. The one relevant and vital qualification is created by s. 35(3) which calls for a serial number registration:

35(3) A security interest in goods that are equipment and are of a kind prescribed by the regulations as serial number goods is not registered or perfected by registration for the purposes of subsection (1), (6) or (7) unless a financing statement relating to the security interest and containing a description of the goods by serial number is registered.

I read s. 35(3) as qualifying s. 35(1), and prevailing over it. That matters in this case. First Calgary made the first correct registration, but that gave no serial numbers. It appears to have been a valid registration, for one can file certain blanket registrations against large amounts of the debtor's assets, without recording any serial number: ss. 26(1)(b) and 28 of the regulations (Alta. Reg. 234/90, as amended by Reg. 342/91). If only s. 35(1) of the Act existed, First Calgary (and hence its receiver the respondent) would win. But (ignoring one error) the appellant made the first registration with a serial number.

Section 35(3) says that if the goods are serial number goods, one looks to the first registration giving serial numbers, not to the first registration. It is conceded that these are serial number goods, so that provision applies. Therefore, the appellant wins that priority test with respect to all four pieces of equipment (ignoring for the moment one mistake in one serial number and in the debtor name).

Counsel for the respondent was eloquent in pointing out to us that stopping there could create great unfairness. He said that some of his client's searches had not revealed some of the appellant's registrations, and that at times it may be difficult or impossible to learn the serial numbers of equipment. And the Act does allow blanket security without giving serial numbers, as noted above. He said that reasonable notice is the aim of the statute, and that we should seek to give effect to that aim.

Though the results may seem unfair in certain fact situations, I cannot interpret the Act that way. The legislature knows how to leave priority questions alone so that common law and equity will govern. And it knows how to modify common law and equity in part only. It repealed legislation of that type and replaced it with the *Personal Property Security Act* which very plainly says that priority flows from registering first in a certain way. That leaves no room for the old common law and equitable doctrines of priority, from notice or otherwise. There may possibly be exceptions, e.g., for fraud, trusts, estoppel, hindering another's registration, or the like, but I cannot think of any which would apply here, and none was suggested in argument.

And of course I say nothing about s. 30 on consumer goods worth under $1,000, temporarily perfected interests, etc.

The aim of giving notice is not necessarily best served by making priority flow from notice. It can also be accomplished by setting up a registry, making priority date from registration, and letting mortgagees register and shoppers search. Furthermore, that system produces much more certainty. What is the first registration is usually very clear and, when it is not clear, it is usually a question of law. But notice is a difficult fact question which often requires a trial to establish. So even if the respondent is right about the aims of the scheme, the statutory scheme of priority does not make any use of notice as such.

Therefore I put no weight on the evidence in the appeal book about who knew of the other party's competing interest, or when.

Had there been no errors in any registration, that would be enough to decide the appeal. But there were errors, so one must go further.

D. *Amending registration*

It was not seriously disputed before us that errors can be cured by registering an amended registration. Sections 44(3), (4) of the Act permits that:

44(3) An amendment to a registration may be made by registering a financing change statement at any time during the period that the registration is effective, and the amendment is effective from the date the financing change statement is registered to the expiry of the registration being amended.

(4) When an amendment of a registration is not otherwise provided for in this Part, a financing change statement may be registered to amend the registration.

If that occurs before anything else happens, the original error becomes irrelevant. The old legislation had elaborate provisions for court orders, and provisions about rights acquired in the interval. The new legislation seems simpler. I cannot find anything qualifying the effect of amended registrations, and none was suggested to us (apart from the general notice arguments described above).

Therefore, in my view, an amended registration simply counts as a registration. Those parts of the original registration which are valid in law count from when they were made, and those which are not, count from the date of filing the amended registration. And s. 35 still governs priorities.

Now one must turn to the individual registrations.

E. *Loader and rammer*

These were registered initially on different dates by the appellant's assignor, but nothing turns on that. Both registrations gave the correct serial number and description of the machinery, and both at first gave the wrong name for the debtor. But in each case the appellant filed an amending registration giving the correct debtor name. And in each case, that occurred before First Calgary registered any serial numbers: First Calgary's original registration was by name alone. Therefore, as discussed, s. 35 gives the appellant priority over each of these two items.

F. *Dozer*

Here again the debtor's name was wrong at first in the appellant's chain of registration, but was corrected before First Calgary registered any kind of serial number. What distinguishes this item is an error in the serial number registered by the appellant's assignor. That error was not corrected at any material time. The serial number consists of three letters, followed by a space, and a string of eight digits. In the appellant's registration the digits and two of the letters were right, but the third letter was wrong.

Which errors invalidate is governed by s. 43(6), (7) of the Act:

43(6) The validity of the registration of a financing statement is not affected by a defect, irregularity, omission or error in the financing statement or in the registration of it unless the defect, irregularity, omission or error is *seriously misleading*.

(7) Subject to subsection (9), where one or more debtors are required to be disclosed in a financing statement or where collateral is consumer goods of a kind that is prescribed by the regulations as serial number goods, and there is a *seriously misleading* defect, irregularity, omission or error in

(a) the disclosure of any debtor, other than a debtor who does not own or have rights in the collateral, or

(b) the serial number of the collateral, the registration is invalid.

(Emphasis added.) Clearly the key phrase is "seriously misleading." So not every error invalidates, nor even every misleading error. Only seriously misleading ones do. That is strong language. It should not be watered down, or limited to trivial faults: see *Elmcrest Furniture v. Price Waterhouse (216200 Alberta Ltd.)* (1985), 5 PPSAC 22 at p. 25, 41 Sask. R 125.

Nor can we say that serial numbers are so detail-specific that any error in one must automatically be "seriously misleading." Section 43(7) says:

... where ... there is a seriously misleading defect, irregularity, omission or error in ...
(b) the serial number of the collateral, the registration is invalid.

This plainly suggests that there can be an error in the serial number which is not seriously misleading, i.e., that minor errors in the serial number do not affect validity.

In my view, an error in describing a chattel would make a registration "seriously misleading" in *either* of two situations:

(i) it would likely prevent a reasonable search under a reasonable filing or registration system from disclosing the existence of the registration, or
(ii) it would make a person who did somehow become aware of the registration think that it was likely not the same chattel.

We heard no evidence about whether the manufacturer's scheme of numbering allowed another dozer with the serial number registered, nor indeed the significance (if any) of the one wrong letter in the serial number.

We were treated to a good deal of evidence about what actual searches by the parties did or did not reveal about this registration, either as an exact match or an inexact match. And we were referred to a number of official government publications. These reveal that the government has chosen a computer and a certain computer program to register financing statements and to search for them. Evidently the computer has been told that certain pairs are equivalent, and that other things might be equivalent and should be listed as an inexact match. Some of the decided cases go into that sort of thing also.

However, this case should not be won or lost on such computer programming. It is the job of the court to interpret and apply the law: *Re Logan* (1992), 15 CBR (3d) 121 at p. 132, 4 PPSAC (2d) 200, 73 BCLR (2d) 377. Law means the *Personal Property Security Act*, and the regulations lawfully made under it. The legislature gave power to make regulations (s. 71) only to the Lieutenant-Governor in Council. (Alta. Reg. 234/90, s. 2(1), purports to subdelegate setting forms to the Attorney-General, who adopted some by Alta. Reg. 295/90, but they do not deal with the present question.) And no regulation has effect unless filed as an Alberta Regulation: *Regulations Act*, RSA 1980, c. R-13, s. 2(3). The various manuals have not been so registered as regulations as far as I know, and I am confident that the computer program has not. The legislature should not and did not delegate any legislative powers to the computer programmer: *Logan* case at p. 132. Indeed, I do not believe that there is even any legislative provision that this Act is to be carried out by using a computer (though s. 11(3) of the regulations incidentally mentions a computer).

If the courts held otherwise, consider the possibilities. It is safe to take notice of the fact that computer programs sometimes cannot see similarities because of what to a human are extremely tiny differences. A computer program which allowed for no equivalents would not retrieve a registration if a space or a comma were different, so the most trivial error would render a search useless. Unless someone tells it, a computer sees no similarity between "Number," "No.," and "#." Nor between a zero and a capital O. Nor between numeral one and small L, although on a typewriter they are usually identical. Spaces, hyphens or commas are treated as a distinct character. These seem totally different to such a computer: 0012345, OO12345, and 12345. Unless all such things are programmed out, to make manuals or programs govern would let the computer programmer repeal s. 43(6).

Section s. 50(b) [*sic*] of the regulations allows the registrar to reply to a search by giving information "corresponding to search criteria similar to those" requested. That implies that full precision is not always contemplated. It would appear that Alberta's computer programmer has told the computer about some equivalents, for "inexact matches" are sometimes indeed disclosed. But what will show up as an inexact match depends on the choices made by the programmer, and whether he made any slips in implementing his choices. Therefore, part (i) of the test given above should not bog down in the minutiae of the computer searching program.

The law is not set by private or government manuals telling the public how to search. Such manuals have no force of law. And their counsel is one of caution. They doubtless give good advice, but even when they touch on law and not computers, they reflect the law; they do not make it. To rely on them is to argue in circles or even backwards.

If the legislators wanted it otherwise, they should have enacted criteria for what is misleading and what is not. Then all Albertans could learn them, not merely those who have become familiar with the interior byways of the particular computer program in use at the moment.

Still less should priority in law turn on the results of an actual search. For all we know, it might have been influenced by keyboarding or programming errors. That is not an imaginary concern. In a recent case, the registration was perfect, but a proper search disclosed no trace of it, because of an error by registry staff in keyboarding a letter and an apostrophe: *Re Clinton's Flowers & Gifts Ltd.* (1993), 108 DLR (4th) 448, 5 PPSAC (2d) 11, 14 OR (3d) 24 (CA).

Furthermore, s. 43(8) says that an error can be "seriously misleading" without "proof that anyone was actually misled by it." I decline to look at actual search results.

At first, this conclusion may seem unfair to persons searching with an eye to buying or taking new security. It suggests that they may search and find nothing, yet there may be an undisclosed encumbrance which the curative section cures. Would it be fairer to them to say that any encumbrance which does not turn up in a search is bad? I cannot take that view of the law, for these reasons:

1. The legislature adopted the "seriously misleading" test. The registration might contain only a trivial error, or no error whatever (*Re Clinton's*, *supra*).
2. It is just as important to try to be fair to the encumbrancer who first registers; it may not be his fault that the search failed.
3. Making results of actual searches govern would still further delegate power to decide what is seriously misleading. All these people would then have power to invalidate a registration:

(a) computer programmers, and their assistants, and
(b) clerks who keyboard or scan the original registration, and
(c) clerks who enter the later searches, and
(d) clerks who report the later searches.

That cannot be the law.

In the present case, there was no error in the first two characters of the serial number, nor in any of its numerals. I cannot imagine any workable filing and retrieval system, manual or computer, which would not reveal the existence of this particular mistaken registration in response to an accurate search for the correct one. Any system which did not would not be reasonable. Where there are this many correct characters and only one which is wrong, the system should be designed to show this. Computer search programs which will retrieve an entry despite a discrepancy in one character are common. And the long string of numbers was correct. A serial number search here did in fact disclose this registration as an "inexact match." The only conclusion I draw from that, is that it was and is possible to design a program to overcome that one small error: *cf. Chrysler Credit Canada Ltd. v. Webber* (1994), 6 PPSAC (2d) 106, 18 Alta. LR (3d) 117, 49 ACWS (3d) 662.

Whether one numeral misstated, especially in a short serial number, would be seriously misleading is a different question which one need not decide today.

That deals with part (i) of the "seriously misleading" test. As for part (ii), I have no hesitation. Any reasonable human being comparing these two serial numbers (correct and mistaken) would immediately think it likely that one was merely a mistaken transcription of the other. The error is small, and a moment's reflection shows that it might be an error of dictation, since the right and the wrong letter rhyme. The fact that (by the relevant time) the name of the debtor was correctly registered would reinforce that conclusion.

Therefore, at the relevant time the appellant's registration was not seriously misleading. So by statute, the error is to be disregarded: s. 43(6). The appellant has the prior right to the dozer.

G. *Excavator*

Here the serial number was right all along, but the name of the debtor was wrong, and was never corrected.

1. Name error

The former *Companies Act*, RSA 1980, c. C-20, s. 87, used to require that a company display its correct name legibly on its premises and on its advertisements, cheques, invoices, orders and bills. For anyone hoping to maintain limited liability, that was also good advice. The reference to premises seems to have been dropped when the *Business Corporations Act*, SA 1981, c. B-15, was substituted. Section 10(9) of that new Act to some extent allows use of a different name. But a shorter version of old s. 87 is found in new s. 10(8), and it expressly prevails over s. 10(9). So I have doubts whether an Alberta corporation can enter into written transactions under a different name. But it is not necessary to decide that today.

The debtor here had followed a practice likely to confuse. It was incorporated as a numbered company, but apparently carried on business as M.S.T. Trucking Co., which "trade name" did not resemble its true name in any respect.

Section 17(5)(a) of the regulations under the *Personal Property Security Act* expressly deals with registering the name of a debtor corporation giving security. It says to give "the name of the body corporate." It is arguable that that means the name on the certificate of incorporation, not a trade name or nickname (aside from puzzles about translating between languages, or between alphabets). (Of course a common abbreviation, or a small spelling error, might well not be "seriously misleading.") Again it is unnecessary to decide that, for that is not what happened here.

The appellant wisely filed amended registrations with respect to the other three items of equipment. The amended registrations gave the debtor corporation's correct name of incorporation and also in a separate blank listed its trade name. So one was expressly shown to be an alias for the other. Obviously that is proper. Had that been done for this last item, the excavator, that would have solved the problem.

But it was not done, and we must look at the original registration. It listed the debtor as "M.S.T. Trucking Co. 366551 Alberta Inc." So it parked the trade name and the real name hard beside each other, in the parking spot reserved for the debtor's name. There was nothing, not even a comma, to separate the two: see the verification of registration on v. 2, p. 375 of the appeal book.

Section 12(2)(a) of the regulations forbids giving more than one name on a line, for obvious reasons. I do not think that it is at all decisive, but in fact neither searches of the company name nor a search of the trade name, revealed this registration at all, not even as an inexact match.

If these were not serial number goods, or if the registration had not given the correct serial number, I would have no hesitation in saying that registration (never corrected) fails part (i) of my test for "seriously misleading." It is a six-word name. The first three words bear no resemblance whatever to the company's real name. And the last three bear no resemblance whatever to the trade name.

Such registrations would create grave problems for any filing or retrieval system. It is common to see different companies with similar or overlapping names. For example, Acme Tool Canada Ltd. may be a subsidiary or sister company to Acme Tool Inc. And Smith Restaurant Ltd. may be the old name for Smith Holdings Ltd., which has sold the business to a different company, Smith Restaurant (1994) Ltd. They are different persons in law. There is no rule that the identifying word in a company name need precede the descriptive one, nor that both are needed. Nor need the word "Company" or "Corp." appear in a specified place, or at all.

Furthermore, it is much easier to learn the exact official name of a corporation than it is for a natural person. It is notorious that few people use the exact full name found on their birth certificate, but that is not true of companies.

I say nothing about how to treat errors or variations in names of individuals. That is a distinct topic not in issue here.

There is a huge volume of personal property security registrations, and so some mechanical scheme must be used, be it computer, or a manual system such as a card index, etc. It would be difficult to devise a system which would reveal a name registration when one half of it (several words) was totally wrong. No matter whether one searched the trade name or the true company name, that was the task facing any searcher or system designer here. And what if the registrar did devise a system of indexing or retrieval which would reliably bring up all such registrations (i.e., those where several words do not match in any degree whatever)? Any search would then catch in its net a large number of totally unrelated companies. In other words, a host of false matches. For example, how many companies must have names ending in "Business Enterprises Ltd.," or ending in "(Northern Alberta) Ltd."? How many societies or companies have names beginning with "Calgary and District"? How many bodies are named "Northern Alberta _____ Society"?

A person wishing to search cannot design his own computer search of the registry, such as "give me all the registrations containing word A and word B but not word C." One has to give a specific company name, the registrar does his standard search, and then reports what matches (if any) it turned up: see Form 14 (Alta. Reg. 295/90).

It is less easy to decide whether part (ii) of my test for "seriously misleading" is met. In the present case, even if a name search had somehow revealed the wrong registration, if there were no serial number registered, the searcher would not be confident that the two names were probably the same company. He would be uncertain. After all, he might have never done business with the debtor company, and know that it used a trade name not resembling its real name. On the other hand, the names of Alberta numbered companies always begin with the number, and trade names do not use the word "Ltd." or "Inc.." It may be that this would not be "seriously misleading" under test (ii).

Therefore, the name fails part (i) of the test for seriously misleading. Though it may well pass part (ii), it must pass both. The name is seriously misleading.

2. Serial number search

This item (the excavator) comes within the definition of serial number goods. Does that change the result? That means that priority is set by priority of serial number registrations, but it does not mean that one must register by serial number for all purposes. The Act says the contrary. And the searcher need not be a person with a competing secured interest, or even a person proposing to become a secured creditor of any kind. Nor need he be a person proposing to acquire just one specific chattel, or even proposing to secure an ownership interest in any or all chattels. He may be proposing to become, or continue to be, an unsecured creditor. He may have an exact idea of the make and model and year and appearance of each of the debtor's chattels, but be unable to secure accurate, or any, serial numbers for them.

Therefore, if the name of the debtor is seriously misleading taken alone, it does not cease to be so because the description of the chattel, complete with serial number, is accurate. And that is so whether or not these are serial number goods.

That is doubly so because the regulations, s. 17, require that one always register the debtor's name, in contrast to the serial number of the chattel (as discussed above). And the Act expressly permits one to search by name: see s. 48(1)(a). If a correct serial number registration cured a hopelessly defective name registration, then any name search would be an empty hope: see *Kelln (Trustee of) v. Strasbourg Credit Union Ltd.* (1992), 89 DLR (4th) 427 at p. 440, [1992] 3 WWR 310, 100 Sask. R 164 (CA); *General Motors Acceptance Corp. of Canada, Ltd. v. Trans Canada Credit Corp.* (1994), 6 PPSAC (2d)

216 at pp. 219-20, 147 AR 333, 15 Alta. LR (3d) 425 (Master), and cases cited: *Re Rose* (1993), 110 DLR (4th) 86, 23 CBR (3d) 58, 16 OR (3d) 360.

Therefore, in my view the defect in the appellant's registration of the excavator is fatally defective, and the respondent has priority with respect to it.

H. *Security over equity only?*

The appellant argues that even if First Calgary and the respondent have security over any item, their security only extends to what the debtor had to encumber, or what he could honestly encumber. The appellant says that its rights were preserved by conditional sales contracts, and so the debtor only had an equity built up by payments, but did not have title. The appellant kept title. It argues that the debtor could not encumber the title of the appellant or its assignor as unpaid vendor.

That argument is academic and need not be considered with respect to the first three chattels, because the appellant's registration gives it priority with respect to each of them.

With respect to the last item, the excavator, it is necessary to see whether the appellant has a conditional sales contract or similar reservation of title. The affidavit and the factum of the appellant do not say that it does. I have examined the copy of the document in the appeal book; it does not say anything like that. So respecting the excavator, this argument is also academic. But it sounds to me dubious, given the basic scheme of the Act.

I. *Conclusion*

The appellant Case has priority over the Volvo Loader, the Case Rammer, and the Case Dozer. First Calgary has priority over the Case Excavator. The appeal should be allowed as to the first three items. The respondent receiver supported the position of First Calgary and attacked Case's position throughout, and in the main failed. It would be too difficult to untangle separate items of costs, and too much work to give the appellant three-quarters costs and set off against that one-quarter costs, and tax all that. On the other hand, the appellant's successful arguments were new before us, and were not made before the master or the chambers justice.

HETHERINGTON JA: I have read the judgment of Mr. Justice Côté in this case, and agree with the final conclusions which he has reached. However, I disagree with his reasoning in the following respects.

Dozer

When the appellant registered a financial statement to protect its security interest in the dozer, it did not use the correct serial number. The correct serial number was GBE0001839. The one used by the appellant was GBC0001839. If it was seriously misleading, this error would prevent the appellant from claiming priority for its security interest in the dozer, under s-ss. (6) and (7) of s. 43 of the *Personal Property Security Act*, SA 1988, c. P-4.05. Was it seriously misleading?

Mr. Justice Côté says that an error in the serial number of a chattel would be seriously misleading in either of two situations, that is, if

(i) it would likely prevent a reasonable search *under a reasonable filing or registration system* from disclosing the existence of the registration, or

(ii) it would make a person who did somehow become aware of the registration think that it was likely not the same chattel.

(Emphasis added.) I would omit from the first alternative the words emphasized.

In my view, whether an error in the serial number of a chattel is seriously misleading or not must be determined with regard to the facts of the case. The nature of the registration and search system in place at the relevant times is one of those facts. Whether a search using the *correct* serial number of the chattel would have produced information about the security interest in the chattel registered using an *incorrect* serial number is a second. Whether a search of the debtor's name would have produced this information is a third. There may be others.

In relation to the dozer, a search using the *correct* serial number produced information about the registration of the appellant's security interest using the incorrect serial number. It showed it as a match "closely approximating your search criteria." A search of the debtor's name also produced information about this security interest, as did a search of the name under which the debtor carried on business. In these circumstances, Mr. Justice Côté's first test, as I would amend it, has surely been satisfied.

I agree with Mr. Justice Côté that the difference in the two serial numbers is so small that any reasonable person would have thought that they referred to the same chattel. Mr. Justice Côté's second test is also met. The appellant's error in relation to the dozer was not, therefore, seriously misleading.

Excavator

When the appellant registered a financing statement to protect its security interest in the excavator, it showed the debtor as M.S.T. Trucking Co. 366551 Alberta Inc. This was not correct. The correct name of the debtor was 366551 Alberta Inc. That company carried on business as M.S.T. Trucking Co. Was this error seriously misleading? If so, it would prevent the appellant from claiming priority for its security interest in the excavator under s-ss. (6) and (7) of s. 43 of the *Personal Property Security Act*.

The two tests described above can be used in relation to an error in describing the name of a debtor. Any reasonable person who became aware of the registration of the appellant's security interest in the excavator would know that the name shown for the debtor was a combination of the company name and the name under which it carried on business. The second test is clearly met.

The first test is another matter. Neither a search of the name of the debtor, 366551 Alberta Inc., nor a search of its trade name, M.S.T. Trucking Co., produced information about the security interest of the appellant in the excavator. A search of the serial number would, of course, have produced this information. However, I agree with Mr. Justice Côté, for the reasons given by him, that this fact does not prevent an error in the name of the debtor from being seriously misleading. I agree with Mr. Justice Côté that his first test is not satisfied. The appellant's error in the name of the debtor in the financing statement was seriously misleading.

It follows that the appellant cannot claim priority for its security interest in the excavator because of s-ss. (6) and (7) of s. 43 of the *Personal Property Security Act*.

CONRAD JA concurs with HETHERINGTON JA.

Appeal allowed in part.

NOTES AND QUESTIONS

1) As indicated in the *Case Power* decision, the Acts based on the CCPPSL model approach errors in registrations differently from the OPPSA. They generally provide for three types of searches: individual debtor name searches, business debtor name searches and serial number searches. See, e.g., SPPSA s. 48(1). A search using the correct name of an individual debtor, a business debtor or a serial number will disclose exact matches and "close similar matches." What close similar matches are disclosed depends upon the computer program used in the particular registry in which the search is conducted.

2) An important and apparently controversial issue is the relevance of "close similiar matches" listed on a search result obtained when the correct name of the debtor is used as the search criterion. Clearly, the system for disclosure of close similar matches was designed to ameliorate the harsh consequences of a failure to record precisely the debtor name or serial number of the collateral. In "Saskatchewan and Manitoba Personal Property Security Handbook" (Carswell, 1994) at 344 (footnotes omitted) Professors Cuming and Wood describe what role disclosed close similar matches should play in the determination of whether or not a registration is seriously misleading:

1. A search result using the debtor's name or serial number in the form prescribed by the regulations should be performed. It is often impossible to determine if an error is seriously misleading in the absence of a search result, since it will not be known if the defective registration was disclosed as a close similar match.

2. There should be a presumption that a defective registration is seriously misleading if the debtor name or serial number is not disclosed as a close similar match.

3. If a search result using the debtor's name in the form prescribed by the regulations discloses a close similar match containing the correct surname of an individual debtor or a surname with only minor differences in spelling from the correct surname together with both:

   (a) a first name alone or a first name with a middle initial very similar to the correct name of the debtor; and

   (b) the correct address of the debtor at the date of the search;
the registration should not be considered to be seriously misleading.

4. If a search result using the debtor's name in the form prescribed by the regulations discloses a close similar match containing a business debtor name with only minor differences from the business debtor name together with the correct address of the debtor at the date of the search, the registration should not be considered to be seriously misleading.

5. If a search result using the correct serial number of serial number goods discloses a close similar match that has the correct make or manufacturer's name, model and type of collateral, the registration should not be considered to be seriously misleading.

[A] defective registration, obtained using the debtor's name in the form prescribed by the regulations, that is not revealed as either an exact or similar match, should always be considered to be seriously misleading. However, a defective registration revealed as a similar match may or may not be seriously misleading depending on the closeness of the match and the number of other similar matches disclosed. A two-step process is involved in the case of a close similar match of a debtor name. A searching party is expected to review the list of close similar matches on a search result. If there is a very close similarity disclosed, the searching party should conduct a further search of these names in order to reveal the address of the debtor recorded on the registration.

To what extent does the approach suggested by Cuming and Wood differ from that applied by the Alberta Court of Appeal in *Case Power*? Note that Côté JA concluded: "Still less should priority in law turn on the results of an actual search." If this is so, why did he point out that in connection with the name of 366551 Alberta Inc. that "in fact neither searches of the company name nor a search of the trade name, revealed this registration at all, *not even as an inexact match*" (emphasis added). Côté JA readily accepted that a result of his approach is that a registration might be valid (i.e., not seriously misleading) even if it is not disclosed as a close similar match when the correct name of the debtor is used as the search criterion. But how does this square with his conclusion that "[a] person wishing to search cannot design his own computer search of the registry such as 'give me all the registrations containing word A and word B but not word C.' One has to give a specific company name, the registrar does his standard search and then reports what matches (if any) it turned up." If the searching party must rely on what is given to him or to her, should not the information given be central to the issue as to whether or not the registration is seriously misleading?

3) Côté JA concluded that to give effect to what is disclosed on a search result, when making the determination as to when a registration is seriously misleading, would "delegate" to certain people the power to make the determination. In the list of such persons he included computer programmers and their assistants; clerks who "keyboard or scan original registrations," "clerks who enter the later searches" and "clerks who report the later searches." However, the matter is not so simple and the anwers are not so obvious. No doubt it is the computer program that provides the disclosure of close similar matches and to this extent, the designer of the program determines what is disclosed as a close similar match. However, how does one formulate a test for determining when a searching party must go beyond use of the correct name of the debtor? Does the test provided by Côté JA ("reasonable search under a reasonable filing or registration system") provide any predictability or consistent outcomes? What is a "reasonable search"; how many and what variations in the correct name of the debtor does it require?

The suggestion that registry clerks can affect the outcome of a determination as to whether or not a registration is seriously misleading is based on a misunderstanding as to how a registry works. Assume that the registering party included an incorrect name of the debtor on the financing statement but the name was in a form that would ordinarily be disclosed as a close similar match when the correct name of the debtor is used as the search criterion. Assume further that the name was incorrectly key edited with the result that it was entered into the data base in a form such that it would not be disclosed as a close similar match when the correct name of the debtor is used as the search criterion. The APPSA (and most of the other Acts based on the CCPPSL model) provides a solution that accommodates the effect of the error on the status of the registration as being or not being seriously misleading. The legal effect of the error on the part of the registry would be that the financing statement tendered for registration by the secured party would not be registered. (Under the APPSA, registration occurs when the information on the financing statement is entered into the data base and not, as in Ontario, when a time is assigned by the registrar.) The result of the error would be that the security interest to which the tendered financing statement refers would be unperfected. Under s. 52(1)(b) the secured party would have a right of recovery from the registry for damages suffered as a result of the key edit clerk's mistake. Consequently, there is no need to ignore what is revealed as a close similar match in order to protect secured parties from the errors of key edit clerks. An error in a particular search result does not affect the question as to what is not a seriously misleading error in a registration. In any event, the chances of there being an error in a search result (such that the result does not disclose a close similar match generated by the computer program) are very small since search results are printed by computer using information drawn from the registry data base. In the rare situation where there is human intervention in the production of a printed search result which produces an error, APPSA s. 52(1)(b) gives a right of recovery to anyone who requested the search result and who suffers loss as a result of reliance on the search result.

4) The Alberta Court of Appeal is not alone in its refusal to allow the computer program of a personal property registry to play a central role in the determination of what is a seriously misleading registration. See cases cited in the decision and *Steinbach Credit Union Ltd. v. Manitoba Agricultural Credit Corp.*, [1992] 1 WWR 448 (Man. CA). Section 47(3) of the new MPPSA (not yet in force) was apparently inserted to reverse the effect of the *Steinbach* decision. The section provides that an error in the spelling of a debtor's name "invalidates the registration ... if a search of the registry under the correct name of the debtor would not reveal the registration."

Adelaide Capital Corp. v. Integrated Transportation Finance Inc.
(1994), 16 OR (3d) 414 (Gen. Div.)

R.A. BLAIR J:

Background and Overview

Integrated Transportation Finance Incorporated ("ITFI") and Integrated Transportation Services Incorporated ("ITS") made voluntary assignments in bankruptcy on April 13, 1993. Prior to their bankruptcies, ITFI and ITS were in the business of leasing truck trailers to various end users in Ontario and elsewhere in Canada.

By orders of this court dated April 5, 1993 and April 14, 1993, Deloitte & Touche Inc. ("Deloitte & Touche") was appointed as interim receiver of the two companies at the instance of certain secured creditors, pursuant to s. 47.1 of the *Bankruptcy and Insolvency Act*, RSC 1985, c. B-3. Deloitte & Touche is also acting as trustee in bankruptcy of the defendant companies.

In its capacity as interim receiver, Deloitte & Touche has taken steps to manage and operate the businesses of the companies, to assume possession and control of their assets, and to verify the existence of numerous trailers which are the subject of competing claims by various creditors. By order dated July 14, 1993, Mr. Justice Rosenberg established a procedure by which the various priority disputes that have arisen—and which relate primarily to claims regarding a large number of the truck trailers leased out on long-term and short-term leases by ITFI and ITS—could be determined.

The dispute in question in this proceeding relates to competing claims between Greyvest Leasing Inc. ("Greyvest") and North American Trust Company ("NAT") to 87 such trailers.

Facts

Greyvest seeks the following relief

1) An order directing the interim receiver to deliver up to Greyvest the vans and trailers listed in Schedule "A" to the notice of motion, together with the proceeds of all lease payments or sales proceeds collected by it, as interim receiver, and interest earned thereon;

2) An order authorizing and directing Greyvest to administer and dispose of those assets; and,

3) An order declaring that Greyvest is the owner of the assets in question, or, alternatively, declaring that Greyvest has a first-ranking security interest in the assets in question.

The 87 trailers or vans are the subject of four lease agreements entered into between Greyvest (formerly known as Greyhound Leasing & Financial of Canada Ltd.) and ITFI between December 1986 and August 1990. Financing statements were registered under the *Personal Property Security Act*, RSO 1990, c. R.10 ("PPSA"), and its predecessor.

SECURED CREDITOR	TYPE	DATE OF REGISTRATION	ACT
Greyvest	Lease (50 Units)	Jan. 12 or 20, 1987	PPSA (E, O) and (E, B, D, O)
Greyvest	Lease (25 Units)	Dec. 2 or 16, 1987	PPSA (E, O) and (E, O)
NAT	Debenture	Feb. 1, 1990	PPSA (I, E, A, O)
Greyvest	Lease (10 Units)	June 1, 1990	PPSA (I, E, O)
Greyvest	Lease (2 Units)	Aug. 13, 1990	PPSA (E, O, MV)
NAT	—	Nov. 16, 1990	PPSA (I, E, A, O)

There is an initial question to be determined as to whether the leases in question require a registration under the PPSA to preserve Greyvest's claim to priority over the chattels which are their subject matter. Depending on the answer to that question, the dispute between the parties turns, in large part, on the question of priorities based on registration. In that respect, the [foregoing] chart, summarizing the competing transactions as relied on and presented to the court by counsel, may be helpful. In the column entitled "Act" the letters "E," "I," "A," and "O" refer to collateral description "boxes" on a financing statement relating to "equipment," "inventory," "accounts" and "other," respectively.

In terms of the dispute regarding priority by registration, the following additional facts are important to note as well.

As the foregoing table indicates, the financing statements registered by Greyvest in January and December 1987 variously described the collateral in question, in the collateral classification section, as "equipment" (E), "book debts" (BD), and "other" (O). The box in the section for "inventory" (I) was not marked.

It is common ground that the trailers in question were not "equipment," but rather were "inventory" in the hands of ITFI, and there is authority for the proposition that the marking of the category "other" has the effect of *excluding* consumer goods, inventory, equipment or accounts, unless they, themselves, have been marked: *Re Laverty* (1982), 3 PPSAC 1, 47 CBR (NS) 109 (Ont. SC). Greyvest's later registration in June of 1990 (the "June 1990 Greyvest Registration"), did designate "inventory" as well as "equipment," "accounts" and "other" on the collateral classification line of the financing statement.

The February 1990 NAT Registration was for a period of one year, and was allowed to expire from the registry unrenewed. It contained the following description in the optional collateral description segment with respect to the collateral: "50 new Roussy Aluminum 53' High Cube Tandem Axle Vans Serial # [50 serial numbers followed]." The November 1990 NAT Registration had all boxes checked off on the collateral classification line, but the optional description lines were not completed.

The Issues

The issues to be determined can be summarized as follows:

1) Are the leases between Greyvest and ITFI the sort of leases which do, or do not, require registration under the PPSA for priority purposes?

2) Can the misclassification of the collateral in the 1987 Greyvest registrations be "cured" by the application of s. 46(4) of the PPSA, such as to preserve Greyvest's priority to the initial 75 trailers?

3) Does the February 1990 NAT Registration prevail, or is it limited in its effect to the "50 Roussy trailers" described in the optional collateral description section of the financial statement, by virtue of s. 46(3) of the PPSA?

4) What is the effect of the expiry without renewal of the February 1990 NAT Registration?

5) Can Greyvest rely upon the June 1990 Greyvest Registration, which did classify the collateral as "inventory," to perfect its earlier security interests in the 1987 leases, by virtue of s. 45(4) of the PPSA which now allows one registration to perfect several security interests?

6) Conversely, if the error in classification of the collateral in the 1987 registrations can be corrected by the operation of s. 46(4) of the PPSA, can Greyvest rely upon those registrations as its "root of title" for all subsequent registrations as well?

7) In any event, does Greyvest have priority with respect to the 12 units covered by the June 1990 and August 1990 Greyvest Registrations?

8) Finally, if NAT has priority by registration on any of the units, is it estopped from asserting that priority because Greyvest relied upon a statement made by Mr. McCleary of NAT to Mr. Micallef of Greyvest to the effect that NAT was not making a claim to any of Greyvest's trailers?

[The Court concluded that the leases were "security leases" that required registration.]

Misclassification of Collateral

Greyvest registered six financing statements in 1987 which are pertinent to these proceedings. They all precede any registration by NAT.

The first two registrations, dated January 12 and 20—which related to a transaction respecting 50 trailers—classified the collateral variously as "equipment," "book debts" and "other," with no optional general collateral description given.

In December 1987, four financing statements were registered, two on December 2 and two on December 16. These registrations relate to a transaction involving 25 trailers. One of the December 2 registrations classified the collateral as "equipment" and "other" but went on to give the following general collateral description: "Registration made respecting assignment and agreement for lease schedules 13310—1, 2 and 3 assigned by debtor to secured party." One of the December 16 registrations classified the collateral as "equipment," "book debts" and "other," with, in addition, a general collateral description which stated: "Registration made respecting assignment & agreement for lease schedule 13610 assigned by debtor to secured party." The optional collateral descriptions in the latter two cases would appear to relate to that aspect of the overall transaction whereby Greyvest took an assignment of the leases between ITFI and the end users as security for the transaction. The second December 16 registration is identical to the first December 2 registration described above except for the name of "Secured Party."

What is apparent from the foregoing is that the 1987 Greyvest registrations do not mark "inventory" as collateral being secured. It is common ground, and counsel for Greyvest concedes, that the collateral is inventory in the hands of ITFI, and should have been classified as such in the financing statement. Mr. Dunphy submits on behalf of Greyvest, however, that this "error" can and should be cured by the operation of s. 46(4) of the PPSA. Pursuant to that section:

46(4) A financing statement or financing change statement is not invalidated nor is its effect impaired by reason only of an error or omission therein or in its execution or registration unless a reasonable person is likely to be misled materially by the error or omission.

In my view, this argument cannot succeed with respect to the Greyvest registrations in January 1987, or with respect to one of the registrations made on December 2, 1987 (No. 871202 1013 49 5597), or with respect to one of the registrations made on December 16, 1987 (No. 871216 0947 43 9742); but it is entitled to succeed with respect to the first registration on that latter date (No. 871202 1013 49 5596) and with respect to the other registration on December 16, 1987 (No. 871216 0947 9744). My reasons for coming to these conclusions are the following.

The trailers which were the subject matter of the financings that triggered these registrations were inventory in the hands of ITFI and would properly have been classified and described as such in the financing statement. They were not.

The January 1987 registrations variously classify the collateral as "equipment," "book debts" and "other," without anything in the general description section of the financing statement to reflect, refine, expend or limit the type of collateral involved. There is simply nothing in the filing to notify a person doing a search under the PPSA that Greyvest is claiming *any* security interest in the inventory of the debtor. In my opinion, this admitted error is one which is likely to mislead a reasonable person materially and, therefore, is one which invalidates or impairs the effect of the financing statement.

• • •

For the foregoing reasons, I conclude that the two January 1987 financing statements, the December 2, 1987 financing statement (bearing No. 871202 1013 49 5597), and the December 16, 1987 financing statement (bearing No. 871216 0947 43 9742), are not curable by the operation of s. 46(4) of the PPSA, and are accordingly invalid and ineffective to establish a security interest in the trailers in question, in priority to the claim of NAT.

The same is not the case with respect to the remaining December 1987 financing statements. Neither refers specifically to "inventory," but each contains a general description of the collateral in lines 13 to 15 of the financing statements. A reasonable person doing a search and reading the general description of the collateral provided is not likely to be misled materially, in my view, as to the nature of the collateral in which the security interest is being claimed. In the case of the December 2 financing statement (No. 871202 1013 49 5596), it is those assets listed in the "agreement for lease schedule 13610— 1, 2 and 3 assigned by debtor to secured party." In either event, there can be no mistake that Greyvest is claiming a security interest in whatever is listed on those schedules. A subsequent creditor doing a search is thus put on notice to make enquiries in order to clarify precisely what the nature of that security interest is and over precisely what collateral priority is claimed, if it wishes to position itself with regard to that prior security claim.

In August 1990, Greyvest registered a financing statement with respect to a two-trailer transaction. This registration did not classify the collateral as "inventory" in the collateral classification section, but did have a description in the general description section and a reference to vehicle identification numbers. It is therefore effective to protect Greyvest's interest in the two trailers which were the subject matter of that transaction: see *Re 533812 Ontario Ltd.* (1985), 52 OR (2d) 750, 23 DLR (4th) 270, 5 PPSAC 128 *sub nom. Touche Ross Ltd. (Trustee in Bankruptcy) v. Ford Credit Canada Ltd.*, 58 CBR (NS) 49 (SC), affirmed (1987), 7 PPSAC xxxii, 64 C.B.R. (NS) 80n (Ont. CA).

This interpretation is consistent with the purpose of the PPSA, which is to give notice of prior claims to a creditor subsequently providing financing to the debtor, and sufficient information as to the collateral in question to put the creditor on inquiry as to whether that collateral is the same as the collateral over which it, too, is seeking security. Professor Richard H. McLaren, in his text *Secured Transactions in Personal Property in Canada*,

2nd ed. (Toronto: Carswell, 1989), at p. 20-11 of vol. 2, describes the purpose of the PPSA in these terms:

The personal property security registration system has a dual purpose. First, it provides the necessary mechanism to permit the step required for perfection in s. 19(b) to be accomplished. Secondly, it provides readily available information to prospective credit grantors and purchasers of certain forms of collateral. In connection with this latter purpose, the registry only contains enough information to enable a person searching the system to know who to contact to obtain information regarding the transaction.

● ● ●

The purpose of the Act's registration system is to provide a registration mechanism *and information concerning collateral subject to a secured transaction.*

While the system is known as "a notice filing system," and imposes on the credit-grantor/searcher the obligation to make inquiries to determine the details of the secured transaction from the parties thereto, certain minimal information must be contained in the financing statement by statute and regulation. Section 46(2) of the PPSA declares that "every financing statement ... shall be in the prescribed form" (Form 1). Section 3 of O. Reg. 372/89 prescribes the contents of financing statements, and includes as a mandatory requirement:

3(1) ...
    (f) the classification of the collateral as consumer goods, inventory, equipment, accounts or that the classification is other than consumer goods, inventory, equipment or accounts or any combination thereof;

A general description of the collateral, in lines 13 to 15 of the financing statement, is optional under the regulations (s. 3(11)).

Where the legislature and the Lieutenant Governor-in-Council have made it a mandatory requirement to classify the collateral, the accurate completion of that exercise can only be considered a material part of the information to be provided. Therefore, a creditor seeking the protection of perfection by registration of a financing statement under the PPSA is impressed with an obligation to provide at least a sufficient indication of the collateral in which it is claiming a security interest to alert a subsequent searcher, who is about to provide credit to the same debtor, that the collateral in which the new credit grantor is claiming an interest *may* be subject to a prior claim. Where—as in the case of the January 1987 and December 1987 registrations referred to above—the financing statements give no indication whatever that "inventory" is covered, and in fact indicate the contrary by the marking of the "other" category, that information is lacking. Where the general collateral description is sufficient to direct the searching creditor to the collateral in question, the financing statement is adequate.

The February 1990 NAT Registration

NAT's predecessor, First City Trust Company, provided financing to ITFI, secured by the NAT Debenture dated January 26, 1990. The NAT Debenture contained a fixed charge in respect of various trailers listed (none of which is listed among the Greyvest assets), but also granted a floating charge over all of the assets, property and undertaking of ITFI. A financing statement was registered with respect to this security interest on February 1, 1990.

The financing statement classified the collateral by marking the boxes for all of "inventory," "equipment," "accounts" and "other." It went on, however, to provide the following general description on the collateral secured in the optional section on lines 13 to 15:

50 new 1990 Roussy aluminum 53' high cube tandem axle vans serial # [the financing statement then went on to list the serial numbers of all 50 trailers].

I think it apparent, from the language of s. 46(3) of the PPSA, that the February 1990 NAT Registration is limited in the priority it provides to the 50 Roussy trailers listed in it. Section 46(3) says:

46(3) Except with respect to rights to proceeds, where a financing statement or financing change statement sets out a classification of collateral *and also contains words that _appear_ to limit the scope of the classification,* then, unless otherwise indicated in the financing statement or financing change statement, the secured party may claim a security interest perfected by registration *only in the class as limited.* (Emphasis added.)

Mr. Wigley argued, on behalf of NAT, that completion of the general collateral description portion of the financing statement is an optional, almost gratuitous, exercise, and that by virtue of the check in the "other" box in the classification section, the financing statement "otherwise indicated" that the secured party's interest was not limited to the 50 trailers listed.

I do not agree.

Filling in the general collateral description portion of the financing statement is optional under the PPSA. Having chosen to fill in that portion, however, the secured creditor risks limiting the collateral that is protected by perfection through registration to something less than what may, in fact, be encompassed by the security instrument, if words are used which fail to make it clear that something other than what is described on lines 13 to 15 is also caught by the registration. Here, the general description appears to limit the scope of the registration to the collateral delineated—50 Roussy trailers specifically set out by serial number: see McLaren, *supra*, at p. 20-41 in note 60.

Thus, the February 1990 NAT Registration is valid to perfect NAT's interest in the 50 Roussy trailers only. However, since it is common ground that those trailers do not overlap with the Greyvest assets, it is not valid to perfect a security interest ahead of Greyvest in any of the trailers which are at issue in these proceedings.

Effect of the Expiry of the February 1990 NAT Registration

There was some argument about whether the February 1990 NAT Registration, which expired without renewal on February 1, 1991, could be sustained *for purposes of continuous registration* by the November 1990 NAT Registration.

In view of my conclusion, set out above, that the February 1990 NAT Registration is limited in its scope to the 50 Roussy trailers listed therein, which are not amongst the trailers in dispute in these proceedings, this issue is academic. I would have thought, however, that s. 21 of the PPSA would operate to provide *for continuous perfection.* Mr.

Dunphy's attempt to distinguish between "continuous registration" and "continuous perfection" is interesting, but in the end not determinative, because it is *continuous perfection* under the PPSA which counts to preserve a creditor's priority position. The fact that the February 1990 NAT Registration subsequently drops by the wayside because of non-renewal is simply the very kind of situation, I would think, that s. 21 is designed to catch.

The June 1990 Greyvest Registration

Greyvest registered a financing statement on June 1, 1990 as a result of a transaction involving 10 trailers. In this instance, the box for "inventory" in the collateral classification section was checked off, as well as the boxes for "equipment," "accounts" and other." In addition, the general collateral description section was filled in with the words: "Re equipment schedule number 02 to lease agreement number 308700 and the proceeds thereof."

I have come to the following conclusions regarding this registration, having regard to the issues outlined earlier in these reasons:

  (i) the registration is effective to give Greyvest priority over NAT with respect to the trailers listed in the schedule referred to in its general collateral description section (i.e., the 10 trailers which were the subject matter of the immediate transaction), because the February 1990 NAT Registration is not effective to give that priority to NAT, for the reasons outlined above;

  (ii) for those same reasons, the June 1990 Greyvest Registration is limited in its scope to the equipment listed in the schedule referred to;

 (iii) even if I am in error regarding (ii) above, the June 1990 Greyvest Registration, which does classify the collateral as "inventory," cannot operate to perfect Greyvest's security interest in the original 1987 leases through the magic of s. 45(4) of the PPSA.

The June 1990 Greyvest Registration gives priority to the trailers listed ...

The first conclusion regarding the June 1990 Greyvest Registration does not require much elaboration. I have already found that the February 1990 NAT Registration does not give NAT priority over any trailers which are part of the disputed assets, but is restricted to the 50 trailers listed therein. Therefore, the June 1990 Greyvest Registration operates to perfect Greyvest's interest in whatever assets are encompassed therein.

Those assets, in my view, are simply the 10 trailers which, I am told, are the assets listed in the schedule to the lease agreement No. 308700 referenced in the general description section.

... but is limited in scope to those trailers listed ...

The same analysis that limited the scope of the February 1990 NAT Registration to the 50 Roussy trailers set out in the general description section of that financing statement limits the scope of the June 1990 Greyvest Registration to the assets listed on "equipment schedule number 02 to lease agreement number 308700 and the proceeds thereof."

A creative argument can be, and was, made by counsel to the effect that the reference to *"equipment* schedule" and "proceeds thereof" *otherwise indicate*—in the language of s. 46(3)—that a security interest is perfected in more than meets the eye, i.e., in collateral which is "inventory" or "other" than inventory or equipment. The purpose of the PPSA is to provide notice and information about a priority claim to collateral subject to a secured transaction, however. To my mind, the reasonable person who is searching the index should not be required to be creative and to perform a labyrinthine lawyer-like analysis of the language used by the creditor seeking to preserve its priority. Where the thrust of what meets the eye in the general description of the collateral *"appear[s]* to limit the scope of the classification," as it does here, "the secured party may claim a security interest perfected by registration only in the class as limited": s. 46(3).

... and cannot operate to perfect Greyvest's 1987 security interests

Should I be wrong in coming to this conclusion, I need to address an additional argument advanced by Mr. Dunphy with respect to the June 1990 Greyvest Registration. He submitted that Greyvest was entitled to rely upon that registration, which did classify the collateral correctly as "inventory," to perfect its earlier security interest in the 1987 leases, by virtue of s. 45(4) of the PPSA. That section, a new provision in the 1989 PPSA, permits one registration to perfect several security interests. It states:

45(4) Except where the collateral is consumer goods, one financing statement may perfect one or more security interests created or provided for in one or more security agreements between the parties.

While this section has no predecessor in the former PPSA, it appears to give statutory recognition to a theme that had developed in the case law under the former PPSA. In a number of decisions, the court had held that a single financing statement could serve to preserve priority for a *subsequent* loan made by the same lender to the same debtor, provided the subsequent loan was not a separate and distinct transaction but was linked to the former arrangement in a way that the two could be said to be "one transaction or an on-going related transaction": *Re Better* (1989), 74 CBR (NS) 76, 9 PPSAC 158 (Ont. SC), *per* Deputy-Registrar Browne (as he then was). See also *West Bay Sales Ltd. v. Hitachi Sales Corp. of Canada* (1978), 20 OR (2d) 752, 88 DLR (3d) 743 (SC); *Trans Canada Credit Corp. v. Royal Bank* (1985), 5 PPSAC 1, 38 Sask. R 274 (QB); *General Motors Acceptance Corp. of Canada v. Bank of Nova Scotia* (1986), 55 OR (2d) 438, 6 PPSAC 53 (CA); *Hongkong Bank Of Canada v. National Bank of Canada* (1990), 73 OR (2d) 28, 1 PPSAC (2d) 73 (HCJ); *Royal Bank v. Agricultural Credit Corp. of Saskatchewan* (1991), 2 PPSAC (2d) 338, 96 Sask. R 264 (QB).

The financial transactions between Greyvest and ITFI in 1987 and later in 1990 are not sufficiently linked to one of the financing statements to perfect the security interests reflected in the others. All related to the financing of trailers, but there otherwise appears to be no connection between the transactions. The end lessees are different in each case. Nothing in the documentation ties the transactions together. Each evolved out of separately negotiated term sheets intended to cover specific collateral—50 trailers, 25 trailers, 10 trailers and 2 trailers. In short, it appears that each was a "stand alone" transaction. Consequently, in my view, the provisions of s. 45(4) of the PPSA cannot operate to enable the June 1990 Greyvest Registration to perfect Greyvest's security interests in the earlier 1987 lease arrangements.

There is another reason for this same result. Although it does not say so on its face, s. 45(4) was not intended, in my opinion, to permit a financing statement to perfect a security interest created or provided for in an earlier security agreement between the parties. Certainly, the predecessor case law which held that a single financing statement could perfect a security interest or interests in more than one security arrangement did so in the context of an earlier financing statement and later security agreements, not the reverse.

In *West Bay Sales Ltd.*, *supra*, for example, Mr. Justice Henry dealt with a situation where a general financing statement had been filed which purported to secure the assignment of the benefit of a conditional sale contract of inventory *"now or hereafter* held for sale or lease as inventory and proceeds thereof" (emphasis added). Shipments of equipment were made under conditional sales agreements to the debtor, but further financing statements were not registered with respect to each individual conditional sale contract. Henry J concluded that *successive* registration of new financing statements as the inventory turned over would add nothing new to the information contained on the general financing statement, and were unnecessary (see p. 755). See also *Royal Bank v. Agricultural Credit Corp. of Saskatchewan*, *supra*, at pp. 346-47.

This makes sense to me. It is one thing to permit the registration of a financing statement to perfect a security interest which arises *subsequently* and with respect to the nature of which notice has already been given. It is quite another thing to extend that protection *retrospectively* to breathe life into a previously unperfected security interest. The PPSA contains a mechanism for correcting errors or omissions in, or for amending or making other changes to, financing statements. The mechanism consists in the filing of a financing *change* statement. Had s. 45(4) been intended merely to perform such a function, there would have been no need to enact it. I do not see its purpose as that of assigning to the financing statement the role already attributed to the financing change statement.

The Priority Dominoes

It follows from the foregoing analysis that the priority dominoes in this proceeding fall into place in the ensuing fashion:

a) Greyvest has priority over NAT with respect to the 25 trailers which are the subject matter of the December 1987 registrations;

b) Greyvest has priority over NAT with respect to the 12 trailers which are the subject matter of the June and August 1990 registrations;

c) NAT, however, has priority over Greyvest with respect to the 50 trailers which are the subject matter of the January 1987 registrations, because those registrations are ineffective for purposes of perfection by registration, and because NAT has registered a financing statement on November 16, 1990 which covers ITFI's inventory.

Order accordingly.

NOTES AND QUESTIONS

1) Most of the issues that arose in the *Adelaide* case are peculiar to the OPPSA. The Acts based on the CCPPSL model adopt a very different approach to collateral description in a registration.

2) For a criticism of most of the conclusions reached by the court, see Ziegel, "Commentaries—Characterization of Equipment Leases and Other PPSA Problems" (1994), 24 *CBLJ* 141.

3) Blair J notes that the OPPSA provides for a "notice registration" system and not a document filing system of the kind prescribed in the registry statutes that were replaced by the Act. However, not all notice registration systems are the same with respect to collateral description in the financing statement. The various systems fall somewhere on a spectrum of specificity. At one end of the spectrum are the PPSAs which require item descriptors: VIN for motor vehicle, consumer goods collateral (Ont.) and serial numbers for consumer goods or equipment collateral in the form of motor vehicles, trailers, boats, aircraft, road construction equipment, tractors and combines (e.g., Alta., BC, Sask.). At the other end of the spectrum is the Bank Act, SC 1991, c. 46 which requires no collateral description whatever in the notice of intention that is registered under ss. 427(4)-(5). The policy behind VIN or serial number description requirements is examined in *Re Lambert, supra*, and the notes and questions following the case.

What is the policy underlying the legislative requirements for including in a registration non-specific descriptors for inventory and most types of equipment? Is the approach embodied in the Bank Act not the most logical one in the context of a notice registration system? The notice indicates the existence or possible existence of a security interest in the personal property of the debtor. That is its sole function. Whether or not a security agreement exists, and, if so, its details, can be obtained from the secured party. This type of system could function quite nicely in the context of a PPSA. (See OPPSA s. 18.) However, the PPSAs are more than mere notice registration systems; some form of description of the collateral is required by every Act. What is the function of this description? Why should failure to include it invalidate a registration? Note that in *Adelaide*, the court accepted as an adequate collateral description nothing more than a reference to equipment listed in a schedule to the security agreement. Does this decision serve the policy behind the requirements of the Ontario regulations that a collateral description be included in the registration? How different is this from the system contained in the Bank Act?

4) The OPPSA regulations applied by the court *require* a registering party to do precisely what the regulations to the Acts based on the CCPPSL model *prohibit* a registering party from doing. For example, s. 28(3) of the Alberta Personal Property Regulations, Alta. Reg. 234/90 as am., provides that a description of collateral is inadequate "if it describes collateral as consumer goods or equipment without further reference to the kind of collateral." Section 28(2)(d) provides that a description of collateral as inventory is valid only while the collateral is held by the debtor as inventory. Should the debtor change the use of the collateral from inventory to consumer goods or equipment, the registration becomes invalid. These restrictions on the use of the terms "consumer goods," "equipment" and "inventory" are an aspect of the general approach of the Acts based on the CCPPSL model under which collateral is to be described by "item or kind" (i.e., specifically or generically).

The Acts do, however, allow the use of broad generic descriptions such as "goods," "intangibles," etc., and the use of "all present and after-acquired personal property" as a collateral description. Restrictions on the use of the terms "consumer goods," "equipment" and "inventory" are apparently based on the fact that these terms do not describe kinds of goods, only the use to which goods are being put at the relevant time. They are "terms of art" in the context of the Acts and may have meanings that would surprise someone not acquainted with the system. This could affect both registering and searching parties. For example, the cows of a dairy farmer are "equipment" under the PPSAs and can be described as such under the OPPSA. The drafters of the Acts based on the CCPPSL model obviously concluded that this type of description would be very misleading to someone who is not acquainted with the categorization system of goods under the Act. What problems of collateral description in this context are faced by registering parties under the Ontario system?

5) Very significant disparities exist between the OPPSA and the Acts based on the CCPPSL model with respect to the requirements for description of proceeds collateral. Taking simplicity to its ultimate, the OPPSA gives a perfected security interest in proceeds without requiring the secured party to register a description of the proceeds claimed. (See OPPSA s. 25, and also the exceptions in ss. 25(5) and 28(5).) So long as a financing statement in the prescribed form is registered with respect to the primary collateral, the secured creditor need do nothing more to perfect his or her security interest in proceeds. This means that a secured creditor who has taken a security interest in inventory and who has marked the inventory box on the financing statement has a perfected security interest in proceeds collateral such as accounts, chattel paper or non-inventory goods. There is no need to describe the proceeds collateral even though it takes a form different from that of the original collateral. Is this feature of the Act likely to be a problem for third parties who are interested in buying or taking a security interest in personal property of the debtor? What justification is there for requiring that original collateral be described in the registration but not proceeds collateral?

6) The Acts based on the CCPPSL model require a registering party claiming an interest in proceeds to provide an item or kind description of the proceeds just as he or she would be required to do if the proceeds were original collateral. The only exception allowed is in a case where the proceeds are in the form of "cash proceeds," or in the same form as the original collateral, in which case no specific additional proceeds description is required. See, e.g., SPPSA s. 28(2). Does this approach destroy the basic concept of proceeds? Are secured parties induced by these requirements to claim proceeds as original collateral?

7) Note importantly that in *Adelaide* the court rejected the argument that the June 1990 Greyvest registration was sufficient to perfect the Greyvest security interest in the 1987 leases. The court concluded that OPPSA s. 45(4) applies only where (i) "a subsequent loan is made by the same lender to the same debtor"; and (ii) "the subsequent loan was not a separate and distinct transaction but was linked to the former arrangement in a way that the two could be said to be 'one transaction or an on-going related transaction.' " Do you agree with this interpretation and the reasoning to support it? Are they consistent with the language and history of s. 45(4) as reflected in the Ontario Advisory Committee's Report? Compare the approach taken by the court with respect to the February 1990 and

November, 1990 NAT registrations. One of the cases relied upon by the court in reaching its conclusion with respect to the Greyvest registrations was the decision of the Saskatchewan Court of Queen's Bench in *Royal Bank v. Agricultural Credit Corp. of Saskatchewan* (1991), 96 Sask. R 264. However, this decision was reversed by the Saskatchewan Court of Appeal [1994] 7 WWR 305. The Court concluded that a single registration can perfect security interests created under separate security agreements. The decision implicitly rejects the conclusion in the *Adelaide* case. Of course, to the extent that a registration relates to a prior transaction, it is effective to perfect a security interest arising under that transaction from the date of the registration.

Amendments to a Registration

Heidelberg Canada Graphic Equipment Ltd. v. Arthur Andersen Inc.
(1992), 4 PPSAC (2d) 116 (Ont. Gen. Div.)

[Heidelberg,which had sold equipment to Kennedy Park Ltd. held a registered security interest in "inventory, equipment, accounts and other" of Kennedy Park. When this security interest was assigned to the Chase Manhattan Bank of Canada (Bank), the Bank registered a financing change statement. When Kennedy Park got into financial trouble, Rob and Lisa Thomas (Thomas) loaned the company money and took and registered a security interest in its assets, including its accounts. When further funding was required Thomas contacted a representative of the Bank and convinced her that the Bank should "remove its registration" with respect to the accounts of Kennedy Park. Apparently, the Bank mistakenly assumed that it did not have a security interest in the accounts. The financing statement (FCS#1) that was used for this purpose indicated that it was amending the initial registration. When the Bank realized that it had a security interest in the accounts, it registered another financing change statement FCS#2 which also provided for an amendment to the initial registration, this time adding back the accounts as collateral.

No interests in the assets of Kennedy Park Ltd. arose between the registration of FCS#1 and FCS#2.

When Kennedy Park made an assignment in bankruptcy, its trustee, acting also as receiver under the Thomas security agreement, attacked the Bank's security interest in the accounts.]

FELDMAN J: At issue in this application is the validity of the security taken by the applicants over the equipment and accounts receivable of the bankrupt, Kennedy Park, and the priority of that security as against the trustee in bankruptcy and two debentures in favour of the two individual respondents. There are three main issues.

(1) Chase Manhattan Bank of Canada ("Chase") registered (i) a financing change statement ("FCS#1") deleting the reference to "accounts" in order to accommodate subordination of its position to a potential new lender for Kennedy Park, and as a result of an error in its understanding of its security and of the effect of such registration; two days later it registered (ii) another financing change statement ("FCS#2") purporting to restore its registration over accounts.

What was the effect of each of those registrations, and in particular:

(a) did the first financing change statement discharge or merely unperfect the security interest in accounts;

(b) did the second financing change statement reinstate or reperfect the security;

(c) if so, is s. 30(6) of the Personal Property Security Act, RSO 1990, c. P.10 ("PPSA" or "new PPSA") applicable to maintain Chase's priority over the registered debentures of the respondents?

(2) Did the amalgamation of the debtor company, Kennedy Park, require Chase to register a financing change statement?

• • •

(i) *Effect of FCS#1*

On its face, FCS#1 does not purport to be a discharge or partial discharge of the security over accounts, but rather a correction of a perceived original error in registration against accounts. It is clear that s. 56(1)(b) contemplates either payment or performance of certain of the obligations under the security agreement before a financing change statement evidencing a partial discharge may be demanded. No payment or performance was made here. This was not a discharge in the sense of a release of security for satisfaction of part of the obligation.

The *Weiss* case, referred to by the respondent, dealt with an interpretation of specific sections of the Bank Act, RSC 1970, c. B-1. In the case of *Re Dante Boutique Shoes Ltd.* (1982), 2 PPSAC 27, 40 CBR (NS) 19, 131 DLR (3d) 243 (Bktcy.), where based on a misunderstanding, the Bank did register a financing change statement in the form of a discharge, Henry J held that the effect under the then PPSA was that the bank's security ceased to be perfected and could only be reperfected if the curative provisions of the Act applied. There was no suggestion that the registration of the discharge had the effect of releasing the security as between the debtor and the secured party. Neither did the registration of FCS#1 have that effect.

The respondents' second argument is that the effect of the first financing change statement was that the registration against accounts "ceased to be effective," using the language of ss. 51 and 52 of the PPSA, and therefore under s. 52(2), Chase could only perfect again by registering a financing statement and not a financing change statement.

In my view, a review of the overall scheme and structure of the PPSA, and in particular Part IV, reveals that the registration system is built on the concept of the registration of a financing statement which may cover more than one type of collateral. Changes can be made to the contents of the financing statement during its life which is its "registration period." However, only a financing statement has a registration period. A financing change statement can only be registered to have effect during the balance of the registration period of the financing statement to which it relates (see, for example, ss. 48(5) and 49), or it may extend or reduce that period (s. 51(2)). The registration period that relates to each category of collateral is the registration period of the financing statement. The financing statement is like a tree, and the financing change statements are like its branches; the branches have no separate lifespan; their lifespan is the lifespan of their tree.

Therefore a financing change statement is not intended under the PPSA to affect the registration period of one of the claimed categories of collateral within the financing statement. I am reinforced in this view by the reference in s. 51(3) to a discharge, but not to a partial discharge, as being one way of ending the registration period of a financing statement. When the PPSA refers in s. 52 to a registration which "has ceased to be effective," it refers to the expiry of the registration period of the financing statement, or its discharge by registration.

Although one argument is that the first financing change statement had no effect because it did not fit within a specific section of the Regulations or of the PPSA, it is clear that Chase intended it to have effect, and anyone doing a search would conclude that Chase was claiming no interest in accounts. It is a case where the security interest in accounts ceased to be perfected. By s. 53 of the PPSA, FCS#1 was effective from the time of its registration.

(ii) *The effect of FCS#2*

The respondents have argued that even if the security of Chase in accounts only became unperfected, it could only be reperfected by registration of a financing statement and not a financing change statement. Section 45(1) mandates as follows:

45.—(1) In order to perfect a security interest by registration under this Act, a financing statement shall be registered.

The respondent also relies on s. 52(2):

(2) Where a security interest has been perfected by registration and the registration has ceased to be effective, the security interest may be perfected again by the registration of a financing statement.

However, there are specific situations where registration of a financing change statement is used to perfect the security again when it has become unperfected, specifically under s. 48 where the debtor has transferred the collateral or changed its name and a further registration is required to reperfect after the creditor learns of these events.

Again, it follows the form of the registration scheme that where the financing statement remains alive, any changes or amendments are to be done by way of a financing change statement. It is only when the financing statement either does not yet exist or no longer exists, that a new financing statement is required.

Section 49 of the Act is consistent with this structure. It provides two basket categories of circumstances where a financing change statement may be used to modify a financing statement during its life (registration period). I can see no impediment in the Act to using a financing change statement under s. 49 to reperfect a security interest if the circumstances of subss. (a) or (b) exist.

I also note that s. 49 is not a "saving provision" in that it does not confer any priority. Under s. 53, a financing change statement is effective from the time of its registration. It is only in the case where the financing change statement is used to reperfect that s. 30(6) must be considered. So that, for example, if the original financing statement did not include in line 10 an "x" in the collateral designation for inventory, and that was added by a financing change statement at a later date, the secured interest in inventory would only be perfected from the date of registration of the financing change statement, and not from the original registration date of the financing statement.

I am satisfied that s. 49(b) is applicable in this case. The only possible sections within Part IV which may be considered to provide for the same amendment are ss. 45(l) and 52(2). The first of those sections deals with the need for an original registration of a financing statement, and in my view does not mean that individual categories of collateral cannot be perfected later by a financing change statement. Such an interpretation would contradict the specific references in s. 48 to the use of a financing change statement to reperfect where security has become unperfected. Section 52(2) is not applicable because the registration has not ceased to be effective within the meaning of that subsection as discussed above.

The applicability of s. 49(a) depends upon the meaning of the terms "error or omission" as used in that section. The curative section of the PPSA, s. 46(4), also contains the terms "error or omission," and reads as follows:

(4) A financing statement or financing change statement is not invalidated nor is its effect impaired by reason only of an error or omission therein or in its execution or registration unless a reasonable person is likely to be misled materially by the error or omission.

Under the former PPSA, the curative section (s. 47(5)) limited the errors to clerical errors, and that phrase was narrowly interpreted by the Courts. The new section has deleted that restriction and arguably allows for a broad interpretation of the meaning of "error or omission," within the context of the mechanism of the section.

The section on its face is aimed at the type of error which would have invalidated the financing statement or financing change statement in which it appeared. That would include errors in filling out the form which caused it to be out of conformity with the Regulations, but which, if overlooked, would leave the form with its intended effect. These would include, for example, errors in the spelling of the debtor's name or date of birth.

The section preserves the validity and effectiveness of the registration "unless a reasonable person is likely to be misled materially by the error or omission." In other words, the form is valid in spite of the error, and the court may so declare. However, the section does not provide for correction of an error. Correction is not necessary where the curative provision applies, because the section treats the form as being effective to carry out what it purports to do on its face. (See, however, *Canamsucco Road House Food Co. v. Lngas Ltd.* (1991), 2 PPSAC (2d) 203 (Ont. Gen. Div.), where the section was applied to allow the creditor to correct an error retroactively by filing a financing change statement.)

If the terms "error or omission" in s. 49(a) have the same meaning as in s. 46(4), then the purpose of s. 49(a) would be to provide a mechanism to correct such errors when the secured creditor becomes aware of them, so that there will be no further risk that someone may be materially misled. Again, the correction is only effective from the time of registration of the financing change statement. Before that, the creditor must rely on the curative section.

On the other hand, there are no interpretive constraints contained within s. 49(a) itself, to limit the types of errors or omissions that can be corrected or may be intended to be corrected under that section. From a conceptual point of view, I can see no reason why any error, including errors made deliberately but only recognized as errors afterwards, and including the error of registering the document at all, should not be able to be corrected under this section, when no retroactive priority is accorded by the section.

Because I have held that FCS#2 was properly registered under s. 49(b), I do not need to decide the scope of applicability of s. 49(a) in this case.

(iii) *Application of s. 30(6)*

In my view, s. 30(6) applies to deem the Chase security over accounts to be continuously perfected from the time it was first perfected by the financing statement.

Although it is initially attractive to reason that because the section uses the phrase "becomes unperfected," it was only intended to apply to the situations referred to in s. 48 where that phrase is also used, it is equally arguable that if that limitation had been intended by the Legislature, it would have included that paragraph as a subparagraph of s. 48, or it could have referred to s. 48 within s. 30(6).

Security interests can also become unperfected in other ways, as is demonstrated in this case, and there is no reason to limit the application of s. 30(6), placed as it is within a general list of rules of priority, unless such a limitation is required by the PPSA.

Section 30(6) deems a security interest that was unperfected for a period, to have been continuously perfected from the time of its first perfection except as against persons who "acquired rights in all or part of the collateral" during the period. Chase submits that to give this section any meaning and effect, it cannot be said that a security interest ranking behind the one in question which moves up in priority in respect of the collateral, thereby "acquires rights" in the collateral, because then the section would have no remedial effect.

The argument made by counsel for the respondents is that the sections which it replaces from the prior Act (ss. 53(1)(c) and (d) of the old PPSA), protected from their ambit the rights acquired by any person "by an act or thing done by him during the period," which required a positive act by any such person. However, the language of the new PPSA is passive and therefore can include rights acquired without any positive action by the affected person including just by moving up in priority.

Counsel argues further that the section should be read narrowly, and that it is only intended to cut out a person referred to in s. 30(1) para. 1 who has registered a financing statement during the hiatus period but before its security agreement is signed and therefore before it is perfected, but whose priority would otherwise run from the time of its registration.

Ingenious though this argument is, I cannot give effect to it. I agree with the statement of Montgomery J in *Weber v. Royal Bank* (1984), 4 PPSAC 242 at 246 (Ont. HC), referring to the predecessor section, s. 53(1)(c) of the old PPSA:

In my view, s. 53(1)(c) is remedial in nature. I give it the broad interpretation that the Legislature intended.

The respondents' interpretation would give a very limited effect to the section and would provide scant remedial effect for secured parties who become unperfected, including by the effect of the PPSA itself in s. 48, while a subsequently secured party may receive a windfall benefit.

The purpose of the section is to preserve the original priority positions when security is reperfected. The section only protects a creditor who acquires some new rights in the collateral during the unperfected period. On the evidence, nothing transpired with respect to the collateral during Chase's unperfected period. Because the respondent debenture holders acquired no new rights in the collateral during the period, nor did any new creditor acquire any such rights, thereby raising the issue of priority as between the three of them. I need not consider further.

(d) *Conclusion*

The Chase security was properly reperfected on February 2, 1990 by the registration of the financing change statement, so that its security is effective against the trustee in bankruptcy. The Chase security also maintains its priority in relation to the subsequent debenture security of the respondents.

(2) THE EFFECT OF THE AMALGAMATION OF THE DEBTOR

On June 1, 1989 Kennedy Park Print & Litho Ltd., an Ontario company, amalgamated with its parent, B.L. United Enterprises Inc. The parent had no liabilities, and its only assets were shares of Kennedy Park. The name of the amalgamated company is the same as the original debtor, Kennedy Park Print & Litho Ltd.

Two issues are raised with respect to the amalgamation.

(1) Was there a transfer of the collateral from the debtor to the amalgamated company within the meaning of s. 48, requiring the registration of a financing change statement by Chase after it learned of the amalgamation, in order to maintain perfection or to reperfect its security interest? (There was also a factual issue raised as to whether and if so when Chase learned of the amalgamation in order to trigger s. 48.)

(2) More fundamentally, does Chase have any security over accounts receivable generated by the amalgamated company, as its security agreement is only signed by the amalgamating company, the original Kennedy Park, as debtor? Nor did Chase ever register a financing statement against the amalgamated company as debtor.

Both of these issues seek to examine again the nature of the transaction and transformation known as amalgamation, and in particular, whether in any sense and for any purpose, the amalgamated company is considered to be a new or separate entity from the amalgamating companies.

The issue raised by the second question is most conceptually intriguing. Counsel for the respondents argues that the original debtor company can give security over its own future accounts receivable, but it cannot grant security over the future accounts receivable of another company. The clause that makes the agreement binding on successors and assigns of the debtor does not assist; the effect of that clause is that a successor company must abide by the obligations of the debtor contained in the contract—but it does not nor can it create new obligations of a successor company such as pledging that company's future accounts receivable.

Does this analysis also apply in the case of amalgamation? Will an original debtor company bind the future accounts receivable of an amalgamated company of which it becomes one of the amalgamators, by binding its own future accounts receivable?

The effect of the amalgamation of corporations has been considered and determined by the Supreme Court of Canada in *R. v. Black & Decker Manufacturing Co.*, [1975] 1 SCR 411, 15 CCC (2d) 193, 13 CPR (2d) 97, 43 DLR (3d) 393, 1 NR 299, and in *Witco Chemical Co. v. Oakville (Town)*, [1975] 1 SCR 273, 43 DLR (3d) 413, 1 NR 453, and its conclusions have been most recently discussed and affirmed in this Court in the decision of Henry J in *Loeb Inc. v. Cooper* (1991), 5 OR (3d) 259, 3 BLR (2d) 8 (Gen. Div.).

Those cases hold that the amalgamating companies do not end their lives with amalgamation, but continue to exist in the amalgamated company. There is no "old" company extinguished or "new" company created. There is no transfer of the assets of the amalgamating companies to the amalgamated company; this is indicated by the use of the term "continues" in the statute together with the statement that the amalgamated company "possesses all the property" of the amalgamating companies. In respect of those two terms Dickson J said the following in *Black & Decker* at p. 417 SCR:

> If corporate birth or death were envisaged, one would have expected to find, in the statute, some provision for transfer or conveyance or transmission of assets and not simply the word "possesses," a word which reinforces the concept of continuance ...

(The Canada Corporations Act, RSC 1970, c. C-32 and the Ontario Business Corporations Act, RSO 1990, c. B.16 (the "OBCA") contain the same language; the Canada Business Corporations Act, RSC 1985, c. C-44 contains similar language.)

In the *Loeb* case, Henry J addressed the issue of transfer of assets and liabilities in the context of whether a lease was assigned without consent by an amalgamating company to the amalgamated company upon amalgamation. He found that it was not, applying the Supreme Court of Canada cases referred to and rejecting the contrary analysis of the Saskatchewan Court of Queen's Bench decision in *Crescent Leaseholds Ltd. v. Gerhard Horn Investments Ltd.* (1982), 26 RPR 121, [19831 1 WWR 305, 141 DLR (3d) 679, 19 Sask. R 391 (QB).

In my view, the law is settled that upon amalgamation there is no transfer of assets or liabilities and therefore specifically there is no transfer by the debtor of its interest in the secured collateral upon amalgamation. Consequently s. 48 of the PPSA does not apply.

Although the second question raised by the respondents is not quite so clearly settled, to accede to the argument would be to start the law down the same path from which the Supreme Court diverted it in the two 1975 decisions, because the argument requires a finding that the amalgamated company is a "new" company, not the debtor.

The full reconciliation of the concept behind amalgamation has often been recognized as difficult. As Kelly JA said in *Stanward Corp. v. Denison Mines Ltd.*, [1966] 2 OR 585 at 592, 57 DLR (2d) 674 (CA) [aff'd [1968] SCR 441, 67 DLR (2d) 743]:

> While it may be difficult to comprehend the exact metamorphosis which takes place, it is within the Legislature's competence to provide that what were hitherto two shall continue as one.

Section 179(b) of the OBCA deals with the status of existing contracts of amalgamating companies: the amalgamated company is "subject to" the *contracts*, liabilities and obligations of each of the amalgamating companies. In my view, the use of the phrase "subject to" is significant. When a corporation is *subject to* a contract, it is not just bound by the contract and bound by its terms, as a successor or assignee of the original debtor;

rather it is as a party to the contract, so that the amalgamating company stands in the shoes of the debtor for the purpose of contracts entered into by the debtor. Again, this is consistent with the concept that the original debtor company continues its existence within the amalgamated company, and that the amalgamated company is not a new company.

Therefore the amalgamated company named Kennedy Park is subject to the security agreements signed by the amalgamating company, Kennedy Park, with Heidelberg and which were assigned to Chase. There is no new "debtor." Consequently, the accounts receivable of the amalgamated Kennedy Park constitute part of the collateral over which Chase has a perfected security interest. As well, no new financing statement nor financing change statement need be registered.

In light of the decision on the legal question raised, it is unnecessary to make a finding as to whether and if so when Chase learned of the amalgamation.

• • •

CONCLUSION

The attack by Arthur Andersen Inc. as trustee in bankruptcy of Kennedy Park and as receiver on behalf of Lisa Thomas and George Schwartz, on the security of Heidelberg and Chase fails on all grounds.

Application allowed.

NOTES AND QUESTIONS

1) Are you convinced that the distinction between discharge and "unperfect" which the court used is sound? Feldman J stated that "[t]here was no suggestion that the registration of the discharge had the effect of releasing the security between the debtor and the secured party. Neither did the registration of FCS#1 have that effect." Is there a difference between "discharge of a registration" and discharge of a security interest"? Has the court confused the two? Could the court have reached the conclusion it ultimately did without having to draw this distinction?

2) Under the Acts based on the CCPPSL model, the changes in the registration (deleting and then adding back accounts) would have been treated as amendments to the registration. See, e.g., BCPPSA s. 44(3), which provides that "[a]n amendment to a registration, whether the registration is valid or invalid, may be made by registering a financing change statement at any time during the period that the registration is effective and the amendment is effective from the date the financing change statement is registered to the expiry of the registration being amended."

3) Note particularly the comments of the court with respect to the relationship between OPPSA s. 49(a) and 46(4). Assume that the original registration was "invalid" in that it does not pass the test of s. 46(4) (e.g., it does not contain the correct name of the debtor). Can this registration be amended to make it valid, or is it necessary to register a new financing statement containing the correct name of the debtor? See BCPPSA s. 44(3) set out in 2), *supra*.

4) In *Heidelberg* the court concluded that s. 30(6) "only protects a creditor who acquires some new rights in the collateral during the unperfected period." Surely this statement must be taken in context; the section is not limited in its effect to rights of creditors. Are the categories of the "persons" referred to in the section broader and more numerous than the persons mentioned in s. 20 who have priority over an unperfected security interest? What if the person acquiring an interest during the period of unperfection is a buyer of the collateral who was aware at the time of the purchase that the collateral was subject to the unperfected security interest? Do the categories of persons referred to in s. 30(6) include a secured party holding a security interest that, prior to the period of unperfection, was subordinate, who (with or without knowledge of the unperfected security interest), makes an additional advance to the debtor during the period of unperfection? What is the position of a subsequent secured party who registers a financing statement during the period of unperfection, but who does not take a security interest in the debtor's property until after the prior security interest has been perfected?

5) What is the status under the OPPSA of a registration that has been discharged by the registry as a result of fraudulent or unauthorized conduct on the part of the debtor or someone else? Is a discharge legally effective only when it is authorized by the secured party?

6) The Acts based on the CCPPSL model approach the problem that arose in *Heidelberg* and the problems raised in 4) and 5), *supra*, quite differently. See, e.g., SPPSA s. 35(7), which provides that where a registration (i) lapses as a result of a failure to renew the registration, or (ii) is discharged without authorization or in error and the secured party registers the security interest not later than 30 days after the lapse or discharge, the lapse of discharge does not affect the priority status of the security interest in relation to a competing perfected security interest that, immediately prior to the lapse or discharge, had a subordinate priority position, except to the extent that the competing security interest secured advances made or contracted for after the lapse or discharge and prior to the registration. See also SPPSA s. 51.

7) OPPSA s. 30(6) and its counterparts in CCPPSL jurisdictions give rise to an important question of interpretation. Consider the following scenario: Prior to lapse of his registration SP 1 had priority over SP 2 because of prior registration. After SP 1's registration lapsed, SP 3 perfected a security interest in the same collateral. Can it be assumed that the renewal of SP 1's registration under s. 30(6) restores SP 1's priority over SP 2? If it does, a circular priority problem results: SP 1 over SP 2 over SP 3. For a discussion of the issues involved in the context of the former OPPSA, see Lysaght and Simmonds, "The Lapsed Registration Problem under the Ontario Personal Property Security Act" (1979-80), 4 *CBLJ* 442. Circular priority problems of the kind that this scenario exemplifies are not without solution. Consider the following situations:

Situation 1
SP 1 has a claim for $1,000
SP 2 has a claim for $1,000
SP 3 has a claim for $1,000
On disposition the collateral is worth $1,000

One approach is to break the circle by looking at the risk each party undertook. SP 2 knew he would be subject to a prior claim of $1,000 when he entered into the security agreement. The same applies to SP 3. In view of the fact that the collateral does not exceed $1,000 in value, the total amount should be paid to SP 1 since to do so would not subject SP 2 and SP 3 to any losses they did not expect to incur when they entered into their security agreements.

Situation 2
SP 1 has a claim for $1,000
SP 2 has a claim for $1,000
SP 3 has a claim for $1,000
On disposition the collateral is worth $2,000

If the above-noted approach is used, SP 1 gets $0; SP 2 gets $1,000; and SP 3 gets $1,000.

This approach has been criticized because SP 1 takes the entire amount when the value of the collateral ranges from 0 to X and thereafter as the value increases beyond X, SP 1's share decreases toward 0. When that point has been reached SP 1 receives nothing until SP 2 and SP 3 have been paid in full. In Situation 1 above, SP 1 got the entire proceeds of the disposition of the collateral. However, if the sale of the collateral had yielded $2,000, SP 1 would get nothing. Point X is reached where the value of the collateral is $1,000. See generally Gilmore, *Security Interests in Personal Property* 1965, volume II, chapter 13. Circular priority problems can also arise in other PPSA contexts. See e.g. *Rich-Wood Kitchens Ltd. v. National Trust Co., infra*, chapter 7.

CHAPTER FIVE

Perfected and Unperfected Security Interests and Rules of Priority

Part III is the longest part of the OPPSA and deals with many of the most complex issues in modern chattel security law. The Part begins with a description of the meaning of perfected security interest (s. 19) and the procedural means of achieving perfection (ss. 21-27), both topics that have been previously discussed in chapter 3. Located between the perfection provisions is s. 20, which spells out the important consequences of a security interest *not* being perfected. Much of the rest of Part III is taken up in prescribing the priority rules that govern competing security interests in a wide variety of situations (ss. 30-35). A security interest that is perfected does not necessarily prevail over other non-security interests. The secured party may have expressly or impliedly authorized the disposition of the collateral (s. 28(1)). Even when he has not, rules of mercantile convenience dictate circumstances when third party rights should override even a perfected security interest. These rules appear in ss. 28-29.

The pre-PPSA registration statutes were invariably much leaner and usually confined themselves to establishing a registration requirement and to spelling out the consequences of non-compliance. A distinctive feature of Part III of the OPPSA is that it provides, in addition, a compendium of reasonably systematized priority rules. Previously these had to be elicited from a conflicting mass of common law, equitable and statutory rules which often differed, depending on the nature of the collateral or the particular security device being used.

SUBORDINATION OF UNPERFECTED SECURITY INTERESTS

Introduction

Section 20 of the OPPSA is a modern version of the sections in the pre-PPSA registration statutes spelling out the consequences of non-registration. Almost invariably they provided that an unregistered security agreement (bill of sale or chattel mortgage, conditional sale, assignment of book debts, or corporate security) was "void" against subsequent purchasers and mortgagees for value and without notice of the prior security interest, and against execution creditors and a trustee in bankruptcy or other creditors' representative.

Section 20 is not easy reading but, if the refinements are ignored, its provisions have a familiar face. Put simply, an unperfected security interest is "subordinated" to four classes of competing claimants, *viz.* (1) those who have a perfected security interest in the same collateral and who are expressly given priority over the unperfected security interest under the OPPSA or any other Act; (2) execution creditors and such like; (3) a trustee in bankruptcy and other creditors' representative; and (4) a transferee of the collateral. Is there a common bond between these classes? Is it based on actual or assumed prejudice resulting from the undisclosed security interest? How is an execution creditor prejudiced? A trustee in bankruptcy? Is it wise for a creditor to give unsecured credit because the debtor does not appear to have given an existing security interest? Has the common law's long standing hostility to concealed liens and against the preferred treatment of one creditor over other creditors also helped to shape s. 20? What is the difference between s. 20 treating an unperfected security interest as subordinated and pre-PPSA declarations that it was "void"? (In practice, the courts held that "void" meant "voidable" and that repossession and disposition of the collateral by the secured party cured the failure to register. See *In re Shelley Films*, [1963] 1 OR 431 (CA).)

Section 20 is a revised version of old s. 22, as can be seen from the following comparison:

Comparison of s. 22 of the old Act and s. 20 of the new OPPSA

Old Section 22

22.—(1) Except as provided in subsection (3), an unperfected security interest is subordinate to,

    (a) the interest of a person,

        (i) who is entitled to a priority under this or any other Act, or

        (ii) who, without knowledge of the security interest and before it is perfected, assumes control of the collateral through legal process, or

        (iii) who represents the creditors of the debtor as assignee for the benefit of creditors, trustee in bankruptcy or receiver; and

    (b) the interest of a transferee who is not a secured party to the extent that he gives value without knowledge of the

New Section 20

20—(1) Except as provided in subsection (3), until perfected, a security interest,

    (a) in collateral is subordinate to the interest of,

        (i) a person who has a perfected security interest in the same collateral or who has a lien given under any other Act or by a rule of law or who has a priority under any other Act, or

        (ii) a person who assumes control of the collateral through execution, attachment, garnishment, charging order, equitable execution or other legal process, or

        (iii) all persons entitled by the Creditor's Relief Act or otherwise to participate in the distribution of the property over which a person described in subclause (ii) has assumed control, or the proceeds of such property;

    (b) in collateral is not effective against a person who represents the creditors of the debtor, including an

Old Section 22 (cont.)

    security interest and before it is
perfected,

           (i) of chattel paper, documents
of title, securities, instruments or
goods in bulk or otherwise, not in
the ordinary course of the business
of the transferor and where the
transferee receives delivery of the
collateral, or

           (ii) of intangibles.

    (2) The rights of a person under
subclause (1)(a)(iii) in respect of the collateral
are referable to the date from which his status
has effect and arise without regard to the
personal knowledge of the representative if
any represented creditor was, on the relevant
date, without knowledge of the unperfected
security interest.

    (3) A purchase-money security interest
that is registered before or within ten days
after the debtor's possession of the collateral
commences has priority over,

New Section 20 (cont.)

    assignee for the benefit of creditors and a
trustee in bankruptcy;

        (c) in chattel paper, documents of
title, securities, instruments or goods is
not effective against a transferee thereof
who takes under a transfer that does not
secure payment or performance of an
obligation and who gives value and
receives delivery thereof without
knowledge of the security interest;

        (d) in intangibles other than
accounts is not effective against a
transferee thereof who takes under a
transfer that does not secure payment or
performance of an obligation and who
gives value without knowledge of the
security interest.

    (2) The rights of a person,

        (a) who has a statutory lien referred
to in subclause (1)(a)(i) arise,

           (i) in the case of the
bankruptcy of the debtor, at the
effective date of the bankruptcy, or

           (ii) in any other case, when the
lienholder has taken possession or
otherwise done everything
necessary to make the lien
enforceable in accordance with the
provisions of the Act creating the
lien;

        (b) under clause 1(b) in respect of
the collateral are to be determined as of
the date from which the person's
representative status takes effect.

    (3) A purchase-money security interest
that is perfected by registration,

        (a) in collateral, other than an
intangible, before or within ten days
after,

           (i) the debtor obtains
possession of the collateral, or

Old Section 22 (cont.)   New Section 20 (cont.)

                                        (ii) a third party, at the request
of the debtor, obtains possession of
the collateral,

whichever is earlier; or

     (b) in an intangible before or within
ten days after the attachment of the
security interest in the intangible,

     (a) an interest set out in subclause
(1)(a)(ii) or (iii); and

     (b) transfers in bulk or otherwise,
not in the ordinary course of business,
occurring between the security interest's
attaching and its being registered.

has priority over,

     (c) an interest set out in subclause
(1)(a)(ii) and is effective against a person
described in clause (1)(b); and

     (d) the interest of a transferee of
collateral that forms all or part of a sale
in bulk within the meaning of the Bulk
Sales Act.

The following notes and cases are designed to explain the meaning of the different parts of s. 20 and the reasons for the changes from the old section.

Subordination to Perfected Security Interests (S. 20(1)(a)(i))

New s. 20(1)(a)(i) has been expanded to cover three types of persons: (1) persons with a perfected security interest; (2) those who hold a statutory or common law lien; and (3) persons who are given priority under any other Act. The reasons for subordinating an unperfected security interest in the first and third cases are reasonably self-evident. However, giving priority to all perfected security interests appears to conflict with new ss. 33(1) and (2). What is the reason for preferring all lienholders over an unperfected security interest? Is it assumed to prejudice the lienholder whose lien arises before the security interest is perfected? How is a government agency that is given a statutory lien for monies owing to it by the debtor prejudiced by an unperfected security interest? "Lien" is not defined but presumably means the right to retain or seize all or some of the debtor's assets and to sell them to satisfy the debtor's obligation to the lienholder. Note too s. 20(2) on the time of attachment of a statutory lien. The reason is explained in Ontario *Supplementary Report*, 1986, at 31, Commentary, para. 2.

Execution Creditors, etc. (S. 20(1)(a)(ii) and (iii))

The new Act amplifies the existing provision to make it clear that remedies of self-help are excluded and that the execution creditor's state of knowledge with respect to the unperfected security interest is no longer relevant. The reasons for these changes are as follows (Advisory Committee's Report, 1984, at 41, paras. 3-4):

3. Subclause 1(a)(ii), as worded at present, accords priority to an execution creditor only where he acts without knowledge of the unperfected security interest and before its perfection. The references to knowledge and the time of perfection have been deleted. The corresponding

provision in the Uniform, Manitoba and Saskatchewan Acts does not contain a test involving knowledge. The execution creditor should be protected because he puts effort and expense into obtaining judgment and proceeding to execute. The secured party who neglects to perfect his security interest should not be able to prejudice the rights of the execution creditor by simply notifying him of the existence of the security interest. The words "time of perfection" are an unnecessary duplication since, by its opening words, subsection (1) only applies to unperfected security interests.

4. A second proposed amendment to subclause 1(a)(ii) sets out examples of various legal processes by which a judgment creditor may assume control of the collateral. The purpose of the amendment is to make it clear that distress and self-help are excluded as means of assuming control of collateral and thereby achieving priority over an unperfected security interest. The present Act is unclear as to whether an execution creditor who assumes control of collateral may, by reason of s. 69, escape his obligation to share ratably with other creditors under the Creditors' Relief Act. Subclause 1(a)(iii) of the Draft Act makes it clear that the scheme of the Creditors' Relief Act takes priority over the rights of the individual seizing creditor.

Why does knowledge of an unperfected security interest remain relevant in s. 20(1)(c) and (d)? *Cf.* the priority rules in ss. 30 and 33, discussed below in this chapter and in chapter 6, where knowledge is irrelevant. For a critical discussion of these issues, see Felsenfeld, "Knowledge as a Factor in Determining Priorities under the Uniform Commercial Code" (1967), 42 *NYU L Rev.* 246. "Knowledge" is defined in s. 69 of the Act.

Meaning of "Is Subordinate To" (S. 20(1)(a)), Constitutional Questions and Other Issues

1) In *International Harvest Credit Corp. of Can. v. Touche Ross Ltd.* (1986), 6 PPSAC 138, the Saskatchewan Court of Appeal experienced considerable difficulties applying the meaning of "is subordinate to" to s. 20(1)(d) of the Saskatchewan Act in the context of an unperfected deemed security lease. Bell's Dairy Limited went bankrupt having in its possession five vehicles on lease from IHCC. The trustee in bankruptcy took possession of the vehicles and refused to release them to IHCC. The trustee took the position, among other defences, that, by failing to perfect its interest in the leases, IHCC had lost the right to recover the vehicles from the trustee.

IHCC responded that s. 20(1)(d) of the Saskatchewan Act only provided that an unperfected security interest was subordinate "to the interest of" a trustee, that a trustee under the Bankruptcy Act [see now BIA, s. 71(2)] only acquires such rights to the debtor's property as the debtor itself has. Under the present leases Bell's Dairy only had possessory rights so long as it complied with the terms of the lease. Consequently, these were the only rights that devolved on the trustee.

The Court of Appeal (speaking through Cameron JA) rejected the argument. In a long and elaborate judgment, Cameron JA traced the history of the provisions in the Saskatchewan Act which deem one-year plus leases to be security leases whether they were so in fact or not. He concluded that "is subordinate to" should be given the same meaning as "is void" under the pre-PPSA provincial registration statutes. He was also satisfied, on the basis of well established doctrine, that a trustee wears several hats and represents the interests of the bankrupt's creditors as well as succeeding to the bankrupt's property rights.

Could the question before the court not have been answered more simply? Under the Saskatchewan Act (as under the Ontario Act) the debtor is deemed to be the beneficial owner of the property in which the secured party obtains (or retains) a security interest. See s. 2 of the Ontario Act. This concept is fundamental in all PPS legislation. Under the Saskatchewan Act a one-year plus lease is treated as a security lease, from which it follows that the lessor acquires the status of a secured party and the lessee becomes the beneficial owner of the leased property in the same way as the lessee under a true security lease does. Hence when the Saskatchewan Act subordinates the lessor's rights to the trustee's interests it is the *entirety* of the lessor's rights that are being subordinated and the trustee is entitled to deal with the leased property free of the lessor's claims. This reasoning may seem artificial and contrived but the artificiality derives from the treatment of one-year plus leases as security leases. Once this hurdle is overcome, applying s.20(1)(d) becomes straightforward.

In Ontario, the Advisory Committee which drafted the new Ontario Act was sufficiently impressed with the difficulty of applying the "is subordinate to" test to a trustee in bankruptcy that the wording was changed to read "is not effective against" a trustee in bankruptcy. See s. 19(1)(b).

2) *Constitutional Issues*. In *Paccar Financial Services v. Sinco Trucking* (1989), 57 DLR (4th) 439, a constitutional challenge was launched against s. 20(1)(d) of the Saskatchewan Act on the grounds that it invaded the exclusive federal jurisdiction in matters of bankruptcy and insolvency (Constitution Act, s. 91(21)). The Saskatchewan Court of Appeal rejected the challenge and took the position that s. 20(1)(d) was merely an incidental part of a broader provision dealing with the consequences of an unperfected security interest. The Court also found there was no conflict between s. 20(1)(d) of the Saskatchewan Act and the Bankruptcy Act, and that therefore the paramountcy doctrine did not apply to give primacy to the federal provisions. The Court relied in part on an earlier decision of the Supreme Court of Canada, *Robinson v. Countrywide Factors Ltd.*, [1978] 1 SCR 573, in which the Supreme Court had upheld the constitutional validity of the Saskatchewan Fraudulent Preferences Act (now RSS 1978, c. F-21) even though there were conflicting provisions in the Bankruptcy Act.

The Court in *Sinco Trucking* could also have invoked the following long-standing provision in the Bankruptcy and Insolvency Act (BIA):

72.(1) The provisions of this Act shall not be deemed to abrogate or supersede the substantive provisions of any other law or statute relating to property and civil rights that are not in conflict with this Act, and the trustee is entitled to avail himself of all rights and remedies provided by that law or statute as supplementary to and in addition to the rights and remedies provided by this Act.

The constitutional position was also raised by the secured parties in *Re Lambert*, *supra*, chapter 4, but the Ontario Court of Appeal found it unnecessary to address the issue. In an article in the *Canadian Bar Review* published in 1992 ("The Conflict Between Canadian Personal Property Security Acts and the Federal Bankruptcy Act: The War is Over" (1992), 71 *Can. Bar Rev.* 77), which excited secured parties at the time, Roman and Sweatman argued that recent decisions of the Supreme Court of Canada supported their claim that it was not competent for the provincial PPS Acts to invalidate unperfected security interests against a trustee in bankruptcy. The decisions they relied on were *Deputy*

Minister of Revenue v. Rainville, [1980] 1 SCR 35; *Deloitte Haskins and Sells Limited v. Workers' Compensation Board*, [1985] 1 SCR 785; *FDBD v. Commission de la Santé et de la Securité du Travail*, [1988] 1 SCR 1081; and *British Columbia v. Henfrey Samson Belair Ltd.*, [1989] 2 SCR 24. These cases involved the interpretation of the pre-1992 versions of ss. 136 and 67 of the BIA and whether there was a conflict between these provisions and provincial legislation conferring priority status on provincial government lien claims. The Supreme Court held that there was a conflict and that the provincial claims were only entitled to the ranking accorded them in the BIA. In a reply to Roman and Sweatman ("Personal Property Security and Bankruptcy: There Is No War—A Reply to Roman and Sweatman" (1993), 72 *Can. Bar Rev.* 44), Prof. Ziegel argued that the Supreme Court decisions were easily distinguishable and that there is no conflict between provisions such as s. 20(1)(b) of the OPPSA and the BIA. On the contrary, he noted, s. 72(1) of the BIA (cited above) makes it clear that Parliament intended provincial law to continue to apply unless it directly conflicted with the BIA provisions. Further treatment of the constitutional position will be found in chapter 12 of this casebook.

3) *Creditors' Representatives.* With respect to the types of creditors' representatives enumerated in s. 22(1)(a)(iii) of the old Act, Catzman et al. observe (at 114):

> Trustees in bankruptcy and assignees for the benefit of creditors are persons whose powers derive from The Bankruptcy Act, or statutes like The Assignments and Preferences Act. "Receiver" is a generic term. Status as a receiver does not depend on what the person is called. It depends on his having the attributes characteristic of a receiver in chancery, to wit, he must be an officer judicially appointed and responsible to the Court, with the object of preserving property pending litigation to decide the rights of the parties, but a person such as a liquidator under The Winding-Up Act, or The Corporations Act, who is of that kind is a receiver in the present context, although not so styled. Conversely one without judicial warrant for his appointment though called a receiver is not.

Does s. 20(1)(b) of the new Act change the essential meaning of old s. 22(1)(a)(iii)? Is it correct to say, as Catzman implies it is, that a court appointed receiver always represents the interests of all the debtor's creditors as distinct from the interests of a single creditor?

4) *Time from which status of representative takes effect (new Act, s. 20(2)(b)).* The rights of a creditors' representative "are to be determined as of the date from which the person's representative status takes effect." Under s. 71(1) of the Bankruptcy Act, RSC 1985, c. B-3, "[t]he bankruptcy shall be deemed to have relation back to and to commence at the time of the filing of the petition on which a receiving order is made or of the filing of an assignment with the official receiver." The effect of this section on old s. 22(2) was held to be that "the date from which the status of the trustee has effect is the date of filing of the petition": *Re Hillstead Ltd.* (1979), 103 DLR (3d) 347, at 349 (Ont. SC in Bkcy). In this case, registration of a financing statement after the filing of the petition in bankruptcy but before the receiving order came too late to save the security interest from subordination to the trustee in bankruptcy.

5) *Delayed Perfection of Security Interest.* Section 47(3) of the old Act provided that a financing statement had to be filed within 30 days of the execution of the security agreement, otherwise the filing was ineffectual. This time the filing requirement, which used to be common in the pre-PPSA registration statutes, does not appear in Article 9. It

was retained in the 1967 Ontario Act on the recommendations of the Ontario Law Reform Commission. The Commission was afraid that a free filing period would encourage secret liens and collusive agreements between a debtor and a secured party not to file a financing statement until the debtor was about to go bankrupt—but still in sufficient time to enable the secured party to comply with the Act.

In a 1980 interim draft bill, the Advisory Committee recommended the abolition of the time filing requirement on the grounds that it caused more trouble than it was worth. Nevertheless, on the insistence of the Ministry of the Attorney General, the draft bill contained a complex "shelter period" provision to protect the debtor's creditors from the effects of a delayed filing. The provision was much criticized by the profession and it was deleted from the 1984 draft bill prepared by the Advisory Committee. The Committee replaced it with a new s. 20(4), which read as follows:

20.—(4) A security interest that attached more than sixty days before the effective date of the bankruptcy of the debtor and that was perfected less than thirty days before that date shall be deemed to be unperfected as against the trustee in bankruptcy.

This provision, too, was later deleted when it was discovered that the Ministry of the Attorney General no longer insisted on any kind of shelter period. Was the deletion of s. 20(4) a wise decision? Will it encourage the mischiefs feared by the OLRC in 1964? In practice, delayed filings usually occur because the secured party forgot to file the financing statement promptly or because the first filing was defective in some respect and the defect only came to light shortly before the debtor's bankruptcy.

The Americans have long been concerned with delayed perfection of security interests on the eve of the debtor's bankruptcy (sometimes referred to as "pocket liens") and with security interests given for amendment debts. Such security interests were treated as voidable preferences in s. 60(a) of the pre-1978 Bankruptcy Act. For the current provisions see Bankruptcy Code 1978, 11 USC s. 547. The reviewable transactions and preference provisions in the successive bills for the revision of the Canadian Bankruptcy Act have also contained a new provision making the time of registration (where registration is required to make the transfer effective against third parties) the deemed date of transfer where the registration is not made within 30 days of the actual date of the transfer. See e.g., Bill S-14, 27-18 Eliz. II, 1978-79, s. 183. However, no revised Act has been adopted so far and the important amendments to the BIA adopted by Parliament in 1992 (SC 1992, c.27) did not include this provision. (What does this tell us about secured creditors' influence in the drafting of bankruptcy legislation?)

Transferees Other Than Secured Parties (S. 20(1)(c))

Section 22(1)(b) of the old Act only protected the interest of a transferee "to the extent that" she gave value without knowledge of the security interest and before it was perfected. The impact of the "to the extent that" restriction is illustrated by the following case.

Royal Bank of Canada v. Dawson Motors (Guelph) Ltd.
(1981), 39 CBR (NS) 304 (Ont.)

[For the facts of the case, see *supra*, chapter 4 in "Notes" following *Re West Bay Sales*. The following extract only deals with the court's interpretation of s. 22(1)(b).]

MCNEELY CO. CT. J.: Section 22 of the [old] Personal Property Security Act deals with priorities between an unperfected security interest and a transferee of the collateral. So far as relevant it reads as follows:

22.—(1) ... an unperfected security interest is subordinate to ...
    (b) the interest of a transferee who is not a secured party to the extent that he gives value without knowledge of the security interest and before it is perfected ...

It is clear that on 15th August the Royal Bank's security interest was unperfected and that Dawson Motors had no knowledge of the security interest. The parties to this action having agreed that Dawson Motors "became owners of the collateral on the evening of August 15th" the plaintiff's security interest as chattel mortgagees would be subordinate to the interests of the defendant to the extent that the defendant gave value before the security interest was perfected.

Since at 8:47 a.m. on 16th August the plaintiff's security interest became perfected by registration, the value given by the defendant at 1:00 p.m. on 16th August, consisting of the transfer of the Chevrolet vehicle and the $1,800 cheque, is of no avail to the defendant so far as s. 22 is concerned.

To succeed in his claim for priority the defendant must establish that it gave value before 1:00 p.m. on 16th August and if it can do this it will enjoy a priority limited to the value so given. The "value" alleged by the defendant is the promise by Dawson Motors to transfer the Chevrolet and to pay the $1,800. This promise was given on 15th August.

I have already found that one reason why the transfer of the Chevrolet and the payment of the $1,800 was to take place on 16th August was to enable Dawson Motors to make a Personal Property Security Act search. It is implicit in the argument of the defendant that notwithstanding the fact that Dawson Motors was fixed with notice of the plaintiff's security interest at 8:47 a.m. on 16th August, the defendant was free to complete the transaction by turning over the entire consideration to Mr. Woods at 1:00 p.m. on 16th August because its original promise to do so was made on 15th August 1979 before it was fixed with notice of the security interest. There is no doubt on the evidence that Mr. Woods was perpetrating a fraud in selling the Thunderbird and that the defendant's promise to Mr. Woods would be unenforceable by Woods once the defendant had notice of the prior security interest. The argument advanced on behalf of the defendant in this case, if valid, would lead to the absurd result that Dawson Motors, even after having notice of the security interest and hence of the fraud, could assist Mr. Woods in completing the fraudulent transaction by turning over the Chevrolet and the $1,800 and could do this without harmful consequences to either itself or Woods because it was being done pursuant to the then unenforceable promise made to Woods before perfection of the security interest.

It is clear to me that the promise made by Dawson Motors to Mr. Woods does not in the circumstances of this case constitute "value" within the meaning of s. 22(1) of the

Personal Property Security Act of a type capable of subordinating the security interest of the plaintiff to the interest of Dawson Motors: Catzman, the learned author of Personal Property Security Law, at 116 expresses the view that a wholly executory promise not accompanied by any change of position is insufficient to form the basis of a priority under s. 22 of the Personal Property Security Act. With this view I am in respectful agreement. A claim for damages was also asserted by the plaintiff but no evidence was led with respect to it and no damages were in fact proved. The claim for damages is accordingly dismissed. The plaintiff is entitled to its costs of this action against the defendant.

Application granted.

NOTES

1) The court's interpretation of the meaning of "to the extent that" is supported by pre-Code negotiable instruments law and, now, UCC 3-303(a). See Ziegel, "Comment" (1981-82), 6 *CBLJ* 507. In other words, s. 22(1)(b) only protected reliance interests. Given facts like those in *Dawson Motors*, is this a desirable result, or should a distinction be drawn between constructive notice of a perfected security interest and actual knowledge thereof? If the transferee has paid the agreed price for the collateral before the security interest is perfected, must he surrender the collateral on being reimbursed for his actual outlay? What is the position if the current market price of the collateral is higher than the value he paid for it?

2) To avoid these complications, "to the extent that" is deleted in new s. 20(1)(c). See Ontario Report, 1984, at 42, para. 6. Has it resolved all the constructional difficulties of old s. 22(1)(b)? In the light of *Dawson Motors* is it conceivable, where a transferee has only paid part of the purchase price before the security interest was perfected, that a court would still restrict the purchaser's priority to the extent of his actual investment? If the answer is no, who would be entitled to the balance of the purchase price?

3) Why do s. 20(1)(c) and (d) distinguish between a transfer of tangible and non-tangible collateral? Why is delivery of the collateral in the former case regarded as essential if the transferee is to receive priority over the unperfected security interest? Compare s. 20(1)(c) and the wording of OPPSA s. 28(1) with the decision in *Tanbro Fabrics Corp. v. Deering Milliken Inc.* (1976), 350 NE 2d 590 (NYCA), reproduced, *infra*, in chapter 9.

BASIC PRIORITY RULES

The pre-PPSA priority rules between competing consensual security interests were a complicated amalgam of common law, equitable and statutory rules. However rational in their historical and doctrinal origins, these are difficult to justify in the context of modern financing arrangements. More particularly, the common law placed primary emphasis on the locus of legal title and therefore gave priority to the person who held it unless he was estopped from denying the authority of the person in possession of the collateral to deal with it or unless he had failed to comply with an applicable registration requirement. The priority of equitable security interests was generally governed by the order of their creation, but this rule was qualified in at least three respects. *First*, as has been noted earlier (*supra*, chapter 1), an equitable security interest could be defeated by a purchaser for value and without notice of the legal interest (recall *Joseph v. Lyons* (1884-85), 15 QBD 280 (CA)). *Second*, floating charges were governed by their own priority rules which turned as much on the distinctive character ascribed to the security device by the courts as to its equitable origins. In the *third* place, under the rule in *Dearle v. Hall*, where there were successive assignments of the same chose in action (and originally such assignments were only recognized in equity) priority went to the assignor who first gave notice of his assignment to the debtor.

The PPSA replaces this disparate set of rules with a much better integrated and functionally oriented regime of rules. This is not to say that they work effortlessly and that their fairness and efficiency will necessarily commend themselves to all. We begin with the basic priority rules in s. 35 of the OPPSA. Although the section describes them as only operating where no other provision applies, it is best to treat them as the starting point for an understanding of the Act's priority structure. The rules in s. 35 may be paraphrased as follows:

a) *Rule of First to Register.* If the competing security interests have all been perfected by registration, then the order of registration determines the order of priority (s. 30(1)). The time of attachment or perfection of the interest is not relevant.

b) *Rule of First to Register or to Perfect by Other Means.* If one security interest is perfected by registration and the other security interest is perfected by other means, then if registration occurs first that security interest will take priority. The converse rule applies if the non-registration perfection precedes registration (s. 30(1)2(i)).

c) *Rule of First to Perfect.* If both security interests are perfected without registration, then the security interest which is perfected first takes priority (s. 30(1)2(ii)).

d) *Rule of First to Attach.* If none of the competing security interests have been perfected, they rank according to the order of attachment (s. 30(1)4).

PROBLEM

January 1   A advances $50,000 to X against the security of goods but does not register a financing statement or take possession of the collateral.

January 7   B advances $25,000 to X secured by the same goods and takes possession of them.

January 8   A registers a financing statement with respect to his rights in the collateral.

When did each security interest attach? When was it perfected? Between A and B, who prevails in the priority contest as to the goods? Would B's knowledge on January 7 of A's interest affect your answer? Would your answer be different if B had registered a financing statement on January 7 and had not taken possession of the goods?

What is the justification for the first to file rule? Is it based on the need for certainty between competing interests or on the need for predictability and safety by the party who first registers? See further Jackson and Kronman, "Secured Financing and Priorities Among Creditors" (1979), 88 *Yale LJ* 1143, at 1161-69, also partly reproduced later.

The new priority rules differ in one important respect from the old rules. Section 35(1) of the old Act read:

35.—(1) If no other provision of this Act is applicable, priority between security interests in the same collateral shall be determined,

(a) by the order of registration, if the security interests have been perfected by registration;

(b) by the order of perfection, unless the security interests have been perfected by registration; or

(c) by the order of attachment under subsection 1 of section 12, if no security interest has been perfected.

The important differences are between s. 30(1)2 of the new Act and s. 35(1)(b) of the old Act. The Report of the Advisory Committee, 1984, at 52-53, explains the reasons for the changes in s. 30(1) as follows:

1. This section [s. 30(1)] is derived from s. 35 of the present Act. Subsection (1) has been completely revised in order to clarify the basic rules which govern all priority disputes between perfected security interests in the same collateral which are not otherwise governed by another provision in the Act. The first rule is a restatement of s. 35(1)(a) of the present Act. The second rule contains the only change in policy. Under present s. 35(1)(b) when one competing security interest has been perfected by registration and a second security interest has been perfected by possession, the first secured party to perfect its security interest prevails. Under the proposed second rule the result may be reversed. The secured party who registers a financing statement before the perfection of the possessory security interest will have priority even though its security interest is perfected afterwards. The effect of the new rule is that the competing security interests will rank according to whether perfection or registration occurs first. The theory is that a creditor who intends to take a security interest and perfect by possession can learn of the existence of the other security interest by doing a personal property security search. This change in principle has been made in the interest of achieving uniformity with s. 33(1) of the Uniform Act and s. 9-312(5)(a) of the Uniform Commercial Code.

2. The principle contained in s. 35(1)(b) of the present Act is still retained for the purposes of determining priority between two security interests perfected otherwise than by registration (the third rule in subsection (1)). Where there is a priority contest between two competing possessory security interests, the first to be perfected will rank first. The fourth rule is substantially the same as s. 35(1)(c). The order of attachment governs priority between two unperfected security interests in the same collateral.

(The provisions in s. 30 dealing with future advance clauses will be dealt with later in this chapter.)

Re-examine the Problem above. Would your answers be the same if the competing priorities were governed by s. 30(1)?

The Robert Simpson Company Ltd. v. Shadlock and Duggan
(1981), 31 OR (2d) 612 (SC)

GRAY J: The issue is whether priority as between competing security interests in the same collateral security is determined under The Personal Property Security Act by whoever perfects or registers first or whether actual notice may defeat a claim to priority based on prior registration or prior perfection.

It was agreed that if priority is determined only by registration or perfection, the Plaintiff has no claim in law but if the doctrine of actual notice prevails, the Defendant cannot succeed on the application to strike out the Plaintiff's Statement of Claim. Between February 18th, 1976 and June 24th, 1976, pursuant to eleven Conditional Sale Contracts, the Plaintiff sold to the debtor certain chattels for installation at a motel property. On or about June 4th, 1976 an employee of the Plaintiff put the Defendants on notice of the Plaintiff's security interest.

On June 14th, 1976 the debtor mortgaged the motel to the Defendants and also on the same date by Chattel Mortgage mortgaged the Chattels and equipment in the motel, including the Plaintiff's Chattels, to the Defendants. The Defendants' Chattel Mortgage was registered under The Personal Property Security Act on June 17th, 1976, but the Plaintiff did not register its Conditional Sales Contracts under that Act until February 7th, 1978.

The relevant sections of The Personal Property Security Act are [ss. 1(k), 1(y), 12(1), 21, 22(1)(a), 25(1), 25(2), 35(1), and 36(3)].

• • •

The submission made by Counsel for the Defendants in summary form was that the only section of The Personal Property Security Act which applied was Section 35 and this section has provided for a test of priorities with the result that the so-called doctrine of actual notice cannot prevail. It was further argued that the Plaintiff had a purchase-money security interest, that Section 21 defines when a security interest is perfected and that Section 25 covers the question of perfection by registration.

The thrust of this argument was that if no other provision of The Personal Property Security Act is applicable the provisions of Section 35 apply since both security interests were registered with the result that priority would be determined by Section 35(1)(a) by the order of registration if the security interests have been perfected by registration.

The submission made by Counsel for the Plaintiff was that the legislation did not specifically abolish the doctrine of actual notice. My attention was directed to Section 22(1)(a) wherein it is clear that an unperfected security interest is subordinate to the interest of a person who is entitled to a priority under The Personal Property Security Act or any other Act. To decide who is entitled to priority it is necessary to peruse Section 35(1). It was said that subsections (a) and (b) had no application because under (a) both security interests were registered and under (b) both were perfected. In other words Section 35(1)(a) and (b) are of no assistance in resolving the issue in this application because here the contest is between one perfected and one unperfected security interest. The question really involves whether the Defendants are entitled to a priority under Section 22(1) of The Personal Property Security Act. The conclusion I was invited to reach was that the only purpose of requiring registration was to give notice to third parties and that if in fact a third party has acquired knowledge of the security interest then the underlying requirement has been met.

I reserved judgment on this application because the legislation is relatively new and the academic writers have indicated that there are conflicting policy arguments with an unresolved problem.

It was said that there is an omission in Section 35(1) which could easily have been rectified by the legislative draftsman so that the case at bar could have been covered. It was also said, with some force, that the doctrine of actual notice is deeply rooted in our law and that one of the well known rules of statutory interpretation is that the provisions of the common law cannot be changed without an express statutory provision to that effect.

I have considered the following cases:

> *Re Jung and Montgomery*, [1955] 5 DLR 287.
> *Pitcher v. Shoebottom*, [1971] 1 OR 106.
> *Re Dominion Stores Ltd. and United Trust Co.* (1973), 42 DLR (3d) 523.
> *United Trust Company v. Dominion Stores*, [1973] 2 SCR 915.

These cases generally stand for the proposition in cases involving The Land Titles Act, R.S.O. 1970, c. 234 as amended that "the doctrine of actual notice as to all contractual relations and particularly the law of real property has been firmly based in law since the beginning of equity. Such a cardinal principle of property law cannot be considered abrogated unless the legislative enactment is in the clearest and most unequivocal of terms." This latter phrase was used by Spence J in delivering the majority decision in the Supreme Court of Canada in *United Trust Company v. Dominion Stores* (*supra*).

I have come to the conclusion that this application should succeed. The provisions of The Personal Property Security Act to some extent flow from the earlier provisions of the U.S. Uniform Commercial Code. Although the language is different it is interesting to compare Section 9-312 of the UCC with Section 35 of The Personal Property Security Act. The language is similar and notice makes no difference [*Bloom v. Hilty* (1967), 234 A.2d 860].

In my view nothing in Section 35 says anything about lack of knowledge being a prerequisite for its operation.

In an action in The County Court of the Judicial District of Ottawa-Carleton between *The Bank of Nova Scotia Plaintiff and Dilauri Chevrolet Oldsmobile Ltd. and Craig Edward Schwartz, Defendants*, the plaintiff bank with prior registration succeeded even though it had notice. Judge E.E. Smith made the following statement:

It is argued that as between the two claimants in this case, the Bank of Nova Scotia and Dilauri Chevrolet Oldsmobile Ltd., a subsequent registration by the Bank ought not to be allowed to prevail where there was actual notice. It is conceded that Dilauri's failure to comply with the Act was innocent and in no way misled the Bank.

If I were to accede to the argument, it seems to me that I would be reading into this rather comprehensive piece of legislation something which was (deliberately—the concept of actual notice being well known to the drafters) omitted and in the process thwarting many of the obvious purposes of the legislation.

In the present case I adopt that reasoning and that language.

I would also adopt the language of Lord Cozens-Hardy MR in *Re Monolithic Building Company; Tacon v. The Company*, [1915] 1 Ch. 643, at 556-66 [who,] quoting James LJ in an earlier case, said:

I think it would be dangerous to engraft an equitable exception upon a modern Act of Parliament.

and at 666:

Both parties stood on their legal rights—neither of them was misleading the other. It is not consistent with the policy of the Legislature to import fine equitable distinctions into these cases, and I am therefore of opinion that the argument founded on the knowledge of the judgment creditor cannot prevail.

I have likewise reviewed Sections 36 and 37 [new Act, ss. 34-35] and have concluded that the special priority rules thereunder have no connection with this application. The Plaintiff's submission depends on looking to see a fixed time for registration but there is nothing in The Personal Property Security Act that fixes the time when the Court looks to see if there has been registration. This is a new statute which should be dealt with upon its own merits rather than some considerations which might apply to The Land Titles Act. Sections 22 and 36(3) contemplate knowledge but it is my view that this appears in The Personal Security Act for two situations and I draw the inference that the actual notice principal doesn't therefore apply elsewhere in the Act.

Prof. R.H. McLaren in his textbook *Secured Transactions in Personal Property in Canada*, Vol. 1, 1979, at 6–2 states the general or residual rule [of] Section 35 thus: "The general rule of priority is built around the key concepts of attachment and perfection. No other statute has ever attempted to state even a single priority rule let alone one of such general application as s. 35. If no special priority rule governs then the rules of subs. (1) are used to resolve competing claims in the same collateral. ... The three rules of s. 35 disregard the pre-Act law and its reverence for legal title to the collateral and application of the equitable principle of good faith and notice."

I adopt the foregoing and am reinforced in my view by the judgment of Laskin CJ in *United Trust v. Dominion Stores (supra)* albeit a dissenting judgment.

Judgment for defendant.

NOTE

For a judgment to the same effect, see *National Trailer Convoy of Can. Ltd. v. Bank of Montreal* (1980), 1 PPSAC 87 (Ont., Saunders J).

In the Matter of Bruce A. Smith
(1971), 326 F. Supp. 1311 (US DC Minn.)

LARSON DISTRICT JUDGE: On or about April 14, 1969, one Bruce A. Smith purchased a 1968 Plymouth automobile from Southtown Chrysler in Minneapolis, Minnesota. At that time he executed a conditional sales contract which was assigned by the seller to the

First National Bank of Minneapolis. Neither the seller nor assignee filed a financing statement evidencing the security interest.

In July of 1969 Community Credit Co. lent Mr. Smith money. Mr. Smith at that time executed a chattel mortgage on the Plymouth automobile in favor of the lender. The lender filed a financing statement evidencing the chattel mortgage on July 14, 1969, with the Hennepin County Register of Deeds. At the time of this transaction Community Credit Co. had actual knowledge of the unperfected security interest of the First National Bank of Minneapolis in the automobile.

Bruce A. Smith was duly adjudicated a bankrupt on May 7, 1970, after the filing of a voluntary petition in bankruptcy. The trustee in bankruptcy is given the power of a perfect lien creditor by Section 70(c) of the Bankruptcy Act. He therefore takes priority over and is entitled to avoid the unperfected security interest of the First National Bank of Minneapolis.

Pursuant to the order of the Referee in Bankruptcy the automobile was sold to Community Credit. The sale proceeds are held by the trustee subject to the claim of security interest by Community Credit.

The trustee, however, chose to exercise the option made available to him by Section 70(e)(2) of the Bankruptcy Act. That provision permitted him to preserve the Bank's interest for the benefit of the estate and to assert it against the subsequent lien taken by Community Credit.

There is no dispute that the Bank's security interest is not good against the trustee in bankruptcy. Since it was not perfected either by possession or filing, it remains subject to the rights of the trustee as a perfected lien creditor. The trustee by preserving the Bank's interest and asserting it for the benefit of the estate steps into the shoes of the Bank. His rights are determined by what position the Bank would have been in had there been no bankruptcy proceedings.

The situation presented is one involving conflicting security interests in the same collateral. Community Credit holds a security interest perfected by filing. The Bank's interest is prior in time but is unperfected either by filing or possession. It is conceded by all parties that Community Credit as holder of the perfected security interest would prevail if it had not had actual knowledge of the Bank's prior unperfected interest. Hence the issue raised before the Referee in Bankruptcy and which now faces this Court is whether actual knowledge on the part of Community Credit of the Bank's prior interest prevents it from achieving priority which would have otherwise been obtained by being the first to file. The Referee answered this question in the affirmative and gave priority to the Bank's lien.

The portion of the Minnesota Uniform Commercial Code which governs this situation is MSA §336.9-213(5) [UCC §9-312(5)].

In all cases not governed by other rules stated in this section (including cases of purchase money security interests which do not qualify for the special priorities set forth in subsections (3) and (4) of this section), priority between conflicting security interests in the same collateral shall be determined as follows:

   (a) In the order of filing if both are perfected by filing, regardless of which security interest attached first under section 336.9-204(1) and whether it attached before or after filing;

   (b) In the order of perfection unless both are perfected by filing, regardless of which security interest attached first under section 336.9-204(1) and, in the case of the filed security interest, whether it attached before or after filing; and

(c) In the order of attachment under section 336.9-204(1) so long as neither is perfected.

This provision nowhere makes lack of knowledge (good faith) a requirement for obtaining priority. The statute on its face provides for a race to the filing office with actual knowledge of a prior unperfected security interest apparently being irrelevant if one perfects first by filing. Such an approach by the Uniform Commercial Code would clearly be a change in the pre-existing law. Under precode commercial law, actual notice of an earlier unperfected interest in the property would prevent the second interest from obtaining priority. This was true even if the second interest was perfected first by filing.

The change would be one effected by omission rather than an affirmative statement of change. It is the absence of any reference to knowledge or good faith which raises the presumption that it is not relevant. There is no positive statement in Section 336.9-312(5) that knowledge of the earlier interest has no bearing on priority. Under these circumstances, a conclusion that knowledge is not a factor in establishing priorities under Section 336.9-312(5) is predicated on the underlying assumption that the omission of any reference to knowledge was a deliberate one. The Referee in Bankruptcy refused to make that assumption. He came, in fact, to the opposite conclusion, namely, that the absence of any reference to knowledge was unintentional on the part of the code draftsmen. Hence, the instant controversy is *casus omissus* and must be interpreted in light of the common law. As was previously noted, the common law made good faith a critical factor in achieving priority.

The Referee, in reaching his decision that the omission was unintentional, relied heavily on Professor Grant Gilmore's interpretation of the drafting history of Section 9-312(5) of the UCC. II.Gilmore, Security Interests in Personal Property §34.2 (pp. 898-902) 1965. Professor Gilmore acknowledges that Article 9 appears to have discarded good faith as a factor in determining priorities under Section 9-312 of the UCC. However, he makes an argument that the result is not clearly an intentional and deliberate one on the part of the draftsmen. Professor Gilmore's analysis fairly questions whether or not the elimination of the good faith provision was a calculated one on the part of the draftsmen of the UCC. However, this Court feels that the Referee in Bankruptcy's reliance on that analysis to imply a good cause provision in Section 9-312(5) is misplaced.

It is true that Professor Gilmore suggested implying a good cause provision as one way of approaching Section 9-312(5). To the contrary he also pointed out that there were some good reasons for disregarding knowledge and creating a race to file situation. One is the protection of the integrity of the filing system. *Gilmore*, at 901-2. It is desirable that perfection of interests take place promptly. It is appropriate then to provide that a secured party who fails to file runs the risk of subordination to a later but more diligent party. In this regard it should be pointed out that filing is of particular importance with respect to notice to other parties. It is agreed that where the later party has actual notice there is no need to rely upon a filing to notify him of a prior interest. The problem, however, cannot be analyzed in this narrow context. Some parties may rely on the record in extending credit and obtaining a security agreement in collateral. Although they will prevail over the unperfected prior interest in time if a dispute arises, it is entirely possible that they wanted to avoid the dispute altogether. In other words, they may not have relied on ultimately prevailing in the event of a dispute but they may have relied on the complete absence of a prior interest perfected or otherwise out of which a dispute could arise. The only way this kind of record expectation can be protected is by prompt perfection of all security interests.

Professor Gilmore also recognizes the fact that a good faith requirement creates evidentiary problems.

[T]he presence or absence of "knowledge" is a subjective question of fact, difficult to prove. Unless there is an overwhelming policy argument in favour of using such a criterion, it is always wise to discard it and to make decision turn on some easily determinable objective event—, as for example, the date of filing. *Gilmore*, at 502.

The only way to effectively produce the above result is to make "knowledge" irrelevant and rely solely on perfection to establish priority.

Finally, Professor Gilmore admits that Example 2 in the official comment to Section 9-312(5) seems to indicate that the apparent result was intended. It reads as follows insofar as relevant:

Example 2. A and B make non-purchase money advances against the same collateral. The collateral is in the debtor's possession and neither interest is perfected when the second advance is made. Whichever secured party first perfects his interest (by taking possession of the collateral or by filing) takes priority and it makes no difference whether or not he knows of the other interest at the time he perfects his own.

Subsections (5)(a) and (5)(b) both lead to this result. It may be regarded as an adoption, in this type of situation, of the idea, deeply rooted at common law, of a race of diligence among creditors. ...

The comment is not directly in point because it deals with knowledge at time of perfection and not at the time of attachment. Subsections (5)(a) and (5)(b), however, give priority whether perfection is before or after attachment. Thus, if attachment came after perfection, knowledge at time of perfection would also mean knowledge at time of attachment. Presumably Example 2 would control in that situation also (although it is not certain since under Example 2's facts, attachment was clearly prior to perfection). This conclusion is supported by Example 1.

Example 1. A files against X (debtor) on February 1. B files against X on March 1. B makes a non-purchase money advance against certain collateral on April 1. A makes an advance against the same collateral on May 1. A has priority even though B's advance was made earlier and was perfected when made. It *makes no difference whether or not A knew of B's interest when he made his advance.* ... (Emphasis added.)

This example makes clear that once priority has been achieved by being the first to file, that priority will not be destroyed as to an advance made with the knowledge that a second party has made a prior advance secured by a perfected security interest in the same collateral. This is the case, apparently, even if it is the first advance made under the prior perfected agreement. Similar treatment should be accorded any interest which attached after filing.

It can be seen from the foregoing that Professor Gilmore's position is not an unequivocal one. Furthermore, Professor Gilmore himself admits that the Code Comment to Section 9-312(5) tends to indicate that the drafters of the code were aware of and intended that knowledge be irrelevant in determining priorities under that section. Under these circumstances this Court feels that the conclusion of the Referee in Bankruptcy that good faith should be read into Minn. Stat. Ann. 336.9-312(5) is unwarranted.

There are some other practical reasons why this Court feels constrained to reverse the Referee in Bankruptcy. First of all, there are other commentators who have argued that the elimination of the good faith provision was intentional. *See* Felsenfeld, Knowledge as A Factor in Determining Priorities Under the Uniform Commercial Code, 42 *NYU L Rev.* 246, at 248-50 (1967).

Secondly, the assumption of most of the commentators has been that Section 9-312(5) operated without regard to knowledge of the perfecting party of a prior unperfected security interest. *See* Coogan, Hogan, Vagts, Secured Transactions Under the UCC 177. The Minnesota Code Comment referring to Section 9-312(5) says:

Notice of a prior security interest does not invalidate a subsequent interest which is otherwise entitled to priority under this subsection. ... This changes prior Minnesota law as to security interests in the nature of chattel mortgages and conditional sales, since subsequent mortgagees under prior law had the burden of proving "good faith" (i.e., lack of notice) as against prior mortgagees or conditional vendors whose mortgages or conditional sales contracts are filed. ...

It is clear that the assumption of the Minnesota legislature when they adopted the code was that it changed prior law.

Finally, all those cases which have dealt with the problem indicate by holding or dicta that knowledge is irrelevant to the operation of Section 9-312(5). *Bloom v. Hilty*, 427 Pa. 463, 234 A. 2d 860 (1967); *First National Bank and Trust Company of Vinita, Okla. v. Atlas Credit Corp.*, 417 F. 2d 1081, at 1082, fn. 1, 1083 (10th Cir. 1969); *In re Gunderson*, 4 UCC Rep. 358, 358-59 (DC Ill. 1967).

The attitude of the commentators and the weight of recorded decisions clearly indicated that knowledge could be disregarded in the operation of Section 9-312(5). The instant situation is evidence that there has been reliance on the apparent meaning of the statute as it has been interpreted by commentators and the courts.

To permit the decision of the Referee in Bankruptcy to stand would be to disrupt substantially expectations under Section 9-312(5). Furthermore, it would create a split in authority and destroy the uniformity the code seeks to achieve. This is not to say that if the current interpretations were clearly contrary to the intent of the drafters that a split in authority would not be appropriate. That, however, is clearly not the situation presented. The only individual who seriously asserts that the elimination of a good faith requirement was unintentional is Professor Gilmore and his position is not an unequivocal one.

Under the circumstances this Court cannot permit to stand a decision which goes against the weight of authority and reasonable expectations under the statute. The decision of the Referee in Bankruptcy must therefore be reversed.

Decision of referee reversed.

NOTES

1) In *Bank of Nova Scotia v. Gaudreau* (1984), 48 OR (2d) 478, the Bank of Nova Scotia ("BNS") financed the conditional sale of an automobile to G, then residing in Hull. G also procured a loan for a company he owned from the Ottawa branch of the National Bank of Canada ("NBC"). G subsequently moved the car to Ottawa but the BNS did not

discover this fact until after the 60-day period had expired under s. 7(1) of the OPPSA. In the meantime, the manager of the NBC branch became concerned about the delinquent state of the company's loan and he prevailed upon G to give the bank a mortgage on the car to secure repayment of the loan. The mortgage was timeously perfected by registration. Mr. Justice Sutherland found that the manager had previously been told by G about the outstanding conditional sale agreement. He also held that the manager must have known about the common provision in the conditional sale agreement prohibiting G from disposing or encumbering the vehicle without the seller's permission.

The BNS sued the NBC in tort for conversion and for inducing G's breach of contract with the BNS. Mr. Justice Sutherland rejected both claims. He held, following Gray J's "touchstone" judgment in *Shadlock*, that the NBC's priority under s. 35(1)(a) of the old Act was not affected by its knowledge of the prior security interest held by the BNS even if, as contended, the manager's conduct had amounted to bad faith. In his fully articulated view, both knowledge and good faith were irrelevant in applying the priority rules in s. 35(1). He also held that since the Ontario Legislature clearly intended to confer priority on the person first to file, despite his knowledge of the earlier security agreement, it would be anomalous to allow a tort action for inducing a breach of contract based on a provision in the same agreement. To do so, he thought, would be to undermine the statutory priority scheme.

Is it correct to say that obtaining a security interest in collateral subject to a prior security interest amounts to bad faith? Is the creation of more than one security interest in real and personal property not commonplace in Canada? Note too that the debtor's power to create successive security interests is expressly recognized in UCC 9-311 and s. 39 of the (new) Ontario Act.

Was s. 33 of the old Act [now s. 30(1)] a complete answer to the allegation that NBC's manager had induced Gaudreau to commit a breach of contract? Is it in any event true to say that he "must" have known about the prohibitory provision because he knew there was a conditional sale agreement between the parties? See further Ziegel (1985), 10 *CBLJ* 131, at 162. Section 66(1) of the Alberta Act requires all rights, duties, and obligations under a security agreement or under the Act to be exercised in good faith and in a commercially reasonable manner. Section 66(2) goes on to provide:

66.(2)—A person does not act in bad faith merely because the person acts with knowledge of the interest of some other person.

Subsection 2 was presumably added to endorse the decision in *Gaudreau*. What does "merely" mean in s. 66(2)? What additional factors are necessary to show bad faith?

2) *In re Smith, supra*, argues, as many others have argued, that to require the first person to file to be without knowledge of the prior unperfected security interest would undermine the integrity of the registration system. Not all Canadian lawyers and judges share this sentiment—in fact, some would argue that results such as those in *Robt. Simpson Co. v. Shadlock* shock the conscience and give a bad odour to the new legislation. Do you agree? Consider the pros and cons of the two arguments as canvassed in the following passage:

First, while the first to file rule is largely novel in the chattel security field it has long been a familiar feature in several of the provincial land registry systems. Second, the filing requirements under the PPS Acts are generally so easy to comply with, and the benefits conferred by the Acts on secured parties so generous, that there is little excuse ordinarily for a secured party not meeting the statutory perfection requirements. Third, the pre-PPSA registration statutes did not consistently apply a reliance test as the basis for protecting third parties. For example, execution creditors and creditors' representatives were entitled to ignore unperfected security interests whether or not they had prior notice of them. Again, unregistered security interests were subordinated to the claims of subsequent purchasers and mortgagees even though they had not searched the register and had not been misled by the absence of registration. Fourth, reversion to a reliance system of priorities would accentuate the problem of circular priorities where, there being more than one subsequent secured party, one of them has notice of the prior security interest and the other has not. Finally, if being informed about an intervening security interest freezes the priority of the secured party who has filed first, this will defeat an important purpose of a notice filing system, which is to assure the first filer that his security interest will enjoy priority subject only to such exceptions as are spelled out in the legislation.

Against these considerations (and others I have not mentioned) there must be balanced arguments such as the following that favour the reinstatement of the traditional purchaser without notice principle. First, the PPS Acts are not consistent in their approach. The good faith purchaser for value without notice doctrine has been retained at least in part in s. 22 of the [old] Ontario Act and its counterparts in the other PPS jurisdictions. It is also retained in many of the other priority provisions involving the claims of subsequent transferees of the collateral. Second, as has already been noted, compliance with the registration requirements of the PPS statutes is not as simple and straightforward as its proponents suggest. Further, reperfection requirements may be imposed on a secured party without his even being aware of the event triggering the requirement. *BNS v. Gaudreau* is a good example of the latter type of situation. Finally, it cannot be correct to say that the rationale for excluding the traditional good faith purchaser test is a desire to maintain the integrity of the registration system since notice of a prior security interest is irrelevant for the purpose of applying the general priority provisions for competing security interests *regardless* of the method of perfection followed by a secured party.

(Ziegel (1985), 10 *CBLJ* 163-64.)

James Talcott Inc. v. Franklin National Bank of Minneapolis
(1972), 194 NW 2d 775 (S. Ct. Minn.)

RONALD E. HACHEY JUSTICE: This is an appeal taken from a summary judgment in favor of defendant, Franklin National Bank of Minneapolis. The action was commenced for the recovery of possession of several motor vehicles, or their value, in which plaintiff, James Talcott, Inc., claimed a superior security interest.

The case was heard on stipulated facts. On February 20, 1968, Noyes Paving Company, hereinafter referred to as "debtor," entered into a conditional sales contract with Northern Contracting Company, as seller, covering the purchase, on an installment basis, of two dump trucks and other construction equipment. On that same day, the seller assigned, without recourse, the conditional sales contract to plaintiff, together with all sums payable thereunder and all right, title, and interest in and to the equipment covered by the contract. On February 21, 1968, a financing statement was filed with the secretary of state naming

Noyes Paving Company as debtor, Northern Contracting Company as secured party, and James Talcott, Inc., as assignee of the secured party. The financing statement covered the following items of property: "Construction Equipment, Motor Vehicles."

On May 1, debtor entered into an equipment lease with defendant bank covering one dump truck; and on May 31, a similar lease agreement was entered into between the same parties covering two additional dump trucks and other equipment. Each lease provided that debtor, if not in default, could purchase the leased goods at the end of the lease term for the sum of $1. Defendant did not at that time file a financing statement regarding the equipment described in the two lease agreements.

During the latter part of the year 1968, debtor experienced difficulty in making payments on the conditional sales contract. On January 30, 1969, debtor and plaintiff entered into an agreement extending the time for payment. In consideration of the extension granted, debtor gave plaintiff a security interest "in all goods (as defined in Article 9 of the Uniform Commercial Code) whether now owned or hereafter acquired." An attached schedule merely repeated in substantially identical form the list of goods attached to the original conditional sales agreement. The new agreement went on to provide that the security interest was granted to secure the payment of all loans, advances, debts, liabilities, obligations, covenants, and duties owing by debtor to plaintiff, including, without limitation, any debt, liability, or obligation owing from debtor to others which plaintiff may have obtained by assignment or otherwise. No additional financing statement was filed in connection with the extension agreement of January 30. At that time, plaintiff did not know of the existence of the motor vehicles and other equipment listed in defendant's two equipment leases and did not rely upon their existence in entering into the extension agreement.

Following the date of the extension agreement, debtor ran into more financial difficulty and defaulted in payments with respect to both the conditional sales contract and the equipment leases. On May 21, 1970, copies of the leases were filed by defendant bank as financing statements with the secretary of state. Sometime during May 1970, defendant repossessed the equipment in question and this action ensued. The precise date on which defendant made the repossession is not clear from the record. The parties agreed that it took place during the month of May 1970. All of the equipment was located with exception of one item. By agreement between plaintiff and defendant, the equipment was sold, and the proceeds were placed in a special account pending the outcome of this case.

The issues on appeal are: (1) Whether an equipment lease which gives the lessee the right to acquire title to the equipment for $1 upon compliance with the lease terms is a "security agreement" within the meaning of Article 9 of the Uniform Commercial Code (Minn. St. 336.9-101, et seq.); (2) whether debtor had sufficient ownership of the leased equipment so that it became secured property under the extension agreement with plaintiff; (3) whether the description of the secured property, as it appeared in the extension agreement, was sufficient to meet the requirements of Art. 9 of the Uniform Commercial Code; (4) whether the financing statement filed at the same time the first security agreement was assigned to plaintiff was sufficient to protect a security interest in the property covered by the extension agreement; and (5) which security interest was entitled to priority.

[Hachey J answered questions 1 to 3 in the affirmative and continued:]

4. Was the financing statement, filed at the time the first security agreement was assigned to plaintiff, sufficient to reflect a security interest in the property covered by the extension agreement?

Defendant argues that plaintiff did not perfect its security interest in the equipment covered by the second security agreement (the extension agreement of January 30, 1969) because of the failure to file an amendment to the financing statement. The trial court also followed this line of reasoning in arriving at its decision that plaintiff had not perfected its security interest.

Section 336.9-402(1) provides that "[a] financing statement may be filed before a security agreement is made or a security interest otherwise attaches." This is what happened in the instant case. The financing statement filed February 21, 1968, met all requirements of the code since it described by type ("Construction Equipment, Motor Vehicles") not only the property covered by the original sales agreement which was assigned to plaintiff but also the property, which likewise consisted of motor vehicles and constructional equipment, financed by defendant. The code does not require a reference in the financing statement to after-acquired property. Section 336.9-402(4) states:

The term "financing statement" as used in this article means the original financing statement and any amendments but if any amendment adds collateral, it is effective as to the added collateral only from the filing date of the amendment.

A careful reading of that section does not compel a finding that the financing statement must be amended when the security agreement is altered.

Section 336.9-204(3) specifically approves the inclusion of after-acquired property in the security agreement. It states:

… [A] security agreement *may* provide that collateral, whenever acquired, shall secure all obligations covered by the security agreement. (Italics supplied.)

That section permits the inclusion of after-acquired property in a security agreement, but it does not require such inclusion in all cases where subsequent collateral is to be added. When §§336.9-402(1) and 336.9-204(3) are read together, it is clear they sanction the essential elements of the transaction in the instant case. The financing statement was filed February 21, 1968, and described the type of goods covered as "Construction Equipment, Motor Vehicles." It was sufficient to give notice of the security agreement entered into on February 20, 1968, and was also sufficient to give notice of the second security agreement of January 30, 1969. As pointed out herein, §336.9-402(1) specifically permits the filing of a financing statement in advance of the making of the security agreement itself.

The whole purpose of notice filing would be nullified if a financing statement had to be filed whenever a new transaction took place between a secured party and a debtor. Once a financing statement is on file describing property by type, the entire world is warned, not only that the secured party may already have a security interest in the property of that type (as did plaintiff in the property originally financed), but that it may later acquire a perfected security interest in property of the same type acquired by the debtor in the future. When the debtor does acquire more property of the type referred to in the financing statement already on file, and when a security interest attaches to that property, the perfection is instantaneous and automatic. §336.9-303(1).

Different fact situations may arise resulting in different arrangements between the secured party and the debtor, all within the contemplation of the code. For instance, in their initial dealings they may contemplate either a number of financing transactions, all secured by the property to which the security interest originally attaches, or they may create a single obligation from the debtor to the secured party, to be secured by property the debtor then owns and additional property that he will later acquire. Furthermore, a transaction between the parties may involve a combination of both of these. Even where the parties originally contemplate a single debt, secured by a single item of property or a single group of items, the secured party and the debtor may enter into further transactions whereby the debtor obtains additional credit and the secured party is granted more security. The validity of such arrangements as against creditors, trustees in bankruptcy, and other secured parties has been widely organized by many courts. See, *DuBay v. Williams*, 417 F. 2d 1277 (9 Cir. 1969); *Grain Merchants of Indiana, Inc. v. Union Bank & Sav. Co.*, 408 F. 2d 209 (7 Cir.), certiorari denied sub nom. *France v. Union Bank & Sav. Co.*, 396 US 827, 90 S. Ct. 75, 24 L. Ed. 2d 78 (1969); *Rosenberg v. Rudnick*, 262 F. Supp. 635 (D. Mass. 1967).

Using future-advance clauses and using after-acquired property clauses in the original security agreement are not the only means by which perfected security interests can be obtained in subsequently contracted obligations or in goods the debtor may later come to own. There is nothing exclusive about §336.9-204(3, 5). Parties may use future-advance and after-acquired clauses, and they are a great convenience. But, if they are not used, there is nothing in the code which prevents the parties from accomplishing the same result by entering into one or more additional security agreements.

Upon a review of decision law in other jurisdictions it would appear that there is a difference of opinion as to perfection and priority of a later advance where it was not made pursuant to the original security agreement but pursuant to a later agreement which may or may not have satisfied the requirements of the code as to security agreements. The better view holds that, where originally a security agreement is executed, an indebtedness created, and a financing statement describing the collateral filed, followed at a later date by another advance made pursuant to a subsequent security agreement covering the same collateral, the lender has a perfected security interest in the collateral not only for the original debt but also for the later advance. The instant matter involves a parallel situation. See, *In re Rivet*, 299 F. Supp. 374 (ED Mich. 1969).

The error of the trial court in the instant matter was apparently prompted by its reliance on §336.9-402(4), which provides that any amendment adding collateral to a financing statement is effective as to the added collateral only from the filing date of the amendment. As has been pointed out, however, the financing statement originally filed was broad enough to cover the after-acquired collateral. If, for instance, the equipment leases between debtor and defendant had included items which did not fall within the description "Construction Equipment, Motor Vehicles" (for example, machine tools), then it would have been necessary, in order for the plaintiff to perfect its security interest in such different goods, to file either a new financing statement or an amendment to the original one. In either event, the effective date would have been the date of filing.

5. *Priority*

As has been pointed out, the record is not clear as to what date defendant repossessed the equipment. The exact date the conflict arose would be helpful in determining which portion of §336.9-312 should be applied in determining priorities.

From an examination of the record, it is clear that §336.9-312(4) is inapplicable inasmuch as defendant's security was not perfected within the allotted time thereunder—that is, no financing statement had been filed at the time that the debtor received the equipment or within 10 days thereafter. Had a financing statement covering the equipment leases been filed at the time the transaction between debtor and defendant took place or within 10 days thereafter, defendant would have had priority under this section of the code. Unfortunate as it may be for defendant, this did not take place; hence, §336.9-312(4) does not govern despite the bank's later filing.

Turning our attention to §336.9-312(5), we must determine whether paragraph (a) or paragraph (b) governs. Again, the date that the dispute arose is not clear. The parties have agreed that it arose sometime during the month of May 1970. Hence, whether the filing of the financing statement (equipment leases) by defendant was prior to or subsequent to the repossession date is not established. It then follows that §336.9-312(5)(a) may or may not be applicable. That section provides in part:

> (5) In all cases not governed by other rules stated in this section ... , priority between conflicting security interests in the same collateral shall be determined as follows:
>> (a) In the order of filing if both are perfected by filing, regardless of which security interest attached first ... and whether it attached before or after filing.

With certain exceptions not applicable in the case at bar, a security interest is perfected when a financing statement is filed. Therefore, a reading of paragraph (a) leads us to the conclusion that, if a dispute arises over priority of perfected security interests (both having been perfected by filing before the dispute arose), then the order of filing of the financing statement governs. We are aware of the date that defendant filed its financing statement (May 21, 1970), but, again, the record is not clear as to the date that the dispute arose (i.e., the date of repossession). Defendant might have filed first and then repossessed, or it might have repossessed first and, upon being confronted with a dispute over priorities, decided to file forthwith. As we have said, if defendant filed first and then repossessed, §336.9-312(5)(a) governs.

Conversely, if the dispute arose first and thereafter the bank filed, then paragraph (a) of §336.9-312(5) is inapplicable, and we direct our attention to paragraph (b), which gives the following alternative method of determining priorities under this subsection:

> In the order of perfection unless both are perfected by filing, regardless of which security interest attached first under section 336.9-204(1) and, in the case of the filed security interest, whether it attached before or after filing.

Defendant's security interest did attach first, but (assuming it was filed after repossession) it was not perfected. Plaintiff's security interest attached later—actually after its filing had occurred. But neither of these factors is material in the application of the first-to-perfect rule. Accordingly, when the conflict arose (still assuming it was before defendant had filed) plaintiff was entitled to priority. Once plaintiff's priority had been acquired, no subsequent filing by defendant (more than 10 days after debtor received possession) could alter the situation. Moreover, even if §336.9-312(5)(a) should apply, plaintiff would still have priority under the first-to-file rule as its filing preceded defendant's by many months.

In passing, it could be said that plaintiff is to receive an unearned windfall, being the beneficiary of a security interest in property of which it wasn't even aware. Unquestionably, defendant bank, through misunderstanding of the applicable provisions of the code, will suffer a substantial loss. By its own failure to conform to and comply with very simple and obvious provisions of the code, it has found itself entangled in other provisions which are admittedly more complex but which are absolutely essential to the whole concept of notice filing. The fundamental purpose of Art. 9 of the code is to make the process of perfecting a security interest easy, simple, and certain. It was intended to be a complete reversal of prior chattel security law and to rid the unaware of the traps of requirement of specific types of acknowledgments, technical affidavits of consideration, selection of specific proper forms, and other pitfalls that were not uncommon. The code very simply and briefly provides for a notice-filing procedure with a minimum of information required to be publicized in a filed financing statement. All that is required is a minimal description, and it may be by type or kind. The statement need not necessarily contain detail as to collateral, nor any statement of quantity, size, description or specifications, or serial numbers. No preciseness is required with respect to whether the collateral exists at the time of filing or is to be acquired thereafter, and no statement of charges, payment schedule, or maturity date need be included in the statement. The first to file shall prevail. Although there are a few exceptions, they are very clearly and definitely stated. To affirm here would amount to a limitation upon the efficacy of the first-to-file rule, which is basic and essential to the certainty that Art. 9 seeks to achieve. Moreover, to hold that plaintiff was required to file an additional financing statement to cover the extension agreement of January 30, 1969, would have a disastrous effect upon financing transactions.

Reversed and remanded for further proceedings.

NOTES

1) *Talcott* should be contrasted with the earlier Rhode Island Superior Court decision in *Coin-O-Matic Service Co. v. Rhode Island Hospital Trust Co.* (1966), 3 UCC Rep. Serv. 1112, reproduced below.

2) How would *Talcott* be decided under the OPPSA? (So far as the Ontario registration requirements are concerned, refresh your memory by re-reading the relevant parts of chapter 4, *supra*, OPPSA ss. 45(3) and (4), and the editors' criticisms of R.A. Blair J's interpretation of these provisions in *Adelaide Capital Corp. v. Inegrated Transportation Finance Inc.*, *supra*, chapter 4.) What could and should the Franklin National Bank have done to preserve the priority of its purchase money security interest? Should the Bank have made a search of the registry records? Should it have sought a waiver or subordination agreement from Talcott? For the effectiveness of subordination agreements, see OPPSA s. 38 and *Euroclean Can. Inc. v. Forest Glade Invts. Ltd.* (1985), 4 PPSAC 271 (Ont. CA), *infra*, chapter 8.

3) Do the facts in *Talcott* suggest that the first to file rule is too generous to the first filer? If so, how would you change it?

PROBLEMS

1) D, a hardware wholesaler, buys small electrical appliances on conditional sale from S. S registers a financing statement in which an "x" appears inside the "inventory" box. The statement contains no other description of the collateral. D seeks a line of credit from its bank (B) on the security of the rest of its inventory. B refuses to grant the credit unless S first files a financing change statement restricting its collateral to small appliances. Can D force S to do this? Do the Ontario regulations provide for optional descriptions? See O. Reg. 372/89, s. 3(1), 27(1) and form 1. *Cf.* new Act, s. 46(3), which provides that:

(3) Except with respect to rights to proceeds, where a financing statement or financing change statement sets out a classification of collateral and also contains words that appear to limit the scope of the classification, then, unless otherwise indicated in the financing statement or financing change statement, the secured party may claim a security interest perfected by registration only in the class as limited.

2) Suppose in Problem 1, B had procured a copy of the conditional sale agreement between D and S, would it be safe for B to give the line of credit without further assurances from S?

SECURITY FOR FUTURE ADVANCES

Chattel security agreements providing for future as well as present advances by the creditor are commonplace, indeed essential, in those situations where the creditor agrees to make a revolving line of credit available to the debtor, usually up to an agreed ceiling. As noted in chapter 3, the common law recognized the validity of future advance clauses but their precise status under the provincial bills of sale legislation was unclear. Section 13 of the OPPSA expressly validates them.

Section 13 does not concern itself with the priority conflicts that arise where there are competing security interests and one of the secured parties makes more than one advance. The materials that follow focus on this issue, distinguishing for this purpose between the common law position, the position under the old Act, and the changes adopted in the new Act and also in force in other jurisdictions.

G.L. Blackburn
Mortgages to Secure Future Advances
(1956), 21 *Mo. L Rev.* 209, at 213-15 (footnotes omitted)

Mortgages to secure future advances generally fall into one of four broad categories of form. In the first type the instrument makes no mention of future advances but rather takes the form of a mortgage absolute on its face which states a definite sum which is secured thereby. Actually only a portion of this stated amount is lent to the mortgagor, and, by oral agreement or a written collateral agreement, the parties manifest their intentions with reference to future advances.

In the second category, the instrument is drafted so as to expressly provide for the making of future advances. This type distinguishes itself, however, in that the mortgagee, by the terms of the agreement, contractually binds himself to make these subsequent advances. This form is generally referred to as a mortgage to secure "obligatory future advances."

In the third type, the mortgage will also provide expressly for the making of future advances, but the making of these advancements is strictly within the discretion of the mortgagee. Such a device is termed a mortgage to secure "optional future advances," but currently is becoming more familiarly known as an "open end" mortgage. Instruments purporting to secure optional advances are generally drawn either as "limited" or "unlimited." The unlimited type makes no mention of the total amount or limit which may ultimately be advanced and secured. The limited form is drafted with a provision providing a maximum amount of advances to be made and secured; or it may be limited as to the time during which such advances shall be made as well as limited in amount. Furthermore, where a mortgage on its face states it is to secure future advances or loans up to a stated maximum, it is valid only up to that amount, but it may be made a continuing security so that when advances have been made up to the limited amount and these are partially or totally repaid, the mortgage will continue as security for further loans within the prescribed limits.

The fourth and final classification of future advances is, in a sense, both optional and limited, but here the limitation is one of purpose wherein it is provided that the mortgagee may, at his own option, and without the consent of the mortgagor, make such advances or expenditures as are necessary to protect his interest or preserve the value of the security. Provisions for the payment of taxes, insurance, repairs, and prior liens are typical.

P.F. Coogan
The New UCC Article 9
(1972-73), 86 *Harv. L Rev.* 477, at 505-7

The term "future advances" is not self-defining—future to what extent? Does the term include all advances subsequent to the date of the original filing? Subsequent to the date of the security agreement? Or is it only subsequent to the date upon which a full-fledged security interest attached and was perfected?

• • •

The [1962] Article 9 does not clearly distinguish between future advances made at the option of the secured party and those made pursuant to the secured party's commitment. A future advance made pursuant to an honest-to-goodness commitment should be treated the same as an actual advance: the secured party had parted with value by incurring an obligation that must be honored even if it proves inconvenient to do so. Lenders sometimes commit themselves to make certain future advances without regard to what the debtor's credit standing will be at the time the advance is actually made. More likely, the lender and debtor agree that the lender's obligation to make any further advance is subject to a set of carefully thought-out conditions aimed at assuring the lender that the debtor's credit position will support the advance when it is actually made and at assuring the debtor that credit will ordinarily be available to him.

The distinction between advances under commitment and optional advances no doubt must arise out of the nature of the conditions which will and will not excuse the lender's performance. Clearly, a lender's commitment to make a future advance which excuses performance if he dislikes the way the debtor has parted his hair on the day the latter asks for the advance is not a real commitment. It is quite a different matter, however, if the lender's commitment to make an advance is excused only if the debtor's balance sheet, audited by an independent accountant, shows that the debtor's net current asset-debt ratio has fallen below an agreed-upon, reasonable standard.

The revised Code attempts with apparent success to distinguish between a real and a phony commitment in new paragraph 9-105(1)(k):

An advance is made "pursuant to commitment" if the secured party has bound himself to make it, whether or not a subsequent event of default or other event not within his control has relieved or may relieve him from his obligation.

Note especially the last clause. Suppose a building construction lender is excused under a security agreement from making further advances if any part of his debtor's assets are subjected to a lien obtained by legal or equitable proceedings involving a claim of $50,000 or more, and a creditor with such a claim levies. The lender, after surveying both his own position as a substantial creditor of the debtor and the probable strength of the lien creditor's claim, decides that he, as an existing creditor, and the debtor will both be worse off if he elects to take advantage of his "out." He consequently makes the advance to complete the building. Under proposed 9-105(1)(k) the lender's advance is entitled to the advantages of one made pursuant to a commitment, notwithstanding the out of which he did not take advantage.

The following case describes the priority of future advances at common law.

West v. Williams
[1899] 1 Ch. 132 (CA)

LINDLEY MR: A first mortgagee, whose mortgage is taken to cover what is then due to him, and also further advances, cannot claim the benefit of his security for further advances in priority to a second mortgagee of whose mortgage he had notice before the further advances were made. This rule was ultimately established in the well-known case of *Hopkinson v. Rolt*, 9 HLC 514, 11 ER 829. In that case the first mortgagee had not agreed to make further advances. We have to consider whether the same rule applies when he has agreed to do so. Kekewich J has held that it does not. This point is of great general importance, and I have carefully considered it, and have come to a conclusion different from that of the learned judge. *Hopkinson v. Rolt*, 9 HLC 514, was commented upon and explained by the House of Lords in *Bradford Banking Co. v. Briggs*, 12 App. Cas. 29, and in *Union Bank of Scotland v. National Bank of Scotland*, 12 App. Cas. 53. These three cases show very clearly that the principle which underlies the rule established in *Hopkinson v. Rolt* is simply this, that an owner of property, dealing honestly with it, cannot confer upon another a greater interest in that property than he himself has. The rule rests on no technicality of English law; it is based on the plainest good sense, and it is as much the law of Scotland as the law of England. When a man mortgages his property he is still free to deal with his equity of redemption in it, or, in other words, with the property itself subject to the mortgage. If he creates a second mortgage he cannot afterwards honestly suppress it, and create another mortgage subject only to the first. Nor can any one who knows of the second mortgage obtain from the mortgagor a greater right to override it than the mortgagor himself has. On the other hand, the first mortgagee has no right to restrain the mortgagor from borrowing money from some one else, and from giving him a second mortgage, subject to the first. Even if the first mortgagee has agreed to make further advances on the property mortgaged to him, the mortgagor is under no obligation to take further advances from him and from no one else, and if the mortgagor chooses to borrow money from someone else, and to give him a second mortgage, the mortgagor thereby releases the first mortgagee from his obligation to make further advances. Whatever prevents the mortgagor from giving to the first mortgagee the agreed security for his further advances releases the first mortgagee from his obligation to make them. A plea of exoneration and discharge before breach would be a good defence at law to an action by the mortgagor against the first mortgagee for not making further advances. If, notwithstanding his release, the first mortgagee makes further advances, with notice of a second mortgage, he is in no better position than any one else who does the like.

NOTES AND QUESTIONS

1) The notice of the intervening interest which defeats the first mortgagee's priority at common law in respect of the future advances is "notice which gives him real and actual knowledge, and so affects his conscience." Protection is given to the first mortgagee "until he is made aware of a change, not by the hypothetical operation of an instrument registered subsequent to his, but by a reasonable communication of the fact by the one who comes in under the subsequent instrument." See *Pierce v. Canada Permanent Loan and Savings Company* (1894), 25 OR 671, 676 (Ch. D.). This was not the universal pre-Code rule in the United States. In *West v. Williams*, *supra*, the intervening interest between the first mortgage and subsequent advances was that of a second mortgagee. The rule in *Hopkinson v. Rolt* also applies where the intervening interest consists of a judicial lien. See *Falconbridge on Mortgages* (4th ed., 1977), at 163.

2) Several of the provincial Registry Acts now both affirm and modify the rule in *Hopkinson v. Rolt* to the extent of excluding it where the mortgagee has committed himself to make future advances. See, e.g., Registry Act, RSO 1990, c. R.20, s. 73, and *cf.* English Law of Property Act, 1925, s. 94. See also Law Reform Commission of British Columbia, *Mortgages of Land: The Priority of Further Advances*, WP No. 47 (1985).

3) There were no specific provisions in the old Act dealing with the priority of future advances. Their position was thus determined according to the general rules of ss. 22 and

35. However, the application of these provisions to future advances was not straightfor-ward. Consider the following: where a lender makes successive advances against the same collateral, when does her security interest attach? Does she have one security interest securing a floating debt, or does she have several security interests in the collateral, each of which secures a particular advance? These questions were relevant in determining priori-ties under ss. 22 and 35(1)(b) and (c) [now ss. 20 and 30(1)2 and 3]. (Why not under s. 35(1)(a)?)

Professor Gilmore argued for one security interest which attaches at the time value is first given and was not disturbed by the adverse effect of his view on the position of an intervening judgment creditor who assumes control of the collateral through legal process between the time of the security agreement and the making of an optional future advance. Gilmore, *Security Interests in Personal Property*, volume 2 (1965) 933 *et seq.* Gilmore's view was that where a future advance is made after the assumption of control through legal process by the judgment creditor, "... the debtor's assets have not been depleted: the ... advance balances the diminution of his equity in the machinery [subject to the security interest]. The [judgment creditor] will ... receive less from the sale of the machinery than he would have received before [the advance was made], but his chance of collecting his claim from the debtor's remaining assets (which now include the ... advance) is as good as ever; presumably it is better than ever since the debtor now has a new supply of working capital": *id.*, at 939. Do you agree?

PROBLEM

On September 1 Debtor gives S a non-possessory security interest in specified machinery owned by him pursuant to a security agreement containing a future advance clause (i.e., a term under which the collateral also secures future advances). The security agreement contains no commitment as to the giving of future advances. S registers a financing statement and advances $5,000. On September 15 Debtor borrows $1,000 from C and signs a security agreement covering the same machinery. A financing statement is duly registered. On September 25, S advances $500 to Debtor. Debtor defaults on September 30 without making any repayment. The machinery is worth $6,000. Consider the following questions:

1) How much will be collected by S? What could C have done to protect himself? See ss. 38 and 50.

2) Suppose C is not an intervening lender but either a buyer of the collateral or a judgment creditor assuming control thereof through legal process on September 15. How will this affect your answer to (1)?

3) Suppose C does not register a financing statement but perfects his security interest by possession. Will this affect your answer to (1)?

4) Suppose the September 25 advance was made by S pursuant to a commitment given by him to the debtor in the September 1 security agreement. Will this affect any of your previous answers?

Coin-O-Matic Service Co. v. Rhode Island Hospital Trust Co.
(1966), 3 UCC Rep. Ser. 1112 (RI Superior Ct.)

LICHT J: This matter is before the court on an agreed statement of facts. The following is a summary of the facts which will help place the case in proper perspective.

On July 11, 1963, Munroe Doroff purchased a motor vehicle from Warwick Motors, Inc., on a time payment basis (Exhibit "A"). The security agreement representing the purchase was assigned to the Rhode Island Hospital Trust Company. The security agreement did not have any provision for after-acquired property or future advances. It described the collateral as one Chevrolet Station Wagon Greenbrier 1963. The financing statement filed July 16, 1963 contained a reference to the same Chevrolet Greenbrier Station Wagon (Exhibit "B").

On October 2, 1964 Doroff became indebted to Coin-O-Matic Service Company in the sum of $5,600.00 represented by a promissory note and secured by a security agreement (Exhibits "C" and "D"). A financing agreement was filed October 23, 1964 (Exhibit "E"). On November 13, 1964, Doroff owed the Hospital Trust Company $302.77 on the security agreement of July 11, 1963 and on that date Rhode Island Hospital Trust Company loaned Doroff the sum of $1,000.00 from which sum he paid to Rhode Island Hospital Trust Company $302.77 in full satisfaction of his July 11, 1963 obligation. Rhode Island Hospital Trust Company thereupon cancelled the old agreement. Doroff executed a new promissory note secured by a security agreement (Exhibit "F"). A new financing statement was filed on November 17, 1964 (Exhibit "G"). On December 7, 1964 Doroff went into bankruptcy. It was stipulated that the value of the motor vehicle at the time it came into Rhode Island Hospital Trust Company's possession was $1,200.00. It was further stipulated that the automobile was used in Doroff's business and there is no question that the automobile was part of the collateral given to Coin-O-Matic Service Company, the plaintiff.

• • •

The defendant contends that its original financing statement was sufficient not only to protect the original conditional sales agreement but the subsequent agreement despite the fact that there intervened a security agreement between Doroff and Coin-O-Matic and a filed financing statement in connection therewith.

The issues raised require a consideration of the Uniform Commercial Code. There is no dispute that the word "equipment" used in the security agreement between Doroff and Coin-O-Matic was within Section 6A-9-109(2).

Section 6A-9-312 provides in part:

(5) In all cases not governed by other rules stated in this section (including cases of purchase money security interests which do not qualify for the special priorities set forth in subsections (3) and (4) of this section), priority between conflicting security interests in the same collateral shall be determined as follows:

(a) in the order of filing if both are perfected by filing, regardless of which security interest attached first under §6A-9-204(1) and whether it attached before or after filing;

The defendant relies wholly upon what it considers the compelling literal meaning of the language of the section. That is to say, that having entered into a security transaction which covered the 1963 Chevrolet Greenbrier Station Wagon and having filed a financing statement it comes ahead of the plaintiff who had a security interest in the same collateral but whose filing of a financing statement was subsequent in time to the original filing and ahead of defendant's second filing. Obviously with respect to the original transaction there is no dispute that the prior filing of the financial statement would govern. But the defendant carries its argument a step further and contends that the original financing statement is an umbrella which gives the defendant a priority with respect to its second security transaction notwithstanding that the plaintiff's security interest was established in point of time prior to defendant's second security transaction.

The defendant contends that as long as there is a financing statement on file the whole world is given notice that the debtor is obligated; that there is a security interest in the particular collateral and that the debtor may at any time after the original transaction become further indebted and enter into an additional security agreement with respect to the collateral. In support of this position the defendant cites a colloquy between Peter Coogan, a member of the Permanent Editorial Board of the Uniform Commercial Code, and a member of the bar at a panel discussion conducted under the auspices of the American Bar Association in August of 1963. The following is the colloquy which is of such interest that the court in order to place the matter in its proper perspective sets it forth as follows:

Mr. Kripke: Before you go on, let us take a hard case. Let us suppose you had this original mortgage for a dollar and then you have another intervening contractual chattel mortgage, and Sydney has no future advance clause but takes a third mortgage instrument for the half million dollars on the same property and there has already been an intervening filing with respect to it. Now where does Sydney rank?

Mr. Coogan: Let's see if I follow you—

Mr. Kripke: You have an original chattel mortgage for a dollar, perfected by a notice which says "industrial equipment." You have an intervening chattel mortgage for another lender on the same equipment for a hundred thousand dollars, let us say. Then Sydney takes a third piece of paper, a chattel mortgage on the same piece of equipment—one never in the original contemplation of the parties. Where do their parties rank?

Mr. Coogan: Sydney comes ahead of everybody. This is an illustration of the first-to-file rule. Where two security interests have both been perfected through filing, and no specific priority rule applies the priorities date from the time of the filing.

Mr. Kripke: You mean the original notice determines priorities as of its date even for a transaction that was not contemplated at the time?

Mr. Coogan: That is correct.

Mr. Kripke: It would cover an advance which was not even covered by a future advance clause?

Mr. Coogan: That is correct. (19 *Bus. Law* 20, 52 (1963))

It will be observed as already noted that the original conditional sales agreement between Doroff and Warwick Motors, Inc. which was assigned to the defendant has no provision for future advances.

Section 6A-204, subsection (5) provides:

Obligations covered by a security agreement may include future advances or other value whether or not the advances or value are given pursuant to commitment.

Defendant contends that this provision merely permits a lender to include a provision for future advances in the original security agreement and that when this is so provided it obviates the necessity of executing subsequent security agreements with respect to future advances as long as the financing statement covering the collateral in question is prior in time and additional security agreements are obtained with each new loan. This is, according to the defendant, the thrust of Mr. Coogan's remarks to which reference has already been made. If this is so, it places a lender in an unusually strong position vis-à-vis the debtor and any subsequent lenders. In fact, it gives the lender a throttle hold on the debtor. For example, a debtor borrows $25,000.00 from a lender to be paid over a three-year period without any right of anticipation. The security is the equipment of the debtor. No provision is made for future advances. The financing statement is filed. The debtor reduces the obligation to $12,500.00 and now seeks to borrow an additional $5,000.00. The original lender is not interested in making a second loan. The debtor is in no position to pay off the loan without borrowing from another lender. The original lender does not desire to liquidate the obligation except in strict accordance with the agreement. Under the theory advanced by the defendant the original debtor cannot borrow from the second lender because no second lender can safely advance the money as long as there is a possibility that a future advance by the original lender would have priority in the collateral over the second lender. The interpretation contended for by the defendant does not appear to this court to be necessary for the protection of lenders nor does it seem necessary for facilitating commercial transactions. Defendant's counsel does not deny that this is so but contends that it makes no difference because Section 6A-9-312(5)(a) gives the original lender such protection. Counsel for the defendant concedes a difference in a case in which the lender is paid off, the balance on the original transaction is reduced to zero and in which the financing statement is not terminated by a termination agreement as provided in Section 6A-9-404 but it distinguishes the instant case from such a situation. The termination statement section provides in part as follows:

Termination Statement.—(1) Whenever there is no outstanding secured obligations and no commitment to make advances, incur obligations or otherwise give value, the secured party must on written demand by the debtor send the debtor a statement that he no longer claims a security interest under the financing statement, which shall be identified by file number. ...

It seems, however, that the defendant, notwithstanding his recognition of a differenmce in the illustration put forth, should nevertheless take the position that as long as the financing statement is not terminated the lender is protected even when the original balance is liquidated, provided that additional funds are loaned and a new security agreement is entered into between the original lender and debtor. In such a case the original lender would come ahead of an intervening security transaction in which a financing statement had been filed for the same collateral. But why should the law be so interpreted to produce such a result? In all of these cases a lender can protect himself against the situation involved herein by providing in the original security agreement for future advances. In other words, the conclusion urged upon this court by the defendant is not required in the interest of facilitating commercial transactions particularly in the light of the fact that the Code provides for future advances in Section 6A-9-204(5). Comment 8, under this section, is as follows:

8. Under subsection (5) collateral may secure future as well as present advances when the security agreement so provides. At common law and under chattel mortgage statutes there seems to have been a vaguely articulated prejudice against future advance agreements comparable to the prejudice against after-acquired property interests. Although only a very few jurisdictions went to the length of invalidating interests claimed by virtue of future advances, judicial limitations severely restricted the usefulness of such arrangements. A common limitation was that an interest claimed in collateral existing at the time the security transaction was entered into for advances made thereafter was good only to the extent that the original security agreement specified the amount of such later advances and even the times at which they should be made. In line with the policy of this Article (Chapter) toward after-acquired property interests this subsection validates the future advance interest, provided only that the obligation be covered by the security agreement. This is a special case of the more general provision of subsection (3).

And Example 4 under 6A-9-312 is as follows:

Example 4. On February 1 A makes an advance against machinery in the debtor's possession and files his financing statement. On March 1 B makes an advance against the same machinery and files his financing statement. On April 1 A makes a further advance, under the original security agreement, against the same machinery (which is covered by the original financing statement and thus perfected when made). A has priority over B both as to the February 1 and as to the April 1 advance and it makes no difference whether or not A knows of B's intervening advance when he makes his second advance.

The case falls under subsection (5)(a), since both interests are perfected by filing. A wins, as to the April 1 advance, because he first filed even though B's interest attached, and indeed was perfected, first. Section 9-204(5) and the Comment thereto should be consulted for the validation of future advances. Section 9-313 provides for cases involving fixtures.

It will be observed that under this example the advance is made pursuant to the original security agreement, meaning thereby that the original security agreement contains a future advance provision. The author directs attention to §9-313 in order to protect a lender in the case of future advances.

This is a case of first impression. No case has been cited to this court but counsel informed the court that there is no decided case involving the precise issue presented herein.

• • •

The provisions of the Code with respect to notice is, in the judgment of this court, helpful in the matter of interpreting §9-312(5).

Section 9-402 [OPPSA, s. 45] provides for the financing statement and the filing.

Section 9-208 [OPPSA, s. 18] provides that a debtor may request information from the lender as to the amount due on the obligation and the collateral covered by the security agreement. If the secured party, without reasonable excuse, fails to comply with the request he is liable for any loss caused to the debtor thereby and if the debtor has properly included in his request a good faith statement of the obligation or a list of the collateral or both, the secured party may claim a security interest only as shown in the statement against persons misled by his failure to comply.

If the Code gives the lender an interest in the collateral for future advances even though no provision is made for such future advances, then the information secured by the debtor and given to a subsequent lender is of little value because the second creditor surely could not rely upon the information. If the defendant's interpretation of the Code is correct, there seems to be hardly any substantive reason why the original lender should be bound to comply with the borrower's request for information concerning a correct statement of the outstanding balance and the collateral covered under the security agreement.

It should be observed that the defendant and the original debtor believed that the original conditional sales transaction was a single transaction and did not provide for future advances by virtue of the original financing statement. This is clear from an examination of the agreed statement and the exhibits attached thereto. When, on November 15th, Doroff's balance with the Hospital Trust was $302.77 on the security agreement of July 11, 1963, and when, on that date, the defendant loaned Doroff $1,000.00 which paid off the original balance and the old agreement was cancelled, Doroff executed a new promissory note secured by a new security agreement and a new financing statement was filed with the Secretary of State on November 17, 1964.

It would seem to this court that without a consideration of the meaning of §9-312(5) this case might properly be decided on what the parties themselves did and what the parties themselves intended. Insofar as Doroff and the Rhode Island Hospital Trust Company were concerned these parties intended an entirely new transaction when the additional loan was made and they considered the original transaction as terminated. They did not intend to affect an intervening creditor. Certainly Doroff, although he subsequently went into bankruptcy, might well have not agreed to a new transaction if such new transaction was to have the effect of cutting out the intervening creditor. What these parties intended was a completely separate transaction and the claim now that the defendant is entitled to the protection of the original financing statement comes, in the judgment of this court, as an after-thought.

It is the considered judgment of the court after a careful consideration of the agreed statement of facts and the applicable provisions of the Commercial Code that particularly in this case the defendant is not entitled to rely upon the original financing statement in order to bring its subsequent loan ahead of that of the intervening creditor. This is said not because of the application of the principles of estoppel or waiver but because the parties surely are not prohibited under the Code from treating their transactions as separate and unrelated transactions. See 6A-1-102(2) and 6A-1-201(3).

Section 6A-9-312(5) deals with priority between conflicting security interests in the same collateral and gives a priority in the order of the filing but that obviously does not relate to separate and distinct security transactions. Moreover, a careful examination of 6A-9-312 and the other applicable provisions of the Code lead to the conclusion that the reasonable interpretation of 6A-9-312 is that a security agreement which does not provide for future advances is a single transaction and in the case of subsequent security agreements there is required a new financing statement. That is to say, a single financing statement in connection with a security agreement when no provision is made for future advances is not an umbrella for future advances based upon new security agreements, notwithstanding the fact that involved is the same collateral.

Judgment for plaintiff.

NOTES AND QUESTIONS

1) Was *Coin-O-Matic* a future advances case? How would it be decided under the OPPSA? Is Judge Licht's interpretation of the Code provisions consistent with the Supreme Court of Minnesota's decision in *James Talcott Inc. v. Franklin National Bank of Minneapolis, supra*, this chapter? Is a future advance distinguishable from a "future transaction"? *Coin-O-Matic* was not followed in subsequent US decisions and was strongly criticized by commentators. Revised Article 9 (1972 version) provides in 9-312(7): "If future advances are made while a security interest is perfected by filing or the taking of possession, the security interest has the same priority for the purpose of subsection (5) with respect to future advances as it does to the first advance." (Subsection (5) corresponds to PPSA s. 35(1).) It has been said that "[b]y new subsection (7) the draftsmen have made explicit what was implicit to all reasonable men under the old 9-312(5), namely, that future advances made while the security interest is perfected by filing or by the taking of the possession relate back to the original date of filing or taking of possession": J. White and R. Summers, *Handbook of the Law Under the Uniform Commercial Code* (1972), at 913. (See also the 2nd edition (1980), at 1042.)

Article 9 further provides in §9-301(4) that,

(4) A person who becomes a lien creditor while a security interest is perfected takes subject to the security interest only to the extent that it secures advances made before he becomes a lien creditor or within 45 days thereafter or made without knowledge of the lien or pursuant to a commitment entered into without knowledge of the lien.

A "lien creditor" is the Code equivalent to a person whose interest is governed by OPPSA s. 20(1)(a)(ii) and (b). UCC 9-307(3) provides that a buyer not in the ordinary course of business "takes free of a security interest to the extent that it secures future advances made after the secured party acquires knowledge of the purchase, or more than 45 days after the purchase, whichever first occurs ..."

Would *Coin-O-Matic* and the problem preceding it be decided differently under these provisions?

2) The new Ontario Act follows the Article 9 1972 revisions in clarifying the priority status of future advances, and in giving future advances made while a security interest is perfected the same priority as the security interest has with respect to the first advance. Note in particular the following Ontario provisions:

s. 1. "future advance" means the advance of money, credit or other value *secured by a security agreement* whether or not such advance is given pursuant to commitment; [Italics added. What is the significance of the italicized words? [ed.]]

s. 30. ...

(3) Subject to subsection (4), where future advances are made while a security interest is perfected, the security interest has the same priority with respect to each future advance as it has with respect to the first advance.

(4) A future advance under a perfected security interest is subordinate to the rights of persons mentioned in subclauses 20(1)(a)(ii) and (iii) if the advance was made after the secured party received written notification of the interest of any such person unless,

(a) the secured party makes the advance for the purpose of paying reasonable expenses, including the cost of insurance and payment of taxes or other charges incurred in obtaining and maintaining possession of the collateral and its preservation; or

(b) the secured party is bound to make the advance, whether or not a subsequent event of default or other event not within the secured party's control has relieved or may relieve the secured party from the obligation.

The other provincial Acts contain similar though not identical provisions.

3) What is the justification for giving a secured party priority with respect to future advances whether or not there is a commitment to make them? Is it sufficient to say that the debtor always has the option of paying off the secured party and of requiring him to file a financing change statement? Suppose the debtor cannot afford to pay off the secured party but wants to be able to use the collateral to secure an advance from another lender. Should he be free to do so or should the second lender be obliged to seek a waiver from the secured party or to agree to make his loan sufficiently large to pay off the first lender?

PRIORITY OF REPERFECTED SECURITY INTERESTS [S. 30(6)]

Section 30(6) is new. It did not appear in the 1984 or 1986 draft bills prepared by the Minister's Advisory Committee but was added at a later date by the Ministry's officials. It was obviously intended to replace s. 53(1)(c) of the old Act and, like s. 53(1)(c), is designed to prevent a later secured party gaining a windfall because an earlier secured party has failed to reperfect a security interest after the original registration lapsed for some reason. However, s. 30(6) is considerably broader than s. 53(1)(c) and it raises difficult questions of interpretation and policy, such as the following (for a detailed discussion, see Ziegel & Denomme, *op. cit.*, § 30.5, pp. 236-39):

1) Does it apply where the security interest was originally perfected by possession, and if not, why should a distinction be drawn between a security interest perfected by registration and a security interest perfected by other means?

2) Does subs. (6) apply where the original registration occurred outside Ontario and there was a gap in re-registration after the collateral was brought into Ontario? (On these conflict of laws aspects refresh your memory by again examining s. 5 of the Ontario Act.)

3) Does subs. (6) apply where the secured party reperfects by taking possession of the collateral and does not file an amended financing statement?

4) Must the secured party reperfect within a given time? Should there be a time limit?

5) What is the meaning of "if a person acquired rights in all or part of the collateral during the period when the security interest was unperfected"? On this, see Feldman J's judgment in *Heidelberg Canada Graphic Equipment Ltd. v. Arthur Andersen Inc.* (1992), 7 BLR (2d) 236 (Ont.), reproduced in and discussed, *supra*, chapter 4.

6) Finally and not least, given the importance which the Act elsewhere attaches to continuous perfection, what is the justification for making an exception to the policy in this case?

CHAPTER SIX

The Purchase-Money Security Interest Priority

Purchase-money security interests (PMSIs) constitute a singularly important exception to the priority rules in s. 30. "Purchase-money security interest" is defined in s. 1(1). Note that unlike the conditional sale at common law, the definition is not confined to a seller retaining title to secure the purchase party of the collateral but equally extends to a lender granting a loan to a buyer to enable her to pay cash to the seller. As a result, the purchase-money lender enjoys the same status as the conditional seller under the OPPS legislation for priority as well as other purposes. It will also elevate his status under other Acts that distinguish between purchase-money and non-purchase-money security interests. See, e.g., *Dube v. Bk. of Montreal* (1986), 5 PPSAC 269 (Sask. CA); and *Rodger v. Bk. of Montreal* (1986), 6 PPSAC 76 (Sask.). This is a far cry from the common law where only the conditional seller could be sure of maintaining his primacy over all other consensual security interests created by the buyer (whether created before or after the conditional sale), the theory being that since the buyer did not have title under a conditional sale the most he could pledge was his equity or special interest in the goods. *Cf.* R.M. Goode, *Commercial Law* (1982), at 779-82.

Sections 33(1) and (2) of the OPPSA provide respectively that a PMSI in inventory or its proceeds and a PMSI in other types of collateral or its proceeds has priority over any other security interest in the same collateral. (The Act distinguishes between inventory and non-inventory collateral because of the nature of inventory financing and its particular requirements.) The economic reason usually given for according priority to the purchase money financer is that he is making it possible for the debtor to add to her stock of assets and therefore deserves to be preferred. A more sophisticated explanation is given by Jackson and Kronman in the following extracts from their very influential article.

Jackson and Kronman
Secured Financing and Priorities Among Creditors
(1979), 88 *Yale LJ* 1143, at 1165-75
(footnotes omitted)

Two general characteristics of the purchase money priority should be noted at the outset. First, the special priority for purchase money lenders is linked logically to the recognition of security interests in after-acquired property. This follows from the definition of a purchase-money security interest. To qualify as a purchase money lender, a creditor must make an "enabling" loan—a loan that makes it possible for his debtor to acquire rights in property that he did not previously have. If a debtor already owns a particular asset, he may of course use it to secure any number of loans, but no creditor making an advance against the property will be eligible for purchase money status.

Since, by definition, a debtor cannot own the property securing a purchase money loan before the loan itself is made, a prior creditor can only claim an interest in such property through an "after-acquired property clause" in his security agreement, which extends his security interest to assets that subsequently become part of the debtor's estate. It is therefore not surprising that in the chattel security field the idea of a special priority for purchase money lenders did not emerge until courts had finally accepted the notion that a debtor can validly encumber property he does not yet own.

A second striking characteristic of the purchase money priority is its limitation to loans that can be traced to identifiable, discrete items of property. Loans made for unrestricted purposes such as general use in the course of the debtor's business have never been accorded purchase money status, even if the loan can be shown to have increased the value of the debtor's estate or, more particularly, the value of the collateral securing a prior creditor's claim. Before a creditor can assert the rights of a purchase money lender, he must demonstrate that his loan has been used by the debtor to acquire a specific and identifiable asset. This limitation, which historically has been incorporated in the definition of a purchase money security interest, is today embodied in the tracing requirement of section 9-107.

These introductory remarks suggest three related issues that we shall address in the following sections in a way that builds upon and is consistent with the general theory already developed. The close link between purchase money priority and security interests in after-acquired property makes it logical to begin by considering why a debtor and his creditor would ever agree to include an after-acquired property clause in their contract. We then discuss the special difficulties created by an after-acquired property clause, difficulties that might explain the establishment of an overriding priority for purchase money lenders. Finally, we attempt to explain the limitation of purchase money status to those creditors who can trace their loans to identifiable items of property.

2. *The After-Acquired Property Clause*

It is sometimes assumed that the principal function of an after-acquired property clause is to decrease the riskiness of a particular claim by expanding the pool of collateral that secures it. If this were the only advantage of such a clause, however, it is hard to see what incentive the parties to a credit transaction would have to include an after-acquired property clause in their contract. For while the clause makes one creditor's claim less risky, it simultaneously increases the riskiness of loans made by the debtor's other creditors. In fact, in the absence of transaction costs, we would expect these effects to exactly offset one another, leaving the total cost of credit to the debtor unchanged; what the debtor gained by having the interest rate on one loan reduced, he would lose in increased payments to his remaining creditors.

When transaction costs are taken into account, however, both the advantages of an after-acquired property clause and a basis for predicting when such a clause will be used emerge more clearly. If the collateral securing a loan is a type of property, such as inventory or receivables, that is turned over rapidly in the ordinary course of the debtor's business, both the debtor and his creditor are likely to view an after-acquired property clause as a cost-saving device. In a case of this sort, the clause saves the parties the expense of writing a new contract, or rewriting their original one, whenever individual items of collateral are liquidated and replaced by new items of the same kind. Because it allows transaction cost savings, a legal regime that recognizes the validity of after-acquired property clauses is more efficient than one that does not.

3. *Situational Monopoly and the Purchase Money Priority*

Although the after-acquired property clause saves costs, it also creates what economists call a "situational monopoly," in that a creditor with a security interest in after-acquired property enjoys a special competitive advantage over other lenders in all his subsequent dealings with the debtor. In our view, the purchase money priority is best thought of as a device for alleviating the situational monopoly created by an after-acquired property clause. Therefore, when a debtor and his creditor have an incentive to include such a clause in their contract, they are also likely to favor the inclusion of a provision empowering the debtor to create an overriding purchase money priority in subsequently acquired assets. These principles may be illustrated by a hypothetical case.

$$\bullet \quad \bullet \quad \bullet$$

Despite the transaction costs savings it offers, then, the after-acquired property clause gives a competitive advantage to the creditor in whose favor it is written. It also works to the disadvantage of the debtor by raising the cost of future credit above what it would be in the absence of the clause, because the advantaged creditor can exploit his monopoly power at any time after the clause is written. Consequently, if we assume that the debtor cannot override an after-acquired property clause by giving later lenders a purchase money security interest, we can expect him to insist upon and, if the credit market is competitive, to obtain a reduction in the interest rate on C1's original loan sufficient to offset the expected increase in the cost of subsequent credit attributable to C1's situational monopoly. The magnitude of this reduction will depend upon how large a premium the parties think the creditor making the original loan will be able to extract in future transactions as a result of the after-acquired property clause. Their estimates regarding the size of this premium will depend, in turn, on the frequency with which they expect the debtor to require additional extensions of credit and, most importantly, on their predictions concerning the bargaining power each party is likely to exert in negotiations over the price term in any subsequent credit transaction.

Suppose now that the parties are free to include a provision in their contract empowering the debtor to override an after-acquired property clause by giving later lenders purchase money priority. By including this provision, the parties can often blunt the situational monopoly created by an after-acquired property clause. In the absence of such a clause, a purchase money provision would of course be superfluous. But when an after-acquired property clause has been included in the contract, the purchase money provision often ensures that the debtor will be able to obtain future loans on nearly competitive terms—whether from the original lender or from some other supplier of credit. To return to the hypothetical case, if the debtor can give C2 a purchase money security interest in the new inventory, the monitoring costs associated with the $1,000 loan will be the same for both creditors, just as they would be the same if C1's original contract with the debtor did not contain an after-acquired property clause in the first place.

Although a purchase money provision blunts the situational monopoly that would otherwise be created by an after-acquired property clause, it does not annul the savings in transaction costs that a clause of this sort makes possible. The debtor and C1 are still relieved of the need to rewrite their contract whenever one item of collateral is replaced by another. This explains why the parties to a credit transaction might prefer a contract that contained both sorts of provisions to one that contained neither. But when coupled with an after-acquired property clause, a purchase money provision weakens the situational monopoly that the creditor would enjoy in its absence, and we would therefore expect the price of a contract with both terms to be higher than one that contained only an after-acquired property clause.

One might think that the parties would be indifferent between a contract that contained an after-acquired property clause together with a purchase money provision and a contract that contained only an after-acquired property clause but also had a lower price term. The second package, however, is almost certain to be more costly to negotiate since it requires the parties to determine how much the price term must be reduced to compensate the debtor for the adverse effects of the creditor's situational monopoly—a determination that cannot be made without assessing a host of future contingencies and evaluating the relative bargaining strength of the parties themselves. Since both parties have an interest in avoiding protracted and expensive negotiations, they will agree to include a purchase money provision in their contract whenever they have independently decided to include an after-acquired property clause in order to reduce transaction costs. Inclusion of a purchase money provision leaves the parties in the same position they would have been in if they had simply reduced the contract price to reflect the cost to the debtor of the situational monopoly created by an after-acquired property clause, without involving the additional negotiation expenses that a price reduction would entail. The purchase money provision in Article 9 merely legislates a standard contract term that the parties would be likely to adopt in its absence.

For the sake of clarity, the foregoing argument ignores a number of complicating factors. There is, however, one factor that is sufficiently important to mention at this point. In developing a rationale for the purchase money priority, we have stressed the competitive advantage created by an after-acquired property clause, and have suggested that the special priority afforded purchase money lenders may be viewed as a device for blunting this advantage. Even if his contract with the debtor does not contain an after-acquired property clause, however, a prior lender may nevertheless enjoy an advantage over his competitors. The very fact that he has made a previous loan to the debtor and is already engaged in monitoring the debtor's behavior is likely to give the prior lender, C1, an informational advantage over later lenders such as C2. The cost of initially acquiring certain basic information about the debtor may be viewed as a start-up cost that every creditor will have to incur. Having already incurred this cost, C1 can extend credit to the debtor on more advantageous terms than can a creditor who is dealing with the debtor for the first time. This undoubtedly explains, at least in part, why debtors engage in "repeat" transactions with particular creditors rather than shifting frequently from one supplier of credit to another.

If C1 enjoys an informational advantage of this sort, however, it is due to his pre-existing relationship with the debtor and not to the presence of an after-acquired property clause in their credit agreement. Furthermore, it is difficult to see how this informational advantage could be eliminated at reasonable cost, or why the parties would want to prevent C1 from acquiring such an advantage in the first place. Although it is true that the information C1 acquires in the course of his dealings with the debtor may give him a competitive advantage over other creditors in bidding for subsequent loans, the debtor is not likely to view this as a detriment at all. He is more likely to think of C1's information as a capital asset that both parties can potentially exploit to their mutual advantage.

NOTE

The definition of purchase-money security interest (hereafter PMSI) in the Act is critically important, particularly where it is a lender who is claiming a PMSI status. If the lender fails to satisfy the definitional requirements *as well as* the requirements in ss. 33(1) and (2), the lender's claim will be defeated. Antecedent competing secured parties have a strong incentive to challenge a PMSI claim so as to protect their ranking under s. 30(1). (For a detailed examination of the definition see Ziegel & Denomme, *op. cit.,* §1.23, pp.25-30).

To satisfy the requirements of limb (b) of the definition the secured party must be able to show:

(1) that its value was given for the purpose of enabling the debtor to acquire rights in or to the collateral;
(2) that the secured party's value was given for the purpose of enabling the debtor to acquire rights in the collateral; and
(3) that the value was in fact so applied.

Each of these requirements is contentious, has attracted much litigation in the United States, and is attracting an increasing amount of attention in Canada.

Agricultural Credit Corporation of Saskatchewan v. Pettyjohn and Pettyjohn
[1991] 3 WWR 689 (Sask. CA)

[In 1981, Mr. and Mrs. Pettyjohn applied for a loan from ACCS to buy cattle, and these were to serve as security for the loan. The loan was approved, subject to the stipulation that the Pettyjohns were not to sell any of the cattle without the previous written consent of ACCS. In fact, ACCS made the loan monies available only after the Pettyjohns had purchased the cattle.

The Pettyjohns purchased additional cattle and irrigation equipment in 1984, after receiving approval for a further loan agreement from ACCS. Since there was again a delay in ACCS making the monies available, the Pettyjohns borrowed the money with which to pay for these items from the Bank of Montreal. When the Pettyjohns received the ACCS funds, they used them to pay off the Bank of Montreal loan.

In 1986 and 1987, the Pettyjohns sold all of the cattle derived from the two ACCS loans and invested the proceeds in a new breed of cattle (Watusi cattle). The sales took place without the knowledge or consent of ACCS. Since the debtors were in default with their payments, ACCS sought to repossess the Watusi cattle, claiming they represented the proceeds from the sale of the earlier cattle financed by ACCS. Under the Saskatchewan Farm Security Act, the Watusi cattle were exempt from seizure unless ACCS had a PMSI in them.

There were therefore two principle issues before the Saskatchewan Court of Appeal: (1) whether ACCS had a PMSI in the 1984 cattle; and (2) assuming they did, whether the Watusi cattle represented the proceeds from the sale of the earlier cattle. The following extract only deals with the first issue.]

SHERSTOBITOFF JA (Vancise JA concurring):

Procedural history

The Pettyjohns made the required payments on their various loans with the ACCS until December 1987. Upon default, ACCS attempted to realize on its security. The Pettyjohns then declared bankruptcy, and claimed that their present Watusi cattle were exempt from seizure under the Saskatchewan Farm Security Act, SS 1988-89, c. S-17.1 ["SFSA"]. Under the SFSA, both parties acknowledge that the Watusi cattle are exempt from seizure unless ACCS had a PMSI in those cattle.

On March 13, 1990 Geatros J directed a trial to determine the issue of whether ACCS had a PMSI in the Watusi cattle. The trial took place on May 8 and 9, 1990 before Barclay J. On August 27, 1990 Barclay J issued reasons including that ACCS did not have a PMSI in the Watusi cattle.

With reference to 1981 and 1984 loans and cattle purchases, the trial judge found as a fact that the cattle purchases took place before funds were advanced. He then concluded, as a matter of law, that a PMSI was not created in these circumstances.

As a result, I am convinced that ACC did not truly advance moneys to the respondents for them to purchase cattle, as the cattle had already been purchased by the respondents prior to the advance of the loan funds. Therefore, it has not been established that ACCS has a purchase money security interest claim in that it has not been shown that "value was applied to acquire such rights" as enunciated by Gerein J in *Royal Bank v. Pioneer Property Mgmt. Ltd.*, [1987] 2 WWR 445, 53 Sask. R 228 (QB).

The test under s. 2(gg)(ii) for a PMSI can be conveniently broken down into three requirements. The first requirement is that the lender has taken a security interest in the property. The second is that the lender has given value for the purpose of enabling the debtor to acquire rights in the property. The third requirement is that the value has in fact been used to acquire those rights.

Although the trial judge did not make any finding of fact with respect to the first requirement, that of a security interest, it is clear on the evidence that ACCS did take a security interest in the 1981 and 1984 cattle.

In dealing with the second and third requirements, the trial judge focused on the advance of the loan moneys as being the value in question. In doing so, the trial judge defined value too narrowly. The PPSA defines value in broad terms:

2. In this Act:

(gg) "value" means any consideration sufficient to support a simple contract and includes an antecedent debt or liability.

ACCS contends that the final loan approval letter which was sent to the Pettyjohns can be treated as a unilateral contract and a binding commitment to advance credit, so that it was itself value given to the Pettyjohns satisfying the second and third requirements.

A number of American cases have considered the issue of what constitutes value in similar, though not identical, legislative schemes. These cases have concluded that value is given where a lender makes a binding commitment to extend credit, notwithstanding the fact that the loan advances occur later. For instance, in *Thet Mah & Assoc. Inc. v. First Bank of North Dakota (NA), Minot*, 336 NW 2d 134, 36 UCC Reporting Service 649 (North Dakota SC, 1983), the court makes the following comments with respect to "value" under the uniform commercial code (at p. 653):

For purposes of the uniform commercial code, a person gives value for rights if he acquires them in return for a binding commitment to extend credit, and generally for any considerations sufficient to support a simple contract.

It is notable that the language used by the court is very similar to the language in our PPSA.

A similar conclusion was reached in *US v. Cahall Bros.*, 674 F.2d 578 (CA 6th Circ., 1982). However the statutory language in that case was more specific than is our PPSA: see also *Honea v. Laco Auto Leasing Inc.*, 454 P.2d 782, (CA, 1969), and *State Bank & Trust Co. of Beeville v. First Nat. Bank of Beeville*, 635 SW 2d 807, 33 UCC Reporting Service 1775 (Texas CA, 1982).

Although, in some cases, the American "binding commitment" test is based on more specific statutory language than is contained in the PPSA, the test itself is entirely congruent with the language of the PPSA. A binding commitment is, by definition, consideration sufficient to support a simple contract. It is, therefore, value in the eyes of the PPSA.

It is not entirely clear whether the loan approval letters issued in 1981 and 1984 themselves create a binding commitment, and it is not in the end necessary to decide that.

• • •

The final loan approval and letter of eligibility between them make it clear that the Pettyjohns were invited to rely on the letter of final loan approval. Thus, at least at the point when the Pettyjohns, in essence, accepted this offer by relying on the final loan approval in making their purchases on credit and/or with the aid of interim financing, ACCS became subject to a binding commitment to extend credit. This represents value given by ACCS to the Pettyjohns. The trial judge ought, therefore, to have approached the second and third requirements for a PMSI with this form of value in mind. Since the trial judge did not approach it on this basis, we must now make our own findings of fact in relation to these requirements.

The purpose for which ACCS gave value in the form of a binding commitment to extend credit to the Pettyjohns is easily ascertained, since it is set out in the letter of final approval itself. It is clear that the purpose of the value given was to enable the Pettyjohns to acquire rights in the property in question.

It is equally clear that the Pettyjohns did, in fact, use this value in order to obtain those rights. In one case, the Pettyjohns bought the cattle on credit, and then used the loan advances to pay off the credit. In another case, the Pettyjohns obtained interim financing from the Bank of Montreal in order to purchase cattle, and used the loan advances from ACCS to pay back the Bank of Montreal. In both cases, the whole course of the transaction indicates unequivocally that the Pettyjohns used the binding commitment from ACCS to supply credit as the ultimate source of value with which to acquire their rights in the 1981 and 1984 cattle.

On this basis, the claim of the ACCS to a PMSI in the 1981 and 1984 cattle is established.

Even on the basis that the value given by ACCS was the advance of the loan moneys, rather than the final loan approval, the claim of ACCS to a PMSI could be established.

The purpose of the PPSA as a whole is to simplify commercial transactions and to make the law governing them accord with practical commercial realities. Analyzed in this light, the second requirement for a PMSI, whether value was given for the purpose of enabling the debtor to acquire rights in the chattels, does not present a problem. The whole series of events leading up to the 1981 and 1984 loans and purchases leads inexorably to the conclusion that the purpose of ACCS in giving value to the Pettyjohns was to enable them to acquire rights in the 1981 and 1984 cattle. This is how the loan application and approval were structured, and was the understanding under which both ACCS and the Pettyjohns operated. The fact that value was given after the purchase does not lead inevitably to the conclusion that its purpose was not to enable the purchase, and looking at the entire series of transactions it is clear that this was in fact its purpose.

The third requirement, that the value have been used to acquire such rights, presents greater difficulties. How can it be said that the moneys advanced were used to acquire rights when the purchase had already taken place and the rights already acquired? It is, however, commercially unreasonable to divide the transactions so minutely. The Pettyjohns used the value given to them to pay off interim financing, but the interim financing had not been obtained as a separate transaction, but always with the view that it would be repaid through the moneys advanced by ACCS. The Pettyjohns used the value given as part of a larger, commercially reasonable transaction to acquire rights in the 1981 and 1984 cattle. The fact that the use of the value given was, due to the nature of the transaction, after the acquisition of rights does not alter the conclusion that the value given was used to acquire those rights.

For all these reasons, the trial judge was mistaken in concluding that ACCS did not acquire a PMSI in the 1981 and 1984 cattle, whether one focuses upon the binding commitment or the actual advances as the value given.

NOTES

1) Compare *Pettyjohn* with the Nebraska Supreme Court decision in *North Platte State Bk. v. Production Credit Assn.*, *infra*, this chapter. Are the two cases distinguishable?

Would the Saskatchewan Court of Appeal have decided the issue differently if there had been a priority contest between the ACCS and an earlier secured party with an interest in the collateral? Did ACCS's commitment to make funds available to the Pettyjohns actually enable them to acquire the cattle? If so, from whom?

2) Presumeably the Bank of Montreal held a PMSI for its advances before it was paid off. Prior to this date, did the BOM and the ACCS both have a PMSI in the cattle? If ACCS had obtained an assignment of the Bank's security interest, would this have given it PMSI status? Even if there was no assignment, could ACCS have claimed to be subrogated in equity to the BOM's security interest? Would this be consistent with the structure and policies of the OPPSA?

3) Meaning of "collateral" for the purposes of the definition.

"Collateral" is very broadly defined in s. 1(1) of the Act but US courts have given it a narrow reading for the purpose of satisfying the definition of a purchase money security interest. In *Northwestern National Bank S.W. v. Lectro System, Inc.,* [262 NW 3d 678, 22 UCC Rep. 199 (1977)] it was held that an advance made to enable the debtor to complete a contract and which was secured against payments due under the contract did not confer a purchase money security interest on the financer. The court reasoned that loaned funds must be intended and actually used for the acquisition of an identifiable asset, and the "performance of a contract" is not an asset. White and Summers note that if the plaintiff's argument had succeeded in *Lectro,* all business loans would qualify as purchase money loans.

The Saskatchewan Court of Appeal came close to sanctioning this result in *Battlefords Credit Union Ltd. v. Ilnicki* [(1991), 82 DLR (4th) 69]. In this case, the credit union made various loans to the defendant farmer over a period of years. Some of the loans were for the purchase of farm equipment; the purpose of the other loans was not clear. The defendant also obtained purchase money loans from other lenders. In 1984, the credit union refinanced all these loans under a consolidation loan which was secured by all of the defendant's machinery and equipment. The Court of Appeal held, approving two lower court decisions to the same effect, that the consolidation loan was a purchase money loan since it enabled the debtor to pay off prior security interests and to increase his own bundle of rights in the collateral. The court did not refer to the contrary American authorities nor did the judgments draw a distinction between a consolidation loan made by a lender holding a PMSI and a consolidation loan made to pay off a purchase money loan made by another lender.

Of even greater concern is the fact that the judgments of Cameron and Vancise JJA show little awareness that their expansive view of a purchase money security interest is not consistent with the history and object of the concept and that it will undermine still further the value of a general security interest held by a prior financer. The *Ilnicki* approach is also inconsistent with the structure of ss. 33(1) and (2) of the Ontario Act, which clearly envisage that the creation of the PMSI's will coincide with the debtor's acquisition of the collateral. In our view, therefore, *Ilnicki* should not be followed in Ontario,* at any rate not where the conflict involves two competing secured parties.

(Ziegel & Denomme, *op. cit.,* pp. 26-27.) Do you share the authors' concerns?

---

* And presumably will not be followed in Ontario if Gotlib J's reasoning in *Greyvest Leasing Inc. v. Canadian Imperial Bank of Commerce, supra,* also appeals to other judges. She said (at p. 269):

(The footnote is continued on the next page.)

Priority of the Inventory Financer (S. 33(1))

Clark Equipment of Canada Ltd. v. Bank of Montreal
(1984), 4 PPSAC 38 (Man. CA)

MATAS JA: Clark Equipment of Canada Ltd. (Clark) and Clark Equipment Credit of Canada Ltd. (Credit) have appealed from an order of Deniset J declaring that the appellants' interest in three pieces of equipment was subordinate to the interest of the Bank of Montreal (Montreal).

The question of priority is determinable under the Personal Property Security Act, SM 1973, c. 5 (also CCSM, c. P35) (the Act) which came into force on September 1, 1978.

Clark is a manufacturer and vendor of equipment. Credit is the financing arm of Clark. Maneco Equipment Co. Ltd. (Maneco) was a distributor of Clark's products. It sold and leased equipment. For the purposes of this litigation the two appellants are treated as one.

In 1977 Montreal made a loan to Maneco. As security, Montreal obtained a demand debenture which was duly registered. Under the terms of the debenture the bank had a floating charge on the assets of Maneco, then owned and after-acquired. The security was continued in force by operation of law (s. 65(2) [am. 1977, c. 28, s. 13] of the Act).

On September 7, 1978, Clark and Credit sent a notice to the bank, pursuant to s. 34(2) [am. 1973, c. 102, s. 7] of the Act, to notify the bank that they had or expected to have a purchase-money security interest in the then owned or after-acquired inventory of Maneco. The appellants filed financing statements in the personal property registry on September 20, 1978, indicating that they held a purchase-money security interest in inventory of Maneco. Maneco and the appellants entered into a new security agreement dated September 26, 1978 (replacing an earlier agreement).

In September 1979, August 1980 and April 1981, respectively, Maneco acquired three pieces of new equipment from Clark that had been manufactured by Clark. Montreal did not advance any funds to Maneco to finance the purchase.

In June 1981, Montreal placed Maneco in receivership. Clarkson Company Limited was appointed the receiver (Clarkson). Clarkson seized the three pieces of equipment in August 1981 and sold them. The sale proceeds are being held pending resolution of the question of priority between Montreal and the appellants.

At the first hearing of the appeal, Montreal contended that the appellants had been doing business with Maneco by way of consolidated accounting and that the appellants had not maintained specific individual accounts for each piece of equipment. The hearing was adjourned.

---

* Continued …

> If a creditor could obtain a PMSI merely by helping a debtor to pay for something of which the debtor had already taken possession then all lenders to debtors who had not fully paid for all property in their possession could obtain PMSI's and take priority over earlier general creditors. That cannot have been the Legislator's intention.

However, although *Ilnicki* cannot be justified for the reasons given by the Court of Appeal, the result may be justifiable on subrogational grounds if the appropriate requirements are met.

Before resumption of argument on the adjourned hearing, the appellants filed additional information to provide more detail about the particulars of the transactions between the appellants and Maneco. The additional material shows the purchase price for each piece of equipment, the course of dealing with the equipment, and how the balances due for each item was determined. Counsel for the appellants confirmed that their claim would be limited to the amount owing for each piece of equipment. Counsel for Montreal agreed that separate accounts had been kept by the appellants.

The learned Chambers Judge held that the appellants had not complied with s. 34(2) of the Act, they did not have a purchase-money security interest, the "first to register rule" prescribed in s. 35 applied, and that Montreal, as the first to register, was entitled to priority.

It will be necessary to examine the provisions of the Act and the security agreement in some detail. We have been greatly assisted in that undertaking by counsel having provided us with a careful exposition of Canadian and American cases and commentaries.

The case for the appellants is founded on their claim that they hold a purchase-money security interest in collateral (i.e., the equipment) and that they are entitled to the special priority prescribed in s. 34(2) of the Act.

One of two kinds of purchase-money security interest defined in the Act is a security interest taken or reserved by a seller to secure payment of the purchase price. The classic example is a conditional sale agreement. (The second kind of security interest is not applicable in this case.) The term "collateral" means property that is subject to a security interest: ss. 1(d), (u) and (aa). [See] Catzman, Personal Property Security Law in Ontario (1976), at 28; McLaren, Secured Transactions in Personal Property in Canada, vol. 1, §§1.02[1][b], 1.02[1][c].

1. In this Act,

• • •

(d) "collateral" means property that is subject to a security interest;

• • •

(u) "purchase-money security interest" means a security interest that is

(i) taken or reserved by the seller of the collateral to secure payment of all or part of its price, or

(ii) taken by a person who gives value that enables the debtor to acquire rights in or use of the collateral, if that value is applied to acquire those rights;

• • •

(aa) "security interest" means

(i) an interest in goods, fixtures, documents of title, instruments, securities, chattel papers or intangibles that secures payment or performance of an obligation, ...

Unless the special priority rules of s. 34 apply, recourse would be made to the general rules set out in s. 35. I adopt McLaren's summary of the effect of s. 35, ibid., §6.01[2][a]:

... The priority is to be determined by the:

(i) order of registration; (known as the first to register rule)

(ii) order of perfection; (known as the first to perfect rule)

(iii) order of attachment; (known as the first to attach rule).

And see *Nat. Trailer Convoy of Canada Ltd. v. Bank of Montreal* (1980), 1 PPSAC 87, 10 BLR 196 (Ont. HC); *Simpson (Robert) Co. v. Shadlock* (1981), 31 OR (2d) 612, 1 PPSAC 272 (HC); and *Roynat Inc. v. United Rescue Services Ltd.*, [1982] 3 WWR 512, 23 Man. R (2d) 290, 2 PPSAC 49 (CA).

In the case at Bar, Montreal registered first and would have priority under s. 35 unless the appellants are entitled to a special priority granted by s. 34(2).

Section 34(2) is designed to permit the purchase of goods and the obtaining of financing from the seller without running counter to the rights of an existing security interest which includes an after-acquired property clause (as Montreal had in this case). McLaren, ibid., §§1.02[1][b], 6.01[3][a]; Clark, Barkley, The Law of Secured Transactions under the Uniform Commercial Code (1980), Warren, Gorham and Lamont, at 3-55.

In order to qualify for the special priority granted by s. 34(2), the creditor must establish first of all that it has a purchase-money security interest in inventory. A purchase-money security interest in inventory will be entitled to special priority if three conditions are met:

(a) Perfection of the purhcase-money security interest at the time the debtor (Maneco) received possession of the collateral;

(b) Notification to a prior security interest holder (Montreal) about the purchase-money security interest before the debtor received possession of the collateral; and

(c) The notification must inform the prior holder that the seller (the appellants) had or expected to acquire a purchase-money security interest in inventory describing the inventory by item or type.

Section 34(2) reads in part [see OPPSA s. 33(1)]: …

And note s. 10 on enforceability of a secured interest. The section reads [see OPPSA s. 11(1)]: …

Clause 1 of the security agreement, headed "Statement of Purpose," says that the parties will have a continuing relationship and, to avoid the need of further documentation, Maneco would grant a security interest in all products, parts, rental contracts and certain chattel paper to secure all liability of Maneco to Clark and Credit.

In cl. 2, the definition section, "products" are said to include "all new equipment and machinery manufactured or offered for sale by CLARK, and used equipment and machinery of the same general type whether or not manufactured or offered for sale by CLARK." "Liability" is defined as "any and all obligations of BORROWER [Maneco] to CLARK or to CREDIT of every kind and description, now existing or hereafter arising, whether arising under this Agreement or otherwise. …" "Collateral" is defined as "Chattel Paper for which value is given by CLARK or CREDIT and any and all Products, Parts and Rental Contracts."

After-acquired property is included in cl. 3, headed "Grant of Security Interest." The clause reads: "To secure payment of Liability, BORROWER hereby grants to CLARK and CREDIT, a security interest in Collateral in the proceeds of each, whether such Collateral is now owned or hereafter acquired by BORROWER."

Clause 5, headed "Request for Loans," authorizes future advances for purchase of Clark products and for other purposes.

Clause 6, "Statements of Account," stipulates that Credit will provide Maneco a separate accounting regularly in respect of acquisition of collateral which has been financed by Credit.

Phraseology consistent with the terms of the security agreement is used in the schedule of collateral attached to the financing statements and in the notification letter referred to, *supra* (at 42-43).

The financing statements identified the type of instrument as a purchase money security interest. So identifying it is not determinative, just as the omission of the phrase in the security agreement is not determinative. The real question, as always, is the substance of the agreement; not what the parties happened to call it.

Inventory is defined in the Act as goods that are held by a person for sale or lease (s. 1(p)). The three pieces of equipment in question were manufactured by Clark, were purchased by Maneco on credit from Clark, and were financed by Credit. The equipment is "inventory."

Montreal argued that the intent of the security agreement entered into between the appellants and Maneco was

to give the Appellants for want of a better expression, a "floating charge" over all of the inventory of Maneco then owned or thereafter acquired whether or not such inventory was manufactured or distributed by Clark and whether or not the purchase of such equipment was financed by Credit. ...

It was also argued by Montreal that the appellants must be denied the status of holder of a purchase-money security interest because they encompassed too wide a field in their security agreements ("add-on" or "cross collateral" clauses, in American terminology). Counsel for Montreal referred us to several American decisions which are consistent with this position. He also referred us to decisions which were not in agreement. (See, e.g., *Re Manuel*, 507 F. 2d 990 (1975); *Re Simpson*, 4 UCC Reporting Service 243 (1966); and *cf. Re Conn*, 33 UCC Reporting Service 701 (1982).)

It may be helpful in understanding the Act and agreements made pursuant to its provisions to relate concepts in the Act to more familiar forms of commercial instruments, e.g., conditional sale agreements, or chattel mortgages or floating charges. But it is essential that the principles underlying the use of older forms should not be used to attenuate the principles expressed in the Act.

The Act envisages provisions for future acquisition and for future advances in a security agreement. Section 13 says that a security agreement may cover after-acquired property (with a proviso in s. 14 [re-en. SM 1977, c. 28, s. 2] in respect of consumer goods which is not applicable here). Section 15 permits the securing of future advances. The sections read:

13 Except as provided in section 14, a security agreement may cover after acquired property.

15 A security agreement may secure future advances or other value [*sic*] whether or not the advances or other values are given pursuant to commitment.

Inclusion of the provisions with regard to the "after acquired" goods and "future advances" does not convert the security agreement into a floating charge and does not adversely affect the appellants' claim to a security interest in the equipment. The Act is designed to permit this kind of commercial relationship without the imposition of a need to prepare and file a separate agreement every time a piece of equipment is purchased for inventory on credit.

In several comments gleaned from the American experience reference is made to the problems arising where the Court is expected to unravel the complexity of a melange of accounting records and lists of collateral. That is not the situation before us. Here, the amount owing on each piece of equipment is clear-cut. The proper groundwork is laid for a purchase-money security interest.

The agreement expresses an intention on the part of Clark and Credit to take or reserve a security interest in some equipment, within the ambit of the meaning of "purchase-money security interest" (s. 1(u)(i) of the Act). Other kinds of interests are also included in the agreement. Does the mixture of a purchase-money security interest with other security interests preclude the appellants from claiming a purchase-money security interest in the three pieces of equipment?

The question of severability of a security document was considered by the Supreme Court of Canada in *Rosen v. Anglin*, [1957] SCR 755, 10 DLR (2d) 113. In *Rosen*, the defendant had taken a chattel mortgage covering substantially the whole of the mortgagors' property. The amount of the mortgage was $5,700, but only $3,800 was advanced in cash. The balance covered an antecedent debt. The same goods had been previously mortgaged to the plaintiffs. The defendant had been honestly ignorant of the plaintiffs' mortgage and did not have constructive notice. Cartwright J, at 763 [SCR], (for the majority, Locke J dissenting) applied the principle expressed by Gwynne J in *Campbell v. Patterson; Madder v. S.F. McKinnon & Co.* (1892), 21 SCR 645 and by the Appellate Division of the Supreme Court of Ontario in *Hunt v. Long* (1916), 35 OLR 502, 27 DLR 337, and held that the part of the transaction relating to the $3,800 was severable. Priority was granted to that portion of the chattel mortgage.

• • •

The question of severability was referred to but was not decided in the only Canadian case cited to us on this point under the Act (*Nat. Trailer Convey, supra*). In that case, a vendor of a tractor-trailer unit and a bank which had advanced the down payment for the purchase claimed a security interest in the unit under the Act. At the time of making the arrangement with the bank the purchaser was in debt to the bank. The bank loaned him the amount required for the down payment and reconstituted the loan to include the existing debt plus the new loan. The bank's security interest covered both amounts. The bank filed before the vendor did. Saunders J applied s. 35(1)(a) of the Act and granted priority to the bank. Saunders J held that it was unnecessary to decide whether the interest of the bank was in whole or in part a purchase-money security interest.

I do not find anything in the Act which inevitably precludes the existence of more than one kind of security agreement. In the case at Bar, it is my view that the purchase-money security interest aspect of the agreement can exist with other kinds of security interests and can be effective. I would apply what was said in *Rosen, supra*, and would hold that the preliminary requirement of s. 34(2) (i.e., existence of a purchase-money security interest in inventory) has been established.

The appellants have met the requirements of the Act with respect to perfection, i.e., the security interest attached and all steps required for perfection under the provisions of the Act have been completed (s. 21). The interest had been perfected prior to Maneco receiving possession of the collateral. The provisions of s. 12, with regard to attachment, have been complied with. Under the security agreement the parties intended a security interest to attach upon acquisition of equipment by Maneco from the appellants. Value was given by the sale on credit. Maneco obtained rights to the collateral when it acquired the equipment. The appellants complied with s. 25(1)(b) by registering financing statements on September 20, 1978. The relevant sections read:

• • •

The requisite notice sent by the appellants to the bank on September 7, 1978 (*supra*, at 41) reads as follows:

This is to notify you, pursuant to Section 34(2) of the Manitoba Personal Property Security Act, that the undersigned, jointly and severally, have or expect to acquire a purchase money security interest in the now owned or hereafter acquired inventory of subject business consisting of:

Inventory now owned or hereafter acquired consisting of all new products manufactured or distributed by Clark Equipment of Canada Ltd., including but not limited to (1) industrial lift trucks, industrial tractors, backhoes and loaders, power hand trucks, straddle carriers, industrial material handling vehicles; (2) front end loaders, dozers, scrapers, backhoes, skidders, power cranes and shovels, excavators, crushing plants, conveyors, asphalt plants, and pavers, screening and washing equipment, graders, rollers, tampers and other construction, material handling, road building, earth moving, farm, log handling, compaction and mining equipment; (3) all used products of the same general type as those described in (1) and (2) whether or not manufactured or distributed by Clark Equipment of Canada Ltd.; and (4) all parts, accessories and attachments for any of the foregoing products; and chattel paper arising from the sale, rental or other disposition of any of the foregoing. Proceeds of the collateral are also covered.

Montreal acknowledged having received the notice but argued that the notice was deficient in the way it described the collateral.

Section 10 of the Act requires a description to be sufficient to enable the collateral to be identified. Section 34(2)(c) is more specific and calls for description of inventory by item or type. Two American cases were cited by counsel for the appellants. In *Fedders Financial Corp. v. Amer. Bank & Trust Co. of Pennsylvania*, 9 UCC Reporting Service 894 (1971), it was held that a description of inventory as "air conditioners," etc., was sufficient compliance with the statutory requirements for notification. And in *GAC Credit Corp. v. Small Business Administration*, 8 UCC Reporting Service 952 (1971), it was held that the description "RCA merchandise" was sufficient. The description in the case at Bar goes considerably beyond those general categories. Montreal should not have been in doubt about the kind of collateral. If there were doubts they could have been resolved by a request for further information (s. 20 of the Act). I would hold the notification complies with the Act.

In its factum, Montreal acknowledges that if the appellants could satisfy the requirements of s. 34(2) of the Act, the appellants would be entitled to priority over Montreal. This is in accord with the policy of the Act referred to by McLaren, *supra*. At §6.01[3][a], the learned author says:

The Act will give a purchase-money security party who complies with its requirements, a priority over any person who may claim an interest in the collateral by operation of an after-acquired property clause. The policy behind the rule is one of ensuring that the debtor is always able to obtain credit from a new financier if he wishes to make additional purchases of property. The purchase-money financier is adding to the debtor's pool of assets in which the earlier secured parties have an interest by their agreements. However, they were at the time of their loan satisfied with the security base without the inclusion of any after-acquired (new) collateral. Thus, the new financier is given priority in recognition of the fact that it is his money which has enabled the debtor to increase his pool of assets. The special rule then enables the financier to look to the collateral which he has financed as security for his loan before anyone else's claim to that collateral.

I have concluded that the appellants have complied with all the statutory requirements entitling them to special priority prescribed by s. 34(2) of the Act.

Appeal allowed.

NOTES

1) *Clark Equipment* was decided under the Manitoba equivalent of old Ontario s. 34(2). Would the case have been decided differently under s. 33(1) of the new Act?

2) Note carefully that under s. 34(2) the inventory financer must both perfect his security interest and notify any prior secured party of record of his (proposed?) PMSI in order to secure priority. Why is notification by itself not enough? Is it because the drafters were concerned to maintain the integrity of the registration system? *Cf. Elmcrest Furniture Mfg. Ltd. v. Price Waterhouse* (1985), 5 PPSAC 22 (Sask.), where Wimmer J appears to have disregarded this consideration in upholding the priority of the inventory financer even though its financing statement was seriously defective.

3) Should failure to notify deprive the inventory financer of his priority if the prior secured party makes no advances to the debtor after the debtor receives the new inventory? Compare the standard provision in pre-PPSA registration legislation which only avoided unregistered agreements against a "subsequent" purchaser or mortgagee claiming his interest from or under the debtor. See, e.g., *Liquid Carbonic Co. Ltd. v. Rountree*, [1924] 1 DLR 1092 (Ont. App. Div.).

Re Chrysler Credit Can. Ltd. and Royal Bank of Canada
(1986), 30 DLR (4th) 616 (Sask. CA)

CAMERON JA: This is an appeal [5 PPSAC 64] from an unsuccessful application made by Chrysler Credit Canada Ltd. pursuant to s. 63 of the *Personal Property Security Act*, 1979-80 (Sask.), c. P-6.1, for an order declaring that, as an inventory financier, it had priority over the Royal Bank of Canada, a general financier, to the used-car inventory of an automobile dealer in receivership.

Before the *Personal Property Security Act* came into force on May 1, 1981, the dealer, White Plymouth Chrysler Ltd. of Moose Jaw, operated with a Royal Bank line of credit secured by a general debenture and an assignment of book debts. Both were subordinated, however, to other conventional security held by Chrysler Credit who financed the dealer's purchase of new cars from the manufacturer, Chrysler Canada Ltd.

After the Act came into force both the bank and the finance company were granted new forms of security. A "General Security Agreement" entered into between the bank and White to secure a $200,000 line of credit gave the bank an interest in the entire undertaking of White, and on April 8, 1983, the bank registered a financing statement disclosing an interest in collateral described as (i) "all goods now or hereafter owned or acquired by the debtor, including without limitation, all equipment ... and vehicles," and (ii) "all proceeds, including but not limited to trade-ins ... ."

Chrysler Credit, to secure its revolving line of credit for the wholesale purchase of new cars, entered into an "Inventory and Lease Financing Security Agreement" with White, in which White conveyed to Chrysler Credit an interest in all inventory supplied by the manufacturer, Chrysler Canada Ltd., as well as in the proceeds from the sale of that inventory. Later, on April 13, 1983, five days after the bank had registered in relation to its security, Chrysler Credit registered a financing statement disclosing a purchase-money security interest in (i) "all inventory whether now owned or ... hereafter acquired by the dealer supplied by Chrysler Canada Ltd. to the dealer, including but not limited to ... new and used motor vehicles," and (ii) in "all proceeds ... including but not limited to trade-[ins]. ..."

Following the registration of its financing statement Chrysler Credit served a notice on the bank informing it of the purchase-money security interest being claimed by Chrysler Credit in both the automobile inventory of White and the proceeds to be derived from the sale of that inventory, including trade-ins.

It was White's practice to purchase new cars from the manufacturer by way of conditional sales contract, with Chrysler Credit advancing the wholesale purchase price. Each time the manufacturer shipped a new car to the dealer, the manufacturer would invoice Chrysler Credit for the wholesale price of the car. Chrysler Credit would then pay the invoice, take an assignment of the conditional sales contract, and enter the transaction on a "Wholesale Inventory Sheet." The total indebtedness of White to Chrysler Credit at any given time was recorded on the "Sheet," as was the amount owing from time to time in relation to each transaction.

In late 1983 White encountered financial trouble, and in December of that year was placed into receivership by the bank. On taking over the business the receiver immediately turned over to Chrysler Credit all of the new cars in White's automobile inventory, but declined to part with the used vehicles, not knowing whether Chrysler Credit or the Royal Bank were entitled to them. The sum of the dealers' indebtedness to the bank and to the finance company exceeded the value of the used car inventory, with Chrysler Credit, alone, being owed $155,000 on new cars whose wholesale purchase by White had been financed by loans from Chrysler Credit.

There were 44 second-hand vehicles in stock when the receiver assumed control of the business. Their origins fell into one of three categories:

1. Four were identified as first trades on the sale of new cars—the loans for whose wholesale purchase by White had not been repaid to Chrysler Credit.

2. Thirty-one were first or later trades traceable to the sale of new cars—the loans for whose wholesale purchase by the dealer had been repaid to Chrysler Credit.

3. Nine were incapable of being linked, either directly or indirectly, to the sale of new cars.

By arrangement between the parties, the vehicles were sold and the proceeds of sale deposited in trust with the receiver to await the outcome of these proceedings.

· · ·

By virtue of s. 34(2) of the Act a purchase-money security interest in inventory or its proceeds has priority over any other security interest in the same collateral given by the same debtor, provided the purchase-money security interest is perfected when the debtor receives possession of the goods, and that notice, as required by the subsection, is served upon others having a registered security interest in that type or kind of collateral.

Section 30(b) of the Act provides that a buyer of goods sold in the ordinary course of business of the seller takes free of any security interest therein (except in limited circumstances which are of no concern here). And under s. 28 where collateral is dealt away with the approval of a secured party, the security interest in the collateral extends to the proceeds, and is deemed to be a continuously perfected security interest in all cases where the security interest in the original collateral was perfected by the registration of a prescribed financing statement.

· · ·

It is common ground:

(i) that each of the bank and Chrysler Canada had a perfected security interest in the inventory of the dealer;

(ii) that Chrysler Credit had a purchase-money security interest therein; and

(iii) that having served a s. 34(2) notice upon the bank, Chrysler Credit's interest generally ranked ahead of the bank's.

The issue, then, is the extent of Chrysler Credit's priority: to which of the three categories of used vehicles did it extend?

To begin with, every time White sold a new car to the ordinary course of its business, Chrysler Credit ceased to have any security interest in that car (s. 30(1)). It did, however, have a security interest in such trade as might have been taken in by the dealer—either on the footing the trade formed part of the collateral included in the security agreement (it covered both new and used inventory), or that the trade constituted "proceeds" derived from the sale of the original collateral (s. 28(1)(b)). At the moment it was taken in by the dealer, a trade linked to the sale of a new car (whose wholesale purchase by the dealer had been financed by Chrysler Credit) constituted "proceeds," and at that moment Chrysler Credit clearly enjoyed the same purchase-money security priority in relation to that trade as it enjoyed in respect of the original collateral (s. 34).

That being the case, and there being no exceptions applicable to the facts before us, Chrysler Credit undoubtedly had priority to the first of the three categories of used vehicles.

The second category differs from the first only to the extent that, in each case, the specific advance enabling the dealer to purchase the new car to which the trade was traceable had been repaid. In light of that the bank contended Chrysler Credit had ceased to have a purchase-money security interest in each of these vehicles—it continued to have interest but not a purchase-money security interest—hence its claim no longer enjoyed priority. The bank had registered first.

Similarly, the bank submitted that since none of the vehicles in the third category could be traced, directly or indirectly, to the sale of new or used cars whose purchase by the dealer had been made possible by loans from the finance company, Chrysler Credit did not have a purchase-money security interest in any of the vehicles; it had only an ordinary security interest therein, and, since the bank was first in time, it had priority. Having regard for the definition of "purchase-money security interest" in s. 2(gg) of the Act, I believe the bank is right about this. The real dispute, then, is over the second category of used car inventory.

Clauses 1 to 3 of the "Inventory and Lease Financing Security Agreement" entered into between Chrysler Credit and White are of particular significance. To the extent they bear upon the issue, they read thus (with those portions having the most direct bearing being italicized):

AGREEMENT

1. In consideration of Chrysler Credit extending credit or continuing to extend credit on motor vehicles and related equipment and accessories sold by Chrysler Canada Ltd. to the Dealer or otherwise acquired by the Dealer, (the continuation of such extension of credit to be nevertheless in the sole discretion of Chrysler Credit) and also *to secure the performance and payment of any and all present and future obligations of the Dealer to Chrysler Credit, the Dealer does hereby* grant, bargain, sell, mortgage and *convey a purchase-money security interest to Chrysler Credit in and to the Collateral referred to in paragraph 3 hereof together with all proceeds as* hereinafter defined of any disposition thereof. The security interest created hereby constitutes a first lien on the Collateral and the Dealer shall keep the Collateral free from any other line, encumbrance or security interest other than the interest of a lessee from the Dealer. The Dealer shall keep and maintain such insurance upon the Collateral in such amounts and manner as Chrysler Credit may require, with loss, if any, under such insurance payable to Chrysler Credit or its assignee and the Dealer as their respective interests may appear.

2.(a) The Dealer has requested and *Chrysler Credit hereby grants to the Dealer a revocable, revolving line of credit* for loans (i) to finance its purchases of new motor vehicles ... built in whole or in part by Chrysler Canada Ltd. and of used motor vehicles (all of which are hereinafter collectively called the "Vehicles") ...

(b) Each loan to be made to Dealer hereunder and the related Vehicle or Vehicles in which a security interest is created hereby shall be evidenced by (i) in the case of a Vehicle purchased from Chrysler Canada Ltd., a CHRYSLER CANADA LTD., VEHICLE INVOICE and such loan shall be in the amount set out in said invoice opposite the words "INVOICE TOTAL"; and (ii) in the case of any other Vehicle, such form of document, including a chattel mortgage, approved by Chrysler Credit from time to time and setting forth the amount of the loan ... The Dealer shall from time to time at the request of Chrysler Credit deliver to Chrysler Credit all chattel paper created through the sale or lease of a vehicle or Vehicles, such chattel paper including but not limited to all leases so created. The provisions of this agreement shall apply to each Vehicle and the loan related thereto separately.

SECURITY INTEREST AND COLLATERAL

3.(a) The security interest in the Collateral is granted to secure the performance and payment *of all obligations and indebtedness* of the Dealer to Chrysler Credit arising out of (i) the financing by Chrysler Credit of the purchase by Dealer of Vehicles for lease or sale to other persons or for use as demonstrators of service vehicles by Dealer, and (ii) the financing by Chrysler Credit of the lease of Vehicles by Dealer to other persons, whether now existing or hereafter incurred, and *of every kind and character, direct or indirect, and whether such indebtedness is from time to time reduced and thereafter increased or entirely extinguished and thereafter re-incurred* including without limitation any sums advanced by Chrysler Credit for taxes, assessments and other charges shall not be discharged or impaired by reason only that such Vehicles are refinanced by Chrysler Credit upon the leasing thereon by Dealer to other persons.

(b) The collateral covered by this agreement is as follows: all inventory, whether now owned or now in the possession of the Dealer or hereafter acquired by the Dealer, supplied by Chrysler Canada Ltd. to the Dealer including but not limited to the following types or kinds of property: new and used motor vehicles and related accessories, and all additions and accessions thereto, and substitutions and parts therefore, and all proceeds of every type or kind of such property, including but not limited to trade-in machinery and equipment, cash, notes, chattel paper, goods, contract rights, accounts and any other property or obligations directly or indirectly received when such collateral or proceeds are sold, exchanged, collected, damaged, destroyed, disposed of or otherwise dealt with.

The importance of the instrument creating the security interest is evident on reference to s. 9 of the Act which reads thus:

9. Except as otherwise provided in this or any other Act, a security agreement is effective according to its terms.

Having regards generally for the breadth of the security agreement in issue, and more specifically to the highlighted portions of it, I believe that the parties to the agreement intended Chrysler Credit's security interest to attach to the whole of the new and used car inventory, as well as to the component parts thereof. In other words they intended, I think, to have the whole of the inventory answerable for the whole of the debt, so that as long as any part of the indebtedness remained owing, the inventory remained liable to satisfy it. As between Chrysler Credit and White, then, each of the trades in the second category secured not only one advance—the one relating to the new car to which that trade was traceable—but all of the advances, or in other words, the whole of the indebtedness from time to time outstanding. The trades must be seen as forming part of a class of property, namely, inventory; and it was that class which was used to secure the grant of credit on an ongoing or revolving basis.

This, too, is consistent, I think, with the Act. Before any of the provinces adopted personal property security legislation of the kind now in effect in several Canadian jurisdictions—patterned after that in the United States—Professor Ziegel, in an article entitled "The Legal Problems of Wholesale Financing of Durable Goods in Canada," 41 *Can. Bar Rev.* 54 (1963), made these comments [at 55]:

•   •   •

Having thus identified the problems, Professor Ziegel went on to recommend the following solutions at 56:

First, the financer must be freed from the necessity of having to record every agreement securing an advance made by him. This introduces us to the concept of "notice filing."

Secondly, the recording law must accept one underlying, or master, agreement as sufficient written evidence of the financer's security interest in the goods acquired through his advances. The need for separate instruments evidencing each transaction must be dispensed with.

Thirdly, the agreement must provide, and the law should recognize, the financer's rights to a "cross-over" security, that is to say, all of the trader's stock-in-trade, or at least that part of it which is financed by the financer, both present and future, must secure both present and future advances. Here we enter the realm of the "floating" lien or charge.

Fourthly, the agreement must provide that the financer shall have a security interest in *the proceeds of any sale* to the extent of *any* outstanding advances. The function of a model law here is to ensure that the financer's claim to the proceeds will not come into conflict with any other recording law, such as a bills of sale act, an assignment of book debts act, and so forth.

(Emphasis added.)

In its Report to the Attorney General: Proposals for a Saskatchewan Personal Property Security Act: July 1977, the Law Reform Commission of Saskatchewan suggested that existing law was no longer adequate to accommodate modern commercial practices, and that a new regime, recognizing functional rather than formal differences between security agreements, was required. More specifically it referred to the problems associated with inventory financing and the need for changes in this respect (at XV):

3. THE PROPOSED ACT EMPLOYS NEW CONCEPTS WHICH FACILITATE INVENTORY FINANCING.

Because of the lack of a common conceptual basis for security arrangements, modern forms of secured financing must be designed so as to fit into one of the traditional categories of security devices. However, many of these devices were developed at a time when methods of financing and the circumstances in which the need for security arrangements existed were quite different from what they are at the present time. In other words, the existing system lacks flexibility and fails to recognize techniques and concepts which are required by the business community.

With some notable exceptions, existing chattel security law was developed to facilitate short-term, single-transaction agreements involving fixed security. However, modern stock-in-trade financing frequently involves shifting collateral and open-ended credit arrangements. This type of secured financing requires not only much more flexibility than that permitted by present law, but it also requires the use of concepts which are not now recognized by Saskatchewan law. For example, when a financer gives credit to a merchant on the security of his stock-in-trade, he will want a security interest in present and future-acquired stock ... In addition, he will want a security interest in the proceeds of the stock-in-trade because the stock will eventually be sold to a buyer in the ordinary course of business who will get clear title. The proceeds may be cash, items traded in or accounts arising from the sale of the stock. Since existing law does not recognize the concept of a security interest in proceeds as a form of collateral itself, the only way the financer would be able to get any measure of protection is to use several types of security agreements, with each agreement covering a specific form of collateral that the proceeds may take. In addition, he may have to comply with two or more registry statutes.

The proposed Act frees the parties to a secured transaction from the conceptual straightjackets of existing law by permitting them maximum freedom to employ agreements with form and content most suitable to their circumstances (see section 9). This does not mean that total freedom is contemplated. Some limitations are required if structure is to exist. However, the limitations prescribed by the Act are based on functional or social policy considerations only.

In order to permit needed flexibility in secured wholesale financing, the proposed Act employs the concept of a continuing general lien (see section 12). While this concept is presently the central feature of equitable security devices such as the equitable chattel mortgage, the floating charge and the assignment of future accounts, its full potential has not been realized under existing law. The proposed Act removes the impediments which, until now, have limited the usefulness of the concept. The continuing general lien, unlike the equitable floating charge, is a fixed security interest. Further, a security interest in after-acquired property is given a status fully equivalent to a "legal" interest without the need for specific appropriation by the debtor (see section 13).

The second major feature of modern inventory financing, future advance agreements, is recognized in section 14. The proposed Act (see section 35(5)) rejects the troublesome rule set down in the case of *Hopkinson v. Rolt* (1861), 9 HLC 514, under which a secured party could never safely make advances pursuant to a prior agreement on the assumption that he was fully secured by a mortgage taken on the debtor's assets.

(Emphasis added.)

The commission went on to describe as "one of the most innovative features" of the proposed Act, its notions of proceeds and their treatment, concluding with the observation that under the proposed Act an inventory financier could readily obtain a perfected security interest in the proceeds of his primary collateral, a thing he could do only with great trouble, if at all, under the law as it then stood.

There are two things here which I think merit particular emphasis. The first is the primacy, under the new regime proposed by the commission, of function over form—a purchase-money security interest, whether or not it arises out of conventional forms of contract (conditional sale, chattel mortgage, or whatever) enjoys special priority status. The second is the nature of the security interest in property such as inventory: the secured party enjoys a continuing general lien, fixed rather than floating. Both are consistent with Professor Ziegel's earlier recommendations. And while the Act, either as proposed or enacted, is not altogether explicit about this, I believe, having regard for its wording, for the policy underlying it, and for the commercial necessities alluded to by Professor Ziegel, that the Act recognizes the inventory financier's right to "cross-over" security: all of the dealer's inventory financed by the financier secures all of the advances which enabled the dealer to acquire it. And, of course, that is, as we have seen, what was contemplated in the security agreement in issue in this instance.

This view of the Act appears to be shared by McLaren & de Jong, who in their text *Secured Transactions in Personal Property in Canada, supra*, suggest that should the parties concerned in these transactions desire more refined arrangements than those contemplated by the statute, they may bring them about through subordination agreements (s. 47). The authors say this (at 12-22.2):

… secured parties will frequently desire to make refinements in their priority positions beyond which might be achieved through the Act. The typical situation, as mentioned, will arise between a purchase money financier and a general financier, both securing equipment or inventory. From an accounting or financial perspective the respective financiers may take the view that the unpaid purchase money vendor's collateral is secured by the supplier but the paid-for collateral is security of the general financier. The priority provisions of the Act do not work in such a fashion.

The priority of s. 34(2) and (3) is as a class of collateral contained in a security interest superior to the general financier's claim until full payment of purchase money vendor's accounts owing. The parties may wish to achieve a refinement of the priority by providing that the purchase money financier is to have priority for all collateral which is unpaid. Priority for collateral which is partly paid for is to be divided in the ratio of paid or unpaid collateral. Finally, the paid for collateral will secure the general financier's security interest.

On this view of the Act and the security agreement in issue, Chrysler Credit enjoyed priority over the bank to the second category of used car inventory, as well as to the first.

Accordingly, I would allow the appeal to the extent of declaring that Chrysler Credit enjoyed priority in relation to the first and second categories of used car inventory. The bank's claim in relation to the third category ranked ahead of that of Chrysler Credit.

Appeal allowed in part.

The PMSI Priority in Proceeds

Massey-Ferguson Industries Ltd. v. Melfort Credit Union Ltd.
(1986), 6 PPSAC 120 (Sask.)

WALKER J: This is an application for:

1. An order, pursuant to s. 63(e) of the Personal Property Security Act, SS 1979-80, c. P-6.1 ("PPSA"), declaring that the applicant (herein called "Massey") has a valid purchase money security interest in the parts inventory of the respondent North East Implements Ltd. (herein called "the dealer") which has been seized by the respondent Melfort Credit Union Limited (herein called "the Credit Union").

2. A further order that the Credit Union release to Massey all of the parts inventory which it has seized.

3. A further order pursuant to s. 63(d) of the Act staying the enforcement by the Credit Union of any rights provided in Part V of the Act until such time as the right of the Credit Union to seize and sell the property has been determined.

This is a contest between the applicant inventory financer and the respondent receivables financer—a contest between "goods-credit or supplier credit," on the one hand, and "money-credit or bank credit," on the other.

Massey's "security agreement—inventory" with the dealer is dated March 18, 1981. Its financing statement claiming a purchase money security interest was registered, in the Personal Property Registry, May 1, 1981 against this collateral:

Existing or to be acquired new Massey Ferguson goods including farm and industrial machinery, Massey Ferguson repair parts and Massey Ferguson used machinery of similar type and all proceeds.

Massey sent a notice dated July 8, 1982, to the Credit Union advising it of its purchase money security interest in the inventory of the dealer.

The dealer agreement between the dealer and Massey was terminated effective November 18, 1985. November 19, 1985, the dealer gave Massey a list of its parts inventory as of termination of a value of approximately $100,000. As of December 6, 1985, $106,281.25 was due and owing to Massey from the dealer with respect to the parts inventory supplied by Massey to the dealer. From August 31, 1982 on, Massey supplied parts inventory to the dealer of the total value of $585,742.

On June 18, 1980, the dealer executed a floating and specific charge debenture in favour of the Credit Union. On March 7, 1981, the dealer entered into a line of credit agreement with the Credit Union. The debenture was registered under the Corporation Securities Registration Act June 19, 1980 [superseded by the PPSA]. The debenture later on found its way on to Personal Property Registry under the Act, the registration date being June 19, 1980. The Credit Union says it did not at any time subordinate its interest in the inventory in favour of Massey. The supplementary affidavit has exhibited the financial statements of the dealer for the year ending October 31, 1982, for the purpose of proving "new value."

It is to be noted that the relief asked by Massey and the counterrelief asked by the Credit Union relate only to the inventory as such. It is to be noted also that the Credit Union's opposition to the application is based solely on the position that s. 34(4) not s. 34(2) should govern. There is no reliance on the failure of Massey to meet the conditions of operation of s. 34(2).

Section 34 [of the PPSA] reads:

34(1) Subject to section 28, a purchase-money security interest in:

(a) collateral or its proceeds, other than intangibles or inventory, that is perfected within fifteen days after the day the debtor obtains possession of the collateral; or

(b) an intangible or its proceeds that is perfected within fifteen days after the day the security interest in the intangible attaches;

has priority over any other security interest in the same collateral or its proceeds given by the same debtor.

(2) Subject to section 28 and subsection (4) of this section, a purchase-money security interest in inventory or its proceeds has priority over any other security interest in the same collateral given by the same debtor if:

(3) The notice required in subsection (2) shall: ...

(4) No purchase-money security interest in proceeds of inventory has priority over a security interest in accounts given for new value where a financing statement relating thereto is registered before the purchase-money security interest is perfected or a financing statement relating thereto is registered.

(5) A non-proceeds purchase-money security interest has priority over a purchase-money security interest in proceeds under subsections (1) and (2) in the same collateral if the non-proceeds purchase-money security interest is perfected at the time the debtor obtains possession of the collateral or within fifteen days thereafter.

Massey relies on s. 34(2). The Credit Union relies on s. 34(4), saying that new value was given and that its registration was first in time. Section 34(2) is subject to s. 34(4) on its own terms if s. 34(4) has application.

The Credit Union relied on this extract. R.C.C. Cuming, in ["Second Generation Personal Property Security Legislation in Canada"], 46 Sask. Law Review 5, has this to say of accounts financing [at 38]:

> ... However, there is no uniformity among the three Acts [Ontario and its western counterparts] when the priority dispute is between an inventory financer claiming a purchase money security interest in accounts as proceeds of his inventory and an accounts financer claiming priority on the basis of a prior registration. All three Acts allow an inventory financer to assert a purchase money security interest in proceeds of inventory collateral in which he has a perfected purchase money security interest. [s. 34(2)] Since generally purchase money security interests have priority over any other security interests in the same collateral, [s. 34(2)] an inventory financer with a purchase money security interest and claiming accounts as proceeds will defeat an accounts financer claiming accounts as primary collateral unless the purchase money priority rule is modified in favour of the accounts financer. Such a modification is contained in the Saskatchewan and Manitoba Acts, which provide that a purchase money security interest in proceeds of inventory does not have priority over a security interest in accounts given for new value where a financing statement relating to the latter is registered before the purchase money security interest is perfected or a financing statement relating thereto is registered. [s. 34(4)] ...

> The result is that an accounts financer is given priority over an inventory financer claiming accounts as proceeds if as between the two the accounts financer has registered first.

This extract seems not to favour the Credit Union in present circumstances.

• • •

Massey relies on *Elmcrest Furniture Manufacturing Ltd. v. Price Waterhouse Ltd.* (1985), 5 PPSAC 22, 41 Sask. R 125 (Sask. QB). That case was decided under s. 34(2). In that case the Court held that the holder of a purchase-money security interest had priority over the bank's security interest. The purchase-money security interest holder's priority dated from the time he gave notice to the bank. Section 34(4) did not fall to be considered. The applicant also relies on *Re Fosters Service (81) Ltd.: Terra Power Tractor Co. v. touche Ross Ltd.* (1985), 5 PPSAC 192, 42 Sask. R 102 (Sask. QB). Section 34(4) did not fall to be considered there. Section 34(2) deals with "a purchase-money security interest in inventory or its proceeds," and its priority over "any other security interest in the same collateral given by the same debtor." Section 34(2) is the general rule. Section 34(4) is a narrow exception to it. Section 34(5) is a special rule involving two purchase-money security interests upon which the Credit Union did not rely and which has no application. Does s. 34(4), an exception to the general rule in s. 34(2), apply?

The s. 34(4) exception to the general rule in s. 34(2) is very narrow. This inventory has not been sold. There has been no sale by the dealer of the inventory generating a receivable. There are no proceeds. There are no accounts. Massey is claiming not the proceeds, but the inventory as such. So is the Credit Union. Section 34(4) has no application. There may be other reasons for the non-application of s. 34(4) but I do not find it necessary to go beyond the question of proceeds. This is consistent with *Elmcrest*.

Section 34(4) has no application. Section 34(2) governs. The date of delivery of the first inventory by Massey to the dealer is not clear beyond peradventure. The inference is possible that there was no delivery prior to the notice from Massey to the Credit Union, from the fact that there was inventory in value of $585,742 delivered subsequent to the notice and there is now inventory in value of approximately $100,000, and an account of $106,281.25. The Credit Union did not argue this point in any way. In fact, the Credit Union rested solely on the applicability of s. 34(4) and non-applicability of s. 34(2), in effect conceding that the application was to be decided on which subsection applied with the conditions of those sections being considered to have been met. In result, there will be an order that Massey has a valid purchase money security interest in all parts inventory delivered subsequent to its notice to the Credit Union of July 8, 1982. The Credit Union is ordered to release to Massey that part of the inventory. If the parties cannot agree in this area, the matter may be referred back for further direction.

Order accordingly.

NOTES

The Saskatchewan and Manitoba provisions referred to in Walker J's judgment were much influenced by the amendment to UCC 9-312(3) made by the Article 9 Review Committee favouring the priority of the accounts financer. The Committee justified its position on the following grounds (Final Report, at 225):

Accounts may be financed by some financers without prior involvement in the inventory, and some have argued that one who provides financing at the early inventory stage of the cycle of a business, which involves greater risk, is certainly to be preferred to one who provides financing only at the later stage of the cycle, and that a prior or only claim to inventory must therefore carry through to accounts as proceeds. But others feel that accounts financing is overall more important than inventory financing, and the desirable rule is one which makes accounts financing certain as to its legal position. Even if both competing financers are involved in the inventory, a purchase money priority in inventory may not represent the order of priority in time on accounts, which may be far more important than inventory financing in the particular case. A suggestion that the purchase money priority carry through to accounts if the notice provided by Section 9-312(3) has been given to accounts financers has seeming merit, but in the Committee's view it has two major difficulties: (a) The purchase-money priority as to inventory would be difficult to trace into accounts if the affected inventory was only part of the goods sold. (b) Accounts financing is intricate, and not easily or safely terminated on receipt of an inventory purchase-money notice. Prevailing practice seems to be for accounts financers to require covenants against competitive inventory financing, and to declare a default unless any inventory financer giving a purchase-money notice agrees not to assert a claim to the accounts. The Committee believes that where a financing statement as to accounts financing is filed first (with or without related inventory financing), the security interest in accounts should not be defeated by any subsequent claim to accounts as proceeds of an inventory security interest which was filed later.

Are you persuaded by this reasoning? Does it equally reflect Canadian financing practices? (In Canada, most accounts receivable financing is done by banks and an assignment of accounts is usually taken in conjunction with other collateral.) If the supplier cannot obtain proceeds priority over a prior accounts financer without the latter's consent, will this not re-create the situational monopoly the purchase-money priority provisions were designed to avoid? In practice, would a supplier always appreciate that his inventory priority does not extend to the proceeds? Prof. Cuming provides another explanation for the priority given the accounts financer in the Saskatchewan and Manitoba Acts:

The policy issue involved in this type of priority dispute was debated for some time in the United States. The drafters of the 1972 version of Article 9 removed any doubt arising out of earlier versions of the UCC by amending Article 9-312(3) so as to deny a purchase money status to a security interest in accounts as proceeds of inventory. The result is that an accounts financer is given priority over an inventory financer claiming accounts as proceeds if as between the two the accounts financer has registered first.

It is impossible to justify the approach contained in the Saskatchewan, Manitoba and US legislation on the grounds that accounts financers are more important to the business community than are inventory financers. However, it is possible to justify it on the grounds that it is sensible from both a commercial and equitable point of view if a secured party is to conduct a search of the registry to determine whether or not any priority claims to the potential customer's accounts have been registered. If the search reveals a prior claim, the inventory financer must decide whether or not he would be adequately secured without having as collateral the accounts which are proceeds of his inventory. The decision that the accounts are necessary may, but need not, lead to the conclusion that the potential customer must be turned away. The accounts financer may be prepared to execute a subordination agreement giving the inventory financer priority to the accounts which are proceeds of his inventory. In any event, if priority is given to the accounts financer, the inventory financer is in a position to take measures to avoid loss to anyone simply by refusing to deal with the person seeking further credit. The situation is quite different under the Ontario approach. Every accounts financer who has registered a financing statement and has loaned money to a debtor in Ontario faces the risk of loss of his security to subsequent inventory financers claiming purchase money security interests in the debtor's accounts. There are no measures an accounts financer can take to protect himself. The result is that accounts financers must make sure that any advances they make are fully secured by existing accounts which cannot be traced as proceeds of the sale of a debtor's inventory.

(Cuming (1981-82), 46 *Sask. L Rev.* 5, 38-39)

Do you agree with this reasoning? Could Prof. Cuming's concerns be met by requiring a purchase financer to give notice to a prior accounts financer of record as well as to secured parties claiming a prior security interest in the same collateral? Would an accounts financer not usually know, from the nature of the debtor's business, whether or not the debtor is likely to give a PMSI in the debtor's inventory?

The Non-Inventory Purchase-Money Security Interest (S. 34(3))

North Platte State Bank v. Production Credit Ass'n
(1972), 200 NW 2d 1 (Neb. S. Ct.)

WHITE Chief Justice: ... This case deals with the priority of secured creditors, each having a perfected security interest in the same collateral. For convenience, the plaintiff-appellant, North Platte State Bank, is hereinafter referred to as Bank, and the defendant-appellee, Production Credit Association of North Platte, is hereinafter referred to as PCA.

In August 1967, Gerald S. Tucker received an "operating loan" from PCA, the loan being subject to annual renewal in the month of December. A contemporaneously executed security contained an after-acquired property clause which applied PCA's security interest to, inter alia, "all livestock now owned or hereafter acquired by debtor, whether by purchase, natural increase or otherwise." PCA perfected its security interest by properly filing a financing statement which covered all of the Debtor's livestock, and all subsequent transactions between PCA and Tucker. No other financing statement was filed by PCA.

From November 1967 through January 1968 PCA advanced approximately $70,000 to Tucker, primarily for periodic purchases of cattle. In February 1968, a second security agreement was entered into by Tucker and PCA to cover newly purchased cattle. PCA inspected the Tucker ranch in March and September of 1968 to count the number of head of cattle that had been added by purchase and by natural increase. Still another security agreement was executed by the parties in September to cover the increase in calves.

In October or November of 1968, Tucker approached D. M. Mann, hereinafter referred to as Seller, to purchase certain Angus heifers in the Seller's possession. It should be mentioned that the Seller was merely an agent acting for the true owner of the cattle but this fact has no bearing on a determination in this case. Tucker agreed to purchase as many of the 100 head of cattle as tested pregnant, and the price was $225 per head. The Seller and Tucker agreed that Tucker *was to take delivery of the cattle before January 1, 1969*, but payment and transfer of a bill of sale were to take place after that date. Sometime in November and again in December of 1968, Tucker went to the Bank to discuss opening a line of credit but there was no discussion of a specific loan for any particular purpose.

On November 30, 1968, a trucking company hired by Tucker took 79 head of impregnated Angus heifers from the Seller's ranch and hauled them to the Tucker ranch. PCA had inspected the Tucker ranch earlier in November, and then in December 1968, PCA made a routine search of the security interest filing records in several counties pursuant to a loan renewal scheduled for December but not formally executed until March 24, 1969. PCA did not see any Angus cattle on the Tucker ranch when it inspected in November, and the December search of the records revealed that only the PCA financing statement of August 1967 was on file.

On January 13, 1969, approximately *a month and a half after he took possession of the cattle*, Tucker drew a check on the Bank for $17,775, the total purchase price for the 79 head of cattle. The Seller, payee of the check, mailed the check to the Bank for deposit. The check was returned for lack of funds, but upon the Seller's inquiry, the Bank acknowledge that a loan to Tucker had been discussed and that if Tucker would come in to complete the necessary papers, the loan would be granted and the check would be honored. Because of weather conditions, Tucker was unable to reach the Bank until January 30, 1969. A note advancing $20,000 to Tucker and a security agreement were executed that day and the next day the Bank honored the check presented by the Seller. Near this point in time, the bill of sale dated January 12, 1969, to the cattle was given to Tucker. On February 5, 1969, the Bank filed a financing statement, thus perfecting a security interest in the 79 head of cattle.

PCA became aware of the presence of the Angus cattle on the Tucker ranch sometime in February 1969. Tucker told PCA that the Angus cattle were purchased with the proceeds of a sale of several calves of another breed. Having checked the records in December 1968, and receiving this explanation for the presence of the Angus cattle, PCA saw to it that a loan renewal note was signed by Tucker and a security agreement including, specifically, the 79 Angus cattle, was executed on March 24, 1969.

In December 1969, unable to locate all of Tucker's cattle in which it had a security interest, PCA checked the filing records and found the Bank's financing statement of February 5, 1969. Late in December 1969, after Tucker defaulted on the PCA note of March 24, 1969, PCA took possession of all the cattle on Tucker's ranch, including the 79 head of Angus cattle. After the Bank claimed priority to the Angus heifers, PCA and the Bank agreed to sell the cattle and to hold the proceeds in escrow pending a determination as to the priority of their respective security interests.

• • •

There are two basic questions presented in this case. As we see it, the resolution of either one of these questions will be decisive in the case. The first question is whether the Bank did in fact under the pertinent provisions of the Code have a purchase money security interest in the collateral? The second question is that, if it did have a purchase money security interest in the collateral, did it acquire priority under section 9-312(4), UCC?

Did the Bank have a purchase money security interest?

A purchase money security interest is defined in section 9-107, UCC. It states:

• • •

Tucker and the Seller (agent for Long) made an oral contract for sale sometime in November 1968. Later when the 79 pregnant cows were identified, they were finally delivered to Tucker on November 30, 1968. It is apparent, therefore, that the actual goods contracted for were delivered to the buyer under the previous contract for sale; that Tucker physically received them; and that they were therefore in his legal possession. The ordinary understanding of the term "possession" means that a person has possession when he has physical control of the property. *Boyd v. Travelers Fire Ins. Co.*, 147 Neb. 237, 22 NW 2d 700. The only further question to be determined here is whether the actual physical delivery of the cows and their acceptance by Tucker, the buyer, was affected by the fact that the payment of the price and the delivery of the bill of sale were postponed. It is true that delivery by a seller under a contract for sale can take place prior to the receipt of the goods by the buyer. Receipt is defined by section 2-103(1)(c), UCC, as taking physical possession. It is clear that the tender of delivery by the Seller for Long took place here under section 2-503(1), U.C.C., and the buyer received and accepted the goods on arrival at his ranch. It is not argued and, indeed, it could not be argued, that the postponement of payment and the later delivery of the bill of sale had any effect upon the time that Tucker received legal possession of the goods. The buyer had received the goods under the precise terms of the Code and this receipt was evidenced by his taking of the actual physical possession. It seems quite obvious that when the cows were delivered to Tucker under the contract for sale and were actually physically received by him, they were in his legal possession and we so hold.

We turn now to the question of whether Tucker on November 30, 1968, acquired more rights in the cows than their possession. It appears from the evidence in this case that Tucker acquired title to the cows as well on November 30, 1968. There is considerable colloquy about the understanding of the parties and particularly about the testimony of the

Seller, Long's agent, about what he relied upon in delivering the cows, and what he would have done had the cows not been paid for. What is important is that the Seller said Tucker's word was good enough for him. All of the indications of the oral testimony are that the Seller was relying on Tucker's willingness and ability to make payment of the price and that he was making a sale on open credit. Neither Seller nor Long made any effort to reclaim the goods under section 2-702, UCC, granting an unpaid seller on open account the right to reclaim the goods if he discovers his buyer's insolvency. This right must be exercised within 10 days, it was not so exercised, nor did the Seller nor Long know until long after November 30, 1968, that Tucker had become insolvent.

Whatever the parties may have thought, the provisions of the Uniform Commercial Code govern, and it is clear that title to the cows actually passed to Tucker when they reached his ranch and he received the actual physical possession of them. Section 2-401(2), UCC, says that unless otherwise *explicitly* agreed, title passes to the buyer at the time and place at which the seller completes his performance with reference to the physical delivery of the goods, despite any reservation of a security interest. There is no evidence that the sales agreement, either expressly or impliedly, contained an *explicit* provision or term reserving the title until payment had actually been accomplished. We therefore come to the conclusion that after November 30, 1968, once the cattle reached Tucker's ranch and came into his physical possession, under the completely oral transaction the Seller had no enforceable security interest in them and no other interest of any kind. Title and possession were merged in Tucker, it was an unsecured credit transaction, and no cause of action existed against Tucker except one for the agreed price of the cattle under the terms of the agreement.

What, then, was the nature of the Bank's security interest? We pause to observe that at the moment the cattle reached Tucker's ranch, PCA's perfected security interest immediately attached to the 79 cows. All of the conditions necessary had been met, there was a written security agreement with an after-acquired property clause containing a description sufficiently broad to include the cows, value had been given in the form of the original loan, and subsequent extensions of credit which had been renewed a number of times. As we have seen, Tucker had acquired both possession and title to the cows. At the time of delivery and possession of title to Tucker, on November 30, 1968, the financing statement of PCA was the only financing statement on file.

As we have pointed out, section 9-107(b), UCC, provides that a security interest cannot become a purchase money security interest unless it is taken by a person who by making advances or incurring an obligation gives value to enable the debtor *to acquire rights in or the use of collateral* if such value is in fact so used. Clearly, the Bank could not qualify as the seller of the 79 cows. Obviously, by advancing the $20,000 and taking the mortgage it did not acquire a security interest in the cows. The distinction is vital to the disposition of this case. The money advanced by the Bank enabled Tucker to pay the price to Seller for the cows. But it was not used by Tucker to acquire any rigths in the cows because he already had all the possible rights in the cows he could have with both possession and title.

There is a further and even more fundamental reason why the Bank may not succeed in establishing any priority over PCA in the enforcement of its security interest. This is because that although it filed its statement within 10 days after it made its loan, the filing occurred almost 2 months after the cows had been delivered and the title had passed to

Tucker. At the risk of repetition, we will repeat the basic portion of section 9-312(4), UCC, which states: "... if the purchase money security interest is perfected at the time the *debtor* receives possession of the collateral or within ten days thereafter." (Emphasis supplied.) The application of this plain, simple, and forceful language to the facts in the case at bar seem so obvious as not to require any further argument. However, the Bank argues at length and persistently that Tucker did not become a "debtor" within the meaning of section 9-312(4), UCC, until the money was loaned by the Bank and that, therefore, "debtor" Tucker never had full "possession of the collateral" in the section 9-312(4), UCC, sense until the loan was made by the Bank and the security agreement signed. Therefore, the Bank argues that since it filed a financing statement within 10 days after the execution of the security agreement with Tucker, it qualifies for the special priority of section 9-312(4), UCC.

Manifestly, on January 30, 1969, when the Bank executed the loan, Tucker was a "debtor" of both the Bank and PCA. Section 9-105(1)(d), UCC, provides that unless the context otherwise requires a "debtor" is "the person who owes payment or other performance of the obligations secured, whether or not he owns or has rights in the collateral ... ." Tucker did not or could not receive possession from the Bank and it is uncontrovertible that he became a "debtor" to the Seller on November 30, 1968. While Tucker may not have been the Bank's "debtor" until January 30, 1969, it is inescapable in the context of the Code that he was the "debtor" in the section 9-312(4), UCC, sense when he became a "debtor" to PCA. On November 30, 1968, the time and the only time that he "received" possession, Tucker was a "debtor" of PCA and Seller only. To hold otherwise renders the language of the statute meaningless, and purports a construction wholly unrelated to setting up an ascertainable time standard by which priorities may be established so that a subsequent lender can achieve priority over the first to file. This interpretation is well stated in 2 Coogan, Hogan & Vagts, Secured Transactions Under the Uniform Commercial Code, section 19.02(3)(a), at 1979, wherein it is stated: "The time at which the debtor receives possession starts the running of the ten-day grace period for perfection. Problems will undoubtedly arise as to when the debtor 'receives possession' of the collateral. The Code does not offer a specific definition of the term, but there are indications that actual delivery to the buyer or a third party is crucial. *It is important to realize that this priority rule turns on the more easily ascertained time of receipt of possession and not upon the time the debtor obtains 'rights' in the collateral.*" (Emphasis supplied.)

The very purpose of the 10-day grace period was to relieve from the rigidity of a requirement of a loan first and acquisition second or simultaneousness of receipt of possession and execution of the loan. At the same time the integrity of the transaction had to be guaranteed by an ascertainable standard related to the receipt of possession, and the retroactive granting of priority over the first to file and the first to advance funds. See II Gilmore, Security Interests in Personal Property, s. 29.2, at 782.

• • •

The Bank relies almost completely on the decision of the Court of Appeals in *Brodie Hotel Supply, Inc. v. United States*, 431 F. 2d 1316 (9th Cir., 1970). There are two answers to this contention, besides the analysis and the decision we shave reached on the merits. In the first place, the *Brodie* case is inapposite on the facts. The court reached the correct decision in the *Brodie* case because the purchase money security holder in fact perfected his filing within 10 days after Lyon, the purchaser, obtained possession of the equipment and thereby achieved priority over the lender. The language and the reasoning of the *Brodie* case, however, relied upon by the Bank have been seriously criticized. For a full discussion of this case, see 27 The Business Lawyer, Kennedy, Secured Transactions, 755 at 768 (1972); and Comment, 49 NCL Rev. 849 (1971).

• • •

We therefore hold in this case that the Bank failed to comply with the requirements of section 9-312(4), UCC, because it did not file a financing statement until more than 10 days had passed from the time the cattle came into the "debtor" Tucker's possession. Therefore, the first to file rule of section 9-312(5)(a), UCC, applies, and the original priority of PCA controls.

Judgment affirmed.

Brodie Hotel Supply, Inc. v. US
(1970), 431 F.2d 1316 (CCA 9)

HAMLEY Circuit Judge: Brodie Hotel Supply, Inc. (Brodie), brought this action against the United States to determine which of the parties had priority, under their respective chattel mortgages, to the proceeds of the sale of certain restaurant equipment. The facts were stipulated and the property was sold and proceeds impounded by agreement. The district court granted summary judgment for Brodie and the United States appeals.

In 1959, Brodie sold the restaurant equipment to Standard Management Company, Inc., for use in a restaurant at Anchorage, Alaska. Standard Management went bankrupt. Brodie repossessed the equipment but left it in the restaurant. With the consent of Brodie, James Lyon took possession of the restaurant and began operating it on June 1, 1964. Throughout the summer of 1964, Brodie and Lyon negotiated over the price and terms under which Lyon was to purchase the equipment.

On November 2, 1964, Lyon borrowed seventeen thousand dollars from the National Bank of Alaska and, as security for the loan, which was evidenced by a promissory note, executed a chattel mortgage covering the restaurant equipment. This equipment consisted of 159 separate types of items, including a refrigerator, a dishwasher, an ice cream cabinet, spoons, forks, cups, ladles, pots, pans, and assorted glassware and chinaware. The bank assigned its mortgage to the Small Business Administration (SBA), represented in this action by the United States. On November 4, 1964, the bank filed a financing statement, showing the SBA as assignee.

On November 12, Brodie delivered to Lyon a bill of sale covering the equipment. On the same day Lyon executed a chattel mortgage on the equipment, naming Brodie as mortgagee. This mortgage was given to secure the unpaid purchase price of the equipment. Brodie filed a financing statement on November 23, 1964.

Alaska has adopted the Uniform Commercial Code (Code). Under section 9-312(5)(a) of the Code (Alaska Statutes [AS] 45.05.754(e)(1)), the general rule of priority, if both interests are perfected by filing, is that the secured party who first files a financing statement (in this case SBA as assignee of the bank) prevails, regardless of when his security interest attached. However, there is a special exception for purchase-money security interests in collateral other than inventory. Brodie had such an interest. Under this exception, the purchase-money security interest prevails over conflicting interests in non-inventory collateral if "the purchase money security interest is perfected [i.e., here it was perfected by filing a financing statement] at the time the debtor receives possession of the collateral or within 10 days after the debtor receives possession." AS 45.05.754(d), (Code, 9-312(4)).

On the basis of these stipulated facts, Brodie moved for summary judgment. Brodie contended that although Lyon received possession of the restaurant equipment on June 1, 1964, over five months before Brodie's financing statement was filed, Lyon did not become a "debtor," and the equipment did not become "collateral" until November 12, 1964, when Lyon received the bill of sale and executed Brodie's chattel mortgage. Accordingly, Brodie contended, it was not until November 12, that "the debtor [Lyon] receive[d] possession of the collateral" within the meaning of the statute referred to above. As already indicated, Brodie's financing statement was filed within ten days of that date. The district court agreed with this analysis in granting summary judgment for Brodie.

If, in AS 45.05.754(d), the term "debtor" is given the meaning ascribed to it in AS 45.05.698(a)(4), Brodie was entitled to priority. It was not until November 12, 1964, that Lyon purchased the equipment and became obligated to pay the purchase price. Until that obligation came into being, Lyon was not Brodie's debtor with power to mortgage the restaurant equipment as collateral for the unpaid purchase price.

But the United States argues that in the context of this case the priority statute, AS 45.05.745(d), is ambiguous as to whether "debtor" is used in the sense defined in AS 45.05.698(a)(4), or whether it is used merely to identify an individual in possession, who ultimately becomes indebted to the purchase-money mortgagee. In contending that this "ambiguity" should be resolved in favor of the latter construction, the United States refers to the history and underlying purposes and policies of the Code, the assertedly different language of the prior Uniform Conditional Sales Act, and the fact that, under AS 45.05.770(a) (Code, §9-402(1)) a financing statement may be filed before a security agreement is made or a security interest otherwise attaches, notwithstanding the fact that this section refers to "debtor," "secured party," and "security interest."

We are not persuaded that either recourse to the history or consideration of the underlying purposes of the Code supports the Government's position. In our view, the term "debtor" as it is used in this particular priority statute, AS 45.05.754(d) (Code, §9-312(4)), means "the person who owes payment or other performance of the obligation secured." AS 45.05.698(a)(4) (Code, §9-105(d)). Although Lyon might have been liable for the reasonable rental of the equipment or for its return to Brodie, he did not owe performance of an "obligation secured" by the collateral in question until November 12, 1964, and therefore was not a "debtor" for purposes of AS 45.05.754(d) (Code, §9-312(4)). Brodie's filing was therefore within the ten-day period and Brodie has priority over the conflicting security interest held by SBA.

The Government has urged us to look at the policy and the purposes of the Code to resolve what it considers to be the ambiguous meaning of "debtor." The Code has granted a specially favored position to the holder of a purchase-money security interest in non-inventory collateral. The holder of such an interest need not follow the notice procedures which are prescribed for the holders of purchase-money interests in inventory. AS 45.05.754(c) (Code, §9-312(3)). Such a holder is also given a special priority position. His interest, perfected second, but within the ten-day grace period, will prevail over any previously perfected security interest. This priority exists even though the framers of the Code knew that the holder of the conflicting security interest would be relying on the possession of the collateral and upon the absence of a prior filing. Similarly, the holder of a purchase-money security interest in non-inventory collateral will have priority over a previously perfected security interest which includes the collateral by virtue of an after-acquired property clause. Code, §9-312(4), Official Comment 3. Such a holder therefore is not required to search the files to determine the existence of such a conflicting interest in order to be sure of his priority.

The protection which the Code confers upon a purchase-money interest in non-inventory collateral is not unduly extended by a decision giving priority to Brodie's interest. Although it is true that Brodie could have filed a financing statement as soon as Lyon went into possession and thus protected itself, it is also true that the bank, SBA's assignor, could have protected itself by inquiring into Lyon's interest in the equipment before accepting his chattel mortgage. Due to the favored status given by the Code to the holder of a purchase-money interest in non-inventory collateral, we are not convinced that the trial court erred in refusing to impose this burden on Brodie.

Affirmed.

NOTES

1) Do you agree with the criticism of *Brodie Hotel Supply* referred to in *North Platte State Bank*? Did White CJ not indirectly endorse the 9th CCA's construction of the meaning of "debtor" in UCC 9-312(4) when he justified the court's decision on the ground that the vendor had filed its financing statement within 10 days after Lyon obtained possession of the equipment? Had the US government not argued that the 10 days should be calculated from the time Lyon started to operate the restaurant business and not from the date (November 12, 1964) on which he agreed to buy the equipment?

OPPSA s. 33(2)(a)(i) adopts the reasoning in *Brodie* by requiring the PMSI to be perfected "before or within ten days after (i) the debtor obtained possession of the collateral *as a debtor* ..." (emphasis added).

2) In the light of the decision in *North Platte*, should the PMSI definition be expanded to include the security interest of a lender whose loan enables the debtor to pay off the seller, whether or not the buyer has already acquired title to the goods?

3) Can there be a PMSI in an intangible? If yes, how does s. 34(3) apply to it? *Cf. Re Berman* (1979), 24 OR (2d) 79 (rev'd. on other grounds (1979), 26 OR (2d) 389) and the discussion of the case by Ziegel in (1979-80), 4 *CBLJ* 54, at 69-75. OPPSA s. 32(4)(b) now recognizes that there may be a PMSI in an intangible and provides for its priority. The recognition is also extended in s. 20(3).

4) The PPS Acts do not indicate what evidence is admissible to allow a lender to prove that his loan was used by the debtor to enable him to acquire new collateral. In *Dube v. Bank of Montreal* (1986), 5 PPSAC 269 (Sask. CA), Vancise JA held, *inter alia*, that extrinsic evidence was not admissible to prove the purpose of the loan where the loan agreement itself made no mention of it. Is this a proper application of the parol evidence rule? Is the decision consistent with the purpose of the purchase-money priority? (The court in *Dube* subsequently withdrew the judgment in 5 PPSAC 269 and replaced it with a new judgment omitting any reference to the evidentiary issue.)

5) Can there be more than one PMSI in the same collateral and if there can, how do they rank in relation to each other? In *Polano v. Bk. of Nova Scotia* (1979), 96 DLR (3d) 510 (Ont.), the purchasers of a mobile home obtained loans from two different lenders to enable them to pay for it and gave each lender a chattel mortgage on the home. Both financing statements were registered within 10 days of the execution of the security agreement. Loukidelis DCJ held that each lender held a PMSI but he refused to apply s. 34(3) [now s. 30(2)] to determine the ranking of the security interests. In his view, s. 34(3) did not apply to such a situation. (Do you agree?) Instead, he applied the first-to-register rule in s. 35(1)(a) [now s. 30(1).1], thus giving priority to the lender whose financing statement was registered first.

Is this an appropriate solution? Would it be fairer to prorate the two loans in the ratio which each loan bears to the sum of the two loans? *Cf.* s. 37 of the OPPSA which applies such a solution to security interests held in commingled goods. Should this solution also be applied where the conflict arises between a seller of the collateral and a lender? See the discussion by Ziegel in (1979-80), 4 *CBLJ* 54, at 75-78. The new Act adopts the position that the seller's security interest should be given priority. Section 33(3) provides:

(3) Where more than one purchase-money security interest is given priority by subsections (1) and (2), the purchase-money security interest, if any, of the seller has priority over any other purchase-money security interest given by the same debtor.

Is this a reasonable priority rule?

Protection for the Prepaying Buyer

As noted in volume I of this casebook, chapter 10, a buyer is frequently required to pay all or part of the purchase price before he actually receives the goods. Various commentators have noted that while Article 9 and its Canadian counterparts are very solicitous of the unpaid seller's position where he delivers the goods before being paid, the legislation offers no comparable protection to the prepaying buyer. See Aleck Dadson, "A Fresh Plea for the Financing Buyer" (1985-86), 11 *CBLJ* 171. True, the buyer could ask the seller to give him a security interest in the goods while they were being manufactured but this would almost certainly be subordinated to an inventory financer's PMSI under s. 34(2). Can you suggest a scheme that would give the buyer's prepayment the equivalent of the seller's PMSI?

CHAPTER SEVEN

Fixtures, Accessions, Commingled Goods and Subordination Agreements

INTRODUCTION

This chapter continues with the topic of priority rules dealt with in the previous chapter. Its focus is the conflict that arises when the collateral is deemed to have changed its character because of a transforming event. In the case of fixtures, the change has come about because the goods have been affixed to land. In the case of accessions, a component (the "accessory") has been added to a larger item (the "principal goods") so as to become part of the whole. The commingling of goods involves goods from different sources which lose their separate identity when they are mixed together or when they are used as components or ingredients in the manufacture or production of an entirely new product or mass. Each of these problems was already familiar to Roman law although only in the context of competing ownership rights. The common law was slow to develop rules in this area appropriate to modern financing techniques and in fact never succeeded in developing a comprehensive framework. It was left to UCC 9-313 to 9-315 to provide such a blueprint; the corresponding sections in the OPPSA are ss. 34 to 35 and 37.

FIXTURES

Goods are frequently bought and then, while they are still subject to a security interest, affixed to land. (By "land" we include of course any affixation to a structure or building that is itself treated as having become part of the land.) Alternatively, after the goods have become fixtures, their owner may wish to pledge them separately from the land either because he doesn't own the land or, assuming he does, because he wishes to use the fixture (e.g., a machine cemented to the floor) as collateral together with other equipment and machinery which have not become attached to the land. The term fixture is often used indiscriminately to describe goods that have become attached to land but retain their separate identity and goods that have become an integral part of the land or a building on the land: e.g., bricks in a wall. For the purpose of analyzing the statutory provisions and the case law referred to in this section, it will be helpful to distinguish between the following three categories of goods: (1) those that are on the land to be used for the better enjoyment of the land but have never become physically attached to it; (2) those that have become attached to the land but are not an integral part of it (true fixtures), and (3) those goods that have become an integral part of the land.

259

Nineteenth century Anglo-Canadian law generally favoured realty interests and readily found that goods attached to land had become part of the realty. See, e.g., Blackburn J's judgment in *Holland v. Hodgson* (1872), LR 7 CP 328. This meant that those who had claims to the land (landlords, realty mortgagees, etc.) could also claim the fixtures. There were some exceptions to the rule, of which a tenant's right to remove household or trade fixtures on or before the termination of the tenancy was one of the best known. However, they were not significant enough to allay the misgivings of conditional sellers in the 19th century who realistically anticipated that the goods sold by them would or might become fixtures.

Their response was to include a clause in the security agreement providing that the goods were to remain chattels even if they were affixed to land; surprisingly, early Ontario and Manitoba courts upheld the effectiveness of such clauses. However, the English Court of Appeal rejected such sleights of hand in *Hobson v. Gorringe*, [1897] 1 Ch. 182, and the House of Lords did the same shortly afterwards in *Reynolds v. Ashby*, [1904] AC 466. (Does this suggest that English courts were more realty oriented than Canadian courts?)

Hobson v. Gorringe sufficiently disturbed the burgeoning instalment sales industry in Ontario that they were able to persuade the Ontario legislature to adopt a neutralizing amendment without delay. See Stat. Ont., 60 Vict., c. 3, s. 3 and c. 14, s. 80. This provided that:

(1) Where any goods or chattels subject to the provisions of this Act are affixed to any realty without the consent in writing of the owner of the goods or chattels, such goods and chattels shall notwithstanding remain so subject, but the owner of such realty, or any purchaser, or any mortgagee, or other incumbrancer on such realty, shall have the right as against the manufacturer, bailor or vendor of such goods or chattels, or any person claiming through or under them, to retain the said goods and chattels upon payment of the amount due and owing thereon.

The same provision was reproduced (but without any reference to the seller's consent not having been obtained to the affixation of the goods) in the Uniform Conditional Sales Act adopted by the Canadian Uniformity Commissioners in 1922.

In *Hoppe v. Manners*, [1931] 2 DLR 253, the Ontario Court of Appeal unexpectedly held that, the statutory provision notwithstanding, goods subject to a security interest became part of the realty on their affixation to the land, and that conditional sellers would have to comply with the registration requirements under the Registry Acts if they wished to protect their interests against the claims of subsequent realty interests in the land. This decision led both Ontario and the Uniformity Commissioners to modify substantially their respective provisions. In both cases, the conditional seller was now required to register a copy of the conditional sale agreement in the appropriate land registry office as well as in the conditional sales registry. It was also made clear that the seller's right to remove the goods on default did not apply to "building materials" or to fixtures which could not be removed without substantial injury to the land. On all the above, see further Goode and Ziegel, *Hire-Purchase and Conditional Sale* (1965), at 173-78; and W. J. Tremeear, *A Treatise on the Canadian Law of Conditional Sales of Chattels and of Chattel Liens* (1899), at 116-19.

The PPS legislation in Canada has introduced some important changes to the treatment of security interests in fixtures. Section 34 of the OPPSA is based on the 1962 version of UCC 9-313 and reproduces s. 36 of the old Act with only minor amendments. Note in particular the following features: (1) s. 34 distinguishes between security interests created *after* as well as before the chattels became fixtures (the pre-PPSA conditional sales Acts only covered pre-affixation security interests); (2) a similar distinction is drawn between interests in real property created before and after affixation of the chattels; (3) if the security interest in the chattel is created *before* affixation it prevails over the claim of any person with an interest in the real property; (4) if the security interest in the chattel is created *after* affixation it is subject to existing interests in the real property; (5) in both (2) and (3) a security interest in the fixture is subordinated to the interests of subsequent purchasers and mortgagees of the real property without knowledge of the security interest. Section 54 provides for the filing of a notice in prescribed form in the land registry office and that such notice constitutes deemed knowledge of the security interest for the purpose of s. 34(2) of the Act; (6) if the secured party wishes to seize and remove the fixture he must reimburse any encumbrancer or owner of the real property for the cost of repairing "any physical injury" caused by the removal but excluding any diminution in the value of the real property caused by the removal of the chattel; and (7) a person with an interest in the real property may retain the fixture on paying the balance owing under the security agreement.

The following case illustrates the interplay between the various rules of s. 34.

Cormier v. Federal Business Development Bank
(1983), 3 PPSAC 161 (Ont. Co. Ct.)

SALHANY Co. Ct. J: At issue in this application is who is entitled to possession of five items of machinery and equipment which are situate on the premises owned by the applicants and which had been leased to Country Squire Auto Body Limited under an oral lease which expired on February 17, 1983, when Country Squire made an assignment in bankruptcy. The Federal Business Development Bank claims priority under a chattel mortgage dated September 11, 1979, on four of those items. The Continental Bank claims priority and seeks to recover the fifth, namely, a Black Hawk Power-Cage Serial No. BHYPC 35, which it sold to Country Squire pursuant to a conditional sales contract dated the 2nd of July 1980. On July 15, 1982, a chattel mortgage in writing was given to the Toronto-Dominion Bank on all five items of equipment. However, the Toronto-Dominion Bank has not entered an appearance in this application or taken any position with respect to its entitlement to recover any of the items covered by its security.

The facts are not in dispute and have been settled by an agreed statement prepared by the parties. They may be summarized as follows:

1. The applicants are the owners in joint tenancy of the lands and premises at 6 Forwell Road in Kitchener pursuant to a deed registered on March 8, 1968. Located on that property is a commercial building containing 16,000 square feet.

2. In 1977, the applicants rented the premises to Country Squire Auto Body Limited to operate an automobile and truck body repair business. No written lease was ever executed by the parties. Initially, only part of the premises was rented but later Country Squire expanded its business to occupy the entire building for the annual rental of $5,900.

3. Apparently the principals of Country Squire, Thomas and Barbara Stoliker, had expressed to the applicants a desire to purchase the premises at some time in the future. On May 15, 1981, this intention was formalized by a deed registered on that day conveying the

property to Thomas and Barbara Stoliker. The purchaser price was $543,500 payable $7,500 by way of cash, the assumption of a first mortgage of $96,500 and the balance of $439,500 secured by way of a second mortgage given by the Stolikers to the applicants. Country Squire continued to rent the premises from the Stolikers upon the same terms.

4. In February of 1983 the second mortgage went into default. As a result, the Stolikers gave a quitclaim of the property to the applicants by a deed which was registered on February 17, 1983. At the same time, the lease to Country Squire was terminated by mutual agreement.

5. During the period that Country Squire was a tenant of the premises, the machinery and equipment which are the subject-matter of this application were installed on the premises. Those items are as follows:

    (a) an Ingersoll Rand Temprite Air Make Up unit;
    (b) a Bearcat frame straightener;
    (c) a Binks spray booth;
    (d) a Bee Line Optoflex alignment machine; and
    (e) a Black Hawk Power-Cage Serial No. BHYPC 35.

6. The Ingersoll Rand Temprite Air Make Up unit was installed by Country Squire with the knowledge and consent of the applicants prior to October 1977. The unit consists of two parts. The first performs a heating function and consists of a propane furnace mounted to the outside of the roof of the building, together with ducts leading from the furnace into the spray area. The second performs an exhaust function and consists of vents about 3 1/2 feet in diameter leading from the floor to the roof.

7. The Bearcat frame straightener was installed on the premises by Country Squire with the knowledge and consent of the applicants in November 1978. It is a machine 25 feet long, 12 feet wide and weighs approximately five tons. Its purpose is to straighten the frame on small and medium sized vehicles. To install the machine it was necessary to remove an area of the original poured concrete floor and a new floor of 6-inch thick concrete was installed. This machine is fastened to the floor by 4 one-half-inch diameter lag bolts. Concrete pedestals were added at the contact points and a pit was constructed underneath the machine in order to enable a man to stand while working beneath the machine. The cost of installation was approximately $28,000 paid entirely by Country Squire. There was no discussion of any future restoration of the premises.

8. The Binks spray booth was installed on the premises by Country Squire with the knowledge and consent of the applicants in November of 1979. It measures 33 feet long by 14 feet in width and is secured to the floor by sixty-five 5/16-inch diameter lag bolts. A cement block pedestal was also added to the floor to accommodate the spray booth. Exhaust fumes from the booth are vented to the outside of the building through a vent measuring 3 1/2 feet in diameter, extending from the booth through the roof of the building.

9. The Bee Line Optoflex alignment machine was installed by Country Squire with the knowledge and consent of the applicants on November 23, 1979, and is used to align the wheels of automobiles and trucks. It consists of two parts: a machine upon which the vehicles are driven measuring 15 feet by 12 feet and a screen measuring 16 feet by 5 feet upon which the alignment of a vehicle's wheels may be measured. It weighs approximately two tons. To install it, it was necessary to remove an area of the original poured concrete floor measuring

17 feet by 18 feet and then lower the floor 2 feet below the original floor level and install a new floor of 6-inch thick reinforced concrete. The machine and screen are fastened to the floor each by four 3⁄4-inch lag bolts. A pit deep enough to permit a man to stand while working was also constructed beneath the machine. The cost of installing the machine, including the price, was approximately $55,000 which was paid entirely by Country Squire. Country Squire never discussed future restoration of the premises with the applicants.

10. The Black Hawk Power Cage was installed by Country Squire with the knowledge and consent of the applicants over a two-week period in June of 1980. The machine is 36 feet in length, 12 feet in width, and weighs approximately five tons. It is used to straighten frames on large vehicles, trucks, buses and trailers. To install the machine, it was necessary to remove an area of the existing concrete floor measuring 20 feet by 43 feet. The floor was then lowered two feet below the original floor level and a new floor of 6-inch thick reinforced concrete was installed. Extensive renovations were then carried out to the building to accommodate the machine. This involved removing 11 wood trusses from the roof and replacing them with seven steel girders above the area of the machine. Two steel runners were also added to the ceiling to permit pulleys to be used along each side of the machine. Six steel I-beams were mounted on concrete pillars and placed around the area to support the weight of the roof. The purpose of this construction was to install various pulleys which are not essential to the operation of the cage. The cage itself is fastened to six 1-inch diameter lag bolts. Additional changes were also made to an overhead door and furnace duct work and electrical systems to accommodate the machine. The cost of installation, exclusive of the price of the machine, was approximately $29,000 which was paid by Country Squire. There was no discussion between Country Squire and the applicants about the future restoration of the premises. In addition to the construction work carried out to accommodate the machinery, Country Squire also constructed a concrete block room in a corner of a bay housing the Bearcat, Optoflex and Black Hawk machines in order to house an air compressor necessary to run the machinery. The compressor itself is secured to the floor by four bolts.

11. On September 24, 1979, the Federal Business Development Bank filed a financing statement under the Personal Property Security Act pertaining to their chattel mortgage dated September 11, 1979. It covered, *inter alia*, the first four items which are the subject-matter of this application. That registration was amended on March 6, 1981, to record a change of the debtor's name and was renewed on August 26, 1982. The chattel mortgage was to secure the principal sum of $55,000.

12. On July 24, 1980, the Continental Bank of Canada filed a financing statement under the Personal Property Security Act pertaining to their conditional sale contract dated July 2, 1980, on the Black Hawk Power-Cage. That financing statement was to secure the sum of $113,266 made up of the principal amount of $78,115 and financing charges of $35,151.

13. Following the quitclaim deed, the Federal Business Development Bank made an arrangement to pay the applicants' occupation rent of $1,058 per month pending the resolution of the dispute as to entitlement to the machinery. Rent has been paid since March of 1983 to date.

It was argued on behalf of the applicants that all of the machinery and equipment had been affixed to the realty in such a manner that it should be considered part of the realty.

Since there was no agreement to the contrary, the respondents, who were claiming through the tenant, had no right to remove these fixtures unless they could establish that they had priority under the Personal Property Security Act, RSO 1980, c. 375 (PPSA).

The respondents' position, on the other hand, was that this machinery and equipment was never really affixed to the realty except for the purpose of steadying the equipment and permitting it to be used properly. It was further argued that, even if it was found to be affixed to the realty and became part of the freehold, nevertheless it could be severed because it was for the purpose of carrying on a trade, in which case it ceased to be "fixtures." Upon resuming its character as chattels, it could be removed by the respondents provided that such removal could be effected without serious injury to the freehold and before the expiration of the term, unless the time for removal was extended by agreement. It was further submitted that even if the machinery and equipment constituted fixtures within the meaning of the PPSA, then their security interest on the machinery and equipment gave them a claim in priority to that of the applicants under the Act.

The general rule at common law was that whatever was affixed to the freehold became part of it and subject to the laws governing the freehold. Over the years a number of exceptions arose to alleviate the harsh results of this inflexible doctrine. These exceptions were in relation to chattels which were used for the purpose of carrying on a trade or of domestic convenience or ornament. Such chattels, though affixed to the realty, could still be severed in which case they ceased to be "fixtures" and resumed their character as chattels. In such instance, they could be removed by the tenant or his assigns provided that such removal could be effected without serious injury to the freehold and provided that the tenant removed them before the expiration of the tenancy or before any time for removal which had been extended by agreement between the parties: see Canadian Law of Landlord and Tenant by Williams and Rhodes (5th ed.), at 3-10, 13-30; Canadian Law of Real Property by Anger and Honsberger (1959), at 463-65, 485; Report of the Ontario Law Reform Commission on "Landlord and Tenant Law" (1976), c. XIV.

In the course of their argument, counsel referred to a number of authorities supporting their contention that the machinery and equipment in question were or were not fixtures. It is apparent from a review of these decisions that often the decision reached by the Court depended on the particular facts before it. In *Stack v. T. Eaton Co.* (1902), 4 OLR 335 (CA), the leading case in Ontario, five rules were laid down to assist the Court in determining what constituted a fixture:

1. Articles not otherwise attached to the land than by their own weight are not to be considered as part of the land, unless the circumstances are such as to show that they were intended to be part of the land.

2. Articles affixed to the land, even slightly, are to be considered part of the land unless circumstances are such as to show that they were intended to continue to be chattels.

3. The circumstances necessary to be shown to alter the *prima facie* character of the articles are circumstances which show the degree of annexation and the object of such annexation, which are patent for all to see;

4. The intention of the parties affixing the article to the soil is material only so far as it can be presumed from the degree and object of the annexation; and

5. Even in the case of tenant's fixtures put in for the purpose of trade, they form part of the freehold, with the right, however, to the tenant, as between him and his landlord, to

bring them back to the state of chattels again by severing them from the soil, and they pass by a conveyance of the land as part of it subject to this right of the tenant.

In *Argles v. McMath* (1894), 26 OR 224 (HC), affirmed, 23 OAR 44, Armour CJ stressed the distinction that had to be drawn between fixtures which he described as fixtures in the primary sense and were irremovable and fixtures in the secondary sense of the term which were removable. Fixtures in the secondary sense of the term included fixtures affixed to the freehold for the purpose of trade or of domestic convenience or ornament and gave to the tenant qualified property rights in them. See also *Carscallen v. Moodie* (1858), 15 UCQB 304 (CA).

I am satisfied on the material before me that the five pieces of machinery and equipment which are the subject matter of this application were for the purpose of carrying on a trade. Even if it can be said that these articles were "affixed to the land even slightly" and thus were "to be considered part of the land" within Rule 2, I am of the view that the tenant or the assignee of the tenant was entitled "to bring them back to the state of chattels again by severing them from the soil" (Rule 5).

Counsel for the respondents submitted that, when Country Squire went into default on the security agreements held by the respondents, this enabled them to step into the shoes of Country Squire as assignees (*Devine v. Callery* (1917), 40 OLR 505, 38 DLR 542 (CA)) or as successors in interest (*Gillett v. Lawrence's Ltd.*, [1922] 2 WWR 584, 14 Sask. LR 438 (CA)) and to sever the fixtures from the land and to remove them as chattels. Thus, it was argued that this enabled the respondents to sever and remove the machinery and equipment in the same way that Country Squire would have been able to do had they not given up their lease to the applicant.

In my view, the fact that there has been a default under a chattel mortgage or conditional sales agreement does not automatically make a secured creditor an assignee or a successor in interest of the debtor in the absence of some agreement in writing or otherwise transferring the debtor's interest to the creditor. This submission also ignores the fact that the PPSA and its predecessor statutes such as the Conditional Sales Act, RSO 1970, c. 76 (but not the Chattel Mortgages Act) have sought to settle the competing interests of landlords and secured creditors to fixtures. Accordingly, it is important to consider the provisions of the PPSA to determine whether the priority rules in that Act resolve the competing interests to the parties in this application.

Section 2(a) of the PPSA makes the Act apply:

(a) to every transaction without regard to its form and without regard to the person who has title to the collateral that in substance creates a security interest, including, without limiting the foregoing.

(i) a chattel mortgage, conditional sale, equipment trust, floating charge, pledge, trust deed or trust receipt, and ...

Section 36 [now s. 34] of the Act provides:

36.—(1) Subject to subsection (3) of this section and notwithstanding subsection 34(3), a security interest that attached to goods before they became fixtures has priority as to the goods over the claim of any person who has an interest in the real property.

(2) Subject to subsection (3), a security interest that attached to goods after they became fixtures has priority over the claim of any person who subsequently acquired an interest in the

real property, but not over any person who had a registered interest in the real property at the time the security interest attached to the goods and who has not consented in writing to the security interest or disclaimed an interest in the goods as fixtures.

(3) The security interest referred to in subsections (1) and (3) are subordinate to the interest of,

(a) a subsequent purchaser or mortgagee for value of an interest in the real property;

(b) a creditor with a lien on the real property subsequently obtained as a result of judicial process; or

(c) a creditor with a prior encumbrance of record on the real property in respect of subsequent advances,

if the subsequent purchase or mortgage was made or the lien was obtained or the subsequent advance under the prior encumbrance was made or contracted for, as the case may be, without actual notice of the security interest.

(4) If a secured party, by virtue of subsection (1) or (2) and subsection (3), has priority over the claim of a person having an interest in the real property, he may on default, subject to the provisions of this Act respecting default, remove his collateral from the real property if, unless otherwise agreed, he reimburses any encumbrancer or owner of the real property who is not the debtor for the cost of repairing any physical injury excluding diminution in the value of the real property caused by the absence of the goods removed or by the necessity for replacement, but a person so entitled to reimbursement may refuse permission to remove until the secured party has given adequate security for any reimbursement arising under this subsection.

(5) A person having an interest in real property that is subordinate to a security interest by virtue of subsection (1) or (2) and subsection (3) may, before the collateral has been removed from the real property by the secured party in accordance with subsection (4), retain the collateral upon payment to the secured party of the amount owing under the security interest having priority over his claim.

Subsection 34(3) [now s. 33(2)] referred to in s. 36(1) provides that:

(3) A purchase-money security interest in collateral or its proceeds, other than inventory, has priority over any other security interest in the same collateral if the purchase-money security interest was perfected at the time the debtor obtained possession of the collateral or within ten days thereafter.

• • •

Unfortunately, the term "fixture" is not defined in the Act. Thus no distinction is made between a fixture "in the primary sense" which may not be severed from the freehold and a fixture "in the secondary sense" which may be severed if it is for the purpose of carrying on a trade or of a domestic convenience or ornament. If the term "fixture" as used in the Act is intended to cover all fixtures, even ones which may be severed and removed by the tenant, then the provisions of s. 36 would apply insofar as the rights of the parties are concerned. On the other hand, if the term "fixtures" was restricted to only those which cannot be severed, then the provisions of the PPSA would not apply and the competing claims of the parties would have to be settled by the common law.

In my view, the word "fixtures" was intended to cover all chattels attached to the land by the tenant whether they are removable or not. Since the common law has always regarded trade, domestic or ornamental fixtures as "fixtures" until the tenant exercised his right of severance and removal, it seems to me that it must have been the intention of the Legislature to include all chattels attached to the land even if they are subject to severance. I find support in that view from the inclusion of s. 36(4) of the Act. It is incomprehensible to me that the Legislature would give to a secured creditor a right to remove fixtures not generally severable from the freehold beyond the term of the tenancy and not that same right to fixtures which are severable. That was the view reached by the Ontario Court of Appeal in *Hoppe v. Manners*, 66 OLR 587, [1931] 2 DLR 253, dealing with the meaning of fixtures under the Conditional Sales Act and supports the conclusions which I have reached.

Turning now to the claim of the respondents, the agreed statement of facts indicates that the Ingersoll Rand Temprite Air Make Up unit and the Bearcat frame straightener were affixed to the property prior to the chattel mortgage, and the Binks spray booth and the Bee Line Optoflex alignment machine subsequent thereto. Applying the conditions set out in s. 12 defining the time of attachment, I find that attachment occurred on September 11, 1979, when the chattel mortgage was executed at which time the principal funds were advanced to the tenant. Thus s. 36(1) gives the Federal Business Development Bank priority with respect to the last two items over the claim of any person who has an interest in the property and who is not a person mentioned in subs. (3). At that time the applicants were the owners of the property and therefore their claim to those two items is subordinate to the claim of the Federal Business Development Bank by s. 36(1). Nor does s. 36(3) assist the applicants. Even if they did become the registered owners after the receipt of the quitclaim deed, it can be hardly said that they were a subsequent purchaser for value without actual notice of the security interest. On the other hand, because the applicants were the registered owners of the property when the first two items became fixtures, I am of the view that s. 36(2) gives them a claim in priority to that of the Federal Business Development Bank unless they "consented in writing to the security interest or disclaimed an interest in the goods as fixtures." Since there has been no such consent or disclaimer, I find that the applicants are entitled to retain these two items.

The Black Hawk Power-Cage was installed and became a fixture in June of 1980 prior to the execution of the conditional sales agreement on July 2, 1980. However, I am of the view that the date of the execution of a conditional sale contract is not necessarily determinative of when attachment occurred under s. 12. As was noted by Arnup JA in *Rogerson Lbr. Co. v. Four Seasons Chalet Ltd.* (1980), 29 OR (2d) 193, 1 PPSAC 160, 12 BLR 93, 36 CBR (NS) 141, 113 DLR (3d) 671 (CA), the provision for retention of title in the vendor is not invalidated by the PPSA unless there is an agreement in writing and registered pursuant to the Act as there was under s. 10(b) of the Conditional Sales Act, RSO 1970, c. 76.

As indicated earlier, s. 12 [now s. 11(2)] requires three conditions to exist before attachment occurs:

1. the parties must intend it to attach;
2. value must be given; and
3. the debtor has rights in the collateral.

I am prepared to concede that the validity of a conditional sales agreement is not dependent upon there being an agreement in writing. Thus, there may be instances when the parties may agree orally that a security interest will attach immediately even though the agreement is subsequently formalized by a document in writing. However, there is no indication in the agreed statement of facts that Country Squire had any meeting with the Continental Bank prior to June of 1980 from which it can be inferred that it was intended that the security interest was to attach at that time. Nor is there any indication when the sum of $2,000 was paid by Country Squire as a down payment which would enable me to find that value was given before installation of the Black Hawk Power-Cage. I am simply asked to infer that such arrangements took place prior to installation; otherwise Country Squire would not have been in a position to purchase the equipment. It is equally consistent, however, that the arrangements for financing were made immediately after installation, that is, when the contract was signed. In the absence of any such evidence, the only conclusion that I can come to on the evidence is that the security interest attached when the conditional sales agreement was signed on July 2, 1980. Since the Black Hawk Power-Cage became a fixture prior to that time, s. 36(2) gives the applicant a prior claim over that of the Continental Bank.

In view of the foregoing reasons, the applicants are entitled to the Ingersoll Rand Temprite Air Make Up unit, the Bearcat frame straightener, and the Black Hawk Power-Cage serial No. BHYPC 35. The respondent, Federal Business Development Bank, is entitled to receive the Binks Spray Booth and the Bee Line Optoflex alignment machine upon payment of the costs of removal pursuant to s. 36(4).

Counsel may speak to me to arrange a time to present their submissions on the cost of removal at which time the issue of costs may also be spoken to.

ADDENDUM

SALHANY Co. Ct. J: Mr. Earnshaw has applied pursuant to Rr. 528 and 529 requesting that I reconsider my findings as to who is entitled to recover the Black Hawk Power-Cage. In my reasons delivered October 25, 1983, I determined that as between the plaintiffs and the Continental Bank of Canada, the plaintiffs had priority under the Personal Property Security Act.

Mr. Earnshaw, on behalf of the Federal Business Development Bank, points out that there must have been a misunderstanding because his notice of motion specifically seeks a determination as to his client's entitlement to the Black Hawk Power-Cage even though the agreed statement of facts may not clearly set out that such a claim has been asserted.

Mr. Bumstead agreed that this was his understanding but says that this matter should be more properly dealt with by way of appeal. However, he concedes that he was contacted the day following the release of my judgment and advised that he intended to have this issue clarified when the matter resumed for determination of the remaining issues raised in the notice of motion. I am satisfied that no prejudice will result to the plaintiffs by a determination of this issue at this stage of the proceedings, and I will proceed to do so.

On p. 171 of my earlier decision, I held that s. 36(1) of the Personal Property Security Act gave the Federal Business Development Bank priority with respect to any chattel installed on the property after attachment occurred on September 11, 1979, over the claim of any person who had an interest in the property and who was not a person in s. 36(3) of the Act. I also held that since the applicants were the owners of the property at the time of attachment their claim was subordinate with respect to any chattels attaching after that time. Thus, it follows that although the applicants have a claim in priority over the

Continental Bank of Canada to the Black Hawk Power-Cage, that claim is subordinate to the claim of the Federal Business Development Bank. Accordingly, the Federal Business Development Bank will also be entitled to recover the Black Hawk Power-Cage.

Order accordingly.

NOTES

1) "Fixture" is not defined in s. 36 of the old Act or s. 34 of the new Act. Does this mean that it retains its common law meaning or should the courts be willing to find even more readily than they were before that a chattel has become a fixture? How relevant is it for this purpose, (a) that the secured party is given a broad right under s. 34(3) to remove the fixture subject only to making good any physical damage, and (b) that s. 34 requires him, as the holder of a security interest in a fixture, to register his claim in the Land Registry Office? It will be noted that in *Cormier's* case Salhany Co. Ct. J approved the common law test of a fixture.

2) The definition of "personal property" in s. 1(1) of the OPPSA expressly excludes "building materials that have been affixed to the realty." This exclusion also appeared in the Ontario Conditional Sales Act and in the Uniform Conditional Sales Act. "Building materials" is not defined but a frequently cited exposition is that by O.E. Lennox, Assistant Master, in *Alexander v. McGillivray* (1931), 41 OWN 407-8:

When the term "building materials" is used [in the Act], the ordinary ingredients such as lumber, mortar, brick and stone are the first to suggest themselves as logical illustrations. But on further consideration there are a great many other things that go into the construction of a building which do not come under these headings, which nevertheless are integral parts of the whole construction, as compared with other articles which are mere adjuncts or appendages. In determining what is building material it is necessary to consider the entire construction. Certain equipment that by itself would appear to come under the classification of a chattel, may in the general construction of a building become so closely interlinked and identified with other materials generally described as building material, that they must for all practical purposes be considered as building materials, within the meaning of s. 8. It would seem that, in determining this question, similar principles must be applied as in dealing with the question of fixtures. The degree and the object of the annexation must be considered. No doubt the distinction here should not be so finely drawn as in the case of fixtures, but the underlying principle is the same.

Not surprisingly, courts have reached different conclusions in applying his test. Thermos windows in a building (*Rockett Lbr. Building Supplies Ltd. v. Papageorgiou* (1979), 30 CBR (NS) 183 (Ont.)) and an electric motor truck scale to be used in a seed mill (*Chas. A. Hare Ltd. v. Payne* (1982), 2 PPSAC 93) have been characterized as building materials for the purposes of s. 36; on the other hand, a furnace (*Collis v. Carew Lbr. Co.*, [1930] 4 DLR 996 (Ont. CA)) and even an elevator installed in an apartment building (*Montreal Trust Co. v. Goldaire Rentals Ltd.*, [1967] 1 OR 40) were not so regarded under the earlier legislation. In *Manning v. Furnasman Heating Ltd.* (1985-86), 5 PPSAC 67 (Man. CA), Sullivan JA, at 77-78, also appears to have been influenced in his conclusion that a furnace had become part of the structure by the fact that the supplier could have filed a lien under the Builders' Liens Act, SM 1980-81, c. 7, s. 35. Why should this affect a secured party's rights under the OPPSA? What are the advantages to the secured party claiming under the PPSA rather than under a construction lien Act?

CIRCULAR PRIORITIES AND SECTIONS 34(1) AND (2)

The problem of circular priorities has been previously discussed in the context of s. 30(6), (*supra*, chapter 4). It can also arise in contests between a fixture security interest and two or more realty interests as shown by the facts in *GMS Securities and Appraisals Limited v. Rich-Wood Kitchens Limited* ((1995), 21 OR (3d) 761 (CA), rev'g (1991), 2 OR (3d) 58 (Div. Ct.)).

D gave NT a construction mortgage in the amount of $111,000 on June 8, 1986. D granted a second mortgage to Darcon (vendor of the land on which the house was to be built) on August 20, 1986. NT made advances on its mortgage on the following dates:

August 7, 1986	$ 35,000
August 22, 1986	$ 22,150
October 10, 1986	$ 16,050
November 19, 1986	$ 11,880
December 12, 1986	$ 4,500
January 5, 1987	$ 10,620
TOTAL	$100,200

On September 8, 1986, D entered into a conditional sales contract with RWK for installation of kitchen and other cabinets in the home for $4,266. The cabinets were delivered on October 17, 1986, and installed on December 13, 1986. RWK only registered a notice of its security interest in the Land Registry Office on March 31, 1987. On March 17, 1987, D granted a third mortgage to GMS for services rendered. D defaulted in payments on the mortgage to NT, and NT sold the home for $141,973.97. The issue before the Ontario courts was the ranking of RWK's claim *vis-à-vis* the first and third mortgages. McDermid LJSC, relying on ss. 36(1) and (3)(c) of the old Ontario Act, held that RWK's security interest had priority over NT's first mortgage, with the exception of the final advance made on January 5, 1987, and that NT should pay off RWK out of its share of the proceeds of sale of the home. He reasoned that GMS, as a subsequent mortgagee without notice of RWK's security interest, had priority over NT's mortgage, that RWK had priority over NT (with the exception of the January 5, 1987, advance), and that NT had priority over GMS's third mortgage pursuant to the terms of the Mortgages Act and the Registry Act. McDermid LJSC did not try to resolve the circular priorities arising between RWK and GMS.

On appeal, Potts J, speaking for the Divisional Court, held that McDermid LJSC had erred in referring twice to s. 36(3) of the old Act to determine the priorities of RWK *vis-à-vis* NT and GMS, and that s. 36(3) ceased to apply once RWK's priority had been determined *vis-à-vis* NT. He thought that the result reached by the lower court was patently unjust and would "make a mockery" out of the PPS registry system.

Potts J further reasoned that s. 36 was only intended to resolve priority conflicts between a PPS interest and a realty interest, and was not meant to resolve conflicts between realty interests such as arose between NT's and GMS's mortgages in the present case. He was also of the view that the effect of s. 69 of the old Act (s. 73 in the new Act) was to resolve any conflict between the PPSA and the Mortgages Act and Registry Act in NT's favour.

The Court of Appeal reversed the Divisional Court's judgment. Speaking for the court, Labrosse JA rejected the various proposals put forward by the parties for resolving the circular priority problem because each of them was in conflict with a provision of the PPSA, the Mortgages Act or the Registry Act. He thought, however, that the following solution was consistent with the existing legislation and the commercial expectation of the parties:

By virtue of s. 36(4) of the PPSA, Rich-Wood, under certain terms, could have removed its fixtures from the real property. Under ss. (5), National Trust, having an interest subordinate to that of Rich-Wood, could have retained the fixtures upon payment to Rich-Wood of the amount owing under the security interest having priority over that part of its mortgage. The material before us does not reveal that the parties took any of the steps outlined in either ss. (4) or (5). However, National Trust did sell the property and has since held in trust $5,539.03, the amount of the Rich-Wood claim plus interest. It was on this basis that National Trust was able to exercise its power of sale and receive full payment of its mortgage. The material also reveals that National Trust paid off the second mortgage to Darcon Leaseholds Ltd., in circumstances where Rich-Wood had priority over this mortgage.

Having regard to the right of the fixture financier to remove its fixture pursuant to s. 36(4), National Trust converted that right when it sold the property pursuant to the power of sale and therefore National Trust should pay Rich-Wood the amount of its claim out of its share of the proceeds of the sale. Accordingly, I see nothing unfair in requiring National Trust to pay Rich-Wood the amount of its claim and then stand in the shoes of Rich-Wood for the purpose of recovering this amount. However, for that purpose, National Trust can only stand after GMS, which has priority over Rich-Wood by virtue of s. 36(3)(a). This solution does not offend the relevant provisions of the PPSA. Not only does it give effect to the priorities under both the PPSA and the registry system of priority registration, but it is equally consistent with the reasonable commercial expectations of the parties. The practical results of this order of priorities can be best illustrated by way of an example. Assuming that the proceeds from the sale under power of sale were $140,000, that National Trust's last advance was $10,000, the balance of its first mortgage $98,000, Rich-Wood's interest $5,000, and GMS's mortgage $30,000, the results are:

National Trust		$ 10,000
National Trust	from this amount, Rich-Wood is paid $5,000	98,000
GMS		30,000
National Trust	National Trust, standing in place of Rich-Wood, gets the balance of the proceeds and suffers a loss of $3,000	2,000
		$140,000

Accordingly, the priorities are:
1. National Trust: amount of last advance
2. National Trust: balance of mortgage, from which amount owing to Rich-Wood is to be paid
3. GMS: amount of its mortgage
4. National Trust: amount of Rich-Wood claim.

• • •

PROBLEM

A has a security interest in all of D's equipment. Some of the equipment has become fixtures in D's plant. On February 1, A registered a financing statement in the chattel security registry but failed to file a notice pursuant to s. 54 of the OPPSA. B also acquired a security interest in the same fixtures and properly filed its financing statement and s. 54 notice, both on April 15. On April 30, D gave C a mortgage on its land which was duly registered in the land registry office. As between A, B and C, whose security interest ranks first under the PPSA?

ACCESSIONS

The rules in s. 35 of the OPPSA (corresponding to those in UCC 9-314) are intended to mirror the fixtures rules in s. 34. Are the situations in fact identical? Consider the following example. D Co. buys an airplane for cash. Subsequently D Co. decides to install an improved radio communications system in the aircraft. D Co. finances the acquisition of the equipment by giving F a purchase money security interest in it. F duly registers a financing statement. Still later, D Co. sells the aircraft to T but fails to disclose the outstanding security interest in F's favour. T made a search in the PPS registry but found no financing statement involving the aircraft.* T made no other searches. Should it have anticipated that there might be financing statements involving accessories in the aircraft? Suppose T subsequently sold the aircraft to U believing it had clear title to it. Should F be entitled to assert its security interest against U even though U knew nothing about it and would not have discovered it by searching the registry under T's name? The reader will note that the example involves the familiar A-B-C-D problem previously discussed in chapter 4 but that it is made more complicated because of the possibility of separate security interests existing against discrete parts of a larger chattel.

The common law rules on security interests in accessions were unsettled, as is shown by the conflicting views expressed in the case that follows. Which of the views has been adopted in s. 35?

---

* There have been discussions between federal and provincial officials and agreement in principle was reached in 1985 on the desirability of establishing a national registry for security interests in aircraft coupled with uniform provincial legislation. To date, however, these plans have not matured into legislative action. See Joel Cuperfain, "A Canadian Central Registry for Security Interests in Aircraft: A Good Idea but Will it Fly?" (1991), 17 *CBLJ* 380.

Industrial Acceptance Corp. v. Firestone Tire & Rubber Co.
(1968), 8 DLR (3d) 770 (Alta. AD),
rev'd. on appeal (1971), 17 DLR (3d) 229 (SCC)

SMITH CJA: The appellant appeals from the judgment of Cullen DCJ, who held that the respondent was entitled to maintain its security on tires on a truck purchased under a conditional sale agreement which was assigned by the vendor to the appellant.

One Vanderlinden purchased the truck under conditional sale agreement and the vendor assigned its interest in that agreement to the appellant. Vanderlinden, according to the concession of both counsel, replaced the tires on the vehicle with tires purchased by him from the respondent under conditional sale agreements. Upon Vanderlinden making default under the agreement providing for the sale of the truck, the truck was seized by the appellant. Thereupon the respondent claimed the tires under its conditional sale agreements.

The dispute was heard and determined by the trial Judge in a summary way upon an agreed statement of facts.

The facts are clear and the point at issue is a narrow one: does the doctrine of accession apply so as to cause the tires to have become part of the truck and thus available as part of the security of the appellant?

This is an ancient principle which apparently comes to us from Roman law. Interesting articles on the subject are found in 9 *Aust. LJ* 50, 27 *Mod. LR* 505, at 507, Crossley Vaines, *Personal Property*, 4th ed., at 383, 39 *Aust. LJ* 408 and 5 *University of Western Aust. L Rev.*, at 496 *et seq.*

The principle has been applied to materials and equipment worked into ships as well as to parts and tires which have been built in or attached to motor cars.

Crossley Vaines summarizes the legal position at 385 as follows:

To this and similar problems a more precise answer may be found in the many Commonwealth and American decisions which deal with accession in relation to motor vehicles. The right of accession gives the property in the whole to the owner of the principal chattel, which is probably that which is the greater in value, and the degree of annexation sufficient to constitute an accession may be decided in the light of various tests: (1) that of "injurious removal"—can there be a separation of the original chattels without destroying or seriously injuring the whole?; (2) that of "separate existence"—has the incorporated chattel ceased to exist as a separate chattel?; or again, (3) would the removal of the incorporated chattel destroy the utility of the principal chattel? Yet another test has been suggested as one particularly suited to English law because of its flexibility and by virtue of its association with realty, namely the test of the degree and purpose of annexation.

So far as a ship is concerned I refer to *Seath & Co. v. Moore* (1886), 11 App. Cas. 350, and the statements of Lord Watson at 380-81, as follows:

The English decisions to which I have referred appear to me to establish the principle that, where it appears to be the intention, or in other words the agreement, of the parties to a contract for building a ship, that at a particular stage of its construction, the vessel, so far as then finished, shall be appropriated to the contract of sale, the property of the vessel as soon as it has reached that stage of completion will pass to the purchaser, and subsequent additions made to the chattel thus vested in the purchaser will, accessione, become his property.

There is another principle which appears to me to be deducible from these authorities and to be in itself sound, and that is, that materials provided by the builder and portions of the fabric, whether wholly or partially finished, although intended to be used in the execution of the contract, cannot be regarded as appropriated to the contract, or as "sold," unless they have been affixed to or in a reasonable sense made part of the corpus. That appears to me to have been matter of direct decision by the Court of Exchequer Chamber in *Wood v. Bell*, 6 E & B 355. In *Woods v. Russell*, 5 B & Al. 942 the property of a rudder and some cordage which the builder had bought for the ship was held to have passed in property to the purchaser as an accessory of the vessel; but that decision was questioned by Lord Chief Justice Jervis, delivering the judgment of the Court in *Wood v. Bell*, 6 E & B 355, who stated the real question to be "what is the ship, not what is meant for the ship," and that only the things can pass with the ship "which have been fitted to the ship and have once formed part of her, although afterwards removed for convenience." I assent to that rule, which appears to me to be in accordance with the decision of the Court of Exchequer in *Tripp v. Armitage*, 4 M & W 687.

Cases in which parties in the position of the respondent have succeeded as against the party holding security on the vehicle are: *Lewis v. Andrews & Rowley Pty. Ltd.* (1956), 56 SR (NSW) 439; *Bergougnan v. British Motors Ltd.* (1930), 30 SR (NSW) 61; *Goodrich Silvertown Stores v. McGuire Motors Ltd.*, [1936] 4 DLR 519; *Dawson v. Floyd Dunford Ltd.*, [1961] OWN 225, and *Rendell v. Associated Finance Pty. Ltd.*, [1957] VR 604.

An opposite conclusion was reached by the Court of Appeal of Saskatchewan in *Regina Chevrolet Sales Ltd. v. Riddell*, [1942] 3 DLR 159, [1942] 2 WWR 357. The view of that Court, as stated in the [DLR] headnote, was that: "Tires are an integral part of a truck necessary to its proper working, and as such when used to equip a truck become by accession the property of the person who has the property in the truck." In that case the rival claimants were the vendor of the truck under a conditional sale agreement and the chattel mortgagee of the tires on the truck which were not the original tires and which had been sold by the mortgagee to the purchaser of the truck.

After consideration of the general nature of the doctrine of accession, *Seath v. Moore*, *supra*, and *Goodrich Silvertown Stores v. McGuire Motors Ltd.*, *supra*, Macdonald JA, delivering the judgment of the Court, said at 162-63:

In this case the tires were in my opinion practically available for the purpose for which they were manufactured, only as parts of the truck; for it seems to me that the truck must be regarded not as a mere aggregation of separate parts, but as a working unit into which the several parts have been integrated and harmonized.

Learned counsel for the defence referred to *Goodrich Silvertown Stores v. McGuire Motors Ltd.*, [1936] 4 DLR 519, where there are references to a number of American decisions supporting his contention that the tires did not pass to the plaintiff, though they were on the truck which was the property of the plaintiff. The ground on which these decisions are based seems to be that tires can be detached from a truck without injury to it, are not integral and permanent parts of a truck but merely temporary and separable attachments.

With all due respect it seems to me that the ground on which the decisions are based is too narrow. Even the engine could easily be removed without doing damage to the rest of the car. I am of opinion that the question is whether tires are necessary parts of the truck as a machine capable of operating as intended. This I would answer in the affirmative. ...

I agree with the reasoning and conclusion of the Saskatchewan Court of Appeal and in the language used by Crossley Vaines that the "utility of the principal chattel" would be destroyed by the removal of the tires and that this is a sound reason for coming to the conclusion in the circumstances of this case that the tires have become subject to the security of the appellant.

[On appeal to the Supreme Court of Canada ...]

LASKIN J: The issue in this appeal is whether the assignee of the conditional seller of a truck, which it repossessed upon the buyer's default, may retain the tires then mounted on the truck as against the claim of the unpaid conditional seller of the tires to priority.

Nothing turns on either registration or non-registration of the respective conditional sale contracts, nor on notice of them apart from registration. There is nothing unusual about the relevant facts. The conditional buyer of the truck, which was a used truck when he bought it under a conditional sale contract, subsequently purchased other tires for it from the appellant, again under a conditional sale contract. Eight months after the truck was purchased, it was seized by the respondent for default in payments thereon. As a result of interpleader proceedings, an adjudication on the competing claims of the appellant and the respondent was made in favour of the appellant by Cullen DCJ. His determination was reversed by the Appellate Division of the Supreme Court of Alberta, which relied mainly on a utility conception of the doctrine of accession, which it held to be applicable, and on the exposition of that doctrine by the Saskatchewan Court of Appeal in *Regina Chevrolet Sales Ltd. v. Riddell*, [1942] 3 DLR 159, [1942] 2 WWR 357.

It is common ground that the tires are removable without physical injury to the body of the truck or to any of its constituent parts. The appellant urges this factor as the governing principle in the application of the doctrine of accession between competing security claimants. The respondent contends for a principle of integral convenience or utility in invoking the same doctrine. The authorities cited by opposing counsel reveal that the doctrine of accession has yielded different results in the same fact situations. This has been because of the attempt, on the one hand, to give it a consistent meaning, regardless of the purpose for which it is invoked or of the relationship of the litigating parties; and because of the attempt, on the other hand, to give it a functional direction to take account of the purpose to be served and of the character of the claims for which its support is sought. I can make a compendious reference to these authorities, Canadian, Australian and American, by noting an article by A.G. Guest, "Accession and Confusion in the Law of Hire Purchase," 27 *Mod. L Rev.* 505 (1964).

The present case is unembarrassed by any suggestion that the accessory chattels have lost their identity. Nor are we concerned with an accession to the title of the purchaser of a fabricated product, be it a ship or other chattel, by the maker thereof. Again, we are not concerned with the enhancement of a security holder's position in some way. In my opinion, whatever be the rationale of the doctrine of accession in taking effect in the foregoing situations, it ought not to be applied to the present case where removable and identifiable accessory chattels are claimed by the holder of an original title thereto, retained as security for their value, against the prior security title holder of the principal chattel.

There is no justification for a conclusion in this case that would give the respondent a windfall against a third party who has reserved title. I know of no policy of commercial dealing in chattels of the kind in question here that would warrant subordination of the claim of their title holder to that of another who has given no value for them. The respondent is not a subsequent purchaser of the principal chattel, and it cannot even urge here that as such a purchaser for value and without notice of the security claim to the tires it is entitled to retain them as accessories to its purchase.

It was submitted on behalf of the respondent that a decision adverse to its claim of accession would mean that numerous searches for possible conditional sale agreements, covering separable automobile parts, would become necessary, and thus hamper commercial dealing in the sale and purchase of automobiles. This might be so in the case of dealings with private sellers. It is hardly likely if business is done with reputable retailers.

The result I would reach here is consistent with the apparent factual situation in *Regina Chevrolet Sales Ltd. v. Riddell, supra*, albeit the exposition of the law there may have gone further than was necessary on the facts. In that case, the conditional buyer of a truck purchased other tires for it, which he obtained on credit without the seller reserving a security title. Some months later, the seller of the tires was given a chattel mortgage on them by the buyer. In subsequent litigation between the conditional seller of the truck and the chattel mortgagee of the tires, the former prevailed. This is easily explicable on the ground that title to the tires mounted on the truck had passed to the buyer upon purchase, and they thereupon came under the security title of the conditional seller of the truck. The buyer could only mortgage them thereafter subject to that conditional seller's prior claim. Counsel for the respondent conceded that under the exposition of the law in the Saskatchewan case, which he supported, the buyer of the tires, although liable for their price, could resist their seizure by their conditional seller for default in payment. I cannot agree with a view of the doctrine of accession that would produce such a result.

Appeal allowed.

NOTE

How would *Firestone* have been decided under the OPPSA? Note the open ended definition of "Accessions" in s. 1(1). Would this make a difference? There has been no significant case law so far on the treatment of accessions under the PPS legislation in Canada.

COMMINGLED GOODS (SECTION 37)

What the marginal note to s. 37 of the OPPSA describes as a section concerned with "commingled goods" in fact covers substantially more. The section equally applies "if the goods are so manufactured, processed, assembled, or commingled that their identity is lost in the product or mass." It therefore applies to such familiar examples as flour, sugar and eggs that are combined to make a cake, iron ore that is converted into steel, and components that are assembled into a machine. See UCC 9-315, Official Comment, s. 3. As the following case shows, a claim to proceeds (s. 25; proceeds are discussed *infra*, chapter 9) and a claim under s. 37 can easily coincide. Whether or not they do, s. 37 raises difficult problems of construction and application.

In the Matter of San Juan Packers, Inc.
(1983), 696 F.2d 707 (CCA 9)

PER CURIAM: This is a dispute between a secured creditor of a bankrupt food processor and a secured creditor of farmers from whom the food processor bought vegetables. The food processor, San Juan Packers, Inc., bought cans on credit from a can manufacturer, National Can Corporation, and granted the can manufacturer a floating lien on all of its inventory. In late summer, 1976, the food processor bought vegetables from many farmers, including the three involved in this litigation. These three farmers had obtained financing from Peoples State Bank and had granted the bank a security interest in their crops and the "proceeds" thereof.

The food processor filed a petition in bankruptcy after it had received the farmers' vegetables and processed and sold a portion of them, but before it had finished paying all purchase price installments due the farmers. Not having been paid by the food processor, the farmers did not pay the bank. The bank brought this adversary proceeding in bankruptcy court against all of the food processor's secured creditors to establish the priority of the bank's security interest in the farmers' vegetables and in the cash proceeds thereof. The parties agreed to the sale of all vegetables in the food processor's possession and creation of a fund from the proceeds to satisfy any judgment that might arise from this action.

The bankruptcy court found for the bank, and the can manufacturer appealed to the district court, which affirmed. The can manufacturer appeals to this court, advancing three contentions.

I.

The can manufacturer first contends that money received by the food processor for the farmers' vegetables is not "proceeds" to which the bank's security interest attached under its security agreements with the farmers.

The Uniform Commercial Code (UCC) provides that "[p]roceeds includes whatever is received when collateral or proceeds is sold, exchanged, collected or otherwise disposed of." Section 9-306(1). Under this definition, the money the food processor received for the farmers' vegetables is "proceeds" unless the vegetables ceased to be collateral when purchased by the food processor.

" 'Collateral' means the property subject to a security interest ..." Section 9-105(1)(c). "Except where ... Article [9] otherwise provides, a security interest continues in collateral notwithstanding sale ... by the debtor unless his action was authorized by the secured party ..." Section 9-306(2). Since the can manufacturer does not dispute the bankruptcy court's finding that the bank did not authorize the sale free of its security interest, and Article 9 does not otherwise provide, it would appear that the bank's security interest continued in the vegetables after their sale to the food processor, that the vegetables remained "collateral," and that whatever was received by the food processor when the vegetables were sold is "proceeds."

The can manufacturer points out that section 9-306(2) provides that a security interest continues, "notwithstanding sale ... *by the debtor* and ... in any identifiable proceeds including collections *received by the debtor*" (emphasis supplied), and argues that the bank's security interest was not saved by section 9-306(2) when the vegetables were sold and cash received by the food processor rather than by the farmers because the farmers and not the food processor were the "debtors." But under §9-105(1)(d), the food processor *is* the "debtor":

> (1) In this article, unless the context otherwise requires:
>   (d) "Debtor" means the person who owes payment or other performance of the obligation secured, whether or not he owns or has rights in the collateral ... *Where the debtor and the owner of the collateral are not the same person, the term "debtor" means the owner of the collateral in any provision of the Article dealing with the collateral*, the obligor in any provision dealing with the obligation, and may include both where the context so requires.

(emphasis supplied).

Official Comment 2 to section 9-105 makes it clear that an owner of the collateral is a "debtor" whether he acquired his rights in the collateral at the time the security interest was created or at a later date:

> In all but a few cases the person who owes the debt and the person whose property secures the debt will be the same. Occasionally, one person furnishes security for another's debt, and *sometimes property is transferred subject to a secured debt of the transferor which the transferee does not assume*; in such cases, under the second sentence of the definition, the term "debtor" may, depending on the context, include either or both such persons.

(emphasis supplied).

The can manufacturer protests that under this view the bank could follow these vegetables into the hands of the ultimate consumer. But this is precisely what the plain language of the UCC requires. *See* B. Clark, The Law of Secured Transactions under the Uniform Commercial Code ¶8.4[3][a], at 8-22 to -23 (1980); R. Henson, Secured Transactions under the Uniform Commercial Code 143-44 (1979); *cf. Garden City Production Credit Ass'n. v. Lannan*, 186 Neb. 668, 186 NW 2d 99 (1971) (plaintiff's security interest in livestock continued through unauthorized sale by farmer and resale by farmer's transferee). As a practical matter, of course, it would be difficult for the secured party to identify its collateral far down a chain of purchasers.

Cases relied upon by the can manufacturer did not consider section 9-105(1)(d). *See Get It Kwik of America, Inc. v. First Alabama Bank*, 361 So. 2d 568 (Ala. Civ. App. 1978); *Beneficial Finance Co. v. Colonial Trading Co.*, 4 UCC Rep. Serv. (Callaghan) 672 (Pa. Ct. of Common Pleas 1967).

II.

The can manufacturer's second argument is that by the terms of section 9-306(2) the bank's security interest continued only in "identifiable proceeds" and was lost because the food processor mixed together vegetables purchased from various farmers making it impossible to identify vegetables, or proceeds from the sale of vegetables remaining in the food processor's possession, as attributable to any particular farmer.

Section 9-315 of the UCC requires rejection of this argument. The bank had a perfected security interest in the farmers' vegetables, and those vegetables became part of a mass of vegetables in the hands of the food processor, so commingled that their identity became lost in the mass. By the express terms of section 9-315(1), where collateral loses its identity by commingling or processing, the security interest continues in the mass or product—and it is not disputed that the proceeds in the fund established in this case can be traced to commingled vegetables in the hands of the food processor.

Cases relied upon by the can manufacturer involved nonfungible goods that did not lose their identity when commingled with other goods. *See Howarth v. Universal C.I.T. Credit Corporation*, 203 F. Supp. 279 (WO Pa. 1962); *Chrysler Credit Corporation v. Bank of Wiggins*, 358 So. 2d 714 (Miss. 1978).

III.

Finally, the can manufacturer argues that if section 9-315 is applied, the can manufacturer was entitled to share in the fund since the can manufacturer had a security interest in the vegetables in the food processor's possession grown by farmers other than the three in whose crops the bank had a security interest, and by the terms of section 9-315 each party whose collateral is commingled in the mass is entitled to a ratable share of the proceeds of the sale of the mass.

The bank resists application of section 9-315 on the ground, relied upon by the district court, that section 9-315(1) "requires the attachment of two security interests to the product or mass." The attachment of two security interests to the product or mass is an explicit condition only to the operation of section 9-315(2), not section 9-315(1). Moreover, this condition to the application of section 9-315(2) was satisfied because both the bank's interest in the vegetables of the three farmers with whom the bank had its security arrangement and the can manufacturer's security interest in the other vegetables in the food processor's inventory attached to the mass of each variety of vegetables when the vegetables of the same variety purchased from various farmers were commingled.

The bank contends further that section 9-315 does not apply because the vegetables were not sufficiently processed. The statute, however, refers to processing *and* commingling, both in the caption of the section and in section 9-315(1)(a). "Commingled" is not a term of art in this context; it simply means "to mix together," *Webster's Third New International Dictionary* 457 (1961), or "[t]o put together in one mass." *Black's Law Dictionary* 246 (5th ed., 1979). As the bank points out, Official Comment 3 to section 9-315 refers to commingling flour, sugar and eggs into cake mix, a process involving more than mere mixing, but there is no indication that the drafters meant to exclude simple mixing of fungible goods.

Application of section 9-315(2) does not, however, completely resolve this case. It is not clear from the record whether vegetables of the bank's three farmers were sold between the time these vegetables were delivered to the food processor and the time the food processor filed a bankruptcy petition. If such sales occurred and proceeds were not dissipated before bankruptcy, they are available to the secured parties subject to the provisions of section 9-306(4). Proceeds of sales made under the supervision of the bankruptcy court are, of course, not subject to section 9-306(4). Furthermore, there may be more than one section 9-315(2) ratio for each mass of vegetables because additional deliveries from farmers other than the three having security arrangements with the bank were subject to the can manufacturer's security interest; when such deliveries were added to the various masses of corn, peas, and carrots, the proportion of the security interest in each mass to which the can manufacturer was entitled increased.

The judgment appealed from is therefore vacated, and the case is remanded for further proceedings:

(1) to determine what proportion of each mass of the various vegetables was sold by the food processor prior to its bankruptcy;

(2) to apportion the available proceeds, if any, from such sales between the bank and the can manufacturer in accordance with sections 9-315(2) and 9-306(4); and

(3) to apportion the proceeds of sales made under the bankruptcy court's supervision between the bank and the can manufacturer in accordance with section 9-315(2).

Grant Gilmore
Security Interests in Personal Property
Vol. II, at 851-53 (footnotes omitted)

Section 9-315(2) establishes the priorities when, under subsection (1), "more than one security interest attaches to the product or mass." We may assume that (with one exception) it will be a rare case in which two or more secured parties deliberately and with malice aforethought put themselves into a §9-315(2) situation. The subsection (2) priority rule will apply principally to cases where the debtor has without authority processed or commingled collateral belonging to different secured parties; in view of the overlap between §9-314 and §9-315, the rule could conceivably be exploited by the supplier of parts or accessories who found his rights under §9-315 more attractive than his rights under §9-314. Finally (this is the exception previously referred to) the rule will become relevant in cases of conflicting purchase-money and after-acquired (or non-purchase-money) interests in manufacturing inventory.

The subsection (2) rule is that security interests which attach to a product or mass "rank equally according to the ratio that the cost of the goods to which each interest originally attached bears to the cost of the total product or mass."

Since subsection (1) allows only previously perfected interests to "continue" in the product or mass, only such interests share under subsection (2). Nowhere in the Article is any light shed on the meaning of "rank equally": presumably any interest entitled to share would have the rights given to a secured party on default by Part 5; if one such secured party repossessed and sold the product, he would no doubt be under a duty to account for the proceeds to his fellows. Perhaps wisely, the draftsmen made no attempt to explore the complications of "rank equally"; the courts will have to do it for them.

The secured parties who rank equally do not of course share equally: they share, as the Comment puts it, "ratably." How they share depends on the meaning of the subsection (2) formula, which is notably obscure. The formula is geared not to value or obligation but to "cost," and cost seems to mean "cost to the debtor" (not how much the secured party has advanced but how much the debtor has invested). The formula requires that two different costs be ascertained. The first is the "cost of the goods to which each interest originally attached"; presumably this means their purchase price. The second is "the cost of the total product or mass"; presumably this means (in the case of a product) the cost of raw materials plus labor and overhead. When we have ascertained these costs, the formula tells us that the secured parties share "according to the ratio" between the costs. We may inquire into the meaning of "according to the ratio" by working out an example.

Assume the case of the debtor who manufactures candy from sugar and chocolate. Secured party A has financed the acquisition of the sugar by advancing the entire purchase price; secured party B has done likewise for the chocolate. For simplicity's sake assume the following figures:

Cost of sugar (A)	3
Cost of chocolate (B)	5
Labor and overhead	2
Cost of candy	10

If there is a foreclosure sale of the candy, the formula tells us that A and B will share in the proceeds "according to the ratio" of $3/10$ to $5/10$. If the candy sells for 10, this works out properly: A gets 3; B gets 5; since both A and B have been paid in full, the residue goes either to the debtor or his trustee in bankruptcy. Suppose, however, that the candy sells for less than 8—to make the arithmetic simple, say that it sells for 5. If the formula means that A gets $3/10$ of 5 and B gets $5/10$ of 5, the result is that A gets $1\frac{1}{2}$ and B gets $2\frac{1}{2}$, with the residue (1) going as before to debtor or trustee in bankruptcy. This result seems wrong, since neither A nor B has been paid in full and, until they have been, nothing should go back to the debtor or over to his unsecured creditors through the trustee. (The foregoing comment assumes that a secured party who has financed raw materials and claims a security interest in the product is entitled, up to the amount of his advance, to the full value of the product.) The correct result, if the candy sells for 5, is for A and B to divide the proceeds in the proportion of 3-to-5: A should get $3/8$ of 5 (or $1\frac{7}{8}$); B should get $5/8$ of 5 (or $3\frac{1}{8}$); there is no residue and there should be none unless the candy sells for more than enough to pay both A and B in full. It would be clear that this is the result contemplated by §9-315(2) if the formula read: according to the ratio that the cost of the goods to which each interest originally attached bears to the sum of the costs of all goods which have become part of the product and which were originally subject to security interests entitled to rank equally in the product under this subsection. Or if it read: according to the ratio that the cost of the goods to which each security interest to the ratio that the cost of the goods to which each security interest originally attached bears to the cost of the total product or mass (excluding, however, from the total cost any costs which represent labor, overhead or the cost of goods not subject to security interests entitled to equal rank under this subsection).

Another weakness in the formula becomes apparent if we vary our hypothetical case by assuming (at whatever damage to the quality of the candy) that A made an advance of 3, which represented 50 per cent of the cost of the sugar, and B made an advance of 5, which represented 100 per cent of the cost of the chocolate. If the candy is sold and A and B are to share ratably in the proceeds, it would seem that they ought to share in a 3-to-5 ratio. However, since the formula is geared to cost of goods, the apparent result is that they will share in a 6 (for A) to 5 (for B) ratio. A, who has advanced less than B, gets a greater share of the proceeds. If cost means the purchase price to the debtor, the formula leads to an inequitable result whenever the advances made by the secured parties represent different percentages of the costs to the debtor.

NOTES

1) In *Borden (U.K.) Ltd. v. Scottish Timber Products Ltd.*, [1979] 3 WLR 672 (CA), the plaintiff company sold large quantities of chipboard resin to the defendant company. The sales contract contained a reservation of title clause in the plaintiff's favour. The resin supplied was used by the defendant in its manufacturing process, in conjunction with other ingredients, to form a "glue mix." The glue mix was then blended with various grades of wood chippings and pressed together to form the end product, chipboard.

The defendant became bankrupt and, at the time of bankruptcy, was indebted to the plaintiff for a very large sum of money arising out of the supply of resin. Because it had retained title to the resin until it was paid for, the plaintiff claimed to be entitled to trace the resin into the chipboard and to have a charge on the chipboard for the amount of the outstanding indebtedness. The trial judge allowed the claim; the English Court of Appeal reversed his order.

Bridge LJ, who delivered the main judgment in the Court of Appeal, gave three principal reasons. The first was that the plaintiff was not entitled to a tracing remedy in equity because there was no fiduciary relationship between the parties. The plaintiff had supplied the resin knowing and intending that the defendant would use it in the manufacture of chipboard. The defendant was not acting as the plaintiff's agent in conducting its manufacturing operations. Secondly, the earlier decision of the Court of Appeal in the *Romalpa* case (*Aluminium Industrie Vaassen B.V. v. Romalpa Aluminium Ltd.*, [1976] 1 WLR 686) was distinguishable because there the buyer had expressly agreed to hold the aluminium foil and the proceeds from the sale thereof as bailee for the seller. Moreover, the foil retained its identity and had never become admixed with goods of a different character.

The third reason given by Bridge LJ was that the tracing remedy was in any event not available under the rule *In re Hallett's Estate* (1880), 13 Ch. D 696, where there is "a mixture of heterogeneous goods in a manufacturing process wherein the original goods lose their character and what emerges is a wholly new product." He continued at 683-84:

Some extreme examples were canvassed in argument. Suppose cattle cake is sold to a farmer, or fuel to a steel manufacturer, in each case with a reservation of title clause, but on terms which permit the farmer to feed the cattle cake to his herd and the steelmaker to fuel his furnaces, before paying the purchase price. Mr. Mowbray concedes that in these cases the seller cannot trace into the cattle or the steel. He says that the difference is that the goods have been consumed. But once this concession is made, I find it impossible to draw an intelligible line of distinction in principle which would give the plaintiffs a right to trace the resin into the chipboard in the instant case. What has happened in the manufacturing process is much more akin to the process of consumption than to any simple process of admixture of goods. To put the point in another way, if the contribution that the resin has made to the chipboard gives rise to a tracing remedy, I find it difficult to see any good reason why, in the steelmaking example, the essential contribution made by the fuel to the steel manufacturing process should not do likewise.

These are the principal considerations which have led me to the conclusion that the plaintiffs are not entitled to the tracing remedy which they claim. But I am fortified in that conclusion by the further consideration that if the remedy were available in such cases, a most intractable problem could, and in many cases would, arise in quantifying the proportion of the value of the manufactured product which the tracer could claim as properly attributable to his ingredient. In the instant case, a breakdown of the actual costings of chipboard over a period of seven months to July 29, 1977, has been agreed, attributing 17 per cent of the total cost to the cost of resin, subject to a reservation with respect to wastage and over-usage. But one can well see that in many cases where the cost of materials and labour involved in a particular production process were constantly fluctuating, it might be quite impossible to assign a proportion of the total cost properly attributable to one particular ingredient with any certainty at all. ...

2) How would *Scottish Timber Products* be decided under s. 37 of the OPPSA? The United Kingdom has no registration requirements for conditional sale or hire-purchase agreements and, prior to the decision in the *Romalpa* case discussed in Bridge LJ's judgment *supra*, it was not customary for inventory to be sold in the United Kingdom subject to conditional sale terms with a proceeds clause. The implications of *Romalpa* are explored in a wider setting by Prof. Goode in "The Right to Trace and Its Impact in Commercial Transactions" (1976), 92 *LQ Rev.* 360 and 528 (Pts. I and II).

SUBORDINATION AGREEMENTS

Subordination agreements and subordination clauses in security agreements are very common. Their validity is expressly recognized in s. 38 (s. 39 in the old Act) of the OPPSA. A subordination agreement occurs when a senior secured party agrees to subordinate its security interest to the security interest of a junior secured party. The senior secured party is not acting out of a spirit of altruism; rather, it is in its interest not to foreclose the debtor's access to other sources of credit. A subordination agreement may also be reached when the secured parties are not sure about their priority positions (e.g., an accounts receivable financer and an inventory financer) or are concerned about an overlap in the collateral covered by their respective agreements.

A subordination clause differs from a subordination agreement in that it appears in the security agreement between the secured party and the debtor; other secured parties are not privy to it although they are expected to benefit from the clause. Such clauses are common in floating charge agreements and in medium- and long-term secured debentures. The following Alberta decision reviews the earlier Canadian case law on s. 38 of the OPPSA and its counterpart in the other Acts, and discusses many of the important issues raised by the statutory provision.

Chiips Inc. v. Skyview Hotels Ltd.
(1994), 116 DLR (4th) 385 (Alta. CA)

FOISY JA:

Facts

The respondents in this appeal are: Skyview Hotels (in receivership); Ernst & Young Inc. (the receiver); and a group of companies holding five mortgages and debentures (all dated January 31, 1988) against the real and personal property of Skyview.

The mortgages and debentures are in the aggregate principal sum of $25 million. They contain a fixed charge on lands and fixtures, and a floating charge on all other assets. A representative sample of these instruments is reproduced at p. 32 of the Appeal Book. The mortgages and debentures were registered in the corporate registry on February 29, 1988. As a result of the enactment of the *Personal Property Security Act*, SA 1988, c. P-4.05 (hereinafter PPSA), these interests were reregistered in the personal property registry on June 23, 1992. *Per* s. 75(3) of the PPSA these interests were perfected and maintained their February 29, 1988 registration date.

The appellant, Chiips Inc., was a supplier for the refurnishing of six floors of the Skyline Plaza Hotel pursuant to a conditional sales agreement dated November 14, 1991. Skyview paid for the goods using 16 post-dated cheques, each in the amount of $38,197.01, to be used as a security deposit toward the contract. The appellant shipped a number of loads of furniture between December of 1991 and March of 1992.

On May 14, 1992, a receivership order was granted as a result of a default by Skyview under the mortgages and debentures. Ernst & Young was appointed receiver and manager. The appellant received notice of this order on May 19, 1992, and gave notice to the receiver on May 21, 1992, when Skyview failed to pay for the goods supplied by the appellant. The amount outstanding at that date was $257,163.58.

On June 5, 1992, the appellant filed a financing statement under the PPSA with respect to its conditional sales agreement. One last load of furniture was shipped after the registration of the financing statement; that shipment was received on July 14, 1992. The respondents were not aware of the fact that the appellant had not perfected its security interest prior to the receivership order.

At the initial priority dispute which was heard by Master Alberstat on January 28, 1993, Chiips argued that s. 40 of the PPSA gave it priority due to certain purported subordination clauses in the mortgages and debentures. The response to this was that the debenture holders' reregistration gave them priority as perfection dated back to February 29, 1988. Master Alberstat determined that the debenture holders had priority to all but the last shipment (the fact that Chiips had registered its security interest prior to the last shipment resulted in "super priority" because the charge was in the nature of a purchase money security interest *per* s. 34 of the PPSA). On April 7, 1993, an appeal to the justice was dismissed with costs.

• • •

Analysis

A. *Subordination clauses as contemplated by the PPSA*

Section 40 of the PPSA specifically provides for the use of subordination clauses in security agreements. The section reads as follows:

40. A secured party may, in a security agreement or otherwise, subordinate his security interest to any other interests and the subordination is effective according to its terms between the parties and may be enforced by a third party if the third party is the person or one of a class of persons for whose benefit the subordination was intended.

This provision of the Act is very important as it allows debtors to carry on their businesses effectively. The significance of the section lies in the fact that, under the PPSA regime, it is relatively simple for a secured creditor to take and perfect a very broadly based security interest: Cuming & Wood, *Alberta Personal Property Security Act Handbook*, 2nd ed. (Toronto: Carswell, 1993) at p. 301. Because the debtor has to be given some ability to carry on business (e.g. acquire goods on credit), the Act allows a secured creditor to subordinate its interest to other creditors with whom the debtor must deal on an ongoing basis. The reasoning behind the enactment of s. 40 was succinctly stated by Philp J in *Royal Bank of Canada v. Gabriel of Canada Ltd.* (1992), 3 PPSAC (2d) 305 at p. 309, 40 ACWS (3d) 512 (Ont. Ct. (Gen. Div.)): "... s. 38 of the PPSA conferred a statutory right on a secured party to waive the priority given him by the PPSA and a corresponding right on the beneficiary of such a waiver ... to enforce it."

Because of the provision for subordination clauses, the Act will not prevent a subsequent credit grantor from claiming priority over a prior secured creditor where the latter has agreed to subordinate its claim. The question is whether the alleged subordination clause actually had that effect.

B. *What is the effect of cls. 4.05 and 6.01(c) of the debentures?*

The appellant argues that the debentures contained subordination clauses which validly gave Chiips priority over the debenture holders pursuant to s. 40. There are two clauses in the debenture agreements which the appellant says amount to subordination clauses; they read as follows (AB pp. 38, 42-3):

4.05 *Possession, Use and Release of Mortgaged Property*
Until the Security becomes enforceable, the Company may dispose of or deal with the subject matter of the floating charge provided for in Section 4.01(b) hereof in the ordinary course of its business and for the purpose of carrying on the same; provided that the Company shall not, without prior written consent of the holder, create, assume or have outstanding, except to the Holder, any mortgage, charge or other encumbrance on any part of the Mortgaged Property ranking or purporting to rank or capable of being enforced in priority to or *pari passu* with the Security, other than,
        (a) any mortgage, lien or other encumbrance upon property, created or assumed to secure all or any part of the funds required for the purchase of such property. ...

• • •

6.01 The Company covenants and agrees with the Holder that, so long as this Debenture is outstanding, the Company shall not:

• • •

(c) create or permit any mortgage, charge, lien or other encumbrances on any part or all of the Mortgaged Property ranking or purporting to rank in priority to or *pari passu* with the Security in order to secure any monies, debts, liabilities, bonds, debentures, notes or other obligations other than this Debenture and the Series of Mortgages and Debentures referred to in Section 8.01(n) hereof which are intended to rank in priority as *pari passu* with this Debenture; provided, however, that this covenant shall not apply to, nor operate to prevent, and there shall be permitted:

(i) the assuming or giving of purchase money mortgages or other purchase money liens on property acquired by the Company or the giving of mortgages or liens in connection with the acquisition or purchase of such property or the acquiring of property subject to any mortgage, lien or encumbrance thereon existing at the time of such acquisition; provided that such purchase money mortgages or purchase money liens shall be secured only by the property being acquired by the Company and no other property of the Company; ...

In order to determine whether the above clauses amount to subordination on the part of the debenture holders as contemplated by s. 40, it is useful to refer to two Ontario decisions. The decisions in question are helpful yet not determinative; in both cases the court analyzes clauses to determine whether an interest is subordinated, but both clauses are different from the clauses in the case at bar.

In *Euroclean Canada Inc. v. Forest Glade Investments Ltd.* (1985), 16 DLR (4th) 289, 54 CBR 65, 4 PPSAC 271 (Ont. CA) (the Supreme Court of Canada refused leave to appeal on June 3, 1985 [reported DLR *loc. cit.*, [1985] 1 SCR viii, 55 CBR (NS) xxxvii]) the court was asked to determine priorities between a debenture holder and a subsequent conditional seller who had failed to register his interest. The debenture contained the following clause which the court found had the effect of giving priority to the conditional seller (at p. 297):

(e) Not Encumber—*The Corporation shall not, without the consent in writing of the Holder, create any mortgage,* hypothec, charge, lien or other encumbrance upon the mortgaged property or any part thereof *ranking or purporting to rank in priority* to or in *pari passu* with the charge created by this Debenture, *except that the Corporation may give mortgages or liens in connection with the acquisition of property* after the date hereof or may acquire property subject to any mortgage, lien or other encumbrance thereon existing at the time of such acquisition *and any such mortgage, lien or other encumbrance shall rank in priority to the charge hereby created.*

(Emphasis added.) Houlden JA, at p. 299, decided that the conditional sale by Euroclean gained priority over the debenture as a result of the above clause:

By cl. (e), Brazier was permitted to give mortgages or liens in connection with the acquisition of property. ... The purchase of the laundry equipment from Euroclean clearly comes within this wording; and if property is acquired in this way, the subordination clause provided that the mortgage, lien or other encumbrance is to rank in priority to the charge created by the debenture.

and at p. 302:

Euroclean, by reason of s. 39, is, in my opinion, entitled to enforce the provisions of cl. (e) against Mady and, consequently, is entitled to priority over Mady's security interest.

The respondents in the case at bar argue that s. 40 makes it clear that the wording of any purported subordination clause is critical in assessing the rights of the parties. The decision of *Euroclean* is used to support this position as the clause in that case makes it abundantly clear that purchase money charges "shall" rank in priority to the debenture. The respondent puts forward the case of *Sperry Inc. v. Canadian Imperial Bank of Commerce* (1985), 17 DLR (4th) 236, 55 CBR (NS) 68, 50 OR (2d) 267 (CA), in support of its argument that case law indicates that nothing short of a clause like the one in *Euroclean* will act to validly subordinate the prior creditor's claim.

The priority dispute in *Sperry* was between a bank holding a general security interest with an equipment dealer and a manufacturer/supplier of farm equipment who had a prior registered security interest with the dealer. Both of the creditor's registrations lapsed and the bank claimed that it had priority because their security interest re-attached before the supplier had renewed its financing statement. The bank's security agreement contains the following clauses (at pp. 239-40):

1. As a general and continuing collateral security for payment of all existing and future indebtedness and liability of the undersigned [Allinson] to Canadian Imperial Bank of Commerce (the "Bank") wheresoever and howsoever incurred and any ultimate unpaid balance thereof, *the undersigned hereby charges in favour of and grants to the Bank a security interest in the undertaking of the undersigned and all property of the kinds hereinafter described of which the undersigned is now or may hereafter become the owner* and which, insofar as the same consists of tangible property, is now or may hereafter be in the place or places designated in paragraph 14 hereof; and the undersigned agrees with the Bank as hereinafter set out.

• • •

4. *Ownership of Collateral*
The undersigned represents and warrants that, except for the security interest created hereby and except for purchase money obligations, the undersigned is, or with respect to Collateral acquired after the date hereof will be, the owner of Collateral free from any mortgage, lien, charge, security interest or encumbrance. "Purchase money obligation" means any mortgage, lien or other encumbrance upon property assumed or given back as part of the purchase price of such property, or arising by operation of law or any extension or renewal or replacement thereof upon the same property, if the principle amount of the indebtedness secured thereby is not increased.

Though the result was in favour of the equipment supplier on other grounds, the court, *per* Morden JA, at pp. 243-4, held that the above clauses in the bank's general security agreement fell far short of showing an agreement by the bank to subordinate its security interest to that of the supplier. The learned appeal justice supported this finding using the specific wording in the subordination clause found in *Euroclean*.

Looking at these two cases as outlined above, we are not in much better a position for determining whether the clauses in the case at bar amount to a valid subordination of the debenture holders' interests to the conditional seller. The subordination clause in *Euroclean* was included in the security agreement for the express purpose of putting the interest of a purchase money security holder ahead of the interests of the debenture holders. The court found this to be the intention based on the clear and unambiguous wording of cl. (e). Conversely, the court in *Sperry* found that the clauses fell far short of the clear and unambiguous wording of the clause in *Euroclean*, and were therefore not read as having the effect of subordinating the bank's interest to that of the supplier.

Given the above two decisions, we know two things: first, where a general security holder specifically states that a subsequent security holder "shall rank in priority to the charge hereby created," that subsequent holder will be entitled to enforce the provisions of that agreement *per* s. 40 of the PPSA. Second, clauses in security agreements which fall far short of that type of express wording (for example the impugned clauses in *Sperry* did not mention the word "priority") will not be enforceable under s. 40.

These decisions represent opposite ends of a spectrum: at one end we have a clause directing exactly who will be given priority and, at the other, a clause which mentions nothing about priority. Consequently we are left with very little direction as to what should result in cases where the alleged subordination clauses fall somewhere in between, as in the case at bar. We therefore look to other authority, which, though not directly deciding the point, address it none the less. There are a number of cases which are of assistance in this regard; they are outlined below.

The discussions of the courts in the following two cases lead to a positive inference by this court that the alleged subordination clause in the case at bar acts to validly give priority to Chiips.

The case of *CIBC v. International Harvester Credit Corp. of Canada* (1986), 6 PPSAC 273 (Ont. CA), involved a debtor who had entered into a fixed and floating charge debenture with CIBC. Later, the debtor entered into a conditional sales agreement for nine trucks. The security interests were registered, but the bank's registration preceded the vendor's. At trial the vendor was given priority over the trucks because there were subordination clauses in the bank's security agreement. The clauses were virtually identical to the clauses in this case; they read as follows (at pp. 274-5):

2.1 As security for the due payment of all moneys payable hereunder, the Corporation as beneficial owner hereby:

(a) grants, assigns, conveys, mortgages and charges as and by way of a first fixed and specific mortgage and charge to and in favour of the Bank, its successors and assigns all machinery, equipment, plant, vehicles, goods and chattels now owned by the Corporation and described or referred to in Schedule A hereto and all other machinery, equipment, plant, vehicles, goods and chattels, hereafter acquired by the Corporation; and

(b) charges as and by way of a first floating charge to and in favour of the Bank, its successors and assigns, all its undertaking, property and assets, both present and future, of every nature and kind and wherever situate including, without limitation, its franchises.

In this Debenture, the mortgages and charges hereby constituted are called the "Security" and the subject matter of the Security is called the "Charged Premises."

2.2 *Until the Security becomes enforceable, the Corporation may dispose of or deal with the subject matter of the floating charge in the ordinary course of its business and for the purpose of carrying on the same provided that the Corporation will not, without the prior written consent of the Bank, create, assume or have outstanding, except to the Bank, any mortgage, charge, or other encumbrance on any part of the Charged Premises ranking or purporting to rank or capable of being enforced in priority to or pari passu with the Security, other than any mortgage, lien or*

other encumbrance upon property, created or assumed to secure all or any part of the funds
required for the purchase of such property or any extension or renewal or replacement thereof
upon the same property if the principle amount of the indebtedness secured thereby is not
increased, or any inchoate liens for taxes or assessment by public authorities.

(Emphasis added.)

The italicized portion of cl. 2.2 above is the same as cl. 4.05 in the case at bar. At trial
the learned judge held that by reason of ss. 2.1 and 2.2 of the debenture, the bank had
subordinated its security interest to the seller (4 PPSAC 329 at p. 336). The appellate court
allowed the bank's appeal based on the fact that the trucks in question were the subject of
the fixed charge as stated specifically in sch. A of the debenture agreement; the subordination clause only applied to the floating charge. In overturning the lower court's decision,
Brooke JA states the following (at p. 276):

In my opinion, the subordination provision in the debenture does not apply to the nine trucks as
they form part of the fixed charge. I think the subordination clause is limited to the floating
charge which, it is conceded, did not apply to the trucks. While the drafting of the clauses leaves
much to be desired, I think it makes provision only as to the manner of the floating charge until it
becomes enforceable. For that period of time it provides that Prospect can deal with the subject
matter of the floating charge in the ordinary course of its business provided that it cannot
encumber any part of that property except where necessary to finance the purchase of its property
and then only to the extent provided for in the clause.

The second case, a recent decision of the Alberta Court of Queen's Bench, is
Transamerica Commercial Finance Corp., Canada v. Imperial TV & Stereo Centre Ltd.
(October 12, 1993), Edmonton No. 9303-12285 (QB) [now reported 22 CBR (3d) 297, 6
PPSAC (2d) 99, [1994] 1 WWR 506]. That case involved a determination of priority
between the holder of a floating charge debenture and the holder of a purchase money
security instrument. The subordination clause was outlined by Nash J as follows (at p. 2)
[p. 299 CBR]:

Imperial, by the terms of the Debenture, agreed not to assume any other charges against the assets
of the company, without the prior written consent of the Credit Union, that would have priority
over the Credit Union's debenture unless, *inter alia* (The Subordination Clause):

The same be given to or *in favour of the bankers of [Imperial]* on the security the accounts
receivable or the inventory of [Imperial] to secure current loans required for the usual
purposes of the business of [Imperial] and whether given pursuant to the provisions of the
Bank Act or otherwise.

(Emphasis added.)

The court accepted the decision of the Court of Appeal in Ontario in *Euroclean* and
applied it in giving effect to subordination clauses where applicable. However, the
subordination clause outlined above only applied where the party giving new credit was a
bank; Transamerica was held not to be a bank. The following finding is made in relation to
that point (at p. 10) [p. 304 CBR]:

When the subordination clause is given its plain and ordinary meaning, I am satisfied that the
parties to the Debenture intended that "bankers" not mere "creditors" or "lenders" were to be
entitled to enforce the subordination clause and rank above or equal to the Credit Union.

It would therefore appear, from the above cases, that the Ontario Court of Appeal and the Alberta Court of Queen's Bench accept that subordination clauses can be enforced against the prior security holder if the collateral in question is subject to that subordination (*International Harvester*) and if the subsequent creditor is of the kind contemplated in the subordination clause (*Transamerica*).

Applying these cases here, it is my view that the clauses in the debenture are subordination clauses; the only questions remaining are whether the furniture was subject to the subordination, and whether Chiips was the kind of creditor that was contemplated by the clause. The furniture is certainly the subject of the floating charge rather than the fixed charge as indicated by cl. 4.01 which outlines the security taken by the debenture holders. Further, the subordination clauses in the debenture agreement are silent with respect to who the subsequent creditor might be; if the debenture holders had intended to limit the granting of priority to a particular group of creditors, they should have outlined this limitation in the agreement. As no such limitation exists it is open for this court to find that the subordination clause may be enforceable by Chiips as against the debenture holders.

The policy rationale for finding that the clauses in question should be enforceable by Chiips is one of commercial reality. The whole purpose for including these kinds of clauses in security agreements is to "remove any obstacles the debtor might encounter in acquiring new collateral for the conduct of his business:" see Ziegel, "The Scope of Section 66A of the OPPSA and Effects of Subordination Clause: *Euroclean Canada Inc. v. Forest Glade Investments Ltd.*" (1984), 9 CBLJ 367 at p. 372. Clauses such as those in this case are intended to confer priority on purchase money security interests; without this clause the debtor would not be able to purchase goods on credit as the potential creditor would not be able to get any sort of security from the debtor.

I think it is clear that the clauses gave Skyview the right in the ordinary course of business to grant security to its suppliers (in the form of purchase money security interests) which would have priority over the floating charge in the debentures. At the time the debentures were granted, the law was clear that the language used in the debentures acted to subordinate the floating charge to a conditional sale or purchase money charge: see *Savin Canada Inc. v. Protech Office Electronics Ltd.* (1984), 8 DLR (4th) 225, 27 BLR 93, 53 CBR (NS) 234 (BCCA); the debenture holders ought to have known then that the provisions had that effect. Clearly, the parties intended that the floating charge would be subordinated to allow Skyview to carry on its business.

It is interesting to note that it is possible under the Act to prove a subordination in fact without the existence of a specific subordination agreement: see *Greyvest Leasing Inc. v. Canadian Imperial Bank of Commerce* (October 28, 1993), Toronto No. C11119 (Ont. CA) [now reported 5 PPSAC (2d) 187, 43 ACWS (3d) 466], and *Royal Bank of Canada v. Tenneco Canada Inc.* (1990), 66 DLR (4th) 328, 9 PPSAC 254, 72 OR (2d) 60 (HCJ). I do not need to discuss this possibility here because the subordination clauses themselves are enough to give Chiips priority over the debenture holders with respect to the furniture supplied.

Having found that the clauses in the case at bar amount to a valid subordination of the debenture holders' interests, it is now necessary to decide two issues: whether the lack of registration on the part of Chiips affects the subordination agreements, and whether the fact that Chiips was not a party to the debenture agreements has any affect on the enforceability of the subordination clauses.

C. *Does s. 40 require registration:*

This issue was examined very carefully in *Euroclean* with the majority of the court holding that registration is not necessary in the enforcement of a subordination agreement. Houlden J referred to an academic comment by Ziegel, *op. cit.*, which was a case comment on the lower court decision. In that article, at p. 372, Ziegel made the following criticism of the trial judge's findings:

Fitzpatrick J went on to hold however that cl. (e) also conferred no priority on Euroclean's security interest unless it had been perfected in time. This is a much more debatable conclusion. The learned judge said:

I find that there was nothing in the provision or elsewhere which rebutted the presumption that the parties intended Mady's security interest to attach, nor does the provision give priority to Euroclean's security interest. The fact that Brazier was permitted by the debenture it gave to Mady to take the equipment from Euroclean, subject to a security interest which would have ranked ahead of Mady's had it been registered in time, does not give any priority to Euroclean's security interest when it was not registered in time.

There are several difficulties about this passage. First, it reads into cl. (e) a requirement of registration not to be found in it. Had there been such a requirement cl. (e) would have conferred no benefit on Euroclean since Euroclean would have been entitled to priority in any event pursuant to s. 34(3) of the OPPSA. Second, the court's reasoning ignores the purpose of cl. (e) ... cl. (e) is intended to confer priority on purchase money security interests ("PMSI"). That being the case, what difference does it make to the debenture holder whether or not the purchase money security interest has been perfected? Lack of perfection does not prejudice him since he has agreed to the PMSI-holder's priority in advance.

The appellate court agreed with Ziegel's analysis of the trial judgment. The court specifically finds, at p. 300, that the failure to make timely registration does not affect the claimant's right to enforce a subordination clause. This finding of the Ontario Court of Appeal was adopted by Nash J in *Transamerica* at p. 8 [p. 302 CBR].

This situation in the case at bar is very similar to the facts in *Euroclean*: there was no requirement in the subordination clauses that the subsequent interest has to be registered in order to claim priority. Had there been such a requirement, Chiips would not have had to rely on the subordination agreements as it would have had "super priority" as a PMSI-holder under s. 34 of the PPSA. Accordingly, enforcement of a subordination agreement does not require that the subsequent creditor register his interest.

D. *Does enforcement of a subordination clause require that the claimant be a party to the original agreement?*

At common law (see *Greenwood Shopping Plaza Ltd. v. Beattie* (1980), 111 DLR (3d) 257, [1980] 2 SCR 228, 10 BLR 234), Chiips, because it was is not a party to the debenture agreement might not be able to enforce the clause. I say "might" because the position at common law is not clear. Section 40 of the PPSA removes any doubt regarding the common law with respect to privity:

> 40. A secured party may, in a security agreement or otherwise, subordinate his security interest to any other interest, and the subordination is effective according to its terms between the parties and *may be enforced by a third party if the third party is the person or one of a class of persons for whose benefit the subordination was intended.*

(Emphasis added.)

The cases considering s. 40 have similarly come to the conclusion that the section allows third parties to enforce subordination agreements: see *Euroclean*, and *Royal Bank v. Gabriel*. The effect of the enactment of s. 40 is clearly explained by Houlden JA in *Euroclean* at pp. 301-2:

> In my opinion, s. 39 is intended to confer a statutory right on a secured party to waive the priority given him by the PPSA and to confer a corresponding right on the beneficiary of such a waiver to enforce it, *even though he is not a party on the agreement which created it or has no knowledge of its existence.*

(Emphasis added.)

This reasoning was adopted and applied by Philp J in *Royal Bank v. Gabriel* at p. 309. There is no other reasonable interpretation of s. 40 but that in order to enforce a subordination agreement, the subsequent creditor need not be a party to the contract.

This court's finding that there is no registration requirement or privity requirement for PMSI-holders to enforce subordination clauses is completely in line with the rules of statutory interpretation. The principle is stated clearly in *Subilomar Properties (Dundas) Ltd. v. Cloverdale Shopping Center Ltd.* (1973), 35 DLR (3d) 1 at p. 5, [1973] SCR 596: "It is of course trite law that no legislation whether it be by statute or by-law should be interpreted to leave parts thereof mere surplusage or meaningless."

To hold that either registration or privity is required would have the effect of rendering s. 40 meaningless. If registration is required, there is no need for s. 40 whether the PMSI-holder is a party to the agreement or not because "super priority" would already have been achieved via s. 34. If privity is required, there is no need for s. 40; as stated by Houlden J in *Euroclean* at p. 301, it would be "bootless" as it would have the effect of adding nothing to the common law.

E. *Conclusion*

For the above reasons, the appeal by Chiips should be allowed. As PMSI-holders Chiips is entitled to enforce the subordination clause and claim priority over the furnishings supplied. The funds which have been set aside pursuant to the order of Moshansky J, should be released to the appellant.

Appeal allowed.

[Harrendence JA wrote a separate concurring judgment; Hetherington JA dissented on the ground that he was not satisfied that the debenture provisions were sufficiently specific to satisfy the statutory requirement for a subordination clause.]

NOTES

1) There is some difference in wording between s. 40 of the Alberta Act and s. 38 of the Ontario Act; is the difference important or is the Alberta version merely an expansion of what is implicit in s. 38? The Alberta version also appears in the PPS Acts of the other Western provinces.

2) Foisy JA correctly notes (as Houlden JA had done before him in *Euroclean Canada Inc. v. Forest Glade Investments*) that s. 38 dispenses with the common law privity requirement as a precondition of the beneficiary's entitlement to invoke a subordination provision. Was this a wise step? Ziegel & Denomme, *op. cit.*, § 38.1, point out that UCC 9-316 is worded much more restrictively ("Nothing in this Article prevents subordination by agreement by a person entitled to priority"), and that, according to Gilmore, the section was not intended to deal with the validity or interpretation of subordination agreements but was simply intended to make it clear that the Article 9 priority rules can be varied by agreement. Is this a case where the Ontario drafters' misreading of the Code's intention led to a felicitous result, given the fact that American law has long abolished the privity doctrine whereas, regrettably, it is still in force in Canada?

3) *Euroclean* settled the point that the beneficiary of a subordination clause is not required to perfect its security interest before it can invoke the clause, but it does not settle another issue which troubled American lawyers in the 1960s. This was whether a subordination clause or subordination agreement creates a security interest given by the senior creditor in favour of a junior creditor and must therefore be perfected under the Article 9. To ensure that the courts would not reach this conclusion, UCC 1-209 was added in 1966 making it clear that a subordination clause does not create a security interest. See Ziegel & Denomme, *op. cit.*, § 38.5. The OPPSA does not contain a similar provision, so in Canada the point is still arguable.

4) In *Euroclean*, Houlden JA referred to the view expressed by Mr Maddaugh in the LSUC *Special Lectures 1982*, at 361-62, that there is nothing in the Ontario Act to prohibit a generalized subordination given in advance and that mere use of the term "floating charge" in describing the security interest in the security agreement may implicitly carry with it a generalized subordination—"that is, the consent of the secured party to the debtor to deal with the charged collateral in the ordinary course of his business free of, or subordinate to, the lien represented by that charge."

Do you agree? Is this construction consistent with the explicit language of s. 11(2) of the Act? (Mr Maddaugh was writing before the adoption of the 1989 Act which added s. 11(2).) See the discussion of s. 11(2) in chapter 3, *supra*, and the case law there cited. Granting that floating charge language in a security agreement must at least impute some sort of licence to the debtor to carry on the business, is it the same as saying that the secured party agrees to postpone its security interest *in its entirety* to a future crystallizing event? Would this not restore the common law position which s. 11(2) was at pains to reverse? Mr Maddaugh was prescient, however, in anticipating that some Canadian courts would construe the debtor's licence to carry on business as implicitly subordinating the licensor's security interest to non-consensual security interests arising by operation of law during the debtor's business activity. See, e.g., *Royal Bank v. Sparrow Electric Corp.* [1994] 9 WWR 338 (Alta.), reproduced in chapter 9, *infra*.

CHAPTER EIGHT

Liens Arising by Statute or Rule of Law and Priority Conflicts

In addition to having to consider its position *vis-à-vis* other consensually secured creditors, a secured party must also take into account another critically important source of competition—the claims of creditors whose liens or similar *in rem* claims arise by statute or operation of law and not as the result of any agreement with the debtor. Two recessions between 1982 and 1992—the second the most serious recession since the war—have made many creditors, who are not able to bargain for consensual security, acutely aware of their vulnerability if the debtor goes bankrupt without having paid them.

Broadly speaking, such creditors fall into two groups. The first group comprises creditors who are given a possessory (and, frequently, non-possessory) lien on the debtor's chattels at common law or by statute for services rendered or materials supplied to the debtor. The second group comprises liens and deemed trusts, almost invariably created by statute, in favour of federal and provincial government departments, agencies and commissions for monies owing to them by the debtor.

Liens in Favour of Private Creditors

Well-known examples of these are a repairer's lien for work and materials bestowed on goods entrusted to her, an innkeeper's lien for a guest's unpaid bill, and a warehouse person's lien for stored goods. For examples of statutory recognition and regulation of such liens, see the Repair and Storage Liens Act, RSO 1990, c. R.25; the Innkeeper's Act, RSO 1990, c. I.7, ss. 2-3, and the Mining Act, RSO 1990, c. M.14, s. 106. See generally R.A. Wood and M.I. Wylie, "Non-consensual Security Interests in Personal Property" (1992), 30 *Alta. L Rev.* 1056, esp. at 1066-71. Technically speaking, a landlord's right to levy distress on its tenant's goods is not regarded as a lien though it becomes a lien once the right is exercised: see *Commercial Credit Corp. v. Harry D. Shields Ltd.* (1981), 1 PPSAC 99, aff'd 1 PPSAC 301 (Ont. CA), *supra*, chapter 2.

The general common law rule is that a lienor can acquire no greater rights in the chattel than the lienee himself has. This rule is, or was, subject to several exceptions: (1) where the debtor has implied or express authority to contract for the services giving rise to the lien rights. See *Gen. Securities Ltd. v. Brett's Ltd.* (1956), 19 WWR 385 (BC), for a review of the earlier authorities and, generally, Goode and Ziegel, *Hire-Purchase and Conditional Sale* (1965), at 180-85; (2) in the case of an innkeeper, his lien extended to all chattels in his guest's possession whether or not the guest owned them, the reason being that the law "compelled an innkeeper to receive the guest and the goods and, regardless of their ownership, the innkeeper was given little opportunity to inquire as to title": *Bank of Montreal v. 414031 Ontario Ltd.* (1983), 2 PPSAC 248, 250 (Ont.); and (3) at common law the landlord's right of distress likewise extended to any goods in the tenant's possession whether or not they belonged to the tenant.

In many of the provinces the landlord's right has been modified by statute. In Ontario, for example, s. 31(2) of the Landlord and Tenant Act, RSO 1990 c. L.7, limits the landlord's right of distraint to the tenant's goods and chattels but exempts from this restriction the claim of a person "whose title is derived by purchase, gift, transfer or assignment from the tenant ... or by way of mortgage or otherwise, nor to the interest of the tenant in any goods or chattels on the premises ... under a contract for purchase, or by which he may or is to become the owner thereof upon performance of any condition ... ." The Saskatchewan Landlord and Tenant Act, RSS 1978, c. L-6, as am., contains a similar provision but *excludes* from the landlord's reach a "purchase money security interest" defined in the same way as in the SPPSA. See *Dube v. Bk. of Montreal* (1985-86), 5 PPSAC 269 (Sask. CA).

The common law did not give employees a lien on their employer's assets for unpaid wages or other benefits (can you guess why not?) but this omission is now repaired in the Employment Standards and other legislation, federal and provincial. For Ontario, see the Employment Standards Act, RSO 1990, c. E.14, the Pension Benefits Act, RSO 1990, c. P.8, and the OPPSA, s. 30(7) and (8). Section 427(7) of the Bank Act also confers a priority in favour of employees for unpaid wages over a bank's s. 427 security interest, although the priority only applies where the employer has gone bankrupt.

At common law and under the provincial sale of goods Acts, unpaid sellers have a possessory lien and a (largely theoretical) right of stoppage of the goods while in transit (see volume I of this casebook, chapter 11), but these rights come to an end once the goods reach the buyer. Thereafter the seller is limited to suing for the price of the goods unless it has retained a consensual security interest. Here again the federal Parliament has intervened to assist unpaid suppliers who are perceived not to be capable of adequately protecting their own interests. See Bank Act, s. 427(7)(b) (growers and producers of agricultural products), and BIA, ss. 81.1 and 81.2. The BIA amendments were added in 1992 and are considered below in chapter 14.

Position of Liens Under PPS Legislation

Section 4(1)(a) of the OPPSA (in common with the other PPS Acts) provides that the Act does not apply to "a lien given by statute or rule of law, except as provided in ... Section 31 ... ." Section 31, which is based on UCC 9-310, confers priority over a perfected security interest in favour of the lien of a person who in the ordinary course of business furnishes materials or services with respect to the goods in his possession "unless the lien is given by an Act that provides that the lien does not have such priority."* In other words,

---

* The quoted words were wrongly transposed in old s. 32, so that it read "unless the lien is given by an Act *that does not provide* that the lien has such priority" (italics added). The error has been corrected in s. 31 of the new Act.

the presumption is that the lien has priority over any consensual security interest, including a PMSI. The common law position was not quite as favourable to the lienholder, but the practical results were or are about the same under either regime. See Ziegel & Denomme, *op. cit.*, §§31.2-3.

Section 31 has so far spawned no significant litigation and the courts have experienced little difficulty in giving it its intended meaning. See, e.g., *Algoma Truck & Tractor Sales Ltd. v. Blais* (1981), 1 PPSAC 319 (Ont.). What is the rationale of s. 32? Is it based on the premise that a secured party should not be enriched at the expense of a repairer who has increased the value of the collateral? Is the increase in value necessarily the same as the amount of the lien claimant's bill?

There has been some discussion about the significance of s. 4(1)(a) being limited to liens. Prof. MacLaren has suggested, for example, that if a right of seizure or detention of the debtor's assets does not technically amount to a lien (he uses the landlord's right of distraint as an example) then "it may be" subject to the PPS legislation. See MacLaren, *Secured Transactions in Personal Property*, volume 1, para. 6.03[2][a][iii] (1986). Is this correct? Are not all non-consensual claims implicitly excluded by the terms of s. 2? What does it mean to say that a right of distraint may be subject to the PPSA?

Repair and Storage Liens Act (Ont.)*

There is not a comfortable fit between the RSLA and s. 31 of the OPPSA. It is clear the RSLA drafters intended the RSLA to supersede s. 31 although the RSLA does not say so explicitly and although the drafters appear to have overlooked the effect of s. 73 of the OPPSA. For the purposes of the following summary it will be assumed that there is no difficulty in maintaining the supremacy of the RSLA in the unlikely event that a conflict is found between the RSLA and the OPPSA.

Scope of the Act. The Act applies to a repairer and storer of an article. "Repairer," "storer" and "article" are each broadly defined. There is no requirement that a repairer or storer must be acting in the course of its business when providing the services (a condition, as we have seen, of the lienholder acquiring property under s. 31 of the OPPSA) or that the repair or storage will enhance the value of the article.

Possessory and non-possessory liens. Both repairer and storers are given possessory and non-possessory lien rights in respect of their claims. There is, however, an important difference between the priorities conferred on repairers' and storers' liens. If the other requirements discussed below are satisfied, a repairer's possessory lien has priority over the interests of all other persons. A storer's lien, on the other hand, is limited to the unpaid amount owing in respect of the 60-day period calculated from the date the article was received under the following circumstances. The circumstances are (1) that the storer knows or has reason to believe that possession of the article was received from a

---

* The following passages are copied from Ziegel & Denomme, *op. cit.*, §§ 31.4-31.4.3. All footnotes have been omitted.

person other than its owner or a person having the owner's authority, and (2) that within 60 days of receiving the article the storer has failed to give notice of the lien to every person whom the storer knows or has reason to believe is the owner or has an interest in the article.

A possessory lien comes to an end, and cannot be revived, if possession of the article is surrendered to or lawfully comes into the possession of the owner or other eligible person. The possessory lien is then replaced by a non-possessory lien for the unpaid amount, which, it is clear, arises automatically on surrender of possession.

Priority of possessory and non-possessory liens and conditions of enforceability. There are also important differences in the priority accorded to possessory and non-possessory liens. A possessory lien has priority over the interests of "all" other persons in the article. This language is broad enough to subordinate a secured party's interest not only where the debtor is in possession with the secured party's consent but equally so where a transferee from the debtor gave the goods for storage or repair and even where the goods were stolen from the debtor. It remains to be seen whether the courts will seek to avoid such extravagant results, as they have in other areas raising similar issues.

A non-possessory lien too has priority over the interest in the article of any other person, but it is subordinated to three classes of person: (1) the holder of a possessory lien even where the non-possessory lien has been registered; (2) the holder of a non-possessory registered lien where the lien holder gave up possession to a prior registered lien holder; and (3) a buyer from a person selling the article in ordinary course of business where the repair or storage services giving rise to the non-possessory lien were rendered at the request of the seller or its agent.

A non-possessory lien is only enforceable if it satisfies two requirements. First, the lien claimant must obtain a signed acknowledgement of indebtedness. This requirement apparently enures for the benefit of all persons, including the lien debtor. Second, the lienholder must register a claim for lien. This condition only enures for the benefit of "third parties," a disturbingly loose expression that is not defined. The perfection requirement is comparable to s. 20 of the OPPSA, but there are important differences in consequences. An unperfected lien claim under the RSLA is only subordinated to the rights of those persons who have acquired a right against the article *after* the non-possessory lien has arisen. The RSLA has no separate priority rule, comparable to s. 30 of the OPPSA, governing competing consensual and non-consensual non-possessory lien interests. A consequence of this omission is that a secured party will derive no benefit from its prior registration under the OPPSA unless it can show that in addition to its registration it had acquired a right to the article before the non-possessory lien was perfected.

Governmental Liens

There are a large number of such liens and they have given rise to a very large body of complex litigation and much non-curial discussion and debate. See, *inter alia*, Law Reform Commission of British Columbia, *Report on the Crown as Creditor: Priorities and Privileges* (1982); Baird, "Priority of non-PPSA Secured Creditors," in D.E. Baird and F. Bennett, *Handbook on the Personal Property Security Act* (1982), chapter 5; *Study Committee on Bankruptcy and Insolvency Legislation* (1970), at 122 *et seq*; *Canada, Report of the Advisory Committee on Bankruptcy and Insolvency* (Ottawa 1986), at 77-79; W.A. Bogart, "Statutory Claims and Personal Property Security Legislation: A Proposal" (1983), 8 *CBLJ* 129; and Anne E. Hardy, *Crown Priority in Insolvency* (Carswell, 1986).

There is no consistency in the statutory language conferring a preferred status on the governmental claim. Often it is described as a lien on the debtor's assets, in which case it may be a "first lien," a "special lien," a "lien and charge," or a "lien ... payable in priority over all liens, charges or mortgages." Bogart, *op. cit.*, at 134-35. Where a debtor is required to make deductions from a payroll (e.g., pursuant to income tax or unemployment insurance requirements) or to collect taxes from a third party (e.g., with respect to sales taxes) and to remit them to the government, a popular statutory device is to create a "deemed" trust in respect of amounts that should have been remitted but were not. See e.g., Income Tax Act, SC 1970-71-72, c. 63, s. 227(4) as am., Canada Pension Plan Act, RSO 1985, c. C-8, s. 23(3)-(4) as am. and Unemployment Insurance Act, RSO 1985, c. U-1, s. 57(2)-(3).

Another feature of the ITA, which has caused secured creditors much anguish (and greatly incensed the members of the Alberta Court of Appeal), is s. 224(1.2) entitling the Crown to attach monies owing to the debtor by a third party where the debtor has failed to remit deductions to National Revenue Canada. Such an attachment overrides any prior perfected security interest given by the debtor.

Further complications arise because the status of such preferential claims may vary depending on whether the issue arises (a) before, or (b) after the debtor's bankruptcy. If before bankruptcy, then the claim will be governed by the applicable provincial or federal law. If after, then the Bankruptcy and Insolvency Act, RSC 1985, c. B-3 as am., will have the final word. Before the 1992 amendments, s. 136(1) of the BIA established the order of priority of claims, other than those by secured creditors, and, in s. 136(1)(j) (formerly s. 107(1)(j)) conferred priority on claims of the Crown. The Supreme Court of Canada held that s. 136(1)(j) reduced a governmental lien, even one that is registered, to the status of a preferred creditor. See *Deputy Min. of Revenue v. Rainville*, [1980] 1 SCR 35. There was, however, much uncertainty about the status of deemed trusts, which was only put to rest by the Supreme Court in 1989 in *British Columbia v. Henfrey Samson Belair Ltd.* [1989] 2 SCR 24, reproduced, *infra*, in chapter 17. The 1992 amendments made important changes to the status of deemed trusts in bankruptcy and the ranking of Crown claims. See *infra*, chapter 17.

The following is a very limited sampling of recent case law interpreting the scope of non-consensual statutory liens outside bankruptcy and their ranking *vis-à-vis* consensual security interests. The bankruptcy priority rules are considered in chapter 17, *infra*.

Leavere v. Port Colborne (City)
(1995), 22 OR (3d) 44 (CA)

The judgment of the court was delivered by GALLIGAN JA: These appeals, which were argued together, raise the same issue. It is whether a municipality distraining a taxpayer's chattels for arrears of business taxes is entitled to those chattels as against a creditor of the taxpayer who has a registered perfected security interest in those same chattels.

The specific facts of the two cases are different but for the purposes of the appeals there is no material distinction between them. Each of the appellants loaned money to the taxpayers and took back security agreements giving them security interests in the taxpayers' chattels. The appellants perfected their security interests by proper registration pursuant to the provisions of the *Personal Property Security Act*, RSO 1990, c. P.10 (the "PPSA"). Later, when the taxpayers fell into arrears in the payment of business taxes, each municipality, acting pursuant to s. 400(2) of the *Municipal Act*, RSO 1990, c. M.45, levied the unpaid taxes by distress upon the taxpayer's chattels by taking possession of them. They were the same chattels to which the appellants' perfected security interests related.

It is the position of the appellants that, because their security interests were perfected by registration before the municipalities levied by distress, the provisions of the PPSA give them priority over the municipalities' claims for arrears of business taxes. It is the contention of the respondent municipalities that the PPSA does not apply to these circumstances and that their levies by distress entitle them to recover their claims for arrears of business taxes out of the chattels. Both judges in motions court, from whose decisions these appeals are taken, decided the issue in the municipalities' favour.

The appeals raise two main issues. The first is whether the PPSA applies to the municipalities' claims. The second is the determination of priorities if the PPSA does not apply. I will deal with the issues separately.

A. *The Applicability of the PPSA to the Municipalities' Claims for Arrears of Business Taxes*

The resolution of this issue requires a consideration of three statutory provisions. They are s. 400(2)(a) of the *Municipal Act*, and ss. 4(1) and 20(1)(a)(i) of the PPSA. Those provisions are as follows:

The Municipal Act
   400(2) Subject to section 399, in case of taxes that are not a lien on land remaining unpaid for twenty-one days after demand or notice made or given under section 392, 395 or 399 or, where a longer period has been authorized under subsection 399(6) such taxes remain unpaid at the expiry of that period, the collector or, where there is no collector, the treasurer may alone or by an agent, subject to the exemptions provided for in subsection (4), levy them with costs by distress,
        (a) upon the goods and chattels of the person taxed wherever found within the county in which the municipality lies for judicial purposes.

The Personal Property Security Act
   4(1) This Act does not apply,
        (a) to a lien given by statute or rule of law, except as provided in subclause 20(1)(a)(i) or section 31.

• • •

20(1) Except as provided in subsection (3), until perfected, a security interest,
    (a) in collateral is subordinate to the interest of,
        (i) a person who has a perfected security interest in the same collateral or who has a
    lien given under any other Act or by a rule of law or who has a priority under any other
    Act. …

As s. 4(1) states, the PPSA does not apply to a lien given by statute or by a rule of law except as provided in the two provisions named therein. It is common ground that unpaid business taxes fall within the provisions of s. 400(2) of the *Municipal Act*. Section 400(2)(a) authorizes the municipality to levy unpaid business taxes "by distress" upon the goods and chattels of the person taxed.

There are two issues which must be decided in order to determine whether the PPSA applies to a municipality's levy of unpaid taxes by distress against a taxpayer's chattels:

1. Does a levy by distress by unpaid business taxes result in a lien upon the chattels either under a statute or by a rule of law?
2. If so, is such a lien excepted by one of the statutory exceptions contained in s. 4(1)(a) of the PPSA?

I will deal with the two issues in that order.

1. *Does a levy by distress of unpaid business taxes result in a lien upon the chattels either under a statute or by a rule of law?*

[See *Commercial Credit Corp. v. Harry D. Shields Ltd., supra*, chapter 3, ed.]

2. *Is the lien upon the taxpayer's chattels, resulting from the exercise of the right of distress, excepted by the provisions of s. 4(1)(a)?*

The exceptions referred to in s. 4(1) are s. 20(1)(a)(i) and s. 31. It is common ground that s. 31 has no application to these appeals. The provision of the PPSA with which the courts were concerned in *Commercial Credit*, s. 3(1)(a), did not have an exception similar to that contained in s. 20(1)(a)(i) of the present Act. The result in *Commercial Credit* was that, because the lien was one given by a rule of law, the PPSA did not apply to it. The lienholder, the landlord, succeeded notwithstanding the prior perfected security interests registered under the PPSA. Therefore, unless the exception in s. 20(1)(a)(i) has the effect of making all of the PPSA applicable to these liens, that case is decisive. I will, therefore, examine whether the exception applies to these cases.

Before considering s. 20(1)(a)(i) I note that s. 20(3) does not apply to these cases. To facilitate the understanding of s. 20(1)(a)(i) I delete the words referring to s. 20(3) and rewrite the provision so that it reads as follows:

Until perfected, a security interest in collateral is subordinate to the interest of
    (a) a person who has a perfected security interest in the same collateral;
    (b) a person who has a lien given under any Act in the same collateral;
    (c) a person who has a lien given by a rule of law; and
    (d) a person who has a priority in the collateral under any other Act.

In order to simplify even more the reading of the provision I will make reference only to the lien given by a rule of law because it is the only one of those interests which is relevant to these appeals. The provision then reads that, until perfected, a security interest in collateral is subordinate to the interest of a person who has a lien given by a rule of law.

It was Mr. Swartz's neat submission that when the legislature used the words "until perfected" it meant that once it was "perfected" the security interest would have priority over the interest of the person with the lien. He said that, because his client's security interest was perfected, the PPSA applied to the extent of giving it priority over the municipality's lien.

I am unable to read the provision in that fashion. Reading s. 20(1)(a)(i) with s. 4(1)(a) leads me to conclude that the legislature intended the Act to apply only to the extent of specifically determining what would happen in the event of a contest between an unperfected security interest and a lien given by a rule of law. At common law priorities were determined in accordance with the chronological order of the encumbrances. Authority for the common law rule is found in *Spence on Equitable Jurisdiction of the Court of Chancery* (1850), vol. 2 at p. 727, where the following appears:

It has already been stated that the general rule, though not without exceptions as will presently appear, is, that statutes, judgments, and recognizances, at law and in equity, and equitable charges of every kind, in equity, all rank according to their dates: therefore, in the absence of particular circumstances, the successive periods of their execution or attainment constitute the order in which they will be directed to be satisfied.

(Footnote omitted.)

Accordingly, if there were no s. 20(1)(a)(i), in the event that an unperfected security interest predated the exercise of a right of distress it could be argued that the unperfected security interest would have priority over the lien given by rule of law. I read the exception provided for in s. 4(1)(a) as an expression of legislative intent that in all cases an unperfected security interest is to be subordinate to the interest of a person who has a lien given by a rule of law. It is my view that the exception was enacted to deal specifically with the problem of a competition between such a lien and an unperfected security interest. I cannot read the provision as going any further than that.

I conclude, therefore, that the exception provided for in s. 20(1)(a)(i) is simply inapplicable in the circumstances of these two cases. The opening words of s. 4(1)(a) are applicable and the PPSA does not apply to the liens which the municipalities have on the taxpayers' chattels in these cases. Since the exception in s. 20(1)(a)(i) is not applicable, it is my opinion that this issue is determined by the decision in *Commercial Credit*. In that case this court held at pp. 703-04 that the landlord's lien need not be registered in accordance with the PPSA. Because the PPSA does not apply to liens given by a rule of law, that Act does not apply to give the holders of perfected security interests priority over the liens of these municipalities which are liens given by a rule of law.

The appellants also contend that there is a conflict between the provisions of s. 400(2) of the *Municipal Act* and the provisions of the PPSA and rely upon s. 73 of the PPSA. Section 73 of the PPSA provides that when there is a conflict between one of its provisions and a provision of any general or special Act (other than the *Consumer Protection Act*) the provisions of the PPSA prevail. This argument can be answered shortly. Section 73 of the

PPSA is identical with the provisions of s. 68 which were in force at the time *Commercial Credit* was decided. In that case this court held that, because the PPSA did not apply to the lien given by a rule of law, s. 68 had no application to the case. That is the precise situation in these cases. Section 73 being a part of the PPSA cannot apply because the PPSA itself does not apply to these cases. That contention cannot succeed.

During argument counsel for the respondents argued that the PPSA did not apply for another reason. Section 2 provides that the PPSA applies to "every transaction ... that ... creates a security interest." It was contended that a lien given by a rule of law was not a "transaction" and therefore the PPSA could not apply to it. In view of the fact that I have concluded on other grounds that the PPSA does not apply, I do not think it necessary to address that interesting argument.

For the reasons set out above, it is my opinion that the provisions of the PPSA do not apply to the municipalities' liens in these cases.

B. *The Priorities Between the Appellants and the Municipalities in the Absence of the PPSA*

Because I have concluded that the provisions of the PPSA do not apply to the municipalities' liens in these cases it is necessary to determine the priorities in the absence of that Act.

It appears to have been accepted in *Commercial Credit, supra*, that, if the PPSA did not apply, the lien given by a rule of law had priority over the chattel mortgage. The applicability of that assumption to this case is challenged because the appellants contend that if the PPSA does not apply then the common law rule, that encumbrances rank in the order of their coming into existence, must be applied. They say that the application of that rule in these cases requires that their security agreements be given priority over the municipalities' liens for the simple reason that they came into existence before the liens were created. So far as I can tell a similar argument does not appear to have been made in *Commercial Credit*. In my view, therefore, it is appropriate that the issue now be addressed.

I think that the issue can be dealt with fairly shortly. In the earlier part of these reasons I noted that the rule at common law, to which there were exceptions, was that priorities were determined in accordance with the chronological order of the encumbrances. For the purposes of this discussion I will assume that a lien given by a rule of law is an encumbrance upon the property to which it attaches, so that if the common law rule is applicable it would apply to a conflict between such a lien and a security agreement which is obviously an encumbrance upon the property subject to it.

There is no need for any detailed examination of the exceptions to the rule which existed at common law. What has always been recognized is that the common law rule could be displaced by the provisions of a statute. It often is. There is, in my opinion, a statutory provision the effect of which is to give the municipalities' liens priority over the appellants' security interests. It is s. 400(2)(c)(ii) of the *Municipal Act*:

400(2) Subject to section 399, in case of taxes that are not a lien on land remaining unpaid for twenty-one days after demand or notice made or given under section 392, 395 or 399 or, where a longer period has been authorized under subsection 399(6) such taxes remain unpaid at the expiry of that period, the collector or, where there is no collector, the treasurer may alone or by an agent, subject to the exemptions provided for in subsection (4), levy them with costs by distress,

(c) upon any goods and chattels in the possession of the person taxed where title to them is claimed,

    (i) by virtue of an execution against the person taxed,

    (ii) by purchase, gift, transfer or assignment from the person taxed, whether absolute or in trust, or by way of mortgage or otherwise.

An analysis of that provision shows that a municipality may levy by distress upon the chattels in the possession of the person taxed where title is claimed by someone who has obtained title from the person taxed "by way of mortgage or otherwise." The appellants' claims to the chattels in question are based upon their security agreements. The security agreements between the appellants and the persons taxed, upon which the appellants' claims to the chattels are founded, are not called mortgages. Strictly speaking it could be said that the appellants' security agreements with the persons taxed are not "mortgages" within the meaning of s. 400(2)(c)(ii). The reason that they are not called mortgages is that the PPSA does not speak of mortgages but of security agreements and these documents were prepared with the intention of complying with the provisions of the PPSA. The definition of security agreements in the PPSA is wide enough to include mortgages and these security agreements are so similar to mortgages in purpose and effect that I think they must be included in the word "otherwise" found in the provision. It follows that the statute authorized the levy by distress against the chattels covered by the appellants' security agreements. I am unable to read s. 400(2)(c)(ii) in any fashion other than clearly expressing a legislative intent that municipalities are entitled to levy by distress upon chattels in the possession of a person taxed even though the chattels are subject to security agreements.

As I pointed out in the earlier section of these reasons the statute itself does not create a lien. The municipalities' liens arose when the municipalities took possession of the chattels in the exercise of their statutory power to distrain. Because the statute authorizes distress upon chattels subject to security agreements I am constrained to conclude that the lien which arises upon the exercise of that right must take priority over the security agreements. It would, in my view, amount to an absurdity if the statute authorized distress upon chattels covered by security agreements but did not intend as well that the lien created by the exercise of the right of distress was to have priority over the security agreement. The power to distrain upon chattels subject to security agreements would be rendered nugatory if the security agreements were not required to rank behind the liens which had arisen by rule of law. The legislature cannot have intended that the statutory right, which it granted, to distrain on such chattels was to be without effect.

It is my opinion, therefore, that s. 400(2)(c)(ii) should be read as giving the municipalities' liens priority over the appellants' security agreements. Thus the common law rule cannot apply to give the appellants' security agreements priority over the municipalities' liens.

• • •

Appeals dismissed.

NOTE

The Court of Appeal's willingness to read s. 400(2) so broadly to accommodate municipalities is surprising on two grounds. The first is that the Supreme Court held in *Board of Industrial Relations v. Avco Financial Services*, [1979] 2 SCR 699 that, in the absence of very clear language to the contrary, a provision conferring priority on a statutory tax lien is only deemed to be prospective in its effect and is not to be read as overriding existing interests. Galligan JA does not refer to this well-established canon of construction. The second reason is that conferring retroactive priority on a tax lien undermines the carefully conceived priority structure of the OPPSA and makes it very difficult for secured parties to predict how their security will fare in practice. Municipalities (like other government agencies claiming a superpriority lien) will no doubt respond that a tax lien is the only effective weapon at their disposal to ensure collection of what is owing to them and that it would not be fair to give preferred treatment to consensually secured creditors at the expense of other tax payers. For an oft-cited article supporting the Crown's position along these lines see M. Shanker, "The Worthier Creditors (And a Cheer for the King)" (1975-76), 1 *CBLJ* 340.

Royal Bank v. Sparrow Electric Corp.
[1994] 9 WWR 338 (Alta.)

AGRIOS J: This is the third application to determine the priority of approximately $625,000 being held in trust by a Receiver pending the completion of all Court proceedings. The first application was by the Receiver for advice and direction, while the subsequent applications were by the plaintiff. The two claimants are Revenue Canada for unpaid employee source deductions and the Royal Bank of Canada ("the Bank") as a security holder.

Counsel for the Bank has explained the two previous decisions are to be the subject of an appeal and accordingly, as a matter of convenience to everyone concerned, this application was heard at this time on the understanding that the appeal of the trilogy of decisions could conveniently be heard at one time. I agree with counsel that this makes good sense.

In the first application, the issue related to certain security documents held by the Bank, principally a general security agreement. The second application was for a pro rata distribution of the monies being held by the Receiver after some $600,000 had been released to the Bank. In both decisions Revenue Canada succeeded and, notwithstanding the ablest of arguments, both written and oral, on behalf of the Bank, I have once again held in favour of Revenue Canada.

This application is concerned with security granted under s. 178 (now s. 427) of the *Bank Act*, RSC 1985, c. B-1 ("Bank Act security"), and claims by Revenue Canada for unpaid employee source deductions under s. 227(4) and (5) of the *Income Tax Act*, SC 1970-71-72, c. 63, as amended ("the ITA"). These provisions in the ITA concern the deemed statutory trust created for employee withholdings. The issue here is whether the *Bank Act* security or the deemed statutory trust take priority in the distribution of proceeds of the inventory of a company in receivership or bankruptcy.

Background

The facts are well set out in the Memorandum of Argument of both counsel and I will assume that a reader will review these decisions in dated order and endeavour not to repeat all the background information.

Briefly, the Bank's claim against Sparrow Electric Ltd. ("Sparrow") in April 1994 amounted to $1,607,458.70. Revenue Canada's claim for source deductions amounted to $625,990.86 exclusive of interest. Sparrow's indebtedness as of the date of the receivership amounted to in excess of $5.1 million. Clearly, there are not sufficient assets to satisfy both the claims of the Bank and Revenue Canada. The asset in issue is a fund realized by Sparrow's receiver from the sale of inventory. As mentioned, the sum of about $600,000 from this fund has previously been paid by the Receiver to the Bank to apply on the indebtedness. The parties now contest their respective claims for the balance of approximately $625,000. As Mr. Rutman, counsel for the Bank, succinctly stated, the essence of the dispute between the Royal Bank of Canada and Revenue Canada is:

(a) Revenue Canada alleges that the deemed statutory trust entitles it to proceeds from the inventory of Sparrow prior to payment of any claims to an assignee of security under the *Bank Act*; and

(b) The Bank asserts that the *Bank Act* Security entitles it to receive the proceeds from the inventory of Sparrow prior to Revenue Canada.

The issue, to once again use Mr. Rutman's words: Is a Bank holding security granted under s. 427 of the *Bank Act* entitled to priority over Revenue Canada in relation to the inventory of a company in receivership or bankruptcy notwithstanding the deemed statutory trust created under s. 227(4) and (5) of the *Income Tax Act*?

For the reasons set out in this judgment I hold that the Bank is not entitled to priority over Revenue Canada.

The Bank Act Security and the Relevant Provisions of the Bank Act and the Income Tax Act

Copies of the *Bank Act* security granted by Sparrow to the Bank are set out in the materials. Counsel notes the security is composed of three components, being:

(a) an application of credit and promise to give security under s. 178 and warehouse receipts and/or bills of lading;

(b) the general assignment itself;

(c) an agreement as to loans, advances and security therefor.

The applicable sections as noted in the Memorandum of Argument are found in paras. 12, 13 and 14 and are attached for convenience's sake as App. 1 to this judgment.

The applicable sections of the *Bank Act* relied on by counsel are ss. 427(2), 435(2), 432, 434(2) and 428(1), and are once again for convenience's sake, attached as App. 2 [not published] to this judgment.

Revenue Canada relies on s. 153 of the *Income Tax Act* and s. 227(4) and (5) of the *Income Tax Act* which are also attached as App. 3 [now published] to this judgment.

The Bank's Claim

There is considerable authority for the arguments advanced on behalf of the Bank by Mr. Rutman. It is difficult to find fault with his premises which are as follows. The effect of *Bank Act* security, it is submitted, is to vest in the Bank all the right and title to the property covered by the security and its proceeds. The Bank is the owner of the inventory. Security granted by a borrower to a Bank under s. 427(2) (formerly s. 178(a)) vests in the Bank the same rights and powers with respect to inventory as if the bank had acquired a warehouse receipt or bill of lading which described the inventory. No act or law is to be construed as ever having intended to prevent a Bank from acquiring and holding an absolute title to any mortgaged property (s. 34(2) of the *Bank Act*).

The Plaintiff, in its memorandum, makes specific reference to a 1986 article by Professor W.D. Moull entitled "Security Under Sections 177 and 178 of the Bank Act" which is contained in a special banking issue of the Canadian Bar Review, 65 Can. Bar Rev. 242. Certain passages which I will refer to shortly have been approved by the Supreme Court of Canada in *Bank of Montreal v. Hall*, [1990] 1 SCR 121 [[1990] 2 WWR 193]. Professor Moull in his introduction notes that these sections provided Canadian chartered banks with special powers and established forms of security interest that are unique to chartered banks and no other financial institutions might have resort to them. He comments that these unique provisions probably assisted the chartered banks in acquiring their positions as Canada's dominant commercial lenders. They provide that banks could take security over raw materials, work in progress, and wholesale inventories.

In *Bank of Montreal v. Hall (supra)* La Forest J notes that the nature, rights and powers vested in the Bank by the delivery of the security interest has been the object of some debate. Argument centres on whether the security interest should be likened to a pledge or bailment, or whether it is more in the nature of a chattel mortgage. He finds the most precise description of the interest is that given in Professor Moull's article. In the article Moull suggests that the effect of the interest is to vest title of the property in the Bank when the security interest is given. Professor Moull's article reads as follows [p. 251]:

The result, then, is that a bank taking security under section 178 effectively acquires legal title to the borrower's interest in the present and after-acquired property assigned to it by the borrower. The bank's interest attaches to the assigned property when the security is given or the property is acquired by the borrower and remains attached until released by the bank, despite changes in the attributes or composition of the assigned property. The borrower retains an equitable right of redemption, of course, but the bank effectively acquires legal title to whatever rights the borrower holds in the assigned property from time to time.

Because of its scope and flexibility, some commentators have suggested that section 178 security is in the nature of a floating charge. This can be misleading, however. Because the bank effectively acquires legal title, section 178 security is really in the nature of a fixed charge on the present and after-acquired property of the borrower assigned to the bank. One attribute that section 178 security may be said to share with a floating charge is its application to all property of a specified class held by the borrower from time to time. But while a floating charge may apply to all property of a specified kind held by the borrower from time, it does not affix itself specifically upon any particular item of property until it crystallizes upon default by the borrower.

Conversely, a section 178 security is a fixed charge on each item of assigned property held from time to time whether or not the loan is in default. This gives a bank significantly greater rights than it would hold under a floating charge debenture on inventory.

I agree with Mr. Rutman's submission that characterization of *Bank Act* security as a floating charge is incorrect and superficial. Professor Moull notes that the usual practice is for the Bank to grant the borrower a general licence to dispose of the secured property in the ordinary course of business of the borrower. He anticipates what has now come to be referred to as a fixed security interest with a licence to sell in the ordinary course of business. Later in his article Professor Moull does make reference to s. 178 and provincial security interests and government claims. See p. 259. He states:

The federal Crown's claim in respect of its taxes will also attach only to the equity of the taxpayer and its assets, except where express provisions require some other result.

An example of such an express provision may be found in the *Special War Revenue Act*, SC 1915, c. 8 (5 Geo. V), as amended SC 1922, c. 47 (12-13 Geo. V), s. 17. It specifically provided that liability to the Crown was a first charge notwithstanding the provisions of the *Bank Act*.

From my review of the article, the issue raised in this application is not specifically dealt with by Professor Moull. It would be difficult to argue with Mr. Rutman's plethora of authorities clearly holding that *Bank Act* security amounts to a transfer of ownership in property, and almost all the cases cited by Mr. Rutman support the proposition of the pre-eminence of the *Bank Act* security over other claims. I will not review all of the authorities cited by Mr. Rutman. His points are well made and authoritative indeed. However, they do not answer the issue raised by Revenue Canada, namely, while ownership rights are transferred, these rights are not absolute.

Revenue Canada's Claim

Both counsel agreed that only two Canadian cases specifically deal with this priority issue. The first was a trial decision in Alberta in 1989, *Royal Bank v. Canadian Aero-Marine Industries Inc.*, 67 Alta. LR (2d) 172 [[1989] 5 WWR 355] (QB), and the second, a trial decision in Saskatchewan, *Ford Motor Co. of Canada v. Manning Mercury Sales Ltd. (Trustee of)* (9 May 1994), (Sask. QB) [reported [1994] 6 WWR 372]. After a careful review of Justice McDonald's decision in *Canadian Aero-Marine*, I agree with Mr. Lema: Justice McDonald's decision does not consider the issues raised here. His reasoning is restricted to an interpretation of s. 178 Bank security as being limited to a "revolving line of credit." As a result, Justice McDonald holds that Bank security claim is limited to that part of the claim based on the revolving line of credit and for that claim there is priority over the statutory trust in favour of Her Majesty.

In the more recent decision, *Ford Motor Co. of Canada v. Manning Mercury Sales Ltd. (Trustee of), supra,* Justice Halvorson of the Saskatchewan Court of Queen's Bench faces the issues raised in this case and holds in favour of Revenue Canada and adopts the reasoning (as did I in *Royal Bank of Canada v. Sparrow Electric Corp.*, "Pt. 1" [reported 19 Alta. LR (3d) 183]) of the British Columbia Court of Appeal, *British Columbia v. Federal Business Development Bank ("FBDB"),* [1988] 1 WWR 1. He concludes that the

Bank's charge was subject to a licence permitting the borrower to deal with the inventory in the ordinary course of business. That permission included all the usual incidents of dealing with inventory, to paraphrase *FBDB*. One incident was the payment of wages and the statutory deemed trust arising therefor which obliged the borrower to remit source deductions. Mr. Lema refers to this decision as well as to a number of others "as an emergent set of cases which give recognition to a court that notwithstanding a specific security, if the borrower can sell inventory by reason of a licence to sell such inventory is exposed to the normal incidents of business which includes statutory trusts for income tax deductions."

The development of this line of cases begins with an analysis of just what a deemed trust actually is. This was addressed in several cases cited by Mr. Lema, including *Re Deslauriers Construction Products Ltd.*, [1970] 3 OR 599 (CA) and *RoyNat Inc. v. Ja-Sha Trucking & Leasing Ltd.*, [1992] 2 WWR 641 (Man. CA). In *RoyNat, supra*, Twaddle JA noted, at p. 647, that:

> The deemed trust arising on the appointment of a receiver is not a trust at all. It is a mechanism for tracing. Her Majesty has a statutory right of access to whatever assets the employer then has, out of which to realize the original trust debt due to Her.

This distinction is important in ascertaining what kind of interest Revenue Canada has in the property. The characterization of the deemed trust as a mechanism for tracing is important here because it relieves Revenue Canada of the requirement to trace the unremitted source deductions. The deductions having been made, even if only notionally, are deemed to exist, and to exist separate and apart from the estate of the bankrupt.

The nature of the Bank's interest under s. 427 security has, as discussed earlier, been said to transfer ownership to the Bank. Revenue Canada has argued that the Bank's interest under s. 427 is a floating charge that did not crystallize until the Receiver was appointed. Alternatively, they argue the charge is a fixed one with a licence to sell. I do not think it is necessary to determine whether the interest is fixed or floating. As discussed by McLachlin JA in *FBDB, supra*, by Twaddle JA in *RoyNat, supra*, and Halvorson J in *Ford Motor Co. of Canada, supra*, that characterization is not relevant. Madam Justice McLachlin in *FBDB* notes [p. 41]:

> Whether the charge is regarded as floating or fixed, it does not entitle FBDB to priority over the Crown's lien. If the charge is floating, as I think it is, no priority arises. On the other hand, if it were to be regarded as fixed, the licence to sell in the ordinary course of business must be taken as encompassing the ordinary incidents of business, including statutory liens arising as a result of sales tax, with the result that FBDB's charge is subject not only to the title of purchasers but to the lien for tax arising from sales.

Also in *FBDB* Madam Justice McLachlin discusses the rationale underlying this approach, noting that it would be unfair and inconsistent to allow the borrower to avoid the usual obligations of doing business, when he is able to take the benefits [pp. 38-39]:

> The courts have recognized that to hold otherwise would be unfair and inconsistent. It would be unfair and inconsistent to permit a debentureholder to grant to a debtor the right to carry on business, while insulating him from the usual legal incidents of doing business, such as seizure and sale by creditors and liens incidental to the business imposed by statute.

The Bank argues that, by virtue of s. 427 of the *Bank Act*, its ownership of the assets is absolute. However, the Bank cannot acquire from the borrower any more rights in the property than the borrower has. I repeat Professor Moull's statement [p. 251]:

The result, then, is that a bank taking security under section 178 effectively acquires legal title to the *borrower's interest* in the present and after-acquired property assigned to it by the borrower ... the bank effectively acquires legal title to whatever rights the borrower holds in the assigned property from time to time. [Emphasis added.]

This point was also made by Carruthers J in *Armstrong v. Canadian Admiral Corp. (Receiver of)* (1986), 53 OR (2d) 468 (SC), affirmed (1987), 61 OR (2d) 129 (CA), leave to appeal to SCC refused (1988), 87 NR 398, at p. 479:

It is clear that when a bank first takes the goods of a manufacturer as security under s. 178 and the goods are then in existence, the bank cannot receive any greater right or title to those goods than the manufacturer itself possessed.

In *Armstrong*, the Ontario High Court of Justice was dealing with a competition between *Bank Act* security and a statutory trust for vacation pay under s. 15 of the *Employment Standards Act*, RSO 1980, c. 137. Carruthers J found that since Admiral, the bankrupt debtor, had no right or title to the deemed trust created under the Act, it could not assign it to the Bank, and therefore found in favour of the plaintiffs. Section 15 of the *Employment Standards Act* is similar to the provisions of the ITA in the case at bar.

However, the *Employment Standards Act* also states that the trust "becomes a lien and charge upon the assets of the employer." Does the existence of the statutory lien have a significantly different effect than the imposition of the deemed trust, without provision for a lien upon the property? I do not think so. The deemed trust is not dependent upon the characterization of the security interest. It is, as the previous cases have suggested, a mechanism for tracing, whether or not funds are actually separate and apart, or even where only notional deductions have been made. The same principles apply. If the borrower had not granted any security interest to the Bank, its interest would be subject to "the normal incidents of business." It would own its inventory subject to paying wages and paying withholdings.

The situation would appear to be even clearer, where the issue is not the inventory assets themselves, but the proceeds of their sale. If Sparrow had not given security to the Bank, it is clear that the proceeds of the sale of the inventory would be subject to the deemed trust. If Sparrow has no rights in that portion of the proceeds, how can it transfer that portion to the Bank?

Conversely, if the Bank owns the inventory and sells it itself, in the ordinary course of business, it would also pay wages, and make and remit deductions. Its interest in the inventory would be limited by these requirements. It would be inconsistent to hold that simply by granting the debtor the right to deal with the property in the ordinary course of business, that the normal consequences of ordinary business could be avoided.

Madam Justice McLachlin in *FBDB* examines the effect that the licence to sell has on the interest transferred to the Bank by the security. She suggests that the licence to deal must impliedly encompass all the incidents of sale, from the transfer of title to sales tax [p. 40]:

When FBDB gave Arcite the power to sell the mortgaged goods in the ordinary course of business, FBDB must be taken to have tacitly accepted that it would cede its priority not only to bona fide purchasers for value, but to other persons who might acquire rights incidental to such sales. The Crown is such a person.

She also suggests that the licence to deal gave the borrower the ability to do all things necessary in order to sell the property, including collecting sales tax.

Similarly here, the licence to deal between the Bank and Sparrow must be taken to have included the ability to deal in the ordinary course of business, including the ability to pay wages and deduct withholdings. Those withholdings have been, at the least, notionally deducted. Therefore the deemed trust exists in relation to the property. The withholdings never formed part of Sparrow's estate. The deemed trust provisions of the ITA do away with the need to trace the funds. The Bank has no right to property that was not Sparrow's. Therefore the proceeds of the inventory are first impressed with the deemed trust in favour of Revenue Canada, as the withholding of payroll deduction is a normal incident of doing business in the ordinary course.

Mr. Lema, in appropriate tradition, raised a case not cited by the Bank's counsel which on the face of it supports the Bank's position. In 1990 our Court of Appeal in *Canadian Imperial Bank of Commerce v. Klymchuk* (1990), 74 Alta. LR (2d) 232 [[1990] 5 WWR 214], held that *Bank Act* security had priority over the Canadian Wheat Board's statutory lien for advances made under the *Prairie Grain Advance Payments Act*. The decision followed the Supreme Court of Canada in *Bank of Montreal v. Hall (supra)*. Our Court held that the Banks had acquired all right and title to the grain in question as legal owners.

However, the distinguishing feature is that the borrowing farmers were not entitled to sell the grain without the prior consent of the lending Banks.

I accept Mr. Lema's argument that because of this significant difference, the case is distinguishable. In the *Klymchuk* case the Wheat Board's advance only attached upon delivery of the grain. The grain producer could not deliver title and possession without the Bank's consent. In contrast here, the Bank had given the borrower authority to sell and deliver. The licence to deal principle was not argued.

● ● ●

Revenue Canada having priority.

NOTE

Royal Bank involved a contest between a s. 427 Bank Act interest and a claim for unremitted deductions, but Agrios J's reasoning is just as apt to trump a security interest under the OPPSA and the other provincial Acts. How persuasive is McLachlin JA's dictum in *British Columbia v. FBDB*, which is the basis of Agrios J's decision? If the implied licence rationale protects sales taxes, what other claims does it also shelter? Claims of suppliers of goods and services rendered to the debtor in the conduct of the debtor's business? Employee claims? Is there a logical limit? Is MacLachlin JA not reintroducing the English floating charge learning through the backdoor? Is this consistent with the structure of the PPS legislation and ss. 427 and 428(1) of the Bank Act? If the implied licence concept can be carried this far, why was it necessary for Parliament to add s. 427(7) to the Bank Act?

Re Canoe Cove Manufacturing Ltd.
(1994), 25 CBR (3d) 260 (BC)

THACKRAY J: This is a priority dispute over the receivables of the bankrupt, Canoe Cove Manufacturing Ltd.

In 1991 Canoe Cove failed to remit Goods and Services Tax pursuant to the *Excise Tax Act*. In 1992 and 1993 it granted a general assignment of book debts and security to the Bank of Montreal pursuant to s. 427 of the Canada *Bank Act*. The assignment contained the following paragraph:

THE PRESENT ASSIGNMENT and transfer shall be a continuing collateral security to the Bank for payment of all and every present and future indebtedness and liability of the undersigned to the Bank and any ultimate unpaid balance thereof with interest.

The agreement between Canoe Cove and the Bank pursuant to s. 427 of the Canada *Bank Act* contained the provision that "all proceeds of the security in the property shall be continuing collateral security for the payment of such debt or liability and also for the payment interest thereon."

In 1993 the Goods and Services Tax ("GST") office learned of the assignment. Further, that the Bank had allowed Canoe Cove to deal with its book accounts in the ordinary course of business by collecting on its own accounts receivable, depositing the funds into its own bank accounts and meeting its financial obligations for payroll, overhead and inventory.

On January 12, 1994 the Goods and Services Tax office assessed Canoe Cove as being liable for $35,349.21 for tax. On January 13 a Requirement to Pay notice was issued pursuant to s. 317(3) of the *Excise Tax Act* and delivered to the British Columbia Minister of Finance. Service on the Minister of Finance was carried out because the GST office had learned the Ministry of Forests was liable to Canoe Cove for an amount in excess of the claimed tax.

On January 7, 1994 Coopers & Lybrand was appointed agent by the Bank of Montreal pursuant to the general assignment of book debts. On January 25 a petition for a receiving order in bankruptcy was filed against Canoe Cove. The value of the receivables was approximately $170,000, but Canoe Cove was indebted to the Bank in an amount in excess of $300,000.

A receiving order in bankruptcy was pronounced on February 9 with an effective date of bankruptcy on January 25, 1994. Coopers & Lybrand was appointed Trustee in Bankruptcy.

On March 8 the GST office received a cheque from the British Columbia Minister of Finance in the amount of $35,349.21.

The issue is whether or not GST has a priority over the claim of the Trustee pursuant to s. 317(3) of the *Excise Tax Act*. That section reads as follows:

(3) Notwithstanding any other provision of this Part, any other enactment of Canada other than the *Bankruptcy and Insolvency Act*, any enactment of a province or any law, where the Minister has knowledge or suspects that a particular person is or will become, within ninety days, liable to make a payment

(a) to a tax debtor, or

(b) to a secured creditor who has a right to receive the payment that, but for a security interest in favour of the secured creditor, would be payable to the tax debtor,

the Minister may, by a letter served personally or by registered ... mail, require the particular person to pay forthwith, where the moneys are immediately payable, and in any other case, as and when the moneys become payable, the moneys otherwise payable to the tax debtor or the secured creditor in whole or in part to the Receiver General on account of the tax debtor's liability under Division V, *and on receipt of that letter by the particular person, the amount of those moneys that is required by that letter to be paid to the Receiver General shall, notwithstanding any security interest in those moneys, become the property of Her Majesty in right of Canada and shall be paid to the Receiver General in priority to any such security interest.*

[my italics]

Section 317(4) defines "secured creditor" as:

a particular person who has a security interest in the property of another person or who acts for or on behalf of the particular person with respect to the security interest, and includes a trustee appointed under a trust deed relating to a security interest, a receiver or receiver-manager appointed by a secured creditor or by a court on the application of a secured creditor, a sequestrator and any other person performing a similar function.

Section 317(4) defines "security interest" as:

any interest in property that secures payment or performance of an obligation, and includes an interest created by or arising out of a debenture, mortgage, hypothec, lien, pledge, charge, deemed or actual trust, assignment or encumbrance of any kind whatever, however or whenever arising, created, deemed to arise or otherwise provided for.

The applicant, Coopers & Lybrand, submitted that Parliament intended, by having the exclusion to the *Bankruptcy and Insolvency Act* in s. 317(3), that the *Excise Tax Act* would not interfere with the distribution scheme found in the *Bankruptcy and Insolvency Act*. It contended that this is clearly indicated by comparing this section to s. 224(1.2) of the *Income Tax Act*. This section does not make any special provision for the *Bankruptcy and Insolvency Act*. It reads as follows:

[Idem]

(1.2) Notwithstanding any other provision of this Act, the *Bankruptcy Act*, any other enactment of Canada, any enactment of a province or any law, where the Minister has knowledge or suspects that a particular person is or will become, within 90 days, liable to make a payment

(a) to another person (in this subsection referred to as the "tax debtor") who is liable to pay an amount assessed under subsection 227(10.1) or a similar provision, or

(b) to a secured creditor who has a right to receive the payment that, but for a security interest in favour of the secured creditor, would be payable to the tax debtor,

the Minister may, by registered letter ...

[The section then reads in the same terms as s. 317(3) of the *Excise Tax Act*.]

The applicant contended that in keeping with the comments in *Quebec (Deputy Minister of Revenue) v. Rainville* (1979), (sub nom. *Re Bourgault*) 105 DLR (3d) 270 (SCC), "Parliament intended to put all debts to a government on an equal footing" excepting cases where it is provided otherwise. This case, and three others cited by the Trustee, form what it submitted are a "quarter" that clearly establish that the distribution scheme in the *Bankruptcy and Insolvency Act* prevails in a bankruptcy. Further, that only clear and unambiguous federal legislation to the contrary can alter this distribution in favour of a Federal Crown claim.

The Trustee thereby contended that the *Excise Tax Act* accords priority to the *Bankruptcy and Insolvency Act* and that Parliament did not intend to alter the distribution scheme under that Act. The Trustee said that if Parliament had intended GST to take priority it would not have included the reference to the *Bankruptcy and Insolvency Act* in s. 317(3) of the *Excise Tax Act*.

The Trustee submitted that this application turns on statutory interpretation. In particular on an interpretation of s. 317(3) of the *Excise Tax Act. Canada Trustco Mortgage Corp. v. Port O'Call Hotel Inc.*, January 18, 1994 (Alta. CA) [now reported at 24 CBR (3d) 257] [hereinafter "*Re Country Inns*"] provides a starting point for an analysis of the issue. The Court set out the issue as follows [p. 260]:

A panel of this Court heard three appeals together. In each, one party is Her Majesty in Right of Canada, as represented by the Minister of National Revenue (here called the MNR). And in each case the other party is a Bank or the Alberta Treasury Branches. Each appeal is a priority contest between the MNR's garnishee summons, and a general assignment of book debts to the Bank or Treasury Branch.

For some years, the *Income Tax Act* and the *Excise Tax Act* have let the MNR garnish debts payable to persons who owe certain kinds of tax. The Act allows the MNR to issue his own garnishee summons without having to go to any court or get any kind of court judgment. (The Act calls it a "letter" but it works like a garnishee summons.) The wording of the two statutes on this point is very similar.

If A owes money to B, who owes income tax to the MNR, then the MNR can serve such a garnishee summons on A. After that, if A has not yet paid B, he has to pay the MNR instead of paying B. However, if B assigns this debt (or all his receivables) to a Bank before the garnishee summons arrives, is A to pay the MNR or to pay that Bank? That was the question in *Lloyds Bank* and the question in these three appeals.

If the two statutes said nothing about priority, the answer would be obvious. Garnishee summonses are always presumed to attach only what the (tax) debtor could honestly assign, and so the Bank would prevail over the MNR. That would also follow from the wording of the two statutes, for after the debt is assigned, A no longer owes anything to B. A owes the debt to the Bank alone.

But where certain types of income tax assessment are involved, the two statutes provide that the MNR is to have a special type of priority.

The Court then set forth s. 224(1.2) and (1.3) of the *Income Tax Act* and "emphasized" the words italicized in s. 317(3) of the *Excise Tax Act, supra.*

Then the Court continued with a "history" [pp. 261-262]:

The emphasized words were not present in 1989. In that year, this Court decided *Lloyds Bank Canada v. International Warranty Co.* (1989), 97 AR 113, 68 Alta. LR (2d) 356, 76 CBR (NS) 54 (CA), leave denied (1989), 102 AR 240 (SCC). The argument of the Crown then and now, was that the subsection just quoted gives the Crown priority over assignments of book debts to other creditors, whenever the assignment was created.

In the *Lloyds Bank* case, our Court held that if the arguments then made by the MNR were right, the *Income Tax Act*'s words about priority would take away without compensation the property of the innocent Bank. It is a principle of statutory construction that if a statute fairly permits two interpretations, the courts will pick the one which does not do that. Our Court found that the words of the *Income Tax Act* as they then stood (without the words emphasized above) were not clear enough to produce that confiscatory result. So the Bank won and the MNR lost.

Then the two statutes were amended by Parliament to add the words emphasized in the quotation above. Doubtless the MNR hoped that this would reverse the effect of the *Lloyds Bank* decision and maybe some other similar decisions.

The Court then said that where the amendments apply they "reverse our *Lloyds Bank* decision and give the MNR priority ..." [p. 262]. It said that where a bank had acquired money after a breach of trust by a taxpayer, "these sections are simply expropriation without compensation from a totally innocent bystander. But where the statute is clear and the *Charter* or *Bill of Rights* is not pleaded, we cannot stop the Minister's expropriation without compensation" [p. 263].

The case then proceeds to interpret s. 224(1.2) of the *Income Tax Act*. It said that a "precondition" is that the Minister of National Revenue must believe or suspect that the intended recipient of the letter is liable, or will soon become liable, to make a payment to a tax debtor or secured creditor. Therefore, all that follows in the subsection is subject to that precondition.

The Court noted that "secured creditor" is defined in the Act as "a particular person who has a security interest in the property of another person. ..." There had been a general assignment of book debts which transferred legal title to the bank. It was therefore held that the bank was not a "secured creditor" because it did not have any interest "in the property of another person."

The Minister of National Revenue argued that the tax debtor still had an equity of redemption and that the debtor would get the receivables back from the bank if the loan were repaid. The Court rejected this submission. it said that the only property of the debtor was the equity of redemption "and the MNR does not claim that" [p. 264]. Furthermore, the loan was larger than the receivables "purportedly garnished." The equity of redemption was therefore valueless.

In the alternative the Court held that subss. (1.2) and (1.3) of the *Income Tax Act* are ambiguous and "in case of ambiguity, the Court will take the construction which does not confiscate innocent persons' property without compensation, as discussed by this Court in the *Lloyds Bank* case, *supra*: [p. 266].

In the case at bar the Trustee submitted that *Re Country Inns* is analogous and should be applied. It contended that in that the debtor owes over $300,000 and the receivables are only worth $170,000, there is no real "equity of redemption."

The Attorney General submitted that *Re Country Inns* is wrongly decided in that it does not accord with the plain reading of s. 317(3) of the *Excise Tax Act*. The submission is in part as follows:

26. It is respectfully suggested that *Country Inns* suggests a restrictive interpretation of a "security interest" which is equivalent to rewriting the definition of a "security interest" by adding to the end of the provision "except such interests as involve a transfer of title to a debtor's assets." The definition "secured creditor" in this provision is sufficiently wide to encompass the holder of a general assignment of book accounts.

27. As indicated, s. 317(4) *Excise Tax Act* defines a "secured creditor" as a person who has security interest in the "property of another person." The phrase "property of another person" is sufficiently broad to include property, such as book accounts which the debtor has transferred to the lender for security purposes. It must be interpreted as referring to property that, absent the security interest, is the property of the person giving the security interest."

I agree with these submissions of the Attorney General. In addition, a review of the leading cases on s. 317(3) of the *Excise Tax Act* and its equivalent *Income Tax Act* section prior to "the amendments" support the conclusion that the amendments were intended to include such an appropriation. The judgment of Forsyth J in *Canada Trustco Mortgage Corp. v. Port O'Call Hotel Inc.* (1992), 15 CBR (3d) 143 (Alta. QB), at pp. 148-149, summarizes the pre-amendment case law and the effect of the amendment:

In *Lloyds Bank Canada v. International Warranty Co.* (1989), 76 CBR (NS) 54, 68 Alta. LR (2d) 356, [1990] 1 WWR 749, 60 DLR (4th) 272, 97 AR 113, [1990] 2 CTC 360, the Alberta Court of Appeal was considering s. 224(1.2), as it then read ... Stratton JA, who delivered the judgment of the court, stated at p. 362 [Alta. LR]:

Following the decisions in *Lamarre* and *Royal Bank* I am of the view that the proceedings under s. 224(1.2) are at the most a form of extra-judicial attachment which could bring the funds in question into the custody of Revenue Canada. The section falls short of effecting the transfer of property in the funds or establishing priority of Revenue Canada's claim. Something further is required to accomplish either purpose.

That decision was followed by the British Columbia Court of Appeal in *Concorde International Travel Inc. v. TJ Travel Services (British Columbia) Inc.* (1990), 80 CBR (NS) 1, 47 BCLR (2d) 188, 72 DLR (4th) 405. In that decision, Hinkson JA, after referring to the decision of the Alberta Court of Appeal in *Lloyd's Bank Canada, supra*, went on to state at p. 409 [DLR]:

In my opinion, s. 224 styled as it is "Garnishment" deals in s-ss. (1) and (1.2) with the mechanics of garnishment. The Minister in serving a demand pursuant to that section must be proceeding upon the basis that he asserts a tax debtor's liability to him. That justified garnishing the funds in the hands of a creditor of the tax debtor. But, I am unable to see in that section any provision that would have the effect of transferring the property in the funds to the Minister or establishing a priority of Revenue Canada's claim. That was the point dealt with by the Alberta Court of Appeal.

On the other hand, the Saskatchewan Court of Appeal expressly did not follow the Alberta Court of Appeal's decision in *Lloyd's Bank* in the case of *Royal Bank v. Saskatchewan Power Corp.* (1990), 73 DLR (4th) 257, [1991] 1 WWR 1, 86 Sask. R 259, 1 PPSAC (2d) 171, (sub nom. *Royal Bank v. Canada*) [1991] 1 CTC 532. The position taken by the Saskatchewan Court of Appeal was followed in a Nova Scotia trial decision *Touche Ross Ltd. v. Minister of National Revenue* (1990), 71 DLR (4th) 648, (sub nom. *Re Century 21—Crown Real Estate Ltd.*) [1991] 1 CTC 505 (TD). In short, it can be seen that there have been conflicting judicial interpretations of the identical section of the *Income Tax Act* prior to its amendment.

Turning back to the *Excise Tax Act*, which is the statute in question in these proceedings, the first issue I propose to deal with is whether or not the amendment to that section which followed these conflicting decisions had the effect of clarifying the situation.

Forsyth J then states the amendment before continuing [p. 149]:

I am satisfied that the secured lenders as I have labelled them fall within the definition of secured creditor with security interests as defined in s. 317(4) of the *Excise Tax Act*. I am accordingly satisfied that the words "something further," as set out in the quote from Stratton JA, that was required to accomplish the purpose apparently intended has been met by the amendment to the section.

Also cited by the Attorney General was the decision in *Berg v. Parker Pacific Equipment Sales*, 15 February 1991 (BCSC) [reported [1991] 1 CTC 442]. Robinson J said that to describe s. 224(1.2) of the *Income Tax Act* as "draconian" "is apt." However, after a review of several authorities he concluded [pp. 444-445]:

Despite the sympathy with which one must feel for an entity believing itself to have carefully effected a security interest, there is, in my view, no interpretation of this section which can now favour the secured creditor in priority to the claim of Revenue Canada. It should further be noted that any expression of sympathy for the secured creditor is, at least to some extent, countered by the position taken by counsel for Revenue Canada that the funds over which it claims priority is for the exclusive benefit of employees of the tax debtor, who has failed to remit to Revenue Canada, moneys deducted from its employees for tax purposes.

The Attorney General further noted that the phrase "property of the bankrupt" under the *Bankruptcy and Insolvency Act* has been found to include property subject to a security interest irrespective of whether legal title of the property remains in the bankrupt or is transferred to the security holder. This argument flows from *Québec (Commission de la santé & de la sécurité du travail) c. Banque fédérale de développement* (1988), (sub nom. *Federal Business Development Bank v. Québec (Commission de la santé & de la sécurité du travail)* 50 DLR (4th) 577 (SCC), which was stated by Rothstein J in *R. v. National Bank of Canada* (1993), 18 CBR (3d) 35 (Fed. TD), at p. 50, to stand for the proposition, "that the term 'property of the bankrupt' in the *Bankruptcy Act* covers property which is the subject of security in favour of a secured creditor, irrespective of the form in which the security is taken. Whether or not legal title to the property remains with the bankrupt or has been transferred to the security holder is not of importance as long as an equity of redemption remains with the bankrupt or his trustee."

In that I have concluded that pursuant to s. 317(3) Revenue Canada could appropriate the book debts, the next question is whether or not the exclusionary words "other than the *Bankruptcy and Insolvency Act*" which appear solely in the *Excise Tax Act* bring into play other considerations, including the priority sections set out in the *Bankruptcy Act*. Again, I agree with Forsyth J's conclusions in *Canada Trustco, supra*, at pp. 150-151:

Section 136 of the *Bankruptcy Act* establishes a priority regime in relation to the property of the bankrupt. It does not purport to address the distribution of property other than that of the bankrupt ... Section 136 of the *Bankruptcy Act* commences as follows:

136.(1) Subject to the rights of secured creditors, the proceeds realized from the property of a bankrupt shall be applied in priority of payment as follows. ...

I am satisfied that by the virtue of the requirements to pay which had been served prior to the *Bankruptcy Act* coming into effect, the situation is that the secured lenders are not assisted by the opening words of that section. At the time of bankruptcy secured lenders' property entitlement to the moneys in question had already been lost. Accordingly, the excepting out of the provisions of the *Bankruptcy Act* in s. 317(3) of the *Excise Tax Act* does not assist the secured creditors in this instance.

The Trustee submitted that the *Bankruptcy and Insolvency Act* scheme of priorities should take precedence over Revenue Canada's claim under the *Excise Tax Act*. It contended that s. 317(3) of the *Excise Tax Act* specifically excludes itself from affecting priorities established under the *Bankruptcy and Insolvency Act* and that this is made clear from the fact that s. 224(1.2) of the *Income Tax Act* has no such exclusion. This is consistent with the *Bankruptcy and Insolvency Act* in that various government source deductions maintain their "super priority" status under s. 67(3) of the *Bankruptcy and Insolvency Act* while the Goods and Services Tax does not.

The Trustee cited a number of cases to support the proposition that, in the case of a bankruptcy, the priority scheme established under s. 136 of the *Bankruptcy and Insolvency Act* prevails. Under the *Bankruptcy and Insolvency Act* an assignment of book debts in favour of a secured creditor takes priority over any Crown claims notwithstanding any statutory preference to the contrary apart from those Crown claims otherwise referred to in s. 136. *R v. National Bank* (1993), 18 CBR (3d) 35 (Fed. TD), summarizes this area of the law.

However, in my opinion the position of the Attorney General is correct in that the *Excise Tax Act* now provides for an explicit transfer of property from the "particular person" to the government upon receipt of a "demand letter." Therefore, the monies owing were no longer the property of the Bankrupt at the time of the bankruptcy and are not subject to the *Bankruptcy and Insolvency Act*'s scheme of distribution.

The Trustee submitted that Parliament intended, by having the exclusion to the *Bankruptcy and Insolvency Act* in s. 317(3) of the *Excise Tax Act*, that the *Excise Tax Act* would not interfere with the distribution scheme found in the *Bankruptcy and Insolvency Act* upon the bankruptcy of a tax debtor. In my opinion s. 317(3) is specifically phrased so as to overcome the rights of a secured creditor and the distribution scheme of the *Bankruptcy and Insolvency Act*. The case law showed confusion over the exact nature of the government's interest under a s. 317(3) claim and the government clarified this by stating it was a transfer of property to the government upon receipt of a demand letter.

The *Excise Tax Act* legislation does seem harsh to the extent that it allows the government to usurp a secured creditor's security for a tax debtor's previously incurred tax liability. However, a debtor should not be allowed to conduct business yet remain immune from the normal incidents of the legal process, such as liability for the Goods and Services Tax. To the extent Revenue Canada's claim is for Goods and Services Tax incurred through ongoing business after the security agreement was in place, this legislation does not seem unjust. The bank, as a secured creditor, should not be entitled to any more than the tax debtor would have been entitled to had it not assigned its book debts.

Revenue Canada by way of the Goods and Services Tax therefore has priority over the claim of the Trustee in connection with the Requirement to Pay issued to the British Columbia Minister of Finance pursuant to s. 317(3) of the *Excise Tax Act*.

Order accordingly.

NOTE

As will be noted, Thackray J refused to follow the Alberta Court of Appeal's decision in *Canada Trustco Mortgage Corp. v. Port O'Call Hotel* (1994), 24 CBR (3d) 257 (currently on appeal to the Supreme Court of Canada). The Court of Appeal, in a passage not reproduced by Thackray J, distinguished between a security interest in the nature of a charge and a security interest in the form of an assignment of the debtor's title in book debts to the lender. The court further reasoned that where, at the time of the Crown's attempted attachment under ITA s. 224(1.2), the debtor was seriously in default and the amount of the outstanding loan greatly exceeded the assigned book debts, the debtor no longer had an interest in the collateral and the book debts belonged absolutely to the bank. Is this reasoning persuasive? Is it consistent with the provisions in Part 5 of the OPPSA and the clear intent of s. 224(1.2)?

The Search for an Integrated Solution

There have been a variety of proposals over the years to resolve the conflict between Crown liens and consensual security interests. One solution, much favoured by secured creditors, is simply to abolish preferred status altogether for Crown claims. This is in effect what s. 86 of the BIA, added in 1992, does in the bankruptcy context. Another approach, put forward by Prof. Bogart ((1983), 8 *CBLJ* 129), is to require all Crown liens to be registered in the PPS registry and to give them the priority accorded to consensual security interests, and no more. How workable is this solution? So far it has made no apparent impression on provincial authorities but it did influence the drafters of s. 87 of the 1992 amendments. This provides in substance that a Crown lien created under federal or provincial legislation has no effect unless it is registered and that, when registered, it shall rank after all previously perfected security interests. These provisions are further considered below in chapter 17, as well as important exceptions to ss. 86-87.

CHAPTER NINE

Transfer of Collateral: Sellers and Buyers in the Ordinary Course of Business

In previous chapters we have examined the interaction between secured parties and general creditors and their representatives, and among secured parties themselves. In the present chapter we focus on a variety of situations in which policy dictates conferring good title to the collateral on a transferee even though there is a prior perfected security interest in the collateral.

The classic example of such a situation is the title conferred by a sale in ordinary course of inventory where the seller (manufacturer, wholesaler, retailer) has previously given a security in the goods (OPPSA s. 28(1)). Equally important, however, is the protection conferred on holders in due course of negotiable instruments, documents of title and securities under s. 29, and on ordinary course purchasers of chattel papers and instruments under ss. 28(3) and (4).

An inventory financer typically expects to be paid out of the proceeds of sale of the inventory whose acquisition it has financed, and s. 25 of the Ontario Act explicitly recognizes and supports this expectation. Indeed, without it it would be difficult to justify cutting off the inventory financer's security interest in the original collateral. Important questions arise, however, with respect to the perfection of security interests in proceeds and the traceability of proceeds in the form of cash where the cash has become commingled with other funds in the debtor's bank account.

These issues, too, as well as some related problems, are examined in this chapter. The chapter concludes with a revisiting of the status of the English-style floating charge under the OPPSA, having regard to the provisions of the new legislation examined in this and in the preceding chapters.

SALES IN ORDINARY COURSE (SECTION 28(1))

Camco Inc. v. Olson Realty (1979) Ltd.
(1986), 50 Sask. R 161 (CA)

[The issue in this case was whether buyers of household appliances, who purchased them with their condominium units, obtained good title under the Saskatchewan equivalent of OPPSA ss. 28(1) and (2). Section 30(1) of the Saskatchewan Act reads:

30.(1) A buyer or lessee of goods sold or leased in the ordinary course of business of the seller or lessor takes free of any perfected or unperfected security interest therein given by or reserved against the seller or lessor or arising under section 29, whether or not the buyer or lessee knows of it, unless the secured party proves that the buyer or lessee also knows that the sale or lease constitutes a breach of the security agreement.

Muxlow was a real estate developer and manager in Saskatchewan. It developed a condominium project in Regina (the "Cedar Meadows" project) comprising 171 units, which were expected to be sold as a tax shelter. Each unit came equipped with four kitchen appliances, i.e., washer, dryer, refrigerator and stove. All 171 units were sold to individual buyers under a purchase and sale agreement.

The appliances were purchased by Muxlow from Camco, an appliance manufacturer, on conditional sale terms, Camco did not know that Muxlow intended to resell the appliances. Conditions 3 and 4 of the conditional sale agreement provided:

3. The purchaser warrants that as of the date hereof the purchaser is not purchasing the equipment for the purpose of reselling same or any part thereof except that the same be sold with the building in which it is a chattel and then only after the Vendor has been paid in full hereunder.

4. The property in and title to the equipment shall not pass to the purchaser, but shall remain in the vendor until the total unpaid purchase price and any other amounts payable to the vendor by the purchaser have been paid and the purchaser has performed all his obligations pursuant to the Agreement.

Camco duly perfected its security interest by registration under the Saskatchewan PPSA. The individual buyers of the condominium units were not aware that the appliances were subject to a conditional sale agreement. Most unit buyers did not retain their own solicitors but used the legal services provided by Muxlow, which were included in the unit price.

The trial judge, applying s. 30(1), found in favour of the unit buyers. On appeal Camco argued (i) that there were no sales of the appliances to the unit buyers, and (ii) that the sales were not made in the ordinary course of Muxlow's business.]

TALLIS JA (for the Court): I first turn to the appellant's contention that the respondents were not "buyers" of the appliances from Muxlow. As a starting point I observe that the Act does not define "buyer" or "sale." Whether the respondents are "buyers" within the intendment of s. 30(1) is essentially a question of fact for the trial court and that court's determination of the issue should not be disturbed unless the standards of appellate review mandate such intervention.

The appellant asserts that the Condominium Purchase and Construction Agreement with each of the respondent unit purchasers creates the relationship of principal and agent with respect to the appliances. While paragraph 3 of the agreement does appoint Muxlow as agent for certain purposes, the stipulated facts do not support the contention that Muxlow acquired the appliances for the respondents as their agent with the result that no actual sale of the appliances by Muxlow to the respondent unit purchasers took place. Paragraph 5 stipulates that the appliances are included in the purchase price. Muxlow purchased the appliances from the appellant in 1982 and thereafter sold the appliances to the respondent purchasers as and when sales of the condominium units were made.

In this case we have the passing of title to the appliances from the seller (Muxlow) to each of the respondents for a stipulated price. Furthermore, the appliances were delivered to the respondent buyers prior to Muxlow's default under the agreement with the appellant. Accordingly I do not find it necessary or desirable to address technical passage-of-title rules in the factual context of this case. Whether one should look to passage-of-title provisions in other legislation such as the Sale of Goods Act, RSS 1978, c. S-1, when dealing with issues under s. 30(1) of the Act is left open for future consideration.

The conclusion of the learned trial judge on this issue comports with commercial reality and is fully supported by the evidence. I therefore reject this ground of appeal.

Buyer of Goods Sold in the Ordinary Course of Business of the Seller

I now consider the question whether the respondent buyers attained the status of buyers of goods sold in the ordinary course of business of the seller (Muxlow)—a question which involves the application of s. 30(1) and its effect on the appellant's perfected security. For convenience I again recite s. 30(1) of the Act: [see above].

• • •

Speaking generally in the context of this case, this provision is an exception to the priority rules under the Act. It protects such a buyer from a security interest *created by his seller* even though the security interest is perfected and the buyer knows of its existence, unless the buyer also knows that the sale was in violation of the security agreement. Thus, the protective value of "perfection" of a security interest is subject to an important qualification: the security interest remains good against the debtor himself and various third party claimants but not good against certain bona fide purchasers—the buyer of goods sold in the ordinary course of business of the seller. In this case the respondent buyers were not aware of the appellant's security interest. As their good faith is not in issue, I do not need to consider the scope of any such limitation. Furthermore, this case is limited to a consideration of a perfected security interest.

In my opinion s. 30(1) represents an outgrowth of the notion that a "buyer in the ordinary course of trade" should take free of a security interest. In our commercial law the holder in due course of negotiable instruments, the bona fide purchaser of negotiable instruments, the bona fide purchaser of investment securities and various other bona fide purchasers have been accorded privileges—with the result that they sometimes acquire rights better than the rights of some kinds of claimants who did not authorize or approve of the sale or transfer. Thus a special kind of bona fide purchaser of goods is described in s. 30(1)—he must buy goods sold in the ordinary course of business of the seller. Under such circumstances the secured party has no claim against the buyer: he must look to the seller only for satisfaction. The statutory protection extended to such a buyer undoubtedly rests on principles of justice and commercial utility. In many cases the collateral involved is of such a kind that the debtor's ability to dispose of it in the usual course of business may be important so that he can continue his business as a going concern and thereby pay his indebtedness to the secured party. Such a consideration would apply with equal force to authorized sales. But even if this is not so—the security agreement may stipulate to the contrary—the secured party who permits a businessman to have possession of the goods, runs the risk that the buyer taking from the businessman may qualify as a "buyer of goods sold in the ordinary course of business of the seller."

Furthermore one can discern a public policy consideration in the legislation which favours the safeguarding of sales transactions over the safeguarding of secured transactions in such a case. In most cases the seller will pay the secured party but whether he does or does not is of no concern to a person with the status of buyer under s. 30(1). This result is desirable where the buyer is an uninformed consumer buyer.

Learned counsel for the parties appearing on this appeal accordingly focused primary attention on the question who is a "buyer of goods sold in the ordinary course of business of the seller." The Act does not define such a buyer. (This may be contrasted with s. 1-201(9) of the *Uniform Commercial Code* which provides in the relevant part:

"Buyer in ordinary course of business" means a person who in good faith and without knowledge that the sale to him is in violation of the ownership rights or security interest of a third party in the goods buys in ordinary course from a person in the business of selling goods of that kind but does not include a pawnbroker.)

So in considering this issue one must consider the express words of the statute in the context of the functional design and legislative intent of the Act. Since considerable argument centered on the point, I first consider an ancillary issue of law—whether s. 30(1) applies only to security interests in inventory.

•   •   •

While this section is primarily applicable to inventory, I am of the opinion that it is not so limited. It is true that s. 30(1) requires that the buyer buy goods "in the ordinary course of business of the seller" and that such goods would often be inventory of the seller. But there is no explicit language in this section that limits it only to security interests in inventory. Furthermore, I do not find any such intent by implication. In each case the critical question is not whether the applicances are classifiable as inventory but whether the buyer is a buyer of goods sold "in the ordinary course of business of the seller." On this branch of the case I refer to *Hempstead Bank v. Andy's Car Rental System Inc.*, 312 NYS (2d) 317, at 321, where Martuscello J, speaking for the Supreme Court, Appellate Division, said:

Similarly, while the Official Comment to section 9-307 indicates that that section applies primarily to sales from "inventory," it does not indicate that every sale from inventory is protected thereby. Indeed, section 9-307 itself does not even employ the word "inventory." The major consequences of the classification of Andy's cars as inventory is the manner in which any security interest therein is required to be perfected (see UCC ss. 9-302 to 9-305). It would seem, therefore, that the critical question here is not whether the cars are classifiable as inventory, but whether Andy's was "in the business of selling goods of that kind."

I also observe that s. 9-307(1) of the *Uniform Commercial Code* provides:

"A buyer in ordinary course of business" (subsection (9) of Section 1-201) other than a person buying farm products from a person engaged in farming operations takes free of a security interest created by his seller even though the security interest is perfected and even though the buyer knows of its existence.

Until 1956, this subsection read as follows:

In the case of inventory, and in the case of goods as to which the secured party files a financing statement in which he claims interest in proceeds, a buyer in ordinary course of business takes free of a security interest even though perfected and even though the buyer knows of the terms of the security agreement.

Having concluded that s. 30(1) is not limited only to security interests in inventory, I now turn to the appellant's attack on the trial judge's finding that the respondents are buyers under s. 30(1) of the Act. First the appellant submits that the court should take judicial notice of the ordinary manner in which the appliances in question are normally sold. Learned counsel submitted that such appliances are normally sold in retail outlets that deal with such types of chattel. This branch of the argument involved a consideration of security interests in inventory which I have previously discussed. As a further point, the appellant submits that generally a purchaser of realty does not purchase major appliances with realty for a global consideration. Conversely the seller of realty does not normally sell appliances with the realty. Under such circumstances the appellant contends that one who purchases appliances in such an abnormal manner is not a buyer within the intendment of s. 30(1). Consequently such a buyer bears the responsibility of first checking the registry of liens against personal property and if he fails to do so, then he must bear any consequent loss.

The appellant, in asking this court to overturn the trial court's conclusion, asserts that s. 30(1) contemplates an inquiry as to the normal manner in which goods of this type are sold. This suggested approach is probably an outgrowth of the language used in s. 30(1) of the Ontario Personal Property Security Act which provides:

● ● ●

In discussing this Ontario subsection, the learned author of McLaren, *Personal Transactions in Personal Property in Canada* (1979), states at pages 10-31:

A seller will be considered to be dealing in the ordinary course of business if he normally deals in the class of items in which the goods fall and the terms of sale are the same as usually found in that type of business. General commercial practice appears to be the guiding criterion. Factors such as whether or not the transaction is one that is normally entered into by people in the seller's business, where the transaction is executed, the nature of the buyer, the quantity of goods sold, and the price obtained, are proper considerations in determining whether a sale complies with the requirements of s. 30(1).

This approach was also discussed in Catzman et al., *Personal Property Security Law in Ontario* (1976), where the learned authors state at pages 144-145:

The person whose conduct is claimed to come under the description must be engaged in carrying on a business, that business must involve as subjects of traffic things of the class in which the item dealt in falls, and the basis of dealing must be on the normal terms of dealing with that class of items in that type of business. General commercial practice rather than the dealer's particular operating methods is the criterion.

Purchasers

All three subsections speak only of purchasers in the ordinary course of business. Such transactions as mortgages or pledges, even though in ordinary course of business, are not included. The USUCC which speaks of "buying" (the Act substitutes "purchasing") in ordinary course of business specifies that it "may be for cash or by exchange of other property or on secured or unsecured credit and includes receiving under a pre-existing contract for sale, but does not include a transfer in bulk or as security for or in total or partial satisfaction of a money claim."

As to goods, a purchaser's protection under this section arises when the seller sells within the meaning indicated by the foregoing quotation. As to chattel paper or a non-negotiable instrument, there must be such a sale (since the provisions apply only as to purchasers) and additionally the purchaser must take possession. Thus, for goods title passage suffices but for chattel paper and non-negotiable instruments it must be supplemented by a transfer of possession.

Aside from goods, chattel paper, and non-negotiable instruments, there are no special rules about purchasers in ordinary course of business. Thus, for example, dealings in documents of title or securities are not affected by this section.

Whose Course of Business

For goods, the inquiry is whether the seller sells in the ordinary course of business. For chattel paper and instruments, only a purchaser taking possession in the ordinary course of his business receives the protection.

The market for chattel paper and instruments is financial institutions. To be entitled to extraordinary protection, they can fairly be required to show that they were following accepted business practices of such institutions.

The market for goods is the public at large buying for a variety of purposes, non-business as well as business, and a buyer should not be called on to show more than that he bought in the same way as the seller's customers generally.

This question was also canvassed by Linden J, in *Fairlane Boats Ltd. v. Leger et al.* (1980), 1 PPSAC 218, at 222:

Thus in deciding whether a transaction is one that is in the ordinary course of business, the courts must consider all of the circumstances of the sale. Whether it was a sale in the ordinary course of business is a question of fact. (See the Ziegel article, supra, at p. 86.) The usual, or regular type of transaction that people in the seller's business engage in must be evaluated. If the transaction is one that is not normally entered into by people in the seller's business, then it is not in the ordinary course of business. If those in the seller's business ordinarily do enter into such agreements, then, even though it may not be the most common type of contract, it may still be one in the ordinary course of business.

Linden J then went on to articulate the relevant factors in determining the question (at 222 and 223):

... where the agreement is made. If it is at the business premises of the seller it is more likely to be in the ordinary course of business. If it is away from the business premises of the seller, in suspicious circumstances for example, a court may hold that it is not in the ordinary course of business.

The parties to the sale may also be significant, although certainly not controlling. If the buyer is an ordinary, everyday consumer, the likelihood of his being involved in a sale in the ordinary course of business is greater. If the buyer is not an ordinary consumer, but a dealer or financial institution, then the court may take this out of the ordinary course of business, but not necessarily so because dealers and others too may, in proper circumstances, receive the benefit of the provision.

The quantity of the goods sold must also be considered, although this too is not definitive. If there is only one or a few articles sold in the ordinary way, the court is more likely to hold this to be a sale in the ordinary course of business. On the other hand, if a large quantity of items are sold, many more than are sold in the ordinary course of business, and perhaps forming a substantial proportion of the stock of the seller, then the court is less likely to consider it to be in the ordinary course of business.

The price charged for the goods must also be examined, thus if the price charged is in the range of the usual market price, courts are more likely to consider the sale in the ordinary course of business, whereas if the price is unduly low, the courts may hold that this is not a transaction in the ordinary course of business.

In my opinion, these authorities from Ontario, while helpful, must be read with caution. The Ontario Provision is materially different from the Saskatchewan one because of the addition in the Saskatchewan provision of the words "*of the seller.*" These words in our legislation must be considered with the usual regard for rules of statutory interpretation. Accordingly, I would not fasten on such authorities as *Fairline* for a conclusive definition or approach in our jurisdiction. In my opinion, the trial court in deciding this issue in Saskatchewan, must consider the business of the particular seller rather than limit the inquiry to the ordinary course of business in the trade or industry as a whole.

Since the question whether a buyer is a buyer under s. 30(1) is a question of fact, I would not attempt to articulate an all inclusive definition of what is a sale of "goods in the ordinary course of business of the seller." I do however hold that the trier of fact should consider whether the person was a person in the business of selling goods of that kind and whether the transaction(s) took place in the ordinary course of that business. And in my opinion the court should give a generally liberal interpretation to the phrase "buyer of goods sold in the ordinary course of business of the seller," in order to carry out the purpose of s. 30(1)—to protect the buying public in cases where the secured party furnishes goods which are sold to the public by the debtor in the regular course of the debtor's business. This comports with the underlying philosophy of the provision to protect the security interest so long as it does not interfere with the normal flow of commerce.

In my opinion, the conclusion of the learned trial judge on this issue is fully supported by the evidence. In this case the seller was involved in an economic enterprise—he was selling condominium units on a systematic basis—and this fact was known to the appellant as evidenced by the project report. The trial court was not here concerned with an isolated transaction. The mere fact that the seller was engaged in the selling of appliances as an incident to his primary business of selling condominium units does not preclude the operation of s. 30(1).

I accordingly reject the appellant's second ground of appeal.

• • •

Appeal dismissed.

NOTES

1) Do you agree with the above decision? The agreed statement of facts shows that most unit buyers did not retain their own solicitors, as legal services were provided by the developer and were included as part of the purchase price. Should this matter? Would it have made a difference if the buyers had retained their own solicitors to search and report on the status of title of the condominium units they were buying? Were the appliances installed in the condominium units as fixtures? (Recall the provisions in ss. 34 and 54 of the Ontario Act with respect to the perfection of security interests in fixtures.) Should the answer to this question affect the buyers' position?

2) What is the rationale for the rule in OPPSA s. 28(1)? Is it an implicit holding out by the seller's financer that the seller is authorized to sell the goods in his possession or is it the unreasonableness of expecting buyers to search the seller's title and to enquire of the secured party whether the sale meets with its approval? If the second explanation is the correct one, what should be the answer to the following hypothetical?

C, a consumer, buys a vehicle on conditional sale. The security interest is properly perfected. Later C trades in the vehicle to D, a car dealer, in part payment for the purchase of a new vehicle. C warrants that there is no outstanding lien against the trade-in. In fact, money is still owing under the original conditional sale. D sells the trade-in to B, who buys the vehicle in good faith. Does B get a clear title under s. 30(1) and, if not, why not?

3) Section 28(1) has a considerable ancestry both at common law and under earlier legislation. The common law used concepts of implied and ostensible authority or estoppel to reach conclusions favourable to the buyer while statutory precedents were (or are) found in the provincial Factors Acts, ss. 25(1) and (2) of the British Sale of Goods Act and their Canadian counterparts and, most pertinently, in the so-called traders' provisions in the Conditional Sales Acts. See further Ziegel, "The Legal Problems of Wholesale Financing of Durable Goods in Canada" (1963), 41 *Can. Bar Rev.* 54, at 76-84.

4) In the context of secured financing, the common law position first evolved in the 19th century when courts were called upon to decide the effect of a debtor giving a security interest on his stock-in-trade. The effect of the decisions is summed up in the following passage from McRuer CJ's judgment in *Insurance and Discount Corp. v. Motorville Car Sales*, [1953] OR 16, at 30, aff'd [1953] OWN 828 (CA): "The irresistible conclusion from all these cases is that a trader who mortgages his stock-in-trade under a chattel mortgage has implied authority or licence to deal with the mortgaged goods, but that authority is limited to dealing with them in the ordinary course of his business, and nothing more."

While this test sounds favourable to the buyer's position, in fact it falls markedly short of a simple estoppel or ostensible authority test as the decision itself shows.

Express or implied authority was also the basis of the traders' provisions. These were of two kinds. The earlier version was first adopted in Ontario in 1892 and it provided, and continued to provide, that where goods were delivered to a person "for the purpose of resale by him in the course of business" and were resold by him in the ordinary course of his business, then "the property in and ownership of such goods passes to the purchaser notwithstanding that this Act has been complied with." See Conditional Sales Act, RSO 1960, c. 61, ss. 2(3) and (4).

The other and more common version appeared in the Uniform Conditional Sales Act which, as revised in s. 8 of the 1955 revised Act, read:

Where a seller of goods expressly or impliedly consents that the buyer may sell them in the ordinary course of business and the buyer so sells the goods, the property in the goods passes to the purchaser from the buyer notwithstanding the other provisions of this Act.

5) It will be seen that neither version goes as far as s. 28(1) of the OPPSA or its Code source, UCC 9-307(1). Wherein lies the difference? Does s. 28(1) protect the buyer even though the secured party would not have approved the sale and even expressly forbade it? See *Ford Motor Credit v. Centre Motors of Brampton* (1982), 38 OR (2d) 516.

Section 28(2) extends the principle of s. 28(1) to a person who leases goods from a lessor acting in ordinary course of his business. However, neither "buyer" nor "ordinary course of business" is defined, unlike UCC 1-201(9), which provides an extensive definition of "Buyer in ordinary course of business." Note too that while s. 28(1) denies its protection where the buyer knows that the sale constitutes "a breach of the security agreement," UCC 2-201(9) requires the buyer to be without knowledge that the sale to him is "in violation of the ownership rights or security interest of a third party." Is the difference in language significant? Suppose the buyer, a discount store, knows that the secured party has forbidden the seller (a wholesaler, let us assume) to sell the goods to discount stores. Does this deprive the buyer of protection under s. 28(1)? Under UCC 1-201(9)? See *O.M. Scott Credit Corp. v. Apex Inc.* (1964), 198 A. 2d 673 (RISC).

6) Note carefully that s. 28(1) and UCC 9-307(1) only apply to a buyer *of goods* in ordinary course. What principles should be applied to a sale of *non*-goods in ordinary course, e.g., the sale of a mortgage by a mortgage broker? *Cf. In re Urman* (1983), 3 PPSAC 191, reproduced *supra* in chapter 2. Should s. 30(1) be applied analogically or must the court fall back on common law principles?

Royal Bank of Canada v. 216200 Alberta Ltd.
(1987), 51 Sask. R 147 (CA)

VANCISE JA: The issue on this appeal is whether a perfected security interest under the Personal Property Security Act, SS 1979-1980, c. P-6.1, covering all present and after-acquired inventory of a retail vendor, takes priority over the claims of persons who, in the ordinary course of business, have placed a deposit or made a partial payment on goods in the possession of the vendor or prepaid all or a portion of the purchase price of goods not in the possession of the vendor.

I

The respondent 216200 Alberta Ltd. owned and operated The Sofa Factory and The Waterbed General Store in both Saskatoon and Prince Albert, and carried on business as a furniture retailer. In July of 1982, it granted a debenture to the appellant, securing all its present and future assets. The debenture was registered pursuant to the provisions of the Personal Property Security Act, SS 1979-80, c. P-6.1, creating a security interest in all present and after-acquired property of 216200 Alberta Ltd.

The respondent, 216200 Alberta Ltd. defaulted under the debenture and on April 22, 1983, Sirois J made an order appointing Price-Waterhouse Ltd. as receiver and manager (the receiver) of all property and operations of 216200 Alberta Ltd.

Prior to the appointment of the receiver, a number of people had paid all or a portion of the purchase price on furniture they intended to purchase from 216200 Alberta Ltd. In some instances the furniture was in the possession of the vendor, and in others it had been ordered but had not arrived on the date of the appointment of the receiver. Subsequent to receivership, Mr. Justice W.R. Matheson, on May 5, 1983, ordered that the receiver be permitted to deliver to customers personal property in the possession of the receiver for which they had paid the full purchase price.

The appellant brought an application in chambers pursuant to s. 56 of the Personal Property Security Act to obtain a declaration in connection with the following four classes of transactions:

Class One
The status of the claims of persons who have paid the full purchase price for personal property, but the personal property is not in the possession of the defendant.

Class Two
The status of the claims of persons who have paid part of the purchase price for personal property in the possession of the defendant.

Class Three
The status of the claim of persons who have paid part of the purchase price for personal property not in the possession of the defendant.

Class Four
The status of claims of persons to whom cash refunds are owed by the defendant.

The learned chambers judge found that with respect to classes one and three, persons who paid the whole or part of the purchase price to 216200 Alberta Ltd. for goods not in its possession, had paid the money in trust, and with respect to class four, the refunds or rebates were to be held in trust for the purchasers and accordingly all such moneys, paid or due, took priority over the security interest of the appellant. She also found that purchasers under class two who had paid a deposit on goods which were in the possession of the vendor were entitled to priority over the interests of the appellant because they purchased the goods in the ordinary course of business pursuant to the provisions of s. 30(1) of the Act.

II

Priority of a buyer of goods sold in the ordinary course of business pursuant to s. 30(1):

As a general rule, the holder of a perfected security interest has an interest in the secured property and the proceeds from the sale in priority to the interests of unsecured creditors of the debtor, and subsequent purchasers of property take subject to the security agreement. A principal exception to this rule is contained in s. 30(1) which provides as follows:

[See *Camco Inc. v. Olson Realty*, *supra*, for terms of s. 30(1).]

• • •

In order to determine whether or not the exception applies to the second class of transaction, one must determine whether the purchaser is a "buyer" of goods sold in the ordinary course of business. If the person who paid a portion of the purchase price or placed a deposit on goods in the possession of 216200 Alberta Ltd. is not a buyer in the ordinary course of business, the person does not take priority over the secured party but is merely an unsecured creditor whose interest is subordinate to that of the appellants who had a perfected security interest.

The Act does not define "sale" or define "buyer in the ordinary course of business." The Act adopts a generic and functional approach to personal property and is a complete code for granting of security in consensual commercial transactions. Title is not relevant for the purpose of determining whether or not an agreement is a security agreement under the Act. That is, however, a different question from determining whether or not someone is a buyer of goods sold in the ordinary course of business. The appellant contends that before any security can be obtained by a buyer in the ordinary course of business, there must be a sale as contemplated by the provisions of the Sale of Goods Act, RSS 1978, c. S-1. It contends that the priority extends only to "buyers of goods sold in the ordinary course of business," that the word "sold" encompasses the concept of a completed sale, and that to determine whether or not there has been a sale one must have reference to the provisions of the Sale of Goods Act. It contends that title must pass before there can be a sale as contemplated by the section. The alternate approach is that title need not pass, in the strict legal sense, but that the "sale" or "contract to buy" must be made in the ordinary course of business. If "the sale" passes that test, then priority extends to the buyer of the goods. The determination of that issue does not appear to have been dealt with in Canada. There are two approaches which have been taken in the US. One is represented by *Herman v. First Farmers' State Bank of Minier*, 392 NE 2d 344 (1979); 26 UCCR 1350 (Illinois Appellate Court). In that case, the Court considered the application of paragraph 9-307(1) of the Uniform Commercial Code which is equivalent to s. 30(1) of the Personal Property Security Act. That article reads as follows:

• • •

The Code in para. 2-402(b) states that if a contract of sale provides for the delivery by the seller to the buyer, title does not pass until delivery has been made. Notwithstanding that proviso, the Court held that "technical passage of title rules" should not be used to defeat the claim of a buyer in the ordinary course of business. The Court preferred to rely on the ordinary course of business requirement as determining the exception, rather than the question of title. The Court held that whether a person was a buyer in the ordinary course of business is not determined by title, but rather by whether there has been a completed sale in the ordinary way. Transference of title was found to be irrelevant for the purpose of determining whether the sale was ordinary or typical of the trade. It should be noted, however, that there is a difference between s. 30(1) of the Act and para. 9-307(1) of the Code. Section 30(1) speaks of a buyer of goods "sold in the ordinary course of business," while para. 9-307(1) refers only to "a buyer in the ordinary course of business." The question arises as to whether or not the addition of the phrase, "goods sold in the ordinary course of business," imports a further element into the question of the determination of priority under the Act. The code defines "buyer" as "a person who buys or contracts to buy goods." It would appear that it is not necessary, having regard to that definition, for one to actually complete a sale, or for title to pass, before one could be a "buyer" in the ordinary course of business under the Code.

The second line of cases in the US contemplates the actual passage of title before one is entitled to the exemption provided under para. 9-307(1). The case of *Chrysler Corp. v. Adamatic, Inc.*, 208 NW 2d 97 (1973) (Wisconsin Supreme Court) is an example of that approach. There, the question posed by the Court was whether one can be a buyer in the ordinary course of business before a sale has occurred. They concluded that a contract to sell and a contract of sale are not synonymous, and because title had not passed to the buyer he was not a "buyer" in the ordinary course of business. They took the position that a completed sale was necessary before one could become a buyer, notwithstanding that certain inequities might result.

I am of the opinion that before a buyer can take property free of the security interest of the appellant, he must establish that there has been a sale and that he is a buyer in the ordinary course of business. The application of the provisions of the Sale of Goods Act, while not being specifically referred to in s. 30, must be referred to to determine whether or not there has been a sale. Section 3(4) of the Sale of Goods Act [Ont. SGA, s. 2(3)] defines "sale" as follows:

3(4) Where under a contract of sale the property in the goods is transferred from the seller to the buyer the contract is called a sale; but where the transfer of the property in the goods is to take place at a future time or is subject to some condition thereafter to be fulfilled the contract is called an agreement to sell.

Goods are sold when title passes to the buyer and sections 18, 19 and 20 are relevant for the determination of that issue. The import of those sections is that no title passes to the buyer in unascertained goods until the goods are ascertained and appropriated to the sale. When there is a sale of specific or ascertained goods, title passes when the parties intend it to pass. Unless a different intention appears from the documentation, s. 20 sets out the rules for ascertaining the intention of the parties as to the time at which the property or the goods is to pass to a buyer. Rule 1 covers a situation where there is an unconditional sale of a specific item in a deliverable state. Title passes at the time of the making of the contract. Where there was a sale of a specific item of furniture in the possession of 216200 Alberta Ltd., which was in a deliverable state and identified in some fashion as being the goods purchased, title passed on the making of the contract, notwithstanding that the full amount of the purchase price had not been paid. The purchaser, in those circumstances, is entitled to priority over the appellant's security agreement. He is entitled to either the goods, on the payment of the balance of the purchase price, or the return of that portion of the purchase price paid, if the sale was made in the ordinary course of business.

In those cases where there was furniture of the type described in the contract of sale but which was not identified as belonging to the buyer, there has been no appropriation of the goods of this sale as contemplated by s. 19. Title did not pass, the buyer is an unsecured creditor, and the security interest of the appellant takes priority.

The second element which must be satisfied before the buyer obtains the goods free of the security interest of the appellant is whether the sale was "one in the ordinary course of business."

• • •

In my opinion, a sale, in the ordinary course of business, includes a sale to the public at large, of the type normally made by the vendor in a particular business where the basic business dealings between buyer and seller are carried out under normal terms and consistent with general commercial practice. It does not include private sales between individual buyers.

Here the sales of goods of the kind normally sold by the vendor were made at its premises, to members of the public at large, under normal terms and conditions of sale of retail merchants. The sales were clearly sales to buyers in the ordinary course of business.

The two indicia for sale in the ordinary course of business have therefore been met. Those persons who paid part of the purchase price for goods in the possession of the vendor which were in a deliverable state, and identified in some fashion as being the goods purchased, have priority over the security interests of the appellant. Those persons are entitled to the goods, on payment of the balance of the purchase price, or if the goods have been sold, to a return of the amount paid.

Before turning to the remaining classes of transaction, there is one specific case which was argued on the appeal by the respondent John Beattie that must be dealt with, because it does not fit within the four classes of transaction outlined in the notice of motion. Mr. Beattie was given leave to file additional material particularizing his claim on the hearing of this appeal. Briefly stated, on March 11, 1983, he purchased a Simmons hide-a-bed from 216200 Alberta Ltd., on condition that the vendor could supply a matching sofa. The hide-a-bed was in stock, identified and appropriated to the sale. Mr. Beattie gave a salesman of 21620 Alberta Ltd. a cheque for the full amount of the purchase price of the Simmons hide-a-bed. The cheque was marked "not to be cashed until instructed." The invoice bore the notation "if unsuitable will cancel." Notwithstanding these instructions, the cheque delivered to 216200 Alberta Ltd. by Mr. Beattie was negotiated. He was ultimately advised that the manufacturer no longer had fabric to match the hide-a-bed and requested the return of his money. He was promised a refund but did not receive it before 216200 Alberta Ltd. was put into receivership. The appellant claims priority over the claim of Mr. Beattie by reason that the sale was conditional and had not been completed prior to receivership. It contends that all he is entitled to is a refund and as such is an unsecured creditor. I do not agree with that position. The sale of the sofa was completed. Title to the property passed to Mr. Beattie and at the time of receivership the goods were still being held for him by reason that he had not received the refund. As between the appellant as holder of a security interest and Mr. Beattie, a bona fide purchaser for value pursuant to s. 30(1) of goods ascertained and appropriated, he must be taken to have priority.

III

The priority between the appellant and those persons in classes one, three and four are the most difficult to reconcile. It is necessary, in my opinion, to separate classes one and three from class four. The persons in class four are persons entitled to receive a rebate or refund. 216200 Alberta Ltd. was simply indebted to them. They have no perfected interests in the property of 216200 Alberta Ltd., and as between themselves and the appellant are unsecured creditors. It follows that the appellant must in those circumstances take priority.

The persons in classes one and three claim a priority on the basis of a trust relationship which, they contend, gives them a priority over the perfected security interests of the appellant. Shortly stated, they contend that the money paid to 216200 Alberta Ltd. was paid in trust on condition that it be applied on the purchase price on goods to be ordered. None of the goods had arrived or were in the possession of 216200 Alberta Ltd. at the date of receivership. They contend that the money did not become the property of 216200 Alberta Ltd., and as such could not form part of the assets which were covered by the security interest of the appellant. Batten CJQB found:

The moneys so paid over were not intended to become the property of the defendant. The defendant was given the money to ensure that the money would be available as consideration for an agreement for sale should such an agreement be entered into at a later date—when the required merchandise was acquired and made available to the purchaser and approved by the purchaser at which time an agreement to purchase would be entered into. The purchaser would, at that time, pay over the purchase moneys and probably authorize the defendant to retain the deposit as part of the purchase price.

The fundamental question which must be answered is whether the security interest of the appellant to personal property in the possession of the vendor which was perfected under the provisions of the Act can be defeated by an unregistered interest in trusts. That question involves both a legal and policy decision.

The policy of the Act can be divined from the comments made by the Saskatchewan Law Reform Commission in Tentative Proposals for the Saskatchewan Personal Property Security Act at 7:

Any modern personal property security legislation must embody a system designed to protect innocent third parties who might otherwise suffer loss as a result of dealing with a person who has given a security interest in his property. The Commission has concluded that a system which avoids deception in cases where security transactions are involved can be employed with equal effectiveness in cases where certain types of non-security agreements create the same type of deception. It is totally unrealistic to attempt to bring within the scope of the Act every kind of transaction in which deception results from a separation of interest and appearance of interest. However, it is realistic to include in the perfection system of the Act certain types of transactions which because of their commercial importance are likely to continue to produce significant disruption if left out.

The scheme of the Act is to register the security interest as to both goods and proceeds. Any scheme which permits trust classes or devices outside the Act will cause commercial uncertainty and produce disruption in commercial transactions. Here, such facts as are contained in the material are relatively straightforward. The buyers paid all or a portion of the purchase price for furniture which 216200 Alberta Ltd. was to order for them. After the money was paid but before the goods were appropriated to the sale, 216200 Alberta Ltd. was placed in receivership by the appellant. The appellant claims to be entitled to all the personal property of 216200 Alberta Ltd. in priority to the persons who paid all or a portion of the purchase price of goods to be ordered. The contract of sale was made in the ordinary course of business as previously defined, but was for future goods.

How does one categorize the transaction here? Is it one where the purchasers paid a deposit, or part-payment of the purchase price, or a transaction where the purchaser paid money to the vendor in trust not to be applied or used until the happening of certain events, or is it an implied or constructive trust because of the unjust enrichment of the vendor?

The money was paid to 216200 Alberta Ltd. in the ordinary course of business and it became the property of the vendor. In order to determine whether it is impressed with a trust, one must examine the intention of the parties advancing the money. Here there was no evidence that they intended the money to be held in trust. It was not impressed with an express trust and it was not to be kept separate and apart from other funds of 216200 Alberta Ltd. It is possible for the funds to be categorized as a trust in some other way, as for example a constructive trust where the money, the title to which is in 216200 Alberta Ltd., in reality is the property of the purchasers. The constructive trust has been utilized as a remedy for injured parties when there has been an unjust enrichment. There is no evidence that that was the situation here. The sale was one made in the ordinary course of business, utilizing an accepted commercial mode of sale.

In my opinion, the money was paid as a deposit or a partial payment for the purchase price of future goods. The purchaser, in the ordinary course, would be entitled to return of the amount paid to 216200 Alberta Ltd. in the event of default. It is a payment made to secure the transaction and is a debt due from 216200 Alberta Ltd. to the proposed purchasers in the event of default. As between the appellant, as the holder of a perfected security interest, and the persons in the class of transaction described in one and three, the appellant takes priority.

The suggestion has been made that the depositors ought to have protection and take priority over a commercial lender such as the appellant, because the commercial lender is far better able to protect itself from loss and to absorb the loss should one occur. That may be true, but in the circumstances of this case, if such protection is to be provided it is for the legislators to provide and not the courts. It would be relatively easy for the legislature to provide that moneys paid in the circumstances described here would be deemed to be held in trust for the purchaser so as to give it priority over a security interest. The device of a deemed trust and charge has been utilized by the legislature in the Education and Health Tax Act, RSS 1978, c. E-3, to ensure just such a priority.

In the result, the appellant will have priority with respect to those classes of transaction described as one, three and four, but not over the transaction described in two or over the Beattie transaction.

Appeal allowed in part.

NOTES

1) *Royal Bank v. 216200 Alberta Ltd.* should be read in conjunction with the materials in chapter 10 of volume I of this casebook on the sales rules for the transfer of title. As will be noted, the underlying issue in the present case was to what extent the Saskatchewan counterpart to s. 28(1) of the Ontario Act can or should be used to protect prepaying buyers.

2) There have been a number of cases in the United Kingdom over the past 15 years raising the question whether a buyer of fungible goods from a merchant holding them in bulk obtains a property interest in the bulk before the seller has actually segregated or otherwise identified the particular goods to satisfy the buyer's purchase. The issue came to a head with the Privy Council's recent decision *In re Goldcorp Exchange Ltd.*, [1995] AC 74 (reproduced in chapter 10 of volume I of this casebook) on an appeal from New Zealand. Goldcorp was a dealer in bullion and gold coins, including Canadian maple leaf coins ("maples"), and through intensive advertising persuaded many New Zealand investors to buy millions of dollars worth of coins and bullion. Most of the buyers never took delivery of their purchases and Goldcorp never set aside any particular gold bars or coins out of the stock they carried in bulk form to satisfy the contracts. Goldcorp also gave a floating charge on its assets to a bank. Goldcorp became insolvent and the bank appointed a receiver under its debenture. The issue before the Privy Council was whether the investors had a legal or equitable interest in the bullion and gold coins in the receiver's possession. Speaking for the Privy Council, Lord Mustil said they did not. He also refused to grant the investors relief on a theory of a remedial constructive trust. See further J. Beatson, "Proprietary Claims in the Law of Restitution" (1995), 25 *CBLJ* 66 and Donovan Waters, "Proprietary Relief: Two Privy Council Decisions—A Canadian Perspective" (1995), 25 *CBLJ* 90. Since Canadian law *does* recognize remedial constructive trusts the position is more flexible under Canadian law than it is under English law although significant difficulties remain in Canada where there is a competing secured party or the debtor is in bankruptcy. See Prof. Waters' article, *supra*.

3) As explained in the notes to this part of volume I, chapter 10, *supra*, various suggestions have been made over the years for protecting prepaying buyers who do not receive the goods they have paid for. In 1987, the BC Law Reform Commission recommended the adoption of a statutory lien in favour of *consumer buyers* (LRC 93, 1987) and this recommendation was given effect to in 1993 by the addition of Part 9 to the BC Sale of Goods Act. For the details see volume I, chapter 10, *supra*, and Arthur Close, QC, "The British Columbia Buyer's Lien—A New Consumer Remedy" (1995), 25 *CBLJ* 127. The Part 9 lien covers monies held by the seller in an account with a "savings institution" as well as inventory in the seller's possession corresponding in description with the goods for which the buyer has prepaid. Although the buyer's lien is non-possessory the buyer is not obliged to give notice of it under the BC PPSA. Is this consistent with the policy of the Act? How will the seller's inventory and accounts receivable financers be able to protect themselves from such secret liens?

Spittlehouse v. Northshore Marine Inc. (Receiver of)
[1994] 18 OR (3d) 60 (CA)

[The judgment of the court was delivered by Grange JA, dismissing the appeal and concurred in by Doherty and Weiler JJA.]

GRANGE JA: This is an appeal from the order of Keenan J declaring the plaintiffs to be the owners of a certain boat manufactured in Singapore and transported to New Jersey and apparently now in Ontario awaiting the result of this appeal.

The plaintiffs entered into a contract with the defendant Northshore Marina for a Grand Banks 46-foot classic boat for the selling price of $555,000. They have paid 90% of the purchase price and are more than willing to pay the balance upon delivery of the boat as provided in the contract of sale "in the water at Port Credit, Ontario."

The difficulty is two-fold. First, the defendant Transamerica Commercial Finance Corporation has a perfected security interest in all the assets of Northshore including this boat and secondly, the contract of sale provided that "title to the above described equipment shall be transferred to the buyer when the buyer has made payment in full for the equipment."

At some time in the course of delivery of the boat, an official of Northshore Marine advised Transamerica of certain defalcations on its (Northshore's) part including its failure to pass on trust moneys. As a result of this information and a general default on payments by Northshore to Transamerica, the latter perfected its security, appointed the Receiver and through it seized the boat in question. This action resulted.

The claim of the defendants is simply stated. Transamerica has a perfected security against the boat. The plaintiffs have no title to the boat having a contractual not a property interest and can rank only as unsecured creditors against the estate of Northshore. It is conceded that there will be little recovery for those unsecured creditors.

The judge of first instance recognized that the result claimed by the defendants would "produce a result that is manifestly unjust." He accepted "with great reluctance" that the *Sale of Goods Act* rules for ascertaining the passing of title could not be invoked in the plaintiffs' favour but found the plaintiffs to have an equitable interest in the boat which was not defeated by the reservation of title. He considered but felt he did not have to decide whether the plaintiffs were the beneficiaries of a resulting trust of the boat.

In my view, the whole issue is readily resolved by the provisions of s. 28(1) of the *Personal Property Securities Act*, SO 1989 which provides as follows:

28.(1) A buyer of goods from a seller who sells the goods in the ordinary course of business takes them free from any security interest therein given by the seller even though it is perfected and the buyer knows of it, unless the buyer also knew that the sale constituted a breach of the security agreement.

There is no question that in the contract between the plaintiffs and Northshore the latter was acting in the ordinary course of business. It was a dealer in boats and its business was to sell them. The plaintiffs were seeking to buy a boat, indeed the very boat that was the subject of the contract. They had no knowledge of the security agreement between Northshore and Transamerica much less of any breach of that agreement (if indeed there was a breach). The only possible problems are whether the plaintiffs were buyers of the boat and Northshore was the seller. In my opinion they indubitably were.

There is no definition of "buyer" or "seller" in the *Personal Property Security Act* but the transaction between the plaintiffs and Northshore was in common parlance clearly a sale. It is what used to be called a conditional sale and was governed by what was called the *Conditional Sales Act* replaced by the *Personal Property Security Act of 1976* the forerunner of the present Act. The Act is replete with reference to "sales," "purchasers" and "sellers" in reference to the transaction between the conditional vendor and the conditional purchaser. This transaction is a sale with title withheld until the purchase price is fully paid. It is a device to protect the seller until full payment is made and no more. It is valid to the extent that the purchasers cannot demand the transfer of title until all of the purchase price is paid.

This conclusion might seem contrary to that reached by the Saskatchewan Court of Appeal in *Royal Bank of Canada v. 216200 Alberta Ltd.*, 33 DLR (4th) 80, the only Canadian case on the subject I can find. The Court was concerned with the priorities between a secured interest holder and certain customers of an insolvent furniture dealer. Saskatchewan had a section of their PPSA almost identical with ours. When dealing with the status of the claims of persons who have paid part of the purchase price for personal property in the possession of the seller, the court stated:

I am of the opinion that before a buyer can take property free of the security interest of the appellant, he must establish that there has been a sale and that he is a buyer in the ordinary course of business. The application of the provisions of the Sale of Goods Act, while not being specifically referred to in s. 30, must be referred to to determine whether or not there has been a sale. Section 3(4) of the Sale of Goods Act defines "sale" as follows:

3(4) Where under a contract of sale the property in the goods is transferred from the seller to the buyer the contract is called a sale; but where the transfer of the property in the goods is to take place at a future time or is subject to some condition thereafter to be fulfilled the contract is called an agreement to sell.

Goods are sold when title passes to the buyer and ss. 18, 19 and 20 are relevant for the determination of that issue. The import of those sections is that no title passes to the buyer in unascertained goods until the goods are ascertained and appropriated to the sale.

The court reached its conclusion after examining two lines of cases in the United States under Article 9.307(1) of the *Uniform Commercial Code* (similar to our s. 28(1) of the PPSA and s. 30 of the Saskatchewan Act) and specifically approved the case of *Chrysler Corp. v. Adamatic, Inc.* (1973), 208 NW 2d 97, a decision of the Wisconsin Supreme Court which held that a "buyer" was not a "buyer" within the meaning of the Code until title had passed. That decision was in effect reversed by the very court that pronounced it in *Daniel v. Bank of Hayward* (1988), 425 NW 2d 416 in which it was said at pp. 420-21 in words equally appropriate, in my view, to the case at bar:

... The cases and commentaries that have considered the issue since *Chrysler* have generally been critical of the reasoning the court employed in *Chrysler*. ... We conclude that we erred in relying on the date of transfer of title as the date on which a purchaser becomes a buyer in ordinary course of business. Reliance on the concept of title is contrary to the thrust of the *Uniform*

Commercial Code and the commentary. The drafters of the *Uniform Commercial Code* tried to avoid giving technical rules of title a central role in furthering the policies of the *Uniform Commercial Code* [cite omitted]. Although title issues may be of significance in determining some issues under the Code, we conclude that reliance on title to interpret s. 409.307(1) is an unduly narrow and technical interpretation.

In my opinion, the *Sale of Goods Act* is not relevant or material to the resolution of our problem. Here, there was a sale with a seller and a purchaser who between them agreed that title in the goods would not pass until all purchase money was paid. The agreement between them states "the dealer agrees to sell and the buyer agrees to purchase" and refers "to the equipment being purchased" and that such equipment "is being sold." It cannot be regarded as anything but a sale. The *Sale of Goods Act* may affect the time when property in the goods passes but it cannot change what is clearly a sale in another Act into something it is not.

For these reasons, I would not follow the *Royal Bank* case. The plaintiff may take advantage of s. 28(1) of our Act upon tendering the balance of the purchase price and I would dismiss the appeal accordingly.

Appeal dismissed.

NOTE

Grange JA's reasoning in *Spittlehouse* is criticized in a comment by Prof. Ziegel, although he supports the actual result. See Comment (1995), 24 *CBLJ* 457. Among others, Prof. Ziegel makes the following points: (1) Justice Grange was mistaken in ignoring the definitions of "contract of sale," "buyer" and "seller" in the Ontario Sale of Goods Act since the SGA is a basic component of Ontario's commercial law and there is no other source to provide a meaning for these terms where they appear in the OPPSA or in other contexts; (2) the American decisions on UCC 9-307(1) [Article 9's counterpart to s. 28(1)] have to be handled with great circumspection since the property provisions in Article 2 of the Code are not the same as in the SGA. In particular, UCC 2-501 recognizes a special property interest in the buyer's favour on identification of the property to the contract and before full title has been transferred to the buyer; (3) there is no reason to believe that preference for the line of American cases represented by *Chrysler Corp. v. Adamatic* was an essential part of the decision in *Royal Bank*.

Prof. Ziegel concludes, however, that the decision in *Spittlehouse* could have been justfied on other grounds. First, a conditional sale agreement is treated as a security agreement under the OPPSA [s. 2(1)], so it is clear that a buyer under such an agreement is treated as the beneficial owner of the goods and should be so treated for the purposes of s. 28(1). Second, UCC 1-201(9), in defining "buyer in ordinary course of business," explains that "buying" may be for cash or on secured or unsecured credit. This again makes it clear that a buyer is protected under s. 28(1) against the inventory financer's claim even though the seller is retaining a security interest in the goods. This result is also fair since the inventory financer will be able to claim the proceeds from the sale in the seller's hands (OPPSA, s. 25) although admittedly difficulties arise where the goods remain in the seller's hands and the inventory financer does not know that they have been sold. This problem is addressed in part in the case that follows.

Tanbro Fabrics Corp. v. Deering Milliken Inc.
(1976), 39 NY 2d 623 (CA)

BREITEL Chief Judge: In an action for the tortious conversion of unfinished textile fabrics (greige goods), plaintiff Tanbro sought damages from Deering Milliken, a textile manufacturer. Tanbro, known in the trade as a "converter," finishes textile into dyed and patterned fabrics. The goods in question had been manufactured by Deering, and sold on a "bill and hold" basis to Mill Fabrics, also a converter, now insolvent. Mill Fabrics resold the goods, while still in Deering's warehouse, also on a bill and hold basis, to Tanbro.

Deering refused to deliver the goods to Tanbro on Tanbro's instruction because, although these goods had been paid for, there was an open account balance due Deering from Mill Fabrics. Deering under its sales agreements with Mill Fabrics claimed a perfected security interest in the goods.

At Supreme Court, Tanbro recovered a verdict and judgment of $87,451.68 for compensatory and $25,000 for punitive damages. The Appellate Division, by a divided court, modified to strike the recovery for punitive damages, and otherwise affirmed. Both parties appeal.

The issue is whether Tanbro's purchase of the goods was in the ordinary course of Mill Fabrics' business, and hence free of Deering's perfected security interest.

There should be an affirmance. Mill Fabrics' sale to Tanbro was in the ordinary course of business, even though its predominant business purpose was, like Tanbro's, the converting of greige goods into finished fabrics. All the Uniform Commercial Code requires is that the sale be in ordinary course associated with the seller's business (§9-307, subd. [1]). The record established that converters buy greige goods in propitious markets and often in excess of their requirements as they eventuate. On the occasion of excess purchases, converters at times enter the market to sell the excess through brokers to other converters, and converters buy such goods if the price is satisfactory or the particular goods are not available from manufacturers. Both conditions obtained here.

Tanbro and Mill Fabrics were customers of Deering for many years. Goods would be purchased in scale on a "bill and hold" basis, that is, the goods would be paid for and delivered as the buyers instructed. When the goods were needed, they were delivered directly where they were to be converted, at the buyers' plants or the plants of others if that would be appropriate. Pending instructions, the sold and paid for goods were stored in the warehouses of the manufacturer, both because the buyers lacked warehousing space and retransportation of the goods to be processed would be minimized.

Mill Fabrics, like many converters, purchased greige goods from Deering on credit as well as on short-term payment. Under the sales notes or agreements, all the goods on hand in the seller's warehouse stood as security for the balance owed on the account. Tanbro was familiar with this practice. It was immaterial whether or not particular goods had been paid for. If the goods were resold by Deering's customers, Deering obtained for a period a perfected security interest in the proceeds of resale for the indebtedness on the open account (Uniform Commercial Code, §9-306, subds. [2], [3]).

Deering's sales executives advised Tanbro's that it had discontinued production of a certain blended fabric. Upon Tanbro's inquiry, the Deering sales executives recommended to Tanbro that it try purchasing the blended fabric from Mill Fabrics, which Deering knew had an excess supply. Ultimately, Tanbro purchased from Mill Fabrics through a broker 267,000 yards at 26 cents per yard. Tanbro paid Mill Fabrics in full.

During October and November of 1969, approximately 57,000 yards of the blended fabric was released by Deering on Mill Fabrics' instructions and delivered to a Tanbro affiliate. There remained some 203,376 yards at the Deering warehouse.

In early January of 1970, Tanbro ordered the remaining fabric delivered to meet its own contractual obligation to deliver the blended fabric in finished state at 60 cents per yard. Deering refused.

By this time Mill Fabrics was in financial trouble and its account debit balance with Deering at an unprecedented high. In mid-January of 1970, a meeting of its creditors was called and its insolvency confirmed.

As noted earlier, under the terms of the Deering sales agreements with Mill Fabrics, Deering retained a security interest in Mill Fabrics' "property" on a bill and hold basis, whether paid for or not. This security interest was perfected by Deering's continued possession of the goods (Uniform Commercial Code, §1-201, subd. [37]; §9-305). Tanbro argued that if it had title by purchase its goods were excluded from the security arrangement which was literally restricted to the "property of the buyer," that is Mill Fabrics. In any event, unless prevented by other provisions of the code, or the sale was not unauthorized, Tanbro took title subject to Deering's security interest.

Under the code (§9-307, subd. [1]) a buyer in the ordinary course of the seller's business takes goods free of even a known security interest so long as the buyer does not know that the purchase violates the terms of the security agreement. As defined in the code (§1-201, subd. [9]) "a buyer in ordinary course" is "a person who in good faith and without knowledge that the sale to him is in violation of the ownership rights or security interest of a third party in the goods buys in ordinary course from a person in the business of selling goods of that kind but does not include a pawnbroker. 'Buying' may be for cash or by exchange of other property or on secured or unsecured credit and includes receiving goods or documents of title under a preexisting contract for sale but does not include a transfer in bulk or as security for or in total or partial satisfaction of a money debt." Critical to Tanbro's claim is that it purchased the goods in the ordinary course of Mill Fabrics' business and that it did not purchase the goods in knowing violation of Deering's security interest.

Under the code whether a purchase was made from a person in the business of selling goods of that kind turns primarily on whether that person holds the goods for sale. Such goods are a person's selling inventory. (Uniform Commercial Code, §1-201, subd. [9]; §9-307, subd. [1]; Official Comment, at par. 2.) Note, however, that not all purchases of goods held as inventory qualify as purchases from a person in the business of selling goods of that kind. The purpose of section 9-307 is more limited. As indicated in the Practice Commentary to that section, the purpose is to permit buyers "to buy goods from a dealer in such goods without having to protect himself against a possible security interest on the inventory" (Kripke, Practice Commentary, McKinney's Cons. Laws of NY, Book 62½, Uniform Commercial Code, §9-307, p. 491, par. 1). Hence, a qualifying purchase is one made from a seller who is a dealer in such goods.

A former Mill Fabrics' employee testified that there were times when Mill Fabrics, like all converters, found itself with excess goods. When it was to their business advantage, they sold the excess fabrics to other converters. Although these sales were relatively infrequent they were nevertheless part of and in the ordinary course of Mill Fabrics' business, even if only incidental to the predominant business purpose. Examples of a nonqualifying sale might be a bulk sale, a sale in distress at an obvious loss price, a sale in liquidation, a sale of a commodity never dealt with before by the seller and wholly unlike its usual inventory, or the like (see *National Bank of Commerce v. First Nat. Bank & Trust Co. [Tulsa]*, 446 P. 2d 277, 282 [Okl.]; *cf. Sternberg v. Rubenstein*, 305 NY 235, 239, 112 NE 2d 210, 211; *Whitmire v. Keylon*, 12 UCC Rept. Serv. 1203, 1206-1207 [Tenn.]).

The combination of stored, paid for goods, on a hold basis, and the retention of a security interest by Deering makes commercial sense. Mill Fabrics' capacity to discharge its obligation to Deering was in part made possible because it sold off or converted the goods held at the Deering warehouse. Mill Fabrics, as an honest customer, was supposed to remit the proceeds from resale or conversion to Deering and thus reduce, and eventually discharge its responsibility to Deering. Thus, so long as it was customary for Mill Fabrics, and in the trade for converters, to sell off excess goods, the sale was in the ordinary course of business. Moreover, on an alternative analysis, such a sale by Mill Fabrics was therefore impliedly authorized under the code if its indebtedness to Deering was to be liquidated (see Official Comment to §9-307, par. 2; *Draper v. Minneapolis Moline*, 100 Ill. App. 2d 324, 329, 241 NE 2d 342).

All subdivision (1) of section 9-307 requires is that the sale be of the variety reasonably to be expected in the regular course of an on-going business (see *Newton-Waltham Bank & Trust Co. v. Bergen Motors*, 68 Misc. 2d 228, 230, 327 NYS 2d 77, 81, affd., 75 Misc. 2d 103, 347 NYS 2d 568; *cf. First Nat. Bank, Martinsville v. Crone*, 301 NE 2d 378, 381 [Ind. App.]). This was such a case.

• • •

Order of Appellate Division affirmed.

NOTES

1) *Tanbro Fabrics* triggered a lively debate between those who thought it was wrongly decided and those who defended it as correctly interpreting the intent of UCC 9-307(1). Prof. Kripke falls into the first category. See Kripke, "Should Section 9-307(1) of the Uniform Commercial Code Apply Against a Secured Party in Possession?" (1977), 33 *Bus. Lawyer* 2607.

Prof. Kripke accepts the fact that the buyer need not obtain possession of the goods in order to secure the protection of UCC 9-307(1), but he argues that 9-307(1) was never intended to apply to a case where the secured party has retained possession of the goods as security for the debtor's obligation. He reasons as follows (*ibid.*, at 159-60):

The difference between a possessory security interest perfected by virtue of the possession and a non-possessory security interest perfected by filing is more than a difference between alternate methods of perfecting the security interest, which methods Article 9 treats equally, in general.

The fact of possession in the secured party, the pledge relationship, means that the secured party has taken the goods out of the hands of the debtor (or withheld them from the debtor) and thus has made it impossible for the debtor to take any advantage from his apparent ownership of the goods as evidenced by possession or to exhibit them or to deliver them upon sale. Until this case I believe that it was always assumed that possession of the secured party protected him from being surprised by a sudden devastation of his security through sales by the debtor to buyers in the ordinary course of business. For this reason, even though the Code facilitated perfection by filing of security interests on shifting inventories, some secured parties demanded warehouse arrangements through field warehousemen, thus exerting a physical control over the goods. Until this case, I believe it was thought that this precluded the debtor from selling the goods out to a buyer in ordinary course of business, thus leaving the secured party to try to recoup from the proceeds if he could find and obtain them from a debtor to whom the secured party had refrained from entrusting them. Field warehousing arrangements are widely used even though the lenders frequently perfect the security interests by filing. The possession of the goods by field warehousemen is not just a means of perfection, which can be accomplished by filing, but it adds something else. Or at least it was thought to do so until now.

It is, of course, true that when a buyer in ordinary course of business buys goods "from a person in the business of selling goods of that kind" (section 1-201(9)), the buyer's entitlement to the protection of section 9-307(1) cannot be precluded—so long as the debtor is in possession of the goods by the secured party and debtor contracting, or purporting to contract, that the debtor does not have liberty of sale. It does not follow that the same result should apply when possession of the goods has been withheld from the debtor (and apparent ownership denied to him) for the very purpose of protecting the seller's normal right to payment before he surrenders the goods, sections 2-507, 2-511. ...

Are you persuaded by this reasoning or do you agree with Mr. Birnbaum's reply that Prof. Kripke is confusing the position of a buyer who knows there is an outstanding security interest with the position of a buyer who knows the seller is selling *in violation* of the inventory financer's interest?

2) Prof. Kripke's concession that UCC 9-307(1) does not require the buyer to take possession of the goods is not made by other scholars. The late Prof. Robt. Braucher's recollection was that Karl Llewellyn thought it obvious that there could be no "buying" without the buyer receiving delivery of the goods. See Baird and Jackson, *Security Interests in Personal Property* (1984), at 767. Prof. Skilton, on the other hand ((1974), *Wis. L Rev.* 1, at 20), thought that the omission in UCC 1-201(9) to the need for delivery of the goods was deliberate. See also "Comment" (1981), 60 *Neb. L Rev.* 848 and *cf.* the provisions in Ontario SGA, s. 25(2) and the Factors Act, s. 2(1), both of which require transfer of possession. Is the secured party prejudiced by the buyer's not taking possession of the goods?

3) *Protection of private buyers of goods or motor vehicles.* As will have been noted, OPPSA 28(1) only protects buyers in ordinary course, not those buying privately. There is, however, a modest trend in the Canadian legislation to protect private buyers of goods or of a motor vehicle in limited circumstances even though there is a prior perfected security interest. The following are important examples:

a) *Goods brought into the province from another jurisdiction.* Section 5(2) of the Ontario Act allows the holder of an extraprovincial perfected security interest in goods 60 days to reperfect the security interest in Ontario after the goods are brought into the province (or 15 days after she received notice of the removal of the goods, whichever is earlier). The 60-day grace period does not apply where a buyer or lessee acquired the goods in Ontario *as consumer goods*, in good faith, and without knowledge of the prior security interest. (The Western provincial Acts do not restrict the exception to transferees of consumer goods.)

b) *Section 20(3)*. The 10-day grace period allowed by the subsection to the holder of the PMSI in collateral to perfect the security interest does not apply to a bona fide purchaser of the collateral who gives value and receives delivery of the collateral without knowledge of the security interest.

c) *Section 30(2) of the Saskatchewan Act*. (A similar provision appears in the Alberta and British Columbia Acts.) Section 30(2) protects a bona fide buyer or lessee of goods bought for *consumer or farming use* (whether or not the sale or lease occurs in the seller's ordinary course of business), but this exception does not apply to (a) a motor vehicle, (b) fixtures, or (c) goods whose purchase price exceeds $500 or, in the case of a lease, whose retail market price exceeds $500.

d) *OPPSA, s. 28(5)*. This exception enures for the benefit of the buyer of any motor vehicle classified as equipment of the seller unless the vehicle identification number (VIN) appears on the registered financing statement. A comparable provision, applying to motor vehicles claimed as proceeds, appears in s. 25(3). (Under the Ontario PPS Regulations VINs are only mandatory for consumer vehicles.) This exception was incorporated in the new Act at the request of the Ontario registry officials to make it possible in every case for the purchaser of a vehicle to check for prior security interests by checking against the vehicle's VIN. "Motor vehicle" is broadly defined in the Regulations and includes tractors, bulldozers, and other self-propelling equipment.

Do the above exceptions have a common rationale? Do they go far enough? Do they go too far? Do they overcome the "A-B-C-D" problem?

TRANSFEREES OF INSTRUMENTS, DOCUMENTS OF TITLE AND SECURITIES

Jacob S. Ziegel
"Perfection by Registration, Instruments, Securities, Documents of Title, and the Personal Property Security Act 1989"
(1989), 15 *CBLJ* 242 (footnotes omitted)

One of the many important changes introduced in the recently adopted Personal Property Security Act 1989 in Ontario (the "new Act") is the rule in s. 23 that a security interest in any type of collateral may be perfected by registration. This means *inter alia* that a security interest in instruments, securities, letters of credit and advices of credit, and in negotiable documents of title may be perfected by registration. This was not possible under the earlier Ontario Act ("old Act") where the general rule was that a security interest in these types of collateral could only be perfected by taking possession of the collateral.

Some banking and securities lawyers have queried how the new provisions will affect "overnight loans" and other well established forms of short term financing in the securities and banking industry. The short answer is that they will not be adversely affected but before explaining why this is so I should explain why the perfection rules were changed in the new Act. The earlier rules were largely borrowed from Article 9 of the Uniform Commercial Code where perfection by registration of a security interest in instruments, securities and letters of credit is not allowed because the "universal" American practice is for the secured party to take possession of the collateral. This is not true in Canada where it has long been the practice for a fixed and floating charge to embrace all of the debtor's assets, and for the secured party to allow the debtor to remain in possession of the collateral until the floating charge is crystallized. This difference was first pointed out by the Committee of the Canadian Bar Association that drafted the Uniform Personal Property Security Act 1982, and it led the Committee to change the Code rule to permit perfection by registration in all cases. The Minister's Advisory Committee in Ontario on the Personal Property Security Act agreed with the CBA Committee's reasoning and as a result s. 23 was introduced in the new Act.

Still, it may be asked, if perfection by registration is not intended to affect the rights of third parties dealing in good faith with instruments, securities and documents of title, why should the secured party bother filing a financing statement? The answer is because it will protect the secured party against the claims of unsecured creditors of the debtor and in particular against the claims of a trustee in bankruptcy. This result comes about because s. 9(1) of the new Act provides (as did the old Act) that except as provided "by this or any other Act" a security agreement is effective according to its terms between the parties to it and against third parties. The rights of third parties are spelled out in Part III of the Act. An unperfected security interest is subordinated, *inter alia*, to the claims of a lien creditor and a trustee in bankruptcy (s. 20(1)(a) and (b)). If the security interest has been perfected paras. 1(a) and (b) do not apply and the secured party's interest prevails unless there is another provision in the Act protecting the rights of unsecured creditors and of a trustee in bankruptcy. There is no such provision.

The Position of Bona Fide Transferees

It is otherwise in the case of designated types of consensual transferees. The old Ontario Act already contained a substantial group of provisions in ss. 27, 30 and 31 permitting qualified transferees to override an existing perfected security interest. The new Act (ss. 25(1), 28 and 29) has substantially expanded the list in favour of transferees of instruments, negotiable documents of title, and securities. Before dealing with the new provisions, a word needs to be said about two exceptions carried forward from the old Act.

1. *Section 25(1)(a)*. This familiar provision (previously s. 27(1)(a)) states that where the collateral gives rise to proceeds the security interest continues in the collateral, "unless the secured party expressly or impliedly authorized the dealing with the collateral." Suppose an investment dealer has given a bank a general security interest in all of its assets and that the dealer continues to buy and sell its inventory of securities as before. Will the purchasers acquire a good title free of the bank's security interest? If the security agreement expressly authorizes the dealer to continue to carry on business the answer will be obvious: "yes."

The same conclusion should follow if the security agreement purports to create a fixed and floating charge over the dealer's assets in the bank's favour. The common law distinction between a fixed and floating charge is abolished in s. 11(2) of the new Act and, unless the parties have otherwise agreed, a security interest in the nature of a floating charge is deemed to attach as soon as the usual prerequisites of attachment (a security agreement, value, and the debtor's having rights in the collateral) have been satisfied. Notwithstanding the explicit language of s. 11(2), a very plausible argument can be made that by describing its interest as a floating charge the bank has implicitly authorized the dealer to continue with its business. This is because some meaning must be given to the use of the words "floating charge" in the security agreement.

Even if the words floating charge do not appear in the agreement, transferees have other cards up their sleeve. I am not aware of any reported PPSA jurisprudence in Canada construing the meaning of "impliedly authorized the dealing with the collateral" in s. 25(1)(a). However, there is abundant jurisprudence at common law and under the "dealer's" provision in the old Conditional Sales Acts holding that a dealer who has given a chattel mortgage on his inventory or who has bought inventory on a conditional sale basis has implied authority to dispose of the inventory in the ordinary course of business. The same reasoning, it seems to me, is apposite where the debtor's "inventory" consists of shares, bonds, instruments or whatever. If the secured party knows that the investment dealer is continuing to deal with its securities and does nothing to stop the dealer, the transferees will be in a still stronger position. The secured party will then be estopped from denying its consent whether or not there was any implied consent. Section 72 of the new Act expressly preserves the principles of law and equity as applicable to secured transactions unless inconsistent with the express terms of the Act. Estoppel is of course a basic common law principle.

2. *Section 28(1) (formerly s. 30(1))*. Section 28(1) of the new Act is a classic embodiment of the estoppel principle and illuminates the point made in the preceding paragraph. True, subsec. (1) speaks only of a buyer of "goods" from a seller who sells the goods in the ordinary course of business but there is no reason to read "goods" so literally. If the collateral constitutes inventory in the debtor's hands then, in the interests of security of transactions, buyers should be entitled to assume that the dealer is authorized to dispose of them in ordinary course.

Sections 25(1)(a) and 28(1) are two general provisions in the new Act enuring in the transferee's favour. I must now deal with the three new provisions specifically directed to the protection of purchasers of instruments, negotiable documents of title, and securities. These are as follows.

3. *Section 28(4)*. This reads:

(4) A purchaser of collateral that is an instrument or negotiable document of title has priority over any security interest therein perfected by registration or temporarily perfected under section 23 or 24 if the purchaser,

(a) gave value for the interest purchased;

(b) purchased the collateral without knowledge that it was subject to a security interest; and

(c) has taken possession of the collateral.

Section 28(4) is borrowed from s. 28(7) of the Uniform Act and has its counterpart in Article 9. The rationale of subsec. (4) is that a purchaser of negotiable or quasi-negotiable paper should not be obliged to search the PPS registry before consummating a transaction because that would defeat the essential qualities of these types of collateral. If the secured party does not have sufficient confidence in the integrity and solvency of the debtor then it should not leave the collateral in the debtor's possession.

Subsection (4) has a substantial number of technical components. "Purchaser" and "purchase" are defined in s. 1. The important point to note is that they have much broader meaning than the layperson's understanding of the terms. In particular, "purchaser" includes a secured party. In other words, a lender making a secured loan to the debtor can override a prior perfected non-possessory security interest in an instrument or negotiable document, provided the lender takes possession of the collateral and satisfies the other requirements of subsec. (4).

"Instrument" is defined in s. 1 and again has a wider meaning than might at first be supposed. It covers not only negotiable money obligations under the federal Bills of Exchange Act but also "any other writing that evidences a right to the payment of money and is of a type that in the ordinary course of business is transferred by delivery with any necessary endorsement or assignment." A debenture made payable to order or to bearer is a good example, assuming it does not fall within the definition of "security" in s. 1. "Document of title" is defined in s. 1 but not "negotiable document of title." Ontario does not have a documents of title Act corresponding to Article 7 of the Uniform Commercial Code but some guidance may be derived from the definition of "negotiable receipt" in s. 1(e) of the Warehouse Receipts Act and from the other provisions in the Act dealing with the negotiation of warehouse receipts.

A transferee under s. 28(4) must satisfy three requirements to override the prior security interest. First, he must have given value. "Value" is defined in s. 1 as any consideration sufficient to support a simple contract. Unlike UCC 9-308 and s. 28(3) of the Ontario Act, subsec. (4) does not require the giving of *new* value. The second requirement is that the transferee must have purchased the collateral "without knowledge" that it was subject to a security interest. "Knowledge" is defined in s. 69 of the Act. In practice s. 69(c) is likely to be the applicable paragraph. It provides that, in the case of a corporation, the knowledge must have come to the attention of a senior employee of the corporation with responsibility for matters to which the information relates "under circumstances in which a reasonable person would take cognizance of it." To translate this test into a concrete situation, the fact that counsel in the lender's legal department knows that the debtor has given a prior general security interest to Financial Institution X will not defeat the lender's specific loan to the debtor against the possessory security of a negotiable bill of lading or warehouse receipt if the loan manager was not aware of the prior security interested. It is *his* state of knowledge, not counsel's, that is relevant if only the loan manager was involved in making the loan decision and completing the transaction.

Finally, s. 28(4)(c) requires that the purchaser must have taken possession of the collateral. The Act does not define what constitutes possession but s. 22 makes it clear, for purposes of perfecting a security interest, that possession must be by the secured party or on its behalf "by a person other than the debtor or the debtor's agent." It seems safe to assume that possession will be given at least this much meaning in s. 28(4).

4. *Section 28(6)*. This subsection applies to the *bona fide* purchaser of a security and is the counterpart for securities of s. 28(4). Its terminology is slightly different because the drafters were anxious to maintain conceptual and terminological consistency with Part VI of the Business Corporations Act, 1982 ("OBCA"). Unhappily the marriage is not entirely successful and the Ontario drafters might have been better off to follow the lead of UCC 8-313, 8-321 and 9-302(1)(f) in letting Part VI deal exclusively with the creation and perfection of security interests in security.

Leaving aside this general observation, the following more technical features of s. 28(7) should be noted. The definition of "security" in s. 1 of the new Act is substantially the same as the definition in s. 53(1)(u) of the OBCA although there appears to be at least one, probably unintended, difference between the definitions. Second, s. 28(8) of the new Act provides that "bona fide purchaser" in subsecs. 6 and 7 has the same meaning as in s. 53(1)(d) of the OBCA. It is there defined as meaning

(d) ... a purchaser for value, in good faith and without notice of any adverse claim,

(i) who takes delivery of a security certificate in bearer form or order form or of a security certificate in registered form issued to him or endorsed to him or endorsed in blank,

(ii) in whose name an uncertificated security is registered or recorded in records maintained by or on behalf of the issuer as a result of the issue or transfer of the security to him, or

(iii) who is a transferee or pledgee as provided in section 85;

"Adverse claim" is defined in OBCA s. 53(1)(a). The definition does not expressly refer to a security interest but it may safely be assumed that the reference in the definition to a "particular adverse person is the owner of or has an interest in the security" is broad enough to include a security interest.

In the third place, s. 28(6) tracks s. 28(4) of the new Act as well as s. 69(1) of the OBCA in requiring the *bona fide* purchaser to take possession of the security to qualify as a purchaser. The requirement creates difficulties in the case of an uncertificated security since the whole purpose of a central depository for securities is to avoid the need for the handling of security certificates. Arguably, the definition of *bona fide* purchaser in OBCA s. 53(1)(d), coupled with the provisions in s. 85(1), is broad enough to dispense with the need for delivery in the case of uncertificated securities. It is understood in any event that a small amendment will be made to the OBCA in the next series of OBCA amendments to make it clear that a notation of the transfer or pledge on the records of the depository will be equivalent to delivery of the security itself.

5. *Section 28(7)*. This entirely new provision was added at the committee stage of the new Act to meet the concerns of lawyers who were worried about the effect on its rights of a purchaser under s. 28(6) who knows that the debtor has given a prior non-possessory security interest to a secured party. It was argued that this should not preclude a professional lender to or buyer from, say, an investment dealer, acquiring a superior interest in the collateral, and the analogy was invoked of the protection afforded under s. 28(1) of the new Act to a person buying goods from a dealer who sells them in the ordinary course of his business.

The Minister's Advisory Committee thought the argument was plausible and agreed to the amendment. However, it appears that s. 28(7) goes farther than s. 28(1). Section 28(1) requires the seller to be selling the goods "in the ordinary course of business." This obviously means the dealer's business. Section 28(7) only requires *the purchaser* to purchase the security in the ordinary course of business. This appears to refer to the purchaser's business and not the debtor's business. Can the difference be justified? Should the purchaser be protected even though the debtor is not a dealer in securities and the purchaser knows of the prior security interest? It seems to me the difference can only be justified if it can fairly be argued that the professional purchaser of a security should always be entitled to assume that a debtor has implied authority to deal with the security as long as he confines his dealings to a professional purchaser.

6. *Section 29.* Section 29 is not new—it is only a modified version of s. 31(1) of the old Act—but a reference to it is necessary to round out the discussion of the s. 28 provisions. Section 29 provides *inter alia* that the rights of a holder in due course of a bill, note or exchange under the BOE "are to be determined without regard to this Act." There is clearly some overlap between this provision and s. 28(6) since, as has been noted, the definition of security in s. 1 of the new Act includes instruments governed by the BOE. The overlap could have been avoided by limiting s. 28(6) to non-negotiable instruments, but it is harmless. Assuming there is a difference in the practical effect of ss. 28(6) and 29 (which is doubtful), the BOE should prevail since the federal government has paramount jurisdiction over negotiable instruments. "Holder in due course" is defined in part in s. 56 of the BOE as a holder who took the bill in good faith and for value and without notice, at the time the bill was negotiated, of any defect in title of the person who negotiated the bill to him. "Defect in title" is not defined in the Act and, curiously, the leading Canadian text on bills of exchange does not indicate whether a subsisting security interest amounts to a defect in title.

Even if astonishingly it were not so, it would surely be held that the debtor's negotiation of a bill in violation of the express or implied terms of the security agreement would be bad faith negotiation under BOE, s. 56(2), and notice of it would deny the transferee the status of a holder in due course. It is a thoroughly well established proposition of bills of exchange law that notice under s. 56 means actual notice of the debilitating facts or wanton disregard of such circumstances as would have enabled the transferee to learn the true facts. Constructive notice or negligent behaviour is not sufficient.

Section 29 does not provide, as did s. 31(2) of the old Act, that registration under the Ontario Act is not such notice as to affect the rights of persons mentioned in subsec. (2). Subsection (2) was deleted because the drafters felt it was redundant, and it was redundant because the new Act has not retained the constructive notice provision in old s. 53. (The provision did not apply in any case to instruments, letters of credit, advices of credit, or negotiable documents of title.) Even if the provision had been retained, it is unlikely that it could have changed the meaning of "notice" in a federal Act.

Conclusion

The reader may feel that a sledge hammer has been used in this Comment to crack a relatively small nut. Perhaps so, but on examination the nut turns out to have a large number of wrinkles. Legal nuts usually do. In any event, it should be abundantly clear that purchasers of instruments, negotiable documents of title, and securities are very adequately protected under the Personal Property Security Act 1989.

TRANSFER OF CHATTEL PAPER (SECTION 28(3))

"Chattel paper" is defined in OPPSA s. 1 as meaning "one or more than one writing that evidences both a monetary obligation and a security interest in or a lease of specific goods." Typical examples of chattel paper are conditional sales and chattel mortgages that are generated when goods are sold on credit by a retailer and the seller retains a security interest in the goods. The Code explains commercial practices with respect to such paper:

... Such paper has become an important class of collateral in financing arrangements, which may—as in the automobile and some other fields—follow an earlier financing arrangement covering inventory or which may begin with the chattel paper itself.

Arrangements where the chattel paper is delivered to the secured party who then makes collections, as well as arrangements where the debtor, whether or not he is left in possession of the paper, makes the collections, are both widely used, and are known respectively as notification (or "direct collection") and non-notification (or "indirect collection") arrangements. In the automobile field, for example, when a car is sold to a consumer buyer under an installment purchase agreement and the resulting chattel paper is assigned, the assignee usually takes possession, the obligor is notified of the assignment and is directed to make payments to the assignee. In the furniture field, for an example on the other hand, the chattel paper may be left in the dealer's hands or delivered to the assignee; in either case the obligor may not be notified, and payments are made to the dealer-assignor who receives them under a duty to remit to his as-signee. The widespread use of both methods of dealing with chattel paper is recognized by the provisions of this Article, which permit perfection of a chattel paper security interest either by filing or by taking possession.

(UCC 9-308, Official Comment, para. 1.)

The common law does not recognize chattel paper as a separate category of specialty; instead it insists on disaggregating such paper into its component parts of an interest in goods (the seller's retention of title) and a chose in action (the buyer's debt) and applying separate rules to the transfer of each. See e.g., *Re George Inglefield*, [1933] 1 Ch. 1 and *Olds Discount Co. Ltd. v. John Playfair Ltd.*, [1938] 3 All ER 275. See further Ziegel, "Wholesale Financing of Durable Goods ..." (1963), 41 *Can. Bar Rev.* 54, at 110-14. (Recall the similar problems with respect to realty mortgages discussed, *supra*, in chapter 2.) The following case illustrates the problem in a modern setting.

In the Matter of Leasing Consultants, Inc.
(1973), 486 F.2d 367 (CCA 2)

JAMESON District Judge: Respondent-Appellant, First National City Bank (Bank), ap-peals from an order of the district court affirming, on a petition for review, the order of a referee in bankruptcy directing the Bank to turn over to the Petitioner-Appellee, George Feldman, Trustee in Bankruptcy (Trustee) of Leasing Consultants, Incorporated (Leas-ing), the proceeds from the sale of equipment which had been leased by Leasing, located in New York, to Plastimetrix Corporation, located in New Jersey. The leases covering the equipment had been assigned to the Bank as security for a loan to Leasing.

The district court held, 351 F. Supp. 1390, on the basis of stipulated facts, that the perfection by the Bank by filing and possession in New York of its security interest in the lease/chattel paper was not a perfection of the Bank's security interest in Leasing's reversionary interest in the leased property, located in New Jersey. Consequently, the Trustee's lien was held superior to the Bank's unperfected security interest in the leased equipment.

Summary of Facts

In March and June of 1969 Leasing entered into eight leases with Plastrimetrix covering heavy equipment. The leased equipment was at all relevant times located in New Jersey. Leasing filed financing statements with the Secretary of State of the State of New Jersey covering each transaction, each statement bearing the legend; "THIS FILING IS FOR INFORMATIONAL PURPOSES ONLY AS THIS IS A LEASE TRANSACTION."

On December 15, 1969 Leasing entered into a "Loan and Security Agreement" with the Bank for the financing of its business of purchasing and leasing equipment. The agreement provided in part for the assignment of "a continuing security interest in the lease(s) and the property leased" as collateral security for advances and loans not to exceed 80% of aggregate unpaid rentals.

Pursuant to the security agreement Leasing borrowed money from the Bank in December, 1969 and February, 1970 and assigned as collateral security the eight Plastrimetrix leases, each assignment covering all moneys due or to become due under the lease and the "relative equipment" described in the lease. The lease documents were delivered to the Bank.

On December 30 and 31, 1969 the Bank filed financing statements against Leasing with the Secretary of State of the State of New York and the Registrar of the City of New York, Queens County, where Leasing had its principal place of business. No financing statements were filed by the Bank in New Jersey; nor did the Bank take possession of the leased equipment.

On October 14, 1970 Leasing was adjudicated bankrupt by the United States District Court for the Eastern District of New York. On October 30, 1970 Plastimetrix filed a petition under Chapter XI of the Bankruptcy Act in the United States District Court for the District of New Jersey.

The leases were in default and an offer was made to purchase the Bank's interest in the property for $60,000. On May 21, 1971 the Trustee, the Bank, and the purchaser entered into a stipulation providing for acceptance of the offer and execution of bills of sale by the Trustee and Bank covering all "right, title and interest" in the property, and that the sum of $60,000 "be substituted for the Property" and the "respective rights of the Trustee and of the Bank ... be impressed upon and relegated to said fund of $60,000 with the same priority and to the same extent as they now have against the Property."

The Trustee petitioned the Referee in Bankruptcy for an order directing the Bank to turn over to the Trustee the sum of $60,000. Under stipulated facts the Trustee and Bank agreed that the question presented was solely one of law—involving the construction of Article 9 of the Uniform Commercial Code—and that the precise issue was:

Was the Bank required to file a financing statement against the Bankrupt with the Secretary of State of New Jersey in order to perfect a security interest in the leases assigned to it and the equipment leased thereunder by the Bankrupt to Plastrimetrix?

The Referee answered in the affirmative and ordered the Bank to turn over the $60,000, with interest, to the Trustee. On review the district court affirmed.

Decision of District Court

As the district court recognized, the aim of Article 9 of the Uniform Commercial Code, relating to "Secured Transactions," is "to provide a simple and unified structure within which the immense variety of present-day secured financing transactions can go forward with less cost and with greater certainty." Uniform Commercial Code, §9-101, Official Comment. The drafters of this article eliminated many distinctions among security devices based on form alone. On the other hand, distinctions based on the type of property constituting the collateral were retained. *Id.*

Based on the stipulation of counsel, the court assumed that the agreements between Leasing and Plastrimetrix were "true leases" and not "conditional sales agreements" or devices intended to create only a security interest. Accordingly the court found that the Bank acquired "a security interest in both the right to receive rental payments under the lease and in the reversionary interest in the underlying equipment."

The court held, and the parties agree, that the leases themselves were "chattel papers" (UCC §9-105(1)(b)) and that the Bank's security interest in the chattel paper was perfected by filing financing statements in New York and taking possession of the leases. UCC §9-304(1), 9-305, and 9-102(1).

The court held further: "By contrast, the machines themselves constituted 'equipment' located in New Jersey and hence, for perfection purposes, came within the scope of the New Jersey requirements." The Bank having failed to perfect its interest in the reversion in New Jersey, the court concluded that the Trustee "—a lien creditor within the meaning of Uniform Commercial Code §9-301(3)—has priority over an unperfected security interest under §9-301(1)(b)."

Emphasizing the distinction between rights under the chattel paper and the reversionary interest in the equipment, the court quoted from Professor Levie as follows:

In one situation the purchaser of a security agreement may have an advantage over the purchaser of a lease. Where [he] purchases equipment leases, he takes only an assignor's interest in the equipment lease itself. If [he] wishes to be secured by an interest in the goods as well, he must obtain a security interest ... [in the goods] and perfect it. Levie, Security Interests in Chattel Paper, 78 Yale LJ 935, 940 (1969).

The district court concluded:

The distinction between the rights represented by the lease and those represented by the reversionary interest in the equipment is a real one, supported by logic and precedent. To ignore the distinction contributes neither to clarity nor uniformity under the Uniform Commercial Code. Moreover, it may mislead third party creditors. The simple solution for a bank in the situation of petitioner is to file notices as to its interest in the reversion in accordance with the law of the state where the equipment is located.

Contentions of Appellant

Appellant Bank contends that (1) whether the leases be considered "true leases" or security devices, the filing of the security interest in New York (where lessor and the chattel paper were located) covered all of the lessor's rights in the rentals and related equipment wherever located, without a separate filing against the equipment; or (2) alternatively, if a distinction is recognized between a "true lease" and a security device, appellant is entitled to an evidentiary hearing to determine whether the instruments were "true leases" or security interests in the equipment through the device of a lease; and (3) in any event, Leasing in fact had no "reversionary" interest in the property leased to Plastrimetrix.

Failure to File Financing Statement in New Jersey

In contending that the filing and physical possession of the lease instruments in New York were sufficient to cover the leased equipment located in New Jersey, appellant argues that the "reversionary interest" of Leasing is "an intangible interest, sited at Leasing's domicile in New York, and not in New Jersey." If the reversionary interest in the equipment were characterized as a "general intangible," the Bank's security interest in the equipment would have been perfected when it filed with the New York Department of State and in the county in which Leasing had a place of business. NY UCC §§9-103(2), 9-104(1)(c) (McKinney 1964).

The policies of the Code, however, militate against such an interpretation. We agree with the district court that the reversionary interest is an interest in "goods" rather than an interest in intangibles, and that to perfect the security interest in the reversionary interest in the equipment it was necessary to file a financing statement in New Jersey where the equipment was located. NJ Stat. Anno. 12A:9-A102(1) (1962), 9-302, 9-401(1)(c) (Supp. 1972).

Obviously the leased property itself is "goods." We conclude, as did the district court, that the future reversionary interest is likewise an interest in goods, whether it represents "equipment" or "inventory" collateral. The drafters of the Code classified collateral mainly according to the nature or use of the underlying entity, rather than the character of its ownership at any given time. Significantly, the examples of "general intangibles" given in the Official Comment to §9-106 are all types of property that are inherently intangible. And several Code sections and comments suggest that a collateral interest in "goods" remains such even when the goods are leased. See §§9-103(2); 9-109(4) and Official Comment 3; 9-304(3); NY UCC 9-109, Practice Commentary 2 (McKinney 1964) (Kripke).

We conclude accordingly that if the instruments were "true leases," the security interest in the leased equipment was not perfected because of the failure of the Bank to file financing statements in New Jersey.

Were Lease Instruments "True Leases"?

In view of our holding that under a true lease the filing of a financing statement in New Jersey would be required, the determination of whether the lease instruments were "true leases" or security agreements is critical. If the agreements were true leases, Leasing was the owner of the equipment. If they were disguised security agreements, Plastrimetrix was the owner, and the filing and possession of the agreements in New York would protect the security interest of the Bank.

In assuming that the agreements between the lessor and lessee were in fact "true leases" the district court relied upon a provision in a stipulation of the parties that, "At all times relevant hereto the Bankrupt [Leasing] owned the leased equipment, subject to the claims and interests of the Bank thereto and therein as appears from the exhibits attached to the stipulation."

This stipulation was made prior to submission of the petition to the Referee in Bankruptcy and apparently before the parties were aware that the distinction between a true lease and a security device would be crucial to a determination of this case. It may well be, as appellant argues, that the Bank and Trustee had simply agreed that Leasing was the owner of the equipment, "*vis-à-vis* the Bank [and not *vis-à-vis* Plastrimetrix], subject to the rights of the Bank," and that, "Neither the Bank nor the Trustee knew all of the real, complete, underlying agreements between Leasing and Plastrimetrix," necessarily involved in determining the nature of the agreements.

In contending that the record supports the conclusion that the agreements were "true leases," appellee relies upon the lease agreements, stipulation of the parties, and the "assumption" of the district court based upon the stipulation. Appellee then argues that the question of whether the agreements were true leases was first raised on appeal and that the case must be decided on the record now before the court. In its reply brief, however, appellant quotes from the brief it submitted to the district court, reading in part: "If this Court concludes the distinction is determinative, it cannot be determined from the Statement and Supplemental Statement, whether the Plastrimetrix leases are leases intended as security devices (hence security agreements) or are true leases.

Whether a lease is intended as security is to be determined by the facts of each case ... ." UCC §1-201(37). In making this determination the court may properly consider "factors outside of the lease as well as the contents of the lease itself ... ." *In Re Walter Willis, Inc.*, 313 F. Supp. 1274, 1278 (ND Ohio 1970), aff'd, 440 F.2d 995 (6 Cir. 1971).

We conclude that the case should be remanded for a determination by the district court, following an evidentiary hearing, whether the lease instruments were in fact "true leases" or lease devices intended as security. ...

NOTES

1) *Leasing Consultants* has attracted substantial criticism but also has its defenders. See "Comment" (1975), 84 *Yale LJ* 1722; Clark, "Abstract Rights versus Paper Rights under Article 9 of the Uniform Commercial Code" (1975), 84 *Yale LJ* 445; and Jackson, "Embodiment of Rights in Goods and the Concept of Chattel Paper" (1983), 50 *U Chi. L Rev.* 1051. Note carefully that *Leasing Consultants* was decided under the 1962 version of Article 9 whose definition of chattel paper did not extend to true chattel leases. (The same was true of the old Ontario Act.) The 1972 revision (UCC 9-105) remedied this defect; the same correction is made in s. 1, "chattel paper," in the new Ontario Act. Leaving aside the definitional issue, is there any justification for disaggregating true lease chattel paper while maintaining the unity of security lease chattel paper?

2) As previously noted, s. 28(3)(b) of the Ontario Act protects a purchaser of chattel paper which represents the proceeds from the sale of inventory, whatever the state of his knowledge. This rule was adopted in the Code to enable a dealer to get a better deal for "lucrative" chattel paper generated by a sale and to prevent an inventory financer from monopolizing access to it. Prof. Kripke justified the rule in the following letter to one of the authors of this casebook:

The policy of the second sentence of 9-308 was never vigorously debated. The persons who might have debated it were the representatives of finance companies who were in the committees, and there were several of us who would not have hesitated to be vocal. However we saw no reason to debate this. Either rule could be justified with arguments of policy, and I actually think the present rule is the better one. In purely mercenary terms, the situation is that the banks have taken a strong position in the automobile installment finance industry in the United States; and, among the finance companies, General Motors Acceptance Corporation almost exclusively dominates the business available to finance companies for General Motors cars, which are about half of all the cars sold. The other finance companies are interested in getting some retail paper by "sniping," which means that the dealer will occasionally sell them an item of retail paper rather than sell it to the inventory financer who gets the bulk of his paper. True, this practice works both ways and other people are able to snipe against the inventory position of CIT, Commercial Credit or any of the other independents. But on balance the rule which permits them freedom to snipe gives them access to more potential dealer business than the opposite rule could do.

The rule does help the dealer somewhat because he can shop his paper around to finance companies who will take more speculative paper than the larger ones who do the inventory financing. This gives him a certain freedom of action in his sales, where otherwise he would not dare make a sale that the inventory financer would not approve in advance. Where the dealer does make some higher speculative sales of this nature, the finance company may condone diversion of the paper to other outlets; but apart from this, of course the dealer will lose his inventory finance source if the finance company does not get a fair penetration of retail paper.

(Kripke to Ziegel in letter dated 21/8/61, cited in 41 *Can. Bar Rev.* 54, at 116, n. 289.)

Competition for the purchase of retail chattel paper appears to be much less in the 1980s than it was in the 1950s and 1960s, and appears never to have been as keen in Canada as it was in the United States. Assuming the soundness of the underlying policy of s. 28(3)(b), is there a danger of its being abused by dishonest dealers and does it not conflict with the policy of s. 25 discussed later in this chapter?

THE RIGHT TO FOLLOW PROCEEDS (SECTION 25)

One of the many innovative features of Article 9 (and therefore also of the Canadian legislation) is that it spells out clearly the secured party's right to follow the proceeds where the debtor has disposed of the collateral, with or without the secured party's consent. This is of great practical importance in the inventory financing context where, as we have seen, the debtor will usually be able to pass good title to the collateral to a third party if the goods are sold in the ordinary course of the debtor's business pursuant to ss. 28(1) and (2). The common law and equitable rules concerning the secured party's right to follow the proceeds were both complex and uncertain and depended in part on the terms of the security agreement and in part on the identifiability of the proceeds. Unhappily, as we shall see, not all of these difficulties have been resolved in s. 25 of the Ontario Act or its Western provincial counterparts.

The following non-exhaustive materials deal with three key aspects of s. 25: (1) the nature and source of the secured party's claim to proceeds; (2) what it must do to perfect her security interest in the proceeds; and (3) the extent to which the proceeds can be followed by the secured party. For a detailed treatment of the status of proceeds under the PPS legislation see R.C.C. Cuming, "Protecting Interests in Proceeds: Equity and Canadian Personal Property Security Acts" in Waters (ed.), *Equity, Fiduciaries and Trusts*, Carswell, 1993); and Ziegel & Denomme, *op. cit.*, §25.

Nature and Source of the Claim to Proceeds

The following decision of the Supreme Court of Canada, although decided under s. 88 (now s. 178) of the Bank Act, still remains important in illuminating and clarifying the conceptual significance of the right to trace in s. 25.

Flintoft v. Royal Bank of Canada
[1964] SCR 631

JUDSON J: The contest in this litigation is between a bank holding security under s. 88(1)(b) of the *Bank Act*, RSC 1952, c. 12, substituted 1953-54, c. 48, and a trustee in bankruptcy of the bank's customer concerning the ownership of certain uncollected debts owing to the customer at the date of bankruptcy. These debts arose from the sale by the customer of goods covered by the bank's security. The trustee says that he is entitled to collect these debts for administration under the *Bankruptcy Act*, RSC 1952, c. 14, because an assignment of book debts held by the bank was void for lack of timely registration. The bank says that the fact that these debts arose from the sale of the goods covered by the bank's security gives them to the bank notwithstanding the failure of the assignment of book debts. There is no dispute about the facts. It is admitted that the bank's security under s. 88(1)(b) was a valid security and that the assignment of book debts held by the bank is void for want of timely registration.

The judge of first instance declared that the trustee in bankruptcy was entitled to all book debts of the bankrupt unpaid at the date of bankruptcy. The Manitoba Court of Appeal held that to the extent that the book debts of the customer outstanding at the time of the bankruptcy represented debts owing to the customer for goods sold and covered by the bank's s. 88 security, these accounts went to the bank. Freedman JA dissented and would have held that the proceeds of these sales must come under the assignment of book debts, that the bank could only claim in its capacity as holder of this assignment and that, therefore, its claim failed.

My opinion is that the majority judgment is correct. By agreement in writing between bank and customer an express trust of these accounts was created in favour of the bank in the following terms:

The proceeds of all sales by the Customer of the property or any part thereof, including, without limiting the generality of the foregoing, cash debts arising from such sales or otherwise, evidences of title, instruments, documents and securities, which the Customer may receive or be entitled to receive in respect thereof, are hereby assigned to the Bank and shall be paid or transferred to the Bank forthwith, and until so paid or transferred shall be held by the Customer in trust for the Bank. Execution by the Customer and acceptance by the Bank of an assignment of book debts or any additional assignment of any of such proceeds shall be deemed to be in furtherance hereof and not an acknowledgment by the Bank of any right or title on the part of the Customer to such book debts or proceeds.

In addition to the creation of the trust, the agreement rejects in advance any suggestion that the bank's right to these accounts will depend upon a valid assignment of book debts. This agreement does no more than set out the terms upon which a bank as holder of s. 88 security permits a customer to sell the property of the bank in the ordinary course of business.

The property rights of the bank are defined by ss. 88(2) and 86(2) of the Bank Act. Under s. 88(2) the bank gets the same rights and powers as if it had acquired a warehouse receipt or bill of lading in which the property was described. Under s. 86(2) it acquires all the rights and title of the customer.

• • •

Section 88 is a unique form of security. I know of no other jurisdiction where it exists. It permits certain classes of persons not of a custodier character, in this case a manufacturer, to give security on their own goods with the consequences above defined. Notwithstanding this, with the consent of the bank, the one who gives the security sells in the ordinary course of business and gives a good title to purchasers from him. But this does not mean that he owns the book debts when he has sold the goods. To me the fallacy in the dissenting reasons is the assumption that there is ownership of the book debts in the bank's customer once the goods have been sold and that the bank can only recover these book debts if it is the assignee of them.

We are not concerned here with the rights of a purchaser for value without notice of the proceeds of the sale of the bank's security. It is true that s. 63 of the *Bankruptcy Act* avoids in favour of the trustee the assignee of book debts held by the bank because of defective registration. Subject to this, the trustee has no higher rights than the bankrupt and he takes the property of the bankrupt merely as a successor in interest and not as an innocent purchaser for value without notice. He takes the property of the bankrupt subject to the express trust created by the agreement noted above, which, in my opinion, cannot be characterized as an assignment of book debts in another form. When these debts, the proceeds of the sale of the s. 88 security, come into existence they are subject to the agreement between bank and customer. As between these two the customer has nothing to assign to the bank. The actual assignment of book debts which was signed does no more than facilitate collection. Any other assignment, whether general or specific, of these debts by the customer to a third party would fail unless the third party was an innocent purchaser for value without notice.

In *Union Bank of Halifax v. Spinney and Churchill* [(1907), 38 SCR 187], the proceeds of the sale of the bank's security came into the hands of Spinney, a third party, who was a guarantor of the customer's account with the bank. The proceeds were in the form of drafts drawn in favour of the guarantor instead of the bank, as they should have been. Spinney took with knowledge that the drafts were in payment for meal, ground from corn, on which the bank held security and he was held liable to account. I can find in the report no mention of any written agreement similar to the one in existence in the present case but it is clear that the oral understanding between bank and customer was to the same effect. Any other understanding would be inconceivable in commercial dealings. Why would any lender who lends for the purpose of enabling another to acquire and manufacture goods, permit the sale of goods on which he holds security except on terms that the borrower must bring in the proceeds of the sale of those goods?

Re Goodfallow, Traders' Bank v. Goodfallow [(1890), 19 OR 299] is a similar case. The contest there was between the bank and the administrator of the deceased customer. The customer was a miller who had given a warehouse receipt to the bank. At the date of his death there was found to be a shortage of wheat which had commenced shortly after the warehouse receipt had been given. During the period of shortage some of the wheat had been converted into flour and sold. The proceeds were paid to the administrator, who was compelled to pay the money to the bank. The ratio of the judgment of Boyd C is contained in the following short extract from his reasons: "As long as the 'product' of this wheat can be traced, whether it be in flour or in money, it is recoverable by the bank as against the deceased and his administrator."

Again, I can find in the report no mention of any agreement in writing, but even in its absence the principle is plainly to be spelled out that if you sell my goods with my consent, it is on terms that you bring me the money in place of the goods. Although the bank's customer does not sell as agent for the bank, he does not sell free of the bank's claim to the proceeds. There is an analogy with the case where goods are consigned to a factor to be sold by him and reduced to money. There has never been any doubt of the right of the owner to trace the money or any other form of property into which the money has been converted. (Underhill's Law of Trusts and Trustees, 11th ed., p. 561.)

The only other case to which I wish to refer is *Banque Canadienne Nationale v. Lefaivre et al.* [[1951] Que. KB 83, 32 CBR 1], where the Quebec Court of Appeal, on facts which cannot be distinguished from those of the present case, anticipated the judgment of the Manitoba Court of Appeal. In the Quebec case the bank and customer had executed an agreement in the following terms:

Art. 5: dans le cas de vente par le client des effets, en tout ou en partie, le produit de cette vente y compris les espèces, les effets de commerce, les billets à ordre, titres et valeurs qui en seront la considération de même que les créances contre les acheteurs, appartiendront à la banque à qui ils devront être immédiatement versés ou remis, et jusqu'à ce versement ou cette remise le client ne les détriendra qu'en fidéicommis pour la banque. L'exécution par le client et l'acceptation par la banque des transports de dettes de livres seront censés résulter de la présente convention et ne constitueront pas une reconnaissance de la part de la banque que le client a des droits ou un titre quelconque à ces dettes de livres.

The contest was between the bank and the trustee in bankruptcy of the customer. The trustee contended that the accounts of the customer representing the proceeds of the sale of the s. 88 security were part of the assets of the bankrupt estate because they had not been validly transferred to the bank in accordance with Art. 1571 of the *Civil Code*. It was held that the use of the words "en fidéicommis" was merely an attempt to translate the English expression "in trust." The majority judgment is founded squarely on the ground that the claims against the buyers of the goods became the property of the bank by virtue of its s. 88 security and never were the property of the customer so as to be affected by the assignment in bankruptcy.

Appeal dismissed.

NOTES

1) As will be noted, Judson J in *Flintoft* takes the position that the inventory financer's right to the proceeds arises from the nature of inventory financing even if the agreement itself is silent on the subject. As he says (*supra*), "even in its absence [i.e., of a proceeds clause in the security agreement] the principle is plainly to be spelled out that if you sell my goods with my consent, it is on terms that you bring me the money in place of the goods." (For a controversial criticism of these aspects of the judgment see Cuming and Wood (1986), 65 *Can. Bar Rev.* 267, at 296-301.) The same position generally obtained under prior American law. See UCC 9-306, Official Comment, para. 2. The point is significant because in *GMAC v. BNS* (1986), 55 OR (2d) 438 (CA), reproduced below, the court made much of the fact that the financing agreement between GMAC and its dealer contained no trust or proceeds clause and did not require the dealer to pay the proceeds from the sale of the collateral (motor vehicles) into a separate account.

Are these valid distinctions? What is the difference between saying a secured party acquires an automatic security interest in proceeds and the requirement that the debtor must agree to hold the proceeds on trust for the secured party? Does "on trust" here mean anything more than that the debtor is not free to deal with the proceeds as he sees fit? Does the difference reside in the fact that a trustee is a fiduciary whereas a debtor under s. 25 is not so referred to? Does a trust clause confer a stronger right to trace than is conferred under s. 25(2)? See further Ziegel, "The Legal Problems of Wholesale Financing ..." (1963), 41 *Can. Bar Rev.* 54, at 96-102, and the notes below following *GMAC v. BNS*.

Perfection of Security Interest in Proceeds

Massey-Ferguson Industries v. Bank of Montreal
(1983), 44 OR (2d) 350, 3 PPSAC 209 (HC)

O'BRIEN J: This action involves a dispute between two creditors of a farm equipment company placed in receivership for the defendant bank.

The dispute requires a consideration of the *Personal Property Security Act*, RSO 1980, c. 375, and raises two issues:

(1) The right to trace proceeds of a sale of goods secured under the *Personal Property Security Act*;

(2) An interpretation of s. 27 of the Act when proceeds from the sale of goods secured under the Act are deposited in a debtor's general bank account and mixed with other funds.

The plaintiff (Massey) appointed Guelph Equipment Company Ltd. (Guelph) as one of its dealers in 1976. The Bank of Montreal (the Bank) was banker for Guelph.

The contractual arrangements between Massey and Guelph were contained in two documents, a dealer sales and service agreement (ex. 2) and a security agreement—inventory and financing statement (ex. 3). The financing statement was registered on April 5, 1976, in compliance with the *Personal Property Security Act*.

The two contracts between Massey and Guelph provided Massey would supply its farm equipment to Guelph without payment, but retain a security interest in it. Guelph agreed to advise Massey of all sales of Massey's equipment and to obtain financing agreements from the purchasers, satisfactory to Massey, or obtain payment for the equipment and hold it in trust for Massey in a separate account.

Guelph made banking arrangements with the Bank, opened a current account and obtained an operating line of credit secured by a general assignment of book debts and a floating charge against inventory. The Bank registered its secured interest under the *Personal Property Security Act*, June 26, 1978.

The Bank transferred money from Guelph's current account to itself in payment of the interest on loans made by the Bank and in part payment on loans. The Bank admits that after Massey's security agreement was registered under the *Personal Property Security Act* it withdrew more money from Guelph's account than is now claimed by Massey.

The Bank placed Guelph into receivership in March, 1981. Massey then discovered Guelph had failed to notify Massey of sales of Massey's equipment and had deposited proceeds from those sales in its own account.

The matter proceeded to trial on an agreed statement of fact. The statement contained a schedule showing the names of the purchasers of that equipment and the amounts Guelph received from them, which Guelph then deposited in its current account. Those amounts total $32,071.18, and is the amount [*sic*] claimed in this action.

The Bank admits Massey had a prior claim regarding its equipment as a result of prior registration under the *Personal Property Security Act*. The Bank argues that priority was lost when the equipment was sold. The Bank argues Massey was required to register a fresh statement under the *Personal Property Security Act* with respect to the proceeds to protect its claim to those proceeds. The Bank further disputes the right of Massey to identify and trace the sale proceeds when mixed with Guelph's own funds in its current account.

The Bank raised the argument of laches and delay on the part of Massey, but the matter was not seriously argued at trial as it appeared Massey had no knowledge of Guelph's default under the contract with Massey until the receiver was appointed in March, 1981, and there was no significant delay by Massey after that.

Massey relies on ss. 27 and 34(2) of the [old] *Personal Property Security Act*, which are as follows:

27(1) Subject to this Act, a security interest in collateral that is dealt with so as to give rise to proceeds,

(a) continues as to the collateral, unless the secured party expressly or impliedly authorized such dealing; and

(b) extends to the proceeds.

(2) The security interest in proceeds is a perfected security interest if the security interest in the collateral is perfected but it ceases to be a perfected security interest and becomes unperfected after ten days after receipt of the proceeds by the debtor unless,

(a) a financing statement in the prescribed form in respect of the collateral is registered; or

(b) the security interest in the proceeds is perfected before the expiration of the ten day period.

but there is no perfected security interest in proceeds that are not identifiable or traceable.

• • •

Massey claims the proceeds in this case are "identifiable and traceable" within the meaning of the word as used in s. 27(2)(b) and within the meaning of those words at common law and equity.

Massey also relies on regulations made under the *Personal Property Security Act*, O. Reg. 879/75, s. 3(1)(a)(iii), which is as follows:

3(1) A financing statement,
(a) shall set out,

• • •

(iii) the classification of the collateral as consumer goods, inventory, equipment, book debts or that the classification is other than consumer goods, inventory, equipment, or book debts or any combination thereof ...

Massey relies on its financing statement which, in the appropriate box on the required form, shows the collateral classification to be "inventory." In another place on the financing statement form there is a space for general collateral description; Massey inserted the following words:

EXISTING OR TO BE ACQUIRED NEW MF GOODS INCLUDING FARM, INDUSTRIAL, CONSTRUCTION MACHINERY, LAWN TRACTORS, SNOWMOBILES, REPAIR PARTS AND MF FINANCED USED MACHINERY OF SIMILAR TYPE, AND ALL PROCEEDS

It can be argued, as the defendant does in this case, that s. 27 of the *Personal Property Security Act* is silent or ambiguous in the manner in which it deals with proceeds from the sale of goods secured under the Act. The argument is, when the collateral goods are sold, the protection of the Act vanishes and the proceeds are protected under the Act for only 10 days, unless a further financing agreement describing the proceeds is registered within that time.

This point is well-considered in *Secured Transactions in Personal Property in Canada* (1979), by R.H. McLaren, vol. 1, §4.02[3]. The author (counsel for the plaintiff in this case) argued at trial, as he does in his book, that, on the basis of the mischief rule of statutory interpretation, any gap in the statute should be filled in by implying the original security interest remains perfected when proceeds are created, if it was perfected just prior to the creation of the proceeds interest. The author points out the failure to accept such interpretation results in the impossibility of a perfected interest in proceeds ever arising.

Conclusions

(1) I accept the argument of Mr. McLaren and conclude s. 27 of the *Personal Property Security Act* does apply and protects these proceeds without the requirement of a fresh registration. In my view, this conclusion does not require torturing the statute at all. If support is needed for this conclusion, it is found in the wording in Massey's registered financing statement where specific reference is made to the type of equipment involved "AND ALL PROCEEDS."

(2) I conclude the proceeds in this case are identifiable and traceable by reason of the schedule attached to the agreed statement of facts, which lists the name of each customer, a brief description of the machine sold, the amount of the cheque received in down payment, and the date of its deposit.

• • •

(3) I also conclude the funds in this case are identifiable and traceable as those terms were used at common law and equity.

The concepts of tracing and identification of funds is [*sic*] carefully considered in the book *Restitution* by Fridman and McLeod (1982), at 570-4. At 571 it is noted common law judges insisted money, like any other property, had to be identifiable before a proprietary claim could be brought. The common law judges held payment into a bank did not, in itself, defeat a proprietary claim. Reference is made to *Banque Belge pour l'Etranger v. Hambrouck*, [1921] 1 KB 321.

The learned authors point out the precise scope of the common law rule remains uncertain. The courts struggled with the problem created when the money in dispute became intermingled with that of the defendant so that it was impossible to trace or follow it. The learned authors consider the decision of the English Court of Appeal in the *Banque Belge* case and point out the different approaches taken by the three members of the court. Only the decision of Atkin LJ, at 335, suggested a plaintiff could utilize common law rules for tracing if the plaintiff's money had been mixed with other money in a bank account. Atkin LJ considered it important for the court to be able to see if the money in the bank account was the product of, or a substitute for, the original thing.

The authors then deal with the question of tracing in equity and the general position of the English courts as it is stated in *Re Diplock*, [1948] 1 Ch. 465 at 532, affirmed [1951] AC 251 *sub nom. Ministry of Health v. Simpson et al.* (HL), as authority for the rule that for a plaintiff to follow property in equity he must establish a fiduciary relationship between himself and the defendant or some other third person who came into possession of the property. Applying that rule to this case, I note contracts between Massey and Guelph provided Guelph would obtain payment for Massey's equipment and hold these payments in trust for Massey in a separate account. In considering the difficult concepts of tracing and identifying funds, I am assisted by the decision of the Ontario High Court of Justice in *Goodbody et al. v. Bank of Montreal et al.* (1974), 4 OR (2d) 147 at 151, 47 DLR (3d) 335 at 339, which held money can be traced in equity, and whether the wrongful holder mixes it with his own money and retains it or places it in a bank or even invests it in personal securities, the true owner of the money is still given a first charge on the whole of the money or securities.

Relying on these authorities, I conclude Massey is able to identify and trace the precise amount claimed in this action, $32,071.18.

Judgment for plaintiff.

Central Refrigeration & Restaurant Services Inc. v. Canadian Imperial Bank of Commerce
(1986), 5 PPSAC 262 (Sask. CA)

TALLIS JA: This is an appeal from a judgment in Queen's Bench under s. 59(2) of the *Bankruptcy Act*, RSC 1970, c. B-3, which allowed the respondent bank's claim to the proceeds from two cheques delivered before its assignment in bankruptcy to Central in payment of certain accounts receivable. The issue on this appeal is whether, in the absence of a claim to *proceeds* of collateral in the financing statement, the respondent's perfected security interest under a general assignment of *accounts* entitles it to the proceeds of the cheques in priority to the trustee's alleged "interest" under s. 20(1)(d) of the *Personal Property Security Act*, SS 1979-80, c. P-6.1 (PPSA).

The facts are not in dispute. Therefore I recite only those material facts that are necessary to deal with the issues raised on this appeal. For several years before its assignment in bankruptcy on November 23, 1983, Central was a customer of the respondent bank. On March 26, 1981, Central executed a "General Assignment of Accounts, etc." in favour of the bank. This assignment contained, *inter alia*, the following paragraphs:

1. FOR VALUABLE CONSIDERATION the undersigned Central Refrigeration and Restaurant Services Inc. of 811–2nd Ave. North, Saskatoon, Saskatchewan, hereby assign(s) and transfer(s) all debts, accounts, claims, moneys and choses in action which now are or which may at any time hereafter be due or owing to or owned by the undersigned and also all securities, bills, notes and other documents now held or owned or which may be hereafter taken, held or owned by the undersigned or anyone on behalf of the undersigned in respect of the said debts, accounts, claims, moneys and choses in action or any part thereof and also all books and papers recording, evidencing or relating to said debts, accounts, claims, moneys and choses in action or any part thereof (all of the foregoing being herein called "assigned premises") to CANADIAN IMPERIAL BANK OF COMMERCE (herein called the "Bank") as a general and continuing collateral security for payment of all existing and future indebtedness and liability of the undersigned to the Bank wheresoever and howsoever incurred and any ultimate unpaid balance thereof, and as a first and prior claim upon the assigned premises.

• • •

5. All moneys collected or received by the undersigned in respect of the assigned premises shall be received as trustee for the Bank and shall be forthwith paid over to the Bank.

On April 1, 1981, a financing statement under the PPSA was filed by the respondent bank describing the collateral as "General Assignment of Account." No reference was made in this financing statement to the proceeds of collateral. On April 28, 1983, this financing statement was renewed for a period of five years.

When Central made its assignment in bankruptcy on November 23, 1983, Mr. McLean, its president, turned over to the trustee five uncashed and uncertified cheques (totalling $9,787.41) that his company had received in payment of certain accounts receivable of the company. On this appeal, our attention was focused on two significant cheques—the first was a cheque from Slider's Restaurant for $1,502.32 dated *November 21, 1983* and received on that date, and the second, a cheque from Empire Meat Packer for $7,073.57 dated and received on November 22, 1983. The respondent did not press its claim with respect to the other cheques. At the date of the bankruptcy, Central owed the sum of $26,877.79 to the respondent bank.

The trustee negotiated these cheques and retained the proceeds pending the administration of the bankrupt's estate. The respondent claimed the funds under its perfected security but the trustee disallowed the claim on the principal ground that the respondent's financing statement did not include proceeds within the meaning of s. 2(ee) of the PPSA and therefore it could not claim the proceeds of the cheques in priority to the trustee's claim on behalf of the bankrupt's creditors. Wright J allowed the bank's claim. In his written reasons he stated, *inter alia*:

The trustee's contention misconceives not only the effect of *The Personal Property Security Act* but the factual situation here existing. The cheques received by Central were property covered by the Assignment and the Financial Statement. When Central delivered them to the trustee, the trustee took them subject to the rights the bank enjoyed against Central. The later conversion of the cheques into cash did not change that fact. The bank did not need to claim the proceeds of the collateral in this case. The bank is entitled to the funds in question including any interest earned on them during the time they have been held by the trustee.

The trustee attacked this conclusion and reiterated his position that the financing statement was ineffective as against the trustee's interest because it did not include "proceeds" of the collateral. The trustee argued that an application of three definitions in the PPSA mandates a finding that the cheques and the money derived from their cashing are *cash proceeds*. He relied on the following definitions:

2. In this Act:

• • •

(b) "account" means any monetary obligation not evidenced by chattel paper, an instrument or a security, whether or not it has been earned by performance;

• • •

(u) "instrument" means a bill of exchange, note or cheque within the meaning of the *Bills of Exchange Act* (Canada), or any other writing that evidences a right to the payment of money and is of a type that in the ordinary course of business is transferred by delivery with any necessary endorsement or assignment, but does not include:

• • •

(ee) "proceeds" means identifiable or traceable personal property in any form or fixtures derived directly or indirectly from any dealing with the collateral or proceeds therefrom, and includes insurance payments or any other payments as indemnity or compensation for loss of or damage to the collateral or proceeds therefrom, or any right to such payment, and any payment made in total or partial discharge of an intangible, chattel paper, instrument or security; and money, cheques and deposit accounts in banks, credit unions, trust companies or similar institutions are cash proceeds and all other proceeds are non-cash proceeds.

The trustee contends that since "instrument" is defined to include cheque, and since instrument is excluded from the definition of "account," the only logical conclusion is that the cheques are included in the definition of "proceeds" and are excluded from the definition of "accounts." Therefore, in order to have a perfected security interest in these cheques as cash proceeds of the collateral, the respondent was required to register a financing statement which covers the original collateral and *proceeds therefrom*: see s. 28(2) of the PPSA.

The respondent bank argues, however, that the description of "General Assignment of Accounts" in its registered financing statement is sufficient to secure payments whether by cheque or otherwise with respect to the bankrupt's accounts. Since it has a perfected security interest in the "accounts" it has a perfected security interest in cheques tendered as payments on these accounts and therefore has priority over the trustee because of the provisions of s. 20(2)(a) of the PPSA.

Several American writers in dealing with secured transactions under the Uniform Commercial Code lean in favour of the principle that payments on account are proceeds: See G. Gilmore, *Security Interests in Personal Property*, Vol. II, 676; R.D. Henson, *Secured Transactions under the Uniform Commercial Code* (2nd ed., 1979), at 198, and Coogan, Hogan and Vagts, *Secured Transactions Under the Uniform Commercial Code*, Vol. 1C (Bender's Uniform Commercial Code Service 1982), at 2482. Whether an uncertified cheque is merely a conditional payment of indebtedness which leaves the account intact until the cheque is honoured is an open question.

Assuming, without deciding, that the two cheques dated November 21 and 22, 1983, respectively, and delivered as payment on account do not fall within the definition of "account" under the PPSA, the appellant still faces a formidable hurdle. Under s. 50(4) of the Bankruptcy Act, the interest of the bankrupt's creditors is determined as at the date of bankruptcy—November 23, 1983. Section 28(2) and (3) of the PPSA provides:

28.(2) A security interest in proceeds is a continuously perfected security interest if the interest in the original collateral is perfected:

(a) by the registration of a financing statement which covers the original collateral and proceeds therefrom and contains a prescribed description;

(b) by the registration of a financing statement which covers the original collateral and proceeds, where the proceeds are of a type or kind which fall within the description of the original collateral;

(c) by the registration of a financing statement which covers the original collateral and proceeds therefrom, where the proceeds are cash proceeds.

(3) In a case other than one mentioned in subsection (2), a security interest in proceeds is a continuously perfected security interest if the interest in the original collateral was perfected, and *the security interest in the proceeds remains perfected for a period of 15 days after receipt of the proceeds by the debtor* but becomes unperfected thereafter, unless the security interest in the

proceeds is otherwise perfected by any of the methods and under the circumstances prescribed in this Act for original collateral of the same type or kind.

[Emphasis added by the court—eds.]

Under these provisions the respondent bank had 15 days from the date of receipt of each of these cheques by the debtor Central in which to perfect its security interest in these "proceeds." The trustee argues that the interim perfection for 15 days is retrospectively lost if the registration does not occur within the grace period. We disagree with this interpretation becaue the clear language of the section does not support the view that the temporary perfection is invalidated retrospectively if registration does not take place. We hold that the respondent bank had a perfected security interest in the cheques during the crucial 15 day period following receipt of those cheques by the debtor. This interest ranks in priority to the interest of the bankrupt's creditors (as represented by the trustee) because the determinative date of November 23, 1983, was well within the 15 day period as defined in s. 28(3). On this branch of the case we find it helpful to refer to the following passages from Jacob S. Ziegel and Ronald C.C. Cuming, "The Modernization of Canadian Personal Property Security Law" (1981), 31 *UTLJ* 249 at 278:

Unlike Article 9, the Canadian acts expressly adopt the rules of tracing in determining what constitutes proceeds. In addition, the Saskatchewan Act and the draft revised model act go further than does Article 9 in requiring public disclosure of an interest in proceeds other than cash proceeds. Under these acts, a security interest in proceeds is temporarily perfected for a short period of time after the debtor obtains possession but ceases to be perfected thereafter unless the secured party takes possession or registers a financing statement describing the proceeds by type or kind.

In this case the cheques were received by the debtor Central either one or two days before its bankruptcy assignment. The respondent bank's temporarily perfected security interest under s. 28(3) secures an advance made before the interest of the creditors arises and therefore is entitled to priority under s. 20(2)(a) of the PPSA.

We accordingly affirm the respondent bank's claim to the proceeds of the two cheques.

The respondent bank also relied upon the trust clause contained in paragraph 5 of its security agreement. The trustee argued that the trust clause was ineffective against a trustee's interest under s. 20(1)(d) of the PPSA. In view of our conclusion, we do not find it necessary to deal with this argument. This matter is left open for future consideration.

Appeal dismissed.

NOTES

1) O'Brien J's decision in *Massey-Ferguson Industries* is discussed by Alpert in a lucid article, "Perfection and Tracing of Proceeds under the PPSA" (1984), 9 *CBLJ* 467. The obscurity of the language in old s. 27(2)(a) is due to an amendment adopted in 1973 without prior consultation with the profession. It is generally agreed that O'Brien J's construction is correct and that grammatically "in respect of the collateral" in s. 27(2)(a) must have referred to the same collateral alluded to in the second line of s. 27(2). The ambiguity is resolved in new s. 25(2).

2) This constructional point does not dispose of the wider policy issue of what perfection requirements should be imposed in respect of security interests in proceeds. There are three main alternatives: (a) to impose the same requirements as would apply if the proceeds were original collateral; (b) to dispense with any new perfection requirements so long as the security interest in the original collateral is and remains perfected; and (c) to adopt a modified version of solution (b) and to require reperfection of the proceeds claim if the form or place of perfection of the original collateral is not apt or appropriate for perfecting the proceeds interest.

UCC 9-306 was amended in 1972 so as to adopt solution (c). UCC 9-306(3) reads:

(3) The security interest in proceeds is a continuously perfected security interest if the interest in the original collateral was perfected but it ceases to be a perfected security interest and becomes unperfected ten days after receipt of the proceeds by the debtor unless

(a) a filed financing statement covers the original collateral and the proceeds are collateral in which a security interest may be perfected by filing in the office or offices where the financing statement has been filed and, if the proceeds are acquired with cash proceeds, the description of collateral in the financing statement indicates the types of property constituting the proceeds; or

(b) a filed financing statement covers the original collateral and the proceeds are identifiable cash proceeds; or

(c) the security interest in the proceeds is perfected before the expiration of the ten day period.

Except as provided in this section, a security interest in proceeds can be perfected only by the methods or under the circumstances permitted in this Article for original collateral of the same type.

As will be seen from *Central Refrigeration & Restaurant Services, supra*, this approach has been implemented with important modifications in the Saskatchewan Act and in UPPSA 1982.

The Ontario Advisory Committee favoured solution (b) subject to some modest qualifications. See OPPSA, s. 25.

The Advisory Committee appears to have been influenced by the fact that the Ontario Regulations only require the secured party to tick off a box in the financing statement identifying the *class* of collateral (viz. "consumer goods," "inventory," "equipment," "book debts" and "other"), and that a searching party would be no wiser if the secured party were required to tick off a new box entitled "proceeds." Does this prove the need for better descriptive requirements than presently obtain under the Ontario regulations?

PROBLEM

D buys a car on conditional sale from SP in Winnipeg. SP duly perfects its security interest. Subsequently D brings the vehicle to Hamilton and uses it as a trade-in on the purchase of a new car. SP becomes aware of D's actions only after the trade-in has occurred. Can SP claim a security interest in the new vehicle? What must it do in order to perfect the security interest in Ontario?

Tracing of Proceeds

General Motors Acceptance Corp. v. Bank of Nova Scotia
(1986), 55 OR (2d) 438 (CA)

BY THE COURT: In this action four issues arose under the *Personal Property Security Act*, RSO 1980, c. 375 (PPSA). They are as follows:

(1) Did General Motors Acceptance Corporation have a perfected security interest in the nine motor vehicles, the proceeds of the sale of which by the dealer to his customers form the subject-matter of the action?

(2) If the answer on issue 1 is yes, did such interest extend to the proceeds of sale?

(3) If the answer on issue 2, is yes, did it have priority over the bank's security interest?

(4) Were the proceeds derived from the sale of the motor vehicles identifiable or traceable within the meaning of s. 27(2) of the PPSA?

The relevant facts which give rise to the issues are as follows. In 1976, GMAC agreed to provide new vehicle financing for the dealer under the name Roger Hunter Motors Ltd. There was no written general financing agreement between these companies. GMAC registered a financing statement on April 1, 1976. The general collateral description included, *inter alia* "motor vehicles of whatever year ... held for sale or lease as inventory including proceeds thereof ... ."

On or about January 1, 1981, Hunter changed its name to Jim Morrison Chevrolet-Oldsmobile Inc. GMAC learned of the change of name on or before January 5, 1981. The original registration had been renewed by a financing change statement registered on March 19, 1979. On February 2, 1981, GMAC filed a new financing statement in which Morrison Ltd. was named as the debtor describing the same collateral as that described in the financing statement registered on April 1, 1976.

In February, 1981, the bank extended an operating line of credit of $150,000 to Morrison by way of a demand loan. On February 5, 1981, Morrison executed a general assignment of book debts and a general security agreement in favour of the bank. On February 9, 1981, the bank registered two financing statements in respect of its two security agreements. Although s. 1 of one statement indicated that the collateral classification included inventory, s. 2 in each case was completed to indicate motor vehicles were not included in the collateral. By letter dated June 22, 1981, in answer to an inquiry from GMAC dated June 17, 1981, the bank's manager advised GMAC that its credit line was secured by a general assignment of book debts and a security agreement over inventory, excluding new auto inventory.

On February 24, 1981, GMAC registered a financing change statement indicating the change in name of Hunter Ltd.

On July 31, 1981, General Motors of Canada Ltd. sold to the dealer the nine new motor vehicles by conditional sales contracts the financing for which was provided by GMAC to whom the contracts were assigned. The vehicles were sold by the dealer to its customers in the ordinary course of business and the proceeds were deposited in the dealer's current account with the bank. Financing statements were not registered with respect to the nine motor vehicles.

[The court answered the first issue in GMAC's favour and continued:]

• • •

Issue No. 2

The bank submitted that the nine conditional sales contracts did not by their terms purport to assign unto GMAC the proceeds received by the dealer from its customers and accordingly GMAC could not claim the proceeds. All parties agreed that the relationship between GMAC and the dealer was that of a debtor and creditor. In our opinion this submission cannot prevail because s. 27(1)(b) of the PPSA specifically provides that a security interest in collateral that is dealt with so as to give rise to proceeds extends to the proceeds. This provision is, of course, subject to s. 27(2) which provides there is no perfected security interest in proceeds that are not identifiable or traceable.

Issue No. 3

It was the submission of the bank that, even if the proceeds were identifiable or traceable and accordingly GMAC had a perfected security interest in motor vehicles and their proceeds, the bank had priority by reason of perfecting its security interest by registration of financing statements on February 9, 1981. It was the bank's position that GMAC's security interest became unperfected 15 days after it learned of the dealer's change of name, by reason of the provisions of s. 49(2) of the PPSA. The bank submitted that the financing statement registered by GMAC on February 2, 1981, did not have the effect of perfecting its security interest as of that date because it did not comply with s. 49(3). It is the bank's submission that GMAC's interest was not perfected again until it registered the financing change statement on February 24, 1981, and was therefore subordinate to the bank's prior perfected security interest.

In our view of this matter we need not decide whether GMAC's security interest, which had become unperfected, was reperfected before the bank perfected its security interest because the financing statements registered by the bank did not purport to relate to the collateral security in which GMAC claimed an interest, *viz.*, the motor vehicles which the dealer purchased for resale. Accordingly, GMAC would have priority over any security interest claimed by the bank under the provisions of the PPSA.

Issue No. 4

It was the submission of the bank that the proceeds derived from the sale of the motor vehicles were not identifiable or traceable within the meaning of s. 27(2) of the PPSA. If the bank is correct in this submission, then GMAC would not have a perfected security interest in the proceeds and the answer given with respect to issue No. 3 becomes irrelevant.

Proceeds are identifiable when they continue to exist in their original form. They are traceable if they are converted into a substituted form which can be located and determined to be the substitution for the original proceeds.

In the present case the dealer received cheques in payment for the motor vehicles and those cheques were deposited in its current account with the bank in the ordinary course of business. In law that merely establishes a debtor-creditor relationship between the bank and the dealer. Even if one regards the cheques as the equivalent of funds, those funds were commingled with other funds received by the dealer from other sources and deposited in its current account and further commingled with the bank's own funds and the funds of the bank's other customers deposited with it.

It is common ground that the dealer drew cheques upon its current account indiscriminately to pay its various creditors. The bank provided a revolving line of credit to the dealer. By agreement the bank would at the end of each business day deduct from the current account any amount standing to the credit of the dealer in excess of $5,000. Such excess would reduce the amount owing by the dealer on its line of credit. If at the end of a business day, the dealer's current account had a balance of less than $5,000 or was in a deficit position, the bank would credit the account from the revolving line of credit with an amount sufficient to restore the balance to $5,000. We view these deductions and additions as acts done in the normal course of business. Furthermore the dealer deposited the proceeds of the car sales into the current account and paid GMAC by cheques drawn on that account in the ordinary course of business. The conditional sales agreements assigned to GMAC did not assign the proceeds of the dealer's sale of the motor vehicles to GMAC nor did it require the dealer to hold such proceeds separate and apart from other funds or to hold the proceeds in trust from GMAC. In that regard this case is readily distinguishable from *Massey-Ferguson Industries Ltd. v. Bank of Montreal* (1983), 44 OR (2d) 350, 4 DLR (4th) 96, 24 BLR 117. In the present case no fiduciary relationship existed between GMAC and the dealer which might enable GMAC to trace the funds into the hands of the bank by the application of equitable principles. At the time the bank paid to itself out of current account the sum of $25,000 to reduce the dealer's indebtedness, it was not aware of the indebtedness of the dealer to GMAC with respect to the individual motor vehicles or any claim of prior right by GMAC to funds in the bank. GMAC's claim against the bank must fail on the grounds that the proceeds of the sale of the motor vehicles were not identifiable or traceable in its hands.

The appellants submitted on the basis of various American authorities, that we should apply the "lowest intermediate balance" rule the effect of which is that where proceeds are commingled with other funds in a bank account, the proceeds are deemed to be the last out of the account for purposes of determining the whereabouts of the proceeds. We are of the view that the rule is not applicable where the deposits into an account and withdrawals therefrom are made in the ordinary course of business and where, as in this case, the amount withdrawn by the bank from the dealer's current account was done in the ordinary course of its business with the dealer: see *Anderson, Clayton & Co. v. First American Bank of Erick*, 614 P. 2d 1091.

• • •

Appeal dismissed.

NOTES

1) What is the ratio of the court's decision in *GMAC* with respect to issue 4? Is it that equitable tracing rules only apply where the security agreement contains a proceeds clause and that GMAC's security agreement with Morrison contained none? Or is it based on the proposition that a secured party cannot trace funds disbursed by the debtor in the normal

course of business? If the first ratio is the correct one, what is the meaning of the following concluding clause in s. 27(2), "but there is no perfected security interest in proceeds that are non-identifiable *or traceable*"? (Emphasis added.) Is it in any event consistent with the objectives and structure of the PPSA to apply different tracing rules depending on whether or not magical trust language has been used in the security agreement? *Cf.* Catzman et al., *Personal Property Security Law in Ontario*, at 137, in referring to the tracing rule under s. 27(2): "The rule is as wide, and as narrow, as the corresponding rule for following a trust fund." In the new OPPSA, the requirement of the identifiability or traceability of proceeds has been transferred from old s. 27(2) to the new definition of "proceeds" in s. 1.

2) The court's assertion in *GMAC v. BNS* that the "lowest intermediate balance" rule (i.e., the right to trace proceeds in a commingled account) does not apply to deposits into and withdrawals from an account in the ordinary course of business appears to be based on American precedents but their invocation here raises various difficulties:

a) The case relied on by the court, *Anderson Clayton & Co. v. First American Bank of Erick* (1980), 614 P.2d 1091 (Oakl. S. Ct.) actually held that the bank was not entitled to rely on the ordinary course of business rule since it knew the plaintiff (a supplier of hog feed to the bank's customer) had a proceeds claim to the monies in question—in fact, the bank had previously entered into an agreement with the plaintiff subordinating its security interest in the hogs to the plaintiff's security interest for all monies owing by the customer for feed supplied by the plaintiff!

b) The "ordinary course" rule appears to be based, at least in part, on statutory rules which have no counterpart in Ontario and on an unexplained dictum in UCC 9-306, Official Comment, para. 2(c). See further Skilton, "The Secured Party's Rights in a Debtor's Bank Account under Article 9 of the Uniform Commercial Code," [1977] *So. Ill. ULJ* 120, esp. at 144 *et seq.*

c) Most importantly, O'Leary J's trial findings, not reversed on appeal, clearly showed that the Bank was well aware of GMAC's status as Morrison's vehicle financer before Morrison's account was frozen, and that Morrison had told the BNS branch manager on several occasions in late July or early August that he was "in conversion" with GMAC in failing to remit monies owing to it arising from the sale of the vehicles in question.

d) In the light of this evidence, one would have expected the court to have referred to s. 206(1) of the Bank Act and the considerable body of case law interpreting the subsection. Section 206(1) provides that "A bank is not bound to see to the execution of any trust, whether express, implied or constructive, to which any deposit made under the authority of this Act is subject." It is clear from the jurisprudence that s. 206(1) cannot be read literally and that it does not apply where the bank knowingly participated in the misapplication of property subject to a trust or to fiduciary obligations or should have realized that the customer was breaching such obligations. See Crawford and Falconbridge, *Banking and Bills of Exchange*, 8th ed., at 538 *et seq.* and authorities there cited. The facts in the present case appear to have been particularly adverse to the bank since, apart from its knowledge of GMAC's role, it benefited directly from debiting Morrison's account in respect of the monies owing to the bank.

GMAC v. BNS therefore leaves many questions unanswered and cannot be regarded as a satisfactory precedent. See the Comment in (1987-88), 13 *CBLJ* 177. It also raises some wider questions. Should an inventory financer be allowed to trace proceeds if it knowingly acquiesces in the debtor paying the proceeds into his general account? Should it insist on the dealer opening a separate account for proceeds? Is this always practicable? What should a bank do when it knows (and usually it will know) that a dealer is receiving inventory or accounts receivable financing from another source? Should it refuse to extend any credit of its own or should it reach an understanding with the other financer? Why was the latter course not followed in the present case?

Flexi-Coil Ltd. v. Kindersley District Credit Union Ltd.
(1993), 107 DLR (4th) 129 (Sask. CA)

JACKSON JA:

Introduction

This judgment concerns a secured transactions priority dispute between a lender and an inventory supplier following the bankruptcy of their mutual customer: a retail farm equipment dealer. The lender and the supplier both claim priority to cheques deposited by the customer to a revolving account in negative balance and to funds deposited by electronic transfer to the same account. After a trial, the learned judge held that the lender took priority over the inventory supplier. I agree with the trial judge's conclusion, but respectfully disagree with his reasons.

Facts

Churchill Farm Equipment Ltd. was a farm equipment dealer. The owners of Churchill tried to transfer control of their successful business to their son. Several disastrous business decisions later, Churchill declared bankruptcy. Flexi-Coil Ltd. was a long-time Churchill supplier and the Kindersley District Credit Union was Churchill's banker. The dispute in this case is between Flexi-Coil and the credit union over $86,659 which had been deposited in Churchill's account and applied to the line of credit supporting the account. Following deposit of this amount, Churchill wrote cheques to other creditors completely drawing on the line of credit.

The legal relationship between Flexi-Coil and Churchill was governed by a standard security agreement executed October 30, 1981. The security agreement covered the inventory supplied by Flexi-Coil plus any proceeds generated from the sale of the inventory. Flexi-Coil's security interest was duly registered in the personal property registry.

Churchill opened a bank account with the credit union early in 1984. The account was created with an operating line of credit of $150,000 payable on demand, which was increased in March, 1984, to $175,000. A loan agreement in this amount was executed and secured by a security interest on land and all stock and equipment. Churchill did not grant a security interest to the credit union with respect to any of the collateral or proceeds claimed by Flexi-Coil. As will be apparent, the competition in this case is between Flexi-Coil as a proceeds-secured creditor and the credit union as an unsecured creditor.

Operations between Flexi-Coil, Churchill and the credit union worked this way. As Churchill sold Flexi-Coil's machinery, it would deposit the cheques in its credit union account. (In some cases the funds were electronically transferred *via* another deposit-taking institution.) In due course, Churchill would pay Flexi-Coil the amount owed by cheques drawn on the same account. Flexi-Coil was aware of this practice. Credit union personnel testified it knew nothing of the secured relationship between Flexi-Coil and Churchill; it was not their policy to conduct searches at the personal property registry even when registering their own security interests at the personal property registry.

Churchill began to have severe financial problems in the fall of 1984. From October 31, 1984 to January 28, 1985, $249,276.16 was deposited or transferred into Churchill's credit union account. Of this amount, sales of Flexi-Coil's equipment accounted for $86,659, of which approximately $28,249 was deposited by electronic transfer. During this time, the credit union honoured cheques written by Churchill in the total amount of $225,524.88 and, in so doing, Churchill used its line of credit which had been credited, in part, as a result of cheques received from the sale of Flexi-Coil's inventory, *i.e.*, Churchill paid other creditors rather than paying Flexi-Coil. On January 8, 1985, Churchill attempted to pay Flexi-Coil $102,054.43 by writing cheques on its account in the usual way. These cheques were returned by the credit union for non-sufficient funds. Subsequently, Churchill made an assignment in bankruptcy.

Flexi-Coil sued the credit union for $86,659 which represented the amounts deposited with the credit union that Flexi-Coil claimed belonged to it. It claimed that amount as "identifiable or traceable proceeds" under the *Personal Property Security Act*, SS 1979-80, c. P-6.1 (the "PPSA") arising from Churchill's sale of Flexi-Coil's inventory.

Decision of the trial judge [98 Sask. R 124, 30 ACWS (3d) 1069]

The trial judge found for the credit union on two alternative grounds: (i) the security agreement did not extend to the moneys Churchill deposited with the credit union because Flexi-Coil allowed Churchill to deposit such moneys in the ordinary course of business; and (ii) Flexi-Coil implicitly subordinated its interest by its actions and, therefore, s. 39 of the PPSA conferred a higher priority on the credit union. In my respectful opinion, the trial judge's decision cannot be sustained on these grounds.

It was not open to the trial judge to conclude the security agreement did not extend to the moneys deposited with the credit union simply because Flexi-Coil allowed Churchill to deposit such moneys in its current account. Section 28(1)(a) of the PPSA provides that, where collateral is dealt with or otherwise gives rise to proceeds, the interest in the collateral is extinguished by an authorized dealing. No such words qualify the secured party's right to the proceeds: s. 28(1)(b) states that, where collateral gives rise to proceeds, the security interest in the collateral "extends to the proceeds." The purpose of s. 28(1)(b) is to ensure, in such circumstances, the security interest continues in such proceeds. To hold otherwise would be contrary to the fundamental basis of *Transamerica Commercial Finance Corp., Canada v. Royal Bank of Canada* (1990), 70 DLR (4th) 627, 79 CBR (NS) 127, 84 Sask. R 81 (CA), which gave priority to the proceeds-secured party over a lender with respect to funds deposited into a current account with the lender.

On the issue of whether Flexi-Coil subordinated its interest in the proceeds to that of the credit union, one begins by reviewing s. 39 of the PPSA:

39. A secured party may, in the security agreement or otherwise, subordinate his security interest to any other security interest.

To support his conclusion, the trial judge referred to a clause in the security agreement which allowed the debtor to use the collateral in its possession in any manner not inconsistent with the agreement. He found that, by allowing Churchill to deposit the cheques with the credit union, Flexi-Coil had [at p. 128] "implicitly subordinated its interest in the proceeds to the interest of Kindersley as banker for Churchill, and as *otherwise* allowed for in s. 39."

In deciding this issue, the trial judge relied on *Euroclean Canada Inc. v. Forest Glade Investments Ltd.* (1985), 16 DLR (4th) 289, 54 CBR 65, 4 PPSAC 271 (Ont. CA). *Euroclean* involved a competition between a perfected floating charge debenture holder and a subsequent unperfected conditional sales vendor. A clause in the floating charge allowed the debtor to "give mortgages or liens in connection with the acquisition of property" after the execution of the floating charge. The Ontario Court of Appeal held that this was an agreement to subordinate the interest of the debenture holder to the interest of those in the position of the conditional sales vendor.

With all due respect to the trial judge, *Euroclean* does not apply to the case at bar. The purpose of s. 39 is to give a third party, who is not party to a subordination agreement, the right to rely on such an agreement as its intended beneficiary. There was no agreement between Churchill and Flexi-Coil to the effect that Flexi-Coil would subordinate its interest in proceeds to others. Clause 4 of the security agreement between Flexi-Coil and Churchill provided that Churchill could "use the collateral in any manner not inconsistent with this agreement," but it would have been inconsistent with the security agreement for Churchill to have "used" the proceeds so that the security interest in the proceeds would be lost.

Whether it is even possible for a secured party to subordinate its security interest by a course of conduct is doubtful, but need not be decided in this case as the course of conduct was insufficient to give rise to such an inference. Flexi-Coil was not aware Churchill was applying the proceeds from the sale of Flexi-Coil equipment as payment on a line of credit, nor did Flexi-Coil acquiesce in Churchill paying the proceeds from the sale of its inventory to another creditor. The terms of the consignment or sale agreements between Churchill and Flexi-Coil required payment by the 10th of the month, or immediately if it was a sale out of existing inventory or a special order. It was simply easier for Churchill to deposit the cheques written to it (which represented the full purchase price) and to write new cheques to Flexi-Coil for Flexi-Coil's portion of the purchase price. One cannot infer Flexi-Coil had subordinated its interest in the proceeds by acquiescing in this practice. To infer an implicit subordination would seriously affect inventory suppliers.

As part of his reasoning, the trial judge pointed to s. 51 of the PPSA which provides that registration of a security interest in the personal property registry is not constructive notice or knowledge of its contents to third parties. It is unclear what the trial judge meant by this reference. At this point, it is sufficient to say the purpose of s. 51 was to remove the possibility of registration being held to constitute constructive notice in priority competitions. Where knowledge is a factor in determining priority under the PPSA, only actual knowledge is relevant: see, *e.g.*, ss. 21 and 67(3) of the PPSA.

Arguments on appeal

Although the trial judge's decision cannot be supported on the grounds listed above, the credit union argued the result could be sustained on other grounds. The credit union agreed the cheques and electronically transferred funds were proceeds of Flexi-Coil's inventory but argued, first, it took the cheques free and clear of Flexi-Coil's security interest as: (i) a *bona fide* purchaser for value; (ii) a purchaser under s. 31(3) of the *Personal Property Security Act* [OPPSA, s.29]; or (iii) a holder in due course under ss. 73 and 165(3) of the *Bills of Exchange Act*, RSC 1985, c. B-4. Secondly, the credit union argued the deposit of the cheques did not create second-generation proceeds because, when the cheques were deposited, the account was in negative balance. It argued that electronically transferred funds should be treated in the same way as cheques. Following initial argument, the credit union put forward two additional arguments, namely: (i) if second-generation proceeds were created, they were set off against the money owed to the credit union on the line of credit; and (ii) the doctrine of change of position protected the credit union when funds were readvanced on the line of credit.

Flexi-Coil advanced that the credit union took the cheques subject to Flexi-Coil's interest, but fundamentally, when the cheques and funds were deposited, there existed a right to payment as the proceeds of its collateral. In other words, Flexi-Coil would have us find that when the credit union advanced further funds on the line of the credit, it advanced its own funds and not the proceeds belonging to Flexi-Coil.

Operation of the account

The credit union's and Flexi-Coil's arguments are dependent on an analysis of the process at the credit union when the cheques and electronically transferred funds were deposited. Credit union personnel testified as to the operation of Churchill's account: when cheques were presented for payment, they were accompanied by a deposit slip, initialled or signed by Churchill, directing the credit union to "credit" the current account; when the funds were electronically transferred, a similar document was prepared by the credit union. An official with the credit union testified the credit union's system was on-line, and, when cheques were deposited, the account would be credited automatically. If the account was in a debit balance, *i.e.*, any of the $175,000 drawn down, the crediting of the account reduced the amount owing on the line of credit and Churchill was immediately given the right to reborrow that amount. If the account was in a credit balance, *i.e.*, none of the $175,000 drawn down, the amount paid in would augment the account. This latter state of affairs never occurred with Churchill. Throughout the life of the account, the line of credit was always significantly drawn down. The automatic process was conditional on the cheques ultimately being honoured by the drawee banks. If a deposited cheque was not honoured for some reason, the previous debit balance would be increased by the amount of the dishonoured cheque the next working day. It was possible for cheques written by Churchill on the account to be honoured before deposits cleared since credit was "immediately" given when cheques were deposited.

There were no agreements showing how the operating account worked. There was a "Loan Agreement" and a "Line of Credit Agreement" but these did not specifically address the revolving nature of the account. Credit union personnel testified the revolving account operated on the basis of custom for such accounts.

One exhibit at trial was a document entitled "Member's Statement of Accounts" which was introduced in evidence to show, by example, how the account operated. This document, produced by the credit union's computerized system, showed the state of Churchill's current account in relation to the line of credit for a one-month period. As of the beginning of the month, the "Balance" column showed a negative balance as it did throughout the account's existence. When a deposit was made, it would be shown in a column headed "Credits/Principal" and the "Balance" column would be reduced by such amount. This indicated that the deposit and the negative balance were in essence "netted" to display a lower negative balance as of the moment the cheques or funds were deposited.

Issue: Whether the cheques were taken by the credit union free of Flexi-Coil's interest

(a) Bona fide purchaser for value

I turn then to the credit union's first argument: that the interest of Flexi-Coil was defeated when the cheques were deposited into Churchill's bank account because the credit union was a *bona fide* purchaser for value without notice. The basis of this claim is that Flexi-Coil must be able to trace its proceeds into the hands of the credit union, and to do so, it is argued, Flexi-Coil must rely on the equitable rules of tracing. At equity, a person seeking to trace property would not be successful if the property came into the hands of a *bona fide* purchaser for value. It has been said this rule did not form part of the common law rules of tracing, which permitted a plaintiff to follow money as long as the funds were not mingled in a bank account. In Fridman's *Restitution* (1992), at p. 417, the author stated:

The distinction between legal and equitable titles and between tracing at common law and in equity is of considerable importance. One reason for this is that a common law proprietary claim may not be defeated by the fact that the defendant acquired the property in good faith and for value; he may still not be able to assert a title that is superior to that of the original legal owner. Only if the common law recognizes a situation in which title may be lost involuntarily, for example, through estoppel or under the provisions of a Factors Act, will the owner at law lose his proprietary rights. In contrast, if the plaintiff's claim is based on equitable title, he may be defeated should the defendant be a *bona fide* purchaser for value without notice of that title.

Clearly, this bar to tracing in equity extends to situations where it is not goods, but money or its equivalent which is transferred to the third party for value without notice. As stated by Denning J in *Nelson v. Larholt*, [1947] 2 All ER 751 (KB), at p. 752:

The relevant legal principles have been much developed in the last 35 years. A man's money is property which is protected by law. It may exist in various forms, such as coins, Treasury notes, cash at bank, cheques, or bills of exchange, but, whatever its form, it is protected according to one uniform principle. If it is taken from the rightful owner, or, indeed, from the beneficial owner, without his authority, he can recover the amount from any person into whose hands it can be traced unless and *until it reaches one who receives it in good faith and for value and without notice of the want of authority.*

(Emphasis added.) See also, *Re Cohen & Lyons*, [1927] 1 DLR 577 at pp. 581-2, 8 CBR 23, [1927] 1 WWR 162 (Alta. CA).

Section 28(1)(b) of the PPSA [OPPSA, s.25(1)] provides: "Subject to the other provisions of this Act, where collateral is dealt with or otherwise gives rise to proceeds, the security interest therein ... (b) extends to the proceeds." Section 2(ee) [OPPSA, s.1(1)] of the PPSA defines "proceeds" to mean "identifiable or traceable personal property in any form ... derived directly or indirectly from any dealing with the collateral or proceeds therefrom." The PPSA provides no further guidance for determining when an asset is identifiable or traceable so as to be proceeds, but this court has interpreted this clause on several occasions. A sampling of such cases is: *Canadian Imperial Bank of Commerce v. Marathon Realty Co.* (1987), 40 DLR (4th) 326, [1987] 5 WWR 236, 57 Sask. R 88; *Transamerica, supra; Agricultural Credit Corp. of Saskatchewan v. Pettyjohn* (1991), 79 DLR (4th) 22, 1 PPSAC (2d) 273, [1991] 3 WWR 689; and *Indian Head Credit Union v. Andrew* (1992), 97 DLR (4th) 462, 7 BLR (2d) 196, [1993] 1 WWR 673.

Vancise JA in *Transamerica*, at pp. 633-4, accepted Professor Donovan Waters' analysis of what constitutes identifiable and traceable proceeds as taken from "Trusts in the Setting of Business, Commerce, and Bankruptcy" (1983), 21 Alta. Law Rev. 395 at pp. 431-4. Based on this article, Vancise JA concluded: "... 'identifiable' refers to the ability to point to the particular property obtained by the debtor as a result of the dealing with the collateral, while 'traceable' refers to the situation where the collateral is commingled with other property so that its identity is lost." In *Transamerica*, cheques were deposited into a bank account in positive balance. The bank had applied the credit to an existing indebtedness without the debtor's authorization. The proceeds-secured party was permitted to trace into the account to defeat the bank's claim. Vancise JA held the right to trace under the PPSA was not limited by equity's requirement of a fiduciary relationship between the debtor and the secured party: see p. 634.

In *Indian Head Credit Union*, this court gave priority to the credit union as the proceeds-secured party over the Royal Bank. The collateral claimed as proceeds was a term deposit purchased with the proceeds of a cheque made payable to the debtor as compensation for the destruction of cattle, the original collateral covered by the credit union's security interest. The cheque was deposited by the debtor into his account at the bank. He subsequently purchased a term deposit with the amount on deposit and used the term deposit as security for a new loan from the bank. The case turned essentially on the finding that the bank knew the cheque was proceeds of the cattle, but the credit union was able to trace its security interest to the term deposit and defeat the bank which claimed the term deposit as its security.

In *Pettyjohn*, the issue was whether certain cattle were traceable as proceeds of other cattle. The debtor, under a security agreement with the Agricultural Credit Corp. of Saskatchewan, argued that when he paid down his debt on a revolving line of credit at his bank with proceeds from the sale of the first herd of cattle, ACCS lost its purchase-money security interest. Subsequently, the debtor purchased other cattle (using the same bank account) which ACCS now claimed as proceeds of the first cattle. There had been numerous deposits and withdrawals to the account, rendering it difficult to identify, with certainty, a direct link between the paying down of the debt and the withdrawal of funds to purchase the second herd. The court, however, developed a fundamental equivalency test based on a close and substantial connection to find the second herd proceeds of the first.

From these cases, one concludes that the secured party's right to trace proceeds is a statutory right not dependent on finding a fiduciary relationship between the debtor and the secured party claiming proceeds. Furthermore, the mingling of funds in a bank account with other funds does not prevent a successful proceeds claim; the funds remain traceable. When one reads these cases with *Re Diplock*, [1948] 1 Ch. 465 (CA); affirmed [1951] AC 251 *sub nom. Ministry of Health v. Simpson* (HL), the leading case on tracing in equity, it is clear this court has not simply adopted the common law or equitable rules of tracing to determine when a secured party can trace under the PPSA, but rather, has developed rules based on the PPSA which are uniquely designed to achieve the flexibility and certainty required by the PPSA. To such an end, the courts, in resolving disputes which invoke the right to trace, should use the common law and equitable rules as their base but, as far as possible, seek to found solutions on the statute and its underlying policy. It is especially important to look to the PPSA to determine whether the statute provides a rule in this case where the right to follow, at common law, may not be restricted by the purchase for value of the cheques, but at equity the right to trace would be. Clearly, it is open to the credit union to make additional arguments based on equitable principles as contemplated by s. 64(5) of the PPSA which reads as follows:

64(5) The principles of the common law, equity and the law merchant, except insofar as they are inconsistent with the express provisions of this Act, supplement this Act and continue to apply.

However, where the issue is addressed almost conclusively by the statute, it is preferable to look to the applicable priority rule in the PPSA which is s. 31(3). This eliminates, on this point at least, the necessity of determining whether the common law or equitable rules would allow tracing in these circumstances: see R.M. Goode, "The Right to Trace and its Impact in Commercial Transactions—I" (1976), 92 Law Q. Rev. 360.

(b) Purchaser under s. 31(3)

Section 31(3) of the PPSA [OPPSA, S.28(4)] provides in relevant part as follows:

31(3) A purchaser of an instrument ... has priority over any security interest in the instrument ... perfected under section 25 [the registration section] ... if the purchaser:

(a) gave value for his interest;

(b) acquired the instrument ... without notice that it was subject to a security interest; and

(c) took possession of the instrument ...

The cheques deposited to the credit union were instruments (see s. 2(u) of the PPSA), Flexi-Coil's interest was perfected by registration under s. 25 of the PPSA and the credit union took possession without notice of Flexi-Coil's prior security interest. "Purchaser" is defined by s. 2(hh) of the PPSA as "a person who takes by purchase." "Purchase" is defined by s. 2(ff) of the PPSA to include "taking by sale, lease, discount, negotiation, mortgage, pledge, lien, issue or reissue, gift or any other voluntary transaction creating an interest in personal property." Section 2(qq) defines "value" as "any consideration sufficient to support a simple contract and includes an antecedent debt or liability." Thus, the issues remaining are, when the cheques were deposited: (i) was the credit union a purchaser; and (ii) did it give value?

To determine whether the credit union was a "purchaser" requires some consideration of its status when it took the cheques. Crawford and Falconbridge, *Banking and Bills of Exchange*, 8th ed. (Toronto: Canada Law Book Inc., 1986), at pp. 1041-3 and Ogilvie, *Canadian Banking Law*, at pp. 584-5 discuss the status of a "collecting bank." Whether a deposit-taking institution acts as principal or agent, they conclude, is a question of fact. Ogilvie at pp. 584-5 said:

... it is necessary to establish the legal status enjoyed by a bank when it collects a cheque, both at common law and pursuant to section 165(3) of the *Bills of Exchange Act* ...

At one time it was fundamental to determine whether the bank was acting as a collecting bank or a discounting bank. When it was simply a collecting bank, it did not acquire property in the cheque but where it was a discounting bank, it permitted the customer to draw against the funds in the cheque prior to final clearance and received payment of the funds on its own account. A bank also became a discounting bank where it reduced an existing overdraft by the amount of the cheque before sending it for clearance ...

Thus Ogilvie would conclude that, when a cheque is deposited to a revolving account in negative balance, the collecting bank acts as a discounting bank in relation to the cheque.

Both texts acknowledge that a collecting bank which receives notice a cheque has been dishonoured is entitled to reverse provisional credit. But if the customer has already drawn upon the account (such that the reversal does not fully compensate the bank), the bank retains rights in the cheque even if partial recovery from the account has been made. The collector is entitled to proceed against the drawer of the cheque, its own customer or the payee: see Ogilvie, at p. 589 and Crawford and Falconbridge, at pp. 1056-7. This right exists whether the collector is a principal or agent by virtue of s. 165(3) of the *Bills of Exchange Act*, and arises simply by reducing an overdraft: see Crawford and Falconbridge, at p. 1756.

I note also that Crawford and Falconbridge at pp. 1443-51 and Baxter's *The Law of Banking*, 3rd ed., at p. 73, would accord the credit union the status of a holder for value.

It is not necessary to determine the credit union's exact status as a holder or collecting bank. It is only necessary to determine whether it acquired an interest to bring it within s. 2(ff) and (hh) of the PPSA. When Churchill presented a cheque, accompanied by a deposit slip, to the credit union, one must infer Churchill gave the cheque to the credit union in order to reduce the balance: see *Kimmel v. Bean*, 75 P. 1118 (SC Kan., 1904) at p. 1121; and *Agard v. Peoples Nat. Bank of Shakopee*, 211 NW 825 (SC Minn., 1927). Conceptually, it cannot be otherwise. The value of a cheque could not create a positive balance in the account as the credit union waited for some further direction, from Churchill, to credit the account while at the same time interest continued to accrue on the outstanding balance on the line of credit. After reducing the overdraft, immediate credit was given. That the credit could be reversed is irrelevant. Based on the above statements which describe a collecting bank's rights and status, the credit union's reduction of Churchill's debt and the grant of further credit gave the credit union a sufficient interest in each cheque to make it a purchaser for the purpose of s. 31(3).

As indicated, when the cheques were deposited, the account was immediately credited and Churchill was able to write cheques on the account equivalent to the amount of the cheques deposited, subject to the $175,000 limit. Based on the definition of value, value was given in exchange for the cheques when the amount owing on the line of credit was reduced and, of course, when the right to draw additional funds was made available. Thus, the credit union took the cheques free and clear of the interest of Flexi-Coil when the cheques were deposited by virtue of s. 31(3).

Having reached this conclusion, it is unnecessary to consider the credit union's third argument on this point.

Issue: Whether second-generation proceeds were created

In considering this issue, it is helpful to return again to the definition of "proceeds" in s. 2(e) of the PPSA. From this definition, one concludes proceeds must have the following characteristics: (i) the proceeds must be personal property; (ii) the proceeds must be identifiable or traceable; and (iii) the proceeds, which must arise from a commercial dealing, can be derived either from a dealing with the original collateral or other proceeds. It is this third feature which makes it necessary to ask whether a dealing with the cheques resulted in another "generation" of proceeds to which Flexi-Coil's interest attached.

It is possible to describe a fourth feature of proceeds under the PPSA: the debtor must have an interest in the personal property *claimed as proceeds*. Versions of the PPSA, more recent than Saskatchewan's, contain an express statement to that effect in the proceeds definition: see, *e.g.*, the *Personal Property Security Act*, SBC 1989, c. 36, s. 1(1), definition "proceeds." The absence of an express statement does not permit a secured party to claim, as proceeds, collateral in which the debtor has no interest. On this point, see R.C.C. Cuming, "Protecting Security Interests in Proceeds: Equity and the Canadian Personal Property Security Acts" (a paper prepared for the Second International Symposium on Trusts, Equity and Fiduciary Relationships, University of Victoria, British Columbia, January 20-23, 1993), at pp. 6 and 15:

A security interest, whether in original or proceeds, collateral can attach only to personal property in which the debtor has a proprietary interest. Quite apart from the conceptual consistency which the limitation preserves, there is an important public policy reason for it. One of the more difficult policy issues endemic to the Personal Property Security Acts is the position of remote third parties who cannot protect themselves through a search of the registry. The problems associated with the use of the debtor name as the appropriate registration-search criterion would be multiplied if the Acts were to recognize that a security interest extends to personal property in which the debtor did not acquire an interest.

• • •

... statutory tracing is more limited than tracing in Equity in that it applies only where the debtor has acquired rights in the personal property that is claimed as proceeds.

Flexi-Coil claimed: (i) the deposit of the cheques created a right to payment which was an account or an intangible belonging to Churchill which was attached by its interest; or, in the alternative, (ii) when the cheques passed through the clearing process, the funds generated belonged to Churchill and were at that time applied to reduce the debt. This argument is based on Professor Goode's article referred to above at pp. 379-80:

If T [Churchill] receives a cheque to which O [Flexi-Coil] is entitled to possession and, though accountable to O at common law, gives the cheque for collection to his own bank to be credited to his account, the right to follow has to be looked at in relation not to one asset but to three.

The three assets referred to are: (i) the cheque; (ii) the chose in action, namely, the claim which the customer acquires against his or her bank when the account is credited; and (iii) the money representing the proceeds of the cheque. The credit union argued that no proceeds within the meaning of the PPSA were created after the cheques were deposited. In advancing its position, the credit union relied heavily on the account's status as a revolving one in negative balance.

(a) Proceeds in the form of an account or an intangible

To assess whether an account or an intangible was created when the cheques were deposited, it is necessary to compare the relationship between a banker and a depositor when an account is in overdraft to that relationship when an account is in positive balance. With respect to the former relationship, Ogilvie, *Canadian Banking Law*, said at p. 464:

As long as an account is in funds, the customer is the creditor of the banker. However, once an account has a negative balance or a deficit, the relationship is reversed and the banker becomes the creditor of the customer. An account in overdraft is legally characterized as a loan which is granted to the customer.

As to what happens when a deposit is made to an account in overdraft, reference may also be made to *M'Lean v. Clydesdale Banking Company* (1883), 9 App. Cas. 95 (HL). In this case, a drawer of a cheque stopped payment on a cheque already deposited to an overdrawn account. When the cheque was credited to the payee's account, the court found the deposit of the cheque extinguished the sum overdrawn, to that extent therefore giving the bank priority.

This is to be contrasted with the situation when a cheque is deposited to an account in positive balance. Again, taking from Ogilvie at p. 463:

The indebtedness of the bank created when a deposit is made would appear to come into existence at the time of the deposit being made. Where a deposit is made in cash, the time when the indebtedness of the bank would appear to arise is when the customer's account is credited either by a passbook entry or by inputting through a computer terminal to a computerized account record where the account does not carry a passbook. This is so whether the deposit is made in person or through a banking machine. Where the deposit is made by negotiable instrument, the position is less clear since an entry either in a passbook or a computerized record is provisional until the instrument is cleared. It is arguable that the indebtedness arises when the instrument is paid in by the customer and a provisional credit is made because in most cases the provisional credit will be cleared and in the event that is not the case other legal remedies are available to permit a bank to recover funds drawn by the customer against the uncleared deposit.

Thus, when a cheque is deposited with a deposit-taking institution when an account is in positive balance, the debtor-creditor relationship between the institution and the depositor gives rise to a monetary obligation on behalf of the bank. Under s. 2(b) of the PPSA a "monetary obligation not evidenced by chattel paper, an instrument or a security" is an account. The account which comes into existence when a cheque is deposited to an account in positive balance is the proceeds of a dealing with the cheque. This is the basis upon which the proceeds-secured party was able to trace the proceeds of the cheques into the deposit account in *Transamerica*. Similarly, in *Indian Head Credit Union*, the bank argued it was entitled to priority because, when it sold the term deposit to Mr. Andrew, it was a holder of money under s. 31(1) of the PPSA and, therefore, knowledge of the credit union's interest was irrelevant. Madam Justice Gerwing said this at p. 477:

The Bank in seeking to protect itself by s. 31(1), that is, as a holder of money, overlooks the two stages in the transaction. The Bank in taking the cheque from Andrew clearly received an instrument. His account was then credited with the amount of the cheque. This placed Andrew and the bank in a debtor-creditor relationship. The Bank did not acquire "money" from Andrew, within the definition of that term in s. 2, and not having "acquired the money" is not within s. 31(1). It acquired an instrument which may have been subsequently converted. The Bank cannot, by purporting to ignore the sequential legal steps in the deposit of the cheque and the crediting of the account, place itself within a section which was not designed to cover this situation.

Counsel for Flexi-Coil argued the "Member's Statement of Accounts," referred to above, was evidence the deposit of the cheques gave rise to an "account" within the meaning of the PPSA. It was argued that, based on *Transamerica* and *Indian Head*, the deposit of the cheques gave rise to a monetary obligation on the part of the credit union in favour of Churchill, thus giving rise to a debtor-creditor relationship sufficient to be personal property. The significant difference between the two cases above and the case before us is, in this case, there never was a point at which Churchill could have called for the proceeds of the cheque to be paid to him. The account was never in positive balance. Churchill had directed his account be credited. Since it was in negative balance, the result was a netting of the two amounts. When an account is in overdraft, based on Ogilvie's analysis, no property right arises. The customer is the debtor of the deposit-taking institution.

I accept the credit union's argument that the reference to "Credit" in the "Member's Statement of Accounts" was not a "credit" in the sense it represented an amount available to Churchill or proceeds available to Flexi-Coil. Rather it was merely a form of bookkeeping. The credit union was required to deposit the amount to that account by Churchill's direction on the deposit slip, and since the account was in negative balance, it was required to apply the funds to the amount owing. It never existed as a positive amount in the account for even a fraction of time. Churchill's right to the amount represented by the cheque was dependent on the credit union honouring its agreement to re-advance the equivalent amount under the line of credit. Once Churchill directed the credit union to credit the account, when in negative balance, there were no proceeds of the cheque to which Churchill was entitled or to which Flexi-Coil's security interest could attach.

When the cheques were deposited, the credit union's only obligation to Churchill was to credit the overdraft and then make further credit available up to the $175,000 limit, provided the line of credit agreement was not otherwise in default. Following the making of a deposit, Churchill could not have sued the credit union and recovered the deposit. The credit union's obligation to credit the account is not an intangible to which a security interest can attach to permit recovery by forcing a payment from the credit union to Flexi-Coil. Churchill's only right after making the deposit was to have the account balance credited. If Flexi-Coil attached this right, it could be in no better position than Churchill.

(b) Proceeds in the form of funds from the clearing process

That brings us to Flexi-Coil's second argument on second-generation proceeds: the funds generated through the clearing process were collected for Churchill's account and were applied at that time to reduce its indebtedness. Flexi-Coil's counsel argued that, when the cheques were honoured by the payee banks, the funds which came to the credit union were Flexi-Coil's proceeds converted by the credit union. This argument, too, must fail. When the cheques were deposited, Churchill's debt was reduced. It is true this process was subject to reversal if a cheque was dishonoured, but if a cheque was honoured, the funds were collected for the credit union's account and not for Churchill: see the above quote taken from pp. 584-5 of Ogilvie. Value had already been given to Churchill in exchange for the cheques when the outstanding balance was reduced.

Clearly, the funds need not be in existence to sustain a proceeds claim. In *Transamerica* and *Indian Head Credit Union*, there were no proceeds left as such because the lenders had applied the funds to their customers' debts. In *Transamerica*, cheques were deposited and subsequently applied to reduce the indebtedness to the bank, and, yet, a third party was allowed to trace into the account and subsequently pursue the bank for the equivalent of the amount that had been in the account. Similarly, in *Indian Head Credit Union*, a cheque was deposited with the bank and the proceeds were used to purchase a term deposit and subsequently claimed by the bank as its security. But, in those cases there had been proceeds in which the debtor, and therefore the proceeds-secured party, had an interest and those proceeds had been appropriated by the lender. Here, the credit union took the first-generation proceeds, *i.e.*, the cheques, free and clear of the interest of Flexi-Coil. Churchill received value for those cheques. After the cheques passed through the cheque-clearing process, there were no proceeds in which Churchill, and therefore Flexi-Coil, had an interest.

In passing I should refer to the only case directly on point which is *C & H Farm Service Co. of Iowa v. Farmers Savings Bank*, 449 NW 2d 866 (Iowa SC, 1989). This case concerned a competition between a proceeds-secured party and a bank. The proceeds-secured party, C & H, had taken a security interest in the Schellhorns' crops. Some grain was sold and the cheques deposited to the Schellhorns' chequing account at the bank. At all material times, the account was in negative balance. The bank continued to honour the overdraft which was credited by the deposit of further cheques. The Iowa District Court found for the bank on the basis that the proceeds were not identifiable because the account was in negative balance. That court reasoned that, if the account had always been in positive balance, the Schellhorns could have always paid other creditors and no claim would lie against the bank for converting the proceeds. The Iowa Supreme Court reversed the District Court's decision and found for the proceeds-secured party. The Supreme Court found the Schellhorns' overdrafts were not paid from identifiable cash proceeds deposited to the Schellhorns' account, but from the bank's own funds. The Supreme Court said this at p. 876:

Rather, various creditors of the customer presented cheques to the bank for payment from an account which had an overdrawn, or debit balance. *The bank paid these cheques out of its own funds*. In effect, the bank loaned Schellhorns enough money to cover the amount of the grain for deposit and applied those proceeds to reduce the debit balance of Schellhorns' account, it was simply satisfying Schellhorns' antecedent debt to it with proceeds in which C & H had a security interest ... the bank paid cheques to other creditors of its customer with its own funds and then paid itself with proceeds in which a secured party, C & H, had a security interest.

(Emphasis added in original.) The Supreme Court said, when the bank paid Schellhorns' cheques in overdraft, the bank became Schellhorns' creditor and accepted the risk of an unsecured loan. It concluded that, when cheques were deposited, the bank set off what it owed the Schellhorns against that which the Schellhorns owed the bank on the overdraft. The Supreme Court said the bank could not do this, and went on to say at pp. 876-7, that the bank could not loan money to Schellhorns by paying Schellhorns' overdrafts and then expect to "jump over" C & H's priority to identifiable proceeds of C & H's collateral.

Another case dealing with a somewhat similar fact situation is *General Motors Acceptance Corp. of Canada Ltd. v. Bank of Nova Scotia* (1986), 6 PPSAC 53, 55 OR (2d) 438 (CA). In this case, which also involved a revolving line of credit and a proceeds-secured party seeking to trace, the court found for the bank largely because the payments were made in the ordinary course of business. This case may very well be confined to its own facts. I note, in this regard, the analysis by J.S. Ziegel, "Tracing of Proceeds under the Ontario Personal Property Security Act: *General Motors Acceptance Corp. of Canada, Ltd. v. Bank of Nova Scotia*" (1987-88), 13 *CBLJ* 177.

Counsel for the credit union is to be commended for drawing the court's attention to the *C & H Farm Service* case as it appears to be adverse in interest, but I find the case to be distinguishable. On a review of the facts, it appears the bank decided on its own to create the overdraft. There is also a suggestion of knowledge of the proceeds-secured party's interest. The language used in the case is strong, but it does not address the facts in the case before us: (i) the credit union had no knowledge of Flexi-Coil's interest; and (ii) the deposit was made to a revolving account in negative balance. In so far as it addresses this case, I prefer the analysis of the lower court.

Finally, it is worth noting that, if counsel for Flexi-Coil were correct, a deposit-taking institution would stand as its customers' guarantor with respect to customers' obligations to proceeds-secured parties. For example, in the *Pettyjohn* case, *supra*, the Pettyjohns banked with the Bank of Montreal. Their deposit account interacted with a line of credit. Whenever the balance of the account went below zero, funds in multiples of $5,000 were automatically borrowed, by agreement, against the line of credit and deposited into the account. Whenever the account balance rose above $5,000, funds in multiples of $5,000 were automatically withdrawn to make payments on the line of credit. As Sherstobitoff JA found at p. 32, the chequing account was itself only a conduit leading to the line of credit. In the case at bar, the credit union stands in the same position as the Bank of Montreal in the *Pettyjohn* case. If Flexi-Coil is correct in its position, ACCS could have also sued the Bank of Montreal in *Pettyjohn* to recover the money applied to the line of credit but which were the proceeds of the sale of cattle in which ACCS had an interest. This cannot have been the intention of the legislature.

Having concluded that no second-generation proceeds were created, it is not necessary to consider the credit union's arguments with respect to set-off and change of position.

Electronic transfer of funds

Counsel for Flexi-Coil pointed out that s. 31 of the PPSA does not deal with electronic transfers of funds and therefore, whatever decision is reached in relation to the cheques, Flexi-Coil must succeed in relation to the credit transfers. These transfers occurred without the use of money or an instrument as defined in the PPSA or the *Bills of Exchange Act*: see Falconbridge and Crawford, *op. cit.*, at pp. 1011-27. Counsel for the credit union argued it would be inconsistent as a matter of policy, to accord a different legal status to credit transfers than that given to money or cheques. It was submitted that a medium of payment such as electronic transfers, accepted by the banking system as a substitute or equivalent for money or cheques, should receive the same treatment at law.

When the PPSA was drafted, credit transfers were relatively new and therefore they are not referred to in the PPSA. What then should be the result? The credit union's proposal is entirely consistent with s. 31(1), (2) and (3) of the PPSA. There is a great deal of merit to the credit union's position. Arguably, these sections, in so far as they deal with matters in federal jurisdiction, were not needed and merely restate the federal law. The goal of these sections is to leave money and cheques largely free from security interests to preserve the integrity of the payment system in Canada which now includes credit transfers. Churchill initiated these credit transfers, in the ordinary course of business, and they were treated by the credit union in the same way as the cheques. When a credit transfer was made, it was immediately applied to reduce the account balance. After the transfer occurred, no second-generation proceeds were created. Accordingly, it is my opinion the credit transfers and the cheques should be treated alike judicially and priority given to the credit union with respect to the credit transfers as well.

Miscellaneous points

There are two miscellaneous matters which require comment. The first is the effect of this decision on secured parties who finance inventory. On this point, different public policy objectives of the PPSA collide. One goal of the PPSA is to provide security for those who finance inventory. It is expected inventory will be sold and proceeds will be generated. Prior to the enactment of the PPSA, the status and security of proceeds claims were beset with problems. These are documented in J.S. Ziegel and R.C.C. Cuming, "The Modernization of Canadian Personal Property Security Law" (1981), 31 *UTLJ* 249. The PPSA significantly addresses these problems. In this case, it may appear as a matter of policy Flexi-Coil, the inventory supplier, should win. However, there are two policy reasons which support a resolution of this case to the contrary. The first is the need to maintain certainty within the banking system. Clearly, s. 31(3) of the PPSA is designed to achieve that end. It, like the other subsections in s. 31, is an exception to the general priority provisions of the PPSA. The second is the need to preserve the debtor's right to pay its creditors. The PPSA recognizes this need in s. 31(1) and (2). As a matter of practical analysis, what Churchill did here was direct a payment to its creditor. At the end of the day it is the latter two policy considerations which govern in this case.

As an extension of this point, it was urged upon us that a result in favour of the credit union would significantly affect the priority given to inventory suppliers; that lending institutions would simply require their customers to deposit all retail cheques to accounts in negative balance to avoid the claims of inventory suppliers. This was of concern to the court, but since the court did not have before it any evidence of such dealings, this issue is best left to another day without further comment.

The second miscellaneous matter concerns the "Loan Agreement" and the "Line of Credit Agreement" between the credit union and Churchill referred to earlier. Under the loan agreement, the credit union granted a loan to be paid in full on March 23, 1985, or on demand. The agreement provided that the deposit account could be charged with payments as they matured. The line of credit agreement provided that Churchill granted to the credit union "a lien against any monies on deposit." If Churchill defaulted in any payment due under the line of credit agreement, the credit union had the authority to exercise its lien on the deposit account. Following the initial hearing of the appeal, the court requested further submissions as to the effect of this clause on the operation of the revolving credit account. After reviewing these submissions, I accept that this clause in the line of credit agreement merely reflects s. 34 of the *Credit Union Act*, 1985, SS 1984-85-86, c. C-45.1. The intention of the clause was to grant a lien on sums in positive balance and is not pertinent.

Appeal dismissed.

PRIORITIES WITH RESPECT TO REPOSSESSED OR RETURNED GOODS

OPPSA s. 27 deals with the competing interests that may arise where goods subject to a security interest are sold in ordinary course by the debtor and then are repossessed by the debtor or are returned to him by the buyer, e.g., because the goods are defective or of the wrong kind or because the buyer cannot afford or does not wish to keep them. The competing interests that may arise are (a) between the debtor and a prior secured party; (b) between the debtor and the transferee of chattel paper or an account generated under the prior sale; and (c) between the prior secured party and a transferee of chattel paper or an account.

There was little Canadian case law on these questions under the prior law, and the courts had difficulty getting a firm handle on the conceptual and policy issues. See, e.g., *Commercial Finance Corp. v. Capital Discount Corp.*, [1931] 1 DLR 1007 (Ont. CA); and *Globe Financial Corp. v. Sterling Securities*, [1932] 1 WWR 347 (Sask. CA). Section 29 of the Act was based on UCC 9-306(5) but it was so compressed that it was difficult to disentangle its various elements. The Advisory Committee therefore decided to replace it with the more clearly drafted s. 29 of the Uniform Act.

Section 27(1) regulates the rights to the returned/repossessed goods between the debtor and the prior secured party; s. 27(3) does the same with respect to the rights of the transferee of chattel paper or an account. Section 27(5) states when the transferee of an account is deemed to have acquired a perfected security interest in the goods for the purpose of resolving priority disputes and implicitly refers the reader to the basic priority rules in ss. 30 and 33 of the new Act to determine an actual contest. (Assuming the contest is with a prior inventory financer of the debtor, whose security interest will have priority?) The Code's position is different. UCC 9-306(4)(c) provides that the unpaid transferee's security interest is subordinate to the inventory financer's security interest. Can you suggest why the inventory financer is being preferred?

Finally, s. 27(6)(a) of the new Act regulates contests between the inventory financer and the transferee of chattel paper in terms of the priority rules applying to the chattel paper itself (as to which see s. 28(3) of the new Act). Section 27(6)(b) deals with priority conflicts between the transferee and other secured parties claiming an interest in the goods.

Note that s. 27, like UCC 9-307(4), has nothing to say about the rights of a transferee of an instrument. Presumably this is due to an oversight. What rules should be applied? Section 27 also does not answer the question whether the buyer who has returned the goods is discharged from further liability to the transferee of the account or chattel paper. To what extent does s. 40 answer the question? How would the common law answer it?

THE FLOATING CHARGE REVISITED

Now that we have completed our study of the attachment, perfection and priority provisions of the PPS Acts and the special provisions protecting ordinary course purchasers and holders in due course, we are in a better position to evaluate the status of the English-style floating charge under the new legislation and to assess the consequences of its having been converted into a fixed charge with an implied licence to the debtor to carry on business. How do these consequences compare with the rights of third parties under the equitable floating charge? Have the PPS drafters been too generous in their treatment of floating charges?

Jacob Ziegel
"Recent and Prospective Developments in the Personal Property Security Area and the Recommendations of the Ontario Advisory Committee"
in *Special Lectures of the Law Soc. of Upper Can. 1985*, 1, at 11-17
(footnotes omitted)

There can be no doubt that the existing Act, and equally the draft Act, apply to floating charges since floating charges are expressly included in the enumeration of security interests covered by the Acts. Even without this explicit authority, the Ontario Court of Appeal has recognized the existence of a floating charge governed by the Ontario Act on at least two occasions. What is not so clear is what conceptual changes the Ontario Act has wrought in the equitable creation. The question has attracted attention from a variety of authors and, while there is substantial consensus on some of the answers, others remain conjectural. Except in one respect, the draft Act does not advance the position and the lawyer has no alternative but to work through the answers in light of the general concepts underlying the legislation and the specific provisions to be found on it.

A good beginning is to isolate the distinctive features of the floating charge at common law and then to see how many of them have survived the enactment of the Ontario Act. There are at least two theories of the floating charge. The first, the older one, treated a charge on shifting assets as a specific charge but subject to an implied licence in favour of the debtor to deal with the collateral in the ordinary course of business. This theory has fallen into disfavour since the turn of the century. It would be a serious mistake, however, to dimiss it as only of historical interest since it may well have been resurrected in the Ontario Act.

The other theory of the floating charge—the dominant one—is the one so picturesquely described by Lord Macnaghten in *Governments Stock and Other Securities Investment Co. Ltd. v. Manila Railway Co.*, [1897] AC 81 (HL): the floating charge is not a specific charge and does not attach in its incipiency to any particular assets of the debtor. Instead it hovers over all the debtor's assets included in the security agreement in their varying forms until a crystallizing event occurs converting the floating charge into a fixed charge.

From the beginning, the decisional law has affirmed the debtor's right to carry on business in the normal way and to dispose and even encumber the collateral. What is less clear is whence the debtor derives this power. Under the older theory of the floating charge it was based on an implied licence. Under the second theory, it is inherent in the nature of the floating charge. Since the secured party has no interest in any particular item in the debtor's floating assets, it is reasoned, and is not entitled to interfere in the operation of the debtor's business prior to crystallization, the debtor must be free to carry on business as before. This approach explains why it is necessary, and customary, for the standard secured debenture to prohibit the creation of subsequent security interests ranking in priority to or *pari passu* with the floating charge. However, it fails to explain why third parties should be bound by such restrictive covenants (whether or not they know of them) and why the debtor's powers of disposition should be restricted to those made "in the course of his business," whatever this may mean. I mention these uncertainties not for academic reasons but to indicate that the Ontario Act, and equally the draft Act, will have performed a valuable role if they put the answers to these questions on a sounder conceptual footing than that on which they rest at present.

What then is the status of the floating charge under the personal property security legislation? The commentators generally agree that it depends on when the security interest created by the agreement is deemed to attach. Section 12(1) of the existing Act provides that it attaches when value has been given, the debtor has rights in the collateral, and when "the parties intend it to attach." Ordinarily, the third requirement creates no difficulties since the agreement will usually provide that the debtor "hereby" gives or agrees to give the secured party a security interest in the described collateral.

If the agreement refers to the creation of a floating charge, using these very words, should this make a difference? I would argue not since the Act does not recognize inchoate or floating security interests in the English sense, or a security interest that has a quasi-immediate existence but only crystallizes on a future occasion. Under all the Canadian personal property security acts, a security interest either has attached or it has not. There is no half-way house. Likewise, contrary to the impression created in some recent judgments, the Ontario Act recognizes only one type of security interest, the type created by the Act itself. The Act recognizes no distinction between legal and equitable interests.

These points may be conceded and yet it may be argued that the use of floating charge terminology in the security agreement indicates the parties' intention to postpone attachment of the security interest until a later date. It is difficult to see why a secured party should intend a result that is so inimical to his interest. This is particularly so since there is nothing in the Act that prevents the secured party from giving the debtor permission to carry on his business without requiring the secured party to postpone attachment of the security interest. However, the Ontario Advisory Committee, like the Uniform Act Committee before it, anticipated the contrary argument being made and has met it.

Section 11(2) of the draft Act provides that a security interest, "including a security interest in the nature of a floating charge," attaches when the other prerequisites have been satisfied and the debtor has rights in the collateral, "unless the parties have agreed to postpone the time for attachment, in which case the security interest attaches at the agreed time." In my view, this formulation leaves little room for argument about the parties' intention and should be interpreted as having the same effect as section 11(1) of the Uniform Act on which it is based. The latter provides that the security interest attaches when the debtor has rights in the collateral unless the security agreement contains a term that "expressly" provides that it shall attach at a later time.

Once it is determined that the security interest has attached to the collateral and that the secured party has done what is necessary to perfect the security interest (almost invariably by registering a financing statement), then his general position *vis-à-vis* third parties should be straightforward. It falls into two parts. With respect to third parties other than competing secured parties, section 22 of the Ontario Act tells us indirectly that a perfected security interest is *not* subordinated to their claims. Section 22 is substantially retained in the draft Act (section 20). Subject to what is said hereafter, I know of no reason why this rule should not also apply to floating charge type security interests. So far as competing secured parties are concerned, their ranking is determined by the priority provisions in the Act and, where no special rule is applicable, by the residual first to file rule in section 35(1)(a) where both security interests have been perfected by filing.

Obviously these general principles must be relaxed if the debtor's business is not to come to a standstill, and we must see how the Ontario Act accommodates this need. (Here again the draft Act introduces no basic changes.) Two provisions are of particular importance. Section 27(1) provides that, where collateral is dealt with so as to give rise to proceeds, the security interest continues as to the collateral unless the secured party expressly or impliedly authorized such dealing. The concept of an implied consent has deep roots in Anglo-Canadian common law and conditional sales legislation. The earlier jurisprudence, as well as the Code case law under UCC 9-306, should prove helpful in providing answers as to when such dealing is authorized where the security agreement fails to address itself to the issue or does so inadequately. One would rarely expect difficulties where a disposition of inventory is involved.

So far as dealings with other types of collateral are concerned, a court is likely to be influenced by the scope of the collateral covered by the agreement, by the duration of the security agreement, and by what the parties must be assumed to have seen as necessary to enable the debtor to carry on business. Whatever the answer in a particular case, it must still be based, in my view, on the secured party's imputed consent. It is this requirement that distinguishes section 27(1)(a) from the common law approach relating to floating charges.

The other important provision that bears on the debtor's freedom of action is section 39, reproduced as section 38 in the draft Act. This provides that a secured party may, "in the security agreement or otherwise," subordinate his security interest to any other security interest. While the meaning of "or otherwise" is not constrained by the *ejusdem generis* rule it can safely be asserted that it was not intended to dispense with the secured party's consent to be subordinated. Section 39 rests on substantially the same conceptual basis as section 27(1)(a) but is seemingly more exacting in its evidentiary requirement of the secured party's consent, and no doubt for good reason.

At least one commentator also sees an important office in section 9 of the Ontario Act in reintroducing a large measure of floating charge law. I do not subscribe to this view. Section 9 is based on UCC 9-201 and was inserted to affirm the parties' freedom of contract and to repudiate such American common law restrictions as the rule in *Benedict v. Ratner*, 268 US 353 (2nd Circ. 1925). Since the Americans never adopted the English type of floating style they could hardly have had it in contemplation. There are two other factors which should make us very cautious is using section 9 as a source of floating charge law. The first is that section 9 states a contractual rule whereas the English floating charge rules rest on a theory of security interests fundamentally at variance with the structure of the Ontario Act and equally of the draft Act. The other factor is that since sections 27(1)(a) and 39 deal specifically with two of the most important facets of the debtor's rights of disposition and to create security interests ranking in priority to the floating charge, section 9 adds nothing new and should not be construed so as to undermine their consensual thrust.

Apart from sections 27 and 39 and their counterparts in the draft Act, there are several other important provisions that protect the third party dealing with the debtor whether or not the secured party has consented to it. The familiar section 30(1) (section 28(1) in the draft Act) protects buyers of goods in ordinary course (now enlarged in the draft Act to include a lessee of goods), section 30(2) covers purchasers of chattel paper, and section 30(3) purchasers of a non-negotiable instrument. Again, section 31 preserves the existing position with respect to the rights of bona fide purchasers of negotiable instruments, documents of title, and securities. Although in terms section 30(1) is restricted to buyers of goods, the Ontario Court of Appeal has intimated its readiness to extend it—presumably by analogy—to buyers of intangible types of inventory, and this is a welcome development.

Sections 30(2) and (3) and section 31 apply to secured parties as well as to buyers acquiring an interest in the collateral. This ensures that banks and other financial institutions will continue to be free to accept negotiable and near-negotiable instruments and documents as collateral for advances without having to worry about outstanding non-possessory security interests. With respect to other types of collateral, under the draft Act purchase money lenders and conditional sellers will continue to enjoy the same priority as under the existing provisions and without having to rely on waivers or subordination clauses in the floating charge agreement.

The upshot of this protracted discussion is that third parties will enjoy a substantial measure of protection under the new Act as they do under the present one, but it may not be as broad as it is at common law because of the conceptual differences between the equitable floating charge and its statutory counterpart. The practical differences will turn to a large extent on the terms of the security agreement. If it contains no express restrictions, then the courts may be expected to imply a broad licence for the debtor to continue to carry on business much as before so long as it does not jeopardize the secured party's general security.

If there are restrictions, third parties will be bound by them unless they can bring themselves under the protective umbrella of one of the statutory provisions to which I have referred. They will be bound, not because they will be deemed to have notice of the restrictions but because they will not be able to rely on the secured party's implied consent to the impugned dealing. Solicitors for debtors and secured parties will be well advised to scrutinize future security agreements carefully to ensure that the agreement accurately reflects their intentions and, in the debtor's case, his business needs.

One class of creditors that will be less well off under the new statutory regime is unsecured creditors who seek to levy execution against the debtor's assets. This is because they will be faced with a perfected security interest and because it is unlikely that the security agreement will contain a subordination clause in their favour. On the face of it, this may appear harsh but the reality is otherwise. If they are voluntary creditors they will be deemed to know of the security interest and therefore are conscious risk-takers in extending unsecured credit to the debtor. If they are involuntary creditors, the difference between the common law position and the position under the PPSA legislation is only marginal. This is because the common law only protects a judgment creditor if he has completed his execution before the floating charge has crystallized. The case law amply shows that it is unlikely that the floating charge holder will stand by idly and watch his security being eroded by the claims of execution creditors.

I recognize, of course, that employees and other types of unsecured creditors will be concerned about their vulnerable position in an era when employers are likely to be left with a diminishing cushion of free assets. The problem is not a new one and existed as much under the prior law of chattel security as it does under the new. It attracted much attention in the discussions on the new bankruptcy bill and will no doubt continue to do so, but it is not a problem that was created by the introduction of personal property security legislation. What it does suggest is the need to rethink the general relationship between secured and unsecured creditors and the retention of a cushion of assets to satisfy the claims of at least some types of general creditor.

CHAPTER TEN

Enforcement of the Security Interest

INTRODUCTION

The enforcement of a security interest is dealt with in Part V of the PPSA. The provisions of this Part govern four stages: (1) debtor's default, (2) taking possession of tangible collateral by the secured party, (3) retention or disposition of the collateral by the secured party or its redemption by the debtor, and (4) post-disposition relationship (*viz.* the debtor's right to any surplus or the creditor's right to claim for any deficiency).

Consistent with the general approach of the PPSA, the remedies are roughly the same, irrespective of the type of transaction by which the security interest was created. While the PPSAs indicate clearly that their provisions were not intended to be exhaustive (see, e.g., OPPSA s. 72), there is little room for the invocation of non-statutory law in post-default situations. The common law and equitable rules and the principles of the law merchant continue to apply interstitially, but they are not sources of significant structural rules applicable to the enforcement of security agreements.

The Act limits the power of the parties to specify in the security agreement what rights and remedies the security party has in the event of default by the debtor. See, e.g., OPPSA s. 59(5). Accordingly, provisions of a security agreement which purport to modify substantially or to excuse the secured party from compliance with the requirements of Part V are of no effect. However, under the OPPSA (but not the Acts based on the CCPPSL model) the parties may by agreement determine the standards by which the rights of the debtor and the duties of the secured party are to be measured, so long as such standards are not manifestly unreasonable (OPPSA s. 59(5)).

The Canadian approach to the regulation of secured creditors' rights in the event of default by debtors departs markedly from the approach in Article 9. Part V of the PPSA contains an elaborate set of detailed rules which, for the most part, must be complied with by a secured party or receiver enforcing a security interest. These rules are supplemented (but in Ontario, only in part) by the overriding requirement that the secured party must act in a commercially reasonable manner. Professor Gilmore described the US approach in the following way: "Despite the considerable amount of wordage, however, Part 5, rejecting the [Uniform Conditional Sales Act] approach of detailed statutory regulation, opts for a loosely organized, informal, anything-goes type of foreclosure pattern, subject to ultimate judicial supervision and control which is explicitly provided for. ... The key provision in Part 5 is that the secured party's disposition of the collateral must be in all respects 'commercially reasonable.' This term is deliberately left undefined. ... In substance,

Article 9 remits to the courts the task of determining standards and refrains from fashioning a statutory rule. ... Nor does the statutory term imply that a single monolithic standard has been, or must be established."* The "anything-goes" approach of Article 9 has apparently been less than successful. The authors of the 1992 Permanent Editorial Board Study Group on Article 9 made several recommendations designed to tighten up Part 5. For example, they recommend that Section 9-504 be revised to provide quite specific guidance as to time that must elapse between the date that notice is given to the debtor and the date of disposition of the collateral. Further, they recommend that the section be revised to include a form of notification and to provide that timely use of the form is sufficient to comply with the secured party's duty to send reasonable notification of disposition of the collateral.†

Another important difference between the PPSAs and their US counterpart is the extent to which discretionary judicial supervision of the exercise of post-default rights and duties is provided for in the legislation. See OPPSA s. 67(1). Section 9-507 of the Uniform Commercial Code provides for judicial intervention only when a secured party is not proceeding in accordance with the statute. However, US courts do not have the broad powers of Canadian courts to reorder the statutory rights and obligations of secured parties and debtors.

Note on Election of Remedies

The PPSAs provide that the rights of the secured party under Part V are cumulative and that a security interest does not merge in a judgment for the debt obtained against the debtor. (OPPSA ss. 58 and 59(7).) These provisions must be read in the light of consumer protection measures that prescribe "seize or sue" or "seize only" regimes. See, e.g., BCPPSA s. 67.

A feature peculiar to the OPPSA may well create considerable difficulties in interpretation. Section 59(7) provides that "a security agreement does not merge ... because the secured party has levied execution ... on the collateral." Under the pre-OPPSA law, a secured creditor was deemed to have waived its security and to have elected to rely solely on rights as an execution creditor when collateral is seized and sold under a writ of execution issued by the creditor. See *Trans Canada Credit Ltd. v. Foubert*, [1961] OR 57 (CA). This approach very likely continues to apply in all other common law jurisdictions in Canada. The basis for this conclusion is that money levied under an execution is shared rateably among all creditors who have issued and delivered to the sheriff writs of execution or creditors' certificates during a specified period after the date of the levy. See Creditors' Relief Act, RSO 1990, c. C.45, s. 5. Once the system that provides for this sharing has been invoked by the actions of the secured creditor, the secured creditor should not be able to terminate it by seeking to exercise the *in rem* rights of the a secured creditor.

---

* G. Gilmore, *Security Interests in Personal Property* (1965), Volume II, at 1183.

† Permanent Editorial Board for the Uniform Commercial Code, *Report of the Study Group, Uniform Commercial Code Article 9* (December 1, 1992), 231.

The problem of interpretation of s. 59(7) involves the meaning of the words "has levied execution ... on the collateral." The bulk of judicial authority supports the position that, in the context of the law of executions, "levy" means to collect, or obtain money by seizure. See *Benjamin Moore Co. v. Finnie*, [1955] 1 DLR 557 (Ont. Co. Ct.). Of course, it would be absurd to conclude that the Ontario Legislature intended that a secured party could issue a writ of execution, authorize seizure of the collateral under the writ and, after sale by the sheriff, exercise its rights under Part V to seize the collateral in the hands of the buyer from the sheriff. The buyer could rely on s. 25(1)(a) of the OPPSA for protection in such a situation. However, it would not be egregious to suggest that the Legislature intended to allow a secured party to circumvent the Ontario Creditors' Relief Act by claiming a security interest in the amount levied through a sheriff's sale. This amount would be proceeds of the secured party's original collateral, and under s. 25(1)(b), the secured party's security interest in the original collateral would extend to the proceeds.

However, any extension of the secured party's interest in the money levied would produce some very troublesome consequences. If, for example, the sheriff distributes money levied on the collateral to several execution creditors who have filed writs or certificates, can the secured party demand that these creditors return the amounts received by them from the sheriff? In such a case, is the sheriff liable to the secured party for interfering with the secured party's rights in the collateral?

PROCEDURAL AND SUBSTANTIVE LIMITS ON THE EXERCISE OF ENFORCEMENT RIGHTS

Waldron v. Royal Bank
(1991), 4 WWR 289 (BCCA)

ANDERSON JA: This appeal concerns two major issues:

(1) Was it necessary for the Royal Bank of Canada (the "Bank") to give the plaintiffs a reasonable time for payment prior to the enforcement of collateral security given in accordance with s. 178(1)(b) of the Bank Act, RSC 1985, c. B-1, to secure payment of a demand loan?

(2) [...]

The plaintiffs, Mr. and Mrs. Waldron (appellants), live in Crescent Spur, BC, which is approximately 100 miles southeast of Prince George. Mr. Waldron is a contractor and heavy equipment operator engaged in logging and road building. In 1984, Mrs. Waldron began to operate a ceramics business in Prince George under the name "The Blue Unicorn." Financing was obtained from the Bank (respondent). In 1985, as the business grew, more financing was necessary and some security was given. The business continued to grow, its indebtedness mounted, and in April, 1986, the Bank agreed to refinance the indebtedness. The plaintiffs signed a demand note for the amount owing and gave security, including an assignment under s. 178 of the Bank Act.

On 26th May 1986 Mrs. Waldron was admitted to hospital in McBride, British Columbia. ... On 12th June 1986 Mr.Waldron caused to be placed in the local Prince George newspaper an advertisement for a "Moving Out Sale" for the Blue Unicorn. ... Mr.

Waldron asked Mr. Karpes to oversee the financial operation of the business. He authorized him to receive some of the receipts of sales from the business for the purposes of paying certain business expenses through Mr. Karpes' trust account.

Mr. Waldron intended to close the Prince George operation of the Blue Unicorn for at least the summer of 1986. The summer was the slow season for the ceramics business. Mrs. Waldron was about to be discharged from hospital and would require some time to convalesce. Mr. Waldron intended to move all of the assets of the Blue Unicorn from its location on 3rd Avenue in Prince George to Crescent Spur by the end of June 1986.

On 17th June 1986 the management of the Royal Bank decided to act. It wrote a letter dated 17th June 1986 addressed to Ron Waldron Contracting operating as the Blue Unicorn, at the address on 3rd Avenue in Prince George. The letter was marked for the attention of Ron Waldron and Peg Waldron. A copy of the letter was sent to Mr. Waldron's accountant, Karpes & Company.

The bank gave the letter to the defendant Classic Bailiffs Ltd. with instructions to deliver the letter to the business address of the Blue Unicorn in Prince George. The bank also instructed the bailiff to seize all of the assets of the business by having the locks on the premises changed.

The letter of 17th June reads, in part, as follows:

We hereby make formal demand for payment of the entire amount due and owing by you, which sum is to be paid upon presentation of this letter. ...

Under Section 178 of the Bank Act, should payment not be made upon demand, the Bank will take such action as necessary to protect its security.

Mr. Bohn and another employee of the defendant Classic Bailiffs Ltd., Eileen Milliken, attended at the business premises of the Blue Unicorn on the afternoon of 17th June.

The bank's letter addressed to Mr. Waldron and the Blue Unicorn was handed to an employee of the business, Mrs. Mary Armella. Mr. Bohn then read the contents of the letter to her. The landlord and a locksmith attended at the business premises. The locks on the door were changed. Both keys to the door were given to Mr. Bohn.

The defendant relies upon the terms of the demand promissory note, and upon para. 6 of the loan agreement [which provided that "in the event of failure by the Customer to make due payment to the Bank of any debt or liability or part therefore" the Bank could without demand realize on its security "in such manner and upon such terms and conditions as the Bank deems best"].

● ● ●

In my view, for the reasons which follow, the judgment of Estey J in *Lister v. Dunlop* applies to the facts of the case on appeal and should have been followed by the learned trial judge.

The judgment of Estey J in *Lister* v. *Dunlop* reads in part as follows, at pp. 288-9, CBR:

The principal difference between the courts below was on the right of the company and the Listers to reasonable notice from Dunlop when enforcing its claims under the note, the debenture and the guaranties. Both courts below agreed that the debtor had the right to reasonable notice but, as quoted above, the majority of the Court of Appeal found that the debtor must ask for time to make the payment claimed to be due and none was asked for by the plaintiff-appellants. The facts of the demand have been set out. The debenture and note signed and delivered by the company provide for payment "on demand." By its terms the debenture further provides that the principal and interest shall "forthwith become due and payable" on the happening of any of 19 specified events such as a default in payment of interest and principal by the company. The security thereby constituted by the debenture likewise becomes enforceable at the same time. The guaranty by the Listers is performable upon "notice in writing" delivered personally or by mail.

The rule has long been that enunciated in *Massey v. Sladen* (1868), LR 4 Ex. 13 at 19, 38 LJ Ex. 34: the debtor must be given "some notice on which he might reasonably expect to be able to act." The application of this simple proposition will depend upon all the facts and circumstances in each case. Failure to give such reasonable notice places the debtor under economic, but nonetheless real duress, often as real as physical duress to the person, and no doubt explains the eagerness of the courts to construe debt-evidencing or creating documents as including in all cases the requirement of reasonable notice for payment.

• • •

LAMBERT JA: ... Mr. Justice Anderson has dealt with the appeal comprehensively and I propose to deal only with those points on which my opinion about the applicability of the principle in *Lister v. Dunlop* to this case particularly rests.

• • •

The principle in *Lister v. Dunlop* is that a person from whom a seizure is being made under a security instrument is entitled to receive such notice of the proposed seizure as is reasonable in the circumstances. The principle may also apply to other seizures but it is not necessary in this case to determine whether that is so.

It is possible for the principle in *Lister v. Dunlop*, [1982] 1 SCR 726 to be limited, modified or eliminated by constitutionally enacted legislation. Subject to that, it is my opinion that the principle applies to the realization of all security interests where a person's property is being taken away by the security holder.

I turn first to the general language in which the principle has been expressed. In *Lister v. Dunlop* itself Mr. Justice Estey, for the Supreme Court of Canada, referred, at p. 746, to the application of the principle in relation to "debt-evidencing or creating documents." In *Canadian Imperial Bank of Commerce v. Prosser* (1982), 41 NBR (2d) 656 (NBCA), Mr. Justice Stratton said, at p. 661, that the principle was applicable to "instruments creating a debt." In *Whonnock Industries Ltd. v. National Bank of Canada* (1987), 16 BCLR (2d) 320, Mr. Justice Seaton, for this Court, said, at p. 323, that the *Lister* case "established the Canadian law on the question of the reasonable time for payment of a demand loan."

The *Lister* case has been applied to a number of different types of security instruments. In the *Lister* case itself the security interest was created by a demand debenture. In *Jim Landry Pontiac Buick v. CIBC* (1987), 40 DLR (4th) 343 (NSSC) Chief Justice Glube treated the principle as applicable to a conditional sale agreement and to a chattel mortgage. *West City Motors Ltd. v. Delta Acceptance Corp. Ltd.* (1963), 40 DLR 818; [1963] 2 OR 683 (Aylen J, Ont. HC) and *Camway Trucking Ltd. v. Toronto Dominion*

Bank (11 March, 1988; Nos. 13227A/82, 7579/82, 1488/87) (Holland J, Ont. HC) were cases where the security interest was a chattel mortgage. In *Barclay Construction Corporation v. Bank of Montreal* (1989), 41 BCLR (2d) 239 (BCCA) and in *Bank of British Columbia v. Rivard* (CA005333; 11 March, 1987) (BCCA), this Court treated the principle as applicable, within its scope, to assignments of book accounts. In *Proud v. National Bank of Canada* (1985), 57 Nfld. and PEIR 14 (PEICA), the principle was applied to a seizure under a pledge agreement.

In my opinion the *Lister* principle applies, in accordance with its scope, subject only to contrary legislation, to all security interests where a person's property may be taken away by the security holder.

The *Lister* principle is a principle about giving reasonable notice before a seizure. The mischief which the principle was designed to remedy, from its earliest origins, was the possibility that a person might suffer serious harm from an unanticipated seizure that was not necessary.

The *Lister* principle is not a principle about the law of negotiable instruments or about whether presentment or demand must precede an action on a bill or note; nor is it a principle about the steps that must be taken to make a debt become due or become payable. There is no need for any requirement of reasonable notice in those areas of the law. It is the realization of security, collateral or otherwise, which raises the call for fairness to which the law has responded.

• • •

The call for fairness in the enforcement of security instruments responds to the same fundamental demands as those which have resulted in the constitutional protection against unreasonable seizure conferred and confirmed by s. 8 of the Canadian Charter of Rights and Freedoms.

The Applicability of the Principle in Lister v. Dunlop as a Question of Fact

In *Mister Broadloom Corporation (1968) Ltd. v. Bank of Montreal* (1979), 25 OR (2d) 198; (1978), 32 CBR (NS) 241 (Ont. HC), Mr. Justice Linden, at p. 208, referred to several factors, the last of which was "any other relevant factors." Two of the preceding six factors were the risk to the creditor of losing his money or his security, and the potential ability of the debtor to raise the money required to pay off the debt in a short period.

In *Whonnock Industries Ltd. v. National Bank of Canada* (1987), 16 BCLR (2d) 320, Mr. Justice Seaton, for this Court, said this at p. 333:

In determining whether a debtor was given a reasonable time, two of the factors to be considered are the risk to the creditor of losing his money and security and the potential ability of the debtor to raise the money required in a short period. A number of cases suggest that where the debtor is in a hopeless position such that the creditor's security is at risk, a shorter period of time for the debtor to make arrangements is sufficient.

Mr. Justice Seaton mentioned three cases where a shorter period was considered. They are: *Royal Bank v. Cal Glass* (1979), 18 BCLR 55, *CIBC v. Quesnel Machinery* (1985), 62 CBR (NS) 91, and *Cripps (Pharmaceuticals) Ltd. v. Wickenden*, [1973] 2 All ER 606

(Ch. D). As Madam Justice McLachlin said in *CIBC v. Quesnel Machinery* at p. 93, reasonable notice may range from a few days to no time at all.

In cases where there is no reasonable ground for thinking that the debtor is dishonest, and the security is not in any significant way at immediate risk, the debtor should probably have a few days to try to obtain alternative financing before any seizure occurs. The debtor should be told how many days are to be allowed. As Mr. Justice Seaton said in *Whonnock*, at p. 329, the judgment of Mr. Justice Aylen in *West City Motors Ltd. v. Delta Acceptance Corp.* (1963), 40 DLR 818 (Ont. HC), at p. 824, seems to have been the source of later references to "a few days." Of course, if the background is such that a reasonable person in the creditor's position would think that, through dishonesty or for any other reason, the security is in immediate peril, then the creditor may well be justified, under the *Lister* principle, in making an immediate seizure. But even in such cases, there should be a pause, after the security is protected by seizure, to allow the debtor to have an opportunity to raise the money to redeem the security, before the security is finally realized and disposed of, if such a pause is reasonably possible.

The basic question about the legal nature of the principle in *Lister v. Dunlop* is whether it is a principle about the interpretation of security instruments, or a principle that governs seizures under security instruments no matter what they say.

In my opinion, the principle governs seizures under security instruments no matter what they say; it overrides any terms of a security instrument that conflict with the principle. In reaching that conclusion, I am following the unanimous judgment of the Ontario Court of Appeal in *Kavcar Investments Ltd. v. Aetna Financial Services Ltd.* (1989), 62 DLR (4th) 277, where Madam Justice McKinlay, in delivering the judgment of a division composed of Mr. Justice Blair, Mr. Justice Robins and herself, said, at p. 280:

I consider that the decision of the Supreme Court of Canada in *Lister v. Dunlop,* and the cases that have been decided since, preclude a creditor from realizing on security which secures an indebtedness payable on demand, *regardless of the wording of the security document,* unless a period of time which is reasonable in the circumstances has been given to the debtor to satisfy the demand.

(Madam Justice McKinlay's emphasis.)

There are statements in the cases to the effect that the *Lister* principle is a rule guiding the interpretation of security instruments. I do not propose to set them out. I think that they are obiter dicta and I have found none in a context which indicates that the question of whether the principle was a guide to interpretation or an independent rule of law was being considered. On the other hand, the key words were emphasized by Madam Justice McKinlay in *Kavcar* to show that they represented an important and considered conclusion of law.

I should also add that in my opinion the cases applying the *Lister* principle illustrate, from the words in the security instruments, that the principle cannot be one of interpretation. Time and again the words used are words such as "immediately," "forthwith," or "instantly." In the leading case of *Massey v. Sladen* (1868), LR 4 Exch. 13 the words in the instrument were: "… instantly on demand, and without any delay on any pretence whatsoever … ." It cannot be consistent with words like that to decide that the *Lister* principle is only a guide to interpretation.

If the *Lister* principle is, as I think it is, an independent rule of law about seizures, then the principle must rest on one or both of two grounds. They are, from the common law side, the ground that a term of a security instrument that is contrary to the *Lister* principle is void as being contrary to public policy, and is severable; and, from the equity side, the ground that a term of a security instrument that is contrary to the *Lister* principle is unconscionable, and is severable. So those are the two grounds, public policy and unconscionability.

I think that either of those two grounds would be adequate for the task. Indeed, I think that they overlap and that they can properly be thought of as together providing the foundation for the rule that a contractual term can not abrogate the *Lister* principle. As to the overlapping nature of the grounds of public policy and unconscionability, I refer to the judgment of Lord Diplock in *Schroeder v. Macaulay*, [1974] 3 All ER 616 (HL) where he says, at p. 623:

It is, in my view, salutary to acknowledge that in refusing to enforce provisions of a contract whereby one party agrees for the benefit of the other party to exploit or to refrain from exploiting his earning power, the public policy which the court is implementing is not some 19th century economic theory about the benefit to the general public of freedom of trade, but the protection of those whose bargaining power is weak against being forced by those whose bargaining power is stronger to enter into bargains that are unconscionable.

• • •

Finally, on the question of the legal nature of the *Lister* principle, I mention the decision of Madam Justice L'Heureux-Dube, for the Supreme Court of Canada, in *Houle v. Canadian National Bank* (20634; 22 November 1990). In that case the Bank had rights under the terms of its security instrument to recall its loan on demand and to realize on its security without delay and without notice. The Supreme Court of Canada decided that under the civil law of Quebec a seizure without reasonable notice was an abuse of contractual rights and that the civil law of Quebec provided a rule in very much the same terms as provided in the common law under the *Lister* principle.

It is clear from the reasons of the Supreme Court of Canada in *Houle v. Canadian National Bank* that the principle in the civil law of Quebec is not a principle of interpretation of a security instrument but a principle which overrides any contrary provision in the security instrument. I think that the common law principle is similar in its legal nature.

• • •

Since I have decided that the *Lister* principle is a principle in relation to seizures and not a principle about the interpretation of security instruments, and since I have decided that it applies to securities under paras. 178(1)(a) and 178(1)(b) of the Bank Act, it is my opinion that the *Lister* principle was applicable in this case to this seizure and that the Bank should be considered to have acted in violation of that principle if it seized the property of the plaintiffs without reasonable notice to them. Whether it did so must be determined by the trial judge when the remaining issues are tried.

Appeal allowed.

NOTES

1) In *Kavcar Investments v. Aetna Financial Services Ltd.* (1989), 62 DLR (4th) 277 (Ont. CA), McKinlay JA observed at p. 285:

At p. 17 of its reasons in *Lister v. Dunlop* the Supreme Court refers, for "a modern summation of the rule and its particular application," to the trial decision in *Mister Broadloom Corp. (1968) Ltd. v. Bank of Montreal* (1979), 25 OR (2d) 198, 101 DLR (3d) 713, 7 BLR 222 (HCJ), and *Royal Bank of Canada v. Cal Glass Ltd.* (1979), 18 BCLR 55, 9 BLR 1 (SC).

In the *Mister Broadloom* case, Linden J found as a fact that the bank creditor reasonably, though mistakenly, apprehended a high risk of default and demanded payment of the debtor's indebtedness to the bank in the amount of $600,000. He found that the debtor had the ability to raise the funds within a few days, but that the debtor did not inform the creditor of this ability or ask for time to arrange for payment. For this reason, he found that the appointment of a receiver to take possession of the assets of the plaintiff within approximately one hour of the demand was reasonable on the facts of the case and did not constitute an unlawful seizure.

Prior to the hearing of an appeal to the Ontario Court of Appeal in the *Mister Broadloom* case, the Supreme Court of Canada decision in *Lister v. Dunlop* was released. *Mister Broadloom* was reversed by the Ontario Court of Appeal, 44 OR (2d) 368, 4 DLR (4th) 74, 49 CBR (NS) 1, based on the Supreme Court decision in *Lister v. Dunlop*. The court held that the fact that the debtor did not inform the creditor of his ability to satisfy the demand within a few days, or ask for time to do so, did not render the seizure lawful, since, on the facts in that case, a reasonable time was not afforded to the debtor to meet the demand. Leave to appeal to the Supreme Court of Canada was denied. Consequently, it appears that the only consideration left in such cases is the question of whether or not the creditor has given the debtor a reasonable time to satisfy the demand. It is clear that the question of "reasonable time" must be looked at in the light of all of the facts and circumstances in the individual case (*per* Estey J in *Lister v. Dunlop*, at p. 16). In the process of his analysis of the facts in the *Mister Broadloom* case, Linden J stated that it was his opinion that the current law of Ontario required a creditor to allow his debtor a reasonable time to pay a demand debt before seizing assets pledged as security, but he went on to say [at p. 208 OR, p. 723 DLR]:

Despite this principle, there may still be cases where "all the creditor has to do is give the debtor time to get it from some convenient place": see Goff J, in *Cripps v. Wickenden, supra*, at p. 616. But the circumstances of such a case, where only a few minutes is permitted, will be such as to lead the Court to the conclusion that it is reasonable in the situation.

Thus, a reasonable time must always be allowed, but, in assessing what length of time is reasonable in a particular fact situation various factors must be analyzed: (1) the amount of the loan; (2) the risk to the creditor of losing his money or the security; (3) the length of the relationship between the debtor and the creditor; (4) the character and reputation of the debtor; (5) the potential ability to raise the money required in a short period; (6) the circumstances surrounding the demand for payment; and (7) any other relevant factors.

The Supreme Court of Canada in *Lister v. Dunlop* did not discuss reasonableness in terms of the ability of the debtor to raise funds, but merely talked about the requirement of payment being made within a reasonable time. ... However, the tacit approval of the Supreme Court of Canada in *Lister v. Dunlop* of the factors to be considered, listed by Linden J in the *Mister Broadloom* case, as well as this court's decision in *Mister Broadloom*, seems to indicate that a reasonable time in Canadian law means a reasonable time in which to *raise* money to satisfy a demand—otherwise the fifth factor listed by Linden J would be meaningless. ...

There is an obvious incongruity in such a development in the law: it is unlikely that a demand for payment will be made on a financially sound debtor, and the worse the financial condition of the debtor the more difficult and time-consuming it will be to raise funds. Does this mean that the more hopeless a debtor's financial plight, the more time he must be given to satisfy a demand for payment? Obviously this cannot be the law. However, since the financial condition of the debtor is almost always the most important concern of the creditor, taking that factor into consideration must mean that the more hopeless a debtor's plight, the less time he need be given to satisfy a demand for payment. Despite this apparent incongruity, such a conclusion seems just for at least two reasons: first, if the assets secured are of insufficient value to satisfy the indebtedness, the creditor's loss increases daily, and second, if the debtor would be unable to raise funds even if given time, then time will avail the debtor nothing.

Given what was said by the Supreme Court in *Lister v. Dunlop*, and given the results in the numerous cases which have been decided since, I am of the view that the law in Canada at the present time requires that a debtor, following a proper demand for payment, must be allowed a reasonable time to raise the necessary funds to satisfy the demand. What constitutes reasonable time will depend on the circumstances, but will generally be of very short duration. In addition, it is clear from the reasons of the Supreme Court of Canada in *Lister v. Dunlop* that the debtor need not ask for a reasonable time to pay. Reasonable time must be given by the creditor, whether or not asked for by the debtor.

• • •

I do not accept Aetna's argument that some types of default permit enforcement of the security without any demand for payment being made. In my view, the law has developed to the point where, regardless of the wording of a debenture security, it cannot be enforced without first, the making of a demand, and second, the giving of a reasonable time within which to pay the indebtedness.

2) The BCPPSA was not the applicable law in *Waldron* and the OPPSA was not mentioned by the Ontario Court of Appeal in *Kavcar*. Part V of the PPSA becomes operative upon default by the debtor (OPPSA section 59). Default is defined as "the failure to pay or otherwise perform the obligation secured when due or the occurrence of any event whereupon under the terms of the security agreement the security becomes enforceable" (OPPSA s. 1(1)). Apparently the parties to a security agreement are free to define what amounts to default so long as the standards such as those of OPPSA s. 59(5) are met. Further, the Act provides that "upon default the secured party may take possession of the collateral" (OPPSA s. 62). Does the *Lister v. Dunlop* principle apply in a case where the security agreement provides that the debtor is "in default" upon the happening of some specific event identified in the agreement? Is there not a conflict between the *Lister* principle and s. 59(5) which gives a statutory right to seize the collateral when the debtor is in "default"?

3) The Acts based on the CCPPSL model require that when exercising rights under Part V, a secured party (including a receiver) must act "in good faith and in a commercially

reasonable manner." See, e.g., SPPSA s. 65(3). Perhaps this type of provision can be seen as embodying the *Lister v. Dunlop* principle. However, there is no equivalent provision in the OPPSA. Are these standards implicitly included in the Act?

4) *Kavcar* is discussed in Ziegel, "The Enforcement of Demand Debentures—Continuing Uncertainties" (1990), 69 *Can. Bar Rev.* 718. Prof. Ziegel is particularly critical of the court in *Kavcar* transforming the requirement of notice from a constructional issue (interpretation of the parties' agreement) into a rule of law, and of McKinlay JA emphasizing that the parties' agreement cannot deprive the debtor of the right to a period of notice before the debenture becomes enforceable. In view of the continuing uncertainties, Prof. Ziegel recommends that the PPS Acts be amended to entitle the debtor, subject to several exceptions, to a fixed period of notice before the secured party enforces its default remedies.

5) Under s. 244(1)-(2) of the Bankruptcy and Insolvency Act, RSC 1985, c. B-3, as am. SC 1992, c. 27, a secured creditor (broadly defined in s. 2 of the Act) who intends to enforce security in all or substantially all of inventory, accounts or other property of an insolvent debtor (also broadly defined) acquired by the debtor for use in a business carried on by it, must give a notice of its intention. A period of at least 10 days must elapse between the date the notice is sent and the date of enforcement of the security interest. While the matter is not totally free from doubt, it is very likely that the section will be intepreted by the courts as applying to secured parties who use receivers to enforce security agreements. The inclusion of this provision in the BIA was not intended to codify the rule in *Lister v. Dunlop*. The 10-day pre-seizure notice is to give to the debtor an opportunity to file a notice of intention to make a reorganization proposal under s. 50.4 of the Act. However, if a secured party gives the requisite 10-days' notice, can it be satisfied that the requirements of *Lister v. Dunlop* have been met?

6) A secured party may encounter other procedural bars or delays in the enforcement of a security interest as part of business reorganization systems. See BIA, s. 69(1); Companies' Creditors Arrangement Act, RSC 1985, c. C-36, s. 11.

7) The secured party is permitted to include in the security agreement an acceleration clause, whereby on default in payment of any part of the obligation secured the entire amount becomes due immediately. Note, however, that if the contractual right to accelerate the maturity of the entire obligation arises whenever the secured party is or deems itself to be insecure, such a right is exercisable "only if the secured party in good faith believes and has commercially reasonable grounds to believe that" the prospect of payment or performance is impaired (OPPSA s. 16). Does an election to accelerate involve a demand for payment, thereby invoking the *Lister* principle?

8) Do the Part V rights of reinstatment and redemption, examined later in this chapter, provide an acceptable statutory substitute for the protection provided by the *Lister* principle?

9) The PPSA may not be the only source of statutory regulation of rights and obligations associated with enforcement of security interests. In some jurisdictions, the defaulting debtor is given the power to invoke judicial intervention in the seizure of collateral. See, e.g., Unconscionable Transactions Relief Act, RSO 1990, c. U.2, s. 2(d).

10) Section 23(1) of the Ontario Consumer Protection Act, RSO 1990, c. C.31, provides:

23.(1) Where a buyer under an executory contract has paid two-thirds or more of the purchase price of the goods as fixed by the contract, any provision in the contract, or in any security agreement incidental thereto, under which the seller may retake possession of or resell the goods upon default in payment by the buyer is not enforceable except by leave of a judge of a county or district court.

What is the policy of this section? Why does it apply only to secured instalment sales contracts and not to secured loan transactions? Note that the equivalent provision in the BCPPSA s. 58(3)(4) applies to both secured sales and secured loan transactions. Why does s. 23(1) apply only to situations where there has been a "default in payment"? Can a secured party circumvent it by claiming to take possession of the collateral pursuant to its statutory right under OPPSA s. 62? While OPPSA s. 73 defers to the Consumer Protection Act, is there a conflict between the two Acts in this context? Apparently it is not an offence to seize goods after more than two-thirds of the price is paid. See *R v. IAC Ltd.*, [1970] 2 OR 407 (Prov. Ct.). If so, what remedy is available to the debtor to ensure compliance?

Andrews v. Mack Financial (Canada) Ltd.
(1987), 46 DLR (4th) 731 (Sask. CA)

VANCISE JA (for the Court, allowing the appeal): Mack Financial Services (the appellant) seized a 1985 Mack truck in order to satisfy the outstanding arrears under a security agreement securing the purchase price of the truck. It exercised rights to repossession granted to it under the security agreement and The Personal Property Security Act, SS 1979-80, c. P.1. The respondents applied, pursuant to s. 63 of the Act, for an order setting aside the seizure and an order preventing the appellant from realizing on its collateral. The chambers judge set aside the seizure and granted certain additional relief, including extending the time for payment under the security agreement.

The issues raised on this appeal all pertain to the rights given to the Court of Queen's Bench under s. 63 of the Act to grant relief to a debtor. Those issues can be stated in the following terms:

(1) Does the Court have the power or authority to set aside a seizure made pursuant to the terms of a security agreement and s. 48 of the Act?

(2) Does the Court have the power or authority to order the alteration of the terms of a security agreement, including the dates of payment, or the time of payment?

(3) If the answer to question (2) is "Yes," did the chambers judge properly exercise his discretion in this case?

III. Facts

On July 9, 1985, Saskatoon Mack Sales Ltd. sold a 1985 Mack truck bearing serial number 2M2N1876FC009604 to Alma Andrews, one of the respondents. On the same date, Saskatoon Mack Sales assigned its interest to Mack Financial (Canada) Ltd., the appellant.

Pursuant to the terms of the contract, the respondent agreed to pay 12 monthly instalments of $3,000.00, commencing August 15, 1985, and thereafter 30 monthly instalments of $1,913.93. The security agreement provides that title and ownership of the truck remain with the appellant and do not pass to Andrews until all amounts payable, including principal, interest and other specified charges, are fully paid.

The security agreement prohibits the sale of the truck without the prior written consent of the appellant. The respondent Trotchie alleges that he purchased the truck from the respondent Andrews with the knowledge and consent of the appellant. The appellant, however, contends that it had no knowledge of, nor did it consent to the sale, and, as a result, the security agreement is in default. It contends it was first informed of the sale in December 1986 when repairs to the truck were being discussed. Indeed, all payments received under the contract were received from the respondent Andrews, including payments received after the alleged sale.

On October 18, 1986, the truck was involved in a single-vehicle accident near Hearst, Ontario. The damage to the truck was appraised by appraisers in Ontario at $38,055.26, and by SGI in Saskatchewan, at $30,000.00. At the time of the accident, the respondent Andrews was in arrears for the months of August, September and October in the total amount of $5,741.79.

At the date of the accident, the respondents estimated the value of the truck to be approximately $75,000.00. The appellant estimates the value is $60,000.00. The balance owing under the contract as at March 5, 1987 was $50,963.46, exclusive of late charges and repossession expenses.

The respondent Trotchie advised the appellant of the accident and the parties discussed repairing the truck. A number of alternatives were examined, but the appellant was adamant that the arrears under the contract would have to be brought up to date before anything could be done. Trotchie advised in late November or early December 1986 that the respondents could not pay the arrears.

On or about November 13th, the truck was returned to Saskatchewan by Cory Smith, an employee of the respondent, and was taken to Smith's farm near Swanson, Saskatchewan. Trotchie refused to advise the appellant of the whereabouts of the truck, in spite of repeated requests to do so. On December 29th or 30th, the appellant retained bailiffs in Alberta and Saskatchewan to search for the truck. In early January 1987, Trotchie advised the appellant of the following:

(1) that he was hiding the truck and would not disclose the location;

(2) that he intended to "strip" the truck, put on a "glider kit," alter the serial number, and sell it;

(3) on January 5th he advised the appellant that he was in the process of removing the engine and transmission and that he would return only the frame to the appellant.

On January 8, 1987, the appellants applied ex parte pursuant to s. 63 of the Act for an order that the respondents deliver up the truck pursuant to the provisions of their security agreement and the Act. Mr. Justice Goldenberg ordered them to deliver up the truck within 24 hours. The respondent Trotchie was served with the order on January 9th, and would not disclose the whereabouts of Andrews. On January 16th, an order for substitutional service on the respondent Andrews was granted and the respondent was substitutionally served that date.

The respondents failed to comply with the order of January 8, 1987, and the appellants brought an application for contempt returnable on January 28, 1987. On January 23, 1987, the respondents through their solicitors advised the appellant of the truck's location and the motion for contempt was withdrawn.

After some difficulty with the respondent Smith, the tires of the truck were physically repossessed on February 11, 1987, and the truck was physically repossessed and delivered to Great West Auto Body in the City of Saskatoon, on February 27, 1987. The truck is undergoing repairs and the appellant intends to sell it to satisfy the indebtedness under the contract.

The respondents brought the motion under s. 63 prior to the appellant taking any action to realize on its collateral.

The chambers judge granted an order pursuant to s. 63 in the following terms:

Upon the application of James Neumeier, Counsel on behalf of the Applicants, and upon hearing Counsel on behalf of the Applicants and Respondent, and upon hearing read the pleadings and proceedings had and taken herein, and the Affidavits of the Parties herein all filed, it is hereby ordered that the following terms under s. 63 of The Personal Property Act are just and reasonable for all parties concerned:

1. That relief is granted to the Applicants from the consequences of s. 59 of the Act, the Mack Financial's seizure of the 1985 Mack Truck is set aside.

2. That the truck is to be repaired by Saskatchewan Government Insurance, with such directions from the Applicants and Mack which SGI may require at its discretion.

3. That the Applicants shall pay Mack, on the 15th day of the month following completion of the repairs on the truck, the arrears of payments were due [*sic*] at the time of the accident.

4. That in the event the Parties are unable to agree on such arrears within 14 days of this date, then the Court will determine such arrears on the basis of the material that has been presented.

5. That upon payment of the arrears, the truck shall be delivered to the Applicants who shall assume control over it.

6. That the Applicants shall commence making payments according to the tenor of the conditional sales contract on the 15th day of the second month following delivery of the truck to them, until the entire purchase price and interest, is paid.

7. The motion shall be spoken to again on Wednesday, April 15, at 9:00 a.m., at which time it shall be determined whether the claim of Cory Smith is still an issue, and in the event that it is then representations will be received to the end that his claim will be resolved.

Section 63 provides as follows:

63. Upon application by a debtor, a creditor of a debtor, a secured party, any person who has an interest in collateral which may be affected by an order under this section or a receiver or a receiver-manager, whether appointed by a court or pursuant to a security agreement and after notice has been given to any person that the judge directs, a judge or court may:

(a) make any order, including binding declarations of right and injunctive relief, that is necessary to ensure compliance with this Part of section 17;

(b) give directions to any party regarding the exercise of his rights or discharge of his obligations under this Part or section 17;

(c) relieve any part from compliance with the requirements of this Part of section 17, but only on terms that are just and reasonable for all parties concerned;

(d) stay enforcement of rights provided in this Part or section 17 under any terms and conditions that the judge, in his discretion, considers just and reasonable;

(e) make any order necessary to ensure protection of the interests of any person in the collateral;

(f) make an order requiring a receiver or receiver-manager, or a person by or on behalf of whom he is appointed, to make good any default in connection with the receiver's or receiver-manager's custody, management or disposition of the collateral of the debtor or to relieve such person from any default on such terms as the court thinks fit, and to confirm any act of the receiver or receiver-manager.

It will be noted that the Court is given broad powers under s. 63, including the right to make declarations of rights, grant injunctive relief, or make any order required to ensure compliance with Part V and s. 17 of the Act. Professor Ronald C.C. Cuming, commenting on s. 63 in an article entitled "Second Generation Personal Property Legislation in Canada" (1981-82), 42 *Sask. Law Rev.* 5, stated at p. 41:

A feature peculiar to the Saskatchewan Act is wide judicial control over the exercise of default rights and remedies. Under the Ontario and Manitoba Acts, deviation from the prescribed structure is not permitted. This is not the case in Saskatchewan. The Saskatchewan Act gives to the courts a wide range of powers including the power to make binding declarations of rights, to issue injunctions, to give directions to parties regarding the exercise of rights or discharge of obligations, to relieve from compliance with Part V of the Act, to stay enforcement of default rights and remedies, and to make orders for the protection of any person's interest in collateral. The decision to give such broad discretionary jurisdiction to courts entails some risk. If this power is exercised without care, it may result in a great deal of disruption in business financing transactions. If, however, it is exercised within the spirit of the legislation, it can be a very constructive method of avoiding the difficulties which are endemic to the detailed and inflexible system prescribed by personal property security legislation.

• • •

The appellant concedes that s. 63 gives the Court broad powers to intervene in the specific areas set out in Part V, but contends that the section should be narrowly interpreted so as to ensure that the scheme of rights, priorities, and remedies established under the Act is not altered. In effect, it contends that the power should be used sparingly to protect rights and to guarantee compliance with the requirements of Part V, but that the purpose of the section is not to disturb or interfere with rights contained in either the contract or the Act. MacLeod J, in *Clarkson Co. Ltd. v. Chrysler Credit Canada Ltd.* (1984), 3 PPSAC 275 at 279, considered s. 63 and found its purpose to be as follows:

The Court may make an order under s. 63(d) or (e) to protect the interests of any party, but this section is to protect parties, not deprive them of their rights. The rights of a prior secured party should be disturbed only where appropriate grounds are shown.

He did not elaborate on what those special grounds would be.

The appellant exercised its right to possession by applying to the Court of Queen's Bench pursuant to ss. 63(a) and (e) to obtain an order directing the respondents to deliver up the collateral. It had effected a lawful seizure, and was in the process of realizing on its collateral when the respondents obtained the order from the chambers judge.

The appellant contends that ss. 63(d) and (e), under which the judge purportedly made his order, were not available to the judge on this application by reason of the fact that the appellant had not exercised and was not exercising any "rights provided in ... Part [V] or section 17"—to use the language of subsection (d)—but was exercising a contractual right to possession granted in the security agreement. More particularly, the appellant contends it had not exercised and was not exercising any right of possession under s. 58 of the Act. Instead, it exercised the right of possession contained in Schedule "A" to the contract, which, in part, reads as follows:

... If the unpaid balance or any other sum due under this contract becomes due and payable, Seller [Mack Financial (Canada) Ltd.], its successors and assigns and its and their agents may, without demand or notice, exercise any or all of the following remedies to the extent not prohibited by law either alternatively or cumulatively, namely: (a) Seller may sue Buyer immediately for the entire remaining balance owing including interest and all other charges owing hereunder; and (b) Except as hereinafter expressly provided, Seller may forthwith take possession of the property or any part thereof, including all equipment, attachments or accessories thereto, without legal process and retain or sell the property as hereinafter set forth. ...

• • •

In my view, to the extent that any contractual right of possession coincides with the statutory right of possession under s. 58, the two rights must be read and treated as one and the same right. The contractual right must be read and treated as an affirmation of the statutory right and not as an independent and separate right. To the extent that the contractual right of possession does not coincide with the statutory right of possession the former must be read and treated as varying the statutory right (given the words "unless otherwise agreed" contained in s. 58(a) a variation is permissible). The statutory right so varied persists. Unless, the two rights are read this way, s. 63, in an important respect, would be waived by the simple device of including a separate right of possession in the contract, thus enabling the security holder to rely upon the contractual right to the exclusion of the statutory right. A waiver of s. 63 is expressly prohibited by s. 56(8) of the Act, except as provided by ss. 61 and 62 which are not relevant here. It follows that s. 56(8), in effect, precludes the reading and treating of a contractual right in any other way but as an affirmation of the statutory right in the manner I have outlined. In the result, I find that the appellant's submission that ss. 63(d) and (e) were not available to the judge must fail. That, however, does not end the matter. It is now necessary to determine what powers the judge has under those subsections and whether the judge in the present case acted within those powers.

On the issue of the scope of s. 63, the appellant submits that the purpose of the section is to ensure compliance with Part V, and to provide a summary procedure for ensuring that the rights of the respective parties are protected, and, to that end, the rights of the respective parties are circumscribed. I agree with that submission.

Section 63 provides a mechanism for ensuring that a commercially just result will be obtained. It gives the Court the power to relieve any party from compliance with the strict scheme established in Part V, in circumstances where strict compliance would produce a detrimental commercial result, as, for example, where a debtor has absconded and it is not possible to serve the requisite notices. The Court also has the power to stay enforcement of rights after default, to make orders for the protection of any person's interest in the collateral, and to make orders requiring receivers to make good any default. The pervading purpose is for the protection of rights and interests between the secured party and the debtor.

• • •

The provisions of s. 63 are designed to protect the debtor's equity as well as preserve the secured party's right to realize on his collateral. The main limitation on the secured party's right to dispose of the collateral is the requirement that he proceed in good faith and in a commercially reasonable manner.

Where the secured party proceeds or is about to proceed without meeting these requirements, it is essential to the debtor and other creditors that a remedy be available. This remedy will be particularly important when it is applied prospectively, before the unreasonable disposition has occurred. Pursuant to s. 63(a) a concerned party may obtain injunctive relief to ensure compliance with Part V or s. 17. Under this clause the court could certainly restrain a sale of the collateral, and in an extreme case, it could order that the disposition be carried out under judicial supervision, or under specified terms and conditions.

The section does not authorize the Court to set aside a seizure properly made in accordance with the rights granted to the appellant, except where there has been non-compliance with s. 17 or this part of the Act. In so ordering, the chambers judge was in error.

One must now consider whether or not the Court has the power to order the alteration of the contract entered into between the parties. In my opinion, the section does not authorize the court to rewrite or change the substance of an agreement entered into between the parties. It can, and indeed should, exercise the power granted to it to prevent a secured creditor from acting in a commercially unreasonable manner, by failing, for example, to comply with the notice requirements or taking possession of collateral when the security agreement is not in default.

The respondents contend that s. 63 can be used by the Court to prevent the secured creditor from realizing on its security and to grant the debtor additional time to pay so as to ensure that its interest or equity in the collateral is preserved. In effect, they submit one of the objects of the section is to provide consumer protection or debtor relief. When Part V, which includes s. 63, is read in its entirety, it is apparent that an elaborate mandatory scheme has been constructed to ensure a commercially reasonable result when a security agreement is in default. Part V is designed to protect the interests of both the secured creditor and the debtor. To accede to the submission of the respondents would be to substitute a scheme based on concepts of consumer protection or debtor relief focussing primarily, if not exclusively, upon the debtors' right for a scheme intended to protect both parties, the creditor as well as the debtor. It would amount to the substitution of a consumer protection scheme without imposing any statutory criteria or guidelines for the judge to follow. It would amount to a scheme vesting a judge with unfettered discretion to decide whether or not contractual rights conferred upon a creditor should be altered to the latter's detriment. I am not prepared to accept that was the intention of the legislators.

In my opinion, s. 63 was not designed to permit a trial judge to rewrite or change the substance of the contractual rights between the parties. The section gives the trial judge the right to stay proceedings on conditions, if necessary, in order to protect the respective rights of the parties. One of the conditions could be to give the debtor additional time to reinstate the contract. While on its face that is an alteration of the contract, it is not, in my opinion, an alteration of the substance of the contract. It would not be advisable to set out the circumstances under which such a stay could be granted, nor to specify the terms and conditions of such stay. Those must be determined by an examination of the facts in each case. As Professor Cuming has noted, the powers granted under s. 63 should be exercised reasonably within the spirit of the legislation.

To accede to the submissions of the respondents would be to deprive the secured party of its rights and to create rights which do not exist under Part V and which do not exist under the contract. The chambers judge erred in making an order to alter the terms of the contract.

What then should be the result here? The respondent Andrews was in arrears under the terms of the security agreement and, by virtue of the terms of the security agreement and the Act, the appellant had the right to take possession of the truck. It took possession pursuant to an order granted by a judge of the Court of Queen's Bench and was therefore lawfully in possession of the truck. In order to resolve the issue, it is not necessary to get into the question of whether or not the respondent Andrews was in default under the security agreement by virtue of having sold the truck to Trotchie without permission. At the time of repossession, Andrews and/or Trotchie, or both, lost her or their possessory right to the truck. They were only entitled, subject to the right of redemption provided for in s. 62 of the Act, to any surplus after the appellant had complied with the provisions of Part V and realized on its security in a commercially reasonable manner.

In my opinion, even if the respondents had applied for a stay to give them time to bring up the arrears, I would not have made the order asked for. There are no appropriate circumstances set out in evidence which would justify making such an order. The evidence established that the respondents were unable to bring the agreement up to date in December 1986, and nothing in the material indicates that their financial condition has changed or that they could bring the arrears up to date. In effect, they wanted an order postponing the payments until the truck could again earn money to make the payments, and an order extending the time for payment. In my opinion, the chambers judge did not have the power to make such an order.

Appeal allowed.

NOTES AND QUESTIONS

1) Note the observations of the Court with respect to the way in which contractual provisions dealing with seizure rights are to be interpreted. The PPSA provides only very limited scope for the contractual modification of the rules of Part V (and s. 17) to the extent that they specify the obligations of the secured party. See OPPSA s. 58(5). The OPPSA contains a provision not found in the other Acts. Under s. 59(4) the parties may set out in

their security agreement "standards by which the rights of the debtor and the duties of the secured party are to be measured, so long as those standards are not manifestly unreasonable having regard to the nature of the rights and duties." However, this power is subject to s. 58(5). What scope, if any, does s. 59(4) give to the parties? The section assumes the existence of statutory "duties" which are subject to varying standards of performance. Can the parties change by agreement the standard of the duty to dispose of the collateral in a commercially reasonable manner prescribed by s. 63(2)? Can the agreement vary the standard of performance of the common law duty to avoid a breach of the peace when seizing collateral? See OPPSA s. 62(a). What other duties might be subject to different standards of performance? What is the difference between a standard that is "unreasonable" and one that is "manifestly unreasonable"?

2) Has the Saskatchewan Court of Appeal in *Andrews* emasculated SPPSA s. 63? Should the absence of a general reinstatement right in the OPPSA induce Ontario courts to give a broader interpretation to the scope of OPPSA s. 67(1)?

3) Note that the OPPSA s. 67(1) contains no equivalent to SPPSA s. 63(d) (as set out in *Mack*) which empowers a court to "stay enforcement of rights provided in [Part V] under any terms and conditions that ... [are] ... just and reasonable." Can one assume that this omission was intentional? Must one conclude that the Ontario Legislature was quite prepared to allow a court to relieve a secured party from compliance with Part V (see also s. 67(1)(f)) but was not prepared to allow a court to stay a secured party's enforcement rights? Does s. 67(1) in this respect simply mirror the approach taken by the Saskatchewan Court of Appeal?

4) There is another context in which a court may use discretionary jurisdiction to affect the rights of a secured party. Marshalling is a principle of equity that would apply in the following situation: SP1 has a first priority security interest in Item A and Item B but the debt secured can be satisfied through seizure and sale of either item. SP2 has a second priority security interest in Item B. If SP1 chooses to seize B, the result will be that SP2 loses his or her security but if SP1 chooses to seize A, Item B is available to SP2. The effect of the principle is that either SP1 is forced to realize against A and leave B to SP2 or SP2 is subordinated to SP1's rights in A when SP1 seizes B. As to the applicability of the principle in the context of the PPSA, see *National Bank of Canada v. Makin Metals Ltd.*, [1993] 3 WWR 318 (Sask. CA) and MacDougall, "Marshalling and the Personal Property Security Acts: Doing Unto Others ..." (1994), 28 *UBC LR* 91. The application of marshalling in the context of the PPSA is not without difficulties. Assume that SP2's security interest in B is unperfected. SP1 seizes B and SP2 is subrogated to SP1's interest in A. Is the policy of OPPSA s. 20(1)(b) (i.e., unperfected security interests are subordinate to a trustee in bankruptcy) frustrated if, at the time of the marshalling order, the debtor is a bankrupt? If marshalling were allowed, the rights of the debtor's unsecured creditors to share in the proceeds of the disposition of B would depend upon the whim of SP1 in choosing to proceed against B and not A. The effect of marshalling would be to give SP2 a perfected security interest in A when all SP2 had was an unperfected security interest in B.

EXERCISE OF THE RIGHT TO TAKE POSSESSION

The PPSA gives the secured party upon default by the debtor under the security agreement, "unless otherwise agreed, the right to take possession of the collateral by any method permitted by law" (OPPSA s. 62(a)). The section incorporates any limitation on seizure of collateral prescribed by federal law or provincial law.

Regina v. Doucette
(1960), 25 DLR (2d) 380, [1960] OR 407 (CA)

SCHROEDER JA (for the court): … The respondents were duly licensed as bailiffs by the Municipality of Metropolitan Toronto after having received a certificate of qualification in accordance with the provisions of the Bailiffs Act, RSO 1950, c. 30. Under the terms of such licence they were entitled to engage in the business or calling of bailiffs but they were not clothed with any official status as peace officers or as duly authorized officers of any Court. Persons so licensed are frequently engaged by merchants or finance companies to repossess merchandise sold under the terms of conditional sales agreements and when thus engaged they are acting in a private and unofficial capacity as the authorized agents of the vendor of the goods in question or of his assignee.

The facts giving rise to the indictment laid against the respondents arose out of a seizure made by them on the afternoon of November 6, 1959, at or about the hour of 4.30 p.m. at the apartment of one John Chappell contained in a building known and described for municipal purposes as No. 2110 Dundas St. West. Chappell occupied a small second storey apartment at that address with his wife and five young children. The respondents had driven to the premises in a station wagon for the purpose of repossessing a television set which had been purchased by Chappell under the terms of a conditional sales contract. The purchaser, Chappell, stated in evidence that the vendor had accepted an old television set in part payment of the purchase-price and that he had paid approximately $15 in cash. A copy of the contract which has been filed does not indicate that any allowance was made for a used television set, but it is not disputed that at the time of the seizure the payments due under the agreement were in arrear.

Only Doucette and McNutt entered the premises in the first instance. The front door leading to the ground floor hall was opened to them by Chappell's 11-year-old-son who called to his father to advise him that some men wished to see him. The visitors did not wait for an invitation to enter Chappell's apartment but immediately proceeded to ascend the stairs. Chappell's evidence is that there was a small gate stretched across the hall entrance to his apartment and placed at the head of the stairs. He stated that the two respondents, while still standing on the stairway, advised him of the purposes of their visit; that they had not at that time passed the gate to enter the upstairs hallway. He then advised them that he would not permit them to take the television set until a policeman could be summoned. He stated that one of the two men then unfastened the gate and pushed him back across the upstairs hall into the living room where the television set was kept. There is a conflict in the evidence upon this point, both Doucette and McNutt having testified that they had not observed the gate referred to; that they did not see Chappell until they entered the living room of the apartment; and that when they announced their intention of repossessing the television set, Chappell stated plainly and emphatically that he objected to their doing so, and when no favourable reaction occurred he attempted to push Doucette out of the room. It is not disputed that Chappell at that time requested his wife to go out to telephone the police and at the same time ordered these two men, Doucette and McNutt, to leave his premises and to remain downstairs until the arrival of the police. They, however, refused to comply with this request and persisted in remaining in the apartment. A fight then occurred between Chappell and Doucette in which McNutt endeavoured to intervene. At this point the third respondent, Dongen, a sturdy man about 6 ft. in height and weighing 240 lbs. entered the room, unbidden by anyone, and his mere presence apparently sufficed to terminate the fighting. One thing that emerges clearly from the evidence is the fact that Chappell had made it abundantly clear that he protested against the presence of these men on his premises; that he objected to the removal of the television set of which he was at the time in peaceable possession under a claim of right, and that he made it very plain that if they attempted to remove it before the arrival of the police he would resist their efforts. In all the circumstances Chappell's suggestion that they desist for carrying out the seizure until the police were called, emanating from a man who had serious doubts as to his legal rights in this affair, was not unreasonable. Notwithstanding this one of the three accused men scoffingly declared that they would be gone before the police arrived. Then, while Chappell was leaning on the television set, Doucette disconnected the electric plug and Dongen seized the instrument and carried it towards the stairs, followed by Doucette and McNutt. The latter acting as a rear guard, walked backwards with his fists raised in order to hold off Chappell, who was apparently following the trio in a threatening manner. McNutt then pushed forward past Doucette who was on the upper steps, and assisted Dongen in carrying the television set down the remaining steps. Doucette who was then last in line, believing that Chappell was about to strike him, directed a hard blow at Chappell's mouth which felled him to the floor. The three bailiffs left the premises carrying the television set with them before the police could arrive on the scene.

The learned trial Judge made no express findings of fact and disposed of the case in these few words:

With respect to the charge of assault in the second indictment, I am satisfied there that the complainant was the author of his own misfortune and that also will be dismissed.

It is not easy to discern precisely what the learned Judge meant by these words. ... I cannot think that the learned trial Judge gave proper consideration to the legal rights and obligations of the respondents in attempting to carry out their object and to the corresponding rights and obligations of the complainant, Chappell. Since there appears to be a popular misconception in the minds of many people, particularly in the minds of persons engaged in the business or calling of licensed bailiffs as to the extent of their rights and privileges, it may serve a useful purpose to review the law bearing upon the issues directly involved in this case.

It should be made clear at the outset that the recaption or resumption of possession of goods by the act of the owner through an agent or bailiff acting under his written authority, is not a lawful execution of any process against lands or goods, or is not the making of a lawful distress or seizure within the meaning of s. 110(c) of the Cr. Code which is directed against resistance to or wilful obstruction of any person engaged in the performance of such acts. This is placed beyond question by the decision of the Court of Appeal in *R v. Shand* (1904), 8 Can. CC 45, 7 OLR 190.

The limitations upon the right of an owner to repossess his goods without process of law are stated clearly and succinctly in 3 *Blackstone's Commentaries* at 4-5, from which I quote:

Recaption or *reprisal* is another species of remedy by the mere act of the party injured. This happens when any one hath deprived another of his property in goods or chattels personal ... in which case the owner of the goods ... may lawfully claim and retake them wherever he happens to find them, so it be not in a riotous manner, or attended with a breach of the peace. The reason for this is obvious; since it may frequently happen that the owner may have this only opportunity of doing himself justice: his goods may be afterwards conveyed away or destroyed; ... if he had no speedier remedy than the ordinary process of law. If therefore he can so contrive it as to gain possession of his property again without force or terror, the law favors and will justify his proceeding. But as the public peace is a superior consideration to any one man's private property; and as, if individuals were once allowed to use private force as a remedy for private injuries, all social justice must cease, the strong would give law to the weak, and every man would revert to a state of nature; for these reasons it is provided that this natural right of recaption shall never be exerted where such exertion must occasion strife and bodily contention, or endanger the peace of society.

•   •   •

It is very clear that whatever rights the vendor or his assignee or their authorized agent might have had under the terms of the conditional sales contract (the purchase-money being in arrear and unpaid) to enter upon Chappell's premises to resume possession of the goods in question, it would be illegal for them to take such possession by force. *Traders Bank of Canada v. G & J Brown Mfg. Co.* (1889), 18 OR 430, cited by counsel for the respondents is authority for this proposition. In *Re Nu-Way Meat Market Ltd. & Grobstein & Commercial Acceptance Corp.* (1940), 22 CBR 46, 46 Rev. de Jur. 418, it was held that the liquidator might claim possession of a truck sold to a debtor under suspensive conditions of property, where the vendor had taken possession of it by force and deceit since the winding-up, and had neglected to furnish the liquidator with the detailed account of what was still owed by the debtor; whatever the terms of the deed, no one had the right to take the law into one's own hands.

Reference may also be made on this point to *Devoe v. Long*, [1951] 1 DLR 203, at 225-26, 26 MPR 357, a judgment of the Appeal Division of the Supreme Court of New Brunswick.

The right to resort to self-help was again discountenanced in *Nilan v. McAndless* (1912), 8 DLR 169, where at 171, Macdonald J stated:

He was not justified, however in taking the law in his own hands when he found that he could not get peaceable possession. His proper course was to obtain possession by legal means.

There must be reasonable limits imposed upon the right of self-help assumed and asserted by private individuals in order to preserve peace and tranquility and to avoid the evil consequences which are bound to flow from insistence upon a right to use private force. Under s. 39 of the Cr. Code, the peaceable possessor of movable property under a claim of right is protected from criminal responsibility (although not from civil responsibility) for resisting its taking even by the person legally entitled.

The principle which must govern in cases of this kind was stated in clear and unmistakable terms by Osler JA, in *R v. Shand*, 8 Can. CC at 52-53, 7 OLR, at 196-97, from which I quote the following excerpt:

> The law is the same where goods are improperly detained by one in defiance of his agreement to yield them up to the owner with or without demand. If the owner can acquire possession peacably he may do so. If he attempts to take it forcibly and in a riotous manner as was done in the case before us, he becomes himself a breaker of the law, as much so as one who attempts to take possession of real property by a forcible entry, contrary to 5 Rich. II., stat. 1, ch. 8, even when it has been agreed that he was to re-enter; *Edwick v. Hawkes* (1881), 18 Ch.D 199; and see *Beddall v. Maitland* (1881), 17 Ch.D 174. If resistance is offered or possession refused he should have recourse to his action, and the code, sec. 144, would then have its full force in making unlawful any resistance to seizure made in due course of law. That is what is meant by a lawful seizure. It was never intended to enlarge the civil rights or powers of individuals, or to convert a breach of contract or resistance to private force into a criminal offence.

• • •

It follows logically that if a person enters premises lawfully in the first instance for the purpose of resuming possession of his movable property and subsequently abuses his authority, he becomes in law a trespasser. It is rather singular that three bailiffs had to descend upon the complainant to repossess a chattel which could be borne by one man, unless it was their purpose to make a display of might, against which the complainant's lone opposition, whether right or wrong, could scarcely be expected to prevail. That these men abused their authority after gaining entrance to the premises is too plain for discussion. Once it was made clear to them, as indeed it was, that they would not be suffered to remove the television set without resistance, they grossly exceeded and abused their rights when they persisted in carrying out their project of abducting the television receiver, using force for the purpose if necessary. They thus became trespassers even if their original entry was lawful, a point which, on the evidence, is itself not free from doubt.

The learned Deputy Attorney-General contends that by force of the provisions of s. 38(2) of the Cr. Code alone, quite apart from the actual physical force applied by the respondents to the person of the complainant, they must be held to have committed an assault without justification or provocation. Section 38(2) reads:

> (2) Where a person who is in peaceable possession of movable property lays hands upon it, a trespasser who persists in attempting to keep it or take it from him or from any one lawfully assisting him shall be deemed to commit an assault without justification or provocation.

Also by s. 38(1) the person in peaceable possession of such property is justified in preventing a trespasser from taking it if he does not strike him or cause him bodily harm.

In my view of the facts, the conduct of the respondents towards the complainant Chappell while exercising their purported right to repossess the television set in question by force is in itself sufficient to support a charge of common assault against them. I agree, however, that if it were necessary for the Crown to rely upon the provisions of s. 38(2) of the Cr. Code, those provisions might successfully be invoked against the respondents.

Appeal allowed.

NOTES AND QUESTIONS

1) The issue before the court in *Doucette* was the criminal liability of the secured creditor's agents. Does a decision that the conduct of the accused was criminal also mean that the seizure was a violation of the debtor's property rights or that the secured creditor could be held liable in conversion? What criminal or civil liability would a secured creditor incur if, without the knowledge of the debtor but after being told by the debtor to stay off his property, the secured creditor took possession of collateral in the form of an automobile which was parked in the debtor's driveway at the time of repossession? (Assume that the security agreement expressly gave the secured party a right to effect seizure in this way.) See generally, D. Paciocco, "Personal Property Security Act Repossession: The Risk and the Remedy," in *Debtor-Creditor Law*, M. Springman and E. Gertner, eds., 1985, chapter 8, at 365.

2) What alternative measures are available to a secured creditor in cases where self-help repossession is likely to result in a breach of the peace? See Courts of Justice Act, SO 1990, c. C.43, ss. 117(1), 177(1) and 211. See also OPPSA s. 67(1), *Andrews v. Mack Financial Services*, *supra* and *Costly v. Pioneer Credit Union* (1992), 2 PPSAC 212 (Sask. QB).

3) Where the collateral is an intangible, chattel paper or an instrument, enforcement of the security interest is quite easy. See OPPSA s. 61. However, s. 244 of the Bankruptcy and Insolvency Act may apply.

4) With respect to the custodial obligations of the secured party while in possession of the collateral (whether after seizure or when the security interest has been perfected by the secured party being in possession of the collateral), see OPPSA s. 17.

5) The repossessory rights of a secured party on the debtor's bankruptcy are governed by conflicting provisions in the BIA which have engendered strong differences of opinion among courts. See BIA ss. 69.4 and 81, *R. v. Ford Motor Credit of Canada* (1990), 78 CBR (NS) 266 (Ont.) and the earlier cases there referred to, and *infra*, chapter 17. An automatic stay on repossessory rights also applies under BIA ss. 69 and 69.1 where a debtor gives notice of intention to file a proposal under s. 50.4 or files such a proposal under s. 62(1). These stays are essential to allow an insolvent debtor an opportunity to develop a plan for the reorganization of its business.

Under s. 11 of the CCAA a court has wide ranging power to order a stay of proceedings, and such orders are made readily (and usually *ex parte*) on the debtor's application. These provisions give a distressed debtor some leverage in renegotiating the terms of security agreements with its creditors.

VOLUNTARY FORECLOSURE

Angelkovski v. Trans-Canada Foods Ltd.
[1986] 3 WWR 723 (Man. QB)

WRIGHT J: The primary issue in this case is whether the defendant, by taking possession of chattels given as security under a chattel mortgage, after default by the plaintiff, and utilizing the chattels in a certain way, thereby terminated any rights the defendant may have had to any other claim for the moneys secured.

The principal of the defendant is one Patrick Cory. The defendant at one time owned and operated the Red Barn Restaurant, 882-884 Main Street, Winnipeg. In 1978 the restaurant was sold to the male plaintiff (Angelkovski) and a partner. The balance of the purchase price was secured by a chattel mortgage of all the chattels in the restaurant, in the amount of $155,230, repayable $2,500 per month with interest at 12 per cent per annum.

Collateral security in the form of a promissory note for the same amount and on the same terms was also provided by the purchasers. As additional security Angelkovski and his co-plaintiff, his wife, gave the vendor a real property mortgage on their home for $55,000, also repayable at $2,500 a month and on the same interest terms as the other security.

After making the payments required through September 1978 to December 1981 the plaintiff and his partner defaulted, and on or about 20th January 1982 the defendant had a bailiff seize the chattels under the chattel mortgage. The seizure was effected by padlocking the premises, which were leased, per authority provided in the chattel mortgage.

Subsequently in March a sale of some sort was organized through the bailiff but proved abortive. Very little evidence was presented as to this sale. It was not suggested that any other effort was made to sell the chattels until the following July.

Following the abortive bailiff's sale the defendant took control of the premises and the chattels. Cory decided to reopen the restaurant, and in the name of the defendant applied for and by June obtained a new liquor licence and opened for business.

Cory had to make some repairs to certain of the chattels and to clean up and partially redecorate the premises. In a letter dated 26th August 1982, to the plaintiff's solicitor, his lawyers said the cost of the work was about $3,150.

Cory continued to operate the restaurant until 4th January 1983, when a fire occurred in the restaurant and the chattels were destroyed.

In the meantime the plaintiffs had issued a statement of claim dated 17th August 1982, but not served until 1st September 1982. As indicated at the outset of these reasons, the main allegation in the claim was that the defendant by its action elected to receive the chattels in full satisfaction of the debt owed, and therefore the plaintiffs had (and have) no further obligation to the defendant.

The exact amount outstanding on the chattel mortgage as of the date of seizure was not precisely established at trial, but as of 29th February 1982 it was no more than $112,179.71 and perhaps it was less.

If it were not for the provisions of the Personal Property Security Act (Manitoba) (which I will come to shortly), the law in Manitoba in respect of this issue would be, in my opinion, the same as the general law applicable to chattel mortgage seizures in Ontario.

Subject always to any special provisions in a particular chattel mortgage (which does not apply in the instant case) in Ontario the courts have held that if it can be demonstrated a chattel mortgagee has appropriated the pledges to his own use, following default by the mortgagor and a proper seizure, he must then be found to have taken them for the debt: *McDonald v. Grundy* (1904), 8 OLR 113; *Gladman v. Hothersall*, [1936] OWN 358 (HC); *Miller v. Budreau*, [1954] OWN 274 (HC); and *Greenberg v. Rapoport*, [1970] 2 OR 349, 10 DLR (3d) 737 (HC).

• • •

To the extent any of the cases that I have cited above in support suggest a chattel mortgagee cannot sell the pledged goods without losing his right to claim for any deficiency I am not in agreement. Most chattel mortgages provide for a right of sale, either public or private, and protect the mortgagee's right to sue for any deficiency. There is provision to that effect in the present chattel mortgage. There is also a clause confirming the defendant's right to utilize the chattels for his own use if desired, which serves to protect the defendant (the mortgagee) from any further claim by the mortgagor relative to the chattels in the event that the defendant (mortgagee) decides to take the chattels in satisfaction of the debt. Whether the defendant here had done this or not is a question of fact to be determined at least in part by identifying his intention and purpose after seizure.

If the facts show the defendant intended to reopen the restaurant to sell the chattels as part of an ongoing business in order to improve their sale value, with the primary purpose of recovering the balance of the debt owing, then I do not think an appropriation of the chattels can be found. On the other hand if it can be concluded the defendant reopened the restaurant with the essential purpose of operating it himself, or of reselling it, so as to make more money than the amount owing on the debt, with no intention of accounting to the plaintiff and his partner for any surplus, then the court could reasonably conclude the chattels were appropriated in full satisfaction of the debt.

From the facts, I have decided in favour of the second alternative.

• • •

If it were not for the provisions of the Personal Property Security Act (the PPSA), the plaintiffs would be entitled to a declaration that they have no further obligation to the defendant in connection with the original debt. However, the PPSA, which applies to chattel mortgages, provides as follows:

61(1) At any time before the secured party has disposed of the collateral by sale or exchange or contracted for the disposition under section 58 or before the secured party shall be deemed to have irrevocably elected to retain the collateral in satisfaction of the obligation under subsection (2) of section 60, the debtor, or any person other than the debtor who is the owner of the collateral, or any secured party in possession, may, unless he has otherwise agreed in writing after default

(a) redeem the collateral by tendering fulfillment of all obligations secured by the collateral; or

(b) reinstate the security agreement by paying the sums actually in arrear, exclusive of the operation of any acceleration clause, or by curing any other default by reason whereof the secured party intends to dispose of the collateral;

together with a sum equal to the reasonable expenses of retaking, holding, repairing, processing, preparing the collateral for disposition and in arranging for its disposition, and, to the extent provided for in the security agreement, the reasonable solicitor's costs and legal expenses.

This subsection brings into play s. 60(2) which in turn relates to s. 60(3). These two subsections provide that a secured party in possession of the collateral may, after default, propose to retain the collateral in satisfaction of the obligation secured, upon giving notification to that effect to the debtor. If the debtor objects within 15 days, the secured party must proceed in such a manner as to protect any realized surplus for the debtor, on the disposition of the collateral. If there is no objection within the 15 days, the collateral is no longer subject to any claim of the debtor.

In this context I interpret s. 61(1) to mean that until there has been compliance with the provisions of s. 60(2) and (3) the debtor retains the right to redeem. In other words, the statute makes it *impossible* for the secured party to appropriate the collateral for his own use free and clear of any claim of the debtor unless s. 60(2) and (3) has been followed. The effect of these statutory provisions then is to preclude any actual or deemed appropriation of the collateral according to the general law principles I earlier identified. The intention and objective of the secured party is no longer of importance. That does not mean to say a secured party does not have to account for the chattels and may be subject to a claim by the debtor for damages in that regard (*cf.* s. 62(2)), but—be that as it may—unless there has been compliance with the procedure under s. 60(2) and (3), the secured party is free to pursue any perceived deficiency.

Counsel for the plaintiffs submitted that it can be inferred from the evidence in the present case the defendant gave the notification required under s. 60(2) to the debtor. Counsel pointed out that the definition of notification in the PPSA simply means "coming to the attention of the debtor" [s. 1r], and argued Angelkovski had that kind of notification. However, I disagree. It may be possible to infer Angelkovski knew the defendant was retaining the collateral but I do not believe the evidence is at all clear he knew the purpose was to retain it *in satisfaction of the obligation secured*. I think in view of the wording in s. 60(2) and (3) the notification should be in clear and precise terms. In any event, I am unable to conclude on the preponderance of evidence that the debtor had the required notification.

The plaintiffs are not entitled therefore to a general declaration that they have no further obligation to the defendant.

• • •

NOTES AND QUESTIONS

1) Rather than selling seized collateral, a secured party may "propose to retain the collateral in satisfaction of the obligation secured." See OPPSA s. 65(2). The secured creditor's right to keep the collateral in return for cancellation of the debt arises by default if the persons who are entitled to object (see OPPSA s. 65(2)) fail to do so within the prescribed time and in the prescribed manner. See OPPSA s. 65(6).

2) Under the OPPSA (but not under the Acts based on the CCPPSL model), where the collateral is consumer goods and the debtor has paid at least 60 percent of the "indebted-

ness secured," the secured party is not entitled to retain the collateral if the debtor "has not signed, after default, a statement renouncing or modifying his rights under the Part." See OPPSA s. 65(1). The section appears to require a general renunciation of "rights under this Part." Would a specific surrender of rights under s. 65(1) not be sufficient? Consider the cumulative effect of OPPSA s. 65(1) and s. 23 of the Ontario Consumer Protection Act, *supra*.

3) Someone other than the debtor may have an interest in seeing that the collateral is sold and not retained by the secured party. A subordinate security interest is extinguished along with that of the debtor when the debtor's rights in the collateral are surrendered. See OPPSA s. 65(6). However, under ss. 65(2)-(3) a person with a security interest in the collateral can force a sale of it only if the collateral is other than consumer goods or, if consumer goods, only when more than 40 percent of the secured indebtedness remains owing. What justification is there for this distinction?

4) What is the result under OPPSA s. 65(7) if a person buys the collateral in good faith for value before the expiry of the period mentioned in subsection (6)?

5) The court in *Angelkovski* found that there had been an appropriation of the collateral by the secured creditor to its own use, yet also found the debtor still liable for a deficiency (reduced by any amount of damages the debtor could establish he has suffered as a result of the defendant's illegal conduct). The court made no mention of the Manitoba equivalent of OPPSA s. 17(5). Should it have?

6) Do you agree that the legislative purpose of OPPSA s. 65 is to prevent a debtor from relying on the common law rule that a secured creditor which appropriates collateral to its own purposes is treated at the election of the debtor to have taken the collateral in full satisfaction? Is there any way OPPSA s. 65 can be read so as to preserve this aspect of the common law?

7) How does OPPSA s. 65 operate in the context of a situation in which the secured party wishes to retain *some* of the collateral in return for cancellation of *part* of the obligation secured?

REDEMPTION AND REINSTATEMENT

Bank of Nova Scotia v. Sherstobitoff
(1987), 64 Sask R 293 (QB)

WRIGHT J: The applicant and his mother signed a promissory note in favour of the Bank. They agreed to pay the Bank $6,189.15 by monthly instalments. The note stated:

If you fail to pay any instalment when it is due, we can require any one of you to pay at once the unpaid balance of the total amount you have borrowed and all interest owing.

They also signed what was described as a "chattel mortgage" under which they gave a security interest to the respondent in two motor vehicles. It contains these terms:

7. Total balance due. We can require that the total balance of the promissory note and anything else you owe us under this chattel mortgage be paid at once, without prior notice or demand, if any of the following events take place:

(1) You fail to pay an instalment of the promissory note on time; or

(2) You fail to pay when we ask any amount we are entitled to charge you for making repairs, maintaining insurance or clearing claims against the property; or

(3) You break any of your promises under this chattel mortgage; or

(4) You become insolvent or bankrupt; or

(5) The property is destroyed or substantially damaged; or

(6) The property is seized in any legal proceeding; or

(7) Anything else happens that we believe endangers your ability to pay or that we believe endangers the property in any way ...

8. Enforcing our rights. We may enforce our rights to be paid the total balance due by:

(1) Suing you for what you owe; or

(2) Taking possession of the property, or both. If we take possession, you can regain possession by paying us the total amount you owe along with our reasonable legal and other expenses of taking and maintaining your property. If you don't regain possession, we can sell the property at either a public or private sale. We will give you at least 20 days notice of the date, time and place of any public sale or of the date after which any private sale will be made. We will then give you the amount left after we subtract the total amount you owed us plus our reasonable legal and other expenses of taking, maintaining and selling the property ("all our costs") plus any amount which we are required to pay to another secured party. If there is a balance still owing to us after we have sold the property and subtracted the total amount you owed us plus all our costs, you must pay us that amount.

Pauline Sherstobitoff also signed a demand promissory note in which she agreed to repay the bank $12,000. The bank sued to recover both debts and also seized the vehicles pursuant to the Personal Property Security Act. The seizure occurred on August 25, 1987, at which time it delivered a notice to the Sherstobitoffs in the following form:

NOTICE OF SALE OR OTHER DISPOSITION

You are hereby notified that the Bank intends to dispose of the following collateral pursuant to a Scotia Plan Chattel Mortgage dated the 5th day of December, 1986 with Barry and Pauline Sherstobitoff (the "debtor"), who is in default.

(a) Collateral subject to disposition:

1976 Lincoln, serial #F6Y89A867509F
1979 Ford, serial U15HLEE6999

(b) Disposition will be by:

Private sale, lease or otherwise after the 16th day of September, 1987.

(c) The amount required to satisfy the obligations secured is $4,720.14 with a per diem rate of interest thereafter of $1.6676.

(d) We estimate the Bank's expenses of retaking, holding, repairing, processing, or preparing for disposition and disposing of the collateral and any other reasonable expenses authorized by the security agreement and not prohibited by law will be $150.00

(e) The amount actually in arrears is $1,187.45.

(f) You may redeem the collateral by paying to the Bank at its Wildwood Mall Branch the amounts mentioned in paragraphs (c) and (d) above at any time prior to the Bank entering into a contract for the sale or other disposition of the collateral.

(g) The debtor may re-instate the security agreement by paying the amount or curing the default mentioned in paragraph (e) above and by paying the amount mentioned in paragraph (d) above to the Wildwood Mall Branch at any time prior to the Bank entering into a contract for the sale or other disposition of the collateral.

(h) Unless the amounts mentioned in paragraphs (c) and (d) above are paid as aforesaid and the collateral is redeemed or unless the amounts mentioned in paragraphs (d) and (e) are paid as aforesaid and the security agreement is re-instated, the collateral will be sold or otherwise disposed of by the Bank and the debtor will be liable for any deficiency resulting from such sale or other disposition of the collateral.

At this point, the bank offered two options, redemption and reinstatement.

The respondent signed judgment against the applicant on September 1, 1987 for the first debt. On September 3, 1987 he tendered the actual arrears to the bank's solicitors relying on s. 62(1)(b) of the Act and the notice he had first received. The Bank refused to reinstate the security and insisted upon payment of the entire debt.

On September 14, 1987, it delivered a second notice which stated:

NOTICE UNDER THE PERSONAL PROPERTY SECURITY ACT: PROVINCE OF SAS-KATCHEWAN

TO: BARRY SHERSTOBITOFF AND PAULINE SHERSTOBITOFF; of Prince Albert, Saskatchewan, respectively (hereinafter called the Debtors);

FROM: THE BANK OF NOVA SCOTIA, Adjustment Centre, of 2nd Floor – 119 – 4th Avenue South, Saskatoon, Saskatchewan (hereinafter called the Secured Party).

AND TO: All other parties appearing to have an interest in the collateral subsequent to that of the secured party.

TAKE NOTICE that the secured party has directly or by its agent taken possession of and intends to dispose of the following items (hereinafter called the "collateral"):

Item: 1976 Lincoln Mark IV Automobile Serial #:F6Y89A867509F

Item: 1979 Ford Ranger XLT Motor Vehicle Serial #:V15HLEE6999

1. The secured party holds security in the collateral and has the right to take possession and dispose of the same by virtue of a security agreement executed by the debtors and in favour of the secured party dated December 5, 1986 (hereinafter called the security agreement).

2. Particulars of what is owing under the security agreement as of September 1, 1987, are as follows:

Total Owing:	$4,831.25
Daily Interest after the above date:	$.6618
Actual Arrears:	$4,831.25

The total amount owing under your security agreement is due because your indebtedness has been reduced to a judgment.

3. The secured party has taken possession and intends to dispose of the collateral because payments were in arrears and now the total amount owing is due under a judgment issued in Queen's Bench Action 2995 of 1987. In addition, the security agreement is in default because Barry Sherstobitoff has also attempted to conceal the collateral from The Bank of Nova Scotia when attempting to exercise its right to possession of the collateral upon default, thereby endangering the collateral and the Secured Party's interest therein.

4. An estimate of the reasonable costs incurred by or on behalf of the secured party including what it has cost the secured party to take possession, hold, repair, process, prepare the collateral for disposition and dispose of the same is $150.00 plus storage charges after August 26, 1987, at the rate of $4.00 per day ($2.00 per day, per vehicle).

5. If the debtors pay all arrears and all actual costs referred to and estimated in paragraph 4 hereof as of the date of payment, and remedy any other breach of the security agreement, the debtors may reinstate the security agreement.

6. If anyone entitled to receive this notice pays to the secured party the total amount owing on the security agreement plus all actual costs referred to and estimated in paragraph 4 hereof as to the date of payment, that person making payment will be entitled to redeem the collateral.

7. Unless the security agreement is reinstated or the collateral is redeemed in accordance with paragraphs 5 or 6 of this notice, the collateral will be disposed of as follows:

_____ × _____ by private sale to be held after October 4, 1987;

8. If the net sale proceeds, after payment of any prior claim and deduction of all costs incurred by or on behalf of the secured party, do not pay the entire amount that is owing to the secured party, the debtors will be liable for any deficiency.

This was the bank's formal assertion of its right to all the indebtedness.

Section 62 states:

62.(1) At any time before the secured party has disposed of the collateral or contracted for such disposition under section 58 or before the secured party is deemed to have irrevocably elected to retain the collateral under section 61:

(a) any person entitled to receive a notice of disposition under subsection 59(4) may, unless he has otherwise agreed in writing after default, redeem the collateral by tendering fulfilment of all obligations secured by the collateral;

(b) the debtor may, unless he has otherwise agreed in writing after default, reinstate the security agreement by paying the sums actually in arrears, exclusive of the operation of any acceleration clause, or by curing any other default by reason whereof the secured party intends to dispose of the collateral;

together with a sum equal to the reasonable expenses of retaking, holding, repairing, processing and preparing for disposition and any other reasonable expenses incurred by the secured party.

(2) Unless otherwise agreed, the debtor is not entitled to reinstate a security agreement:

(a) more than twice, if the security agreement or any agreement modifying the security agreement provides for payment in full by the debtor within 12 months after the day value was given by the secured party;

(b) more than twice in each year, if the security agreement or any agreement modifying the security agreement provides for payment by the debtor during a period of time in excess of one year after the day value was given by the secured party.

Subparagraph (1)(b) is not found in comparable Canadian legislation. It is akin to relief from forfeiture and intended to permit debtors to recover property seized as a result of default provided actual arrears and certain costs are paid. A debtor's right to do so is limited. The section specifically provides that accelerated arrears need not be paid, unless the debtor agrees to do so after default. Sherstobitoff did not do so. Taking judgment against him does not constitute an agreement. That is especially so as the applicant disputed his indebtedness to the bank before the bank signed judgment over his objections. If he had consented to judgment, a different result might have followed. There will be an order reinstating the personal property security upon payment of the actual arrears now owing and the expenses referred to in s. 62(1)(b). If there is any difficulty between the parties in settling the amount that is owing, there will be a reference to the local registrar to settle the amount.

The applicant also sought to set aside the default judgment entered against him. His affidavit evidence is contradicted in several important areas in the affidavits of the respondent's officers. Counsel declined to examine on the affidavits. He has not satisfied the burden imposed upon him and his application in this respect is dismissed.

The applicant will have the costs of the application as he has been substantially successful in these proceedings.

Application allowed.

NOTES AND QUESTIONS

1) The Acts based on the CCPPSL model (other than BCPPSA) give all defaulting debtors (whether consumers or businesses) the right to "reinstate the security agreement by paying the sums actually in arrears, exclusive of the operation of any acceleration clause, or by curing any other default by reason whereof the secured party intends to dispose of the collateral." (See, e.g., SPPSA s. 62(1)(b)(iii).) Section 62(3) of the BCPPSA gives an automatic right of reinstatement where the collateral is consumer goods and in other situations gives power to a court to "relieve the debtor from the consequences of the default or stay enforcement of any provision of a security agreement providing for acceleration of the payment or performance upon default by the debtor." Under all of the CCPPSL Acts, there are limits placed on the number of times a debtor may reinstate.

2) There is no provision in the OPPSA giving a general right to cure a default. OPPSA s. 66(2) gives a very narrow right only in the context of consumer transactions. Compare this restricted approach with the Ontario position involving mortgages of real property where the debtor is entitled to remedy a default at any time before final judgment has been granted against him (Mortgages Act, RSO 1990, c. M.40, s. 22). Is there any justification for this difference?

3) What are the social and economic arguments for and against a broad right of reinstatement? Most reputable credit grantors give their debtors the right to reinstate after failure to meet one or more payments. Why is it necessary to give statutory rights of reinstatement?

4) OPPSA s. 66(1) provides that the debtor (and other specified persons) may "redeem the collateral by fulfilment of all obligations secured by the collateral" and payment

of the secured party's costs. How would this provision operate in the context of the following situation: SP has a security interest in D's (debtor's) car. D owes SP $10,000 but the car is worth $5,000. Upon D's default, SP seizes the car and gives D the requisite notice of its intention to sell the car. D tenders $5,000 plus SP's seizure costs and demands the return of the car claiming his right of redemption. Can SP insist on being paid the full $10,000 even though only $5,000 of the debt owing by D is the "obligation secured by the collateral"? Would SP's position as a secured party be negatively affected if D were allowed to redeem by paying the value of the collateral? How much would SP recover if it refused to return the car and proceeded to sell it? What would be the net result if D bought the car at the sale? What justification is there for allowing SP to insist on selling the car and incurring the extra costs of sale which must be paid by D?

DISPOSAL OF THE COLLATERAL

Copp v. Medi-Dent Services Ltd.
(1991), 2 PPSAC (2d) 114 (Ont. Gen. Div.)

HOILETTE J: The relevant facts, which are distilled from the material filed, are hereafter briefly summarized.

Starting in early 1984 Doctors Copp and Piccininni established a dental practice in premises located at College Park here in Toronto.

At the commencement of their practices Doctors Copp and Piccininni formed a management company, Dentistry and Anaesthesia Management Limited, which company has, at all material times held the lease to the premises occupied by the two dental practices as well as the leases to virtually all the equipment used by the dentists in their respective practices. So far as the equipment is concerned there are five leases, numbered 376770, 378711, 381615, 381616 and 391287.

Acrimony, it is not an exaggeration to say, has been the dominant characteristic of the relationship between the two dentists since about early 1987.

The acrimony between the two dentists reached one of its peaks when in the summer of 1989 Dr. Piccininni stopped making his share of the payments due under the leases to Medi-Dent. Dr. Copp for some time contributed more than his agreed upon share in order to maintain the leases in good standing but when the impasse between him and Dr. Piccininni remained unresolved he too held back on his payments. The result was that the leases fell into default. In consequence of the default, Medi-Dent served notice of intent to sell, pursuant to s. 63(4) and (5) of the *Personal Property Security Act*, SO 1989, c. 16 (PPSA). The notice of intent to sell, dated April 18, 1990, reports arrears in the amount of $31,151.97 on the leases, and concludes, among other things that,

Unless the Collateral is first redeemed, the Collateral will be disposed of by private disposition or public sale after May 14, 1990.

It is common ground that the above notice of intent to sell was served upon Dentistry and Anaesthesia Management Limited, Dr. Copp and Dr. Piccininni, on or about the date it bears, April 18, 1990. Dr. Piccininni responded to the notice of intent to sell by instructing his solicitors on or about April 20, 1990 to redeem the security. The result was an agreement of purchase and sale, dated May 15, 1990, entered into between Dr. Piccininni and Medi-Dent for the purchase of the leased property for a purchase price of $31,151.97; the amount of the arrears outstanding on the leases. The agreement provided for, among other things, a closing date of May 15, 1990 (clause 3); and, in clause 6(a) that:

(a) The Purchaser acknowledges that this Agreement is subject to the expiry of the redemption period provided to the Debtor under the Leases and the *Personal Property Security Act*.

A companion bill of sale to the agreement of purchase and sale forms Exhibit "C" to the affidavit sworn by Dr. Piccininni, and a release, executed on behalf of Medi-Dent Services, forms Exhibit "D" to Dr. Piccininni's affidavit.

Dr. Copp, seemingly because of the long-standing dysfunctional relationship between him and Dr. Piccininni, suffered a form of decision-making paralysis and it was not until May 14, 1990 that his solicitors, acting on his instructions, contacted Medi-Dent with a view to pursuing the redemption. It is not explicit from the material filed if May 14, 1990 was the date of Dr. Copp's instructions to his solicitor; what is clear, however, is that it was at the eleventh hour, having regard to the May 14, 1990, redemption deadline. Suffice it to say that the last minute attempts by Dr. Copp's solicitor, Mr. David Wingfield, to make meaningful contact with Medi-Dent or their solicitors, proved abortive. The letter, Exhibit "A" to Mr. Wingfield's affidavit, sworn May 29, 1990, among other things, speaks of his abortive attempt at communicating with Medi-Dent and confirms their telephone conversation of May 17, 1990, in which he was informed of the sale of the security that had been consummated on May 15, 1990.

The following other points are worth mentioning: The sale to Dr. Piccininni was without notice to Dr. Copp, there was no appraisal, independent or otherwise, of the items sold, and there was no advertisement of the securities sold in any relevant publications. Finally, the only independent opinion of value is that reported by one Roy Brown, who in his affidavit describes himself as a "professional business valuator specializing in valuing medical and dental practices. I have been so engaged for over 17 years." Mr. Brown's affidavit, sworn September 13, 1990, forms Tab 1 to the "supplementary application record" and the report itself, dated June 25, 1990, though not formally made an exhibit in these proceedings, was filed without objection. The report places a value of $79,030.00 on the dental equipment that is in issue.

•   •   •

Fundamental to a resolution of the issues raised, in my view, is a determination as to whether or not the sale consummated between Dr. Piccininni and Medi-Dent was a "commercially reasonable transaction."

Steele J in his oral reasons for judgment in the unreported decision in *National Bank of Canada v. Marguis Furs Ltd.*, December 3, 1987, Doc. No. 780/86, Ont. HC, summarized the applicable test at page 5 of his reasons:

Generally there are two tests that may be applied to the conduct of a sale as referred to by the Court of Appeal in *Wood v. Bank of Nova Scotia et al.*, 14 RPR 1. One is the less stringent test which is that the creditor who sells must act in good faith. The plaintiff has clearly complied with that test. The other test is the more stringent one, that the creditor must take reasonable care that the proper value is obtained. While it is not a trustee for the debtor it cannot act negligently in the sale. I adopt the principle as stated in *Debor Contracting Ltd. v. Core Rentals Ltd. and Parks*, 44 CBR 9 (a *Mechanics' Lien action*) that the creditor must "act a role somewhat akin to that of an agent or fiduciary for the purpose of a sale." This is a higher standard than that referred to in *Kimco Steel Sales Ltd. v. Latina Ornamental Iron Works Ltd.*, 1984 3 PPSAC 237, at page 241 where the test was that the sale be in good faith and not be in a recklessly improvident manner calculated to result in a sacrifice of the equipment.

In my opinion, the proper test under the PPSA is the more stringent one that I have enunciated.

Whether a sale is commercially reasonable is a *question of fact in every case.* ...

In the particular case Steele J found that the test had been met, but the point should be made that on the facts before him, without canvassing the details, there had been advertisements in several locations and in relevant publications aimed at the relevant market.

In the instant application I have no difficulty in concluding that not even the most generous test of reasonableness could be met. There was no attempt at advertisement or publicity. What we had was a private sale to a party clearly adverse in interest to the joint debtor. Those circumstances are aggravated by the fact that there was no attempt at obtaining any opinion of value of the security, let alone an independent appraisal. The only measure of the sale price was the amount of the debt outstanding to the lessor and when one considers that the only independent evaluation places a value on the security more than twice the amount of the sale price, the conclusion is inescapable, in all the circumstances, that the impugned transaction was not a "commercially reasonable" one.

The foregoing reasons are sufficient to dispose of this application favourably to the applicant. There are, however, other equitable considerations which fortify me in that conclusion. They are:

1. Neither of the parties has come to this Court with perfectly clean hands.
2. Regardless of the true nature of the relationship between Doctors Copp and Piccininni, which it is not here necessary to decide, it was such, in my view, as to carry with it certain moral, if not legal, obligations such as not to allow one to score what, in my view, was clearly an unfair victory over the other. Equitable considerations dictate that Dr. Piccininni should not be allowed to profit from what was essentially a private, if not secret, deal between him and Medi-Dent.

• • •

There is an obvious need for an accounting between the two dentists, in respect of which, if they cannot arrive at an agreement, I am prepared, upon further representation, to order a reference.

The moving party should be indemnified by the respondents in respect to any loss consequential upon what was not a proper "disposition" under the provisions of the PPSA.

[The court granted an order containing, *inter alia*, a declaration that the transfer of the collateral to Dr. Piccininni is not a disposition under the PPSA and that Dr. Piccininni "continues to have duties to the secured party to the collateral."]

Application granted.

NOTES AND QUESTIONS

1) A secured creditor who has seized collateral may elect, or may be required, to sell the collateral. Under OPPSA s. 63(3) the secured creditor may delay disposition for such period of time as is commercially reasonable. Failure of the secured party to proceed expeditiously or properly is remediable by court order. See OPPSA s. 67.

2) The Acts based on the CCPPSL model dispense with the notice of sale where the collateral consists of foreign currency. See, e.g., BCPPSA s. 59(17)(b.2). Where the collateral consists of domestic currency, disposition makes no sense; the money is simply applied to the obligation secured. These provisions are designed to permit immediate sale of foreign currencies without notice since the collateral is of a type which has an established market value and can be readily sold.

OPPSA s. 67(3)(c) excuses the notice, where, *inter alia*, "the collateral is of a type customarily sold on a recognized market." The provision does not provide guidance as to what constitutes a "recognized market." Experience in the United States with a very similar provision has generated considerable litigation and differences in judicial opinion as to the meaning of this term. The prevailing view is that a "recognized market" is one in which neutral market forces, as opposed to competitive bidding, determine the price, and where the prices paid in actual sales of comparable property are currently available by quotation. See, e.g., *Cottan v. Heppner*, 9 UCC Rep. Serv. 805 (Utah SC, 1989). Accordingly, bonds and commodities trading on public exchanges would be types of collateral sold on "recognized markets." Where the collateral is fungible property sold on national or international exchanges, its market value can be determined immediately by reference to quoted prices for property of the same kind without the need to offer the particular items of collateral for sale at the highest price.

While the test is easy to state, it is more difficult to apply in peripheral situations. For example, it is possible to determine on the basis of published information the "value" of an automobile of specified make, model, age and condition. However, the prevailing US view is that automobiles do not fall within the exception. See, e.g., *Community Management Association v. Tousley,* 505 P.2d 1314 (Colo. Ct. App., 1973). In each case the outcome will depend upon whether or not at the date of seizure it is possible to get a reliable indication of the market value of the collateral at the place of its location without offering it for sale. If there are factors in the local market that affect the price, there is no "recognized market" for the collateral in the sense in which the term is used in the Act. The Acts based on the CCPPSL model provide that a notice is unnecessary where "the collateral is a security or instrument that is to be disposed of by sale on an organized market that handles large volumes of transactions between many different sellers and many different buyers." See, e.g., SPPSA s. 59(16)(e). Does this provision remove the uncertainty associated with the Ontario formulation?

3) The disposition "may be by public sale, private sale, lease or otherwise" (OPPSA s. 63(2)). Under OPPSA s. 63(9)-(10) it would appear that the position of a *bona fide* purchaser of the collateral varies depending upon whether the sale has or has not been conducted in accordance with the section, and, in the latter case, whether the sale is a public sale or is otherwise than a public sale. But are the standards of ss. 63(10)(a) and 63(10)(b) different? If so, which is the more demanding?

4) Under OPPSA s. 63(2), "every aspect of the disposition" of the collateral by the secured party must be "commercially reasonable." How is this standard to be applied in the following situations?

(a) The evidence establishes that if the collateral had been held for two months longer, a higher sale price would have been obtained because of predictable increased demand for the type of goods involved. The secured party did not hold the collateral because it had a cash flow problem and was in need of cash at the date of the sale.

(b) The evidence establishes that if the secured party had incurred the not unreasonable expense of transporting the collateral to a place some distance from the place of seizure and had offered it for sale there, a higher sale price for the collateral would have been obtained.

(c) The evidence establishes that if the secured party had spent small amounts of money to make the collateral more presentable for sale, a higher sale price would have been obtained. See OPPSA s. 63(1) and *Donnelly v. International Harvester Credit Corp. Ltd.* (1982-83), 2 PPSAC 290, at 298 (Ont. Co. Ct.).

5) In *Copp*, the court accepted the proposition, as an aspect of a commercially reasonable sale, that the collateral's "proper value is obtained." There is generally a difference between the wholesale price and retail price of goods. Assume a bank seizes a car and sells it to a used car dealer at "wholesale price." Has the standard been violated if it is established that, had the bank advertised the car for sale and sold it privately a higher price would have been obtained?

6) The right to recover damages for non-compliance with Part V is set out in OPPSA s. 67(2). How does one characterize the "illegal" conduct of a secured party who does not comply with Part V? Does the party's non-compliant seizure and/or sale of the collateral amount to conversion? If so, is the measure of damage recoverable different from that suggested by s. 67(2)? Could the court award punitive damages?

7) OPPSA s. 67(1)(f) has no counterpart in the CCPPSL Acts. Note that it gives power to a court to require "a secured party to make good any default in connection with the secured party's custody, management or disposition of the collateral of the debtor." What does this add? Is this another source of remedy for the debtor that provides a different measure of recovery or recover under different circumstances than is provided by s. 67(2)? Note also that the section gives power to the court to "relieve the secured party from any default on such terms as the court considers just, and to confirm any act of the secured party." Does this mean that a court can deny a debtor the recovery in an action brought under s. 67(2)?

8) The PPSA provides a statutory right to a "deficiency" (i.e., the difference between the debt owing and the net amount recovered on sale of the collateral). See, e.g., OPPSA s. 64(3). The right to a deficiency has become an issue in the context of cases where there has been non-compliance with Part V. The question that has been debated in the cases is whether or not (and, if so, to what extent) failure to comply with a requirement of Part V results in a loss or diminution in the amount payable by the debtor as a deficiency. The legal position in Ontario with respect to the right to recover a deficiency was clarified by the Court of Appeal in *Bank of Montreal v. Featherstone* (1989), 9 PPSAC 139. In a *per curiam* judgment, the Court stated at 142-43:

In our opinion, the failure of the respondent to give the s. 59(5) notice to the appellants does not result in its being deprived of the right to claim the deficiency owing. Each side before us has relied on the judgment of this Court in *Royal Bank v. J. Segreto Construction Ltd.* (1988), 63 OR (2d) 502, 8 PPSAC 43, 38 BLR 134, 67 CBR (NS) 168, 47 DLR (4th) 761, 25 OAC 297 in support of its position on this issue. In our view the reasoning in this decision supports the respondent. In holding that the bank in that case had no right to claim the deficiency owing because of failure to comply with s. 59(5), the Court indicated that this conclusion would have been otherwise if the bank had "shown [a] contractual right to sue for the deficiency" (at p. 509). The Court contrasted the case where the creditor is obliged to rely upon the statute as the basis of its right to recover the deficiency. In the present case the respondent relies upon its contractual right to sue for the deficiency. In the light of this conclusion it is not necessary to pursue the issue further as to whether the right to claim the deficiency in the present case could be based on common law principles. In this respect it may be noted that at common law it was only in the case of a conditional sale contract that the creditor, in the absence of an agreement to the contrary, was not entitled to recover the deficiency upon the repossession and resale of the property sold. See *Delta Acceptance Corp. v. Redman* (1966), 2 OR 37 at 46-7, 55 DLR (2d) 481 (CA).

Accordingly, it is our opinion that failure to give notice does not of itself afford a defence to the claim for a deficiency. In some circumstances it may give rise to an award of damages under s. 63(2) of the Personal Property Security Act. No claim for such an award is made in this case. This is understandable in light of the trial Judge's findings, which are not challenged by the appellants, that the appellants suffered no damages as a result of the failure to give notice and that the respondent acted reasonably in selling the assets.

(Note that *Featherstone* was decided under the old Ontario Act.)

9) Is the distinction between a right to a deficiency given by statute and one given by contract justifiable on any grounds? Should a secured party which ignores the debtor's rights under Part V be in a better position because the secured party happens to have included a "boiler plate" deficiency clause in its security agreement?

10) It will be noted that, in *Featherstone,* the Court of Appeal concluded that, in some circumstances, the failure to give a notice to the debtor may result in a successful claim for damages. See also OPPSA s. 67(2). What are these circumstances likely to be? Must the debtor show that, if he or she had received the notice, steps would have been taken that would have avoided the loss to the dealer? In jurisdictions like Ontario, which give only a very limited right of reinstatement, the only meaningful steps would likely be to redeem the collateral by paying the total amount owing under the security agreement. How often would the debtor be able to establish that he or she had sufficient resources to redeem the collateral? If a debtor simply loses the use of the collateral (but does not go the expense of replacing it), what damages has the debtor suffered? If the collateral was sold for its fair market value, would the debtor suffer anything other than nominal damages? Note that the value of the collateral would have been applied by the secured party to the debt with the result that the net position of the debtor would not have changed. See the final sentence of the comment in the *Featherstone* case, *supra.* Does it follow from the aforesaid that in many cases a secured party can ignore a debtor's rights under Part V with impunity? For further discussion of these and related issues, see Ziegel, Comment (1988-89), 3 *BFLR* 196.

Where the collateral is consumer goods, the debtor need not prove actual damages to recover $500. See OPPSA s. 67(2). Can a court "relieve a secured party" under section 67(1)(f) so as to deny the debtor his or her right of recovery of $500 under s. 67(2)?

11) The Acts based on the CCPPSL model have not completely severed the link between compliance with Part V and the recovery of a deficiency. In addition to providing for "deemed damages" in an amount prescribed by regulations as a penalty for non-compliance with specified provisions of the Act (a remedy also given in OPPSA s. 67(2) where the collateral is consumer goods), ss. 67(3) and (4) of the APPSA provide:

(3) In an action for a deficiency, the defendant may raise as a defence the failure on the part of the secured party to comply with the obligations of section 17, 18, 60 or 61, but non-compliance shall limit the right to a deficiency only to the extent that it has affected the right of the defendant to protect his interest in the collateral or has made accurate determination of the deficiency impracticable.

(4) Where a secured party fails to comply with obligations in section 17, 18, 60 or 61, the onus is on the secured party to show that the failure,

(a) where the collateral is consumer goods, did not affect the debtor's ability to protect his interest in the collateral by redemption or reinstatement of the security agreement, or otherwise, or

(b) did not make the accurate determination of the deficiency impracticable.

Does this provision place an impossible burden of proof on the secured party? If you were advising a secured party, what measures would you suggest be taken to enable your client to meet the burden of s. 67(4)(a) if the need to do so arises.

12) Whether the right to deficiency, even on compliance with the "commercially reasonable" requirement, should exist at all, has been a hotly debated issue in Canada and the United States: see, e.g., British Columbia Law Reform Commission, *Working Paper No. 4, Deficiency Claims and Repossession* (May 1971); and P. Shuchman, "Profit or Default: An Archival Study of Automobile Repossession and Resale" (1969-70), 22 *Stan. L Rev.* 20. Arguments against the right to deficiency point to the potential for abuse, the unfortunate position of the debtor who is forced to pay for goods he or she no longer enjoys, and the ability of the business community to internalize losses as well as to screen debtors. The anti-deficiency lobby has won many adherents. Such a provision has been adopted in British Columbia, Manitoba, Quebec, Newfoundland and the Northwest Territories. In British Columbia, the "seize or sue" principle is also applied to PMSI or non-PMSI secured lenders as well as to PMSI sellers. See BCPPSA s. 67. In Saskatchewan, subject to a few enumerated exceptions, a secured seller is only allowed to repossess the goods (i.e., he or she cannot elect to sue): see the Limitation of Civil Rights Act, RSS 1979, c. L-16, s. 18.

13) When the amount of a deficiency is calculated, must the secured creditor account for any unearned interest charges resulting from acceleration of payments under an instalment credit contract? The debtor's right to a rebate on prepayment was recognized in Ontario in *Delta Acceptance Corp. Ltd. v. Redman*, [1966] 2 OR 37 (CA) where "all members of the Court agree[d] ... that, notwithstanding the terms of the conditional sale contract which provided for accelerated payment of all charges upon default, no amounts for unearned finance charges may be recovered" (*id.*, at 485, per McGillivray JA).

"Whether this passage correctly sets out the views of all members of the Court in that case, or whether in some way the statement is to be regarded as *obiter*, is now academic, because later in the same year the legislature passed the Consumer Protection Act, 1966 ..."; *Industrial Acceptance Corp. Ltd. v. Keeler Ford Sales Ltd.* (1971), 18 DLR (3d) 257, at 264, [1971] 2 OR 465 (CA), *per* Arnup JA. See now Consumer Protection Act, RSO 1990 c. C.31, s. 28. What is the position apart from such a statutory provision? Can the creditor's claim to unearned interest be treated as an unenforceable penalty or does it depend on whether or not the interest is pre-computed and becomes part of the principal debt? See *The Protector Endowment Loan and Annuity Co. v. Grace* (1880), 5 QBD 592 (CA); *cf. Warner v. Carina* (1974), 2 NSWLR 301.

ENFORCEMENT OF SECURITY INTERESTS BY RECEIVERS AND RECEIVER-MANAGERS AND PART V OF THE PPSA

Introduction

Generically, receivership involves the appointment of a person who is given the power to take possession or control of property of another for the benefit of a third person. Receiverships are used in many situations, the most significant of which are:

- as a method to enforce a judgment by appointing a receiver to take control and liquidate specified property of the judgment debtor. In this context, the receiver is appointed by and acts on the instructions of the court.
- as a method of taking control of property for the purposes of protecting it from destruction or dissipation pending the completion of proceedings (a specific example of this is found in s. 46 of the Bankruptcy and Insolvency Act, RSC 1985, c. B-3 as am. 1992, c. 27. However, the use of this type of receivership is not confined to bankruptcy. For example, a receiver can be appointed to preserve property of an estate pending probate or administration or to protect the interest of disabled persons. Here again, receivers in this category are appointed by the court.
- a mechanism for enforcement of security interests in real and personal property. It is this use of the receivership that is the focus of the following materials.

The appointment of receivers originated in the latter part of the 16th century as a remedy of the Courts of Chancery. The remedy was designed to provide a means whereby property could be preserved pending judicial determination of conflicting claims. Occasionally, it was used to supplement common law and statutory judgment enforcement remedies. The use of receivers to enforce mortgages was developed by Chancery as a special feature of equitable mortgages that compensated for the absence of a right in the mortgage (a right enjoyed by legal mortgagees) to take possession of the mortgaged property. After the merger of the equity and common law courts in 1873 under the Supreme Court of Judicature Act, the power to appoint a receiver was no longer purely within equitable jurisdiction. See now Courts of Justice Act, RSO 1990, c. C.43, s. 114(1).

Originally, court appointed receivers only had authority to receive or take possession of property and to dispose of it in accordance with the powers vested in them. However, by the beginning of this century, the judicial practice of appointing a receiver and manager (now frequently referred to as a receiver-manager) developed so as to permit receivers to take over and manage the business of a debtor. This became particularly useful and common where the entire undertaking (all of the property) of a business corporation was taken as security under an equitable floating charge.

The practice of making provision in security agreements for the extra-judicial appointment of a receiver also developed during the 19th century and was later expanded to include receiver-managers.

Until the advent of modern legislation (circa 1965) dealing with receivers and receiver-managers, a clear distinction existed between court appointed receivers (CAR) and receiver-managers and privately appointed receivers (PAR) and receiver-managers. While some aspects of this distinction remain, it is no longer as significant as it once was. See the discussion, *infra*.

Standard Trust Co. v. Turner Crossing Inc.
(1993), 4 PPSAC (2d) 238 (Sask. QB)

MATHESON J: The defendant, Turner Crossing Inc. ("Turner"), has applied for an order setting aside the appointment by the plaintiff of a receiver and manager of the business of Turner.

Turner acquired property in the City of Regina in February 1989, for the purpose of constructing a shopping mall complex. The project was to be financed by Standard Trust Company. Agreements were executed as security for the funds to be advanced, consisting of a first real property mortgage in the amount of $5,646,000; a second participation mortgage; a purchase money security agreement; and an assignment of leases and rental.

Phase I of the shopping mall complex was completed by March 1991. However, problems developed with respect to Phase II. Turner has alleged Standard Trust Company refused to provide additional funding. In any event, on May 2, 1991, Standard Trust Company was ordered by the Ontario Court of Justice to be wound up, and Ernst & Young Inc. was appointed permanent liquidator.

In November 1991, the liquidator informed Turner that it was in default under the mortgage. The alleged default was apparently not remedied, and on December 23, 1991, the liquidator appointed a "Receiver and Manager of the business of Turner Crossing Inc." The plaintiff then applied for, and was granted, leave to commence this action, wherein the principal claims are for judgment against the defendants and foreclosure of the mortgaged premises.

The defendants filed a statement of defence, and Turner filed a counterclaim against the plaintiff. The defendants did not really deny that they were in default under the mortgage, but one of the assertions in the counterclaim is that the appointment of the receiver and manager was unlawful.

• • •

The plaintiff purported to appoint the receiver and manager pursuant to the purchase-money security agreement and assignment of leases and rental. However, in the event that the appointment was not authorized by those documents, the plaintiff has argued that it had a statutory right to appoint a receiver and manager.

There is no disagreement between the parties with respect to the basic facts. Turner has acknowledged that it executed the security agreements and that it defaulted in making the payments required of it pursuant to the first real property mortgage. If, in those circumstances, the plaintiff was entitled by statute to appoint a receiver and manager, the resolution of that question entails only the interpretation of the appropriate statute, or statutes, which is solely a matter of law. But the form of appointment states that it was made pursuant to a purchase money security agreement and assignment of leases and rental. It must first be determined from the provisions of those documents whether the appointment was authorized. The documents speak for themselves.

• • •

Division VIII of the Business Corporations Act, RSS 1978, c. B-10 (also CCSS, c. B-10), encompassing ss. 89 to 96, is entitled "Receivers and Receiver-Managers." There is no provision in any of those sections empowering a creditor to appoint a receiver or receiver-manager. It is quite clear from the initial words of s. 91—"if a receiver-manager is appointed by a court or under an instrument"—that the functions and duties of receivers and receiver-managers, set out in the Act, related to court appointments or those made pursuant to agreements between the debtor and creditor.

The plaintiff has suggested that s. 56 of the Personal Property Security Act, SS 1979-80, c. P-6.1 (also CCSS, c. P-6.1) ("PPSA") empowered it to appoint the receiver and manager. However, subs. (1) of s. 56 states that "A security agreement may provide for the appointment of a receiver or a receiver-manager and, except as provided in this Act, prescribe his rights and duties." Subsection (2)(a) of s. 56 states that a court may appoint a receiver or a receiver-manager. No right is given to a creditor, by that statute, to appoint a receiver or receiver-manager.

The appointment of the receiver and manager was in the following terms:

STANDARD TRUST COMPANY, by its liquidator, ERNST & YOUNG INC., being the registered holder of a security interest under a Purchase Money Security Agreement and an Assignment of Lease(s) and Rental with Turner Crossing Inc. both dated February 24, 1989, in favour of STANDARD TRUST COMPANY (the "Security Agreements") and which said security interests were registered under the provisions of The Personal Property Security Act of Saskatchewan on the 29th day of May, 1989 as Instrument Number 03258370, hereby appoints McClocklin Real Estate Corp. with an office in the City of Saskatoon, in the Province of Saskatchewan, pursuant to the powers conferred upon STANDARD TRUST COMPANY, *to be the Receiver and Manager of the business of Turner Crossing Inc.* with full power and secured by the Security Agreements upon the terms and with and subject to the powers, provisions and conditions in the Security Agreements.

(Emphasis added)

A notice of appointment of receiver and manager was filed with the Director of Business Corporations on February 3, 1992, as required by s. 96(a) of the Business Corporations Act. That requirement is not without significance, because s. 91 of the Business Corporations Act states:

91. If a receiver-manager is appointed by a court or under an instrument, the powers of the directors of the corporation that the receiver-manager is authorized to exercise may not be exercised by the directors until the receiver-manager is discharged.

The purchase-money security agreement does not contain any provision whereby Turner agreed, upon default, that the plaintiff would be entitled to appoint a receiver, or a receiver and manager, of any assets of Turner. Counsel for the plaintiff so acknowledged, but stated that the authority for the appointment of the receiver and manager was derived from the assignment of leases and rentals ("the assignment").

The assignment contains the following clause:

3. THAT at any and all times when there shall be default under any of the provisions contained in the mortgage, *the Assignee shall be entitled to* enter into possession of the mortgaged premises and collect the rents and revenues thereof and distrain in the name of the Assignor for the same, and *appoint its agents to manage the mortgaged premises* and pay such agents reasonable charges for their services and charge the same to the account of the Assignor; and that any agents so appointed by the Assignee shall be and are hereby authorized and empowered;

(a) To make any lease or leases of the mortgaged premises or any part thereof, for not more than three years, at such rental or rentals and in all other respects on such terms as the Assignee in its discretion may direct or agree to;

(b) *To manage generally the mortgaged premises* to the same extent as the Assignor could do;

(c) Without derogating from the generality of the foregoing:

(i) To collect the rents and revenues and give good and sufficient receipts and discharges therefor, and in their discretion distrain in the name of the Assignor for such rents;

(ii) To pay all insurance premiums, taxes, necessary repairs, renovations and upkeep, carrying charges, rental commissions, salary of janitor or caretaker, cost of heating, and any and all payments due on the mortgage to the Assignee;

(iii) To accumulate the rentals in such agents' hands in a reasonable amount to make provision for maturing payments of interest and principal on the mortgage, and for the payment of taxes, insurance, heating, repairs, renovations and upkeep and other expenses or carrying charges connected with the mortgaged premises.

(Emphasis added)

The foregoing is the clause pursuant to which the receiver and manager was appointed. The plaintiff has submitted that the authorization granted to it to appoint agents "to manage the mortgaged premises" is synonymous with an authorization to appoint a receiver or a receiver and manager.

The distinction in law between a receiver and manager was set out by Jessel MR in *Re Manchester & Milford Railway Co.; Ex parte Cambrian Railway Co.* (1880), 14 Ch. D 645, 49 LJ Ch. 365, 42 LT 714 (CA) when he was considering the meaning of an agreement to "the appointment of a receiver and, if necessary, of a manager." At p. 653 Ch. D he pointed out that a "receiver" is a term which was well known in the Court of Chancery, as meaning a person who receives rents or other income. But a receiver did not have the power to manage the business of the debtor. He stated that if it was desired to continue the trade of the debtor, it was necessary to appoint a manager, or a receiver and manager.

In Frank Bennett, *Receiverships* (1985), it is stated, at p. 109:

The appointment of a receiver will usually coincide with the appointment of a manager. In this dual role, the receiver and manager may operate the debtor's business pursuant to the terms of his appointment. Initially, such terms may authorize the receiver and manager to preserve the debtor's business. Subsequently, the receiver and manager may be authorized to liquidate or sell the business as a going concern.

If the security instrument does not charge the debtor's goodwill, only a receiver can be appointed. However, *if the security instrument covers all the debtor's property and effects whatsoever*, the court will infer that the goodwill was included in order to permit the appointment of a receiver and manager.

(Emphasis added.)

The terms "receiver" and "receiver and manager," and the differences between the two terms, obviously have a distinct meaning in law. Both the Business Corporations Act and the PPSA distinguish between the two terms. But the assignment contains no reference whatever to an entitlement granted to the plaintiff, upon Turner's default, to the appointment of either a "receiver" or a "receiver and manager." The authority was confined to the plaintiff collecting rents and revenues from "the mortgaged premises" and to the appointment of agents to manage the "mortgaged premises." Instead of exercising the powers granted to it in the terms of the assignment, the plaintiff purported to appoint a "Receiver and Manager of the business of Turner Crossing Inc." Nowhere in either the appointment, or notice of appointment which became a matter of public record, is it stated that the authority of the appointee is confined to the "mortgaged premises."

The material on file does not reveal the extent of the business of Turner. Nevertheless, one can imagine the furore which would be created if an international developer defaulted in payment of but one mortgage, but then was faced with the appointment of a receiver and manager of its "business," notwithstanding that the mortgagee's rights were confined to the mortgaged premises.

The notice of appointment of receiver and manager, filed with the Director of Business Corporations, is even more misleading than the notice of appointment itself:

NOTICE IS HEREBY GIVEN pursuant to Section 96 of The Business Corporations Act that on the 23rd day of December, 1991, STANDARD TRUST COMPANY, by its liquidator, ERNST & YOUNG INC., appointed McCLOCKLIN REAL ESTATE CORP. *as Receiver and Manager of the business of TURNER CROSSING INC. with full power and authority over all of the premises, chattels and undertakings of TURNER CROSSING INC.,* pursuant to the terms of a Purchase Money Security Agreement and Assignment of Lease(s) and Rental (the "Security Agreements") given by TURNER CROSSING INC., in favour of STANDARD TRUST COMPANY both dated February 24, 1989, and which security interests were registered under the provisions of The Personal Property Security Act of Saskatchewan on the 29th day of May, 1989, as Instrument Number 03258370.

(Emphasis added.)

On the basis of the wording contained in clause 3 of the assignment, it seems quite incredible that anyone could have, other than deliberately, drafted the appointment of receiver and manager, and notice of appointment, in the terms which they contain. However, that is a question which will no doubt be pursued at trial if Turner proceeds with its counterclaim. In the meantime, Turner is effectively prevented from carrying on business by virtue of the clearly unlawful appointment of a receiver and manager of its "business." To allow that situation to continue until trial, when there was no legal justification whatever for the appointment of the receiver and manager, would be patently unjust.

There will therefore be an order setting aside the appointment of the receiver and manager and vacating the notice of appointment of receiver and manager filed with the Director of Business Corporations.

Application granted.

NOTES AND QUESTIONS

See OPPSA s. 60 and definition of "secured party" in s. 1(1). Note that s. 60 refers to both "document appointed receivers (and receiver-managers)" and court appointed receivers (and receiver-managers) but the definition of "secured party" refers only to "receivers and receivers and managers." Must a court appointed receiver (hereafter read as including a receiver-manager unless otherwise indicated) comply with the requirements of Part V applicable to secured parties unless the CAR obtains an order under s. 67(1)(b) or (d)? Is there any reason why a court appointed receiver should be exempt from these requirements? For further discussion of this issue in the context of the Acts based on the CCPPSL model, see notes following the next case.

Ostrander v. Niagara Helicopters Ltd.
(1974), 40 DLR (3d) 161 (Ont. HC)

[Ostrander was the founder and principal shareholder of the defendant corporation. The defendant borrowed money from Roynat Limited and gave as security a debenture under a trust deed arrangement encumbering its assets. Upon default, Roynat appointed Bawden as receiver-manager of the defendant. Roynat sold most of the assets of the defendant after receiving two tenders.

Ostrander brought an action to regain possession of the defendant and to set aside the sale of its assets. He alleged improper conduct on the part of Bawden. As part of his case, Ostrander argued that Bawden was acting in a fiduciary capacity with respect to the defendant and that his conduct amounted to a breach of trust. In dealing with this aspect of the case Stark J observed:]

My decision might well be otherwise if I had come to the conclusion that Bawden as receiver-manager was acting in a fiduciary capacity. I am satisfied that he was not. His role was that of agent for a mortgagee in possession. The purpose of his employment was to protect the security of the bondholder. Subsequently his duty was to sell the assets and realize the proceeds for the benefit of the mortgagee. Of course he owed a duty to account in due course to the mortgagor for any surplus; and in order to be sure there would be a surplus he was duty bound to comply with the full terms of the conditions of sale set out in the debenture, to advertise the property and to take reasonable steps to obtain the best offer possible. Certainly he owed a duty to everybody to act in good faith and without fraud. But this is not to say that his relations to Ostrander or to Niagara or to both were fiduciary in nature. A very clear distinction must be drawn between the duties and obligations of a receiver-manager, such as Bawden, appointed by virtue of the contractual clauses of a mortgage deed and the duties and obligations of a receiver-manager who is appointed by the Court and whose sole authority is derived from that Court appointment and from the directions given him by the Court. In the latter case he is an officer of the Court; is very definitely in a fiduciary capacity to all parties involved in the contest. The borrower, in consideration of the receipt by him of the proceeds of the loan agrees in advance to the terms of the trust deed and to the provisions by which the security may be enforced. In this document he accepts in advance the conditions upon which a sale is to be made, the nature of the advertising that is to be done, the fixing of the amount of the reserve bid and all the other provisions contained therein relating to the conduct of the sale. In carrying on the business of the company pending the sale, he acts as agent for the lender and he makes the decisions formerly made by the proprietors of the company. Indeed, in the case at hand, Mr. Bawden found it necessary to require that Ostrander absent himself completely from the operations of the business and this Ostrander consented to do. As long as the receiver-manager acts reasonably in the conduct of the business and of course without any ulterior interest, and as long as he ensures that a fair sale is conducted and that he ultimately makes a proper accounting to the mortgagor, he has fulfilled his role which is chiefly of course to protect the security for the benefit of the bondholder. I can see no evidence of any fiduciary relationship existing between Ostrander and Bawden. Mr. Papazian in his able argument put it very forcibly to the Court that the duties and obligations of a receiver-manager appointed by the Court and a receiver-manager appointed under the terms of a bond mortgage without a Court order, were in precisely the same position, each being under fiduciary obligations to the mortgagor. I do not accept that view and I am satisfied that the cases clearly distinguish between them. A good example of the obligation placed upon the Court-appointed receiver-manager is provided by *Re Newdigate Colliery, Ltd.*, [1912] 1 Ch. 468. That case was authority for the proposition that it is the duty of the receiver and manager of the property and undertaking of a company to preserve the goodwill as well as the assets of the business, and it would be inconsistent with that duty for him to disregard contracts entered into by the company before his appointment. At 477 Buckley LJ described the duties of the Court-appointed receiver and manager in this way:

The receiver and manager is a person who under an order of the Court has been put in a position of duty and responsibility as regards the management and carrying on of this business, and has standing behind him—I do not know what word to use that will not create a misapprehension, but I will call them "constituents"—the persons to whom he is responsible in the matter, namely, the mortgagees and the mortgagor, being the persons entitled respectively to the mortgage and the equity of redemption. If we were to accede to the application which is made to us, and to allow the receiver and manager to sell the coal at an enhanced price, the result would be that the enhanced price would fall within the security of the mortgagees and they would have the benefit of it; but, on the other hand, there would be created in favour of the persons who had originally contracted to purchase the coal a right to damages against the mortgagor, the company, with the result that there would be large sums of damages owing.

Lord Justice Buckley then continued with language which further accentuates the difference between the two classes of receiver-managers [at 447-48]:

It has been truly said that in the case of a legal mortgage the legal mortgagee can take possession if he choose[s] of the mortgaged property, and being in possession can say "I have nothing to do with the mortgagor's contracts. I shall deal with this property as seems to me most to my advantage." No doubt that would be so, but he would be a legal mortgagee in possession, with both the advantages and the disadvantages of that position. This appellant is not in that position. He is an equitable mortgagee who has obtained an order of the Court under which its officer takes possession of assets in which the mortgagee and mortgagor are both interested, with the duty and responsibility of dealing with them fairly in the interest of both parties.

It appears to me unfortunate that the same terms "receiver-manager" are customarily applied to both types of offices, when in fact they are quite different. The difference is well pointed out in the case of *Re B. Johnson & Co. (Builders) Ltd.*, [1955] 1 Ch. 634, where it was held that a receiver and manager of a company's property appointed by a debenture holder was not an officer of the company within the meaning of the *Companies Act*. The language of Evershed MR, at 644, is in point:

The situation of someone appointed by a mortgagee or a debenture holder to be a receiver and manager—as it is said, "out of court"—is familiar. It has long been recognized and established that receivers and managers so appointed are, by the effect of the statute law, or of the terms of the debenture, or both, treated, while in possession of the company's assets and exercising the various powers conferred upon them, as agents of the company, in order that they may be able to deal effectively with third parties. But, in such a case as the present at any rate, it is quite plain that a person appointed as receiver and manager is concerned, not for the benefit of the company but for the benefit of the mortgagee bank, to realize the security; that is the whole purpose of his appointment ...

Again, at 662, Lord Justice Jenkins stated:

The company is entitled to any surplus of assets remaining after the debenture debt has been discharged, and is entitled to proper accounts. But the whole purpose of the receiver and manager's appointment would obviously be stultified if the company could claim that a receiver and manager owes it any duty comparable to the duty owed to a company by its own directors or managers.

•   •   •

The duties of a receiver and manager for debenture holders are widely different from those of a manager of the company. He is under no obligation to carry on the company's business at the expense of the debenture holders. Therefore he commits no breach of duty to the company by refusing to do so, even though his discontinuance of the business may be detrimental from the company's point of view. Again, his power of sale is, in effect, that of a mortgagee, and he therefore commits no breach of duty to the company by a bona fide sale, even though he might have obtained a higher price and even though, from the point of view of the company, as distinct from the debenture holders, the terms might be regarded as disadvantageous.

In a word, in the absence of fraud or mala fides (of which there is not the faintest suggestion here), the company cannot complain of any act or omission of the receiver and manager, provided that he does nothing that he is not empowered to do, and omits nothing that he is enjoined to do by the terms of this appointment. If the company conceives that it has any claim against the receiver and manager for breach of some duty owed by him to the company, the issue is not whether the receiver and manager has done or omitted to do anything which it would be wrongful in a manager of a company to do or omit, but whether he has exceeded or abused or wrongfully omitted to use the special powers and discretions vested in him pursuant to the contract of loan constituted by the debenture for the special purpose of enabling the assets comprised in the debenture holders' security to be preserved and realized.

Similar principles are to be found in the case of *Deyes v. Wood et al.*, [1911] 1 KB 806.

Action dismissed.

NOTES AND QUESTIONS

1) The traditional approach to the role of a CAR is that, as an officer of the court, a court appointed receiver takes possession and control not only for the benefit of the secured party but as well for the benefit of other creditors with a claim to the property. *Royal Bank v. Vista Homes* (1984), 57 CBR (NS) 124 (BCSC). The receiver's authority derives from the order appointing the receiver (and from legislative provisions applicable to receiverships). A document appointed receiver is basically an agent of the secured party appointing the receiver. The receiver draws authority to act from the security agreement (and from legislative provisions applicable to receiverships).

2) Each type of receivership has advantages and disadvantages. The advantages of a document appointed receiver include speed, efficiency and the control that the secured party can exercise through the receiver. Since no court order is required, a receiver can be appointed immediately upon the debtor's default under the security agreement. However, this does not mean that the collateral can be seized immediately. See BIA, ss. 243(2) and 244 and *Kavcar Investments Ltd. v. Aetna Financial Services Ltd.* (1989), 62 DLR (4th) 277 (Ont. CA). The judicial appointment of a receiver under Ontario law requires an interlocutory application to a court as part of an action brought against the debtor. This may involve delay and expense. (Under the Acts based on the CCPPSL model, a receiver may be appointed by a court on application without the need to commence an original action against the debtor. See, e.g., BCPPSA s. 66(1).) Since the receiver is acting under the instructions and authority of the court, the receiver and the secured party are shielded (although not completely immune) from liability and attack by those who disapprove of the conduct of the receiver. But see OPPSA s. 67(2).

3) It is possible for a receiver, initially appointed under a security agreement, to be appointed by a court. However, when this occurs, the receiver's authority derives solely from the court and he or she cannot revert to acting under the terms of the security agreement. *Price Waterhouse Ltd. v. Creighton Holdings Ltd.* (1984), 54 CBR (NS) 116 (Sask. QB).

4) The traditional distinction between court appointed and privately appointed receiverships may be breaking down. This is particularly so in the provinces whose PPSAs are based on the CCPPSL model (see *infra*). However, the erosion may also be happening in Ontario. Note that OPPSA s. 60(2) applies to "with respect to a receiver or receiver and manager, however appointed." In other words, it applies to both a CAR and a PAR. Are the

powers given to the court by OPPSA s. 60(2)—especially ss. 60(2)(b) and (d)—consistent with the traditional view of the position of a PAR as agent of the secured party? If a CAR is subject to the same standard of conduct when dealing with the collateral (e.g., s. 60(2)) as is a PAR, does the reasoning used in *Ostrander* have any relevance in the context of a receivership to which the OPPSA applies?

5) The homogenization of rules applicable to court appointed and privately appointed receivers has gone much further in provinces whose PPSAs are based on the CCPPSL model. Most of these Acts contain extensive regulatory provisions applicable to receivers. See, e.g., BCPPSA ss. 64-66. This legislation sets out the minimum qualifications for receivers, basic bookkeeping and extensive disclosure requirements and gives to the court wide supervisory jurisdiction over receivers. The PPSA regulatory scheme applies to receivers of both personal and real property. (See Law and Equity Act 1979, BC Stat., c. 224, s. 60, added, 1989, c. 36.) While there may be some doubt on the matter, taken at face value the legislation appears to subject all receivers, whether court appointed or privately appointed, to the requirements of Part V. By the same token, all receivers are subject to the overriding obligation to exercise and discharge their duties and obligations under the security agreement and under the Act or any other applicable law "in good faith and in a commercially reasonable manner." See BCPPSA s. 68(1). This suggests that the standard of conduct of a receiver in these provinces is the same whether the receiver is court appointed or privately appointed. The same approach appears to be incorporated in the BIA, RSC c. B-3 as amended 1992, c. 27, adding ss. 245-252, esp. s. 247. Further, the extensive disclosure and reporting requirements of the PPSAs apply to all receivers. See, e.g., BCPPSA s. 65(2).

6) It is standard practice to insert in a security agreement providing for the appointment of a receiver a clause similar to the following:

Any receiver or receiver-manager appointed hereunder shall be deemed to be the borrower's agent and the borrower shall be solely responsible for his act, defaults and remuneration.

In *Peat Marwick Ltd. v. Consumers' Gas Co.* (1978), 83 DLR (3d) 450 (Ont. HC), a receiver-manager sought an injunction against the defendant utility company requiring it to supply gas to the business under the receiver-manager's control. The company in receivership was indebted to the defendant which was the reason why the defendant refused to supply additional gas to it. Under s. 59 of the Public Utilities Act, RSO 1970, c. 390, the defendant was entitled to cut off supply to any person who neglects to pay the amount owing for the supply of gas. It was argued by the receiver-manager that he was representing the charge holder who had appointed him and not the defendant company and, therefore, s. 59 provided no basis for the defendant's refusal to supply gas to the company under his control. In rejecting the receiver-manager's argument, Osler J observed:

In *Ostrander v. Niagara Helicopters Ltd. et al.* (1973), 1 OR (2d) 281, 40 DLR (3d) 161, 19 CBR (NS) 5, Stark J points out that a receiver, not Court appointed, is called the agent of the company but is, in fact, the agent for the mortgagee or other creditor in possession. In practice, however, the debenture in such cases, as here, provides expressly that the receiver shall be deemed to be the agent of the company. Obviously, this is done for the purpose of making it apparent to third parties that the receiver has authority to deal with and manage the affairs of the company. That being so, it is not surprising that the defendant in the present case should look to the receiver for payment of its account and refuse to enter upon a new contract unless it is paid. This was the result in two English cases dealing with similar situations under very similar legislation, namely: *Re Smith*, [1893] 1 QB 323; and *Paterson v. Gas Light & Coke Co.*, [1896] 2 Ch. 476.

See also *Sperry Inc. v. Canadian Imperial Bank of Commerce* (1985), 50 OR 267 (CA), *supra*, chapter 3. In this case the court concluded that when a receiver-manager took possession, this could not amount to perfection by possession under former OPPSA s. 24 since, by the terms of the security agreement, the receiver-manager was the agent of the debtor.

7) An additional reason for the inclusion of agency clauses is to protect the secured party which appoints the receiver or receiver-manager from liability for misconduct or negligence of the receiver or receiver-manager. To the extent the agency clause is recognized as protecting the secured creditor in this way, the secured creditor has the best of all worlds: the receiver or receiver-manager must act in its interests, but it is insulated from liability for the misconduct of the receiver or receiver-manager. The Acts based on the CCPPSL model, in effect, have addressed this practice, although there is some ambiguity in the way in which this was done. For the purposes of this matter, the SPPSA is taken as representative of these Acts.

8) SPPSA s. 56(1), which precludes a debtor from waiving rights and remedies against the "secured party" given by Part V, expressly applies to a "receiver." It is clear, therefore, that a debtor cannot waive Part V rights and remedies against a receiver. However, since the section applies as well (and principally) to secured parties, it would appear to deny efficacy to an agency clause (see, *supra*) designed to protect the secured party from the misconduct of a receiver appointed by the secured party. However, SPPSA s. 64(8)(e) provides that upon application of an interested person, a court may

(e) notwithstanding anything contained in a security agreement or other document providing for the appointment of a receiver, make an order requiring a receiver, or a person by or on behalf of whom the recevier is appointed, to make good any default in connection with the receiver's or receiver-manager's custody, management or disposition of the collateral of the debtor or to relieve such person from any default or failure to comply with this Part.

The implication of the provision is that ordinarily a secured party is not liable for the misconduct of a receiver appointed by it (to the extent the misconduct relates to custody, management and disposition of the collateral), but that, in appropriate circumstances, a court may hold the secured party responsible. If, as a result of SPPSA s. 56(1), a secured party is liable for a receiver's non-compliance with Part V, there is no need for s. 64(8)(e). If agency clauses are effective apart from s. 64(8)(e), there would appear to be little scope for the application of the final part of the provision giving a court power to exonerate the secured party from liability the misconduct of the receiver amounting to non-compliance with Part V.

9) Another approach to the rationalization of SPPSA ss. 56(1) and 64(8)(e) is to conclude that, as a result of s. 56(1), a debtor cannot waive his or her rights against the secured party when the receiver appointed by the secured party has failed to comply with Part V. Under this approach, the role of s. 64(8)(e) would be to give to the court power to

require the secured party to make good the receiver's default even for misfeasance for which the secured party would not otherwise be liable. This could include making the secured party liable for the misconduct of a CAR in cases where the receiver acted under the instructions of the secured party and not those of the court. The balance of s. 64(8)(e), under which the court can relieve the secured party from liability for default of a receiver, could be invoked where the court concludes that it is not reasonable to require the secured party to answer for the receiver's failure to meet the requirements of Part V.

10) The aforegoing comments should be compared with OPPSA s. 67(1)(f). Does this provision apply to receivership in the same way as does SPPSA s. 64(8)(e)? If so, the first mentioned "secured party" must be the secured party and the second mentioned "secured party" must be the receiver appointed by the secured party.

LESSORS' DEFAULT RIGHTS

The discussion up to this point has been concerned with the enforcement rights of a secured party holding a true security interest as defined in the PPSAs. However, as noted, *supra*, in chapter 2, equipment leases not amounting to security agreements are widely used as alternative financing vehicles with the result that the lessor's enforcement rights are not governed by Part V of the PPSAs. (This is also true in jurisdictions with Acts based on the CCPPSL model which deem one year-plus leases to be security agreements for most purposes of the Act.) However, because of the hybrid nature of such leasing agreements, the Anglo-Canadian courts have experienced much difficulty in determining the scope of the lessor's claim to damages at common law on the lessee's default. In Canada, the issue is now, for the most part, resolved by the decision of the Supreme Court of Canada in the following case.

Keneric Tractor Sales Ltd. v. Langille
(1988), 79 NR 241 (SCC)

WILSON J: The issue in this appeal is how damages are to be calculated for breach of a lease of chattels. Central to this issue is whether the reasoning of this Court in *Highway Properties Ltd. v. Kelly, Douglas and Co.*, [1971] SCR 562; 17 DLR (3d) 710, a case dealing with the method of calculation of damages for breach of a lease of land, should be extended to cover leases of chattels.

1. The Facts

The appellants, Eric and Paul Langille are farmers. During the summers of 1981 and 1982 the respondent Keneric Tractor Sales Limited ("Keneric") leased ten pieces of farm equipment to the Langilles. The 1982 leases called for ten semi-annual payments over a five-year period. The sum of these semi-annual payments was equal to 120% of the original purchase price. A separate agreement gave the Langilles an option to purchase the equipment for 25% of the original purchase price. The option was exercisable at the end of the five year period. If the option was not exercised the equipment would revert back to Keneric. The 1982 leases were structured the same way but the semi-annual payments were higher and the option to purchase was set at 30% of the original purchase price.

Keneric has bought the farm equipment in question from Allis-Chalmers Canada Inc., the manufacturer. In order to finance the purchases the leases taken from the Langilles were assigned to Allis-Chalmers Credit Corporation of Canada, Ltd. Keneric guaranteed the Langilles' performance under the leasing agreements and agreed to act as agent for the recovery of amounts due to Allis-Chalmers Credit Corporation.

In March 1983 the Langilles advised Keneric that they would have trouble making the lease payments. Negotiations failed to resolve the problem. The Langilles defaulted under the leases and Keneric seized the equipment. After due notice Keneric sold the seized equipment. Keneric then commenced the present action claiming damages resulting from breach of the leases.

• • •

3. The Issue

Counsel for the appellants submit that the Nova Scotia Court of Appeal erred as to the proper method of assessing damages for default under the equipment rental agreements. Two sub-issues must be examined in order to determine the principal issue. These are (a) what are the general rules governing damages for breach of a lease of chattels? and (b) did the resale by Keneric satisfy its duty to mitigate its damages?

(a) The General Rules

The most recent discussion of the relevant law is found in the Manitoba Court of Appeal's decision in *Canadian Acceptance Corp. Ltd. v. Regent Park Butcher Shop, supra*. That case involved the lease of a cash register. After the lessee failed to make several payments the lessor repossessed and sold the cash register. A clause in the leasing contract stipulated a particular level of damage payable upon breach. The Court of Appeal held that the sum stipulated in the clause was not a genuine pre-estimate of liquidated damages and therefore the clause was a penalty and unenforceable. The court then examined the case law dealing with the damages recoverable for breach of a chattel lease.

Dickson J (as he then was), speaking for the Court examined the Canadian case law on the subject and concluded at p. 314:

There being no uniform pattern emerging from the Canadian decisions we feel free to approach the matter afresh according to our best judgment. It is our considered opinion that the rationale of the series of cases beginning with *Bridge v. Campbell Discount Co. Ltd.*, [1962] 1 All ER 385, provides the proper approach and we propose to apply it. In one of the cases of that series, *Financings Ltd. v. Baldock*, [1963] 1 All ER 443, Lord Denning MR said at p. 445:

> It seems to me that, when an agreement of hiring is terminated by virtue of a power contained in it and the owner retakes the vehicle, he can recover damages for any breach up to the date of termination, but not for any breach thereafter, for the simple reason that there are no breaches thereafter. I see no difference in this respect between the letting of a vehicle on hire and the letting of land on a lease. If a lessor, under a proviso for re-entry, re-enters on the

ground of nonpayment of rent or of disrepair, he gets the arrears of rent up to date of re-entry and damages for want of repair at that date, but he does not get damages for loss of rent thereafter or for breaches of repair thereafter.

And at p. 446:

In applying this principle, I asked counsel for the plaintiffs: What were the breaches by the hirer up to the termination of the hiring? He could only point to the simple failure to pay the two instalments of rent. In these circumstances, the only moneys which the plaintiffs can recover are those two instalments which are in arrear and unpaid with the interest thereon. If the plaintiff could prove damages for breach of contract to repair, they could recover them, but no more ...

    If, however, there is no repudiation, but simply, as here, a failure to pay one or two instalments (the failure not going to the root of the contract and only giving a right to terminate by virtue of an express stipulation in the contract), the owners can recover only the instalments in arrear, with interest, and nothing else; for there was no other breach in existence at the termination of the hiring.

Thus, a lessor who terminates a chattel lease by virtue of a provision in the lease allowing him to do so is limited in his remedies to the rent due at the time of the termination plus any proceeds from resale.

Both *Regent Park* and *Baldock* on which Dickson J relied proceed by analogy to the common law of damages for breach of a lease of land. As Dickson J pointed out at p. 315 of his reasons:

If a landlord re-enters land for nonpayment of rent he may bring an action for arrears of rent on the express or implied covenant to pay rent but he cannot recover rent falling due after the date of re-entry. No authority has been given us to show why the position of a lessor of a chattel should be stronger than that of a lessor of land.

Indeed, if the law in this area is to be coherent and principled it would make good sense to abolish artificial legal distinctions between leases of land and leases of chattels. However, the pursuit of consistency today mandates a different result in this case because the decision of this Court in *Highway Properties* has intervened and shifted the jurisprudential foundation upon which the *Regent Park* decision was based.

In *Highway Properties* the Court addressed the issue of the landlord's right to damages flowing from the repudiation of a lease of shopping centre space by a tenant. The landlord claimed both for the loss suffered to the date of repudiation and for the prospective loss resulting from the tenant's failure to carry on business in the shopping centre for the full term of the lease. An application of the traditional approach reflected in *Regent Park* would have defeated the second half of the landlord's claim. Laskin J, speaking for the whole Court, noted at p. 570 that up until that point:

The developed case law has recognized three mutually exclusive courses that a landlord may take where a tenant is in fundamental breach of the lease or has repudiated it entirely, as was the case here. He may do nothing to alter the relationship of landlord and tenant, but simply insist on performance of the terms and sue for rent or damages on the footing that the lease remains in force. Second, he may elect to terminate the lease, retaining of course the right to sue for rent accrued due, or for damages to the date of termination for previous breaches of covenant. Third, he may advise the tenant that he proposes to re-let the property on the tenant's account and enter into possession on that basis.

What was not possible at common law before *Highway Properties* was for the landlord to terminate the lease, relet the property, and make a claim for damages that included a claim for unpaid future rent less the actual rental value of the unexpired period.

Highway Properties changed this. Laskin J examined the applicable English, Australian and American authorities. He paid particular attention to the decision in *Buchanan v. Byrnes* (1906), 3 CLR 704 (H. Ct. Aust.). In that case the tenant, in breach of covenant, abandoned hotel property which he had leased. The landlord succeeded in a claim for damages over the unexpired term of the lease despite the surrender. The approach to the damages issue taken by the High Court is summarized in two passages from the judgment (the first from the reasons of Griffith CJ at p. 715 and the second from the reasons of Barton J at p. 719):

Then the question arises—to what damages is he entitled? There is a covenant the performance of which will extend over a term of 15 years, and it is unequivocally broken. The natural damage is the loss likely to be sustained by the plaintiff during the period for which the covenant ought to be kept; just as in the case of a contract to engage a servant for a term of years, paying him monthly wages. If the contract is unequivocally broken by the employer, the servant can bring an action at once. He cannot, of course, recover anything in the form of wages; he recovers damages, which are assessed usually upon the basis of the wages that he would have received; but he must on the other hand give credit, and the jury must give the employer credit, for whatever the servant might reasonably be expected to have earned during the period for which the contract would have been in existence. Prima facie, the damages, therefore, would be the value of the term to the lessor, that is, the difference between the benefit which he would have derived from the premises being kept as a going hotel for 15 years at the agreed rent, being kept in repair, and so on, and the value of the premises as they were thrown on his hands.

But it is said that the conduct of the plaintiff in resuming possession under the circumstances estops him from suing upon the covenants. It must not be taken to hold that it has that effect as to the covenant to pay rent. But, however that may be, can it estop him as to the other covenants which relate to the keeping the premises as an inn throughout the term, and the doing of the other things necessary for that purpose? Conduct, to constitute an estoppel, must have caused another to believe in the existence of a certain state of things, and have induced him to act on that belief so as to alter his own position. How can that be said to be the effect of the plaintiff's conduct, when the act of the defendant, so far from having been induced by it, has preceded it? In my judgment the doctrine of estoppel cannot be applied against the plaintiff ...

Laskin J noted that *Buchanan v. Byrnes* was applied by the Supreme Court of Australia in *Hughes v. N.L.S. Pty., Ltd.*, [1966] WAR 100. He concluded at pp. 575-576:

The approach of the High Court of Australia commends itself to me, cutting through, as it does, artificial barriers to relief that have resulted from overextension of the doctrine of surrender in its relation to rent. Although it is correct to say that repudiation by the tenant gives the landlord at that time a choice between holding the tenant to the lease or terminating it, yet at the same time a right of action for damages then arises; and the election to insist on the lease or to refuse further performance (and thus bring it to an end) goes simply to the measure and range of damages. I see no logic in a conclusion that, by electing to terminate, the landlord has limited the damages that he may then claim to the same scale that would result if he had elected to keep the lease alive.

Laskin J then expressly adopted the Australian approach.

The Court in *Highway Properties* justified its decision by an appeal to both principle and practicality. In principle it made no sense to regard a commercial lease of land as "simply a conveyance and not a contract." This historical anomaly could only be corrected by assessing damages in breach of land lease cases on general contract principles. Practicality supported the change as well since the new approach avoided the potential for multiplicity of actions inherent in the old approach. Both these factors suggest that the same change should be made in the law applicable to breaches of chattel leases.

In addition to these two considerations the need for consistency within the law militates in favour of a change in the rules relating to breach of chattel leases. As was noted in both *Baldock* and *Regent Park* there is no essential difference between a lease of land and a lease of chattels that is material to the ascertainment of damages on breach. They are both contracts. Thus the spirit of *Regent Park*—the harmonizing of the law relating to the leasing of chattels with the law relating to the leasing of land—is best given effect today by a different result in a chattel lease case. The damages flowing from the breach of a chattel lease, like the damages flowing from the breach of a land lease, should be calculated in accordance with general contract principles. To the extent that *Regent Park* reflects a different approach it should not be followed.

Counsel for the appellants, however, point out that *Highway Properties* was a case of express repudiation by the lessee. The present case, they argue, is distinguishable in that there was no express repudiation. Assuming that the appellants could establish the factual basis for this distinction, is there any reason why the rule laid down in *Highway Properties* should not logically extend to all cases involving a lawful termination by the lessor?

In order to answer this question we must go back to first principles in the law of contract. If a party to a contract breaches a term of sufficient importance the other party has the right to treat the contract as terminated and consider himself discharged from any future obligations under it: *Pigott Construction Co. v. W.J. Crowe Ltd.* (1961), 27 DLR (2d) 258 (Ont. CA), at pp. 269-272; *Alkok v. Grymek*, [1968] SCR 452, at p. 456; *Hongkong Fir Shipping Co. v. Kawasaki Kisen Kaisha Ltd.*, [1962] 2 QB 26 (CA), *per* Diplock LJ at pp. 65-66, 71; *Cehave N.V. v. Bremer Handelsgesellschaft n.b.H. The "Hansa Nord,"* [1976] QB 44 (CA). An identical right arises where one party to a contract by words or conduct indicates to the other party that he does not intend to perform his contractual obligations. In the latter instance the first party is said to have repudiated the contract: see Sir W.R. Anson, *Law of Contract* (26th ed. by A.G. Guest), pp. 470-484; G.C. Cheshire, C.H.S. Fifoot and M.P. Furmston, *Law of Contract* (11th ed. 1986), pp. 521-533. The question at hand is whether the assessment of damages in a case of termination based on breach of a term of the contract should be any different from the assessment of damages in a case of termination based on repudiation.

Laskin J in *Highway Properties* seemed to assume that the answer to this question was no. His analysis in that case focussed on the "courses that a landlord may take where a tenant is in fundamental breach of the lease or has repudiated it entirely." I would respectfully agree with Laskin J that damages should be assessed in the same way in both cases. Repudiation may be triggered by either the inability or the unwillingness of a party to perform his contractual obligation. The same is true of a breach of contract that gives rise to a right to terminate; it may be the result of inability or unwillingness to perform. The breach and the repudiation are merely subdivisions within a general category of conduct, i.e., conduct which gives the innocent party the right to treat the contract as terminated. Thus, there is no conceptual difference between a breach of contract that gives the innocent party the right to terminate and the repudiation of a contract so as to justify a different assessment of damages when termination flows from the former rather than the latter. General contract principles should be applied in both instances.

The trial judge in this case correctly found that the Langilles' default constituted a breach of lease that gave Keneric the right to terminate. Keneric accepted the breach and terminated the leases. It is not necessary to determine whether the Langilles also repudiated the leases. For the reasons given above such a finding would make no difference to the assessment of damages.

Before returning to the particular facts of this case it might be useful to comment on *Humphrey Motors, supra*, which was referred to by Jones JA in his dissenting opinion in the Court of Appeal. As noted above, this case involved a conditional sale. The buyer defaulted and the vendor repossessed the truck and resold it. This Court held that the resale by the vendor had "rescinded" the contract and the vendor therefore had no claim for the deficiency on the resale. In my opinion this case is not good law today as it relies on an out-moded concept of rescission.

The modern view is that when one party repudiates the contract and the other party accepts the repudiation the contract is at this point terminated or brought to an end. The contract is not, however, rescinded in the true legal sense, i.e., in the sense of being voided *ab initio* by some vitiating element. The parties are discharged of their prospective obligations under the contract as from the date of termination but the prospective obligations embodied in the contract are relevant to the assessment of damages: see *Johnson v. Agnew*, [1980] AC 367: [1979] 1 All ER 883 (HL), and *Moschi v. Lep Air Services Ltd.*, [1973] AC 331; [1972] 2 All ER 393 (HL). Such is the law for contracts generally and it is this law which should apply equally to breaches of chattel leases.

• • •

Appeal dismissed.

NOTES

Justice Wilson's assertion that there is no conceptual distinction between the innocent party's right to terminate the agreement and claim damages because of repudiatory conduct by the guilty party and a right to claim damages because of a termination clause in the agreement is not supported by the English authorities, and is not consistent with the English Court of Appeal's reasoning in *Baldock*. Nevertheless, Justice Wilson's position has been justified on the ground that the British approach in the hire-purchase cases is artificial and provides no meaningful protection to consumers. Justice Wilson's approach to the measurement of damages is also unusual since it relies on the first rather than the second rule for the measurement of damages in *Hadley v. Baxendale*. See Ziegel, "Measurement of Damages for Breach of a Chattel Lease: The Supreme Court of Canada Liberalizes the Rules," [1988] *Lloyd's Marit. & Coml. Law Quart.* 276. Part 5 of Article 2A of the Uniform Commercial Code contains a much more sophisticated and refined series of rules for measuring the lessor's damages where the equipment has been repossessed by the lessor.

CHAPTER ELEVEN

Suretyships

KINDS AND CHARACTERISTICS OF SURETYSHIP CONTRACTS

The body of law falling generally under the heading of suretyship* deals with contracts under which one person (the surety) has agreed to answer for an existing or future liability of another person (the principal, i.e., primary obligor) to a third person (the creditor).† The liability assumed by the surety is in addition to the liability of the principal debtor and not in substitution for it. The liability can be in the form of a personal guarantee or the provision of a security interest in property of the surety or both. (See the definition of "debtor" in the personal property security Acts.)

In some specific situations, parties can stand in the relationship to each other of principal and surety without there being an express contract of suretyship between them. For example, an accommodation party who accepts a bill of exchange is a surety for the payment by the drawer. See Bills of Exchange Act, RSC 1985, c. B-4, s. 54. A principal-surety relationship can also be created by statute in furtherance of specific public policy initiatives. See, e.g., Small Business Loans Act, RSC 1985, c. S-11; Canada Student Loans Act , RSC 1985, c. S-23.

Very little of the basic law of suretyship in a domestic context is in statutory form. In the international context there are several codes of non-binding rules dealing with various aspects of suretyship and payment mechanisms. The International Chamber of Commerce (ICC) has been particularly active in preparing and encouraging the use of these codes. See, e.g., Uniform Customs and Practice for Documentary Credits (UCP 500-1992 revision) which deal with primary liability undertakings; and Uniform Rules for Contract Bonds (ICC 524), which deal with guarantee bonds.

There are two main categories of contracts of suretyship: contracts of guarantee and contracts of indemnity. The two types of contract have much in common. For this reason they are often, but inaccurately, lumped together under the label "guarantees." However, there are important differences between them. It is not always easy to determine whether a relationship is that of guarantee or indemnity. Often form contracts contain wording that gives the contracts some of the characteristics of both.

---

* See generally, K. McGuiness, *The Law of Guarantee: A Treatise on Guarantee, Indemnity and the Standby Letter of Credit* (Toronto: Carswell, 1986).

† Although the term "creditor" is used, the obligations owing by the principal to the creditor may involve something other than the payment of money.

Contracts of Guarantee

A contract of guarantee is one in which the surety (the guarantor) assumes responsibility for the due performance by the principal of existing or future obligations (specific or non-specific) owing by the principal to the creditor if the principal fails to discharge these obligations. The effect of the contract may be limited in time or open-ended. A distinguishing feature of a guarantee contract is that the guarantor's liability only arises when the principal fails to perform the obligations; the guarantor's liability is always ancillary, or secondary, to that of the principal, who remains primarily liable. It follows from this that the existence and extent of the guarantor's liability is directly proportional to the existence and extent of the principal's obligations. This is known as the principle of co-extensiveness. Accordingly, the guarantor is usually not liable if the underlying obligations is void or unenforceable or ceases to exist. There are, however, exceptions to the principle of co-extensiveness.

A second distinguishing feature of a guarantee contract is that it is the only category of suretyship contract subject to the writing requirement of the Statute of Frauds, 1677. Section 4 of the Statute requires a writing, signed by the guarantor, evidencing the existence of a guarantor contract.

Contracts of Indemnity

A contract of indemnity, unlike a contract of guarantee, provides for primary, not secondary, liability of the surety (indemnifier). The liability is wholly independent of any liability between the principal and the creditor (unless the indemnifier also assumes joint liability with the principal). It is generally understood, as between the principal and the surety, that the former is primarily liable; however, this does not affect the relationship between the creditor and the indemnifier. Co-extensiveness is not a feature of an indemnity contract with the result that the creditor is protected against the possibility that the underlying obligation of the principal is void or becomes unenforceable. Generally, the discharge of the principal, or any variation or compromise of the creditor's claim against the principal, will not necessarily affect the liability of the surety.

Credit Foncier Trust Co. v. Zatala Hldg. Inc.
(1986), 4 BCLR (2d) 25 (CA)

McLACHLIN JA: This is an appeal from an order dismissing Credit Foncier's claim that David Ready was liable as covenanter on a mortgage granted by Credit Foncier to Titan Electric.

The facts may be summarized as follows. On 12th October 1979, Credit Foncier granted a mortgage to Zatala Holdings Inc., now known as Titan Electric Ltd. Mr. Ready was a shareholder in Titan Electric. He was included on the covenant in the mortgage. Some time before 12th October 1982, Mr. Ready sold his shares in Titan Electric. The mortgage matured 1st October 1982. Credit Foncier made an offer to Titan Electric to renew the mortgage at a higher rate of interest on 30th September 1982. The offer was accepted by Titan Electric on 10th October 1982. Credit Foncier did not consult or advise

Mr. Ready of the renewal agreement, of which Mr. Ready remained ignorant until some time later.

Titan Electric defaulted on its mortgage in June 1984. The plaintiff Credit Foncier sued not only Titan Electric but Mr. Ready on the covenant contained in the original mortgage. Mr. Ready then applied to have the claim against him struck out. The chambers judge acceded to that request. It is from that decision that this appeal is brought.

A transcript of the judge's reasons is not available. However, counsel agree that the basis of the judge's dismissal of Credit Foncier's claim against Mr. Ready, was the judge's conclusion that Mr. Ready was a surety with respect to the obligations of the mortgagor, Zatala Holdings Inc., and as such, was discharged from any obligation on the mortgage because of the renewal agreement, based on the decision of the Supreme Court of Canada in *Holland-Can. Mtge. Co. v. Hutching; Holland-Can. Mtge. Co. v. Royal Trust* Co., [1936] SCR 165, [1936] 2 DLR 481 [Alta.].

The main issue is whether the chambers judge erred in holding that Mr. Ready was a guarantor for surety and not a principal debtor or indemnitor. The appellant, Credit Foncier, concedes that if Mr. Ready is a guarantor, then *Holland* applies and he is not liable. This is because it is well settled that sureties who guarantee a contract are released from all liability if the parties to the contract effect a material variation in it which is not approved by the sureties. As Lord Westbury put it in *Blest v. Brown* (1862), 4 De GF & J 367 at 376, 45 ER 1225, in a passage cited with approved [*sic*] in *Holland* [p. 172]:

it must always be recollected … in what manner a surety is bound. You bind him to the letter of his engagement. Beyond the proper interpretation of that engagement you have no hold upon him. He receives no benefit and no consideration. He is bound, therefore, merely according to the proper meaning and effect of the written engagement that he entered into. If that written engagement is altered in a single line, no matter whether it be altered for his benefit, no matter whether the alteration be innocently made, he has a right to say. "The contract is no longer that for which I engaged to be surety: you have put an end to the contract that I guaranteed, and my obligation, therefore, is at an end."

The same rule does not apply to a person primarily liable on the obligation. In *Prospect Mtge. Invt. Corp. v. Van-5 Dev. Ltd.* (1985), 68 BCLR 12 at 23, this court, per Esson JA, held that *Holland* did not apply to covenantors, as opposed to mere sureties. If a surety does not consent to changes in the primary obligation, his liability is discharged. However, a covenanter who is primarily liable on the obligation remains liable on the covenant, notwithstanding material changes to the agreement to which he is not a party and to which he does not agree.

The question, then, is whether Mr. Ready is a mere surety. The mortgage document in its preamble and closing describes him as a "covenanter." The only portion of the document which deals with Mr. Ready's obligation is the following:

The loan hereby secured is made at the request of the covenanter and in consideration thereof the covenanter doth hereby covenant, promise and agree to and with the mortgagee that he will at all times pay or cause to be paid to the mortgagee, the principal monies, interest and other monies hereby secured, at the time or times respectively appointed therefor, and that he will observe and perform or cause to be observed and performed, all the covenants, terms, provisos, stipulations and conditions herein contained on the part of the mortgagor to be observed and performed and that he will at all times indemnify, protect and save harmless the mortgagee form (sic) all loss, costs and damage in respect of this mortgage and every matter and thing herein contained, and that no extension or extensions granted by the mortgagee to the mortgagor for payment of the monies thereby secured, or for the doing, observing or performing of any covenant, agreement, matter or thing herein contained to be done, observed or performed by the mortgagor, and that no taking of any further security from the mortgagor, nor any other dealings between the mortgagee and the mortgagor shall in any way modify, alter, vary or otherwise prejudice the mortgagee or effect the liability of the covenanter in anywise under this covenant, which shall continue and be binding upon the covenanter, his heirs, executors, administrators, successors and assigns as well after as before default, and as well after as before maturity of this mortgage until the said monies are fully paid and satisfied, and the mortgagee shall not be bound to exhaust its recourse against the mortgagor or any other persons before enforcing its rights against the covenanter.

In many respects this provision resembles the primary obligation found in the *Prospect Mtge.* case. The loan is stated to have been made at the request of the covenanter, "in consideration of which the covenanter gives his promise." The promise itself is couched in absolute and primary terms; the covenanter agrees that he will "at all times pay or cause to be paid to the mortgagee the principal monies, interest and other monies hereby secured ... ." The covenanter agrees to "observe and perform or cause to be observed or performed, all the covenants, terms, provisos, stipulations and conditions herein contained on the part of the mortgagor to be observed, performed ... ." Finally, both the mortgage in this case and in *Prospect*, contain a clause which states that no indulgences, time extensions, taking further security from the mortgagor, "nor any other dealings between the mortgagee and mortgagor shall in any way, modify, alter, vary or otherwise prejudice the mortgagee or affect the liability of the covenanter ... ."

On the other hand, the covenant in this case, unlike that found in *Prospect Mtge.*, includes a proviso that the covenanter will "at all times indemnify, protect and save harmless the mortgagee from all loss, costs and damage in respect of this mortgage. ..." Moreover, the covenant in *Prospect* provided expressly that the covenantors gave their covenants "as primary obligors and not as guarantors." No such clause is found in the mortgage in this case.

Mr. Ready contends that the reference in the covenant to his obligation to indemnify and save harmless the mortgagee makes him a mere surety or guarantor with the result that *Holland* applies and he is discharged from liability on the renewed agreement. The appellant on the other hand, relies on the legal distinction between a guarantor or surety on the one hand, and an indemnitor on the other. In essence, the distinction is this. A surety or guarantor is liable only if the principal debtor defaults. An indemnitor, on the other hand, is primarily liable to pay, even in the absence of default by the debtor.

The distinction is set out in *Jowitt's Dictionary of English Law*, 2nd ed. (1977), vol. 1, p. 959:

[An indemnity] differs from a guarantee (q.v.), which is required to be evidenced by writing by the Statute of Frauds, 1677, s. 4, in that a guarantee contemplates the primary liability of a third person, whereas an indemnity gives to the person to whom it is made the immediate right to look for satisfaction to the person by whom it is made. An indemnify [sic] may be illustrated by "if you will supply goods to A, I will see you paid"; a guarantee by "If A does not pay you, I will."

In the clause under consideration in this case, there is nothing which makes Mr. Ready's obligation as covenanter conditional on the default of the mortgagor. He may be sued on the mortgage debt at any time. He has given the mortgagee his own primary undertaking to repay the mortgage debt and otherwise abide by the mortgage covenants. The fact that he additionally agrees to indemnify and save harmless the mortgagee against the defaults of the mortgagor does not, in my view, detract from his clear and unambiguous assumption of a primary obligation to the mortgagee. The agreement to indemnify is a primary assumption of responsibility, not a conditional guarantee. Having so covenanted, Mr. Ready cannot bring himself within the special rules which give additional protection to mere sureties, who have not bound themselves to pay the creditor in any event and enter into their obligation of guarantee merely as a secondary accommodation of another.

These considerations lead me to the conclusion that Mr. Ready was not a mere surety, as were the guarantors in *Holland*. I would allow the appeal and reverse the order of the chambers judge below, striking out Credit Foncier's claim against Mr. Ready. The matter is remitted to the trial division for determination of the issue of novation.

Appeal allowed.

NOTES

1) It is sometimes necessary to draw a distinction between a suretyship contract, which gives rise to legal obligations, and a "letter of comfort" which does not. For example, in *Kleinwort Benson Ltd.* v. *Malaysia Mining Corp. Bhd.*, [1989] 1 All ER 785 (CA) a parent company, as part of an arrangement to make financing available to its subsidiary, gave to the plaintiff bank two "letters of comfort." Each of the letters stated that "It is our policy to ensure that the business (of the subsidiary) is at all times in a position to meet its liabilities to you under the [loan] arrangement." The Court of Appeal held that the letters did not amount to a suretyship contract; they were nothing more than a statement of present fact regarding the parent company's future conduct. The court pointed out that its decision depended in part on the wording of the letters (no words of promise were used) and in part on the fact that the letters were given after the parent had refused to enter into a contract of suretyship.

2) The *standby letter of credit* is a legal technique providing for personal liability by a third party as a method of securing performance of a contract. See generally, L. Sarna, *Letters of Credit* (Toronto: Carswell, 1984). Generally, a letter of credit is an undertaking by a financial institution to pay a sum of money to the person to whom the undertaking is addressed or to accept or purchase a bill of exchange drawn or held by that person. The standby letter of credit is frequently used in the construction industry and in other commercial contexts in place of performance guarantees.

The obligation under a standby letter of credit is not connected to the underlying contract and, as such, is not in the nature of a guarantee. A letter of credit does not involve indemnification; if the issuer is to recover from the customer of the issuer, separate contractual arrangements must be made. See *Westpac Banking Corp. v. Duke Group Ltd.* (1995), 20 OR (3d) 514. However, there is no obligation to pay when there is fraudulent conduct on the beneficiary's part with respect to the tendering of the documents or in the underlying transaction. See *Bank of Nova Scotia v. Angelica-Whitewear Ltd.*, [1987] 1 SCR 59.

3) A guarantee contract may usefully be compared with an insurance contract where the loss is payable to someone other than the insured. There are important differences between them, one of them being that insurance contracts are subject to elaborate statutory regimes while guarantee contracts are not.

The Contract

Hoon v. Bank of Nova Scotia
[1966] SCR 405

[The issue before the Court was whether the Bank had given consideration for the promise of the guarantor.]

In the spring of 1959 Haro Holdings Ltd., hereinafter referred to as "Haro," was building an apartment house in Vancouver. Dunsmuir Construction Ltd., hereinafter referred to as "Dunsmuir," was the construction contractor and Modern Aluminum Ltd., hereinafter referred to as "Modern Aluminum," was the supplier of aluminum materials to Dunsmuir for use in the building. These three companies banked with the respondent at its Columbia and Hastings streets branch. All three were short of working capital and were indebted to the bank. In early April, 1959, Dunsmuir owed the bank about $28,400 by way of overdraft and $20,000 on a demand loan and Modern Aluminum owed the bank $20,000 on a demand loan but had a credit balance in its current account of $4,133.44. At this time the appellant was engaged in negotiations looking to obtaining control of the three companies.

The appellant met with Summers on April 9 and 10, 1959. As to what occurred at these meetings the learned trial judge accepted the evidence of Summers which he summarized as follows at p. 563:

There was some discussion as to the bank advancing $75,000 to Dunsmuir and Modern Aluminum. Mr. Summers asked for the defendant's personal guarantees, the defendant agreed to give guarantees and he signed the guarantees without the bank making any commitment to make further loans to Dunsmuir or Modern Aluminum.

The two guarantees were signed on April 10, 1959. They were on printed forms prepared by the bank. The opening paragraph of that relating to Dunsmuir reads as follows:

In consideration of the bank's agreeing to deal with Dunsmuir Construction Ltd. (hereinafter called "the customer") in the way of its business as a bank, the undersigned hereby guarantees payment to the bank of the liabilities whether direct, contingent or otherwise which the customer has incurred or is under or may hereafter incur or be under to the bank, whether arising from dealings between the bank and the customer, or from other dealings or proceedings by which the bank may become in any manner whatever a creditor of the customer.

The guarantee relating to Modern Aluminum is the same except that "the customer" is Modern Aluminum Ltd. instead of Dunsmuir Construction Ltd.

Following the signing of the guarantees the bank refused to honour outstanding cheques of Dunsmuir unless cash were deposited to cover them, although up to that time the account had been allowed to become overdrawn. Four days after the signing of the guarantees the bank transferred $5,000 from the account of Modern Aluminum in part payment of the demand loan, thereby reducing that loan to $15,000 and creating an overdraft in the account of $866.56. On April 23, Summers told the appellant that the bank would not advance further moneys to either Dunsmuir or Modern Aluminum on the basis of the security that had been offered by the appellant. On April 24, the bank demanded payment in full of the indebtedness of Dunsmuir and Modern Aluminum and, on April 27, demanded payment thereof from the appellant under the guarantees.

On the following day, April 28, there was a stormy interview between the appellant and Summers. The bank demanded further securities for the indebtedness of Dunsmuir, Modern Aluminum and Haro as the price of postponement of immediate payment. After some days of discussion an arrangement was completed by May 12, 1959; Haro gave further security for its own indebtedness and gave guarantees, secured by mortgages on the equity of redemption in the apartment building, of the indebtedness of Dunsmuir and Modern Aluminum; in return the bank agreed to a postponement of payment until April 29, 1960.

On either May 11 or May 12 (Mr. Summers was not sure on which of these days), the appellant signed a letter dated May 8, 1959, which is Ex. 5. Mr. Summers said that it was one of a number of documents prepared by the bank's solicitor and presented to the appellant for signature. It is dated at Vancouver, BC and reads as follows:

The Manager,
The Bank of Nova Scotia,
Hastings & Columbia Branch,
Vancouver, BC

Dear Sir:

Re: Haro Holdings Ltd., Dunsmuir Construction Ltd., Modern Aluminum Ltd.

In confirmation of discussions between myself and the Bank of Nova Scotia with regard to loans made by the Bank to the three companies named above, I agree that any or all of the following measures be carried out in order to improve the Bank's security position and I will cause the companies concerned to execute and deliver to the Bank all necessary documents to implement the following steps:—

(1) That Haro Holdings Ltd. guarantee to the Bank the indebtedness of Dunsmuir Construction Ltd. and Modern Aluminum Ltd.

(2) That Haro Holdings Ltd. furnish to the Bank by way of additional security for loans to Haro Holdings Ltd., a mortgage payable on demand with interest at 6% per annum over Lot 20, Block 32, District Lot 185, Group 1, New Westminster District, Plan 92.

(3) That Haro Holdings Ltd., in support of its guarantee for the indebtedness of Dunsmuir Construction Ltd. and Modern Aluminum Ltd. furnish the Bank by way of additional security with a further mortgage over the aforesaid property, such mortgage to be payable on 29th April, 1960 with interest at 6% per annum.

(4) That Haro Holdings Ltd. deliver to the Bank and to Great-West Life Assurance Company a letter under seal in accordance with the copy attached hereto and initialled by me,

(5) That Haro Holdings Ltd. will furnish the Bank with a letter of undertaking to execute and deliver the mortgages referred to in paragraphs (2) and (3).

I acknowledge that the acquisition by the Bank of the foregoing securities or any of them shall in no way affect my liability as guarantor of the indebtedness to the Bank of Dunsmuir Construction Ltd. and Modern Aluminum Ltd.

Yours truly,

[Sgd.] N.S. Hoon

• • •

It appears to me to be implicit in the reasons of the learned trial judge that he would have dismissed the action if it were not for the effect which he ascribed to the arrangements completed on May 12, 1959, in connection with which the letter, Ex. 5, quoted above, was signed by the appellant. In this I think he would have been right. The finding of fact, fully supported by Summers' own evidence, that the respondent (which acted throughout its dealings with the appellant through its manager Summers) had no intention of dealing with Dunsmuir or Modern Aluminum in the way of its business as a bank would have been fatal to the respondent's claim. The case would have been indistinguishable from the decision of the judicial committee in *Royal Bank v. Salvatori* [1928] 3 WWR 501 (PC).

The language of the guarantee under consideration in that case did not differ in any material particular from that in the case at bar. The facts were very similar. In the *Salvatori* case following the execution of the guarantee by the defendant the bank left the account of the debtor firm open but refused to extend further credit to it. Lord Atkinson who delivered the judgment of the board said, at pp. 508-9:

> Their Lordships do not think that the language of this deed is so ambiguous as the appellants contend that it is, but if it be so, then they think that the key to its construction is that laid down by Lord Blackburn. *Weir River Commrs. v. Adamson* (1878) 2 App. Cas. 734, at 763, 47 LJQB 193. In the report he expressed himself thus:
>
>> Though no doubt the principles of construction of statutes laid down by this House in the present case must have an important effect on those who have to construe that or any other enactment. My Lords, it is of great importance that those principles should be ascertained; and I shall therefore state, as precisely as I can, what I understand from the decided cases to be the principles on which the Courts of law act in construing instruments in writing; and a statute is an instrument in writing.
>>
>> In all cases the object is to see what is the intention expressed by the words used. But from the imperfection of language, it is impossible to know what that intention is without inquiring farther, and seeing what the circumstances were with reference to which the words were used ...
>
> Adopting that rule of construction, it is impossible in their Lordships' view, having regard to the circumstances out of which the deed of guarantee arose and in reference to which its language was used, to suppose that what was intended was that these broken and insolvent traders, the firm, should get no help from the bank beyond leaving their account open, merely continuing to carry the liability, as Connell phrases it. The learned Judge, Mr. Justice Adrian Clark, said that the words continuing to deal with Antoni Brothers in the way of its business as a bank must involve some bona-fide fresh transaction between the parties. Their Lordships concur with him in this view. They think it is impossible to confine these words to merely keeping the account of this

firm open, that is, merely receiving payment from anyone who chooses to pay in money to the bank to the firm's credit. The deed really contains two covenants or contracts, one being the consideration for the other, the first covenant being that if the bank continue to deal with the firm as their customer in the way of its business as a bank, the guarantor will pay to the bank the $40,000 at the times and in the manner specified and do the other things he has undertaken to do. The bank have failed to perform this covenant, they have not continued to deal with the firm as their customer in the way of their business as a bank. The guarantor has not received the consideration, i.e., the whole of the consideration upon which his covenant was based. He is therefore not bound to perform that covenant by reason of this failure.

In the case at bar, the intention of the respondent, far from being to deal with Dunsmuir and Modern Aluminum as customers, was to terminate that relationship immediately upon receiving the guarantees from the appellant and by April 24, 1959, it had done so.

The real question on which there has been a difference of opinion in the court of appeal is as to whether the arrangement completed on May 12, 1959, altered this position in favour of the respondent. In my opinion, it did not. The transaction then carried out, while it involved a number of documents, was a simple one. It was the case of a creditor pressing its debtors for payment of the balances due at the time when it had, for all practical purposes, put an end to its relationship of banker and customer with them and agreeing to give an extension of time for payment on the furnishing of additional securities. It did not, in my opinion, constitute a *bona fide* fresh transaction between the parties as banker and customer. The essential point is that the respondent did not grant an extension of time for payment by the two debtor companies as consideration for the obtaining of the guarantees from the appellant. What it did do was to demand and obtain additional security as the price for postponement of the enforcement of its claim for payment.

It remains to consider whether the situation is affected by the concluding paragraph of the letter, Ex. 5, signed by the appellant. The letter has been quoted in full above and as a matter of convenience I repeat the final paragraph:

I acknowledge that the acquisition by the Bank of the foregoing securities or any of them shall in no way affect my liability as guarantor of the indebtedness to the Bank of Dunsmuir Construction Ltd. and Modern Aluminum Ltd.

Without having recourse to the maxim, *verba chartarum fortius accipiuntur contra proferentem*, I am of opinion that this letter does not assist the respondent. Its purpose is to retain matters *in statu quo*. It neither increases nor diminishes the liability of the appellant. That liability, whatever it may be, is "in no way" affected. I have already expressed my view that the liability did not exist.

Appeal allowed.

NOTES

1) Forbearance to sue is good consideration for a suretyship contract. However, how much forbearance (i.e., the time between the execution of the contract and the date action is brought on it) is required? See *Nikaldi Sportswear Inc.* v. *Mear* (1977), 5 BCLR 79 (Co. Ct.).

2) The Statute of Frauds 1677, s. 4 provides that:

no action shall be brought ... whereby to charge the defendant upon any special promise to answer for the debt default or miscarriage of another person ... unless the agreement upon which such action shall be brought or some memorandum or note thereof shall be in writing and signed by the party to be charged therewith or some other person hereunto by him lawfully authorized.

The writing requirement applies only to guarantee contracts and not to indemnity contracts. Failure to comply with the formalities of the Statute results in the contract of guarantee being unenforceable, but not void. Consequently, the defence of non-compliance must be specially pleaded by the defendant and oral agreements may be raised in set-off as a defence to a related claim. See *Lucas v. Dixon* (1889), 22 QBD 357 (CA).

3) The note or memorandum required by the Statute of Frauds need not be a contract by itself and does not have to be executed contemporaneously. It can be in several documents if the total required evidence of the obligation is in writing containing the requisite signature authenticating the writing. See *Re Hoyle* [1893] 1 Ch. 84 (CA).

4) A guarantee that is given as an incident of a wider economic relationship between the guarantor and the principal creditor need not comply with the Statute of Frauds. For example, the Statute of Frauds would not apply where an owner, by promising subcontractors that he would pay them if the contractor fails to pay, induced the subcontractors, who were threatening to abandon the work, to continue. See *John C. Love Lumber Co. v. Moore*, [1963] 36 DLR (2d) 609 (Ont. CA). In *Pullano v. Yellowhead Timber Ltd.* (1995), 93 BCLR 76 (CA) Donald JA (speaking for the Court) stated at p. 83: "While many of the cases dealing with the wider interest exception discuss the existence of a separate agreement or transaction between the guarantor and creditor, I do not believe that proof of such an agreement is an essential element of the exception. At the heart of the exception lies the pursuit of an objective beyond that of simply guaranteeing the debt; in other words the guarantee is incidental to a larger purpose sought to be accomplished by the promisor."

Canadian Imperial Bank of Commerce v. White
(1975), 61 DLR (3d) 185 (Alta. CA)

McGILLIVRAY CJA (for the court): The principal question which falls to be decided in this appeal concerns the duty of disclosure that a bank owes to a guarantor at the time the bank takes a guarantee.

The Canadian Imperial Bank of Commerce, the respondent and plaintiff herein, to whom I shall hereafter refer as "the Bank" has as its customer D.J. Studios Ltd., to which company I shall hereafter refer as "the Company."

The Company operated the business of photography of school children on a commercial basis, and in November of 1970, it applied to the Bank for a loan of $62,000.

According to the application for loan, which is dated November 10, the shareholders of the Company [had loaned substantial sums of money to the Company] ...

• • •

The guarantor is a farmer and the farm where he lived at all times material was in the Vulcan area, some 250 miles from Edmonton. The guarantor was the brother of Mr. D.J. White, who was the principal officer of the Company. Mr. D.J. White resided in Edmonton, and the headquarters of the Company was Edmonton.

The Company's dealings in the fall of 1970 were with the CN Tower branch in Edmonton of the Bank.

The guarantor was also a director of the Company, but his evidence is that he did not attend directors' meetings and knew little of the Company's operation.

As mentioned, in November of 1970, the Company applied to the CN Tower branch of the Bank in Edmonton for a total credit of $62,000 in order to carry on. At this time the Company had given notes to the Bank totalling $20,000, it had in addition an overdraft of between $17,000 and $18,000, and in addition to this, the three shareholders mentioned were indebted to the Bank in the sum of $22,200.

The Company was informed that it did not have sufficient security to justify a loan, and Mr. D.J. White volunteered to obtain a guarantee from his brother, Mr. Terrance F. White, the appellant. The guarantee was prepared and sent to the Vulcan branch of the Bank, where the guarantor did business, and the guarantor attended at the branch and executed the guarantee on November 16, 1970.

By a memorandum dated November 17, 1970, the credit requested was authorized by the regional general manager of the Bank, who, in authorizing it, wrote:

Referring to your communication of November 13th with regard to the guarantee of T.F. White for full liability, our position would appear adequately protected and accordingly we authorize the credit on the clear understanding that the existing loans to D.J. White and D. Potter and D. Hiller will now be assumed by the Company within the limit recorded and there will be no further authorized excesses in loans accorded to the participants without our prior approval.

A substantial part of the claim advanced by the Bank in this action arises out of this guarantee. It was argued first that the guarantee was given without consideration. This is dealt with fully by the learned trial Judge, and I agree with him that the argument is without merit. It is evident that the Bank continued to carry the Company.

The second argument for the guarantor is that the guarantee was invalid owing to the failure of the Bank to disclose to the guarantor the condition that certain of the shareholders' loans were to be repaid out of the new credit extended to the Company.

The appellant complains that he understood his guarantee was intended to put the Company on its feet, and that with his guarantee, the Company would have operating capital. It is argued that if the $22,200 in loans made by the other shareholders had not been paid off, the Company would have had substantially more working capital, and that with this money, it might not have gone under, as it ultimately did. It is argued on behalf of the guarantor that he was certainly not signing a guarantee with the intent that out of the moneys it generated, some of the loans of other shareholders would be paid, so that, in effect, the liability for these loans would be transferred from the other shareholders to him. The appellant says he was quite unaware that such loans made to the Company by the other shareholders were to be paid off as a condition of the loan, and he only learned that this had occurred after the litigation had commenced.

The learned trial Judge said this:

I accept the defendant's evidence that he did not know of this condition of the loan nor indeed did he know that the said loans were repaid until the date of the examination for discovery in this action, however, I point out that such knowledge was at all times available to him as a director of the company.

It is clear from the guarantor's own evidence that any information he obtained, he obtained from his brother. The Bank gave him no information directly, nor did he request any. The question arises—was there a duty of disclosure on the part of the Bank? There is no question here of fraud, or even of innocent misrepresentation, unless it can be said that the failure to disclose when there is a duty to disclose, may amount to innocent misrepresentation.

In *Actionable Misrepresentation*, by Spencer Bower and Turner, 3rd ed. (1974), at pp. 102-3, the authors state:

89. Lastly, there are cases which are usually classed as belonging to the province of non-disclosure, pure and simple, and not to that of misrepresentation, but which, nevertheless, certain very learned authorities have preferred to treat as examples of positive misrepresentation to be implied from silence. It has been held that the mere entering into any ... matters which would be considered unusual and abnormal in such transaction, amounts to a representation that there are no such matters, and therefore (if it be proved that in fact such matters did exist, and that the transaction was not of the regular and normal description which from the representor's silence the representee was entitled to expect), a false representation.

In Rowlatt on *Principal and Surety* it is stated at p. 155:

A creditor must reveal to the surety every fact which under the circumstances the surety would expect not to exist; for the omission to mention that such a fact does exist is an implied representation that it does not.

The authority quoted for this statement is *Hamilton v. Watson* (1845), 12 Cl. & Fin. 109, 8 ER 13139 (HL). In that case the debtor was indebted to the bank. He was granted a new cash account, which was guaranteed. The new amount of this account was used to pay the previous debt. When the surety signed the bond in question he was not aware of the previous debt, nor was any information on the subject given him by the bank. The surety contended that the suretyship was void as the circumstances of the previous dealings between the parties had not been communicated to him.

Lord Campbell said [at pp. 118-20]:

My Lords, I am of the same opinion. Your Lordships must particularly notice what the nature of the contract is. It is suretyship upon a cash account. Now the question is, what, upon entering into such a contract, ought to be disclosed? and I will venture to say, if your Lordships were to adopt the principles laid down, and contended for by the appellant's counsel here, that you would entirely knock up those transactions in Scotland of giving security upon a cash account, because no bankers would rest satisfied that they had a security for the advance they made, if, as it is contended, it is essentially necessary that every thing should be disclosed by the creditor that is material for the surety to know. If such was the rule, it would be indispensably necessary for the bankers to whom the security is to be given, to state how the account has been kept: whether the debtor was in the habit of overdrawing; whether he was punctual in his dealings; whether he performed his promises in an honourable manner; for all these things are extremely material for the surety to know. But unless questions be particularly put by the surety to gain this information, I hold that it is quite unnecessary for the creditor, to whom the suretyship is to be given, to make any such disclosure; *and I should think that this might be considered as the criterion whether the disclosure ought to be made voluntarily, namely, whether there is anything that might not naturally be expected to take place between the parties who are concerned in the transaction, that is, whether there be a contract between the debtor and the creditor, to the effect that his position shall be different from that which the surety might naturally expect, and, if so, the surety is to see whether that is disclosed to him.* But if there be nothing which might not naturally take place between these parties, then, if the surety would guard against particular perils, he must put the question, and he must gain the information which he requires. *Now, in this case, assuming that there had been the contract contended for, and that that had been concealed, that would have vitiated the suretyship.* There is no proof, nor is there any allegation that there was any such contract. There is, therefore, neither allegation nor proof, and what then does the case rest upon? It rests merely upon this, that at most there was a concealment by the bankers of the former debt, and of their expectation, that if this new surety was given, it was probable that that debt would be paid off. It rests merely upon non-disclosure or concealment of a probable expectation. And if you were to say that such a concealment would vitiate the suretyship given on that account, your Lordships would utterly destroy that most beneficial mode of dealing with accounts in Scotland.

In *London General Omnibus Co., Ltd. v. Holloway*, [1912] 2 KB 72 at p. 79, Vaughan Williams LJ commenting on *Hamilton v. Watson* said:

Lord Campbell, it is true, takes as his example of what might not be naturally expected an unusual contract between "editor and debtor whose debt the surety guarantees, but I take it this is only an example of the general proposition that a creditor must reveal to the surety every fact which under the circumstances the surety would expect not to exist, for the omission to mention that such a fact does exist is an implied representation that it does not. Such a concealment is frequently described as "undue concealment."

Now, looking at the facts of this case, can it be contended that the condition of the loan, namely, that the loans in the total sum of $22,200 which the Bank manager had made to shareholders because he could not, without authority, make the loan directly to the Company, be repaid by the Company, is such an unusual transaction that the guarantor should have been so informed by the Bank? In the consideration of the existence of any such duty, these facts should be borne in mind. First, in the documentation which accompanied the application for loan by the Company, it is contemplated that some of the short-term shareholders' loans would be repaid by the loan. Secondly, it is clear that the guarantor was getting such information as he required, not from the Bank at all, but from his brother. Thirdly, there must be considerable question as to whether the Company's position after repayment of the short-term loans of $22,200 was, in fact, different from what the guarantor expected. The following questions and answers appear in his examination for discovery:

74. Q. Did you ask him at that time if the company was in fact already indebted to the bank?
A. Oh yes, this was—

75. Q. Did he—

A. What he was saying, was a certain figure owing to the bank and this had to be covered before he could get additional help and get this thing moving.

76. Q. Did he mention that specific figure that was then owing to the bank?

A. Sixty-two thousand I believe it was, sixty-two. Which is the figure that I always had in mind, sixty-two thousand.

In short, by this answer the guarantor appears to have understood that the loan was really intended to do no more than cover the outstanding debts to the Bank, which would then enable the Bank to further carry the Company. Fourthly, to the knowledge of the Bank he had not looked to them for information, and, indeed, he was to the knowledge of the Bank a director of the Company. Fifthly, it is clear that the loans of $22,200 had from the outset been treated by the Bank and the Company as short-term financing for the Company.

It seems to me that in the light of these facts and the authorities, that there was no duty on the Bank to advise the guarantor as to what they were proposing as a condition of the loan. In my view there was nothing about the transaction that was unusual. Had the Bank required that as a condition of granting the credit, certain shareholders who had made loans to the Company be paid by the Company, thereby constituting some sort of preference, and thereby doing something which could hardly be expected by one of the other shareholders who was a guarantor, the position might then be different. Here, however, the only shareholder loans which were repaid were short-term loans which were in addition to the loans made by the shareholders originally to the Company, and they were loans which were only made through the shareholders because the Bank manager would have exceeded his authority in granting the money directly to the Company. I think it can be fairly said that all the Bank sought was the consolidation or regularization of three banking situations the notes in the amount of $20,000; the overdraft of between $17,000 and $18,000, and the borrowings by the shareholders from the Bank for the Company in the amount of $22,200.

The case of *Westminster Bank Ltd. v. Cond* (1940), 46 Corn. Cas. 60, is in point. In this case the plaintiff bank had given an overdraft to a customer, which overdraft was secured by two guarantors and the deposit of life insurance policies. The customer wanted to increase his overdraft, but the Bank would not do this without a further guarantor. The defendant became a guarantor. He was unaware of the fact that the customer was already overdrawn. He had an interview with the manager of the branch. He asked the manager his opinion as to the customer's prospects, and the manager advised that in view of the salary the customer was making, he thought he would be able to repay the overdraft within a reasonable time. The prospective guarantor and defendant did not ask the manager whether the customer was already overdrawn and the manager did not disclose the fact. Later the customer became insolvent, and the bank called upon the guarantor, who refused to pay. He contended that although he did not ask the bank manager the specific question as to whether the customer was overdrawn, it must have been apparent to the manager that he was unaware of the fact, and that he would have regarded it as material in considering whether he should grant the guarantee or not. He contended that under these circumstances the manager was under a duty to disclose the fact to him.

Mr. Justice Tucker said this at p. 71:

In all the circumstances of this case I am unable to find anything which made it, in my view, the duty of Mr. Mason (the bank manager) to disclose to Mr. Cond (the guarantor) that there was this existing fully secured overdraft. He was not asked a specific question with regard to it, and in all the circumstances of this case, I do not think that anything took place which put that duty upon the bank manager.

Similarly, in the case at bar, I am of the view that the Bank was not in breach of any duty to the guarantor (the appellant), and this defence fails.

Appeal dismissed.

NOTES

1) In *Bank of Montreal v. Intracom Investments Ltd.* (1982), 42 NBR (2d) 696 (QB), aff'd 47 NBR (2d) 391 (CA), the court held that, where co-owners had agreed to guarantee the debts of a company, the creditor's failure to disclose to one of the owners that the guarantee of the other was unacceptable was a failure to discharge the disclosure obligation.

2) Under the Alberta Guarantees and Acknowledgment Act RSA 1980, c. G-12, ss. 3-4, a guarantee given by an individual "has no effect" unless the person appears before a notary public, acknowledges to the notary public that he executed the guarantee and signs the notary certificate. The notary must issue a certificate "after being satisfied by examination of the person entering into the obligation that he is aware of the contents of the guarantee and understands it." Is this statute likely to do more harm than good? Is a notary public likely to have sufficient legal knowledge to explain adequately the various aspects of a guarantee contract of the kind currently in use by lending institutions?

3) A guarantee obtained from a bank customer by a bank manager who stood in a fiduciary relationship with the customer is unenforceable since it is in breach of the fiduciary duty owed to the customer. See *Bank of Montreal v. Jakoujian* (1986), 32 BLR 177 (Ont. Dist. Ct.). However, such a fiduciary relationship does not arise merely out of a long period of dealing between the customer and the bank. See *Bank of Nova Scotia* v. *Strauss* (1992), 80 Man. R (2d) 260 (QB).

Contribution Between Co-Sureties

Manu v. Shasha
(1983), 41 OR (2d) 685 (CA)

ROBINS JA (for the court): This appeal concerns the right of a surety who has paid more than his proportionate share of a common liability to compel contribution from a co-surety.

The factual background to the issue in dispute is essentially this. In early 1978, the appellant/plaintiff, Sami Manu, and the respondent/defendant, Jack Shasha, agreed, by way of a homemade handwritten document, to incorporate a company to carry on a computerized bookkeeping business. The company was to be known as Manusha Investments Limited; its share capital was to be divided equally between the parties; their capital investment was to be equal; and if the capital contributed by them was not sufficient to purchase the computer necessary for the business operation, they agreed to seek a loan from the Bank of Montreal for that purpose.

The company was incorporated in February, 1978, by a solicitor retained by the respondent, and was organized by him in such a way that the respondent became its sole shareholder and director, notwithstanding that the parties were to be equal in all respects. Office space was leased; each contributed $3,000 by way of capital; and the company began business, as agreed, under the day-to-day direction of the respondent. The Bank of Montreal was appointed the company's banker.

Consistent with their agreement, the parties arranged a bank loan of $42,000 to finance the company's purchase of a computer. The bank required that they personally guarantee the loan and, accordingly, on March 23, 1978, they each executed the bank's standard form "guarantee for indebtedness of an incorporated company" jointly and severally guaranteeing Manusha Investments Limited's indebtedness to the limit of $42,000 and interest. As further collateral security the bank took a chattel mortgage on the computer and the appellant's personal pledge of a $25,000 term deposit. As between the parties, it is undisputed that they were to be equally liable under the guarantee.

Shortly thereafter a dispute arose which eventually led to the liquidation of the company's assets. At the outset, the dispute centred on the state of the corporate records and the fact that they did not disclose the appellant as either a shareholder or director, although he was named in the banking resolution as the company's sole signing officer. The appellant complained about the fact that his true position was not reflected in the corporate records and the respondent, who did not then and never has denied the equality of their positions, sought to meet the complaint by instructing the company's solicitor to prepare such documents as were necessary to properly reflect the respective holdings. These documents were completed in April, 1978, but were not executed. It would appear that while the appellant purported to complain about the state of the corporate records, in reality he had become dissatisfied with the deal itself and wished out, or if that were not possible, wished a new agreement prepared this time with proper legal advice.

The situation between the parties deteriorated progressively; there were mutual recriminations and, to make the story short, their hostility finally reached the point where the appellant refused to sign any cheques. Consequently, the rent was not paid, the landlord re-entered the company's premises, the respondent discontinued his management and, in no time at all, the company was out of business.

Not unexpectedly, the bank required payment of its loan. The computer, the company's only real asset, was sold and the proceeds were paid to the bank but unfortunately were insufficient to satisfy the indebtedness. As of January 26, 1979, the balance owed to the bank was $18,842.47, and that sum was paid out of the $25,000 term deposit the appellant had personally pledged as collateral. So, by the time the fiasco was over, each of the parties had lost his $3,000 capital investment and the appellant was out a further $18,842.47.

This action was then brought by the appellant Manu to recover, as against the respondent Shasha, one-half of the total amount he was required to pay to the bank by reason of the personal guaranty (i.e., $9,421.24) and, as against the company, the full amount. The latter claim is obviously of no practical consequence and no argument was addressed to it on this appeal. The respondent counterclaimed seeking recovery of his $3,000 capital loss and damages and now cross-appeals against the dismissal of that claim.

The appellant's action is founded on the long established proposition that where a co-surety has paid the debt of a principal debtor, or more than his proportionate share, and is unable to recover against the principal debtor, the co-surety is entitled to contribution from his fellow co-sureties to equalize the burden.

Contribution does not depend upon agreement, but upon an equity arising from the fact of the existence of co-sureties for the same debt owed to the same creditor. The underlying principle of equity is that the creditor's remedies against the co-sureties should be applied so as to apportion the burden rateably, and if the remedies have been applied otherwise the court will correct the inequity between the co-sureties: *DeeHng v. Earl of Winchelsea* (1787), 2 Bos. & Pul. 270, 126 ER 1276; *Rowlatt on the Law of Principal and Surety*, 4th ed. (1982), pp. 152-3; 20 Hals., 4th ed. pp. 120-1, paras. 220-2; and Goff and Jones, *The Law of Restitution,* 2nd ed. (1978), pp. 211-22. Under the *Mercantile Law Amendment Act*, RSO 1980, c. 265, s. 2(3):

2(3) No co-surety ... is entitled to recover from any other co-surety ... more than the just proportion to which, as between themselves, the last mentioned person is justly liable.

The respondent does not challenge the legal basis upon which the claim is asserted; nor does he deny that as between the appellant and himself it was intended that they be liable in equal degree as co-sureties of their company's indebtedness to the bank. But, the respondent argues, the appellant, by his conduct, had disentitled himself to the right to contribution he would otherwise have had; his refusal to sign cheques caused the company's failure; he is to blame for the loss; and, that being so, the argument concludes, he does not come to court with clean hands and is not entitled to obtain equitable relief by way of contribution and thus derive advantage from his own wrong.

• • •

With deference, we are of the view that the mutual rights of the sureties in this case are not to be determined simply by resort to the maxim that a plaintiff in equity must approach the court with clean hands. In our opinion, the surety here who was compelled to pay more than his proportionate share of a common liability is not to be debarred on that ground alone from obtaining contribution from his co-surety.

• • •

The fact that the appellant, in the course of his business relationship with the respondent, engaged in conduct which may be described as deliberate or reckless, or as motivated by an ulterior purpose, is not in itself a sufficient ground upon which to deny the appellant, as surety, his well-recognized right to contribution. The more important question is whether the conduct provides the co-surety (here the respondent) with a cause of action. If it does, the co-surety would be entitled to redress for the damages resulting from the conduct, and the claim for contribution would in effect be reduced accordingly. If, however, the conduct is non-actionable, its characterization as "unclean hands" ought not to compel the dismissal of an action of this nature and the consequent discharge of the co-surety from payment of his share of the common debt, and particularly so in the circumstances of this case where the conduct complained of is not directly connected with or referable to the guarantee or the obligations of the parties as sureties based on which relief is sought: see, generally, *Snell's Principles of Equity,* 27th ed. (1973), pp. 32-3; Spry, *supra,* pp. 213-33; 16 Hals., 4th ed., pp. 875-6, para. 1305.

The matter may be tested in another way. If the situation between the parties were reversed to the extent that the respondent rather than the appellant had been required to pay the company's indebtedness to the bank, he certainly would be entitled to compel the appellant to equalize the burden of the guarantee by contributing his one-half share. But he would not be entitled, simply because of the questionable conduct, to shift the entire burden to the appellant and relieve himself of any payment on the guarantee, which is, of course, the effect of the judgment in appeal. Before the appellant could be required to pay more than the amount for which he was responsible as a co-surety, the respondent would have to establish that the conduct gave rise to a cause of action and prove his damages; and that action would be separate and distinct from the action between sureties. The conduct involved in this case was not aimed at the guarantee or at the respondent in his capacity as a guarantor; nor was it directed towards the relief sought in this suit or devised to derive any advantage as a surety. Such connection as the conduct may have with the subject-matter of the action is not sufficient to warrant invoking the clean hands maxim and thereby defeating the claim for contribution. Those rights and liabilities that may flow from the impugned conduct fall to be determined independent of the rights and liabilities of the parties as co-sureties. The rights of sureties are mutually enforceable and it would be patently incongruous if they were to be determined differently depending on which surety was called upon to pay the debt and bring the action.

With deference to the able argument of counsel for the respondent we are not persuaded that the *Mercantile Law Amendment Act* supports the application of the maxim in this case by its reference in s. 2(3) to the "just proportion" to which, as between themselves, co-sureties may be "justly liable." The just proportion to which recovery is limited by that section is the proportion of the total debt for which a given co-surety is responsible. That proportion and responsibility for it will depend on a number of factors (e.g., agreement between co-sureties, insolvency of one of them, relationship with principal debtor; and see, generally, Rowlatt, *supra,* pp. 153-60), none of which are pertinent to the present circumstances. Whether in other situations among co-sureties the maxim may properly be invoked is not a matter for determination here.

That leaves the question of the nature of the appellant's conduct or, more specifically, whether it was such as to provide the respondent with a cause of action for damages. That matter was dealt with by the trial judge. The respondent, as indicated earlier, counterclaimed for the loss of his $3,000 investment and for general damages.

• • •

We are all of the view that the trial judge correctly concluded on the record before him that the respondent had failed to establish a cause of action entitling him to maintain his counterclaim. While the appellant's conduct was not nice and doubtless would have warranted a winding-up of the company, the evidence does not establish that his acts constituted him guilty of any breach of contract or other actionable wrong vis-à-vis the respondent. It follows on the view we take of the parties' respective rights as co-sureties, that the respondent has likewise failed to establish any legal basis upon which he is entitled to resist the appellant's claim for contribution and, accordingly, each of them must pay his proportionate share of the liability they jointly assumed in signing the bank guarantee.

Appeal allowed.

NOTES

1) Section 5 of the Mercantile Law Amendment Act (1856), 19 & 20 Vict., c. 97 provides:*

5. Every person who, being surety for the debt or duty of another, or being liable with another for any debt or duty, shall pay such debt or perform such duty, shall be entitled to have assigned to him, or a trustee for him, every judgement, specialty or other security which shall be held by the creditor in respect of such debt or duty, whether such judgement, specialty or other security shall or shall not be deemed at law to have been satisfied by the payment of the debt or the performance of the duty, and such person shall be entitled to stand in the place of the creditor, and to use all of the remedies, and, if need be, and upon a proper indemnity, to use the name of the creditor, in any action, or other proceedings, at Law or at Equity, in order to obtain from the principal debtor, or any co-surety, co-contractor, or co-debtor, as the case may be, indemnification for the advances made and loss sustained by the person who shall have so paid such debt or performed such duty, and such payment or performance so made by such surety shall not be pleadable in bar or any such action or other proceeding by him; provided always that no co-surety, co-contractor, or co-debtor shall be entitled to recover from any other co-surety, co-contractor, or co-debtor, by the means aforesaid, more than the just proportion to which, as between those parties themselves, such last-mentioned person shall be justly liable.

2) Co-sureties are free to agree between themselves on what portion of the indebtedness guaranteed will be borne by each. However, this agreement does not affect the rights of the creditor to recover the total amount from one of them. When the entire benefit resulting from the suretyship accrues to one of the sureties, that surety has no right of contribution. See *Bater v. Kare*, [1964] SCR 206.

3) A and B are co-sureties for a debt owing by C to D. A obtains "back-up" security for his liability from X. Should B have a right of contribution from this security when C defaults and A and B pay D? See *Goodman v. Keel*, [1923] 2 WWR 789 (Alta. CA).

4) A, B and C are co-sureties for a debt owing by C to D. Upon C's default, A pays the debt and claims contribution from B and C. Before paying his share, C becomes insolvent. Can A recover from B one-third or one-half contribution of the amount paid by her to D? See *Re Price* (1978), 85 DLR (3d) 554 (NSTD).

---

* See also The Mercantile Law Amendment Act, RSM 1987, c. M-120, s. 2; Law and Equity Act, RSBC 1979, c. 224, s. 30; Mercantile Law Amendment Act, RSO 1990, c. M.10, s. 2.

Release and Discharge

Bank of Nova Scotia v. Neil
(1968), 65 WWR 215 (BCCA)

ROBERTSON JA: This is an appeal from a judgment dismissing an action brought against the endorser of a promissory note in the circumstances which I shall outline. Town & Country Distributors Ltd. (which I shall call "Town & Country") was controlled by a man named Cronin. Town & Country banked with the appellant, whose manager was named Livingstone. At the request of Cronin, the respondent went with Cronin to see Livingstone to arrange for Town & Country to borrow $2,000 working capital from the appellant. Livingstone said that the bank would make the advance. Before the respondent signed anything Livingstone had a private discussion with him, explained that Town & Country was operating on a close margin and pointed out to the respondent his responsibility as endorser of a note. In return for an advance of $2,000 Town & Country then gave the appellant its note, which was dated at Vernon on October 27, 1959, and in which Town & Country promised to pay $2,000 to the appellant, on demand, with interest at six per cent per annum. On the back of the note were stamped the words "Pay to the order of the Bank of Nova Scotia," and under this Cronin and the respondent signed their names. They also signed their names under the following words stamped on the back of the note:

I hereby waive presentment, protest and notice of dishonour and guarantee payment of the within note.

The defendant said that his endorsements on the note were intended to be a form of continuing security. The appellant advanced further sums aggregating $3,300 to Town & Country and on July 29, 1960, took a note for that amount. Before so doing it did not give any notice to the respondent or obtain his consent. Upon that indebtedness there were paid on August 30, 1960, the sum of $1,050 and on September 6, 1960 the sum of $1,570, leaving a balance owing of $1,680. Some time after the note for $3,300 had been taken, Town & Country suffered a loss by fire and the plaintiff took an assignment from Town & Country of the proceeds of the insurance which it was to recover in respect of that loss. Following that the appellant advanced further sums aggregating $6,330 to Town & Country and on January 17, 1961, took a note for that amount. Before so doing it did not give any notice to the respondent or obtain his consent. The debt of $6,330 added to the previous balance of $1,680 made a balance owing on the second and third notes to the appellant by Town & Country of $8,010. On November 8, 1962, the proceeds of the fire insurance amounting to $8,127.75 (after satisfying a prior claim of another bank) were paid to the plaintiff. Of the insurance moneys the plaintiff applied $8,010 to extinguish the liability of Town & Country on the second and third notes and applied the balance of $117.75 on the note for $2,000 which the respondent had endorsed, thus reducing the principal thereof to $1,882.25. This, with interest, the plaintiff sued to recover.

• • •

The learned trial judge then referred to *Drinkle v. Regal Shoe Co.* (1916) 10 WWR 448, 34 WLR 690, 23 BCR 24, affirming (1915) 7 WWR 194, 29 WLR 509, 20 BCR 314, a decision of this court and, after disposing of another defence, said:

On the issue that an additional large loan was made by the Plaintiff to the principal debtor without notification to the Defendant the Defendant is released and the action fails.

From that judgment the plaintiff has appealed.

• • •

NORRIS JA:

• • •

In giving judgment the learned trial judge said:

The risk is one that was assumed by the Plaintiff; certainly the Defendant was prejudiced by the Plaintiff's failure to notify him of the second large advance; had this large advance not been made the Plaintiff would have no difficulty in securing payment of the balance due from the principal creditor out of the insurance money.

• • •

Reading the judgment as a whole I understand the learned judge to mean, although he did not say it in terms, that this being a case of suretyship the rule in *Devaynes v. Noble; Clayton's Case* (1816) 1 Mer. 572, 35 ER 781, is to be applied in favour of the surety as though the debtor had made an appropriation of the insurance moneys to the account which had been guaranteed by the surety even although such an appropriation had not been made. Such an argument may be derived from the obligation imposed on the principal debtor of indemnifying the surety which would make it inequitable for a creditor to appropriate a security for the guaranteed debt to the payment of any other debt and thus throw the whole liability on the surety. This right does not rest upon contract but on the general principles of equity. However, there is in the absence of appropriation no presumption that moneys paid in are to be allocated to the unsecured rather than the secured portion. Where the guarantee is a continuing one, the surety has no right to control the appropriation of payments in, so long as (in this case) the banker deals with the accounts in the ordinary way of business: *Deeley v. Lloyds Bank Ltd.* [1912] AC 756, at 768, 81 LJ Ch 697. See also *Royal Bank v. Slack* [1958] OR 262, reversing [1957] OWN 235 (CA).

In *Re Sherry, London & County Banking Co. v. Terry* (1884) 25 Ch D 692, 53 LJ Ch 404, Lord Selborne LC said at p. 703:

A surety is undoubtedly and not unjustly the object of some favour both at law and in equity, and I do not know that the rules of law and equity differ on the subject. It is an equity which enters into our system of law, that a man who makes himself liable for another person's debt is not to be prejudiced by any dealings without his consent between the secured creditor and the principal debtor. If, therefore, it could be shown that what has been done here was done without the consent of the surety in prejudice of an implied contract in his favour, I quite agree that he ought not to suffer from it. But there being no express contract, on what ground is it to be said that there is an implied contract? I am unable to find any such contract, unless we are to hold that the mere fact of suretyship takes away from the principal debtor and the creditor those powers which they would otherwise have of appropriating payments which are not subject to any particular contract with the surety. Now it seems to me that although there may not be a case in the books in every respect precisely the same as this, the cases of *Kirby v. Marlborough (Duke)* (1813) 2 M & S 18, 105 ER 289, before Lord Ellenborough in 1813, and *Williams v. Rawlinson* (1825) 3 Bing 71, 3 LJOSCP 164, 130 ER 440, before the Court of Common Pleas in 1825, govern it *a fortiori*.

And at p. 705:

It appears to me that the principle of those cases shows, if it were necessary to have authority for the purpose, that the right of appropriation of payment to an account not guaranteed is not taken away by a contract of this kind. Consequently this appeal must be allowed and the judgment of the Vice-Chancellor reversed.

And see also Cotton LJ at pp. 705-6:

As far as I see, the only implied contract is that the account shall be carried on in accordance with the general practice of bankers; and that really answers what has been suggested, that this case does not differ from an attempt by a bank to make a new account during the lifetime of the surety, that is to say, before the guarantee terminates. The balance which the surety guarantees is the general balance of the customer's account, and to ascertain that, all accounts existing between the customer and the bank at the time when the guarantee comes to an end, must be taken into consideration. So that it would be impossible for the bank to say, to the prejudice of the surety, "We carry these sums which have been paid by the customer not to an account of which we ascertain the balance, but to a new account, and we refuse to bring those sums to the credit of his banking account to the relief of the surety." That is quite a different thing, and would be an improper dealing, improper in this sense, that it would prevent the balance of the account from being ascertained in accordance with the terms of the guarantee. But here the account to which these payments have been appropriated is one which, according to the contention of the surety, is not guaranteed in any way, being an account after the death of the surety, and there being nothing in the contract relating to the mode in which the bank was to deal as regards that account, there is nothing to prevent the bank from acting as they have done.

The rule in *Clayton's Case, supra*, has been summarized by McRuer CJHC in *Canada Fishing Tackle & Sports Ltd. v. Dawe* [1960] OWN 499, 25 DLR (2d) 487, at pp. 489-90, as follows:

The general rule applicable to cases involving the doctrine of appropriation was formulated in *Devaynes v. Noble; Clayton's Case* [*supra*], at p. 608. Where an account is carried between two parties as a banking account there is no room for any other appropriation than that which arises from the order in which the receipts and payments take place, and are carried into the account. Presumably, it is the sum first paid in, that is first drawn out. It is the first item on the debit side of the account, that is discharged, or reduced, by the first item on the credit side. The appropriation is made by the very act of setting the two items against each other. Upon that principle, all accounts current are settled, and particularly cash accounts.

This rule, although adopted in all subsequent cases, is not an invariable rule of law but the circumstances of the particular case may warrant the Court in coming to a conclusion that the parties did not intend that it should apply.

In discussing this case four principles applicable to the doctrine of appropriation were laid down in *Simson v. Ingham* (1823) 2 B & C 65, 1 LJOSKB 234, 107 ER 307:

(1) As a general rule a party who pays money has a right to apply the payment as he sees fit. Thus, if there are several debts due from the debtor to the creditor the debtor has a right to say to which of those debts the payment shall be applied.

(2) If the debtor does not make a specific application at the time of payment, the right of application generally devolves on the creditor.

(3) Where one of several partners dies and the partnership is in debt and the surviving partners continue their dealings with a creditor and the latter joins the transactions of the old and new firm in one account, then the payments made from time to time by the surviving partners are applied to the old debt. This is based on the presumption that the parties have consented that the entire account should be considered as one debt.

(4) Entries in the books of the creditor without any communication of the fact of the entry to the debtor does not constitute an election by the creditor to treat the payment in accordance with the entry.

• • •

Middleton J discussed the doctrine of *Clayton's Case* in *Thomson v. Stikeman* (1913) 29 OLR 146, at 158, affirmed 30 OLR 123 (CA), where he pointed out that *Clayton's Case* had not established an inflexible rule which could not be excluded by the conduct of the parties, and he quoted the words of Lord Atkinson in *Deeley v. Lloyds Bank Ltd.* [*supra*], at 771, which I repeat:

> The rule laid down in *Clayton's Case* is not a rule of law to be applied in every case, but rather a presumption of fact, and this presumption may be rebutted in any case, by evidence going to show that it was not the intention of the parties that it should be applied.

Reference may also be made on this point to the judgment of Lord Denman CJ in *Henniker v. Wigg* (1843) 4 QB 792, at 793, 1 Dav & Mer 160, 114 ER 1095.

Counsel for the defendant in advancing his argument, based on the doctrine or rule in *Clayton's Case*, mistakenly assumes that Sir W. Grant had laid down in that case a rigorous and adamantine rule which no circumstances could displace, but that proposition, as has been shown, is not supported by the authorities.

It is well established, too, that the dealings between a principal debtor and his creditor with relation to the question of appropriation are binding upon a surety: *Harvey v. McKay* (1905) 5 OWR 711. In Rowlatt on Principal and Surety, 2nd ed., at 122, this proposition is supported by references to *City Discount Co. v. McLean* (1874) LR 9 CP 692, at 698, 43 LJCP 344; *Re Mayor; Ex parte Whitworth* (1841) 2 Mont D & De G 164, at 169; *Riroy v. Marlborough (Duke)* (1813) 2 M & S 18, 105 ER 289, and *In re Sherry; London & County Banking Co. v. Terry* (1884) 25 Ch D 692, 53 LJ Ch 404. From these decisions the learned author deduces the following principle:

> The question whether payments made by the principal debtor, not being dividends in his bankruptcy, are to be appropriated in discharge or reduction of the guaranteed or some other indebtedness, is one which, in the absence of special agreement between the creditor and the surety must be determined as if it arose merely between the creditor and the principal debtor, a surety having no right of his own to dictate either to the creditor or the debtor how payments made by the latter are to be appropriated.

I am in respectful agreement with the principles enunciated in these cases.

In the appeal at bar the appellant bank made an appropriation of the insurance moneys to the later unsecured indebtedness and there is nothing in the evidence of anything that would indicate that there was any contract that the rule in *Clayton's Case* was to be waived in favour of the surety. In the absence of such contract the surety is at law in no better position than the debtor who made no appropriation of the insurance moneys to affect the appropriation made by the bank.

Appeal allowed.

Benge v. Hanna
(1980), 100 DLR (3d) 218 (Man. QB)

WILSON J: The parties were two of several co-sureties of a continuing account secured by way of chattel mortgage in favour of the creditor, which debt was eventually retired at the cost of the guarantors save only the defendant, who defaulted. Plaintiff took an assignment of the guarantee and sues upon this, to claim from the defendant the latter's proportionate share of the amount paid.

Defendant concedes the right of contribution, as a principle of law, but denies application of the rule in the instant case because of the conduct of the creditor, whose disabilities passed to the plaintiff with assignment of the guarantee. And, says the defendant, his guarantee was forfeit because the creditor, after notice of the insolvency of the principal debtor, continued to advance moneys on the account secured by the guarantee, allowed moneys of the principal debtor to be diverted from the account of the creditor, and permitted assets caught by the chattel mortgage to be transferred to unsecured creditors, thereby negligently failing to realize upon the security.

• • •

[The defendant Hanna was a shareholder of Turtle Mountain Farm Equipment Ltd.]

To finance its operations the company established lines of credit with the Canadian Imperial Bank of Commerce at Killarney, secured by way of an assignment of receivables, and with International Harvester of Canada, resting upon the guarantee signed by the parties, ex. 3. From this last, it appears that business was being carried on by the new company as early as April 16, 1969, although the charter did not issue until March of 1970. A further line of credit was established with Killarney Credit Union Society Limited, secured by the chattel mortgage and guarantee which form the basis of the plaintiff s action here, ex. 3.

Initially, borrowings from the credit union were limited to $15,000; and see the company's by-law 4, enacted when the company was first organized. By-law 5, enacted September 18, 1971, and signed by the defendant himself as president, expanded the line of credit with the credit union to $30,000.

The original by-law 5, filed in the company's minute book, is the only record of the due creation of that authority. Unchallenged as it was, however, for present purposes it must be presumed that in fact by-law 5 was duly enacted, and the company executed in favour of Killarney Credit Union its chattel mortgage (ex. 3) accordingly, charged upon all the inventory, parts and equipment of the mortgagor company, including future purchases, naming three specific pieces of equipment.

Not content with the mere covenant of the company secured in that way, the mortgagee credit union asked for and received the written joint and several personal guarantees of the four proprietors of the borrower company. That guarantee, signed September 18, 1971, and annexed to the chattel mortgage to which it refers, records that the guarantors and each of them, *inter alia*:

... will at all times pay or cause to be paid to the Mortgagee, its successors and assigns, the mortgage monies hereby secured at the time or times respectively appointed therefor, and that we will observe and perform, or cause to be observed or performed, all the covenants, terms, provisos, stipulations and conditions herein contained on the put of the said mortgagor to be observed and performed, and we will, at all times, indemnify, protect and save harmless the mortgagee from all loss, costs and damage in respect of the advance of the mortgage monies and every matter and thing herein contained, and that no release or releases of any portion or portions of all the mortgaged property; and *no indulgence shown by the mortgagee* in respect of any default by the mortgagor which may arise under this mortgage, and that *no extension or extensions granted by the mortgagee to the mortgagor* for payment of the mortgage monies hereby secured or for the doing, observing or performing of any covenant, agreement, matter or thing herein contained, to be done, observed or performed by the mortgagor, *nor any other dealings between the mortgagor and mortgagee, shall in anywise modify, alter, vary or in anywise prejudice the mortgagee or affect our liability in anywise under this covenant*, which shall continue and be binding on us and as well after as before default and after as before maturity of this mortgage, until the said mortgage monies are fully paid and satisfied. NOTWITHSTANDING anything herein contained to the contrary, the liability of Richard Melville Ruberry and Edward Fedorowich is limited and restricted in each case to one-seventh of the said indebtedness from time to time owing hereunder: (My emphasis.)

Unhappily, Turtle Mountain did not prosper.

• • •

Whatever the hardship to its creditors the company was producing precious little for its proprietors too, and, in late May or early June of 1972, defendant told the plaintiff that unless he could get more money, he—the defendant—was going to get out. And, says defendant, he "resigned" from the company on July 5, 1972.

And, says the defendant, by so resigning not only did he dissociate himself from what might be done thereafter by the board of directors, but his own responsibility vis-à-vis the financial condition of the company must be fixed as of the date of his resignation. This last, I think, goes too far.

Having embarked with the others for this corporate enterprise, of which he was to be the chief executive, it would be a strange turn of affairs if, by his "resignation," and with no evidence of bad faith, negligence, or gross mismanagement on the part of his erstwhile associates and co-directors, his own fate is not bound up with that of the rest, as the company of which they are all shareholders continued in business.

• • •

Worsening of Turtle Mountain's affairs was confirmed by the action of the Canadian Imperial Bank of Commerce in closing its account and calling upon the guarantors to settle the outstanding overdraft, when defendant accepted his responsibility as a surety and joined with the plaintiff in paying his share of that debt. On March 21, 1973, ex. 13, International Harvester gave notice of the termination of its franchise and demanded payment of its own account, whereby defendant was exposed to his responsibility as a guarantor of that account.

Anticipating a like demand under his guarantee to Killarney Credit Union, on March 27, 1973—and for the first time—the defendant wrote to that creditor, ex. 21, giving notice of his resignation as a director and president of the debtor company as from July 15, 1972, his offer to surrender his shares "as they have requested" (of which request there was no evidence at all) and pointing out that he believed Turtle Mountain to be insolvent, so that "I will not participate in any further dealings of the company."

At that date—March 27, 1973—the credit union account stood at $23,239.46, ex. 23.

The other directors, and particularly the plaintiff, were not equally prepared to simply walk away from the situation, and continued their efforts to wring what income or other salvage might be won from the floundering Turtle Mountain Equipment Ltd. With the co-operation of International Harvester and Killarney Credit Union, the latter continued to carry the company until September 5, 1973, when the credit union demanded of the four guarantors payment of its account, no later than October 1, 1973, ex. 4. And, September 8th, the credit union advised the balance due was $26,975.68, ex. 35, some $3,600 more than when the defendant advised that creditor of his withdrawal from the debtor company's affairs.

During the intervening six months or so the account, active indeed as from the ledger sheets (ex. 23) appears, had fluctuated between a high of $31,239.51 to a low at one point on May 8, 1973, of $11,294.70, rising that same date upon entry of three more transactions to $24,763.51. All of this reflecting the efforts, directed by the plaintiff, to bring the company clear of debt.

By October 23, 1973, when the credit union gave formal notice of suit, the balance due was $26,233.94 of which defendant's share was $9,369.26. In the action which followed the guarantors Fedorowich and Ruberry paid their own respective shares of the debt, leaving a balance of $14,435.34, paid by the plaintiff by way of his cheques $8,605.45 paid April 16, 1974, and $5,829.89 November 12, 1976. Plaintiff now looks to the defendant for one-half of that sum, $7,217.67, with interest.

As earlier noted, defendant concedes the right of one joint surety to recover from the other the latter's proper share of the amount paid by the first to extinguish the joint liability; and see 18 Hals., 3rd ed., p. 484, para. 890, and 12 CED (Western), 2nd ed., p. 282.

The protest here is that the defendant is not responsible for any part of the debt after his "resignation" from the company, certainly no more than his share of what was due on March 27, 1973, when the account stood at $23,239.46, or better still, his share of the lowest balance after that date, $11,294.70.

Defendant treats as fortuitous the fact that, by the efforts of the others, the International Harvester account was fully cleared, so that he was free of liability under his guarantee to that creditor. And he would have it that upon his repeated notices of resignation, and in particular his advice to Killarney Credit Union of March 27, 1973, the company should have gone into voluntary liquidation. At least, he says, the credit union, upon receipt of his letter, should have inferred a withdrawal of his guarantee, and wound up its account at once.

In his evidence before me and upon examinations for discovery, ex. 32, Qq. 153 and 171, defendant admitted that he did not, at any time, advise the credit union, in so many words, that he would no longer be responsible as a guarantor.

"It perhaps might be hardly equitable for a banker or merchant to go on making advances after receiving a distinct notice from the guarantor that he would not be further liable": per James LJ in *Lloyd's v. Harper* (1880), 16 Ch. D 290 at p. 314.

But, assuming the right to withdraw from a guarantee (and none was written into the guarantee here) notice to such effect must be expressed in clear terms; and see *Dickson v. Royal Bank of Canada* (1975), 66 DLR (3d) 242, [1976] 2 SCR 8349, 13 NSR (2d) 672, where the headnote [DLR], I think, correctly presents the opinion of Ritchie J, for the Supreme Court, that:

Where by the terms of a guarantee a guarantor may determine his liability in respect of future advances "by notice in writing" to the creditor, such a notice must be in clear and explicit terms. It is not sufficient for the guarantor's solicitor to express a "wish" that no further funds be advanced or to write that he "would like the guarantee to be withdrawn." Although no set form of words is required, commercial rights are not normally exercised by mere expression of a wish or preference, and it is of obvious importance that a creditor in such circumstances should be left in no doubt as to his position.

In *Dickson*, the surety unsuccessfully argued that the statement "that is what we wish" in answer to the question "is the guarantee being determined?" was not enough.

And, again assuming a right to withdraw, and further assuming exercise of that right without equivocation, withdrawal from or cancellation of the guarantee is effective only when that notice is accompanied by payment of the full amount then due or owing. *Royal Bank v. Stems,* [1924] 3 DLR 1050; *Starrs v. Cosgrave Brewing & Malting Co. of Toronto* (1885), 12 SCR 571, per Gwynne J, at pp. 5934; *Burgess v. Eve* (1872), LR 13 Eq. 450.

In *E.A. Towns Ltd. v. Harvey et al*, [1945] 2 DLR 782, 61 BCR 416 [affirmed [1946] 2 DLR 72, 62 BCR 168], Coady J considered that, where the guarantee was by its nature not revocable and there was no express provision that it could be revoked, notice of the surety's death was not sufficient to terminate the guarantee, affirmed with the opinion of Kerwin J, [1946] 4 DLR 160 (SCC). That decision, perhaps, does no more than recognize the remarks of Fry J in *Lloyd's v. Harper, supra*, at p. 303, that "A guarantee, like every other contract, must be construed reasonably; it must be construed by the words used, but also with regard to the surrounding circumstances."

And here, given the language of the guarantee—and this could hardly be stronger, as to the right of the creditor to look to the sureties and each of them regardless of the lender's indulgence of the primary debtor or dealings between them of any kind—it seems to me that this guarantee was not revocable.

Nor do I consider the efforts of the defendant's erstwhile associates to disentangle the company's affairs, as an alternative to liquidation or winding-up, must be looked upon as something not contemplated by the guarantee. If the company had no need of financial assistance there would have been no need to arrange that line of credit; and if every borrower/lender association of this sort must be interrupted when times run against the borrower, the Courts would be clogged with the multitude of liquidation or winding-up matters so called for. The question of whether to wrestle one's way through the bad times, or simply to cast away the venture, calls for a nice appreciation of all of the factors involved. And again, absent bad faith and carelessness, the validity of that business decision, as a response to the company's problems, is not to be tested simply by the ultimate success in restoring the position of the debtor.

Defendant insists the company was insolvent, in which case the creditor should have put it into bankruptcy, or it could have gone into voluntary liquidation. Experience in such matters does nothing to seriously impugn the opinion of the credit union manager that, given the administration, legal and accounting costs involved, the net recovery would be well below what could be expected from an orderly winding-down of the company's affairs, as here occurred.

True, "Where, however, the creditor has assets or securities in his hands (the surety having no connection with them) which may be applied by the creditor in reduction of the debt secured, any improper or careless dealing in respect of such securities may discharge the surety to the extent of the loss occasioned thereby": *O'Gara v. Union Bank of Canada* (1893), 22 SCR 404 at p. 435.

No doubt; but here, there was no evidence of careless or improper handling of assets otherwise available to the creditor, or other dealings between the borrower company and creditor Killarney Credit Union to the prejudice of the defendant.

In support of his argument defendant pleads s. 4 of the *Mercantile Law Amendment Act*, RSM 1970, c. M120:

4. Giving time to a principal debtor, or dealing with or altering the security held by the principal creditor, does not of itself discharge a surety or guarantor; in such cases a surety or guarantor is entitled to set up the giving of time or dealing with or alteration of the security as a defence, but the defence shall be allowed in so far only as it is shown that the surety has thereby been prejudiced.

Assuming that rule not to have been avoided by the terms of the guarantee, so long ago as *Blackwood v. Percival* (1902), 14 Man. R 216, where the equivalent rule appeared as s. 36(r) of the *King's Bench Act*, at pp. 221-2, Bain J held that "The onus of proving that he has been prejudiced must rest on the surety; and, as I understand the Act, he must show that he has suffered pecuniary loss or damage as the reasonably direct and natural result of the creditor having given the extension of time; and the defence will avail him to the extent of the loss or damage he can prove.": approved by Mathers CJKB in *National Land & Loan Co. v. Rat Portage Lumber Co.* (1917), 36 DLR 97 at p. 105, [1917] 3 WWR 269 at p. 277.

Finally, defendant voices his distrust of, disagreement with, the values at which the company's assets were disposed of, and the fact that to a significant extent they found their way into the reactivated Killarney Farm Equipment Ltd. But again, defendant's displeasure or disappointment aside, there was no evidence, none at all, to show prejudice to the defendant in what was done. Indeed, plaintiff and the others might have been heard to challenge the attitude and actions of the defendant himself in leaving them to their fate, and returning to his own former occupation as a salesman of farm equipment with a franchise area which included—and so competed with—that of the company of which he had, but days before, been the president, and the officer in charge of sales.

And, of the plaintiff's negotiations for settlement (whereby the claim, as finally paid, was less than the amount originally claimed) defendant is somewhat in the position of the defendant in *Stewart et al. v. Braun et al.*, [1925] 2 DLR 423, [1925] 1 WWR 871. In that case, as here, the defendant declined to attend meetings called for the purpose, or otherwise offer assistance or even express his opinions as to the resolution of differences between the lender and the primary debtor. In which circumstance, thought Dysart (then) J, the plaintiff having in good faith settled with the creditors, defendant was bound by the amounts so negotiated.

The defendant referred me to *Bater et al v. Kare*, [1964] SCR 206. There, the two original co-sureties went into business in 1956 upon terms that Bater would secure a bank loan of $50,000, Kare to advance to the new company up to $50,000 in cash, and Kare paid that amount into the company accordingly. In 1958 the line of credit with the bank was increased to $80,000, at which time the bank took the signatures of each of them, Bater and Kare, as guarantors. In 1960 Kare sold out to Bater at $29,850, being his equity at that time in the company. Bater died, and his executors paid off the bank overdraft of $59,034.21, whereof $50,000 was payable by Bater under his initial contract with Kare, so that Bater's estate claimed indemnity from Kare for his share of the difference of $9,034.21.

Not so, said Cartwright (then) J. The bank never did call on Kare under his guarantee, and in any event, Kare having sold out his interest in the business, settlement of the bank's debt did not bring any benefit to him, so that, p. 211, "From the date of Kare's withdrawal, as between Bater and Kare, the whole benefit resulting from the suretyship was Bater's." And, p. 212 "The rule that the one who gets the whole benefit must bear the whole burden is equally applicable in equity."

That is not what occurred in the instant case where, throughout, the defendant was a shareholder in the debtor company, and through the efforts of those who remained with the ship his own guarantee to International Harvester was liquidated. The equities here, with respect, are not at all equivalent to those considered in *Bater*.

• • •

Judgment for plaintiff.

NOTES

1) The general rule is that a continuing guarantee of future advances will be interpreted as being of unlimited duration. However, certain guarantees are limited in time even if there is no express statement in the guarantee contract to this effect. Clearly, fidelity guarantees will normally be viewed as being limited to the current principal's employment where a term contract for employment is involved, or to the period for which an office holder remains in office. What would be the result where, although at the time the contract was executed a single term was contemplated, the term was renewed several times and the liability arises during one of the subsequent terms?

2) Where a guarantee covers the liability of the principal during a specified period, it is important to determine whether the guarantee covers only liabilities accruing during that

period or whether it extends to liabilities which arise after the period ends as a result of transactions entered into during the period.

3) Section 19 of the Partnership Act, RSO 1990, c. P.5 provides as follows:

19. A continuing guaranty or cautionary obligation given either to a firm or to a third person in respect of the transactions of a firm is, in the absence of agreement to the contrary, revoked as to future transactions by any change in the constitution of the firm to which, or of which, the guaranty or obligation was given.

Since the basic rule of the section is merely declaratory of the common law, it applies as well to an incorporated partnership and a sole proprietorship. See *Canfor Ltd. v. Carpet Centre* (1980), 26 Nfld. & PEIR 343 (Nfld. TD).

4) Death or incapacity due to insanity of the surety does not necessarily terminate liability under a continuing guarantee. However, when the creditor receives notice of the death or insanity, there is no further liability unless the guarantee contract provides otherwise. See *Toronto Dominion Bank v. Brot*, [1958] OR 152 (HC); *Bradford Old Bank v. Sutcliffe*, [1918] 2 KB 833 (CA).

5) What should be the effect of death or insanity of a co-surety (communicated to the creditor) on the future liability of the other surety under a continuing guarantee? Release of one of a number of joint or joint and severable co-sureties by the creditor results in the release of the other co-sureties unless the creditor has reserved its rights against the co-sureties. See *Re EWA Ltd.*, [1901] 2 KB 642 (CA).

Royal Bank v. Girgulis
[1979] 3 WWR 451 (Sask. CA)

BROWNRIDGE JA (for the court): This is an appeal from the judgment of Noble J [[1977] 6 WWR 439] in which he allowed the plaintiff's claim against the defendant for the sum of $10,000 and interest at 8 per cent based upon a guarantee in writing dated 23rd August 1968.

On that date the defendant, while in the main office branch of the plaintiff, came upon a casual acquaintance by the name of Dr. D. Hiliopoulos, whom he had met at church and whom he knew to live in a small place outside Minot, North Dakota. A conversation ensued in which Hiliopoulos told the defendant that he would like to buy $10,000 in convertible bonds based on a tip he had received from a friend in Minneapolis, Minnesota but he did not have the money. The defendant suggested that Hiliopoulos ask the bank to loan him the money and for this purpose took him to the counter and asked to see the manager. Since he was out, one of the assistant managers waited on them. The defendant introduced the prospective customer to the assistant manager and explained that he wished to borrow $10,000 to purchase convertible bonds but the specific bonds that Dr. Hiliopoulos had in mind were not mentioned. As a result the defendant was asked to and did, in fact, sign a guarantee which obligated him to repay the plaintiff if the borrower defaulted up to the limit of $10,000 and interest at 8 per cent per annum.

The loan was to be repaid by payment of $5,000 on 1st September 1969, and the balance by 1st March 1970. Dr. Hiliopoulos was to lodge the convertible bonds with the plaintiff as security. He did not do so and he eventually defaulted on the loan. In the meantime, he disappeared and neither the bank nor Mr. Girgulis was able to find him because he had apparently moved from his residence in Crosby, North Dakota, where he lived at the time the loan was made. Three defences were raised before the learned trial judge.

The first submission was that because of the inequality of the bargaining power as between the plaintiff and the defendant there was a duty cast upon the plaintiff to fully explain the terms of the guarantee or insist that the defendant get independent advice. This was not done and, therefore, the defendant argued that the transaction was unconscionable and he relied upon such cases as *Cymbaluk v. Lewicki*, [1973] 3 WWR 169 (BC); *McKenzie v. Bank of Montreal* (1976), 12 OR (2d) 719, 70 DLR (3d) 113 (CA); and *Lloyds Bank v. Bundy*, [1951] QB 326, [1974] 3 All ER 757 (CA).

Noble J held that these cases were clearly distinguishable from the case at bar. Although Mr. Girgulis is 83 years old and came from his native Greece in 1912, with a public school education and limited understanding of the English language, he has been a highly successful businessman, particularly with investments, and had for many years been in almost daily contact with this branch of the Royal Bank of Canada. He is indebted to the said bank for about $235,000 for which the bank is holding securities valued at approximately $300,000. The learned trial judge said [p. 444]:

... there is no evidence that the defendant was induced or influenced into signing the guarantee form by either the words or actions of the bank's officers. While it is true that he did not understand all the words of the form, it is clear from the evidence that he understood the nature of the guarantee document because he had done it many times before.

I do not believe the defendant "understood the nature of the guarantee document because he had done it many times before." Mr. Girgulis said this was the first time he had ever seen the "Guarantee and Postponement of Claim" form, Ex. P.1, which he was asked to sign in this case. He said that he was used to signing or endorsing a note which is quite different from the sweeping terms of this guarantee, which covers all debts and liabilities, present or future, direct or indirect, absolute or contingent, matured or not, at any time owing by Dr. Hiliopoulos and permitting the bank to grant time, renewals, extensions, etc., all without limiting or lessening the liability of Mr. Girgulis.

Mr. Girgulis has a limited understanding of the English language and it is not disputed that the form was neither read nor explained to him. Indeed, the whole transaction took only about three minutes. I am satisfied that if he had fully understood the document he never would have signed it.

It is clear that Mr. Girgulis understood and appreciated that he was guaranteeing the loan to Dr. Hiliopoulos but he thought he was being asked to guarantee the loan on an entirely different basis from that set out in Ex. P.1. He believed that it was a single transaction—for the purpose of enabling Dr. Hiliopoulos to buy $10,000 of convertible bonds which were to be lodged with the bank as security. That, to my mind, is something quite different from being asked to sign a continuing guarantee in the form of Ex. P.1 which enabled Dr. Hillopoulos to carry on a continuing investment Program and enabled the bank to default in taking the required security.

Mr. Girgulis has been a valued customer of the bank since 1912, and the uncontradicted evidence is that he trusted the bank completely. He simply signed Ex. P.1 as directed by the bank officer without question and without reading it or understanding its implications. As I have said, that document contemplated an entirely different agreement between the parties than actually existed according to the evidence of Girgulis, the terms of the loan agreement as shown by the bank's "Character File Card," Ex. D.1, and as found by the learned trial judge. Under these circumstances there may well be good reason to infer that the bank officer knew of Mr. Girgulis' mistake, or innocently misrepresented the facts to induce his signature, thus satisfying all of the elements of unilateral mistake as in *Royal Bank v. Hale* (1961), 30 DLR (2d) 138 (BC), and *Royal Bank of Can. v. Oram*, [1978] 1 WWR 564 (BCSC). However, I prefer to rest this judgment on another ground, as hereinafter explained.

The second submission made to the learned trial judge was that the plaintiff's officials, in dealing with the defendant at the time the guarantee was executed, failed to disclose material facts to the defendant, namely, that they did not know the borrower, Dr. Hiliopoulos; and, secondly, that the defendant would be required to pay, should the borrower default. It was argued that this non-disclosure was an implied misrepresentation which entitled the defendant to repudiate the contract. On this point, counsel relied upon *Niagara Dist Fruit Growers Stock Co. v. Stewart* (1896), 26 SCR 629; *Davies v. London & Prov. Ins. Co.* (1878), 8 Ch. 469; and *MacKenzie v. Royal Bank*, [1934] AC 468, [1934] 2 WWR 620, [1934] 4 DLR 1 (PC).

These cases hold that a contract of guarantee, like any other contract, is liable to be avoided if induced by material misrepresentation of an existing fact, even if made innocently. Here, the learned trial judge found no evidence to suggest that the plaintiff made any such representations or implied representations to the defendant and, therefore, the submission was rejected. With the exception of the form of the guarantee document, I am in agreement with his finding on that point.

The third submission made below was that it was a condition precedent to the guarantee being used by the plaintiff bank that the convertible bonds to be purchased with the loan would be lodged by Dr. Hiliopoulos with the plaintiff as security and, since they were not, the condition failed and the guarantee is unenforceable. Here counsel relied upon *Standard Bank v. McCrossan*, 60 SCR 655, [1920] 3 WWR 846, 55 DLR 238; and *Molsons Bank v. Cranston* (1918), 44 OLR 58, 45 DLR 316 (CA).

In rejecting this defence, the learned trial judge said [p. 446]:

However the evidence does not suggest, even by inference, that the plaintiff would undertake to see that the securities were purchased and lodged before the guarantee would take. Even the defendant admits there was no discussion whatsoever with the officer of the bank at the time the guarantee document was signed. All the evidence indicates is that the convertible bonds would be lodged as security for the loan to Dr. Hiliopoulos. There is a suggestion in the evidence that the convertible bonds were not even discussed until after the guarantee was signed, and the plaintiff bank's understanding was only that the bonds would be lodged as security when issued.

The learned trial judge said that the defendant may well have thought that the bank would advance the moneys through the agency which was selling the convertible bonds on behalf of Dr. Hiliopoulos and have them sent directly to the bank to be held as security because this was the method the bank always used with the defendant when he borrowed from them to buy securities. He also said that "there was no meeting of the minds as between the defendant and the plaintiff's officers to the effect that the guarantee was conditional" [p. 447].

Although Noble J held that the purchase and deposit of the bonds with the bank was not a condition precedent to the validity of the guarantee, he did find that [p. 442]: "The terms of the loan were that Dr. Hiliopoulos was to lodge the convertible bonds with the plaintiff as security." There is no doubt that the deposit of the bonds with the bank was a term of the loan agreement and that the loan was made "for the purchase of the above bonds."

Ex. D.1, from the bank records shows the original entry:

August 23, 1968. New $10,000. Demand 8%—total loans $10,000. Collateral Security:—
Guarantee, Form 812 in the amount of $10,000. signed by W.H. Girgulis. (To be lodged $10,000. in convertible bonds when issued.) This gentleman was introduced to us by our valued client, W.H. Girgulis and the loan was made, at his request, *for the purchase of the above bonds.* A $5,000. reduction will be provided on September 1, 1969 and full liquidation by March 1, 1970.

(The italics are mine.)

Instead of making sure that the said bonds were deposited as security, the bank continued to deal with Dr. Hiliopoulos without them and even granted further loans, as the entry on Ex. D.1, shows:

February 6, 1969. New demand $4,000. 8¼%. Total loans $14,000. Collateral Security: Guarantee Forms 812 in the amount of $10,000. signed by W.H. Girgulis. *Stocks and/or bonds* with of p.m.v. of $10,000. New funds granted for investment purposes. In addition to the above, the doctor has a loan of $5,500. at our Albert & 25th Branch covered by marketable securities to be delivered by Richardson's.

(The italics are mine.)

Mr. Girgulis never agreed to guarantee any advance of new funds to enable Dr. Hiliopoulos to carry on a continuing investment program and the bank officer who dealt with Mr. Girgulis was not called to challenge his evidence.

On behalf of the plaintiff, Mr. Steranka testified that the bank never did receive the bonds which were to be deposited as security by Dr. Hiliopoulos but instead on 17th April 1969 received from him 500 shares of Riley Data which had a value of $7,500. Thus, the next entry on Ex. D.1 is as follows:

May 2, 1969. Loans $14,000. Collateral Security: Form 812, Guarantee for $10,000. signed by W.H. Girgulis, 500 shares Riley Data, p.m.v. $7,500.

Mr. Steranka was asked on his examination for discovery about the entry on 6th February 1969 as to stocks and/or bonds with a prime market value of $10,000. Counsel undertook to provide an answer to this question, which he did at the trial in the following words:

With respect to the character card notation on February 6, 1969 that we are holding stocks and/or bonds with prime market value of $10,000, the bank has searched all its records and confirmed that there was no other security held on that date, and they therefore assumed that the $10,000 mentioned relates to the Riley Data shares which were forthcoming at that time, although same were not received until April 17, 1969.

In 18 Hals. (3d) 506, para. 926, it is stated:

Any departure by the creditor from his contract with the surety without the surety's consent, whether it be from the express terms of the guarantee itself or from the embodied terms of the principal contract, which is not obviously and without inquiry quite unsubstantial, will discharge the surety from liability whether it injures him or not, for it constitutes an alteration in the surety's obligations.

From the bank's own documents it is clear that on or about 6th February 1969, the bank made a new agreement with Dr. Hiliopoulos which altered the original loan agreement:

(1) by making a new advance to Dr. Hiliopoulos of $4,000 at a new interest rate of 8 1/4%;

(2) by expressly or impliedly waiving the deposit of $10,000 of convertible bonds which, under the terms of the original loan agreement, were to be deposited as security; and

(3) by expressly or impliedly agreeing to accept shares of stock instead of the convertible bonds.

The said shares of stock were, as early as 2nd May 1969, worth only $7,500 and at the time of the trial were worth only $400.

All of these items constitute a substantial departure by the creditor from its contract with the surety.

These alterations in the original agreement were made by the bank without the knowledge or consent of the defendant and the result is that he, as surety, is discharged. *In Holland-Can. Mtge. Co. v. Hutchings; Holland-Can. Mtge. Co. v. Royal Trust Co.,* [1936] SCR 165 at 172, [1936] 2 DLR 481, Davis J, on behalf of the court, said:

A surety has always been a favoured creditor in the eyes of the law. His obligation is strictly examined and strictly enforced. "It must always be recollected," said Lord Westbury in *Blest v. Brown* (1862), 4 De GF & J 367 at 376, 45 ER 1225 (LC), ... "in what manner a surety is bound. You bind him to the letter of his engagement. Beyond the proper interpretation of that engagement you have no hold upon him. He receives no benefit and no consideration. He is bound, therefore, merely according to the proper meaning and effect of the written engagement that he entered into. If that written engagement is altered in a single line, no matter whether it be altered for his benefit, no matter whether the alteration be innocently made, he has a right to say, 'The contract is no longer that for which I engaged to be surety: you have put an end to the contract that I guaranteed, and my obligation, therefore, is at an end.'"

Apart from an express stipulation to the contrary, where the change is in respect of a matter that cannot "plainly be seen without inquiry to be unsubstantial or necessarily beneficial to the surety," to use the language of Rowlatt, The Law of Principal and Surety, 2nd ed. (1926) p. 102, the surety, if he has not consented to remain liable notwithstanding the alteration, will be discharged whether he is in fact prejudiced or not. *Holme v. Brunskill* (1878), 3 QBD 495 (CA).

This case is also authority for the proposition that the guarantee and postponement of claim on which the bank relies may be effective as to extending the time for payment to Dr.

Hiliopoulos and still be binding upon the surety, but it is wholly ineffective in attempting to bind Mr. Girgulis on the substantial changes made by the bank on the original agreement.

In *Rose v. Afterberger*, [1970] 1 OR 547 at 552, 9 DLR (3d) 42 (CA), Laskin JA (as he then was) discussed three different situations and, in my opinion, the present case falls within the second group, namely, cases in which the contract of guarantee is made on the footing that certain security, by whomever provided, is to be taken and kept by the creditor for the surety's benefit but there is default by the creditor uncomplying with this condition. This is considered a breach of the very terms on which the surety agreed to give the guarantee and the result is that the surety is discharged.

The third situation is where security is taken at the time of or after the guarantee but without it being a condition of the guarantee, and the creditor improperly disposes of the security. In such cases, the surety cannot be relieved beyond the value of the security lost to him. This was submitted by counsel for the appellant as an alternative argument. However, on the facts of the present case, the security, which was to have been worth $10,000, is now worth only $400, so that for all practical purposes the surety lost the benefit of the entire security.

Appeal allowed.

Direct Leasing Limited v. Chu
[1976] 6 WWR 587 (BCSC)

MURRAY J: The plaintiff in this action is an Ontario corporation registered as an extra-provincial corporation in British Columbia. It sues the three defendants as guarantors of three leases covering a number of floating docks on the Fraser River. All of the contracts are identical in form and amount and all of the guarantees are identical except as to the dates on which they were executed. The lessees in each contract were corporations named LaRonde Leasing Ltd. and Captain's Cove Marina Ltd. The latter corporation is in bankruptcy.

Each of the three leases was for a term of 84 months and the schedule of payments in each case called for a payment of $3,900 on 1st December 1973, followed by six annual payments of $11,970 and a final payment of $7,980 on 1st April 1980. On the back of each contract were a number of printed terms of which the following are of importance:

• • •

I set out immediately hereunder a copy of one of the guarantees which form the subject matter of this action:

This is the personal guarantee of DODD QUAN CHU for the Lease Agreement dated—November 15, 1973.

For valuable consideration, the receipt whereof is hereby acknowledged the undersigned Guarantor hereby unconditionally guarantees full and absolute performance of the within contract, and particularly all payments to be made thereunder and without restricting the generality of the foregoing, should the Lessee default in any payments by the Lessee to be made to the Lessor, the Guarantor undertakes and agrees to make such payments forthwith upon demand.

IN WITNESS WHEREOF THE GUARANTOR HAS EXECUTED THIS GUARANTEE THIS 15th DAY OF November 1973.

WITNESS   GUARANTOR

                                              JAMES F. RICHARDSON
                                              BARRISTER & SOLICITOR
                                              26th FLOOR, TORONTO-DOMINION BANK TOWER
                                              700 WEST GEORGIA ST.
                                              VANCOUVER, BC

At the time the leases and guarantees were executed the docks had already been constructed at the behest of the lessees and concurrently with the execution of the leases and guarantees the plaintiff acquired title to the docks from the manufacturer. The plaintiff paid the manufacturer a total of $150,000 for the three docks.

The relationship of the defendants to the lessees is of considerable importance in this case. LaRonde Leasing Ltd. owned two-thirds of the issued shares of Captain's Cove Marina Ltd. The defendants each owned 25 per cent of the issued shares of LaRonde Leasing Ltd. The defendant Allan was a director of, and the president of, LaRonde Leasing Ltd. The defendant Chu was a director of LaRonde Leasing Ltd. and the defendant Gray was an officer and director of that company. The defendants Gray and Allan were also shareholders in and officers and directors of Captain's Cove Marina Ltd.

The lessees paid the rental payments due under the leases in December 1973. When the time came for payment of the annual instalments due on 1st April 1974, the lessees did not make the payments on the due date. The failure to make these payments led to certain conversations between one Derrick Ellis, representing the plaintiff, and the defendants Gray and Allan. The defendant Chu was not a party to the discussions and alleges that, as a result of these conversations, an agreement was reached between the plaintiff and the lessees which varied the lease and accordingly as such variation took place without his consent he was discharged from his liability under his guarantee.

• • •

The contention of the defendant Chu is that the alleged agreement constitutes a variation of the interest rate set forth in para. 18 of the leases and not having consented to this variation he is discharged.

I find on the evidence that there was an agreement to vary the interest rate but in the circumstances of this case I also find that the defendant Chu is not discharged. In making this finding I refer to the decision of Hawkins J in the case of *York City and County Banking Co. v. Bainbridge* (1880), 43 LT 732, where he says at p. 734:

It was next contended that the effect of the transaction in March 1875 was to give time to the principal debtor without the assent of the surety. I do not adopt that view. It is quite true the rate of interest was increased but there was no agreement to allow any specified time nor indeed any time at all to the debtor for payment. The agreement was to pay 6 per cent. if the bank forbore to press, but there was no moment of time when they might not have sued him upon the note. It is true there was abstinence, but it was mere abstinence as favour, not as obligation, and for that simple voluntary abstinence it was that the increased rate of interest was paid.

This case was followed and approved by the Appeal Division of the Nova Scotia Supreme Court in the case of *Oxner v. Bank of Montreal* (1967), 61 DLR (2d) 599, affirmed without written reasons 70 DLR (2d) 719n (Can.).

When the annual payments for the year 1975 came due on 1st April of that year they were not paid and further discussions were held between Ellis and the defendants Gray and Allan representing the lessees. The defendant Chu alleges that these discussions led to an agreed variation of the leases which discharged him. On the basis of the testimony of the witness Ellis I find that at some time after 1st April: 1975 and prior to 9th July, 1975 the plaintiff and the lessees entered into an agreement whereby the plaintiff agreed to accept a minimum of $1,500 per week or whatever sum the lessees could collect from boat owners who were mooring to the docks (whichever sum was the greater) until the marina was sold and the whole balance owing was paid off. I further find that there is no evidence that the defendant Chu knew of or consented to this variation of the leases. I refer in this connection to the judgment of Bull JA in *Bausch & Lomb Optical Co. Ltd. v. Moresby Developments Ltd.,* [1975] 3 WWR 324, 52 DLR (3d) 622 (BCCA), where he says at pp. 329-30:

A helpful and, in my opinion, accurate view of the relevant law is contained in the following passages from the old textbook De Colyar, Law of Guarantees, 1887, at p. 278, as follows:

> A variation of the terms of the original contract made between the principal debtor and the creditor will, generally speaking, discharge the surety. And this is the case, whether such variation be, first, of the original agreement between the principal debtor and the creditor; or, secondly, of the original agreement between the surety and the creditor ...
>
> There are two states of facts under which a surety is discharged by a variation of the contract between the principal debtor and the creditor. For, 1st, any material variation of the terms of the contract between the creditor and the principal debtor will always discharge the surety; and 2ndly, a variation of those terms which is not material, will also discharge the surety if it clearly appears that he became surety on the faith of the original contract, or if he has made these terms part of his own contract. And if notice were given to the surety of the terms of the contract between the creditor and the principal debtor, and after such notice he executed the guarantee, he is held to have become surety on the faith of the original agreement. And where the surety has made the terms of the original contract between the creditor and the principal debtor part of his own contract, any variation will discharge the surety, because it amounts to a breach of the creditor's contract with the surety and not merely to a breach of the creditor's contract with the principal debtor.

• • •

I find that the defendant Chu was discharged. The action against him is dismissed with costs.

Action dismissed.

NOTES

1) A material variation is one that alters the business effect of the relationship in such as way as to affect the risk. The general approach is that alterations to the contract between the principal debtor and the creditor are presumed to be material unless it is established by the plaintiff that their result is insubstantial or beneficial to the surety. See *Holme v. Brunskill* (1878), 3 QBD 495; *Bell v. National Forest Products Ltd.* (1964), 47 WWR 449 (BCSC). A risk of prejudice to the surety is enough without proof of actual prejudice. *Pioneer Trust Co. v. 220263*, [1989] 4 WWR 668 (Alta. CA).

2) Should the material variation rule apply where the surety agreed to act as a surety at a time when she only had a vague idea of the terms of the contract under which the obligation being guaranteed would arise or where the guarantee is given in connection with "general dealings" between the principal debtor and the creditor? Should a material alteration that turns out to be beneficial to the surety (although this may not have been apparent at the time it was made) result in discharge of the surety?

3) A very common type of variation in the contractual relationship between the principal debtor and the creditor is the creditor giving to the principal debtor extra time to discharge the obligation. Generally speaking, an enforceable agreement, made after the principal debtor's liability arises, to give additional time to the debtor to perform is treated as a material alteration and discharges the surety without proof that the surety has been prejudiced. Why should this be the case? How does it affect the risk the surety has assumed? However, as noted in the *Direct Leasing* case, *supra,* mere delay on the part of the creditor to pursue his or her rights against the principal debtor or a non-contractual indulgence or forbearance does not have this result. See *Pittsburgh-Westmorland Coal Co. v. Jamieson* (1910), 16 OWR 758 (HC), aff'd (1910), 17 OWR 61 (CA).

4) Legislation in some provinces (not including Ontario) has addressed the effect of giving time to the debtor without the consent of the surety. To what extent does this legislation modify or merely codify the common law? For example, paragraph 18 of s. 45 of the Saskatchewan Queen's Bench Court Act, RSS 1978, c. Q-1 provides:

(18) Giving time to a principal debtor, or dealing with or altering the security held by the principal creditor, shall not of itself discharge a surety or guarantor; in such cases a surety or guarantor shall be entitled to set up such giving of time or dealing with or alteration of the security as a defence, but the same shall be allowed insofar only as it shall be shown that the surety has thereby been prejudiced.

See also Law Mercantile Amendment Act, RSM 1987, c. M120, s. 4.

5) Difficult conceptual issues arise where the creditor gives to the debtor extra time to pay and, at the same time, reserves his or her rights against the surety. In *Latcham v. Canadian Imperial Bank of Commerce* (1988), 50 DLR (4th) 724 (Ont. HC), Fitzpatrick J, in *obiter dicta,* stated that it was contrary to fundamental principles of the law of suretyship to hold that, in these circumstances, the surety is not discharged. See *Mahamt Singh v. U Ba Yi*, [1939] AC 601 (PC). The reservation, if effective, converts the promise of the creditor to give the extra time to pay into a covenant not to sue, which is not a binding release. The principal debtor knows that the surety may be called upon to pay and, when payment is made, may well exercise his rights to recover from the principal debtor. Consequently, the principal debtor gains no legal benefit from the creditor's release. The

reservation need not be communicated to the surety. See *Re Armitage, ex parte Good* (1877), 5 Ch. D 46 (CA).

What happens when the guarantee agreement gives the creditor the right to discharge the debtor without affecting the surety's obligations and the creditor discharges the principal debtor entirely? (See, e.g., the clause designed for this purpose in the Bank of Montreal guarantee agreement set out in part in *Bauer v. Bank of Montreal* (1980), 110 DLR (3d) 424 (SCC), *infra.*) Is the surety released? Does the surety cease to be a guarantor? Has the surety implicitly waived his or her right of indemnification against the principal debtor?

If the right of identification is not implicitly waived, what is the position of the principal debtor? If she has contracted for a discharge from the creditor, does the reservation not make the contract illusory since the surety, when required to pay the creditor, can claim back against the principal debtor? See *Commercial Bank of Tasmania v. Jones*, [1893] AC 313 (PC) and comments on this decision in *Perry v. National Provincial Bank*, [1910] 1 Ch. 464 (CA).

6) A breach by the creditor of the contract between the creditor and the principal debtor discharges the surety only to the extent that the surety's rights of subrogation under the guarantee contract are affected. See *Pax Management Ltd. v. Canadian Imperial Bank of Commerce*, [1992] 6 WWR 289 (SCC).

Bauer v. Bank of Montreal
(1980), 110 DLR (3d) 424 (SCC)

McINTYRE J (for the court): This appeal raises the question of the effect upon the liability of a guarantor to the creditor when the creditor, by reason of its dealing with security for the debt, has rendered it impossible to deliver the security to the guarantor upon the guarantor paying the debt.

Bauer, defendant at trial and appellant in this Court, hereinafter referred to as the guarantor, was in March of 1971, the principal officer and major shareholder of a company known as Grey Electronics Supply Limited, hereinafter referred to as the company. The company was a customer of the respondent bank. The bank was prepared to advance or to continue to allow the company an operating credit of up to $50,000 upon receiving an assignment of the company's book accounts and the guarantee of the indebtedness by the guarantor. The guarantee was signed on the bank's standard form on March 29, 1971, and the assignment of book accounts was executed later on April 7, 1971. Despite the difference in date, it is common ground that the two dispositions formed part of the same transaction. In December of 1971, the guarantor sold his interest in the company to one David Walling. The bank would not, however, release him from his liability under the guarantee and it remained in effect. The company ran into serious difficulty and in August of 1974, it went into bankruptcy. The amount then owing by the company to the bank came to $36,165.73. In the bankruptcy proceedings, the bank claimed preference relying upon its assignment of book accounts. The trustee, however, contested this claim successfully (see *Re Grey Electronics Supply Ltd.* (1974), 52 DLR (3d) 532, 6 OR (2d) 308, 20 CBR (NS) 88 (SC)) on the basis that the assignment had not been registered by the bank. The bank had attempted to register and in fact had done so but in the wrong county. The result of this failure, which was entirely the responsibility of the bank, was that the assignment was held to be void against the trustee. The assigned accounts, for whatever value they possessed, became available to general creditors and were of little if any value to the guarantor in reducing his obligation or recouping his loss under the guarantee. At trial before Galligan J, the bank's action was dismissed [76 DLR (3d) 636, 15 OR (2d) 746, 25 CBR (NS) 1931]. The trial Judge held [p. 639] that a creditor was under an obligation to safeguard "securities given to him in the same condition as when the guarantee was given and if registration is necessary to make the security valid and effective, then the creditor must properly register the securities." He went on to hold that where a creditor fails to preserve the security, and it therefore became unavailable for delivery to the guarantor upon payment of the debt, the guarantor would be relieved wholly or partially from his liability depending on the extent of the injury suffered. He held as well that since the bank had not met the onus of showing to what extent the guarantor was prejudiced by the loss of the accounts, the guarantor was entitled to be fully discharged. On appeal by the bank, the Court of Appeal [85 DLR (3d) 752, 19 OR (2d) 425, 28 CBR (NS) 207] per Arnup JA, agreed with the trial Judge upon his disposition of the case as it was presented to him but allowed the appeal on a new point not raised or argued at trial.

As has been stated earlier, the guarantee was on the bank's standard form which is used regularly for this purpose. It provided for a continuing guarantee by the guarantor of all indebtedness of the company to the bank from time to time owing up to $50,000 and provided as well:

It is further agreed that said bank, without exonerating in whole or in part the undersigned, or any of them (if more than one), may grant time, renewals, extensions, indulgences, releases and discharges to, may take securities from and give the same and any or all existing securities up to, may abstain from taking securities from, or from perfecting securities of ... the customer.

The inclusion of this provision in the guarantee raised the only point considered of significance in the Court of Appeal and Arnup JA for the Court dealt with it in these words [p. 755]:

In the circumstances of this case, the words "perfecting securities" in the guarantee included registration of the assignment of book debts in the right place. The guarantee contains in express terms an agreement by the signatory, with the bank that the bank may abstain from perfecting securities without exonerating in whole or in part the guarantor. In our view, this language precisely covers the situation that arose, and accordingly it was not open to the defendant to assert, by way of defence, the alleged negligent dealing with the securities by the bank.

The duty of a creditor holding security for the performance of the obligations of a debtor or a surety is clearly established. The creditor, in the absence of agreement to the contrary with the debtor or the surety, must protect and preserve the security and be in a position, unless excused by other agreement, to return or reassign the security to the debtor or surety on repayment of the debt. The principle was aptly stated in *Traders Finance Corp. Ltd. v. Halverson* (1968), 2 DLR (3d) 666 (BCCA) at p. 672, by Bull JA, where he collected various authorities on the point. As well Robertson CJO, in *Household Finance Corp. Ltd. v. Foster et al.*, [1949] 1 DLR 840, [1949] OR 123 (Ont. CA), reviewed several authorities on the point at p. 845 DLR, pp. 132-3 OR, after having said at DLR *loc. cit.*, p. 131 OR, regarding the position of an endorser of a note who had no contract with the payee:

There was no contractual relationship between them with respect to the mortgage security given the appellant by the Fosters, the principal debtors. Such right or interest as the respondents had in that security rested, not upon contract, but on the rule of equity by which, upon payment of the debt, the surety is entitled to benefit of every security held by the creditor, even though neither contracted for by the surety, nor known to him, and even though not existing until after the surety became bound.

There are other authorities and writings to the same effect: see *Jamesway v. Krug* (1932), 41 OWN 146 (Ont. HC); *Bryans v. Peterson* (1920), 53 DLR 429, 47 OLR 298 (CA), as well as 28 Hals., 4th ed., p. 152, para. 280 *et seq.*, and *Snell's Principles of Equity*, 27th ed. (1973), pp. 462-3. It was upon a recognition of this principle, and without having the clause above-quoted referred to him, that Gailigan J exonerated the guarantor at trial.

Despite this rule, it is open to the parties to make their own arrangements, and a surety is competent to contract himself out of the protection of the equitable rule requiring preservation of his security. If authority is needed for such a proposition, it may be found in *Rose v. Aftenberger et al.* (1969), 9 DLR (3d) 42 at p. 47, [1970] 1 OR 547 (CA) at p. 552, where Laskin JA, as he then was, speaking for the Ontario Court of Appeal, said:

The law is that sureties are entitled to the benefits of any security taken by a creditor who has their promise to pay the debt of the principal obligor, unless the sureties have contracted them-selves out of this right or are estopped from asserting it. In this connection, it is immaterial when the security was taken or whether the guarantor knew of it at the time.

See as well Holden, *Securities for Banker's Advances*, 2nd ed., p. 197 *et seq.*, where the question is discussed and reference is made to *Perry v. National Provincial Bank of England*, [1910] 1 Ch. 464 (CA). It was upon this basis that the Court of Appeal allowed the appeal and imposed liability on the guarantor.

In this Court, the appellant argued several points. In summary, his argument embraced four principal propositions. He contended in the first place that the clause in the guarantee relied upon by the Court of Appeal was an exemption or exclusion clause, and as such it should be construed *contra proferentem,* that is, against the bank whose standard printed form embodied the guarantee. He then contended that the bank could not rely on the clause because it was unusual, onerous, and unreasonable.

• • •

The clause in question is not an exemption clause in my opinion. It is no more than a provision which varies the ordinary terms of a guarantee and which gives the bank the right to deal with security provided by the debtor with greater freedom than would be otherwise permissible. This is a provision by which the guarantor has contracted himself out of the equitable right he would have possessed in the absence of this term and he has, as a term of the contract between the bank and himself, given the bank affirmative rights in this regard. That a guarantor in this situation is fully competent to so dispose of his affairs is beyond question: see the words of Laskin JA, as he then was, in *Rose v. Aftenberger*, *supra*, quoted above and *Perry v. National Provincial Bank of England, supra,* particularly the words of Cozens-Hardy MR, at p. 471. The clause in question here is just such a provision as that referred to in the *Perry* case. It must be construed according to the general rules of construction and the appellant may not, in my view, call in aid any special rules applicable in an approach to an exemption clause.

When the whole guarantee is examined, it becomes clear at once that the consideration for the guarantee was the bank's continuation of the line of credit it had advanced to the company. As part of the transaction, the company had agreed to give and had given the assignment of book debts. The clause in question gave the bank powers which it could exercise or not as it chose in dealing with that security. The principal bone of contention here turned on the words permitting the bank to abstain from perfecting or registering securities. "Abstain" meant, it was said, to voluntarily or knowingly refrain from registration. The bank had then not abstained from registration for it had tried unsuccessfully to do so and had negligently failed. Therefore, it was said that upon a strict construction of the clause in question it had not brought itself within its terms and the guarantee should be void. I am not able to accept this argument. I do not consider that the reason or motive for the bank's non-registration alters the case. The bank was under a duty not to damage the position of the guarantor or act to his prejudice beyond the terms of the agreement but the clause is clear in that it provides that a failure to perfect security or to register will not impair the bank's position. This ground of appeal must fail.

To the argument that the clause was onerous and unreasonable and that the bank could not rely upon it, various arguments were advanced. It was stressed that the guarantee was on a standard bank form, that it was drawn by a party seeking to rely upon the clause, that there was inequality between the parties, and that the clause was unusual in nature. I can find no merit in this position. While it is, of course, true that the guarantee was on the bank's standard form, it is difficult to say that the clause was unusual. It was the one the bank always used and the guarantor, an experienced businessman, admitted that he had signed three previous guarantees to the bank on the same form and that he knew the general scope and purpose of the guarantee and what it would require of him. The guarantor was a customer of the bank; he had been for some years. While I suppose it could be said that there is always a degree of inequality between borrower and lender, banker and guarantor, there was no such inequality here that would void the arrangements. Nor, in my opinion, can it be said that there was any unreasonableness in the arrangement. This contract concluded between the bank and the guarantor was an ordinary commercial transaction carried out between the bank and an experienced businessman in the same manner and upon the same terms as are employed daily in such matters. The contract created no unusual or onerous burden in ordinary commercial terms. I can find no merit in this argument.

Appeal dismissed.

First City Capital Ltd v. Hall
(1993), 99 DLR (4th) 435 (Ont. CA)

ABELLA JA (for the court): This is an appeal by the defendant, Karen Hall, from a judgment awarding First City Capital Ltd. ("FCC") $207,313.16, pursuant to Hall's general guarantee.

Hall and the second defendant at trial, Shadde de Haan, were the sole shareholders and officers of Karsha Holdings Ltd. Between April, 1982 and December 1983, Karsha Holdings entered into seven leases of word processing equipment with FCC. Both Hall and de Haan executed personal guarantees in favour of FCC. In January, 1985, while the leases were in good standing, Hall sold her interest in Karsha Holdings to de Haan and resigned as an officer.

In June, 1985, all seven leases went into default. In the same month, Karsha Holdings defaulted under a security agreement held by the Royal Bank of Canada. Because FCC had failed to perfect five of the leases pursuant to the provisions of the Personal Property Security Act, RSO 1980, c. 375, as amended ("PPSA"), the Royal Bank claimed priority over FCC, and its receiver seized the equipment referred to in the leases.

FCC then sued Hall and de Haan on their guarantees for the amount owing under the seven leases as of June, 1985, namely, $108,758.37, plus annual interest at the rate of 24%.

The trial judge concluded that these were not true leases, but were conditional sale agreements and therefore subject to the requirements of the PPSA, a conclusion not disputed in this appeal. He described FCC as "asleep at the switch, and indeed negligent" [67 OR (2d) 12 at p. 19, 13 ACWS (3d) 276].

However, the trial judge went on to exonerate FCC based on the language of para. 1 of the guarantee, which states in part [at p. 15]:

Guarantor shall pay all the foregoing amounts and perform all of the foregoing terms, covenants and conditions notwithstanding that the Lease or any of the Other Agreements shall be void or voidable as against Lessee or any of the Lessee's creditors, including a trustee in bankruptcy of Lessee, by reason of any fact or circumstance including, without limiting the generality of the foregoing, failure by any persons to file any document or to take any other action to make the Lease or any of the Other Agreements enforceable in accordance with their respective terms.

This language, the trial judge held, relieved FCC from any duty to protect its security. In his words [at p. 16]:

The guarantor [Hall] having authorized or excused the guarantee for a failure to file any document or take any other action, in effect waived her right to insist in equity that ... [FCC] perfect the leases under the *Personal Property Security Act.*

In his view, para. 1 not only "authorized and condoned the failure of ... [FCC] to register the leases under the *Personal Property Security Act,*" it "precluded [Hall] from trying to assert a right to take over the payments under the lease" [at p. 17] pursuant to any subrogation rights found either in the guarantee or s. 2(1) of the Mercantile Law Amendment Act, RSO 1990, c. M.10.

While the trial judge recognized that FCC's failure to comply with the PPSA and register the leases prevented Hall from taking over the leases, he none the less held that any such failure "was authorized under para. 1 of the guarantee" and that, after the default on the part of the lessee, "the rights which [Hall] might otherwise have had were simply no longer available to her" [at p. 18].

The relevant section of the PPSA, RSO 1990, c. P10, states: [s. 20(1)] ... .

The duty of a secured creditor to protect the security is clear. As McIntyre J stated in *Bauer v. Bank of Montreal* (1980), 110 DLR (3d) 424 at p. 426, [1980] 2 SCR 102, 10 BLR 209:

The creditor, in the absence of agreement to the contrary with the debtor or the surety, must protect and preserve the security and be in a position, *unless excused by other agreement*, to return or reassign the security to the debtor or surety on repayment of the debt.

(Emphasis added.) In *Bauer*, the guarantee stated:

It is further agreed that said bank, without exonerating in whole or in part the undersigned, or any of them (if more than one), may grant time, renewals, extensions, indulgences, releases and discharges to, may take securities from and give the same and any or all existing securities up to, may abstain from taking securities from, *or from perfecting securities of* ... the customer.

(Emphasis added.)

There is no doubt that "it is open to the parties to make their own arrangements, and a surety is competent to contract ... out of the protection of the equitable rule requiring preservation of his security": *Bauer, supra*, at p. 427; see also *Central Trust Co. v. Friedman*, [1989] 5 WWR 533, (1989), 67 Alta. LR (2d) 325, 15 ACWS (3d) 438 (QB); *RoyNat Ltd. v. Denis* (1982), 139 DLR (3d) 265, 18 BLR 259, [1982] 5 WWR 509 (Sask. CA); affirming 17 Sask. R 437; *Federal Business Development Bank v. Clements* (1982), 43 AR 155, 24 Alta. LR (2d) 144 (QB, Master). But any such contracting out of the equitable principle that there is no claim on the guarantee if the security is unavailable, must be clear. I am not satisfied that such clarity exists in this case.

In the absence of clear language to the contrary, Hall cannot be presumed to have exonerated FCC from its duty as creditor to protect the security. As guarantor, she is therefore entitled to be discharged to the extent of any prejudice suffered through FCC's negligent breach of the duty as creditor to protect securities held in respect of a guaranteed debt: see K.P. McGuinness, *The Law of Guarantee* (Toronto: Carswell, 1986), at p. 208. Notwithstanding that it had the opportunity at trial to do so, FCC did not prove the extent to which the value of the guarantee exceeded the value of the security lost, an onus it bears as creditor. *Rose v. Aftenberger* (1969), 9 DLR (3d) 42, [1970] 1 OR 547 (CA).

At the appellate level, but not at trial, Hall argued that, unlike the guarantee in *Bauer*, *supra*, para. 1 of the guarantee does not provide a contracting out of the protection of the equitable rule requiring preservation of the security unless, in the words of the guarantee, the "Lease or any of the Other Agreements shall be *void or voidable* as against Lessee or any of the Lessee's creditors" (emphasis added). For ease of reference, the guarantee is repeated with the relevant phrases emphasized [at p. 15]:

Guarantor shall pay all the foregoing amounts and perform all of the foregoing terms, covenants and conditions notwithstanding that the Lease or any of the Other Agreements shall be void or voidable as against Lessee or any of the Lessee's creditors, including a trustee in bankruptcy of Lessee, *by reason of any fact or circumstance* including, without limiting the generality of the foregoing, failure by any person to file any document or to take any other action to make the Lease or any of the Other Agreements enforceable in accordance with their respective terms.

FCC, relying on the same paragraph, argued that these words plus those that follow, namely, "by reason of any fact or circumstance including ... failure by any person to file any document," cover the very contingency experienced by the parties in this situation.

The ordinary grammatical reading of para. 1 of the guarantee is that the guarantor is to pay all amounts and perform all covenants even if the lease is *void or voidable* for any reason. It does not say that the guarantor is to perform all of the terms, even if the lease is *ineffective* for any reason. "Void" and "voidable" have established meanings in the law of contract and the words which follow them must, on a plain reading, be held to modify them.

There was no evidence at trial that these leases were either void or voidable, as those terms are contractually understood; rather, because of FCC's negligence, they were ineffective as against the receiver appointed by the Royal Bank. The failure to perfect securities pursuant to the PPSA renders them subordinate to securities registered under the Act, not void or voidable.

In the alternative, in my view, para. 1 of the guarantee is, at the very least, ambiguous, rendering it amenable to the application of the contra proferentum doctrine which allows an interpretative approach unfavourable to the drafting party: see *Steel Co. of Canada Ltd. v. Allendale Mutual Insurance Co.*, [1977] ILR ¶1-831 (Ont. SC); *Consolidated-Bathurst Export Ltd. v. Mutual Boiler & Machinery Ins. Co.* (1979), 112 DLR (3d) 49, [1980] 1 SCR 888, [1980] ILR ¶-1176. In *Consolidated-Bathurst*, at p. 57, Estey J states:

... it is trite to say that where an ambiguity is found to exist in the terminology employed in the contract, such terminology shall be construed against ... the author.

• • •

If there is any doubt as to the meaning and scope of the excluding or limiting term, the ambiguity will be resolved against the party who has inserted it and who is now relying on it.

Based on the language of para. 1 of the guarantee which appears only to exempt FCC from the duty to protect the security if the lease is void or voidable, and based, in the alternative, on the application of the contra proferentum doctrine, I would allow the appeal, set aside the judgment appealed from, and dismiss the action as against the appellant.

Appeal allowed.

NOTES

1) See the Mercantile Law Amendment Act, *supra*, in the note following *Manu v. Shasha*.

2) What is the difference between an "exemption clause" (which is subject to the *contra proferentem* rule of interpretation applied in *First Capital City*) and what McIntyre J in *Bauer* described as "a provision that varies the ordinary terms of a guarantee and which

gives the bank the right to deal with security provided by the debtor with greater freedom than would be otherwise permissible"?

3) Can the obligations of a surety be affected by the creditor's failure to act in a "commercially reasonable manner" when realizing on its security under Part V of the Personal Property Security Act? To what extent has the ratio in the *Bauer* case been rejected by OPPSA ss. 59(3)-(5) [see section 56 of Acts based on CCPPSL Model]. See, further, Ziegel and Denomme, *The Ontario Personal Property Security Act* (Toronto: Canada Law Book Inc. 1994), 10-11, and Cuming and Wood, *British Columbia Personal Property Security Handbook* (Calgary: Carswell, 1993), 373-75.

4) What protection should a surety have when the security held by the creditor is in the form of shares which have a very volatile market value? Should the creditor be required to sell the shares so as to avoid loss through future possible reduction in value of the shares, or is it entitled to sell them where it is convenient to do so and claim against the surety although the value of the shares has fallen to the point that there is a significant unsecured debt? See *China & South Sea Bank Ltd. v. Tan Soon Gin*, [1990] 1 AC 536 (PC).

5) One of the creditor's rights to which the paying surety is subrogated is the right to bring action against a co-surety. However, the release of a co-surety, even one that is jointly liable to a creditor, does not discharge the other co-surety where the creditor reserves his or her rights against the other co-surety. Why should this be the case? See *Heller-Natofin (Western) Ltd. v. Bender* (1984), 28 Man. R (2d) 66 (QB), aff'd. (1984), 29 Man. R (2d) 315 (CA).

Moose Jaw Credit Union Limited v. Kjarsgarrd
[1982] 3 WWR 543 (Sask. QB)

HALVORSON J: A special case has been stated by the parties pursuant to R. 263 for the opinion of the court. The question concerns the enforceability of a personal guarantee in light of the foreclosure of a mortgage to which it was collateral.

No dispute exists on the facts. The plaintiff loaned money to Bridgeview Properties and Developments Ltd. and took a land mortgage as security. By way of additional security the defendant gave his guarantee. Default occurred under the mortgage and it was foreclosed. After a final order of foreclosure was obtained, the property was sold by the plaintiff and cannot be reconveyed. The defendant was not a party to the foreclosure proceedings.

Can the plaintiff now sue the defendant on his guarantee for the deficiency between the mortgage balance and the sale price? At common law a mortgagee could not sue a mortgagor for the balance owing on the mortgage if the mortgagee disposed of the land after obtaining a final order, unless the mortgagee was in a position to retransfer the property to the mortgagor: see *Rushton v. Indust Dev. Bank*, [1973] SCR 552, 34 DLR (3d) 582 at 589, per Laskin J.

At the root of this is the concept of "once a mortgage, always a mortgage," whereby the parties' rights continue even after the mortgage has been foreclosed. A mortgagor may redeem after final order under exceptional circumstances, because the mortgage is considered unsatisfied so long as the mortgagee retains the land. As well, following final order the mortgagee may yet enforce the mortgagor's covenant to pay, but this will have the effect of opening the foreclosure and revesting in the mortgagor the redemption privilege. However, if the mortgagee as owner in any way alters his relation to the land, he elects to take it and forgoes the debt, but not until then: see Anglin J in *Davidson v. Sharpe*, 60 SCR 72, [1920] 1 WWR 888 at 895, 52 DLR 186.

Counsel cited a number of decisions in support of the plaintiff's position, including *Kleiman v. Bazin* (1970), 73 WWR 252, 10 DLR (3d) 384 (Sask. CA), but none is directly in point. *Kleiman*, for example, was not a case where the same mortgagee first foreclosed and then sued on an indemnity for the deficiency.

On the facts before me the plaintiff would fail at common law if it sued the mortgagor herein on the covenant to pay because the plaintiff has disposed of the property. But is the plaintiff precluded from suing a guarantor of the debt?

In 20 Hals. (4th) 154 it is stated that whatever expressly or implicitly discharges the principal debtor from liability usually discharges the surety also by implication. I conclude that the instant mortgage is extinguished due to the irreversible sale by the plaintiff and the debt obligation is, therefore, at an end. If there is no debt there is nothing to guarantee. This being so, the plaintiff cannot succeed in its claim against the defendant on his guarantee, and the action is dismissed.

To hold otherwise would prejudice the defendant who has a right upon paying the indebtedness to receive the mortgagee's security: see 20 Hals. (4th) 107. In addition, the defendant would be prejudiced because, not being a party, he could not avail himself of the opportunity to participate in the foreclosure or sale. It could also be argued that a suit on the guarantee is merely an oblique method of enforcing the mortgagor's covenant to pay because if the defendant paid under his guarantee, he could claim like indemnity from the mortgagor.

The plaintiff's dilemma could have been avoided had it followed the usual procedure of suing the guarantor in the foreclosure litigation. An order for sale could then be obtained and the guarantor could either be involved in the sale to lessen his loss or to pay out the mortgage and take the security. Alternatively, the plaintiff could have elected to sue on the guarantee prior to initiating or concluding the foreclosure.

There was a suggestion in *Gordon Grant & Co. Ltd. v. Boos*, [1926] AC 781 at 785, [1926] 3 WWR 57 (PC), that it might be possible to place a value upon the foreclosed property and to allow the mortgagee to sue for any balance. This suggestion has not generally been followed and I would not entertain it in the circumstances even if that form of relief were available in view of the potential prejudice to the defendant.

As I have concluded that the plaintiff could not succeed in a common law action, there is no need for me to rule on the defendant's further contention that the *Limitation of Civil Rights Act*, RSS 1978, c. L-16, was improperly waived by the mortgagor thereby providing the defendant with an additional defence under that Act.

It was agreed that if the defendant succeeded on this motion he should have his costs of the action to be taxed on col. 5, and I so order.

Order accordingly.

Effect of Bankruptcy of the Principal Debtor

Re Tuxedo Silver Limited
(1963), 4 CBR (NS) 95 (Man. QB)

ELLIOTT, Registrar: The trustee herein, who appeared on his own behalf as trustee, has disallowed in part a claim filed with him by the appellant in this bankruptcy proceeding. Notice of the disallowance is dated 19th December 1960. Notice of the appeal therefrom was filed on 4th January 1961. The appeal was argued before me on 12th January 1961, pursuant to ss. 149 (1)(n) and 94 of the Bankruptcy Act, RSC, 1952, c. 14.

The claim of Oneida Limited was for $122,364.68. By virtue of security which it held, Oneida Limited was able to recover $37,695 from accounts receivable. It also held a guarantee by one John Epp. Litigation between Oneida and John Epp resulted in a settlement.

The appellant, Oneida Limited, disagrees with the trustee's decision as to the effect of the guarantee and settlement on the balance remaining due to Oneida Limited as an unsecured claim in the estate in bankruptcy. The trustee allows the claim at $69,194.52; the appellant says it should be $91,559.20.

The trustee arrives at $69,194.52 in this way:

The guarantee of John Epp obligated him to pay any indebtedness in excess of $100,000, so that his obligation was to pay Oneida Limited $22,364.68. But Oneida Limited recovered $37,695 from the accounts receivable of the bankrupt. John Epp is regarded as being entitled to share in that recovery and his share was apportioned at $6,889.52 which, if deducted from the $22,364.68 he was obliged to pay, would leave $15,475.16. This $15,475.16, with the $37,695, gives a total recovery of $53,170.16 and leaves an unsecured claim of $69,194.52. This is what the trustee has allowed.

The appellant submits that instead of a total recovery of $53,170.16 the figure should be $30,805.48, leaving the balance of the claim at $91,559.20 unsecured. The amount of $30,805.48 is arrived at by admitting a recovery from the accounts receivable of $37,695 and then deducting therefrom the $6,889.52 which seems to be regarded as John Epp's share of the recovery, leaving $30,805.48.

This appeal was argued on the basis that John Epp has also filed a proof of claim in the bankruptcy. Although the particulars thereof are not stated, I assume the proof was for $22,364.65.

The appellant in argument cited *In re Coughlin & Co.; Guarantee Co. of North America's Claim*, 33 Man. R 499, at 503, 4 CBR 294, [1923] 3 WWR 1177, [1923] 4 DLR 971, 3 Can. Abr. 779, which deals with a guarantee and a bankruptcy, $10,000 having been paid out on the guarantee and a claim having been filed with the trustee in bankruptcy. The court was concerned to guard against "double proof" in the bankruptcy. The late Dennistoun JA stated at p. 505:

It is to be noted that it is the "debt" which is provable. There may be several claimants to the "debt," but there is only one debt, and double proof in respect to it is not permitted.

And at p. 506:

It appears to be well settled, that if it was the intention to guarantee the whole debt with a limitation on the liability of the surety, the latter cannot rank on the debtor's estate until the creditor has been paid in full. The creditor is therefore entitled to get what he can from the debtor's estate and then look to his surety for the shortage.

If on the other hand the surety has guaranteed a part of a debt only, he is entitled on payment of that part to rank against the debtor's estate in respect to it.

The part of the debt which John Epp has guaranteed is only "any indebtedness in excess of the sum of $100,000." The decisions which deal with the guarantee of a part of a debt are not applicable because they are concerned with the part at the low end of the liability scale, not the indebtedness in excess of $100,000.

In Rowlatt on *Principal and Surety*, 3rd ed., a whole chapter is devoted to "Bankruptcy." The text considers English law. It is stated at p. 317:

Payments made to the creditor by the surety and dividends paid in his bankruptcy can, provided no double proof results, be proved for in the bankruptcy of the principal.

The history of the law relating to such proof is reviewed, in part, as follows at pp. 319-20:

Before the statute 49 Geo. III, ch. 121, s. 8, a surety could only prove, and the bankrupt, as against the surety, only got a discharge, in respect of money paid by the surety to the creditor before the bankruptcy. But if the surety paid the whole of the debt after the creditor had proved, he became entitled to the benefit of the creditor's proof, which it was held must not be expunged, but be preserved for the benefit of the surety. In this case justice was done to the surety, who had the benefit of all that the principal's estate would yield towards payment of the debt; but a hardship was inflicted on the principal, who remained exposed to the demand of the surety though his estate had paid a dividend on the debt, of which the surety had had the benefit. On the other hand, if the surety paid the debt after the bankruptcy, but before any proof by the creditor, the creditor could not prove at all, and the surety was wholly deprived of the benefit of any dividend in the bankruptcy, while the bankrupt obtained no discharge. The importance which, in this state of the law, attached to the proof of the creditor being made before the surety paid the debt, induced the Courts of Equity, upon the surety depositing the money, to compel the creditor to prove in the bankruptcy before exacting payment from the surety, and so to ensure to the surety a participation in the estate of the principal, though without, as has been shown, any corresponding relief to the latter. To avoid this circuity in the protection given to the surety, and also to afford relief to the debtor, it was provided by 49 Geo. III, ch. 121, s. 8, re-enacted in 6 Geo. IV, ch. 16, s. 52, and 12 and 13 Vict., ch. 106, s. 173, that a surety paying after the commencement of the bankruptcy the whole of the debt, or part in satisfaction of the whole, should be entitled, if the creditor had proved, to the benefit of his proof and, if the creditor had not proved to prove in his own name, not disturbing past dividends.

In Snell's *Principles of Equity*, 13th ed., it is stated at p. 510:

Where the principal debtor becomes a bankrupt, the creditor and the surety may (each of them) prove in the bankruptcy the creditor in respect of his debt, and the surety in respect of his liability; but this distinction is to be taken, namely, that when the surety is surety for the whole debt, the creditor (and not the surety) shall prove; but when the surety is surety for part only of the debt, and he has paid his part, he may prove in respect of that part, and the principal creditor may prove in respect of the residue, or even, in the general case, in respect of the whole original debt.

Since Oneida Limited has recovered from the accounts receivable of the bankrupt the sum of $37,695, the amount for which it can prove as an ordinary creditor (apart from any question of guarantee) would therefore be $84,669.68. Since the indebtedness does not now exceed $100,000 a question arises as to the liability of the guarantor at the present time. Has the guarantor any right to relief or protection in this bankruptcy, or is his recourse against Oneida Limited to whom he has paid out $22,364.68? These are not questions to be decided on this appeal, for neither the guarantor nor his proof of claim are before me.

In the result the appellant is entitled to have its claim as an unsecured creditor approved at $84,669.68.

NOTES

1) Section 179 of the BIA provides that an "order of discharge does not release a person who at the date of bankruptcy was ... a surety or in the nature of a surety for" the bankrupt. Insolvency of the principal debtor is likely the most frequent reason for a creditor requiring a guarantee contract as a condition of dealing with the debtor.

2) An obvious problem arises when the principal debtor becomes bankrupt: who can prove as an unsecured creditor in the bankruptcy proceeds—the creditor, the surety, or both? Double proof (double dividends) will not be allowed since this would distort the *pari passu* distribution principle of distribution in bankruptcy. The so-called rule against double proof provides that the claim of the surety is a mirror image of the creditor's claim and is contingent until the surety has paid the creditor in full, so that its right to indemnity from the principal debtor arises.

3) What is the result when a surety is liable under the guarantee contract to pay $100 but pays only $25, leaving some of the obligation undischarged? Assume the dividend to be paid out of the estate of the bankrupt debtor is 25% of proven claims. Should the creditor be able to prove for $75 and the surety for $25, or should the surety be barred from proving and the creditor be allowed to prove for $100 and refuse to give to surety any credit for what he or she paid? If the latter approach is allowed, the effect would be to bar the surety from ever recovering indemnity from the principal debtor since the bankruptcy discharge extinguishes any claim by the surety against the debtor. See *Re Sass*, [1896] 2 QB 12 (CA); *Re Fenton (No.2)*, [1932] 1 Ch. 178 (CA). Ordinarily the surety's right to indemnification is based on subrogation. The surety has no right to be indemnified unless the obligation secured has been paid in full.

4) A drawer and an indorser of a negotiable instrument are liable to the holder as if they were sureties of the acceptor, where the acceptor does not pay the instrument on presentation. When the holder has been paid part of the debt represented by the instrument, before she has received a dividend in the acceptor's insolvency, she is only entitled to prove for the balance which she has not received, and the drawer and indorser are entitled to prove for the amount that they paid. See *Re Houlder*, [1929] 1 Ch. 205.

5) Some guarantee contracts contain a suspense account clause giving the creditor the right to keep separate any payment made by the surety until the creditor has received all that is due from the principal debtor. The effect of such a clause is that the creditor is not obliged to give credit, when proving in the principal's bankruptcy, for any amounts in the account unless they have been appropriated to the principal obligation. The same rule applies to any security held by the creditor.

6) Section 95(3) of the BIA provides that a surety or guarantor is a "creditor" for the purposes of ss. 95(1)-(2). These sections give the trustee in bankruptcy the power to have declared "void" a "conveyance or transfer of property or a charge thereon made, every payment made, every obligation incurred and every judicial proceeding taken or suffered by an insolvent person in favour of a creditor ... with a view to giving that creditor a preference over the other creditors" if the preference occurs within three months of bankruptcy.

The purpose of the equivalent provision in the English bankruptcy legislation was explained by Eve J in *Re G. Stanley & Co. Ltd.*, [1925] 1 Ch. 148 at p. 153: "It is common ground that the reference to surety and guarantor was inserted to reverse the effect of two decisions which held that payment to a person whom it was not sought to prefer could not be recovered from him, because there was no fraudulent preference so far as he was concerned nor from the person whom it was sought to prefer, because the payment was not made to him. The result was that a payment to the principal creditor with the intent to prefer the guarantor of the debtor so paid could not be recovered either from the principle creditor or the guarantor ... ."

PART II

Principles of Canadian Insolvency Law

The following chapters round out the discussion of secured transactions law by introducing the student to the principles of Canadian insolvency law.* There is a natural linkage between these two branches of law. A security interest is only as good as the recognition which it receives on the debtor's bankruptcy. If the security interest survives intact the secured party will have little to fear; if the security interest is demoted in bankruptcy or in reorganization proceedings initiated by the debtor or a creditor, its value to the secured party will diminish commensurately. However, secured creditors constitute only one class of creditors and bankruptcy and reorganization proceedings can be very complex. As a result, a proper appreciation of the treatment of secured creditors requires a general understanding of the structure and principles of the Canadian legislation.

The following chapters provide an overview of the key landmarks but lay no claim to comprehensiveness or completeness of treatment of the topic. That role belongs to a full-fledged course on bankruptcy and insolvency law.

---

* Bankruptcy law is the branch of law which deals with the procedure by which a person (the "bankrupt") (who may be a natural or artificial person) may be put into bankruptcy and the consequences that flow from this condition. "Insolvent" is the term used to describe a person who or which is unable to pay the person's debts as they arise, but who has not been put into bankruptcy. The distinction is important because far reaching consequences flow from the status of bankruptcy. A state of insolvency triggers no legal consequences by itself but is a precondition to a debtor being able to invoke the reorganization and extension of payment provisions in the Companies' Creditors Arrangement Act (CCAA) and Parts III and X of the Bankruptcy and Insolvency Act (BIA). Because of the dual role of the Act, the name of the Bankruptcy Act was changed in the 1992 amendments to its present name.

CHAPTER TWELVE

Historical Introduction, Statistics and Modern Objectives

Report of the Study Committee on Bankruptcy and Insolvency Legislation
(Canada, 1970) ("Tassé Report"), sections 1.1-1.3 (footnotes omitted)

Chapter 1
The History of Bankruptcy

An Expanding Concept: The long history of bankruptcy has been one of an expanding concept. From the harsh and merciless treatment of debtors, the law, through many stages, has come to recognize that, while there may be fraudulent debtors from whom society must be protected, an honest bankrupt is not a contradiction of terms. Upon this cornerstone has been built the modern law of bankruptcy.

In primitive societies, the debtor's lot was hard. There was no exception to the rule that he must pay his debts in full. If he could not pay with his property, he paid with his person.

The Code of Hammurabi: Written more than 4000 years ago, the Code of Hammurabi, King of Babylon, contained several actions concerning the relations between debtors and creditors. According to this Code, the creditor was entitled to levy a "distress" or "pledge," called a *nipûtum*, if the debt was not paid when it became due. It was not necessary for the creditor to first obtain judgment, but he was penalized if he wrongfully levied a distress. While oxen of the plough and grain were exempted from seizure, the debtor's wife, a child or a slave could be brought as *nipûtum* to the creditor's house. There they were put to work until the debt was satisfied. In addition to the *nipûtum*, the Code considered the case where the debtor voluntarily surrendered a dependant into bondage by selling him, with or without right of redemption, to a merchant or to the creditor himself. The position of the dependant in the house of his new master seems to be similar to that of the *nipûtum*, but, in the case of a wife or child, the servitude came to an end after three years service. Finally, if the debt of the creditor was not satisfied one way or another, there seems little doubt that the debtor could be adjudicated to him as a bond-servant.

The Law of Ancient Greece: By the end of the 7th Century, BC, in Athens, the new class of mercantile capitalists virtually owned the entire peasant class with mortgages on nearly every small holding in Attica. The peasants could not resist foreclosures on their lands and on their persons, which often were included in their pledges. The poor were in a state of bondage to the rich, both themselves, their wives, and their children. The political situation was critical. In order to avert a revolution, Solon cancelled all existing mortgages and debts, released debtors from bondage and made illegal those contracts in which a person's liberty was pledged.

The Roman Law: When, in the middle of the 5th Century, BC, Rome decided to codify its laws, it sent three commissioners to Greece to study the laws of Solon. The code that resulted is known as the *Law of the Twelve Tables*. Contrary to the spirit of the reform of Solon, the Roman jurists maintained the execution against the person. After the fulfilment of certain formalities, the unpaid creditor had the power to seize the debtor himself. This seizure, called *manus injectio*, gave the creditor authority to bring the debtor to his home and keep him in chains for sixty days. During this period, the debtor, still the owner of his property and a Roman citizen, could try to settle his debts with his creditor. To allow for the possibility of a ransom being paid, the creditor was required to take him three times to the market place giving notice of the amount of the debt each time. Finally, if at the end of sixty days, the creditor was not fully paid, he could, it would seem, put the debtor to death or sell him into foreign slavery. According to certain modern writers, the creditors could even divide between them the body of the debtor. If this was so, there is no proof that such an inhuman treatment was ever applied. It must also be noted that the *paterfamilias* could, as was the case under the *Hammurabi Code*, in order to avoid his slavery, raise money by leasing out the services of the members of his family. In Roman law, this is known as *mancipium*. During the centuries that followed the promulgation of the *Law of the Twelve Tables*, the severity of the *manus injectio* was progressively reduced. By the end of the Republic, the unpaid creditor could still imprison the debtor or make the debtor work for him in satisfaction of the debt but he could no longer put him to death or sell him into slavery.

As Ihéring pointed out, early Roman law only recognized execution against the person:

Ce qu'un individu a acquis au prix de son corps et de sa vie, ou à la sueur de son front, semble devenir une partie de lui-même. Quiconque entame cette propriété doit payer; s'il ne peut restituer, son propre corps répond de ce qu'il a enlevé.

This was the rule under Roman law until the end of the Republic, when the *Edict of the Praetor* alleviated the harshness of the old quiritarian law. About that time, one praetor developed a method of execution against property known as *venditio bonorum*. This fundamental reform, for the first time, established a link between the assets and the liabilities of a person. Moreover, this was in the nature of a procedure for the collective execution against the property of an insolvent or recalcitrant debtor. To quote W.W. Buckland, "It is in effect the Roman equivalent of bankruptcy proceedings."

Thus, by the end of the Republic, Roman law recognized two methods of execution, one against the person and the other against property. The debtor could, however, by the time of Augustus, avoid execution against his person by making a *cessio bonorum*, that is to say, by surrendering to his creditors everything he owned. About three centuries later, the *cessio bonorum* was not available to debtors who had squandered their property or concealed it from their creditors. According to an imperial ordinance of the year 379, this procedure was only allowed when the insolvency of the debtor was due to an act of God. Under Justinian, the use of the *cessio bonorum* had become so widespread that the *Corpus Juris* scarcely mentions imprisonment for debt.

The Italian Cities: As trade and the use of credit developed, the ordinary law of debtor and creditor became inadequate to cope with the problem of the insolvent trader. Towards the end of the Mediaeval [*sic*] Ages, the Italian cities attempted to deal with this problem and new concepts, such as the "act of bankruptcy" were developed by legal writers of the time. It is from the Italian *bancarupta* that the word "bankrupt" is derived. It may be literally translated as "bank broken" or "bench broken." The allusion is said to be the custom of breaking the table of a defaulting tradesman.

The French Law: In France, and elsewhere in Europe, the Roman law, in its ultimate stages, became the basis of the law merchant. The French *Ordinance of 1673* is celebrated as being the first great codification of the law merchant in France. This Ordinance and the *Code de Commerce de 1807* had great influence in most civil law jurisdictions of the world.

The English Law: In England, one of the first insolvency statutes was enacted in 1351. In an attempt to promote commercial integrity, it provided that, if any merchant of the Company of Lombard Merchants acknowledged himself bound in a debt, the Company should answer for it. Apparently, this was by reason of the fact that some of these merchants had, in the past, left the country without paying their debts.

At Common Law, a creditor has to resort to a very expensive, lengthy and cumbersome procedure to obtain an attachment of his debtor's property. Execution cannot be obtained against a debtor's entire estate but only against the property described in the writ. If there was a plurality of creditors, they took the property of the debtor in the order of their attachments. The race was to the swift. The rule was "first come, first served."

The first Bankruptcy Statutes provided a summary method for the collective execution of all of the debtor's property, both movable and immovable. They stressed the rights of creditors. The only concern shown in respect of the debtor was that he should surrender all of his property and that no fraud on his part should go undetected and unpunished. Under the first of these statutes, the property was liquidated and distributed "to every of the said creditors a portion, rate and rate alike, according to the quantity of their debts." The preamble of this statute stated: "where divers and sundry persons craftily obtaining into their own hands great substance of other Mens [*sic*] Goods, do suddenly flee to Parts unknown, or keep their Houses not minding to pay or restore to any [*sic*] their Creditors, their Debts and Duties, but at their own Wills and Pleasures Consume the Substance obtained by credit of other Men for their own Pleasure and delicate Living against all Reason, Equity and good Conscience."

Although the English *Bankruptcy Act* of 1542 was directed against any debtor who attempted to defeat his creditors by fraudulent means, the Act of 1571 restricted bankruptcy to those who were engaged in trade. This distinction was to be maintained for almost 300 years. A debtor who was not in trade and who could not pay his debts was imprisoned until some person paid them for him.

The first English Act showing concern for the rehabilitation of the debtor was enacted in 1705 in the reign of Anne. A debtor who was a merchant could get a discharge of all his debts owing at the time of his bankruptcy provided he surrendered all of this property and conformed to the other provisions of the statute. However, the legislator remained very much aware of the continuing problem of the fraudulent debtor. So, while being given new privileges, the debtor had to be free from fraud and submit himself to the control of the

Court. Evidence of the concern of the legislator that debtors might abuse the privileges given to them was the severity of the penalty for a debtor who did not strictly comply with the law. The penalty, in the past, had been to stand in the pillory or have an ear cut off. The new penalty was hanging. This penalty applied, for example, if the bankrupt failed to surrender himself to the court, committed perjury on his examination or fraudulently concealed his assets.

In the middle of the 18th Century, Sir William Blackstone, commenting on the Law of England, had this to say about bankruptcy:

The Laws of England, more widely, have steered in the middle between both extremes: providing at once against the inhumanity of the creditor, who is not suffered to confine an honest bankrupt after his effects are delivered up; and at the same time taking care that all his just debts shall be paid; so far as the effects will extend. But still they are cautious of encouraging prodigality and extravagance by this indulgence to debtors; and therefore they allow the benefit of the laws of bankruptcy to none but actual traders; since that set of men are, generally speaking, the only persons liable to accidental losses, and to an inability of paying their debts, without any fault of their own. If persons in other situations of life run in debt without the power of payment, they must take the consequences of their own indiscretion, even though they may meet with sudden accidents that may reduce their fortunes: for the law holds it to be an unjustifiable practice, for any person but a tradesman to encumber himself with debts of any considerable value. If a gentleman, or one in a liberal profession, at a time of contracting his debts, has a sufficient fund to pay them, the delay of payment is a species of dishonesty, and a temporary injustice to his creditor: and if, at such time, he has no sufficient fund, the dishonesty and the injustice is the greater. He cannot therefore, murmur, if he suffers the punishment which he has voluntarily drawn upon himself. But in mercantile transactions, the case is far otherwise. Trade cannot be carried on without mutual credit on both sides: the contracting of debts is therefore here not only justifiable, but necessary. And if by accidental calamities, as by the loss of a ship in a tempest, the failure of brother traders, or by the non-payment of persons out of trade, a merchant or tradesman becomes incapable of discharging his own debts, it is his misfortune and not his fault. To the misfortunes, therefore, of debtors, the law had given a compassionate remedy, but denied it to their faults: since at the same time that it provides for the security of commerce, by enacting that every considerable trader may be declared a bankrupt, for the benefit of his creditors as well as himself, it has also to discourage extravagance, declared that no one shall be capable of being made a bankrupt, but only a trader, nor capable of receiving the full benefit of the statutes, but only an industrious trader.

James A. Bayard expressed similar views when speaking in the United States Congress in 1803 against the repeal of the first United States *Bankruptcy Act*, modelled on the English Act:

... the commercial world cannot exist without such an act. Its necessity arises from the nature of trade and does not belong to other classes of citizens. It is founded on the principle that commerce is built on great credits and great credits produce great debts. Owing to the risks arising from these and other circumstances, the most diligent and honourable merchant may be ruined without committing any fault. Not so as to the other classes of citizens; either the cultivators of the soil, the mechanics, or those who follow a liberal profession. They live on the profit of their labor [*sic*], not on profits derived from credit.

In the early part of the 19th Century, a number of statutes were passed for the relief of insolvent debtors who were not engaged in trade and therefore could not be made bankrupt. Originally, the insolvency acts provided only for the release from imprisonment of the debtor. He was not released of his debts and remained liable for their repayment. Later legislation provided for the discharge of persons who were imprisoned for their debts if they surrendered all of their goods for the benefit of their creditors. In 1812, the laws relating to insolvency were administered by a court of record known as the Court for the Relief of Insolvent Debtors. By the *Bankruptcy Act* of 1861, which made persons other than traders subject to bankruptcy law, this Court was abolished and its jurisdiction transferred to the Court of Bankruptcy. In 1869, by the *Bankruptcy Repeal and Insolvent Court Act*, all insolvency statutes theretofore existing were extinguished. Imprisonment for debt was abolished altogether, except in the case of a dishonest person who could pay his debts but refused to do so. The legal distinction between bankruptcy and insolvency was thus all but eliminated.

In the history of bankruptcy, there is much experimentation concerning who should liquidate and supervise an estate. In 1831, for example, the English legislation provided for the joint administration by official assignees and assignees chosen by the creditors. In 1869, the system of administration, at the insistence of the trading community, reverted to a system of creditor liquidation. The creditors chose the trustee who was supervised by a committee of inspectors also chosen by the creditors. Abuses soon arose, however, particularly in regard to the solicitation of proxies, which often permitted a minority of creditors to control and manipulate the administration of an estate in their interests to the prejudice of the majority of creditors.

It was recognized in England that the system of creditor control over the administration of a bankruptcy estate, as provided by the 1869 Act, had failed. The English *Bankruptcy Act of 1883* devised a new system of joint official and creditor control. Although minor amendments have been made to this Act, the system of administration, that it created, has not changed in any material respect. When Joseph Chamberlain, the then President of the Board of Trade, spoke on the second reading of the Bill for the 1883 Act, he explained the philosophy of his new legislation as follows:

He, (Joseph Chamberlain), asked the House to keep in mind two main, and, at the same time, distinct objects of any good Bankruptcy Law. Those were, firstly, in the honest administration of bankrupt estates, with a view to the fair and speedy distribution of the assets among the creditors, whose property they were; and, in the second place their object should be, following the idea that prevention was better than cure, to do something to improve the general tone of commercial morality, to promote honest trading, and to lessen the number of failures. In other words, Parliament had to endeavour, as far as possible, to protect the salvage, and also to diminish the number of wrecks.

His next point was that, with regard to those two most important objects, there was only one way by which they could be secured and that was by securing an independent and impartial examination into the circumstances of each case; and that was the cardinal principle of this Bill. ... What happened when a bankruptcy took place which might easily cause misery to thousands of people and bring ruin on many homes? It was treated as if it were entirely a matter of private concern, and allowed to become a scramble between the debtor and his advisers—who were often his confederates—on the one hand, and the creditors on the other. Meanwhile, the great public interests at stake in all these questions were entirely and absolutely ignored, as there was nobody to represent them, and the practice which was followed in the case of other calamities was, in this case, entirely absent. In the case of accidents by sea and by land—railway accidents, for instance—it was incumbent upon a Government Department to institute an inquiry. There were inquiries in the case of accidents in mines, and of boiler explosions, and sad as those disasters were, they did not, in the majority of cases, cause so much misery as a bad bankruptcy, which brought ruin to many families by carrying off the fruits of their labour and industry. ...

Now, it would be seen that the provision which he had described (a description of duties and responsibilities of the official receiver, the office of which was first created by this Bill) constituted a system which he thought they might fairly call a system of official inquiry, and which went on all fours with a similar system in the matters of accident to which he had referred. He did not think that without some such limited officialism as this any satisfactory inquiry was even possible. No investigation could be worth anything unless it was conducted by an independent and impartial officer. ...

Conclusion: In this chapter we have examined how the insolvent debtor was treated under the laws of several of the civilizations of the ancient world and, in particular, under the law of Rome. Among the modern bankruptcy systems, the only one here studied in any detail was the English system, as it was upon it that the Canadian legislation was modelled.

Over the years, the principles underlying the English Insolvency and Bankruptcy Law changed considerably. While, at the outset, the legislation was of a purely criminal nature, this character has been progressively attenuated as the legal treatment given to debtors became more and more humane. The former "creditors acts," very strict with debtors, eventually recognized the necessity to give the honest and unfortunate debtor a chance to rehabilitate himself. This chance was given to insolvent traders as early as 1705 and, about one century later, extended to all debtors. Finally, after a great deal of experimentation in the field of bankruptcy administration, England opted for a compromise between official and creditor control. As will be seen in the next chapter, the element of officialism in the English system is much greater than in its Canadian counterpart.

Chapter 2
The Canadian Legislation Since Confederation

Principal Milestones: In the hundred years since Confederation, the following Statutes constitute the important milestones of bankruptcy and insolvency legislation:

1869:	*The Insolvent Act of 1869*	32-33 Vic., Can. S. 1869, c. 16
1875:	*The Insolvent Act of 1875*	38 Vic., Can. S. 1875, c. 16
1880:	*An Act to repeal the Acts Respecting Insolvency now in force in Canada*	43 Vic., Can. S. 1880, c. 1
1882:	*An Act respecting Insolvent Banks, Insurance Companies, Loan Companies, Building Societies and Trading Corporations*, later named the *Winding-Up Act* (for insolvent companies)	45 Vic., Can. S. 1882, c. 23
1889:	*The Winding Up Amendment Act, 1889* (extended to solvent companies)	52 Vic., Can. S. 1889, c. 32

1919:	*The Bankruptcy Act*	9-10 Geo. V, Can. S. 1919, c. 36
1923:	*The Bankruptcy Act Amendment Act, 1923* (companies prohibited from making proposals without previously being adjudged bankrupt; office of custodian created; office of official receivers created)	13-14 Geo. V., Can. S. 1923, c. 31
1932:	*The Bankruptcy Act Amendment Act, 1932* (office of Superintendent created)	22-23 Geo., V, Can. S. 1932, c. 39
1933:	*The Companies' Creditors Arrangement Act, 1933*	23-24 Geo. V, Can. S. 1932-33, c. 36
1934:	*The Farmers' Creditors Arrangement Act, 1934*	24-25 Geo. V, Can. S. 1934, c. 53
1943:	*The Farmers' Creditors Arrangement Act, 1943*	7 Geo. VI, Can. S. 1943, c. 26
1949:	*Bankruptcy Act, 1949*	13 Geo. VI, Can. S. 1949 (2nd Session), c. 7
1953:	*An Act to Amend the Companies' Creditors Arrangement Act, 1933* (act restricted to arrangement including an arrangement between a company and its bondholders)	1-2 El. II, Can. S. 1952-53, c.3
1966:	*An Act to Amend the Bankruptcy Act*	14-15 El. II, Can. S. 1966-67, c. 32

The First Insolvency Legislation After Confederation: The Acts of 1869 and 1875 applied only to insolvent traders. From 1874 to 1878 there was a serious depression in Canada resulting in many commercial failures. This caused much public resentment particularly in the rural areas of the country which led to the enactment of *The Insolvency Acts Repeal Act* in 1880. The following quotations from the debates in the House of Commons indicate something of the public opinion of the time and the reasons for the repeal. The anger directed at those who appeared to be acting fraudulently still has a timeliness:

Mr. Colby: Whatever may have been the necessity of the law when it was passed, I think that now it is unquestionably a fact that it has outlived its usefulness and that public opinion is definitely settled and has declared itself in a way that is unmistakeable, in favour of an immediate and summary repeal of the Act ... (the law) became rather a means of escape for the dishonest and designing debtor than a mere means of relief for the honest and unfortunate debtor ... experience has also shown in this country, and in other countries I believe, that the rapacity of assignees, the dishonesty of debtors, the greed of some creditors, the inattention of others, have thwarted the beneficient intentions of the law; and instead of there being an economical and honest administration of assets, the practical operation of the law has been characterized by a wasteful extravagance, and too often by a dishonest administration. I think it is unmistakeably the case in this country where the law has been a long time on the Statute-Book, that it has tended to the demoralisation of trade, and to lower the standard of commercial morality. It has tended to recklessness in trading and in living to extravagance. It has tempted many persons, wholly unsuited for business, to risk their fortune in business enterprises that were little understood by them. The whole effect of the law in recent years has been unfortunate and disastrous. I think, sir, that it is the sentiment of the people of this country, generally, that it has tended, in some considerable degree, if not to create, at all events to aggravate, the commercial distress which has unhappily prevailed in this country.

Mr. Sproule: ... Public opinion has been too strong against the continuance of these laws, which apply to one class of the community only, to prevent their continuance upon the Statutes of our country. They have only held out inducements for parties so disposed to shape their affairs in such a way, even to change from one line to another, so as to enable them to take advantage of the Act, and pay their debts with twenty, thirty or forty cents on the dollar. I believe it is generally recognized that there is not more than one honest trader out of every three or four who have taken the benefit of that act since it was placed on the Statute-Book. It seems strange that if the law was so beneficial, it should have been made applicable only to commercial people, and that all professional men, labourers and mechanics, and all the agricultural classes of the community should be entirely left out from the benefits supposed to accrue from that law ...

By a coincidence that appears not to be accidental, the *Bill to Repeal the Insolvency Acts* was read for the third time on March 4, 1880, while on March 5, 1880, assent was given, in Ontario, to "An *Act to Abolish Priorities of and Amongst Execution Creditors.*" In the discussion in the House of Commons, it was said that the Ontario Bill, which was similar to the law prevailing in Quebec, would provide for the just and equitable distribution of estates and the hope was expressed that other provinces would enact similar legislation.

The Winding-Up Act: It was soon found that, without an *Insolvency Act*, there was no convenient way to wind up insolvent companies. Boards of Trade, in most of the large cities, passed resolutions requesting new legislation. In 1882, the *Insolvent Banks, Insurance Companies and Trading Corporations Act*, later to be known as the *Winding-Up Act*, was enacted.

In some countries, such as England and Australia, the *Bankruptcy Act* applies only to individuals and there is other legislation for the liquidation of insolvent companies. With the existence of the *Winding-Up Act*, this dichotomy could have developed in Canada. However, when the *Bankruptcy Act* of 1919 was enacted, it applied to both individuals and corporations. From 1919 until 1966, there were, in effect, two separate Acts in competition with each other relating to the insolvency of limited liability companies. These two Acts differ in substance and technique. In bankruptcy, for example, the property of the bankrupt vests in the trustee; under the *Winding-Up Act*, title to the property of the company remains in the company, but its control and management are taken from the directors and placed in the liquidator. The *Bankruptcy Act* binds the Crown, while the *Winding-up Act* does not. Under the *Bankruptcy Act*, an act of bankruptcy must be proved to obtain a receiving order, while, under the *Winding-Up Act*, a winding-up order may be obtained if the debtor is insolvent or deemed to be insolvent. Neither banks, insurance companies nor railway companies may be liquidated under the *Bankruptcy Act*, but they may be wound up under the *Winding-Up Act*. The *Bankruptcy Act* is characterized by an administration, for the most part, controlled by creditors, while, under the *Winding-Up Act*, the administration is controlled by the court. This duality is restricted by the amendments to the *Bankruptcy Act* in 1966, which provide in effect that the *Bankruptcy Act* should take precedence over the *Winding-Up Act*. Thus, now, where a petition for a receiving order or an assignment is filed under the *Bankruptcy Act*, in respect of a corporation, the *Winding-Up Act* does not extend or apply to that corporation.

The Period from 1880 to 1919: During the thirty-nine years when there was no federal bankruptcy or insolvency legislation relating to individuals, the only relief available to insolvent individuals was through provincial legislation. There were, in Quebec, articles 763-780 of *The Code of Civil Procedure* and, in the other provinces, the Assignment and Preferences Acts. The first of these Acts was an *Act Respecting Assignments for the Benefit of Creditors* passed by the Ontario Legislature in 1885, some five years after enacting what is now *The Creditors' Relief Act.*

Under provincial legislation, an insolvent debtor makes an assignment of his property to an authorized trustee licensed by the province. The authorized trustee is then required to liquidate the estate under the supervision of inspectors. For this, he is paid a fee from the debtor's estate. What characterizes provincial legislation, and since 1919, distinguishes it from the *Bankruptcy Act* is that a creditor cannot force a debtor to make an assignment; once an assignment is made, there is no provision in the legislation permitting a debtor to make a composition with his creditors and a debtor does not receive a release of his debts or a discharge.

The 1919 Bankruptcy Act: By 1917, there was considerable agitation across the country in support of the enactment of a national *Bankruptcy Act*. A committee of the Canadian Bar Association was created to draft such an act. This, in turn, disturbed some businessmen and authorized trustees licensed by the provinces. They felt that an act drafted by lawyers would provide for some form of court controlled administration instead of the provincial system of creditor control whereby estates were liquidated by the authorized trustees under the supervision of inspectors. One of the largest firms of authorized trustees, the Canadian Credit Men's Trust Association, retained Mr. H.P. Grundy, KC of Winnipeg, and instructed him to draft a Bill based upon creditor control and retaining the essential features of the provincial Assignments and Preferences Acts.

The Bill, based upon Mr. Grundy's draft, was first introduced in the House of Commons on March 27, 1918 as a war measure. On the motion for first reading, it was said:

Mr. Jacobs: ... I think that I can claim for this Bill that it is essentially a war measure at this particular time. We must be prepared when the war comes to a close, to be able to handle the situation which is bound to arise in this country as a result of the long continued struggle and of the readjustments which must be made. ... By this measure it is proposed that the courts shall carefully scrutinize the business dealings and the business relations of traders, and shall make a distinction—shall separate the sheep from the goats. When the court is of the opinion that a debtor has been obliged to assign through misfortune, he shall be given the necessary relief. If, on the other hand, it should be found in scrutinizing his affairs, that he wrecked his own business wilfully, then, of course, he should receive no relief whatever.

The Bill, later referred to a special committee and then reintroduced in the House of Commons during the following session, was enacted in 1919.

The Office of the Custodian Created in 1923: It had been hoped that the system of administration established by the 1919 Act and based upon the practice prevailing under the provincial Assignments Acts would prevent the occurring of the abuses that had helped to discredit the old Insolvency Acts. It was soon found, however, that most of the business under the new Act was not going to the experienced organizations of trustees that had efficiently handled most of the business under the provincial Assignments Acts. The work of a trustee attracted many unqualified and inexperienced persons, and, as there was then not enough business, this resulted in many trustees openly soliciting business and often lead [*sic*] to collusive and inefficient administration of estates.

In an attempt to rectify the abuses surrounding the appointment of trustees, particularly in voluntary assignments where the debtor was nominating his own trustee, the office of custodian was created in 1923. In many respects, the custodian fulfilled several of the functions of the official receiver in England until the first meeting of the creditors. The custodian was in effect the first trustee in every estate. He had to take possession of the property of the debtor and was responsible for its safekeeping until the appointment of the trustee at the first meeting of creditors. In practice, it soon developed that the custodian was invariably appointed trustee. As a result, the office of the custodian served no useful purpose and was ultimately abolished in 1949.

The Office of Superintendent of Bankruptcy created in 1932: The lack of safeguards surrounding the appointment of trustees encouraged the activities of dishonest trustees. There were scandals involving inefficient and collusive liquidations by incompetent and untrustworthy trustees. The supervision of trustees by creditors was ineffectual and the demand grew for some form of government supervision.

At the Annual Meeting of the Canadian Credit Men's Trust Association Ltd., in 1927, attention was called to the office of "Accountant of Court" created under the *Bankruptcy Act* of Scotland. The Accountant, who was appointed by the court on the recommendation of the Crown, had the responsibility to examine the charges and conduct of trustees and inspectors in every proceeding.

In 1929, the late Lewis Duncan, QC, an acknowledged bankruptcy specialist, after comparing the English, French and United States systems, suggested that there was a need in Canada for an adequately staffed bankruptcy department with offices at strategic centres.

In 1932, the office of the Superintendent was created. It was contemplated that the Superintendent would provide an independent, impartial and official supervision of trustees administering estates under the *Bankruptcy Act*. Except for the increased investigatory powers given to it in 1966, the office of the Superintendent has remained unaltered and compares with that of the Inspector General in Bankruptcy established in England in 1883.

The 1949 Bankruptcy Act: The present Canadian *Bankruptcy Act* was enacted in 1949. The intention of the new Act was said to be "to clarify and simplify the legislation." The following extract from Hansard, when the Bill was first introduced in the Senate, explains the history of the Bill and the principal changes:

Hon. J. Gordon Fogo: Honourable senators, it has sometimes been said that legislation in Canada is passed hastily and that those interested and the public in general are not given an opportunity to study its provisions. I do not think that can be said of this Bill F, which appears to have had a rather checkered career. This, I believe, is the fourth time that the bill has been introduced in this honourable House. It was first brought down in the year 1946, in a somewhat different form from the present measure, and was laid over for study for a period during which representations concerning it were made. Subsequently, in 1948, it came up again in a revised form. And, as most honourable senators will remember, it was introduced for a third time at the first session of this year, but unfortunately, owing to early dissolution, consideration of it was not completed. The present bill, I am informed, with very few exceptions, is practically identical with the bill that was before the Senate last session. ... The bill provides a more orderly arrangement of subjects and the language in many sections of the Act has been simplified. One or two of the more notable changes should be mentioned. The bill reinstates a provision which was in the *Bankruptcy Act* of 1919. During the period from 1919 to 1923 the Act contained a provision whereby an insolvent person could make a proposal to his creditors without making an assignment or having a receiving order made against him, and thereby suffering the stigma of bankruptcy. The bill now provides that an insolvent person may make such a proposal without going through the procedure of bankruptcy.

A further change which has been generally accepted as an improvement is a code for the administration of small estates in an economical and inexpensive manner. This section of the bill covers estates with assets of $500 or less, and provides a simplified procedure for their administration.

One other notable innovation of this bill is found in sections 127 to 129, which deal with the discharge of bankrupts. Under the existing legislation it has been necessary for a bankrupt, after the administration was completed, to apply to get his discharge. For various reasons, whether because the debtor did not know he was entitled to do this, or for other reasons, it was not customary for bankrupts to apply to their discharge. Following legislation in other countries—I think in the United States, and perhaps in Australia—this bill incorporates what might be regarded as an automatic application for discharge, because the occurring of the bankruptcy through assignment or receiving order in the first instance is also treated as an application for discharge. The debtor of course has to satisfy the court that he qualifies before he gets his discharge, and the conditions are laid down.

To move on quickly and in a very summary way: there are other miscellaneous provisions which might be mentioned. The new bill vests a greater measure of control in the creditors and inspectors. The powers of the superintendent have been made more explicit. ... The remuneration of trustees has been increased; that is, the maximum remuneration has been enlarged from 5 to 7½ per cent. ... The office of the custodian is eliminated. ...

The 1966 Amendment: During the fifties and early sixties, there was an increasing number of complaints about fraudulent bankruptcies. The complaint was also made that the investigatory machinery was not adequate to cope with the problem. As a result, the *Bankruptcy Act* was amended in 1966 so as to give the Superintendent wider powers of investigation. He may now investigate offences under any Act of Parliament, whether they have occurred before or after bankruptcy.

Many other significant amendments were made in 1966. One relates to non-arms' length transactions, and enables trustees better to deal with the transactions entered into by a debtor to the prejudice of his creditors. Part X of the *Bankruptcy Act* was also enacted. It provides for a system of orderly payment of debts under the supervision of the courts, but it is effective only in provinces where the Lieutenant Governor in Council has requested the Governor in Council to proclaim it in force.

The Companies' Creditors Arrangement Act: Prior to 1914, when most of Canada's financing was done in England, the practice, in issuing securities, was to follow English precedents. As a consequence, almost all trust deeds during this period contained clauses permitting a majority of debenture holders to vary the terms of a trust deed. Sometime later, in the twenties, when financing in the United States became more common, such provisions were no longer included in a great many trust deeds as they were not at that time usual in the United States. When the depression came, many companies needed to be reorganized. Often, to the embarrassment of the directors, it was found that the trust deeds did not contain provisions permitting reorganization by agreement. As a result, without the existence of enabling legislation, there was no way by which such companies could be reorganized.

Some of the reasons for which companies may wish to reorganize are to permit

(1) the extension of the maturity of debentures, with or without increasing the interest rate, when the marketing conditions make the refunding difficult, undesirable or impossible;

(2) a new encumbrance to rank ahead of existing debentures;

(3) the sale of assets to a new company subject to the same debenture;

(4) the release of mortgaged assets to secure new securities;

(5) the trustee to release part of the mortgaged property either unconditionally or upon terms;

(6) the waiver of minor defects.

The Bankruptcy Act of 1919 permitted a limited company to make a proposal to its creditors before a receiving order was made or an assignment filed. There was, however, little protection for the creditors. In many parts of Canada, complaints arose that debtors were bribing their creditors and using fraudulent means to secure their creditors' consent to a proposal and thus to avoid bankruptcy. As a result of the 1923 amendments to the *Bankruptcy Act*, no debtor was permitted to make a proposal unless he had first been declared bankrupt and the first meeting of creditors had been held. The requirement that there first be a bankruptcy before a proposal could be made met with mounting criticism and, as a consequence, the *Companies' Creditors Arrangement Act* was enacted in 1933 to permit a company to make, outside of bankruptcy, an arrangement with its secured and unsecured creditors. Broadly speaking, this Act was modelled upon provisions of the English *Companies Act*.

When the *Companies' Creditors Arrangement Act* received its first reading in the House of Commons, the Honourable C.H. Cahan, the then Secretary of State, said:

(The *Bankruptcy Act* and the *Winding-Up Act*) provide for the liquidation of the company under a trustee in the one case and under a liquidator in the other and the almost inevitable result is that the organization of the company is entirely disrupted, its good will depreciated and ultimately lost and the balance of its assets sold by the trustee or the liquidator for whatever they will bring. There is no mode or method under our laws whereby the creditors of a company may be brought into court and permitted by amicable agreement between themselves to arrange for a settlement or compromise of the debts of the company in such a way as to permit the company effectively to continue its business by its reorganization. ... At the present time, some legal method of making arrangements and compromises between creditors and companies is perhaps more necessary because of the prevailing commercial and industrial depression and it was thought by the government that we should adopt some method whereby compromises might be carried into effect under the supervision of the court without utterly destroying the company or its organization without loss of good will and without forcing the improvident sales of its assets.

The Companies' Creditors Arrangement Act worked well and gave general satisfaction to investors and to companies with secured indebtedness who wished to make arrangements with their creditors. There were, however, abuses of the Act by insolvent companies that used it, instead of the *Bankruptcy Act*, to make arrangements with their unsecured creditors. The *Companies' Creditors Arrangement Act* was never intended for this purpose, as it did not provide an appropriate procedure to give sufficient protection to unsecured creditors against false or misleading statements by the company concerning its affairs, thereby inducing them to accept proposals not in their best interests.

"Debenture holders" did not, however, have to rely solely on this Act for protection. The investing public had other facilities available. Most debentures gave the indenture trustee wide powers to intervene in the affairs of the debtor upon certain conditions. Institutional investors and underwriters that have large blocks of debentures on their hands or in their portfolios would, as a rule, also intervene in order to prevent any serious abuse.

In 1946, Bill A5, the first of the four bills mentioned by Senator Fogo, (*supra*) proposed to bring all corporate reorganizations under a new *Bankruptcy Act* and to repeal the *Companies' Creditors Arrangement Act*. No provision, however, was contained in the Bill for the special problems of the investor creditor, such as the position of the holder of a bearer debenture; for example, there was no provision for representation orders and service was required to be made on all creditors, which, in many cases, is clearly impossible.

The former Dominion Mortgage and Investments Association opposed the repeal of the *Companies' Creditors Arrangement Act*. It suggested, instead, that the abuses concerning it could be remedied if its use were confined to debtors with outstanding issues of debentures and the proposed arrangement affected the debentures or some of them. No further action was taken on Bill A5, although many of the features contained in it were later incorporated in the *Bankruptcy Act* of 1949.

In 1953, the *Companies' Creditors Arrangement Act* was amended, as originally suggested by the Dominion Mortgage and Investments Association, so as to restrict its application to a debtor company that had an outstanding debenture issue and wished to make a proposal with the debenture holders. When the Honourable Stuart S. Garson, the then Minister of Justice, moved the second reading of the Bill, he said:

The *Companies' Creditors Arrangement Act* was passed in 1933. At that time, the *Bankruptcy Act* did not contain adequate provisions for an arrangement between a corporate debtor and its creditors by which the corporate debtor, by getting an extension of its liabilities, could liquidate them, avoid bankruptcy and retain its identity. In other words, if they were going to come under the *Bankruptcy Act* at all they had to go into bankruptcy. The *Companies' Creditors Arrangement Act* was passed to enable these corporate debtors to make an extension of that sort without going into bankruptcy. But it appeared that the *Companies' Creditors Arrangement Act* was passed without too careful regard for the protection of the trade creditors of mercantile concerns going into an arrangement of that sort under this act, and since the arrangements under the *Companies' Creditors Arrangement Act* were not in the hands of an official trustee as under the *Bankruptcy Act*, it was found in a number of cases that the trade creditors' interests were frequently and seriously prejudiced.

As a consequence a Bill was introduced in the house in 1938 to repeal the *Companies' Creditors Arrangement Act* altogether. But this was strongly opposed by the Dominion Mortgage and Investment Association because, amongst other reasons, the laws of the United States prohibit the sale of securities unless there is in existence in relation to them appropriate legislation to enable a majority of stockholders to effect a reorganization of company if the circumstances seem to demand it. Of two conflicting groups who were in disagreement in respect of the legislation, one was this Dominion Mortgage and Investment Association which desired the retention of the *Companies' Creditors Arrangement Act* in order to deal with financial companies whose creditors were secured by a trust deed containing a provision for a trustee for such creditors. On the other hand, was a group of businessmen who were either trade creditors themselves or were opposed to the trade creditors being mulcted under the same act in respect of mercantile liabilities.

The introduction of the present bill is agreeable to both these groups. When the bill was before the other place, I am informed that both groups appeared and were agreeable to its provisions. With the passage of this bill it will leave companies that have complex financial structures, and a large number of investor creditors, able to use the *Companies' Creditors Arrangement Act* for the purpose of re-organization. Moreover they will be able to use it efficiently; because as a rule the terms of their own trust deed provide for trustee of the creditors whose business it will be to look after their interests, a provision of which almost invariably [is] absent in the case of the mercantile creditors. The mercantile companies will be able to use the provision of part III of the new revised *Bankruptcy Act*, which, unlike the *Bankruptcy Act* in force in 1933, has a provision whereby companies may apply for an extension to work out their affairs without incurring the stigma of bankruptcy.

Moreover, this provision of part III of the *Bankruptcy Act* requires the appointment of a trustee in bankruptcy who will look after the interests of the mercantile creditors and who will have supervision of the bankruptcy branch, which proceedings under the *Companies' Creditors Arrangement Act* do not now have.

I do not think there can be great opposition to this because it seems to be an arrangement—the arrangement set out in this bill—which adequately protects the position of the investor creditor, and is not at all unfair to the corporate debtor in either case.

Since its 1953 amendment, the *Companies' Creditors Arrangement Act* has been seldom used. This is by reason of the fact that its application has been restricted and that trust indentures usually now provide machinery for the contractual reorganization of the financial affairs of the debtor company.

The Farmers' Creditors Arrangement Act: This was emergency legislation designed to cope with the economic emergency of the depression. It was considered to be temporary legislation. The preamble to the Act, which explained its purpose, stated:

Whereas in view of the depressed state of agriculture the present indebtedness of many farmers is beyond their capacity to pay; and whereas it is essential in the interest of the Dominion to retain the farmers on the land as efficient producers and for such purpose it is necessary to provide means whereby compromises or rearrangements may be effected of debts of farmers who are unable to pay.

The then Prime Minister, the Right Honourable R.B. Bennett, in the initial debate on the Bill, said:

Bankruptcy proceedings have been regarded with some suspicion not only by farmers themselves, but also by those with whom the farmers deal and the question of whether or not the general provisions of the *Bankruptcy Act* should apply is, of course, an open one. We do not propose, therefore, that the ordinary provisions of the *Bankruptcy Act* should apply, but that for the present—hoping that it will not be for a long period—there should be appointed a special receiver rather than an official receiver such as we now have whose duty will be to assist in arriving at a composition, adjustment or settlement of the outstanding difficulties that confront the farmer.

In 1943, the Judicial Committee of the Privy Council held that the *Debt Adjustment Act*, 1937 (Alberta) was legislation in relation to bankruptcy and insolvency and was *ultra vires*.

This decision served to confirm the decisions of the lower courts on the Saskatchewan *Debt Adjustment Act* and likewise threw grave doubts upon the Manitoba *Debt Adjustment Act.* As a result of this decision, the *Farmers' Creditors Arrangement Act* of 1934 was repealed in 1943 and a new Act under the same name was enacted in its place. On the second reading of the Bill, it was said by the Honourable J.L. Ilsley, the then Minister of Finance:

... As a result (of the decision of the Judicial Committee of the Privy Council), representations were made to the Dominion Government by various delegations, including a delegation from the Saskatchewan conference of representatives of the three prairie province governments and farmers' organization and representatives of the mortgage and investment companies and insurance companies, as well as other individual creditors and debtors. Various representations were made to the government from private citizens of the prairie provinces, including a consider- able number of farmers who represented the point of view of both debtors and vendors of land. The need for a means of adjusting the old and onerous debt loads of depressed farmers in the west was admitted, but various opinions were advanced as to the best method of doing this. I think it is fair to say that general emphasis was put on the importance of safeguarding the credit of western agriculture and ensuring the necessary flow of new capital for the development of the industry. ...

Experience has shown certain limitations on the *Farmers' Creditors Arrangement Act,* 1934 and it was urged upon the government by representatives of both debtors and creditors that these defects should be remedied by new legislation under the bankruptcy jurisdiction of the dominion. Manitoba pressed for the extension of the Act, or similar legislation, to that province as well as to Alberta and Saskatchewan, and indeed, the Saskatchewan conference suggested that there be enacted legislation which would provide for continuous adjustment of farm debts.

The government has given careful consideration to these representations and to the question of the best way of meeting the problem that existed in the three prairie provinces without doing irreparable harm to the credit of western agriculture. After careful deliberation, the government reached the decision that it was inadvisable at this time to reopen the fundamental issues of the western debt problem. To embark upon legislation so highly controversial during the stress of war when the energies of parliament and the country, as a whole, are being taxed by immediate war emergencies, was felt to be unwise. ...

... The government, however, felt it desirable to meet the immediate need of preventing farmers from being dispossessed of their lands when food production was of such vital impor- tance to the nation and to that end an order-in-council was passed following the Privy Council decisions, that provided that in any action by a mortgagee for foreclosure, or by a vendor under an agreement for sale or cancellation of the agreement, the court may stay the action, postpone the payment of any moneys due, vary or extend any order previously made with a view to retaining on the land during the state of war now existing an efficient and industrious farmer and at the same time protecting all other persons having any interest in the land of the debtor.

At the same time the study which has been made of the operation of the *Farmers' Creditors Arrangement Act,* 1934 and of the representations received earlier this year, has induced us to introduce the bill which is now before the house. This bill is designed to rescind the 1934 Act and substitute for it an act which will continue, with important changes the system of farm debt adjustment which has, on the whole, worked successfully in the past.

In the same debate, The Right Honourable J.G. Diefenbaker, in discussing the operation of the Act in Saskatchewan, gave some indication of the extent of the problem when he said:

... Up to April of 1940, there were 5094 proposals made under the act since 1935; secured debts were reduced by $18,547,051 and unsecured debts by $1,926,819 during that period, or an average reduction of 41.9 per cent per farm. In the Province of Saskatchewan there were 142,000 farmers with a debt load in excess of $482,000,000. ...

The Act, which is required to be "read and construed as one with the *Bankruptcy Act*," provides a summary procedure whereby a farmer may make an arrangement with his creditors. Where the farmer and his creditors cannot agree upon the terms of an arrangement, the court is empowered to formulate an arrangement and impose it upon the creditors. In such cases, the secured debt of a farmer can be reduced without the consent of the creditor. Although the Act, which is far reaching and drastic, had the immediate result of helping the hard pressed prairie farmers, there is reason to believe that in the long run the Act worked to the detriment of the farmer. Investors became reluctant to lend money on farm mortgages by fear that a part of the loan might be wiped out through an arrangement under the Act. The long term result of the Act was that almost the only money loaned on farm mortgages came from the Farm Loans Board, created at the time the *Farmers' Creditors Arrangement Act* was enacted.

The *Farmers' Creditors Arrangement Act*, as a practical matter, cannot now be used as it relates only to farmers who have incurred two-thirds of the total amount of their debts before December 15, 1943. No proceedings under this Act have been reported since 1959.

Other Legislation: The *Bankruptcy Act*, The *Winding-Up Act*, The *Companies' Creditors Arrangement Act* and *The Farmers' Creditors Arrangement Act* are the principal but not the only federal statutes relating to bankruptcy and insolvency. There are, for example, special provisions in the *Bank Act* and the *Quebec Savings Bank Act* in reference to insolvent banks. *The Exchequer Court Act* and the *Railway Act* contain sections relating to insolvent railways. In addition to the *Winding-Up Act* by which the winding up of insurance companies is primarily governed, there are special sections concerning insolvent insurance companies in the *Canadian and British Insurance Companies Act* and the *Foreign Insurance Companies Act*.

Conclusion: At the end of this brief description of how the bankruptcy and insolvency system developed in Canada, there are a number of comments that come to mind.

Although, at the outset, the legislation was almost entirely borrowed from England, in the course of time, amendments were made to the original legislation to better adapt it to Canadian conditions and special statutes were passed to meet particular problems. Little attempt was made, however, to integrate new legislation with the existing legislation or to make a single comprehensive Act. The result has been a multiplicity of statutes and systems which often lead to inequity and inefficiency.

With the multiplicity of systems, the debtor and the creditor sometimes have the choice of the system under which to proceed and, under certain circumstances, they can fare better under one system than another. A creditor, for example, may be better protected or may have a higher priority for a dividend under one system than another. Similarly, the penalty provisions applicable to debtors may vary.

Many corporations may be liquidated under either the *Winding-Up Act* or the *Bankruptcy Act*. There are transactions that may be set aside as fraudulent preferences under one of these Acts, which could not be set aside, as such, under the other. However, since the 1966 amendments to the *Bankruptcy Act*, the *Winding-Up Act* does not apply to a corporation, where a petition is filed under the *Bankruptcy Act*. While the opportunity of a debtor or creditor to elect to take proceedings under the *Winding-Up Act*, and thus forestall proceedings under the *Bankruptcy Act*, has been reduced, inequities are still possible. The majority of creditors, for example, may wish to take proceedings under the *Winding-Up Act* to reach a creditor who has received a preference that may be set aside as fraudulent under the *Winding-Up Act*, but not under the *Bankruptcy Act*. The creditor who is alleged to have obtained a fraudulent preference, or a creditor friendly to him, may effectively block the proceedings under the *Winding-Up Act* by making a petition under the *Bankruptcy Act*.

There are situations, however, where no choice is given to the debtor or the creditors as to which statute may be used. A number of statutes apply in whole or in part, for example, to particular debtors, such as banks, insurance companies and railways. This situation may also lead to inequity as both debtors and creditors, under the particular statutes, may, without good reason, fare differently than those who come within the provisions of other statutes.

Moreover, in spite of the multiplicity of systems and statutes, there are a number of debtors whose affairs cannot be liquidated under existing federal legislation. The non-trading corporations, for example, would be in that category. It is not clear, either, whether any of this legislation applies to the winding-up, by reason of their insolvency, of some corporations, such as provincial trust companies and certain building societies.

Finally, the existing legislation may also be criticized for being, to a considerable degree, either rudimentary or out-dated. Much of it was designed when social and commercial conditions were very much different than what they are today. In other cases, legislation designed to meet a particular emergency survived long after the emergency had passed and the conditions changed. The procedure for the liquidation of insolvent railways is a good example of rudimentary legislation. Under present conditions, as a practical matter, special legislation would probably be required to effectively liquidate a railway company by reason of its insolvency, as existing legislation is silent in respect to many matters of importance. The *Farmers' Creditors Arrangement Act* is an example of special legislation inspired by a national emergency that has been long out of date, but which has never been repealed, brought up to date or incorporated into the principal statute.*

Chapter 3
The Present Canadian Legislation

Having briefly traced the history of Canadian bankruptcy and insolvency legislation and how the system developed, we pause in this chapter to shortly describe the system and the manner in which it functions.

Proceedings Under the Bankruptcy Act

Voluntary and Involuntary Bankruptcies: There are two methods by which liquidation of a debtor's property may be initiated under the *Bankruptcy Act*. Firstly, a debtor may voluntarily enter bankruptcy by making an assignment of his property. Secondly, a debtor may be forced into bankruptcy by the petition of a creditor. A debtor who has filed a

---

* The Act has now been repealed. [ed.]

proposal under the Act may also be forced into bankruptcy if the creditors do not give their approval or if the Court either does not ratify or annuls the proposal.

Petition by Creditor: If the debtor has committed an "act of bankruptcy," a creditor may petition for a receiving order. An "act of bankruptcy" may be regarded as an act that raises a presumption that the debtor is either unable to pay his debts or is attempting to avoid their payment. The "act of bankruptcy" most frequently used is that the debtor ceased "to meet his liabilities generally as they become due." The petition is filed with the registrar in bankruptcy. If the debtor consents or if he does not oppose the petition, the registrar may make a receiving order that has the effect of adjudicating the debtor bankrupt. If the petition is opposed, it is heard by a judge.

Interim Receiver: At any time after the filing of a petition, but before a receiving order is made, the court may appoint a licensed trustee to be interim receiver of the property of the debtor, if it is "necessary for the protection of the estate." The interim receiver usually owes his appointment to the recommendation of the petitioning creditor. If a receiving order is subsequently made, the interim receiver, in most cases, is appointed the trustee of the estate.

Assignment by Debtor: A voluntary bankruptcy is commenced by the debtor filing, with the official receiver, a formal assignment of his property with the name of the assignee in blank. It must be accompanied by a sworn statement showing the property of the debtor, a list of his creditors with their addresses, and the amount owed to each. The official receiver must then select a trustee by reference to the wishes of the most interested creditors "if ascertainable at the time," and complete the assignment by inserting therein, as grantee, the name of the trustee. In practice, the trustee is chosen by the debtor who, in the majority of cases, has approached the trustee, before the assignment is filed, to ascertain whether or not he would act as trustee. The trustee, before accepting the appointment, satisfies himself that the proceeds from the realization of the estate will be at least sufficient to secure the payment of his fee. In "no asset cases," cash deposits or third party guarantees are usually required by the trustee.

Official Receivers: The principal duties of the official receivers are to accept and file assignments, to appoint trustees on assignments, to examine all debtors as to their conduct, the causes of their bankruptcy and the disposition of their property, to fix the amount of the bond to be filed by trustees in both voluntary and involuntary bankruptcies and to preside over, or nominate someone else to preside over, the first meeting of creditors.

Each Province of Canada is a bankruptcy district, some of which are divided into bankruptcy divisions. For each division, one or more official receivers may be appointed by the Governor in Council. In Vancouver, Calgary, Edmonton, Toronto, Ottawa, Hull, Montreal and Quebec City, where the volume of bankruptcies is greater than in other parts of the country, full-time federal civil servants have been appointed as official receivers. Elsewhere, the official receivers are usually provincial civil servants, often court officials.

In Canada, the official receiver is not a receiver in the generally accepted meaning of the word. In England, the official receiver is a true receiver. There, in the interval between the making of a receiving order, which is in the nature of an interim order, and the order adjudging the debtor bankrupt, which is the final order, the official receiver is given control of the debtor's property. The debtor, during this interval, is not deprived of the ownership of his property, but is not entitled to deal with it.

First Meeting: At the first meeting of creditors, the appointment of the trustee is affirmed or another is substituted in his place. One or more, but not exceeding five inspectors, are appointed. Such directions are given to the trustee as the creditors may see fit with reference to the administration of the estate. There are seldom subsequent meetings of creditors as the inspectors are considered to represent them.

Inspectors: The first meeting of inspectors takes place, as a rule, at the conclusion of the first meeting of creditors. The inspectors discuss with the trustee how the estate is to be administered. All major decisions of the trustee relating to the liquidation of the property of the debtor must be authorized by them. Each inspector is entitled to be repaid his actual and necessary travelling expenses incurred in and about the performance of his duties and may be paid a fee ranging from $3.00 to $10.00 per meeting, depending upon the size of the estate.

The Trustee: Only a trustee who has been licensed by the Superintendent of Bankruptcy, with the approval of the Minister of Consumer and Corporate Affairs, may be appointed the trustee of an estate. He is an officer of the Court and subject to its direction. His main responsibility is to collect the estate of the debtor, to liquidate it and to distribute the proceeds to the creditors. He does this under the direction and supervision of the creditors who, usually, act through the board of inspectors.

The Role of the Creditors: The underlying principle of the *Bankruptcy Act* is that the creditors should control the administration of an estate in bankruptcy. The theory of creditor control is that, since the assets of the bankrupt are liquidated for the benefit of the creditors, they are in the best position to look after their own interest. As much power as is reasonably possible to give is given to the creditors. They appoint the trustee and may substitute one trustee for another, within the limits of the system requiring trustees to be licensed. In the administration of the estate, the trustee must consider the directions of the creditors, so long as they are not contrary to the Act. Not only is the trustee bound by these instructions in order for his actions to be valid, but, to avoid being subject to personal liability, he generally requires specific authorization for all that he does. In addition, the trustee is required to report to the creditors, at their request, concerning his administration.

Property Available for Creditors: All the property of a debtor at the date of his bankruptcy, or that may be acquired by, or devolved on, him before his discharge, is available for the payment of his debts. The only exception is property that, as against the bankrupt, is exempt from execution or seizure under the laws of the province within which the property is situated and within which the bankrupt resides.

The trustee is required to go beyond mere appearances in identifying and taking possession of the property of the bankrupt. Certain transactions entered into within varying suspect periods may be examined and avoided or reviewed under the *Bankruptcy Act* or the applicable provincial legislation. Examples of such transactions include: (a) certain types of gifts made by a debtor within one year prior to becoming bankrupt; the suspect period is extended to five years where the debtor, at the time of the gift, was unable to pay his debts in full without the aid of the property given away; (b) certain transfers of property, where the intention of the debtor was to defraud his creditors; (c) transfers of property by a debtor to creditors with a view to giving those creditors a preference, where the debtor becomes bankrupt within three months thereafter; the period is extended to twelve months, if the debtor and the creditors are related persons; (d) transactions entered into within twelve months prior to bankruptcy, by a debtor, with persons dealing with him otherwise than at arm's length, may be reviewed and, where it is found that the consideration given or received by the bankrupt was conspicuously greater or less than the fair market value of the property or services concerned in the transaction, judgment may be given to the trustee for the difference.

Claims Against the Estate: All persons to whom the bankrupt is indebted, as of the date of bankruptcy, may prove a claim against the estate of the bankrupt. The trustee may disallow the claim or allow it, in whole or in part, subject to an appeal to the court. A secured creditor may prove a claim, if he surrenders his security to the trustee for the general benefit of the creditors. Where the creditor realizes his security, he may prove for the balance due to him, after deducting the net amount realized. Instead of realizing his security, the secured creditor may assess the value of his security and claim for the difference. The trustee may redeem the security at the value assessed by the creditor or, if the secured creditor takes no action, the trustee may redeem the security by paying the debt.

Distribution of Property: The trustee is required to pay dividends in the course of realizing the property as funds become available, subject to the retention of such sums as may be necessary for the costs of administration. Certain claims are paid in priority to others. After payment of the costs of administration, these claims must be paid in full before a dividend may be paid to the ordinary creditors. The creditors who have a priority include those to whom are owed: (a) wages and salaries for services rendered within three months prior to bankruptcy, to the extent of five hundred dollars in each case; (b) municipal taxes for a two-year period, if they are not secured by a preferential lien on real property, provided they do not exceed the value of the property against which the taxes are imposed; (c) arrears of rent for a period of three months prior to bankruptcy and accelerated rent for three months, if permitted by the lease, provided the total amount does not exceed the realization from the property on the premises under the lease; and (d) claims of the Crown in right of Canada or of any province.

The claims of certain creditors are postponed until the claims of all other creditors are satisfied. These creditors are: (a) a spouse or former spouse of the bankrupt, in respect of a claim for wages, salary, commission or compensation in connection with the business of the bankrupt; (b) a creditor who entered into a reviewable transaction with the bankrupt unless, in the opinion of the trustee or the court, it was a proper transaction; and (c) certain persons claiming under a marriage contract.

Disabilities of Bankrupts: The bankruptcy has the effect of imposing a number of legal disabilities upon the bankrupt until his discharge. Some of the most important of these are that: (a) he may not engage in trade or business without disclosing, to all persons with whom he enters into a business transaction, that he is an undischarged bankrupt, (b) he may not obtain credit, for a purpose other than the supply of necessaries for himself and family, to the extent of five hundred dollars or more, without disclosing that he is an undischarged bankrupt; (c) he may not be a director of a limited liability corporation; and (d) he may not be a senator.

Discharge of Bankrupt: The court has a wide discretion to grant a discharge to a bankrupt. It may refuse a discharge, suspend it for any period, or require the bankrupt, as a condition of his discharge, to pay such moneys, or comply with such other terms, as the court may direct. However, no corporation may obtain a discharge unless it satisfies the claims of its creditors in full.

The discharge releases the bankrupt of all the claims of his creditors in the bankruptcy, except: (a) a fine or penalty imposed by a court; (b) a debt arising out of a bail bond; (c) a debt or liability for alimony, maintenance, or support of a spouse or child, living apart from the bankrupt; (d) certain debts incurred by fraud; (e) a debt for goods supplied as necessaries of life; and (f) a dividend that a creditor would have been entitled to receive on a provable claim not disclosed to the trustee, except where the creditor had notice of the bankruptcy.

Discharge of Trustee: When a trustee has completed the administration of the estate, he is required to apply for his discharge. The court may grant him a discharge if he has accounted, to the satisfaction of the inspectors and the court, for all property that came to his hands. The discharge has the effect of releasing the trustee from all liability in respect of any act done or default made by him in the administration of the property of the bankrupt, and from all liability in relation to his conduct as trustee. For his services, the trustee, unless the court otherwise orders, or the creditors otherwise agree, is entitled to a remuneration not exceeding seven and one-half per cent of the amount realized. In calculating the trustee's remuneration, however, payments made to secured creditors are not taken into account.

Bankruptcy Offences: In order to ensure their full co-operation in the administration of estates, the *Bankruptcy Act* imposes upon bankrupts many duties with penalties for their non-performance. Bankrupts are obliged, for example, to make discovery of and deliver their property to the trustee, to prepare a statement of their affairs, to attend the first meeting of creditors and to examine the correctness of all proofs of claims. The Act also provides that the doing of certain things by the bankrupt, such as a fraudulent disposition of property and the making of a false entry in a statement, constitute an offence. Penalties are also imposed upon inspectors for accepting anything in addition to their fees. There are also a number of offences directed at trustees who abuse their position.

Proposals: A debtor, before or after becoming bankrupt, may make a proposal to his creditors. If the proposal is accepted by a majority in number and three-fourths in value of the creditors present at a meeting of creditors and subsequently ratified by the court, it is binding upon all creditors with provable claims. In the case of a proposal made after bankruptcy, the approval of the court operates to annul the bankruptcy and to revest in the debtor, or such other person as the court may direct, the property of the bankrupt, unless the terms of the proposal otherwise provide.

• • •

The Superintendent of Bankruptcy: Official control of the bankruptcy process is exercised by the Superintendent of Bankruptcy. He is the head of the Bankruptcy Branch of the Department of Consumer and Corporate Affairs. Among other responsibilities, he must investigate allegations that offences have been committed under the *Bankruptcy Act*, where it appears that they would not otherwise be investigated. He also has the responsibility to supervise the administration of all estates to which the Act applies. To do this, he may intervene, as a party, in any matter or proceeding in Court. Every petition for a receiving order is served upon the Superintendent. He may thereby get early notice of a matter that might require investigation. In the same way, every bill of costs of a solicitor is served upon him and, if he considers it advisable, he may intervene on the taxation. The Superintendent also examines every statement of receipts and disbursements and the final dividend sheet prepared by the trustee when the administration of an estate is completed. The Superintendent's comments upon these documents are considered by the Court when the trustee's accounts are passed. It is also the responsibility of the Superintendent to receive applications for licences, and to make recommendations to the Minister for or against the granting of such applications.

Proceedings Under the Winding-Up Act

A winding-up order may be made in respect of any insolvent company. When an order is made, a liquidator is appointed by the court. The property of the debtor corporation is liquidated by the liquidator under the supervision of the court. In the course of liquidation, the debtor corporation may propose to make a compromise or arrangement with its creditors. If an arrangement is accepted by a majority in number representing three-fourths in value of the creditors and subsequently sanctioned by the court, it is binding upon all the creditors, the liquidator and contributories of the company. Special provisions are applicable to the liquidation of banks and insurance companies, which are excepted from the provisions of the *Bankruptcy Act*. Where proceedings have been instituted under the *Bankruptcy Act* in respect of a corporation, the *Winding-Up Act* does not apply to that corporation. With court control of the administration, the procedure, under the *Winding-Up Act*, necessitates more frequent applications to the court than that under the *Bankruptcy Act*.

Proceedings Under the Companies' Creditors Arrangement Act

An arrangement may be made under this Act by a company, only if it has outstanding an issue of debentures and the arrangement includes terms binding the company and the debenture holders. Where an arrangement is proposed, an application is made to the court to direct a meeting of the class or classes of creditors concerned. The court, in its discretion, may also require a meeting of the shareholders. An arrangement is binding upon all of the creditors in the classes concerned, where it has been agreed by a majority in number representing three-fourths in value of the creditors and sanctioned by the court.

NOTES

1) *Historical update*. Following the publication of the Tassé Report the federal government introduced Bill C-60 in 1975. This was a complete revision of the Bankruptcy Act (BA) and adopted most of the Task Force's recommendations. The bill was strongly criticized, on technical and policy grounds, by various bankruptcy constituencies in hearings before the Senate Banking and Commerce Committee and was withdrawn by the government for further review. A revised bill, Bill C-12, was introduced in 1980 but it, and three other bills introduced over the next four years, never emerged from the committee stage in the House of Commons. See further Comment (1982-83) 8 *CBLJ* 374.

The newly elected Mulroney government abandoned in 1984 further attempts to enact a revised Act and opted instead for incremental changes to the BA. To this end the federal government established an advisory committee (the "Colter Committee") composed of insolvency practitioners and trustees to recommend those changes that were deemed to be most urgent. The committee reported in 1986.

The committee's recommendations were largely adopted in Bill C-22, first introduced in the summer of 1991. The bill nearly came to grief over Part I of the bill, which would have enacted a separate Wage Claim Payment Act. The bill was given parliamentary approval in 1992 (SC 1992, c. 27), but only after the government had dropped Part I entirely. The most important changes contained in the 1992 amendments were the following:

a) A totally revised Part III, Division 1, dealing with the reorganization of insolvent business debtors (although, technically speaking, not restricted to business debtors), and a new Division 2 aimed at the composition of consumer debts.

b) A new Part XI requiring secured creditors to give 10 days' notice to the debtor before seeking to repossess the collateral where the collateral comprises all or substantially all of the debtor's assets or all or substantially all of the debtor's inventory or accounts receivable, and subjecting privately appointed or court appointed receivers and receiver-managers to judicial supervision.

c) The substantial recasting of s. 136 (which deals with the ranking of creditors for the purpose of distributing the net assets of the estate) and the elimination of preferred creditor status for Crown claims.

d) The recognition of deemed trusts, established pursuant to federal and provincial tax legislation, of monies collected and deductions made by a taxpayer on behalf of the Crown (BIA s. 67(3)).

e) Introduction of registration requirements for Crown lien claims as a condition of their recognition in bankruptcy (BIA ss. 86-87).

f) Creation of an unpaid seller's right to recover the goods on the buyer's bankruptcy and, in the case of unpaid farmers, fishermen and aquaculturists, to claim a charge on the debtor's inventory for the unpaid amounts.

The 1992 Act (s. 92) requires Parliament to review the BIA three years after the amendments have come into effect. To prepare for this event, Industry Canada established a Bankruptcy and Insolvency Act Advisory Committee (BIAC) in 1993 to consider what further amendments should be recommended. The BIAC in turn established a series of Working Groups to study the various parts of the Act. The most important groups were those dealing with arrangements and proposals, preferences and priorities, consumer bankruptcies, and international insolvencies. Not all the working groups were able to reach a consensus on desirable changes. At the present time (June 1995) it is anticipated that Industry Canada will release a report and draft bill before the end of 1995. Some of the prospective changes will be referred to in subsequent chapters of this casebook.

2) *Non-Canadian developments.* Canada is not alone in feeling the need to modernize its bankruptcy and insolvency legislation. Over the past 20 years many other industrialized countries have felt the same pressure. The United States adopted a revised Bankruptcy Code in 1978, the United Kingdom its Insolvency Act of 1986, and Australia its corporate insolvency legislation of 1992. Germany adopted a new insolvency regime in 1993 and important new legislation was adopted, *inter alia*, in France and Japan.

There were common reasons for this abundance of legislative activity. Much of the legislation being replaced was very old (in the case of the civilian countries some of the legislation was over a hundred years old), and no longer served contemporary conditions. A second reason was that the occurrence of post-war recessions of increasing severity and the collapse of large enterprises made it urgent to seek viable alternatives to straight bankruptcies. Thirdly, with the rapid increase in the number of consumer bankruptcies, there was a significant shift in bankruptcy philosophy from one stigmatizing individual bankrupts, to a philosophy more hospitable to enabling the consumer debtor to wipe the slate clean under prescribed conditions.

Philosophically, in a spectrum of bankruptcy regimes, Canada's laws fall in the middle between the American and British regimes. The American Bankruptcy Code is both more complex and generally more debtor oriented than the BIA and companion Canadian legislation. The British Insolvency Act, 1986, on the other hand, true to its 19th century legacy, is more pro-creditor, and particularly more deferential to secured creditor claims, than either the Canadian or American regimes.

3) *Constitutional position.* Section 91(21) of the Constitution Act entrusts the federal government with exclusive jurisdiction to enact laws in relation to bankruptcy and insolvency. (Note the distinction between "bankruptcy" and "insolvency" and the significance of the distinction.) The apparent exclusiveness of the jurisdiction is misleading, however, since it has to be reconciled with the provincial power to regulate "property and civil rights (Constitution Act s. 92(13)). In practice, therefore, the courts have had to answer three types of questions: (a) what are the limits to the federal government's s. 91(21) powers (i.e., how do you define what is bankruptcy and insolvency legislation); (b) when is provincial legislation *ultra vires* because it is intrinsically "bankruptcy" or "insolvency" in character; and (c) applying the well established concurrency test, if the provincial legislation can be justified as an exercise of the provincial property and civil rights power, when will it be disqualified because it is repugnant to existing federal legislation?

Not surprisingly, the courts have not answered these questions uniformly nor with a consistent voice. One would have thought the courts would tolerate provincial intrusion so long as there was no parallel federal legislation and, conversely, that the judges would look askance at duplicative provisions likely to complicate the administration of insolvent estates. However, neither assertion can be made made with any degree of confidence. For example, in the *Voluntary Assignments Reference*, [1894] AC 189 the Privy Council upheld the Ontario Assignments and Preferences Act but, some sixty years later, struck down Prairie debt moratorium legislation in the *Debt Adjustment Act* case, [1943] AC 356, although it too was not in direct conflict with federal laws. The same observation can be made about the Supreme Court's much later decision in the *Orderly Payments of Debt Act* case [1960] SCR 571. These cases, and others, should be contrasted with the Supreme Court's majority decision in *Robinson v. Countrywide Factors Ltd.*, [1978] 1 SCR 753, also reproduced *infra* in chapter 16, upholding the validity of the Saskatchewan Fraudulent Preferences Act even though its provisions duplicate s. 95 of the BIA. Here, as in other branches of constitutional law, judicial impressions and perceptions of the role of particular policies are as important in determining the outcome of a challenge as the reading of precedents or the bare language of the Constitution Act.

Leaving aside the intermittent constitutional issues, it should be appreciated that provincial (and, where appropriate, federal) substantive law forms an essential backdrop for the BIA. This is because bankruptcy law is primarily adjectival in character and only provides the machinery for creating bankruptcies, administering bankrupt estates, and establishing rules for the ranking of creditors. Section 72(1) of the BIA expressly provides that the Act does not abrogate or supersede the substantive provisions of any other law or statute relating to property or civil rights that are not in conflict with the Act.

Canadian Insolvency Statistics

Insolvency Bulletin
March 1992, Vol. 12(3) pp. 152, 179, 180, 193, 197

Nombre Annuel de Faillites et Variances D'Année en Année
Annual Number of Bankruptcies and Variances from Year to Year
(1966-1990)

Année Year	Consommateurs Consumers		Affaires Business		Total	
1966	1,903		2,774		4,677	
1967	1,549	(−19%)	2,474	(−11%)	4,023	(−14%)
1968	1,308	(−16%)	2,481	(−)	3,789	(−6%)
1969	1,725	(+32%)	2,354	(−5%)	4,079	(+8%)
1970	2,732	(+58%)	2,927	(+24%)	5,659	(+39%)
1971	3,107	(+14%)	3,045	(+4%)	6,152	(+9%)
1972	3,086	(−1%)	3,081	(+1%)	6,167	(−)
1973	3,195	(+4%)	2,934	(−5%)	6,129	(−1%)
1974	6,992	(+119%)	2,790	(−5%)	9,782	(+60%)
1975	8,335	(+19%)	2,958	(+6%)	11,293	(+15%)
1976	10,049	(+21%)	3,136	(+6%)	13,185	(+17%)
1977	12,772	(+27%)	3,905	(+25%)	16,677	(+26%)
1978	15,938	(+25%)	5,546	(+42%)	21,484	(+28%)
1979	17,876	(+12%)	5,694	(+3%)	23,570	(+10%)
1980	21,025	(+18%)	6,595	(+16%)	27,620	(+17%)
1981	23,036	(+10%)	8,055	(+22%)	31,091	(+13%)
1982	30,643	(+33%)	10,765	(+34%)	41,408	(+33%)
1983	26,822	(−12%)	10,260	(−5%)	37,082	(−10%)
1984	22,022	(−18%)	9,578	(−6%)	31,600	(−14%)
1985	19,752	(−10%)	8,663	(−9%)	28,415	(−10%)
1986	21,765	(+10%)	8,052	(−2%)	30,267	(+7%)
1987	24,384	(+12%)	7,659	(−10%)	32,043	(+10%)
1988	25,817	(+6%)	8,031	(+5%)	33,848	(+6%)
1989	29,202	(+11%)	8,664	(+7%)	37,866	(+11%)
1990	42,782	(+47%)	11,642	(+34%)	54,424	(+44%)
1991	62,277	(+46%)	13,496	(+16%)	75,773	(+39%)

Source: Sommaire des statistiques annuelles du Bureau du surintendant des faillites.
Annual Statistical Summary of the Office of the Superintendent of Bankruptcy.

	Tableau 1 Total des Faillites et des Propositions Signalées au Cours de l'Année Civile 1993		Table 1 Total Bankruptcies and Proposals Reported in the Calendar Year 1993	
	Total des *d'actifs*	*Total des* *éléments* *d'actifs*	*Total des* *passifs*	*Total des* *déficits*
Province	*Total of* *Estates*	*Total* *Assets* *$*	*Total* *Liabilities* *$*	*Total* *Deficiency* *$*
T-N/Nfld.	685	22,682,373	44,729,945	22,047,572
N-É/NS	2,230	104,919,223	216,153,971	111,234,748
ÎP-É/PEI	89	3,063,222	10,399,519	7,336,297
N-B/NB	680	25,859,670	56,168,487	30,308,817
Québec	20,719	1,406,418,713	3,216,832,342	1,810,413,629
Ontario	28,329	1,930,313,146	4,623,467,361	2,693,154,215
Manitoba	2,732	115,015,988	248,340,089	133,324,101
Saskatchewan	1,675	72,388,252	127,358,778	54,970,526
Alberta	7,116	335,260,032	557,140,921	221,880,889
C-B/BC	5,011	149,879,478	471,170,480	321,291,002
TN-O/NWT	29	1,599,054	7,953,398	6,354,344
Yukon	2	2,710	25,738	23,028
Canada	69,297	4,167,401,861	9,579,741,028	5,412,339,167

	Tableau 2 Total des Faillites de Consommateurs Signalées au Cours de l'Année Civile 1993		Table 2 Total Consumer Bankruptcies Reported in the Calendar Year 1993	
	Total des *d'actifs*	*Total des* *éléments* *d'actifs*	*Total des* *passifs*	*Total des* *déficits*
Province	*Total of* *Estates*	*Total* *Assets* *$*	*Total* *Liabilities* *$*	*Total* *Deficiency* *$*
T-N/Nfld.	523	10,534,191	17,859,371	7,325,180
N-É/NS	1,592	28,827,538	43,996,450	15,168,912
ÎP-É/PEI	51	1,122,821	2,504,532	1,381,711
N-B/NB	467	8,434,942	15,611,795	7,176,853
Québec	15,707	346,569,744	772,638,923	426,069,179
Ontario	23,153	959,253,951	1,844,681,045	885,427,094
Manitoba	2,358	48,588,237	129,044,527	80,456,290
Saskatchewan	1,206	34,360,712	49,688,774	15,328,062
Alberta	5,337	142,465,663	168,943,215	26,477,552
C-B/BC	4,045	35,190,895	135,651,573	100,460,678
TN-O/NWT	16	324,604	575,747	251,143
Yukon	1	610	6,339	5,729
Canada	54,456	1,615,673,908	3,181,202,291	1,565,528,383

	Tableau 3 Total des Faillites Commerciales Signalées au Cours de l'Année Civile 1993		Table 3 Total Business Bankruptcies Reported in the Calendar Year 1993	
Province	Total des d'actifs Total of Estates	Total des éléments d'actifs Total Assets $	Total des passifs Total Liabilities $	Total des déficits Total Deficiency $
T-N/Nfld.	139	10,223,338	23,938,262	13,714,924
N-É/NS	534	65,900,963	161,443,749	95,542,786
ÎP-É/PEI	36	1,933,986	7,336,943	5,402,957
N-B/NB	197	17,137,470	38,912,454	21,774,984
Québec	4,623	819,678,650	2,012,013,495	1,192,334,845
Ontario	3,984	621,529,167	2,348,228,030	1,726,698,863
Manitoba	266	61,411,465	111,980,710	50,569,245
Saskatchewan	400	33,000,582	68,244,023	35,243,441
Alberta	1,476	170,748,106	355,559,255	184,811,149
C-B/BC	862	59,796,154	248,456,667	188,660,513
TN-O/NWT	9	1,170,000	7,252,792	6,082,792
Yukon	1	2,100	19,399	17,299
Canada	12,527	1,862,531,981	5,383,385,779	3,520,853,798

	Tableau 4 Total des Propositions Déposées au Cours de l'Année Civile 1993		Table 4 Total Proposals Filed in the Calendar Year 1993	
Province	Total des d'actifs Total of Estates	Total des éléments d'actifs Total Assets $	Total des passifs Total Liabilities $	Total des déficits Total Deficiency $
T-N/Nfld.	23	1,924,844	2,932,312	1,007,468
N-É/NS	104	10,190,722	10,713,772	523,050
ÎP-É/PEI	2	6,415	558,044	551,629
N-B/NB	16	287,258	1,644,238	1,356,980
Québec	389	240,170,319	432,179,924	192,009,605
Ontario	1,192	349,530,028	430,558,286	81,028,258
Manitoba	108	5,016,286	7,314,852	2,298,566
Saskatchewan	69	5,026,958	9,425,981	4,399,023
Alberta	303	22,046,263	32,638,451	10,592,188
C-B/BC	104	54,892,429	87,062,240	32,169,811
TN-O/NWT	4	104,450	124,859	20,409
Yukon	0	0	0	0
Canada	2,314	689,195,972	1,015,152,959	325,956,987

Tableau 6
Mises Sous Séquestres
Rapport de l'Année 1993

Table 6
Receiverships
Report for the Year 1993

	Privée / Private	Cour / Court	Total
T-N/Nfld.	30	0	30
N-É/NS	76	0	76
ÎP-É/PEI	5	0	5
N-B/NB	37	1	38
Québec	204	1	205
Ontario	836	29	865
Manitoba	37	5	42
Saskatchewan	55	5	60
Alberta	176	46	222
C-B/BC	99	21	120
TN-O/NWT	7	0	7
Yukon	0	0	0
Canada	1,562	108	1,670

QUESTIONS

What inferences do you draw from the above statistics? What accounts for the rapid growth in consumer bankruptcies over the past 15 years? How much is due to population increases and the growth in consumer credit? How much of it can be ascribed to the two recessions in 1982 and 1990? Do bankruptcies themselves inflict harm on the economy or are they merely *ex post* descriptions of losses that have occurred already?

Modern Bankruptcy Objectives

Thomas H. Jackson
The Logic and Limits of Bankruptcy Law
7-27 (1986) (footnotes omitted)

1. The Role of Bankruptcy Law and Collective Action in Debt Collection

Bankruptcy law and policy have been subject to long-standing debate. This debate is not so much about whether bankruptcy law should exist at all but about how much it should do. All agree that it serves as a collective debt-collection device. Whether, when firms are involved, it should do more is the crux of the dispute. I plan to start by establishing in this chapter what accepted wisdom has already acknowledged—that bankruptcy's system of collectivized debt collection is, in principle, beneficial. Most of this book will then be concerned with exploring how that benefit can be realized and, as importantly, how viewing bankruptcy as a collectivized debt-collection device imposes limits on what else bankruptcy can do well. It is in the latter area that the most conflict arises. It exists because bankruptcy analysts have failed to follow through on the first principles of establishing a collectivized debt-collection system. To show why bankruptcy's principal role limits what other functions it can usefully perform is the objective of this book. Toward that end we shall first examine why bankruptcy law *should* be doing what everyone takes as a given.

Bankruptcy law is a response to credit. The essence of credit economies is people and firms—that can be called *debtors*—borrowing money. The reasons for this are varied. In the case of individuals credit may serve as a device to smooth out consumption patterns by means of borrowing against future income. In the case of corporations and other firms it may be a part of a specialization of financing and investment decisions. And just as the reasons for borrowing are varied, so, too, are the methods. The prototype creditor may be a bank or other financial institution that lends money, but that is only one of many ways in which credit is extended. An installment seller extends credit. So does a worker who receives a paycheck on the first of December for work performed in November. The government, in its role as tax collector, also extends credit to the extent that taxes accrue over a year and are due at the end. Similarly, a tort victim who is injured today and must await payment until the end of a lawsuit extends credit of sorts, although involuntarily and (probably) unhappily. Finally, credit is not extended just by "creditors." First-round purchasers of common and preferred stock of a corporation are also lending money to the debtor. Their repayment rights are distinct (they are the residual claimants), but it is proper to view them, too, as having defined rights to call on the assets of the debtor for payment.

Whatever the reasons for lending and whatever its form, the terms on which consensual credit is extended depend to a substantial extent on the likelihood of voluntary repayment and on the means for coercing repayment. We are not concerned here with the means for getting paid when the debtor is solvent—when it has enough assets to satisfy all its obligations in full—but is simply mean-spirited or is genuinely disputing whether it has a duty of payment (as the debtor might be with our putative tort victim or with a supplier who the debtor believes sold it defective goods). The legal remedies for coercing payment when the debtor is solvent concern the rights of a creditor to use the power of the state in pursuit of its claim. This is a question of debtor-creditor law and one to which bankruptcy law historically has had nothing to add, directly at least.

Bankruptcy law can be thought of as growing out of a distinct aspect of debtor-creditor relations: the effect of the debtor's obligation to repay Creditor A on its remaining creditors. This question takes on particular bite only when the debtor does not have enough to repay everyone in full. Even then, however, a developed system exists for paying creditors without bankruptcy. The relevant question is whether that existing system of creditor remedies has any shortcomings that might be ameliorated by an ancillary system known as bankruptcy law.

To explore that question, it is useful to start with the familiar. Creditor remedies outside of bankruptcy (as well as outside other formal, non-bankruptcy collective systems) can be accurately described as a species of "grab law," represented by the key characteristic of first-come, first-served. The creditor first staking a claim to particular assets of the debtor generally is entitled to be paid first out of those assets. It is like buying tickets for a popular rock event or opera: the people first in line get the best seats; those at the end of the line may get nothing at all.

When the issue is credit, the ways that one can stake a place in line are varied. Some involve "voluntary" actions of the debtor: the debtor can simply pay a creditor off or give the creditor a security interest in certain assets that the creditor "perfects" in the prescribed manner (usually by giving the requisite public notice of its claim). In other cases a creditor's place in line is established notwithstanding the lack of the debtor's consent: the creditor can, following involvement of a court, get an "execution lien" or "garnishment" on the assets of the debtor. Or, sometimes, a place in line may simply be given to a particular claimant by governmental fiat, in the form of a "statutory lien" or similar device.

Although the *methods* for establishing a place in line are varied, the fundamental ordering principle is the same. Creditors are paid according to their place in line for particular assets. With a few exceptions, moreover, one's place in line is fixed by the time when one acquires an interest in the assets and takes the appropriate steps to publicize it. A solvent debtor is like a show for which sufficient tickets are available to accommodate all prospective patrons and all seats are considered equally good. In that event one's place in line is largely a matter of indifference. But when there is not enough to go around to satisfy all claimants in full, this method of ordering will define winners and losers based principally on the time when one gets in line.

The question at the core of bankruptcy law is whether a *better* ordering system can be devised that would be worth the inevitable costs associated with implementing a new system. In the case of tickets to a popular rock event or opera, where there must be winners and losers, and putting aside price adjustments, there may be no better way to allocate available seats than on a first-come, first-served basis. In the world of credit, however, there are powerful reasons to think that there *is* a superior way to allocate the assets of an insolvent debtor than first-come, first-served.

The basic problem that bankruptcy law is designed to handle, both as a normative matter and as a positive matter, is that the system of individual creditor remedies may be bad for the creditors *as a group* when there are not enough assets to go around. Because creditors have conflicting rights, there is a tendency in their debt-collection efforts to make a bad situation worse. Bankruptcy law responds to this problem. Debt-collection by means of individual creditor remedies produces a variant of a widespread problem. One way to characterize the problem is as a multiparty game—a type of "prisoner's dilemma." As such, it has elements of what game theorists would describe as an *end period* game, where basic problems of cooperation are generally expected to lead to undesirable outcomes for the group of players as a whole. Another way of considering it is as a species of what is called a *common pool* problem, which is well known to lawyers in other fields, such as oil and gas.

This role of bankruptcy law is largely unquestioned. But because this role carries limits on what *else* bankruptcy law can do, it is worth considering the basics of the problem so that we understand its essential features before examining whether and why credit may present that problem. The vehicle will be a typical, albeit simple, common pool example. Imagine that you own a lake. There are fish in the lake. You are the only one who has the right to fish in that lake, and no one constrains your decision as to how much fishing to do. You have it in your power to catch all the fish this year and sell them for, say, $100,000. If you did that, however, there would be no fish in the lake next year. It might be better for you—you might maximize your total return from fishing—if you caught and sold some fish this year but left other fish in the lake so that they could multiply and you would have fish in subsequent years. Assume that, by taking this approach, you could earn (adjusting for inflation) $50,000 each year. Having this outcome is like having a perpetual annuity paying $50,000 a year. It has a present value of perhaps $500,000. Since (obviously, I hope) when all other things are equal, $500,000 is better than $100,000, you, as sole owner, would limit your fishing this year unless some other factor influenced you.

But what if you are not the only one who can fish in this lake? What if a hundred people can do so? The optimal solution has not changed: it would be preferable to leave some fish in the lake to multiply because doing so has a present value of $500,000. But in this case, unlike that where you have to control only yourself, an obstacle exists in achieving that result. If there are a hundred fishermen, you cannot be sure, by limiting *your* fishing, that there will be any more fish next year, unless you can also control the others. You may, then, have an incentive to catch as many fish as you can today because maximizing your take this year (catching, on average, $1,000 worth of fish) is better for you than holding off (catching, say, only $500 worth of fish this year) while others scramble and deplete the stock entirely. If you hold off, your aggregate return is only $500, since nothing will be left for next year or the year after. But that sort of reasoning by each of the hundred fishermen will mean that the stock of fish will be gone by the end of the first season. The fishermen will split $100,000 this year, but there will be no fish—and no money—in future years. Self-interest results in their splitting $100,000, not $500,000.

What is required is some rule that will make all hundred fishermen act as a sole owner would. That is where bankruptcy law enters the picture in a world not of fish but of credit. The grab rules of nonbankruptcy law and their allocation of assets on the basis of first-come, first-served create an incentive on the part of the individual creditors, when they sense that a debtor may have more liabilities than assets, to get in line today (by, for example, getting a sheriff to execute on the debtor's equipment), because if they do not, they run the risk of getting nothing. This decision by numerous individual creditors, however, may be the wrong decision for the creditors as a group. Even though the debtor is insolvent, they might be better off if they held the assets together. Bankruptcy provides a way to make these diverse individuals act as one, by imposing a *collective* and *compulsory* proceeding on them. Unlike a typical common pool solution, however, the compulsory solution of bankruptcy law does not apply in all places at all times. Instead, it runs parallel with a system of individual debt-collection rules and is available to supplant them when and if needed.

This is the historically recognized purpose of bankruptcy law and perhaps is none too controversial in itself. Because more controversial limits on bankruptcy policy derive from it, however, less allegorical and more precise analysis is necessary. Exactly *how* does bankruptcy law make creditors as a group better off? To find the answer to that question, consider a simple hypothetical example involving credit, not fish. Debtor has a small printing business. Potential creditors estimate that there is a 20 percent chance that Debtor (who is virtuous and will not misbehave) will become insolvent through bad luck, general economic downturn, or whatever. (By insolvency, I mean a condition whereby Debtor will not have enough assets to satisfy his creditors.) At the point of insolvency—I shall make this very simple—the business is expected to be worth $50,000 if sold piecemeal. Creditors also know that each of them will have to spend $1,000 in pursuit of their individual collection efforts should Debtor become insolvent and fail to repay them. Under these circumstances Debtor borrows $25,000 from each of four creditors, Creditors 1 through 4. Because these creditors know that there is this 20 percent chance, they can account for it—

and the associated collection costs—in the interest rate they charge Debtor. Assume that each party can watch out for its own interest, and let us see whether, as in the example of fishing, there are reasons to think that these people would favor a set of restrictions on their own behaviour (apart from paternalism or other similar considerations).

Given that these creditors can watch out for their own interests, the question to be addressed is *how* these creditors should go about protecting themselves. If the creditors have to protect themselves by means of a costly and inefficient system, Debtor is going to have to pay more to obtain credit. Thus, when we consider them all together—Creditors 1 through 4 *and* Debtor—the relevant question is: would the availability of a bankruptcy system reduce the costs of credit?

This requires us to try to identify what bankruptcy's advantages might plausibly be. Identification of abstract advantages is not, however, the end of the issue. One must also compare those possible advantages with the costs of having a bankruptcy system. Determining whether a bankruptcy system would reduce the cost of credit requires a net assessment of charges.

But first the case for bankruptcy's advantages. The common pool example of fish in a lake suggests that one of the advantages to a collective system is a larger aggregate pie. Does that advantage exist in the case of credit? When dealing with businesses, the answer, at least some of the time, would seem to be "yes." The use of individual creditor remedies may lead to a piecemeal dismantling of a debtor's business by the untimely removal of necessary operating assets. To the extent that a non-piecemeal collective process (whether in the form of a liquidation or reorganization) is likely to increase the aggregate value of the pool of assets, its substitution for individual remedies would be advantageous to the creditors as a group. This is derived from a commonplace notion: that a collection of assets is sometimes more valuable together than the same assets would be if spread to the winds. It is often referred to as the surplus of a going-concern value over a liquidation value.

Thus, the most obvious reason for a collective system of creditor collection is to make sure that creditors, in pursuing their individual remedies, do not actually decrease the aggregate value of the assets that will be used to repay them. In our example this situation would occur when a printing press, for example, could be sold to a third party for $20,000, leaving $30,000 of other assets, but the business as a unit could generate sufficient cash so as to have a value of more than $50,000. As such it is directly analogous to the case of the fish in the lake. Even in cases in which the assets should be sold and the business dismembered, the aggregate value of the assets may be increased by keeping groups of those assets together (the printing press with its custom dies, for example) to be sold as discrete units.

This advantage, however, is not the only one to be derived from a collective system for creditors. Consider what the creditors would get if there were no bankruptcy system (putting aside the ultimate collection costs). Without a collective system all of the creditors in our example know that in the case of Debtor's insolvency the first two creditors to get to (and through) the courthouse (or to Debtor, to persuade Debtor to pay voluntarily), will get $25,000, leaving nothing for the third and fourth. And unless the creditors think that one of them is systematically faster (or friendlier with Debtor), this leaves them with a 50 percent chance of gaining $25,000, and a 50 percent chance of getting nothing. A collective system, however, would ensure that they would each get $12,500.

Would the creditors agree in advance to a system that, in the event of Debtor's insolvency, guaranteed them $12,500, in lieu of a system that gave them a 50 percent chance of $25,000—payment in full—and a 50 percent chance of nothing? Resolution of this question really turns on whether the creditors are better off with the one than the other. There are two reasons to think that they are, even without looking to the question of a going-concern surplus and without considering the costs of an individual collection system. First of all, if these creditors are risk averse, assurance of receiving $12,500 is better than a 50 percent chance of $25,000 and a 50 percent chance of nothing. Even if they can diversify the risk—by lending money to many people—it is probably preferable to eliminate it in the first place. This, then, represents a net advantage to having a collective proceeding.

One other possible advantage of a collective proceeding should also be noted: there may be costs to the individualized approach to collecting (in addition to the $1,000 collection costs). For example, since each creditor knows that it must "beat out" the others if it wants to be paid in full, it will spend time monitoring Debtor and the other creditors—perhaps frequently checking the courthouse records—to make sure that it will be no worse than second in the race (and therefore still be paid in full). Although some of these activities may be beneficial, many may not be; they will simply be costs of racing against other creditors, and they will cancel each other out. It is like running on a treadmill: you expend a lot of energy but get nowhere. If every creditor is doing this, each one *still* does not know if there is more than a fifty-fifty chance that it will get paid in full. But in one sense, unless the creditors can negotiate a deal with each other, the creditors have no choice. Each creditor has to spend this money just to stay in the race because if it does not, it is a virtual certainty that the others will beat it to the payment punch. Of course, a creditor could decide that it did not want to stay in the race, and just charge Debtor at the time of lending the money for coming in last should Debtor become insolvent. Debtor is not likely, however, to agree to pay a creditor that extra charge for having a lower priority provision, because, once paid that extra amount, the creditor may have an incentive to take steps to remain in the race and make money that way. For that reason it may be hard for a creditor to opt out of the race and get compensated for doing so.

These various costs to using an individual system of creditor remedies suggest that there are, indeed, occasions when a collective system of debt-collection law might be preferable. Bankruptcy provides that system. The single most fruitful way to think about bankruptcy is to see it as ameliorating a common pool problem created by a system of individual creditor remedies. Bankruptcy provides a way to override the creditors' pursuit of their own remedies and to make them work together.

This approach immediately suggests several features of bankruptcy law. First, such a law must usurp individual creditor remedies in order to make the claimants act in an altruistic and cooperative way. Thus, the proceeding is inherently *collective*. Moreover, this system works only if all the creditors are bound to it. To allow a debtor to contract with a creditor to avoid participating in the bankruptcy proceeding would destroy the advantages of a collective system. So the proceeding must be *compulsory* as well. But unlike common pool solutions in oil and gas or fishing, it is not the exclusive system for dividing up assets. It, instead, supplants an existing system of individual creditor remedies, and as we shall see, it is this feature that makes crucial an awareness of its limitations.

Note that the presence of a bankruptcy system does not mandate its use whenever there is a common pool problem. Bankruptcy law stipulates a minimum set of entitlements for claimants. That, in turn, permits them to "bargain in the shadow of the law" and to implement a consensual collective proceeding outside of the bankruptcy process. Because use of the bankruptcy process has costs of its own ... , if creditors can consensually gain the sorts of advantages of acting collectively that bankruptcy brings, they could avoid those costs. Accordingly, one would expect that consensual deals among creditors outside the bankruptcy process would often be attempted first. The formal bankruptcy process would presumably be used only when individual advantage-taking in the setting of multiparty negotiations made a consensual deal too costly to strike—which may, however, occur frequently as the number of creditors increases.

... It is possible that the rules specifying when a bankruptcy petition may be filed prevent the commencement of a collective proceeding until it is too late to save the debtor's assets from the self-interested actions of various creditors. Another possibility, however, is that the collective proceeding will begin too soon. Forcing all the creditors to refrain from individual actions (many of which have the effect of monitoring the debtor and preventing it from misbehaving) brings its own costs. Thus, to say that bankruptcy is designed to solve a common pool problem is not to tell us how to design the rules that do that well. These concerns do not, however, undermine the basic insight of what bankruptcy law is all about.

Like all justifications, moreover, this one is subject to a number of qualifications. To say that a common pool problem exists is not to say that individual behavior is entirely self-interested or that legal rules can solve all collective action problems. We often observe people behaving in a cooperative fashion over time even if it appears contrary to their short-run interest. In the credit world, for example, creditors do not always rush to seize a debtor's assets whenever it seems to be in financial trouble. Yet despite this qualification the underlying point remains: sometimes people behave in a self-interested way and would be better off as a group if required to work together. The tragedy of the Texas oil fields in the first half of this century is a notable example of how self-interest led to the depletion of oil that otherwise could have been enjoyed by the group of oil field owners. Creditor relations almost certainly are another area where this essential truth has validity, especially given the fact that creditors may have fewer incentives to cooperate when a debtor is failing than they do when there are greater prospects of repeat dealings with a debtor.

Nor can we be confident that the bankruptcy rules themselves do not create problems. They do, and we will examine later how they should be dealt with. Because these complications play out against a backdrop of basic bankruptcy principles, however, it is preferable for now to make two simplifying assumptions. The first assumption is that insolvency occurs without warning. By this assumption, we eliminate consideration of strategic behavior that is likely to exist when some creditors sense the imminent likelihood of bankruptcy's collective proceeding and attempt to avoid it. ... The second assumption is that bankruptcy proceedings take no time. By this assumption, we can set aside problems that occur through the passage of time and the fact that this passage of time affects various claimants in different ways. We can also set aside the complications that result from a debtor's need to encourage people to deal with it while in bankruptcy and the fact that some of these people may wear both prepetition and postpetition hats. ...

Although imposing these two assumptions is, of course, somewhat unrealistic, doing so clarifies several key features of bankruptcy law. We can later extend our examination by making the inquiry somewhat more realistic. For now, however, it is sufficient to ask whether there is in fact a common pool problem that cannot be solved by creditors contracting among themselves. If the number of creditors is sufficiently small and sufficiently determinate, it may be possible for them to negotiate a solution at the time of insolvency that would avoid many, if not most, of the costs of an individual remedies system, even if they were not bargaining in the shadow of the law. But in cases in which there are large numbers of creditors or the creditors are not immediately known at a particular time (perhaps because they hold contingent or nonmanifested claims), the ability of the creditors to solve the problem of an individual remedies system by an actual agreement may be lost. Bankruptcy provides the desired result by making available a collective system after insolvency has occurred. It is the implications of that view of bankruptcy law that we can now begin to explore.

2. Determining Liabilities and the Basic Role of Nonbankruptcy Law

Bankruptcy provides a collective forum for sorting out the rights of "owners" (creditors and others with rights against a debtor's assets) and can be justified because it provides protection against the destructive effects of an individual remedies system when there are not enough assets to go around. This makes the basic process one of determining *who* gets *what*, in *what order*. *Who* is fundamentally a question of claims, or what shall often be referred to as *liabilities*. *What* is fundamentally a question of property of the estate, or what shall often be referred to as *assets*. At one level there is nothing magical about these basic building blocks. A liability is something that makes you less valuable—that you would pay to get rid of. An asset is something that makes you more valuable—that someone would pay you for.

In looking at all of this, it is helpful to think of bankruptcy as follows. What bankruptcy should be doing, in the abstract, is asking how much someone would pay for the assets of a debtor, assuming they could be sold free of liabilities. The resulting money is then taken and distributed to the holders of the liabilities according to their nonbankruptcy entitlements. Essentially, [the following discussion] simply [fleshes] out this idea against the basic role of bankruptcy law. ... The question [to be] addressed ... is exactly what this means in considering how claimants should be treated in bankruptcy. The basic answer involves seeing the bankruptcy process as protecting, at a minimum, the relative *value* of particular nonbankruptcy entitlements instead of the rights themselves. This is the subject of determining liabilities in bankruptcy and involves the question of how to divide the assets. The question of ... assets is integrally related to the question of liabilities.

The Destructive Effect of Changes of Relative Entitlements in Bankruptcy

Bankruptcy's basic procedures are designed to ameliorate a common pool problem. The key to effective implementation of this goal is to trigger bankruptcy when, and only when, it is in the interests of the creditors as a group. Consider what this means. Insolvency may be an occasion to collectivize what hitherto had been an individual remedies system. It does not, however, justify the implementation of a different set of relative entitlements, unless doing so is necessary as a part of the move from the individual remedies system. It is not just that the need for a collective proceeding does not go hand in hand with new entitlements. It is that the establishment of new entitlements in bankruptcy conflicts with the collectivization goal. Such changes create incentives for particular holders of rights in assets to resort to bankruptcy in order to gain for themselves the advantages of those changes, even when a bankruptcy proceeding would not be in the collective interest of the investor group. These incentives are predictable and counterproductive because they reintroduce the fundamental problem that bankruptcy law is designed to solve: individual self-interest undermining the interests of the group. These changes are better made *generally* instead of in bankruptcy only.

The problem of changing relative entitlements in bankruptcy not only underlies this book's normative view of bankruptcy law but also forms the basis of the bankruptcy system that has been enacted. The Supreme Court made this point in a case that is as important for recognizing it as the actual issue decided is unimportant. The case, *Butner v. United States* [440 US 48], decided in 1979, involved a secured creditor's claim to rents that accrued on the property serving as collateral after the filing of the bankruptcy petition relative to the claims of the unsecured creditors generally. Under relevant state law, as the Supreme Court described it, the debtor was entitled to the rents as long as it remained in possession or until a state court, on request, ordered the rents to be paid over to the secured creditor. In bankruptcy the unsecured creditors of an insolvent debtor can be viewed as the new equity owners of the debtor and hence entitled to what the debtor was entitled to outside of bankruptcy. This gave rise to the conflict between the secured creditor and the trustee, as representative of the unsecured creditors. The issue that the Supreme Court considered in *Butner* was: What should the source of law be (state or federal) in deciding how the secured creditor may realize on the post-bankruptcy rents? The Court saw the source of law as nonbankruptcy and observed that "the federal bankruptcy court should take whatever steps are necessary to ensure that the [secured creditor] is afforded in federal bankruptcy court the same protections he would have under state law if no bankruptcy had ensued." It justified this result as follows:

> Property interests are created and defined by state law. Unless some federal interest requires a different result, there is no reason why such interests should be analyzed differently simply because an interested party is involved in a bankruptcy proceeding. Uniform treatment of property interests by both state and federal courts within a State serves to reduce uncertainty, to discourage forum shopping, and to prevent a party from receiving "a windfall merely by reason of the happenstance of bankruptcy."

In the notion of forum shopping the Supreme Court expressed the fundamental point.

Yet to say that *Butner* denounced changing relative entitlements only in bankruptcy does not end the matter. It is important to understand *why* such rule changes cut against bankruptcy's recognized goal. This requires the separation of two issues that arise when a debtor is in bankruptcy: first, it is necessary to decide what to do with the debtor's assets, and, second, it is necessary to decide who gets them. The principal proposition I wish to establish here is that only by treating the answer to the second question as a nonbankruptcy issue can it be kept from unfavorably altering the answer to the first. To put this another way, in its role as a collective debt-collection device, bankruptcy law should not create rights. Instead, it should act to ensure that the rights that exist are vindicated to the extent possible. Only in this way can bankruptcy law minimize the conversion costs of transferring an insolvent debtor's assets to its creditors.

This point is easiest to demonstrate by examining a case where there is no occasion to use bankruptcy as a response to a common pool problem—where only one person has rights to the debtor's assets. Such a person, the sole owner of the assets, would have no creditors. Irrespective of any thought of bankruptcy, this sole owner would continually re-evaluate his use of the assets. If he were manufacturing buggy whips, at every moment (in theory at least) he would reassess whether this was the best use for those assets. If it was, he would continue; but if it was not, he would stop and either use the assets for some other purpose or sell them, piecemeal or as a unit, to others. This decision would be his alone. And he presumably would make it after determining which action would bring him the most from the assets.

This is, of course, an oversimplification. No person has *full* ownership of assets in the sense that he has absolutely unfettered control over their use. I do not have the right to sell cocaine even if I could make a great deal of money doing so. Similarly, a person making buggy whips may be subject to regulations governing the types of materials he can use, the minimum wages he must pay, or the environmental controls he must observe. These regulations will constrain his decisions and may lead him to choose a different use than he would choose in their absence.

This qualification, however, does not fundamentally undercut the basic point that given an existing array of legal rules, a sole owner would presumably decide to use the assets in the way that would bring him the most. He has, by definition, no need to use bankruptcy to ameliorate a common pool problem because a common pool exists only when there is more than one person with rights. He, accordingly, would be utterly indifferent to bankruptcy policy, unless the debtor's use of it benefited him (by permitting the debtor, for example, to escape an undesirable nonbankruptcy charge). If a charge were placed on assets only in bankruptcy law (such as that a debtor could not go out of business without first protecting employees), this owner would remain free to ignore it by going out of business without using bankruptcy. He would only be obligated to take account of such a charge if it were imposed by nonbankruptcy law.

When rights to assets are spread among a number of people, however, as they almost always are, things change. It then becomes necessary to decide not only how best to deploy the assets but also how to split up the returns from those assets. Because of the diversity of the owners, the deployment question creates a common pool problem. Bankruptcy law exists to solve that problem. But the lessons from the common pool show that the answer to the distributional question should not affect the determination of how to deploy the assets. As a group these diverse owners—bondholders, tort victims, trade creditors, shareholders, and others—would want to follow the same course as a sole owner. It is in the interest of the owners as a *group*, in other words, to keep the distributional question from spilling over into the deployment question.

Bankruptcy law is best approached by separating these two questions—the question of how the process can maximize the value of a given pool of assets and the question of how the law should allocate entitlements to whatever pool exists—and limiting bankruptcy law to the first. This distinction makes clear the relationship between bankruptcy rules and nonbankruptcy rules and provides a principle of bankruptcy policy capable of identifying which nonbankruptcy rules may need to be supplanted.

Because there is perhaps no point in bankruptcy policy that is more easily misunderstood, it is worth proceeding carefully. Let us consider one of the most common views of what bankruptcy law should do. This view is that bankruptcy law exists, in part, to help firms stay in business because of an increased social value and/or the jobs that are saved. In one guise this simply restates the common pool problem—that diverse owners, if unconstrained, will pull apart assets that would be worth more to the group of owners if kept together. Usually, however, the notion of keeping firms in business seems to be meant as an independent policy. For that policy to have independent force, it must mean that, irrespective of the wishes of the owners, a firm's assets should be kept in their current form because somebody—society or workers—is better off.

Incorporating such a policy in a bankruptcy statute, however, would be to mix apples and oranges, if one accepts the view (as everyone seems to) that bankruptcy law also exists as a response to a common pool problem. The question is really one of defining substantive rights. If the group in question—society, or workers, or whatever—deserves such rights, it is counterproductive to locate them only in a bankruptcy statute. Under existing nonbankruptcy law, for example, workers have no substantive entitlements to keep assets in their current form; they are not owners with substantive rights against the assets. For that reason the owners are free to close the business without considering the interests of the workers if doing so brings the owners more money. The fact that those owners have a common pool problem and need to use a collective proceeding to ameliorate it is not a reason to suddenly give a new group—workers—rights that they would not otherwise have and that could be ignored if the bankruptcy process was avoided. The decision whether they should have such rights should not be bankruptcy-specific. It addresses a distributional question as well as a deployment question.

Another way to put this is to note the distinction between saying that something is a problem that Congress should address and saying that something is a problem that Congress should address through bankruptcy law. The first is a federalism question, the second a collective debt-collection question. Whether giving workers substantive rights with regard to how assets are used is desirable, just as whether secured creditors should come ahead of unsecured creditors, is a question of underlying entitlements. Although protecting the victims of economic misfortune who have not been given rights against assets may be an important social and legal question, it is not a question specific to bankruptcy law. However the question is answered, a bankruptcy statute would still be necessary, because answering these substantive questions one way instead of the other does not eliminate the common pool problem. Because the issues of who should have entitlements and how to address a common pool problem are distinct, they should be kept separate in the legal response.

Nor is this simply an academic point. Bankruptcy law cannot both give new groups rights and continue effectively to solve a common pool problem. Treating both as bankruptcy questions interferes with bankruptcy's historic function as a superior debt-collection system against insolvent debtors. Fashioning a distinct bankruptcy rule—such as one that gives workers rights they do not hold under nonbankruptcy law—creates incentives for the group advantaged by the distinct bankruptcy rule to use the bankruptcy process even though it is not in the interest of the owners as a group. The consequences can be seen frequently: many cases are begun where the reason for filing for bankruptcy quite clearly is nothing more than the fact that the entity bringing the case is advantaged because of a bankruptcy rule change. Bankruptcy proceedings inevitably carry costs of their own. When bankruptcy is activated for a rule change that benefits one particular class, the net effect may be harmful to the owners as a group. It is this problem that makes such rule changes undesirable as a matter of bankruptcy law.

Even though a nonbankruptcy rule may suffer from infirmities such as unfairness or inefficiency, if the nonbankruptcy rule does not undermine the advantages of a collective proceeding relative to the individual remedies that exist given those entitlements, imposing a different bankruptcy rule is a second-best and perhaps a counterproductive solution. At bottom, bankruptcy is justified in overriding nonbankruptcy rights *because* those rights interfere with the group advantages associated with creditors acting in concert. If the nonbankruptcy rule—for example, a rule permitting owners to close down a business without considering the plight of workers—is thought undesirable for reasons other than its interference with a collective proceeding, the proper approach for Congress would be to face that issue squarely and to overturn the rule in general, not just to undermine or reverse it in bankruptcy. The latter course is undesirable because, as *Butner* recognized, it creates incentives for strategic "shopping" between the nonbankruptcy and bankruptcy forums.

NOTES

As will be seen from the above extract, Prof. Jackson* holds strong views about the normative roles of bankruptcy law—views that he shares with his frequent collaborator Prof. Douglas Baird, now dean of the University of Chicago law school. The following notes respond briefly to Prof. Jackson's theses from a Canadian perspective.

1) *Bankruptcy law as a solution to the common pool problem.* It is difficult to argue that this objective describes the exclusive, or even dominant, role of the BIA in straight bankruptcies. The case law presented below in chapter 13, in the context of s. 43 of the BIA, shows that Canadian courts are quite willing to entertain a bankruptcy petition to assist the petitioner in enforcing a claim even where there is no evidence that the debtor's bankruptcy will make the debtor's other creditors any better off. Bankruptcy petitions are also frequently brought by secured creditors to protect their security interests, again with scant concern about how it will affect the unsecured creditors' welfare. Often, after satisfying secured and preferred creditors' claims, little if anything is left for distribution among general creditors. As a result, there is little incentive for unsecured creditors to present a petition or to take an active interest in the administration of bankruptcy estates. Do these facts mean that Canadian bankruptcy law is not playing its proper role or do we deduce that *prebankruptcy* law is undermining bankruptcy law by failing to treat all creditor claims equally?

---

* Prof. Jackson has had a distinguished academic career. After graduating from the Yale law school he started teaching at the Stanford law school and then moved to Harvard. He was then appointed dean of the University of Virginia law school and subsequently became provost of the University. He is currently president of the University of Rochester.

2) *The "free start" policy for natural insolvent debtors.* Prof. Jackson appears to approve of this role of modern bankruptcy law. It is a role that Canadian bankruptcy law also shares, although perhaps not quite as enthusiastically, with US law. Is the policy a wise one or is it merely acceptance of the truism that you cannot extract blood from a stone? Does the free start policy encourage consumers to overspend knowing that, if the worse comes to the worst, they can always seek absolution in bankruptcy? Is the free start policy the consumers' equivalent of limited liability for enterpreneurs and shareholders operating behind a corporate veil? (The analogy between the two becomes even closer when it is remembered that directors and dominant shareholders of closely held corporations frequently have to provide guarantees for their companies' loans and for realty leases.) Until well into the 19th century, English (and Canadian) law took a much more punitive view of personal insolvencies, as readers of Charles Dickens's novels know all too well. Many civil law systems still look darkly at personal insolvencies.

In the Canadian context, it is in fact misleading to speak about a "free" start policy. There is no absolute right to a free start. The relevant provisions will be found in BIA ss. 169-180. From these provisions it appears: (1) that six types of debts are not dischargeable at all (ss. 177-78; the debts include alimony claims, fines and penalties, and debts arising out of the debtor's fraudulent conduct); (2) that the court must refuse, suspend or impose terms (s. 172(2)) where any of the wide ranging circumstances described in s. 173 apply (the circumstances include the fact that the debtor's assets are not at least equal to 50 per cent of the debtor's unsecured liabilities, unless the debtor can show that the shortfall arose because of factors for which he cannot justly be held responsible); and (3) that in all other cases, where the debtor's application is opposed, the court has a discretion whether or not to grant an absolute discharge.

In practice, the court will frequently make an order requiring the debtor to make at least partial payments on her debts where the debtor is earning a substantial income. However, it appears to be unusual for the court to require the payments to run for more than three years. The details about the administration of the discharge provisions will be found in Houlden & Morawetz, *Annotated Bankruptcy and Insolvency Act 1994*, H§10-H§22.

3) *Prebankruptcy entitlements should be respected in bankruptcy.* Prof. Jackson is well known (as is Prof. Baird) as a strong proponent of this proposition which, as he explains, flows from the adjectival role of bankruptcy law. Other American scholars, notably Prof. Elizabeth Warren,* take a more communitarian view. They recognize the legitimacy of making adjustments among creditors' claims, particularly where it is necessary for the successful reorganization of the business of a significant employer. Recent French bankruptcy law amendments, as well as other civilian systems, adopt a similar stance. See Axel Flessner, "Philosophies of Business Bankruptcy Law: An International Overview" in Ziegel (ed.), *Current Developments in International and Comparative Corporate Insolvency Law*, chapter 2 (1994). On the other hand, British bankruptcy law has traditionally respected creditors' rights, and especially secured creditors' rights, even more zealously than American bankruptcy law, and this continues to be true in the Insolvency Act 1986.

---

* See Warren, "Bankruptcy Policy" (1987), 54 *U Chi. L Rev.* 775.

Canadian law is a curious pastiche. The ranking of creditors' claims appearing in s. 136, as interpreted by the Supreme Court of Canada, does not follow the ranking under prebankruptcy law. Secured creditors regularly put a debtor into bankruptcy to take advantage of the more favourable treatment accorded them under the BIA. See *infra*, chapter 13, and the "quartet" of Supreme Court cases culminating in *BC v. Henfrey Samson Belair Ltd.* (1989), 59 DLR (4th) 726, *infra*, chapter 17. Obviously, secured creditors see nothing wrong in using bankruptcy law *to improve* their prebankruptcy entitlements (presumably because they regard the provincial and federal Crown and employee superpriority liens provisions as seriously destabilizing), but is it consistent with Jackson's view of the role of bankruptcy law? To use another example, ss. 80.1 and 80.2 of the BIA confer higher rights on unpaid sellers on the buyer's bankruptcy than the sellers enjoy under most of the provincial sales laws; and again, at the other end of the spectrum, Canadian courts have often interpreted their powers under the CCAA generously, to the disadvantage of secured creditors, so as to assist the restructuring of an insolvent company.

Having regard to these and other factors, the conclusion we would draw in the Canadian context is that federal-provincial relations are too complex to admit of easy generalizations and that creditors and debtors regularly seek help from either level of government with scant regard for the bankruptcy principles so strongly espoused by Prof. Jackson.

CHAPTER THIRTEEN

Initiation of Bankruptcy Proceedings

(BIA ss. 13.3, 13.4, 42, 43, 46, 49, and s. 2 "insolvent person")

Re Dixie Market (Nurseries) Limited
(1971), 14 CBR (NS) 281 (Ont. SC)

HOULDEN J (orally): This is a petition for a receiving order. The petitioning creditor is the trustee in bankruptcy of The Dixie Fruit Market Ltd. and Co., a limited partnership. The trustee was instructed by an unanimous resolution of a meeting of the creditors of the bankrupt company to file this petition.

The petitioning creditor's debt is in the amount of $26,335; this represents moneys advanced by the bankrupt company to the debtor. According to Ex. 1, the advances by affiliates as at 30th September 1970 total $27,835.03. None of the witnesses, who have given evidence for the debtor, have been able to explain the discrepancy between the two figures. It may be that some payment was made after 30th September 1970 to the petitioning creditor prior to its bankruptcy.

As at 30th September 1970 it appears that there were certain other accounts payable; however, the evidence given for the defence would indicate that all accounts payable have now been paid apart from the debt owing to the petitioning creditor. There is no dispute about the amount owing to the petitioning creditor. Apparently there was no arrangement for payment of the debt and, in the absence of any arrangement for payment, the law of course is that it must be paid within a reasonable time, depending upon the circumstances: *McGregor v. Curry* (1914), 31 OLR 261 at 269, 20 DLR 706, affirmed 25 DLR 771 (PC); *Owchar v. Owchar*, [1949] 2 WWR 97, [1949] 2 DLR 432 (Sask. CA). The debt was owing as at 30th September 1970 and, in my opinion, a reasonable time for payment has elapsed and as at 11th February 1971, the date of the filing of the petition, it was past due.

Counsel for the debtor submits that the reason for the filing of the petition is to use the Bankruptcy Court as a collection agency. I do not think that this is so. I believe the trustee in bankruptcy is well justified in filing the petition. The assets of the debtor consist of two pieces of property in the Oakville area. These properties were purchased for $60,000 about three years ago, and there are presently outstanding mortgages of $42,000. On the basis of the original purchase price, it will be obvious that there is not sufficient equity to pay the debt owing to the petitioning creditor. Furthermore, there is considerable risk that, if the trust in bankruptcy does not take some positive steps to protect the amount owing to the petitioning creditor, the assets of the debtor may in some way be encumbered to the prejudice of the petitioner. At the present moment, the mortgage payments are up to date although, as appears from Ex. 2, the payment due on the mortgage of Mor Investments Limited was not paid on 1st February 1971. This resulted in a telephone call from the mortgagee, and a letter of 9th February 1971 (Ex. 2) threatening to take legal proceedings.

The rental income from the property is not sufficient to meet the mortgage payments. The taxes on the property, which must be substantial, will soon be falling due and the money will have to be found to pay them.

Turning to the petition, there is no denial of para. 1. As I have pointed out, the debt of the petitioner is admitted so there is no dispute in respect of para. 2. With reference to para. 3, the petitioning creditor has certainly no security. The only paragraph in the petition which is contested, is whether or not the debtor has ceased to meet its liabilities generally as they become due. If there were liabilities to other creditors, there would be a question in this case, as to whether or not the act of bankruptcy has been committed, but this is one of those peculiar situations in which there is only one debt owing and that debt is the amount owing to the petitioning creditor.

Whether or not the failure to pay a single creditor can constitute ceasing to meet liabilities generally as they become due is not an easy question. There have been a number of decisions on this point. However, in this province, the case of *Re Raitblat*, 5 CBR 714, 28 OWN 237, [1925] 2 DLR 1219, affirmed by the Court of Appeal 5 CBR 765, 28 OWN 292, [1925] 3 DLR 446, has decided that a failure to pay a single creditor may constitute ceasing to meet liabilities generally as they become due: see also *Re Freedman*, 4 CBR 499, [1924] 1 DLR 682, reversed on other grounds 5 CBR 47, 55 OLR 206, [1924] 3 DLR 517 (CA) and *Re Glenn* (1941), 23 CBR 81 (Ont.).

I can see no reason why, if there is only a single creditor and there has been a failure to pay that creditor, this cannot constitute ceasing to meet liabilities generally. To hold otherwise would be to deprive the petitioning creditor of the benefits of the Bankruptcy Act, RSC 1952, c. 14. If the creditor in the present case is prevented from using the Bankruptcy Act, he will be required to use the remedies of a judgment creditor—this means that the assets cannot be disposed of for a year and the sheriff will have control of their disposal.

As I have said, the debt is overdue; the debtor has not been able to suggest any way in which it can be paid and in my opinion, it is a proper case for a receiving order to be made. There will, therefore, be a receiving order and Mr. Sprackman will be the trustee. ...

Petition granted.

Re Holmes and Sinclair
(1975), 20 CBR (NS) 111 (Ont. SC)

HENRY J: ... It is clear that the Courts, in Ontario at least, have granted a receiving order on the basis of a default to one creditor in special circumstances. These circumstances are:

(a) The creditor is the only creditor of the debtor; and the debtor has failed to meet repeated demands of the creditor; in these circumstances he should not be denied the benefits of the Bankruptcy Act by reason only of his unique character; or

(b) The creditor is a significant creditor and there are special circumstances such as fraud on the part of the debtor which make it imperative that the processes of the Bankruptcy Act be set in motion immediately for the protection of the whole class of creditors; or

(c) The debtor admits that he is unable to pay his creditors generally, although they and the obligations are not identified.

I find on the evidence that these circumstances do not exist here.

Because this Court has in some of the recent decisions referred to, such as *Dixie Market*, *Polyco* and *King Petroleum*, made a receiving order on proof of failure to meet a liability to a single creditor, it is not to be taken to have established a new principle that a petitioning creditor need only prove default with respect to the debt owing to him. Those decisions in my judgment do not lay down such a principle; they are, as I see it, merely the application to particular facts of the general rule (exemplified by the decision in *Re Elkind; Samuel Hart & Co. v. Elkind, supra*) that when relying on an act of bankruptcy described in s. 24(1)(j) the petitioning creditor must strictly establish that, in the words of the statute, the debtor "ceases to meet his liabilities generally as they become due;" in all of them the Court was influenced either by the existence of other creditors, or of one of the special circumstances I have set out above. In the non-exceptional case, as in the case at bar, that situation cannot be ordinarily proved by having regard to the experience of one creditor only, even though he may be a major creditor. Resort to the statutory machinery of the Bankruptcy Act, rather than to the remedies to enforce a debt or claim in the ordinary courts, is intended by Parliament to be for the benefit of the creditors of a debtor as a class, and the act of bankruptcy described in s. 24(1)(j) is, in my judgment, an act that singles out the conduct of the debtor in relation to the class, rather than to the individual (as is the case under s. 24(1)(e)). It is for this reason that the court must be satisfied that there is sufficient evidence from which an inference of fact can fairly be drawn that creditors generally are not being paid. This requires as a minimum some evidence that liabilities other than those incurred towards the petitioning creditor have ceased to be met. The court ought not to be asked to draw inferences with respect to the class on the basis of one creditor's experience where evidence of the debtor's conduct towards other members of the class could, with reasonable diligence, be discovered and produced. The court's intuition is no substitute for the diligence of the petitioning creditor.

In the case before me, the petitioning creditor has not established conduct of the debtors towards other creditors. I am, in effect, asked to infer that there is a group of creditors who have not been paid. It is not possible to say, on the evidence, whether they exist at all, or are few or numerous, or whether their claims individually or in total are significant or, most important, to say whether the debtors have *ceased* to meet their liabilities *generally*. ...

Petition refused.

Re Public's Own Market (Prince George) Ltd.
(1984), 54 CBR (NS) 222 (BCSC)

HARDINGE LJSC: The applicant Francana Real Estate Ltd. seeks to have the assignment of Public's Own Market (Prince George) Ltd. into bankruptcy set aside or, in the alternative, a declaration that the proceeds of the sale of certain of the bankrupt's assets form a part of the estate of the bankrupt available for distribution to the unsecured creditors including the applicant.

The applicant was the landlord of the bankrupt. As such it claims to be owed approximately $32,000 by way of rent, part of which is claimed to be owed pursuant to a lease entered into between the landlord and the bankrupt on 16th January 1976. The remainder of the landlord's claim is said to arise out of an unwritten month-to-month tenancy.

Prior to the bankruptcy the bankrupt was engaged in the business of selling household furniture and appliances through a retail sales outlet in Prince George. As is common with such businesses it needed working capital. In order to raise the required capital it obtained a loan from the Royal Bank of Canada. To secure the repayment of the loan the bank obtained a debenture from the bankrupt. The debenture created a floating charge on all the assets of the bankrupt and authorized the bank to appoint a receiver of the bankrupt's assets in the event of default. Default occurred and on 10th July 1984 the bank appointed the trustee to be its receiver. Thereupon the bank's charge crystallized.

On 17th July 1984 the trustee (who was then acting in its capacity as receiver under the bank's debenture) was advised of the landlord's claim for rent. In the meantime the trustee had arranged to conduct a sale of the bankrupt's stock of furniture and appliances. The sale was scheduled to take place a few days later. The solicitor for the landlord, in an attempt to secure the payment of the arrears in rent, attempted to negotiate a settlement of his client's claim with the solicitors for the bank. In order, as the solicitor for the applicant at any rate believed, to give the trustee some time to consider the claim for rent, it was agreed the landlord would not take any action by way of distress against the bankrupt's moveable assets prior to 9:00 a.m. on 19th July 1984.

Unknown to the solicitor for the landlord the period of grace was used not to consider the merits of its claim but to prepare an assignment into bankruptcy. The assignment was filed in the office of the official receiver, bankruptcy administration, at 11:00 a.m. on 19th July 1984. The same company that had up to the time of the filing of the assignment been performing the duties of receiver on behalf of the bank was named trustee of the estate of the bankrupt. This situation may have created a conflict of interest but counsel agreed that is not a matter which I need decide on this application.

At about 9:15 a.m. on the date of the assignment the solicitor for the landlord was informed that the assignment had in fact been perfected by filing. In an attempt to protect his client's interests in case the information he had been given should be incorrect, he attended at the bankrupt's place of business accompanied by two representatives of the landlord at about 10:10 a.m. the same day. One of the landlord's representatives then proceeded to levy distress pursuant to a distress warrant. Distress was levied in the presence of a representative of the trustee.

It is not disputed that although the preliminary steps required to levy distress for arrears of rent were carried out before the assignment in bankruptcy took effect, the receipt in the office of the official receiver of the assignment effectively prevented anything further being done to complete the distress proceedings. The trustee proceeded to sell the stock in trade (including those articles against which the landlord had levied distress) by public auction. However, sufficient funds were set aside out of the proceeds of the sale to satisfy the landlord's claim in the event the bankruptcy should be set aside or the landlord declared to be entitled to rank at least as an unsecured creditor in respect of such funds.

Counsel for the landlord advanced ingenious arguments in an attempt to persuade me that the assignment in bankruptcy should be set aside as being made for a fraudulent purpose, or alternatively, to declare that the landlord is a preferred creditor in relation to the realized value of the goods against which distress had been levied. I am not satisfied that either order should be made.

Section 151(1) of the Bankruptcy Act, RSC 1970, c. B-3, authorizes the court to annul a bankruptcy. The section does not specify the circumstances in which such a drastic step should be taken. It merely provides that, "Where, in the opinion of the court ... an assignment ought not to have been filed, the court may by order annul the bankruptcy." Here there is no doubt but that the company was insolvent. Even if, as was alleged, the decision of the directors to file an assignment into bankruptcy could result in a benefit to them in their capacity as guarantors of the company's indebtedness to the bank, that alone does not make the assignment fraudulent.

The facts in the present case bear a significant degree of similarity to those in *Re Gasthof Schnitzel House Ltd. and Sanderson*, 27 CBR (NS) 75, [1978] 2 WWR 756 (BCSC). There the landlord had levied distress against a tenant's goods and had proceeded to realize the value of the goods. The trustee brought a motion to require the landlord to pay the proceeds of the distress sale to him and the landlord brought a counter-motion to have the bankruptcy annulled. Ruttan J held that the fact that this insolvent debtor filed the assignment as a result of the urging of secured creditors, who were jockeying for legal remedies, did not mean the assignment was invalid. Legg J reached the same conclusion in *Re Koprel Ent. Ltd.* (1978), 27 CBR (NS) 22 (BCSC), where he said at p. 25:

It is clear from the authorities cited to me by counsel for the trustee that it is not improper for a creditor in the position of Kolosi, whose rights to the chattels here conflict with a distraint against the same chattels asserted by the receiver-manager of International, to promote a bankruptcy in order to defeat the priority otherwise afforded the distraint of a landlord and permit a security holder in the position of Kolosi to rank ahead of the landlord. This is the combined effect of ss. 107(1)(f) and 112 of the Bankruptcy Act.

The facts in the present case are so similar to those in the two cases cited above that I can find no basis on which I could grant an order annulling the bankruptcy. There was no improper conduct on the part of the bank, its solicitor or the directors of the bankrupt.

The alternative submission of counsel for the landlord is that the act of levying distraint before bankruptcy against the bankrupt's stock in trade had the effect, qua those goods, of removing them for the chattels of the bankrupt to which the bank's security could attach. Accordingly, he submitted that the money realized from the sale of the distrained goods should be distributed by the trustee in accordance with the scheme of distribution set out in s. 107 of the Act.

It was conceded that the alternative submission on behalf of the landlord was novel. No authority was cited to substantiate the submission. The short answer to the proposition seems to be that the bank's floating charge against all the stock in trade of the bankrupt crystallized on 10th July 1984 when the receiver was appointed. Therefore there was nothing against which the landlord could levy distress when it purported to do so nine days later. Further, even if a similar argument was not raised in the *Re Gasthof Schnitzel House Ltd.* and *Re Koprel Ent. Ltd.* cases, *supra*, or the various authorities considered in them, to give effect to the proposition counsel has advanced in the present case would be tantamount to reaching a conclusion diametrically opposed to that reached in the earlier cases. That is not something I am persuaded I should do.

Applications dismissed.

Re Harrop of Milton Inc.
(1979), 92 DLR (3d) 535 (Ont. SC)

HENRY J: The trial of this petition raises several issues that require resolution. The first issue is whether the act of bankruptcy alleged, namely, a general failure to meet liabilities as they become due, is proved to have occurred within the six months immediately preceding the issue of the petition. The second issue is whether the debtor company has any assets or potential assets that could be got in by a trustee appointed under a receiving order. The third is whether the Court ought to make a receiving order to effect the main purpose of the petitioning creditor, which is to realize its security under debentures given to it by the debtor company in priority to the claims of the debtor's landlord.

Most of the facts are not disputed. The debtor Harrop of Milton Inc. owned a restaurant business which was operated by Miss Hedi Nowak from its inception in June, 1975, until March 1, 1978, when it was taken over by a receiver and manager appointed by RoyNat, the petitioning creditor, and debenture holder. Miss Nowak's family had for some years operated a restaurant business in Milton. Miss Nowak's mother assisted her to start her own restaurant after she had gained experience in the family business, by leasing to Miss Nowak an old farmhouse for $1,500 per month from January 15, 1975. The lease was assigned to the debtor company Harrop, and the premises were refurbished and equipped. Miss Nowak is the president and sole shareholder of the company, and she managed the business. Her mother, the landlord, was the secretary of the company.

RoyNat made two loans to Harrop—$100,000 on June 6, 1975, and $30,000 on March 31, 1976, repayable in monthly instalments. The loans were secured by two debentures creating a first floating charge on all the assets of Harrop except inventory and receivables; essentially, the security under the debentures was the lease and the chattels of the company.

By August, 1976, both loans were in default and all payments on them had ceased. In January, 1978, RoyNat sent a Mr. Blair in to assess the commercial liability of Harrop. While he was doing so Mrs. Erna Nowak, who had not been paid any rent under the lease, but who was forbearing until then, by letter of January 17, 1978, purported to distrain for arrears of rent totalling $35,200. The landlord, however, did not remove and sell any assets at that time. On March 1, 1978, RoyNat appointed Mr. Blair's firm receiver and manager under the debentures, and the receiver-manager took over the operation of the business, retaining Miss Nowak as salaried manager. On March 1, 1978, a number of creditors' accounts were outstanding, and the debtor company was unable to pay them; this is not disputed. On November 22, 1978, the landlord Mrs. Nowak gave notice to the debtor company that the goods previously "distrained and impounded" were appraised at $32,638, that she had exercised her right to sell them, and had applied the value against the arrears of rent and costs of distress, leaving a balance outstanding of rental owing of $2,562 to January 15, 1978. The following day, November 23rd, the landlord gave notice to the debtor company, the receiver-manager, and RoyNat of termination and forfeiture of the lease for failure to pay rent and calculated the arrears outstanding as of November 15, 1978, at $2,652 plus $15,000 since accrued, for a total of $17,652. (While the evidence is not clear on the point, I infer that Mrs. Nowak, the landlord, made some arrangement with her son to transfer the chattels to him, and that he is now operating the restaurant under another name.)

On November 27, 1978, RoyNat issued the petition in bankruptcy. The debt alleged in the petition is $156,144.15 which is not disputed, and the security is valued at $135,000 (which, as I have said, represents the lease and chattels).

By way of rounding out the background I add that on November 27, 1978, an interim receiver was appointed by the Registrar *ex parte*. Also on the same day the petitioning creditor RoyNat obtained an interlocutory injunction to restrain the landlord from selling, distraining and interfering with the chattels and fixtures of the debtor company, and from disposing of the proceeds of sale or other disposition thereof until December 12, 1978. On the latter day the matter came on before me, and I refused to continue the injunction or to renew it on the grounds that, at that stage of proceedings, the landlord might quite lawfully distrain for arrears of rent, and might do so at any time up to bankruptcy having regard to the provisions of ss. 17, 50(1) and 51(4) of the *Bankruptcy Act*, RSC 1970, c. B-3, as interpreted in *Re Southern Fried Foods Ltd.* (1976), 12 OR (2d) 12, 67 DLR (3d) 599, 21 CBR (NS) 267. The landlord was not a party before the Court and no substantive claim is as yet made against the landlord in these proceedings. That cannot occur until the receiving order is made and the trustee determines that the landlord has property of the bankrupt in her hands. In these circumstances the Court ought not to award an injunction to prevent the landlord from taking such steps as the law permits. If in the result it turns out that a fraud or other improper act has been done to defeat the trustee and the creditors, that matter should be pursued by the trustee if and when a receiving order is made and a trustee appointed. Those were substantially my reasons for refusing to continue or renew the interlocutory injunction.

The first issue arising at trial of this petition is whether the act of bankruptcy alleged occurred within the six months prior to the filing of the petition on November 27, 1978. There is no dispute that on March 1, 1978, when RoyNat appointed its receiver-manager, debts owing to the petitioning creditor were due and unpaid. I find that as of that date and earlier, the debtor company had ceased to meet its liabilities generally as they became due. Clearly, that is so as of January, 1978, with respect to the loans of RoyNat; and the rent was in arrears with the landlord purporting to distrain. Several other creditors testified at trial. As to these I find as follows:

The debtor owed Milpark Dairy $1,700 in December, 1977. This debt has not been paid. This creditor continued to bill the debtor monthly for this amount until October, 1978, and in July, 1978, turned it over to a collection agency to recover.

The Robert Simpson Co. Ltd. is now owed $15,666.61 by the debtor company, which is the balance of a considerably larger amount owing from the year 1975 for furnishing the restaurant. Efforts to collect commenced in September, 1975, and a number of payments were then made, some substantial, the last of which was made in January, 1978. When the receiver-manager was appointed by RoyNat the creditor obtained judgment against Miss Nowak on her personal guarantee but continued to bill the company monthly for the balance up to November 15, 1978.

The debtor owes at present $4,086.88 for retail sales tax. The last payment on this liability was made in April, 1978, which resulted in the above balance. In June, 1978, the department continued to press its claim against the receiver-manager.

The Royal Bank of Canada has a claim for a balance of $18,935.78. Payment was demanded by letter dated March 1, 1978. At that time the bank decided to proceed against Mrs. Nowak on her personal guarantee and took no further steps to collect from the debtor company because the bank decided that the company had no assets from which to recover.

As I have said, RoyNat appointed the receiver-manager under its debenture on March 1, 1978. On July 17, 1978, RoyNat formally advised the debtor of the default under the debentures, the appointment of the receiver-manager, the balance owing on the two loans and the fact that interest was continuing to accrue.

It is admitted that one creditor, who did not testify, issued a writ against the debtor company in June, 1978.

The amounts of these creditors' claims are not disputed by the debtor company, nor is it disputed that the company has been and now is unable to pay them. I have set out the above facts with respect to the creditor's claim, because Mr. Poultney submits that for purposes of proving the act of bankruptcy these debts are now "stale" since the defaults occurred prior to the six months' period prescribed by the Act, and no serious efforts have been made within that period to enforce payment. He submits that there is, therefore, no current act of bankruptcy to support a receiving order. In support of this position he cites *Brown v. Kelly Douglas Co., Ltd.*, [1923] 2 DLR 738, 3 CBR 812, [1923] 1 WWR 1340 (BCCA); *Re Raitblat*, [1925] 2 DLR 1219, 28 OWN 237, 5 CBR 714 (Ont.).

As I understand those judgments they interpret the Act as meaning that where the act of bankruptcy occurred prior to the six months' period and thereafter nothing was done by creditors with respect to the debts in default for a period of six months or more, the act of bankruptcy ceases to be current and cannot found a receiving order. But in my opinion that does not apply where the debtor has since the initial defaults received continued demands for payment within the six months' period. The rental payments continued to fall due currently, and were not paid. I am quite satisfied that the company was insolvent on and before March 1, 1978, and continued to be so until the petition was filed. There is no suggestion that the creditors who continued to bill the debtor or otherwise press for payment had abandoned their claims; nor is there any suggestion that the debtor was at any time within the six months' period able to pay them. Indeed the evidence is to the contrary: see *Re The Pas Foundation & Excavation Ltd.* (1975), 21 CBR (NS) 154.

In these circumstances I find that the act of bankruptcy occurred not only before March 1, 1978, but was repeated from time to time during the six months' period. The act of bankruptcy is established as required by the statute.

The second issue is whether there are any assets or potential assets that a trustee in bankruptcy could realize for distribution to creditors. Mr. Poultney says there are none, as any chattels were seized and disposed of by the landlord, and the lease has been formally terminated. If there are no assets, he submits that no receiving order should issue as there would be no purpose to a bankruptcy. He relies on the decisions in *Re Moneysworth Chain Stores Ltd. et al., Ex. p. J. & A. Aziz* (1932), 13 CBR 203; *Re Benson*, [1937] OWN 1, 18 CBR 99; *Re Stone* (1925), 57 OLR 640; *Re Dennis* (1978), 27 CBR (NS) 100.

There is no real dispute that the only asset that might be available to a trustee in bankruptcy is the property upon which the landlord purported to distrain. It is Mr. Dolan's position on behalf of RoyNat that the distress is capable of challenge on grounds that possession was not properly taken by the landlord in January, 1978, that the landlord may well have abandoned and lost the right of distress between January and the issue of the petition in November, and that the propriety of the distress is questionable in face of RoyNat's intervention in the affairs of the debtor company immediately beforehand, and having regard to the close family relationship that characterizes the transactions in question.

I am prepared to assume, without deciding, that a trustee in bankruptcy could find grounds to challenge the validity of the landlord's distress, although I obviously am unable to say whether the trustee would succeed. But assuming a trustee could successfully set aside the seizure and disposition of these assets (notwithstanding s. 50(1) of the Act) the evidence before me is that the assets or their proceeds are fully encumbered by RoyNat's debentures, and that there could be nothing available for unsecured creditors. RoyNat in its petition values the security at $135,000 which Mr. Swaine in his evidence says is based on their original value at the time the security was taken. The chattels are no longer new and the landlord in ex. 15 values them at $32,638. In face of RoyNat's undisputed claim for over $156,000 it is clear that there could be no assets available for distribution to the unsecured creditors. I add that no attack is made on the termination of the lease.

The third issue is whether the secured creditor RoyNat ought to be granted a receiving order so that a trustee when appointed may investigate and, if possible, have set aside the distress and disposition of the proceeds for the benefit of RoyNat. There is no question and no dispute that the sole objective of a receiving order in this case is to enable RoyNat to take advantage of the *Bankruptcy Act*, RSC 1970, c. B-3, to recover its security as against Mrs. Nowak, the landlord. Mr. Dolan is quite frank to concede this and to point out that, as a result of a receiving order, the secured creditor RoyNat could obtain priority over the landlord: *Re Polycoating & Films Ltd.*, [1965] 2 OR 698, 51 DLR (2d) 673, 8 CBR (NS) 163 (Ont. CA); whereas if there is no bankruptcy the priority is to the landlord. The purpose of a receiving order, therefore, is really to change the order of priorities as between two competing creditors for the sole advantage of the secured creditor RoyNat, whereas the objective of the *Bankruptcy Act* is to achieve a fair and equitable distribution of the debtor's assets among the unsecured creditors. In two recent decisions in the Bankruptcy Courts of Ontario and British Columbia it has been held that it is not improper for a secured creditor to file a petition or procure an assignment in bankruptcy for the purpose of defeating a landlord's priority, even though no benefit accrues to the unsecured creditors: *Re Develox Industries Ltd.*, [1970] 3 OR 199, 12 DLR (3d) 579, 14 CBR (NS) 132 (Ont.), and *Re Gasthof Schnitzel House Ltd. and Sanderson* (1978), 27 CBR (NS) 75, [1978] 2 WWR 756.

In my opinion I am obliged to follow these authorities in this case, notwithstanding that I have some misgivings. A receiving order will therefore issue.

Judgment accordingly.

Re Gaudet
(1989), 57 DLR (4th) 727 (Ont. SC)

SAUNDERS J (orally): Lloyds Bank Canada petitions the court that Venard J Gaudet ("Gaudet") be adjudged bankrupt and that a receiving order be made in respect of his property.

The petitioner and the debtor have filed an agreed statement of facts and it is therefore unnecessary to set out in detail the background that gave rise to the filing of the petition and the subsequent events. If these reasons are to be published, the statement should be added as an appendix [*post*, p. 735] for the better understanding of the background.

There was additional evidence introduced at the hearing to which reference shall be made to the extent required. There are a number of pending matters relating to Gaudet and his affairs and I therefore intend to say no more about the details of the evidence that I consider necessary to dispose of the issues before me.

It is admitted that there is a debt owing to Lloyds Bank in the amount of at least $1,000. There are the following issues to be decided:

1. Did Gaudet commit an act of bankruptcy within the six months next preceding filing of the petition, which was August 31, 1988; and

2. if Gaudet did commit an act of bankruptcy, should the petition be stayed pursuant to s. 43(11) of the *Bankruptcy Act*, RSC 1985, c. B-3 [formerly s. 25(11) of RSC 1970, c. B-3].

There are two acts of bankruptcy alleged in the petition:

(a) that Gaudet has ceased to meet his liabilities generally as they become due; and

(b) that he has permitted a process issued against him, namely an order of the Supreme Court of Ontario made January 27, 1988, appointing an interim receiver of all his undertaking, property and assets under which certain of his property has been seized, to remain unsatisfied for 14 days after such seizure.

I find on the evidence that prior to January 11, 1988, Gaudet was insolvent and that he has remained insolvent up to the present time. On that date, he had not lived up to his commitments and promises to Lloyds Bank. The bank had become concerned about the situation no later than some time in December, 1987. Gaudet had told the bank that he would come up with a proposal and he had been given until January 13, 1988, to do so. As no proposal was forthcoming and as he remained in default on his commitments, Lloyds

Bank, on January 13th, decided to demand payment of its indebtedness and did so on the following day by letter in which it gave Gaudet until the following January 28th to comply with demand. Gaudet, on or about January 11, 1988, also owed money to other creditors which they alleged were overdue and that circumstance was not disputed.

I find on the admitted evidence together with the uncontradicted evidence that prior to January 11, 1988, Gaudet had ceased to meet his liabilities generally as they became due and that that situation did not change prior to the filing of the petition and indeed continues to the present time.

It is to be noted that s. 42(1) and (3) of the *Bankruptcy Act* does not qualify the act of bankruptcy. The statute simply says that a debtor commits an act of bankruptcy if he ceases to meet his liabilities generally as they become due.

It was submitted that certain events in January, 1988, precluded there being such an act of bankruptcy in the six months next preceding the filing of the petition, which, as previously stated, occurred on August 31, 1988.

On January 11, 1988, the Ontario Securities Commission (the "OSC") made an investigation order in respect of Gaudet and his wife and others pursuant to s. 11 of the Ontario *Securities Act*, RSO 1980, c. 466. On January 13th, the OSC issued a direction pursuant to s. 16(1) of the *Securities Act* directing Lloyds Bank and others to hold all funds and securities which they might have on deposit, under their control or for safekeeping in respect of Gaudet and others until the direction was revoked or there was a consent to release from the OSC. On January 27th, the OSC applied for and was granted an order in the Supreme Court of Ontario pursuant to s. 17 of the *Securities Act* appointing Clarkson, Gordon Inc. as interim receiver of all the undertaking, property and assets of Gaudet, his wife and others.

It was submitted that the effect of the actions instituted by the OSC in seizing and freezing the assets of Gaudet prevented him from making payment out of his assets and that such a circumstance could not constitute the alleged act of bankruptcy, namely ceasing to meet liabilities generally as they became due.

In the situation where a receiver is appointed at the instance of a secured creditor, it has been held that the position of the debtor in so far as liability for the debt is concerned, particularly vis-à-vis an act of bankruptcy, is not altered by reason of the appointment. That was the decision of the Manitoba Bankruptcy Court in the case of *Re Churchill Forest Industries (Manitoba) Ltd.* (1971), 23 DLR (3d) 301, [1972] 2 WWR 178, 16 CBR (NS) 158. That decision was affirmed by the Manitoba Court of Appeal without reasons [25 DLR (3d) 380n, [1972] 4 WWR 122n]. In the course of giving the reasons in the bankruptcy court decision the learned judge said [at p. 305]:

I do not accept the contention that because of the receiving order of January 7, 1971, the debtor could not commit an act of bankruptcy after that date.

And subsequently at p. 306 DLR, p. 186 WWR he said: "The issue is ceasing to meet liabilities generally as they became due, not the reasons therefor."

The reasoning in that case was adopted in the decision of the British Columbia Supreme Court in *Re Sooke Forest Products Ltd.* (1985), 55 CBR (NS) 276. It was also adopted by my colleague Mr. Justice Chilcott when he granted leave to Lloyds Bank to issue the petition now under consideration.

As I understood it, counsel for Gaudet did not take issue with the reasoning in those decisions. Rather, it was submitted that the situation before the court was different from the situation in *Churchill Forest* and in *Sooke*. In those cases a receiver and manager had been appointed by a secured creditor who was seeking to realize his security to satisfy an indebtedness. In such a situation it was submitted that a finding of an act of bankruptcy would be appropriate and the effect of such a finding was to recognize the rights of other creditors. In contrast, the situation before the court here is that the freezing of the assets and the receiving order is expressly for the protection of all creditors and there is no realization necessarily involved.

While I appreciate that there is some distinction as well as some similarities in the two types of process, I am unable to see why the distinction should have a different impact on the issue of whether there has been an act of bankruptcy. From the point of view of the unsecured creditors there is no distinction except perhaps that the logic of the *Churchill Forest* decision is even more compelling when there is, as here, a receivership which allows the debtor to have some say in the treatment of his assets. To repeat, the reason why the debts were not paid, in my opinion, is irrelevant in determining whether there was the alleged act of bankruptcy.

In any event, the evidence is overwhelming that whether or not there had been a s. 17 receivership, there was no ability to pay the liabilities as they became due and no possibility of doing so. If there had been such a possibility, there would have been evidence of it.

The result of giving effect to the submissions made by the debtor would be to allow the debtor to take advantage of the s. 17 order which was granted by the court because of his alleged misconduct.

I find that the petitioning creditor has proved that there was an act of bankruptcy in that Gaudet, within the six months preceding the filing of the petition, ceased to meet his liabilities generally as they became due. Accordingly, there is no need to consider the second alleged act of bankruptcy because nothing further is required to grant the petition other than a consideration of whether there should be a stay. I should add that there was no request to dismiss the petition pursuant to s. 43(7) and in my submission no basis for doing so.

The debtor submits that in the circumstances the petition should be stayed. There is a broad discretion in the court to order a stay. Section 43(11) of the *Bankruptcy Act* provides that:

43(11) The court may for other sufficient reason make an order staying the proceedings under a petition, either altogether or for a limited time, on such terms and subject to such conditions as the court may think just.

Counsel for Gaudet submitted that certain points should be considered and I intend to address the issue of the stay with reference to those points.

The first point was that no substantial or meaningful demand was made on Gaudet while he had effective control of his assets. As I have said, Gaudet was aware of the concern of Lloyds Bank. He was given three weeks to come up with a proposal. He did not do so. There were other creditors, some of whom had started actions to preserve lien rights in property. While the property may have been in the name of Mrs. Gaudet, it was admitted that the claims were also against Mr. Gaudet.

It is abundantly clear that for some time prior to the formal demand of Lloyds Bank that Gaudet was unable to meet his liabilities to the bank and the fact that he had control over whatever assets he had is, in my opinion, of little significance. The evidence does not indicate any real intention of Gaudet to make a substantial payment to the bank in the weeks immediately prior to the formal demand.

The second point was that any meaningful failure to pay liabilities arose after the courts had made it beyond the power of Gaudet to make payment. While, as I have already said, this circumstance is not relevant in determining whether there has been an act of bankruptcy, it is, in my opinion, a proper consideration as to whether there ought to be a stay. If, for example, a debtor had both the ability and the desire to pay its obligations, and was precluded only by the existence of something in the nature of a s. 17 order, there might be a reason to order a stay. Here the evidence shows that there was neither ability nor desire and in the circumstances of this case it is my opinion that this point has little significance.

The third point was that Lloyds Bank was the only creditor petitioning for a receiving order. Furthermore, it was drawn to my attention, in the course of argument, as it was clear from the evidence, that an earlier petition by Lloyds Bank had been dismissed and that Lloyds Bank had been found in contempt for issuing that petition without leave [see *Ontario Securities Com'n v. Gaudet* (1988), 65 OR (2d) 424]. That circumstance apparently was also the basis for the dismissal of the petition. Both the dismissal of the petition and the contempt order are under appeal. There was no suggestion of any creditor opposition to the filing of this petition. Indeed, both the receiver of Osler Incorporated and the receiver of Mr. and Mrs. Gaudet consider bankruptcy to be preferable to the present situation. This point, in my opinion, is of no significance.

The fourth point was that the assets are now under the receiver's control. On that basis, it was submitted that the receiver can monitor the assets and report to the court, presevatory [*sic*] payments can be made, representative creditors can be appointed, and existing powers can be extended to provide for sale or for other remedies.

Again, I think it is of some significance that both receivers say that bankruptcy, in their opinion, would be preferable to the present situation. The present receivership does not provide for an orderly and effective identification and collection of the debtor's assets or for a distribution of those assets. In addition to being inadequate for those purposes, the s. 17 receivership may, in view of the insolvency of Gaudet, not be proper in view of the superior constitutional position of the *Bankruptcy Act* over provincial legislation in dealing with matters of bankruptcy and insolvency.

Furthermore, and most dramatically, the present receivership recognizes a right of Gaudet to his assets and a resort to those assets for personal needs and to discharge certain debts. This results in an adverse and uneven impact on his creditors generally.

Finally, the monitoring may not be working effectively. The court ordered the receiver to make a payment to Gaudet to discharge certain obligations, including those of American Express. The uncontradicted evidence of a representative of American Express was that those moneys did not find their way to that company.

The fifth point was that until such time as there is a realistic chance of distribution, there is no advantage to the bankruptcy process and the making of the receiving order will be an additional cost. As submitted, the rights of the creditors are protected by the filing of the petition which preserves the date for attacking prebankruptcy transactions. Counsel for the debtor does not go so far as to say that bankruptcy may not at some time be an appropriate process but rather that it is premature to make a receiving order at this time.

In every case where there is a bankruptcy following a receivership there is a new party, the trustee, with the consequent additional cost that his participation entails. Nevertheless, in this case it is generally recognized that the unsecured creditors require some established representation and that function would be supplied by a trustee who would be armed with his rights under the *Bankruptcy Act.*

The protection of the creditors given by the existing receivership, for reasons already stated, may perhaps be not only inadequate but also improper on constitutional grounds. In addition there are some further factors which require consideration under this point. First, a trustee in bankruptcy can prosecute claims that Gaudet may now have against others such as, for example, claims against some of the affiliated corporations. Second, a trustee in bankruptcy would be able to ascertain the nature and extent of the assets and then pursue settlements and fraudulent preferences, if that seems to be appropriate. There is evidence of the possibility of substantial claims of this nature. A trustee, with the benefit of the *Bankruptcy Act* is, in my opinion, in a better position than the receiver to attack questionable transactions. Third, some of the assets can now be realized and liquidated. Fourth, the assets of Gaudet will no longer be available for personal expenses. They would also not be available to professional advisors to the extent that they have been. It is recognized that looking at the over-all situation of Gaudet and his wife, the family trust and the related corporations, that to the extent the assets of Gaudet are no longer available, there is a likelihood of greater resort to the assets of the others involved. Fifth, whatever there is to distribute can be distributed in accordance with the scheme of the *Bankruptcy Act* with minimum expense in determining how the administration of the estate is to be effected. That does not ignore that any meaningful distribution may be delayed until some of the serious and substantial issues involved in this matter have either been determined or settled.

The sixth point in support of a stay was that a bankruptcy would preclude Gaudet from adequately defending himself on the serious charges brought against him from several sources. The granting of a receiving order would not affect his right to fully defend the charges against him by the OSC and by the Toronto Stock Exchange. To the extent that the receiver of Osler Incorporated or others might assert personal claims as distinct from property claims, Gaudet would be able to defend those claims. Property claims would be dealt with by the trustee as the property of Gaudet would then be vested in the trustee. Post discharge claims could be fully defended by Gaudet. Unless he had agreed, he would not be bound by any compromise made by the trustee without his consent. That does not completely rule out the possibility of some prejudice. It is not an uncommon circumstance that a bankrupt has to face serious charges that may have in whole or in part contributed to his bankruptcy. That circumstance, in my opinion, should not of itself lead to a stay. The situation might be different if Osler Inc. were to have been the petitioning creditor or if there were other circumstances indicating that the petition was improper or was an abuse of process.

Finally, I consider that s. 7 of the *Canadian Charter of Rights and Freedoms* does not assist on this issue. The matter involved is one of property and, in any event, there was, in my opinion, no denial of fundamental justice. While, no doubt, there is in every case of bankruptcy a loss of self-worth and reputation, that is a factor which, in my opinion, can be given very little weight in dealing with a stay of a petition.

In deciding whether to exercise my discretion, all circumstances must be considered. There are factors going both ways. Looking at the situation as a whole, it is my opinion much better dealt with by the bankruptcy process. Furthermore, I accept the submissions of the petitioning creditor that it is the proper procedure on constitutional grounds. Even if the constitutional issue had not been a factor, I would not have come to a different conclusion. I am of the opinion that the circumstances clearly warrant that there should be no stay.

A receiving order will issue. ...

Order accordingly.

NOTES

1) *Difference between petition and assignment.* There are important differences between a bankruptcy petition brought by a debtor's creditors under s. 43, and an assignment of his property for the benefit of his creditors made by a debtor (who or which may be a natural person or legal entity) pursuant to s. 49. An assignment, it would seem, can be made as of right so long as the debtor-assignor satisfies the requirement of "insolvent person" under s. 2.* No hearing is involved and apparently the Official Receiver has no discretion to refuse an assignment if the paperwork is in order. However, an assignment can be annulled under s. 181 (just as a receiving order can be annulled under the same section), but the basis on which the court can or should exercise its discretion remains unclear. In *Re St. Louis & Peter Co.* (1988), 67 CBR (NS) 176 an assignment was set aside on the ground that it would not benefit the bankrupt and would be detrimental to the only creditor (who would have to pay the costs of the bankruptcy). In *Re Kergan* (1966), 9 CBR (NS) 15 (Ont.), on the other hand, the court refused to set aside the assignment even though the debtor was making monthly payments that were satisfactory to his creditors. Courts have also repeatedly refused to set aside an assignment on the ground that the debtor had no assets available for distribution among the creditors. See, e.g., *Re Linteau* (1944), 26 CBR (NS) 244.

The simplicity of an assignment should be contrasted with the much more complex proceedings involved where a creditor (defined in s. 2) brings an application for a receiving order. Here, even if the creditor proves the debtor's "act of bankruptcy" (defined in s. 2) the court may refuse the receiving order if the court concludes that the debtor is able to pay her debts or that "for other sufficient cause" no order ought to be made. How do we

---

* Note importantly that under the US Bankruptcy Code there is no requirement that the debtor must be insolvent for the purpose of making an assignment or initiating reorganization proceedings under Chapter 11. This dispensation has proven to be a key element in enabling US companies facing mass tort or contract claims to make a Chapter 11 filing and impose an automatic stay on further proceedings. See, e.g., *In re Johns-Manville Corp.* (1984), 36 BR 727. Canadian women with breast implants manufactured by the Dow Corning Corp. have recently felt the impact of these provisions as the result of Dow Corning's decision to file under Chapter 11.

explain this basic difference in procedure? Does it have something to do with the "free start" policy for debtors favoured by the BIA?

2) *Important lessons.* Some important lessons about the perceived role of s. 43 emerge from the cases reproduced earlier in this chapter:

(a) the petition will not be restricted to cases where a receiving order (RO) is necessary to solve common pool problems. *Re Dixie Markets (Nurseries) Lim.* shows that an RO will be made to assist even a single creditor to enforce a judgment debt. (Henry J's judgment in *Re Holmes & Sinclair* takes a more cautious approach but Houlden J's judgment in *Re Dixie Markets* is generally regarded as expressing the better view.)

(b) *Re Harrop of Milton* is a recent authority for the equally well settled proposition that an application may be brought by a secured creditor to advance its own interests regardless of how it affects the debtor's other creditors. (What was RoyNat's reason in *Harrop* for bringing the application?)

(c) *Harrop* also illustrates the common practice of a secured creditor bringing a s. 43 application even though the secured creditor has installed a privately appointed receiver-manager to enforce the security interest. This does not mean that the receiver-manager is displaced on the appointment of the trustee in bankruptcy because there is no such requirement in the BIA. On the contrary, s. 71(2) makes it clear that the vesting of the debtor's property in the trustee is qualified by the (antecedent) rights of the secured creditor. In practice, to reduce costs, the secured creditor's application under s. 43 will frequently designate the receiver-manager as trustee. This practice is expressly sanctioned in s. 13.4 of the BIA but may it not give rise to a conflict of interests given the fact that the trustee will be wearing two hats?

3) *Advantages of bankruptcy order over other execution remedies.* Both *Re Holmes & Sinclair* and *Re Gaudet* demonstrate the superiority of a receiving order over execution orders and conservatory measures, such as a court appointed receiver, available outside bankruptcy. Consider, for example, the powers of a sheriff under the Execution Act, RSO 1990, c. E-29. The sheriff is invested with broad powers to seize the debtor's real and personal property (ss. 10-21), but in most other respects the sheriff's powers fall short of a trustee's powers under the BIA. The sheriff has no power to examine the debtor (*cf.* BIA s. 163(1)); he has no power to carry on the debtor's business for even the shortest period of time (*cf.* BIA ss. 18, 30); he has no power to seize assets outside his jurisdiction (*cf.* BIA, s. 2 definition of "property" and ss. 16(3), 17) or to levy execution after the writ has expired. Likewise, the sheriff has no power to set aside impeachable transactions engaged in by the debtor prior to execution although the execution creditor may be able to do so (*cf.* BIA ss. 90-100).

4) *Consolidation of bankruptcies.* A question of growing importance, domestically and internationally, is whether a court can make a single bankruptcy order for a group of companies, or permit them to make a consolidated application under the CCAA or a consolidated proposal under Part III of the BIA. The effect of such an order is to create a single corpus of assets and liabilities and as a result some creditors will recover more and others less than if there were no consolidation. Such substantive consolidations must be distinguished from procedural consolidations, which are merely mechanisms for the more

efficient administration of related insolvent debtors and involve no collapsing of assets and liabilities.

Substantive consolidation orders are usually sought where the debtor and its creditors have themselves treated the related corporations as a single enterprise (in some cases the creditors may not even have been aware of the multiple legal personalities) or where assets and liabilities of members of the group have been so completely commingled that it would be very expensive to try to disentangle them. (The latter scenario applied to the group affairs of the Bank of Credit and Commerce International (BCCI), which went bankrupt in the early 1990s with unmet liabilities to depositors of about $10 billion. The British courts approved a recommendation from the liquidators that the assets and liabilities of the group be consolidated for greater efficiency.)

American courts have long accepted the doctrine of substantive as well as procedural consolidation, but they have been divided about the tests to be applied in determining when a consolidation order should be made. There are no provisions in Canadian insolvency legislation authorizing consolidation orders. Nevertheless, according to one count, at least 16 plans of arrangement were attempted under the CCAA in the 1980s and early 1990s and several well known ones were approved by the courts. The best known of these is the consolidation order made in the *Northland Properties Ltd.* CCAA proceedings. See (1988), 73 CBR (NS) 175 (BC), affd. [1989] 3 WWR 363 (BCCA) and Ellen Hayes, "Substantive Consolidation under the Companies' Creditors Arrangement Act and the Bankruptcy and Insolvency Act" (1994), 23 *CBLJ* 444.

5) *Jurisdictional issues and international bankruptcies.* Large insolvent enterprises frequently hold assets and have creditors in several jurisdictions, and this raises difficult questions of the conflict of laws and public policy. The important questions are these: (1) when should a Canadian court assume insolvency jurisdiction over a multinational enterprise; (2) if jurisdiction is assumed, whose national law should be applied to determine particular issues; and (3) to what extent will foreign insolvency orders be recognized and enforced in Canada?

The first question is perhaps the easiest to answer. The BIA grounds the court's jurisdiction in the debtor residing or carrying on business in Canada. See BIA, s. 2, definition of "insolvent debtor." In the case of a corporation, the jurisdictional base seemingly is broader and extends to any company incorporated or authorized to carry on business by or under an Act of Parliament or of any province, and any incorporated company, wherever incorporated, that has an office in or carries on business within Canada (BIA, s. 2, definitions of "debtor," "insolvent person" and "corporation.") The CCAA and the Winding-Up Act contain their own jurisdictional criteria. It is well established Anglo-Canadian law that a court is not precluded from making a bankruptcy order because bankruptcy proceedings have already been initiated in another country. Instead, the court may order the trustee to confine her administration to Canadian based assets and to cooperate with the foreign administrator. (The position with respect to concurrent reorganization proceedings is unsettled.)

The second question is complex and equally unsettled. Non-bankruptcy questions, such as the validity of a contract, the commission of a tort or the validity of a security interest, will be determined by the normal conflict of laws rules. "Pure" bankruptcy questions, such as the method for the presentation and calculation of claims and the ranking of creditors, will be governed by the BIA or other applicable legislation. Difficulties arise however because it is a well established conflicts rule that a Canadian court will not enforce foreign tax claims, and will therefore deny them any preferential status in the Canadian administration.

The third question (the recognition and enforcement of foreign insolvency orders in Canada) is the most controversial at the present time. The traditional rule, and one supported by case law, is that the foreign insolvency order will be recognized if, in the case of natural persons, the insolvent was domiciled in the foreign country and, in the case of a corporation, the corporation was incorporated there. The status of foreign reorganization orders remains very unsettled. None of the Canadian insolvency legislation contains rules for the recognition of foreign proceedings. In the absence of statutory rules, a court would be expected to apply the conflict of laws rules of the province where the court is sitting. A draft Canada-US Bankruptcy treaty was negotiated in 1979 but was not proceeded with. Bill C-17 of 1984 contained a series of international bankruptcy rules but these suffered the same fate as the rest of the bill. Working Group III of the BIAC was commissioned to present suitable amendments for inclusion in the second round of amendments to the BIA. The committee presented an ambitious group of provisions in its December 1994 report. However, these encountered stiff opposition and the present prospects are that only wholly innocuous and uncontroversial provisions are likely to find their way into the proposed bill.

See further R.N. Robertson, "Enforcement and Other Problems in International Insolvencies" in *Meredith Memorial Lectures 1985*, p. 266; Grace, "Recognition and Enforcement of Foreign Liquidation Orders in Canada and Australia—A Critical Comparison" (1986), 35 *ICLQ* 664; and Ziegel, "Jurisdiction to Liquidate Foreign Companies and Extraterritorial Effects of Bankruptcy and Liquidation Orders" in Nat. Univ. of Singapore, *Current Developments in International Banking and Corporate Financial Operations* (1989), p. 313.

6) *Consequences of an assignment or receiving order.* The following is a list of the most important consequences:

s. 69.3 Automatic stay of proceedings against bankrupt unless court grants exemption.

s. 70(1) Bankruptcy order takes precedence over all outstanding judgments, execution, etc.

s. 71(1) Bankruptcy order deemed to relate back to time of filing of petition or assignment.

s. 71(2) Subject to limited exemptions in the case of individuals, all of the bankrupt's present and future property vests in trustee, and debtor ceases to have capacity to deal with the property. The trustee may also seek court order to attach future wages and other fee income of the bankrupt (s. 68(1)).

s. 73(2) Sheriff must deliver to trustee any property of the bankrupt in his hands.

s. 73(4) Similar effect of bankruptcy order on outstanding distraint for rent or taxes.

s. 199(a) Offence for undischarged bankrupt to engage in trade or business without disclosing his bankruptcy to the other party; or (b) to obtain credit to a total of $500 or more from any person or persons without disclosing his status.

Do these provisions serve a common purpose?

CHAPTER FOURTEEN

Property of the Estate, Unpaid Suppliers' Right to Recover Goods, and Claims Against the Estate

PROPERTY OF THE ESTATE
(BIA ss. 17, 67, 70-73, 75, 78, 81, 82, 83, 97(3), 135(2) and s. 2 "property")

Introduction

After his appointment, the trustee is expected to apply himself to the following major tasks: (1) to gather in and determine what assets belong to the estate; (2) where the assets are not already in liquid form, to collect any monies owing to the estate and to realize the other assets by selling them piecemeal or as an entirety; and (3) to distribute the net residue of the estate in accordance with the creditors' ranking under s. 136(1).

Section 71(2) provides that on the making of a receiving order or the filing of an assignment, the bankrupt ceases to have the capacity to deal with or dispose of his property and the property forthwith passes to and vests in the trustee. "Property" is comprehensively but non-exhaustively (" 'property' includes ...") defined in s. 2 and covers all forms of property, real and personal, tangible and intangible, present and future, vested or contigent, and whether located in Canada or elsewhere.

However, subject to a variety of exceptions, the Act does not purport to determine what property rights the bankrupt in fact has at the time of bankruptcy which vest in the trustee. This question is determined by provincial and other federal laws pursuant to s. 72(1). Express exceptions recognized in the BIA are (a) property of the bankrupt exempt from execution under applicable provincial law (s. 67(1)(b)); (b) property held by the bankrupt on trust (s. 67(1)(a)); (c) property held subject to a security interest (s. 71(2)); (d) patented articles in the bankrupt's possession where the patent is held by another person (s. 82(1)); and (e) the disposition of copyrights in manuscripts and published works in the bankrupt's possession where the copyright belongs to another person (s. 83). Additionally, (f) s.73 deals with the status of executions and distraints against the bankrupt's property in process at the time of the bankruptcy order but not yet completed.

The 1992 amendments to the BIA added important provisions to the Act affecting property claims against the estate (see ss. 67(2), 67(3), 80.1-80.2, 86-87, and 136(1)). These will be considered hereafter.

On the plus side, in determining the scope of the bankrupt's property rights it is important to bear in mind that ss. 91-101 of the Act confer powerful rights on the trustee to claw back funds and other assets transferred by the debtor under impeachable transactions prior to the bankruptcy. These too will be considered hereafter.

Chicago Board of Trade v. Johnson
264 US 1 (1923)

Mr. Chief Justice TAFT delivered the opinion of the Court: ... Wilson F. Henderson, the bankrupt, a citizen of Chicago, was admitted to membership in the Board of Trade in 1899, and for many months prior to March 1, 1919, was president and one of the principal stockholders in a corporation known as Lipsey and Company, and actively engaged in making contracts on its behalf for present and future delivery of grain on the Board of Trade. In March, 1919, Lipsey and Company became insolvent and ceased to transact business, being then indebted to thirty or more members of the Exchange on its contracts in an aggregate amount of more than $60,000. A corporation is not admitted to membership of the Board, but under the rules it may do business on the Exchange if two of its executive officers, substantial stockholders, are members in good standing and give its name as principal in their contracts. The rules further provide that, if the corporation is accepted as a party to a contract and fails to comply with any of its obligations under the rules, its officers, as members, are subject to the same discipline as if they had failed to comply with an obligation of their own.

Any male person of good character and credit and of legal age, after his name has been duly posted for ten days, may be admitted to membership in the Board of Trade by ten votes of the Board of Directors, provided that three votes are not cast against him and that he pays an initiation fee of $25,000, or presents "an unimpaired or unforfeited membership, duly transferred," and signs "an agreement to abide by the Rules, Regulations and By-Laws of the Association." The rules further provide that a member, if he has paid all assessments and has no outstanding claims held against him by members, and the membership is not in any way impaired or forfeited, may, upon payment of a fee of $250, transfer his membership to any person eligible to membership approved by the Board, after ten days posting, both of the proposed transfer and of the name of substitute.

No rule exists giving to the Board of Trade or its members the right to compel sale or other disposition of memberships to pay debts. The only right of one member against another, in securing payment of an obligation, is to prevent the transfer of the membership of the debtor member by filing objection to such transfer with the Directors.

The membership of Henderson was worth $10,500 on January 24, 1920, when the petition in bankruptcy was filed against him. All assessments then due had been paid and the membership was not in any way impaired and forfeited. On May 1, 1919, Henderson had posted on the bulletin of the Exchange a notice and application for a transfer of his membership. Within ten days, two objections were filed, one of them on account of a debt due from Lipsey and Company. The objections were withdrawn, however, in December, 1919. On January 29, 1920, however, five days after the petition in bankruptcy was filed, members, creditors of Lipsey and Company on its defaulted contracts signed by Henderson, lodged with the Directors objections to the transfer. These objectors were respondents in the District Court and are petitioners here.

Under par. a, § 70 of the bankrupt law of July 1, 1898, c. 541, 30 Stat. 565, the trustee takes the title of the bankrupt (3) to "powers which he might have exercised for his own benefit," and (5) to "property which prior to the filing of the petition he could by any means have transferred or which might have been levied upon and sold under judicial process against him." Petitioners insist that the membership is not property within (5). The Supreme Court of Illinois, from which State this Board of Trade derives its charter, has held, in *Barclay v. Smith*, 107 Ill., 349, that the membership is not property or subject to judicial sale, basing its conclusion on the ground that it can not be acquired except upon a vote of ten Directors, and can not be transferred to another unless the transfer is approved by the same vote, and that it can not be subjected to the payment of debts of the holder by legal proceedings. It is not possible to reconcile *Barclay v. Smith* with the decisions of this Court. In *Hyde v. Woods*, 94 US 523, the bankrupt was a member of the San Francisco Stock and Exchange Board, a voluntary association with an elective membership, and with a right in each member to sell his seat subject to an election, by the Directors, of the vendee as a member. This Court held the membership to be an incorporeal right and property which would pass to the trustee of the bankrupt, subject to the rules of the Board, which required first the payment of all debts due to the members. In *Sparhawk v. Yerkes*, 142 US 1, the conclusion in *Hyde v. Woods* was reaffirmed in respect of seats in the Stock Exchanges of New York and Philadelphia, which were then voluntary unincorporated associations, with the same provision as to membership and preference for the debts of member creditors. In *Page v. Edmunds*, 187 US 596, the question was whether a seat of a bankrupt in the Philadelphia Stock Exchange was property passing to the trustee under subdivision 5 of § 70 of the Bankrupt Act. In that association, no member could sell his seat if he had unsettled claims on the Exchange. In case of insolvency, the seat could be sold, and the proceeds distributed to the member creditors. The Supreme Court of Pennsylvania had held, just as in this case the Supreme Court of Illinois has held, that such membership was not property, and could not be seized in execution for debts of its holder. *Thompson v. Adams*, 93 Pa. St. 55; *Pancoast v. Gowen*, 93 Pa. St. 66. These were the cases relied on by the Supreme Court of Illinois to sustain its view. Referring to the Pennsylvania decisions in *Page v. Edmunds* (p. 603), this Court said:

It is not certain whether the learned court intended to say that the seat was not property at all, or not property because it could not be seized in execution for debts. If the former, we cannot concur. The facts of this case demonstrate the contrary. If the latter, it does not affect the pending controversy. The power of the appellant to transfer it was sufficient to vest it in his trustee.

The Court thus held that the question was to be determined by reference to the language of the Bankrupt Act and that the seat was property "which prior to the filing of the petition he [the bankrupt] could by any means have transferred." It declined to limit the definition of property under subdivision (5) to such as the state courts might hold could be seized in execution by judicial process. Subdivision (3), vesting in the trustee title to powers which the bankrupt might exercise for his own benefit, manifests a purpose to make the assets of the estate broadly inclusive. By a construction not unduly strained, subdivision (3) might be held to include a power to transfer a seat on the Exchange, subject to its rules, if it were necessary.

In *Citizens National Bank v. Durr*, 257 US 99, we held, following the *Hyde*, *Sparhawk* and *Page Cases*, *supra*, that membership in the New York Stock Exchange was personal property, whose situs followed that of the owner, and was taxable where he was domiciled.

Congress derives its power to enact a bankrupt law from the Federal Constitution, and the construction of it is a federal question. Of course, where the bankrupt law deals with property rights which are regulated by the state law, the federal courts in bankruptcy will follow the state courts; but when the language of Congress indicates a policy requiring a broader construction of the statute than the state decisions would give it, federal courts can not be concluded by them. *Board of Trade v. Weston*, 243 Fed. 332.

Counsel for petitioners urges that the *Hyde*, *Sparhawk* and *Page Cases* differ from the one before us, in that the rules of the associations there under consideration provided specifically for a sale of the seat and a preferred distribution of the proceeds to the creditor members, whereas here there is no sale provided for at all, at the instance of the Board or its members who are creditors. Their only protection is in the power to prevent a transfer as long as the member's obligations to them are unperformed. We do not think this makes a real difference in the character of the property which the member has in his seat. He can transfer it or sell it subject to a right of his creditors to prevent his transfer or sale till he settles with them, a right in some respects similar to the typical lien of the common law, defined as "a right in one man to retain that which is in his possession belonging to another, till certain demands of him the person in possession are satisfied." *Hammonds v. Barclay*, 2 East, 235. *Peck v. Jenness*, 7 How. 612, 620. The right of the objecting creditor members differs, however, from the common law lien, in that the latter, to exist and be effective, must deprive the owner of possession and enjoyment, whereas the former is consistent with possession and personal enjoyment by the owner, and only interferes with, and prevents, alienation.

•   •   •

The District Court ordered the transfer and sale of the seat free from all the claims and objections of the petitioners. The view of the court was that, because Henderson had duly posted his intention to transfer in May, 1919, and all the objections of creditor members then filed against such transfer had been settled or withdrawn before the petition in bankruptcy was filed against him, the right of the member creditors to object to the transfer had been lost. The rule which is applicable (Section 2 of Rule X) reads in part as follows:

Every member shall be entitled to transfer his membership when he has paid all assessments due, and has against him no outstanding unadjusted or unsettled claims or contracts held by members of this Association, and said membership is not in any way impaired or forfeited, upon payment of two hundred and fifty dollars, to any person eligible to membership who may be approved for membership by the Board of Directors, after due notice by posting, as provided in Section 1 of this rule. ... Prior to the transfer of any membership, application for such transfer shall be posted upon the bulletin of the exchange for at least ten days when, if no objection is made, it shall be assumed the member has no outstanding claims against him.

We do not think these last words are intended to operate as a statute of limitations against the making of objections before the Board of Directors to such a transfer after the ten days. The effect of the rule is to warrant the Directors in proceeding, after the ten days, to effectuate the transfer on the assumption that no one entitled opposes it, and, if the transfer is completed before objection, those who have been silent are, of course, estopped. But if, at any time before the Directors act, otherwise valid objections are brought to their attention, it is too drastic a construction to hold that delay for ten days after notice has worked a forfeiture. To give the rule such a meaning, the intent should be more clearly expressed. The objections of most of the petitioners herein were filed within five days after the petition in bankruptcy and the Board never has acted on the application for transfer. The objections are therefore valid.

The claims of the petitioners are also attacked on the ground that they were debts of Lipsey and Company and not of Henderson, the bankrupt. There is nothing in this. The rules make the agent of a corporation who is a member and does business and makes contracts in its name on the Exchange, subject to discipline for a default in the obligations of the corporation. This impairs the membership of the agent and prevents transfer under Section 2, Rule X.

Nor is there any weight to the argument that, as the preference claims of petitioners were not asserted until after bankruptcy proceedings were begun, the transfer to the trustee was rendered free from their objection. Such a claim was negatived in *Hyde v. Woods, supra*. The preference of the member creditors is not created after bankruptcy. The lien, if it can be called such, is inherent in the property in its creation, and it can be asserted at any time before actual transfer. Indeed, the danger of bankruptcy of the member is perhaps the chief reason, and a legitimate one, for creating the lien.

We think, therefore, that the District Court and the Circuit Court of Appeals erred on the merits of the case. The claims of the petitioners amount to more than sixty thousand dollars, and these must be satisfied before the trustee can realize anything on the transfer of the seat for the general estate.

● ● ●

Reversed.

NOTES AND QUESTIONS

Would the result have been the same under ss. 2 (definition of "property"), 67 and 71(1) of the BIA? What would be the position if the membership constitution provided that on her bankruptcy a member automatically forfeited her rights of membership and/or the right to assign the membership?

Such provisions are common in a wide variety of agreements and may be objectionable if they deprive the trustee of a valuable asset of the estate. Until the 1992 amendments the Act only marginally addressed the issue by incorporating provincial law governing a landlord's rights after a tenant's bankruptcy. See BIA, s. 146, and Ontario Landlord and Tenant Act, ss. 38-39, and *infra*, chapter 15. As will be seen later (*infra*, chapter 18), in the context of corporate reorganizations under the CCAA the courts frequently make orders under s. 11 of the Act which preclude parties from cancelling existing contracts with the debtor. More carefully circumscribed restrictions on cancellation powers now appear in s. 65.1 of the BIA in relation to proposals under Part III, Division 1, of the Act.

Re Ontario Worldair Limited
(1983), 45 CBR (NS) 116 (Ont. SC),
aff'd. (1984), 48 CBR (NS) 1121 (Ont. CA)

SAUNDERS J: In this application for directions pursuant to s. 16 of the Bankruptcy Act, RSC 1970, c. B-3, the primary issue is whether moneys held by the Mercantile Bank of Canada in an account to the credit of the bankrupt are trust moneys unavailable for distribution to creditors of the bankrupt.

The bankrupt (sometimes referred to as "OWL") operated a charter flight airline. It subleased a Boeing 707 aircraft from Abelag Airways ("A/W") (subsequently and from now on referred to as "Air Belgium"). The sublease dated 20th December 1979 was for a fixed term. The responsibility for maintenance of the aircraft was extensively set out in art. 7 of the sublease. A distinction was drawn in that article between the "Aircraft" and the "Engines." The bankrupt was obliged at its own cost and expense to service, repair, replace worn out parts, maintain, overhaul, and test the aircraft and the engines except that in art. 7.2, Air Belgium was required at its cost and expense to be responsible for the "accomplishment of 'D' check." There was no evidence as to the nature of a "D" check or whether it was related to the aircraft or to the engines or to both. Article 7.6 of the sublease provided:

7.6(a) On termination of this sub-lease and re-delivery of the Aircraft and Engines to A/W;

(i) A/W will pay to OWL the sum of US $35.00 per hour per engine for each hour in excess of the time remaining for scheduled engine overhaul as recorded at the commencement of the sub-lease, or

(ii) OWL will pay to A/W the sum of US $35.00 per hour per engine for each hour less than the time remaining for scheduled engine overhaul as recorded at the commencement of the sub-lease.

(b) OWL agrees to open an account with a bank or trust [*sic*] in Toronto, Ontario in the name of OWL in trust for maintaining Engines on Aircraft Boeing 707/351 serial number 18746.

OWL further agrees to provide A/W monthly with a statement disclosing the deposits and withdrawls [sic] to and from the said trust account.

(c) A/W agrees to obtain and deliver to OWL a bank letter of guarantee or letter of credit in favour of OWL at such time and from time to time, not expiring prior to termination of this sublease, and in such amounts as will be sufficient to cover any credit to OWL for hours remaining for scheduled overhaul in excess of the hours at the time of delivery of the aircraft.

(d) OWL agrees to pay to A/W monthly within 15 days of the dates for payment of rent herein, a further sum equal to the total of all flight hours for the preceding calendar month at US $65.00 per such hour.

Subparagraph (b) would appear to set out a separate and independent understanding between the parties. Subparagraphs (a) and (c) appear to be concerned with a termination adjustment relating to engine overhaul and subparagraph (d) provides for a payment of $65 (US) per flight hour by the bankrupt in addition to rent. It is to be observed that there is no stipulation in subparagraph (b) as to the amount of deposits and withdrawals to be made and that the word "trust" appears three times. No reference was made to any other provision of the sublease which affected or amplified the understanding contained in art. 7.6(b).

By letter dated 30th June 1980 a vice-president of the bankrupt confirmed the following instructions to the Mercantile Bank of Canada.

2) Another separate US dollar Bank Account is required for overhaul reserve requirements under the Air Belgium (formerly Abelag Airways) lease. The account is to be designated OWL— Air Belgium Reserve Account. Monthly reserve requirements are to be transferred to this account, invested and re-invested upon our instructions. Reporting procedures for this account are as set out in my letter to you dated June 27, 1980.

The letter dated 27th June 1980 cannot be found.

By letter dated 2nd July 1980 the vice-president of the bankrupt wrote again to the bank as follows:

The company hereby requests you to open a US dollar account with the above name for the purpose of controlling reserve amounts as determined by Ontario Worldair.

With regard to this account, the following instructions should be put into effect immediately;

(1) At the company's direction the bank will transfer amounts to the above mentioned account.

(2) Investment of the funds in this account will be under the control of Ontario Worldair. Investment income generated will be to the account of Ontario Worldair and will be remitted to the company's general account on maturity of the investments.

(3) A report detailing deposits, withdrawals and all other activity in this account together with details of investments held for the account should be made to the person designated below at the end of each month. A copy of the report should be forwarded to the company.

Mr. R. Nuyens
General Manager
Air Belgium
Vilvoordelaan 192
Brussels, Belgium

I have forwarded a copy of these instructions to Mr. Nuyens of Air Belgium and would appreciate your confirming their implementation to Air Belgium.

Should you require further information please contact me.

The letter indicates that a copy of it was sent to Mr. Nuyens.

The word "trust" is not used in either letter. Under the instructions the deposit of funds was under the control of the bankrupt. The bankrupt was to receive the income from investments. Withdrawals were contemplated and there is no provision with respect to the extent and manner of deposits and withdrawals. So far as the bank was concerned, the only involvement of Air Belgium was the instruction that it was to receive monthly reports detailing deposits, withdrawals and all other activity.

An account was opened in July 1980. Reports were sent by the bank for July and August of that year but copies of them could not be located. A report as at 30th September 1980 was sent by letter dated 16th October 1980. It indicated investments in eight term deposits, none of which had matured, and no withdrawals. There is no evidence of any further report. In November 1980 Price Waterhouse Limited was appointed receiver and manager of the assets of the bankrupt under two debentures and took possession of the aircraft on 5th November 1980, which it turned over to Air Belgium on 10th December 1980. Price Waterhouse Limited also took possession of the Mercantile Bank account. The receiving order in bankruptcy was made on 19th January 1981.

I was referred to nothing in the evidence that would lead to the conclusion that the funds in the bank account were beneficially owned by Air Belgium or that it had any right to compel payment of any part of the funds to it. The obligation to maintain the aircraft was on the bankrupt at its cost and expense. It had the further obligation to make the adjusting payment in art. 7.6(a) if the circumstances called for such payment and the monthly payments called for in art. 7.6(d). If it fulfilled those obligations, any moneys in the bank account credited to Air Belgium would, in effect, have been a double payment unjustly enriching Air Belgium. I was referred to no provision or understanding which would have entitled Air Belgium to resort to the moneys in the account in the event of default by the bankrupt in its obligation under art. 7 or otherwise. The bank account, which was admittedly set up to comply with 7.6(b), in my opinion did no more than provide Air Belgium with some assurance that the bankrupt had the necessary resources to meet its obligations under art. 7.

In Waters, *Law of Trusts in Canada* (1974), p. 5, the learned author, in considering the nature of the trust, states:

Among common lawyers the following definition is generally regarded as being one of the best: "All that can be said of a trust, therefore, is that it is the relationship which arises whenever a person called the trustee is compelled in Equity to hold property, whether real or personal, and whether by legal or equitable title, for the benefit of some persons (of whom he may be one, and who are termed *cestuis que trust*) or for some object permitted by law, in such a way that the real benefit of the property accrues, not to the trustee, but to the beneficiaries or other objects of the trust." Another familiar definition, approved by Romer LJ in *Green v. Russell*, [1959] 2 QB 226 at 241, [1959] 2 All ER 525 (CA), by Cohen J in *Re Marshall's Will Trusts*, [1945] Ch. 217 at 219, [1945] 1 All ER 550, and in Canada by Disbery J in *Tobin Tractor (1957) Ltd. v. Western Surety Co.* (1963), 42 WWR 532 at 542, 40 DLR (2d) 231 (Sask.), is to be found in *Underhill's Law of Trusts and Trustees*, 12th ed. (1970), p. 3:

A trust is an equitable obligation binding a person (who is called a trustee) to deal with property over which he has control (which is called the trust property), for the benefit of persons (who are called the beneficiaries or *cestuis que trust*), of whom he may himself be one, and anyone of whom may enforce the obligation.

An English author [Pettit, *Equity and the Law of Trusts*, 2nd ed. (1970), p. 16] has completed this definition by adding that a trustee may hold property, not for the benefit of persons, but for the furtherance of certain purposes:

or for a charitable purpose, which may be enforced at the instance of the Attorney-General, or for some other purpose permitted by law though unenforceable.

While Air Belgium no doubt derived some benefit from the establishment of the account, in my opinion it cannot be said that the real benefit of the funds accrues to it. It is fundamental that in order for a trust to be validly constituted there must be a clear intention to create it. As pointed out by Waters, the use of the word "trust" is neither conclusive nor indispensable.

In *James F. Lawrie & Co. v. Moffat*, [1951] OWN 461, 31 CBR 197, [1951] 3 DLR 329 (CA), a debtor entered into an agreement with a supplier-creditor under which payment by customers would be deposited in a "Special Trust Account" from which no withdrawals could be made unless the cheque was countersigned by a nominee of the creditor. The agreement between the parties provided that moneys paid into the account should be paid out first to the creditor and then to the debtor with respect to orders which had been filled by the supplier and paid for by the customer. In giving the judgment of the court, Hope JA said at pp. 200-201:

If a trust was created by the agreement, then there is no doubt that in law the judgment of the learned trial Judge is correct, but a review of the agreement itself, and the circumstances leading to its consummation, as disclosed by the evidence, must be examined and on an examination of such circumstances I find it impossible to conclude that the agreement does in fact create a trust. The uncontroverted evidence at the trial discloses that when the agreement was made the debtor was in a "bad financial condition," and that the respondent knew that he was in such condition, and that that was the reason for clause 5 being inserted in the agreement. In my opinion the agreement provides only for some control of the finances of the debtor company by the respondent by having a nominee of the respondent appointed as secretary-treasurer of the debtor company, and a signing officer for banking purposes, and this was a contractual obligation of the debtor, which did not impose a trust upon the funds in question when collected by the appellant. ...

I am satisfied on the evidence in this matter that the agreement in question was not in the nature of a trust, and that if it was it was unlawful. The purpose of the agreement was rather to protect and give a preference to the respondent as against the ordinary creditors of the debtor who was known to the respondent to be in financial difficulties at the time the agreement was completed. The simple device of designating a bank account as a "Special Trust Account" cannot in itself constitute a trust in the face of all the other *indicia* here present.

In my opinion, the evidence here does not disclose an intention to create a trust. It was submitted that the property was under the control of the bankrupt which was consistent with its position as trustee; that the absence of any power in Air Belgium to seize the funds or to appoint a receiver indicated that it already had a proprietary interest in the moneys; and that the existence of the account provided a significant benefit to Air Belgium. The absence of any designation of Air Belgium as beneficiary of the fund or the fact that the income from the account went to the bankrupt, it was submitted, did not necessarily mean that the funds were not trust property. It was pointed out that even though the bankrupt was in serious financial difficulties, moneys in the account were not withdrawn, which it was said showed a recognition by the bankrupt that the funds did not belong to it. Notwithstanding all such submissions, the overriding circumstance seems to me to be that there is nothing in the letters to the bank which indicates an intention to create a trust and that the provisions in the sublease do not indicate that the funds in the account are to be beneficially owned by or available to Air Belgium. It is plain that the funds were owned by and were to be available to the bankrupt to enable it to perform its obligations under art. 7. If default occurred, there are extensive remedies available to Air Belgium in art. 16 but they do not appear to include a resort to the moneys in the bank account. In all circumstances, I am bound to conclude that the moneys in the account were not impressed with a trust for the benefit of Air Belgium.

In my opinion, the moneys in the bank account are not trust funds for the benefit of Air Belgium and to the extent not claimed by Price Waterhouse Limited under the debentures are available for division amongst the ordinary creditors of the bankrupt.

Having reached the foregoing conclusion, it is unnecessary to consider the submissions by the trustee that if there was a trust it is unenforceable because it lacks certainty of objects and, in any event, is invalid as a non-charitable purpose trust. Nor is it necessary to consider whether there is a security interest in Air Belgium which is unperfected under the Personal Property Security Act, RSO 1980, c. 375.

Accordingly, there will be a declaration that the moneys standing to the credit of the bankrupt in account 9013274 of the Mercantile Bank of Canada are not impressed with a trust in favour of Abelag Airways or its successor, Air Belgium, and are available for distribution to the creditors of the bankrupt in the ordinary course subject to the rights of secured creditors. ...

Directions given.

NOTE

The use of trust language in commercial agreements has long been common to ensure that an agent does not misappropriate funds owing to the principal and also to enable the principal to assert a proprietary claim if the agent goes bankrupt before the funds have been remitted. If the language is clear and the other prerequisites of a trust are established, such provisions are quite legitimate and enforceable in bankruptcy. As well, the agent's corporate officers may be held personally liable if they allow the trust funds to be diverted to unauthorized purposes. See *Air Canada v. M & L Travel Ltd.* (1994), 108 DLR (4th) 592 (SCC). Trust provisions have also acquired a sharper bite as a result of the House of Lords' decision in *Barclays Bank Ltd. v. Quistclose Investments Ltd.*, [1970] AC 567; Ziegel & Denomme, *op. cit.*, §2.2.6.2. The status of trust provisions under the Personal Property Security Acts is discussed, *supra*, in chapter 1.

Prior to the Supreme Court's decision in *BC v. Henfrey Samson Belair Ltd.* (1989), 59 DLR (4th) 726 there was much uncertainty whether a deemed trust established under federal and provincial tax legislation in respect of taxes and premiums deducted by an employer, or sales taxes collected for the Crown but not remitted, qualified as trusts under s. 67(1)(a) of the BIA. The Supreme Court held not. This greatly disturbed the Crowns and the new ss. 67(2) and (3) were added in 1992 to address their concerns. These provisions are considered *infra*, chapter 17.

Re Knechtel Furniture Limited
(1985), 56 CBR (NS) 258 (Ont. SC)

SAUNDERS J: This is an application under s. 16 of the Bankruptcy Act for advice and direction as to the interest of the trustee in the surplus under an Employee Pension Plan (the "plan") maintained by the bankrupt, Knechtel Furniture Limited ("Knechtel"). Fasken & Calvin (the "representative") was appointed by the court to represent the interests of the eligible employees, participants, pensioners and beneficiaries under the plan.

The plan was established in 1966. On or about 30th March 1983 Knechtel was placed in receivership by a secured creditor. It was then insolvent. No further contributions were made to the plan after that date. On 7th May 1984 Knechtel made an authorized assignment in bankruptcy. Subsequently, the Pension Commission of Ontario declared the plan to be wound up as at 31st March 1983 and authorized the actuary for the plan to prepare a wind-up report. The report revealed a surplus of $471,300 after all beneficiaries had been fully paid out in accordance with the terms of the plan.

The plan was established under a trust agreement between Knechtel and Royal Trust Corporation of Canada ("Royal Trust"). The plan called for moneys to be contributed by each of Knechtel and the employees, which moneys were to be deposited with Royal Trust for the purposes described in the plan. Contributions by employees were by payroll deduction based on annual earnings. Contributions by Knechtel were based on actuarial opinions and were to be in amounts sufficient to cover current service costs of the future-service pensions and to amortize the past-service liability for past-service pensions. In short, Knechtel was required to "top up" the fund so that full benefits would be available to participants.

Paragraph 4 of art. XV of the plan provided:

4. The Company intends to maintain the Plan in force indefinitely but necessarily reserves the right by action of its Board of Directors to amend, suspend, or discontinue the Plan should future conditions warrant such action in the opinion of the Company.

Paragraph 6 of art. XV provided for what was to take place in the event of termination of the plan and upon complete discontinuance of contributions. An actuarial investigation was to be made and the funds applied to specified purposes as set out in subparas. (i)-(viii). As previously stated, the assets of the fund were sufficient to fully pay out all beneficiaries in accordance with the terms of the plan and to leave a surplus remaining. The Pension Commission has now advised the actuary to distribute the assets to the beneficiaries but to defer distributing the surplus, pending the outcome of this application.

The distribution of surplus was provided for in subpara. 6(ix) of art. XV. It stated:

(ix) All moneys which remain after the purposes enumerated in Paragraphs (i) to (viii) of this Section 6 of Article XV have been accomplished shall be paid over to the Company, its successors or assigns. Provided, however, that in the event that the Company, at the date of dissolution of the Plan, shall have become bankrupt or insolvent, or shall have taken the benefit of any Statute providing for arrangements with creditors, or shall have been wound-up, either voluntarily or by order of the Court, then in such event all moneys which remain after the purposes enumerated in Paragraphs (i) to (viii) of this Section 6 of Article XV have been accomplished shall not be paid over to the Company, its successors or assigns, but shall be allocated to provide equitable increases in the benefits of those persons and in the respective order, enumerated in this Section 6 of Article XV.

The issue on this application is the entitlement to surplus. There is no problem in the interpretation of subpara. 6(ix) of art. XV. The surplus is to be paid over to Knechtel provided that certain events have not occurred at the date of dissolution. If any of the events have occurred, the surplus is to be allocated to provide equitable increases in the benefits of the persons who have already received a distribution under para. 6. One of the events did occur in that Knechtel had become insolvent on 31st March 1983, the date of dissolution of the plan. On a plain reading of the provision of subpara. 6(ix), Knechtel is not entitled to the surplus and it should be paid over to the employee beneficiaries under the Plan. It is the position of the trustee that the provision that the surplus is to be paid to the beneficiaries on the insolvency of Knechtel is void and not binding on the trustee to the extent that it relates to contributions made by Knechtel.

The plan was established and administered under a trust agreement between Knechtel and Royal Trust. Contributions were made to the trust fund by each of Knechtel and the employee participants. The contributions, when made, were impressed by a trust. Knechtel and the participants were the settlors of the fund. The employees were beneficiaries of the fund. Knechtel was also a beneficiary. On termination, after all employee benefits were paid and distributed, Knechtel had a right to surplus unless certain events had occurred.

Counsel for the representative argued that Knechtel had no interest in the fund. While the plan may have been established for the sole benefit of the employees and the surplus provisions might have been inserted as a "housekeeping" measure to deal with a situation that was considered unlikely and remote, I am unable to see how the surplus provision can be ignored or how it can be said in the light of that provision that Knechtel had no interest in the trust fund during the life of the plan and prior to termination.

The trustee submits that the provision in subpara. 6(ix) is unenforceable and not binding on the trustee. An agreement that provides that upon a person becoming bankrupt his property should pass to a third party is void against a bankruptcy trustee as being in violation of the bankruptcy laws. That policy principle applies equally to an agreement that purports to forfeit a person's rights in the event of insolvency. Thus, a settlor of a trust fund of which he is a beneficiary, may not provide that his beneficial interest shall pass to others in the event of insolvency. That is the situation here. The principle is well-established: see *Higinbotham v. Holme* (1812), 19 Ves. 88, 34 ER 451, Chancery Cases 87; *Whitmore v. Mason* (1861), 2 J & H 204, 70 ER 1031; *Re Jeavons; Ex parte MacKay; Ex parte Browne* (1873), 8 Ch. App. 643; and *Re Harrison; Ex parte Jay* (1880), 14 Ch. D. 19 (CA). It has been applied in Ontario: see *Re Hoskins* (1877), 1 OAR 379 (CA); *Re Laing; Ex parte Laing* (1921), 51 OLR 11, 2 CBR 38, 64 DLR 637 (SC); and *Re Ted Weale Ltd.*, [1952] OWN 560, 32 CBR 206, [1952] 3 DLR 839 (SC).

The trustee does not contend that the application of the principle will result in the entire surplus becoming the property of the bankrupt's estate. It is only the interest settled by Knechtel that may not be distributed under subpara. 6(ix). The provision is not void with respect to the contributions settled by the employees: see *MacKintosh v. Pogose*, [1895] 1 Ch. 505 at 511. The trustee is, therefore, only claiming an interest in proportion to the contributions made by Knechtel to the plan. On the basis of the principle, he should succeed in that claim.

Counsel for the representative submits, however, that the trustee has no status to claim against the surplus. The allocation under subpara. 6(ix) is to be made as at the date of dissolution. At that date, the trustee had no status and it is submitted that the allocation must be made without regard to any status later achieved and that the trustee must take its rights as they existed at the date of bankruptcy.

In applying the policy principle on which the trustee relies, the courts have, on several occasions, mentioned that although an agreement or arrangement diverting property in the event of bankruptcy or insolvency may be valid as between the parties, it is void against the trustee on policy grounds. If there had been no bankruptcy, Knechtel, as it had become insolvent on 31st March 1983, could not have claimed the surplus on termination and it would have been allocated to the employee beneficiaries. The trustee's claim is based on the policy principle and may be enforced irrespective of the right of Knechtel existing at the date of bankruptcy. As the surplus fund is available and undistributed, the trustee has status to claim against it.

The representative relied on *Brooke v. Pearson* (1859), 27 Beav. 181, 54 ER 70; and *Re Detmold; Detmold v. Detmold* (1888), 40 Ch. D. 585, where, in each case, a bankruptcy trustee had been denied status where there was a provision alienating an interest conditional upon the event of bankruptcy. Those cases are distinguishable. In each of those cases, the interest had been validly alienated for reasons other than bankruptcy before the bankruptcy occurred. There was, therefore, no interest that the bankrupt could have claimed at the date of his bankruptcy and the trustee in those circumstances had no better right.

The principle relied on by the trustee is that an owner may not qualify his interest in property by a provision that it will pass to a third party in the event of bankruptcy. On the other hand, an owner may agree to transfer property on the condition that the transferee is not bankrupt. That was the situation in *Cox v. Fonblanque* (1868), LR 6 Eq. 482. A legacy was given to Fonblanque "if not an uncertificated bankrupt at the testator's death." Fonblanque was bankrupt at the testator's death and he was held not entitled to the legacy. Counsel for the representative submits that there is a similar situation in this case. He submits that before Knechtel is entitled to the surplus, it must satisfy the condition precedent of not being insolvent. With respect, that view requires a tortuous reading of subpara. 6(ix), but in any event does not assist in determining the issue. The reason that the policy principle is said to apply to this situation is not because Knechtel is the beneficiary of the fund, but because it is the settlor as well. If there had been no contributions by Knechtel, the situation would have been similar to the *Cox* case and the trustee would have had no claim to the fund. Knechtel, however, had a vested interest in the fund subject to divestment in the event of insolvency. It is the divesting provision that is attacked on policy grounds by the trustee.

Counsel for the representative submits that the policy principle should not be extended to the situation in this case. First, because, unlike many of the cases in which it has been applied, the provision with respect to the surplus was not inserted in the plan to defeat creditors. On the contrary, the uncontradicted evidence was to the effect that the provision was inserted to provide additional benefits to employees who would probably suffer great hardship if the plan were to be wound up after Knechtel had become bankrupt or insolvent.

I find it difficult to see why the hardship would necessarily be any less if the plan had been terminated when Knechtel was solvent. The effect on the employees in each case would depend on all the surrounding circumstances.

Second, counsel submits that because the plan was designed to be for the sole benefit of the employees and they received assurances and commitments from management that this would be so. In 1966, Knechtel issued a booklet to employees which said:

21. *What is the future of the Plan?*
The Company expects to continue the Plan indefinitely, but in the event of future legislation or other circumstances, beyond the Company's control, necessarily reserves the right to amend or discontinue the Plan.

In any event, all contributions made by the Company with respect to accrued benefits are irrevocable and must remain in the Trust Fund for the sole benefit of members and their beneficiaries.

The extract from the booklet fails to mention the provision in the plan entitling Knechtel to be paid the surplus except in certain events. I would expect that in 1966 and thereafter, until financial difficulties overtook Knechtel, that not much thought was given to the possible termination of the plan or the distribution of surplus. Nevertheless, there are provisions in the plan dealing with that eventuality that cannot be ignored.

Third, it is said that the policy principle is based on old English cases which are inappropriate in the current social context. Employee pension plans are part of the conditions of modern life and are protected against encroachment by legislation. It is said that the court should be slow to apply principles that would deprive employees of possible pension benefits. While such a view is understandable, it also may be said that the court should not lightly deprive creditors of funds to which they may be entitled. When a business fails, employees and creditors alike may suffer hardship.

In my opinion, the policy principle is sound and the fact that it was pronounced well over a century ago should not affect its validity. If the drafters of the plan had intended the employees to benefit from the surplus and not Knechtel, it would have been an easy matter to have allocated any surplus on termination to the employee participants. As drafted, subpara. 6(ix) has the effect of diverting moneys to the employee beneficiaries that would otherwise have gone to Knechtel. It is a situation where the policy principle may be applicable. The employee participants have received their benefits in full under the plan. If Knechtel had ceased operations without becoming insolvent, those participants would have had no claim to the surplus. The effect of applying the provision in subpara. 6(ix) is to give the employees a right to funds as against the creditors of Knechtel that they would not have had if there had been no insolvency. I am not persuaded that the policy principle should not be applied in this case and in fact, consider that it is proper to do so.

An order should issue declaring that the trustee has an interest in the surplus fund rateably in proportion to the contributions made by the bankrupt to the plan, such percentage contribution to be calculated by the actuary under the plan. If there is any difficulty in complying with this order, either party may apply to the court for further directions.

Both the trustee and the representative should have their costs of this application out of the surplus fund on a solicitor-and-client basis subject, in the case of the representative, to the provisions of para. 3 of the order by which it was appointed.

Directions given.

NOTE

Knechtel may usefully be compared with the recent Alberta decision in *Principal Savings & Trust Co. v. British Columbia* (1994), 26 CBR (NS) 104. This was an action by the liquidator of PST under the federal Winding-Up Act requiring the BC Minister of Finance to release a deposit made by PST under s. 47 of the BC Trust Companies Act as a condition of PST being permitted to operate in British Columbia. Section 47(4) of the Act provided that the Minister was to hold deposits on trust as security for the extra-provincial trust company's depositors and creditors in the Province and the faithful execution of all trusts accepted in the Province. Murray J held (1) that the deposit requirements were *intra vires* the powers of the Province and not colourable bankruptcy legislation; (2) that PST's deposit was not trust money since it did not satisfy the three certainties for the creation of a trust; and (3) that the liquidator was not entitled to the return of the deposit until the statutory conditions for its return had been satisfied.

Do you agree with this reasoning? Does the requirement for a deposit offend the BIA's principle of equality of treatment of creditors. Is there in fact such a principle in the BIA or are the exceptions to it more important than the principle? Is there a difference between a security deposit and requiring, say, a builder to provide a performance bond to guarantee completion of a building?

In re Christian
(1957), 36 CBR 131 (Ont. SC)

SMILY J: This is a declaration that all moneys in the hands of the Sheriff of the County of York standing to the credit of the debtor are property divisible amongst the creditors of the debtor, and directing the said Sheriff to pay the same to William L. Walton as trustee, subject to payment of all proper fees, costs, poundage and expenses, or for such further or other order as the circumstances may require.

I do not think I need reserve this matter because, as I view it, the matter is determined by s. 42 [now s. 73(2)] of *The Bankruptcy Act*. This makes it very clear, in my opinion, that any moneys received by the Sheriff with respect to the property of the bankrupt should be delivered to the trustee less his fees and costs referred to in subs. 1 of that section. To state otherwise is to say that a provision of *The Creditors' Relief Act*, which might indicate a contrary disposition as to moneys received by the Sheriff from the respondent, is in conflict with the provisions of s. 42 of *The Bankruptcy Act* and, of course, if that is so, the provisions of s. 42 must prevail as provided in s. 41(1) and (6) of *The Bankruptcy Act*.

I do not think that the moneys held by the Sheriff, even if the one month has expired, that is, the one month under the provision of s. 5(2) of *The Creditors' Relief Act*, can be said not to be covered by s. 42 but, rather, they do come within that section.

Also, I do not think that the execution creditors, in the circumstances here, that is, with respect to moneys received by the Sheriff, are secured creditors or creditors holding a lien within the meaning of s. 41(1) of *The Bankruptcy Act* and the definition of a secured creditor under s. 2, as they are not moneys representing a debt, due, or accruing due, to the creditor, under a security for a debt due, that is, a creditor holding a mortgage, charge, or lien, as security for a debt due, or accruing due, to him from the debtor. I think, also, they are not moneys under judgments or attachments which have been completely executed by payment to the creditor or his agent as referred to in s. 41(1). If it were otherwise then I think the principle of *The Bankruptcy Act* with respect to the distribution of the property of the debtor among all his creditors would be defeated. Further, I do not think these moneys can be said to be within the provisions of s. 39(a) as being "property held by the bankrupt in trust for any other person." Apart from any other interpretation of that section, clause (a), it seems to me that s. 42 would make it clear that s. 39(a) was not intended to refer to moneys obtained by the Sheriff. It will be noted that s. 42 makes no exception with respect to moneys received by the Sheriff of the property of the bankrupt and, in my view, it concludes the matter quite clearly.

There will, therefore, be an order that these moneys in the hands of the Sheriff are property divisible amongst the creditors of the debtor, and directing the Sheriff to pay the same to the trustee, William L. Walton, subject to payment of all proper fees, costs, and expenses in compliance with *The Bankruptcy Act*.

Order accordingly.

Canadian Credit Men's Trust v. Beaver Trucking Ltd.
(1959), 38 CBR 1 (SCC)

LOCKE J: ... The facts to be considered in dealing with the matter are as follows: On November 5, 1956 the respondent commenced an action against T.L. Cleary Drilling Co. Ltd. for the recovery of the sum of $2,282.50 and caused to be served a garnishing order upon the California Standard Company, a debtor of the Cleary Company. On February 9, 1957 the garnishee paid into the Court of Queen's Bench at Brandon the sum of $2,282.50. On May 13, 1957 default judgment was signed in the action against the Cleary Company for the amount claimed and taxed costs. On June 18, 1957 that company made a voluntary assignment in bankruptcy, in the statutory form, to the Canadian Credit Men's Trust Association Ltd.

On November 18, 1957 the trustee applied for payment out of the amount so paid by the garnishee and which was then in court and, contemporaneously, the present respondent made an application for payment out to it and both motions were by consent heard together by the local judge. By an order dated December 16, 1957 the application by the trustee was dismissed and it was ordered that the amount in court be paid out to the Beaver Trucking Co. Ltd.

Proceedings were stayed on this order, pending an appeal to a judge of the Court of Queen's Bench by the present appellant, and as stated, that appeal was dismissed by Monnin J on February 28, 1958 in a considered judgment. The reasons for judgment of the majority of the Court of Appeal were delivered by Tritschler JA.

Section 41 of *The Bankruptcy Act*, RSC 1952, c. 14 [BIA s. 70(1)], so far as it is relevant to the present appeal, reads: ...

It is in reliance upon the first of these subsections that the trustee claims that the moneys in court should be paid to it for distribution among the creditors. The position taken by the garnishing creditor is that, by reason of the service of the garnishing order upon the California Standard Company in advance of the assignment in bankruptcy, it is a secured creditor within the meaning of that expression in s. 41 and, as such, has priority over the trustee's claim.

The expression "secured creditor" is defined in s. 2(r) [BIA s. 2] of the Act to mean: ...

By Rule 526 of the Queen's Bench Rules, the court is empowered in the matter of a claim such as that of the present respondent to make an order that all debts, obligations and liabilities owing, payable or accruing due from any person who is indebted or liable to the debtor shall be attached. A form of the order which may be made appears as Form 74 in the Appendix to the Rules. The nature of the order, in so far as it might concern the present matter, does not differ from the orders *nisi* authorized by Order 45, Rule 1 of the Rules of the Supreme Court 1883 in England. That rule authorizes the making of an order that all debts owing or accruing due from a third person to the debtor shall be attached to answer the judgment or order.

I refer to these rules since in certain of the cases decided in Manitoba it has been held that a garnishing creditor is, by virtue of the service of a garnishing order, a secured creditor within the meaning of s. 41(1) of *The Bankruptcy Act* (*In re Doyle* (1957), 22 WWR 651, 1957 Can. Abr. 40 and on appeal (1957), 36 CBR 134, 23 WWR 661 at 663, 1958 Can. Abr. 41) though, as pointed out by Adamson CJM, the decision did not turn upon that point.

• • •

In my opinion, the meaning to be assigned to s. 41, as it applies to the present case, is plain. In the clearest terms it is provided that the assignment shall take precedence over a garnishment, except where such has been completely executed by payment to the creditor or his agent. Here, no such payment was made. The moneys were paid into court to the credit of the cause and remain there.

If, as is stated by Farwell LJ in *Galbraith v. Grimshaw*, [1910] 1 KB 339 at 343, the service of a garnishing order creates an equitable charge upon the debt in favour of the garnishing creditor and, if such a charge falls within the definition of a secured creditor in *The Bankruptcy Act*, it must be taken that, since the rights of garnishing creditors have already been dealt with, they are not included in the expression "the rights of a secured creditor" in the concluding words of the subsection.

If there were ambiguity in the language of the first subs. of s. 41, and I think there is none, it would be necessary for us to construe it in the manner directed by s. 15 of *The Interpretation Act* (RSC 1952, c. 158) and to give to it such interpretation as will best ensure the attainment of the object of the Act according to its true intent, meaning and spirit. The purpose of *The Bankruptcy Act* and of all bankruptcy legislation in Canada and in England is to assure that, in the case of insolvent debtors, their assets shall be divided fairly among their creditors, having due regard to the position of persons such as mortgagees who, having advanced moneys upon the security of assets of the debtor, are to be afforded the rights of secured creditors, and to those claims which are by statute entitled to preference.

Section 86 and those sections immediately following it declare the position of secured creditors and define the extent to which they are entitled to priority. Subject to such rights and to preferences to which other claims such as those of the Crown may be declared to be entitled and the costs and expenses of the trustee, it is the purpose of the Act that the creditors shall rank *pari passu* upon the estate. The construction of the Act contended for by the respondent in the present matter would mean that a creditor sufficiently alert to bring an action and attach moneys owing to a debtor on the brink of insolvency may thereby obtain preference over other creditors who refrain from bringing actions, for the amount of his claim in full and not merely for his costs, as provided by s. 41(2). This, in my opinion, is directly contrary to the intent and purpose of *The Bankruptcy Act*, and any such contention should be rejected unless the language of the Act should require it in the clearest terms. ...

JUDSON J (Cartright, Fauteux and Martland JJ concurring): ... Until the concluding phrase of the section [s. 41] "and except also the rights of a secured creditor," words could not be plainer. The claim of the trustee prevails over that of the judgment creditor under any of the execution procedures mentioned unless there has been payment to the creditor or his agent. It is not sufficient that the fund may have been payment to the creditor or his agent. It is not sufficient that the fund may have been stopped in the hands of the garnishee or that it may be in court subject to further order or even subject to payment-out on an order already issued. Nor does it matter when the money was attached or paid into court or what the status of the action may have been when bankruptcy supervened. The only question is—has the execution procedure been completed by payment to the creditor or his agent?

In the judgment under appeal, the Court of Appeal has held that the section has no such operation because a judgment creditor who has caused a garnishee order to be served is a secured creditor. After specific and clear directions concerning the rights of the garnisheeing creditor and the trustee in bankruptcy, it is held that the section has said nothing because the creditor whose position and rights are defined and limited in the first part of the section is the same creditor who is removed from its scope and put within the exception.

Only the plainest language could compel an interpretation which produces this conclusion and I do not think that this compulsion exists in the present case. With all respect to the majority opinion in the Court of Appeal, I agree with the dissenting opinion expressed by Adamson CJ, that the provisions of the section are clear and that even a literal interpretation does not lead to the conclusion reached by the majority. To me the compelling inference is that whoever the secured creditor may be whose rights are excepted from the operation of the section, he is not the attaching or garnisheeing creditor, whose position has already been fully dealt with. The intention that I find plainly expressed is to ensure the distribution of the debtor's property in accordance with *The Bankruptcy Act* and not according to the execution procedures mentioned in the section, all of which are brought to an end when bankruptcy supervenes unless they have been completed by payment.

There are subsequent sections which carry out this intention and reinforce my conclusion. These sections, also, would be without meaning if the judgment under appeal is correct. Although under s. 41(1) the execution creditor must give way to the trustee in bankruptcy, by the next subsection the one who has first attached by way of garnishment or lodged a writ of execution with the sheriff gets his solicitor's bill of costs paid and this is done in accordance with the priorities established in s. 95(9). Next there is provision in s. 42(2) for delivery to the trustee of any property of the bankrupt under execution or attachment, and finally, by s. 43(2), the trustee is enabled to have himself registered as the owner of any land "free of all encumbrances or charges mentioned in s. 41(1)."

My conclusion, therefore, is that judgment creditors who have made use of the execution procedures set out in s. 41(1) are subject to the provisions of *The Bankruptcy Act* unless they have been paid, that they do not come within the class of secured creditors mentioned in the exception, and that they are not secured creditors under *The Bankruptcy Act* as defined in s. 2(r).

• • •

Appeal allowed.

Re Bright
(1981), 33 OR (2d) 219 (SC)

HOLLINGWORTH J: Before me are two notices of motion, one by the trustee in bankruptcy asking that the security claimed to be held by Ida Heather Burns, a creditor of the above-noted bankrupt, be declared null and void as against the said trustee, and the motion by Mr. McCallen, who acts for Ida Heather Burns, for an order vesting in Ida Heather Burns the equity of redemption or other interest which is vested in the trustee in certain properties mentioned in the notice of motion, said properties being shares which were held by the bankrupt in Bright Investments Limited.

It was mutually agreed that Mr. Palmateer's notice of motion should proceed and that, therefore, I am now dealing with the motion by the trustee stating that the security claimed by the respondent is null and void as against the said trustee.

The security consists of the order of the Honourable Mr. Justice Cromarty dated September 23, 1980, pursuant to s. 143(4) of the *Judicature Act*, RSO 1970, c. 228 [now RSO 1980, c. 223, s. 146(4)], which charged that all shares standing in the name of the bankrupt with payment of a judgment in favour of the said Ida Heather Burns, in the County of York, in the Judicial District of York, dated March 7, 1980, in the sum of $31,966.65, together with the sum of $96.50 for costs, plus post-judgment interest at the rate of 15% per annum. As of November 18, 1980, this total amounted to $35,426.22.

It would thus appear that initially Ida Heather Burns was the judgment creditor of the bankrupt but took the further step under s. 143 of the *Judicature Act* of placing a charging order against the assets in which she had become a judgment creditor as a result of the default judgment granted by Cromarty J. She thus succeeded under s. 143(4) of the said *Judicature Act* in causing to be made absolute the order of Anderson J dated August 13, 1980, in which Anderson J granted the charging order judgment *nisi* which as I have indicated Cromarty J made absolute.

The material filed by the bankrupt indicates that the bankrupt had unsecured creditors at the time of his bankruptcy in an amount in excess of $200,000 and the only assets of any consequence that he had were 500 shares of Bright Investments Limited, and one share in Bright Canning Company Limited. It was, of course, the canning company that really went bankrupt and Mr. Bright in the material he submitted, being the questions put to the bankrupt by the Official Receiver under s. 132 of the *Bankruptcy Act*, RSC 1970, c. B-3, indicated that the causes of the bankruptcy were due to bad investments and an excessive use of credit. On p. 5 of the report he stated that the bulk of investments were to purchase Ida Burns & Associates which operated a consumer research and product promotion operation. Due to absentee management and numerous competitive businesses the company could not survive and ceased operation the first part of January, 1980. It went on to say that the final blow came when the creditor, Ida Burns, had his shares seized. I might point out at this stage that the solicitors for Ida Burns served a notice on the Sheriff of the Judicial District of York to sell the shares which I have already mentioned. The Sheriff immediately forwarded them to the trustee and, hence, this application.

As this application is an interesting but rather rare type of application, I have had the opportunity of having argument *in extenso* by both counsel with numerous cases cited, and I shall now endeavour to summarize the arguments of each prior to resolving the question.

Both counsel have relied heavily on s. 50, s-ss. (1) and (2) [now ss. 70(1) and (2)] of the *Bankruptcy Act* and the definition of "secured creditor" found in the definition section under s. 2. In order to understand their arguments it is necessary to quote both of these sections in full and I now proceed to do so.

Precedence of receiving orders and assignments

50(1) Every receiving order and every assignment made in pursuance of this Act takes precedence over all judicial or other attachments, garnishments, certificates having the effect of judgments, judgments, certificates of judgment, judgments operating as hypothecs, executions or other process against the property of a bankrupt, except such as have been completely executed by payment to the creditor or his agent, and except also the rights of a secured creditor.

●   ●   ●

I now turn to the "secured creditor" definition which is contained in s. 2. That reads as follows:

"secured creditor" means a person holding a mortgage, hypothec, pledge, charge, lien or privilege on or against the property of the debtor or any part thereof as security for a debt due or accruing due to him from the debtor, or a person whose claim is based upon, or secured by, a negotiable instrument held as collateral security and upon which the debtor is only indirectly or secondarily liable;

To epitomize, every receiving order takes precedence over the items cited in s. 50 with two exceptions; first, if the creditor or his agent has received payment, and secondly, if the creditor is a secured creditor. It is Mr. Palmateer's position simply that the receiving order takes precedence in this particular case and the exceptions are not applicable because in the first place, there has been no payment to the creditor or his agent, and secondly, the creditor, Ida Burns, is not a secured creditor.

It is Mr. McCallen's submission that Ida Burns is a secured creditor and by the definition section, a "secured creditor" means "a person holding a charge" and that is exactly what she has. It is Mr. McCallen's further submission that although he concedes that as a judgment creditor Ida Burns does not have a claim in preference to a receiving order, because she has a charging order, this puts her in quite a different position and this also indicates that a charging order, being in effect a "charge," comes within the definition of a secured creditor. Both counsel have backed up their submissions with cases which I will now proceed to consider.

Mr. Palmateer begins with a Supreme Court of Canada case, *Canadian Credit Men's Trust Ass'n Ltd. v. Beaver Trucking Ltd.; California Standard Co., Garnishee*, [1959] SCR 31, 17 DLR (2d) 161, 38 CBR 1. ...

It would thus appear that only an execution creditor who has received payment is entitled to priority over the other creditors claiming in bankruptcy.

Mr. Palmateer deals head on with Mr. McCallen's contention that a charging order is a different matter, in that a charging order is a charge and consequently comes under the definition of a "secured creditor" in the *Bankruptcy Act*. Mr. Palmateer quotes from the case of *Re Overseas Aviation Engineering (G.B.), Ltd.*, [1962] 3 All ER 12, in which the Court of Appeal, comprised of Lord Denning MR, Harman and Russell LJJ, by a majority of two to one with Russell LJ dissenting, came to the conclusion that a charging order was in the nature of an execution and consequently should come within the definition of the English equivalent of s. 50 of the *Bankrupt Act*. It should be noted that under s. 50: "Every receiving order ... takes precedence ... over *executions or other process. ...*" (My emphasis.)

There is no doubt that their Lordships were dealing with a different matter than we have before us, in that in the case before them, the charging order concerned land and not shares, but Lord Denning had no trouble dealing with that and stated at pp. 16-7:

... I should have thought it plain that when a judgment creditor gets a charge on the debtor's property, it is a form of "execution," for it is a means of enforcing the judgment. I do not think that *Re Hutchinson* (1885), 16 QBD 515, should be taken to decide the contrary. The reasoning is obscure, and in any event it must be read in the light of later cases. A charging order on shares has since been said to be "in the nature of an execution," see *Finney v. Hinde* (1879), 4 QBD at p. 104, and *Re O'Shea's Settlement, Courage v. O'Shea*, [1895] 1 Ch. at p. 329.

Lord Denning goes on to say:

Sir Raymond Evershed, MR, has gone further and described a charging order on shares as an "execution," see *Re Love, Ex p. Official Receiver v. Kingston-upon-Thames County Court Registrar*, [1951] 2 All ER at p. 1023.

I might state at this point that Mr. McCallen relies heavily on Cave J in *Re Hutchinson*, which case I shall come to in due course, and I have searched in vain for Sir Raymond Evershed's describing a charging order on shares as an "execution" in the *Love* case. There is no doubt that this was stated in *Finney v. Hinde, supra*, specifically by Baron Pollock at p. 104, and it is also interesting to note that the *Finney v. Hinde* case stood squarely on the *Judgments Act*, 1838, c. 110, ss. 14 and 15, which are almost verbatim with our s. 143: see also Lord Halsbury and Lindley LJ in *Re O'Shea's Settlement; Courage v. O'Shea*, [1895] 1 Ch. 325 at p. 329.

It is put another way, and rather succinctly, by Buckley LJ in *Rainbow et al. v. Moorgate Properties Ltd.*, [1975] 2 All ER 821 at p. 825, as follows:

The effect of the petition having been presented ... is that if eventually a winding-up order is made, the plaintiffs will be unable to insist on their charging orders, but if no winding-up order is ever made, and if the charging orders remain in force, the plaintiffs will remain secured creditors of the company.

To put it in a nutshell, Mr. Palmateer's argument is that Ida Burns cannot recover in precedence to the trustee on the basis of being a judgment creditor or an execution creditor or if she has an absolute charging order because of the authorities which I have quoted. A charging order is not mentioned in s. 50 but an execution is and by s. 50(1): "Every receiving order ... takes precedence over ... executions or other process against the property of a bankrupt" unless there are two exceptions; the creditor has been paid (which is not the case here) or the rights of a secured creditor, and Mr. Palmateer argues strenuously that Ida Burns is not a secured creditor. Consequently, the exception clauses are vitiated and the receiving order, as I indicated, has priority.

Mr. McCallen relies principally on two authorities; the first being *Bortoluzzi v. Kaplan*, [1927] 1 DLR 183. The headnote states in this five-man decision of the Manitoba Court of Appeal that:

A creditor holding a charging order against a fund in Court, is a secured creditor within the meaning of the Bankruptcy Act, 1919 (Can.), c. 36.

Let us begin by conceding the fact that the definition of a secured creditor as stated on p. 184 of the report is not different from the definition which I have cited in the *Bankruptcy Act* of today. Let us also concede that s. 11(1) of the Canadian *Bankruptcy Act*, enacted in 1920, is not substantially or of any significant difference in form than s. 50(1) and (2) or s. 41(1) and (2) as cited in the *Canadian Credit Men's* case at the beginning of my legal analysis.

Fullerton JA, at p. 184, says:

I am unable to understand how it can be said that the charging order does not create a charge on the property of the debtor. The order says in so many words that the sum of $2,011.59—admittedly the property of the debtor—shall stand charged with the payment to the appellant of the sum therein named.

He quotes Sir J. Romilly MR in *Montefiore v. Behrens* (1865), LR 1 Eq. 171 at p. 173:

It is impossible to hold that a charging order does not create a charge; in fact, it would be a contradiction in terms if it were otherwise.

Trueman JA is equally emphatic and at p. 186 states:

However ... I cannot deem it to be an execution within s. 11(1) [now s. 50(1)], which plainly in its context refers to the common law writ of execution (see *Re Hutchinson* (1885), 16 QBD 515). Nor can I think that the charging order in question comes within the term "process," wide though the expression obviously was intended to be. Process as there used must in its collocation be akin to attachment or execution, by means of which payment of a judgment debt is enforced by seizure and sale by an officer of the Court of property of the debtor.

Mr. Palmateer, in reply, distinguishes *Bortoluzzi* on three grounds. In the first place he said the charging order covered funds already in Court and, similarly, *Re Coast Mill Works Ltd.* (1956), 5 DLR (2d) 334, 19 WWR 379, 36 CBR 36, which purports to follow *Bortoluzzi*, also deals with funds already in Court. This is a Supreme Court of British Columbia decision rendered by McInnes J and at p. 337, he states baldly [quoting from *Bradford & Greenberg's Canadian Bankruptcy Act, 1951*]:

A person who prior to the authorized assignment obtained a charging order against a fund in court is a secured creditor: *J.J.H. McLean Co. v. Newton*, 36 Man. R 187, 8 CBR 61.

I would point out that the *McLean v. Newton* case is the same case as *Bortoluzzi v. Kaplan* and the appeal, of course, was dismissed and the fund was disbursed as asked. The second group upon which Mr. Palmateer purported to distinguish *Bortoluzzi* was the fact that there was a great difference in wording between s. 11(1) of the *Bankruptcy Act* in 1927 and s. 50(1) of the *Bankruptcy Act* in 1951. He went on to say that the wording was much broader now and this would certainly have an effect on the decisions, in that *Bortoluzzi* was confined to the wording of 1927. The third reason for distinguishing it was because Trueman JA in *Bortoluzzi* relied on *Re Hutchinson* which was a discredited case according to Mr. Palmateer, as a result of Lord Denning's remarks and as a result of the decision of the Court which I have already cited which was followed by *Re a debtor (No. 39 of 1974); Ex p. Okill et al. v. Gething et al.*, [1977] 3 All ER 489, which purported to follow *Re Overseas Aviation Engineering (GB), Ltd., supra*. I think none of these purported distinctions has any cogent validity.

If I may briefly review the quintessence of s. 50 again, it states that: ...

We must first consider whether an execution or other process encompasses a charging order. It has been stated by Trueman JA in *Bortoluzzi*, at p. 186, that he does not deem the charging order concerning a fund in Court in that case:

... to be an execution within s. 11(1), which plainly in its context refers to the common law writ of execution (see *Re Hutchinson* (1885), 16 QBD 515). Nor can I think that the charging order in question comes within the term "process," wide though the expression obviously was intended to be. Process as there used must in its collocation be akin to attachment or execution, by means of which payment of a judgment debt is enforced by seizure and sale by an officer of the Court of property of the debtor.

It is necessary, therefore, in considering *Re Hutchinson, supra*, to look at s. 45 of the English *Bankruptcy Act*, 1883 (UK), c. 52, which reads this way: ...

It will be seen that nowhere in s. 45 is any reference made to "other process." It does mention, it is true, attachment and execution but there is no consideration of "other process." I have come to the conclusion that notwithstanding and with the greatest respect to the judgment of Trueman JA in *Bortoluzzi*, that the term "other process" can definitely include the circumstances of the present case and, consequently, I find *prima facie* that under s. 50(1) the trustee has precedence over the execution creditor because of the wording of the Act and with specific reference to "other process."

But that does not complete the matter. It is necessary to consider the two exceptions to s. 50(1). The receiving order only gets precedence over the "attachments," etc., cited in s. 50(1), unless there has been payment to the creditor or his agent or unless the creditor falls under the aegis of a "secured creditor." There is no argument whatsoever that payment has not been completed; the shares are in the hands of the Sheriff and the Sheriff is awaiting instructions whether they should be sold, given to the trustee, or given to the execution creditor for disposition. I have already mentioned that in the definition s. 2(r) of the *Bankruptcy Act* that a "secured creditor" means "a person holding a mortgage, hypothec, pledge, charge, lien or privilege. ..." It is a question very simply of determining whether or not a charging order is a charge. Again looking at s. 50(1), there is no mention whatsoever of a charge and, indeed, in the definition section of the *Bankruptcy Act* there is no definition of "charge." I have, accordingly, gone to *Jowitt's Dictionary of English Law*,

2nd ed., and at p. 322, a charging order is defined, *inter alia*, as a "charge on the securities of a judgment debtor or a charge on monies in court." The word "charge" is found at p. 321 and includes, *inter alia*, charge as applied to property signifies that it is security for the payment of a debt or the performance of an obligation which includes mortgages and writs of execution, etc. I turn again to *Canadian Credit Men's Trust Ass'n Ltd. v. Beaver Trucking Ltd.; California Standard Co., Garnishee*, [1959] SCR 311, 17 DLR (2d) 161, 38 CBR 1, which is a Supreme Court of Canada decision which I have already alluded to. The [CBR] headnote in that case states:

Judgment creditors who have made use of the execution procedures set out in s. 41(1) [now s. 50(1)] of the Act are subject to the provisions of *The Bankruptcy Act* and *do not come within the class of secured creditors as defined in s. 2(r)* unless they have been paid.

(My emphasis.)

The action in that case indicated that the respondent creditor commenced an action against the debtor and caused a garnishee order to be served on a debtor of the principal debtor. In due course the principal debtor made an assignment in bankruptcy and the question was whether or not the moneys would be paid to the trustee who applied for payment out of the amount paid by the garnishee and which were then in Court. The Supreme Court of Canada refused to do so. The Court had no trouble in finding that in the circumstances of this case there was no secured creditor and because payment had not been made, the first exception of s. 50(1), then s. 41(1), was not applicable and, of course, the matter of a secured creditor concerning a charging order did not come up because no charging order had been taken out. Judson J, speaking for Cartwright, Fauteux and Martland JJ, simply said judgment creditors were subject to s. 41(1) of the *Bankruptcy Act* unless they had been paid, and they did not come within the class of secured creditors mentioned in the exception, and accordingly they were not secured creditors under the *Bankruptcy Act* as defined in s. 2(r).

I finally turn to the passage of Locke J, at p. 316 SCR, p. 164 DLR, pp. 4-5 CBR, which reads as follows:

... it is the purpose of the Act that the creditors shall rank *pari passu* upon the estate. The construction of the Act contended for by the respondent in the present matter would mean that a creditor sufficiently alert to bring an action and attach moneys owing to a debtor on the brink of insolvency may thereby obtain preference over other creditors who refrain from bringing actions, for the amount of his claim in full and not merely for his costs, as provided by s. 41(2) [now s. 50(2)]. This, in my opinion, is directly contrary to the intent and purpose of the *Bankruptcy Act*, and any such contention should be rejected *unless the language of the Act should require it in the clearest terms*.

[Emphasis added.]

I am of opinion that because the word "charge" is not defined in the Act nor are the words "charging order" defined in the Act, that I must be bound by the original purpose of the Act which is, to quote Locke J again: "that the creditors shall rank *pari passu*. ..."

I do not feel that, again to quote the words of Locke J, "the language of the Act" requires me to hold "in the clearest terms" that a charging order places the creditor in the position of a secured creditor and, accordingly, I find that the shares are vested in the trustee and that the security claimed by the creditor, Ida Heather Burns, shall be declared null and void as against the said trustee. ...

Declaration accordingly.

Re Southern Fried Foods Ltd.
(1976), 67 DLR (3d) 599 (Ont. SC)

HENRY J (orally): Prior to this bankruptcy, Southern Fried Foods Limited occupied premises in the City of Toronto which it leased from the respondent Maria Soja, the landlord. The rent fell into arrears and the landlord placed the matter in the hands of Associated Bailiffs and Co. Limited, who, pursuant to a distress warrant, seized the assets located on the leased premises for arrears of rent, and sold them by auction on July 25, 1973. The gross proceeds realized from the sale was $3,416.75. The bailiff withheld a proportion of the proceeds, the accounting for which is subject to question and remitted a cheque for the net proceeds in the amount of $1,800 to the landlord, drawn by the bailiffs on the Toronto Dominion Bank dated August 17, 1973. On August 20, 1973, Southern Fried Foods Limited made an assignment in bankruptcy and the trustee immediately entered into possession of the leased premises. On August 21st, both the landlord and the bailiff had notice of the bankruptcy. The cheque for the net proceeds, which had been presented for payment on August 17th, was certified by the bank on August 23rd, three days after the bankruptcy.

The trustee now applies for an order declaring that he is entitled to the proceeds of the sale of the assets seized and sold from the leased premises, less the proper costs of distress, on the ground that the assignment in bankruptcy takes precedence over the process of seizure and sale by virtue of s. 50(1) of the *Bankruptcy Act*, RSC 1970, c. B-3, which provides [see *supra, Re Bright*]. ...

The trustee's position is that the process of seizure and sale had not been completely executed by payment to the creditor or her agent at the time the bankruptcy occurred, because the bailiffs had given the landlord a cheque which had not by the date of bankruptcy been paid to the landlord by the bank and was not certified by the bank until after the date of bankruptcy. He refers further to s. 51 of the *Bankruptcy Act* [now s. 73] as requiring the proceeds to be paid to him. That section provides in part as follows: [see ss. 73(2), (3) and (4)].

In my opinion, in effecting the seizure and the sale, the bailiff was acting as agent of the landlord and the process had been completely executed at the time the proceeds of the sale were in the hands of the bailiff as the landlord's agent. In these circumstances, that transaction is within the exception in s. 50(1) of the Act and the trustee is not entitled to those proceeds. The disposition of the proceeds becomes a matter entirely between the bailiff as agent and the landlord as principal. The effect of this is to take the transaction out of the purview of s. 51. It does not fall within s-ss. (2) and (3) of that section because the bailiff is not a Sheriff or other officer of the Court. It does not fall under s-s. (4) because the transaction was complete at the time of the bankruptcy and the proceeds ceased to be property of the bankrupt and were not subject to the priority of the assignment by reason of the exception in s. 50(1). Mr. Gringorten referred me to the decision of McDermott J in *Re*

Stan-Don Supply (Sudbury) Ltd., [1968] 2 OR 53, 68 DLR (2d) 125, 11 CBR (NS) 243, in which the headnote [CBR (NS)] appears to support the position taken by the trustee. There, a landlord instructed his solicitor to effect collection of arrears of rent owing by the bankrupt. The solicitor instructed a bailiff to levy distress on the goods and chattels of the bankruptcy; a seizure was made on September 29, 1965, resulting in a sale of auction on October 7, 1965, and the trustee demanded payment from the bailiff who at that time still retained the proceeds of the sale of assets. The proceeds were not delivered to anyone by the bailiff until February 10, 1966, when the bailiff delivered a cheque in that amount payable to the landlord to the landlord's solicitor.

In that case the learned Judge held that the trustee in bankruptcy was entitled to the proceeds from the sale, less the costs of distress. A careful reading of the judgment reveals that the learned Judge did not consider that the process of seizure and sale had been "completely executed by payment to the creditor or in his agent." It seems clear that he considered that the agent of the landlord in the circumstances of that case was the solicitor and that the solicitor had no authority to delegate his agency to the bailiff. It is clear he did not consider what is now s. 50(1) of the *Bankruptcy Act* which gives priority to the assignment was not negatived by reason of the exception and his decision was based squarely on the provisions of what is now s. 51(4), which I have quoted above. In my view, it is implicit in his reasons that he did not consider that the proceeds had found their way into the hands of an agent of the landlord until the cheque was received by the solicitor well after the date of bankruptcy.

In my view, that decision is to be distinguished because as I see the matter the transaction was completed when the proceeds found their way into the hands of the bailiff who as I have held in this case was the agent of the landlord. Unless this view of the interaction of s. 50(1) and s. 51 of the Act is taken, namely, that once the transaction is completed and the proceeds are in the hands of the agent of the landlord, s. 51(4) no longer operates, it would be impossible for the landlord ever to escape a demand from the trustee. In other words, s. 51(4) must be read as being subject to the exception mentioned in the latter part of s. 50(1). I further point out that the matter may well be different if the proceeds were in the hands of a Sheriff or other officer of the Court as contemplated by s. 51(2) and (3). While I do not find it necessary to decide the point, it appears to me that the difference between those subsections and s-s. (4) is that the Sheriff or other officer of the Court is not the agent of the landlord. ...

Application dismissed.

Coopers & Lybrand v. Lumberland Building Materials
(1983), 50 CBR (NS) 150 (BCSC)

CAMPBELL LJSC: This is the hearing of a special case pursuant to British Columbia Supreme Court R. 33. The agreed facts are as follows:

1. The Plaintiff is a licensed Trustee in Bankruptcy and is Trustee in Bankruptcy of the Estate of Trans-Lite Distributors Ltd. ("Trans-Lite") which made an assignment for the benefit of its creditors on July 19, 1982.

2. Lumberland Building Materials Ltd. ("Lumberland") is a corporation duly incorporated under the laws of the Province of British Columbia, with its registered office at 5650 Lougheed Highway, Burnaby, Province of British Columbia.

3. Pursuant to an agreement made between Trans-Lite Distributors Ltd. before it became bankrupt, the Plaintiff, Trans-Lite agreed to sell and the Defendant, Lumberland agreed to buy certain goods, namely building supplies and the Defendant agreed to pay Trans-Lite for the goods.

4. Pursuant to the agreement, Plaintiff sold and delivered building supplies to the Defendant, particulars of which have been given to the Defendant, and, as of July 19, 1982, the sum of $11,613.40 was due and owing from the Defendant to Plaintiff on account thereof before allowing for any claim for set-off by the Defendant.

5. In order to induce purchases from, *inter alia*, the Defendant, the Plaintiff had offered its customers a volume sales rebate program for 1982. Attached as Schedule "A" is a true copy of that offer, which was made to the Defendant.

6. The Defendant purchased goods which qualified under the rebate offer, in the amount of $267,256.00 on or before July 19, 1982.

7. The Plaintiff offered the Defendant, *inter alia*, to share the costs of advertising products regularly sold by the Plaintiff. Attached as Schedule "B" is a true copy of the co-operative advertising offer made by the Plaintiff.

8. The Defendant set off the sum of $6,681.40 from the amount owed by it to the Plaintiff as at July 19, 1982 on account of a claimed volume rebate.

9. The Plaintiff claims that the Defendant was not entitled to set-off the sum of $6,681.40.

Schedule "A" to the special case contains, *inter alia*, the following provision:

Volume earned rebates are based and paid on the plateau achieved by year end. The amount of earned rebate will be paid to you by cheque within sixty (60) days following year end.

The issue is the right of the defendant to set-off against the $11,613.40 owing the plaintiff on the date of bankruptcy the sum of $6,681.40 it says it was entitled to on that date as earned rebate.

Section 75(3) of the Bankruptcy Act, RSC 1970, c. B-3 [now s. 97(3)] provides:

(3) The law of set-off applies to all claims made against the estate and also to all actions instituted by the trustee for the recovery of debts due to the bankrupt in the same manner and to the same extent as if the bankrupt were plaintiff or defendant, as the case may be, except in so far as any claim for set-off is affected by the provisions of this Act respecting frauds or fraudulent preferences.

Section 95(2) and (3) [ss. 121(2) and (3)] provides ... .

The plaintiff says the defendant is not entitled to do so because: (1) there was no rebate due at the date of bankruptcy, i.e. "The amount of earned rebate will be paid ... within sixty (60) days following year end"; and (2) the intervention of the bankruptcy and the lack of crystallization of the amount due destroyed the element of mutuality which is required to permit a set-off.

The defendant says that there is one related agreement as set out in paras. 3 and 5 of the agreed facts which allows the defendant to set off its claim, the amount which can be ascertained, against the plaintiff's liquidated claim and even if there is a loss of mutuality, equity will assist to permit a set-off in the circumstances here.

Section 75 of the Bankruptcy Act clearly allows a set-off and I must here determine whether at law one is permitted on the facts here.

There are two kinds of set-off: legal/statutory and equitable set-off. Legal set-off originated in England by statute, s. 13 of Insolvent Debtors Relief (1728), 2 Geo. 2, c. 22, amended and made effective "for ever" by s. 4 of Set-off (1734-35), 8 Geo. 2, c. 24, and carried forward into the law of British Columbia in 1858 by the predecessor of the present s. 2 of the Law and Equity Act, RSBC 1979, c. 224. Equitable set-off has its origins in equity and does not rest on the statute of 1729. It followed and even extended the law, the courts of equity holding that certain cases were within the equity of the statute, although not within their actual words.

In *CIBC v. Tuckerr Indust. Inc.*, 48 CBR (NS) 1, [1983] 5 WWR 602, 46 BCLR 8, 149 DLR (3d) 172 (CA), Lambert JA, speaking for the court, held that statutory set-off is available only if two conditions are fulfilled, i.e. (1) both obligations must be debts; and (2) both debts must be mutual cross-obligations, and both conditions must be fulfilled at the same time.

The first requirement is that both the plaintiff's and the defendant's claims be for a debt which can be ascertained with certainty at the time of pleading. (See *Royal Trust Co. v. Holden* (1915), 21 BCLR 185, 8 WWR 500, 22 DLR 660 (CA).) Here, the defendant owes the plaintiff the sum of $11,613.40 for goods purchased. This is a liquidated amount and can be ascertained at the time of pleading. On the other hand the defendant claims entitlement from the plaintiff its share of the advertisement costs and the amount of rebate available to the defendant. These are also ascertainable with certainty at the time of pleading and then amounted to $6,681.40. The rebate programme (previously quoted) provides that value earned rebates are based and paid on the plateau achieved by year-end in accordance with the schedule. After the date of bankruptcy, 19th July 1982, the plaintiff could no longer sell any goods to the defendant. Prior to that, between 1st January 1982 and 19th July 1982, the defendant had purchased goods in an amount entitling it to a rebate in the amount it seeks to set off. Clearly then, on 19th July 1982 the debt owed by the plaintiff to the defendant was a liquidated sum which is ascertainable.

The second condition as stated in the *Tuckerr Indust.* case is that there must be cross-obligations.

A set-off is available only between the same parties and in the same right as the claim. A right of set-off cannot be maintained against a plaintiff suing to enforce his demand or against an assignee when the demand which it is sought to set off arises upon an independent contract and is not due at the date of the suit, for in that case it has not become a "debt" so as to be subject to the statute. The right of set-off depends on the existence of the debt due to the defendant and thus the fact of its debtor being a bankrupt does not prevent the set-off arising. The time that both obligations must exist in a bankruptcy situation is at the time of the bankruptcy, i.e., the assignment in bankruptcy or the pronouncement of a receiving order.

Here, on 19th July 1982 there were mutual and cross-obligations between the parties. On that date the defendant owed the plaintiff the amount of goods purchased and the plaintiff owed the defendant the costs of advertisements and the rebate. Even though the latter amounts were not "due" at that time, that does not defeat the defendant's right of set-off. In *Re Agra & Masterman's Bank, Anderson's Case* (1866), LR 3 Eq. 337 (Ch. D.), the court held that if a company goes into liquidation, debts which accrued before the winding-up may be set off against one another.

The plaintiff relies on *Re Debtor (No. 66 of 1955), Ex parte Debtor v. Trustee of Property of Waite*, [1956] 3 All ER 225 (CA), for the proposition that debts have to be due and cannot be merely accruing due at the time of the bankruptcy. A careful reading of that case discloses the court did not say that the debts have to be due at the date of bankruptcy and could not be accruing due. The court only said that there was no debt at all at that time. Thus, I reject the plaintiff's submission on that point.

So long as there is a debt owed to the defendant by the plaintiff before the date of bankruptcy and a corresponding debt from the defendant to the plaintiff, that satisfies the mutual and cross-obligation condition notwithstanding one of the debts was not actually payable at that time. At the time of bankruptcy there were mutual and cross-obligations between the parties. The trustee in bankruptcy is in the same position as the bankrupt. Thus I find that the defendant is entitled to a legal or statutory set-off in the amount claimed.

Even if I am wrong in that conclusion, I find that the defendant is entitled to the right of equitable set-off. In the *Tuckerr Indust.* case the Court of Appeal said that equitable set-off can apply where the cross-obligations are not debts, or where mutuality is lost or never existed. It may also arise where the cross-obligations arise from the same contract, though mutuality has been lost, or where the cross-obligations are closely related, or where the parties have agreed that a right to set-off may be asserted between them, or where a court of equity could otherwise have permitted a set-off.

In *Abacus Cities Ltd. v. Aboussafy*, 39 CBR (NS) 1, [1981] 4 WWR 660, 124 DLR (3d) 150, 29 AR 607 (CA), the court held that with equitable set-off, even though unliquidated amounts could be set off against liquidated amounts and there is no need of mutuality, nonetheless the claim by the defendant has to be related to the claim by the plaintiff against the defendant.

In addition, in equitable set-off cases the party seeking the benefit of it has to show some equitable ground for being protected against his adversary's demand. In *Rawson v. Samuel* (1841), Cr. & Ph. 161, 41 ER 451 (Ch.), cited in the *Abacus* case at p. 7, the court said that the mere existence of cross-demands is not sufficient. In *Equitable Remedies* by Spry, 2nd ed. (1980), the learned author stated at pp. 170-71:

What generally must be established is such a relationship between the respective claims of the parties that the claim of the defendant has been brought about by, or has been contributed to by, or is otherwise so bound up with, the rights which are relied upon by the plaintiff that it would be unconscionable that he should proceed without allowing a set-off. Thus if conduct of the plaintiff is such as to induce the defendant to incur an obligation in favour of the plaintiff, and that conduct itself is fraudulent, negligent or otherwise wrongful so as to give a cause of action to the defendant, the plaintiff will not ordinarily be permitted to proceed until he has made good the material claims of the defendant.

In the circumstances here I conclude that the relationship between the parties is one in which it would be inequitable not to allow the defendant to set off its claims. The rebate programme was offered to induce the defendant to purchase more goods. The defendant had fulfilled all the stipulations and qualified for the rebate programme, thus it is equitable that it be allowed to set off the rebate and the advertisement costs against the debt it owes to the plaintiff.

Even if it could be maintained that the obligation owed to the defendant by the plaintiff was not a liquidated debt or there was lack of mutuality, in my view the defendant is still entitled to equitable set-off because the defendant's claim is closely related to the plaintiff's claim and there exist factors that warrant the defendant's protection against the plaintiff's demand.

Therefore, the defendant is entitled at law and in equity to set off its claim against the plaintiff's claim. ...

Set-off allowed.

NOTE

Set-offs are frequently asserted in claims by a trustee—for obvious reasons, since the debtor wishes to reduce or extinguish the amount payable to the estate. Why does s. 97(3) of the BIA recognize the right of set-off? Is it to maintain mutuality between the cases where the trustee is being sued and those where the trustee is suing, or is it based on a principle of unjust enrichment or an implicit agreement between the parties that set-offs will apply?

The right to claim a set-off can be astutely used by a debtor of the estate by buying at a discount a debt owing by the estate and then setting it off against the purchaser's debt to the estate. See, e.g., *Food Group Inc. v. Peat Marwick* (1988), 67 CBR (NS) 159 (NSSC). Is this practice consistent with the spirit of s. 97(3)?

The law of set-off is very complex and, as Campbell LJSC indicates, different rules govern legal set-offs from those applying to equitable set-offs. The right to legal set-offs is enshrined in Ontario in the Courts of Justice Act, RSO 1990, c. C.43, s. 111. Equitable set-offs continue to be governed by judicially made rules. These were reviewed by the Supreme Court of Canada in *Telford v. Holt*, [1987] 2 SCR 193. For further details see Kelly R. Palmer, *The Law of Set-Off in Canada* (Canada Law Book, 1993).

UNPAID SUPPLIERS' RIGHT TO RECOVER GOODS

Introduction

Since 1970 there has been much discussion about whether the BIA should grant special rights to unpaid suppliers of goods where the buyer has gone bankrupt shortly after receiving the goods. Suppliers argued (the Canadian apparel manufacturers foremost among them) that unscrupulous buyers frequently "loaded up" on inventory in anticipation of the buyer's bankruptcy so that the inventory could be sold after the bankruptcy and the proceeds used to pay off secured loans. This would help the buyer's officers who often gave personal guarantees to the buyer's bank. In the common law provinces, the sale of goods Acts confer a possessory lien in the seller's favour while the goods are under the seller's control, and a right of stoppage if the goods are in transit to the buyer. See *supra* this casebook, volume I, chapter 11. However, these remedies do not assist the unpaid seller once the goods have reached the buyer. The seller could of course retain a security interest until the goods are paid for, or demand prepayment or some other form of guarantee of payment. However, suppliers argued that none of these alternatives were realistic. The first was rejected by suppliers because retaining a purchase money security interest would require the supplier to file a financing statement and give notice to any prior secured party of record with a security interest in the same class of collateral, both requirements which the supplier was ill equipped to handle and which, in any event, would get the buyer into trouble with the buyer's lender bank. The other alternatives were problematic because buyers insisted on a short period of free credit. Suppliers pointed to the old Quebec civil code which gave unpaid sellers a limited right to rescind the contract of sale and recover the goods following the buyer's bankruptcy.

The issue was examined by the Colter Committee in its 1986 report (see *infra* this chapter). The committee was opposed to giving unpaid suppliers any special rights against bankrupt buyers. The federal government was more sympathetic and two new sections were included in the 1992 amendments, ss. 81.1 and 81.2, to meet at least some of the suppliers' concerns. The two sections should be studied carefully in the light of the materials which follow. An excellent analysis of these provisions also appears in R. Klotz, "Protection of Unpaid Suppliers Under the New BIA" (1993), 23 *CBLJ* 161.

Report of the Advisory Committee on Bankruptcy and Insolvency
("Colter Report") (1986), 64-66

Suppliers of Merchandise

Current Law

There are no provisions in the present *Bankruptcy Act* giving special rights to sellers of merchandise to the bankrupt. Subsection 178(6) of the *Bank Act* gives a producer of agricultural products priority over a bank in respect of a specified portion of a claim the producer might have for a product delivered to a manufacturer during the six months preceding the manufacturer's bankruptcy. At the provincial level, the provisions of the Quebec Civil Code permit an unpaid vendor to repossess products delivered to an insolvent buyer. In the common law provinces vendors may register security interests over products delivered to buyers under personal property security legislation. The taking of such security makes the supplier a secured creditor.

Background

The underlying philosophy of any bankruptcy legislation should be equal treatment of all creditors. A strict application of this philosophy would entail a system free of priorities in which each creditor would be entitled to receive a share of the assets of the debtor on a pro rata basis. However, given the existing economic structure, such an approach is unrealistic as it would lead to many restrictions in commercial practice. For example, financial institutions not permitted to take security would demand guarantees so onerous that debtors' access to credit would be reduced. Thus if it is conceded that any amendments are not intended to change the foundation of the existing economy, only changes should be proposed that will permit the fair treatment of all intermediaries while allowing the smooth operation of commerce.

Acceptance of this premise necessitates the existence of security interests. Some creditors, such as financial institutions, have sufficient leverage to require debtors to give them priority. However, some groups do not have the strength to negotiate terms that would guarantee them prior treatment in the event of a bankruptcy. It is widely accepted that workers should receive special treatment under bankruptcy legislation because they are not in a position to negotiate such treatment. The issue before the committee was whether unpaid suppliers of merchandise to insolvent buyers should receive protection under the *Bankruptcy Act* over and above that provided to creditors in general. If so, what should be the extent of that protection and should it include priority over secured creditors?

In Canada, only the Province of Quebec has adopted legislation affording suppliers of merchandise any preferred rights. In all other provinces the rights of creditors have been determined by contractual provisions negotiated between the parties. Some provinces have established a system whereby suppliers of merchandise may give notices entitling them to priority over secured creditors. However, the system is not effective in many cases because the giving of such notices may constitute default under security agreements or is prohibited by such agreements.

Problems

A majority of the committee members, representing the common law provinces, were of the opinion that the existing legislation does not require any reform. Their view was that unpaid suppliers should be treated equally with other classes of unsecured creditors. Any special treatment of unpaid suppliers would deprive other unsecured creditors of assets that would otherwise be available for distribution to them. In addition, it would be inequitable and without justification to distinguish between suppliers who have delivered merchandise within a specified period prior to the insolvency and other suppliers who delivered goods before that period. A minority of the committee members, representing the Province of Quebec, was of the view that, within the existing economic structure, suppliers are not in a position to negotiate with their debtors such terms as would reestablish the appropriate balance of power, given the relevant importance of such suppliers to the survival of their debtors. This fact highlights, in the opinion of the minority group, the need for legislative intervention to guarantee suppliers of merchandise rights commensurate with their importance to the financial health of debtor enterprises.

Many problems have been encountered in the Province of Quebec with respect to the application of legislative provisions dealing with the protection of suppliers and merchandise. The most serious problems involve the identification of merchandise and the procedure for the revendication of goods. These problems have caused significant confusion and have greatly increased the expense involved in administering the assets of an insolvent debtor.

Solutions

There are three options:

• the status quo could be maintained, leaving the onus on the provinces to legislate some form of protection for suppliers of merchandise;

- an amendment to the *Bankruptcy Act* could be introduced to provide suppliers of merchandise with the tools that would enable them to protect themselves against at least part of the losses resulting from the insolvency of their debtors; or
- the *Bankruptcy Act* could be amended to include a provision enabling provinces that have enacted the right of revendication to benefit from certain amendments to be inserted in the *Bankruptcy Act*.

Comment

In the event that either the second or third of the above options should be implemented, the amendment should provide for the following:

- unpaid vendors should be granted the right to be reimbursed for goods delivered within five working days prior to the bankruptcy or receivership on the basis of invoice price and proof of delivery;
- the request for reimbursement must be made within 21 days of the receivership or bankruptcy;
- this right should constitute a priority ranking after the payment of the administration costs and unpaid wages and prior to any payment to a secured creditor;
- this right should be suspended in the event of a reorganization pending the decision on a proposal. If a proposal were accepted by the creditors and approved by the court, the special priority of the unpaid vendor would be abolished.

Recommendation

There should be no change to the *Bankruptcy Act* with regard to the rights of unpaid vendors. Granting special treatment to unpaid vendors would be inequitable and prejudicial to the position of other unsecured creditors. Each province should retain the right, if it deems fit, to grant or maintain secured creditor status to an unpaid vendor. Such treatment would be recognized in the administration of the *Bankruptcy Act* just as the claims of other secured creditors are recognized.

Re Woodward's Ltd.
(1993), 100 DLR (4th) 133 (BCSC), and
Woodward's Ltd., Re
(1993), 17 CBR (3d) 253 (BCSC)
[Unpaid suppliers' applications]

TYSOE J: On December 11, 1992, I granted an interim stay order pursuant to the *Companies' Creditors Arrangement Act*, RSC 1985, c. C-36 (the "CCAA"), in favour of Woodward's Limited, Woodward Stores Limited and Abercrombie & Fitch Co. (Canada) Ltd. (collectively, "Woodward's"). Shortly thereafter a number of Woodward's suppliers of goods and services made applications for various forms of relief. The item of relief that was pursued at the hearing of the applications was the creation of a trust fund for the benefit of the suppliers.

The interim stay order was granted on an *ex parte* basis and it was expressed to expire at 6 p.m. on January 8, 1993, the day on which the hearing of the petition in this matter was intended to take place. The applications of the suppliers first came on for hearing at 4 p.m. on December 17, 1992. The relief requested at that time included: (i) the setting aside or varying of the interim stay order; (ii) the payment of the amounts owing to the suppliers; (iii) the return of the goods provided by the suppliers; and (iv) the creation of the trust fund. Time did not permit the hearing of the applications on that day and the earliest they could be heard was one week later. I adjourned the applications for one week but, as I did not want the adjournment to prejudice any rights that the suppliers may have, I made an interim order that the proceeds from the sale of any goods after December 17th would stand in the place and stead of such goods. When the matter came back on for hearing on December 24th, the parties agreed that the applications could be adjourned until January 8th and heard concurrently with the hearing of the petition.

The hearings began on January 8th and, when it became clear that these and other applications would take several days to be heard, I extended the interim orders until further order of the court with the intent that they would continue until I made my determinations on the various issues to be decided. There appears to be little doubt that there will be an extension of the stay order, and it is the terms of the continuing stay order and the related applications that are in dispute. I will approach the present applications on the basis that the CCAA stay is going to be extended and the issue to be determined is how the suppliers should be treated within this context.

Woodward Stores Limited operates a chain of 59 full line and junior department stores in British Columbia and Alberta. Abercrombie & Fitch Co. (Canada) Ltd. operates two stores in Ontario. Each of these companies is a subsidiary of Woodward's Limited.

Woodward's has been carrying on business for 100 years. Until January 8, 1993, when it terminated 1,200 employees as part of its downsizing strategy, Woodward's had approximately 6,000 employees. Woodward's has been an important part of the economy of western Canada for a long period of time and every effort should be made to facilitate its financial reorganization, which is the stated purpose of the CCAA.

Woodward's suppliers generally support its reorganization but they do not feel that they have been treated fairly in all of the circumstances. The principal complaints of the suppliers are that Woodward's purchased a substantial amount of inventory in the period preceding the commencement of these CCAA proceedings and that Woodward's is proceeding with its reorganization under the CCAA rather than the *Bankruptcy and Insolvency Act*, RSC 1985, c. B-3 (the "B & I Act").

On December 17th, I directed that the monitor appointed by the interim stay order report to the court regarding the inventory purchased by Woodward's during the period prior to the commencement of these proceedings. The monitor has reported that in the 30-day period prior to December 11th Woodward's received goods having an aggregate cost of approximately $30.4 million, of which $27.3 million remains unpaid. The monitor estimates that approximately $4.3 million worth of the goods for which payment has not been made can be identified and were unsold by Woodward's at the time these proceedings were commenced. Identification of goods appears to be a major difficulty because the monitor believes that less than $8 million of the $30.4 [million] worth of goods received within the 30-day period preceding December 11th can be identified by way of Woodward's inventory control system. The suppliers say that they will be able to assist in identifying the goods that were supplied by them.

The reason for the importance of the 30-day period preceding the commencement of these proceedings is s. 81.1 of the B & I Act which came into effect on November 30, 1992. Section 81.1 gives rights of repossession to suppliers of goods similar to the revendication rights that suppliers have previously enjoyed by virtue of the *Civil Code of Lower Canada* in effect in Quebec. In brief terms, s. 81.1(1) provides that suppliers are entitled to the return of goods supplied by them within 30 days of a written demand for repossession that can be given if the purchaser of the goods has gone into bankruptcy or receivership. Two important qualifications are that the goods have not been resold and that the goods are identifiable.

Section 81.1(4) is also relevant because it deals with a situation analogous to these CCAA proceedings, namely, a situation where the purchaser of the goods has filed a notice of intention to file a proposal under the *Bankruptcy and Insolvency Act*. The section provides that the time between the filing of the notice of intention and the date on which the purchaser goes into bankruptcy or receivership is not counted as part of the 30-day period following delivery of the goods within which the supplier must make its demand of repossession. Hence, if the purchaser of the goods files a notice of intention to file a proposal 20 days after the goods are delivered, the supplier can make the written demand for receivership even though the reorganization attempt by means of the proposal may have taken several months. The statute is silent with respect to the resale of goods by the purchaser during the period of reorganization and, all other things being equal, the supplier will lose its right of repossession if the goods are sold during this period.

The suppliers submitted that if Woodward's had proceeded under the B & I Act rather than the CCAA, they could have taken one of two steps to protect their rights. First, they say that an application could have been made for the appointment of an interim receiver under s. 47.1 of the B & I Act and that upon the appointment of the interim receiver the suppliers could exercise their rights under s. 81.1. Second, they say that an application could be made under s. 81.1(8) which allows the court to make any order it considers appropriate if a supplier is aggrieved by an act of the purchaser of the goods and that such an order could direct the creation of a trust fund. The suppliers conclude this aspect of their argument by saying that it would be an abuse if the rights under s. 81.1 could be frustrated by allowing the insolvent company to choose the CCAA over the B & I Act and that the suppliers should therefore be given the protection of the trust fund.

In addition to the potential rights under the B & I Act, the suppliers argued that the trust fund should be created to redress an inequity. They say that other creditors such as Woodward's banker had advance warning that Woodward's would be commencing these proceedings and that they took steps to ensure payment of the indebtedness owing to them. Although the evidence does not support an allegation that Woodward's purchased additional inventory with the knowledge that it would be commencing these proceedings, the suppliers say that Woodward's purposely choose the December 11th date to obtain the stay order because the aggregate of all unpaid amounts for the purchase of inventory would be at its highest on or about that date. An affidavit was filed to the effect that some of Woodward's directors first consulted the monitor about the possibility of commencing CCAA proceedings in October, 1992.

There was not a consensus among the suppliers as to the exact nature of the trust fund that they were requesting be established. All of the suppliers did want the court to make the determination that they were entitled to the moneys in the trust fund if Woodward's is not successful in its reorganization effort. Most of the suppliers suggested that the fund be equal to the total cost of the purchases during the 30-day period preceding December 11th. One supplier wrote a letter requesting that the fund be equal to 90 days' worth of purchases. One supplier of services was represented during the hearing and had filed its own notice of motion. It wanted the fund to provide for services that were purchased by Woodward's as well as the inventory.

The purpose of the stay under s. 11 of the CCAA was first summarized by Wachowich J in *Re Meridian Developments Inc. and Toronto Dominion Bank* (1984), 11 DLR (4th) 576, 52 CBR (NS) 98, [1984] 5 WWR 215 (Alta. QB). At p. 580, Wachowich J said:

> The legislation is intended to have wide scope and allows a judge to make orders which will effectively maintain the *status quo* for a period while the insolvent company attempts to gain the approval of its creditors for a proposed arrangement which will enable the company to remain in operation for what is, hopefully, the future benefit of both the company and its creditors.

And at p. 581, he stated:

> This order is in accord with the general aim of the *Companies' Creditors Arrangement Act*. The intention was to prevent any manoeuvres for positioning among creditors during the interim period which would give the aggressive creditor an advantage to the prejudice of others who were less aggressive and would further undermine the financial position of the company making it less likely that the eventual arrangement would succeed.

In *Quintette Coal Ltd. v. Nippon Steel Corp.* (1990), 80 CBR (NS) 98 (BCSC), the stay order authorized Quintette to pay its trade creditors who were owed less than $200,000 on the basis that these creditors were mostly small local businesses which would face insolvency themselves if they were not paid. Trade creditors which were owed in excess of $200,000 complained that the order did not maintain the *status quo* and they applied to be paid the first $200,000 of the debt owed to them by Quintette. In dismissing the application, Thackray J said the following about the *status quo*, at p. 109:

> While it is a compelling argument to suggest that the status quo should be maintained between *classes* of creditors, I do not believe that I should be blinkered by such a narrow view. The overall design of the CCAA is to preserve the debtor as a viable operation and to reorganize its affairs to the benefit of not only the debtor but also its creditors. With that design in mind, I do not believe that Wachowich J was suggesting that every detail of the status quo would be maintained. Indeed he went on to note that [p. 220] "The intention was to prevent any manoeuvres for positioning among creditors during the interim period."

> What is meant by maintaining the status quo is that the debtor will be able to stay in business, and that they will have breathing space in which to develop a proposal during which time there will be a stay under any bankruptcy or winding-up legislation, a restraint of all actions against the company, and no realization of guarantees or other rights against the company. In this case the order also restrained creditors from exercising any right of set-off.

An unusual case relating to the maintenance of the *status quo* is *Re Alberta-Pacific Terminals Ltd.* (1991), 8 CBR (3d) 99, 26 ACWS (3d) 958 (BCSC). In that case, the owner of the facilities at which the insolvent company carried on business made application for an order compelling the insolvent company to make the ongoing monthly payments under the operating agreement between the parties. The payments were the equivalent of rental payments under a lease. The insolvent company did not have sufficient funds to make the payments, in part because it was making the interest payments on the pre-stay debt of one of its lenders. The company had agreed to make the interest payments in exchange for the agreement of the lender to continue providing an operating credit facility. Huddart J dismissed the application and she said the following about the *status quo* at p. 105:

The status quo is not always easy to find. It is difficult to freeze any ongoing business at a moment in time long enough to make an accurate picture of its financial condition. Such a picture is at best an artist's view, more so if the real value of the business, including goodwill, is to be taken into account. Nor is the status quo easy to define. The preservation of the status quo cannot mean merely the preservation of the relative pre-stay debt status of each creditor. Other interests are served by the CCAA. Those of investors, employees, and landlords among them, and in the case of the Fraser Surrey terminal, the public too, not only of British Columbia, but also of the prairie provinces. The status quo is to be preserved in the sense that manoeuvres by creditors that would impair the financial position of the company while it attempts to reorganize are to be prevented, not in the sense that all creditors are to be treated equally or to be maintained at the same relative level. It is the company and all the interests its demise would affect that must be considered.

This case is unusual because one would normally expect during a reorganization period that ongoing rental payments would be made and that interest on pre-stay debt would not be paid. However, the particular circumstances of the case meant that the preservation of the *status quo* produced a different result. The payment of the interest was considered to be a preservation of the *status quo* because the company required the continuation of the operating credit facility in order to survive an attempt to reorganize. The non-payment of the monthly amounts under the operating agreement was considered to be a preservation of the *status quo* because the company did not have sufficient funds and could not have continued if it had been required to make the payments.

It is my view that the maintenance of the *status quo* is intended to attempt to accomplish the following three objectives:

1. To suspend or freeze the rights of all creditors as they existed as at the date of the stay order (which, in British Columbia, is normally the day on which the CCAA proceedings are commenced). This objective is intended to allow the insolvent company an opportunity to reorganize itself without any creditor having an advantage over the company or any other creditor.

2. To postpone litigation in which the insolvent company is involved so that the human and monetary resources of the company can be devoted to the reorganization process. The litigation may be resolved by way of the reorganization.

3. To permit the insolvent company to take certain action that is beneficial to its continuation during the period of reorganization or its attempt to reorganize or, conversely, to restrain a non-creditor or a creditor with rights arising after the stay from exercising rights that are detrimental to the continuation of the company during the period of reorganization or its attempt to reorganize. This is the objective recognized by *Quintette*

and *Alberta-Pacific Terminals*. The first case to recognize that the maintenance of the *status quo* could affect the rights of non-creditors was *Norcen Energy Resources Ltd. v. Oakwood Petroleums Ltd.* (1989), 72 CBR (NS) 20, [1989] 2 WWR 566, 64 Alta. LR (2d) 139 (QB). This is the objective that takes into account the broad constituency of interests served by the CCAA. As the overriding intent of the CCAA is to facilitate reorganizations, this is the overriding objective of maintaining the *status quo* and it may produce results that are not entirely consistent with the other objectives. The most common example of an inconsistency is a situation where the giving of effect to this objective results in an unequal treatment of creditors.

There are exceptions to the maintenance of the *status quo* but they are not relevant to this case.

Apart from consideration of s. 81.1 of the B & I Act, there is no justification for the creation of the trust fund. It would not serve to maintain the *status quo*. To the contrary, it would give the suppliers an advantage over other creditors of Woodward's. It would not be beneficial to the continuation of Woodward's business during the reorganization period or Woodward's attempt to reorganize. Indeed, it was the position of Woodward's on these applications that the creation of a trust fund in the amount of $30 million would make any reorganization impossible.

I am not prepared to order the creation of the trust fund on the basis of the allegations of events that took place prior to the commencement of these proceedings or on the basis of the timing of the commencement of these proceedings. There is no evidence in this case of fraud that could justify the preservation of assets by way of the creation of a trust fund. If the allegations were proven, it could possibly be argued that there has been an abuse of process or that Woodward's has not come to court with clean hands. But these would not justify the creation of a trust fund for the benefit of the suppliers. The likely result would be that the court would decline to exercise its discretion to afford Woodward's the protection it requires to reorganize and no one is suggesting that Woodward's should not be given an opportunity to attempt to reorganize its business and financial affairs.

That brings me to s. 81.1 of the B & I Act. In order to decide whether the creation of a trust fund will preserve rights of the suppliers, I must consider the rights that exist as a result of s. 81.1. I am reluctant to make definitive comments regarding s. 81.1 because I am not required to make a decision under that section, and I do not wish to constrain another judge who is required in the future to make such a decision. I am particularly sensitive because s. 81.1 has only been in force for one and one-half months and I am not aware of any cases that have considered it. However, I must make some comments about the likelihood of the courts making certain orders in relation to s. 81.1 because I must determine what rights are to be preserved.

I begin by making the observation that on December 11th when these proceedings were commenced, the suppliers had no rights under s. 81.1 that could have been acted upon because Woodward's was not in bankruptcy or receivership. In *Re Westar Mining Ltd.* (unreported, June 16, 1992, BC Supreme Court Action No. A921164, Vancouver Registry) [now reported 14 CBR (3d) 88, [1992] 6 WWR 331, 70 BCLR (2d) 6] Macdonald J was faced with an argument by the Crown that he should not have created a charge against Westar's assets to secure credit being extended during the reorganization period by Westar's suppliers because it would alter the priorities that would prevail in a bankruptcy of Westar. Macdonald J rejected this argument in the following manner at p. 9 [p. 93 CBR]:

But, the company was not in bankruptcy on June 10 when the charge was created. The Crown claims which are not afforded the protection of a statutory lien are not yet preferred. The June 10 order creating the charge does not purport to alter the priorities which will apply between the claims of the Crown and the unsecured trade creditors as at May 14.

The suppliers argue that the rights that I must preserve are the right to crystallize their position under s. 81.1 by way of the appointment of an interim receiver and the right to have the court make an order for the creation of a trust fund pursuant to s. 81.1(8). I must therefore consider the likelihood of the court appointing an interim receiver or making an order for the creation of a trust fund in the event that Woodward's had filed a notice of intention to file a proposal under the B & I Act.

I agree with the submission of Mr. Fitch that s. 81.1 was intended to give suppliers the right to repossess goods that they had sold to the insolvent company if the company is to be liquidated by way of a bankruptcy or a receivership. Parliament directed its mind to the possibility that an insolvent company may first attempt to reorganize its affairs and it enacted s-s. (4) of s. 81.1. Parliament decided that the period of the attempted reorganization should not be counted as part of the 30-day period under s-s. (1) of s. 81.1. Parliament was silent as to the potential appointment of an interim receiver so that the suppliers could exercise their repossession rights during the reorganization period. Parliament was also silent as to the creation of a trust fund to be held for the benefit of the suppliers in the event that the reorganization is not successful. It must therefore be inferred in my view that Parliament intended that the insolvent company could continue to sell its goods in the ordinary course of business and utilize the sale proceeds to continue carrying on business pending its reorganization attempt.

It is my view that the likelihood of a court appointing an interim receiver for the purpose of enabling suppliers to repossess the goods they supplied during the preceding 30-day period is low. The repossession of such goods would be counter-productive to the company's reorganization effort because it would deprive the company of assets it requires to continue carrying on business and to make a viable reorganization proposal. I can envisage a case where the court may be willing to take such a step if it is concerned that the reorganization attempt may not be *bona fide* and the court wishes to have an interim receiver to oversee the collection and disbursement of funds and to preserve the rights of suppliers if it is proven that the reorganization attempt was not *bona fide*. In this case there is no suggestion that Woodward's attempt to reorganize is not *bona fide*. In addition, I have reservations about whether an interim receiver is a receiver within the meaning of s. 243(2) of the B & I Act. An interim receiver is very different from a (permanent) receiver.

Similarly, I believe that the likelihood of a court making an order under s. 81.1(8) for the creation of a trust fund is low. This would again be counter-productive to the attempt of the company to reorganize. I also doubt that it was intended by Parliament that the filing of a notice of intention to file a proposal would be considered to be an act aggrieving a supplier within the meaning of s. 81.1(8) unless, possibly, the filing was not *bona fide*.

I was referred to two Quebec decisions dealing with the CCAA and the revendication rights of suppliers in Quebec. The first case was *Century Industries Inc. v. Enterprises*

Union Électrique Ltée (unreported, April 29, 1992), Que. SC Action No. 500-05-005804-925). I have been provided with a translation of the decision. Archambault J ordered that the proceeds from the sale of any merchandise delivered in the 30 days prior to the service of the application before him be deposited in a trust account and that the moneys in the trust account not be disbursed without further court order. The paragraph containing the reasoning of Archambault J reads as follows (at p. 9):

Le tribunal doit s'assurer que le statu quo est maintenu. Si une ordonnance n'était pas rendue, la requérante pourrait, si les marchandises étaient vendues dans l'intervalle par Union Électrique, perdre ses droits quant a la revendication des marchandises qui furent vendues et livrées a Union Électrique dans les derniers 30 jours. De plus, il serait fondamentalement injuste de permettre a Union Électrique de continuer de vendre ces marchandises qui ne lui appartiennent peut-être pas, au détriment des personnes qui en sont véritablement les propriétaires.

The translation for this paragraph with which I have been provided reads as follows:

The court must ensure that the *status quo* is maintained. If no order were given, the applicant might, if the merchandise was sold by Union Électrique in the interim, lose its rights of revendication of the goods which were sold and delivered to Union Électrique within the last 30 days. Moreover, it would be fundamentally unjust to permit Union Électrique to continue to sell merchandise which perhaps does not belong to it, to the detriment of those who are the true owners.

I do not believe that the last sentence of the above paragraph relates to the right of revendication. In addition to merchandise that had been delivered within the previous 30 days, the applicant had sold goods to Union Électrique by way of conditional sale and title to these goods had not passed to Union Électrique.

I am not familiar with the details of a supplier's right of revendication in Quebec, but I think that there is an important distinction between it and the right afforded by s. 81.1 of the B & I Act. The distinction is that the right of revendication is not dependent upon the bankruptcy or receivership of the purchaser of the goods. Thus, the applicant in the *Union Électrique* case had an existing right to repossess the goods supplied by it at the time the CCAA [proceedings] were commenced. Archambault J was preserving that right when he made the order that he did. In the present case, the suppliers did not have a right to repossess the goods supplied by them at the time these proceedings were instituted.

The second Quebec case took a different approach. In *Steinberg Inc. v. Colgate-Palmolive Canada Inc.* (1992), 13 CBR (3d) 139, a supplier made application for leave under s. 11 of the CCAA to exercise its right of revendication with respect to goods delivered to the insolvent company within the previous 30 days. The Quebec Superior Court dismissed the application. The headnote, which is consistent with the translation of the decision provided to me, reads as follows:

The power conferred on the judge under the Act applies to all proceedings likely to affect the survival of a company. The individual interest of any creditor must be weighed against the objects of the Act and must yield to the collective interests of all creditors. Granting the application would impose on the court an obligation to do the same for all 30-day suppliers. Therefore, an arrangement proposal submitted to the judge at the time of the order might fail before it was presented to all creditors, and might cause the debtor to go bankrupt. It followed that the goods in question should not be allowed to be seized prior to judgment.

This reasoning is similar to my reasoning in concluding that it is unlikely that a court would appoint an interim receiver or order the creation of a trust fund when an insolvent company is attempting to reorganize pursuant to the B & I Act.

The result in the *Steinberg* case is also consistent with the decision of the BC Court of Appeal in *Hongkong Bank of Canada v. Chef Ready Foods Ltd.* (1990), 4 CBR (3d) 311, [1991] 2 WWR 136, 51 BCLR (2d) 84, where the issue involved security under s. 178 of the *Bank Act*. Section 178 security creates a security interest in inventory and the bank has the right to seize and sell the inventory. The right of the bank is therefore similar to the right of revendication enjoyed by a Quebec supplier. If the goods covered by s. 178 security are sold during the period of reorganization, the bank will be prejudiced in the same fashion as a supplier whose 30-day goods are sold during the period of reorganization (except to the extent that proceeds from the sale of inventory are utilized to purchase new inventory which would become covered by the bank's s. 178 security). In *Chef Ready Foods* the BC Court of Appeal held that the enforcement of s. 178 security can be stayed by an order under s. 11 of the CCAA. Gibbs JA said the following at pp. 319-20:

It is apparent from these excerpts and from the wording of the statute that, in contrast with ss. 178 and 179 of the *Bank Act*, which are preoccupied with the competing rights and duties of the borrower and the lender, the CCAA serves the interests of a broad constituency of investors, creditors and employees. If a bank's rights in respect of s. 178 security are accorded a unique status which renders those rights immune from the provisions of the CCAA, the protection afforded that constituency for any company which has granted s. 178 security will be largely illusory. It will be illusory because almost inevitably the realization by the bank on its security will destroy the company as a going concern. Here, for example, if the bank signifies and collects the accounts receivable, Chef Ready will be deprived of working capital. Collapse and liquidation must necessarily follow. The lesson will be that where s. 178 security is present a single creditor can frustrate the public policy objectives of the CCAA. There will be two classes of debtor companies: those for whom there are prospects for recovery under the CCAA; and those for whom the CCAA may be irrelevant dependent upon the whim of the s. 178 security holder. Given the economic circumstances which prevailed when the CCAA was enacted, it is difficult to imagine that the legislators of the day intended that result to follow.

The above passage contains persuasive reasoning why the court is unlikely to appoint an interim receiver or to create a trust fund under the B & I Act if an insolvent company files a notice of intention to file a proposal. The ability to reorganize would be illusory for companies which deal with goods provided on credit by suppliers.

Subject to the point on which I will subsequently invite further submissions, I have concluded that there is likely to be no difference in the approach of the court when dealing with a proposal under the B & I Act from the approach of the court when dealing with a reorganization under the CCAA as they relate to the rights of suppliers. Therefore, there is no special right of suppliers that needs to be preserved by the creation of a trust fund and there is no abuse in Woodward's choosing the CCAA over the B & I Act. In addition, I repeat that the suppliers did not have any right to repossess the goods supplied by them at the time of the commencement of these proceedings. Accordingly, I dismiss the application of the suppliers for an order creating a trust fund for their benefit.

Section 81.1(4) of the B & I Act does attempt to preserve the potential rights of suppliers by providing that the period of reorganization does not count in the computation of the 30-day period under s. 81.1(1). This is consistent with the *status quo* objective of suspending the rights of creditors during the period of reorganization. No submissions were made to me by the parties as to whether I can make an order in these proceedings that has the same effect as s. 81.1(4). It may be possible that I could order that the period during which Woodward's is attempting to reorganize will not be counted as part of the 30-day period under s. 81.1(1) with the result that if Woodward's reorganization attempt is not successful and it goes into bankruptcy or receivership, the suppliers would still have the right to repossess goods supplied by them within the 30-day period preceding the commencement of these proceedings that have not been sold by Woodward's in the meantime. I invite counsel to make submissions in this regard.

As I have concluded that there are no rights of the suppliers that should be preserved other than a potential postponement of the running of the 30-day period under s. 81.1 of the B & I Act, my interim order of December 17th should be set aside as it relates to the proceeds from the sale of goods after December 17th. Counsel for several of the suppliers has requested that he have the opportunity to seek instructions regarding an appeal before the order is set aside. Counsel for Woodward's does not object. I therefore set aside my December 17th, order as it relates to the sale proceeds effective 4:00 p.m. on January 18, 1993, or such later time as I may order.

• • •

January 21, 1993. TYSOE J: In my Reasons for Judgment dated January 14, 1993 [reported at 77 BCLR (2d) 332] I invited counsel to make further submissions with respect to the preservation of the potential rights of suppliers under s. 81.1 of the *Bankruptcy and Insolvency Act* (the "B & I Act"). The issue that I posed in brief terms was whether the Court in these proceedings under the *Companies' Creditors Arrangement Act* (the"CCAA") should produce a result that is the same as the result that would have been created had Woodward's filed a notice of intention to file a proposal under the B & I Act.

As I pointed out in my January 14 Reasons for Judgment, a supplier's right of repossession under s. 81.1 of the B & I Act does not arise until the purchaser of the goods is in bankruptcy or receivership. The stay of proceedings contained in my interim Order dated December 11, 1992 prevents any proceedings being taken that would result in Woodward's going into bankruptcy or receivership. In particular, the stay prevents any of the suppliers from petitioning Woodward's into bankruptcy and thereby crystallizing their potential rights under s. 81.1. The bankruptcy of Woodward's would obviously be inconsistent with its effort to reorganize its business and financial affairs. On the day of the hearing of this issue I pronounced a continuing stay Order and it also prevents the suppliers and any other person from petitioning Woodward's into bankruptcy.

The Court often exercises its discretion in connection with the stay under the CCAA so that the rights of parties are not prejudiced by the effluxion of time during the continuance of a CCAA stay which prevents them from taking steps to preserve their rights. One example arises from the requirement of the BC *Builders Lien Act* that an action for the enforcement of the lien must be commenced within one year of the lien being filed at the Land Title Office. The Court has granted leave for a builders lien claimant to commence the action against a company having the protection of a CCAA stay so that the lien right was not extinguished by the effluxion of time during the course of the CCAA stay.

Another example which is more analogous to the present situation relates to s. 95 of the B & I Act, a provision dealing with fraudulent preferences. Subsection (2) of s. 95 creates a rebuttable presumption that a transaction is fraudulent if it occurs within the three-month period preceding the date of bankruptcy and if it has the effect of giving a preference to one creditor over other creditors. Section 71 of the B & I Act provides that in the case of an involuntary bankruptcy where the bankrupt has been petitioned into bankruptcy, the date of bankruptcy is deemed to be the date on which the petition is filed. The Court in CCAA proceedings has granted leave for a creditor to file a bankruptcy petition in order to preserve the three month presumption period under s. 95 in the event that the reorganization is not successful. In fact, I have granted such leave in these proceedings and one of the creditors has filed a bankruptcy petition against Woodward's (subject to the re-imposition of the stay preventing the bankruptcy petition from being heard). The filing of the bankruptcy petition preserves the *status quo* in the sense that, while the ability of the creditors to pursue a bankruptcy is restrained during the period of attempted reorganization, the effluxion of time during the CCAA stay does not prejudice their rights. If the reorganization attempt is not successful and the company goes into bankruptcy, the bankruptcy will date back to the filing of the petition and the three month presumption period will not have expired during the period of attempted reorganization.

Unfortunately, the filing of a bankruptcy petition does not preserve the potential rights of suppliers under s. 81.1 of the B & I Act. The usual "retroactive effect" or "dating back" of a bankruptcy to the date on which a petition or a proposal is filed does not apply to the potential rights under s. 81.1. Subsection (3) of s. 81.1 effectively states that the date of bankruptcy in the case of an unsuccessful attempt to reorganize is the date on which the proposal is not approved by the creditors or the Court. Thus, even though a bankruptcy petition may have been filed, the date of bankruptcy for the purposes of s. 81.1 is the day on which the reorganization attempt fails and it is not retroactive to the day on which the petition was filed. The reason for this result is obvious—suppliers cannot make the demand of repossession until a bankruptcy occurs and it is known that the insolvent company will not be continuing. This result is consistent with the conclusion I reached in my January 14 Reasons for Judgment in the sense that, until it is known that the reorganization attempt is not successful, the suppliers have no rights under s. 81.1.

In granting a stay under the CCAA to prevent the insolvent company from being petitioned into bankruptcy, the Court is taking a necessary step to allow the company an opportunity to reorganize itself. A stay under the CCAA will almost always prejudice rights of some or all of the creditors. However, the Court should avoid or lessen the prejudice if it can do so without disadvantaging the insolvent company or other creditors. In the two above examples dealing with builders liens and fraudulent preferences, the Courts have imposed the CCAA stay in a manner that avoided or lessened the prejudice to the creditors because the steps permitted by the Court did not have an adverse effect on the company or its reorganization effort (although there may be circumstances where the filing of a bankruptcy petition will have a material adverse effect). In this case, I am preventing the suppliers from petitioning Woodward's into bankruptcy but it is my view that I should endeavour to minimize the prejudice caused to the suppliers as a result of the stay.

Parliament considered the issue of suppliers' potential repossession rights during a reorganization under the B & I Act and it decided to implement s. 81.1(4) of the B & I Act. That subsection essentially provides that the period of attempted reorganization will not count as part of the 30 day period following delivery of the goods in which the supplier is required to give its demand for repossession (that cannot be given until the purchaser of the goods has gone into bankruptcy or receivership).

It is my view that the potential rights of the suppliers under a CCAA reorganization should be preserved in the same fashion as Parliament decided to preserve them under s. 81.1(4) of the B & I Act. If the potential rights are not preserved in this fashion, it would probably lead to abuses of the insolvency legislation. Insolvent companies would attempt to defeat the potential rights of suppliers by utilizing the CCAA and the protection given to suppliers by s. 81.1 would become illusory. A theoretical answer to the potential abuse of the insolvency legislation is that the Court should refuse to exercise its discretion to grant a stay of proceedings under the CCAA if it believes that the insolvent company has chosen the CCAA over the B & I Act in order to defeat the potential rights of suppliers. However, there are other advantages of the CCAA over the B & I Act and it would be very difficult for suppliers to prove that there is an abuse. In my opinion, the Courts should avoid the possible abuse by treating suppliers in CCAA proceedings in the same way that they are treated under the B & I Act.

It is my view that I should lessen the prejudice to the suppliers by making an Order that deems the date on which the goods are considered to be delivered to the insolvent company with the result that the running of the 30 day period under s. 81.1 is suspended during the period of attempted reorganization. In exercising its jurisdiction the Court often makes Orders that deem events to occur in order to produce an appropriate result. In granting the stay of proceedings under s. 11 of the CCAA and thereby preventing the suppliers from putting Woodward's into bankruptcy, I may impose a condition that serves to preserve the positions of the parties. In doing so, I am not creating rights and I am simply imposing the CCAA stay in a qualified manner that preserves potential rights of the suppliers against goods that are not sold during the period of reorganization.

During the course of submissions I suggested that there was another possible alternative to preserve some of the suppliers' potential rights. The alternative was to make my earlier Order of December 17, 1992 a permanent Order. That Order was a temporary Order pending full argument with respect to the position of the suppliers and it provided that the proceeds from the sale of any goods after December 17 will stand in the place and stead of such goods. The Order allowed Woodward's to use the sale proceeds for the purpose of carrying on its business and the expenditure of the monies was deemed to be a reduction in the available proceeds of each sale on a pro rata basis.

If the December 17 Order is made permanent, the suppliers will have rights in the event that Woodward's is not successful in its reorganization and goes into bankruptcy or receivership. Subject to the pro rata reduction, the suppliers would have access to the funds in the possession of Woodward's at the time of the bankruptcy or receivership to the extent that they could identify the funds as representing proceeds from the sale of goods supplied by them in the 30 day period preceding December 17.

I have concluded that the December 17 Order should not be made permanent. I think that the Court should be guided by the provisions of s. 81.1 that Parliament decided to enact to deal with the analogous situation under the B & I Act. The potential rights with which we are concerned were created by the B & I Act and I do not think that it would be appropriate to give added strength to these rights under the auspices of the CCAA (which could ironically lead insolvent companies to select the B & I Act over the CCAA because the rights of suppliers would potentially be weaker in the case of a reorganization under the very statute that created them). It is also noteworthy that Parliament did not give suppliers the right to trace proceeds from the sale of goods that are delivered within the 30 day period preceding the demand for repossession by the supplier and that are resold by the insolvent company prior to the demand being made. ...

Accordingly, I order that, in the event that Woodward's goes into receivership or bankruptcy, each good coming into the possession of Woodward's within the 30 day period preceding December 17, 1992 shall be deemed to be delivered to Woodward's by the supplier of the good on the day that follows the date on which the good came into the possession of Woodward's by the same number of days as there are between December 17, 1992 and the earlier of (a) the date on which Woodward's goes into receivership and (b)(i) the date on which a receiving order is made against Woodward's under the B & I Act or (ii) the date on which Woodward's makes an assignment for the benefit of its creditors pursuant to the B & I Act, as the case may be.

Order accordingly.

[Leave to appeal refused (1993), 105 DLR 517.]

NOTES

1) Do you agree with Tysoe J's reasoning? With the result? Does the fault lie with Parliament in not adequately addressing the status of unpaid suppliers' claims under Part III and the CCAA? Does the result not encourage buyers to give a notice of intention under Part III or to proceed under the CCAA with a view to defeating s. 81.1 claims? Could the problem be addressed by treating unpaid suppliers meeting the s. 81.1 criteria as a special class of creditors for voting purposes on a proposal or arrangement?

2) Why does s. 81.2 treat farmers, fishermen and aquaculturists more favourably than other unpaid suppliers?

3) The available evidence so far is that ss. 81.1 and 81.2 have done little to improve the position of unpaid suppliers. In January 1994, the Bankruptcy Branch of Industry Canada sent 500 questionnaires to trustees to which there were 229 replies. Of the bankruptcies sampled in the replies, there were s. 81.1 claims in only 13 out of 229 cases (5.7%). In those 13 bankruptcies, there were a total of 54 claims with a total value of $438,209. In 9 of the 13 bankruptcies some claimants were at least partially successful. The total value of the goods repossessed was $109,922 or approximately one-quarter of the goods whose release was demanded. There were no s. 81.2 claims at at all. (The above information is taken from an unpublished paper on s. 81.1 by Jeffrey Simser, a part-time Osgoode Hall LLM student, submitted in January 1995.)

CLAIMS AGAINST THE ESTATE
(BIA ss. 121, 124, 127, 135, 148-50)

Introduction

1) Before the trustee can declare a dividend, or an interim dividend, he must of course know, and accept the validity of, the number and value of the claims entitled to share in the net proceeds of the estate. But this is only one aspect of the important role played by claims against the estate. The number of votes that may be cast by a creditor at meetings of creditors depends on the value of its claim (s. 115) and affects creditors' ability to elect inspectors of their choice (s. 116). Still more important, the value of a claim determines voting power at class meetings of creditors and may make all the difference between approval and rejection of a proposal or arrangement under Part III or the CCAA.

2) The eligibility requirements for claims and guidelines for establishing the value of a claim are set forth in ss. 121, 124, 127 and 135. In many estates these issues create no problems, particularly since there is often not enough left in the estate to make it worth while for unsecured creditors to press their claims. Problems arise where the claim is unliquidated or contingent in character. Even more difficult issues arise in the case of mass tort claims (such as those involving asbestosis claims, or claims involving medical devices and implants), where many of the victims may not even be aware of the fact that they have, or may have a claim, and may not be able to bring a claim under applicable provincial law until they can establish an injury and quantify their damages. The cases which follow illustrate some of these problems as well as the innovative approach taken by American courts in resolving deadlocks.

Re F.E.A. Griffiths Corporation
(1971), 15 CBR (NS) 231 (Ont. SC)

HOULDEN J (orally): This is an application for directions pursuant to s. 12(1) of the Bankruptcy Act, RSC 1952, c. 14; however, the parties are agreed that it should be tried as a substantive motion, and I propose to deal with it on that basis.

A proposal was made by the debtor corporation on 4th March 1970 and in due course the proposal was accepted by creditors and approved by the Court. A proof of claim was filed with the trustee by Neonex International Limited in the amount of $13,337.40, representing the balance due on five contracts for the rental of display equipment. In its proof of claim the creditor took the position that its contracts were terminated as of the date of the proposal and its claim represents the payments in arrears prior to the date of the proposal, and rental payments from that date to the termination date of the contracts.

Section 83(2) and R. 91(1) of the Bankruptcy Act confer power on the court to value contingent and unliquidated claims. It is my opinion, that by reason of s. 38(1) of the Bankruptcy Act, these provisions are applicable in respect to contingent and unliquidated claims of creditors in a proposal.

Counsel for the creditor argues that this claim is not a contingent or unliquidated claim. This is a very difficult question, but in view of the conclusion that I have arrived at, I am not called upon to decide it in this application.

In the case of *Re Emil's Furniture & Appliances Ltd.* (1961), 2 CBR (NS) 225 (Ont.) Smily J dealt with a claim of this type. In the note of the case, it is stated that the learned judge permitted the creditor to claim the rental for the unexpired portion of the contract, subject to an allowance for maintenance, for recovery of a lump sum by way of damages in lieu of rental over a period of years, and for salvage value. If the matter were free of authority, I would like to make a similar determination in this case as I believe it is a fair method of dealing with this kind of claim.

In *Neon Products of Canada Ltd. v. Smith* (1961), 8 CBR (NS) 68, the Ontario Court of Appeal also dealt with a claim of this type but arrived at a different result from the *Emil's* case. Unfortunately the *Smith* decision was not reported until 1966 and the report of the case only gives the reasons for judgment of the trial judge, which were affirmed by the Court of Appeal on 11th October, 1961 without written reasons. In the *Smith* case, the Court decided that the creditor was entitled to claim for the payments in arrears and for the balance of the payments due under the contract of leasing without any deduction for salvage, maintenance, etc.

As counsel for the claimant has pointed out, it is trite law that a trustee in bankruptcy stands in the shoes of the debtor and has no higher rights than the debtor, apart from situations such as ss. 60 and 64 of the Bankruptcy Act. The fact that this is a bankruptcy matter is, therefore, not sufficient to distinguish the present application from the *Smith* case.

It is my opinion that the decision of *Neon Products of Canada Ltd. v. Smith, supra*, is binding upon me and that the claimant is entitled to claim for the sum of $13,337.40 without deduction. I wish to make it quite clear, however, that my decision is restricted to the facts of this case, i.e., the lease of display equipment, and different considerations might well apply in the case of leases of other kinds of chattels.

There will, therefore, be an order that Neonex International Limited is an unsecured creditor for the sum of $13,337.40 in the proposal. ...

NOTE

Claims by lessors of equipment for liquidated and unliquidated damages have proved very troublesome over the years in many common law jurisdictions, particularly given common provisions in chattel leases holding the lessee liable for the full balance of the lease payments even if the contract is terminated and the lessor repossesses the chattel before the end of the contractual term. English courts frequently stigmatized such provisions as penalty clauses and refused to enforce them. These precedents were followed in Canada in Dickson JA's influential judgment in *Canadian Acceptance Corp. Ltd. v. Regent Park Butcher Shop Ltd.*, [1969] 3 DLR (3d) 304 (Man. CA).

The position was reviewed by the Supreme Court of Canada in *Keneric Tractor Sales Ltd. v. Langille*, [1987] 2 SCR 562. (See also *supra*, chapter 10 of volume I of this casebook.) The Supreme Court held that even if the liquidated damages clause was not enforceable the lessor was entitled to recover damages at common law on normal expectation and foreseeability loss principles.

Re Carling Acceptance Limited
(1976), 22 CBR (NS) 258 (Ont. SC),
aff'd (1977), 23 CBR (NS) 245 (Ont. CA)

HUGHES J: Carling Acceptance Limited (hereinafter "the company") was, according to a prospectus dated 16th July 1965 drawn in connection with an offer of $1,000,000 unsecured debentures, incorporated by letters patent under the Dominion Companies Act, RSC 1952, c. 53, on 10th July 1964 under the name of Carling Finance Limited as a private company. By supplementary letters patent dated 4th February 1965 its name was changed, and it was constituted a public company. Note 9 to the prospectus contains, *inter alia*, the following statement:

Four of the Directors have each loaned the Company the sum of $25,000.00 and these have been secured by promissory notes bearing interest at the rate of 7% per annum which is repayable semi-annually. The Directors and the Company have entered into a subrogation agreement dated the 16th day of July, 1965 which provides that these loans shall not be repaid until the Company's earned surplus account shall have reached a minimum of $150,000.00.

This agreement, which was indisputably entered into to secure approval of the debenture issue by the Ontario Securities Commission, was made between the company and one Brian H. Wilson of the first part, and Frank C. Patterson, George S. Murray, Lawrence W. Butler and George A. Ault as lenders of the second part, and Price Waterhouse & Co. of the third part. It recites the application to the Ontario Securities Commission by the company for the approval of the prospectus, the fact that the lenders have each loaned to the company the sum of $25,000, the loans being secured by promissory notes, and that these lenders, being also shareholders of the company and four of its five directors, have agreed as follows:

1) The trustees declare that they stand possessed of the said sum of One Hundred Thousand ($100,000) Dollars, the said sum to remain as a part of the working capital of the Company, for the benefit of creditors of the act of bankruptcy during the currency of these presents, to apply the said funds as they may legally be required so to do.

2) The lenders shall not present the individual promissory notes hereinbefore referred to to the Company nor demand payment of the said promissory notes in either case in whole or in part until the Company's earned surplus account shall have reached a minimum of One Hundred and Fifty Thousand ($150,000.00) Dollars and the auditor's certificate to that effect has been forwarded to the Company.

3) The Trustees covenant and agree to continue to stand possessed of the said sum until the Company's auditors have issued a certificate to it certifying that the Company's earned surplus account has reached a minimum of One Hundred and Fifty Thousand ($150,000.00) Dollars and upon receipt of such certificate these presents shall be of no further force or effect.

The operations of the company were not in the end profitable although interest was regularly paid upon the directors' loans, and new notes drawn in the same terms were provided to the lenders in 1971. It may be said here that the notes themselves were unconditional on their face and payable on demand. Then on 12th May 1975 the company made a proposal in bankruptcy approved by the court on 17th June, and Robert E.

Lowe, CA, of Toronto was appointed trustee. In the course of the subsequent proceedings required by statute the lending directors preferred their claims, and on 10th February 1976 the trustee, upon advice that they were not provable, moved before Henry J sitting in bankruptcy to have the question determined. The learned judge referred the question to the judge sitting in weekly court in Ottawa "to determine whether the subordinated claims of Alastair Macdonald, Executor under the Last Will and Testament of Frank Charles Patterson, George S. Murray, Lawrence W. Butler and George A. Ault are provable claims, and if the claims are provable, to value the claims."

It is clear from the report of the trustee that the proposal was made under s. 32 of the Bankruptcy Act, RSC 1970, c. B-3, by the company as an insolvent person and not as a bankrupt, and this distinction, although blurred in some of the authorities, may be of significance in this case. The motion is made pursuant to the provisions of s. 95 [now s. 121] and I quote what appear to be the relevant provisions:

95(1) All debts and liabilities, present or future, to which the bankrupt is subject at the date of the bankruptcy or to which he may become subject before his discharge by reason of any obligation incurred before the date of the bankruptcy shall be deemed to be claims provable in proceedings under this Act.

(2) The court shall, on the application of the trustee, determine whether any contingent claim or any unliquidated claim is a provable claim, and, if a provable claim, it shall value such claim, and such claim shall after, but not before, such valuation be deemed a proved claim to the amount of its valuation.

(3) A creditor may prove for a debt not payable at the date of the bankruptcy and may receive dividends equally with the other creditors, deducting only thereout a rebate of interest at the rate of five per cent per annum computed from the declaration of a dividend to the time when the debt would have become payable according to the terms on which it was contracted.

(4) Where a proposal is made before bankruptcy the claims provable shall be determined as of the date of the filing of the proposal.

(5) The claims of creditors under a proposal are, in the event of the debtor subsequently becoming bankrupt, provable in the bankruptcy for the full amount of the claims less any dividends paid thereon pursuant to the proposal.

Counsel for the trustee took the position that the claims of the directors were not provable since the occasion for presenting their notes had not arisen. Both Mr. Laishley and Mr. Solway relied on the doctrine of frustration, contending that under the circumstances the occasion for presentation and payment could never arise. As to valuation they said that the directors should rank with other creditors and that their claims should be valued at their face value plus interest accrued and unpaid. It was not suggested in argument that the claims might be valued as contingent claims, and indeed such a solution would be fraught with serious difficulty.

I think the question of frustration can be shortly dealt with. The doctrine arises from the decision of Blackburn J applying by analogy the civil law in *Taylor v. Caldwell* (1863), 3 B & S 826, 122 ER 309, where the defendant had agreed to give the plaintiff the use of a music hall. Before the stipulated day of performance it was destroyed by fire. Such a contract was described at pp. 834-35 as "subject to an implied condition that the parties shall be excused in case, before breach, performance becomes impossible from the perishing of the thing without default of the contractor." Much attention has been given to such implied terms as a result of enemy action in two world wars, and the doctrine of frustration has been subsequently extended to embrace situations where performance of a contract becomes impossible because of a change in the circumstances which were contemplated by the parties as the basis of the contract. But the contract between these parties obviously contemplated bankruptcy on the part of the company, and it is clear from the authorities that, where the source of frustration is foreseeable, and a fortiori foreseen, relief from the obligations thereunder cannot be provided: see for example *Can. Govt. Merchant Marine Ltd. v. Can. Trading Co.*, [1922] 3 WWR 197, 64 SCR 106, 68 DLR 544.

If then, as I hold, the contract still subsists, can the directors prove contingent claims? With regard to the distinction maintained in the Bankruptcy Act between a proposal made before bankruptcy and one afterwards, I quote the words of Orde J in *Re McKay; Ex parte McCall Co.* (1922), 2 CBR 462 at 464-65, 52 OLR 466. The learned judge was considering the case of a claim under a contract for the supply of goods over a period which had not yet expired. After holding that the contractor was entitled to file his claim under the whole contract "both in respect of moneys already payable thereunder and in respect of the liability incurred for the performance of the unexpired or uncompleted portion of the contract" he continued:

In cases such as this it is incumbent upon the debtor, the trustee and the compounding creditors to take contracts of this nature into consideration, and if it is necessary for the future conduct of the debtor's business to retain such contracts that matter should be made the subject of special provision as a term of the proposal.

It was argued by counsel for the trustee that there had been no breach of the contract by the debtor, but I do not think that think that the question of breach is involved at all. The right to prove against an insolvent estate is based upon the theory that the debtor's business has come to an end and that all obligations whether already incurred or merely contingent are to be disposed of and cleared off in the bankruptcy proceedings. There is manifestly some inconsistency in applying this theory to compositions and extension under sec. 13 [of the Bankruptcy Act, 1919 (Can.), c. 36] which have for their object the continuance of the debtor's business, but there is, even in such cases, the fundamental object of enabling the debtor to continue business with a clean sheet. Whatever the inconsistencies may be, the scheme of sec. 13 seems to be that the rights and obligations of the debtor and his creditors are to be worked out in cases which come under that section in substantially the same manner as in cases of assignments and receiving orders.

But what is the situation where, as in the claims under consideration, a valuation depends upon such a contingency as is contemplated in the agreement here? The chance of the company's earned surplus account reaching a figure of \$150,000 in the future, assuming it is able as a result of its proposal to continue in business, is not, in my view, measurable by any actuarial computation, and I cannot in conscience refer valuation of these claims to the registrar were I to find them provable. In England s. 30(6) of the Bankruptcy Act, 1914 (UK), c. 59, provides:

(6) If, in the opinion of the court, the value of the debt or liability is incapable of being fairly estimated, the court may make an order to that effect, and thereupon the debt or liability shall, for the purposes of this Act, be deemed to be a debt not provable in bankruptcy.

I have not discovered, nor have been advised of any similar provision in our Bankruptcy Act, but it may be argued that s. 95 contemplates proof of claims only in those cases where they can be valued by the court. In any event, the language of subs. (1), saying that "All debts and liabilities, present or future, to which the bankrupt is subject at the date of the bankruptcy or to which he may become subject before his discharge by reason of any obligation incurred before the date of the bankruptcy," would exclude proof of a claim dependent upon the liability occurring under the provisions of the agreement between the company and the directors quoted above. No doubt the language of this subsection is applicable to the case of a proposal made before bankruptcy by virtue of the provisions of s. 46(1):

46(1) All the provisions of this Act, in so far as they are applicable, apply *mutatis mutandis* to proposals.

There is also an equitable aspect to the situation in which the directors find themselves. They have indeed advanced the money to the company, and these advances, recorded in the company's accounts, exist independently of the notes by which they are secured. Yet, having regard to the purpose of the agreement entered into between them and the company, avowed in the affidavit of George A. Ault filed on the motion, can the directors, in the light of its provisions and of the unequivocal assurance given in the prospectus, be heard to say that they were providing for their own security as well as for that of other creditors of the company? It is contended that their contribution was always expressed to be a loan and not a subscription, and indeed they have been paid interest by the company on this assumption. But, having represented to the public in a prospectus for which they are responsible that the loan was not repayable until $150,000 accumulated in the earned surplus account, they should not, in my view, be now allowed to prove their claims in the same category as other creditors.

For these reasons, and only in connection with this proposal made before bankruptcy, I find that the directors' claims are not to be proved except as to interest on their notes due and unpaid before the date of the proposal. ...

On Appeal

ARNUP JA (for the Court): ... The judgment of Hughes J is primarily concerned with the argument addressed to him that the agreement between the note holders, the company, and others, dated 16th July 1965, had been frustrated. We agree with the reasons for judgment of Hughes J on that issue.

In this court the first point made to us by the appellants is that the agreement terminated prior to any act of bankruptcy by the company. That termination, it is submitted, occurred either when the debentures originally issued were exchanged for new debentures by the vast majority of the debenture holders, or at the latest terminated on 1st July 1973, when the debentures issued originally became due and payable. We do not accept this argument. In our view, it involves reading into the agreement a termination date which is not found within it. The agreement, according to its terms, could not have terminated prior to the company's earned surplus account reaching the sum of $150,000. The note holders agreed that they would not demand payment of their notes prior to the occurrence of that event.

Needless to say, it did not occur, and accordingly the agreement, in our view, was in full force and effect on the date as of which claims of creditors are to be ascertained for the purposes of the proposal.

Appeal dismissed.

US Bankruptcy Code (1978)

s. 101(4) "claim" means—

(A) right to payment, whether or not such right is reduced to judgment, liquidated, unliquidated, fixed, contingent, matured, unmatured, disputed, undisputed, legal, equitable, secured, or unsecured; or

(B) right to an equitable remedy for breach of performance if such breach gives rise to a right to payment, whether or not such right to an equitable remedy is reduced to judgment, fixed, contingent, matured, unmatured, disputed, undisputed, secured, or unsecured;

Bittner v. Borne Chemical Company, Inc.
691 F.2d 134 (CCA 3, 1982)

GIBBONS, Circuit Judge: Stockholders of The Rolfite Company appeal from the judgment of the district court, affirming the decision of the bankruptcy court to assign a zero value to their claims in the reorganization proceedings of Borne Chemical Company, Inc. (Borne) under Chapter 11 of the Bankruptcy Code (Code), 11 USC §§ 1-151326 (Supp. IV 1981). Since the bankruptcy court neither abused its discretionary authority to estimate the value of the claims pursuant to 11 USC § 502(c)(1) nor relied on clearly erroneous findings of fact, we affirm.

I.

Prior to filing its voluntary petition under Chapter 11 of the Code, Borne commenced a state court action against Rolfite for the alleged pirating of trade secrets and proprietary information from Borne. The Rolfite Company filed a counterclaim, alleging, *inter alia*, that Borne had tortiously interfered with a proposed merger between Rolfite and the Quaker Chemical Corporation (Quaker) by unilaterally terminating a contract to manufacture Rolfite products and by bringing its suit. Sometime after Borne filed its Chapter 11 petition, the Rolfite stockholders sought relief from the automatic stay so that the state court proceedings might be continued. Borne then filed a motion to disallow temporarily the Rolfite claims until they were finally liquidated in the state court. The bankruptcy court lifted the automatic stay but also granted Borne's motion to disallow temporarily the claims, extending the time within which such claims could be filed and allowed if they should be eventually liquidated.

Upon denial of their motion to stay the hearing on confirmation of Borne's reorganization plan, the Rolfite stockholders appealed to the district court, which vacated the temporary disallowance order and directed the bankruptcy court to hold an estimation hearing. The parties agreed to establish guidelines for the submission of evidence at the hearing, and, in accordance with this agreement, the bankruptcy court relied on the parties' choice of relevant pleadings and other documents related to the state court litigation, and on briefs and oral argument. After weighing the evidence, the court assigned a zero value to the Rolfite claims and reinstated its earlier order to disallow temporarily the claims until such time as they might be liquidated in the state court, in effect requiring a waiver of discharge of the Rolfite claims from Borne. Upon appeal, the district court affirmed.

II.

[1] Section 502(c) of the Code provides:

There shall be estimated for purposes of allowance under this section—

(1) any contingent or unliquidated claim, fixing or liquidation of which, as the case may be, would unduly delay the closing of the case. ...

The Code, the Rules of Bankruptcy Procedure, 11 USC App. (1977), and the Suggested Interim Bankruptcy Rules, 11 US CA (1982), are silent as to the manner in which contingent or unliquidated claims are to be estimated. Despite the lack of express direction on the matter, we are persuaded that Congress intended the procedure to be undertaken initially by the bankruptcy judges, using whatever method is best suited to the particular contingencies at issue. The principal consideration must be an accommodation to the underlying purposes of the Code. It is conceivable that in rare and unusual cases arbitration or even a jury trial on all or some of the issues may be necessary to obtain a reasonably accurate evaluation of the claims. See 3 *Collier on Bankruptcy* ¶ 502.03 (15th ed. 1981). Such methods, however, usually will run counter to the efficient administration of the bankrupt's estate and where there is sufficient evidence on which to base a reasonable estimate of the claim, the bankruptcy judge should determine the value. In so doing, the court is bound by the legal rules which may govern the ultimate value of the claim. For example, when the claim is based on an alleged breach of contract, the court must estimate its worth in accordance with accepted contract law. See, e.g., 3 *Collier on Bankruptcy* ¶ 57.15[3.2] (14th ed. 1977). However, there are no other limitations on the court's authority to evaluate the claim save those general principles which should inform all decisions made pursuant to the Code.

In reviewing the method by which a bankruptcy court has ascertained the value of a claim under section 502(c)(1), an appellate court may only reverse if the bankruptcy court has abused its discretion. ...

According to the Rolfite stockholders, the estimate which section 502(c)(1) requires is the present value of the probability that appellants will be successful in their state court action. Thus, if the bankruptcy court should determine as of this date that the Rolfite stockholders' case is not supported by a preponderance or 51% of the evidence but merely by 40%, they apparently would be entitled to have 40% of their claims allowed during the reorganization proceedings, subject to modification if and when the claims are liquidated in state court. The Rolfite stockholders contend that instead of estimating their claims in this manner, the bankruptcy court assessed the ultimate merits and, believing that they could not establish their case by a preponderance of the evidence, valued the claims at zero.

[2] We note first that the bankruptcy court did not explicitly draw the distinction that the Rolfite stockholders make. Assuming however that the bankruptcy court did estimate their claims according to their ultimate merits rather than the present value of the probability that they would succeed in their state court action, we cannot find that such a valuation method is an abuse of the discretion conferred by section 502(c)(1).

The validity of this estimation must be determined in light of the policy underlying reorganization proceedings. In Chapter 11 of the Code, Congress addressed the complex issues which are raised when a corporation faces mounting financial problems.

The modern corporation is a complex and multi-faceted entity. Most corporations do not have a significant market share of the lines of business in which they compete. The success, and even the survival, of a corporation in contemporary markets depends on three elements: First, the ability to attract and hold skilled management; second, the ability to obtain credit; and third, the corporation's ability to project to the public an image of vitality. ...

One cannot overemphasize the advantages of speed and simplicity to both creditors and debtors. Chapter XI allows a debtor to negotiate a plan outside of court and, having reached a settlement with a majority in number and amount of each class of creditors, permits the debtor to bind all unsecured creditors to the terms of the arrangement. From the perspective of creditors, early confirmation of a plan of arrangement: first, generally reduces administrative expenses which have priority over the claims of unsecured creditors; second, permits creditors to receive prompt distributions on their claims with respect to which interest does not accrue after the filing date; and third, increases the ultimate recovery on creditor claims by minimizing the adverse effect on the business which often accompanies efforts to operate an enterprise under the protection of the Bankruptcy Act.

124 Cong.Rec. H 11101-H 11102 (daily ed. Sept. 28, 1978) (statement of Rep. D. Edwards of California, floor manager for bankruptcy legislation in the House of Representatives). Thus, in order to realize the goals of Chapter 11, a reorganization must be accomplished quickly and efficiently.

If the bankruptcy court estimated the value of the Rolfite stockholders' claims according to the ultimate merits of their state court action, such a valuation method is not inconsistent with the principles which imbue Chapter 11. Those claims are contingent and unliquidated. According to the bankruptcy court's findings of fact, the Rolfite stockholders' chances of ultimately succeeding in the state court action are uncertain at best. Yet, if the court had valued the Rolfite stockholders' claims according to the present probability of success, the Rolfite stockholders might well have acquired a significant, if not controlling, voice in the reorganization proceedings. The interests of those creditors with liquidated claims would have been subject to the Rolfite interests, despite the fact that the state court might ultimately decide against those interests after the reorganization. The bankruptcy court may well have decided that such a situation would at best unduly complicate the reorganization proceedings and at worst undermine Borne's attempts to rehabilitate its business and preserve its assets for the benefit of its creditors and employees. By valuing the ultimate merits of the Rolfite stockholders' claims at zero, and temporarily disallowing them until the final resolution of the state action, the bankruptcy court avoided the possibility of a protracted and inequitable reorganization proceeding while ensuring that Borne will be responsible to pay a dividend on the claims in the event that the state court decides in the Rolfite stockholders' favor. Such a solution is consistent with the Chapter 11 concerns of speed and simplicity but does not deprive the Rolfite stockholders of the right to recover on their contingent claims against Borne.

III.

The Rolfite stockholders further contend that, regardless of the method which the bankruptcy court used to value their claims, the court based its estimation on incorrect findings of fact. Rule 810 of the Rules of Bankruptcy Procedure permits an appellate court to overturn a bankruptcy referee's findings of fact only when they are clearly erroneous. ... A bankruptcy court may not, however, mask its interpretation of the law as findings of fact. In determining the legal merits of a case on which claims such as those of the Rolfite stockholders are based, the bankruptcy court should be guided by the applicable state law. The determination of such law is of course subject to plenary review. ...

The Rolfite stockholders argue that in assessing the merits of its state court action for the purpose of evaluating their claims against Borne, the bankruptcy court erred both in finding the facts and in applying the law. In reviewing the record according to the standards we have just described, we cannot agree. ...

The court's ultimate finding of fact—that the Rolfite stockholders' claims in the reorganization proceeding were worth zero—must also be upheld since it too is not clearly erroneous. The subsidiary findings of the court plainly indicated that the Rolfite counterclaim in the state action lacked legal merit. Faced with only the remote possibility that the state court would find otherwise, the bankruptcy court correctly valued the claims at zero. On the basis of the court's subsidiary findings, such an estimation was consistent both with the claims' present value and with the court's assessment of the ultimate merits.

District court judgment affirmed.

Note on Meaning of "Claim" and "Creditor" in the Context of Mass Torts

American courts have on several occasions had to wrestle with the meaning of "creditor" and "claim" under the Bankruptcy Code when corporations sought protection under Chapter 11 against current and prospective mass tort claims brought, or liable to be brought against them, by alleged victims of asbestosis (Johns-Manville Corp.) or wearers of the Dalkon Shield (A.H. Robins Co.). According to Baird & Jackson (Douglas G. Baird and Thomas H. Jackson, *Cases, Problems and Materials on Bankruptcy*, 2d ed. 1989, p. 151), writing in 1989, the case law was "conflicting, contradictory, and, from time to time, confused." In one such case, *In re UNR Industries*, 29 Bankr. 741 (Bankr. ND Ill. 1983), appeal dismissed, 725 F.2d 1111 (7th Cir. 1984), Judge Hart refused to appoint a representative to file claims on behalf of individuals who might develop asbestosis from past exposure to products manufactured and sold by UNR, and reasoned as follows (Baird & Jackson, *op. cit.*, 151):

The debtors contend that the putative claimants are holders of contingent claims. Three principles determine the question presented here:

1. A claim of which a bankruptcy court may take cognizance must be one that is recognized by state or federal law. ... The asbestos claims and rights all arise under state law.

2. The existence of a claim turns on when it arose. ... In the case of a claim sounding in tort, it is not the wrongful or negligent act which gives rise to the claim. Instead, no claim arises until the plaintiff suffers an injury. ...

3. The claim of an asbestos plaintiff (including a putative claimant) does not arise under state law until the plaintiff knows or should have known about the injury. ...

Therefore, under the definition imposed in the debtors' Application, the putative claimants—who have been exposed to asbestos some time in their lives but do not now have or do not know that they have an asbestos-related disease—have no claims under state law, and therefore do not have claims cognizable under the Code. Further, by the debtors' own definition the claims of the putative claimants will not have arisen either "at the time of or before the order for relief," 11 USC § 101(9), since a putative claimant is one who does not know that he has an asbestos-related disease.

The Code provision for the possibility of the evaluation and discharge of a *contingent* claim does not change the definition of "claim." It is not true that any conceivable claim is contingent. The contingency must be one that arises out of the prior contractual relationship of the claimant and the debtor. A tort claim does not meet this requirement. Instead, a tort action brought against a debtor is covered by other definitions: it is a "right to payment [not yet] reduced to judgment [which is] unliquidated [and] disputed. ..." 11 USC §101(4)(A).

On appeal, Judge Posner, writing for the Seventh Circuit, did not reach the merits of the case on the ground that Judge Hart's order in which he refused to appoint a representative was not "final" within the meaning of 28 USC § 1291 and hence was not appealable, 725 F.2d at 1118. However, he went on to suggest what his own views of the cognizability of asbestosis claims might be if the issue were before him (Baird & Jackson, *op. cit.*, 152-53):

The practical difficulties of identifying, giving constitutionally adequate notice to, and attempting to estimate the damages of the thousands upon thousands of people who have been exposed to asbestos sold by UNR but have not yet developed asbestosis are formidable, and possibly insurmountable. Yet if any of them have already suffered a tort there would be no basis we can think of for not letting them file claims in this bankruptcy proceeding. And some, at least, probably have suffered a tort. The states differ on whether a cause of action in an asbestosis case accrues upon inhalation ... or not until there is palpable disease ... or the disease is discovered. ... Even in a "discovery" state the cause of action may "exist" before it "accrues"—that is, before the statute of limitations on bringing it begins to run. ... These states postpone the date of accrual of the cause of action not in order to prevent the early filing of claims but in order to lift the bar of the statute of limitations to later filings. Since there is "medical evidence that the body incurs microscopic injury as asbestos fibers become lodged in the lungs and as the surrounding tissue reacts to the fibers thereafter," *Keene Corp. v. Insurance Co. of North America*, 667 F.2d 1034, 1042 (DC Cir. 1981), and since no particular amount of injury is necessary to create tort liability, courts in these states might hold that a tort claim arises as soon as asbestos fibers are inhaled, however much time the victim might have for bringing suit. In any event, some at least of the many thousands of workers who have been exposed to asbestos sold by UNR must have been exposed in states such as Indiana and New York where the cause of action accrues upon inhalation, and their claims against the bankrupt estate—accrued tort claims—would appear uncontroversially to be provable in bankruptcy.

Even in states where exposed workers are not injured in a tort sense till the disease manifests itself, and therefore do not have an accrued tort claim in any sense, and even assuming that an unaccrued tort claim cannot be a "claim" within the meaning of 11 USC § 101(4)(A), ... a bankruptcy court's equitable powers ... just might be broad enough to enable the court to make provision for future asbestosis claims against the bankrupt when it approved the final plan of reorganization. The date on which a person exposed to asbestos happens to develop a diagnosable case of asbestosis is arbitrary. Could it not be argued therefore that a bankruptcy court can and should use its equitable powers, which traditionally "have been invoked to that end that ... substance will not give way to form, that technical considerations will not prevent substantial justice from being done" [*Pepper v. Litton*, 308 US 295, 305 (1939)] (especially, perhaps, in a reorganization case, see *In re Michigan Brewing Co.*, 24 F. Supp. 430 (WD Mich. 1938)), to prevent the liquidation or discharge of the bankrupt before provision is made for such persons? And more than arbitrariness is involved. If future claims cannot be discharged before they ripen, UNR may not be able to emerge from bankruptcy with reasonable prospects for continued existence as a going concern. In that event, and assuming that UNR's going-concern value would exceed its liquidation value, both UNR (which is to say the creditors who will own UNR at the conclusion of the reorganization) and future plaintiffs would be made worse off, and UNR's current creditors would not necessarily be made better off, by the court's failure to act along the lines proposed by UNR. ...

QUESTION

How would these issues be decided under the BIA? Can it be argued that s. 121(1) of the Canadian Act is more broadly worded than USC § 101(4) and (9) in so far as it applies to all debts and liabilities, present and future, to which the bankrupt is subject on the day on which the bankrupt become bankrupt "or to which the bankrupt may become subject before the bankrupt's discharge ... ," or should the court interpret the language, as Judge Posner did in the American context, in the light of the underlying purposes of reorganization and bankruptcy proceedings?

CHAPTER FIFTEEN

Executory Contracts and Leases

(BIA ss. 69.3, 69.4, 18, 30-32, 34, 37-38, 73(4), 146 and
Ontario Landlord and Tenant Act, ss. 38(2), 39)

The term "executory contract" does not appear in the BIA. Nevertheless, it is an important concept and it has great practical significance in the bankruptcy context, particularly when a business seeks to reorganize. For bankruptcy purposes, an executory contract means a contract between the bankrupt (or an insolvent person in the case of a reorganization) and another person where the contract has not been fully performed by the bankrupt or the other party prior to the bankruptcy. It does not include a debt which has accrued prior to the bankruptcy for goods delivered or services rendered by either party. (Can you see why?) The main problems raised by executory contracts are these: to what extent is a trustee entitled to step into the bankrupt's shoes and to complete or require the other party to perform its part of the contract if the trustee deems it in the estate's interest to proceed in this way? Conversely, is the trustee bound by the contract or can she disclaim or repudiate it and if she does will the estate be liable in damages?

Before the 1992 amendments, with one exception, the BIA said little about these issues but left them to be resolved by general principles (which in this case meant primarily provincial law) pursuant to s. 72(1). The exception involved realty leases. Here s. 146 provided, and still provides, that subject to priority of ranking as provided in s. 136 and subject to s. 73(4) (which deals with the effect of the tenant's bankruptcy on a landlord's distraint for unpaid rent) the rights of landlords shall be determined according to the law of the province in which the leased premises are situated. Many of the provincial landlord and tenant statutes do in fact address the question specifically, and often very much in the tenant's favour. So far as other types of contract are concerned, provincial law does not preclude the parties from agreeing on the effect a party's bankruptcy or insolvency proceedings will have on the contract.* Professionally drafted agreements commonly provide that such an event shall entitle the non-bankrupt party to cancel or amend the agreement, demand the return of chattels (in the case of chattel leases or bailments), and claim damages which may be in a liquidated amount.†

Such unilateral powers of cancellation often jeopardize the prospects for a successful reorganization. It was for this reason that s. 65.1 was added in the 1992 amendments

---

* Public utility services are usually governed by their own statutory rules.

† It is generally assumed that BIA s. 69.3, which provides that on the bankrupty of a debtor no creditor has any remedy against the debtor or the debtor's property, does not preclude the other contracting party from
(The footnote is continued on the next page.)

invalidating or regulating such provisions. A new s. 65.2 was also added giving a commercial tenant under a realty lease the power to repudiate the lease on giving the prescribed notice to the landlord. Both ss. 65.1 and 65.2 only apply where a notice of intention to make a proposal or a proposal has been made under Part III of the BIA. They do not apply to proposed arrangements under the CCAA. However, judges regularly use their powers under s. 11 of that Act enjoining cancellation or suspension of performance by the non-insolvent party.

Potato Distributors Inc. v. Eastern Trust Company
(1955), 35 CBR 161 (PEI CA)

TWEEDY J: This is an appeal from a judgment of my Lord the Chief Justice, upon an application by Potato Distributors Incorporated for an order declaring a certain contract to be frustrated and void by reason of bankruptcy of the debtor, or in the alternative, for an order that the trustee in bankruptcy disclaim the said contract as onerous.

The learned Chief Justice refused the application and as to the alternative order sought he held it clearly could not be considered upon the application before him as the above appellant was only a contractor and not a creditor at that time.

Since then, however, Russell Hammill and Russell Ching, two creditors of the debtor, have been added as intervenants. Some objection was made to this procedure, but for the purpose of this appeal it was agreed that the appeal be considered as properly before the Court and that the appeal should be heard and determined upon its merits.

The contract in question is dated April 9, 1955, and is between the debtor of the one part and the appellant of the other part and is for sale and delivery by the debtor to the appellant in each of the years, 1955, 1956, and 1957, of 25,000 bags of certified Number One Canada A Grade Sebago Seed Potatoes and also 1,750 bags of certified Number One Canada A Grade Small Sebago Seed Potatoes, ship's tackle at Summerside, Charlottetown or Souris in Prince Edward Island.

---

† Continued ...

cancelling or suspending an executory contract. The position is not as clear as might be wished. In *Vachon v. Canada Employment and Immigration Commission* (1985), 57 CBR (NS) 113, the Supreme Court of Canada gave a very broad reading to "remedies" in s. 49(1) (the predecessor of s. 69.3) of the pre-1992 Act to prevent the Commission from setting off a debt against a claim for unemployment benefits. (Curiously the judgment does not refer to s. 97(3) of the Act.) However, *Vachon* did not involve an executory contract and Beetz J's judgment for the Court does not discuss their position. Ellen Hayes suggests ("Executory Contracts in Debt Restructuring" (1994), 24 *CBLJ* 44) the distinction lies in the fact that s. 69.3 only applies to "creditors' claims" whereas a contracting party asserting a right of cancellation on the debtor's bankruptcy may not be a creditor as defined in s. 2 of the BIA. The distinction is very subtle and in many cases the cancelling party will also be a creditor. The most satisfactory explanation is probably that s. 69.3 was never intended to apply to executory contracts; had it been otherwise, it would not have been necessary to add s. 65.1 in the 1992 amendments. It is also significant that in the U.S. Bankruptcy Code the automatic stay provision (s. 362) and the executory contract provision (s. 365) appear in different sections.

The date of delivery of said potatoes in each of the said three years was to be during the months of November and December, and the price agreed to be paid by the purchaser appellant to the debtor was $1.75 United States funds per 100 pound bag.

On August 25, 1955, a receiving order was made against the debtor and the respondent was appointed trustee in bankruptcy. No potatoes have been delivered under the contract.

The grounds of appeal are as follows:

1. From the very nature of bankruptcy, performance of a three year contract by the trustee is inapt.

2. More especially is this so where, as in the present case, performance of the contract involves gambling on the potato market.

3. *The Bankruptcy Act* does not contemplate carrying on the business of the bankrupt by the trustees where that business is of a highly speculative nature.

4. Carrying on business by the trustee must be confined to such business as will promote a reasonably speedy winding up of the estate.

5. The undertaking given by the trustee in the present case would be worthless in certain circumstances, and His Lordship therefore erred in refusing the appellant's application upon such an undertaking.

The argument was devoted mainly to s. 10(1)(c) of *The Bankruptcy Act*, 1949, 2nd Sess. (Can.), c. 7 [now BIA s. 30(1)], which reads as follows:

The trustee may, with the permission of the inspectors, do all or any of the following things: ...

(c) carry on the business of the bankrupt, so far as may be necessary for the beneficial administration of the estate.

It was contended by the appellant that the completion of the contract by the trustee is the carrying on of the business of the debtor; business that is not necessary for the beneficial administration of the estate.

Our *Bankruptcy Act* was no doubt modelled after and largely copied from the English Act, 1914, c. 59. An examination of the English cases therefore will be of some assistance in the consideration of this case.

The original *Bankruptcy Act* was enacted by the Dominion Parliament in the Session of 1919 (9-10 Geo. V, c. 36) and was to become operative by Royal Proclamation. A proclamation was issued on December 31, 1919, bringing the Act into force on July 1, 1920.

Various amendments were passed and these were consolidated and revised and the new *Bankruptcy Act* was contained in RSC 1927, c. 11.

What is now s. 10(1)(c) already quoted, was s. 43(1)(b) in RSC 1927, c. 11, and was s. 20(1)(b) of *The Bankruptcy Act*, 1919 and amendments thereto with this variation:

Section 43(1)(b) of RSC 1927, c. 11 reads as follows:

43. The trustee may, with the permission in writing of the inspectors, do all or any of the following things: ...

(b) carry on the business of the debtor, so far as may be necessary for the beneficial winding-up of the same.

From a perusal of the English cases, it would appear that this section of the English *Bankruptcy Act* reads exactly the same way.

However, our *Bankruptcy Act*, 1949, in s. 10 does not require the permission of the inspectors to be in writing; refers to the "debtor" as a "bankrupt" in s. 10(1)(c) and states that the business should be carried on "so far as may be necessary for the beneficial administration of the estate," not "so far as may be necessary for the beneficial winding-up of the business of the debtor."

It is contended by the appellant that "administration" and "winding-up" are the same thing. I realize that the words are used interchangeably in the English cases. Also that Morawetz's 3rd edition of *Bradford & Greenberg's Canadian Bankruptcy Act* at p. 43 states that "Para. (c) corresponds to former para. (b)." I cannot help feeling, however, that there is a difference in meaning in the words of the two sections. One of the dictionary meanings of "administration" is "The management and disposal of the estate of a deceased person."

The dictionary meaning of "wind-up" is to close, conclude, finish.

A very common use of the word administration is in connection with the administration of estates of deceased persons. In that use it does not mean that contracts of the deceased be frustrated or voided or that the administrator should disclaim contracts of the deceased as being onerous.

Neither do I think that Parliament intended this to be the case when it deliberately changed the wording of the section as used in the English Act, *The Bankruptcy Act*, 1919 and *The Bankruptcy Act*, 1927.

However, it is not necessary for the disposition of this appeal that I should determine this point although I must confess it is fascinating and very interesting.

[To deal] now with the main question whether or not by carrying out this contract the trustee is carrying on business not necessary for the beneficial administration of the estate.

I was much impressed with the argument and the cases cited. I am quite prepared to admit too that the pith and substance of this section is whether or not the carrying on of the bankrupt business is necessary for the beneficial administration of the estate. See *In re Wreck Recovery and Salvage Company* (1880), 15 Ch.D. 353, per Jessel MR at p. 360: "Now the word 'necessary' means that it must not be merely beneficial but something more. ... Then it must be for the 'beneficial winding-up' of the business of the company, therefore it must be with a view to the winding-up of the company, not with a view to its continuance."

I am also in agreement with the quotation from the judgment of Macdonald J in *In re Sechart Fisheries Limited* (1929), 10 CBR 565 at 569, [1929] 2 WWR 413, 41 BCR 323, [1929] 4 DLR 536, 3 Can. Abr. 442, where he states: "... in my opinion it is the duty of a trustee to speedily realize the assets, and divide the proceeds among the creditors."

In re Delisle (Colonial Construction Co.), Bonnier and Fels, 23 CBR 333, [1942] Que. SC 72, Abr. Con. 285, and *In re Grobstein and Capra* (1929), 11 CBR 250, 3 Can. Abr. 443, were cited by the appellant as cases showing where it was proper that the business of the bankrupt debtor should be carried on for a time.

The leading English case of *Clark v. Smith*, [1940] 1 KB 126, [1939] 4 All ER 59, while it is very interesting and illuminating, yet is not of much assistance in the present case.

After carefully considering all the above cases and the other cases cited, I cannot reach the conclusion that the trustee in this case is carrying on business of the bankrupt that is not necessary for the beneficial administration of the estate.

The potato business of the bankrupt was only one branch of many other lines of business carried on by it. Among others mentioned were plumbing, feed business, hardware business and many others.

All the trustee is trying to do by carrying out this contract is to endeavour to mitigate the liabilities as much as possible and not try to make a profit.

As so often pointed out, *The Bankruptcy Act* was passed for two main objects: 1. To secure the creditors the best result, i.e., an economical administration, and 2. To enable an honest bankrupt to obtain a discharge and to make a fresh start.

The Bankruptcy Act was passed primarily for the purpose of securing to creditors the wreckage of bankrupt estates, and extricating from an intolerable situation the unfortunate trader who, through no fault of his own, finds himself weighed down with financial burdens which he cannot discharge: *Per* Barry, CJKBD, in *In re Holdengraber; Ex parte Royal Brand Clothing Co.* (1927), 8 CBR 411 at 413, 3 Can. Abr. 662.

"In the performance of his duties a trustee ... should have regard to the fact that his principal duty is to realize the assets of the debtor ... and distribute such assets *pari passu* amongst the unsecured creditors after having satisfied all preferred creditors. ... The trustee cannot carry on the business for the purpose of making a profit for the debtor or with a view of saving the business for him, but only for the purpose of beneficially winding-up the business in the interest of the general body of creditors:" *Per* Maclennan J, in *In re Gareau; Ex parte Joseph Bros.* (1922), 3 CBR 76, 3 Can. Abr. 486.

Here the inspectors instructed the trustee to carry out the contract under consideration.

The whole scope of *The Bankruptcy Act* indicates that in the administration of the estate of a debtor the governing authority shall be the inspectors and not the Court. If, however, they act fraudulently or in bad faith and not for the benefit of the estate, the Court may interfere, but otherwise the policy of the Act is to leave the matter entirely in their hands: *In re J.L. Jacobs & Co.* (1941), 22 CBR 208, Abr. Con. 323.

It is not as though the trustee were entering upon some new project. Here he is trying to do the best possible, guided by the views of his inspectors for the creditors as a body and not for any one group.

I am of the opinion, therefore, that the learned Chief Justice was right in refusing to grant an order declaring the contract to be frustrated and void subject to the express undertaking given by the trustee that no distribution of assets would be made among the creditors until after the date of the completion of the three-year contract with the appellant, and that the assets of the bankrupt in the hands of the trustee would be answerable to the appellant for any damages arising from a breach of the contract.

Appeal dismissed.

[MacGuigan J delivered a short concurring judgment.]

NOTE

Why does the BIA impose the condition that the trustee can only carry on the debtor's business "so far as may be necessary for the beneficial administration" of the estate of the bankrupt (s. 30(1)(c))? Whose interests are being protected? Is it likely the inspectors would encourage the trustee to gamble on the success of continuing in business? Why is the inspectors' business judgment of the merits of the trustee being allowed to carry on the business not sufficient?

In re Gareau (1922), 3 CBR 76 (Que.) shows the advisability of not fettering the inspectors' discretion. The bankrupt was a manufacturer and retailer of woolen clothing (men's suits) and apparently had a large number of orders and cloth in hand at the time of its assignment. With the inspectors' consent, the trustee continued the business. Fifteen stores had been closed and seven more were shortly to be closed. Suits to the value of $390,000 had been manufactured and had realized 67.5% of their inventory value. This was much more than the goods were supposed to be worth at the time of the assignment.

The trustee had also sold suits for a total amount of $1,152,000, had paid all related expenses, paid the secured creditors $88,000 and a dividend of 12.5% to ordinary creditors, and had on hand a further $96,000 for distribution to ordinary creditors, whose remaining claims amounted to $1,112,000. The trustee expected to be able to pay a further dividend of 12.5% to ordinary creditors at the end of the spring season in 1922.

So it is clear that an orderly liquidation of a bankrupt business is much to be preferred over a fire sale.

In re Thomson Knitting Co.
(1924-25), 5 CBR 189 (Ont.), aff'd (1925) 5 CBR 489 (OCA)

FISHER J: The debtor company was incorporated under *The Ontario Companies Act*, RSO, 1914, ch. 178, and carried on business at Bowmanville as wholesale and retail manufacturers of hosiery and designers and dealers in textile products.

Bever & Wolf carried on business in Bradford, England.

In October, 1922, the debtor company ordered from the creditors 5,000 pounds of artificial silk wool, of which 3,240 pounds were delivered. On December 29, 1922, the debtor company ordered 10,000 pounds and only 307 pounds were delivered. On January 5, 1923, the debtor company ordered 10,000 pounds; no delivery was made under this order. On January 13, 1923, the debtor company ordered 2,500 pounds and only 379 pounds were delivered. The wool was to be delivered in instalments.

Exhibits (1) (2) (3) (4) (5) and (6) show the contracts entered into and the correspondence in connection therewith.

Slater & Company were the Toronto agents of the creditors, and it was through these agents that all the orders were obtained.

On September 23, 1923, the debtor company made an authorized assignment and the creditors filed with the trustee the usual declaration proving their claim. The trustee admitted the claim, excepting as to any amount the creditors were claiming damages for, because of the insolvent company's failure to take delivery of the goods as ordered.

The facts and terms of the contracts are not in dispute. The goods were to be paid for, net 60 days from date of invoice.

One of the conditions in all the contracts reads:

If any payment is in arrear, either under this or any other contract, deliveries may be suspended or contract cancelled at our option.

The purchasers confirmed all the contracts in these words:

To Bever & Wolf: We have received your contract dated ... and we hereby accept and confirm.

> Yours Truly,
> (Sgd.) Thomson Knitting Co. Ltd.

The creditors now claim £675-16-5, as damages by reason of the insolvent company's failure to take delivery.

Counsel for both parties agreed that if it was found the creditors were entitled to any damages for breach of contract, they would agree on the *quantum* of damages.

Slater was the only witness called on behalf of the creditors, and he swore that the only reason deliveries were not made was because the insolvent company was unable to make payments for the goods already sold and delivered and for the goods they subsequently requisitioned under their contracts. All the correspondence, excepting that referred to in Exs. (1) (2) (3) (4) (5) and (6), was put in as Ex. (7).

From the correspondence it appears the purchasers were endeavouring, through Slater & Company, to obtain deliveries, and Slater communicated with the vendors. The correspondence indicates the purchasers were always hard-pressed for money. Slater & Company at one time were satisfied the company was in a position to pay and so communicated to the vendors. Slater & Company went even so far as to become personally responsible for a portion of some of the deliveries. They also obtained the personal guarantee of the directors of the debtor company and forwarded it to the vendors; Slater & Company agreeing to be personally responsible, and the guarantee, relieved the situation somewhat, but the vendors were not satisfied with the guarantee and so stated in the correspondence, because there was too much money owing.

It is only necessary to refer to a few of the letters to show the readiness on the part of the vendors to deliver and the desire on the part of the purchasers to obtain delivery and the inability on their part to pay.

• • •

The learned counsel for the trustee does not attack the contracts but contends that as the contracts called for delivery at certain stated periods, if there is any liability, it is at the time a delivery was to be made; that failure by the purchasers to pay does not relieve the vendors from the necessity of delivering, and that, whilst the vendors, on failure to pay, could have cancelled the contracts, not having done so there can now be no claim for damages; that the vendors cannot say "we will refuse delivery" and then claim damages for failure to pay; that the vendors having elected to retain the goods cannot now come into competition, on a claim for damages, with those creditors who had sold and delivered goods to the purchaser and were unpaid when they became insolvent, and that in any event, even if there was a failure to pay, it was the duty of the vendors, if they wished to hold the purchasers liable in damages for breach of contract, to have tendered the goods.

The learned counsel for the vendors contends that as they had not cancelled the contracts, and as they had kept in stock goods for the purpose of fulfilling the contracts when the purchasers called for deliveries, they are entitled to damages for breach of the contracts as of the date of its cancellation.

The questions for determination are: Are these creditors entitled to any damages; and if so, at what time is the damage to be ascertained?

The trustee's contention that the vendors' refusal to make deliveries operated as a rescission of the contracts is not borne out by the facts, as the correspondence clearly indicates there never was any intimation by the purchasers they would and could not pay, but on the contrary the purchasers were repeatedly calling for deliveries, making occasional payments and promising to pay, and as I have stated there was always readiness on the part of the vendors to deliver if payments were made. All the circumstances point to an intention on the part of both vendors and purchasers to have the contract continued. There was only a suspension of deliveries, and I hold the contract was not cancelled, and on these findings *Morgan v. Bain* (1874), LR 10 CP 15, 44 LJCP 47, 31 LT 616, 23 WR 239, relied on by counsel for the trustee, has no application.

A vendor is entitled to consider his contract cancelled on the insolvency of the purchaser if the trustee within a reasonable time after his appointment fails to notify the vendor he intends to adopt the contract, and a reasonable time, in my opinion, would be after the first meeting of creditors, as there is no one, until that meeting is called, authorized to act for the debtor. If a trustee remains silent a vendor is entitled to assume the contract is at an end.

The trustee in this case did not notify the vendors he intended to carry out the contract, and I therefore hold, if the vendors can prove any damages, they will be measured as of the date of the first meeting of creditors.

The law is well settled that a contract for the purchase of goods is not cancelled merely on account of the purchaser becoming bankrupt; see *Boorman v. Nash* (1829), B & C 145, 7 LJKB 150; *Griffiths v. Perry* (1859) 1 E & E 680, 28 LFQB 214, 5 Jur. (NS) 1076. It seems to me the terms of the contracts must govern. The vendors expressly provided, if payments were in arrear for two separate and distinct contingencies, namely, at their option (1) suspension of deliveries and (2) cancellation of their contracts. They could adopt either. The purchasers made their first default under the contracts on or about January 14, 1924, and according to the correspondence, at the solicitation of the purchasers, several deliveries were subsequently made and payments on account received from time to time. The vendors did not know the purchasers were going into insolvency, and they had a right to believe they might be able to pay for the goods purchased, and in order that they could make deliveries instead of cancelling the contracts kept them alive. The purchasers at any time up to the insolvency, if they could have provided for payment of the money, the contracts not having been cancelled, could have compelled the vendors to deliver all the goods covered by the contracts. But the evidence in this case is that the purchasers did not want the contracts cancelled, on the contrary they wanted them continued.

This is not a case where there was only one default by the purchasers (they were always in default) but rather that of a case where the sellers were ready and willing to deliver and were anxious for the buyers to take delivery. There was no object in the vendors tendering the goods, as default had already been made, and the correspondence shows the purchasers could not pay. In such circumstances the vendors were not bound to tender deliveries. See *Ex parte Chalmers; In re Edwards* (1873), LR 8 Ch. 289, 42 LJ Bk. 37, 28 LT 325, 21 WR 349, and at p. 291, Mellish LJ, said:

> The first question that arises is, what are the rights of the seller of goods when the purchaser becomes insolvent before the contract for sale has been completely performed. I am of opinion that the result of the authorities is this—that in such a case the seller, notwithstanding he may have agreed to allow credit for the goods, is not bound to deliver any more goods under the contract until the price of the goods not yet delivered is tendered to him; and that, if a debt is due to him for goods already delivered, he is entitled to refuse to deliver any more till he is paid the debt due for those already delivered as well as the price of those still to be delivered.

And at p. 293:

> I am, therefore, of opinion that, in the present case, when the insolvency of the purchaser had been declared the vendor was not bound to deliver any more goods until the price of the goods delivered in November, as well as those which were to be delivered in December, had been tendered to him.

• • •

There must be a finding that these contracts were outstanding and uncancelled at the date of the debtor company's bankruptcy; and, as the trustee refused to take them over and accept delivery of the goods, there will be judgment in favor of the creditors, and the damages, if any, will be measured as of the date of the first meeting of creditors.

• • •

Judgment for creditors.

Creditel of Canada Ltd. v. Terrace Corp.
(1983), 4 DLR (4th) 49 (Alta. CA)

BELZIL JA: The appellants appeal a judgment against them for $11,991 and costs.

The plaintiff's action in its final form as amended at trial alleged a debt owing by the appellant to Formex Ltd. The debt is alleged to have been assigned by Formex Ltd. to Formex Location Rental Inc., and by the latter to the present respondent, Creditel of Canada Ltd., on October 1, 1980. The assignment from Formex Location to Creditel filed as an exhibit at trial was an assignment of an account or debt receivable. Notwithstanding that the action was pleaded in debt, the judgment awarded was for damages for breach of contract, without amendment of the pleading to fit the evidence. This discrepancy between the award of damages and the pleading in debt was raised before us but apparently not before the trial judge. ...

The assignment from Formex Ltd. to Location Formex Rental Inc. was not filed as an exhibit. It appears from the evidence of Norbert Dubois, an officer of both corporations, that Location Formex Rental Inc. was entirely owned by Formex Ltd., that Formex Ltd. went into bankruptcy on February 23, 1978, and that Formex Location Rental Inc. bought all the assets of Formex Ltd. on September 19, 1979, presumably from a trustee in bankruptcy, although that is not indicated in evidence.

The debt sued for is alleged to be due under an agreement for the fabrication and sale by Formex Ltd. to the appellants of three metal forms for the moulding of pre-cast concrete construction panels for a building being undertaken by the appellants in Edmonton. The trial judge found, correctly on the evidence, that there was one contract for the three forms. That contract is evidenced by quotation from Formex Ltd. submitted to and accepted by the appellants for fabrication of the units as per the appellants' design.

The first two units required modification of the design at extra cost. Responsibility for the additional cost was settled amicably by the parties and the two first units so modified were delivered and likewise specified by the appellants, over and above the modifications made to the first two units. Formex Ltd. sent a quotation to the appellants covering those extra modifications and requested approval of the extra costs by issuance of a supplementary purchase order. The appellants did not formally respond to this request, although it is indicated in evidence that there were telephone consultations between the parties. On February 13, 1978, Formex Ltd. sent a telegram to the appellants reaffirming its quotation for the modified third unit and again requesting a purchase order to cover. On February 27, 1978, Formex Ltd. sent a follow-up telegram to the appellants advising that work on the unit was being delayed pending advice from the appellants. The appellants did not respond because in the meantime they had received information from an employee of Formex Ltd. that Formex Ltd. was in bankruptcy. The trial judge found that the action of Formex Ltd. in delaying completion of the work on the third unit did not amount to a breach disentitling it to payment for work already done on the unit. He attributed fault to the appellants for having failed to supply a purchase order as requested. He awarded judgment to the value of the work done by Formex Ltd. on the third unit.

While the learned trial judge did not specifically qualify the award as one in damages, it obviously must have been so intended. It could not be for the contract debt since the contract remained uncompleted. It could only succeed in damages or *quantum meruit* and then only if the appellants had repudiated the contract by failing to furnish a new purchase order in acceptance of the quotation of Formex Ltd.

The learned trial judge did not take into account the effect on the contract of the bankruptcy of Formex Ltd. That effect is stated concisely as follows in *Re Thomson Knitting Co. Ltd., Ex p. Bever & Wolf*, [1925] 2 DLR 1007 at p. 1008, 56 OLR 625 at p. 631, 5 CBR 489:

> While the bankruptcy did not of itself constitute a breach of the contract, it did not on the other hand cast any further burden upon the vendors. But it had this effect: it entitled the vendors to treat the contract as broken if the trustee did not, within a reasonable time, approbate the contract and call for its completion.

In *Emden and Watson's Building Contracts and Practice*, 6th ed. (1962), the proposition is stated as follows at p. 220:

> *Rights which Pass to Trustee*—Ordinarily the benefits and rights under contracts which would pass as part of the bankrupt's personal estate to his personal representatives if he had died, pass to

the trustee as part of the bankrupt's property, subject to the trustee's right to disclaim unprofitable contracts ...

Election to Perform or Disclaim—As regards those contracts which the trustee can perform, he has an election and may disclaim them, in which cases the persons who have contracted with the bankrupt may prove in the bankruptcy for damages to the value of any injury sustained by them, or the trustee may insist on the contract being performed, and in such case must perform the bankrupt's part of the contract, as and when the bankrupt should have done so himself.

There is no evidence to show that an election to perform was ever made by the trustee in bankruptcy, and certainly no evidence that such an election was ever communicated to the appellants. The issue was never addressed at trial. In these circumstances, the appellants could not be found in breach of the contract for their failure to issue a purchase order to the bankrupt vendor after learning of the bankruptcy. No case was made out by the plaintiff to support an award either in damages or in debt.

Appeal allowed.

Landlord and Tenant Act
RSO 1990, c. L.7, ss. 38, 39

38(1) In case of an assignment for the general benefit of creditors, or an order being made for the winding up of an incorporated company, or where a receiving order in bankruptcy or authorized assignment has been made by or against a tenant, the preferential lien of the landlord for rent is restricted to the arrears of rent due during the period of three months next preceding, and for three months following the execution of the assignment, and from thence so long as the assignee retains possession of the premises, but any payment to be made to the landlord in respect of accelerated rent shall be credited against the amount payable by the person who is assignee, liquidator or trustee for the period of the person's occupation. RSO 1980, c. 232, s. 38(1).

(2) Despite any provision, stipulation or agreement in any lease or agreement or the legal effect thereof, in case of an assignment for the general benefit of creditors, or an order being made for the winding up of an incorporated company, or where a receiving order in bankruptcy or authorized assignment has been made by or against a tenant, the person who is assignee, liquidator or trustee may at any time within three months thereafter for the purposes of the trust estate and before the person has given notice of intention to surrender possession or disclaim, by notice in writing elect to retain the leased premises for the whole or any portion of the unexpired term and any renewal thereof, upon the terms of the lease and subject to the payment of the rent as provided by the lease or agreement, and the person may, upon payment to the landlord of all arrears of rent, assign the lease with rights of renewal, if any, to any person who will covenant to observe and perform its terms and agree to conduct upon the demised premises a trade or business which is not reasonably of a more objectionable or hazardous nature than that which was thereon conducted by the debtor, and who on application of the assignee, liquidator or trustee, is approved by a judge of the Ontario Court (General Division) as a person fit and proper to be put in possession of the leased premises. RSO 1980, c. 232, s. 38(2), *revised.*

39(1) The person who is assignee, liquidator or trustee has the further right, at any time before so electing, by notice in writing to the landlord, to surrender possession or disclaim any such lease, and the person's entry into possession of the leased premises and their occupation by the person, while required for the purposes of the trust estate, shall not be deemed to be evidence of an intention on the person's part to elect to retain possession under section 38.

(2) Where the assignor, or person or firm against whom a receiving order has been made in bankruptcy, or a winding up order has been made, being a lessee, has, before the making of the assignment or such order demised any premises by way of under-lease, approved or consented to in writing by the landlord, and the assignee, liquidator or trustee surrenders, disclaims or elects to assign the lease, the under-lessee, if the under-lessee so elects in writing within three months of such assignment or order, stands in the same position with the landlord as though the under-lessee were a direct lessee from the landlord but subject, except as to rental payable, to the same liabilities and obligations as the assignor, bankrupt or insolvent company was subject to under the lease at the date of the assignment or order, but the under-lessee shall in such event be required to covenant to pay to the landlord a rental not less than that payable by the under-lessee to the debtor, and if such last mentioned rental was greater than that payable by the debtor to the said landlord, the under-lessee shall be required to covenant to pay to the landlord the like greater rental. RSO 1980, c. 232, s. 39(1, 2).

(3) In the event of any dispute arising under this section or section 38, the dispute shall be disposed of by a judge of the Ontario Court (General Division) upon an application. RSO 1980, c. 232, s. 39(3), *revised*.

Re Limestone Electrical & Supply Co. Ltd.
[1955] OR 291 (Ont. CA)

LAIDLAW JA: This is an appeal by the landlord of certain premises known as 255 Bagot Street in the city of Kingston, from an order made by Barlow J on 25th June 1954 in chambers, under the provisions of s. 37(2) of The Landlord and Tenant Act, RSO 1950, c. 199, whereby Ronald M. Grant was approved as a fit and proper person to be put in possession of the premises. Leave to appeal to this Court was granted by order of Wells J dated the 21st September 1954.

The appellant leased the premises to Clarkson Electrical Company Limited on the terms and under the provisions set forth in two documents dated the 31st December 1946 and the 29th August 1949. The name Clarkson Electrical Company Limited was subsequently changed to Limestone Electrical & Supply Co. Limited.

On the 3rd March 1954 Limestone Electrical & Supply Co. Limited made an assignment pursuant to The Bankruptcy Act, RSC 1952, c. 14, and the respondent The Canadian Credit Men's Trust Association Limited was duly appointed as trustee of the estate of the bankrupt.

The manager of the business carried on by Limestone Electrical & Supply Co. Limited for the period from 6th July 1953 until the appointment of the respondent as trustee of the estate of the bankrupt was Ronald M. Grant. On 20th April 1954 Mr. Grant made an offer in writing to purchase from the trustee the assets of the bankrupt. That offer included the following provision: "It is a condition of my agreement to purchase that you assign to me all the right, title and interest of the estate but without warranty or condition in a lease or licence or leases or licences covering premises known as 255 Bagot Street. ..."

On the 6th May 1954 the appellant received from the respondent a notice in writing, pursuant to s. 37(2) of The Landlord and Tenant Act, dated the 30th April 1954, whereby the trustee elected "to retain for the whole or any portion of the unexpired terms and any renewals thereof" the two leases made by the appellant to Clarkson Electrical Company Limited.

By an indenture dated "the   day of May, AD 1954" the trustee and the inspectors of the estate and Ronald M. Grant made an agreement wherein the two leases mentioned above were made exhibits, and it was recited, *inter alia*, that "the Assignor as Trustee in bankruptcy of Limestone Electrical & Supply Co. Limited has elected to retain the aforesaid leased premises for the whole or any portion of the unexpired terms and any renewals thereof," pursuant to s. 37(2) of The Landlord and Tenant Act; that Grant (described in the indenture as "the Assignee") "has offered to purchase from the ... Trustee assets of the estate of the said Limestone Electrical & Supply Co. Limited conditional upon the Assignor assigning to the Assignee all the right, title and interest of Limestone Electrical & Supply Co. Limited in the said lease;" that the assignee covenants to observe and perform the terms of the leases; that "the Assignee agrees to conduct upon the demised premises a trade or business which is not reasonably of a more objectionable or hazardous nature than that which was thereon conducted by the said Limestone Electrical & Supply Co. Limited;" and that the trustee "is desirous of accepting the said offer to purchase and of assigning the said lease." The indenture then sets forth that the trustee assigns to Ronald M. Grant the leased premises, together with the residue unexpired of the term of years in the leases, and after covenants and agreements on the part of the assignee the indenture contains the following provision:

It is expressly understood and agreed that this Indenture and everything herein contained is subject to and conditional upon approval of the Assignee by a Judge of the Supreme Court of Ontario as a person fit and proper to be put in possession of the leased premises aforesaid.

On the 8th June 1954 the respondent trustee served a notice of motion for an order approving Ronald M. Grant as a person fit and proper to be put in possession of the premises, and the order now in appeal was made by Barlow J.

It appears that Mr. Grant was permitted by the trustee to occupy the premises from and after the 23rd April 1954, and he conducted thereon the same business formerly carried on by the bankrupt company. On or about the 30th April he sent to the appellant a cheque for rent for the month of May. The cheque was returned to Mr. Grant with a letter advising him that he was not recognized by the landlord as a tenant and that he was illegally in possession of the premises. On the 3rd June 1954 Mr. Grant again forwarded a cheque to the landlord for rental, and it was again returned to him with the same advice.

The submissions made to this Court by counsel on behalf of the appellant are:

(a) That Section 37(2) of The Landlord and Tenant Act ... is an interference with contractual rights of a landlord and must be strictly construed.

(b) That before an assignee of a lease from a Trustee can be put in possession of the demised premises, the Trustee must elect to retain the demised premises and obtain an order from a Judge of the Supreme Court of Ontario approving of the proposed assignee as a fit and proper person to be put in possession of the demised premises.

(c) On the date the Trustee purported to elect to "retain" the premises the Trustee had already delivered possession to Grant as tenant.

(d) The order appealed from herein provides for the approval of Grant "as a fit and proper person to be put in possession of the premises." The Trustee had put Grant in possession of the premises approximately two months prior to the making of the order.

(e) There is an onus on the applicant to satisfy the Court that Grant is a fit and proper person to be put in possession and there is no evidence of any nature whatsoever in the material filed dealing with the fitness of Grant.

I shall first reproduce s. 37(2) of The Landlord and Tenant Act: [see supra, RSO 1990, c. L-7, s. 38(2)].

That subsection has a twofold purpose and effect. It creates certain rights of an assignee, liquidator or trustee of a bankrupt estate. It also prescribes the procedure and requisites for the acquisition and exercise of such rights. Thus it makes available the following rights to an assignee, liquidator or trustee:

1. To retain leased premises for the purpose of the trust estate for a period of three months after an assignment for the general benefit of creditors, or an order for the winding up of a bankrupt company, or where a receiving order in bankruptcy or authorized assignment has been made by or against a tenant.

2. To retain the leased premises for the whole or any portion of the unexpired term of a lease and any renewal thereof.

3. To assign the lease with rights of renewal, if any.

The procedure and requisites for the acquisition and exercise of the rights created by the subsection, and as prescribed therein, are these:

1. The right to retain the leased premises for the period of three months described above does not depend upon any condition or stipulation, but is unqualified and unconditional.

2. In order to acquire the right to retain the leased premises for any period after the expiration of the three months described above, it is essential to comply with the following statutory requirements:

(a) that the assignee, liquidator or trustee elect by notice in writing to retain the leased premises for the whole or any portion of the unexpired term and any renewal thereof, upon the terms of the lease and subject to the payment of the rent as provided therein;

(b) that such notice be given by the assignee, liquidator or trustee within the period of three months;

(c) that the notice be given before the assignee, liquidator or trustee has given notice of intention to surrender possession or disclaim.

3. If the assignee, liquidator or trustee desires to exercise the right given to him by the subsection to assign the lease with rights of renewal, if any, he is required:

(a) to pay to the landlord all arrears of rent;

(b) to obtain from the proposed assignee (i) a covenant to observe its terms and (ii) an agreement to conduct upon the demised premises a trade or business which is not reasonably of a more objectionable or hazardous nature than that which was thereon conducted by the debtor; and

(c) to make an application to a judge of the Supreme Court for approval of the proposed assignee "as a person fit and proper to be put in possession of the leased premises."

I suppose that s. 37(2) may be properly regarded as an interference with the contractual rights of a landlord, but, be that as it may, I am certain that the assignee, liquidator or trustee must follow the procedure and fulfil the requirements of the subsection before he can acquire the rights available to him thereunder. It is clear in my mind that he has no right in law to transfer or assign to any person any right of possession to the leased premises except in the manner prescribed by the subsection, and upon compliance with the provisions thereof. Thus, if he proposes to retain the leased premises for the whole or any portion of the unexpired term after the expiration of the three months' period described above, and to assign the lease with rights of renewal, if any, he must first give notice in writing within the prescribed time of his election to retain the premises. After he has complied with that requirement, he must follow the procedure and satisfy the further stipulated requirements to exercise the right given by the subsection to assign the lease.

It is argued on behalf of the appellant that the trustee delivered possession of the premises to Ronald M. Grant on or about 23rd April 1954, and could not afterwards elect to retain the premises or assign the leases. Prior to that time the trustee was in possession by virtue of a statutory right and it had no authority or power to transfer a right of possession to any person in any manner otherwise than as prescribed by the statute and subject to the requirements therein. It could not give Grant a lawful right of possession at that time, and Grant did not then obtain such a right of possession from the trustee. Moreover, it seems plain to me that neither Grant nor the trustee intended that Grant should have a lawful right of possession until both parties had done all that was required by s. 37(2). The indenture made "the   day of May, AD 1954," recited that the trustee had elected to retain the leased premises pursuant to s. 37(2) of The Landlord and Tenant Act. It contained the covenant and agreement required by that subsection on the part of the proposed assignee of the lease, and it was understood and agreed by all parties that the indenture and everything contained in it was subject to and conditional upon approval of the assignee by a judge of the Supreme Court of Ontario as required by the subsection.

Neither the agreement for the purchase of the assets of the bankrupt by Grant nor the assignment of the leases to him with the right of possession thereunder came into force or had binding effect unless and until the trustee had taken the necessary steps under the subsection and obtained the required approval of Grant as an assignee of the leases. It is my opinion that the premises continued at all times after the assignment on 3rd March 1954 to be in possession of the trustee, and although Grant had *de facto* occupation of the premises, the possession and right to possession of them remained in the trustee pending the completion of the transaction between the parties.

Counsel emphasized the fact that Grant sent cheques to the landlord for rent for the months of May and June, and that the landlord returned the cheques and refused to recognize Grant as a tenant. There was no relation of landlord and tenant as between the appellant and Grant, and the landlord was quite right in refusing to do anything that might be deemed a recognition of such a relation. The rent for those months was payable to the landlord by the trustee, who was lawfully in possession of the premises. It may be that Grant was simply acting as an agent for the trustee in seeking to make the payments of rent, but, be that as it may, he was not a tenant of the appellant at that time.

Counsel for the appellant argued that "there is no evidence of any nature whatsoever in the material filed dealing with the fitness of Grant." I cannot agree. There was evidence before Barlow J that Grant had made a payment of $1,414 by certified cheque on account of the purchase of the business and that he had undertaken to pay the balance of the purchase-price within five days after acceptance of the offer made by him to the trustee. He had entered into the covenant and agreement required by the statute, and it may properly be assumed that the trustee satisfied itself before deciding to accept the offer and to make a sale to him that he was able to carry out the obligations assumed by him. I think there was evidence from which the learned judge could properly decide that Grant was a fit and proper person to be put in possession of the leased premises. The burden was on the applicant to satisfy the learned judge in respect of that fact, and when the learned judge has stated that he was so satisfied and there is some evidence to support his conclusion, I am not willing to say that he was wrong.

Appeal dismissed.

Re Darrigo Consolidated Holdings
(1987), 63 CBR 216 (Ont. SC)

EBERLE J: There appear to be two issues for resolution in connection with the application, which is brought under s. 38(2) of the Landlord and Tenant Act for approval of the court to certain proposed assignments of leases by the trustee in bankruptcy. There were six properties in issue, six store properties. I understand from counsel that three of them have been resolved; a fourth is on the way to resolution, and an adjournment of it is requested, although perhaps the matter may be resolved before the end of today; but as to the remaining two, there are issues.

These two are two stores located at 900 St. Clair Avenue, and 2715 Lawrence Avenue. The landlords of those two properties oppose giving of the court's approval. Two issues appear to be, first a procedural one, and secondly a substantive one. The procedural one is this. It is said by the landlords s. 38(2) requires that, before even launching an application for approval of the court to a proposed assignment, the trustee in bankruptcy must elect in writing to retain the balance of the lease terms. That submission is based on what was said in *Re Limestone Elec. & Supply Co.*, [1955] OR 291, 35 CBR 20, [1955] 3 DLR 104. It is a decision of the Ontario Court of Appeal, and it is one which concerns me. It is there stated with considerable clarity that the first step must be a written election by the trustee to retain the lease term to be followed then, if such be the facts, by an application to the court for approval of an assignment. That is not the sequence of events in this case.

In this case, the trustee has brought this application without making any such election. He proposes that the order he seeks be made upon condition that the trustee give the necessary notice of election to retain. The statute, it is to be noted, requires that that notice be given within three months of the bankruptcy. That three-month period will expire 4th February next.

As I have said, the procedure, as laid out in the *Limestone* case, concerns me. However, I am satisfied that what was there said about the sequence of these events was not necessary for the decision in that case, and I think, with the greatest of respect, that it is time for a reconsideration.

Undoubtedly, the provisions of s. 38(2) were established for the purpose of protecting and balancing the rights of the several parties who may be involved in such a procedure. I confess, however, that I am unable to see any harm or prejudice to any conceivable party in the trustee seeking approval first. I can see no merit in requiring the trustee first to commit himself and the bankrupt estate to taking over the balance of a lease without having assurance that an assignment may be carried through. I can, on the other hand, see considerable dangers and disadvantages to the bankrupt estate in requiring the sequence of events to be as indicated in the *Limestone* case.

Looking at the present case, I can see no harm whatever to the landlords in the sequence of events proposed in the present case, nor can I see that sequence of events can be likely to have any prejudicial effect upon any party in other matters brought under s. 38(2). I am satisfied that the intention of the requirements set out in s. 38(2) is adequately and properly met by allowing the trustee to seek the court's approval before committing himself and/or the estate to taking over the balance of a lease. However, it goes without question that any approval that may be granted must be conditional upon the trustee giving the appropriate notice, or by some other means ensuring that that part of s. 38(2) will indeed be complied with, and that in its absence there will be no approval. I can see no difficulty in devising appropriate means to accomplish such a result.

Accordingly, in the present case, I hold that the procedure adopted by the trustee does not create any infirmity, nor that the present application is premature. If approval is given it will be conditional upon the trustee giving the appropriate notice in writing to retain the lease and of his election to do so within the limitation period of three months prescribed by s. 38(2).

I turn now to the second objection, which is a substantive one. It is based upon the unsuitability and, particularly, the financial unsuitability of the proposed assignees. Specifically the landlords ask for security, such as by way of a bank letter of credit for the balance of the rental payments which will fall due to them under the two leases in question. Counsel relies for this request upon the decision in *Re FigurMagic Int. Ltd.* (1974), 19 CBR (NS) 310 (Ont. Div. Ct.), where it appears that some security or prepayment of at least part of the balance of the rent was provided for.

I think that the present case should be regarded on the basis of what was said in *Re Griff and Sommerset Mgmt. Services Ltd.* (1978), 19 OR (2d) 209, 26 CBR (NS) 205, 4 BLR 72, 3 RPR 225 (sub nom. *Re Sommerset Mgmt. Services and Yolles Furniture Co.; Re Yolles Furniture Co. (Ont.) and Modernage Furniture Ltd.*), 84 DLR (3d) 386 (CA), concerning the factors which should be considered by a judge asked to approve an assignment of a lease under s. 38(2).

At pp. 219-20 [OR], and continuing on to 221, certain factors are prescribed for the court's consideration. I regard what the court there said about those factors as meaning that they are to be considered in sum, and that, weighing all of them together, approval should or should not be granted, according to the case. I do not read what is said by the court on this subject to have established each of the elements or factors as a precondition to the granting of approval. The operation, as I see it, is a weighing of the various elements.

When one looks at the facts of this case, it is quite clear that the financial position of the proposed assignees is not as sound as many would like it to be. The proposed assignees are incorporated companies which were only recently incorporated and have no business history. The principal behind all of them is Hilda Darrigo, the wife of one of the former partners, and I use that term not in any legal sense, in the Darrigo business. The two brothers have, I am told, had a substantial falling out, and must be very much at loggerheads, for it is said that that produced the bankruptcy. It appears that relations within the family are no better now than they were at the time of the bankruptcy. Mrs. Darrigo, it is said, had some connection with the business before the bankruptcy, although I gather it was not an extensive connection. Her husband has been retained as a consultant on behalf of the assignees if they should obtain the businesses.

The material discloses that the tender made by Hilda Darrigo is the best tender, well above any other, and that among those others was a tender by the other Darrigo brother. The material also discloses that the prices tendered by Mrs. Darrigo are for a going business, and that they are prices and amounts which total well above the break-up value of the assets, if they were to be sold on that basis.

It must be to the benefit of the creditors of the bankrupt company, and particularly the unsecured creditors, that the businesses be disposed of on a going concern basis, and, in any event, that the maximum return be obtained on disposition. It is to be observed that the sale of the businesses on a going concern basis has already received an approval by the court by order made 18th December 1986, which approved the acceptance by the receiver and manager of the property of an offer or offers made by Mrs. Darrigo in trust for company or companies to be incorporated. Such an order does not, of course, render unnecessary the application presently made. However, a refusal of approval of the present application would nullify that part of the order of 18th December 1986.

The landlords' concern at the present time is with respect to the rental payments that would accrue to them during the balance of the two leases. It appears to be clear, however, that if there is default in payment of any of those rental payments the landlords will have their usual remedies, including retaking possession of the property. It is suggested that that may not be as easy in this case, as it might be in some other case, because of the family dispute, and because of the fact that, with respect to each of the properties in this case, the landlord is owned by the wives of the two feuding brothers. In view of the time limit imposed by s. 38(2) upon the trustee electing to retain the leases, it seems to me there is a reasonable probability that, if the present application is not granted, there will be no assignment of the leases, and no recovery of money with respect to these two properties on a going concern basis, and on 4th February the landlords will be entitled to take over these two properties. Whatever difficulty may exist in the future about retaking possession of the properties will certainly exist on 4th February.

In other words, I can see little difference in the landlords' position whether the present application is granted or not. And particularly, I am unable to see any real prejudice to the landlords by the granting of the application. It appears to me that to give the landlords full security, such as by a bank letter of credit, for future rent payments, is to give them a security and an advantage which they do not presently possess. I have been referred to no authority with the possible exception of the *FigurMagic* case, where such an improvement in the landlord's position is mandated, and I am unaware of any ground in principle why the landlord's position should be better upon an assignment subject to a bankruptcy than it was prior to the bankruptcy.

In this case, the interests of the creditors are important, and particularly those of the unsecured creditors. In view of the shortness of time remaining out of the three months, it is most unlikely that any other assignee can be found and the necessary approvals obtained; and that, accordingly, if the present application is refused, there will be a substantial deterioration in the position of the unsecured creditors as compared to their position, if the application is granted.

Accordingly, the best conclusion that I can come to, in endeavouring to consider the interests of the landlords, and of the unsecured creditors, is that the application should be granted.

I referred earlier to the weaknesses in the assignees' financial position, and I keep them in mind. Nevertheless, that is but one of the factors to be considered. I consider as well the other factors mentioned in *Re Griff and Sommerset Mgmt. Services Ltd.* The business reputation of the assignees in the present circumstances is practically non-existent in a technical sense. However, on the other hand, there is the connection of Mrs. Darrigo herself, and of her husband, who has, it need hardly be said, had considerable experience in operating this kind of business. There is no change in the use of the premises. I am satisfied that the facts in evidence establish a reasonable motivation and a reasonable ability on the part of the assignees to honour their covenants, and I see a considerable advantage to the unsecured creditors, without any significant disadvantage, if indeed there is any disadvantage, to the landlords at all.

• • •

Application granted.

Re Vrablik
(1993), 17 CBR (3d) 154 (Ont.)

MALONEY J: This is a motion brought by the Trustee in this bankruptcy for:

1. An Order of the Court determining whether the contingent claim of Donald Raymond Stasiuk, Kathryn Marta Stasiuk, Andrew Findlay Coffey, Roberta Joan Coffey and 705514 Ontario Limited is a provable claim;

2. If the contingent claim is a provable claim then, an Order of the Court valuing the claim;

The reason for the bringing of the motion is that the above-named landlords of the bankrupt tenant are claiming damages in lieu of payments which would otherwise be due under the portion of the lease as yet unexpired at the time of the assignment in bankruptcy made by the tenant on November 16th, 1989.

On June 10, 1988 Melanie Vrablik (the "Tenant") entered into a commercial lease with Donald Raymond Stasiuk, Kathryn Marta Stasiuk, Andrew Findlay Coffey, Roberta Joan Coffey and 705514 Ontario Limited (hereinafter referred to as the "Landlord") as the lessor. The tenant had hoped to establish a fitness and exercise salon. The leased premises were known municipally as 104 North Syndicate Avenue in the City of Thunder Bay. The term of the lease was from July 1, 1988 to June 30, 1993. The monthly rental under the lease was $1,606.67. The tenant was responsible for the payment of municipal taxes, hydro, water and maintenance costs as set out in the lease. On November 16, 1989 the Tenant filed an assignment in bankruptcy (Bankruptcy No. 027144), the Trustee in Bankruptcy of the Estate of Melanie Vrablik being Ignit Stetsko (the "Trustee"). The landlord filed Proof of Claim dated December 11, 1989 in the amount of $99,412.59. A portion of this claim was a preferred claim, being the arrears of rent for a period of three months immediately preceding the bankruptcy of the tenant and the accelerated rent for a period of three months following the bankruptcy of the tenant. The Proof of Claim dated December 11, 1989 disclosed a sum of $13,886.09 as the preferred claim. A revised Proof of Claim dated November 22, 1991 filed by the Landlord reduced that sum to $8,167.41. The Proof of Claim dated December 11, 1989 also disclosed that the landlord has advanced a contingent and unliquidated claim in the amount of $85,526.50 based on the damages the landlord alleges it has sustained as a result of the tenant's default under the lease. The revised Proof of Claim dated November 22, 1991 outlines the landlord's unliquidated claim as follows:

(1)	rent from February 16, 1990 to August 1, 1991 at $1,606.67	$28,116.72
(2)	1989 taxes	$2,949.81
(3)	1990 taxes	$4,685.94
(4)	1991 taxes to August 1, 1991	$3,043.64
(5)	maintenance in 1990	$1,121.95
(6)	maintenance in 1991	$839.08
(7)	shortfall on re-letting August 1, 1991 to June 30, 1993	$5,623.44
		$46,380.58

In summary, the Revised Proof of Claim dated November 22, 1991 lists the landlord's preferred claim at $8,167.41 and the unliquidated claim at $46,380.58. Section 38 of the *Landlord and Tenant Act*, RSO 1990, c. L.7 ("*Landlord Tenant Act*") gives a landlord a preferential lien for the arrears of rent due during the period of three months preceding the assignment in bankruptcy and for three months following the execution of the assignment of bankruptcy:

38(1) In case of an assignment for the general benefit of creditors, or an order being made for the winding up of an incorporated company, or where a receiving order in bankruptcy or authorized assignment has been made by or against a tenant, the preferential lien of the landlord for rent is restricted to the arrears of rent due during the period of three months next preceding, and for three months following the execution of the assignment, and from thence so long as the assignee retains possession of the premises, but any payment to be made to the landlord in respect of accelerated rent shall be credited against the amount payable by the person who is assignee, liquidator or trustee for the period of the person's occupation.

Section 136 of the *Bankruptcy Act*, RSC 1985, c. B-3 ("*Bankruptcy Act*") lays out a scheme of distribution of priorities subject to the rights of secured creditors. It is interesting to note that the preferential lien granted to a landlord in s. 38 of the Ontario *Landlord and Tenant Act*, reflects exactly the lien granted by s. 136(1) of the *Bankruptcy Act* and Parliament in its wisdom has ranked this priority sixth behind various other security interests:

136(1) Subject to the rights of secured creditors, the proceeds realized from the property of a bankrupt shall be applied in priority of payment as follows;

• • •

(f) the landlord for arrears of rent for a period of three months immediately preceding the bankruptcy and accelerated rent for a period not exceeding three months following the bankruptcy if entitled thereto under the lease, but the total amount so payable shall not exceed the realization from the property on the premises under lease, and any payment made on account of accelerated rent shall be credited against the amount payable by the trustee for occupation rent;

The preference provided by the *Bankruptcy Act, supra,* is only to the extent of the availability of property of the bankrupt on the premises at the time of the bankruptcy and is subject to the rights of other secured creditors having a higher priority under the *Bankruptcy Act*. The law is quite explicit in designating the Landlord as a preferred creditor compensating him for his vacant premises and in substitution of his right to distrain. This motion is brought on the basis of the combined strength of s. 121 of the *Bankruptcy Act* and Rule 94 of the *Bankruptcy Rules* which state that when an unliquidated claim is made, the Trustee in Bankruptcy must apply to the Court to determine whether or not the claim is provable, and if provable to have the claim valued. Counsel have all agreed that the central issue is whether or not the contingent, unliquidated claim is provable.

Upon making an Assignment in Bankruptcy or Receiving Order, all of the obligations and rights of the tenant in the lease vest in the Trustee in Bankruptcy as per s. 71(2) of the *Bankruptcy Act*:

71(2) On a receiving order being made or an assignment being filed with an official receiver, a bankrupt ceases to have any capacity to dispose of or otherwise deal with his property, which shall, subject to this Act and to the rights of secured creditors, forthwith pass to and vest in the trustee named in the receiving order or assignment, and in any case of change of trustee the property shall pass from trustee to trustee without any conveyance, assignment or transfer.

The Trustee in Bankruptcy has the right for a period of up to three months from the date of bankruptcy in which to elect whether to retain, assign, surrender or disclaim the lease as per s. 38(2) of the *Landlord Tenant Act* [see *supra*].

The Trustee in this case decided to disclaim and surrendered the lease in question to the landlord on December 11, 1989. Upon this action on the part of the Trustee, all rights and obligations of the Trustee under the lease are terminated as of the effective date of the disclaimer or surrender.

Counsel for the landlord in this matter argues that the landlord possesses a valid claim against the tenant or Trustee for amounts falling due *after* the date of the surrender or disclaimer of the lease. He relies upon the 1971 Supreme Court of Canada decision in *Highway Properties Ltd. v. Kelly, Douglas & Co.*, [1971] SCR 562, 17 DLR (3d) 710 (*"Highway Properties"*) for this proposition. In that case, a major tenant in a shopping centre repudiated an unexpired lease. The landlord resumed possession of the premises and gave notice to the defaulting tenant that it would be held liable for damages suffered by the landlord as a result of the admittedly wrongful repudiation. In deciding whether or not to allow the damages, Laskin J, as he then was, considered the various options open to a landlord when faced with a repudiation of a lease:

1. The landlord may refuse to accept the repudiation of the lease by the tenant. Nothing is done to alter the landlord-tenant relationship. The landlord simply insists on the performance of the terms of the lease and sues for rent or damages as they accrue on the basis that the lease remains in force.

2. The landlord may elect to terminate the lease and retake possession of the premises. In this case, the landlord may sue for rent accrued due, or for damages to the date of termination for previous breaches of the covenant. The landlord may not sue for prospective damages because it is a principle of common law that once the lease is terminated, all obligations under the lease cease to exist.

3. The landlord may advise the tenant that he refuses to accept the repudiation of the lease but that he proposes to re-enter the premises and, unless otherwise directed by tenant, relet the property *on the tenant's behalf* and hold the original tenant liable for any deficiency in rental for the balance of the lease term.

Noting the increasing intermingling of property law with contract law in the area of leasehold estates in land, Laskin J recognized the common law principle that a lease of land for a term of years, under which possession is taken, creates an estate in land. In many situations legislation or a strict literal reading of contractual terms have superseded the common law, for example, the provision of payment of rent in advance, and the provision of re-entry for non-payment of rent or for breaches of other covenants by the tenant. For some reason the courts had stopped short in refusing to apply to leasehold estates in land the contractual doctrine of anticipatory breach and its accompanying principle governing relief upon repudiation of contract. On p. 716 [DLR] he continues after noting that this doctrine has been applied without question to contracts for the sale of land:

I think it is equally open to consider its application to a contractual lease, although the lease is partly executed. Its anticipatory feature lies, of course, in the fact that instalments of rent are payable for future periods, and repudiation of the lease raises the question whether an immediate remedy covering the loss of such rent and of other advantages extending over the unexpired term of the lease may be pursued notwithstanding that the estate in the land may have been terminated.

In allowing a new, fourth alternative—the right of the landlord to sue for prospective damages—Laskin J overruled *Goldhar v. Universal Sections & Mouldings Ltd.* (1963), 36 DLR (2d) 450 (Ont. CA) (*"Goldhar"*). *Goldhar* formulated the doctrine of surrender such that once a lease is terminated, there can be no claim for prospective damages because that claim may only be founded on rights accruing to the tenant under the lease when still alive. Laskin J did not think it fair that, once an election to terminate the lease had been communicated through repudiation, all covenants and potential claims for relief in damages are terminated. At p. 721 [DLR] he made this observation:

> It is no longer sensible to pretend that a commercial lease, such as the one before this Court, is simply a conveyance and not also a contract. It is equally untenable to persist in denying resort to the full armoury of remedies ordinarily available to redress repudiation of covenants, merely because the covenants may be associated with an estate in land.

Counsel for the Landlord has urged that the analysis and decision in *Highway Properties* be adopted in the present case. This would be a grave error in that the present case involves a bankruptcy, which is quite different from an outright repudiation of contract. A bankruptcy is a final and irreversible situation. In fact the Legislature has foreseen the present situation in that it has very distinctly created a comprehensive scheme for administering the leasehold interests of bankrupt tenants. It is not a coincidence that s. 38 of the *Landlord Tenant Act* reflects almost verbatim s. 136(1)(f) of the federal *Bankruptcy Act*. Section 136(1)(f) outlines the priority of a landlord for arrears and accelerated rent as against other secured and unsecured creditors. When it comes to the rights of the landlord and tenant with regards to the repudiation of the lease contract because of the bankruptcy, s. 146 of the *Bankruptcy Act* refers the parties back to the wording of the appropriate sections of the *Landlord Tenant Act* and not to the common law as counsel for the Trustee has stated:

146. Subject to priority of ranking as provided by section 136 and subject to subsection 73(4) [*right to distrain for arrears of rent*], the rights of landlords shall be determined according to the laws of the province in which the leased premises are situated. [insert added]

It has been argued that the "laws of the province" referred to in s. 146 are the common law as well as the statute law and that in this situation the common law right to sue for prospective damages as outlined in *Highway Properties* should be adopted in this case. Despite this argument, the "laws of the province in which the leased premises are situated" are, of course, ss. 38 and 39 of the *Landlord Tenant Act*. As stated above, the combined effect of the *Bankruptcy Act* and the *Landlord Tenant Act* provides a comprehensive scheme for the administration of the leasehold interest of bankrupt tenants, *Re Limestone Electrical & Supply Co.*, [1955] OR 291 (Ont. CA).

Quite often Trustees in Bankruptcy elect under s. 38(2) to assign the lease with the approval of the Ontario Court (General Division). This is the kinder option for the landlord but it is only possible if an assignor can be found and approved by the Court. In an effort to promote fairness in commercial dealings, Trustees in Bankruptcy have been held personally liable for occupation rent during the time of disposal of the bankrupt's assets where there has been no clear agreement waiving such rights between the landlord and the Trustee, *Sasso v. D & A MacLeod Co.* (1991), 3 OR (3d) 472 (Gen. Div.); *Re Auto Experts Ltd.* (1921), 3 CBR 591 (Ont. CA). Nonetheless, where the Trustee legally disclaims the lease as per s. 39(1) of the *Landlord Tenant Act*, the effect of such a surrender is the same as if the lease had been surrendered with the consent of the lessor: *Re Mussens Ltd.* (1933), 14 CBR 479 (Ont. SC) at p. 482; *Cummer-Yonge Investments Ltd. v. Fagot*, [1965] 2 OR 152 (HC), affirmed [1965] 2 OR 157 (note) (CA); *Titan Warehouse Club Inc. (Trustee of) v. Glenview Corp.* (1988), 67 CBR (NS) 204 (Ont. HC). Any cause of action under the lease that arises against a tenant prior to bankruptcy remains a liability of the tenant and is accordingly, a responsibility of the Trustee as per s. 38(1) of the *Landlord Tenant Act*. However, a claim for rent after bankruptcy is restricted to the statutory three months next following the execution of assignment in bankruptcy or for so long as the Trustee elects to retain possession of the property. This is the law of this province. The landlord's claim for damages is therefore not provable in this bankruptcy and the Trustee's motion is hereby determined accordingly, and I am relieved of the necessity of assessing quantum.

Motion determined;
no assessment of quantum.

QUESTIONS AND NOTES

1) *Re Vrablik* should be compared with the Supreme Court's decision in *In re Gingras Automobile Ltee* (1962), 4 CBR (NS) 123 (SCC). In the latter case, the landlord claimed 3 months' arrears of rent and $1,398.22 for the cost of repairs the landlord was entitled to recover under the terms of the lease. The trustee allowed the first claim but disallowed the second. The landlord relied on the provisions of the (old) Quebec civil code giving him a *privilège* for both claims and on C.C. 1994 ranking a landlord's claim seventh among the claims of competing creditors. The Supreme Court held (1) that s. 95(1)(f) (now s. 136(1)(f)) of the BA exclusively determines the landlord's priority; (2) that s. 105 of the BA (now s. 146) only relates to the validity of the landlord's claim and not to its priority; (3) that a landlord is not a secured creditor for the purposes of s. 2 of the Act; and (4) (*semble*), even if the landlord's *privilège* could be so construed, s. 107(1)(f) inferentially denies it that status.

2) Faced with limited rights of recovery under the BIA and provincial law, landlords have sought to work their way around the problem but their success has been divided. In *885676 Ont. Ltd v. Frasmet Holdings Ltd.* (1993), 12 OR (3d) 62, R.A. Blair J held that while disclaimer of a lease deprived the landlord of the right to sue the trustee for damages, the trustee was not entitled to an order restraining the landlord from demanding payment from the issuer of an irrevocable letter of credit (LOC) to cover the landlord's damages. The trustee was concerned because the bankrupt had given security to the issuer of the LOC and release of the security would obviously be jeopardized if the issuer honoured the LOC. On the other hand, in *Peat Marwick Thorne Inc. v. Natco Trading Corp.* (1995), 22 OR (3d) 727 Feldman J held that a landlord could not enforce security given by a tenant to collect future rent or damages under the lease upon the tenant's bankruptcy. Her reasoning was that the security was only as good as the underlying claim and that since the combined effect of the BIA and the Ontario Landlord and Tenant Act was to relieve the estate from further liability if the trustee elected to disclaim, there were no remaining obligations to support the security. She did not question the soundness of the decision in *Frasmet Holdings* and acknowledged that a letter of credit or other security could be so drafted as to survive termination of the lease by the landlord and the landlord's claim for damages. Is this reasoning sound where enforcement of the LOC or security interest will oblige the trustee to make good the third party's loss, as apparently was true in *Frasmet*? Would this not undermine the statutory intent?

3) Why should realty leases be singled out for special treatment in the BIA and why does the BIA defer to provincial legislation in straight bankruptcies and not in the case of Part III proposals (see s. 65.2)? Assuming the appropriateness of allowing the trustee to disclaim a lease, why should the landlord's damages be limited to a preferential claim for 3 months' accelerated rent following the bankruptcy (and then only if the realized amount from the property on the premises is sufficient to cover the claim and subject to a deduction for any amount payable by the trustee for occupation rent)?

These questions received much attention in 1994, in the context of Part III of the BIA, by the Working Group of BIAC studying the desirability of amending s. 65.2. Landlords complained loudly that owners of chain stores were often invoking Part III so that they could disclaim leases and that the results were grossly unfair to them. Do you agree? See further the case law reproduced in chapters 18 and 19, *infra*. What solution would you recommend?

CHAPTER SIXTEEN

Review of
Pre-Bankruptcy Transactions

Concern about insolvent debtors attempting to place assets beyond their creditors' reach goes back to Lord Coke's day and the Statute of 13 Eliz., c. 5 (1577) on fraudulent conveyances. The concern has not abated over the succeeding centuries. On the contrary, the categories of transactions voidable in bankruptcy have grown significantly over the past 150 years. A brief overview of the current Canadian position is provided in the chart at the end of these notes. The following points may be helpful in reviewing the chart as well as in reading the illustrative cases following the chart.

(1) Provincial law is as important in this area as is federal law. In some cases, the provincial source is the exclusive or predominant basis for challenging a prebankruptcy transaction; in other cases, there is substantial overlap between the BIA and the provincial provisions. Where there is no overlap, s. 72 of the BIA appears to envisage continued application of provincial law. This is supported constitutionally by the provincial jurisdiction over property and civil rights (Constitution Act 1867, s. 92(13)).

As previously explained (*supra*, chapter 9), recent cases have upheld the invalidation of unperfected security interests in bankruptcy as a valid exercise of provincial powers. Constitutionally and operationally, the position is much more difficult where the federal and provincial laws cover essentially the *same* ground but are sufficiently different to make it worthwhile for a trustee to rely on one or the other, or both, depending on which system of law is more favourable to the trustee in a particular case. The Supreme Court was deeply divided on this issue in *Robinson v. Countrywide Factors Ltd.*, [1978] 1 SCR 753, *infra*, this chapter, in determining the validity of ss. 3-4 of the Saskatchewan Fraudulent Preferences Act. (Indeed, had Laskin CJ's views prevailed, the general scope for provincial intrusion in this area would have been cut significantly.)

(2) It is not always easy to rationalize the basis for the impeachability of a prebankruptcy transaction. Historically, the two principal bases were: (i) gratuitous transfers made by the debtor with a view to hindering, defeating or delaying creditors' claims (see, for example, the Fraudulent Conveyances Act (Ont.), s. 2); and (ii) payment or other transfers made with a view to preferring one or more creditors over other creditors (BIA ss. 95-96 and Assignment and Preferences Act (Ont.), s. 4(2)). On the other hand, BIA ss. 91 (prebankruptcy settlements) and 101 (declaration of dividends and the like by a

Table of Avoidance and Pre-Bankruptcy Review Provisions

Type of Transaction	LEGISLATION			KEY ISSUES					
	Federal BIA	Provincial FCA	Provincial APA	Debtor's Insolvency	Prescriptive Period	Importance of Parties' Relationship	Debtor's Intention	Presumptions	Protection of Bona Fide Transferee
1. Unperfected Security Interests	Only s. 94, otherwise provincial law applies.	OPPSA s. 20(1)(b)*		N/A	No	N/A	N/A	N/A	N/A
2. Settlement and Conveyances	ss. 2, 91-93	2	4(1)	91(2)	1 yr (5 yrs if insolvent at time of transfer)	No	No	No	BIA 91(3)(b) cf. 98(1)-(3)
				Yes (APA)	No	No	Yes	No	Yes
3. "Fraudulent" Preferences	ss. 95-96 [Note broad reach of s.95(1)]	—	4(2)	Yes	3 m regular 12 m if non-arm's length	No / Yes / No	Yes	Yes [95(2)]	No
				Yes	No		Yes	Yes [4(3)]	See s. 5(1)
4. Reviewable Transactions	s. 100, ss. 3-4	—	—	No / —	12 m [100(1)] / —	Yes / —	No / —	No / —	N/A / —
5. Dividends, Redemptions, and Purchase of Shares	CBCA 118(2) 34(2) 35(2) 36(2)	OBCA 30-32 38(3) 130(2)		Yes	2 yrs (OBCA) (CBCA)	No	N/A	No	N/A
	BIA s.101			Yes	12 m (BIA)				

* No restriction in OPPSA on right to perfect right up to time of bankruptcy.

Abbreviations: BIA – Bankruptcy and Insolvency Act, RSC 1985, c. B-3, as am. 1992, c. 27
FCA – Fraudulent Conveyances Act (Ont.), RSO 1990, c. F.29
APA – Assignment and Preferences Act (Ont.), RSO 1990, c. A.33, as am.

corporation) are not concerned with the debtor's intention vis-à-vis his creditors but seem to rest on the concept that gratuitous transfers are intrinsically objectionable if they are made shortly before bankruptcy. If that is so, why are only *some* types of gratuitous (or partly gratuitous: see BIA s. 100) transfers open to attack?

(3) The rationale for the avoidance of unperfected security interests is also hard to pin down. Historically, they were regarded as a badge of fraud because the debtor was allowed to remain in possession of the collateral. He could thus pass himself off as being more solvent than was in fact the case. With the introduction of registration systems and decreased reliance on appearances, this rationalization has lost much of its persuasiveness. Nevertheless, most creditors would probably still agree that an unperfected security interest should be unenforceable in bankruptcy on the ground that a concealed security interest is akin to a fraudulent preference even though the debtor may have had no intention to prefer the secured creditor.

It will be seen, then, that modern theories of voidable transactions in bankruptcy are complex. They become even more so when the frequently inconsistent statutory provisions are examined in detail. However, this does not dissuade creditors from encouraging trustees to invoke them fully in practice! In this branch of bankruptcy law at least, clawing back assets for the benefit of the estate carries great moral and psychological appeal.

Profile United Industries Ltd. v. Coopers & Lybrand
(1987), 38 DLR (4th) 600 (NBCA)

STRATTON CJNB: This appeal raises two questions: whether a payment made by one related company to another was a "settlement" within the meaning of s. 69 of the *Bankruptcy Act* [now BIA s. 91], RSC 1970, c. B-3; and whether the payment was made in contravention of the *Statute of Elizabeth* (Fraudulent Conveyances Act), 1570, 13 Eliz. I, c. 5.

In 1980 the appellant, Profile United Industries Limited ("Profile"), Associated Freezers of Canada Limited ("Freezers") and Associated Fisheries of Canada Limited ("Fisheries"), were associated companies, all controlled by one Joseph Yvon Robichaud.

Fisheries operated a fish processing plant at Shippegan, New Brunswick. On February 29, 1980, Fisheries sold its fish-processing business to Connors Bros. Ltd. for $3,650,000.00. After the payment of several encumbrances Fisheries' solicitors paid the balance of the sale price in the amount of $578,308.06 to Profile. Profile then proceeded to liquidate Fisheries' remaining assets, collect its receivables and pay its outstanding accounts. Among Fisheries' outstanding accounts was one due Profile of $150,570.04, one due Metrocan Leasing Ltd. of $220,149.79 and one due Excel Packaging Ltd. of $220,071.23. Profile off-set against the sums it received its own account with Fisheries while Freezers assumed payment of the Metrocan account.

When the sale by Fisheries to Connors Bros. took place, Excel Packaging Ltd. had commenced legal action in the courts of Quebec to collect its account with Fisheries. In that litigation Fisheries had counterclaimed against Excel for substantially the same amount as was claimed against it. But the counterclaim was unsuccessful and Excel was awarded judgment against Fisheries for the full amount of its account. On July 23, 1981,

Excel registered its judgments against Fisheries in New Brunswick. The registered judgment was for $238,638.92. On December 11, 1981, Excel petitioned for a receiving order against Fisheries. On January 8, 1982, a receiving order was made and Coopers & Lybrand Limited was appointed trustee of the estate of Fisheries.

The trustee commenced the present action against Profile claiming that the sum of $578,308.06 that was paid to it by Fisheries' solicitors was paid at a time when Fisheries was unable to pay its debts without these funds, that it was paid with intent to defraud the creditors of Fisheries, and in particular Excel, and that such payment contravened the *Statute of Elizabeth* and was therefore void and should be set aside. At the trial of the action a judge of the Court of Queen's Bench made the following findings:

(1) When the payment of $578,308.06 was made to Profile, Fisheries was insolvent;

(2) The payment made to Profile was not an ordinary business transaction but one which prevented Fisheries from paying its debts in a fair and equitable manner;

(3) The sum of $578,308.06 was paid to Profile so that it could control the payment of Fisheries' accounts and thus exclude Excel;

(4) The assumption by Freezers of Fisheries' account with Metrocan Leasing Limited in the amount of $220,149.79 reduced the Trustee's claim by this amount;

(5) As the Trustee did not contest the set-off by Profile of its own account with Fisheries in the sum of $150,570.04 the Trustee's claim was reduced by this amount;

(6) The payment made to Profile was a "settlement" within the meaning of s. 69(1) of the *Bankruptcy Act* and therefore void as against the Trustee;

(7) Additionally the Trustee was entitled to succeed on the basis of the *Statute of Elizabeth*; and

(8) The Trustee was entitled to judgment against Profile for $263,945.20 together with interest at the rate of 10% per annum from October 31, 1983 and to costs of $11,875.00.

Profile has appealed the decision at trial contending that the learned trial judge erred in law in two respects: (1) in finding that the payment to Profile was a "settlement" within the meaning of s. 69 of the *Bankruptcy Act*, and (2) in finding that the payment to Profile was in contravention of the *Statute of Elizabeth*. The trustee has cross-appealed submitting that the trial judge erred in giving credits to Profile in respect of Profile's own account of $150,507.04 and the account of Metrocan Leasing Ltd. in the amount of $220,149.79.

I The Settlement Issue

Section 69 of the *Bankruptcy Act* deals with settlements. The relevant portions of that section provide as follows [see now ss. 91(1) and 2(2)]:

It has been said that the purpose of the section is to prevent a person from making a voluntary settlement of property which would otherwise be available for his creditors if bankruptcy were to ensue within one year after settlement. It does not, however, prevent a person executing a settlement by which he divests himself of property not required for the payment of his debts, even though bankruptcy ensues within five years from the settlement: see Houlden and Morawetz, *Bankruptcy Law of Canada* (Toronto, Carswell Co., 1960), vol. 1, p. F-105.

The term "settlement" is not defined in the present *Bankruptcy Act* although its meaning under the former Act was considered by the Supreme Court of Canada in *Re Bozanich; A.H. Boulton Co. Ltd. v. Trusts & Guarantee Co. Ltd.*, [1942] 2 DLR 145, [1942] SCR 130, 23 CBR 234. In that case Duff CJC, at pp. 147-8 DLR, p. 135 SCR cited with approval the statement that the term "settlement" implies an intention that the property shall be retained or preserved for the benefit of the donee in such a form that it can be traced. In the same case Rinfret J at pp. 151-2 DLR, p. 139 SCR, approved the statement that to qualify as a settlement the end and purpose of the transaction must be a disposition of property to be held for the enjoyment of some other person. He also said this at p. 153 DLR, p. 140 SCR:

I doubt whether an arrangement with a creditor may ever be considered a settlement; and I would incline to the opinion that, generally speaking, "settlement" involves the idea of a clear gift, or that type of cases where provision is made for a trust of some sort. It should not be taken to include an ordinary business transaction between a debtor and a creditor.

In an earlier decision, *Re Cohen and Lyons; Canadian Credit Men's Trust Ass'n Ltd. v. Spivak*, [1926] 3 DLR 942 at p. 952, 7 CBR 655 at pp. 666-7, [1926] 3 WWR 34, *sub nom. Re Cohen and Mahlin* (reversed on other grounds, [1927] 1 DLR 577, [1927] 1 WWR 162, 8 CBR 23), Tweedie J of the Alberta Supreme Court defined the word "settlement" as it then appeared in s. 29 [*Bankruptcy Act*, 1919 (Can.), c. 36] of the Act as follows:

"Settlement" as here used means a disposition of property by the settlor either directly, or through the intervention of a trustee, for the benefit of the person on whose behalf the settlement is made, subject to such restrictions and conditions as to the retention of the settled property in its original form, or in the case of money as to the investment thereof, as may be imposed by the settlor. The retention of the property in some form is contemplated and not intermediate alienation of consumption, the use and enjoyment thereof to be in accordance with the terms of the disposition.

In Waters, *Law of Trusts in Canada* (Toronto, Carswell 1974), the learned author discusses the question "what is a settlement." He writes at p. 255:

A settlement has ... been interpreted as a disposition of property by the settlor, either directly or through the intervention of a trustee, for the benefit of the person on whose behalf the settlement is made, but with the contemplation, even if there is no intermediate trustee, that the property in some form shall be retained, its use and enjoyment being determined by the terms of the settlement.

This means that, though the property actually transferred may be varied as a trustee would handle an investment portfolio, nevertheless the essence of the disposition is the retention of property earmarked for the settlement so that continued enjoyment by the beneficiary may be secured. An acid test of whether property was so earmarked is whether at the time of the application to set the disposition aside the alleged property çan be traced.

In *Re Geraci* (1970), 12 DLR (3d) 314 at p. 316, [1970] 3 OR 49, 14 CBR (NS) 253 (CA), the term "settlement" as used in the *Bankruptcy Act* of 1952 was defined as a "disposition of property to be held, either in original form or in such form that it can be traced, for the enjoyment of some other person." In a later case, *Re Barnett* (1983), 43 AR

215 at p. 218, 46 CBR (NS) 211, Hope J of the Alberta Court of Queen's Bench defined a "settlement" in these terms:

A "settlement" is a voluntary disposition of property to and for the benefit of an individual with the intention that it be retained by that individual either in its original form or in such form that it can be traced.

In the present case, the learned trial judge, citing what was said by Rinfret J in the *Bozanich* case concluded that the money paid by Fisheries' solicitors to Profile was a settlement within the meaning of s. 69(1) of the Act because it was a trust of some sort. As he put it:

The payment to Profile was far from an ordinary business transaction but one where Profile and another related company, Freezers [*sic*] were using the payment to pay debts. They received the payment and used it for that purpose—a trust situation.

With respect, I am unable to agree that the payment to Profile in this instance was a settlement within the meaning of s. 69 of the *Bankruptcy Act*. It is clear that there never was any intention that Profile was to retain the funds which it had received. What in fact occurred was nothing more than a business arrangement whereby Profile paid Fisheries' creditors. Indeed the evidence was that in the payment of Fisheries' accounts Profile expended $111,969.69 more than it received. I would, therefore, conclude that the arrangement which occurred did not come within the term "settlement" as defined because Fisheries neither reserved to itself any beneficial interest in the funds nor did Profile retain or preserve the funds for the benefit of Fisheries.

Moreover, even if the payment in issue could be taken to be a settlement, I do not think that s. 69(1) of the Act can have application. That section provides that if a settlor becomes bankrupt within one year from the settlement, such settlement is void against the trustee. The term "bankrupt" is defined in s. 2 of the *Bankruptcy Act* as follows:

"bankrupt" means a person who has made an assignment or against whom a receiving order has been made or the legal status of such a person;

The evidence in the present case was that the impugned transaction took place February 29, 1980 and that the receiving order against Fisheries was made January 8, 1982. In view of the definition of the term "bankrupt," for s. 69(1) to apply the receiving order had to be made within one year of the settlement, i.e., by February 28, 1981. The receiving order in the present case was more than nine months late. Thus, s. 69(1) cannot have application.

But, in my view, if the payment in issue were a settlement, s. 69(2) of the Act could have application. That section provides that where a settlement occurs more than a year before the date of bankruptcy but within five years, the settlement "is void against the trustee if he can prove that the settlor, was at the time of making the settlement, unable to pay all his debts without the aid of the property comprised in the settlement." The inability to pay all debts without the aid of the property comprised in the settlement as mentioned in s. 69(2) has been held to mean not being able to meet obligations generally as they become due: see *Re Cyr* (1982), 45 CBR (NS) 195 (Alta. QB).

In the present case, the trial judge was satisfied that Fisheries was insolvent on February 29, 1980. He said:

There is ample evidence that at the time of the payment to Profile that [Fisheries] was insolvent. Its debts exceeded $1,000. In addition, it was unable to meet its obligations as they became due and its current obligations were not being paid in the ordinary course of business.

In view of the findings of the trial judge, I think it could be said that the trustee has met the onus of establishing that Fisheries was unable to pay all its debts without the aid of the funds here in issue and accordingly s. 69(2) of the Act could have had application.

As previously stated, however, I would accept the submission of Profile that the payment by Fisheries' solicitors to it was not a "settlement" within the meaning of s. 69 of the *Bankruptcy Act*. I would accordingly give effect to this ground of appeal.

II The Statute of Elizabeth

Profile contends that the payment of $578,308.06 to it by Fisheries' solicitors did not contravene the *Statute of Elizabeth* because, it argues, the statute does not prohibit a debtor from preferring one creditor to another. Indeed, Profile further submits that even though a debtor may know that a judgment is pending against him or that what is at issue is a substantial portion of the proceeds of sale of the debtor's principal asset yet the statute is not necessarily offended when all creditors save one are paid. There is support for this submission in 17 Hal., 3rd ed., pp. 656-7, para. 1267, where it stated:

Unlike the bankruptcy laws, the statute does not prohibit a debtor preferring one creditor to another, and therefore a conveyance executed in favour of one or some only of the creditors of the grantor may be bona fide and valid, notwithstanding that the grantor knows at the time that execution is about to be issued against him, or that he is insolvent, and even though the conveyance comprises the whole of the grantor's property. Such an alienation will, however, be avoided if it is a mere cloak to secure a benefit to the grantor, and the fact that one creditor obtains an advantage will not of itself prevent a transaction from being avoided.

It has been said that the *Statute of Elizabeth* was merely declaratory of what was previously the common law of the land. The purpose of its enactment is described in *Kerr on Fraud and Mistake*, 7th ed. (1952), at p. 298, as follows:

The statute 13 Eliz. c. 5, was made for the protection of creditors. It provided, in effect, that all conveyances and dispositions of property real or personal, made with the intention of delaying, hindering, or defrauding creditors, should be null and void as against them, their heirs, etc., and assigns. It also provided that nothing therein contained should extend to any estate or interest made on good consideration and bona fide to any person not having, at the time, any notice of such fraud.

The question whether the *Statute of Elizabeth* was in effect in Nova Scotia and the relationship between that enactment and the *Assignments and Preferences Act*, RSNS 1967, c. 16, was widely canvassed by Mr. Justice Hallett of the Nova Scotia Supreme Court in *Bank of Montreal v. Crowell et al.* (1980), 109 DLR (3d) 442, 37 NSR (2d) 292, 34 CBR (NS) 15. In that decision Hallett J concluded that it had been decided many years ago that the law set forth in the *Statute of Elizabeth* was applicable and necessary in that province and therefore in force. In this respect I would observe that there are as well decisions by New Brunswick courts that have adopted the statute as the law of this province: see, for example, *Bank of Montreal v. Vandine et al.*, [1953] 1 DLR 456, 33 MPR 368 (CA). Hallett J also states the following conclusion to which I too would respectfully subscribe (p. 449):

> In my opinion, the *Assignments and Preferences Act*, although it deals with the same subject-matter as the Statute of Elizabeth (fraudulent conveyances), does not repeal the Statute of Elizabeth by implication. The Statute of Elizabeth enables an attack on conveyances made by solvent persons while the *Assignments and Preferences Act* deals with insolvent persons and the matter of preferences which are not subject to attack under the Statute of Elizabeth. The two Acts are not inconsistent or repugnant. I am satisfied that effect can be given to both statutes at the same time and there is therefore no repeal by implication: *Craies on Statute Law*, 7th ed. (1971), p. 366; *Bank of Montreal v. Reis et al.*, [1925] 3 DLR 125, [1925] 2 WWR 169.

I would observe that the *Assignments and Preferences Act*, RSNB 1973, c. A-16, was not raised as an issue either at the trial of this action or on the hearing of the appeal.

It is to be noted that the *Statute of Elizabeth* makes a distinction between voluntary conveyances and *bona fide* transfers for consideration. Section 6 of the statute provides that the statute does not extend to any conveyance made upon good consideration and "bona fide lawfully conveyed" to any person not having notice or knowledge of the fraud or collusion against the creditors. The applicable rule is stated in 17 Hals., 3rd ed., p. 654, at para. 1261, as follows:

> For creditors to be in a position to impeach an alienation of property by their debtor they must prove, in addition to fraudulent intent on the part of the grantor, either that the alienation was not made for valuable consideration or upon good consideration, or that the grantee was privy to the fraud. Otherwise the grantee will be entitled to the protection given by the provision, even where a creditor is in fact defeated by the grant.

The decision in *Bank of Montreal v. Vandine et al.* cited previously involved a conveyance that was made for valuable consideration. In the judgment of Harrison J in that case it was stated at p. 460 DLR, p. 373 MPR:

> Two questions have to be determined under the *Statute of Elizabeth*—(1) Whether the conveyance in question was made by the debtor with the intent "to delay, hinder or defraud" his creditors; and (2)—If there was such intent, whether the party buying such property participated in such fraudulent intent.

When a transaction is entered into for good and valuable consideration the burden of proving that it was made in fraud of creditors is upon those who seek to set the transaction aside. Although it is recognized that there can be no hard and fast rule as to what constitutes a fraudulent transaction, since the decision in *Twyne's Case* (1601), 3 Co. Rep. 80b, 76 ER 809, the existence of certain unexplained circumstances have sometimes been looked upon as "badges of fraud" so as to take the case out of the protection afforded to a *bona fide* purchaser. Two of the categories mentioned that have some relevance to the present case are the generality of the transfer, i.e., the inclusion therein of substantially all of the debtors' property, and the transfer of assets *pendente lite*. But overall what must be determined in each case as a question of fact is whether a concurrent intent on the part of the parties to defraud a creditor has been established by a preponderance of evidence.

In the instant case it was established that Fisheries sold its only substantial revenue producing asset, i.e., its fish-processing plant, and diverted the net sale proceeds to Profile in an effort to avoid payment to Excel which had sued it. While it is true that Profile undertook to collect Fisheries' receivables and to pay its outstanding accounts it is also true that Profile, Fisheries and Freezers were associated companies, all controlled by Mr. Robichaud. And as the trial judge took pains to point out, although he was present at the trial, Mr. Robichaud did not testify. In all of the circumstances, the trial judge categorized the diversion of Fisheries' funds to Profile as an unusual business transaction and one which prevented Fisheries from paying its debts in a fair and equitable manner at a time when it was insolvent. More importantly, he also found that Profile shared Fisheries' desire to exclude Excel from the payment of debts. As he put it:

> The balance of the purchase price was paid to a related company, Profile, so that it could choose which of [Fisheries] debts to liquidate. It might be natural that the management of Profile would not want to pay the Excel account which was thought to have caused [Fisheries] downfall.

The learned trial judge therefore concluded that the trustee was entitled to succeed on the basis of the *Statute of Elizabeth* because, he said, as a result of the impugned transaction there were no funds left for Excel "as Profile chose to pay other creditors instead." In my opinion, the trial judge's conclusion is substantiated by the evidence. I would respectfully agree with him that there was present here a shared intention on the part of Fisheries and Profile to delay, hinder or defraud Excel, a potential judgment creditor. Adopting the language of Halsbury, the diversion of Fisheries' funds to Profile "was a mere cloak to secure a benefit" to Fisheries and under the *Statute of Elizabeth* it was void.

• • •

Appeal allowed in part.

Re Yewdale
(1995), 121 DLR (4th) 521 (BCSC)

TYSOE J: Approximately five months prior to her bankruptcy, Mrs. Yewdale converted her investment portfolio into two annuities under which she designated her grandchildren as beneficiaries. The trustee in bankruptcy has applied for a declaration that the annuities were void as against it. Mrs. Yewdale resists the application and has filed a cross-application to allow her to receive monthly payments sufficient to cover her living expenses.

Background facts

Mrs. Yewdale had a most unfortunate motor vehicle accident in June, 1990. Her car was involved in a collision with a motorcycle ridden by Darren Gervais. Mr. Gervais was seriously injured in the accident and he suffered permanent brain damage which, among other things, made him unable to walk. He sued Mrs. Yewdale and she disputed liability.

The trial of Mr. Gervais' claim took place in January, 1993 and judgment was, [sic] reserved. On April 23, 1993 the trial judge determined the issue of liability against Mrs. Yewdale [see *Gervais (Guardian ad Litem of) v. Yewdale* (1993), 39 ACWS (3d) 972]. Damages were agreed to in the amount of approximately $4.2 million. Mrs. Yewdale was ill when the judgment was rendered and she was not informed of the decision until the beginning of June, 1993.

At the time of the accident, Mrs. Yewdale was an 82-year-old widow. Her husband had died in 1973 and he had left her the family home and substantial investments. At the time of the trial, the investment consisted of stocks and bonds having a value of approximately $760,000.

In the latter part of June, 1993, Mrs. Yewdale caused her investment to be liquidated, and she applied for two annuities with two insurance companies, Manufacturers Life and Standard Life. The aggregate cost of the annuities was approximately $705,000. The annuities were each guaranteed for a certain period of time in the sense that if Mrs. Yewdale died during that period, the monthly payments of $9,600 would be paid for the rest of the period to the beneficiaries named by Mrs. Yewdale. Her two grandchildren were irrevocably appointed as the beneficiaries.

Mrs. Yewdale had liability insurance with the Insurance Corporation of British Columbia ("ICBC") in the amount of $1 million and it paid this amount to Mr. Gervais. Mrs. Yewdale did not have sufficient assets to pay the remaining $3.2 million of the judgment against her, and she made an assignment into bankruptcy on November 30, 1993.

Mrs. Yewdale has commenced an action against ICBC and her former solicitors in connection with the judgment against her. She is claiming that ICBC acted in bad faith and that her former solicitors were negligent. The trial is scheduled for February, 1995.

Discussion

Numerous submissions were made to me. I will deal separately with each submission.

• • •

(b) *Exempt Status*

Section 67 of the *Bankruptcy and Insolvency Act,* RSC 1985, c. B-3, amended SC 1992, cc. 1 and 27 (the "Act"), provides exemptions for certain types of property. The exempted property is excluded from the bankrupt's estate and is not available for division among the creditors. The relevant portion of s. 67 reads as follows:

67. The property of a bankrupt divisible among his creditors shall not comprise

• • •

   (b) any property that as against the bankrupt is exempt from execution or seizure under the laws of the province within which the property is situated and within which the bankrupt resides ...

It is conceded by the trustee that the annuities purchased by Mrs. Yewdale are exempt from execution under s. 147 of the BC *Insurance Act* RSBC 1979, c. 200, because qualifying relatives were designated as beneficiaries under the annuities.

The trustee challenges the annuities under s. 91(1) of the Act. It says that the acquisition of the annuities with the designation of beneficiaries was a "settlement" and is void because it was done within one year preceding the date of bankruptcy. I will set out s. 91 in its entirety because reference will be made to all three of its subsections:

91(1) Any settlement of property, if the settlor becomes bankrupt within one year after the date of the settlement, is void against the trustee.

(2) Any settlement of property, if the settlor becomes bankrupt within five years after the date of the settlement, is void against the trustee if the trustee can prove that the settlor was, at the time of making the settlement, unable to pay all his debts without the aid of the property comprised in the settlement or that the interest of the settlor in the property did not pass on the execution thereof.

(3) This section does not extend to any settlement made
    (a) before and in consideration of marriage;
    (b) in favour of a purchaser or incumbrancer in good faith and for valuable consideration; or
    (c) on or for the spouse of children of the settlor of property that has accrued to the settlor after marriage in right of the settlor's spouse or children.

Two of the terms used in s. 91 are defined in s. 2 of the Act. The terms "property" and "settlement" are defined as follows:

"property" includes money, goods, things in action, land and every description of property, whether real or personal, legal or equitable, and whether situated in Canada or elsewhere, and includes obligations, easements and every description of estate, interest and profit, present or future, vested or contingent, in, or arising out of or incident to property;

• • •

"settlement" includes a contract, covenant, transfer, gift and designation of beneficiary in an insurance contract, to the extent that the contract, covenant, transfer, gift or designation is gratuitous or made for merely nominal consideration;

It is to be noted that the definition of "settlement" was added to the Act at the time of substantial amendments to the legislation in 1992. The Act previously had another definition of "settlement," but it had been removed at the time of amendments made in 1949.

There are numerous authorities dealing with the effect of s. 91 on assets of a bankrupt which have been converted from non-exempt to exempt assets prior to the bankruptcy. However, these authorities present a difficulty because the one relevant British Columbia case reaches a different result.

The authorities begin with the decision of the Ontario Court of Appeal in *Re Geraci* (1970), 12 DLR (3d) 314, 14 CBR (NS) 253 *sub nom. Swallow v. Geraci*, [1970] OLR ¶ 1-343, [1970] 3 OR 49. In that case, the bankrupt had designated his wife as beneficiary in an existing insurance policy and the designation made the policy an exempt asset. The trustee in bankruptcy attacked the transaction as being a settlement under the predecessor to s. 91 (then s. 60) and as being a fraudulent conveyance under provincial legislation. The Ontario Court of Appeal held that the designation of the beneficiary was a settlement void against the trustee. The court also stated, without providing reasons, that the designation of beneficiary was void under the provincial fraudulent conveyance legislation.

The court ruled that the designation of beneficiary was a settlement within the ordinary definition of the word. In doing so, it relied on the broad definition of "property" in the Act. The court then went on to consider the interplay between s. 60 and s. 39 (the predecessor to s. 67) in the following passage (at pp. 318-19):

> If a settlement of property which comes within s. 60(1) of the *Bankruptcy Act,* both as to substance and as to time, is none the less to be taken as exempt, by virtue of s. 39(b), from the claims of a bankrupt's creditors merely because it would enjoy that exemption under provincial law apart from s. 60(1), the result would be to make s. 60(1) completely nugatory. I cannot conceive that to have been the intent of Parliament. The proper rule of construction is to harmonize all sections of an enactment and this is achieved in the present case by applying s. 39(b) in the light of s. 60(1) and not despite s. 60(1). I would, therefore, hold that property settled by a bankrupt within a year before his bankruptcy includes property rendered exempt from execution or seizure, under the laws of the relevant Province, as a result of the settlement.

Before I turn to the British Columbia decision which reaches a contrary conclusion, I should refer to an earlier case of this court which considered *Geraci* and which was relied on in the later decision. In *Sovereign General Insurance Co. v. Dale,* [1989] 2 WWR 338, 32 BCLR (3d) 226, 13 ACWS (3d) 254, a creditor challenged the purchase of an exempt annuity (with the designation of a beneficiary) by the judgment debtor. The debtor was not bankrupt and the creditor was attempting to utilize the provincial fraudulent conveyance legislation. Gibbs J held that the transaction could not be set aside as a fraudulent conveyance because the purchase of the annuity with the debtor's wife as beneficiary did not constitute a disposition of property.

In reaching his conclusions, Gibbs J noted that the bankruptcy cases were not helpful to him because they turned in large part on the broad definition of "property" in the Act. He considered *Geraci* as a result of the alternate ruling of the Ontario Court of Appeal that the designation of beneficiary was void under the provincial fraudulent conveyance legislation. Gibbs J expressed the opinion that this alternate ruling constituted *obiter dicta,* and he came to the independent conclusion that the naming of the wife as beneficiary was not a disposition of property.

The British Columbia case which reached a different conclusion from *Geraci* with respect to the interplay between ss. 67 and 91 was *Re Sykes* (1993), 18 CBR (3d) 148, 80 BCLR (2d) 368, 38 ACWS (3d) 436 (SC). That case involved the acquisition of an exempt annuity (with the designation of a beneficiary) by the bankrupt shortly before his bankruptcy. The trustee in bankruptcy sought to have the transaction declared void under s. 91. The chambers judge referred to the decision of *Geraci* and *Sovereign General Insurance,* and he noted that Gibbs J in the *Sovereign* case did not follow *Geraci.* The chambers judge reached his conclusions as follows (at p. 153):

> The reasoning in the *Geraci* case seems to tag onto s. 167(b) [*sic*] words such as "unless the disposition of the property referred to amounts to a settlement referred to in s. 91." That comes close to judicial legislation.

To give effect to *Geraci* in the present case would make available to creditors that which Gibbs, J denied them. As that result would be anomalous I hold that the annuity contract in the hands of the trustee in the present case is exempt from creditors' claims.

The chambers judge in *Sykes* did not refer to three Saskatchewan decisions which expressly or impliedly follow the conclusion in *Geraci* with respect to the interplay between ss. 67 and 91. There has since been a fourth such decision by the Saskatchewan courts. These four Saskatchewan decisions are *Camgoz (Trustee of) v. Sun Life Assurance Co. of Canada* (1988), 70 CBR (NS) 131, 35 CCLI 256, 70 Sask R. 70 (QB); affirmed 72 CBR (NS) 319, 13 ACWS (3d) 243 (CA); *Klassen (Trustee of) v. Great West Life Assurance Co* (1990), 1 CBR (3d) 263, 48 CCLI 40, [1991] ILR ¶ 1-2715 *sub nom. Deloitte & Touche Ltd. v. Great West Life Assurance Co.* (QB); *Royal Bank of Canada v. Oliver* (1992), 11 CBR (3d) 82, 9 CCLI (3d) 98, [1992] 4 WWR 54 (QB); *Royal Bank of Canada v. North American Life Assurance Co.* (1994), 115 DLR (4th) 536, 26 CBR (3d) 1, 4 CCPB, 1 *sub nom. Ramgotra (Trustee of) v. North American Life Assurance Co.* (CA).

• • •

It is my opinion that the view expressly or impliedly accepted in *Geraci* and the four Saskatchewan cases is to be preferred over the reasoning in *Sykes*. I adopt the reasoning as expressed in *Oliver* (at p. 92):

There is ample judicial authority for the proposition that even if an asset is exempt under provincial legislation (and thereby not part of the bankrupt's property available to his creditors under s. 67(b) of the Act), if it was obtained by means of a settlement within the ambit of s. 81, it is void against the trustee. No matter how securely an exemption is entrenched in law, the exemption itself cannot validate an otherwise void or voidable transaction. In other words, a valid exemption cannot be acquired by means of a void transaction. Property obtained in such manner is deemed to be property available to the trustee under s. 67. Sections 67(b) and 91 of the Act must accordingly be read together; *Camboz*, supra.

While s. 67(b) does provide an exemption for insurance annuities, it cannot be viewed in isolation. An asset can only be properly exempted under s. 67(b) if the transaction creating the asset is valid. If the transaction is void under s. 91 (or any other provision), the exempted asset must be considered to revert to its form prior to the invalid transaction. If its prior form was not an exempted asset, s. 67(b) is not applicable.

In *Sykes*, the chambers judge seems to have been principally influenced by the fact that the result would be opposite *Sovereign Life* if he followed *Geraci*. With the greatest of respect, it should not matter that the Act produces a different result than the provincial fraudulent conveyance legislation. There are many occasions where the result is different under the Act (*e.g.,* priorities). Indeed, in the *Sovereign Life* case itself, Gibbs J acknowledged that the result would have been different under the Act as a result of its broad definition of "property."

In addition to *Sykes,* counsel for Mrs. Yewdale relied on the decision in *China Software Corp. v. Leimbigler* (1990), 4 CBR (3d) 185, 45 CPC (3d) 41, 23 ACWS (3d) 805 (BCSC), as support for the proposition that s. 147 of the *Insurance Act* has been given very wide and sweeping application to protect the interest of the insurance policy beneficiary.

In that case the court declined to appoint a receiver of an annuity which was exempt under s. 147. I do not see how this case assists Mrs. Yewdale. Like *Sovereign Life,* it only concerned provincial legislation and there was no consideration of s. 91 of the Act.

(c) *Requirement of intent*

There can be little doubt, that apart from a consideration of Mrs. Yewdale's intention, the conversion by Mrs. Yewdale of her investment portfolio into the two annuities (with the designation of beneficiaries) is a type of transaction which can be a settlement within the meaning of the Act. The current definition of "settlement" did not exist at the time of the decisions in *Geraci, Camgoz, Klassen* and *Oliver,* but the courts in those cases had little difficulty in deciding that similar transactions were settlements. In *Ramgotra,* the Saskatchewan Court of Appeal made the observation that the result in *Camgoz* has been codified by the present definition of "settlement" which specifically makes reference to a designation of a beneficiary in an insurance contract.

Counsel for Mrs. Yewdale submits that the transaction is not a settlement because she did not acquire the annuities with the intent of creating an exempt asset. Mrs. Yewdale has sworn an affidavit stating that she converted the investments into the annuities on the advice of a friend, because her declining health did not permit her to pay the required attention to her financial affairs. She deposed that she never discussed with her friend the protection of her assets from creditors, and that she did not know the annuities could qualify as exempt assets until several months after their acquisition.

Her counsel submits that the definition of "settlement" is the definition adopted by the Supreme Court of Canada in the 1942 decision of *Re Bozanich* [1942] 2 DLR 145, [1942] SCR 130, 23 CBR 234, and that this definition requires the intention of the settlor to be proven. In *Bozanich,* the Supreme Court of Canada held that, although the version of the *Bankruptcy Act* of the time contained a broad definition of "settlement" which included any conveyance or transfer of property, Parliament did not intend to enlarge the meaning of "settlement" as the courts of England had interpreted the word. Duff J stated the English interpretation as follows (at p. 148):

> In the treatise on Bankruptcy and Insolvency in the 2nd edition of Halsbury [vol. 2, para. 487] by Lord Justice Luxmoore it is stated that the term "settlement" "implies an intention that the property shall be retained or preserved for the benefit of the donee in such a form that it can be traced."

Counsel points out that two very recent decisions have held that the definition of "settlement" accepted in *Bozanich* continues to be the definition to be applied by our courts (*Ramgotra* and *Goertz Estate (Trustee of) v. Goertz* (1994), 26 CBR (3d) 222, [1994] 8 WWR 250, 122 Sask. R. 93 (QB)).

With respect, counsel for Mrs. Yewdale is confusing two different types of intention. The intention referred to in the definition accepted in *Bozanich* is the intention that the property be retained or preserved in traceable form for the benefit of a third party. It is a different intention than the intention to put property beyond the reach of creditors.

Counsel for Mrs. Yewdale relied on *Ramgotra* in support of his submission. However, after referring to *Bozanich,* the Saskatchewan Court of Appeal in that case went on to consider whether the transfer of funds into an exempt asset constituted a settlement. Jackson JA (at p. 545 *Ramgotra*) relied on the following passage from *Geraci* (at p. 316):

I think there emerges from the authorities a definition of the ordinary meaning of "settlement" that it is a disposition of property to be held, either in original form or in such form that it can be traced, for the enjoyment of some other person; and that the designation of a beneficiary of an insurance policy is such a disposition. ...

Jackson JA goes on to note an important distinction from *Geraci* (at p. 546). He notes that it is the act of designating the beneficiary that effects the settlement and that it is not the conversion of non-exempt property to exempt property which constitutes a settlement. In other words, the intention of creating exempt property is irrelevant to a determination of whether the transaction is a settlement.

The other decision relied on by counsel for Mrs. Yewdale, *Goertz*, also fails to support his position. Although the court in that case did refer to the definition of "settlement" from *Bozanich*, there was no suggestion that it is necessary under s. 91 to prove an intention to prejudice creditors. To the contrary, Klebuc J specifically held that the trustee did not need to prove an intent by the bankrupt to defeat or prejudice his creditors (at p. 236).

In *Oliver*, the court addressed the issue of the intention of the bankrupt to defeat creditors. Baynton J said the following (at p. 90):

The absence of good faith or of an intent to defraud is not an element or a characteristic of the legal concept of a "settlement." Such considerations are irrelevant. This is clearly established by the case law, *Camgoz*, and by the wording of s. 91(3) that excludes certain settlements from the operation of s. 91. The wording of that exclusion clearly indicates that the fact the transaction constituting the settlement was made in good faith does not "undo" the settlement, but simply excludes the settlement from the operation of s. 91. It is the effect of the transaction on the settlor's estate rather than the nature of his intent that is the essence of a settlement.

The intent required by the definition of "settlement" accepted by *Bozanich* is the intent that property be retained or preserved in traceable form for the benefit of a third party. By designating her grandchildren as beneficiaries, Mrs. Yewdale clearly intended to benefit her grandchildren in the event of her death prior to the expiry of the guaranteed period. Her intention may be inferred from her act of designating the beneficiaries. There is no evidence suggesting a different intention.

(d) *Section 91(3) applicability*

Counsel for Mrs. Yewdale submitted that s. 91 does not apply to the acquisition of the annuities because s. 91(3)(b) provides that the section does not extend to settlements made in good faith and for valuable consideration. He says that the transactions were made in good faith because Mrs. Yewdale did not acquire the annuities for the purpose of protecting her assets against creditors. He submits that there were two types of valuable consideration. The first type of consideration was that Mrs. Yewdale's grandson, Mr. Layker, gave up his job in 1990 to look after her. Between the two dates for the hearing of this application, Mrs. Yewdale swore an affidavit stating that the designation of Mr. Layker as a beneficiary under the annuities was partially done in consideration of his past assistance and the assistance she trusted he would provide in the future.

The second type of consideration was the moneys used to acquire the annuities. I was referred to the following passage from *Oliver* (at p. 100):

> To qualify as an exclusion, the transactions must be bona fide and for valuable consideration. Although there is no question that the annuity RRSPs constitute valuable consideration for the term deposit RRSPs and the money that they replaced, the remaining bona fide requirement has not been made out.

Counsel for Mrs. Yewdale says that in the present case the *bona fide* requirement has been made out. As this hearing has not been a trial where the aspect of *bona fides* could be tested, I must proceed on the assumption that the *bona fide* requirement has been met.

The exclusion in s. 91(3)(b) is for settlements made "in favour of a purchaser or incumbrancer in good faith and for valuable consideration." On a literal interpretation of this phrase, neither Mrs. Yewdale nor her grandchildren are purchasers or incumbrancers. While one may use the phraseology that Mrs. Yewdale "purchased" the annuities, it cannot be said that the settlement was made in favour of a purchaser. The settlement was the designation of her grandchildren as beneficiaries under the annuities. The designation of beneficiaries was not made in favour of Mrs. Yewdale. The designation was in favour of the grandchildren, but they cannot be considered to be purchasers or incumbrancers with any stretch of the imagination.

However, counsel for Mrs. Yewdale is not mistaken that s. 91(3)(b) was utilized in *Oliver* as a potential exclusionary provision in respect of a conversion of an RRSP to an annuity. How was this done?

The problem facing Baynton J in the *Oliver* case was that he envisaged a scenario which he considered inequitable. He was concerned that everyone who went bankrupt within five years of acquiring exempt property by way of a settlement on themselves would lose the exemption even though they were not insolvent at the time of acquisition and even though they acquired it legitimately.

Baynton J noted that the concept of "settlement" has only recently evolved to transactions involving the settlement of property on oneself. He felt that the wording of s. 91(3), when applied to this new concept of "settlement," could produce inequities and he concluded that he should "apply the new developments with counterbalancing qualifications to avoid the inequitable consequences that can otherwise arise." Baynton J did this by interpreting "purchaser" in s. 91(3)(b) as including a person who exchanges property by means of a *bona fide* transaction for value.

The reasoning of Baynton J is *obiter dicta* because he held that the transactions in that case were not proved to be *bona fide*. More importantly, however, he expressly limited his interpretation of s. 91(3)(b) to a case under s. 91(2) where the bankrupt was solvent at the time of the transaction (at p. 98): "The counterbalancing qualification of good faith will not apply to other types of settlements, (i.e., s. 91(1) settlements or s. 91(2) settlements made when insolvent)." The present case involves s. 91 because the annuities were acquired within the one-year period preceding bankruptcy. Although it is not necessary for me to find that Mrs. Yewdale was insolvent, it does appear that in June, 1993, she could not have paid all her debts without the aid of the annuities.

Therefore, the counterbalancing qualification introduced by Baynton J in the *Oliver* decision has no application to the present case. I give the exclusion in s. 91(3)(b) its literal interpretation, and I conclude that the exclusion is not available.

• • •

Conclusion

In the result, the conversion of Mrs. Yewdale's investment portfolio into the two annuities (with the designation of beneficiaries) is void as against the trustee. The trustee is entitled to have Manufacturers Life and Standard Life return the amounts paid into the annuities subject, of course, to a reduction for the annuity payments made to date by them. In other words, they are to pay the trustee the present values of the annuities.

• • •

Declaration accordingly.

NOTES

Re Yewdale (*supra*) is only the latest in a series of cases involving the issue of when the conversion of assets by a debtor from a non-exempt to an exempt status prior to bankruptcy amounts to a voidable settlement for the purposes of s. 91 of the BIA and is therefore impeachable even though the assets would otherwise be protected under s. 67(1)(a) of the Act.

The Ontario Court of Appeal's decision in *Re Geraci* (1970), 12 DLR (3d) 314, has long been interpreted as meaning that such a conversion of assets amounts to a settlement. However, in Prof. Cuming's view* this is a serious mistake—a mistake which, he argues, has been put right in Jackson JA's recent careful analysis of the position in *Royal Bank of Can. v. North American Life Assurance Co.* (*"NALAC"*) (1994), 115 DLR (4th) 536 (Sask. CA).

Prof. Cuming argues, first, that a bare conversion of assets from non-exempt to exempt status cannot be a settlement under s. 91 since the conversion itself does not vest assets in anyone. As Jackson JA observes in *NALAC* (at 546), to say that conversion of non-exempt property to exempt property effects a settlement "mistakes the consequence of this type of settlement from the act which effects it."

Prof. Cuming's second point is that historically s. 91 was only meant to apply where property was transferred or held on trust for a donee, and not to a case where the debtor converts assets from one form to another while still remaining the sole beneficiary of the property or otherwise retaining control over it. In any event, he points out, where the settlement involves a donee, s. 67(1)(a) of the BIA does not apply and it makes no difference how the property is characterized in the donee's hands under provincial law.

Third, Prof. Cuming is also critical—again relying on Justice Jackson's judgment— on the much expanded meaning earlier courts have given to the concluding words in s. 91(2) ("or that the interest of the settlor in the property did not pass on the execution thereof"), to overcome the requirement in the first part of s. 91(2) that the trustee must be able to prove that the settlor was unable to pay all her debts without the aid of the property

---

* R.C.C. Cuming, "Section 91 (Settlements) of the Bankruptcy and Insolvency Act: A Mutated Monster" (1995), 25 *CBLJ* 235.

comprised in the settlement. Thus the pre-*NALAC* courts held that the "or" alternative applies where the bankrupt is the beneficiary under the settlement or otherwise retains control over the property. Jackson JA shows in *NALAC* (at 549-56) that this was not the intended role of the "or" exception and that, coupled with the courts' willingness to treat a conversion of assets from non-exempt to exempt status as a settlement, it leads to very unfair results for bankrupt debtors.

Prof. Cuming's overall conclusion is that it should be left to Parliament to decide whether the provincial exemptions recognized in s. 67(1)(a) are too generous, and he believes that the courts have badly skewed s. 91 by reading in their own prescriptions of desirable public policy.

Other lawyers disagree with Prof. Cuming's and Justice Jackson's reading of s. 91(2). They argue that the effect of the 1992 amendment of "settlement" in s. 2 of the BIA to include the designation of a beneficary in an insurance contract justifies the broader reading of s. 91(2), at least where the settlor was insolvent at the time of the designation. *NALAC* is on appeal to the Supreme Court of Canada, so we may look forward to a resolution of this conflict in the reasonably near future.

An important issue that was not addressed in either *Yewdale* or *NALAC* is the significance of the fact that the 1992 definition of "settlement" makes no reference to the settlor's intention in making the contract or transfer. At common law a settlement "implies an intention that the property shall be retained or preserved for the benefit of the donee in such a form that it can be traced" (*Re Bozanich* [1942] SCR 130, 23 CBR 234, 237, a leading case). Lisa Caplan argues in a case comment on *NALAC* in (1994), 26 CBR (3d) 1, that the omission of intention is highly significant. She states that the test is no longer how the bankrupt intended the property to be held, but whether the property was dealt with in such a manner as to put it beyond the creditors' reach.

She recognizes that if the intention test is removed there is nothing to distinguish a settlement from an outright conveyance or gift and that conveyances which would normally be subject to scrutiny under provincial conveyance legislation will also be caught by s. 91 of the BIA. This consequence does not dismay her since she favours uniform rules for the avoidance of pre-bankruptcy transactions over the fragmentary results brought about by the concurrent operation of federal and provincial avoidance provisions.

Hopefully the Supreme Court will address the definitional issue when hearing the *NALAC* appeal. Regrettably, current plans of the federal government for further amendments to the BIA do not include a review of s. 91 and the other voidable transaction provisions in the Act.

Optical Recording Laboratories v. Digital Recording Corp.
(1990), 1 OR (3d) 131 (CA)

GRIFFITHS JA (for the Court): On the petition of the respondent creditor, Granger J, by judgment dated August 27, 1989 [now reported 69 OR (2d) 628, 75 CBR (NS) 216 (SC Bkcy.)], adjudged the appellant debtor bankrupt and issued a receiving order against it finding that the appellant had committed acts of bankruptcy contrary to ss. 42(1)(b) and 42(1)(g) of the *Bankruptcy Act*, RSC 1985, c. B-3 (as amended). The appellant appeals from the receiving order, contending that the trial judge erred in finding the particular acts of bankruptcy. The respondent cross-appeals, contending that the trial judge erred in failing to go further and find that the appellant had committed, in addition, an act of bankruptcy under s. 42(1)(c) of the Act by creating a fraudulent preference.

The facts

The facts are set out at length in the reasons of the learned trial judge. The following is a summary of those facts pertinent to this appeal.

The appellant, Optical Recording Laboratories Inc. (Laboratories), had a sister company, Optical Recording Corporation (ORC). Mr. G. John Adamson owned all of the common shares of John Adamson Associates Limited which controlled Laboratories and ORC. Adamson was the directing mind of both Laboratories and ORC.

On March 28, 1985 the respondent, Digital Recording Corporation Inc. (Digital), sold a complete experimental facility known as a document storage development system (DSDS) to Laboratories for $21,500,000 of which $2,730,000 was paid in cash and the balance of $18,770,000 was secured by a promissory note made by Laboratories in favour of Digital. The promissory note provided that instalment payments on account of principal and interest would not commence until March 28, 1990 unless there was a default on the part of Laboratories in which case the whole of the principal amount outstanding together with accrued interest thereon would be due and payable immediately. Default under the note would include the following:

1. If Laboratories failed to pay any instalment payment within five days of the due date; or

2. If Laboratories became bankrupt or involved in an insolvency proceeding; or

3. If Laboratories defaulted on any obligation of $100,000 or more which gave the holder of such obligation the right to accelerate payment thereof.

Pursuant to the agreement of March 28, 1985, Laboratories received from Digital the "hard assets," that is, the technology and hardware necessary to undertake research and to develop new products with the DSDS. At the same time as the sale to Laboratories, there was a separate transaction wherein Digital assigned to ORC the patent rights to the technology involved in the DSDS. Under this separate arrangement, ORC was to pay to Digital a certain percentage of royalties received.

On August 31, 1987, Mr. Eli Jacobs (principal shareholder of Digital), Laboratories and ORC entered into a credit arrangement whereby Jacobs was to provide Laboratories and ORC with a line of credit up to $500,000 (US). Laboratories and ORC were jointly and severally liable under this agreement and were, pursuant to the agreement, required to pay monthly interest payments on the principal amount owing.

By January 1988, Laboratories and ORC were indebted to Jacobs under the credit arrangement in the amount of $650,000 (US). On February 12, 1988, Jacobs served Laboratories and ORC with a notice of default under the credit agreement and instituted an action in New York State to recover the amount owing. Jacobs, on behalf of Digital, also took the position that this default under the credit agreement constituted an event of default under the promissory note in that Laboratories had defaulted on an obligation of $100,000 or more. On March 8, 1988, Digital instituted proceedings in the Supreme Court of Ontario against Laboratories for $18,770,000 plus accrued interest owing on the note.

On April 12, 1988, the action brought by Jacobs in New York State was settled and the amount owing under the credit agreement was satisfied when ORC paid approximately $761,000 (US) or $960,000 (Cdn.) directly to Jacobs. Laboratories purported to treat this payment by ORC as a loan to it by ORC. On May 13, 1988, Laboratories executed a general security agreement in favour of ORC purporting to secure the $761,000 US.

On June 30, 1988, Laboratories entered into an asset sale agreement with ORC pursuant to which Laboratories purported to sell all its assets to ORC except the DSDS and a term deposit held in trust for Revenue Canada, for $1,922,000. The terms of the sale were $200,000 cash, assumption of $360,000 of Laboratories' debt and satisfaction of the $1,362,000 of debt owing by Laboratories to ORC.

On July 1, 1988, Laboratories terminated all its employees, who were immediately rehired by ORC. Laboratories' research business was then carried on by ORC on premises formerly occupied by Laboratories, using the same employees and facilities to carry on the business previously pursued by Laboratories.

On August 8, 1988, Digital petitioned Laboratories for a receiving order. The trial judge granted the order, holding that Laboratories had committed acts of bankruptcy contrary to what are now ss. 42(1)(b) and 42(1)(g) of the *Bankruptcy Act*. Those subsections read:

42(1) A debtor commits an act of bankruptcy in each of the following cases:

• • •

(b) if in Canada or elsewhere he makes a fraudulent conveyance, gift, delivery or transfer of his property or of any part thereof;

• • •

(g) if he assigns, removes, secretes or disposes of or attempts or is about to assign, remove, secrete or dispose of any of his property with intent to defraud, defeat or delay his creditors or any of them. ...

The learned trial judge declined to make a finding that Laboratories had committed an act of bankruptcy pursuant to s. 42(1)(c) which reads:

(c) if in Canada or elsewhere he makes any conveyance or transfer of his property or any part thereof, or creates any charge thereon, that would under this Act be void as a fraudulent preference.

The findings of the trial judge

The findings of the trial judge may be summarized as follows:

1. That Digital was a creditor of Laboratories within the meaning of s. 2 of the *Bankruptcy Act*, that is, Digital was a person having a claim "preferred, secured or unsecured, provable as a claim" under the Act.

2. That the issue of whether the entire sum owing under the promissory note was due must await the trial of the Supreme Court action in Ontario brought by Digital against Laboratories and in which Laboratories denied liability under the promissory note and counterclaimed for damages. The trial judge ruled that, until the issue of what was due

under the promissory note was settled in the Supreme Court action, he was not prepared to find that Laboratories had committed a fraudulent preference within the meaning of s. 42(1)(c) of the *Bankruptcy Act* since proof of the insolvency of Laboratories at the time of the transfer is an essential requisite under s. 95 of the Act. For the same reasons, the trial judge was not prepared to find that Laboratories had committed an act of bankruptcy within the meaning of s. 42(1)(j) of the *Bankruptcy Act*, that is, had ceased to meet its liabilities generally as they became due.

The general security agreement dated May 13, 1988 and the asset sale agreement dated June 30, 1988 were both fraudulent and constituted acts of bankruptcy within ss. 42(1)(b) and (g) of the *Bankruptcy Act*.

The trial judge found on the evidence that Adamson clearly intended in both instances to protect the assets of Laboratories from "attack by Digital" [p. 635 OR]. He concluded [p. 637 OR] that the "timing of the actions" by Laboratories corroborated the expressed intent of Adamson to protect the assets of Laboratories and defeat Digital, the major creditor.

With respect to the asset sale agreement of June 30, 1988, the trial judge found that the alleged consideration for this transaction, wherein Laboratories purported to sell not only its hard assets but also its potential ability to generate income from the DSDS, was totally inadequate and that this alleged consideration did not "in any manner (breathe) legitimacy into the agreement" [p. 639 OR].

The trial judge found that, by hiring the former employees and taking over Laboratories' former premises, ORC would continue to use the DSDS and research developed by Laboratories. The trial judge said [p. 637 OR] that he was "convinced beyond any doubt that the transfer was fraudulent and an act of bankruptcy within s. 42(1)(b)" of the *Bankruptcy Act*.

Attack on the findings of the trial judge

On this appeal, counsel for Laboratories submitted that the trial judge erred in concluding on the evidence that the two transactions constituted fraudulent conveyances. It is submitted that the general security agreement of May 13, 1988 and the asset sale agreement of June 30, 1988 were each entered into for *bona fide* business purposes and for good consideration.

In arriving at his conclusions, the trial judge made findings of fact that, in my view, were open to him to make on the evidence and an appellate court should not interfere with those findings. The trial judge expressly rejected the position of Laboratories that all of its actions were legitimate business actions and were not fraudulent within the meaning of the *Bankruptcy Act*. The trial judge found, on the testimony of John Adamson, the directing mind of both Laboratories and ORC, that his object in both transactions under attack was to ensure that if the principal sum on the promissory note was due, the income-producing assets developed by Laboratories would be protected from attack by Digital. He found, in effect, that the timing of the transactions and the lack of "good and valuable consideration" raised general suspicion as to the *bona fides* of the transactions. The question of whether both transactions were entered into with an intent to defraud creditors is one of fact, to be decided in the particular circumstances of the case. Here, the trial judge concluded in effect that the actions of Laboratories were intended to denude it of all its revenue-producing assets, so that the principal creditor, Digital, could not be repaid. This conclusion was justified on the evidence. The first ground of appeal must fail.

Whether the "conveyances" constitute fraudulent conveyances in law

Counsel for Laboratories submitted as a central ground of appeal that the trial judge erred in law in making a finding under the *Bankruptcy Act* that the two transactions in question constituted fraudulent conveyances. Counsel submitted that a fraudulent conveyance within the meaning of s. 42(1)(b) of the *Bankruptcy Act* and a fraudulent preference within the meaning of s. 42(1)(c) are mutually exclusive categories. Counsel argued that a fraudulent conveyance is a conveyance to a person who is not a creditor of the transferor. A fraudulent preference, it was submitted, by contrast is a conveyance to a person who is a creditor. ORC was a creditor to some extent at the material time and therefore, it was argued, the conveyance to that company would not qualify as a fraudulent conveyance but should only be considered as a possible "fraudulent preference" within the meaning of s. 42(1)(c).

Counsel for Laboratories submits that in order for a conveyance to be considered a fraudulent preference under s. 95 of the *Bankruptcy Act*, the party challenging the conveyance must prove at the outset that the transferor, Laboratories, was insolvent at the time the conveyance was made. It is submitted that Digital failed to satisfy the trial judge that Laboratories was insolvent at the date of the conveyances and, therefore, the transactions would not constitute fraudulent preferences under the Act.

The only authority that counsel for Laboratories cited in support of the proposition that ss. 42(1)(b) and (g) of the *Bankruptcy Act* apply only where the transfer or conveyances are made to a third party that is not a creditor, was the following statement contained in the report of the Ontario Law Reform Commission on the *Enforcement of Judgement Debts and Related Matters* (Toronto, 1983), Part IV:

Conceptually, and for the purposes of this chapter, a distinction may be drawn between a fraudulent conveyance and a fraudulent or unjust preference. A fraudulent conveyance is a transfer by the debtor of his property to a third party other than a creditor, whereas a fraudulent preference is a payment by the debtor to one or more, but not all, of his creditors, the transferee or transferees being preferred thereby. While the language of the *Fraudulent Conveyances Act* would seem to comprehend both fraudulent conveyances and fraudulent preferences, the orthodox view is that the Act is restricted to the voiding of fraudulent conveyances.

No case authority was cited for the above proposition. In my view, the distinction drawn by the authors of the Law Reform Commission report between fraudulent conveyances and fraudulent preferences was drawn solely for the purpose of the discussion that followed in the ensuing chapter.

Although the *Bankruptcy Act* is the governing federal legislation, it has long been recognized that creditors are entitled to make use of the rights and remedies provided under provincial legislation to the extent that such legislation is not in conflict with the *Bankruptcy Act*: see *Re Panfab Corp.*, [1971] 2 OR 202, 15 CBR (NS) 20, 17 DLR (3d) 382 (HCJ), at p. 207 OR *per* Houlden J.

The two provincial statutes that operate concurrently in the area of fraudulent transfers are the *Fraudulent Conveyances Act*, RSO 1980, c. 176 and the *Assignments and Preferences Act*, RSO 1980, c. 33.

There is no definition of "fraudulent conveyance" in the *Bankruptcy Act*. Under the *Fraudulent Conveyances Act*, a debtor makes a "fraudulent conveyance" if he makes a "conveyance" of property "with intent to *defeat, hinder, delay or defraud* creditors or others of their just and lawful actions" (s. 2) (emphasis added). By s. 1(a), the term "conveyance" includes a "charge" on the debtor's property and, accordingly, the general security agreement of May 13, 1988 executed by Laboratories in favour of ORC would qualify as a "conveyance."

The provisions of the *Fraudulent Conveyances Act* defining a fraudulent conveyance in no way limit such transaction to conveyances to third parties other than creditors. In my view, there is no rational reason to read into the legislative definition such a restrictive interpretation. The legislation, being remedial, should be given a liberal construction.

The author C.R.B. Dunlop, in his textbook *Creditor-Debtor Law in Canada* (Toronto: Carswell, 1981), at p. 513, states the purpose of fraudulent conveyance legislation as follows:

> The purpose of the Statute of Elizabeth and of the Canadian Acts based on it, as interpreted by the courts, is to strike down all conveyances of property made with the intention of delaying, hindering or defrauding creditors and others except for conveyances made for good consideration and bona fide to persons not having notice of such fraud. *The legislation is couched in very general terms and should be interpreted liberally.* Lord Mansfield concluded that the common law had always been strongly against fraud in every shape and that the Statute of Elizabeth *"cannot receive too liberal a construction, or be too much extended in suppression of fraud." Relying on this policy, the courts have interpreted the statute to include any kind of alienation of property made with the requisite intent, the form of the transaction being immaterial.* Similarly the legislation has been held to invalidate a conveyance of any kind of exigible or attachable property of the debtor, so long as it is of some real value.

(Emphasis added)

In my view, in determining whether a conveyance is fraudulent under s. 42(1)(b) or (c) of the *Bankruptcy Act*, it is irrelevant whether the transfer was made to a creditor. Instead, what is germane to such an inquiry is the genuineness of the conveyance. To this end, s. 3 of the *Fraudulent Conveyances Act* precludes the impeachment of a conveyance "upon good consideration and *bona fide* to a person not having at the time of the conveyance to him notice or knowledge of the intent set forth" in s. 2 (i.e., to defeat, hinder, delay or defraud creditors). If the argument of Laboratories were correct, debtors could avoid a finding of fraudulent conveyance under the *Fraudulent Conveyances Act*, even though they conveyed assets intending to defeat, hinder or delay their creditors, so long as the recipient of the conveyance was a creditor for any amount, no matter how nominal. In my view, if such a limitation were intended, then it would surely have been expressly stipulated in the legislation.

This second ground fails and, accordingly, the appeal must be dismissed.

The cross-appeal

In the cross-appeal, counsel for Digital submits that the learned trial judge erred in failing to find that the sale under the asset sale agreement of June 30, 1988 from Laboratories to ORC was a transfer of property between a debtor and a creditor made within three months of the date of the petition for the receiving order. Counsel argues it was therefore void as a fraudulent preference under s. 95 of the *Bankruptcy Act* because (a) Laboratories was insolvent at the time of the transfer; (b) the transferee, ORC, was a creditor; and (c) the transfer had the effect of giving that creditor a preference over other creditors such as Digital.

There is no question that conditions (b) and (c) are satisfied in the light of the findings of the trial judge. As the trial judge said [pp. 634-35 OR]:

If the sum of $18,770,000 plus accrued interest was due when ORL (Laboratories) entered into the asset sale agreement, such agreement would have been a transfer by an insolvent company providing a creditor with a preference and therefore deemed fraudulent and void, as made within three months of the bankruptcy.

However, the trial judge declined to make a finding that the sum of $18,770,000 was owing on the promissory note at the material time and that Laboratories was therefore insolvent. He directed his mind to s. 42(1)(j) of the *Bankruptcy Act* which provides:

42(1) A debtor commits an act of bankruptcy in each of the following cases:

• • •

(j) if he ceases to meet his liabilities generally as they become due.

The trial judge held that the issue of whether or not the sum of $18,770,000 was a liability that had become due must await the outcome of the Supreme Court action brought by Digital against Laboratories for recovery of that sum under the note. In that respect, he said [p. 632 OR]:

That action, however, is for a determination as to whether or not the actions of ORL (Laboratories) constituted a default under the promissory note and thereby rendered the total amount owing, not whether Digital has a claim against ORL. The unliquidated amount of damages ORL alleges are due to it under the counterclaim cannot be set off against Digital's claim and do not affect Digital's status as creditor. Accordingly Digital has status to bring this petition.

Counsel for Digital submits that the trial judge erred in limiting his consideration to the issue of whether Laboratories was insolvent in the sense that it had ceased to meet its liabilities generally as they became due as at May 13, 1988 under s. 42(1)(j) of the *Bankruptcy Act*. Counsel submits that the 1987 and 1988 financial statements filed at trial demonstrate that Laboratories had approximately $400,000 of assets at the time and liabilities in excess of several million dollars made up substantially of the debt owing to Digital. It was submitted that the trial judge should have directed his attention to the definition of "insolvent person" as defined by s. 2 "insolvent person" (c) of the Act as follows:

"insolvent person" means a person who is not bankrupt and who resides or carries on business in Canada, whose liabilities to creditors provable as claims under this Act amount to one thousand dollars, and

• • •

(c) the aggregate of whose property is not, at a fair valuation, sufficient, or, if disposed of at a fairly conducted sale under legal process, would not be sufficient to enable payment of all his obligations, due and accruing due.

In my respectful view, the learned trial judge erred in failing to make a finding of insolvency within the meaning of the definition in s. 2 "insolvent person" (c). At the material time of the petition, the financial statements filed in the proceedings clearly established that the liabilities of Laboratories far exceeded its assets. In its evidence at trial, Adamson admitted that the obligation of $18,770,000 plus interest *was owing* but disputed whether it was due. In the Supreme Court action brought in Ontario, the counterclaim of Laboratories was for a sum of approximately $200,000 damages. Whatever success Laboratories might enjoy in the pending Supreme Court action, it seems to me improbable that its liabilities on the promissory note, which are now in excess of $23,000,000, would be reduced to a point where its assets at any fair valuation would be sufficient to meet those liabilities. It must not be overlooked, as well, that the trial judge earlier found that Laboratories was a "creditor" of Digital and this finding could only be supported on the basis that money was owing to Digital under the promissory note.

Accordingly, I would allow the cross-appeal and vary the judgment below to include a finding that the appellant committed an act of bankruptcy as well, contrary to s. 42(1)(c) of the *Bankruptcy Act* by making a conveyance of its property and creating a charge thereon that would, under the *Bankruptcy Act*, be void as a fraudulent preference.

• • •

*Appeal dismissed with costs;
cross-appeal allowed without costs.*

Blaine L. Hudson, Trustee v. Benallack
[1976] 2 SCR 168

The judgment of the Court was delivered by DICKSON J:

I

This appeal raises a question of statutory construction which, one should think, would not cause difficulty, but which has indeed given rise to an abundance of conflicting legal opinion and a thoroughly obfuscated state of the law. The question is whether the words "with a view to giving such creditor a preference" contained in s. 73(1) of the *Bankruptcy Act*, RSC 1970, c. B-3, require only an intention on the part of the insolvent debtor to prefer or a concurrent intent on the part of both debtor and creditor. Sections 73 and 74 of the Act [BIA s. 95] read as follows:

• • •

Any conveyance or transfer of property or payment made by an insolvent person in favour of any creditor with a view to giving such creditor a preference over other creditors is deemed fraudulent and void as against the trustee in bankruptcy if the insolvent person becomes bankrupt within three months thereafter or within twelve months where the insolvent person and the preferred creditor are related persons.

II

In the present case the transaction impugned is the assignment on March 1, 1972, by G.S. & D. Construction Ltd. to the respondents, John Alexander Benallack and Lillian M. Benallack, of the assignor's interest, as purchaser, in an agreement for sale of certain lands in the City of Calgary. The consideration for the assignment was stated to be $15,250. At the time the assignor company was indebted to the assignees in the amount of $15,000 with interest and this indebtedness was used to offset the purchase price of the assignor's interest in the agreement of sale. All of the issued shares of G.S. & D. Construction Ltd. were owned by George Bayard Benallack and Shirley Edna May Benallack, the son and daughter-in-law respectively of the respondents. G.S. & D. Construction Ltd. made an assignment in bankruptcy on June 27, 1972, within the 12-month period mentioned in s. 74 of the Act, and the appellant Hudson was named as trustee. The learned Chambers Judge, Cullen J, made a number of findings, of which the following are of moment:

1. On March 1, 1972, the date of the assignment, the bankrupt company was an insolvent person within the meaning of the *Bankruptcy Act*;
2. The bankrupt and the respondents were related persons within the meaning of the Act and s. 74 applied;
3. The respondents received a preference over other creditors as a result of the assignment;
4. The bankrupt intended to give the respondents a preference over its other creditors.

Cullen J held against the need for concurrent intent and declared the assignment to be void as against the trustee in bankruptcy. The Appellate Division of the Supreme Court of Alberta reversed.

III

On the question whether proof of concurrent intent on the part of the debtor and creditor must be shown before the transaction can be set aside, there is, as I have indicated, a wide divergence of opinion. There are many decisions in which it has been held that concurrent intent must be proved; others in which it has been held that the Court is concerned only with the intent of the debtor; and still others in which the point has been left unresolved.

IV

Although the Courts of the country appear divided, more or less evenly, on the need for a concurrent intent before invalidating a transaction, the textbook writers and commentators do not evidence such divergence of opinion. The editors of Duncan & Honsberger, *Bankruptcy in Canada*, 3rd ed., p. 485, point out that s. 64 (now s. 73) makes no reference to the view of the creditor and that the cases in England and in the other Dominions on corresponding sections in Bankruptcy Acts contain no references to the view of the creditor, the view of the debtor alone being considered. The editors of Houlden & Morawetz, *Bankruptcy Law of Canada*, Cumulative Supplement, 1974, at p. 83, say:

In view of the plain meaning of Sec. 73, the concurrent intent of both debtor and creditor is not necessary to show a fraudulent preference. The intention of the debtor alone is to be considered.

and in Bradford & Greenberg's *Canadian Bankruptcy Act*, 3rd ed., p. 163, the authors cite "an intention on the part of the debtor to prefer" as one of the two circumstances constituting a fraudulent preference. See also 2 CED (Ont. 3rd) 15-334: "The intention of the debtor alone is to be considered" and *Comment* in (1958-59), 37 CBR 153, and *Notes on Section 64 of the Bankruptcy Act* by Professor Réginald Savoie in (1967), 9 CBR (NS) 1.

V

If this Court is free to decide the issue of concurrent intent untrammelled by earlier decisions, there would seem to be at least three reasons why we should not engraft upon s. 73 of the *Bankruptcy Act* an additional concept, that of concurrent intent: first, the policy of the *Bankruptcy Act*; second, the history of the Act; third, the language of s. 73.

The object of the bankruptcy law is to ensure the division of the property of the debtor rateably among all his creditors in the event of his bankruptcy. Section 112 of the Act provides that, subject to the Act, all claims proved in the bankruptcy shall be paid *pari passu*. The Act is intended to put all creditors upon an equal footing. Generally, until a debtor is insolvent or has an act of bankruptcy in contemplation, he is quite free to deal with his property as he wills and he may prefer one creditor over another but, upon becoming insolvent, he can no longer do any act out of the ordinary course of business which has the effect of preferring a particular creditor over other creditors. If one creditor receives a preference over other creditors as a result of the debtor acting intentionally and in fraud of the law, this defeats the equality of the bankruptcy laws.

The cognizance of the creditor or its absence should be irrelevant. One can sympathize with the rationale of concurrent intent, which is the desire to protect an innocent creditor who accepts payment of a debt in good faith, but it is hard to reconcile this point of view with the language of the statute, with the history of bankruptcy legislation, and with the right of other innocent creditors to equal protection.

VII

I come now to consider the decision of this Court in *Benallack v. Bank of British North America*. The case has stood on the books for seventy years. Many judges have considered it controlling on the question of concurrent purpose as applied to s. 73(1) of the *Bankruptcy Act*. I approach the case, therefore, with the respect to which those considerations entitle it, but I must at once observe that the case was decided in 1905, some fourteen years before the enactment of the Canadian *Bankruptcy Act* in 1919. It concerned a Yukon Ordinance having to do with preferential assignments, c. 38 of the Consolidated Ordinances of the Yukon Territory 1902. To permit comparison with s. 73(1) of the *Bankruptcy Act*, I will give the Ordinance in its entirety:

An Ordinance respecting Preferential Assignments.

1. Every gift, conveyance, assignment or transfer, delivery over or payment of goods, chattels or effects or of bonds, bills, notes, securities or of shares, dividends, premiums or bonus in any bank, company or corporation made by any person at any time when he is in insolvent circum-

stances or is unable to pay his debts in full or knows that he is on the eve of insolvency with
intent to defeat or delay or prejudice his creditors or to give to any one or more of them a
preference over his other creditors or over any one or more of them or which has such effect shall
as against them be utterly void.

2. Every such gift, conveyance, assignment, transfer, delivery over or payment whether made
owing to pressure or partly owing to pressure or not, which has the effect of defeating, delaying
or prejudicing creditors or giving one or more of them a preference shall as against the other
creditors of such debtor be utterly void.

3. Nothing in this Ordinance shall apply to any deed of assignment made and executed by a
debtor for the purpose of paying and satisfying rateably and proportionately and without preference or priority all the creditors of such debtor their just debts or any *bona fide* sale of goods or
payment made in the ordinary course of trade or calling, to innocent purchasers or parties.

The wording of the Ordinance differs from that of s. 73(1) of the *Bankruptcy Act*; in
particular s. 3 introduces concepts of *bona fides* and "innocent purchasers or parties" not
found in s. 73(1).

The action in the 1905 *Benallack* case was brought to set aside several instruments,
consisting of a chattel mortgage, land transfer and book debt assignments, in favour of a
bank, as being void against creditors under the Ordinance. The bank was ignorant of the
true financial condition of the debtor. Idington J, who delivered the unanimous judgment
of a five-man Court, after referring to the cases of *Stephens v. McArthur*, and *Gibbons v.
McDonald*, said:

> And if a fraudulent preference to whom is the having such a purpose to be attributed?
>
> Is it enough to shew that the assignor may have had such an intent?
>
> Must not the assignee as well as the assignor be a party to the fraudulent intent?
>
> Such would seem to be the result of a long line of decisions upon which the commercial world
> has had a right to act for a long time past. And though there may not have been any express
> decision on the point upon this legislation in this Court the late Chief Justice, Sir William Ritchie,
> in *Gibbons v. McDonald*, at page 589 indicates that in his view there must be
>
> a concurrence of intent on the one side to give and on the other to accept a preference over
> other creditors.
>
> Counsel for the appellants properly conceded that the evidence here did not show knowledge
> on the part of the bank such as would enable us to find this concurrence of purpose.
>
> Until the legislature obliterates the element of intent in such legislation and clearly declares
> that, quite independently of intent, the preferential result or effect of the transaction impeached is
> to govern, it will be exceedingly difficult to arrive at any other conclusion in cases of this kind.
> The results that might flow from such legislation ought not to be brought about without such
> purpose being most clearly expressed by the legislature.

The case is unsatisfactory, if I may, with respect, say so, in that none of the "long line of
decisions" upon which Idington J relies is identified and no reasons are given for
concluding that the intent to which the Ordinance refers must be entertained by the creditor
as well as the debtor. In the later case of *Salter & Arnold, Ltd. v. Dominion Bank, supra*, as
I have already mentioned, Duff J observed that whatever else may be said about the
intention to give a preference envisaged by s. 31 (now s. 73) "it must be an intention

entertained by the debtor." These words have been interpreted by some judges to mean that the intention with which one is concerned is only that of the debtor. I think, however, that we must give effect to the words of Duff J "whatever else may be said about it." What Duff J intended, in my opinion, was merely to leave the matter open, just as Cartwright J, as he then was, did in the penultimate paragraph of his judgment in *Velensky v. Canadian Credit Men's Trust Association Limited* (reported in 38 CBR 162 as *In re Bernard Motors Ltd.*). The paragraph in question, for some reason, was not printed in the report of the case in the Supreme Court Reports but is contained in the 38 Canadian Bankruptcy Reports, p. 167 and reads:

Before parting with the matter, I wish to observe that Bridges J suggests a doubt as to whether if he were untrammelled by authority he would hold that, on the true construction of s. 64, to render void a preference in fact it is necessary that there be an intention on the part of the creditor to be preferred as well as an intention on the part of the debtor to prefer. In *In re Blenkarn Planer Ltd.* (1958), 37 CBR 147, 26 WWR 168, 14 DLR (2d) 719, 1958 Can. Abr. 55, Ruttan J examines a number of decisions and expresses the opinion that the view of the debtor alone has to be considered. I mention this for the purpose of making it clear that in the case before us this point does not require decision and I express no opinion upon it.

I have concluded that a finding of concurrent intent is not necessary in order to set aside a payment as a fraudulent preference under s. 73 of the *Bankruptcy Act*. I do not believe that the decision of this Court in *Benallack v. Bank of British North America* is authoritative in interpreting s. 73 of the *Bankruptcy Act*. However similar may be the wording, I do not think that a phrase in a provincial or territorial Ordinance of three paragraphs dealing with preferential assignments and having a particular legislative history and jurisprudence should govern the language of a federal Act of some 213 sections dealing with bankruptcy and having an entirely different legislative history and jurisprudence.

One must recall that fraudulent preference statutes and fraudulent conveyance statutes outside of the bankruptcy laws have generally contained a section exempting from the application of the statute any assignment or payment or *bona fide* sale of goods made in the ordinary course of trade to innocent purchasers. Such saving provisions are contained in our provincial fraudulent preference statutes and in each of the cases relied on in the 1905 *Benallack* judgment a similar statute was under consideration. These statutes required consideration of the knowledge or *bona fides* of the creditor. Under the law relating to bankruptcy the rule has been different, as the English authorities cited earlier in these reasons will confirm.

I am further of the view that s. 3 of the Yukon Ordinance plays the same role in the interpretation of the Ordinance as the proviso to s. 92 of the English Act of 1869 played in *Butcher v. Stead*, requiring consideration of the knowledge and intent and privity of the creditor; but there is no counterpart of s. 3 of the Ordinance to be found in s. 73(1) of the *Bankruptcy Act*. Section 75(1) of the Act, which protects certain transactions, is the only section in which the *bona fides* of the creditor emerges. Section 75(1) is very limited in scope. It is expressly made "Subject to the foregoing provisions of this Act ... with respect to the avoidance of certain settlements and preferences ..." and only comes into operation when s. 73(1) does not apply. Section 75(1) in express terms calls for double intent whereas s. 73(1) does not.

Our duty is to construe the language of s. 73 of the *Bankruptcy Act* within the ambit
and policy of that Act; if we go to the words of the statute we find that what is to be
considered as fraudulent and void is:

"Every conveyance ... of property" (i.e., the assignment in favour of respondents) "... made by
any insolvent person" (i.e., G.S. & D. Construction Ltd.) "in favour of any creditor" (i.e. the
respondents) "... with a view to giving such creditor a preference ..."

It seems to me plain from the quoted words that the view, the only view, with which
s. 73(1) of the Act is concerned is that of the insolvent person making the conveyance and
we should not be diverted to any other conclusion by reliance upon a case in which a
different statute in different language was construed. Whether or not a conveyance or
payment is a fraudulent preference depends entirely on the intention of the debtor. The trial
judge has found against the respondents on this point.

• • •

Appeal allowed.

Thomas Flynn & Sons Construction (Toronto) Limited v.
Laporte and Optimum Contracting Limited
(1990), 78 CBR (NS) 158 (Ont. SC)

REID J: Plaintiff was a subcontractor for Lap-Ron Construction Ltd., a company owned
by defendant Laporte, on a substantial contract to outfit ice cream parlours in southern
Ontario for Ontario Dairy Products Limited. Ontario Dairy ran into financial difficulties,
and in 1982 could not pay Lap-Ron's outstanding account. This in turn caused Lap-Ron
difficulty in paying its creditors.

By the summer of 1982, Lap-Ron owed plaintiff $19,563.96 on the Ontario Dairy
contract. On 10th September 1982, after repeated requests for payment, plaintiff issued a
specially endorsed writ of summons against Lap-Ron and Ontario Dairy claiming payment
of $23,029.74 (the first action). On 27th January 1983 plaintiff moved successfully for
judgment against Lap-Ron for part of its claim in the amount of $15,205.96. This judgment
remains unsatisfied.

On 7th June 1983 a judgment debtor examination of Laporte as president of Lap-Ron
revealed to plaintiff for the first time the existence of Optimum, a company of which
Laporte is as well the president and sole shareholder. That revelation led to the present
action (this action) being commenced on 21st September 1983.

The writ of summons in the first action had been served on Lap-Ron on 20th
September 1982. On 1st October 1982 Laporte caused two written agreements to be made
between Lap-Ron and Optimum. The first transferred Lap-Ron's office equipment to
Optimum for a consideration of $2,200. The second transferred other Lap-Ron assets,
including a truck, a van, two saws and a planer for a consideration of $3,350. Laporte
executed both agreements on behalf of both companies and his secretary witnessed them.
The agreements provided for payment by 30th June 1983 and 1st March 1983 respectively.
On 15th December 1982 Laporte caused another written agreement to be made, again

under his signature for both parties, transferring to him personally Lap-Ron's company car, a 1981 Oldsmobile Cutlass, in consideration of $1 and his assumption of the obligation to pay the balance owing on its purchase. This vehicle later appeared on the books of Optimum.

Lap-Ron made an assignment in bankruptcy on 8th June 1984.

On 10th July 1985 plaintiff obtained an order enabling it to continue this action pursuant to s. 20 [now s. 38] of the Bankruptcy Act, RSC. The order reads, in part:

> 1. THIS COURT ORDERS THAT Thomas Flynn & Sons Construction (Toronto) Ltd. are hereby authorized and may proceed with an action commenced in the Supreme Court of Ontario in the Judicial District of York at Toronto bearing action number 10110/83 in its own name and at its own expense and risk for the purpose of obtaining an Order setting aside certain conveyances made by the within bankrupt to Ronald Laporte and Optimum Contracting Limited.

The order went on to provide for other creditors to join in the action with plaintiff if they saw fit. None did.

Plaintiff relies principally on s. 2 of the Fraudulent Conveyances Act, RSO 1980, c. 176. Sections 1 to 4 of that Act read:

• • •

Plaintiff relies also on ss. 4(1) and 12(1) of the Assignments and Preferences Act, RSO 1980, c. 33, which read:

• • •

The foregoing provisions are referred to hereafter for convenience as "the legislation."

Plaintiff makes the following claims for relief in para. 12 of its statement of claim:

a) such amounts as may be found appropriated or due to Lap-Ron Construction Limited by the Defendants or either of them;

b) interest on any sums found to be appropriated or wrongly given preference by the Defendants to any other creditor and the amounts to which the other Creditors or Defendants were given preferences;

b.1) a declaration that the conveyance of any and all assets or property of Lap-Ron Construction Limited to Optimum Contracting Limited is void;

b.2) a declaration that the conveyance of any assets and property of Lap-Ron Construction Limited to Optimum Contracting Limited, including the ongoing business of Lap-Ron Construction Limited, be set aside;

b.3) damages in the amount of $30,000.00;

c) exemplary and punitive damages in the amount of $25,000.00;

d) pre-judgment interest on the aforesaid sums pursuant to the relevant provisions of the Judicature Act, RSO 1980, c. 223 and the relevant amendments thereto;

e) post-judgment interest on the aforesaid sums pursuant to the relevant provisions of the Judicature Act, RSO 1980, c. 233 and the relevant amendments thereto;

f) their costs of this action.

It was overwhelmingly established in evidence that the written conveyances were part of a scheme contrived by Laporte, when he realized that Lap-Ron was insolvent or about to be, to defeat Lap-Ron's creditors. Laporte testified that as a result of Ontario Dairy's failure to pay Lap-Ron's account, Lap-Ron was unable to pay its creditors. Laporte entreated his creditors for indulgence, but that strategem failed, for Ontario Dairy continued to default and ultimately became bankrupt on 8th June 1984. By September 1982 Lap-Ron was clearly no longer viable. Laporte embarked on a course of action which allowed it to die by taking on new business in the name of Optimum, a company he had incorporated in 1972 but which had been inactive since 1977. He held creditors at bay with promises of payment.

To ensure that services essential to the operation of Optimum, such as the telephone, would continue, Laporte paid, or arranged for payment, of what Lap-Ron owed for them. He was thus able, in effect, to continue Lap-Ron's business under Optimum's name by paying Lap-Ron's debts to such of its suppliers and for such of its services as were necessary to the operation of Optimum. The fact that there are many companies able to do plaintiff's kind of work meant that plaintiff was not essential to Optimum's business operations. That made it possible for Laporte to choose not to pay its account, or, for that matter, the accounts of other non-essential unpaid subcontractors. Being able to pick and choose, Laporte paid some subcontractors and continued to use them, but plaintiff was not in that fortunate group. Probably because of Laporte's repeated assurances that they would be paid, none of Lap-Ron's creditors initiated bankruptcy proceedings. Laporte was thus able to continue this policy of diverting Lap-Ron business to Optimum. Without the burden of Lap-Ron's debt Optimum flourished. It was not until 8th June 1984 that Laporte finally consigned Lap-Ron to bankruptcy, and killed it off.

It is clear that the written agreements of 1st October and 15th December were made when Lap-Ron was insolvent and with the intent to defeat or prefer creditors. They thus fall clearly within the legislation.

The legislation is not confined by its terms to written conveyances. Indeed, s. 1(a) of the Fraudulent Conveyances Act refers to a conveyance "in writing or otherwise." This is significant because the largest transfers were not made by written conveyances. When Laporte saw that Lap-Ron would not be able to carry on he did nothing really more than take down Lap-Ron's sign and hoist Optimum's. He carried on the same business from the same premises with the same phone number, the same customers, the same office equipment, the same employees, some of the same suppliers, and some of the same subcontractors. The most important asset of the business was no doubt his own services, which he simply applied to the interests of Optimum instead of Lap-Ron. Lap-Ron's entire inventory, stock-in-trade, and work-in-progress was taken over by Optimum, and thus transferred just as effectively as if there had been written conveyances for every asset, signed, sealed and delivered. Sales secured by Lap-Ron were credited to Optimum. No consideration was given for anything transferred outside the written agreements. The evidence of the value of what was transferred outside the written agreements differed somewhat. The witness Delaney's evidence was that Lap-Ron had inventory in the amount of some $3,000 and sales of $13,300 which were transferred in effect to Optimum (the costs associated with these sales were left in Lap-Ron). While the unaudited books prepared by Laporte's secretary and her testimony and Laporte's are at odds with Delaney's conclusions, I accept Delaney's evidence. I found Laporte's credibility questionable. His secretary's obvious loyalty in my opinion might well have affected her objectivity.

Since it is clear that by written and "silent" transfers Laporte caused every asset possessed by Lap-Ron to be conveyed to Optimum because Lap-Ron could no longer pay its creditors and for the purpose of defeating creditors, all of the transfers are void. The definition of conveyance in the legislation is wide enough to include transfers made without consideration.

[The court calculated the plaintiff's total damages to be $30,415.64 and continued:]

The relief available under s. 2 of the Fraudulent Conveyances Act and s. 4(1) of the Assignments and Preferences Act is the return of the property conveyed. However, s. 12(1) of the latter enables the plaintiff to recover the proceeds of disposition or realization where the property has been disposed of or realized. It is obvious that the inventory and the sales conveyed have been realized, and plaintiff is therefore entitled to recovery from Optimum against Lap-Ron's debt to the extent of $16,300, the value of the wrongfully transferred inventory and sales. Interest should be added to that amount from 1st October 1982, a date I deem to be the date of the transfers as evidenced by the first written agreement, for I find that Laporte was carrying on Lap-Ron's business under Optimum's name by at least that date. The rate shall be the prime rate in the month preceding the month on which the action was commenced in accordance with s. 36 of the Judicature Act, RSO 1980, c. 223, i.e., 11 per cent, from the date the cause of action arose, 1st October 1982, to the date of judgment, 12th February 1990. The per diem interest owing is thus $4.91 (11 per cent/365 × $16,300). 2690 days have passed since the cause of action arose. Thus, $16,300 plus $13,217.90 ($4.91 × 2690) in interest is owing, for a total value of property fraudulently conveyed of $29,507.90. Plaintiff is also entitled to post-judgment interest on the $16,300 according to s. 137(1)(c) of the Courts of Justice Act, 1984, as amended.

Plaintiff is entitled to judgment in accordance with the foregoing. Plaintiff is as well entitled to an order setting aside the written conveyances. With respect to the latter, the amount plaintiff would be entitled to recover from Optimum towards what it is owed cannot be determined on the evidence placed before me. A reference would be required. If plaintiff desires to proceed in this way it may apply for directions.

I do not think that a case has been made out for exemplary or punitive damages.

• • •

Order accordingly.

Donald A. Robinson v. Countrywide Factors Ltd.
[1978] 1 SCR 753

The judgment of Laskin CJ and Martland, Dickson and de Grandpré JJ was delivered by

THE CHIEF JUSTICE (dissenting): There are two issues in this appeal which is here by leave of this Court. The first is whether a certain transaction and, in particular, a certain debenture, granted on a debtor's stock-in-trade in pursuance of the transaction between the debtor and the respondent creditor, was a fraudulent preference that was impeachable under ss. 3 and 4 of *The Fraudulent Preferences Act*, RSS 1965, c. 397; and the second is whether, if it was so impeachable, those provisions of the provincial Act were *ultra vires* as an invasion of exclusive federal power in relation to bankruptcy and insolvency or, alternatively, were inoperative in the face of the preference provisions of the *Bankruptcy Act*, RSC 1970, c. B-3.

The appellant is trustee in bankruptcy of Kozan Furniture (Yorkton) Ltd. pursuant to a receiving order of November 19, 1968. On November 19, 1966, Kozan entered into a transaction with a pressing creditor, the respondent, whereby it sold certain stock-in-trade to a third person (payment being made to the respondent which reduced Kozan's indebtedness accordingly) and also agreed to give the respondent a debenture on its stock-in-trade for its remaining indebtedness. The debenture was executed on or about March 20, 1967, and duly registered. After the receiving order against Kozan was made, proceedings were taken by the appellant trustee in bankruptcy to set aside the transaction of November 19, 1966, as constituting a fraudulent preference under the provincial *Fraudulent Preferences Act* and to recover the money paid to the respondent and to annul the debenture.

MacPherson J found that Kozan was insolvent at the time of the transaction of November 19, 1966, that there was a concurrent intention of Kozan and the respondent to give and receive a preference, and that, consequently, both the payment made to the respondent and the debenture constituted fraudulent preferences under the provincial statute and were hence impeachable. On appeal, this judgment was set aside on the view of the majority of the Saskatchewan Court of Appeal that the appellant had failed to prove that Kozan was insolvent on November 19, 1966. The trial judge was not called upon to deal with any constitutional issue, and the majority of the Court of Appeal did not have to do so in view of its finding on insolvency. Hall JA who dissented supported the trial judge's finding of insolvency, and in a one sentence assertion, in reliance upon *Re Panfab Corp. Ltd.*, he rejected the contention that *The Fraudulent Preferences Act* was *ultra vires*.

I would not interfere with the findings of the judge of first instance that Kozan was insolvent at the material time and that Kozan intended to give and the respondent intended to receive a preference. This is the view of my brother Spence who, in exhaustive reasons, also concluded that *The Fraudulent Preferences Act* as a whole was not *ultra vires* nor was either s. 3 or s. 4 inoperative in the face of the *Bankruptcy Act*. I have a different opinion on the constitutional issue in this case, as appears from what now follows. That issue does not invite this Court to pronounce on the validity of provincial legislation dealing with fraudulent conveyances or with fraudulent transactions in general. Thus, to take as an example the *Fraudulent Conveyances Act*, RSO 1970, c. 182, nothing said in these reasons is to be taken as impugning the validity of that or similar enactments. They do not, *ex facie*, depend on proof of insolvency or on bankruptcy. In so far as any of the case law, some of it canvassed by my brother Spence, relates to such legislation and carries it into a consideration of the validity of provincial preference legislation which depends, as do ss. 3 and 4 of the Saskatchewan *Fraudulent Preferences Act*, on a condition of insolvency, I find it inapt for the determination of the constitutional question in this appeal.

Sections 3 and 4 aforesaid are in the following terms: ...

Sections 8, 9, 10 and 11, to which each of the foregoing provisions is subject, do not affect the constitutional issue, being concerned with *bona fide* sales or payments to innocent purchasers, to valid sales for consideration and to protection of security given up by a creditor. The present cases does not involve ss. 8 to 11.

I approach the question of validity on principle and on authority. So far as principle is concerned, the starting point is in relevant words of the *British North America Act*, namely s. 91(21), "bankruptcy and insolvency," as they relate to s. 92(13), "property and civil rights in the Province." The elucidation of the meaning and scope of s. 91(21), as of the meaning and scope of any other heads of legislative power, can hardly ever be a purely abstract exercise, even where an attempt is made at neutral definition; but I see no reason why judicial pronouncements, especially at the appellate level where they are those of the Court, should not be considered as throwing light upon the integrity of the head of power in the scheme of the *British North America Act* as a whole.

Four things stand out. First, s. 91(21) is an exclusive federal power; second, it is a power confided to the Parliament of Canada notwithstanding anything else in the Act; third, it is a power, like the criminal law power, whose ambit, did not and does not lie frozen under conceptions held of bankruptcy and insolvency in 1867: see the *Farmers' Creditors Arrangement Act* reference, *Attorney-General for British Columbia v. Attorney General for Canada*, at pp. 402-403; and, fourth, the term "insolvency" in s. 91(21) has as much an independent operation in the reservation of an exclusive area of legislative competence to the Parliament of Canada as the term "bankruptcy"; see *Canadian Bankers Association v. Attorney-General of Saskatchewan*, per Rand J, at p. 46.

The view taken by the Privy Council and by this Court as to the meaning of "insolvency," as well after as before the abolition of Privy Council appeals, has been a uniform one. Lord Thankerton, speaking for the Privy Council in the *Farmers' Creditors Arrangement Act* reference, *supra*, at p. 402, expressed it as follows:

> In a general sense, insolvency means inability to meet one's debts or obligations; in a technical sense, it means the condition or standard of inability to meet debts or obligations, upon the occurrence of which the statutory law enables a creditor to intervene with the assistance of a Court, to stop individual action by creditors and to secure administration of the debtor's assets in the general interest of creditors; the law also generally allows the debtor to apply for the same administration.

This definition was referred to with approval in the majority judgment of the Supreme Court of Canada delivered by Kerwin CJC in *Reference re Validity of the Orderly Payment of Debts Act, 1959 (Alta.)*, at p. 576. Earlier in *Reference re Alberta Debt Adjustment Act*, at p. 40, Duff CJC speaking for all but one of the members of the Court took as an additional ground for invalidating the challenged provincial legislation in that case that the powers of the provincial statutory tribunal set up under that legislation would normally "come into operation when a state of insolvency exists"; and he continued: "It is not too much to say that it is for the purpose of dealing with the affairs of debtors who are pressed and unable to pay their debts as they fall due that these powers and duties are created." If it is for Parliament alone to deal with insolvency, indeed to define it where it chooses to do so and to leave it otherwise to judicial definition, there can be no argument about unlawful invasion of provincial power in relation to property and civil rights. A limitation upon such power necessarily inheres in the federal catalogue of powers in s. 91, and it was recognized as early as 1880 in *Cushing v. Dupuy*, at p. 415, in respect of the federal bankruptcy and insolvency power.

I refer to two other propositions before turning to what I consider to be the relevant cases. First, there is the well-recognized proposition that federal abstinence from legislation in relation to an exclusive head of legislative power does not leave that legislative area open to provincial action: see *Union Colliery Co. v. Bryden*, at p. 588. The principle of our Constitution as it relates to legislative power is not one of simple concurrency of authority subject only to a variable doctrine of paramountcy. Exclusiveness is central to the scheme of distribution, save as to a specified number of concurrent powers, such as those in s. 95. It is only under the umbrella of the doctrine of exclusiveness that the relative scope of federal and provincial authority is assessed, the assessment being carried forward to determine whether there is preclusion or supersession where both federal and provincial legislation are in competition. This brings me to the second point. I take the same view here that was taken by Duff CJC in the *Alberta Debt Adjustment Act* reference and I adopt his words at p. 40, namely that although the motives of a provincial Legislature may be laudable ones, it is precluded from seeking to realize its object by entering into a field not open to it.

Attorney-General of Ontario v. Attorney-General for Canada, generally known as the *Voluntary Assignments* case, stands as the general support for provincial legislation that is challenged in the present case. It concerned only one section, s. 9, of the *Ontario Assignments and Preferences Act*, RSO 1887, c. 124, first enacted in 1885 by 1885 (Can.), c. 26. That section was as follows:

> An assignment for the general benefit of creditors under this Act shall take precedence of all judgments and of all executions not completely executed by payment, subject to the lien, if any, of an execution creditor for his costs, where there is but one execution in the sheriff's hands, or to the lien, if any, of the creditor for his costs, who has the first execution in the sheriff's hands.

This Act replaced the earlier pre-Confederation legislation found in CSUC 1859, c. 26, under the title *The Indigent Debtors Act*, which was continued in the post-Confederation legislation of Ontario as *An Act respecting The Fraudulent Preference of Creditors by persons in insolvent circumstances*, and included in RSO 1877, c. 118. What is significant in this earlier legislation is that (as set out in s. 2 of RSO 1877, c. 118) it dealt with "any person being at the time in insolvent circumstances or unable to pay his debts in full, or knowing himself to be on the eve of insolvency." The substituted Act of 1885 continued the reference to insolvency in respect of preferences, but it also introduced new provisions respecting assignments for the benefit of creditors and these provisions, as was noted in the *Voluntary Assignments* case, were not predicated on insolvency and, indeed, were to a large degree separated from the preference provisions of the Act, as is reflected in s. 3 of RSO 1887, c. 124.

Certainly, as the Privy Council noted, the challenged provision, s. 9, had to be taken in the context of the entire Act. There is no doubt, as well, that the issue of validity was recognized as arising at a time when there was no federal bankruptcy or insolvency legislation in force, the only such legislation, the *Insolvency Act* of 1875 having been repealed in 1880 by 1880 (Can.), c. 1. The majority of the Ontario Court of Appeal, to which the question of the validity of s. 9 had been referred, found that it was *ultra vires* as invading exclusive federal power in relation to bankruptcy and insolvency; see *Re Assignments and Preferences Act, Section 9*. The reversal of this judgment by the Privy Council was accompanied by an acknowledgement of the broad scope of federal power under s. 91(21) when affirmatively exercised but it was held that this power was not invaded by an enactment relating to an assignment that was purely voluntary.

The explanation for this result is found in two passages of the Privy Council's reasons. First, "it is to be observed that an assignment for the general benefit of creditors has long been known to the jurisprudence of this country and also of Canada, and has its force and effect at common law quite independently of any system of bankruptcy or insolvency, or any legislation relating thereto" (at p. 198). Second, "the operation of an assignment for the benefit of creditors was precisely the same, whether the assignor was or was not insolvent. ... The validity of the assignment and its effect would in no way depend on the insolvency of the assignor, and their Lordships think it clear that the 9th section would equally apply whether the assignor was or was not insolvent" (at p. 199). What is evident, therefore, from that case is that, unlike the situation here, the operation of the provincial enactment did not depend on insolvency and the Privy Council was willing to treat s. 9 as having an object that was independent of it. This may even be a supportable view today, albeit there is a range of existing federal legislation dealing with bankruptcy and insolvency. I should note, however, that the majority judgment of this Court in *Reference re the Validity of the Orderly Payment of Debts Act, 1959 (Alta.)*, at pp. 576-577, Kerwin CJC referring to the *Voluntary Assignments* reference, said "it is doubtful whether in view of later pronouncements of the Judicial Committee it would at this date be decided in the same sense, even in the absence of Dominion legislation upon the subject of bankruptcy and insolvency."

The later pronouncements of the Privy Council include its judgment in the *Alberta Debt Adjustment Act* reference, as well as in the *Farmers' Creditors Arrangement Act* reference, *supra*. Equally important is the judgment of this Court in *Canadian Bankers Association v. Attorney-General of Saskatchewan*, dealing with the validity of provincial moratorium legislation. It was in line with the decision in the *Alberta Debt Adjustment Act* reference in finding an invasion of federal power in relation to bankruptcy and insolvency. I think it enough, for present purposes, to refer to what Locke J, speaking for the majority of the Court, said, at p. 42:

> Power to declare a moratorium for the relief of the residents of a Province generally in some great emergency, such as existed in 1914 and in the days of the lengthy depression in the thirties is one thing, but power to intervene between insolvent debtors and their creditors irrespective of the reasons which have rendered the debtor unable to meet his liabilities is something entirely different.

Although judgments of the Privy Council and of this Court (and I add to those already cited *Royal Bank of Canada v. Larue*) have recognized the broad power of Parliament to embrace in its legislation in relation to bankruptcy or insolvency provisions which might otherwise fall within provincial competence, I know of no case in those Courts, other than *Ladore v. Bennett*, where provincial legislation has been sustained, either in the absence of or in the face of federal legislation, when such provincial legislation depends for its operation only upon insolvency. *Ladore v. Bennett* can best be explained as involving municipal reorganization and hence as being concerned with the amalgamation and financial restructuring of units of local government for which the provincial Legislature has a direct responsibility, albeit some of the municipalities involved in the legislatively-directed reorganization were insolvent. It is, indeed, a special case of a piece of special legislation enacted in pursuance of the power conferred by s. 92(8) of the *British North*

America Act, and I do not regard it as offering any lead to continuing legislation relating to private debtors and their creditors.

It is plain to me that if provincial legislation avowedly directed to insolvency, and to transactions between debtor and creditor consummated in a situation of insolvency, can be sustained as validly enacted, unless overborne by competent federal legislation, there is a serious breach of the principle of exclusiveness which embraces insolvency under s. 91(21). This Court so held in a series of cases where the encroachment on the federal bankruptcy and insolvency power was less obvious than that exhibited here. I refer, of course, to the *Alberta Debt Adjustment Act* reference, *supra*, to the *Canadian Bankers' Association* case, *supra*, and to the *Orderly Payment of Debts Act 1959 (Alta.)* reference, *supra*. It would be a curious reversal of the proposition, enunciated in *Madden v. Nelson and Fort Sheppard Railway Co.*, namely, that you cannot do indirectly what you cannot do directly, to hold that the Province can do directly what it cannot do indirectly.

The case put forward by the appellant and by the intervening Provinces which supported him goes even farther. It is contended that notwithstanding the existence of federal bankruptcy legislation dealing with preferences, the challenged provincial legislation can still operate in respect of a particular preference which is given outside of the time limits within which the federal control operates, so long at least as the provincial provision is not more stringent.

I do not follow this line of reasoning, especially on the submission of greater or lesser stringency. The relevant federal provision is s. 73 of the *Bankruptcy Act* [see now s.95] which reads as follows: ...

This provision cannot be taken in isolation. The *Bankruptcy Act* is a code on the subject of bankruptcy and insolvency, defining what is an act of bankruptcy, who is an insolvent person, prescribing what are vulnerable settlements as well as what are vulnerable preferences, declaring what is comprised in a bankrupt's estate, providing for priorities in distribution and for rateable distribution. It provides also, as in the present s. 31(1), for the making of an assignment by an insolvent person for the benefit of creditors as well as providing by s. 24(1)(a) that it is an act of bankruptcy to make an assignment for the benefit of creditors whether the assignment is or is not authorized by the *Bankruptcy Act*. In short, apart from the question whether provincial legislation predicated on insolvency is *ipso facto* invalid, I see no room for any assertion that such provincial legislation can continue to have operative effect in the face of the scope of the *Bankruptcy Act* embracing both bankruptcy and insolvency in its provisions.

It is worth a reminder that there is no common law of bankruptcy and insolvency, and hence it cannot be said that there was an existing common law course of decision which was being embraced by provincial legislation. The common law did not distinguish the fraudulent from the insolvent debtor; it was through legislation that such a distinction was made. If a provincial Legislature wishes to proscribe fraudulent transactions, it is compelled by the *British North America Act* to ensure that its legislation dealing with such transactions does not focus on insolvency.

● ● ●

I wish now to address myself to an issue which, I think, has influenced the approach by single judges to the constitutional question in this case, and wrongly so. That issue is the undesirability of interfering with what appeared to be a practical way of reaching as many alleged preferences in fraud of creditors as possible, to use provincial legislation where federal legislation did not reach far enough, and to use provincial insolvency legislation if nothing else was available. Hence, the approach by way of construction, albeit a dip into a constitutional area was inevitable, avoiding a direct constitutional confrontation. There are cases even in this Court and on this very subject which have proceeded on a straight construction basis to examine whether operative effect can be given to provincial legislation in the face of a federal enactment. Two examples are *Traders Finance Corp. Ltd. v. Levesque*, and *Produits de Caoutchouc Marquis Inc. v. Trottier*. I do not regard either of these cases as requiring a decision on constitutional grounds. The *Traders Finance* case concerned a largely procedural matter, namely, whether the failure of a trustee in bankruptcy to impeach a preference illegal under the *Bankruptcy Act*, precluded a suit by a creditor to that end. The *Trottier* case dealt with the effect of the *Bankruptcy Act* on the extent of a landlord's claim to rank as a preferred creditor.

• • •

I conclude, therefore, as follows. Provincial legislation which purports to provide for impeachment of preferences to creditors given by a person who is then insolvent, where insolvency is the *sine qua non* of impeachability, is invalid as a direct invasion of exclusive federal power in relation to bankruptcy and insolvency. Hence, ss. 3 and 4 of Saskatchewan *Fraudulent Preferences Act* are *ultra vires*. Moreover, in so far as these sections prescribe an impeachment period which enables a creditor to set aside a preference made beyond the period fixed by the *Bankruptcy Act*, and hence not impeachable under that Act, it interferes with the operation of the *Bankruptcy Act* and is, indeed, repugnant to it. It must be remembered that where, as in the present case, there has been a receiving order, the intrusion of provincial legislation relating to transactions entered into by an insolvent, must interfere with the rateable distribution of the bankrupt's property according to the scheme of distribution prescribed by the *Bankruptcy Act*. Whether that scheme is faulty in the view of a Court is immaterial; the correction must come from the responsible Legislature. No more under bankruptcy and insolvency law than under the criminal law can a Province make unlawful what is lawful under valid federal legislation, nor make lawful what is unlawful under valid federal legislation.

• • •

SPENCE J (for the majority): ... I have dealt with what, in my view, are the main cases upon the subject in Canada. Upon considering them *all*, as well as the decision of the Judicial Committee in *A.G. of Ontario v. A.G. for Canada, supra*, I have come to the conclusion that the better view is to confine the effect of what is now s. 73 of the *Bankruptcy Act* to providing for the invalidity of transactions within its exact scope. To that extent, the Parliament of Canada, by valid legislation upon "bankruptcy" and "insolvency," has covered the field but has refrained from completely covering the whole field of transactions avoided by provincial legislation. I am of the opinion that the enactment in 1949 of the provisions now found in s. 50(6) of the *Bankruptcy Act* is a plain indication that Parliament recognized that provisions in provincial statutes dealing with preferential transactions were still valid provincial enactments in reference to "property" and "civil rights" and were valuable aids to trustees in bankruptcy in attacking the validity of such transactions and should be available to the said trustees in bankruptcy.

I am assisted in coming to this conclusion by the view which I believe was behind the Lord Chancellor's reasons in *A.G. of Ontario v. A.G. for Canada, supra*, that the words "bankruptcy" and "insolvency" in s. 91, para. 21, of the *British North America Act* were aimed at legislative schemes which had the purpose of governing the distribution of a debtor's property amongst his creditors. There may well be, and there are, provisions in such legislative schemes, i.e., the *Bankruptcy Act*, dealing with "property" and "civil rights." Such provisions are properly ancillary to the bankruptcy and insolvency legislation, and to the extent to which they do overcome existing valid provincial legislation and bar future provincial legislation *contra* thereto but do not purport to extend beyond that point to invalidate other valid provincial legislation upon "property" and "civil rights."

• • •

BEETZ J: I have had the advantage of reading the opinions of the Chief Justice and of Mr. Justice Spence. I agree with Mr. Justice Spence. To his reasons for judgment I would however like to add some of my own.

The power to repress fraud by avoiding fraudulent conveyances and preferences is an indisputable part of provincial jurisdiction over property and civil rights. The risk of fraud is increased when a debtor finds himself in a situation of impending or actual insolvency and, in my view, provincial laws can, without undergoing a change in nature, focus upon that situation as upon a proper occasion to attain their object. Given their purpose, they do not cease to be laws in relation to property and civil rights simply because they are timely and effective or because Parliament could enact similar laws in relation to bankruptcy and insolvency.

Insolvency has been defined by Lord Thankerton in the *Farmers' Creditors Arrangement Act* reference, *Attorney-General for British Columbia v. Attorney-General for Canada*, at p. 402:

In a general sense, insolvency means inability to meet one's debts or obligations; in a technical sense, it means the condition or standard of inability to meet debts or obligations, upon the occurrence of which the statutory law enables a creditor to intervene, with the assistance of a Court, to stop individual action by creditors and to secure administration of the debtor's assets in the general interest of creditors; the law also generally allows the debtor to apply for the same administration.

The primary meaning of "insolvency" in s. 91.21 of the Constitution is insolvency in the technical sense, not in the general sense. This Lord Thankerton made just a few lines after the passage quoted above: with respect to the jurisdiction of Parliament under s. 91.21, he referred to "... the statutory conditions of insolvency which enabled a creditor or the debtor to invoke the aid of the bankruptcy laws. ..."

There is no common law of bankruptcy and insolvency in the technical sense, but the disruptions resulting from insolvency in the general sense had of necessity to be taken into account by general legal systems such as the common law and the civil law. Insolvency lies at the core of those parts of the common law and of the civil law which relate to such matters as mortgage, pledge, pawning, suretyship and the securing of debts generally which are implicitly or explicitly predicated on the risk of insolvency and which produce their full effect when the risk has been converted into reality; so it is with the rules which determine the rank of privileges and hypothecs or which ordain that an insolvent or bankrupt debtor shall lose the benefit of the term (art. 1092 of the Quebec *Civil Code*). Some of the most fundamental principles of the civil law are expressed in arts. 1980, 1981 and 1982 of the Quebec *Civil Code*:

Art. 1980. Whoever incurs a personal obligation, renders liable for its fulfilment all his property, moveable and immoveable, present and future, except such property as is specially declared to be exempt from seizure.

Art. 1981. The property of a debtor is the common pledge of his creditors, and where they claim together they share its price rateably, unless there are amongst them legal causes of preference.

Art. 1982. The legal causes of preference are privileges and hypothecs.

Although not expressly referred to, insolvency forms the web of these articles; there would be little need for them, particularly the last two, were it not for insolvency. But I cannot be persuaded that they are not laws relating to property and civil rights.

When the exclusive power to make laws in relation to bankruptcy and insolvency was bestowed upon Parliament, it was not intended to remove from the general legal systems which regulated property and civil rights a cardinal concept essential to the coherence of those systems. The main purpose was to give to Parliament exclusive jurisdiction over the establishment by statute of a particular system regulating the distribution of a debtor's assets. However, given the nature of general legal systems, the primary jurisdiction of Parliament cannot easily be exercised together with its incidental powers without some degree of overlap in which case federal law prevails. On the other hand, provincial jurisdiction over property and civil rights should not be measured by the ultimate reach of federal power over bankruptcy and insolvency any more than provincial competence in relation to the administration of justice can be determined by every conceivable and potential use of the criminal law power. This, I believe, is the general import of the *Voluntary Assignments* case, *Attorney-General of Ontario v. Attorney-General for Canada*. The Judicial Committee declared that the validity of the provision it had to consider and of the assignments made under the authority of that provision did not depend on the insolvency of the assignor: an assignment was also open "to any debtor who might deem his insolvency doubtful. ..." All that one can say is that legislation of the type considered in the *Voluntary Assignments* case presents little interest for prosperous persons; it is of concern chiefly to debtors in strained circumstances whose solvency is, at best, uncertain. It should be noted that the impugned voluntary assignments enactment did not only deal with assignments: it also provided that an assignment for the general benefit of creditors should take *precedence* of all judgments and of all executions not completely executed by payment.

I am reinforced in those views by a consideration of the *Civil Code of Lower Canada, 1866*, in light of *An Act Respecting Insolvency*, 1864 (Can.), c. 17. Both were enacted at a time when Confederation was being discussed. The French title of *The Insolvent Act of 1864*, was "*l'Acte concernant la faillite, 1864*," the word "faillite" being the one now currently used to translate the word "bankruptcy." In spite of its English title, the Act was in fact a bankruptcy act. It applied to all persons in Upper Canada and to traders only in Lower Canada and it contained detailed provisions relating to fraudulent conveyances and preferences. Nevertheless, the *Civil Code* comprised a section of nine articles (arts. 1032 to 1040 incl.), entitled "Of the Avoidance of Contracts and Payments made in Fraud of Creditors," applicable to traders and to non-traders alike except where *The Insolvent Act* was to prevail. The legislative history of those articles was set forth by Mr. Justice Pigeon in *Gingras v. General Motors Products of Canada Ltd.* Some have been amended. It will suffice to quote a few of them as they then read:

1034. A gratuitous contract is deemed to be made with intent to defraud, if the debtor be insolvent at the time of making it.

1035. An onerous contract made by an insolvent debtor with a person who knows him to be insolvent is deemed to be made with intent to defraud.

1036. Every payment by an insolvent debtor to a creditor knowing his insolvency, is deemed to be made with intent to defraud, and the creditor may be compelled to restore the amount or thing received or the value thereof, for the benefit of the creditors according to their respective rights.

1037. Further provisions concerning the presumption of fraud and the nullity of acts done in contemplation of insolvency are contained in The Insolvent Act of 1864.

Article 17.23 of the *Code* defines "bankruptcy" ("faillite") as meaning "the condition of a trader who has discontinued his payments"; insolvency was left undefined, the word being clearly used by the *Code* in the general sense. Even though articles 1034, 1035 and 1036 are predicated on insolvency, the Commissioners appointed for codifying the laws of Lower Canada in civil matters would have been astonished had they been told that those articles formed no part of the civil law: except perhaps for art. 1036 which appears to be an improvement of relatively modern origin (although it was not considered new law), such provisions were derived from a division of Roman law called Paulian law and, from time immemorial, had constituted a pivot of the civil law system. Other provisions of the *Code* are of the same nature and also depend on insolvency, such as art. 803 (revocation of a gift made by an insolvent debtor), and art. 2023 (hypothec consented to by an insolvent debtor). Other provisions still, although not expressly predicated on insolvency are related to insolvency and to the protection of creditors, for instance, art. 655 (the creditors of an heir who renounces a succession to their prejudice can have the renunciation rescinded and accept the succession in his stead).

The constitutional validity of such provisions is not in issue: they antedate Confederation and were continued by s. 129 of the Constitution. The only issue which could arise with respect to them is whether they are in conflict with federal law. But the content and integrity of the *Civil Code* are indicative of the extent of provincial jurisdiction over property and civil rights: *Citizens Insurance Company of Canada v. Parsons*, at pp. 110 and 111. The fact that there existed a statutory scheme of bankruptcy and insolvency to which the *Code* explicitly referred as to a distinct and specific body of law, without curtailing for that reason its own normal ambit, illustrates how the respective domains of property and civil rights and of bankruptcy and insolvency were viewed during the very period when the federal union was being discussed; it also reveals how it was intended that the distribution of powers should operate with respect to those domains.

In the *Alberta Debt Adjustment Act* reference, in *Canadian Bankers Association v. Attorney-General of Saskatchewan*, and in *Reference re Validity of the Orderly Payment of Debts Act, 1959* (Alta.), the various provincial laws found *ultra vires* were predicated upon insolvency. But they went further and set up elaborate statutory schemes involving one or more of the following features: the denial of creditors' access to courts or the restriction of their right to enforce their claims, the establishment of administrative boards, mediation, composition, arrangements, moratoriums, consolidation orders, staying of proceedings and the relief of debtors from liability to pay their debts. No such features are to be found in the presently impugned Saskatchewan statute where all that is at stake is the avoidance of fraudulent acts for the better enforcement of civil obligations. Some doubt was expressed in the *Orderly Payment of Debts Act, (1959) (Alta.)* reference at pp. 576 and 577 as to whether the *Voluntary Assignments* case would have been decided in the same way at a later date even in the absence of federal legislation on the subject of bankruptcy and insolvency. But even if this doubt was not expressed in an *obiter dictum*, I would regard it as questioning not the general principles enunciated in the *Voluntary Assignments* case, but their application in that particular instance. Accordingly, I do not think that those previous decisions of the Judicial Committee and of this Court preclude my abiding by my conclusions: laws provincial in their purpose, object and nature as those under attack cannot be rendered *ultra vires* because of virtual federal paramountcy: they can only become inoperative in case of actual repugnancy with valid federal laws.

On this latter point, I believe the test of repugnancy to be applied in this case should not differ from the one which was admitted in *Provincial Secretary of Prince Edward Island v. Egan; O'Grady v. Sparling*, and *Ross v. The Registrar of Motor Vehicles et al.*: provincial law gives way to federal law in case of operational conflict. Even if the test be one of conflict of legislative policies entailing no operational inconsistency and depending solely "upon the intention of the paramount Legislature" as was said by Dixon J, in a passage of *Ex p. McLean*, at p. 483, quoted by Mr. Justice Pigeon in the *Ross* case (at p. 15), I am of the view that s. 50, subs. (6) of the *Bankruptcy Act* provides a clear indication that Parliament, far from intending to depart from the rule of operational conflict, did in fact aim at the highest possible degree of legal integration of federal and provincial laws: attacks upon transactions within the three-month period provided by s. 73 of the *Bankruptcy Act* constitute a minimum but the trustee in bankruptcy is entitled to avail himself of all other rights and remedies provided by provincial law "as supplementary to and in addition to the rights and remedies provided by" the *Bankruptcy Act*.

Standard Trustco Ltd. (Trustee of) v. Standard Trust Co.
(1993), 13 OR (3d) 7 (Gen. Div.)

[The bankrupt, Trustco, was a holding company whose major creditors consisted of two groups of unsecured lenders. Trustco was the parent company of STC, a federally incorporated trust company regulated by the Office of the Superintendant of Financial Institutions (OSFI). Deposits made by members of the public with STC were insured by the CDIC. As of August 1990, Trustco had a $73,823,000 investment in STC.

OSFI was concerned about STC's financial condition. In July 1990, OSFI told Trustco and STC that it required an immediate capital injection of $25 million, and made it clear that if this was not done it might decide to seize STC's assets as well as taking other measures to protect STC's depositors.

Because of this pressure, Trustco's directors decided to transfer to STC a portfolio of mortgage assets allegedly worth $25 million in exchange for a $12.5 million promissory note and 1,250,000 common shares with a par value of $10 per share. The directors were acting in good faith and were not aware that either STC or Trustco was insolvent. The transaction was structured with the assistance of OSFI and CDIC, and Trustco's unsecured lenders were also advised about it. In the months that followed Trustco attempted to find a purchaser of its interest in STC but, before an agreement could be consummated, some of Trustco's lenders petitioned Trustco into bankruptcy.

Trustco's trustee in bankruptcy claimed that the August 3, 1990, transactions were reviewable transactions under ss. 3 and 100 of the BIA, and he expressed the opinion (as required under s. 100) that the value of the assets transferred to STC was $25m and that the value of the consideration given in return was nil because STC was insolvent in August 1990.

STC moved for summary judgment dismissing the action. STC argued, *inter alia*, that s. 100 did not apply to trust companies or did not apply to this particular transaction, or that if s. 100 did apply the court should exercise its discretion and deny relief.]

FARLEY J:

Statutory Interpretation:

Let me now turn to the question of statutory interpretation. Mr. Lamek was quite candid in his observation that this definitional approach had not met with conspicuous success in the cases and he agreed with the thrust of *Re Owen* (1990), 69 DLR (4th) 356 (Ont. SC), that a judge in an interpretation situation should not have to produce an absurdity (see pp 377-80). On the other hand he submitted that one should give the words meaning that would give sense and practicality to the system involved. Turning to the words of the Act:

100(1) Where a *person* who has sold, purchased, leased, hired, supplied or received property or services in a reviewable transaction becomes bankrupt within twelve months of the transaction, the court may, on the application of the trustee, inquire into whether the bankrupt gave or received, as the case may be, fair market value in consideration for the property or services concerned in the transaction.

(Emphasis added.)

A reviewable transaction is defined in s. 3(1) of the Act as follows:

3(1) For the purposes of this Act, *a person* who has entered into a transaction *with another person* otherwise than at arm's length shall be deemed to have entered into a reviewable transaction.

(Emphasis added.)

"Person" and "corporation" are defined in s. 2 of the Act as follows:

"person" includes a partnership, an unincorporated association, *a corporation*, a cooperative society or an organization, the successors of a partnership, association, corporation, society or organization, and the heirs, executors, administrators or other legal representatives of a person, according to the law of that part of Canada to which the context extends;

• • •

"corporation" includes any company incorporated or authorized to carry on business by or under an Act of Parliament or of any province, and any incorporated company, wherever incorporated, that has an office in or carries on business within Canada, *but does not include* building societies having a capital stock, or incorporated banks, savings banks, insurance companies, *trust companies*, loan companies or railway companies;

(Emphasis added.)

STC submits that because a trust company is expressly excluded from the definition of "corporation," it cannot therefore be a "person" within the statutory definition of that term and thus cannot be a person party to a s. 100 reviewable transaction. I note specifically that this must be *restricted to the system envisaged by the legislation.* It is clear that the system envisaged by the Act would disintegrate if the financial institutions mentioned as excluded under the definition of "corporation" were not to be treated as being capable of being creditors under the Act. This would be an absurdity. In this regard see *Re Selkirk Spruce Mills Ltd* (1958), 37 CBR 11 at pp. 13-14, 25 WWR 598 (BCSC); *Re Fischel* (1991), 84 DLR (4th) 236 at pp. 238-41, 119 NBR (2d) 61 (CA); *Re Owen, supra,* at pp. 377-80. I believe the New Brunswick Court of Appeal in *Fischel* at p. 239 made the valid distinction:

It is important to look at the purpose of the definition of the word "corporation." It was defined as such so that the institutions listed could not be petitioned into bankruptcy: see *Re Inverness Railway and Collieries Ltd.* (1922), 65 DLR 139 at pp. 145-7, 3 CBR 271, [1923] 1 WWR 937 (NSCA); affirmed in part *sub nom. Royal Bank of Canada v. Eastern Trust Co.,* [1923] 1 DLR 498, [1923] SCR 177, 3 CBR 724, WWR *loc. cit., per* Brodeur J. at p. 503.

I note in passing that the version of the Act in effect for the *Inverness* case was the *Bankruptcy Act,* SC 1919, c. 36, as amended by SC 1920, c. 34, where the lead-in to the definitional section was:

2. In this Act *unless the context otherwise requires or implies,* the expression ...

(Emphasis added.)

This may be contrasted with the lead-in of the Act in question: "In this Act ... ." I think that the deletion of "unless the context otherwise requires or implies" may possibly strengthen STC's definitional case. On the other hand the Quebec Court of Appeal in *Re Parc Commémoratif de Montréal* (1980), 114 DLR (3d) 600, determined at p. 608 that the definition of "person" in the version of the Act under question in *Inverness* was changed in 1921 and so included at the time of that decision "a corporation *as restrictively defined in this section*" (emphasis added). Under the current Act, the emphasized words have been deleted. In any event, it appears to me that the thrust of the definitional sections was to preclude a trust company from being petitioned into a bankruptcy (or making a proposal) wherein the trust company was the *object of the exercise;* that should be left to the *TCA* (or

equivalent provincial legislation) and the *WUA*. However, in the s. 100 situation we could
have a case where the trust company was in effect the complainant. In the instant case it
appears that possibly a trust company has been the recipient of a conspicuous discrepancy
benefit (although I would stress this has not yet been proved). It is only in this context that
a trust company is subject to scrutiny under s. 100. It seems to me that the consequences of
adverse determination are far different from the consequences that would flow with
respect to a trust company being petitioned into bankruptcy, *etc.* Under s. 100, if the matter
goes against a company (including a trust company) then judgment will be given against
that company to the extent of the conspicuous discrepancy so found. The transaction is not
reversed; it is simply a situation where a lawsuit has been brought and action has been
taken against a company in the same way that a lawsuit could be brought against a trust
company for a breach of contract, negligence, or another cause of action. This is clearly
different from a situation whereby, being the subject of an insolvency question, STC is
being wound up pursuant to the *WUA* and is not being dealt with pursuant to the
bankruptcy petition provisions under the Act.

• • •

Discretion

Let us then turn to the last element in question: Should I exercise my discretion pursuant to
s. 100(1) and (2) of the Act?
     STC's position is that even if the presence of a trust company as a party to a
reviewable transaction does not preclude the application of s. 100, an inquiry by the court
into the transaction and provision of a remedy is not mandated. By the express language of
s. 100(1), whether there should be an inquiry into the relative values of the consideration
exchanged is a matter for the discretion of the court. Even if the court should make inquiry
and find that the value of the consideration given by the bankrupt was "conspicuously
greater" than that of the consideration it received, still, by the express words of s. 100(2),
the giving of judgment to the plaintiff trustee for the difference in value is again a matter
for the court's discretion. STC submitted that the areas of discretion are totally separate
and distinct from the discretion which Houlden JA was called upon to exercise on the
trustee's application for leave to launch the s. 100 proceeding. In fact, Houlden JA said at
p. 664 of leave decision: "If there is a discretion conferred by s. 100(1), that discretion
belongs to the judge hearing the application by the trustee to set aside the reviewable
transaction." He went on to say at the same page that that same judge (and not himself)
should determine whether Trustco got "fair market value" for the assets it sold to STC.
     What is the nature of this distinction? In *Clarkson Co. v. White* (1979), 102 DLR (3d)
403 at pp. 410-11, 32 CBR (NS) 25 (NSCA), the court said:

> In my opinion, s. 78 [now s. 100] of the *Bankruptcy Act* was intended to permit the trustee to
> have reviewable transactions between the bankrupt and persons not dealing at arm's length made
> within one year of the bankruptcy without adequate consideration set aside. Once all of the
> conditions have been established as required by the legislation, then, although the remedy is in
> the permissive form, the Court has a duty to grant some judgment against any or all of the
> persons named in the section so that an asset improperly removed from the company may be
> restored for the benefit of its creditors. The section of the Act involved does not leave the Judge

with an unfettered discretion to grant or withhold the remedy on the grounds of fairness to the people concerned but indicates that the trustee has a right to judgment upon satisfying the requirements established by the legislation.

It is up to businessmen, knowing this, to avoid making gifts or transfers without consideration to related persons. It is quite true that none of the parties involved at the time of the purchase of the shares by TMA envisaged the possibility of bankruptcy within the next 12 months, but the subject of the write-off was brought up and all parties should have been on their guard when extinguishing a debt of $26,650 without consideration.

One of the purposes of the *Bankruptcy Act* is to prevent the transfer of assets of a bankrupt to related persons during the year prior to the bankruptcy without adequate consideration, and when such a transaction has been established it is, in my opinion, the duty of the Judge presiding at the hearing to enable the trustee to recover the value of the asset for the benefit of creditors and judgment should be given accordingly.

There is nothing in s. 78, as there is in s. 79, which says that the disposal of an asset of the company must be made at a time when the company is insolvent or made in such a manner as to contribute to the insolvency before that asset can be recovered by the trustee. The only qualification is that the asset be disposed of without consideration to a related person within 12 months immediately prior to the bankruptcy. *I can find in the section no statutory discretion vested in the trial judge which would permit him to refuse judgment to the trustee on the ground of unfairness. Once the trustee has shown the Court that the transaction falls within the prohibition of s. 78, it is, in my opinion, the duty of the trial Judge to give judgment, against the related company or against the directors as being privy to the transaction, or against both.*

(Emphasis added.)

STC submitted that courts may properly consider legislative debate in interpreting legislation in issue between the parties to an action. One should not rush off to read the legislative debates but rather one should approach this area very carefully. In this regard, I was advised that s. 100 was introduced into the Act by the 1967 amendments. Do the House of Commons debates at the time provide insight into the legislative intent behind the enactment of s. 100? I was directed to the speech of the Honourable L.T. Pennall, Solicitor General, when moving the second reading of the bill (s. 17), where he said, *inter alia:*

It will be possible for the court to review transactions which would not come within what may be called moral practices.

• • •

The Bill will incorporate in the Bankruptcy Act the technique used in the Income Tax Act matters. It will provide that where a person has sold etc., or purchased etc. property or services to or from another person with whom the first mentioned person was not dealing at arm's length, and within 12 months of such transaction the first mentioned person becomes bankrupt, *the court upon application will have power to review the transaction to inquire whether the consideration was conspicuously excessive or inadequate and to give judgment to the trustee for the difference between such consideration and the fair market value of the property or services.*

(Emphasis added.)

On June 16, 1966, the Honourable Lucien Cardin, Minister of Justice, was said to have defined to some extent what immoral business practices s. 100 was designed to address:

Another important amendment has to do with reviewable transactions. We have received numerous representations in recent years regarding certain transactions involving related persons or a closely held corporation and its directors or shareholders in contemplation of bankruptcy. *For example*, in contemplation of bankruptcy the corporation would pay exorbitant salaries or expense allowances to officers of the company, or the debtor would sell at an unreasonably low price some of his assets to persons or corporations who in some way control the debtor. While transactions of this kind may, under the present state of the law, be legal they do not on many occasions come within what may be called moral business practice.

The amendments—clauses 1 and 12 of the bill—incorporate in the Bankruptcy Act the concept of "at arm's length" which is used in income tax matters. The court will have the power, on the application of the trustee, to review transactions between the debtor and related persons that have taken place within the 12 months preceding the bankruptcy. *If the court finds, after having inquired into the matter, that the consideration for the transaction was conspicuously excessive or inadequate, it will give judgment to the trustee for the difference between such consideration and the fair market value of the property or services.*

(Emphasis added.)

I think it important to note that both the speeches of the Solicitor General and the Minister of Justice indicated (as *per* my emphasis) that if there is a conspicuous difference in the value of the consideration between non-arm's length of parties [*sic*] then the court should give judgment for the difference to the trustee. The Minister of Justice did not define immoral business practices (not a defined term of or found in the Act in any event) but merely gave examples which are not all-inclusive. Further it is quite clear that the Act does not contain any language suggesting intent as one would expect from the Minister's reference to "in contemplation of bankruptcy." The sin here is a conspicuous discrepancy when the parties are not acting at arm's length. I do not think that the Nova Scotia Court of Appeal in *Clarkson, supra,* would have found much nourishment in Hansard for the benefit of the defendant if Hansard had been quoted to it. I do not find Hansard to be of assistance to STC in this case. See also *Henfrey* (BCCA), *supra,* at pp. 64-65 CBR, and *Lagden Equipment Ltd. (Trustee of) v. Lagden* (1989), 77 CBR (NS) 285 (Que. SC), when Gomery J said, at pp. 288-89:

It is not relevant to proceedings based upon s. 100 to determine when or if the respondents knew or suspected that the bankrupt would be unable to discharge its liabilities. The relevant criteria for determination by the court to enable it to exercise its jurisdiction are:

(1) Was the transaction a reviewable one?

(2) Did it take place within 12 months preceding the bankruptcy?

(3) Was the consideration received conspicuously less than the fair market value of the property concerned?

(4) Was the respondent privy to the transaction?

Issues of good or bad faith do not arise, except insofar as they may assist the court in deciding what was in fact the fair market value of property, or whether or not a party was aware of or privy to the transaction.

I am of the view that Houlden and Morawetz, *supra*, at p. 4-111, correctly captured the intent of the legislation:

Once all the conditions have been established as required by the legislation, then, although the remedy is in the permissive form, the court has a duty to grant some judgment against all or any of the persons named in the section so that an asset improperly removed from the company may be restored for the benefit of its creditors. The section of the *Act* involved does not leave the judge with an unfettered discretion to grant or withhold the remedy on the grounds of fairness to the people concerned but indicates that the trustee has a right to judgment upon satisfying the requirements established by the legislation.

In my view the only "restoration" possible is that the judgment not reverse the transaction but merely that the trustee of the bankruptcy [*sic*] ("complainant") company be "made whole" by receiving a judgement for the conspicuous difference (*i.e.,* a topping-up "restoration").

However, as STC pointed out, a bankruptcy court is invested with equitable jurisdiction. A bankruptcy proceeding is a proceeding in equity. A bankruptcy court can and, in appropriate cases, should apply equitable doctrines such as laches. STC submitted that the uncontradicted facts of this case, taken together with equitable principles and appropriate policy considerations, provide clear and ample support for the court to decline to inquire into the transaction pursuant to s. 100 of the Act. This submission was based upon the following points:

(a) *No improper removal of assets*

STC asserted that s. 100 of the Act captures transactions where there has been an improper removal of assets from a bankrupt to another with whom the bankrupt is not dealing at arm's length. I believe it would be better expressed as s. 100 capturing transactions between parties which are not at arm's length whereby there is a conspicuous disparity in the exchange ratio of the consideration given and received. STC submitted that an investment by a holding company in its wholly owned subsidiary is not an improper removal of assets from the holding company. To which I reply—quite so, provided there is no conspicuous discrepancy. Under a s. 100 regime there is the requirement that persons in bankruptcy must look over their shoulders backwards a year to see if the "*quid*" they get bore a reasonable relationship to the "*quo*." Creditors of the operating company must bear the risk of the capital in that company being "illusory," at least to the extent of investments made by the holding company within one year prior to the bankruptcy of the parent holding company; to protect themselves in such a situation it would seem that prudent creditors not lend on the strength of such "new capital" until they have satisfied themselves there is no conspicuous discrepancy in values.

It may well be true that (i) the investment was made in good faith with public notice in advance and with full disclosure to creditors on completion; (ii) it was not tainted with fraud or any other form of questionable commercial conduct; (iii) there is no evidence of an intention to defeat, hinder or obstruct creditors; and (iv) the investment was made in response to a regulatory requirement and was deemed necessary to protect what was thought to be a much larger pre-existing investment. I do not see that these are reasons which would require me to exercise my discretion in these circumstances as it appears to me that what should bear on my judgment is the degree of difference in value. In the circumstances of the particular case was it appropriate to find that there was a conspicuous difference? The aspect of good or bad faith of the parties is irrelevant except in so far as a determination in this area may assist the court in deciding what was the fair market value of the exchanged goods or services and whether or not a party was aware of or privy to the transaction: see *Lagden, supra.* The question of conspicuous difference of course is one to be left to the trial judge based upon the evidence which may be forthcoming at trial.

(b) *The role of the regulators*

Next STC submitted that OSFI and CDIC are central to the origin, structure and aftermath of the injection and therefore their respective positions and systemic policy considerations must be taken into account in the exercise of the court's discretion. Both OSFI and CDIC discharge their public duties in reliance upon the permanence of the injection. OSFI issued compliance directions to ensure that the injection would stay in place. CDIC altered its position, potentially to its detriment, by agreeing to guarantee STC's liability to its clearing bank. CDIC also exposed itself to a greater loss than would have been the case had STC's deposit insurance been terminated in August 1990. STC then questioned the appropriateness of a s. 100 action where the recipient of the benefit is a trust company which is under regulatory supervision and moral suasion. It went on to say the s. 100 action seeks to reverse an injection by a parent corporation of what is regarded, for regulatory purposes, as a form of capital into a regulated public financial institution which is a recipient of funds of depositors. The effective reversal of such an injection of capital is sought on grounds not available to the parent holding company itself. If depositors, regulators and insurers cannot rely on injections of capital into financial institutions by owners of those institutions, obvious and significant policy and practical problems will arise. While I wholeheartedly agree with the proposition and its conclusion, I do not find it persuasive. It seems to me that such a course of action would be to impart without any authority some form of Crown immunity (once removed) to STC when it may well be questionable whether the Crown itself would enjoy such. A future must be based on a firm foundation. The regulators of necessity must look out first, foremost and always to those which they regulate and the creditors of those regulated entities. To the extent that new capital is required, they cannot do a Nelson's blind eye and be oblivious to the danger of the holding company not being able to sustain such a reverse transfusion with the result that it goes bankrupt or that the recipient of the transfusion will still expire and bring down the holding company with it. If that happens within the year then the regulators have merely robbed Peter to pay Paul since the trustee of the bankrupt holding company will be able to make a s. 100 claim. Why should not the creditors (and shareholders) of a bankrupt holding company in these circumstances look to the benefit of the trustee being able to make such a claim? Why should they be deprived of the benefit of s. 100? I can think of no reason. If the regulators feel that this type of situation should not have that protection then it would seem incumbent on them to push for a change in the legislation. However, it does not seem to me that s. 100 contemplates that the reviewable transaction be reversed; there is merely a judgment (which is not a secured obligation) for the conspicuous difference. Would not the trustee, if successful, merely rank with other unsecured creditors of STC?

• • •

Application for summary judgment rejected.

CHAPTER SEVENTEEN

Ranking of Creditors and Distribution of Proceeds

(§§ 2 (definition of "secured creditor"), 136, 137, 67(2)-(3), 137-141, 69.3, 81, 86-87; Bank Act, §427(7) and Employment Standards Act, Part XIV.1 and 2 (Ont.))

From the creditors' perspective, no bankruptcy topic is more controversial than the ranking of creditors' claims in the distribution of the bankrupt's estate—understandably so since the creditors are fighting over their share in what is almost invariably a seriously depleted estate. Under the BIA (ss. 136-141), creditors' claims are ranked in the following order:

(1) secured creditors' claims;*
(2) preferred creditors (s. 136(1));
(3) ordinary unsecured creditors (s. 141); and
(4) deferred creditors (ss. 137-140).

"Secured creditor" is defined in s. 2 of the BIA and quintessentially embraces consensual secured claims, including those regulated by the provincial PPS Acts and s. 427 of the Bank Act. The definition also appears to include non-consensual secured claims arising by operation of law at common law or by statute. Section 136(1) of the pre-1992 BIA classified and ranked preferred claims in the following order:

(a) in the case of a deceased bankrupt, reasonable funeral and testamentary expenses relating to the deceased;

(b) costs of administration of the estate;

(c) levy payable under s. 147;

(d) wages, salaries and commissions payable to employees during the three months preceding bankruptcy up to $500 and expenses of travelling salesmen up to $300;

(e) municipal taxes that do not constitute preferred liens or charges against the real property of the bankrupt;

---

* Technically speaking, secured creditors do not share in the proceeds of the estate at all since they are entitled to withdraw the secured assets from the estate pursuant to s. 69.3 and to realize the assets themselves. This is why s. 71 provides that the debtor's property passes to the trustee "subject to the rights of secured creditors" and why s. 136(1) provides that "*Subject to the rights of secured creditors*, the proceeds realized from the property of a bankrupt shall be applied in priority of payment as follows … ."

(f) landlords for rental arrears up to three months preceding the bankruptcy and accelerated rent for three months following bankruptcy if provided for in lease;

(g) fees and expenses under s. 70(2) [i.e., costs of garnishments and executions not completed at time of bankruptcy order];

(h) amounts owing under workmen's compensation legislation and the unemployment insurance and income tax Acts for deductions required to be made and remitted to the Crown;

(i) monies received from insurance claims for injuries to bankrupt's employees; and

(j) claims of the Crown in right of Canada or any province notwithstanding any statutory preference to the contrary.

The deferred claims are listed in ss. 137-140 and cover (a) claims under reviewable transactions (s. 131(a)); (b) wage claims of spouse or former spouse (s. 137(2)); (c) wages and other compensation claims by the bankrupt's close relatives (s. 138); and (d) "silent" partners of the bankrupt (s. 140).

The practical results emerging from this order of priorities in the distribution of the bankrupt's estate are shown in the tables following this introduction. Contraintuitively, they appear to show that preferred creditors led the list with an overall rate of recovery of 49% of their claims. However, the figure is misleading because of the large distorting effect of the trustee's claim for expenses and the trustee's fee.* If the trustee's expenses and fees are excluded, the recovery rate for the other preferred creditors would have been approximately 16%—well below the 49% for all preferred creditors. This also means, as one would expect, that secured creditors ranked first with an overall recovery rate in this sample of 43%. Unsecured creditors came last with a recovery rate of 5%.

Among the preferred creditors, the federal and provincial Crowns and wage earners have long felt that they deserved to be treated much better. (Disagreement among the bankruptcy constituencies about how their claims should be treated was one of the reasons for the long delay between 1975 and 1992 in the adoption of bankruptcy reforms.) Rather than waiting for Parliament to revise the BIA, the federal and provincial governments addressed the issue in the Excise Tax Act, the Income Tax Act, the Unemployment Insurance Act, the Canada Pension Plan Act, and the Workers' Compensation Acts by deeming deductions not remitted to the governmental agencies to be held on trust for the Crown and creating a first lien on all the debtor's assets ranking ahead of all other claims. In other cases, where no deductions or collections by the debtor were involved, the legislation created a superpriority lien in favour of the Crown.

Predictably, this led to fierce (and ongoing) litigation. Consensual secured creditors took the position that the governmental agencies were trying to circumvent the ranking prescribed in s. 136(1) of the BIA. The Supreme Court of Canada agreed with the secured creditors and, in a quartet of cases decided in the 1980s, decided that provincial legislation could not be used to by-pass the s. 136(1) ranking by converting Crown claims into lien claims. In the last of the four cases, *British Columbia v. Henfrey Samson Belair Ltd.* (1989), 59 DLR (4th) 726, the Court also held that a deemed trust created under the BC

---

* A trustee usually makes sure, before agreeing to serve, that the net assets of the estate will at least be sufficient to cover the trustee's expenses and fees. Where necessary, they will often be guaranteed by a secured creditor or, less frequently, by a director of the debtor company.

Social Service Tax Act in respect of sales tax collected by the bankrupt, but not remitted to the province, did not qualify as a trust under s. 67(1) of the pre-1992 BIA.

These issues were addressed in detail in the Colter Report. As detailed later in this chapter, the Advisory Committee fully supported the ethos of the Supreme Court judgments and wanted the federal government to go even further by abolishing all government priorities in bankruptcy unless they met the prescribed criteria. The federal government compromised and met the committee's recommendations only partly: see BIA ss. 67(2) and (3), and 86-87, and 136, discussed more fully hereafter.

Wage earners fared very poorly under the pre-1992 BIA, their claims only ranking fourth among preferred creditors. As previously explained (*supra*, chapter 12), the Mulroney government wanted to adopt a Wage Earner Protection Act as part of the Bill C-22 package of amendments but was unable to overcome opposition from within its own caucus. The government therefore contented itself with some marginal improvements on the pre-1992 position by increasing the amount of wages eligible for preferred treatment to $2,000 and the eligible expenses of travelling salesmen to $1,000.

This means that it has been left to other legislation—mainly provincial in character—to fill the void, whether by establishing a contributory compensation fund (as in Manitoba and Quebec) or a fully government funded plan (as in Ontario); by holding directors personally liable for unpaid wages; or by creating a superpriority lien against the employer's inventory and accounts receivable (OPPSA s. 30(7)).

This chapter concludes with a brief survey of the problems of ranking claims for the costs of environmental clean ups under federal and provincial legislation. Until the 1992 amendments, the BIA did not address this issue at all. Under environmental legislation, the occupier of premises or the person in control of a business is typically held responsible for the costs of the clean up, regardless of when the pollution was first caused and whether or not the occupant was at fault. Not surprisingly, such provisions have made lenders very nervous about enforcing security interests against premises suspected of being contaminated, and have made receivers and trustees equally circumspect about accepting office without iron clad indemnities if they are held liable.

As will be seen, Canadian courts have been divided in their interpretation of the impact environmental legislation has on the liability of secured creditors, receivers and trustees. However, the majority of the courts appear to favour a broad application of such legislation without the benefit of exclusions. Section 14.06 of the BIA, as added in 1992, provides personal relief for a trustee where the environmental condition arose before the trustee assumed office or, if it arose subsequent to this date, where it arose through no fault of the trustee. However, this important provision does not give similar immunity to secured lenders or privately appointed receivers, nor does it protect the secured creditor's security.

J.S. Ziegel and W.L. Garton, STATISTICAL PROFILE OF CREDITORS IN BANKRUPTCY (April 1989 Figures)

Table 1
Total Claims—95 "Pure" Business Bankruptcy Files

Claimant	# of claims	% of total # claims	Claimed $	% of total $ claimed	Div. or $ real.	% of total div. or real.	Recovery %
Secured	140	2.9	7,856,442	28.1	3,425,731	60.2	43
Preferred	735	15.4	2,761,305	9.9	1,355,594	23.8	49
Ord. unsec.*	3,907	81.7	17,361,508	62.0	911,979	16.0	5
TOTAL	4,782	100.0	27,979,255	100.0	5,693,304	100.0	20

* Excluding deemed deficiency claims of secured creditors.

Table 2
95 "Pure" Business Bankruptcy Files—All Secured Claims

Claimant: Type	# of claims	% of # claims sub-tot	tot	Claimed $	Avg. claim $	% of $ claimed sub-tot	tot	Div. or $ real.	% of $ real. sub-tot	tot	Recovery %
1-1 Banks	46	32.9	1.0	3,996,434	86,879	50.9	14.3	1,797,805	52.5	31.6	44
1-2 Other fin. inst.	30	21.4	0.6	1,268,264	42,275	16.1	4.5	469,189	13.7	8.2	36
1-3 Sup. of goods	46	32.9	1.0	1,987,416	43,205	25.3	7.1	824,972	24.1	14.5	41
1-4 Services	12	8.5	0.2	20,833	1,736	0.3	0.1	803	0.0	0.0	3
1-7 Others	6	4.3	0.1	583,495	97,249	7.4	2.1	332,962	9.7	5.8	57
SUB-TOTAL	140	100.0	2.9	7,856,442	56,117	100.0	28.1	3,425,731	100.0	60.1	43

Table 3
Preferred Claims—95 "Pure" Business Bankruptcy Files

Claimant: Type	# of claims	% of # claims sub-tot	tot	Claimed $	Avg. claim $	% of $ claimed sub-tot	tot	Div. or $ real.	% of $ real. sub-tot	tot	Recovery %
2-1 Est. admin	95	12.9	2.0	1,054,213	11,097	38.2	3.8	1,051,857	77.6	18.5	99
2-2 Wages up to $500	139	18.9	2.9	42,295	304	1.5	0.2	13,112	1.0	0.2	31
2-3 Mun. taxes	15	2.0	0.3	21,032	1,402	0.8	0.1	5,790	0.4	0.1	27
2-4 Rent	49	6.7	1.0	282,030	5,756	10.2	1.0	62,888	4.6	1.1	22
2-6 WCB ded.	33	4.5	0.7	150,432	4,559	5.5	0.5	30,033	2.2	0.5	19
2-7 UI & CPP ded.	24	3.3	0.5	19,461	811	0.7	0.1	5,764	0.4	0.1	29
2-8 Inc. tax d.a.s.	43	5.8	0.9	369,913	8,603	13.4	1.3	42,084	3.1	0.7	11
2-10 Other fed. claims	41	5.6	0.8	426,303	10,398	15.4	1.5	65,767	4.9	1.1	15
2-11 Other prov. claims	99	13.5	2.0	326,108	3,294	11.8	1.1	45,315	3.4	0.8	13
2-12 Vac. pay trust	197	26.8	4.1	69,518	353	2.5	0.2	32,984	2.4	0.6	47
Sub-Total	735	100.0	15.4	2,761,305	3,757	100.0	9.8	1,355,594	100.0	23.8	49

Table 4
Ordinary Unsecured Claims (excluding deemed deficiency claims of secured creditors)
95 "Pure" Business Bankruptcy Files

Claimant: Type	# of claims	% of # claims sub-tot	% of # claims tot	Claimed $	Avg. claim $	% of $ claimed sub-tot	% of $ claimed tot	Div. or $ real.	% of $ real. sub-tot	% of $ real. tot	Recovery %
3-1 Banks	79	2.0	1.6	1,501,631	19,008	8.6	5.4	8,902	1.0	0.1	1
3-2 Other fin. inst.	55	1.4	1.1	748,936	13,617	4.3	2.7	24,308	2.7	0.4	3
3-3 Sup. of goods	1,803	46.2	37.7	6,798,671	3,771	39.2	24.3	667,267	73.2	11.7	10
3-4 Services	1,047	26.8	21.9	4,096,940	3,913	23.6	14.6	105,831	11.6	1.9	3
3-6 Util.	144	3.7	3.0	131,835	916	0.8	0.5	4,602	0.5	0.1	3
3-7 Wages	65	1.7	1.3	106,672	1,641	0.6	0.4	7,191	0.8	0.1	7
3-8 Indiv. lenders	343	8.8	7.2	3,468,943	10,114	20.0	12.4	75,260	8.2	1.3	2
3-9 Mun. claims	76	1.9	1.6	121,201	1,595	0.7	0.4	11,671	1.3	0.2	10
3-10 Other	267	6.8	5.6	287,971	1,079	1.7	1.0	4,591	0.5	0.1	2
3-11 Rent	27	0.7	0.6	98,708	3,656	0.5	0.4	2,356	0.2	0.0	2
SUB-TOTAL	3,907	100.0	81.7	17,361,508	4,444	100.0	62.1	911,979	100.0	16.0	5

Ranking of Secured Creditors

R. v. Ford Credit Canada Limited
(1990), 78 CBR (NS) 266 (Ont. SC)

AUSTIN J: This case considers the respective rights of a secured creditor and a trustee in bankruptcy. Section 49(1) [now s. 69(1)] of the Bankruptcy Act stays proceedings against a bankrupt. Section 49(2) [now s. 69(2)] says, in effect, that s. 49(1) does not apply to secured creditors. Section 174 [now s. 203] makes it an offence, in certain circumstances, to take property from the bankrupt or the trustee. The issue, in a nutshell, is whether s. 174 applies to secured creditors.

Mr. and Mrs. Szucsko bought a Ford Tempo from Delhi Ford Sales Ltd. on 25th April 1987. The vehicle was taken in Mrs. Szucsko's name. It was financed by Ford Credit Canada Limited. The financing statement filed by Ford under the Personal Property Security Act was in the name of Mr. Szucsko.

The Szucskos made a voluntary assignment in bankruptcy on 30th October 1987. The trustee left the motor vehicle in the possession of Mrs. Szucsko. Mrs. Szucsko listed Ford as a secured creditor for $10,000. The trustee gave notice of the bankruptcy to Ford. Ford filed a proof of claim on 21st December 1987 for $8,626.14 and claimed the vehicle as security.

On 22nd December 1987 the trustee asked Ford for further documentation. Ford demanded the vehicle. The trustee indicated that he was not yet satisfied with the security. The trustee also advised Ford that any repossession would be contrary to the Bankruptcy Act and that if such action were taken, Ford would be charged with theft. Ford seized the car from Mrs. Szucsko on 11th January 1988.

On 21st January 1988 the trustee demanded the return of the vehicle. On 8th February 1988 Ford asked the trustee to pay Ford out or to waive his rights to the vehicle. The trustee did neither.

At some stage Ford applied to the bankruptcy court for a declaration that it had a security interest in the vehicle valid and subsisting in priority to the interest of the trustee. Such a declaration was made on 21st March 1989.

In November 1988 the trustee had a charge laid against Ford under s. 174 of the Bankruptcy Act. That section reads as follows:

174. A person, except the trustee, who, within thirty days after delivery to the trustee of the proof of claim mentioned in section 59, or who, in case no such proof has been delivered, removes or attempts to remove the property or any part thereof mentioned in such section out of the charge or possession of the bankrupt, the trustee or other custodian of such property, unless with the written permission of the trustee, is guilty of an offence and is liable on summary conviction to a fine not exceeding five thousand dollars, or to imprisonment for a term not exceeding two years, or to both.

The charge under the Bankruptcy Act was heard by His Honour Judge P.R. Mitchell in Hamilton on 2nd August 1989. It was dismissed. This is an appeal by the Crown from that dismissal.

In its argument, the Crown relied on three western cases. Their fact situations are very close, if not identical, to the present case. The first of the three is *R. v. Ford Motor Credit Co.*, [1977] 6 WWR 241, 25 CBR (NS) 283 (Man. Prov. Ct.). Klassen Concrete went bankrupt and gave possession of its four motor vehicles to the trustee. The trustee wrote to Ford Credit, which held the conditional sales agreement. The trustee asked Ford to file a proof of claim and the security documents. Ford replied to the effect that its policy was to take possession notwithstanding the bankruptcy. Ford seized the motor vehicles despite the efforts of the trustee. Subsequently, Ford provided a proof of claim and the security documents for the four motor vehicles and the trustee gave releases for two of them to Ford. Ford was charged under s. 174 with respect to the other two and was convicted.

In that case, as in the present case, the Crown relied upon s. 59 [now s. 81] of the Bankruptcy Act. It reads as follows:

59.(1) Where a person claims any property, or interest therein, in the possession of the bankrupt at the time of the bankruptcy he shall file with the trustee a proof of claim verified by affidavit giving the grounds on which the claim is based and sufficient particulars to enable the property to be identified.

(2) The trustee with whom a proof of claim is filed under subsection (1) shall within fifteen days thereafter or within fifteen days after the first meeting of creditors, whichever is the later, either admit the claim and deliver possession of the property to the claimant or give notice in writing to the claimant that the claim is disputed with his reasons therefor, and, unless the claimant appeals therefrom to the court within fifteen days after the mailing of the notice of dispute, he shall be deemed to have abandoned or relinquished all his right to or interest in the property to the trustee who thereupon may sell or dispose of the property free of any lien, right, title or interest of the claimant thereon or therein.

(3) The onus of establishing a claim to or in property under this section is on the claimant.

(4) The trustee may give notice in writing to any person to prove his claim to or in property under this section, and, unless that person files with the trustee a proof of claim in the prescribed form within fifteen days after the mailing of the notice, the trustee may thereupon with the leave of the court sell or dispose of the property free of any lien, right, title or interest of that person thereon or therein.

(5) No proceedings shall be instituted to establish a claim to, or to recover any right or interest in, any property in the possession of a bankrupt at the time of the bankruptcy, except as provided in this section.

(6) Nothing in this section shall be construed as extending the rights of any person other than the trustee.

The defendant relied upon s. 49(2). It reads as follows:

(2) Subject to section 57 and sections 98 to 105, a secured creditor may realize or otherwise deal with his security in the same manner as he would have been entitled to realize or deal with it if this section had not been passed, unless the court otherwise orders, but in so ordering the court shall not postpone the right of the secured creditor to realize or otherwise deal with his security, except as follows:

(a) in the case of a security for a debt due at the date of the bankruptcy or of the approval of the proposal or which becomes due not later than six months thereafter such right shall not be postponed for more than six months from such date; and

(b) in the case of a security for a debt that does not become due until more than six months after the date of the bankruptcy or of the approval of the proposal, such right shall not be postponed for more than six months from such date, unless all instalments of interest that are more than six months in arrears are paid and all other defaults of more than six months standing are cured, and then only so long as no instalment of interest remains in arrears or defaults remain uncured for more than six months, but, in any event, not beyond the date at which the debt secured by such security becomes payable under the instrument or law creating the security, except under paragraph (a).

Kopstein Prov. J held that there was no conflict between s. 49(2) and s. 59. He found that even secured creditors had to comply with s. 59 and that, in seizing the motor vehicles before such compliance, Ford had violated s. 174.

This decision was followed in *R. v. Mathers* (1979), 30 CBR (NS) 133 (Sask. Prov. Ct.). There the creditor held a chattel mortgage and filed a proof of claim which was rejected by the trustee. The creditor then seized the trucks from the possession of the trustee on the premises of the bankrupt. The creditor was charged under s. 174. There, as in the present case, a separate proceeding determined that the creditor did have title to the vehicle. Wedge Prov. J followed Kopstein Prov. J and at p. 138 held that if the security is in the possession of the trustee, a secured creditor must comply with s. 59.

At the same page he held that s. 57 and ss. 98 to 105 "do not derogate from the right of a trustee in possession to demand proper proof of claim before giving up possession or custody."

He said at p. 139 that: "The purpose of the relevant sections of the Bankruptcy Act is to ensure the orderly and speedy settlement of a bankrupt's affairs."

Ford and *Mathers* were followed in *R. v. Bank of Montreal*, 53 CBR (NS) 287, [1985] WWR 259 (Man. Prov. Ct.). The bank held a chattel mortgage on some vehicles and equipment. It filed a proof of claim pursuant to s. 59. The trustee did not take physical possession of the mortgaged items but went to the various farms where they were located and made arrangements to leave them in place. The bank agreed with this arrangement. Norton Prov. J found that the trustee had taken possession.

The bank argued that the Act intended to distinguish between creditors with proprietary interests in the property and those who only had security interests in it. The bank contended that s. 59 only applied where a proprietary interest was claimed and since it had only claimed a security interest, s. 59 had no application.

The learned trial judge gave no effect to that argument. At p. 291, he said:

In my view, s. 174 simply sets forth the time frame in which the removal of the assets from the bankrupt after filing a claim would constitute an offence, or, failing to file a claim, the removal of the property from the possession or charge of the trustee becomes an offence unless done with the prior written permission of the trustee.

He went on to comment that:

Apart from the above conclusion, if such were not the case it might well become possible to defeat what Wedge Prov. J stated in *R. v. Mathers* [p. 13], "The purpose of the relevant sections of the Bankruptcy Act is to ensure the orderly and speedy settlement of the bankrupt's affairs," if a secured creditor could arbitrarily seize its security and make no accounting to the trustee. This is precisely what the bank did in this case.

That decision was appealed to the Manitoba Court of Queen's Bench, 58 CBR (NS) 45, [1986] 2 WWR 573. In dismissing the appeal, Lockwood J said at p. 47 that it was irrelevant whether the bank's interest in the property was proprietary or security because s. 174 does not exclude secured creditors.

It is apparent from the reasons of the learned trial judge that those three cases were presented to him. He chose, however, to follow another line of cases which included *Re Leblanc; Cie Eagle Lumber Ltée v. Rochon* (1966), 11 CBR (NS) 13 (Que.), and *Re Bradford; Household Fin. Corp. v. Davis*, 17 CBR (NS) 171, [1972] 4 WWR 484 (Alta.).

In *Leblanc*, Eagle sold lumber to Rochon and registered a privilege against Rochon's real property for the amount owing. Rochon went into bankruptcy and Eagle issued a writ to enforce its privilege. The trustee then sent Eagle a notice disallowing its claim on the ground that the granting of a privilege constituted a preference under the Bankruptcy Act. Eagle did not appeal the disallowance. In the action the trustee pleaded that the action should be dismissed upon the ground that the disallowance of the claim was final and conclusive. Batshaw J held that, by virtue of s. 40(2), the plaintiff as a secured creditor was entitled to realize upon its security without seeking the permission of the court.

At p. 15, Batshaw J said:

1. It is the policy of the Bankruptcy Act not to interfere with secured creditors except insofar as may be necessary to protect the estate as to any surplus on the assets covered by the security.

2. In the opinion of the court, once the trustee received the plaintiff's writ to enforce the privilege, he should have contested the action on the merits if he wished to challenge its claim as a secured creditor rather than seek to do so through the disallowance of the claim as such.

(These reasons use the numbering of the Bankruptcy Act as it appears in the Revised Statutes of Canada, 1970. They were the relevant numbers at the time the proceedings were launched. They are also the numbers used in most of the cases referred to in these reasons. The s. 40(2) referred to in *Leblanc* was s. 49(2) in the Act of 1970 and is s. 69(2) of RSC 1985.)

In the *Household Fin.* case, the lender took a wage assignment as security for a loan. When the borrower went bankrupt, the lender sent a copy of the assignment to the trustee and at the same time served the employer. The trustee disallowed the claim as contrary to the Bankruptcy Act and then applied to the court for directions. The lender also appealed the disallowance of its claim. At p. 485, Riley J held:

I am of the opinion that there is no such jurisdiction in the trustee to determine whether a claim is secured or not, and that the proper method is to bring the matter before a bankruptcy court by way of notice of motion for advice and directions.

At pp. 487-488, he went on:

To my mind the case authorities are conclusive that if there is a dispute as to whether or not a claim is secured, as there is in this case, the proper procedure of the trustee is to bring an application to the Bankruptcy Court for advice and directions on this issue, but he has no jurisdiction pursuant to s. 106, or any other section of the Bankruptcy Act, to disallow an alleged secured claim or determine by himself the question of the validity of the security.

At first blush, it is difficult to see why Judge Mitchell in the present case chose to follow *Re Leblanc* and *Household Fin.* rather than the reasoning of Kopstein Prov. J in *R.*

v. Ford and the cases which followed. Those latter cases are directly on point and their facts are identical, or almost so, to the present case. *Leblanc* and *Household Fin.*, on the other hand, are factually different and are not directly on point. They deal with the extent, if any, to which a trustee has the power to disallow the claim of a secured creditor. If the rationale of *Leblanc* and *Household Fin.* is pursued, however, it can be seen where conflict will arise with the reasoning in *Ford, Mathers* and *Bank of Montreal*.

Those latter cases hold that a secured creditor must comply with s. 59. If s. 59 is applicable to secured creditors, then s. 59 gives the trustee power to dispute or disallow the claim. According to s. 59(2), the claimant must then appeal if he wishes to preserve his rights. *Leblanc* and *Household Fin.*, however, say clearly that the trustee has no power to disallow the claim of a secured creditor and that there is no obligation on a secured creditor to appeal and that the proper course for the trustee to follow is to apply to the court for advice and directions. How then to reconcile these decisions?

One of the matters discussed on the argument of this appeal was whether Ford's interest was proprietary or security. This question arises by virtue of a distinction drawn between the two kinds of interests in such cases as *Re Festival Singers of Can.* (1980), 32 CBR (NS) 193 (Ont. SC), *Re Shibou* (1982), 42 CBR (NS) 132, 134 DLR (3d) 568 (Man. QB) and *Bank of Montreal*.

The distinction arises from the different language used in ss. 49(2) and 59(1). Section 49(2) refers to a "secured creditor" dealing "with his security." Section 59(1), on the other hand, deals with the situation "where a person claims any property, or interest therein, in the possession of the bankrupt." It is clear that s. 59 is intended to deal with a bailment situation, e.g., where a person leaves his suit with the drycleaner and the drycleaner goes bankrupt. Whether it applies to more than bailments need not be decided here. Section 59 sets out a code or procedure to be followed in those circumstances. The claimant must file a proof of claim. The trustee may allow it or dispute it. If disputed, the claimant may appeal. If he does not, he is deemed to have abandoned the property. The onus of establishing a claim is on the claimant. Section 59 provides the only method of determining such a claim.

It is clear that the procedure to be followed where a security claim only is made is quite different. In the event of a dispute, the trustee's recourse is not to give notice of disallowance but to apply to the court for directions: *Household Fin. v. Davis*. Section 59 does not provide an exclusive procedure for this situation: *Re Leblanc*.

This difference in procedure raises the question whether Parliament intended s. 59 to have any application at all where a security interest only is claimed. Having regard to the language of s. 49(2) and of s. 59, it would appear that Parliament did not.

On its face, s. 49(2) indicates that s. 59 does *not* apply. Section 49(2) says that with certain exceptions, a secured creditor may deal with his security as if this section had not been passed. "This section" refers to s. 49(1). The "certain exceptions" are set out in ss. 57 [now s. 79] and 98 to 105 [now ss. 127-134]. They are commented on below, but none of those sections has any application in the present circumstances. Section 59 is not even mentioned in s. 49(2). On a plain reading of s. 49(2), therefore, it is not subject to s. 59. Since s. 174 is only applicable to the property or property interest referred to in s. 59, it would appear that s. 174 is not applicable to security.

Section 57 deals with property of the bankrupt held by another as a pledge, pawn or other security. In such a case, the trustee may inspect the property and redeem it. On receipt of notice from the trustee, the holder is not to realize the security until the trustee has had an opportunity to inspect, and if he so wishes, to redeem. That section has no application here as the property was in the possession of Mrs. Szucsko at the time of the bankruptcy.

Sections 98 to 105 are under the heading "Proof by Secured Creditors." Section 98(1) says that where a secured creditor realizes his security, he may prove (as an ordinary creditor) for the balance of the debt.

Section 98(2) provides that where the creditor surrenders his security to the trustee, he may file a proof of claim for the whole amount of his claim. Clearly s. 98 has no application to the present circumstances.

Section 99 [now s. 128] provides that where a secured creditor neither realizes nor surrenders his security, he shall, if the trustee so demands, value the security. If he does this, he is entitled to share in the bankruptcy only to the extent that his claim exceeds the stated value of the security. The trustee, for his part, may accept the creditor's valuation and may redeem the security if he so wishes.

Section 100 [now s. 129] deals with the situation where the secured creditor has failed to value his security or the trustee is not satisfied with the creditor's valuation. In either of these events, the trustee may require that the security be put up for sale.

Section 101 [now s. 130] empowers the creditor to require the trustee to elect whether he is going to redeem or require a sale. This was what Ford purported to do on 8th February 1988. No response from the trustee is revealed in the evidence.

Sections 102 and 103 [now ss. 131 and 132] deal with amending the valuation of the security.

Section 104 [now s. 133] provides that if a secured creditor does not comply with ss. 98 to 103, he shall be excluded from any dividend.

Section 105 provides that subject to s. 101, a creditor shall not receive more than 100 cents on the dollar, plus interest.

As noted above, none of ss. 57 or 98 to 105 is directly applicable to the circumstances of the present case. They suggest that a secured creditor may deal with the security as if the Bankruptcy Act had not been passed, subject to certain exceptions, and that a secured creditor need not file any proof of claim, except as an unsecured creditor for any amount by which his claim exceeds the value of his security.

The issue in the present appeal is the same as in the three western cases. That is, whether s. 174 applies to property in the possession of the bankrupt which is security for a debt of the bankrupt.

The Crown argues that s. 174 *is* applicable because it applies to anyone who is "a person," with the sole exception of the trustee. Had it been intended to exempt secured creditors, it is argued, they would have been listed along with the trustee. There can be no doubt that the meaning would have been clearer had secured creditors been so listed. As it is, something must be read in, in order to reconcile s. 49(2) and s. 174. Either s. 174 should be added to the exceptions in s. 49(2) or secured creditors should be added to the exception in s. 174. I would resolve that question as the learned trial judge has done, by finding that s. 49(2) is the more specific section in that it deals only with secured creditors and that "a person" in s. 174 is not intended to include secured creditors.

The Crown argues that s. 174 does not interfere with the operation of s. 49(2), it simply sets forth the time frame in which, after filing a claim, removal of the assets from the bankrupt would constitute an offence. This, it is argued, is to ensure the orderly and speedy settlement of the bankrupt's affairs. Finally, if a secured creditor could arbitrarily seize its security and make no accounting to the trustee, the purpose of the Act would be frustrated.

In my view the "time frame" argument ignores the fact that speed may be very important to the realization of security. It also ignores the specific language of s. 49(2) that, subject to some exceptions, a secured creditor may treat s. 49(1) as if it did not exist. Seizure by a secured creditor is not necessarily "arbitrary"; it may only be done in accordance with the terms of the agreement between debtor and creditor. Nor need there be an absence of accounting. Sections 57, 99 and 100 give the trustee certain rights in this regard.

It is argued as well by the Crown that irrespective of his status under s. 49(2), a secured creditor must always file a proof of claim pursuant to s. 59 in order to get possession when the trustee already has possession. While that would certainly fit in with the "orderly scheme" argument, I do not interpret s. 59 in that manner.

As I read that section, it would apply to goods left with a drycleaner who goes bankrupt, or a car left with a garage for repair where the garage operator goes bankrupt. The claimant would be the real owner of the goods; he is not claiming just a security interest in the goods. He claims both title and possession. In such a case, the trustee does have power to disallow the claim, by virtue of s. 59(2). This is not the situation dealt with in *Household Fin. v. Davis*; that case dealt with a secured claim.

Returning to the decision of Kopstein Prov J in *R. v. Ford Motor Credit*, at the conclusion of his reasons he said:

In my opinion, there is no conflict between s. 49(2) and s. 59. What is dealt with under s. 49(2) in the context of this case is an exception enabling the secured creditor to take action upon his security without awaiting the discharge of the bankrupt. That enabling provision, however, does not negate or nullify the requirement that he first comply with s. 59. That his rights may be prejudiced by the delay involved in compliance with s. 59 appears to be an unavoidable result of s. 59, but such prejudice does not minimize or negate the requirement.

In my view, it is an error to find that a secured creditor must comply with s. 59. As indicated above, s. 59 does not apply to secured claims but to situations where the bankrupt has possession, as, for instance, as bailee.

Some cases appear to have been decided upon the basis of whether the creditor had title to the property in question. In *Re Festival Singers of Can.*, the registrar, Master Ferron, suggested at p. 195 that:

... in cases involving conditional sales agreements title to the property never passed to the bankrupt, and since it remained in the claimant he could properly assert his interest as owner under that section.

He was referring to s. 59 and I understand the registrar to mean that in cases where the creditor claims under a conditional sales agreement, s. 59 applies because the creditor has title. The registrar went on to say, "It is not the case where other security is involved such as under a chattel mortgage." I understand this to mean that, in the case of a chattel mortgage, the creditor does not have title and therefore s. 59 does not apply. But a chattel mortgagee does have title so that, in that respect, he would be in the same position as a conditional vendor: Barron and O'Brien, Chattel Mortgages and Bills of Sale, 3rd ed. (1927), p. 3.

I raise the broader question—was s. 59 intended to apply to situations where the creditor is a conditional vendor or chattel mortgagee?—that is, where the claimant may have title for legal purposes, but is not the "real owner" in practical terms and does not have possession. Clearly, such a claimant is "a person [claiming] any property, or interest therein"—the language of s. 59(1). In my view, however, s. 59 should be limited to the cases where the claimant has *only* a proprietary interest; the person who left his suit with the drycleaner would be an example, as would the man leaving his vehicle with the garage operator for repairs. Where the claimant has a security interest, either in isolation or together with a proprietary interest, then he can rely on his security interest. In this event, he can exercise his rights under s. 49(2) and need not proceed under s. 59. This approach appears to be consistent with the reasoning of Scollin J in *Re Shibou*.

A reason for drawing a distinction between the assertion of a proprietary right and the assertion of a security right lies in the different requirements of a trustee in those two situations. In the case of the suit left with the drycleaner who went bankrupt, the trustee would be entitled to the cost of the cleaning, if it had been done, nothing more. In the case of the assertion of a security interest, however, the trustee must be concerned about the value of the security, whether it will yield money in excess of the claim of the secured creditor, or whether on the other hand there will be a deficiency and a claim by the creditor for that deficiency. To meet these exigencies, the trustee is given the powers and duties set out in s. 57 and in ss. 98 to 105: *Re Festival Singers of Can.*, at p. 195, para. 3. To meet the circumstances of a purely proprietary claim, the trustee is given the powers and duties set out in s. 59.

It was suggested earlier in these reasons that in order to reconcile ss. 49(2) and 174, something had to be read into one or other of them. I would read into s. 174 that it does not apply to property in the possession of the bankrupt which is security for a debt of the bankrupt. To do otherwise is to make s. 49(2) subject to s. 174. To do that is to import into s. 49(2) the code of procedure set out in s. 59. That, it seems to me, is entirely contrary to the apparent objective of s. 49(2).

Whether Ford in the present case had a proprietary interest is irrelevant. It was a secured creditor. It was bound to observe the requirements of ss. 49(2), 57 and 98 to 105. It was not bound to observe the requirements of s. 59. Because s. 59 did not apply, neither did s. 174. The learned trial judge was correct and the appeal should be dismissed.

Appeal dismissed.

NOTES

1) Do you agree with the decision and with Austin J's rationalization of the distinction between ss. 69.3(2) and 81(1)? Is there a meaningful distinction between a security claim and a proprietary claim? If there is, why would Parliament put a trustee in a stronger position vis-à-vis proprietary claimants (e.g., bailors of goods left with the bankrupt for storage or dry cleaning) than towards secured parties? How is the secured party prejudiced

by having to comply with s. 81(1)? Given the unsettled state of the case law, should the conflict not have been resolved in the 1992 amendments to the BIA?

2) Section 362(a)(4) of the US Bankruptcy Code makes it clear that the automatic stay triggered on the filing of a bankruptcy petition (and Chapter 11 filing) also applies to the enforcement of security interests. However, under s. 362(b) the court may grant relief from the stay under the following circumstances: (1) for cause, including the lack of adequate protection of an interest in property of the party in interest; and (2) where the stay applies to an act against property, if (a) the debtor does not have an equity in such property; and (b) such property is not necessary to an effective reorganization.

The meaning of "adequate protection" is explained in s. 361, but the definition has attracted considerable litigation and scholarly discussion because it does not address the issue of the time value of money or its equivalent. See Baird & Jackson, *Cases, Problems and Materials on Bankruptcy*, 2nd ed., pp. 620-23. The American theory of the automatic stay appears to be that secured creditors, as well as other creditors, will be better off if the trustee is allowed to deal with all the assets of the estate. The Canadian theory, on the other hand (embodied in s. 69.3(2)), adopts the view that the secured creditor's bargain (which includes the right to foreclose and sell the collateral on default or other prescribed events) should be respected in bankruptcy as well as outside of bankruptcy. The Canadian position is supported in F.H. Buckley, "A Corporate Governance Theory of Repossessory Rights" (1994), 23 *CBLJ* 96. However, in the light of the American doctrine of adequate protection, is there a practical difference between the Canadian and American positions? As we have noted in other chapters, it is common for a privately appointed receiver (PAR) also to act as trustee of the estate and, where there is no PAR, the secured party may agree to allow the trustee to realize the collateral on its behalf. Frequently, the secured party will have repossessed the collateral before the filing of the bankruptcy petition.

3) An argument that could be made in favour of applying the automatic stay to straight bankruptcies is that it would assist the trustee in valuing the collateral and in determining whether the debtor still has an equity in it. BIA ss. 127-134 address these issues as well as other questions affecting the collateral. Since these provisions are not predicated on the trustee's having possession of the collateral, do they prove that an automatic stay is not essential for the protection of the estate? Or would we argue that the main purpose of the stay is to enable the trustee to determine whether the business can be sold as a going concern? If this is our main worry, why would the debtor not file a notice of intention to make a proposal under Part III.1 and secure the benefit of an automatic stay under s. 69? (Bear in mind that the s. 244 requirement for the secured creditor to give 10 days' notice before enforcing its security is intended to facilitate reorganization under Part III.)

4) As the above mentioned provisions show and as we have also seen in earlier chapters, the BIA supports secured creditors' claims at almost every stage. Is this sound policy? Prof. Cuming argues that it is not,* although he does not tell us by how much he would cut back secured creditors' rights in bankruptcy, and why. The conceptual dilemma that faces all scholars in this area is to reconcile the generous PPS regimes now in force in

---

* R.C.C. Cuming, "Canadian Bankruptcy Law: A Secured Creditors Heaven" (1994), 24 *CBLJ* 17; and *cf.* Ziegel, "The New Personal Property Security Regimes: Have We Gone Too Far?" (1990), 28 *Alta. L Rev.*

most parts of Canada (with their implicit philosophy that secured credit is good for the economy), with the urge to restrict enforcement rights and to demote the priority of consensual security interests when the debtor gets into trouble. This contradiction lies at the root of the conflict between consensual security interests and non-consensual Crown claims and wage earner claims, although the conflict is not limited to these classes.

Note on Equitable Subordination of Creditors' Claims

Starting with *Pepper v. Litton* (1938), 308 U.S. 295 and *Taylor v. Standard Gas & Electric Co.* (1939), 306 U.S. 307, American courts have embraced a doctrine of equitable subordination. The doctrine applies where a claimant, not dealing at arm's length with the bankrupt, has exploited its controlling position by taking unfair advantage of the bankrupt or securing a benefit over the bankrupt's other creditors which would not otherwise have accrued to it. The wrongdoer may be a majority shareholder in a single corporation or it may be a parent corporation in a position to dictate decisions to a subsidiary. The advantage may consist in the dominant shareholder causing the corporation to confess to judgment in the shareholder's favour with respect to a long dormant wage claim (as in *Pepper v. Litton*); or it may involve a parent company causing the subsidiary to declare large dividends in the parent company's favour (as in *Taylor*, *supra*) where the dividends cannot be justified on economic grounds.

Where such inequitable conduct is found, the remedy applied by American courts is to subordinate the wrongdoer's claim, in whole or in part, until the claims of the bankrupt's other creditors have been satisfied. The doctrine is recognized in s. 510(c) of the US Bankruptcy Code, although the section provides no guidance as to when the doctrine should be applied. According to Dean Clark of the Harvard Law School,* the remedy may involve the subordination of all the claims of the controlling party ("full subordination" rule); it may be restricted to a deduction of the unfair benefit received by the insider from the insider's claim ("offset" rule); or the insider's entitlement to share in the proceeds of the estate will be calculated as if no tainted transaction had taken place and the insider is then considered to have received an anticipatory distribution equal to the amount of the unjust benefit previously received by it ("constructive distribution" rule).

Whatever the precise remedy, questions arise of how the equitable subordination doctrine differs from other pre-bankruptcy transactions voidable on the debtor's bankruptcy, and why, given the scope of modern voidable transaction statutory provisions, the doctrine is still needed at all. With respect to the first question, Dean Clark has argued† that the difference resides in the intricate relationship between members of a corporate group not dealing at arm's length with each other. At least from a Canadian perspective, the explanation is not entirely satisfactory. First, the seminal case of *Pepper v. Litton, supra*, did not involve an intricate corporate relationship. Second, ss. 100 and 137 of the BIA

---

* Clark, "The Duties of the Corporate Debtor to its Creditors" (1977), 90 *Harv. L Rev.* 505, 519-20, cited in Baird & Jackson, *op. cit.*, 729.

† Clark, "The Interdisciplinary Study of Legal Evolution" (1981), 9 *Yale LJ* 1238, 1249-50, reproduced in Baird & Jackson, *op. cit.*, at 730-31.

seem to have no difficulty addressing such non-arm's length relationships in a more direct fashion.

Section 100 has been discussed in chapter 16, *supra*. Section 137 provides that a creditor who enters into a "reviewable transaction" (defined in s. 3) "at any time" prior to the debtor's bankruptcy is not entitled to claim a dividend until (a) the claims of other creditors of the estate have first been satisfied, *or* (b) unless the transaction was, in the trustee's or court's opinion, a proper transaction between the parties. Section 140 is also important. This section subordinates the claims of officers and directors of the bankrupt for wages, salary, commission or compensation for work done or services rendered to the corporation "in any capacity."

Given these provisions, does Canadian bankruptcy law need a doctrine of equitable subordination at all? In several recent cases (Iacobucci J in *CDIC v. Canadian Commercial Bank*, SCC, unreported, Nov. 12, 1992, p. 59, referred to in *Max Metro-City Realty Ltd. v. D. & A. Macleod Co.*, [1993] OJ No.87; *Olympia & York Developments Ltd. v. Royal Trust Co.* (1993), 14 OR (3d) 1 (OCA), and *O & Y Dvpts. Ltd. v. Royal Trust Co.* (1993), 17 CBR (3d) 75), the courts found it unnecessary to express an opinion. However, their attention does not appear to have been drawn to the BIA provisions, although these provisions may not have been applicable because some of the cases did not involve BIA proceedings.

Priority of Crown Claims

British Columbia v. Henfrey Samson Belair Ltd.
(1989), 59 DLR (4th) 726 (SCC)

McLACHLIN J: The issue on this appeal is whether the statutory trust created by s. 18 of the British Columbia *Social Service Tax Act*, RSBC 1979, c. 388, gives the province priority over other creditors under the *Bankruptcy Act*, RSC 1970, c. B-3.

Tops Pontiac Buick Ltd. collected sales tax for the provincial government in the course of its business operations, as it was required to do by the *Social Service Tax Act*. Tops mingled the tax collected with its other assets. When the Canadian Imperial Bank of Commerce placed Tops in receivership pursuant to its debenture and Tops made an assignment in bankruptcy, the receiver sold the assets of Tops and applied the full proceeds in reduction of the indebtedness of the bank.

The province contends that the *Social Service Tax Act* creates a statutory trust over the assets of Tops equal to the amount of the sales tax collected but not remitted ($58,763.23), and that it has priority over the bank and all other creditors for this amount.

The chambers judge held that the *Social Service Tax Act* did not create a trust and that the province did not have priority [5 BCLR (2d) 212, 61 CBR (NS) 59]. On appeal the receiver conceded that the legislation created a statutory trust, but contended that the chambers judge was correct in ruling that the province did not have priority because the *Bankruptcy Act* did not confer priority on such a trust. The British Columbia Court of Appeal accepted this submission [40 DLR (4th) 728, 13 BCLR (2d) 346, [1987] 4 WWR 673, 65 CBR (NS) 24, 5 ACWS (3d) 47]. The province now appeals to this court.

The section of the *Social Service Tax Act* which the province contends gives it priority provides:

18(1) Where a person collects an amount of tax under this Act

(a) he shall be deemed to hold it in trust for Her Majesty in right of the Province for the payment over of that amount to Her Majesty in the manner and at the time required under this Act and regulations, and

(b) the tax collected shall be deemed to be held separate from and form no part of the person's money, assets or estate, whether or not the amount of the tax has in fact been kept separate and apart from either the person's own money or the assets of the estate of the person who collected the amount of the tax under this Act.

(2) The amount of taxes that, under this Act,

(a) is collected and held in trust, in accordance with subsection (1); or

(b) is required to be collected and remitted by a vendor or lessor

forms a lien and charge on the entire assets of

(c) the estate of the trustee under paragraph (a);

(d) the person required to collect or remit the tax under paragraph (b); or

(e) the estate of the person required to collect or remit the tax under paragraph (d).

The province argues that s. 18(1) creates a trust within s. 47(a) [now s. 67(1)(a)] of the *Bankruptcy Act*, which provides:

47. The property of a bankrupt divisible among his creditors shall not comprise

(a) property held by the bankrupt in trust for any other person;

The respondents, on the other hand, submit that the deemed statutory trust created by s. 18 of the *Social Service Tax Act* is not a trust within s. 47 the *Bankruptcy Act*, in that it does not possess the attributes of a true trust. They submit that the province's claim to the tax money is in fact a debt falling under s. 107(1)(j) of the *Bankruptcy Act*, the priority to which falls to be determined according to the priorities established by s. 107.*

107(1) Subject to the rights of secured creditors, the proceeds realized from the property of a bankrupt shall be applied in priority of payment as follows:

• • •

(j) claims of the Crown not previously mentioned in this section, in right of Canada or of any province, *pari passu* notwithstanding any statutory preference to the contrary.

Discussion

The issue may be characterized as follows. Section 47(a) of the *Bankruptcy Act* exempts trust property in the hands of the bankrupt from distribution to creditors, giving trust claimants absolute priority. Section 107(1) establishes priorities between creditors on distribution: s. 107(1)(j) ranks Crown claims last. Section 18 of the *Social Service Tax Act* creates a statutory trust which lacks the essential characteristics of a trust, namely, that the property impressed with the trust be identifiable or traceable. The question is whether the statutory trust created by the provincial legislation is a trust within s. 47(a) of the *Bankruptcy Act* or a mere Crown claim under s. 107(1)(j).

---

* Section 107(1)(j) was repealed in the 1992 amendments to the BIA and replaced by new ss. 86-87. [ed.]

In my opinion, the answer to this question lies in the construction of the relevant provisions of the *Bankruptcy Act* and the *Social Service Tax Act*.

In approaching this task, I take as my guide the following passage from Driedger, *Construction of Statutes*, 2nd ed. (1983), at p. 105:

The decisions ... indicate that the provisions of an enactment relevant to a particular case are to be read in the following way:

1. The Act as a whole is to be read in its entire context so as to ascertain the intention of Parliament (the law as expressly or impliedly enacted by the words), the object of the Act (the ends sought to be achieved), and the scheme of the Act (the relation between the individual provisions of the Act).

2. The words of the individual provisions to be applied to the particular case under considera-tion are then to be read in their grammatical and ordinary sense in the light of the intention of Parliament embodied in the Act as a whole, the object of the Act and the scheme of the Act, and if they are clear and unambiguous and in harmony with that intention, object and scheme and with the general body of the law, that is the end.

With these principles in mind, I turn to the construction of ss. 47(a) and 107(1)(j) of the *Bankruptcy Act*. The question which arises under s. 47(a) of the Act concerns the meaning of the phrase "property held by the bankrupt in trust for any other person." Taking the words in their ordinary sense, they connote a situation where there is property which can be identified as being held in trust. That property is to be removed from other assets in the hands of the bankrupt before distribution under the *Bankruptcy Act* because, in equity, it belongs to another person. The intention of Parliament in enacting s. 47(a), then, was to permit removal of property which can be specifically identified as not belonging to the bankrupt under general principles of trust law from the distribution scheme established by the *Bankruptcy Act*.

Section 107(1)(j), on the other hand, has been held to deal not with rights conferred by general law, but with the statutorily created claims of federal and provincial tax collectors. The purpose of s. 107(1)(j) was discussed by this court in *Re Bourgault* (1979), 105 DLR (3d) 270, [1980] 1 SCR 35 *sub nom. Deputy Minister of Revenue v. Rainville*, 33 CBR (NS) 301, Pigeon J, speaking for the majority, stated at p. 278:

There is no need to consider the scope of the expression "claims of the Crown." It is quite clear that this applies to claims of provincial governments for taxes and I think it is obvious that it does not include claims not secured by Her Majesty's personal preference, but by a privilege which may be obtained by anyone under general rules of law, such as a vendor's or a builder's privilege.

If ss. 47(a) and 107(1)(f) are read in this way, no conflict arises between them. If a trust claim is established under general principles of law, then the property subject to the trust is removed from the general distribution by reason of s. 47(a). Following the reasoning of Pigeon J in *Rainville*, such a claim would not fall under s. 107(1)(j) because it is valid under general principles of law and is not a claim secured by the Crown's personal preference.

This construction of ss. 47(a) and 107(1)(j) of the *Bankruptcy Act* conforms with the principle that provinces cannot create priorities under the *Bankruptcy Act* by their own legislation, a principle affirmed by this court in *Re Deloitte, Haskins & Sells Ltd. and Workers' Compensation Board* (1985), 19 DLR (4th) 577, [1985] 1 SCR 785, [1985] 4 WWR 481 (SCC). As Wilson J stated at p. 592:

... the issue in *Re Bourgault* and *Re Black Forest* was not whether a proprietary interest has been created under the relevant provincial legislation. It was whether provincial legislation, even if it did create a proprietary interest, could defeat the scheme of distribution under s. 107(1) of the *Bankruptcy Act*. These cases held that it could not, that while the provincial legislation could validly secure debts on the property of the debtor in a non-bankruptcy situation, once bankruptcy occurred s. 107(1) determined the status and priority of the claims specifically dealt with in the section. It was not open to the claimant in bankruptcy to say: By virtue of the applicable provincial legislation I am a secured creditor within the meaning of the opening words of s. 107(1) of the *Bankruptcy Act* and therefore the priority accorded my claim under the relevant paragraph of s. 107(1) does not apply to me. In effect, this is the position adopted by the Court of Appeal and advanced before us by the respondent. It cannot be supported as a matter of statutory interpretation of s. 107(1) since, if the section were to be read in this way, it would have the effect of permitting the provinces to determine priorities on a bankruptcy, a matter within exclusive federal jurisdiction.

While *Re Deloitte, Haskins & Sells Ltd. and Workers' Compensation Board* was concerned with provincial legislation purporting to give the province the status of a secured creditor for purposes of the *Bankruptcy Act*, the same reasoning applies in the case at bar.

To interpret s. 47(a) as applying not only to trusts as defined by the general law, but to statutory trusts created by the provinces lacking the common law attributes of trusts, would be to permit the provinces to create their own priorities under the *Bankruptcy Act* and to invite a differential scheme of distribution on bankruptcy from province to province.

Practical policy considerations also recommend this interpretation of the *Bankruptcy Act*. The difficulties of extending s. 47(a) to cases where no specific property impressed with a trust can be identified are formidable and defy fairness and common sense. For example, if the claim for taxes equalled or exceeded the funds in the hands of the trustee in bankruptcy, the trustee would not recover the costs incurred to realize the funds. Indeed, the trustee might be in breach of the Act by expending funds to realize the bankrupt's assets. Other difficulties would arise in the case of more than one claimant to the trust property. The spectre is raised of a person who has a valid trust claim under the general principles of trust law to a specific piece of property, finding himself in competition with the Crown claiming a statutory trust in that and all the other property. Could the Crown's general claim pre-empt the property interest of the claimant under trust law? Or would the claimant under trust law prevail? To admit of such a possibility would be to run counter to the clear intention of Parliament in enacting the *Bankruptcy Act* of setting up a clear and orderly scheme for the distribution of the bankrupt's assets.

In summary, I am of the view that s. 47(a) should be confined to trusts arising under general principles of law, while s. 107(1)(j) should be confined to claims such as tax claims not established by general law but secured "by her Majesty's personal preference" through legislation. This conclusion, in my opinion, is supported by the wording of the sections in question, by the jurisprudence of this court, and by the policy considerations to which I have alluded.

I turn next to s. 18 of the *Social Service Tax Act* and the nature of the legal interests created by it. At the moment of collection the trust property is identifiable and the trust meets the requirements for a trust under the principles of trust law. The difficulty in this, as in most cases, is that the trust property soon ceases to be identifiable. The tax money is mingled with other money in the hands of the merchant and converted to other property so that it cannot be traced. At this point it is no longer a trust under general principles of law. In an attempt to meet this problem, s. 18(1)(b) states that tax collected shall be deemed to be held separate from and form no part of the collector's money, assets or estate. But, as the presence of the deeming provision tacitly acknowledges, the reality is that after conversion the statutory trust bears little resemblance to a true trust. There is no property which can be regarded as being impressed with a trust. Because of this, s. 18(2) goes on to provide that the unpaid tax forms a lien and charge on the entire assets of the collector, an interest in the nature of a secured debt.

Applying these observations on s. 18 of the *Social Service Tax Act* to the construction of ss. 47(a) and 107(1)(j) of the *Bankruptcy Act* which I have earlier adopted, the answer to the question of whether the province's interest under s. 18 is a "trust" under s. 47(a) or a "claim of the Crown" under s. 107(1)(j) depends on the facts of the particular case. If the money collected for tax is identifiable or traceable, then the true state of affairs conforms with the ordinary meaning of "trust" and the money is exempt from distribution to creditors by reason of s. 47(a). If, on the other hand, the money has been converted to other property and cannot be traced, there is no "property held ... in trust" under s. 47(a). The province has a claim secured only by a charge or lien, and s. 107(1)(j) applies.

In the case at bar, no specific property impressed with a trust can be identified. It follows that s. 47(a) of the *Bankruptcy Act* should not be construed as extending to the province's claim in this case.

The Province, however, argues that it is open to it to define "trust" however it pleases, property and civil rights being matters within provincial competence. The short answer to this submission is that the definition of trust which is operative for purposes of exemption under the *Bankruptcy Act* must be that of the federal Parliament, not the provincial legislatures. The provinces may define "trust" as they choose for matters within their own legislative competence, but they cannot dictate to Parliament how it should be defined for purposes of the *Bankruptcy Act: Re Deloitte, Haskins & Sells Ltd. and Workers' Compensation Board.*

Nor does the argument that the tax money remains the property of the Crown throughout withstand scrutiny. If that were the case, there would be no need for the lien and charge in the Crown's favour created by s. 18(2) of the *Social Service Tax Act.* The province has a trust interest and hence property in the tax funds so long as they can be identified or traced. But once they lose that character, any common law or equitable property interest disappears. The province is left with a statutory deemed trust which does not give it the same property interest a common law trust would, supplemented by a lien and charge over all the bankrupt's property under s. 18(2).

The province relies on *Re Phoenix Paper Products Ltd.* (1983), 3 DLR (4th) 617, 44 OR (2d) 225, 48 CBR (NS) 113, where the Ontario Court of Appeal held that accrued vacation pay mixed with other assets of a bankrupt constituted a trust under s. 47(a) of the *Bankruptcy Act.* As the Court of Appeal in this case pointed out, the Ontario Court of

Appeal in *Re Phoenix Paper Products Ltd.*, in considering the two divergent lines of authority presented to it, did not have the advantage of considering what was said in *Re Deloitte, Haskins & Sells and Workers' Compensation Board*, and the affirmation in that case of the line of authority which the Ontario Court of Appeal rejected.

• • •

Conclusion

For the reasons stated, I conclude that s. 47(a) of the *Bankruptcy Act* does not apply in this case and the priority of the province's claim is governed by s. 107(1)(j) of the Act. I would decline to answer the alternative question posed by the appellants.

Appeal dismissed.

Report of the Advisory Committee on Bankruptcy and Insolvency
(1988) ("Colter Report"), 76-79

Crown Priority

Current Law

Section 107 of the *Bankruptcy Act* provides that, subject to the rights of secured creditors, the proceeds realized from the property of the bankrupt shall be applied in priority of payment as follows:

- funeral expenses;
- administration costs;
- Superintendent of Bankruptcy's levy;
- wages;
- municipal taxes that are not a lien on land;
- landlord;
- legal costs of first seizing creditor;
- workmen's compensation, unemployment insurance and deductions owing under the *Income Tax Act*;
- injuries to employees not covered by any workmen's compensation acts;
- claims of Crown, provincial or federal, not previously mentioned.

Since the statutory priority under Section 107 ranks behind secured claims, the federal government and most provincial governments have created statutory deemed trusts or deemed liens which were intended to rank in priority to the claims of secured creditors. The federal government has done this in respect of claims for amounts deducted from employees under the *Canada Pension Plan Act*, the *Unemployment Insurance Act* and, in the most recent budget, the *Income Tax Act*. Provinces have created statutory deemed trusts and liens to cover amounts owing for wages and vacation pay. The attempt of the Province of Quebec to create a statutory lien for retail sales tax was rejected by the

Supreme Court of Canada in the case of *Deputy Minister of Revenue v. Rainville (in re Bourgault)*, [1980] 1 SCR 35. Similarly, the Supreme Court of Canada in the recent case of *Deloitte, Haskins & Sells Limited v. Workers' Compensation Board*, [1985] 55 CBR (NS) 241 ruled that the Workers' Compensation Board of Alberta was not entitled to a secured claim in a bankruptcy on the grounds that Section 107(1)(h) of the *Bankruptcy Act* conflicted with the provisions of the *Workers' Compensation Act*, creating a secured claim that rendered the provisions of the latter Act inoperative after a bankruptcy has occurred. This was the most recent of a long series of cases dealing with the validity and priority of statutory deemed trusts and liens. In some instances there are conflicting decisions in different provinces. There is no doubt that while provincial legislation can validly secure debts on the property of the debtor in a non-bankruptcy situation, once bankruptcy occurs Section 107(1) of the *Bankruptcy Act* determines the status and priority of the claims specifically dealt with in that section.

Section 47 of the *Bankruptcy Act*, which excludes from a bankruptcy all property held by the bankrupt in trust for any other person, has also been used to circumvent the provisions of Section 107(1). This is done for the obvious reason that since the property does not belong to the bankrupt, the creditors should have no right to share in it. Both federal and provincial legislation have resorted to a legal fiction to recover certain debts in priority to the claims of secured creditors. They have created the deemed trust where the law grants to the government or the beneficiary of the deemed trust a claim against all the assets of the bankrupt ranking in priority to the claims of secured creditors. This fiction applies even though amounts deducted, which were supposed to have been kept separate and apart, were in fact not so kept. In some cases, a deemed trust is created even where there is no obligation to make a deduction from the wages of the employee, such as the claim for vacation pay under the *Employment Standards Act* of Ontario.

The same priorities apply to proposals under Section 41(4) of the *Bankruptcy Act*. A proposal cannot be approved by the court if it does not provide for the same priority of payment of claims as Section 107 of the *Bankruptcy Act*.

Problems

The proliferation of statutory deemed trusts and liens has created significant uncertainty and confusion in the distribution of a bankrupt's property. The priority attributed to Crown claims, either by way of statutory deemed trusts and liens or under Section 107 of the *Bankruptcy Act*, has reduced the ability of a debtor to make a proposal to its creditors. Frequently, the requirement that claims of the Crown be paid in full before there is any distribution to the unsecured creditors prevents an effective reorganization.

Unsecured creditors often do not take an active interest in the administration of a bankruptcy because all the proceeds of any recovery will go to the Crown as a preferred creditor. The Crown, either federal or provincial, seldom involves itself in the administration of a bankrupt estate. In many instances, a representative of the Crown will not attend the first meeting of creditors or will not act as an inspector. It is also most unusual for the Crown to advance any money to recover assets for a bankrupt estate. Crown corporations also have the advantage of the same priority, and this creates unfair competition against private sector companies in the marketplace.

Options

Option A—Crown Priority

1. Crown priority would be totally abolished, under both federal and provincial jurisdiction, and all claims of the Crown would rank in the same priority as those of unsecured creditors. The elimination of the Crown priority would include all provincial and federal legislation purporting to give a priority, whether by way of security, statutory trust or lien or otherwise for any debt not contractually incurred. The abolishment of priority would include all Crown corporations, either federal or provincial.

2. Any future act of Parliament must make a direct reference to the *Bankruptcy Act* in order to supersede the provisions of the *Bankruptcy Act* dealing with the priority of distribution of a bankrupt's property.

Option B—Crown Priority

1. Under the American Bankruptcy Code, the federal government retains a priority for deductions at source and other amounts owing. However, in the event of a reorganization under Chapter 11, the United States government does not have the right to vote and must accept automatically a six-month payout with interest at the market rate. This priority has not created any particular problem, any lack of interest by creditors or any lack of the possibility of reorganization for the following reasons:

- the amount to be paid is spread out over a period of six months;
- in the United States, the law does not permit a creditor to take a blanket security such as the floating charge that exists in Canada. Thus, there always appear to be free assets with which to pay the government priority and to fund the costs of the reorganization of the debtor, including the creditors' committee.

2. The priority of the Crown, whether by way of secured claim, statutory trust or under Section 107 of the *Bankruptcy Act*, for amounts deducted from the wages of employees would be limited to those amounts deducted from employees' wages during the 90 days prior to the date of bankruptcy. The priority would not apply to the employer's contributions. No other debts due to the Crown, either federal or provincial, would have the right of priority; they would be treated as all other unsecured creditors.

3. In the event that the unsecured and secured creditors accept a proposal for a reorganization, the Crown, either federal or provincial, would be required to automatically accept a 12-month payout of its prior priority claim with interest at the market rate. Interest at market rate would mean the interest charged by the Bank of Canada as the "rediscount rate."

Recommendation

The committee recommends the abolishment of the priority of the Crown in accordance with Option A. The burden of tax left unpaid by the bankrupt should be divided among all the tax-paying public rather than borne by the creditors, who have already suffered losses. Such abolishment should also improve the administration of bankrupt estates since in many instances the Crown does not get involved in such matters, even when it appears to be the only creditor entitled to a dividend. The abolishment of Crown priority should give the unsecured creditors a greater incentive to involve themselves in the administration of bankrupt estates.

NOTES

As noted in the introduction to this chapter, the Committee's recommendation in favour of Option A was not adopted by the federal government in Bill C-22. Instead, the government opted for a compromise solution, the details of which are found in ss. 67(2) and (3), 86-87, and 136(1) of the amended BIA.

Study the provisions closely, and consider the following questions:

1) Do the amendments proceed on a principled basis and if so what is that basis?

2) What is the justification for conferring absolute priority for deemed trusts under s. 67(3)? Should the priority be restricted in time to a short period preceding the bankruptcy, say three months? Should the Crown's priority be prorated with advances made by a secured lender during this or any other period?

3) Is it correct to say that ss. 86-87 have simply abolished all Crown priorities in non-deemed trust cases?

4) What are the strengths and weaknesses of the registration provisions in s. 87? What happens to Crown claims that accrue *after* the date of registration? What is the status of advances made by a secured party with a prior perfected security interest where the advances are made after the date of registration of the Crown claim? Will the OPPSA rules apply?

Section 67(3) of the BIA does not apply to federal government claims for GST amounts collected but not remitted by a taxpayer as required in Part IX of the Excise Tax Act, nor does it apply to provincial sales taxes. In the following unpublished paper, Mr. B.J. Skulski, a senior Revenue Canada officer, argues for removing this anomaly. His paper also canvasses the general merits of giving the Crown priority for source deductions and therefore provides a well argued counterpoint to the position taken in the Colter Report reproduced above.

B.J. Skulski
The Deemed Trust and Enhanced Garnishment Provisions of the *Excise Tax Act* and Their Application in Relation to the *Bankruptcy and Insolvency Act**
(footnotes omitted)

Introduction

This paper addresses the need to reinforce some of the remedies that are available under Part IX of the *Excise Tax Act* and which pertain to the collection of the Goods and Services Tax ("GST"). Currently, the Crown enjoys protected status under the *Income Tax Act* vis-à-vis source deduction amounts and the ability to collect those amounts in the event of

---

* Unpublished paper prepared in 1993 by Mr. Skulski for use by the Preferences and Priorities Working Group of BIAC. The editors are deeply indebted to Mr. Skulski and Revenue Canada for permission to reproduce the paper.

proceedings under the *Bankruptcy and Insolvency Act*. By contrast, under the context of the *Excise Tax Act*, the Crown is restricted and enjoys a limited means for collection of GST arrears.

It is estimated that potential GST losses resulting from insolvency since the implementation of the tax have reached some $130 million. To the extent that these losses represent a significant portion of government shortfalls in revenue generation, it is necessary to explore possible remedies to this problem.

The purpose of this paper is to set out the arguments in favour of according the same rights under the *Bankruptcy and Insolvency Act* in respect of the collection of the GST arrears as are now in place for the recovery of unremitted source deductions under the *Income Tax Act*.

Synopsis of Existing Legislation

Deemed Trusts

Both the *Income Tax Act* and the *Excise Tax Act* contain provisions for deemed trusts to deal with amounts withheld, deducted or collected, which are held for remittance to the Crown. In the case of the deemed trust under the *Income Tax Act*, the remedy provides a measure of protection to ensure the remittance of amounts deducted from employees' remuneration. In the interim period between the time the amounts are deducted and the time they are to be remitted, they are deemed to be held in trust and separate and apart from the person's own moneys notwithstanding that they may be commingled with those other moneys.

In a similar fashion, amounts collected from purchasers on account of GST are deemed to be held in a trust and separate and apart from the person's own moneys until such time as they are remitted to the Receiver General. In both cases, the operative rationale for legislating the deemed trusts is the fact that the amounts withheld, deducted or collected are not the property of the person who withheld, deducted or collected them, but rather are in the temporary possession of that person.

The provisions in the two statutes are similar except for one important difference. The deemed trust under the *Income Tax Act* survives the bankruptcy of the debtor while that in respect of GST amounts collected or collectible prior to bankruptcy is rendered inoperative in the event bankruptcy were to occur.

Section 67 of the *Bankruptcy and Insolvency Act* defines what constitutes property of the bankrupt. True trusts are not the property of the bankrupt. However, amounts secured under a deemed trust form part of the property of the bankrupt unless the trust could be sustained without reference to legislation. An exception is provided for the deemed trust created under the *Income Tax Act* in respect of source deductions, whereby an amount equivalent to the source deductions is deemed to be separate and apart from the assets of the bankrupt. By contrast, the deemed trust established for the collection of GST is not so treated. As a result, claims for GST revenues are included in the estate of the bankrupt, and do not enjoy the priority in ranking amongst creditors. Under the amendments incorporated in the *Bankruptcy and Insolvency Act*, the Crown gave up its priority to payment as a preferred creditor in respect of tax revenues. The preferred status previously afforded the Crown has been repealed. Since the Crown is now an unsecured creditor, it is often left in the position of being unable to recover its claims for GST revenues.

Enhanced Garnishment

In an effort to recover arrears of source deductions or GST in situations where most, if not all, the assets of a tax debtor are pledged as security, both the *Income Tax Act* and the *Excise Tax Act* make provision for enhanced garnishment. These provisions, although perceived as draconian or piratical, are necessary to enable the Minister to garnish amounts otherwise payable to the secured creditor. Once an enhanced garnishment notice is received, the amounts in question become the property of the Crown to the extent of the liability as assessed by the Minister, notwithstanding the prior claim to those amounts by the secured creditor. Again, as in the case of the deemed trusts, the enhanced garnishee under subsection 224(1.2) of the *Income Tax Act* operates "Notwithstanding ... the *Bankruptcy and Insolvency Act*." By contrast, the applicable provision under the *Excise Tax Act* does not contain similar wording. On the other hand, recent reforms in the bankruptcy legislation imposed some restriction on the operation of subsection 224(1.2).

Paragraphs 69(1)(c) and 69.1(1)(c) of the *Bankruptcy and Insolvency Act* bar the Crown from initiating or continuing to use garnishment under subsection 224(1.2) when a stay of proceedings is in effect. However, that prohibition ceases if the tax debtor defaults in the remittance of current source deductions during the stay and proposal stages or if a secured creditor becomes entitled to realize on its security.

A commercial reorganization cannot be approved by the court if source deduction payments occurring after the date of the filing of the notice of intention are not made as they fall due. Similarly, a court cannot, unless Her Majesty consents otherwise, approve a debtor's reorganization plan that does not provide that all arrears of source deductions will be paid in full within six months of acceptance of the proposal.

Taken together, these provisions provide much greater certainty that arrears and current remittances of source deductions under the *Income Tax Act* will be recovered by the Crown during the stay of proceedings. By contrast, arrears of GST are not afforded the same protection and are unlikely to be recovered since the Crown no longer enjoys preferred status and its claims have been relegated to that of an ordinary unsecured creditor. Furthermore, the Crown's ability to recover arrears of GST and to ensure that current GST remittances are made is severely hampered during the period of the stay of proceedings.

The debate about the priority amongst creditors in insolvency situations has been ongoing for a long time and is not likely to be resolved in the near future. Each party feels that it has a unique and justifiable claim to be first in line for distribution of any available proceeds from the estate. This paper does not purport to resolve the debate; it does, however, represent an attempt to present the case for according the deemed trust provisions under the *Excise Tax Act* the same priority and status as that provided to source deductions pursuant to the *Income Tax Act*. As well, a case will be made for an expanded use of enhanced garnishment during insolvency in a manner consistent with that now accorded source deductions.

Arguments Against Upgrading the Crown's Position

Arguments have been advanced to suggest that to allow the federal Crown priority for its tax amounts would have a negative impact with the following results, namely:

   (a) disadvantage to the other creditors;

(b) impact on financing costs;

(c) discrimination against certain secured creditors; and

(d) disruption of the insolvency process.

Disadvantages of Other Creditors

In terms of disadvantaging other creditors, most creditors do, when there is an insolvency, suffer financial loss to a greater or lesser degree. It can be argued that private sector creditors do not have the same resources as does the federal government and are unable to withstand the financial impact of non-payment of debts. Accordingly, the Crown should yield in its claim for payment ahead of the claims of other creditors. In particular, smaller creditors and employees are most likely to suffer as a result of any priority given the Crown. In this regard, the legislative amendments reflected in the *Bankruptcy and Insolvency Act* represent an attempt to ensure that more safeguards are put in place to protect businesses that have supplied the debtor with goods during the period immediately prior to bankruptcy or receivership. Furthermore, to this end, the Crown's preferred status has, as was indicated earlier, been eliminated and the Crown now claims as an ordinary unsecured creditor.

Impact on Financing Costs

It has been argued that if the financial community is to bear additional costs in relation to insolvencies, then the cost of financing would, over time, rise for all borrowers. The argument is premised on the assumption that the financial community must be able to rely on the certainty of its security to recover losses, or otherwise it would have to re-evaluate upward the risk factor associated with lending money.

Accordingly, financial institutions would be forced to closely monitor clients, thereby pushing up the costs of financing which would, in turn, be passed to their clients in the form of higher interest rates. Furthermore, due to the uncertainty arising in the value of their security, lenders may also insist on reducing lending ratios, that is to say they may increase the margin between the money lent and the value of the security. In this respect, lenders would regard labour intensive firms a greater risk than capital intensive companies, and shift money away from them. Consequently, companies that most need credit, because they have a lot of wage earners, might have the greatest difficulty in getting it, thereby undermining the government's job creation objectives.

It is suggested, however, that the foregoing arguments are valid only when the demand for commercial credit outpaces the supply of money available for loan purposes. Indeed, when the demand for credit wanes and the supply of money remains constant or increases, market forces should compel financial institutions to modify their previously stringent lending criteria.

Discrimination Against Certain Secured Creditors

It has been argued that a creditor holding an assignment of accounts receivables or inventory may be treated unfairly vis-à-vis other creditors holding a charge against fixed assets. Enhanced garnishment intercepts moneys otherwise payable to the secured creditor. Likewise the deemed trust is effective against inventory held under a floating charge where it has taken effect prior to the appointment of the receiver or the taking of possession by the receiver. Accordingly, the value of the creditor's security decreases in direct proportion to the amount intercepted by the Crown. In extreme circumstances, the creditor's security position could be eroded to such an extent that the creditor might be left with an unsecured claim. The creditor would, albeit indirectly, have been forced to pay its client's debt to the Crown.

However, insolvency does not occur overnight and secured creditors are invariably aware of any financial difficulties experienced by their clients. Furthermore, steps are usually initiated by secured creditors to protect their interest before the Crown becomes aware of the debtor's problems.

Disruption of the Insolvency Process

The last argument against upgrading the Crown's position for the recovery of GST amounts is that existing special Crown priorities arising from Crown privilege disrupt commercial insolvencies and create difficulties in determining the applicable order of priorities. It has been suggested that insolvency practitioners are unable to effectively administer insolvent estates due to the Crown's legislated priorities.

It is argued that the objective in insolvency legislation should, in addition to rehabilitation of the debtor, include provision for the fair allocation of loss over all classes of creditors. In this regard, such existing remedies as the deemed trust and enhanced garnishment under the *Income Tax Act* undermine the integrity of the bankruptcy process to the extent that they specifically override the process. On the other hand, in order to minimize the disruption caused to the orderly administration of insolvent estates as a result of the use of the deemed trust and enhanced garnishment, a directive has been issued from the Office of the Superintendent of Bankruptcy which includes details of an administrative agreement that has been negotiated concerning the application of those remedies.

Arguments for Upgrading the Crown's Position

There are a number of arguments in favour of according the recovery of GST arrears the same priorities as are presently allowed the collection of source deductions in insolvency situations. The remittance of GST amounts under the *Excise Tax Act* and under the *Income Tax Act* represents a vital component of Canada's voluntary compliance system of taxation. The integrity of this voluntary system of compliance is dependant on the concept of amounts being held in trust for the Crown and on the ability of the Minister to recover arrears by the enhanced garnishment. In this regard, these two cornerstones need to be preserved as much as possible, even in insolvency situations.

The following points favour providing the deemed trust and enhanced garnishment provisions of the *Excise Tax Act* with the same priority as are afforded source deductions under the *Income Tax Act*, namely:

(a) unjust enrichment;
(b) strategic bankruptcy;
(c) Crown unable to choose its debtors;
(d) favourable to corporate directors;
(e) reduction of propensity towards rigorous enforcement;

(f) pervasive nature of floating charge security;

(g) back door vs. front door remedies; and

(h) requirement to refund unremitted amounts.

Unjust Enrichment

Where funds belonging to a third party were mixed with moneys subject to a general assignment of book debts, it has been held that the third party was entitled to those funds. The secured creditor, in this case a bank, having knowledge of its customer's business operations, knew or ought to have known that its customer collected a portion of the funds as an agent for the third party.

Similarly, arrears of GST are amounts that never belonged to the insolvent debtor. Instead, these are amounts that were collected by the person as a result of a legislative requirement to act as an agent for the Crown and to charge and collect GST on taxable sales. Embedded in the accounts receivable assigned to the secured creditor are GST amounts to which the secured creditor should not be entitled. To allow these amounts to form part of the security of the secured creditor would constitute unjust enrichment. Accordingly, it is suggested that it would be unjust, with respect to GST arrears, not to give to the Crown the benefits which flow from the recognition of a right of property in view of the special relationship between the parties involved.

Strategic Bankruptcy

Failure to ensure that either enhanced garnishment or the deemed trust under the *Excise Tax Act* survive bankruptcy enables bankruptcies to be orchestrated in order to allow secured creditors to gain strategic advantage. For example, if a business experiencing financial difficulty has not kept current its GST remittances and a receiver is appointed, the deemed trust continues and the receiver is jointly and severally liable for remitting the arrears to the extent of the assets under his or her control.

On the other hand, if a business owing a substantial sum of GST arrears is petitioned into bankruptcy by a secured creditor, the Crown's claim is effectively downgraded to that of an ordinary unsecured creditor with the result that the secured creditor gains what otherwise in receivership would have been paid to the Crown. This practise of manipulating the bankruptcy process to avoid GST obligations fuels business failure, and denies opportunity for possible orderly reorganization of the affairs of troubled businesses.

Government Unable to Choose Its Debtors

Financial institutions and other creditors that extend credit to a business typically have the opportunity to undertake a risk analysis. Varying levels of risk result in varying degrees of control, the imposition of certain conditions and financial implications. Ultimately, if the risk is considered too high, no credit is extended. Under the existing voluntary compliance scheme of taxation, the Crown, not unlike a tort claimant, is unable to choose the businesses with which it deals, nor is it able to discriminate amongst businesses according to the risk they represent. These are prerogatives reserved for private sector creditors and lenders.

For these reasons, the Crown is more likely to be faced with situations where it is owed money by persons who are experiencing financial difficulty. Allowing the deemed trust to survive bankruptcy is one method of reducing the Crown's risk exposure and avoiding more stringent requirements which would impact on all persons required to remit GST, regardless of whether they represent a risk of insolvency.

Favourable to Corporate Directors

When a corporation becomes bankrupt, and there are GST amounts outstanding, directors of that company may become personally liable for those outstanding amounts. In order to avoid being liable for those amounts, directors must demonstrate that they have exercised "due diligence" in the performance of their duties. This defence requires that the director demonstrate some active involvement in ensuring compliance.

The ability of the Crown to look toward the directors to cover amounts owing by the corporation can lead to considerable financial exposure for the directors. Provision for greater recovery of GST arrears from the bankrupt company would lessen the potential burden on directors.

Reduction of Propensity Towards Rigorous Enforcement

The existing lack of uniformity between the enhanced garnishment provisions of the *Income Tax Act* and the *Excise Tax Act* puts pressure on the frequency and timeliness of the usage of the enhanced garnishee to collect GST arrears. This pressure is directly attributable to the fact that the enhanced garnishee under the *Excise Tax Act* is, unless it is issued prior to the bankruptcy, rendered ineffective. Such pressure on the Crown to protect its revenues can precipitate insolvency with the attendant loss of jobs and financial hardship on unsecured creditors.

While the business and insolvency communities would prefer a hands-off approach, the Crown requires some assurance that its revenue collection will not be compromised. Aligning the respective enhanced garnishment provisions would accomplish this to the extent that the rigorous propensity towards frequent and early (sometimes possibly premature) usage of the enhanced garnishee under the *Excise Tax Act* would be diminished.

Pervasive Nature of Floating Charge Security

The pledging of assets under a floating charge debenture has the effect of rendering those assets judgment proof vis-à-vis unsecured creditors. This is all the more so as against involuntary creditors who do not have the opportunity to pick their debtors or do credit risk assessments. It should be noted that the courts have, albeit in a different context, taken a somewhat jaundiced view of the pervasive nature of floating charge security. However, it is too useful a form of security to be dismissed lightly. But, the recipient of such security should remain aware of its detrimental effect on other creditors and should not be surprised at the Crown's response. Indeed, the unfortunate reality is that small creditors generally still do not recover anywhere near the full amount of the debt due to them since most assets are pledged to secured creditors, leaving little for the other creditors. Hence, any priority given the GST deemed trust and enhanced garnishee would therefore have minimal effect, if any, on small creditors. In this respect, the deemed trust and enhanced garnishment provisions represent a unique response to the abusive and pervasive nature of floating charges. Such recourse is unavoidable given the Crown's status as an involuntary creditor vis-à-vis unremitted GST amounts.

Back Door vs. Front Door Remedies

If potential losses cannot be safeguarded against with the result that significant revenue leakage continues to occur, the Crown may have to explore other options to ensure that revenues are collected. This could lead to even more stringent measures than that which have already been enacted. For example, remedial options for ensuring that GST remittances are kept current might involve a requirement to keep amounts collected in a trust account, or possibly that a security bond based on a percentage of past or projected sales, be posted. Recognizing that certain compliance problems are inherent to such remedies, an alternate [sic] approach might be to hold financial institutions responsible for ensuring that those businesses, to whom they advance moneys, make their GST remittances. In other words, any financial institution extending a line of credit to a business would become jointly and severally liable for GST amounts that are not remitted as and when required by the business in question. Rationale for such a risk allocation is reflected in the earlier comments pertaining to unjust enrichment, strategic bankruptcies and the pervasive nature of floating charge security.

Requirement to Refund Unremitted Amounts

Due to the nature of the net tax calculation for GST, businesses are able to claim input tax credits on a tax payable basis. There is no requirement for the tax to have been remitted. Furthermore, a business which determines that it will not be able to recover an account receivable, that includes a GST component, is permitted to adjust its net tax calculation to reverse a previous entry accounting for that amount as tax collectible. As a result, the business writing off the bad debt is not disadvantaged by the GST component that was not collected, whereas the Crown may, at the next tier, have to pay out or reduce an amount owing for which it has not received offsetting revenue.

Conclusion

While it is recognized that the private sector is the motor which drives the economy, it must also be appreciated that the Crown has a part to play vis-à-vis its responsibilities for taxation. The Crown's mandate involves redistribution of the wealth to all sectors of the economy in all four corners of Canada. In this regard, the tax regime overlaps the role of the private sector in the economy. Given that both parties find themselves in the market, albeit for different reasons, it is inevitable that both would be affected by the same economic down turns. Hence, in the event of insolvency, both are exposed to the risk of loss. A recognition of this relationship is evidenced by the fact that the Crown's historic claim to preferred status in bankruptcy has been repealed. However, GST revenues, like source deductions under the *Income Tax Act*, are not comparable to trade debts. In both cases, they constitute third party funds which never belonged to the insolvent debtor. For this reason, it is suggested that the collection of GST arrears receive similar treatment as that accorded the recovery of source deductions under the *Income Tax Act* and the *Bankruptcy and Insolvency Act*.

Protection of Wage Earners

Report of the Advisory Committee on Bankruptcy and Insolvency
("Colter Report") (1986), 20-34.

Current Law

Under Section 107(1)(d) of the *Bankruptcy Act* a wage earner is entitled to a preferred claim, in an amount not exceeding $500, for arrears of wages for services rendered during the three months prior to the bankruptcy. In addition, a travelling salesman is entitled to a preferred claim for disbursements not exceeding $300 incurred during the same period. These preferred claims rank behind the claims of all secured creditors. Various provincial statutes also provide wage protection for employees. For example, the Employment Standards Act of Ontario and the Labour Standards Code of Nova Scotia provide that amounts owing for vacation pay constitute deemed trusts and liens. The Labour Standards Code of British Columbia creates a statutory lien for unpaid wages. Similar legislation exists in Alberta, Saskatchewan, Manitoba and Newfoundland. Under Section 178(6) of the *Bank Act*, if a bank enforces security granted pursuant to that Act and a bankruptcy ensues, the arrears of wages owing to the employees for services rendered within three months prior to the date of bankruptcy rank in priority to the claim of the bank.

Problems

The present *Bankruptcy Act* does not provide satisfactory protection to employees whose employer goes bankrupt. In many instances there are insufficient assets to satisfy the claims of secured creditors, leaving no funds available to pay the claims for wages. The requirement that secured claims be satisfied first usually produces a long delay in the payment of wage claims. Provincial legislation has also been ineffective. In some cases, there is no adequate protection for arrears of wages and only vacation pay is protected. In other cases, the court has held that the deemed trusts or liens created by provincial statutes rank behind various categories of secured creditors. The determination of the respective priorities of wage claims and secured claims under provincial legislation has generated considerable litigation. The rights of employees to priority under the *Bank Act* are somewhat illusory, because they do not apply when a bank enforces a security agreement (such as a debenture) that is not covered by the *Bank Act*. Also, the employees' rights only arise when a bankruptcy has occurred; in many instances a bank will realize on its security without formal bankruptcy proceedings.

Background

The Tassé Committee's report, published in December 1970, recommended that wage claims should take priority over all other claims, including all types of secured claims. This recommendation, which has become known as "super priority," was incorporated into Bill C-60 when it was introduced into the House of Commons on May 5, 1975. It provided that a claim for wages up to a maximum of $2,000 would be entitled to be paid in full out of the assets of the bankrupt in priority to the claims of all secured creditors. In its report dated December 1975, the Senate Committee recommended that consideration be given to the creation of a government-administered fund under the authority of the *Bankruptcy Act* out of which unpaid employee wages could be paid forthwith after the bankruptcy of the employer. The claim for unpaid wages would cover wages in arrears to a limit of $2,000 and would not include vacation pay, severance pay and fringe benefits.

In Bill C-12, the employee was entitled to a preferred claim for wages up to a maximum amount of $2,000 for arrears of wages plus an additional $500 for pension plan and other employee benefits. However, the preferred claim for the wage earner would have been subordinate to the claims of secured creditors. In its report on Bill C-12, the Senate Committee reaffirmed its support for a wage earners' protection fund.

In 1981 a committee chaired by Raymond Landry, the present Dean of Law at the University of Ottawa and a former Superintendent of Bankruptcy, was asked to recommend ways of protecting wage earners in the event of their employer's bankruptcy. In its October 1981 report, the Landry Committee recommended, as an interim solution, that a wage earner protection fund be established for a period of three years. It would pay claims for arrears of wages up to a maximum of $1,000 and would be financed from the Consolidated Revenue Fund.

Bill C-17, which received its first reading in the House of Commons on January 31, 1984, contained basically the same provisions for wage earners as Bill C-12. However, amendments tabled on May 28, 1984 provided that in the event of a bankruptcy or receivership, a claim for wages up to a maximum of $4,000 would rank in priority to the claims of all secured creditors.

Other Jurisdictions

Province of Manitoba

The Province of Manitoba has created a fund, called the Payment of Wages Fund, under the *Payment of Wages Act*. The fund may pay to an employee, in respect of unpaid wages, an amount not exceeding $1,200 per calendar year. The fund will apply when wages remain unpaid although all reasonable and necessary efforts have been made to collect them. When the employee has received money from the fund the Director of the Employment Standards Division of the Ministry of Labour and Manpower can institute proceedings against the employer to recover the amount of the unpaid wages. In the fiscal year 1984-1985 the following moneys were advanced to unpaid wage earners from the Payment of Wages Fund.

Fiscal Year—April 1984 to March 1985

	Number of Employers	Number of Employees	Amount Paid	Amount Recovered
Bankruptcies	20	177	$84,722.53	$81,292.77
Receivership	19	309	189,328.94	135,918.71
Closures	72	238	114,035.78	12,572.14
Business Still Operating	21	41	23,661.38	9,199.18
Total	132	765	$411,748.63	$238,982.80

Construction Board of Quebec

In 1975, the Construction Board of Quebec created a fund to protect the construction employees under the *Loi sur les relations de travail dans l'industrie de la construction* (LRQCR 20). The fund provides protection for all employees working in the construction industry for payment of wages, in cases of bankruptcy, insolvency, liquidation, or in a proposal. The fund is financed by the employer (two cents an hour worked per employee).

Province of Ontario

The final report of the Commission of Inquiry into Wage Protection in Insolvency Situations was recently submitted to the Minister of Labour of Ontario by Mr. Donald J.M. Brown, QC, Commissioner. Although the Committee has not had adequate time to fully study this report, its recommendations included *inter alia* that:

- A fund be established, to be administered by the Director of Employment Standards of the Province of Ontario, out of which claims of employees for unpaid wages and vacation pay should be paid.
- The limit to claims from such a fund should be one-year's accrued vacation pay and three pay periods of unpaid wages.
- Separation and termination pay claims should not be reimbursed by the fund.
- The fund should be financed by the Consolidated Revenue Fund of the Province of Ontario or alternatively by increasing the Personal Property Security Act registration fees for non-consumer security registrations.
- The Director of Employment Standards should be empowered to licence or authorize trustees in bankruptcy to act as his agent to facilitate speedy payments of unpaid wages.

In addition, the study concluded the following:

1. Ideally, the federal government should accept responsibility for legislation relating to wage protection in insolvency situations. In the absence of federal action, however, a province does have legislative competence and has open to it most of the techniques necessary to ensure that employees do not bear the loss of unpaid wages.

2. In many instances, the present laws are ineffective in protecting employees from unpaid wages, and a wide cash flow gap exists since unemployment insurance does not commence from the date of the last wage payment; rather, the "waiting period" of two weeks commences with the first day of unemployment.

3. The extent of unpaid wages in 1982-83 was estimated to be not more than six million dollars, excluding unpaid fringe benefits, severance and termination payments not made. While this figure, even if an estimate is added for unpaid fringe benefits, is relatively minor when viewed from the perspective of the annual budget of the Province, its impact on the individuals affected was substantial.

European Countries

A number of the largest countries in Western Europe, including England, France and Germany, have recognized the need to protect employees upon the insolvency of their employer. Each of them has determined that the most effective method of providing this protection is by the establishment of a wage earner protection fund. A summary of the employees entitled to protection, the coverage afforded by each of the funds and the costs associated with such funds is set out in Table 1. Our investigation has determined that the major problems resulting from the fund are administrative ones. However, they appear to have been overcome in those cases where the trustee of the insolvent employer is responsible for filing the claims and distributing the payments to the employees. In each instance, the annual contribution per employee is a relatively low amount; in Denmark, for example, it was $5 in 1984. This was the case even though coverage under the fund included severance pay and the maximum payment per claim was $8,700.

In England, with a population of 56,400,000 and a work force of 18,800,000, the authorities are budgeting in the 1985-86 fiscal period for 70,000 claims totalling £42,000,000 ($84,000,000). In England the maximum payment out of the fund per claim for arrears of wages and holiday pay is £2,156 (approximately $3,780). In addition, payments of up to £1,848 (approximately $3,240) are permitted for severance pay.

In Germany the wage earner protection fund is administered by the Unemployment Insurance Fund. In 1984, with a population of 62,000,000, there were 166,987 claims aggregating 665,000,000 DM (approximately $345,000,000). The fund covers three months' arrears of wages and fringe benefits with no maximum limit on a claim.

Policy Considerations

To the fullest extent possible, the provisions of the *Bankruptcy Act* should protect the rights of employees to any amount owed them by their bankrupt employer. Payment of such claims should be both certain and prompt. The administration of any system for the payment of the claims should be simple and inexpensive. Any priority attributed to wage claims should not severely prejudice the availability of credit to business enterprises in Canada.

• • •

Solutions

Super Priority

One potential solution is super priority, which involves granting wage claims priority over all other claims, including all types of secured claims. This solution has the advantage of not involving any government funding or the establishment of any form of administrative system to pay the claims. The courts would deal with any disputes or problems.

Under super priority there is no absolute certainty that the wages owed by the bankrupt will be paid. The available assets of the bankrupt may not cover the amount claimed. There may also be a significant delay in the payment of wage claims, because the sale of the bankrupt's assets may occupy a lengthy period of time. It has been proposed that the trustee of the bankrupt estate should be empowered to borrow funds for the purpose of paying the claims of wage earners. However, the assets of the bankrupt may not be readily convertible into cash and a lender may be reluctant to make loans against them. The time required to satisfy a lender as to the realizable value of the assets may also delay payment of wage claims.

Serious difficulties may arise in the administration of the super priority proposal, such as the allocation of the burden among the secured creditors. A very complicated formula for allocating the liability to pay wage claims will be necessary. It has been suggested that the trustee should be entitled to use moneys on hand or in a bank or other depository to pay wages. If additional moneys are required, the trustee should also be entitled to borrow money and grant to the lender of that money a security interest in all or any part of the property of the bankrupt, whether or not the property is subject to an existing security interest. Such borrowing would then rank ahead of claims of all other secured creditors.

In principle, this sounds very simple. However, it must be realized that there are many different types of security interests, and the allocation of the burden of paying wage claims among the various secured creditors is a complicated task. The courts will be clogged with cases attempting to determine the respective priorities of various classes of secured creditors. According to the complicated formula proposed, it would be necessary to determine the amount that was in fact realized from the assets (or the amount that was deemed to be realized from the assets) in respect to the particular property. This means that whether or not an asset had been sold, it would have to be evaluated, which may be extremely difficult in the case of unmarketable assets.

The creation of a super priority may impose an unexpected burden on a secured creditor. The mortgagee of a property originally used as a warehouse but then converted to a labour-intensive business facility may find that the claims of unpaid employees take precedence over its mortgage. Super priority, as proposed, would impose a burden on many small secured creditors, such as an electrician who may file a mechanics' lien for moneys owing to him by a contractor or a garageman who has repaired a truck owned by a bankrupt. It is anticipated that super priority will reduce the credit available to a labour-intensive industry. If super priority is enacted into law, a lender who normally advances against fixed assets such as buildings and equipment will take into account the possibility of wages being unpaid in the event of a bankruptcy before determining the amount of credit to be extended.

Modified Priority

It has been proposed that wage earners be granted modified priority for their unpaid claims in the event of a bankruptcy. This would involve granting the wage earner a statutory priority for arrears of wages that would rank in priority to the claims of secured creditors holding security on the current assets of the bankrupt, these being assets that would normally be realized within one year, such as cash, temporary investments, inventory and receivables. Like super priority, this solution does not involve any government funding or the creation of an administrative body to supervise its implementation, and all disputes would be dealt with by the courts. The administrative problems of dealing with priority would be reduced, since fewer creditors take security on current assets.

The modified priority proposal however has problems similar to those of super priority. Paying wage claims out of current assets, which may be of limited realizable value, would reduce the likelihood of payment. This problem could arise in the case of a construction company or a courier service. There may also be a greater delay in payment of wage claims. After a bankruptcy, accounts receivable are difficult to collect for many reasons, including the fact that warranty service may be unavailable. In addition, an inventory of partially manufactured goods may be difficult to sell at a reasonable price. With only accounts receivable and inventory available as security, a lender may be reluctant to advance funds to pay wage claims.

Wage Earner Protection Fund

Another solution is the establishment of a wage earner protection fund from which to pay the claims of unpaid employees of an insolvent employer. The creation of such a fund would ensure the prompt, certain payment of the employees' wage claims. To avoid the creation of a new bureaucracy, an existing administrative system could be used. The trustee of the bankrupt estate or the receiver could perform the same duties as those required of them under the present *Bankruptcy Act* when funds are available for distribution to employees of a bankrupt company. The unnecessary time-consuming and expensive litigation resulting from the problem of allocation and priority would be avoided.

The major deterrent to the implementation of a wage earner protection fund has been a lack of consensus on how the fund should be financed, chiefly because there are no reliable Canadian estimates of potential claims. However, the committee has reviewed the total amounts of claims paid by the funds established in the European countries and is of the opinion that the financial experience of such funds provided a realistic basis for estimating the amount of the Canadian claims which would be made against a wage earner protection fund.

There have been various alternatives suggested for financing such a fund. Some of these are as follows:

• contributions from all employers based on the number of employees;
• contributions from employees;
• payment out of the Consolidated Revenue Fund;
• a levy on secured transactions when security is placed;
• a levy on the gross realization by all creditors after a bankruptcy or receivership has occurred.

Contributions by employers

The obligation to pay wages is that of the employer. It is only because an employer has failed to meet its obligation that the fund will be called upon to pay the wages of employees. Since it is impossible to determine in advance which employer will fail, it is fair and equitable that all employers should be required to make a modest contribution to the wage earner protection fund.

Contributions by employees

The purpose of a wage earner protection fund is to provide protection for employees. Since they are the beneficiaries of the fund, it is also fair and equitable that employees be required to make a modest contribution to the fund.

Payment out of the Consolidated Revenue Fund

This involves financing the fund from the general revenue pool of the government at a time when the government is attempting to reduce the deficit.

Levy on secured transactions

Such a levy could be applied to the taking of security such as debentures, mortgages and conditional sale contracts when such security is taken. Whether it would be constitutionally correct for the federal government to impose such a levy is a significant legal question.

Levy on gross realization by all creditors, secured and unsecured

In the event of a bankruptcy or a receivership a statutory levy could be imposed on the realization by all creditors, secured and unsecured. Any creditor realizing the assets of the debtor would be required to make a payment to the Superintendent of Bankruptcy to finance the wage earner protection fund. A secured creditor would be entitled to receive the full amount of its claim plus the levy if there was sufficient value in the property subject to the security.

Miscellaneous

Other issues relating to wage priority must also be resolved. These are:

- who is included in the definition of "employee";
- which type of claim should be granted priority;
- should there be a time limit restricting the claims entitled to priority;
- what should be the maximum amount of the priority claim;
- should the priority claim include claims for vacation pay, pension and other employee benefits; and
- should severance pay be granted priority?

Recommendations

Wage Earner Protection Fund

It is recommended that a wage earner protection fund be established because no other solution ensures prompt and certain payment to employees. The fund should be financed by contributions from employers and employees. Such financing spreads the burden of paying the claims of employees among all employers and employees and avoids any impact on a particular lender. A lender to a labour-intensive industry would not deem it necessary to restrict the amount of credit it would otherwise extend. Thus there would be no impact on current lending practices.

Specific Details

Definition of "employee"

The definition should include an individual (other than a related party as defined in sections 108(2), 109 and 110 of the *Bankruptcy Act*) who is employed by or was, or has been, on the payroll of the insolvent employer prior to the date of the bankruptcy and should include sales agents who are on the payroll of the company.

Monetary entitlement

The employee as defined above should be entitled to the following:

- arrears of gross salaries, commission and wages earned within the six months preceding the insolvency;
- arrears of vacation pay earned within the 12 months preceding the insolvency;
- arrears of all amounts withheld from the employee such as pension benefits and union dues, the whole to a maximum of $2,000 per employee; and
- arrears of expenses incurred by the employee on behalf of the employer to a maximum of $1,000 per employee in the two months preceding the insolvency.

Administration of the Fund

The fund established by the government should be administered by the Unemployment Insurance section of the Department of Employment and Immigration.

Bankruptcy

In the event of a bankruptcy where a receiver has not been previously appointed, the trustee should be required to prepare a special preferred claim on behalf of all employees. The trustee should then determine whether the assets that are not subject to claims of secured creditors would immediately realize sufficient funds to satisfy the proof of claim. If, in the trustee's opinion, the assets would not be sufficient for an immediate realization to pay the special preferred claim of the employees, a proof of claim should be filed with the Unemployment Insurance section, which should forward to the trustee sufficient funds to cover the amounts owed to the employees. The trustee should effect immediate payment to the employees, making such normal deductions as income tax, unemployment insurance and pension benefits. The trustee, as the available assets of the bankruptcy are realized, should be obliged to reimburse the fund after payment of the trustee's fees and other expenses of administration.

Receivership

In the event of the appointment of a receiver, the receiver should immediately be obliged to prepare a special preferred claim on behalf of all employees. This claim should be filed with the Unemployment Insurance section, which should forward to the receiver sufficient funds to cover the amounts owed to the employees.

Payment of Costs of Trustee or Receiver

The fees and expenses of the trustee or receiver resulting from processing the special preferred claims of the wage earners should also be paid by the fund. The amount of such fees should be set on a sliding scale by regulation.

Financing of the Fund

Contributions to the wage earner protection fund should be collected monthly from employers and employees. Although in the European countries the financing is largely accomplished through contributions by employers only, it is our view that the employees, as the beneficiaries of this system, should contribute their fair share.

The ultimate objective will be to have a fund which is self-financing. Funding should come from monthly contributions of employers and employees, recoveries by the fund as a special preferred status creditor under Section 107 of the *Bankruptcy Act* and recoveries from directors in specified limited circumstances. Based on the experiences of other countries, it is clear that there is a wide variance in claims experience which results from differences between countries in the details of each wage protection plan and wide swings which have occurred in economic conditions. In reviewing all available information, we would not anticipate that claims against such a fund would exceed $50 million on an annual basis. It would be our recommendation that this target funding from employer and employee contributions be arranged at the outset to be adjusted up or down based on subsequent experience. As there are approximately 12,100,000 employees in Canada at the present time and assuming that the contributions were split on a 50-50 basis between employers and employees, this would result in an additional per employee charge of approximately $2.07 per annum.

To minimize the impact on any particular employer or employee, we recommend that all employees and employers, including governments, contribute to the fund.

As previously noted, the fund should be subrogated as a special preferred status creditor under Section 107 of the Bankruptcy Act ranking immediately after the costs of administration. This, together with any recoveries from directors as proposed in the section dealing with directors' and officers' liability, will reduce the amounts which employers and employees will be required to contribute to the fund.

Severance Pay

The committee recommends that amounts due to employees for severance pay remain as unsecured claims ranking with other unsecured claims of the bankrupt, notwithstanding any provincial legislation to the contrary. There should be no special preferred status for severance pay claims, since granting such status would increase the contributions to the wage earner protection fund, and reduce the assets available for distribution to other creditors.

NOTE

As noted in the introduction to chapter 17, Bill C-22 sought to implement the Advisory Committee's recommendation for the establishment of a wage earners' protection fund. Regrettably the Mulroney administration lacked the political will to overcome resistance to this part of the bill and, though the federal government promised to give the matter further study, it seems to have died a quiet (or not so quiet) death. Instead, for the most part, it has been left up to the provinces to fill the slack. The following statutory provisions contain Ontario's answer as enacted in 1991.

The Employment Standards Amendment Act
SO 1991, c. 16

Part XIV.1
Employee Wage Protection Program

58.1(1) The Employee Wage Protection Program is hereby established.

(2) Except for the purposes of section 58.7, when an employee is compensated by the Program, the wages for which the employee may receive compensation are,

(a) regular wages, including commissions, overtime wages, vacation pay, holiday pay, termination pay and severance pay;

(b) amounts that are deemed to be wages under subsection 32(4);

(c) compensation awarded under sections 45, 48 and 51, clause 56(3)(b) and section 56.2 in so far as the compensation is awarded for loss of earnings and for termination pay and severance pay; and

(d) such additional payments as may be prescribed by regulation.

(3) The vacation pay for which an employee may be compensated is the greater of the minimum vacation pay provided in subsection 28(2) and the amount contractually agreed to by the employer and the employee or his or her agent.

(4) The amount of holiday pay for which an employee may be compensated from the Program is the greater of the amount for the holidays at the rate as determined under this Act and the regulations and the amount for the holidays at the rate as contractually agreed to by the employer and the employee or his or her agent.

(5) The overtime wages for which an employee may be compensated are the greater of the amount of overtime pay provided in section 24 and the amount contractually agreed to by the employer and the employee or his or her agent.

(6) The amount of termination pay for which an employee may be compensated is the amount as provided by subsection 57(14).

(7) The amount of severance pay for which an employee may be compensated is the amount as provided by subsection 58(4).

58.2(1) The Minister shall appoint a person to administer the Program.

(2) The Program Administrator may exercise the powers conferred and shall perform the duties imposed on him or her under this Act.

(3) The Program Administrator may delegate any of his or her powers and duties to a person employed at the Ministry.

(4) The Program Administrator, in the name of his or her office, may bring any proceedings he or she considers necessary in relation to the Program and he or she may respond to any proceedings in that name.

58.3 The Program Administrator and any person employed at the Ministry to whom his or her powers and duties have been delegated shall not be required to testify in a civil proceeding or in a proceeding before any other tribunal respecting information obtained in the discharge of the Program Administrator's duties under this Act.

58.4(1) An employee is eligible for compensation from the Program if,

(a) where the employer is insolvent, the employee has caused a claim for unpaid wages to be filed with the receiver appointed by a court with respect to the employer or with the employer's trustee in bankruptcy and the claim has not been paid;

(b) an employment standards officer has made an order that the employer pay wages to the employee, unless the employer has applied to have the order reviewed or the amount set out in the order has been paid;

(c) an employment standards officer has made an order that the directors pay wages to the employee, unless the employer has applied to have the order reviewed or the amount set out in the order has been paid; or

(d) a referee acting under section 56, 68 or 69 or an adjudicator acting under subsection 67(3) has made, amended or affirmed an order that wages are owed to the employee and the amount set out in the order has not been paid.

(2) If an employee has been paid wages pursuant to an order and the employee is still owed wages under the order, the employee is eligible for compensation from the Program for the balance of wages owed to the limit of the recovery set out in section 58.8.

(3) For purposes of this Act, any claim described in clause (1)(a) that has been verified by the Program Administrator is deemed to be an order.

58.5(1) Despite section 58.4, employees who are entitled to the protection of a lien under the Construction Lien Act are only eligible for compensation from the Program if they have used their best efforts to preserve their lien claim.

(2) If the Program Administrator is satisfied that such employees could not get sufficient information to preserve their rights, were unable to preserve them or were unaware of their rights, he or she may allow the employees to be compensated from the Program in the same manner as any other employee.

(3) If an employee who is entitled to the protection of a lien is compensated by the Program, the Program Administrator may require the employee to subrogate his or her rights in the lien to the Program Administrator, or may require the employee to assign any judgment arising from the lien claim to the Program Administrator.

58.6(1) If a trade union has entered into a settlement agreement with an employer over severance pay under subsection 58(18), and the employer has paid the severance pay agreed to, an employee is not eligible for compensation for severance pay from the Program.

(2) Despite subsection (1), an employee is eligible for compensation for severance pay from the Program if an employment standards officer has made an order under subsection 65(1) with respect to the severance pay and it has not been paid and the employer has not applied to have the order reviewed.

58.7(1) An employee who has entered into a settlement of compromise of wages under clause 65(1)(b) and who has received the amount agreed upon is not eligible for compensation from the Program for the wages that were the subject of the settlement or compromise.

(2) Despite subsection (1), an employee is eligible for compensation from the Program for the wages that were the subject of the settlement or compromise if an employment standards officer has made an order under subsection 65(1) with respect to those wages and they have not been paid and the employer has not applied to have the order reviewed.

58.8 The maximum amount of compensation, before deductions made under subsection 58.9(3), that an employee may receive from the Program in respect of his or her employment with an employer is $5,000 or such greater amount as is prescribed.

58.9(1) An employee who is eligible for compensation from the Program may be compensated when wages are due and owing and the Program Administrator has verified that the wages are owing and their amount.

(2) Upon approving compensation for the employee, the Program Administrator shall apportion from the compensation in such manner as may be prescribed among the types of wages described in subsection 58.1(2).

(3) Upon approving compensation for the employee, the Program Administrator shall deduct from the compensation such amounts as are required to be deducted by a law of Canada or of Ontario.

58.10(1) If an employer has made an application for review under section 68, the Program Administrator may approve compensation only if the referee acting under section 68 affirms or amends the order such that the employer is found to be liable to pay the wages.

(2) If an employment standards officer has made a report that an employer may have failed to pay wages owed to an employee and the Director appoints a referee to hold a hearing under section 69, the Program Administrator may approve compensation from the Program only if the referee acting under section 69 orders that the employer pay the wages.

(3) If, during a hearing under section 69, the referee finds that the employees are entitled to wages or there is an undisputed portion of wages and he or she makes an interim order before the hearing is completed that those wages are owed, the Program Administrator may approve compensation from the Program in the amount of the interim order.

(4) If, during a hearing under section 68, the referee finds that there is an undisputed portion of wages to which the employees are entitled and he or she amends or affirms the order to the extent of those wages before the hearing is completed, the Program Administrator may approve compensation from the Program in the amount of the interim order.

58.11 If an employee applies for a review under subsection 67(2), the Program Administrator may approve compensation only if the adjudicator conducting the review makes an order that the employee is entitled to the wages or amends the order of the employment standards officer such that the employee is entitled to wages.

58.12 If the compensation received from the Program exceeds the wages to which the employee was entitled, the Program Administrator, on the basis of the prescribed criteria, may seek repayment of the excess amount.

58.13 (1) If the Program Administrator recovers from a person liable to pay an amount greater than the compensation that the employee received from the Program, he or she shall pay the excess amount to the employee.

(2) For the purposes of this section, the excess amount is the amount the Program has recovered up to the amount owed under the order less the compensation already received by the employee.

58.14(1) The Program Administrator is subrogated to all the rights of an employee who is compensated by the Program and may bring an action against the employer, or any other person who is liable, for administration costs as determined under clause 65(1)(c) and for wages or may use the provisions of this Act to collect the amount.

(2) The Program Administrator may accept an assignment of a judgment obtained by an employee in respect of wages as described in subsection 58.1(2) and the Program Administrator may exercise the rights of the employee under the judgment.

58.15 Where money may be received by an employee under this Part, or may be collected from a person who is liable to pay, interest may be collected on the money as prescribed.

58.16 If the employee and employer enter into an agreement for the purpose of increasing the amount of compensation the employee is eligible to recover from the Program, the Program Administrator may decide to limit the compensation to the amount as determined under the employment contract before the agreement was made.

58.17 The Minister, with the approval of the Lieutenant Governor in Council, may enter into agreements with the Government of Canada related to the payment of compensation under this Part and the administration of compensation if employees are entitled to compensation for wages under an Act of the Parliament of Canada.

58.18(1) Except as provided in the Family Plan Act and in this section, no amount payable as compensation under this Part is capable of being assigned.

(2) The Program Administrator may deem that an assignment is made if the prescribed conditions are met and the prescribed restrictions are not breached.

(3) The number of deemed assignments respecting an employee that a person may present in any period may be restricted.

(4) Deemed assignments of compensation are limited to additional payments as described in clause 58.1(2)(d).

(5) Deemed assignments may only be made to a prescribed person or to a person who is a member of a prescribed class of persons.

Part XIV.2
Liability of Directors

58.19(1) In this Part, "director" means a director of a corporation and includes a shareholder who is a party to a unanimous shareholder agreement.

(2) This Part applies to shareholders described in subsection (1) only to the extent that the directors are relieved, under subsection 108(5) of the Business Corporations Act or subsection 146(5) of the Canada Business Corporations Act, of their liability to pay wages to the employees of the corporation.

(3) This Part does not apply to directors of corporations to which Part III of the Corporations Act applies or to which the Co-operative Corporations Act applies.

(4) This Part does not apply to directors, or persons who perform functions similar to those of a director, of a college of a health profession or a group of health professions that is established or continued under an Act of the Legislature.

(5) This Part does not apply to directors of corporations,

    (a) that have been incorporated in another jurisdiction;

    (b) that have objects that are similar to the objects of those types of corporations referred to in subsection (3); and

    (c) that are carried on without the purpose of gain.

58.20(1) The directors of an employer are jointly and severally liable for wages as provided in this Part if,

    (a) where an employer is insolvent, the employee has caused a claim for unpaid wages to be filed with the receiver appointed by a court with respect to the employer or with the employer's trustee in bankruptcy and the claim has not been paid;

    (b) an employment standards officer has made an order that the employer is liable for wages, unless the amount set out in the order has been paid or the employer has applied to have it reviewed;

    (c) an employment standards officer has made an order that a director is liable for wages, unless the amount set out in the order has been paid or the employer or the director has applied to have it reviewed; or

    (d) an adjudicator acting under subsection 67(3) or a referee acting under section 68 or 69 has made, amended or affirmed an order that the employer is liable for wages or that the directors are liable for wages and the amount set out in the order has not been paid.

(2) Despite subsection (1), the employer is primarily responsible for an employee's wages but proceedings against the employer under this Act do not have to be exhausted before proceedings may be commenced to collect wages from directors under this Part.

(3) The wages that directors are liable for under this Part are wages, not including termination pay and severance pay as they are provided for under this Act, under a contract of employment, or under a collective agreement and not including amounts that are deemed to be wages under this Act.

(4) The vacation pay that directors are liable for is the greater of the minimum vacation pay provided in subsection 28(2) and the amount contractually agreed to by the employer and the employee or his or her agent.

(5) The amount of holiday pay that directors are liable for is the greater of the amount for the holidays at the rate as determined under this Act and the regulations and the amount for the holidays at the rate as contractually agreed to by the employer and the employee or his or her agent.

(6) The overtime wages that directors are liable for are the greater of the amount of overtime pay provided in section 24 and the amount contractually agreed to by the employer and the employee or his or her agent.

(7) The directors of an employer corporation are jointly and severally liable to the employees of the corporation for all debts not exceeding six months' wages, as described in subsection (3), that become payable while they are directors for services performed for

the corporation and for the vacation pay accrued while they are directors for not more than twelve months under this Act and the regulations made under it or under any collective agreement made by the corporation.

(8) Directors are liable to pay interest as prescribed on outstanding wages for which they are liable.

(9) A director who has satisfied a claim for wages is entitled to contribution in relation to the wages from other directors who are liable for the claim.

58.21(1) Directors are liable to the Employee Wage Protection Program for compensation awarded under section 58.7 to the extent and in the circumstances described in this section.

(2) A director shall be liable for wages, as described in subsection 58.20(3), to the extent of the settlement or compromise unless,

(a) at the time of or after the settlement or compromise, the employer becomes insolvent and the director knew or ought to have known of the insolvency when the settlement or compromise was agreed to; or

(b) the settlement or compromise was made as the result of fraud or coercion on the part of the employer and the director knew or ought to have known of it.

(3) A director shall only be held liable for an amount in excess of the settlement or compromise when, on the grounds set out in subsection (2), an employment standards officer makes an order assessing such greater amount.

(4) Nothing in this section increases the maximum liability of a director under this Act beyond the amounts set out in subsections 58.20(7) and (8).

58.22(1) If an employment standards officer makes an order against an employer under section 65 that wages be paid, he or she may make an order to pay wages, as described in subsection 58.20(3), against some or all of the directors of the employer and may serve a copy of the order on them together with a copy of the order to pay against the employer.

(2) Within fifteen days of service of the order or in such longer period as the Director may for special reasons allow, a director may apply under section 68 to have the order against them reviewed or to have a finding that he or she is a director reviewed.

(3) For the purposes of a review provided for in subsection (2), a reference in section 68 to "employer" shall be deemed to read as a reference to "director."

(4) Despite subsection 68(1), a director is not required to pay the wages to the Director in order to apply for a review under that subsection.

(5) If the directors do not comply with the order or do not apply to have it reviewed, the order becomes final and binding against those directors even though a review hearing is held to determine another person's liability under this Act.

(6) If an employer is insolvent and the employee has caused a claim for unpaid wages to be filed with the receiver appointed by a court with respect to the employer or with the employer's trustee in bankruptcy, and the claim has not been paid, the employment standards officer may issue an order to pay wages as described in subsection 58.20(3) against some or all of the directors and shall serve it on them.

(7) Subsections (2), (3), (4) and (5) apply with necessary modifications to an order made under subsection (6).

(8) Nothing in this section increases the maximum liability of a director beyond the amounts set out in subsections 58.20(7) and (8).

58.23(1) An employment standards officer may make an order to pay wages as described in subsection 58.20(3) against some or all of the directors of an employer who were not the subject of an order under subsection 58.22(1) or (6), and may serve it on them,

(a) after an employment standards officer has made an order against the employer under section 65 that wages be paid and they have not been paid and the employer has not applied to have the order reviewed;

(b) after an employment standards officer has made an order against directors under subsection 58.22(1) or (6) and the amount has not been paid and the employer or the directors have not applied to have it reviewed;

(c) after an adjudicator has made, amended or affirmed an order against an employer under section 67 that an amount be paid and the amount has not been paid; or

(d) after a referee acting under section 68 or 69 has made, affirmed or amended an order that the employer or the directors owe wages to the employee.

(2) A director who is served under subsection (1) and who considers himself or herself aggrieved by the order may, within fifteen days of its service or such longer period as the Director may for special reasons allow, apply to have it or the finding that he or she is a director reviewed by way of a hearing.

(3) An application for review shall be made in writing to the Director and shall specify the grounds for the application.

(4) The review shall be heard as soon as is practicable by a referee selected by the Director from the panel of referees.

(5) The directors who are served, the employment standards officer from whose order the application for review is taken and such other persons as the referee may specify are parties to the application for review and, on the review, the directors served shall be the applicants and the employment standards officer and such other persons specified by the referee, if any, shall be the respondents.

(6) On a review, the referee may substitute his or her findings for those of the employment standards officer who issued the order being reviewed and may amend, rescind or affirm the order against any or all of the directors who were served.

(7) A decision of the referee under this section is final and binding upon the parties to the review and on such other parties as the referee may specify and is not subject to a review under section 68.

(8) Nothing in this section increases the maximum liability of a director beyond the amounts set out in subsections 58.20(7) and (8).

58.24 At the discretion of the Director, a director who is subject to an order under section 58.22 or 58.23 may be ordered to pay the wages in trust to the Director.

58.25(1) In the event of a conflict between the limitation period set out in subsection 82(1) and a limitation period in any other Act, the limitation period in subsection 82(1) applies unless the provision in the other Act states that it is to prevail over that subsection.

(2) If a judgment has been obtained against the employer or a certificate has been filed under section 73, a director from whom the Program Administrator has recovered is entitled to an assignment of the judgment or certificate to the extent of the amount that has been recovered from that director after the Employee Wage Protection Program and the employees have fully recovered the wages that were owed.

58.26(1) A director may be served by prepaid registered mail addressed to his or her last known address or may be served personally.

(2) If the document that was mailed under subsection (1) is returned and the director is not served personally, the Director may appoint an adjudicator to consider the manner of service.

(3) The adjudicator may order that service be effected in such manner as he or she considers appropriate in the circumstances.

58.27 Any director who fails to comply with an order of an employment standards officer and who has not applied for a review of it or who fails to comply with an order of an adjudicator or a referee is guilty of an offence and is liable on conviction to a fine not exceeding $50,000.

58.28(1) No provision in a contract, in the articles of incorporation or the by-laws of a corporation or in a resolution of a corporation relieves a director from the duty to act according to this Act or relieves him or her from liability for breach of it.

(2) An employer may indemnify a director, a former director and the heirs or legal representatives of a director or former director against all costs, charges and expenses, including an amount paid to satisfy an order under this Act or paid in respect of a certificate issued under this Act, reasonably incurred by the director in respect of any civil or administrative action or proceeding to which he or she is a party by reason of being or having been a director of the employer if,

(a) he or she has acted honestly and in good faith with a view to the best interests of the employer; and

(b) in the case of a proceeding or action that is enforced by a monetary penalty, he or she had reasonable grounds for believing that his or her conduct was lawful.

58.29 No civil remedy that a person may have against a director or that a director may have against any person is suspended or affected by this Part.

• • •

NOTES

Easily the most controversial aspects of the ESA amendments are the provisions imposing personal liability on directors for unpaid wages. This liability is also imposed in long-standing federal and provincial business corporations Acts: see for example, CBCA s. 119, and OBCA s. 131. Some provincial employment standards Acts also hold directors liable for severance and termination pay. Directors may also incur personal liability under pension benefits legislation if the corporation fails to maintain its contributory payments to an employee pension benefits plan. For the details see Chartrand, "Labour and Insolvency in the 1990s" (1994), 24 *CBLJ* 193.

Trustees in bankruptcy may also be caught in the liability net. In *Re St. Mary's Paper Inc,* (1994), 15 OR (3d) 359, affd. (1994), 107 DLR (4th) 715 (Ont. CA), it was held that the trustee, by retaining the employees after bankruptcy and making contributions to the pension fund, was liable for *all* deficiencies in the pension plan under the Ontario Pension Benefits Act.

The proliferation of directorial liability has caused much concern in the corporate community and among scholars. See Chartrand, *supra*, and Daniels, "Must Boards Go Overboard? An Economic Analysis of the Effects of Burgeoning Statutory Liability on the Role of Directors in Corporate Governance" (1994), 24 *CBLJ* 229. Faced with the corporation's insolvency, directors have resigned *en masse* in recent high profile cases. It is becoming increasingly common for large companies to establish trust funds to cover prospective liabilities to employees and/or indemnities for directors. However, these may run into difficulties under the voidable preference provisions of the BIA if they are established too close to the corporation's bankruptcy and are retroactive in character. In *Re Westar Mining* (1992), 14 CBR (3d) 95 and 101 (BC) the courts refused to sanction continuing payments into a trust fund after the initiation of reorganization proceedings under the CCAA on the ground that this would prejudice Westar's other creditors and give preferred treatment to one class of creditors.

In short, the whole position cries out for clarification and some clear enunciation of public policy!

Environmental Problems

Diane Saxe
Lender's Liability for Provincial Environmental
Protection Requirements—Recent Developments
(1992), 14 CBR (3d) 197

Under Canadian environmental statutes, provincial regulators have broad-ranging powers to order private parties to do work to prevent, control or clean up pollution. Do such orders have priority over the prior claims of other creditors, especially secured creditors, when the party responsible becomes insolvent? If so, under what circumstances? Fortunately, recent cases offer some clues.

1. Environmental protection orders where the debtor is not bankrupt

The leading case on the relationship between environmental protection orders and insolvency outside a bankruptcy is *Canada Trust Co. v. Bulora Corp.* (1981), 39 CBR (NS) 152. The Ontario Court of Appeal held that a receiver-manager was obliged to comply with a provincial administrative order necessary in the public interest, prior to paying the claim of the secured creditor who had appointed him. In that case, the assets of the debtor (who was not bankrupt) included a residential subdivision. The fire marshall ordered the debtor to tear down certain of the homes, because there were fire hazards to nearby residents. As the secured creditor's claim exceeded the value of the estate, there were no funds available to pay for the demolition except those owed to the secured creditor. The creditor had a prior, perfected, legitimate claim to the funds. On the other hand, failure to demolish the houses could endanger the lives and property of all other residents of the subdivision. The court held that the urgent need to protect public safety took priority over the rights of the creditor. The receiver-manager was required to comply with the order prior to paying the secured creditor.

Several more recent cases have continued to give lenders grounds for concern. In *King (Township) v. Rolex Equipment Co.* (1992), 90 DLR (4th) 442 (Ont. Gen. Div.), environmental cleanup costs were given precedence over the claims of a completely innocent mortgagee who was out of possession. In that case, a purchaser bought land (giving a large mortgage back to the unsuspecting vendor) and dumped solid, non-hazardous waste on it. The land was not a certified waste disposal site. The Township obtained a mandatory order against the purchaser requiring removal of the waste. Instead, the purchaser abandoned the land. Shortly thereafter, the mortgagee obtained default judgement on the mortgage covenant for $1.4 million. The mortgagee refused to take possession and refused to remove the waste, arguing that this was the responsibility of the regulatory authorities which had allowed the illegal dumping to take place.

The Ministry of the Environment and the township also refused to remove the waste, because they were not certain the costs of removal would be recovered. The township applied to the court for appointment of a receiver to remove the waste and to sell the land, so that the cost of waste removal would take priority over the interests of the secured creditor (mortgagee).

Given the public interest in removal of the waste and given the fact that the property was unsaleable until the waste was removed, the court announced that it was prepared to appoint a receiver and thereby give the costs of waste removal priority over the mortgagee's interests. However, the mortgagee was given 30 days to agree to remove the waste itself, since it might be able to do so less expensively than a government agency.

On the other hand, regulators' bargaining position has been somewhat weakened by *Bank of Montreal v. Lundrigans Ltd.* (1992), 92 DLR (4th) 554 (Nfld. TD), in which the court took an unusually narrow approach to the liability of receivers and secured creditors for pre-existing contamination.

In this case, the bank (a secured creditor of a large diversified company) sought a court order appointing a receiver. The receiver refused to be appointed unless the bank agreed to indemnify it against all claims arising out of the proper performance of its duties as receiver and manager. Due to the open-ended nature of the environmental obligations, the bank was not prepared to provide an unlimited indemnification agreement. The bank was prepared to indemnify the receiver against environmental liability with respect to any particular property over which the receiver assumed control, but only up to the net proceeds realized by the receiver from that particular property. The receiver was prepared to accept this limited indemnification agreement, provided that its own liability be similarly limited by the court order appointing it as receiver. Notice of the proposal order was given to both the provincial and federal governments. Both objected to the limitation of liability.

The chief justice held that he had jurisdiction to appoint the receiver on conditions which limited its liability, due to general statutes which authorize superior courts to make orders on whatever terms they consider just. He then reviewed the environmental provisions of a number of statutes, including the federal Fisheries Act and the Canadian Environmental Protection Act and three Newfoundland statutes. Each of these statutes imposed important environmental liabilities on the "occupant" or the person who "owns" or "has the charge, management and control" of contaminants or contaminated property. The judge agreed that the appointment of a receiver puts him or her in a position to take possession and control of a debtor's property, and that the receiver frequently chooses to acquire such control.

The governments argued that once a person is in control of contaminated property, their liability is unlimited. Under most environmental statutes, anyone in control of contaminated property can be required to clean up that property, regardless of how they came into possession and whether or not they were at fault in causing the contamination. Mr. Justice Hickman ruled, however, that the rules are different for receivers, at least in respect of environmental damage caused prior to the receiver's appointment:

> In my view, the principles of vicarious liability for prior environmental damage or offences cannot be extended to a receiver and manager who is charged with the responsibility of controlling and realizing on all or some of the assets of what is, in essence, a bankrupt company.

• • •

> None of the relevant legislation clearly provides that a receiver and manager shall be personally liable for any environmental contaminant found upon the property that comes into its or his hands. There is nothing in environmental legislation which defines what "charge and control," "authority or having control" or "charge, management or control" over land and assets particularly as it relates to the peculiar responsibilities of a receiver and manager who, upon his appointment, becomes an officer of the court.

> In my view, the appointment of a receiver and manager by the court, and his subsequent assumption of control of all or some of a debtor's assets, does not, under existing legislation, render him liable to pay money or perform work ordered by environmental authorities *in excess of the value of or moneys received from the sale of the individual asset which caused the environmental damage*. Legislation intended to impose unlimited liability on a receiver and manager would have to say so in clear and unmistakable language, which is not the case with existing environmental legislation. [Emphasis added.]

Accordingly, Mr. Justice Hickman appointed the receiver on terms that the receiver had no liability for environmental costs relating to any asset which exceeded the proceeds of sale of that asset. He held that such an order was consistent with the environmental legislation of the federal government and the province as he interpreted them.

This decision, if followed in other jurisdictions, would have important consequences for the handling of environmental costs in a receivership or bankruptcy, and would be much more favourable to secured creditors than the current practice. For example, under the agreements now negotiated by the Ontario Ministry of the Environment with secured creditors who are contemplating going into possession of the property of a company with environmental liabilities, the ministry typically demands that the receiver establish an environmental reserve. The reserve normally includes a large proportion of the value of the contaminated property, such as 50 per cent. In addition, the ministry demands a significant portion of the value of other assets, such as inventory and equipment, whose sale value may far exceed the value of the contaminated site. Under the *Lundrigans* approach, creditors may be entitled to keep the entire value of all valuable personal assets, such as inventory, work in progress, machinery and equipment, and accounts receivable, and offer the ministry only the value (which will often be nothing) of the contaminated land itself.

Unfortunately for creditors, it is not at all certain that the *Lundrigans* case will withstand further judicial scrutiny. The policy considerations which motivated Mr. Justice Hickman are clearly set out in his judgment:

If a receiver and manager is appointed under the terms proposed, then some of the operations of Lundrigans will continue, at least for a time, with the resultant employment of those on the payroll of such enterprises. If, on the other hand, a receiver and manager is not appointed, at this time, the bank, understandably, is not prepared to continue financing the operation of Lundrigans with the result that the entire operations will immediately shut down, all employees will be laid off and the assets and enterprises abandoned, subject only to the bank's continuing security. As a result, there would be no one responsible for any environmental cleanup required as a result of the operations of the various businesses by Lundrigans. This would not be in the public interest.

In my view, it is very much in the public interest that as many of the operations of Lundrigans continue as going concerns in the hope that they may be sold at realistic prices and, hopefully, continue in operation in the future. It is also in the public interest that there be someone to whom governmental authorities may look to for compliance with existing environmental legislation.

While these are undoubtedly worthy motives, the legal reasoning which Mr. Justice Hickman used to achieve this result is very weak. It rests upon his assertion that the imposition of liability on the receiver-manager is a type of vicarious liability. This is wrong. The liability of a person in control of premises to clean up those premises is not a form of vicarious liability. Vicarious liability is "the imposition of liability on one person for the actionable conduct of another, based solely on a relationship between the two persons." Attempts to impose vicarious liability are not entirely unknown in environmental law. However, the liability to clean up contaminated land imposed upon a person with charge, management and control of that land is not a vicarious one. It does not depend upon any real or imagined relationship between the person now in possession and the person who caused the problem (which would be the hallmark of vicarious liability). Instead, liability is based squarely on the present direct relationship of control between the person and the contaminated site. Nor does it depend, directly or indirectly, on fault. Fault-based liability is provided for in different provisions.

Mr. Justice Hickman was therefore wrong in concluding that his order was consistent with existing environmental laws. Nevertheless, it is possible that his decision could be upheld, or followed, on the more direct grounds that the court has jurisdiction to limit a receiver's liability, where this is what justice (and the best interests of society) require.

2. Environmental protection orders in a bankruptcy

Until last year, it was not clear what effect provincial environmental requirements would have in a bankruptcy. There is no doubt that provincial environmental statutes are constitutionally valid within the province, but when they conflict with federal laws such as the Bankruptcy Act, the federal laws prevail. What priority would a provincial environmental protection order have in a bankruptcy?

2.1. Quanta Resources

In the United States, the leading case on the point is *Quanta Resources*. (*Midlantic National Bank v. New Jersey Department of Environmental Protection; Quanta Resources Corp. v. New York (City),* 474 U.S. 494 (1986).) In *Quanta Resources*, the trustee in bankruptcy obtained court approval to abandon premises heavily contaminated with PCBs. This ended both security and fire protection services at the sites, notwithstanding state orders to the contrary. Both sites were in heavily populated areas, where fires or spills of PCBs could have devastating consequences. On appeal, the U.S. Supreme Court held that the trustee should not have been allowed to abandon the sites. Because of the danger to the public which could flow from non-compliance with the state orders, the trustee should have put compliance with the orders ahead of the interests of the creditors. Creditors are better able to protect themselves than are the innocent victims of pollution. The court specifically held that an administrative order under valid state law which requires positive action necessary in the public interest is not a "claim" in the bankruptcy sense, and is not analogous to a mere demand for money.

2.2. Panamericana

This question was addressed by a Canadian court for the first time in *Panamericana de Bienes y Servicios, S.A. v. Northern Badger Oil & Gas Ltd.* Northern Badger Oil & Gas Ltd. was an oil and gas producer. It operated a number of valuable wells. However, it was also the named operator of seven old, disused wells, which could cause significant contamination unless properly decommissioned, as required by provincial law. Northern Badger Oil & Gas Ltd. became insolvent without decommissioning the old wells. Creditors began making their claims. A receiver-manager was appointed by the principal secured creditor, followed shortly by a trustee in bankruptcy.

The receiver-manager operated the business while arranging to realize the assets. However, it did not decommission the wells, despite a formal order to do so issued by the provincial Energy Resources Conservation Board ("E.R.C.B."). Instead, the receiver deliberately arranged a complicated sale of the assets of the estate, designed to ensure that all of the valuable assets were realized for the benefit of the secured creditor, leaving for the trustee in bankruptcy only the burdensome "assets," such as the disused wells. It worked by "selling" all of the assets, but on condition that the purchaser could refuse to accept any asset. This arrangement was made without notice to the E.R.C.B., despite its express request and clear interest, and without drawing the fact to the attention of the court which approved the sale. On the day of closing, the purchaser declined to accept the seven old wells, thus leaving them in the estate.

Most of the funds realized (over one million dollars) were promptly paid to the secured creditors, leaving enough to complete the administration of the estate but not enough to decommission the wells. When all other matters had been completed, the receiver applied to the court for permission to pay remaining funds to the secured creditor, to turn over the unrealized property, including the seven old wells, to the trustee, and to be discharged. The E.R.C.B. moved for an order requiring the receiver to first decommission the wells.

At first instance, Mr. Justice MacPherson upheld the validity of the E.R.C.B.'s order, recognizing that the wells were dangerous in their present condition. However, he held that the receiver was not obliged to comply with it. He characterized the order to properly decommission the wells as a "claim" within the meaning of the Bankruptcy Act, and characterized the E.R.C.B. as a creditor seeking to use provincial law to evade the scheme of priorities set out in the Bankruptcy Act.

> The E.R.C.B. orders in council in form relate to a constitutionally valid objective, that is, abandonment of gas wells. The genuine purpose is to do something beyond the province's

constitutional powers. It is to take money directed, by the Bankruptcy Act, to be paid to a secured creditor, and apply it to another purpose.

The justice pointed out that the E.R.C.B. had the power to decommission the wells at public expense and to file a claim in the bankruptcy to seek to recover its costs. Such a claim would be a normal Crown claim ranking after the claim of the secured creditor. He held that there was no distinction between his kind of claim and an order to do the work. He therefore dismissed the motion of the E.R.C.B., and discharged the receiver, leaving the seven wells to be abandoned at public expense or to be left in their hazardous condition.

The critical point in this decision was the justice's conclusion that there is no difference between an order requiring private parties to do work necessary in the public interest, and an action to indemnify the public for the cost of having done the work, if the Crown does the work itself. It seems clear that an action by the Crown to recover the costs of work done at public expense (as under s. 124(e) of the Environmental Protection Act) is a "claim" as defined by s. 121 of the Bankruptcy Act:

> (1) All debts and liabilities present or future to which the bankrupt is subject.

But is an obligation to comply with the law by doing something necessary in the public interest truly of the same character? The logical conclusion of the justice's argument is that, if a debtor is bankrupt, a trustee or receiver is free to ignore all provincial administrative orders if they would save money by so doing, regardless of the cost to the public or to the environment.

On appeal, Mr. Justice MacPherson's decision was reversed. The unanimous decision of the Court of Appeal adopted the same analysis as in *Quanta Resources.* They held that an obligation to comply with the law, whether a statute or an administrative order, is a "liability," but it is not a "claim" as defined by the Bankruptcy Act. Nor was the E.R.C.B. a "creditor" of the bankrupt estate when it ordered the receiver to properly seal the abandoned wells.

The court held that it did not matter that the debtor, Northern Badger, owned only a 10-per-cent ownership interest in the wells. The receiver, as manager of the wells, had operating control of them, and was therefore bound to obey the provincial law which governed those wells and which required the abandonment. The obligation to properly abandon wells is not a liability owed to the particular government agency which enforces the law; it is a duty owed by all citizens to all of their fellow citizens. A public authority which enforces the law does not thereby become a creditor of those persons bound to obey the law. Accordingly, the E.R.C.B.'s order took priority over the rights of the secured creditor; the receiver was obliged to do whatever was necessary to obey the law before disbursing funds to the bank which had appointed it.

The appeal court also stressed that a court-appointed receiver is a fiduciary on behalf of all parties with an interest in the debtor's property. As such, he is held to the highest standards of propriety and of respect for the law. The receiver's conduct in deliberately diverting all valuable assets for the benefit of the secured creditor, thus ensuring that no funds would be left to decommission the wells, while concealing these facts from the E.R.C.B. did not meet these standards. For this reason, the receiver was ordered to perform the abandonment (at an estimated cost of more than $250,000), notwithstanding the fact that there were no longer sufficient assets in the debtor's estate.

There was no indication in the decision as to whether the deficiency would have to be made up by the receiver personally, or whether he could look to the secured creditor for indemnity.

This decision was followed in *Re Lamford Forest Products Ltd.* (1991), 10 CBR (3d) 137. The British Columbia Supreme Court in Bankruptcy held that the cost of compliance with an environmental protection order has priority over the claims of all secured and unsecured creditors, except for the fee of the trustee. The court made an exception for the trustee because otherwise it would not be possible to appoint trustees in cases involving serious contamination. The court also held that a trustee in bankruptcy is not *personally* liable for cost of complying with an environmental protection order which was issued to the bankrupt before the trustee was appointed. However, the court refused to decide whether and in what circumstances the trustee would have personal liability for breaches of environmental laws committed during administration of the estate.

Protection of trustees from personal liability for pre-existing environmental problems has now become law as part of the recent amendments to the Bankruptcy Act.

These decisions have put everyone in the lending community on notice that they must be concerned about the environmental status of their debtors.

3. Discharging government claims for the cost of cleanup

The *Panamericana* appeal decision left several questions unanswered. It did not disturb the trial ruling that where a government steps in to protect the environment, and then seeks to recover the cost of its work from a bankrupt, its claim is discharged by bankruptcy and is subject to the normal priorities in a bankruptcy. This means that the government's claim would be unsecured and would often go unpaid.

Where pollution occurs before bankruptcy but cleanup occurs afterwards, can a province avoid a discharge of its claim on the grounds that the claim arose after the bankruptcy? Three recent American cases illustrate the competing approaches. Despite their different statutory context, they may be of persuasive value in Canada.

3.1. Jensen

In *Jensen v. California Dept. of Health Services* (U.S. Bank App., 9th Cir., 1991) the state Department of Health Services argued that their cost of cleaning up a contaminated site previously owned by a bankrupt corporation arose post-petition. The department had discovered the presence of the waste only after the corporate bankruptcy, by which time there were no assets available for site cleanup. The individual owners of the company then declared personal bankruptcy and were subsequently discharged. The state partly cleaned up the site and demanded that the individual owners pay for the work done. The individuals then moved for an order of the bankruptcy court declaring that their liability to clean up the site had been discharged.

The court considered three possible times at which the state's claim for the cost of cleanup could have arisen:

- the claim arose when the state acquired a right to payment, i.e., when it performed the cleanup;
- the claim arose when the debtor and the creditor (the state) first established a relationship, i.e., when the state discovered the contamination; or

- the claim arose with the conduct of the debtor on which the claim is founded, i.e., when the contamination occurred.

The choice between the three options illustrated the competing policy goals of environmental law and of bankruptcy law. One of the key goals of environmental law is to ensure that "the polluter pays" so that contamination will be cleaned up by those who caused it, without burdening the public purse. In contrast, one of the key goals of bankruptcy law is to allow debtors a fresh start. The two goals come into direct conflict where a debtor seeks to discharge liability for an expensive cleanup through bankruptcy.

The *Jensen* case was decided by a bankruptcy court. Not surprisingly, it gave priority to the policy goals of bankruptcy law. The court therefore discarded the first and second alternatives as contrary to the overriding goal of granting debtors a fresh start. They pointed out that bankruptcy law frequently discharges rights to payment which are contingent or unmatured, including pre-petition torts. Accordingly, the court held that claims based on pre-petition contamination should be considered to have arisen prior to the petition, and should therefore be discharged by bankruptcy.

3.2. Penn Central

Priority was given to environmental goals in *Re Penn Central Transportation Co.* In that case, the 3d Circuit of the Court of Appeals held that the state's claim could not have arisen before the enactment of the statute on which their claim was based. Penn Central became bankrupt in 1978. Their property was then contaminated as a result of 30 years of pollution. However, in 1978 the U.S. government did not have legal grounds to make a claim in the bankruptcy because there was, at that time, no obligation to clean up contaminated land. The legal obligation to clean up, and the state's entitlement to the costs of cleanup, was not created until 1980, when the Superfund Law (CERCLA) was passed. The court held that the 1978 bankruptcy could not discharge any claims for which the legal basis did not then exist. Accordingly, the post-bankruptcy company was held liable for the cost of cleaning up the pre-bankruptcy pollution.

3.3. Chateaugay

The best effort to reconcile the competing policies is probably found in *Re Chateaugay Corp.* (September 6, 1991). As a general court of appeal, the U.S. 2nd Circuit Court of Appeals found the policy goals of bankruptcy law and of environmental law to be equally compelling. In this contest between equally valid social goals, the court emphasized that a final choice must be made by the legislators. However, the court wisely recognized the immediate need for some tolerable compromise to give guidance to all parties. They chose to do so by drawing a line based on when the pollution occurred. They created a more sophisticated analysis by distinguishing between costs incurred by government to remedy contamination which occurred before bankruptcy, and which presented no ongoing risk, and those orders to control pollution or public danger that continued after the bankruptcy began.

Like the *Jensen* court and the trial judge in *Panamericana*, the *Chateaugay* judges ruled that the goals of bankruptcy law take priority when dealing with what is essentially a money claim: a claim for the cost of cleaning up past contamination which occurred pre-petition. In such cases, all the environmental damage is done, and nothing is at stake except the cost of cleaning it up. Where all that is at stake is money, it is reasonable to give precedence to the law which is designed for the allocation of money.

However, the balancing of legislative goals has a very different result where the state requires the debtor (or the trustee) to take action to control illegal pollution (or public danger from existing pollution) which is ongoing after the petition. The court reasoned that a government could not lawfully accept a sum of money in exchange for permitting illegal pollution to continue. Accordingly, an order requiring cessation of pollution is not a money claim at all. In addition, it belongs to the post-petition period because compliance with it is necessary if the estate is not to break the law after the petition. The court therefore ordered the trustee to pay the costs of preventing ongoing pollution as an administrative expense in priority to secured creditors.

This decision is well reasoned and strikes an equitable balance between valid social goals. It is also reassuringly consistent with the leading Canadian decisions, *Panamericana* and *Canada Trust v. Bulora*. It should therefore be of some assistance to debtors, creditors and trustees in bankruptcy who are struggling to ascertain their positions in the current confusion of the law.

4. Other cases

Since American law so often heralds directions which we follow later, it may also be worth noting two other cases which illustrate the continuing search of governments to find deep pockets to fund environmental cleanups. In *O'Neil v. Q.L.C.R.I.* (32 E.R.C. 1661, 1991; earlier proceeding 738 F. Supp. 623, 1990) the state of Rhode Island and private parties sued the owners and operators of a residential subdivision sewage system for the discharge of raw sewage into a river. In 1991, the state of Rhode Island obtained court permission to add the real estate lender (a credit union) as a defendant, on the ground that the lender "aided and abetted" the pollution. The state alleged that the lender knew of the sewage problem yet lent the system operators money without requiring them to solve the problem. The court held that these facts, if proved, could be enough to make the lender liable.

In another 1991 case, the state of California laid charges against a lawyer acting for a bankrupt biotechnology company, InFerGene Inc. The bankrupt company is alleged to have caused contamination of rented premises in which it had carried on business. The lawyer wrote to the landlord advising that the company was insolvent and would not be performing the cleanup. The state then charged the company, some of its officers and the lawyer with "causing" the abandonment of hazardous waste at an unlicensed site.

5. Conclusion

Lenders and their counsel can no longer afford to be complacent about the environmental exposure of their debtors. No matter how carefully a loan has been secured, registered and protected, the security may be valueless or worse if it is contaminated or a public danger. How, then, can a lender protect itself?

Only a limited amount can be done once a debtor is already insolvent. It is far more cost-effective for lenders to focus on prevention. Prudent lenders will want to insist that their major debtors demonstrate that they have incorporated environmental responsibility into their central system of management. Environmental control should be as important, and as routine, as financial control. The exact system to be adopted varies substantially from company to company, depending on its corporate culture, its economic situation and the exact nature of its problems. At a minimum, lenders should insist that debtors implement a systematic "green plan," which includes environmental policies, properly structured audits, and a methodical system of implementation and follow-up.

• • •

CHAPTER EIGHTEEN

Reorganization of Insolvent Businesses: I The Companies' Creditors Arrangement Act

There is little doubt that over the past twenty years the dominant theme in business insolvencies has revolved around averting business bankruptcies by facilitating business reorganizations* and updating frequently dated laws to provide a modern statutory framework for this purpose. This is not to suggest that the restructuring of insolvent business debtors as an alternative to liquidation is, economically or legally, a modern concept. England adopted legislation as far back as 1870, although it was heavily circumscribed. In the United States, court sanctioned receiverships were widely used in the 19th century to address the problems of insolvent railroads and these generated a large body of complex case law before the introduction of legislation in 1933 and 1938. In Canada, the Bankruptcy Act of 1919 contained a separate part dealing with proposals which was moderately used in practice prior to the 1992 amendments. The main shortcoming of the provisions was that they did not apply to secured creditors. This was one of the principal reasons why, at the height of the Great Depression, Parliament deemed it necessary to adopt the

---

* The term business reorganization is commonly used in Canada and the United States to describe the restructuring of the debts of an insolvent business, but the term is not used in the Canadian legislation. The CCAA speaks of an arrangement, but without defining the term. Part III, Division 1 of the BIA uses the term "Proposal." "Proposal" is defined in s. 2 as "including" a proposal for a composition, for an extension of time or for a scheme of arrangement. "Composition" and "arrangement" are not defined but, given the non-exhaustive definition of "proposal" it probably does not matter. Composition is usually understood to mean an arrangement whereby creditors agree to accept less than full repayment of what is owing to them as contrasted with a proposal for an extension of time, which simply gives the debtor more time to pay the debts. A scheme of arrangement usually implies a more elaborate proposal possibly involving a restructuring of the classes of creditors and equity holders in the debtor corporation coupled with a reduction in the amount that is repayable and the period in which it must be paid. For the purposes of chapters 18 and 19 of this casebook, "reorganization" is used in a non-technical sense to denote any and all of these methods of rescuing an insolvent business.

Companies' Creditors Arrangement Act. The sources of the Act were some skeletal provisions in the English Companies Act of 1929. As drafted, the CCAA was only designed to facilitate the reorganization of large corporations.

Nevertheless, so far as Canada was concerned, two major recessions in the 1980s made it urgent to revise and augment the earlier legislation. The same need was felt in many other countries. In Canada, the 1992 amendments to the BIA greatly expanded Part III of the Act and divided it into Division 1 and Division 2. Division 1 is intended to deal with business proposals although, technically speaking, it is not limited to business insolvents; Division 2 is restricted to consumer proposals and is intended to provide consumer debtors with an alternative to straight bankruptcies. (Part X of the BIA, which was added in 1966, following a Supreme Court of Canada decision invalidating similar Alberta legislation, enables consumer debtors to obtain an extension of time for the repayment of their debts.)

In the United States, chapter 11 of the Bankruptcy Code of 1978, replaces the earlier reorganization legislation and greatly encourages insolvent businesses, especially larger ones, to seek shelter from importuning creditors. In the United Kingdom, the Insolvency Act 1986 contains new provisions for an "administration order" which may lead to a reorganization proposal. Many other industrialized countries, including France, Germany and Australia, have recently revamped their insolvency legislation so as to facilitate corporate reorganizations.

However, it needs to be emphasized that while, broadly speaking, these legislative initiatives share common goals the techniques adopted in the legislation and their commitment to a rescue culture differ widely. It is generally agreed that chapter 11 is the most debtor oriented of the post-war provisions. Because of this, its underlying philosophy and practical effects have engendered a lively controversy among lawyers, economists and bankruptcy scholars. In a much cited 1992 article,* Bradley and Rosenzweig argued that corporate creditors were signficantly worse off than they were under the pre-1978 insolvency regime and that generally chapter 11 was a grossly inefficient and heavily biased solution to corporate debt problems. Bradley and Rosenzweig's factual assertions have been hotly disputed by other scholars.† While there is every evidence that the academic controversy will continue, it has so far had little impact on the US Congress.

The British administration order provisions have proved to be a great disappointment and for the past three years the British government has been actively canvassing suggestions for amendments or alternative solutions.‡ Canadian insolvency practitioners are generally satisfied with the 1992 amendments to the BIA. There is broad agreement that, between the CCAA and Part III, insolvent debtors now have a choice of two very differently structured regimes designed respectively to accommodate the needs of large and medium to small

---

* "The Untenable Case for Chapter 11" (1992), 101 *Yale LJ* 1043. See also Baird, "The Uneasy Case for Corporate Reorganization" (1986), 15 *J Legal Education* 127.

† See Lynn LoPucki (1992), 91 *Mich. L Rev.* 79 and Elizabeth Warren (1992), 102 *Yale LJ* 437.

‡ The provisions suffer from two main difficulties. The first is that holders of fixed and floating charges can opt out of them entirely, and often do; the second is that once an order is made management is displaced and an administrator is put in charge of the debtor company's business. This obviously gives debtor companies little incentive to make use of the administration regime.

sized firms respectively. As the cases reproduced later in this chapter amply show, Canadian courts have given the skeletal provisions of the CCAA a very generous spin so as to produce results not markedly different from those experienced under chapter 11.*

The CCAA differs from Part III because the first is court driven while the latter is rule driven and offers much less scope for judicial discretion. The difference troubles some observers because it allows debtors to choose between the regimes depending on which offers the better advantages in a given context. We shall have occasion in this chapter and in chapter 19 to examine the differences in some detail. Parliament chose to retain both systems in 1992, at least on a trial basis until experience was gained with the Part III provisions. Since then BIAC has recommended the retention of the two systems but with some borrowings from Part III to make the CCAA still more congenial to large corporate debtors.† The federal government is likely to adopt these recommendations in the amending bill expected to be laid before Parliament in late 1995.

Despite their obvious intellectual appeal, it is important not to exaggerate the importance of reorganizations on the overall bankruptcy system. In 1994, there were 11,810 business bankruptcies compared with 743 Division 1 proposals (i.e., proposals amounted to about 6% of the number of bankruptcies). If we assume that only about 50% of proposals were successful the ratio is reduced to a modest 3%. In the same calendar year, there were 1,467 privately appointed and 72 court appointed receivers in relation to the estates of insolvent debtors, for a total of 1,539 receiverships. In other words, there were slightly more than twice the number of receiverships than there were Division 1 proposals. Unfortunately, no statistics are available with respect to the number of CCAA arrangements.

The number of Division 2 consumer proposals filed in 1994 also tells an important story. There were 1,851 such proposals compared with 74,300 consumer bankruptcies or a ratio of about .035:1. Clearly Division 2 does not carry much appeal for the average consumer bankrupt.

Taxonomy of Legislative Issues

In examining and comparing the provisions of Part III and the CCAA (or for that matter the provisions of any other reorganization regime), the student will find it helpful to bear in mind the following taxonomy of legislative issues in determining how the issues are answered by the statutory framework under examination.

I. *The scope of the legislation.* Does it apply to all insolvent business debtors or only to some? Is the debtor's insolvency an essential condition? Should it be? Are all creditors, secured as well as unsecured, caught by the legislation?

II. *Initiation of proceedings.* Is a simple filing by the debtor (or other qualified person) sufficient, or must court approval first be obtained? What are the conceptual and practical effects of the two approaches?

---

* This is also the conclusion of Lynn M. LoPucki & George G. Triantis in "A Systems Approach to US and Canadian Reorganization of Financially Distressed Companies" in Ziegel (ed.) *Current Developments in International and Comparative Corporate Insolvency Law* (1994), ch. 6.

† The issues are examined in Gordon Marantz's memorandum reproduced *infra*, chapter 19.

III. *Supporting documents.* What documents must be filed at the time of, or shortly after, the initiation of the proceedings? What role do they play? If the documents include financial statements how comprehensive are they?

IV. *Conduct of debtor's business.* Is the debtor permitted to carry on business as before? If not, what restrictions are imposed? Does the existing management remain in place and if yes, why?

V. *Role of monitor/trustee.* If there is no mandatory change in management, does the legislation require the appointment of a monitor or trustee to verify financial statements and generally to protect creditor interests before and after approval of the reorganization proposals?

VI. *Stay of proceedings against debtor.* Is such a stay automatic or must it be sought from the court? Are there are any restrictions on the scope of the stay? Can the stay be lifted in favour of petitioning creditors and if so on what grounds?

VII. *Executory contracts.* Does the legislation address this important question and if so in what way? Does the legislation apply to all types of executory contracts or only some? Does it apply to union contracts? Does the legislation merely maintain existing contracts or does it also allow the debtor *to repudiate* existing contracts with or without compensation to the other party?

VIII. *Post-petition financing and administrative expenses.* Does the legislation permit the debtor to raise new capital to enable the debtor to stay in business and if yes, what priority is accorded the new financing? What about administrative expenses incurred during the reorganization proceedings? What priority do they enjoy over the claims of other creditors?

IX. *Classification of creditors.* How are creditors classified for purposes of voting and their treatment in the debtor's proposal? Does it depend on the nature or size of the claim? The existence of security? The treatment of the claim in a straight bankruptcy? The commonality of interests of members of the class?

X. *Voting requirements with respect to proposal.* What degree of majority support is required of the voting creditors?

XI. *Role of court approval of proposal.* Is court approval necessary in addition to creditor approval, and if so why? What criteria is the court required to apply in determining whether to give its approval?

XII. *"Cram down" provisions.* Should the court be entitled to override creditor opposition to a proposal if the court believes the creditors are not acting reasonably?

XIII. *Effect of rejection of proposal.* What is the effect of creditor rejection of a proposal? Does it lead to automatic bankruptcy or only to a lifting of the stay and restoration of the status ante quo?

XIV. *Implementation of proposal.* Who ensures that the terms of an approved proposal are duly implemented? What is the effect of a breach of the proposal terms?

Scope of Materials in Chapters Eighteen and Nineteen

The materials in chapters 18 and 19 do not purport to answer all of the above questions, but the missing answers can often be gleaned from the legislation itself or from a careful reading of the case law. Chapter 18 focuses on the CCAA case law and related materials; chapter 19 on the much less comprehensive and less fully reasoned Part III case law.

Elan Corp. v. Comiskey
(1990), 1 CBR (3d) 101 (Ont. CA)

FINLAYSON JA (KREVER JA concurring): This is an appeal by the Bank of Nova Scotia (the "bank") from orders made by Mr. Justice Hoolihan [(11 September 1990), Doc. Nos. Toronto RE 1993/90 and RE 1994/90 (Ont. Gen. Div.)] as hereinafter described. The Bank of Nova Scotia was the lender to two related companies, namely, Elan Corporation ("Elan") and Nova Metal Products Inc. ("Nova"), which commenced proceedings under the *Companies' Creditors Arrangement Act*, RSC 1985, c. C-36 (the "CCAA"), for the purposes of having a plan of arrangement put to a meeting of secured creditors of those companies.

The orders appealed from are:

(i) An order of September 11, 1990, which directed a meeting of the secured creditors of Elan and Nova to consider the plan of arrangement filed, or other suitable plan. The order further provided that for 3 days until September 14, 1990, the bank be prevented from acting on any of its security or paying down any of its loans from accounts receivable collected by Elan and Nova, and that Elan and Nova could spend the accounts receivable assigned to the bank that would be received.

(ii) An order dated September 14, 1990, extending the terms of the order of September 11, 1990, to remain in effect until the plan of arrangement was presented to the Court no later than October 24, 1990. This order continued the stay against the bank and the power of Elan and Nova to spend the accounts receivable assigned to the bank. Further orders dated September 27, 1990, and October 18, 1990, have extended the stay, and the power of Elan and Nova to spend the accounts receivable that have been assigned to the bank. The date of the meetings of creditors has been extended to November 9, 1990. The application to sanction the plan of arrangement must be heard by November 14, 1990.

(iii) An order dated October 18, 1990, directing that there be two classes of secured creditors for the purposes of voting at the meeting of secured creditors. The first class is to be comprised of the bank, RoyNat Inc. ("RoyNat"), the Ontario Development Corporation ("ODC"), the city of Chatham and the village of Glencoe. The second class is to be comprised of persons related to Elan and Nova that acquired debentures to enable the companies to apply under the CCAA.

There is very little dispute about the facts in this matter, but the chronology of events is important and I am setting it out in some detail.

The bank has been the banker to Elan and Nova. At the time of the application in August 1990, it was owed approximately $1,900,000. With interest and costs, including receivers' fees, it is now owed in excess of $2,300,000. It has a first registered charge on the accounts receivable and inventory of Elan and Nova, and a second registered charge on the land, buildings and equipment. It also has security under s. 178 of the *Bank Act*, RSC 1985, c. B-1, as am. RSC 1985 (3rd Supp.), c. 25, s. 26. The terms of credit between the bank and Elan as set out in a commitment agreement provide that Elan and Nova may not encumber their assets without the consent of the bank.

RoyNat is also a secured creditor of Elan and Nova, and it is owed approximately $12 million. It holds a second registered charge on the accounts receivable and inventory of Elan and Nova, and a first registered charge on the land, buildings and equipment. The bank and RoyNat entered into a priority agreement to define with certainty the priority which each holds over the assets of Elan and Nova.

The ODC guaranteed payment of $500,000 to RoyNat for that amount lent by RoyNat to Elan. The ODC holds debenture security from Elan and secure the guarantee which it gave to RoyNat [*sic*]. That security ranks third to the bank and RoyNat. The ODC has not been called upon by RoyNat to pay under its guarantee. ODC has not lent any money directly to Elan or Nova.

Elan owes approximately $77,000 to the City of Chatham for unpaid municipal taxes. Nova owes approximately $18,000 to the Village of Glencoe for unpaid municipal taxes. Both municipalities have a lien on the real property of the respective companies in priority to every claim except the Crown under s. 369 of the *Municipal Act*, RSO 1980, c. 302.

On May 8, 1990, the bank demanded payment of all outstanding loans owing by Elan and Nova to be made by June 1, 1990. Extensions of time were granted and negotiations directed to the settlement of the debt took place thereafter. On August 27, 1990, the bank appointed Coopers & Lybrand Limited as receiver and manager of the assets of Elan and Nova, and as agent under the bank's security to realize upon the security. Elan and Nova refused to allow the receiver and manager to have access to their premises, on the basis that insufficient notice had been provided by the bank before demanding payment.

Later on August 27, 1990, the bank brought a motion in an action against Elan and Nova (Court File No. 54033/90) for an order granting possession of the premises of Elan and Nova to Coopers & Lybrand. On the evening of August 27, 1990, at approximately 9 p.m., Mr. Justice Saunders made an order adjourning the motion on certain conditions. The order authorized Coopers & Lybrand access to the premises to monitor Elan's business, and permitted Elan to remain in possession and carry on its business in the ordinary course. The bank was restrained in the order, until the motion could be heard, from selling inventory, land, equipment or buildings or from notifying account debtors to collect receivables, but was not restrained from applying accounts receivable that were collected against outstanding bank loans.

On Wednesday, August 29, 1990, Elan and Nova each issued a debenture for $10,000 to a friend of the principals of the companies, Joseph Comiskey, through his brother Michael Comiskey as trustee, pursuant to a trust deed executed the same day. The terms were not commercial and it does not appear that repayment was expected. It is conceded by counsel for Elan that the sole purpose of issuing the debentures was to qualify as a "debtor company" within the meaning of s. 3 of the CCAA. Section 3 reads as follows: ...

The debentures conveyed the personal property of Elan and Nova as security to Michael Comiskey as trustee. No consent was obtained from the bank as required by the loan agreements, nor was any consent obtained from the receiver. Cheques for $10,000 each, representing the loans secured in the debentures, were given to Elan and Nova on Wednesday, August 29, 1990, but not deposited until 6 days later on September 4, 1990, after an interim order had been made by Mr. Justice Farley in favour of Elan and Nova staying the bank from taking proceedings.

On August 30, 1990 Elan and Nova applied under s. 5 of the CCAA for an order directing a meeting of secured creditors to vote on a plan of arrangement. Section 5 provides: ...

The application was heard by Farley J on Friday, August 31, 1990, at 8 a.m. Farley J dismissed the application on the grounds that the CCAA required that there be more than one debenture issued by each company. Later on the same day, August 31, 1990, Elan and Nova each issued two debentures for $500 to the wife of the principal of Elan through her sister as trustee. The debentures provided for payment of interest to commence on August 31, 1992. Cheques for $500 were delivered that day to the companies but not deposited in the bank account until September 4, 1990. These debentures conveyed the personal property in the assets of Elan and Nova to the trustee as security. Once again it is conceded that the debentures were issued for the sole purpose of meeting the requirements of s. 3 of the CCAA. No consent was obtained from the bank as required by the loan terms, nor was any consent obtained from the receiver.

On August 31, 1990, following the creation of the trust deeds and the issuance of the debentures, Elan and Nova commenced new applications under the CCAA which were heard late in the day by Farley J. He adjourned the applications to September 10, 1990, on certain terms, including a stay preventing the bank from acting on its security and allowing Elan to spend up to $321,000 from accounts receivable collected by it.

The plan of arrangement filed with the application provided that Elan and Nova would carry on business for 3 months, that secured creditors would not be paid and could take no action on their security for 3 months, and that the accounts receivable of Elan and Nova assigned to the bank could be utilized by Elan and Nova for purposes of its day-to-day operations. No compromise of any sort was proposed.

On September 11, 1990, Hoolihan J ordered that a meeting of the secured creditors of Elan and Nova be held no later than October 22, 1990, to consider the plan of arrangement that had been filed, or other suitable plan. He ordered that the plan of arrangement be presented to the secured creditors no later than September 27, 1990. He made further orders effective for 3 days until September 14, 1990, including orders:

(i) that the companies could spend the accounts receivable assigned to the bank that would be collected in accordance with a cash flow forecast filed with the Court providing for $1,387,000 to be spent by September 30, 1990; and

(ii) a stay of proceedings against the bank acting on any of its security or paying down any of its loans from accounts receivable collected by Elan and Nova.

On September 14, 1990, Hoolihan J extended the terms of his order of September 11, 1990, to remain in effect until the plan of arrangement was presented to the Court no later than October 24, 1990 for final approval. This order continued the power of Elan and Nova to spend up to $1,387,000 of the accounts receivable assigned to the bank in accordance with the projected cash flow to September 30, 1990, and to spend a further amount to

October 24, 1990, in accordance with a cash flow to be approved by Hoolihan J prior to October 1, 1990. Further orders dated September 27 and October 18 have extended the power to spend the accounts receivable to November 14, 1990.

On September 14, 1990, the bank requested Hoolihan J to restrict his order so that Elan and Nova could use the accounts receivable assigned to the bank only so long as they continued to operate within the borrowing guidelines contained in the terms of the loan agreements with the bank. These guidelines require a certain ratio to exist between bank loans and the book value of the accounts receivable and inventory assigned to the bank, and are designed in normal circumstances to ensure that there is sufficient value in the security assigned to the bank. Hoolihan J refused to make the order.

On October 18, 1990, Hoolihan J ordered that the composition of the classes of secured creditors for the purposes of voting at the meeting of secured creditors shall be as follows:

(a) The bank, RoyNat, ODC, the City of Chatham and the Village of Glencoe shall comprise one class.

(b) The parties related to the principal of Elan that acquired their debentures to enable the companies to apply under the CCAA shall comprise a second class.

On October 18, 1990, at the request of counsel for Elan and Nova, Hoolihan J further ordered that the date for the meeting of creditors of Elan and Nova be extended to November 9, 1990, in order to allow a new plan of arrangement to be sent to all creditors, including unsecured creditors of those companies. Elan and Nova now plan to offer a plan of compromise or arrangement to the unsecured creditors of Elan and Nova as well as to the secured creditors.

There are five issues in this appeal:

(1) Are the debentures issued by Elan and Nova for the purpose of permitting the companies to qualify as applicants under the CCAA debentures within the meaning of s. 3 of the CCAA?

(2) Did the issue of the debentures contravene the provisions of the loan agreements between Elan and Nova and the bank? If so, what are the consequences for CCAA purposes?

(3) Did Elan and Nova have the power to issue the debentures and make application under the CCAA after the bank had appointed a receiver and after the order of Saunders J?

(4) Did Hoolihan J have the power under s. 11 of the CCAA to make the interim orders that he made with respect to the accounts receivable?

(5) Was Hoolihan J correct in ordering that the bank vote on the proposed plan of arrangement in a class with RoyNat and the other secured creditors?

It is well established that the CCAA is intended to provide a structured environment for the negotiation of compromises between a debtor company and its creditors for the benefit of both. Such a resolution can have significant benefits for the company, its shareholders and employees. For this reason the debtor companies, Elan and Nova, are entitled to a broad and liberal interpretation of the jurisdiction of the Court under the CCAA. Having said that, it does not follow that in exercising its discretion to order a meeting of creditors under s. 5 of the CCAA that the Court should not consider the equities in this case as they relate to these companies and to one of its principal secured creditors, the bank.

The issues before Hoolihan J and this Court were argued on a technical basis. Hoolihan J did not give effect to the argument that the debentures described above were a "sham" and could not be used for the purposes of asserting jurisdiction. Unfortunately, he did not address any of the other arguments presented to him on the threshold issue of the availability of the CCAA. He appears to have acted on the premise that if the CCAA can be made available, it should be utilized.

If Hoolihan J did exercise any discretion overall, it is not reflected in his reasons. I believe, therefore, that we are in a position to look at the uncontested chronology of these proceedings and exercise our own discretion. To me, the significant date is August 27, 1990 when the bank appointed Coopers & Lybrand Limited as receiver and manager of the undertaking, property and assets mortgaged and charged under the demand debenture and of the collateral under the general security agreement, both dated June 20, 1979. On the same date, it appointed the same company as receiver and manager for Nova under a general security agreement dated December 5, 1988. The effect of this appointment is to divest the companies and their boards of directors of their power to deal with the property comprised in the appointment: Raymond Walton, *Kerr on the Law and Practice as to Receivers*, 16th ed. (London: Sweet & Maxwell, 1983), p. 292. Neither Elan nor Nova had the power to create further indebtedness, and thus to interfere with the ability of the receiver to manage the two companies: *Alberta Treasury Branches v. Hat Development Ltd.* (1988), 71 CBR (NS) 264, 64 Alta. LR (2d) 17 (QB), aff'd (1989), 65 Alta. LR (2d) 374 (CA).

Counsel for the debtor companies submitted that the management powers of the receiver were stripped from the receiver by Saunders J in his interim order, when he allowed the receiver access to the companies' properties but would not permit it to realize on the security of the bank until further order. He pointed out that the order also provided that the companies were entitled to remain in possession and "to carry on business in the ordinary course" until further order.

I do not agree with counsel's submission covering the effect of the order. It certainly restricted what the receiver could do on an interim basis, but it imposed restrictions on the companies as well. The issue of these disputed debentures in support of an application for relief as insolvent companies under the CCAA does not comply with the order of Saunders J. This is not carrying on business in the ordinary course. The residual power to take all of these initiatives for relief under the CCAA remained with the receiver, and if trust deeds were to be issued, an order of the Court in Action 54033/90 was required permitting their issuance and registration.

There is another feature which, in my opinion, affects the exercise of discretion, and that is the probability of the meeting achieving some measure of success. Hoolihan J considered the calling of the meeting at one hearing, as he was asked to do, and determined the respective classes of creditors at another. This latter classification is necessary because of the provisions of s. 6(a) of the CCAA, which reads as follows:

6. Where a majority in number representing three-fourths in value of the creditors, or class of creditors, as the case may be, present and voting either in person or by proxy at the meeting or meetings thereof respectively held pursuant to sections 4 and 5, or either of those sections, agree to any compromise or arrangement either as proposed or as altered or modified at the meeting or meetings, the compromise or arrangement may be sanctioned by the court, and if so sanctioned is binding

> (a) on all the creditors or the class of creditors, as the case may be, and on any trustee for any such class of creditors, whether secured or unsecured, as the case may be, and on the company.

If both matters had been considered at the same time, as in my view they should have been, and if what I regard as a proper classification of the creditors had taken place, I think it is obvious that the meeting would not be a productive one. It was improper, in my opinion, to create one class of creditors made up of all the secured creditors save the so-called "sham" creditors. There is no true community of interest among them, and the motivation of Elan and Nova in striving to create a single class is clearly designed to avoid the classification of the bank as a separate class.

It is apparent that the only secured creditors with a significant interest in the proceeding under the CCAA are the bank and RoyNat. The two municipalities have total claims for arrears of taxes of less than $100,000. They have first priority in the lands of the companies. They are in no jeopardy whatsoever. The ODC has a potential liability in that it can be called upon by RoyNat under its guarantee to a maximum of $500,000, and this will trigger default under its debentures with the companies, but its interests lie with RoyNat.

As to RoyNat, it is the largest creditor with a debt of some $12 million. It will dominate any class it is in because, under s. 6 of the CCAA, the majority in a class must represent three-quarters in value of that class. It will always have a veto by reason of the size of its claim, but requires at least one creditor to vote for it to give it a majority in number (I am ignoring the municipalities). It needs the ODC.

I do not base my opinion solely on commercial self-interest, but also on the differences in legal interest. The bank has first priority on the receivables referred to as the "quick assets," and RoyNat ranks second in priority. RoyNat has first priority on the buildings and realty, the "fixed assets," and the bank has second priority.

It is in the commercial interests of the bank, with its smaller claim and more readily realizable assets, to collect and retain the accounts receivable. It is in the commercial interests of RoyNat to preserve the cash flow of the business and sell the enterprise as a going concern. It can only do that by overriding the prior claim of the bank to these receivables. If it can vote with the ODC in the same class as the bank, it can achieve that goal and extinguish the prior claim of the bank to realize on the receivables. This it can do, despite having acknowledged its legal relationship to the bank in the priority agreement signed by the two. I can think of no reason why the legal interest of the bank as the holder of the first security on the receivables should be overridden by RoyNat as holder of the second security.

The classic statement on classes of creditors is that of Lord Esher MR in *Sovereign Life Assurance Co. v. Dodd*, [1892] 2 QB 573, [1891-94] All ER 246 (CA), at pp. 579-80 [QB]:

> The Act [*Joint Stock Companies Arrangement Act, 1870*] says that the persons to be summoned to the meeting (all of whom, be it said in passing, are creditors) are persons who can be divided into

different classes—classes which the Act of Parliament recognises, though it does not define them. This, therefore, must be done: they must be divided into different classes. What is the reason for such a course? It is because the creditors composing the different classes have different interests; and, therefore, if we find a different state of facts existing among different creditors which may differently affect their minds and their judgment, they must be divided into different classes.

The *Sovereign Life* case was quoted with approval by Kingstone J in *Re Wellington Building Corp.*, [1934] OR 653, 16 CBR 48, [1934] 4 DLR 626, [1934] OWN 562 (SC), at p. 659 [OR]. He also quoted another English authority at p. 658:

> In *In Re Alabama, New Orleans, Texas and Pacific Junction Ry. Co.*, [1891] 1 Ch. 213, a scheme and arrangement under the Joint Stock Companies Arrangement Act (1870), was submitted to the Court for approval. Lord Justice Bowen, at p. 243, says:
>> Now, I have no doubt at all that it would be improper for the Court to allow an arrangement to be forced on any class of creditors, if the arrangement cannot reasonably be supposed by sensible business people to be for the benefit of that class as such, otherwise the sanction of the Court would be a sanction to what would be a scheme of confiscation. The object of this section is not confiscation. ... Its object is to enable compromises to be made which are for the common benefit of the creditors as creditors, or for the common benefit of some class of creditors as such.

Kingstone J set aside a meeting where three classes of creditors were permitted to vote together. He said at p. 660:

> It is clear that Parliament intended to give the three-fourths majority of any class power to bind that class, but I do not think the Statute should be construed so as to permit holders of subsequent mortgages power to vote and thereby destroy the priority rights and security of a first mortgagee.

We have been referred to more modern cases, including two decisions of Trainor J of the British Columbia Supreme Court, both entitled *Re Northland Properties Ltd.* One case is reported in (1988), 73 CBR (NS) 166, 31 BCLR (2d) 35, and the other in the same volume at p. 175 [CBR]. Trainor J was upheld on appeal on both judgments. The first judgment of the British Columbia Court of Appeal is unreported (16 September, 1988) [Doc. No. Vancouver CA009772, Taggart, Lambert and Locke JJA]. The judgment in the second appeal is reported at 73 CBR (NS) 195, [1989] 3 WWR 363, 34 BCLR (2d) 122.

In the first *Northland* case, Trainor J held that the difference in the terms of parties to and priority of different bonds meant that they should be placed in separate classes. He relied upon *Re Wellington Building Corp., supra*. In the second *Northland* case, he dealt with 15 mortgagees who were equal in priority but held different parcels of land as security. Trainor J held that their relative security positions were the same, notwithstanding that the mortgages were for the most part secured by charges against separate properties. The nature of the debt was the same, the nature of the security was the same, the remedies for default were the same, and in all cases they were corporate loans by sophisticated lenders. In specifically accepting the reasoning of Trainor J, the Court of Appeal held that the concern of the various mortgagees as to the quality of their individual securities was "a variable cause arising not by any difference in legal interests, but rather as a consequence of bad lending, or market values, or both" (p. 203).

In *Re NsC Diesel Power Inc.* (1990), 79 CBR (NS) 1, 97 NSR (2d) 295, 258 APR 295 (TD), the Court stressed that a class should be made up of persons "'whose rights are not so dissimilar as to make it impossible for them to consult together with a view to their common interest'" (p. 8 [of CBR]).

My assessment of these secured creditors is that the bank should be in its own class. This being so, it is obvious that no plan of arrangement can succeed without its approval. There is no useful purpose to be served in putting a plan of arrangement to a meeting of creditors if it is known in advance that it cannot succeed. This is another cogent reason for the Court declining to exercise its discretion in favour of the debtor companies.

For all the reasons given above, the application under the CCAA should have been dismissed. I do not think that I have to give definitive answers to the individual issues numbered (1) and (2). They can be addressed in a later case, where the answers could be dispositive of an application under the CCAA. The answer to (3) is that the combined effect of the receivership and the order of Saunders J disentitled the companies to issue the debentures and bring the application under the CCAA. It is not necessary to answer issue (4), and the answer to (5) is no.

Accordingly, I would allow the appeal, set aside the three orders of Hoolihan J, and, in their place, issue an order dismissing the application under the CCAA … .

DOHERTY JA (dissenting in part):

I Background

On November 2, 1990, this Court allowed the appeal brought by the Bank of Nova Scotia (the "bank") and vacated several orders made by Hoolihan J. Finlayson JA delivered oral reasons on behalf of the majority. At the same time, I delivered brief oral reasons dissenting in part from the conclusion reached by the majority and undertook to provide further written reasons. These are those reasons.

The events relevant to the disposition of this appeal are set out in some detail in the oral reasons of Finlayson JA. I will not repeat that chronology, but will refer to certain additional background facts before turning to the legal issues.

Elan Corporation ("Elan") owns the shares of Nova Metal Products Inc. ("Nova Inc."). Both companies have been actively involved in the manufacture of automobile parts for a number of years. As of March 1990, the companies had total annual sales of about $30 million, and employed some 220 people in plants located in Chatham and Glencoe, Ontario. The operation of these companies no doubt plays a significant role in the economy of these two small communities.

In the 4 years prior to 1989, the companies had operated at a profit ranging from $287,000 (1987) to $1,500,000 (1986). In 1989, several factors, including large capital expenditures and a downturn in the market, combined to produce an operational loss of about $1,333,000. It is anticipated that the loss for the year ending June 30, 1990, will be about $2.3 million. As of August 1, 1990, the companies continued in full operation, and those in control anticipated that the financial picture would improve significantly later in 1990, when the companies would be busy filling several contracts which had been obtained earlier in 1990.

The bank has provided credit to the companies for several years. In January 1989, the bank extended an operating line of credit to the companies. The line of credit was by way of a demand loan that was secured in the manner described by Finlayson JA. Beginning in May 1989, and from time to time after that, the companies were in default under the terms of the loan advanced by the bank. On each occasion, the bank and the companies managed to work out some agreement so that the bank continued as lender and the companies continued to operate their plants.

Late in 1989, the companies arranged for a $500,000 operating loan from RoyNat Inc. It was hoped that this loan, combined with the operating line of $2.5 million from the bank, would permit the company to weather its fiscal storm. In March 1990, the bank took the position that the companies were in breach of certain requirements under their loan agreements, and warned that if the difficulties were not rectified the bank would not continue as the company's lender. Mr. Patrick Johnson, the president of both companies, attempted to respond to these concerns in a detailed letter to the bank dated March 15, 1990. The response did not placate the bank. In May 1990, the bank called its loan and made a demand for immediate payment. Mr. Spencer, for the bank, wrote: "We consider your financial condition continues to be critical and we are not prepared to delay further making formal demand." He went on to indicate that, subject to further deterioration in the companies' fiscal position, the bank was prepared to delay acting on its security until June 1, 1990.

As of May 1990, Mr. Johnson, to the bank's knowledge, was actively seeking alternative funding to replace the bank. At the same time, he was trying to convince the union which represented the workers employed at both plants to assist in a co-operative effort to keep the plants operational during the hard times. The union had agreed to discuss amendment of the collective bargaining agreement to facilitate the continued operation of the companies.

The June 1, 1990 deadline set by the bank passed without incident. Mr. Johnson continued to search for new financing. A potential lender was introduced to Mr. Spencer of the bank on August 13, 1990, and it appeared that the bank, through Mr. Spencer, was favourably impressed with this potential lender. However, on August 27, 1990, the bank decided to take action to protect its position. Coopers & Lybrand was appointed by the bank as receiver-manager under the terms of the security agreements with the companies. The companies denied the receiver access to their plants. The bank then moved before the Honourable Mr. Justice E. Saunders for an order giving the receiver possession of the premises occupied by the companies. On August 27, 1990, after hearing argument from counsel for the bank and the companies, Mr. Justice Saunders refused to install the receivers and made the following interim order:

1. THIS COURT ORDERS that the receiver be allowed access to the property to monitor the operations of the defendants but shall not take steps to realize on the security of The Bank of Nova Scotia until further Order of the Court.

2. THIS COURT ORDERS that the defendants shall be entitled to remain in possession and to carry on business in the ordinary course until further Order of this Court.

3. THIS COURT ORDERS that until further order the Bank of Nova Scotia shall not take steps to notify account debtors of the defendants for the purpose of collecting outstanding

accounts receivable. This Order does not restrict The Bank of Nova Scotia from dealing with accounts receivable of the defendants received by it.

4. THIS COURT ORDERS that the motion is otherwise adjourned to a date to be fixed.

The notice of motion placed before Saunders J by the bank referred to "an intended action" by the bank. It does not appear that the bank took any further steps in connection with this "intended action."

Having resisted the bank's efforts to assume control of the affairs of the companies on August 27, 1990, and realizing that their operations could cease within a matter of days, the companies turned to the *Companies' Creditors Arrangement Act*, RSC 1985, c. C-36 (the "Act"), in an effort to hold the bank at bay while attempting to reorganize their finances. Finlayson JA has described the companies' efforts to qualify under that Act, the two appearances before the Honourable Mr. Justice Farley on August 31, 1990, and the appearances before the Honourable Mr. Justice Hoolihan in September and October 1990, which resulted in the orders challenged on this appeal.

II The Issues

The dispute between the bank and the companies when this application came before Hoolihan J was a straightforward one. The bank had determined that its best interests would be served by the immediate execution of the rights it had under its various agreements with the companies. The bank's best interest was not met by the continued operation of the companies as going concerns. The companies and their other two substantial secured creditors considered that their interests required that the companies continue to operate, at least for a period which would enable the companies to place a plan of reorganization before its creditors.

All parties were pursuing what they perceived to be their commercial interests. To the bank, these interests entailed the "death" of the companies as operating entities. To the companies, these interests required "life support" for the companies through the provisions of the Act to permit a "last ditch" effort to save the companies and keep them in operation. The issues raised on this appeal can be summarized as follows:

(i) Did Hoolihan J err in holding that the companies were entitled to invoke the Act?

(ii) Did Hoolihan J err in exercising his discretion in directing that a meeting of creditors should be held under the Act?

(iii) Did Hoolihan J err in directing that the bank and RoyNat Inc. should be placed in the same class of creditors for the purposes of the Act?

(iv) Did Hoolihan J err in the terms of the interim orders he made pending the meeting of creditors and the submission to the court of a plan of reorganization?

III The Purpose and Scheme of the Act

Before turning to these issues, it is necessary to understand the purpose of the Act, and the scheme established by the Act for achieving that purpose. The Act first appeared in the midst of the Great Depression (SC 1932-33, c. 36). The Act was intended to provide a means whereby insolvent companies could avoid bankruptcy and continue as ongoing concerns through a reorganization of their financial obligations. The reorganization contemplated required the co-operation of the debtor companies' creditors and shareholders: *Re Avery Construction Co.*, 24 CBR 17, [1942] 4 DLR 558 (Ont. SC); Stanley E. Edwards, "Reorganizations Under the Companies' Creditors Arrangement Act" (1947), 25 *Can. Bar Rev.* 587, at pp. 592-93; David H. Goldman, "Reorganizations Under the Companies' Creditors Arrangement Act (Canada)" (1985), 55 CBR (NS) 36, at pp. 37-39.

The legislation is remedial in the purest sense in that it provides a means whereby the devastating social and economic effects of bankruptcy- or creditor-initiated termination of ongoing business operations can be avoided while a court-supervised attempt to reorganize the financial affairs of the debtor company is made.

The purpose of the Act was artfully put by Gibbs JA, speaking for the British Columbia Court of Appeal, in *Hongkong Bank of Canada v. Chef Ready Foods Ltd.*, an unreported judgment released October 29, 1990 [Doc. No. Vancouver CA12944, Carrothers, Cumming and Gibbs JJA, now reported [1991] 2 WWR 136, 51 BCLR (2d) 84], at pp. 11 and 6 [unreported, pp. 91 and 88 BCLR]. In referring to the purpose for which the Act was initially proclaimed, he said:

> Almost inevitably liquidation destroyed the shareholders' investment, yielded little by way of recovery to the creditors, and exacerbated the social evil of devastating levels of unemployment. The government of the day sought, through the CCAA ["the Act"], to create a regime whereby the principals of the company and the creditors could be brought together under the supervision of the court to attempt a reorganization or compromise or arrangement under which the company could continue in business.

In an earlier passage, His Lordship had said:

> The purpose of the CCAA is to facilitate the making of a compromise or arrangement between an insolvent debtor company and its creditors to the end that the company is able to continue in business.

Gibbs JA also observed (at p. 13) that the Act was designed to serve a "broad constituency of investors, creditors and employees." Because of that "broad constituency," the Court must, when considering applications brought under the Act, have regard not only to the individuals and organizations directly affected by the application, but also to the wider public interest. That interest is generally, but not always, served by permitting an attempt at reorganization: see S.E. Edwards, "Reorganizations Under the Companies' Creditors Arrangement Act," at p. 593.

The Act must be given a wide and liberal construction so as to enable it to effectively serve this remedial purpose: *Interpretation Act*, RSC 1985, c. I-21, s. 12; *Hongkong Bank of Canada v. Chef Ready Foods Ltd., supra*, at p. 14 [unreported, p. 92 BCLR].

The Act is available to all insolvent companies, provided the requirements of s. 3 of the Act are met. ...

A debtor company, or a creditor of that company, invokes the Act by way of summary application to the Court under s. 4 or s. 5 of the Act. For present purposes, s. 5 is the relevant section: ...

Section 5 does not require that the Court direct a meeting of creditors to consider a proposed plan. The Court's power to do so is discretionary. There will no doubt be cases where no order will be made, even though the debtor company qualifies under s. 3 of the Act.

If the Court determines that a meeting should be called, the creditors must be placed into classes for the purpose of that meeting. The significance of this classification process is made apparent by s. 6 of the Act: ...

If the plan of reorganization is approved by the creditors as required by s. 6, it must then be presented to the Court. Once again, the Court must exercise a discretion, and determine whether it will approve the plan of reorganization. In exercising that discretion, the Court is concerned not only with whether the appropriate majority has approved the plan at a meeting held in accordance with the Act and the order of the Court, but also with whether the plan is a fair and reasonable one: *Re Northland Properties Ltd.* (1988), 73 CBR (NS) 175 at 182-185 (SC), aff'd 73 CBR (NS) 195, [1989] 3 WWR 363, 34 BCLR (2d) 122 (CA).

If the Court chooses to exercise its discretion in favour of calling a meeting of creditors for the purpose of considering a plan of reorganization, the Act provides that the rights and remedies available to creditors, the debtor company, and others during the period between the making of the initial order and the consideration of the proposed plan may be suspended or otherwise controlled by the Court.

Section 11 gives a court wide powers to make any interim orders: ...

Viewed in its totality, the Act gives the Court control over the initial decision to put the reorganization plan before the creditors, the classification of creditors for the purpose of considering the plan, conduct affecting the debtor company pending consideration of that plan, and the ultimate acceptability of any plan agreed upon by the creditors. The Act envisions that the rights and remedies of individual creditors, the debtor company and others may be sacrificed, at least temporarily, in an effort to serve the greater good by arriving at some acceptable reorganization which allows the debtor company to continue in operation: *Icor Oil & Gas Co. v. Canadian Imperial Bank of Canada* (1989), 102 AR 161 at p. 165 (QB).

IV Did Hoolihan J Err in Holding that the Debtor Companies Were Entitled to Invoke the Act?

The appellant advances three arguments in support of its contention that Elan and Nova Inc. were not entitled to seek relief under the Act. It argues first that the debentures issued by the companies after August 17, 1990, were "shams" and did not fulfil the requirements of s. 3 of the Act. The appellant next contends that the issuing of the debentures by the companies contravened their agreements with the bank, in which they undertook not to further encumber the assets of the companies without the consent of the bank. Lastly, the appellant maintains that once the bank had appointed a receiver-manager over the affairs of the companies on August 27, 1990, the companies had no power to create further indebtedness by way of debentures or to bring an application on behalf of the companies under the Act.

(i) Section 3 and "Instant" Trust Deeds

The debentures issued in August 1990, after the bank had moved to install a receiver-manager, were issued solely and expressly for the purpose of meeting the requirements of s. 3 of the Act. Indeed, it took the companies two attempts to meet those requirements. The debentures had no commercial purpose. The transactions did, however, involve true loans in the sense that moneys were advanced and debt was created. Appropriate and valid trust deeds were also issued.

In my view, it is inappropriate to refer to these transactions as "shams." They are neither false nor counterfeit, but rather are exactly what they appear to be, transactions made to meet jurisdictional requirements of the Act so as to permit an application for reorganization under the Act. Such transactions are apparently well known to the commercial Bar: B. O'Leary, "A Review of the Companies' Creditors Arrangement Act" (1987), 4 *Nat. Insolvency Rev.* 38, at p. 39; C. Ham, "'Instant' Trust Deeds Under the C.C.A.A." (1988), 2 *Commercial Insolvency Reporter* 25; G.B. Morawetz, "Emerging Trends in the Use of the Companies' Creditors Arrangement Act" (1990), Proceedings, First Annual General Meeting and Conference of the Insolvency Institute of Canada.

Mr. Ham writes, at pp. 25 and 30:

> Consequently, some companies have recently sought to bring themselves within the ambit of the CCAA by creating "instant" trust deeds, i.e., trust deeds which are created solely for the purpose of enabling them to take advantage of the CCAA.

Applications under the Act involving the use of "instant" trust deeds have been before the Courts on a number of occasions. In no case has any court held that a company cannot gain access to the Act by creating a debt which meets the requirements of s. 3 for the express purpose of qualifying under the Act. In most cases, the use of these "instant" trust deeds has been acknowledged without comment.

The decision of Chief Justice Richard in *Re United Maritime Fishermen Co-op.* (1988), 67 CBR (NS) 44, 84 NBR (2d) 415, 214 APR 415 (QB), varied on reconsideration (1988), 68 CBR (NS) 170, 87 NBR (2d) 333, 221 APR 333 (QB), at 55-56 [67 CBR], speaks directly to the use of "instant" trust deeds. The Chief Justice refused to read any words into s. 3 of the Act which would limit the availability of the Act depending on the point at which, or the purpose for which, the debenture or bond and accompanying trust deed were created. He accepted [at p. 56 CBR] the debtor company's argument that the Act:

> does not impose any time restraints on the creation of the conditions as set out in s. 3 of the Act, nor does it contain any prohibition against the creation of the conditions set out in s. 3 for the purpose of obtaining jurisdiction.

It should, however, be noted that in *Re United Maritime Fishermen Co-op.*, *supra*, the debt itself was not created for the purpose of qualifying under the Act. The bond and the trust deed, however, were created for that purpose. The case is therefore factually distinguishable from the case at Bar.

The Court of Appeal reversed the ruling of the Chief Justice ((1988), 69 CBR (NS) 161, 51 DLR (4th) 618, 88 NBR (2d) 253, 224 APR 253) on the basis that the bonds required by s. 3 of the Act had not been issued when the application was made, so that on a precise reading of the words of s. 3 the company did not qualify. The Court did not go on to consider, had the bonds been properly issued, the company would have been entitled to invoke the Act. Hoyt JA, for the majority, did, however, observe without comment that the trust deeds had been created specifically for the purpose of bringing an application under the Act.

The judgment of MacKinnon J in *Re Stephanie's Fashions Ltd.*, unreported, Doc. No. Vancouver A893427, released January 24, 1990 (BCSC) [now reported 1 CBR (3d) 248], is factually on all fours with the present case. In that case, as in this one, it was acknowledged that the sole purpose for creating the debt was to effect compliance with s. 3 of the Act. After considering the judgment of Chief Justice Richard in *Re United Maritime Fishermen Co-op., supra*, MacKinnon J held, at p. 251:

> The reason for creating the trust deed is not for the usual purposes of securing a debt but, when one reads it, on its face, it does that. I find that it is a genuine trust deed and not a fraud, and that the petitioners have complied with s. 3 of the statute.

Re Metals & Alloys Co. (16 February 1990) is a recent example of a case in this jurisdiction in which "instant" trust deeds were successfully used to bring a company within the Act. The company issued debentures for the purpose of permitting the company to qualify under the Act, so as to provide it with an opportunity to prepare and submit a reorganization plan. The company then applied for an order, seeking, *inter alia*, a declaration that the debtor company was a corporation within the meaning of the Act. Houlden JA, hearing the matter at first instance, granted the declaration request in an order dated February 16, 1990. No reasons were given. It does not appear that the company's qualifications were challenged before Houlden JA; however, the nature of the debentures issued and the purpose for their issue was fully disclosed in the material before him. The requirements of s. 3 of the Act are jurisdictional in nature, and the consent of the parties cannot vest a court with jurisdiction it does not have. One must conclude that Houlden JA was satisfied that "instant" trust deeds suffice for the purposes of s. 3 of the Act.

A similar conclusion is implicit in the reasons of the British Columbia Court of Appeal in *Hongkong Bank of Canada v. Chef Ready Foods Ltd.* In that case, a debt of $50, with an accompanying debenture and trust deed, was created specifically to enable the company to make application under the Act. The Court noted that the debt was created solely for that purpose in an effort to forestall an attempt by the bank to liquidate the assets of the debtor company. The Court went on to deal with the merits, and to dismiss an appeal from an order granting a stay pending a reorganization meeting. The Court could not have reached the merits without first concluding that the $50 debt created by the company met the requirements of s. 3 of the Act.

The weight of authority is against the appellant. Counsel for the appellant attempts to counter that authority by reference to the remarks of the Minister of Justice when s. 3 was introduced as an amendment to the Act in the 1952-53 sittings of Parliament (House of Commons Debates, 1-2 Eliz. II (1952-53), vol. II, pp. 1268-69). The interpretation of words found in a statute, by reference to speeches made in Parliament at the time legislation is introduced, has never found favour in our Courts: *Reference Re Residential Tenancies Act (Ontario)*, [1981] 1 SCR 714, 123 DLR (3d) 554, 37 NR 138, at 721 [SCR], 561 [DLR]. Nor, with respect to Mr. Newbould's able argument, do I find the words of the Minister of Justice at the time the present s. 3 was introduced to be particularly illuminating. He indicated that the amendment to the Act left companies with complex financial structures free to resort to the Act, but that it excluded companies which had only unsecured mercantile creditors. The Minister does not comment on the intended effect of the amendment on the myriad situations between those two extremes. This case is one such situation. These debtor companies had complex secured debt structures, but those debts were not, prior to the issuing of the debentures in August 1990, in the form contemplated by s. 3 of the Act. Like Richard CJQB in *Re United Maritime Fishermen Co-op., supra*, at pp. 52-53, I am not persuaded that the comments of the Minister of Justice assist in interpreting s. 3 of the Act in this situation.

The words of s. 3 are straightforward. They require that the debtor company have, at the time an application is made, an outstanding debenture or bond issued under a trust deed. No more is needed. Attempts to qualify those words are not only contrary to the wide reading the Act deserves, but can raise intractable problems as to what qualifications or modifications should be read into the Act. Where there is a legitimate debt which fits the criteria set out in s. 3, I see no purpose in denying a debtor company resort to the Act because the debt and the accompanying documentation was created for the specific purpose of bringing the application. It must be remembered that qualification under s. 3 entitles the debtor company to nothing more than consideration under the Act. Qualification under s. 3 does not mean that relief under the Act will be granted. The circumstances surrounding the creation of the debt needed to meet the s. 3 requirement may well have a bearing on how a court exercises its discretion at various stages of the application, but they do not alone interdict resort to the Act.

In holding that "instant" trust deeds can satisfy the requirements of s. 3 of the Act, I should not be taken as concluding that debentures or bonds which are truly shams, in that they do not reflect a transaction which actually occurred and do not create a real debt owed by the company, will suffice. Clearly, they will not. I do not, however, equate the two. One is a tactical device used to gain the potential advantages of the Act. The other is a fraud.

Nor does my conclusion that "instant" trust deeds can bring a debtor company within the Act exclude considerations of the good faith of the debtor company in seeking the protection of the Act. A debtor company should not be allowed to use the Act for any purpose other than to attempt a legitimate reorganization. If the purpose of the application is to advantage one creditor over another, to defeat the legitimate interests of creditors, to delay the inevitable failure of the debtor company, or for some other improper purpose, the Court has the means available to it, apart entirely from s. 3 of the Act, to prevent misuse of the Act. In cases where the debtor company acts in bad faith, the Court may refuse to order a meeting of creditors, it may deny interim protection, it may vary interim protection initially given when the bad faith is shown, or it may refuse to sanction any plan which emanates from the meeting of the creditors: see Lawrence J. Crozier, "Good Faith and the Companies' Creditors Arrangement Act" (1989), 15 *Can. Bus. LJ* 89.

(ii) Section 3 and the Prior Agreement with the Bank Limiting Creation of New Debt

The appellant also argues that the debentures did not meet the requirements of s. 3 of the Act because they were issued in contravention of a security agreement made between the companies and the bank. Assuming that the debentures were issued in contravention of that agreement, I do not understand how that contravention affects the status of the debentures for the purposes of s. 3 of the Act. The bank may well have an action against the debtor company for issuing the debentures, and it may have remedies against the holders of the debentures if they attempted to collect on their debt or enforce their security. Neither possibility, however, negates the existence of the debentures and the related trust deeds.

Section 3 does not contemplate an inquiry into the effectiveness or enforceability of the s. 3 debentures, as against other creditors, as a condition precedent to qualification under the Act. Such inquiries may play a role in a judge's determination as to what orders, if any, should be made under the Act.

(iii) Section 3 and the Appointment of a Receiver-Manager

The third argument made by the bank relies on its installation of a receiver-manager in both companies prior to the issue of the debentures. I agree with Finlayson JA that the placement of a receiver, either by operation of the terms of an agreement or by court order, effectively removes those formerly in control of the company from that position, and vests that control in the receiver-manager: *Alberta Treasury Branches v. Hat Development Ltd.* (1988), 71 CBR (NS) 264, 64 Alta. LR (2d) 17 (QB), aff'd without deciding this point (1989), 65 Alta. LR (2d) 374 (CA). I cannot, however, agree with his interpretation of the order of Saunders J. I read that order as effectively turning the receiver into a monitor with rights of access, but with no authority beyond that. The operation of the business is specifically returned to the companies. The situation created by the order of Saunders J can usefully be compared to that which existed when the application was made in *Hat Development Ltd.* Forsyth J, at p. 268 CBR, states:

> The receiver-manager in this case and indeed in almost all cases is charged by the court with the responsibility of managing the affairs of a corporation. It is true that it is appointed pursuant, in this case, to the existence of secured indebtedness and at the behest of a secured creditor to realize on its security and retire the indebtedness. Nonetheless, this receiver-manager was court-appointed and not by virtue of an instrument. As a court-appointed receiver it owed the obligation and the duty to the court to account from time to time and to come before the court for the purposes of having some of its decisions ratified or for receiving advice and direction. *It is empowered by the court to manage the affairs of the company and it is completely inconsistent with that function to suggest that some residual power lies in the hands of the directors of the company to create further indebtedness of the company and thus interfere, however slightly, with the receiver-manager's ability to manage.* [Emphasis added.]

After the order of Saunders J, the receiver-manager in this case was not obligated to manage the companies. Indeed, it was forbidden from doing so. The creation of the "instant" trust deeds and the application under the Act did not interfere in any way with any power or authority the receiver-manager had after the order of Saunders J was made.

I also find it somewhat artificial to suggest that the presence of a receiver-manager served to vitiate the orders of Hoolihan J. Unlike many applications under s. 5 of the Act, the proceedings before Hoolihan J were not ex parte and he was fully aware of the existence of the receiver-manager, the order of Saunders J, and the arguments based on the presence of the receiver-manager. Clearly, Hoolihan J considered it appropriate to proceed with a plan of reorganization despite the presence of the order of Saunders J. Indeed, in his initial order he provided that the order of Saunders J "remains extant." Hoolihan J did not, as I do not, see that order as an impediment to the application or the granting of relief under the Act. Had he considered that the receiver-manager was in control of the affairs of the company, he could have varied the order of Saunders J to permit the applications under the Act to be made by the companies: *Hat Development Ltd.*, at pp. 268-69 CBR. It is clear to me that he would have done so had he felt it necessary. If the installation of the receiver-manager is to be viewed as a bar to an application under this Act, and if the orders of Hoolihan J were otherwise appropriate, I would order that the order of Saunders J should be varied to permit the creation of the debentures and the trust deeds and the bringing of this application by the companies. I take this power to exist by the combined effect of s. 14(2) of the Act and s. 144(1) of the *Courts of Justice Act, 1984*, SO 1984, c. 11.

In my opinion, the debentures and "instant" trust deeds created in August 1990 sufficed to bring the company within the requirements of s. 3 of the Act, even if in issuing those debentures the companies breached a prior agreement with the bank. I am also satisfied that, given the terms of the order of Saunders J, the existence of a receiver-manager installed by the bank did not preclude the application under s. 3 of the Act.

V Did Hoolihan J Err in Exercising his Discretion in Favour of Directing that a Creditors' Meeting be Held to Consider the Proposed Plan of Reorganization?

As indicated earlier, the Act provides a number of points at which the Court must exercise its discretion. I am concerned with the initial exercise of discretion contemplated by s. 5 of the Act, by which the Court may order a meeting of creditors for purposes of considering a plan of reorganization. Hoolihan J exercised that discretion in favour of the debtor companies. The factors relevant to the exercise of that discretion are as variable as the fact situations which may give rise to the application. Finlayson JA has concentrated on one such factor, the chance that the plan, if put before a properly constituted meeting of the creditors, could gain the required approval. I agree that the feasibility of the plan is a relevant and significant factor to be considered in determining whether to order a meeting of creditors: S.E. Edwards, "Reorganizations Under the Companies' Creditors Arrangement Act," at pp. 594-95. I would not, however, impose a heavy burden on the debtor company to establish the likelihood of ultimate success from the outset. As the Act will often be the last refuge for failing companies, it is to be expected that many of the proposed plans of reorganization will involve variables and contingencies which will make the plan's ultimate acceptability to the creditors and the Court very uncertain at the time the initial application is made.

On the facts before Hoolihan J, there were several factors which supported the exercise of his discretion in favour of directing a meeting of the creditors. These included the apparent support of two of the three substantial secured creditors, the companies' continued operation, and the prospect (disputed by the bank) that the companies' fortunes would take a turn for the better in the near future, the companies' ongoing efforts—that eventually met with some success—to find alternate [*sic*] financing, and the number of people depending on the operation of the company for their livelihood. There were also a number of factors pointing in the other direction, the most significant of which was the likelihood that a plan of reorganization acceptable to the bank could not be developed.

I see the situation which presented itself to Hoolihan J as capable of a relatively straightforward risk-benefit analysis. If the s. 5 order had been refused by Hoolihan J, it was virtually certain that the operation of the companies would have ceased immediately. There would have been immediate economic and social damage to those who worked at the plants, and those who depended on those who worked at the plants for their well-being. This kind of damage cannot be ignored, especially when it occurs in small communities like those in which these plants are located. A refusal to grant the application would also have put the investments of the various creditors, with the exception of the bank, at substantial risk. Finally, there would have been obvious financial damage to the owner of the companies. Balanced against these costs inherent in refusing the order would be the benefit to the bank, which would then have been in a position to realize on its security in accordance with its agreements with the companies.

The granting of the s. 5 order was not without its costs. It has denied the bank the rights it had bargained for as part of its agreement to lend substantial amounts of money to the companies. Further, according to the bank, the order has put the bank at risk of having its loans become undersecured because of the diminishing value of the accounts receivable and inventory which it holds as security and because of the ever-increasing size of the companies' debt to the bank. These costs must be measured against the potential benefit to all concerned if a successful plan of reorganization could be developed and implemented.

As I see it, the key to this analysis rests in the measurement of the risk to the bank inherent in the granting of the s. 5 order. If there was a real risk that the loan made by the bank would become undersecured during the operative period of the s. 5 order, I would be inclined to hold that the bank should not have that risk forced on it by the Court. However, I am unable to see that the bank is in any real jeopardy. The value of the security held by the bank appears to be well in excess of the size of its loan on the initial application. In his affidavit, Mr. Gibbons of Coopers & Lybrand asserted that the companies had overstated their cash flow projections, that the value of the inventory could diminish if customers of the companies looked to alternate sources for their product, and that the value of the accounts receivable could decrease if customers began to claim set-offs against those receivables. On the record before me, these appear to be no more than speculative possibilities. The bank has had access to all of the companies' financial data on an ongoing basis since the order of Hoolihan J was made almost 2 months ago. Nothing was placed before this Court to suggest that any of the possibilities described above had come to pass.

Even allowing for some overestimation by the companies of the value of the security held by the bank, it would appear that the bank holds security valued at approximately $4 million for a loan that was, as of the hearing of this appeal, about $2.3 million. The order of Hoolihan J was to terminate no later than November 14, 1990. I am not satisfied that the bank ran any real risk of having the amount of the loan exceed the value of the security by that date. It is also worth noting that the order under appeal provided that any party could apply to terminate the order at any point prior to November 14. This provision provided further protection for the bank in the event that it wished to make the case that its loan was at risk because of the deteriorating value of its security.

Even though the chances of a successful reorganization were not good, I am satisfied that the benefits flowing from the making of the s. 5 order exceeded the risk inherent in that order. In my view, Hoolihan J properly exercised his discretion in directing that a meeting of creditors should be held pursuant to s. 5 of the Act.

VI Did Hoolihan J Err in Directing that the Bank and RoyNat Inc.
Should be Placed in the Same Class for the Purposes of the Act?

I agree with Finlayson JA that the bank and RoyNat Inc., the two principal creditors, should not have been placed in the same class of secured creditors for the purposes of ss. 5

and 6 of the Act. Their interests are not only different, they are opposed. The classification scheme created by Hoolihan J effectively denied the bank any control over any plan of reorganization.

To accord with the principles found in the cases cited by Finlayson JA, the secured creditors should have been grouped as follows:

—Class 1: The City of Chatham and the Village of Glencoe

—Class 2: The Bank of Nova Scotia

—Class 3: RoyNat Inc., Ontario Development Corporation, and those holding debentures issued by the company on August 29 and 31, 1990.

VII Did Hoolihan J Err in Making the Interim Orders He Made?

Hoolihan J made a number of orders designed to control the conduct of all of the parties, pending the creditors' meeting and the placing of a plan of reorganization before the Court. The first order was made on September 11, 1990, and was to expire on or before October 24, 1990. Subsequent orders varied the terms of the initial order somewhat, and extended its effective date until November 14, 1990.

These orders imposed the following conditions pending the meeting:

(a) all proceedings with respect to the debtor companies should be stayed, including any action by the bank to realize on its security;

(b) the bank could not reduce its loan by applying incoming receipts to those debts;

(c) the bank was to be the sole banker for the companies;

(d) the companies could carry on business in the normal course, subject to certain very specific restrictions;

(e) a licensed trustee was to be appointed to monitor the business operations of the companies and to report to the creditors on a regular basis; and

(f) any party could apply to terminate the interim orders, and the orders would be terminated automatically if the companies defaulted on any of the obligations imposed on them by the interim orders.

The orders placed significant restrictions on the bank for a 2-month period, but balanced those restrictions with provisions limiting the debtor companies' activities, and giving the bank ongoing access to up-to-date financial information concerning the companies. The bank was also at liberty to return to the Court to request any variation in the interim orders which changes in financial circumstances might merit.

These orders were made under the wide authority granted to the court by s. 11 of the Act. L.W. Houlden and C.H. Morawetz, in *Bankruptcy Law of Canada*, 3d ed. (Toronto: Carswell, 1989), at pp. 2-102 to 2-103, describe the purpose of the section:

> The legislation is intended to have wide scope and allows a judge to make orders which will effectively maintain the status quo for a period while the insolvent company attempts to gain the approval of its creditors for a proposed arrangement which will enable the company to remain in operation for what is, hopefully, the future benefit of both the company and its creditors. This aim is facilitated by s. 11 of the Act, which enables the court to restrain further proceedings in any action, suit or proceeding against the company upon such terms as the court sees fit.

A similar sentiment appears in *Hongkong Bank of Canada v. Chef Ready Foods Ltd.* Gibbs JA, in discussing the scope of s. 11, said at p. 7 [unreported, pp. 88-89 BCLR]:

When a company has recourse to the CCAA the court is called upon to play a kind of supervisory role to preserve the status quo and to move the process along to the point where a compromise or arrangement is approved or it is evident that the attempt is doomed to failure. Obviously time is critical. Equally obviously, if the attempt at compromise or arrangement is to have any prospect of success, there must be a means of holding the creditors at bay, hence the powers vested in the court under s. 11.

Similar views of the scope of the power to make interim orders covering the period when reorganization is being attempted are found in *Meridian Developments Inc. v. Toronto-Dominion Bank; Meridian Developments Inc. v. Nu-West Ltd.*, 52 CBR (NS) 109, [1984] 5 WWR 215, 32 Alta. LR (2d) 150, 11 DLR (4th) 576, 53 AR 39 (QB) at 114-118 [CBR]; *Norcen Energy Resources Ltd. v. Oakwood Petroleums Ltd.* (1988), 72 CBR (NS) 1, 63 Alta. LR (2d) 361, 92 AR 81 (QB) at 12-15 [CBR]; *Quintette Coal Ltd. v. Nippon Steel Corp.*, an unreported judgment of Thackray J, released June 18, 1990 [since reported (1990), 47 BCLR (2d) 193 (SC)], at pp. 5-9 [pp. 196-98 BCLR]; and B. O'Leary, "A Review of the Companies' Creditors Arrangement Act," at p. 41.

The interim orders made by Hoolihan J are all within the wide authority created by s. 11 of the Act. The orders were crafted to give the company the opportunity to continue in operation, pending its attempt to reorganize, while at the same time providing safeguards to the creditors, including the bank, during that same period. I find no error in the interim relief granted by Hoolihan J.

VIII Conclusion

In the result, I would allow the appeal in part, vacate the order of Hoolihan J of October 18, 1990, insofar as it purports to settle the class of creditors for the purpose of the Act, and I would substitute an order establishing the three classes referred to in Part VI of these reasons. I would not disturb any of the other orders made by Hoolihan J.

Appeal allowed.

NOTES AND QUESTIONS

1) *Elan v. Comiskey* is a leading case on the requirements for initiating proceedings under the CCAA as well as many other aspects of the Act. It is of particular interest because of the contrasting philosophies of Finlayson and Doherty JJA with respect to the interpretation and fleshing out of the skeletal provisions of the Act. It is fair to say that Doherty JA's strong communitarian approach is much closer to the prevailing judicial sentiment than Finlayson JA's narrower creditor oriented analysis. Are future courts likely to be more restrained in the face of the more rule based approach in the BIA? Will they interpret Parliament's decision to retain both statutory regimes as implicit approval of their creative approach in applying the CCAA provisions—and adding very generous glosses to them?

2) The parliamentary history of s. 3 of the CCAA shows that instant trust deeds and debentures were never contemplated. If they had been, why would Parliament have

bothered with the requirements of trust deeds and debentures to begin with? Were the courts right then to ignore the statutory intent or were they merely correcting a historical anachronism in the face of a serious recession? It is almost certain that the trust deed and debentures requirement will be deleted in the proposed 1995 amendments to the CCAA. They may be replaced with a requirement that only business debtors with assets or liabilities over a minimum threshhold (e.g., $20 million) will be entitled to use the CCAA. Can you see a justification for this two-tiered approach to insolvents' reorganizations?

3) Finlayson JA's judgment raises an important issue about the effect of a receiver-manager being appointed by the secured creditor before the filing of a CCAA application. Is it correct to say that because management's powers are transferred to the receiver-manager this necessarily precludes the debtor's directors from authorizing a CCAA application? Does the security agreement authorizing the secured party to appoint a receiver-manager on the debtor's default contemplate the receiver-manager making a CCAA application? Would it be in the secured party's interest to do so?

Assuming the appointment of a receiver-manager does override the directors' powers, was Doherty JA right in holding that Hoolihan J's order could "suspend" the receiver-manager's powers? Can a court exercise *any* powers under the CCAA (express or implicit) until a proper application has been filed by competent applicants?

The *Quintette* ex parte order which follows is typical of the kind of order frequently made by the court following a s. 4 or s. 5 CCAA application. Examine the order carefully and determine what lessons it teaches us about the courts' interpretation of the CCAA and their willingness to exercise a broad gap-filling function. Consider also the following questions:

1) Do ss. 4-5 authorize the court to make a "holding" order pending the debtor's preparation of a reorganization proposal? (*Cf.* the filing of a notice of intention under s. 50.1 of the BIA.)

2) Why do the courts appoint a monitor under such an order. If the monitor is only a watchdog without managerial or executive powers can he/she do an effective job?

3) Does the ex parte order provide any protection to secured creditors to avoid erosion of their security or use of proceeds from the disposition of collateral (e.g., sale of inventory) for unauthorized purposes? Should the CCAA adopt a doctrine of "adequate protection" of secured creditors' rights similar to that found in s. 362(d) of the US Code?

4) The ex parte order contains a sweeping prohibition of third party proceedings and acts likely to prejudice the rescue operation. How far is it supported by the language of s. 11 of the CCAA? What about prohibitions on cancellation of contracts with the debtor and supension of vital services supplied by utilities and such like? Do they fall within s. 11 as well or are these further examples of judicial creativity? What lessons do we derive from the fact that the executory contract provisions in s. 65.1 and s. 65.2 of the BIA are considerably more circumscribed? (On the influence of s. 65.2 on future court orders affecting the repudation of realty leases, see *Re Dylex Ltd., infra.*)

Re Quintette Coal Limited, Ex Parte Order

British Columbia Supreme Court
June 13, 1990

In the Supreme Court of British Columbia

In the Matter of the Companies' Creditors Arrangement Act
RSC 1985, c. C-36
and
In the Matter of the Company Act, RSBC 1979, c., 59
and
In the Matter of Quintette Coal Limited

Order
Before the Honourable Mr. Justice Thackray
Wednesday, the 13th day of June, 1990

UPON THE EX PARTE APPLICATION of the Petitioner, Quintette Coal Limited, coming on for hearing at Vancouver this day; AND UPON READING the Petition and the Affidavits of Bruce McConkey filed herein; AND UPON HEARING Dave F. Tysoe, Esq., Counsel for the Petitioner herein:

THIS COURT DECLARES that the Petitioner is a corporation to which the Companies' Creditors Arrangement Act, R.S.C. 1985, c. C-36, ("CCAA") applies.

AND THIS COURT ORDERS that the Petitioner be and is hereby authorized to file with this Court within six months of the date of this order or within such other period as this Court may order, a formal plan of compromise or arrangement between the Petitioner and its creditors and (if appropriate) its shareholders (the "Reorganization Plan");

AND THIS COURT FURTHER ORDERS that the Petitioner call meetings of classes of its creditors and (if appropriate) its shareholders (the "Meetings");

AND THIS COURT FURTHER ORDERS that the Petitioner may file the Reorganization Plan and the Notices of the Meetings with this Court by way of Affidavit;

AND THIS COURT FURTHER ORDERS that all proceedings taken or that might be taken in respect of the Petitioner under the Bankruptcy Act and the Winding-up Act or either of them be stayed;

AND THIS COURT FURTHER ORDERS that any further proceeding in any actions, suit or proceeding against the Petitioner be restrained;

AND THIS COURT FURTHER ORDERS that no suit, action or other proceeding shall be proceeded with or commenced against the Petitioner;

AND THIS COURT FURTHER ORDERS that notwithstanding anything herein contained, a defendant in any action, suit or proceeding may hereafter file a counterclaim against the Petitioner and prosecute any such counterclaim or any counterclaim against the

Petitioner pending at the date hereof, provided that any such defendant may not execute on a judgment on any such counterclaim;

AND THIS COURT FURTHER ORDERS that notwithstanding anything herein contained the arbitration proceeding between Nippon Steel Corporation, Nippon Kokan Kabushiki Kaisha, Kawasaki Steel Corporation, Sumitomo Metal Industries Ltd., Kobe Steel Ltd., Nisshin Steel Co. Ltd., Nakayama Steel Works, Ltd., Mitsubishi Chemical Industries Ltd., Godo Steel, Ltd., and Mitsui Mining Company, Limited (the "Japanese Coal Purchasers") and the Petitioner (including, without limitation, any applications for the correction of the arbitral award and for additional arbitral awards) shall not be stayed, but that no steps to have the arbitral award recognized or enforced may be taken;

AND THIS COURT FURTHER ORDERS that the right of any person, firm or company to realize upon or otherwise deal with any right of property of the Petitioner or any security held by the person, firm or company on any of the undertaking, property or assets of the Petitioner be and the same is postponed;

AND THIS COURT FURTHER ORDERS that all creditors of the Petitioner be enjoined from making demand for payment upon the Petitioner or upon any guarantor of an obligation of the Petitioner until further Order of this Court;

AND THIS COURT FURTHER ORDERS that no creditor of the Petitioner may exercise any right of set-off against any debts owed to the Petitioner including, without limitation, monies owed in respect of the sale of the Petitioner's coal to the Japanese Coal Purchasers or any member thereof and monies on deposit with any bank or other accounts of the Petitioner;

AND THIS COURT FURTHER ORDERS that all persons, firms and companies having agreements with the Petitioner whether written or oral for the supply of goods or sevices to the Petitioner (including, without limitation, leases of goods) be enjoined until further Order of this Court from terminating, determining or cancelling such agreements and that such persons, firms and companies shall continue to supply the goods or services pursuant to the provisions of such agreements so long as the Petitioner pays the prices or charges under the agreements for such goods or services incurred after the date of this Order when the same become due in accordance with the payment terms negotiated by this Petitioner from time to time, and without limiting the generality of the foregoing, that all persons, firms and companies be enjoined until further Order of this Court from discontinuing, interfering or cutting off any utility (including telephone service at present telephone numbers), the furnishing of oil, gas, water, heat or spare parts, equipment or other supplies and the supply of transportation, loading, unloading or storage services provided to the Petitioner so long as the Petitioner pays the prices or charges for such goods and services incurred after the date of this Order when the same become due in accordance with the payment terms negotiated by the Petitioner from time to time;

AND THIS COURT FURTHER ORDERS that all persons, firms and companies having other agreements with the Petitioner (including, without limitation, the Japanese Coal Purchasers) be enjoined from terminating, determining or cancelling such agreements without the written consent of the Petitioner or leave of this Court and that all such persons, firms and companies perform and observe the terms, conditions and provisions contained in such agreements on their part to be performed or observed;

AND THIS COURT FURTHER ORDERS that all obligations incurred by the Petitioner after the date of this Order including, without limitation, all obligations to persons, firms and companies who advance or supply goods (including those under purchase orders outstanding at the date of this Order) or services to the Petitioner after the date of this Order (but excluding any interest on the Petitioner's existing loans, other than employee housing loans, and any other obligations incurred prior to the date of this Order) may be paid or otherwise satisfied by the Petitioner and, without limiting the generality of the foregoing, that the Petitioner may pay all wages, source deductions, benefits, severance pay and other monies owing to or in respect of its employees and their housing, property taxes owing by the Petitioner and the indebtedness owed to such of the Petitioner's trade creditors who are owed less than $200,000 as at the date of this Order, whether or not the same are payable or accrue before or after the date of this Order;

AND THIS COURT FURTHER ORDERS that Deloitte and Touche Inc., licensed trustee, be appointed until further Order of this Court as Monitor of the undertaking, property and assets of the Petitioner with the following powers and duties:
  a) generally, to observe and report to the Court on a monthly basis the financial and business affairs of the Petitioner, based upon information to be provided by the Petitioner to the Monitor, and consistent with the efforts of the Petitioner to carry on its business and reorganize and restructure its affairs; and
  b) particularly, to receive the following information from the Petitioner:
      i) monthly sales information;
      ii) monthly summaries of the Petitioner's cash receipts, cash disbursements, short term investments and bank balances;
      iii) monthly inventory balances as between the mine and the Ridley Island coal terminal; and
      iv) monthly financial statements of the Petitioner;
  c) to have access to all books of account of the Petitioner;
  d) to be at liberty to retain or appoint any agent or agents, including legal counsel, and to obtain such assistance from time to time as it may consider necessary in respect of its powers and duties hereunder; and

AND THIS COURT FURTHER ORDERS that the Monitor need not file security with this court for the due and proper performance of its powers and duties as Monitor;

AND THIS COURT FURTHER ORDERS that the Monitor be paid in respect of its remuneration, costs and expenses from time to time subject to the passing of such accounts before this Court and each amount so paid shall constitute an advance against such remuneration, cost and expenses;

AND THIS COURT FURTHER ORDERS that the Monitor shall be entitled to indemnity out of the property and assets of the Petitioner in priority to all creditors of the Petitioner in respect of its remuneration, costs and expenses;

AND THIS COURT FURTHER ORDERS that the Monitor shall report on a monthly basis to the parties who have entered an Appearance herein and the Monitor shall also report to such parties if it believes that there has been a materially adverse change in the operations, business or financial conditions of the Petitioner, provided that in so reporting, the Monitor shall endeavour to minimize the disclosure of confidential information;

AND THIS COURT FURTHER ORDERS that the Monitor do from time to time pass its accounts with this Court and for such purpose the said accounts shall be referred to a Master or Registrar of the Supreme Court of British Columbia;

AND THIS COURT FURTHER ORDERS that an officer of the Monitor be Chairman of the Meetings (the "Chairman");

AND THIS COURT FURTHER ORDERS that the Petitioner be at liberty to serve the Petition, this Order, the Reorganization Plan and Notices of the Meetings by mailing true copies thereof by prepaid post addressed to each of the Petitioner's creditors at their addresses shown on the records of the Petitioner and by publishing a notice thereof in an edition of the Vancouver Province;

AND THIS COURT FURTHER ORDERS that the Chairman shall, in due course, and prior to the final hearing of any application to sanction the Reorganization Plan, render to this Court an Affidavit verifying the actions taken and decisions reached at the Meetings;

AND THIS COURT FURTHER ORDERS that the Petitioner shall remain in possession of its undertaking, property and assets and shall continue to carry on its business and upon approval of the Re-organization [*sic*] Plan to implement the same according to its terms;

AND THIS COURT FURTHER ORDERS that in the event that the Reorganization Plan is not approved by the requisite majority when it is voted upon by the creditors of the Petitioner, the Petitioner shall be adjudged bankrupt and a receiving order under the Bankruptcy Act RSC 1985, c. B-3, shall be deemed to have been made against the Petitioner;

AND THIS COURT FURTHER ORDERS that this Order and any other Orders in these proceedings shall have full force and effect in all provinces and territories of Canada;

AND THIS COURT FURTHER ORDERS that liberty be reserved to any and all persons interested to apply to this Court to set aside or vary this Order or for such further or other Order as they may advise upon forty-eight hours' notice.

Quintette Coal Limited v. Nippon Steel
(1990), 47 BCLR (2d) 193 (SC) and (1990), 51 CBLR (2d) 105 (CA)

THACKRAY J: The motion is for an order setting aside a portion of an ex parte order made by me on 13th June 1990. That order arose by way of a petition from Quintette Coal Limited pursuant to the provisions of the Companies' Creditors Arrangement Act, RSC 1985, c. C-36 (the "CCAA"). In general terms, the petition was for an order permitting Quintette Coal Limited to prepare and present a plan of compromise or arrangement between itself and its creditors within six months and that during that time further proceedings in any action, suit or proceeding against the petitioner be restrained.

In support of that petition, affidavits were filed revealing that the petitioner operates an open pit coal mine in northeastern British Columbia and that pursuant to contracts entered into in 1981, Quintette sells to Japanese coal purchasers approximately five million tonnes of coal per year. The Japanese coal purchasers are the only customers of Quintette. The shipments commenced in January 1984 and under the terms of the agreements are to continue until at least 31st March 1998.

The coal purchase agreements contain price review clauses which allow the price of coal supplied under the agreements to be reviewed at approximately four-year intervals. When agreement could not be reached under the first scheduled price review, the matter was referred to arbitration with the Honourable Nathan T. Nemetz as chairman. The Board of Arbitration rendered its award on 28th May 1990.

Quintette estimated that based on the prices set forth in the arbitration, the amount owing by them to the Japanese coal purchasers for coal supplied from 1st April 1987 to the date of the award was approximately $46 million.

The petitioner revealed that the amounts owed by Quintette to its creditors as of 30th April 1990, is in the approximate amount of $772 million. Of that, $649 million is owed to what was called the 55 Bank Syndicate, $41 million to trade creditors, and $36 million by way of employee housing mortgages. The balance was the $46 million owed to the Japanese coal purchasers.

The order sought was to specifically exclude obligations of Quintette to suppliers of goods and services who were owed less than $200,000. The petition further specifically provided for the order to contain a provision that no creditor of Quintette could exercise any right of set-off against debts owed to Quintette and specifically noted moneys owed by the Japanese coal purchasers to the petitioner. Both of the above noted provisions were contained in the order. The motion with which I am now to deal asked for a declaration that the ex parte order does not affect the arbitration award pursuant to which the Japanese coal purchasers would be paying a lesser amount per tonne for coal than they had been paying as of the time of the award. That matter was conceded by Quintette and this, in effect, confirmed the indebtedness of Quintette to the Japanese coal purchasers in the approximate amount of $46 million.

The motion further asked that the provision of the order regarding set-off be set aside, this allowing the Japanese coal purchasers to realize upon their claim out of purchases of coal which are being made at this time and over the next several months. Before this matter came on for hearing, the Japanese coal purchasers had already commenced this practice of set-off and as a result, the amount owing as of the date of the application was $36,180,876.22.

... The submission of the Japanese coal purchasers, called the Japanese Steel Industry ("JSI"), was that the order should not preclude JSI from setting off overpayments because the arbitration award is the final and binding determination of the contractual rights and thereby constitutes an amendment to the contract, and on the basis that the right to repayment of the overpayments is part of the determination by the arbitration committee.

Counsel argued forcefully that the arbitration award is an amendment to the contract and that this amendment speaks as of 1st April 1987. That is, this is not an award of money to JSI at this time but rather is a ruling at this time that money has been owing by Quintette to JSI from 1st April 1987 and intermittent dates thereafter as coal was provided and payments became due. The ultimate result of that argument by JSI is that any money which they set off was never the property of Quintette and consequently there was no jurisdiction in this court to make any order affecting those funds.

... In summary, counsel for JSI took the position that the set-off provision in the ex parte order further amends the contract between the parties by, in effect, reinstating the old price. Mr. McAlpine stated that the result of this is manifestly unfair because it forces JSI to pay more than is due under the amended contract. He was adamant that the court should confine its consideration of this matter to the contract between Quintette and JSI and not draw any analogy to suppliers of other goods and services who are also creditors of Quintette.

The next branch of JSI's position, although not completely separate from any other part, is that the nature of a set-off is such that the funds to be set off are not a separate category. That is, it is not really a debt of Quintette to JSI but rather the amount in question is encompassed in the overall amount owed by JSI to Quintette. The argument then is that by enjoining a set-off, the court is ordering JSI to make an overpayment in the future for coal deliveries. Counsel concluded this portion of the argument by stating that what is effectively occurring is that JSI is, by this motion, trying to prevent more of its funds from going to Quintette and that the set-off is no more than the retention by JSI of its own asset.

Counsel for JSI argued that the provisions of s. 11 of the CCAA give jurisdiction to restrain "proceedings" but that this does not in any fair sense encompass a set-off which is a well known concept not to be categorized as a proceeding. He categorizes set-off as a defence or shield. In support he referred to Russell on the Law of Arbitration and quotes that "the award may be relied on by way of defence or set-off in circumstances where any other contract debt could be so relied on." Accordingly, he argues that "JSI are entitled to rely upon the award by way of set-off, just as they could where any other contract debt could be so relied on."

In providing authority for the definition of "proceeding," counsel for JSI referred to *Northland Properties Ltd. v. Guardian Trust Co.*, BCCA, Vancouver No. CA009605 [73 CBR (NS) 163]. This was a decision of Hutcheon JA in chambers. He said he found it difficult to include within the word "proceeding" an assignment of rents or an assignment of book debts.

I do not accept that any of the arguments put forth by JSI nor any of the positions taken by them are sufficient to support an order setting aside the set-off provisions of the ex parte order. I find, as submitted by Quintette, that the CCAA does apply to Quintette in this matter pursuant to s. 3 thereof, that this is an appropriate case for restructuring, and that the court has been given broad powers under s. 11 of the CCAA to assist reorganization by granting a stay so that no one creditor is given an advantage over another. I do not accept the argument that the stay provisions of the ex parte order in any way amend the contract between the parties either in its original form or if it has been amended by the arbitration award, in its amended form.

Nor do I accept the proposition that the order forces an overpayment by JSI for future coal deliveries. They are obliged to pay and Quintette is obliged to accept a price set pursuant to the arbitration award or any variation thereof pursuant to any appeal of that award. The award has created a debt owed by Quintette to JSI and I see that as completely distinguishable from the debts incurred by JSI for future coal deliveries. ...

On Appeal

The judgment of the court was delivered by GIBBS JA: ... The primary ground of appeal is stated in the factum of the Japanese companies to be that:

The Learned Chambers Judge erred in holding that the power to stay any "suit, action or other proceeding ... against the company," in s. 11 of the CCAA conferred jurisdiction upon the Court to restrain the JSI from exercising their right to set-off the Overpayments in paying for future coal deliveries.

• • •

... The principal issue on the appeal is whether the prohibition in the impugned paragraph is or is not within the powers vested in the court by s. 11 of the CCAA.

... However, the issue is not be resolved by construing the language of s. 11 in isolation. Maxwell on Interpretation of Statutes, 12th ed. (1969), states the basic rule at p. 47:

It was resolved in the *Case of Lincoln College* that the good expositor of an Act of Parliament should "make construction on all the parts together, and not of one part only by itself." Every clause of a statute is to "be construed with reference to the context and other clauses of the Act, so as, as far as possible, to make a consistent enactment of the whole statute."

And at p. 58 reference is made to "an elementary rule" of construction:

Passing from the external aspects of the statute to its contents, it is an elementary rule that construction is to be made of all the parts together, and not of one part only by itself.

The starting point in the construction is an understanding of the historical setting of the CCAA to the end that s. 11 is read in such a manner as to achieve the object of Parliament.

[Gibbs, JA quoted from the discussion of the history of the CCAA in *Chef Ready Foods v. Hongkong Bank*.]

... It is evident from the above that, providing no violence is done to the words used by Parliament, s. 11 is to be construed so as to confer on the court the power to permit Quintette to continue as a going concern while the attempt at compromise or arrangement or reorganization is being actively pursued. Here Thackray J gave Quintette six months from 13th June 1990, or such longer period as may be ordered, to reach an accommodation with its creditors. As the court pointed out at p. 7 [pp. 88-89] of *Chef Ready*:

... if the attempt at compromise or arrangement is to have any prospect of success, there must be a means of holding the creditors at bay, hence the powers vested in the court under s. 11.

Narrowing the focus of the inquiry somewhat, it is apparent that, with the possible exception of s. 11, the operative provisions of the CCAA apply precisely to the fortunes of Quintette, and to the circumstances which obtain as between Quintette and the Japanese companies. Quintette is a debtor company; the Japanese companies, collectively, are a creditor. Quintette as debtor is proposing a compromise or arrangement with its creditors, including the Japanese companies. The court may sanction and make binding on all creditors, including the Japanese companies, a compromise or arrangement agreed upon by a "majority in number representing three-fourths in value of the creditors, or class of creditors, as the case may be ..." (s. 6). With respect to value, the $36 million 13th June 1990 debt owed to the Japanese companies represents approximately 4¹/₂ per cent of the total of secured and unsecured debt. It would be anomalous indeed if, by denying or restricting cash flow, a 4¹/₂ per cent creditor could frustrate the compromise or arrangement because s. 11 did not apply, whereas if s. 11 did apply so that a stay could be ordered a creditor or creditors of up to 25 per cent could ultimately be forced to defer to the compromise or arrangement agreed upon by the 75 per cent. If the language of s. 11 so confines the court that that result flows the anomalous consequence must be accepted. On the other hand, if there is a reasonable construction which more nearly reflects the intention of the legislators, and avoids the anomaly, it is to be preferred.

The other aid to construction which is appropriate here is the view other courts have taken of s. 11. Maxwell at p. 47 (see above) quotes Sir George Jessel MR as saying, *inter alia*:

... when ... prior judgments tell this present Court, what the object of the Legislature was, the Court is to see whether the terms of the section are such as fairly to carry out that object and no other, and to read the section with a view to finding out what it means, and not with a view to extending it to something that was not intended.

Considering that the CCAA was enacted some 57 years ago there are relatively few reported cases interpreting its provisions. That may be a reflection of the general level of prosperity, with some short term reverses, which has been the Canadian experience for the past 50-plus years. In any event, and whatever the reason, the reported cases indicate that the courts have tended to avoid microscopic parsing of the words and phrases of s. 11 in favour of a broader "purposes" perspective thereby reaching conclusions held to further the objectives of Parliament. Without so stating they have given full effect to the direction in s. 12 of the Interpretation Act, RSC 1985, c. I-21:

12. Every enactment is deemed remedial, and shall be given such fair, large and liberal construction and interpretation as best ensures the attainment of its objects.

The following cases are illustrative of the kind of conduct the courts have found to be within their power to restrain under s. 11: *Re Feifer and Frame Mfg. Corp.*, [1947] Que. KB 348, 28 CBR 124 (CA); *Wynden Can. Inc. v. Gaz Métropolitain Inc.* (1982), 44 CBR (NS) 285 (Que. SC); *Norcen Energy Resources Ltd. v. Oakwood Petroleums Ltd.* (1988), 63 Alta. LR (2d) 361, 72 CBR (NS) 1, 92 AR 81 (QB). The judgments also contain helpful and persuasive observations about the intent and purpose of the Act, as do the following judgments: *Meridian Dev. Inc. v. TD Bank; Meridian Dev. Inc. v. Nu-West Ltd.*, [1984] 5 WWR 215, 32 Alta. LR (2d) 150, 52 CBR (NS) 109, 11 DLR (4th) 576, 53 AR 39 (QB); *Re Ursel Invt. Ltd.*, Sask. QB, 1990 (not yet reported); and *Northland Properties Ltd. v. Excelsior Life Ins. Co. of Can.*, 34 BCLR (2d) 122, [1989] 3 WWR 363, 73 CBR (NS) 195 (CA). And in his judgment in this case Thackray J adopted the approach followed in *Meridian* and *Norcen*. There is a perceptive observation about the attitude of the courts at the end of the case comment following the CBR report of *Norcen*:

The *Norcen* decision is one of the strongest examples to date of the willingness of the courts to permit the CCAA to be used as a practical and effective way of restructuring corporate indebtedness.

By way of brief summary, the subject matter of each of the judgments which has a direct bearing on the scope of s. 11 is as follows: in *Feifer and Frame*, a notice of eviction by a landlord; in *Wynden Can.*, cessation of utility services; in *Meridian*, a letter of credit; in *Norcen*, a replacement of the operator under an oil and gas operating agreement.

To the extent that a general principle can be extracted from the few cases directly on point, and the others in which there is persuasive obiter, it would appear to be that the courts have concluded that under s. 11 there is a discretionary power to restrain judicial or extra judicial conduct against the debtor company the effect of which is, or would be, seriously to impair the ability of the debtor company to continue in business during the compromise or arrangement negotiating period. The power is discretionary and therefore to be exercised judicially. It would be a reasonable expectation that it would be extremely unlikely that the power would be exercised where the result would be to enforce the continued supply of goods and services to the debtor company without payment for current deliveries, whereas it would not be unlikely when the result would be to enforce payment for goods thereafter taken from or services thereafter received from the debtor company, as is the case here. In cases not involving the supply or receipt of goods or services, no doubt judicial exercise of the discretion would produce a result appropriate to the circumstances.

• • •

The one remaining question is whether, to return to an expression used earlier, the order does violence to the words used by Parliament. The critical words in s. 11(b) are "restrain further proceedings in any action, suit or proceeding against the company"; and in s. 11(c) "make an order that no suit, action or other proceeding shall be proceeded with or commenced against the company." either subsection might apply dependent upon the view taken of the withholding conduct by the Japanese companies. But whichever applies the question remains the same and that is whether "proceeding" is to be understood as a legal proceeding only. In *Meridian* Wachowich J held that it was not to be so narrowly construed, as did Forsyth J in *Norcen*. As well, there is a higher court support for a broad construction which would include extrajudicial conduct without the meaning of "proceeding" in this statute. In *Vachon v. Can. Employment & Immigration Comm.*, [1985] 2 SCR 417 ... Beetz J, for the court, held that withholding payment of unemployment insurance benefits, even though authorized by statute, was contrary to the provisions of s. 49 [now s. 69] of the Bankruptcy Act, RSC 1970, c. B-3 [now RSC 1985, c. B-3]. At p. 121 he said:

> The Bankruptcy Act governs bankruptcy in all its aspects. It is therefore understandable that the legislator wished to *suspend all proceedings, administrative or judicial, so that all the objectives of the Act could be attained.* [emphasis added]

With the exception of the first sentence, what Beetz J said in this paragraph reflects precisely the attitude the courts have taken in respect of the CCAA. It must be recognized that s. 49 of the Bankruptcy Act is worded differently and includes the word "remedy." However, it should also be noted that the paragraph quoted above appears at the end of a section of the judgment entitled "General Nature of Stay of Proceedings Imposed by s. 49(1) of the Bankruptcy Act" in which no fine distinction is drawn between "remedy" and "proceeding." The emphasis is on the intention of Parliament and the objectives of the statute. And earlier on p. 121 Beetz J, again in language that applies equally to the CCAA, said:

... in my opinion the courts were right to give, expressly or by implication, a broad meaning to the stay of proceedings imposed by s. 49(1) of the Bankruptcy Act.

There is no rational ground for treating withholding by an arm of government, an "administrative" proceeding, differently than withholding by a private person. Accordingly, the withholding by the Japanese companies is as much a proceeding which can be restrained under s. 11 of the CCAA as was the withholding by the unemployment insurance authorities which was prohibited, except with leave, under s. 49 of the Bankruptcy Act.

The word "withholding" has been used throughout these reasons so as to distinguish from the concept of "set-off." The Japanese companies put their case forward on appeal primarily on the ground that what they were engaged in was set-off and that set-off was not a proceeding. With respect, the argument failed to recognize the difference between set-off in the colloquial sense and set-off in terms of the legal lexicon. Set-off in law is only available as a defence. It has been described as "a shield and not a sword." In respect of the payments due for ongoing coal deliveries Quintette has not sued for the amounts withheld. The Japanese companies have not therefore been put into a position where they could raise the set-off shield. On the contrary, they have had, and wish to continue to have, recourse to set-off, in the colloquial sense, as a sword to achieve a species of extrajudicial execution. The sword is being, and is intended to be, wielded "against the company." As it is a proceeding against the company it is within the power of the court to restrain under s. 11 of the CCAA.

• • •

Appeal dismissed.

Re Dylex Ltd.
(1995), 31 CBR (3d) 106 (Ont. Gen. Div.)

FARLEY J: Cambridge Western Leaseholds Limited ("Cambridge") moved for a determination of the right of the applicants ("Dylex") to proceed with the intended closure of stores at Mill Woods Town Centre, Edmonton and at Lethbridge Centre, Lethbridge. It was indicated at the hearing that the request was to keep the stores open until the *Companies' Creditors Arrangement Act* ("CCAA") plan is voted on (i.e., for a couple of months). Cambridge is the owner-operator of the two shopping centres, both of which are acknowledged to have some operating difficulties re vacancies. Cambridge's position is that Dylex's announced closure of a Tip Top Tailor store on February 18th and a Bi-Way Store on April 8th (both Mill Woods) and a Tip Top Tailor store on February 21st (Lethbridge) would materially affect each shopping centre. These three closures are part of a cross-Canada program of 200 closures including a previous Thrifty's closure on February 26th in Lethbridge.

Allow me to observe that Dylex is under the tight scrutiny of the Royal Bank of Canada ("Royal"), which is the special operating lender to Dylex, whose loan has, in an event of default, the failure to meet projected cash flows. Dylex has multiple stores in many of the shopping centres across Canada and in this respect has been a tenant of some magnitude. Cambridge is part of the Cambridge Leaseholds Limited group, which at the present time, has indicated an interest in making an investment in the Cadillac Fairview group of some hundreds of millions of dollars; thus it appears that Cambridge is financially secure at this time. However, Dylex has demonstrated that it faces severe financial challenges.

In a January 23rd letter following the CCAA order (which allowed store closures) given by Houlden JA on January 11th, Dylex advised various landlords (including Cambridge):

Where any intended store closures or closure in a mall or project has a material effect on the viability of the mall or project, in the view of the applicable landlord, such applicable landlord shall have the right to apply to the court for a determination of the right of [Dylex] to proceed with the intended closure or closures.

Cambridge has availed itself of that opportunity. In essence it is an amplification of or a specific comeback clause. The CCAA order provided as well that landlords' claims for closures would be determined and form part of the claims compromised in the CCAA plan.

The Mill Woods Centre is 442,345 sq. ft. of which 193,701 sq. ft. is represented by 109 ancillary stores (including the subject stores). The present vacancy rate is 26 per cent of the ancillary stores; with the proposed closures this would increase to 34 per cent. The Lethbridge Centre has 338,130 sq. ft. of which the 83 ancillary stores represent 146,547 sq. ft. Presently 26 per cent of the ancillary space is vacant and the proposed closure would increase this to 31 per cent. Both centres apparently suffered from an extended recession in the retail business and competition for other centres in each city.

With restructuring Dylex will not have any Bi-Way stores west of Ontario after April; thus an isolated Bi-Way store may cause management and stocking problems. The Lethbridge Tip Top lease will expire August 31st; it would be inconceivable that Dylex would attempt to extend this lease beyond its expiry. The subject stores have been a financial drain on Dylex, at a time when it is in a tight financial squeeze. Their closure is projected to bring about variable cost savings and an amelioration of some fixed costs (i.e., the elimination of what would normally be regarded as fixed costs in terms of certain overheads).

The two subject centres are experiencing some difficulty; however they were experiencing this difficulty generally before the time of Dylex's troubles. Generally it appears that Cambridge is in a secure financial position although the health of the two centres is less than robust. Of course, vis-à-vis the subject closings, there is always the aspect of the straw which breaks the camel's back. However in many [sic] view a compelling case has not been made out by Cambridge in this regard. Rather what we have are some vague generalities such as the following from the Gordon Harris report:

Competitive regional malls are heavily reliant on anchor stores and high profile national tenants in order to establish the identity and traffic needed to generate sale in the centre. Dylex stores are viewed as highly desirable retail concepts that help shape consumers shopping patterns.

The loss of Dylex tenants at Mill Woods Town Centre will alter, possibly on a permanent basis, shopping patterns away from Mill Woods Town Centre to other major malls in Edmonton.

The loss of BiWay and Tip Top at this time is a damaging blow to a centre which has had difficulty achieving the kind of occupancy and sales performance levels needed to achieve dominance in the local market. Recent sale increases point to a stabilization at Mill Woods Town Centre. The revenue lost as a result of the closures will effectively wipe out the gains in overall CRU sales increases achieved in the past two years.

It is therefore our opinion that the Dylex action will have a significant negative impact upon the ability of Mill Woods Town Centre to maintain its market share, to keep its other tenants, and to retain its customers. These factors will certainly affect the long-term economic viability of Mill Woods Town Centre.

I am therefore of the view that in weighing the balancing of interests in a CCAA context, the nod should continue to be given to Dylex which is a precarious position as opposed to Cambridge which is a sound financial condition although the two subject centres may be less than robust. However this pallor of the two centres is not caused by these three subject closings. I as well note that the one closure in Lethbridge will occur no matter what (barring a complete miracle) on the expiry of that lease on August 31st. Also the Bi-Way closing in Edmonton is not scheduled to take place for almost two months which is the anticipated plan vote time in any event. I am of the view that my discretion should be exercised in favour of Dylex in this situation: see *Meridian Developments Inc. v. Toronto Dominion Bank* (1984), 52 CBR (NS) 109 (Alta. QB), at pp. 113-14; *Norcen Energy Resources Ltd. v. Oakwood Petroleums Ltd.* (1988), 72 CBR (NS) 1 (Alta. QB), at pp. 12-13; *Hongkong Bank of Canada v. Chef Ready Foods Ltd.* (1990), 4 CBR (3d) 311 (BCCA), at p. 318; *Nova Metal Products Inc. v. Comiskey (Trustee of)* (1990), 1 CBR (3d) 101 (Ont. CA), at pp. 119-20; *Re Lehndorff General Partner Ltd.* (1993), 17 CBR (3d) 24 (Ont. Gen. Div. [Commercial List]), at p. 31.

It is clear that s. 11 [s. 6?] of the CCAA gives the power to the court to sanction a plan which includes termination of leases as part of the debtor's plan of arrangement: see *Sklar-Peppler Furniture Corp. v. Bank of Nova Scotia* (1991), 86 DLR (4th) 621 (Ont. Gen. Div.), at p. 625; *Re Armbro Enterprises Inc.* (1993), 22 CBR (3d) 80 (0nt. Bktcy.), at p. 84. In the interim between the filing and approval of a plan, the court has the inherent jurisdiction to fill in gaps in legislation so as to give effect to the objects of the CCAA, including the survival program of a debtor until it can present a plan: see *Re Westar Mining Ltd.* (1992), 14 CBR (3d) 88 (BCSC), at pp. 93-94 and generally *Lehndorff, supra*, at pp. 35-38. While not specifically mentioned in *Re Triangle Drugs Inc.* (1993), 12 OR (3d) 219 (Bktcy.), it was inherent jurisdiction which I was relying on to fill the gap in that legislation, namely the *Bankruptcy and Insolvency Act*, RSC 1985, c. B-3 (as amended by SC 1992, c. 27) ("BIA").

Mr. Arcand freely and voluntarily acknowledges that if he had to meet the test of a mandatory order he would be in difficulty: see *Bramalea Ltd. v. Canada Safeway Ltd.* (1985), 37 RPR 191 (Ont. HC); *Islington Village Inc. v. Citibank Canada* (1992), 27 RPR (3d) 100 (Ont. Gen. Div.), affirmed (November 23, 1992), Doc CA C13327 (Ont. CA); *Chatham Centre Mall Ltd. v. New Miracle Food Mart Inc.* (Farley J, released June 23, 1994) [reported at 40 RPR (2d) 124 (Ont. Gen. Div. [Commercial List])]; and *566719 Ontario Ltd. v. New Miracle Food Mart Inc.* (Farley J, released August 11, 1994) [reported at 41 RPR (2d) 22 (Ont. Gen. Div. [Commercial List])].

Lastly allow me to deal with Cambridge's point that I should import the principles of s. 65.2 BIA into the CCAA proceedings for the purpose of requiring Dylex to satisfy me that without these three closures it would not be able to make a viable proposal. The authority said for this proposition was *Triangle, supra* at p. 222 where in the Cambridge factum it was stated:

25. The philosophy of the CCAA in certain parts has been imported into the BIA. The procedure set out in s. 65.2 of the BIA should be imported into the CCAA.

Firstly let me observe that the 1992 amendments to the BIA regarding reorganizations in particular got into intricate detail, but as pointed out in *Triangle* had an obviously overlooked gap. However the CCAA since its inception has been a skeleton piece of legislation, almost pre-Victorian in style. This history of CCAA law has been an evolution of judicial interpretation. My observation about s. 66(2) BIA in *Triangle* was to the effect that a BIA proposal could be transferred to the CCAA and thus where the BIA was inappropriately silent in the reorganizational regime, it would be appropriate to measure the situation according to the philosophy in the parallel situation under the CCAA. However it should be noted that s. 66(2) BIA is a one way street; there is no similar provision for transferring from the CCAA to the BIA (although I do note that a bankruptcy company would be eligible to file under the CCAA).

Secondly and just in passing I note that I would not think it would be appropriate to view these three stores in isolation vis-à-vis the question of the viability of Dylex (or its plan of reorganization). It appears that the three stores are part of a pre-plan restructuring program package.

• • •

Order accordingly.

NOTE

Dylex Limited is significant for two reasons. First, it shows how boldly courts have interpreted the s. 11 power to authorize repudiation of burdensome leases. Second, it shows the cross-fertilization of CCAA and Part III concepts. Is this likely to be a two-way traffic? Can it be? For example, will courts interpret the s. 50(1.4) provisions on the classification of creditors in the light of the abundant CCAA case law on the same question?

Canadian Imperial Bank of Commerce v. Quintette Coal Ltd.
(1991), 1 CBR (3d) 253 (BCSC)

THACKRAY J:

Background

This Court made an order on June 13, 1990 pursuant to the provisions of the *Companies' Creditors Arrangement Act,* RSC 1985, c. C-36 (the "CCAA") whereby the status quo of Quintette was frozen until December 13, 1990. By that date Quintette was to file with the

Court a plan of financial reorganization. There was a short extension of that date but the plan was filed on December 20, 1990. The filing of the plan came as a surprise to the creditors in that a motion had been filed by Quintette asking for an extension. In anticipation of that application the applicants filed a motion for an order providing for expanded authority for the monitor. In spite of the filing of the plan the applicants have proceeded with their motion.

The original order of June 13, 1990 provided for the appointment of a monitor and the general duties to be assumed by the monitor. It states that on a monthly basis the monitor is to report to the Court the financial and business affairs of the company. Quintette is to provide to the monitor monthly sales information, inventory balances, financial statements and cash summaries. The monitor is required to report monthly to the parties who have entered an appearance and to include in such reports adverse changes in the operation of the company.

One of the provisions of the June 13, 1990 order that has particular relevance is "that the Monitor may from time to time apply to this Court for direction and guidance in the discharge of its duties and powers as Monitor hereunder."

The monitor has filed six reports. These reports outline Court proceedings together with financial data of the operations of Quintette in the immediately preceding period. The banks take the position that the role of the monitor is not very useful in the task of producing a financial plan that has some prospect of satisfying the majority of the creditors. The monitor is acknowledged by all parties to be an agent of the Court. The monitor has not communicated with the Court in any way other than through the filing of its reports. It has never suggested that it could not carry out its appointed task with the powers as set forth in the original order. Nor has it ever asked for "direction and guidance."

Applicants' Position

The applicants want greatly expanded powers and duties for the monitor. In digested form these are that the monitor will have supervision over the preparation and negotiation of the plan, file the plan with the Court, negotiate with all interested parties, co-ordinate the process of approval of the plan, and call and chair meetings of the shareholders and creditors of Quintette.

At the hearing the monitor did not comment upon these suggestions. However, it did have one of its officers sign an affidavit. Mr. William Bakk, senior vice-president of Deloitte & Touche Inc., attested that he does not believe that the June 13 order provides for the monitor to "comment on the contents of any plan of reorganization." He went on to say that if granted the duties and powers requested by the banks "it would be better able than it is now to assist the Court and the parties concerning any plan of reorganization."

It would have been helpful if the monitor had seen fit to enlarge upon Mr. Bakk's statement and let the Court know in what ways expanded powers or duties would be helpful. Counsel for the monitor took no position at the hearing. Other parties who took no position were the Japanese Steel Industry, Ridley Terminals Inc., Kal Tire, Finning Ltd., C. de F.I. and Sumitomo Metal Industries.

In support of the motion were BC Rail and Canadian National Railway. They adopted the applicants' position that the plan as filed is useless but it could form the basis for negotiations. But they see the monitor as useful if it acted as a "monitor/negotiator." They referred to ss. 4 and 5 of the CCAA, which states that where an arrangement is proposed the Court may order a meeting of creditors. They also noted the *Law and Equity Act,* RSBC 1979, c. 224, s. 36. It provides jurisdiction for the Court to appoint a receiver wherever it appears just or convenient. This Court's R. 47 also provides for the appointment of a receiver in any proceeding. The position taken by the banks was that if the Court has jurisdiction to appoint a receiver then surely it can appoint a negotiator. The applicants also submitted that if the Court had the jurisdiction to appoint a monitor on June 13, 1990, then it has the jurisdiction to redefine its duties. But they do not challenge the jurisdiction to make the original order appointing a monitor.

The applicants relied by way of precedent upon an order of Mr. Justice Houlden of the Supreme Court of Ontario in *Re Co-operative Corporations Act, the Companies' Creditors Arrangement Act and United Co-operatives of Ontario,* delivered on August 27, 1984. That order was the original order and it provided that an accounting firm was interim receiver and administrator of the assets and that it was appointed to have general supervisory powers over the preparation and consummation of the "Plan of Compromise." That order was given ex parte and there is no doubt but that it set out a more powerful role for its "monitor." But a distinction that must be recognized is that Mr. Justice Houlden had the company as the applicant.

The CCAA is silent as to appointment of receivers, monitors or arbitrators. Consequently the applicants argued that I should pay heed to words of Mr. Justice Gibbs on statutory interpretation as set forth in *Quintette Coal Ltd. v. Nippon Steel Corp.* BCCA, Vancouver Registry CA012636 [now reported (1990), 51 BCLR (3d) 105]. That is, that I should give the CCAA liberal interpretation to "best ensure the attainment of its objects." As pointed out by Gibbs JA, the CCAA was enacted some 57 years ago and there are few cases interpreting its provisions.

The position of the applicants is that I should show initiative in carrying out the broad objectives of the Act. It is submitted that by so doing there will be some hope of concluding a fiscal reorganization that will be sanctioned by the Court. Section 6 of the CCAA provides that if at a meeting of creditors held pursuant to s. 4 or 5, 75 per cent in value of the creditors agree to a plan then the compromise "may be sanctioned by the court, and if so sanctioned is binding." They quoted from *Reorganizations Under the Companies' Creditors Arrangement Act (Canada)* by David H. Goldman, (1985) 55 CBR (NS) 36. He says that when a plan comes to the Court for sanctioning "the judge will have no jurisdiction to sanction it unless there has been substantial compliance with the words and spirit of the statute." What is being suggested is that with the plan as presented and in the existing climate between the parties the plan will not obtain court sanction.

There is no doubt that over the past 6 months the relationship between Quintette and its creditors has deteriorated. The spirit of cooperation that I saw in the early spring is no longer evident. Counsel are now less open with each other and it was this climate that led, at least in part, to the unannounced filing of the plan. A plan that, according to the banks, is doomed to failure.

Quintette's Position

Quintette opposed the motion. Their position was supported by P. & H. Harnischfeger, Shell Canada, Cummins Diesel, and BC Hydro. They "regretted" that the lenders decided to bring this motion. They said that the plan is conciliatory in nature and that the proposed order would emasculate the power of Quintette to negotiate. Quintette feels that the banks are unhappy because they do not have the control which they usually possess in distress situations. This control has been taken away by the provisions of the CCAA, which contemplates that the company is the one to prepare plans and make proposals. Quintette takes the legal stance that the Court has no jurisdiction to remove this control from the company and give it to the monitor. Their fall-back position is that if the Court does have such jurisdiction, it would be premature to exercise it now.

On this latter point the facts are important. Quintette retained Coopers & Lybrand shortly after the June 13 order. They worked with Quintette in developing a plan. A comprehensive mine plan was finalized in mid-November. The reorganization plan was distributed on November 15, 1990. The JSI replied in a fax communication dated December 6 and stressed that the views contained therein were preliminary. The applicants supplied its "preliminary comments" in a letter dated November 26. A meeting of these parties was held on December 5. CN Rail and BC Rail had a preliminary meeting with the company on December 7. In a letter dated December 4 Ridley Terminals asked for information and as of December 12 a meeting was being arranged. In letters dated in the last week of November, C. de F.I. asked Quintette to apply for an extension of the December deadline. A meeting of the board of directors of Quintette was held on December 10 and it was decided to ask the Court for such an extension in order to allow time for further discussions with its creditors. I believe that they expected to obtain an extension.

The company is of the view that the process of negotiating a plan is not doomed to failure and that more time should be given under the existing format. But Quintette made it clear that this suggestion on their part should not be seen as a retreat from their main position that the Court has no jurisdiction to vest a monitor with powers any greater than those already spelled out.

In support it cited *Re Daon Development Corp.* (1984), 54 BCLR 235, 26 BLR 38, BC Corps. L.G. 78,261 (sub nom. *Re Mac-Rae and Daon Development Corp.)* 10 DLR (4th) 216, wherein Mr. Justice Wallace of this Court said that the Court did not have jurisdiction to vary the plan "in the circumstances which prevail on this application." But the words of Mr. Justice Wallace that are emphasized are that the CCAA "clearly restricts the Court's jurisdiction to sanctioning a compromise or arrangement" which emerges from a creditors' meeting. But as I see it that case dealt with jurisdiction emanating from s. 6 of the Act. That is something for the future in this case. Similarly the reliance which Quintette places upon passages from *Re Northland Properties Ltd.* (1988), 73 CBR (NS) 166, 31 BCLR (3d) 35 (SC) and (1988), 73 CBR (NS) 175 (BCSC). The guidelines contained therein will be useful if and when a plan is presented to the Court for approval.

But in two other *Re Northland Properties Ltd.* decisions there are passages that are applicable. Mr. Justice Trainor in the same volume of the Canadian Bankruptcy Reports [(1988), 73 CBR (NS) 141 at p. 144 referred to *Meridian Developments Inc. v. Toronto-Dominion Bank; Meridian Developments Inc. v. Nu-West Ltd.,* 52 CBR (NS) 109, [1984] 4 WWR 215, 32 Alta LR (3d) 150, 53 AR 39 (QB)]. He noted that Mr. Justice Wachowich said:

This Act, though little used, is one of a number of federal statutes dealing with insolvency. In common with the various other statutes, it envisages the protection of creditors and the orderly administration of the debtor's affairs or assets.

Mr. Justice Wachowich then referred to the words of Duff CJC in *AG Canada v. AG Quebec*, [1934] SCR 659, 16 CBR 1, [1934] 4 DLR 75:

The legislation is intended to have wide scope and allow a judge to make orders which will effectively maintain the status quo for a period *while the insolvent company* attempts to gain the approval of its creditors for a proposed arrangement which will enable the company to remain in operation for what is, hopefully, the future benefit of both the company and its creditors.

Trainor J then said [at 144]:

I adopt that as a statement of the purpose of this legislation.

Quintette has elevated the words which I have underlined to be the operative statement. I doubt that such was in the mind of Mr. Justice Trainor. I expect that he would have no objection to a rewording to read "while the insolvent company and its creditors work together to arrive at an arrangement that will enable the company to remain in operation."

I am fortified in my thinking by further words from Mr. Justice Trainor in another *Re Northland Properties Ltd.* decision at (1988), 73 CBR (NS) 138 [at 140]:

If there is to be an opportunity to reorganize, then that should be given fully to the companies to achieve that purpose. Putting in a receiver and then controlling the receiver by the court is a clumsy, awkward, inefficient way to try to deal with a problem of this kind. I would not endorse it.

Once again Quintette latches onto the suggestion that it is the "companies" that are to be given the opportunity to reorganize. Once again, I reject that as the message from Mr. Justice Trainor. The message that I receive and endorse is that the *parties* must seize the opportunity to work together for the benefit of the parties and in the public interest.

P. & H. Harnischfeger submitted that the Court does not have to expand the role of the monitor. They contend that it is up to the debtor and creditors to come to an agreement and that the Court should not get involved.

Shell Canada and Cummins Diesel said that it would not be helpful to give additional powers to the monitor. They argued the exact opposite of what was contended by the banks, i.e., if additional powers are given to the monitor "the plan is doomed to failure."

Conclusions

I am again going to refer to the words of Gibbs JA, but this time as they appear in *Hongkong Bank of Canada v. Chef Ready Foods Ltd.*, Vancouver Registry CA12944 [now reported [1991] 2 WWR 136, 51 BCLR (2d) 84 (CA), at 88 BCLR]:

The purpose of the CCAA is to facilitate the making of a compromise or arrangement between an insolvent debtor company and its creditors to the end that the company is able to continue in business ... . When a company has recourse to the CCAA the court is called upon to play *a kind of supervisory role* to preserve the status quo and to move the process along to the point where a compromise or arrangement is approved or it is evident that the attempt is doomed to failure.

The definition of "a kind of supervisory role" is the problem. I am going to apply to the task the principles of liberal interpretation of the objectives of the Act. The objectives are clear and have not changed from what was said by the Honourable C.H. Cahan when he introduced the Bill in the House of Commons. He said that it is designed to permit a corporation, through reorganization, from being disrupted and its goodwill lost.

I am hard pressed to decide if the parties as now constituted are the best vehicle to obtain those objectives, or if a strengthened role by the Court through the monitor would be preferable. I am conscious of what was said by Stanley E. Edwards in *Reorganizations under the Companies' Creditors Arrangement Act* (1947) 25 Can. Bar Rev. 587. He listed a significant number of facts that should be known by the Court before it approves a plan and said [at 601]:

It would also be desirable that the proposed plan be carefully analysed in the light of all this information, preferably by a competent expert, and that the result of the analysis indicates that all of the tests of compliance with the words and purpose of the statute were satisfied.

Although he is speaking of the s. 6 step, I find his thoughts appealing. That is, that at some stage an "independent and competent expert" be authorized to review and report upon the plan.

Using the principles and objectives earlier noted, I am of the opinion that the Court has jurisdiction to appoint such a person. Indeed it might be that this has already been done in the person of the monitor. The Court is by statute involved in the process and should seek competent and expert assistance. The need for an objective assessment is directed toward the Court's obligation to protect the public interest. There can be no doubt but that the public of this province has a vital interest in the future of the business now being operated by Quintette.

The questions that remain to be answered are:

1. Should that appointment be now?
2. If so, who should it be?
3. What will be the duties and powers?

I am of the opinion that the appointment should be now. I am also of the opinion that the monitor should occupy the position. I say this because Deloitte & Touche Inc. were chosen by Quintette, there has been no criticism voiced by any party of the choice and the motion is to have the monitor's duties and powers expanded. All of this appears to me to be a vote of confidence in Deloitte & Touche Inc. But on the third question I do not accept that the monitor should, at this time, have the powers as proposed. I am not ruling that those powers or powers akin thereto might not be appropriate at some stage, but I agree with the submissions of Quintette that it would be premature to create such a powerful position at this time.

Earlier I detailed the recent history of events. It can be seen from that history that there has been little time for the parties to negotiate an acceptable solution. At the time of the hearing no party had progressed beyond "preliminary views." I cannot accept the bank's prognostication that "the plan is doomed to failure" when, as late as December 6, 1990, the vice-presidents of the Bank of Montreal and the Canadian Imperial Bank of Commerce said that "we remain ready and willing to resolve our concerns so that the Plan can become a fair and equitable mechanism designed to restructure Quintette and its indebtedness on a viable basis." Quintette and its creditors must be given a fair chance to arrive at a successful solution within the existing framework.

But in view of the stated belief of Mr. William Bakk, senior vice-president of Deloitte & Touche Inc., I am prepared to clarify the role of the monitor. Mr. Bakk said that in his opinion the June 13 order did "not provide for a role for the Monitor to comment on the contents of any plan or reorganization." That power and duty is now vested in the monitor.

The applicants have asked that the monitor have access to personnel books, accounts, records, documents and other property of Quintette which may be required in connection with the preparation of the plan. They have also asked that the monitor be entitled to receive information on a confidential basis and to keep such information in confidence. They also want the monitor to have access to any mining alternatives to the current mining operations. At the hearing Quintette suggested that these matters were probably capable of resolution. I am of the opinion that the monitor should have these documents and information but the monitor has a duty to keep certain information confidential. If any party gives to the monitor information on a confidential basis, then that information shall not be revealed to any other person.

Order accordingly.

NOTE

CIBC v. Quintette is an important discussion of the role of the monitor in CCAA proceedings and the scope of his powers. Why was Quintette opposed to vesting expanded powers in the monitor? In what way would it have hindered negotiations between the parties? Was Quintette right in claiming that s. 3 of the Act intended the debtor to have the carriage of the negotiations and not to relegate the task to a third party?

There is in fact an important precedent under the CCAA for appointing a third party mediator. In the Algoma Steel Corp. reorganization, when Algoma and the banks were unable to reach agreement on the terms of a reorganization, Justice Farley requested Justice Adams to act as mediator at intensive negotiating sessions between the parties and (so rumour has it) urged the parties to keep negotiating until they reached an agreement. (Agreement was ultimately reached with the aid of Justice Adams.)

The US Bankruptcy Code allows the bankruptcy judge to appoint an "examiner" to conduct investigations, make recommendations to the court, and perform such other tasks as the court may request. In the Maxwell Communication Corp. reorganization, Judge Brozman in New York appointed an examiner to act as facilitator and harmonizer between the UK administrators of the parent company and management of the US based subsidiaries. Closer to home, in the Olympia & York reorganization, when difficulties arose between the Canadian liquidator of the parent corporation and American creditors of O & Y's US subsidiaries, Judge Garrity Jr. appointed Cyrus Vance to act as examiner with a view to resolving the impasse between the parties.

We conclude chapter 18 with two leading cases dealing with the classification of creditors for CCAA purposes. Getting the classification right is of critical importance to the debtor since otherwise the plan may not secure the necessary amount of support under s. 6 of the

Act. Conversely, the amount of leverage exercisable by a creditor will depend on its dominant role in a class of creditors, and this in turn will hinge on the classification scheme approved by the court. *Norcen* and *Woodward's* are of prime importance because they confirm a major shift from the pre-war English and Canadian cases, which had emphasized commonality of interest as the hallmark of a class, to a more flexible standard which favours the non-proliferation of classes in order to facilitate successful reorganizations. Examine again the BIA provisions and see whether they permit a similar degree of flexibility.

Norcen Energy Resources Limited v. Oakwood Petroleums
(1988), 72 CBR (NS) 20 (Alta. QB)

FORSYTH J: On 12th December 1988 Oakwood Petroleums Limited ("Oakwood") filed with the court a plan of arrangement ("the plan") made pursuant to the Companies' Creditors Arrangement Act (Canada), RSC 1970, c. C-25 [now RSC 1985, c. C-36] ("CCAA"), as amended, ss. 185 and 185.1 [now ss. 191 and 192] of the Canada Business Corporations Act, SC 1974-75-76 [now RSC 1985, c. C-44] as amended, and s. 186 of the Business Corporations Act (Alberta), SA 1981, c. B-15, as amended.

On 16th December 1988 Oakwood brought an application before me for an order which would, *inter alia*, approve the classification of creditors and shareholders proposed in the plan. I would note that the classifications requested are made pursuant to ss. 4, 5 and 6 of the CCAA for the purpose of holding a vote within each class to approve the plan.

Since my concern primarily is with the secured creditors of Oakwood, I shall set out, in part, the sections of the CCAA relevant to the court's authority with respect to compromises with secured creditors:

5. Where a compromise or arrangement is proposed between a debtor company and its secured creditors or any class of them, the court may ... order a meeting of such creditors or class of creditors. ...

6. Where a majority in numbers representing three-fourths in value of the creditors, or class of creditors, as the case may be, present and voting either in person or by proxy at the meeting or meetings ... held pursuant to sections 4 and 5 ... agree to any compromise or arrangement ... [it] may be sanctioned by the court, and if so sanctioned is binding on all the creditors. ...

The plan filed with the court envisions five separate classes of creditors and shareholders. They are as follows:

  (i) The secured creditors;
  (ii) The unsecured creditors;
  (iii) The preferred shareholders of Oakwood;
  (iv) The common shareholders and holders of class A non-voting shares of Oakwood;
  (v) The shareholders of New York Oils Ltd.

With the exception of the proposed class comprising the secured creditors of Oakwood, there has been for the moment no objection to the proposed groupings. I add here that shareholders of course have not yet had notice of the proposal with respect to voting percentages and classes with respect to their particular interests. With that caveat, and leaving aside the proposed single class of secured creditors, I am satisfied that the other classes suggested are appropriate and they are approved.

I turn now to the proposed one class of secured creditors. The membership of and proposed scheme of voting within the secured creditors class is dependent upon the value of each creditor's security as determined by Sceptre Resources Ltd. ("Sceptre"), the purchaser under the plan.

As a result of those valuations, the membership of that class was determined to include: the Bank of Montreal, the ABC noteholders, the Royal Bank of Canada, the National Bank of Canada and the HongKong Bank of Canada and the Bank of America Canada. Within the class, each secured creditor will receive one vote for each dollar of "security value." The valuations made by Sceptre represent what it considers to be a fair value for the securities.

Any dispute over the amount of money each creditor is to receive for its security will be determined at a subsequent fairness hearing where approval of the plan will be sought. Further, it should be noted that all counsel have agreed that, on the facts of this case, any errors made in the valuations would not result in any significant shift of voting power within the proposed class so as to alter the outcome of any vote. Therefore, the valuations made by Sceptre do not appear to be a major issue before me at this time insofar as voting is concerned.

The issue with which I am concerned arises from the objection raised by two of Oakwood's secured creditors, namely, HongKong Bank and Bank of America Canada, that they are grouped together with the other secured creditors. They have brought applications before me seeking leave to realize upon their security or, in the alternative, to be constituted a separate and exclusive class of creditors and to be entitled to vote as such at any meeting convened pursuant to the plan.

The very narrow issue which I must address concerns the propriety of classifying all the secured creditors of the company into one group. Counsel for Oakwood and Sceptre have attempted to justify their classifications by reference to the "commonality of interests test" described in *Sovereign Life Assur. Co. v. Dodd*, [1892] 2 QB 573 (CA). That test received the approval of the Alberta Court of Appeal in *Savage v. Amoco Acquisition Co.* (1988), 59 Alta. LR (2d) 260, 68 CBR (NS) 154, 87 AR 321, where Kerans JA, on behalf of the court, stated [pp. 264-65]:

> We agree that the basic rule for the creation of groups for the consideration of fundamental corporate changes was expressed by Lord Esher in *Sovereign Life Assur. Co. v. Dodd*, [supra] when he said, speaking about creditors:
>
> > ... if we find a different state of facts existing among different creditors which may differently affect their minds and their judgments, they must be divided into different classes.

In the case of *Sovereign Life Assur. Co.*, Bowen LJ went on to state at p. 583 that the class:

> ... must be confined to those persons whose rights are not so dissimilar as to make it impossible for them to consult together with a view to their common interest.

Counsel also made reference to two other "tests" which they argued must be complied with—the "minority veto test" and the "bona fide lack of oppression test." The former, it is argued, holds that the classes must not be so numerous as to give a veto power to an otherwise insignificant minority. In support of this test, they cite my judgment in *Amoco Can. Petroleum Co. v. Dome Petroleum Ltd.*, Calgary No. 8701-20108, 28th January 1988 (not yet reported).

I would restrict my comments on the applicability of this test to the fact that, in the *Amoco* case, I was dealing with "a very small minority group of [shareholders] near the bottom of the chain of priorities." Such is not the case here.

In support of the "bona fide lack of oppression test," counsel cite *Re Alabama, New Orleans, Texas & Pac. Junction Ry. Co.*, [1891] 1 Ch. 213 (CA), where Lindley LJ stated at p. 239:

The Court must look at the scheme, and see whether the Act has been complied with, whether the majority are acting *bona fide*, and whether they are coercing the minority in order to promote interests adverse to those of the class whom they purport to represent. ...

Whether this test is properly considered at this stage, that is, whether the issue is the constitution of a membership of a class, is not necessary for me to decide as there have been no allegations by the HongKong Bank or Bank of America as to a lack of bona fides.

What I am left with, then, is the application to the facts of this case of the "commonality of interests test" while keeping in mind that the proposed plan of arrangement arises under the CCAA.

Sceptre and Oakwood have argued that the secured creditors' interests are sufficiently common that they can be grouped together as one class. That class is comprised of six institutional lenders (I would note that the ABC noteholders are actually a group of ten lenders) who have each taken first charges as security on assets upon which they have the right to realize in order to recover their claims. The same method of valuation was applied to each secured claim in order to determine the security value under the plan.

On the other hand, HongKong Bank and Bank of America have argued that their interests are distinguishable from the secured creditors class as a whole and from other secured creditors on an individual basis. While they have identified a number of individually distinguishing features of their interests vis-à-vis those of other secured parties (which I will address later), they have put forth the proposition that since each creditor has taken separate security on different assets, the necessary commonality of interests is not present. The rationale offered is that the different assets may give rise to a different state of facts which could alter the creditors' view as to the propriety of participating in the plan. For example, it was suggested that the relative ease of marketability of a distinct asset as opposed to the other assets granted as security could lead that secured creditor to choose to disapprove of the proposed plan. Similarly, the realization potential of assets may also lead to distinctions in the interests of the secured creditors and consequently bear upon their desire to participate in the plan.

In support of this proposition, the HongKong Bank and Bank of America draw from comments made by Ronald N. Robertson, QC, in a publication entitled "Legal Problems on Reorganization of Major Financial and Commercial Debtors," Canadian Bar Association—Ontario Continuing Legal Education, 5th April 1983, at p. 15, and by Stanley E. Edwards in an earlier article, "Reorganizations under the Companies' Creditors Arrangement Act" (1947), 25 *Can. Bar Rev.* 587, at p. 603. Both authors gave credence to this "identity of interest" proposition that secured creditors should not be members of the same class "unless their security is on the same or substantially the same property and in equal priority." They also made reference to a case decided under c. 11 of the Bankruptcy Code of the United States of America which, while not applying that proposition in that given set of facts, accepted it as a "general rule." That authority is *Re Palisades-on-the-Desplaines; Seidel v. Palisades-on-the-Desplaines*, 89 F. 2d 214 at 217-18 (1937, Ill.).

Basically, in putting forth that proposition, the HongKong Bank and Bank of America are asserting that they have made advances to Oakwood on the strength of certain security which they identified as sufficient and desirable security and which they alone have the right to realize upon. Of course, the logical extension of that argument is that in the facts of this case each secured creditor must itself comprise a class of creditors. While counsel for the HongKong Bank and Bank of America suggested it was not necessary to do so in this case, as they are the only secured creditors opposed to the classification put forth, in principle such would have to be the case if I were to accept their proposition.

To put the issue in another light, what I must decide is whether the holding of distinct security by each creditor necessitates a separate class of creditor for each, or whether notwithstanding this factor that they each share, nevertheless this factor does not override the grouping into one class of creditors. In my opinion, this decision cannot be made without considering the underlying purpose of the CCAA.

In *Norcen Energy Resources Ltd. v. Oakwood Petroleums Ltd.*, [63 Alta. LR (2d) 361], after canvassing the few authorities on point, I concluded that the purpose of the CCAA is to allow debtor companies to continue to carry on their business and that necessarily incidental to that purpose is the power to interfere with contractual relations. In referring to the case authority *Re Companies' Creditors Arrangement Act; A.G. Can. v. A.G. Que.*, [1934] SCR 659, 16 CBR 1, [1934] 4 DLR 75, I stated at pp. 24 and 25 [p. 15]:

It was held in that case that the Act was valid as relating to bankruptcy and insolvency rather than property and civil rights. At p. 664, Cannon J held:

> Therefore, if the proceedings under this new Act of 1933 are not, strictly speaking, "bankruptcy" proceedings, because they had not for object the sale and division of the assets of the debtor, they may, however, be considered as "insolvency proceedings" *with the object of preventing a declaration of bankruptcy and the sale of these assets*. If the creditors directly interested for the time being reach the conclusion that an opportune arrangement to avoid such sale would better protect their interest, as a whole or in part, provisions for the settlement of the liabilities of the insolvent are an essential element of any insolvency legislation. ...

I went on to note:

The CCAA is an Act designed to continue, rather than liquidate companies. ... The critical part of the decision is that federal legislation pertaining to assisting in the continuing operation of companies is constitutionally valid. In effect the Supreme Court of Canada has given the term "insolvency" a broad meaning in the constitutional sense by bringing within that term *an Act designed to promote the continuation of an insolvent company.* [emphasis added]

In this regard, I would make extensive reference to the article by Mr. Robertson, QC, where, in discussing the classification of creditors under the CCAA and after stating the proposition referred to by counsel for the HongKong Bank and Bank of America, he states at p. 16 in his article:

An initial, almost instinctive, response that differences in claims and property subject to security automatically means segregation into different classes does not necessarily make economic or legal sense in the context of an act such as the CCAA.

And later at pp. 19 and 20, in commenting on the article by Mr. Edwards, he states:

However, if the trend of Edwards' suggestions that secured creditors can only be classed together when they held [sic] security of the same priority, that perhaps classes should be sub-divided into further groups according to whether or not a member of the class also holds some other security or form of interest in the debtor company, *the multiplicity of discrete classes or sub-classes might be so compounded as to defeat the object of the act.* As Edwards himself says, the subdivision of voting groups and the counting of angels on the heads of pins must stop somewhere and some forms of differences must surely be disregarded.

In summarizing his discussion, he states on pp. 20-21:

From the foregoing one can perceive at least two potentially conflicting approaches to the issue of classification. On the one hand there is the concept that members of a class ought to have the same "interest" in the company, ought to be only creditors entitled to look to the same "source" or "fund" for payment, and ought to encompass all of the creditors who do have such an identity of legal rights. *On the other hand, there is recognition that the legislative intent is to facilitate reorganization, that excessive fragmentation of classes may be counter-productive and that some degree of difference between claims should not preclude creditors being put in the same class.*

It is fundamental to any imposed plan or reorganization that strict legal rights are going to be altered and that such alteration may be imposed against the will of at least some creditors. When one considers the complexity and magnitude of contemporary large business organizations, and the potential consequences of their failure it may be that the courts will be compelled to focus less on whether there is any identity of legal rights and rather focus on whether or not those constituting the class are persons, to use Lord Esher's phrase, "whose rights are not so dissimilar as to make it impossible for them to consult together with a view to their common interest. ..."

If the plan of reorganization is such that the creditors' particular priorities and securities are preserved, especially in the event of ultimate failure, *it may be that the courts will, for example in an apt case decide that creditors who have basically made the same kinds of loans against the same kind of security, even though on different terms and against different particular secured assets, do have a sufficient similarity of interest to warrant being put into one class and being made subject to the will of the required majority of that class.* [emphasis added]

These comments may be reduced to two cogent points. First, it is clear that the CCAA grants a court the authority to alter the legal rights of parties other than the debtor company without their consent. Second, the primary purpose of the Act is to facilitate reorganizations and this factor must be given due consideration at every stage of the process, including the classification of creditors made under a proposed plan. To accept the "identity of interest" proposition as a starting point in the classification of creditors necessarily results in a "multiplicity of discrete classes" which would make any reorganization difficult, if not impossible, to achieve.

In the result, given that this planned reorganization arises under the CCAA, I must reject the arguments put forth by the HongKong Bank and the Bank of America, that since they hold separate security over different assets, they must therefore be classified as a separate class of creditors.

I turn now to the other factors which the HongKong Bank and Bank of America submit distinguishes them on individual bases from other creditors of Oakwood. The HongKong Bank and Bank of America argue that the values used by Sceptre are significantly understated. With respect to the Bank of Montreal, it is alleged that that bank actually holds security valued close to, if not in excess of, the outstanding amount of its loans when compared to the HongKong Bank and Bank of America whose security, those banks allege, is approximately equal to the amount of its loans. It is submitted that a plan which understates the value of assets results in the oversecured party being more inclined to support a plan under which they will receive, without the difficulties of realization, close to full payments of their loans.

The problem with this argument is that it is a throwback to the "identity of interest" proposition. Differing security positions and changing security values are a fact of life in the world of secured financing. To accept this argument would again result in a different class of creditor for each secured lender, with the possible exception of the ABC noteholders who could be lumped with the HongKong Bank or Bank of America, as their percentage realization under the proposed plan is approximately equal to that of the HongKong Bank and Bank of America.

Further, the HongKong Bank and Bank of America also submit that since the Royal Bank and National Bank of Canada are so much more undersecured on their loans, they too have a distinct interest in participating in the plan which is not shared by themselves. The sum total of their submissions would seem to be that, since oversecured and undersecured lenders have a greater incentive to participate, it is only those lenders, such as themselves with just the right amount of security, that do not share that common interest. Frankly, it appears to me that these arguments are drawn from the fact that they are the only secured creditors of Oakwood who would prefer to retain their right to realize upon their security, as opposed to participating in the plan. I do not wish to suggest that they should be chided for taking such a position, but surely expressed approval or disapproval of the plan is not a valid reason to create different classes of creditors. Further, as I have already clearly stated, the CCAA can validly be used to alter or remove the rights of creditors.

Finally, I wish to address the argument that, since Sceptre has made arrangements with the Royal Bank of Canada relating to the purchase of Oakwood, it has an interest not shared by the other secured creditors. The Royal Bank's position as a principal lender in the reorganization is separate from its status as a secured creditor of Oakwood and arises from a separate business decision. In the absence of any allegation that the Royal Bank will not act bona fide in considering the benefit of the plan of the secured creditors as a class, the HongKong Bank and Bank of America cannot be heard to criticize the Royal Bank's presence in the same class.

In light of my conclusions, the result is that I approve the proposed classification of secured creditors into one class. ... .

Application granted.

Re Woodward's Ltd.
(1993), 20 CBR (3d) 74 (BCSC)

TYSOE J [in chambers]:

Introduction

The Petitioners ("Woodward's") apply for an order approving the classes of creditors designated in their plan of arrangement under the *Companies' Creditors Arrangement Act*, RSC 1985, c. C-36 (the "CCAA") filed on April 7, 1993 (the "Reorganization Plan"). Woodward's proposes to hold meetings of these classes of creditors during the first part of May 1993 for the purpose of voting on the Reorganization Plan.

The classes of creditors designated by the Reorganization Plan are Secured Creditors, Noteholders, Landlords and General Creditors. Each of these terms is defined in the Reorganization Plan. There is no issue as to the appropriateness of classes of secured creditors, noteholders, landlords and general creditors. The question is whether or not there should be additional classes.

The definitions in the Reorganization Plan of the classes of creditors are as follows:

"*Secured Creditors*" means the Secured Trustee as holder of the Secured Notes;

"*Noteholders*" means the A & F Debentureholders, the Stores Debentureholders, the 9% Noteholders and the 10% Noteholders;

"*Landlord*" means any landlord, head lessor, sublessor or owner of premises which has entered into any Lease with any member of the Woodward's Group and includes any mortgagee or successor in title of such premises who has taken possession of such premises or is collecting rent in respect of such premises as well as any party who has taken an assignment of rents or assignment of lease in respect of such premises, whether as security or otherwise; provided, however, that if more than one person would otherwise come within this definition of Landlord in respect of any particular Lease, the rights and claims of all such persons in respect of such Lease will be dealt with collectively under this Plan and each reference herein to such Landlord shall be construed as a collective reference to all such persons;

"*General Creditors*" means all persons with unsecured claims for any Indebtedness against Woodward's Group as at the General Creditor Meeting Date, including the Pre-Filing Trade Creditors, Employee Creditors, the Landlords and the Equipment Financiers but, for the Landlords and the Equipment Financiers, only to the extent of their claims to be dealt with in the General Creditor class as provided herein, and specifically excluding Post-Filing Trade Creditors, the Noteholders and the holders of the Unaffected Obligations.

The additional classes that have been proposed are as follows:

(a) employees of Woodward's that have been terminated since the commencement of these proceedings on December 11, 1992 (these employees made a formal application for separate classification);

(b) Royal Trust Corporation of Canada which holds a debenture creating a fixed charge against certain equipment purchased by Woodward's with the financing provided by Royal Trust;

(c) equipment financiers (which could include Royal Trust);

(d) creditors of Woodward Stores Limited (the "Operating Company") that hold the guarantee or joint covenant of its holding company, Woodward's Limited (the "Holding Company");

(e) one or more classes of landlords whose leases are being repudiated.

There is the potential that two parties having agreements to lease with Woodward's will want to make submissions that they should be in a separate or different class. These parties were only served with the Petition in this proceeding recently and it was agreed that my ruling would not affect their ability to make submissions at a subsequent time. It was also agreed that General Electric Capital Canada Inc. would not be bound by my ruling and could make submissions that it should be in a separate or different class or that it should be considered to be a holder of an Unaffected Obligation.

I will return to the positions of the various parties but I think it will be useful to first review the authorities setting forth the general principles applicable to the issue of creditor classification.

General Principles

The starting point of the case authorities is the decision of the English Court of Appeal in *Sovereign Life Assurance Co. v. Dodd*, [1892] 2 QB 573 (CA) where Lord Esher said the following at pp. 579-80 in relation to the meeting of creditors to consider a plan of arrangement under the *Joint Stock Companies Arrangement Act*:

[See extract in Finlayson JA's judgment in *Elan v. Comiskey, supra* this chapter (ed.).]

Bowen LJ made the following comments at p. 583: ... .

There has been some jurisprudence over the years regarding creditor classification but, like the jurisprudence on other issues under the CCAA, it has intensified over the past five to ten years. One of the earlier cases of the present wave of jurisprudence dealing with creditor classification is *Norcen Energy Resources Ltd. v. Oakwood Petroleums Ltd.* (1988), 72 CBR 20 (Alta. QB). In that case Forsyth J rejected the argument that different secured creditors should be placed in separate classes because they held separate security over different assets or because the relative values of their security were different. The Court rejected the "identity of interest" approach, which involves each class only containing creditors with identical interests. Instead, the Court followed the approach which I will call the "non-fragmentation" approach. This approach avoids the creation of a multiplicity of classes by including creditors with different legal rights in the same class as long as their legal rights are not so dissimilar that it is not possible for them to vote with a common interest. This is essentially the approach that was suggested by Bowen LJ in the passage from the *Sovereign Life* quoted above (although his words have been incorrectly attributed to Lord Esher in at least one case authority and one article).

The approach taken in the *Oakwood Petroleums* case has been specifically adopted by the BC Court of Appeal in *Northland Properties Ltd., Re* (sub nom. *Northland Properties Ltd. v. Excelsior Life Insurance Co. of Canada*) (1989), 73 CBR (NS) 195 (BCCA). In the lower court decision in that case the Court considered the similarities and dissimilarities of various mortgagees holding mortgages against different properties and concluded that they should be in the same class. Dealing with the points of dissimilarity, Trainor J said as follows at p. 192 of (1988), 73 CBR (NS) 175 (BCSC):

The points of dissimilarity are that they are separate properties and that there are deficiencies in value of security for the loan, which vary accordingly for particular priority mortgagees. Specifically with respect to Guardian and Excelsior, they are both in a deficiency position.

Now, either of the reasons for points of dissimilarity, if effect was given to them, could result in fragmentation to the extent that a plan would be a realistic impossibility. The distinction which is sought is based on property values, not on contractual rights or legal interests.

After the Court of Appeal in *Northland Properties* quoted the above passage, it said the following (at p. 203):

I agree with that, but I wish to add that in any complicated plan under this Act, there will often be some secured creditors who appear to be oversecured, some who do not know if they are fully secured or not, and some who appear not to be fully secured. This is a variable cause arising not by any difference in legal interests, but rather as a consequence of bad lending, or market values, or both.

As the BC Court of Appeal has specifically adopted the reasoning in *Oakwood Petroleums*, the approach which I have called the "non-fragmentation" approach is the one to be followed in British Columbia. As will be seen shortly, the "non-fragmentation" approach has also been preferred over the "identity of interest" approach by the Ontario courts.

There have been two recent cases that are particularly relevant because they deal with employees, landlords and equipment lessors in circumstances that are similar to the situation at hand. The first of these cases is *Sklar-Peppler Furniture Corp. v. Bank of Nova Scotia* (1991), 8 CBR (3d) 312 (Ont. Gen. Div.) where one of the proposed classes consisted of all creditors other than two secured creditors, including holders of unsecured debentures, terminated employees, landlords whose leases had been repudiated and equipment lessors whose leases were to be repudiated (although the report does not specifically say it, I assume that the proposed class also included the general trade creditors). The Court rejected the argument of one of the landlords that there should be a separate class of creditors consisting of the landlords and the equipment lessors. Borins J utilized the "non-fragmentation" approach as illustrated by the following passage on pp. 317-18:

In my view, an important principle to consider in approaching ss. 4 and 5 of the CCAA is that followed in *Re Wellington Building Corp.*, 16 CBR 48, [1934] OR 653, [1934] 4 DLR 626 (SC), in which it was emphasized that the object of ss. 4 and 5 is not confiscation but is to enable compromises to be made for the common benefit of the creditors as creditors, or for the common benefit of some class of creditors as such. To this I would add that recognition must be given to the legislative intent to facilitate corporate reorganization and that in the modern world of large and complicated business enterprises the excessive fragmentation of classes could be counter-productive to the fulfilment of this intent. In this regard, to approach the classification of creditors on the basis of identity of interest, as suggested by counsel for H & R Properties, would in some instances result in the multiplicity of classes, which would make any re-organization difficult, if not impossible, to achieve. In my view, in placing a broad and purposive interpretation upon the provisions of the CCAA the court should take care to resist approaches which would potentially fragment creditors and thereby jeopardize potentially viable plans of arrangement, such as the plan advanced in this application.

The other recent decision is *Grafton-Fraser Inc. v. Canadian Imperial Bank of Commerce* (1992), 90 DLR (4th) 285 (Ont. Gen. Div.). In that case Houlden JA approved the classification of creditors into secured creditors, landlords and unsecured creditors. It appears from the report that the plan contemplated that some leases would be repudiated and there would be rent reductions in respect of certain of the continuing premises. I am told that the final plan of Grafton-Fraser Inc. did not include the landlords with continuing leases at reduced rental rates in the same class as the landlords whose leases were repudiated, but the decision of Houlden JA appears to be predicated on the fact that the two types of landlords would be in the same class. It had been argued that the landlords should be in the same class as the unsecured creditors. Houlden JA felt that it was appropriate to have the landlords in a separate class for two reasons; namely, there would be great difficulty in ascertaining the amounts of the claims of the landlords and the plan enjoined the landlords from exercising their contractual and statutory remedies.

Before I apply the general principles outlined above to the circumstances of this case, I wish to add some comments regarding the classification of creditors. The case authorities focus on the differences in the legal rights of the creditors in determining whether their interests are sufficiently similar or dissimilar to warrant creditors being placed in the same class or separate classes. I agree that it is the legal rights of the creditors that must be considered and that other external matters that could influence the interests of a creditor are not to be taken in account. However, it is my view that the legal rights should not be considered in isolation and that they must be considered within the context of the provisions of the reorganization plan. It would be appropriate to segregate two sets of creditors with similar legal interests into separate classes if the plan treats them differently. Conversely, it may be appropriate to include two sets of creditors with different legal rights in the same class if the plan treats them in a fashion that gives them a commonality of interest despite their different legal rights. In addition, when the Court is assessing whether there is a sufficient commonality of interest to include two sets of creditors in the same class, it is necessary in my view to examine their legal rights within the context of the potential failure of the reorganization plan. The treatment of the two sets of creditors under the plan should be compared to the rights they would have in the event of the failure of the plan (i.e., bankruptcy or other liquidation).

Terminated Employees

The first set of creditors that submitted that it should be in a separate class is the group of former employees of Woodward's who were terminated after December 11, 1992, the date of commencement of these CCAA proceedings. These former employees all have claims against Woodward's for damages as a result of Woodward's failure to give them reasonable notice of termination. The Reorganization Plan includes the terminated employees in the class of General Creditors which also includes the trade suppliers and other unsecured claims of the Operating Company. The Reorganization Plan proposes that the General Creditors receive 37% of the principal amounts of their proven claims.

The two counsel acting for former employees on this application submitted that their clients should comprise a separate class of creditors for several reasons. They say that the terminated employees are largely middle-aged, long service employees with limited education who have little prospect of finding alternate employment. They point to the fact that the courts recognize the difference between a contract of employment and an ordinary commercial contract. They further make reference to the fact that the trade suppliers will be selling merchandise to the reorganized company and that they will have a potentially continuing relationship which may influence the manner in which they vote on the plan. Finally, they say that the trade suppliers have the ability to "write off" their losses and that they will receive different income tax treatment in respect of their losses than the terminated employees.

In arguing that the terminated employees should form their own class, counsel relied on the article *Reorganizations under the Companies' Creditors Arrangement Act* (1947), 25 *Can. Bar Rev.* 587 by Stanley E. Edwards. This article has been relied upon extensively by the courts in interpreting the CCAA. However, the article has not been followed with respect to the classification of creditors. Mr. Edwards proposes the "identity of interest" approach which was not been adopted by the Alberta, British Columbia and Ontario courts. The preferred approach is the "non-fragmentation" approach.

The legal rights of the terminated employees are the same as the legal rights of the trade suppliers. They are both creditors with unsecured claims against the Operating Company (the secured and preferred amounts payable to employees under provincial legislation and the *Bankruptcy and Insolvency Act* have already been paid to the terminated employees). In a bankruptcy or other liquidation they would both receive the same pro rata amount of their claims. They are to receive the same pro rata amount of their claims under the Reorganization Plan.

The fact that there is a recognized difference between contracts of employment and ordinary commercial contracts is not relevant because the contracts of employment of the terminated employees have come to an end. The terminated employees have claims for damages against Woodward's for wrongful dismissal. Once the amount of damages for an employee has been agreed upon or determined by the Court, the difference between the two types of contracts becomes historical and the employee has the same rights as any other unsecured creditor. The differences between the two types of contracts may result in the employees receiving higher amounts of damages but the differences do not warrant the terminated employees being entitled to a higher distribution than the other unsecured creditors.

I am satisfied that there is a sufficient commonality of interest between the terminated employees and the other members of the General Creditors class that they should be included in the same class.

Equipment Financiers and Royal Trust Corporation of Canada

It is convenient to deal with the submissions of the equipment lessors and Royal Trust at the same time because if Royal Trust is not put in a class of its own, its alternate position was that it should be included in a class with the equipment lessors.

The term "Equipment Financiers" is defined in the Reorganization Plan. In brief, the term means any person who has provided financing for the acquisition or installation of office equipment or trade fixtures and who has retained a security interest by way of a lease or a security instrument. Woodward's has notified or will be notifying certain equipment financiers that it no longer requires their equipment. These equipment financiers will then have a claim against Woodward's for damages resulting from the repudiation of their contractual arrangements. It is these equipment financiers who wish to be in a separate class. The Reorganization Plan proposes that the terminated equipment financiers be treated as General Creditors and that they receive 37% of the amounts of their claims. The amount of each claim would presumably be the discounted value of future payments owing by Woodward's to the equipment financier less the present value of the equipment.

Most of the equipment financiers are parties that bought the equipment and are leasing it to Woodward's on a normal type of term lease. The equipment financiers who are lessors include National Bank Leasing, North American Trust Company and Royal Bank Leasing. Royal Trust also falls within the definition of "Equipment Financier" but it is not a lessor. It financed the acquisition by Woodward's of certain equipment by way of a traditional financing arrangement. It loaned money to Woodward's on a term basis and it took security in the form of a debenture creating a fixed charge against the equipment that it financed.

In other contexts under the CCAA the treatment of equipment leases in relation to the treatment of security documents causes me considerable doubts. Should equipment leases be treated the same as security instruments in all or some cases? Does it make a difference whether the lease is classified as an operating lease or a capital lease? Should the extent of depreciation of the subject asset be taken into account? Fortunately these questions can be left for another time because they do not need to be resolved in order to deal with the classification issue.

Lessors and debentureholders do have different legal rights but the question to be answered is whether the different rights result in a lack of commonality of interest. In bankruptcy a lessor is entitled to retake possession of the leased goods upon default and, if the lease is worded properly, the lessor is entitled to prove as an unsecured creditor for its damages. In the case of a debentureholder in a bankruptcy situation, the debentureholder has the right to cause the charged assets to be sold and it is entitled to prove as an unsecured creditor for the deficiency on its loan. In most cases the damages of the lessor and the deficiency on the debentureholder's loan will be equivalent; namely, the difference between the present value of the monies that are owed and the value of the leased goods or the charged assets. Hence, the rights of an equipment lessor and the rights of a debentureholder with a fixed charge on financed equipment in a bankruptcy situation are roughly the same. The equipment lessors and Royal Trust are being treated the same under the Reorganization Plan. Therefore, there is a sufficient commonality of interest for Royal Trust to be included in the same class as the equipment lessors.

Some submissions were made with respect to the priority between Royal Trust and The R-M Trust Company which is the sole Secured Creditor under the Reorganization Plan. I do not accept the contention that Royal Trust has priority over The R-M Trust Company on any of Woodward's assets other than the ones that are covered by the fixed charge in favour of Royal Trust.

The question then becomes whether the equipment financiers (including Royal Trust) belong in a separate class or in the class of General Creditors. This is an example of why the legal rights of the parties must be examined within the context of the Reorganization Plan. In isolation the rights of the equipment financiers and the rights of unsecured creditors are very different. But the treatment of the two groups in the Reorganization Plan could affect their interests.

If the Reorganization Plan provided that Woodward's was to retain the financed equipment and the equipment financiers were to be paid the same proportion of their indebtedness as the unsecured creditors, the equipment financiers would be entitled to be included in a different class from the unsecured creditors. They would be losing their proprietary or security rights in the equipment and they would be receiving the same pro rata distribution as unsecured creditors who do not have the same rights. However, that is not what the Reorganization Plan is proposing.

The Reorganization Plan does not affect any of the proprietary or security rights of the equipment financiers. Woodward's is allowing the equipment financiers to fully exercise those rights outside of the Reorganization Plan. All the Reorganization Plan is purporting to affect are the claims of the equipment financiers for damages or the deficiencies on loans. These claims are unsecured claims and there is no reason why they should be treated any differently than the claims of unsecured creditors. There is a sufficient commonality of interest between the unsecured creditors and the equipment financiers with respect to their unsecured claims for damages or the deficiencies on loans. It is appropriate to include the equipment financiers in the class of General Creditors with respect to these claims.

This classification of the equipment financiers is consistent with the decision in *Sklar-Peppler, supra,* where the Ontario Court of Justice approved the grouping of equipment lessors in the same class as the unsecured creditors.

Holders of Guarantees or Joint Covenants

The class of General Creditors is comprised of creditors of the Operating Company. However, at least two of these creditors hold a guarantee or joint covenant of the Holding Company. National Bank Leasing holds a guarantee from the Holding Company and the debenture held by Royal Trust is a joint debenture from the Operating Company and the Holding Company. For ease of reference I will refer to a creditor holding a guarantee or joint covenant of the Holding Company as the holder of a guarantee and such reference shall also include the holder of a joint covenant.

The Holding Company does not own any tangible assets. Other than the shares in the Operating Company, the only asset owned by the Holding Company is an inter-company account owed to it by the Operating Company. This inter-company account means that upon the bankruptcy or other liquidation of the Operating Company, the Holding Company would be an unsecured creditor entitled to share on a pro rata basis in distributions to the unsecured creditors of the Operating Company. If the Holding Company was also to be liquidated, the money received on account of the inter-company receivable would be distributed to the creditors of the Holding Company, including creditors of the Operating Company with guarantees from the Holding Company and other unsecured creditors if sufficient monies were available to fully satisfy the secured and preferred creditors of the Holding Company. The result is that unsecured creditors of the Operating Company with guarantees from the Holding Company may receive more money than the other unsecured creditors of the Operating Company in the event of bankruptcies or other liquidations of the two companies.

On April 16, 1993 the Monitor appointed in these proceedings issued a report confirming that upon a liquidation of the two companies, the unsecured creditors of the Holding Company would receive a distribution. The Monitor estimates a liquidation distribution for the unsecured creditors of the Holding Company to be in the range from 2% to 12%.

The distinction between the interests of the unsecured creditors of the Operating Company and the interests of the unsecured creditors of the Holding Company is recognized in the classification of the creditors in the Reorganization Plan. The unsecured creditors of the Holding Company are included in the class of Noteholders which is a different class from the General Creditors, the class that includes the unsecured creditors of the Operating Company. It is proposed in the Reorganization Plan that the Noteholders receive 32% of their indebtedness.

The Reorganization Plan ignores the fact that the holders of guarantees are unsecured creditors of both companies. It proposes that they receive the same 37% proportion of their indebtedness as the other General Creditors and their status as creditors of the Holding Company is not reflected.

In view of the fact that the holders of guarantees do have different legal rights from the other members of the class of General Creditors, it is necessary to decide whether the rights are so dissimilar that they cannot vote on the Reorganization Plan with a common interest. It was submitted by counsel for Woodward's that there is a common interest because the holders of guarantees will still receive more under the Reorganization Plan that they will be paid upon a liquidation of the two companies. I do not think that this is sufficient to create a commonality of interest with the other members in the class of General Creditors who have lesser legal rights. To the contrary, I believe that this is an example of what Bowen LJ had in mind in the *Sovereign Life* case, *supra*, when he used the term "confiscation." By being a minority in the class of General Creditors, the holders of guarantees can have their guarantees confiscated by a vote of the requisite majority of the class who do not have the same rights. The holders of guarantees could be forced to accept the same proportionate amount as the other members of the class and to receive no value in respect of legal rights that they uniquely enjoy and that would have value in a liquidation of the two companies.

The passage from *Sklar-Pepper* quoted above made reference to the decision in *Re Wellington Building Corp., supra* [(1934), 16 CBR 48 (Ont. SC)]. In that case the Court was asked to approve a scheme of arrangement under the CCAA that had one class of secured creditors which included bondholders, lienholders, third mortgagee and fourth mortgagees. The Court refused to approve the scheme on the basis that there should have been more than one class of secured creditors. Kingstone J said the following at p. 54 of 16 CBR:

… it was necessary under the Act that they should vote in classes and that three-fourths of the value of each class should be obtained in support of the scheme before the Court could or should approve of it. Particularly is this the case where the holders of the senior securities' (in this case the bondholders') rights are seriously affected by the proposal as they are deprived of the arrears of interest on their bonds if the proposal is carried through. It was never the intention under the Act, I am convinced, to deprive creditors in the position of the bondholders of their right to approve as a class by the necessary majority of a scheme propounded by the company which would permit the holders of junior securities to put through a scheme inimicable to this class and amounting to confiscation of the vested interest of the bondholders.

In *Re 229531 BC Ltd.* (1989), 72 CBR (NS) 310 (BCSC) the Court refused to approve a plan of arrangement under the CCAA for numerous reasons. One of the reasons was that a guarantee held by one creditor was to be released as a result of the reorganization plan and the creditor was to receive the same proportionate distribution as all of the other unsecured creditors. In other words, the guarantee was being confiscated by the vote of other creditors who did not enjoy the same rights as the creditor which held the guarantee.

If it was clear that no monies would be available to unsecured creditors upon a liquidation of the Holding Company, the legal rights of the holders of the guarantees would have no practical value and there would then be no objection to their inclusion in the class of General Creditors. There is also a point where the prospects of the unsecured creditors of the Holding Company receiving any monies upon its liquidation would be so uncertain that the commonality of interest between the holders of the guarantees and the other members of the class of General Creditors would not be affected. However, I am not satisfied in this case that such prospects are so uncertain that the holders of guarantees should be forced to be in the same class as the other unsecured creditors of the Operating Company. In making this statement, I note that the unsecured creditors of the Holding Company are to receive 32% of their indebtedness under the Reorganization Plan.

I should stress that it is important in my view that there is only one difference between the rights of the holders of the guarantees and the rights of the other members of the class of General Creditors. It is clear that the one additional right enjoyed by the holders of the guarantees is not being given any value under the Reorganization Plan. The result could be different if the other members of the class of General Creditors had additional rights that were not enjoyed by the holders of the guarantees. There could be a trade-off between the rights that were not commonly shared and the groups could have a sufficient commonality of interest to be included in the same class. Here, there is no potential trade-off between the two groups and the one additional right of the holders of the guarantees is being confiscated without compensation.

Counsel for Woodward's suggested that the issue of the guarantees be left to the fairness hearing (i.e., the hearing to consider the sanctioning of the Reorganization Plan). As I believe that the holders of guarantees have a sufficiently different legal right to warrant a separate classification, it follows that I would consider the Reorganization Plan to be unfair to them if they are included in the class of General Creditors. I should not order meetings for the creditors to vote on the Reorganization Plan when I know that those meetings would be fruitless because I would refuse to approve the outcome of the meetings.

Landlords

Counsel for Triple Five Corporation Limited submitted that there should be two classes of landlords, one class consisting of landlords with anchor tenants whose leases are being repudiated and the other class consisting of the remaining landlords. Counsel for Bucci Investment Corporation and Prospero International Realty Inc. submitted that there should be three classes of landlords, one class consisting of landlords with anchor tenants whose leases are being repudiated, a second class consisting of landlords without anchor tenants whose leases are being repudiated and the third class consisting of the remaining landlords.

Counsel for Triple Five Corporation Limited put forward three reasons in support of his position. A fourth reason was also put forward initially but it was withdrawn and reserved for the fairness hearing. The three reasons are as follows:

(a) a repudiation of a lease by an anchor tenant will cause the landlord to be in breach of other contractual obligations and the consequences of such a repudiation go beyond the liquidated damages that result from the repudiation of a lease by a tenant other than an anchor tenant;

(b) there is no precedent for the selective repudiation of leases under the CCAA and Woodward's has chosen not [to] utilize the proposal provisions of the *Bankruptcy and Insolvency Act* that now has a procedure for the repudiation of leases;

(c) Zellers Inc. (and its parent, The Hudson's Bay Company) is a stranger to the relationship between Woodward's and its creditors and its involvement in Woodward's reorganization (by way of a merger with the reorganized company) requires a higher degree of fairness.

In my view, none of these reasons is a valid justification for the creation of a separate class of landlords:

(a) the additional consequences of a repudiation by an anchor tenant flow from external considerations and the different consequences to different landlords does not result from different legal rights existing between the landlords and Woodward's. As was held in *Northland Properties, supra*, separate creditor classification must be based on a difference in legal interests or rights;

(b) *Sklar-Peppler, supra*, and *Grafton-Fraser, supra*, are both examples of reorganizations involving repudiations of leases. The fact that the *Bankruptcy and Insolvency Act* now specifically provides for the repudiation of leases does not mean that a reorganization involving lease repudiation cannot be attempted under the CCAA and it certainly does not mean that there should be separate classes of landlords;

(c) the aspect of fairness is a matter to be considered on the application for the Court to sanction the Reorganization Plan. The application is commonly called the fairness hearing. There is nothing in the involvement of Zellers Inc. that requires the creation of separate classes for landlords.

Counsel for Bucci and Prospero did not put forward any independent grounds for the creation of separate landlord classes. His point was that if there was justification for the creation of a separate class for landlords with anchor tenants whose leases were being repudiated, there was equal justification for the creation of a separate class for the other landlords whose leases were being repudiated.

There was one point that bothered me about the grouping of all the landlords into a single class. In addition to including landlords whose leases were being repudiated, the class includes landlords who are having their leases partially repudiated by the unilateral reduction in the amount of leased space and landlords who are having the rent under their leases unilaterally reduced. Both of these two groups of landlords would be having a continuing relationship with Woodward's. Unlike the trade suppliers, the continuing relationship between these landlords and Woodward's is based on legal rights. I was concerned that the continuing legal relationship between these landlords and Woodward's may give them a different interest from interests of the landlords whose leases are being wholly repudiated. For example, the continuing landlords may be more willing to vote in favour of the Reorganization Plan because they will be able to recoup some of their losses from the profits generated out of the continuing relationship with Woodward's. The answer to my concern is that the rent under all of the continuing leases is to be adjusted to market rent. The landlords whose leases are being repudiated will also be leasing their premises to new tenants at market rent. Accordingly, the landlords with continuing leases will not have any advantage over the other landlords and there will be sufficient commonality of interest to include all of the landlords in one class.

During submissions I queried whether the landlords should be included in the class of General Creditors. At first blush a landlord whose lease is being repudiated is in the same position as the other unsecured creditors of the Operating Company. The reason why it is appropriate for the Landlords to be in a different class is that they receive different treatment under the Reorganization Plan. The General Creditors are to be paid an amount equal to six months' rent. One reason for the different treatment is the fact that it is very difficult to properly quantify the claims of the Landlords and the efforts of the Landlords to mitigate their damages will not be known prior to the implementation of the Reorganization Plan. This rationale was accepted in *Grafton-Fraser, supra*, where the Court approved a separate classification for the landlords. Another justification for the different treatment is the fact that the *Bankruptcy and Insolvency Act* provides that landlords whose leases are repudiated are entitled to compensation equal to six months' rent.

In the *Grafton-Fraser* case, *supra*, the Court approved a landlord class which, at least at the time of the decision, appeared to include both landlords with repudiated leases and landlords with continuing leases at reduced rental rates.

It is my view that there is sufficient commonality of interest among the landlords for all of them to be included in a single class. I am reinforced in my decision by the positions of the other landlords represented by counsel at the hearing. Mr. Kuhn, Mr. Knowles and Mr. Mitchell, who each represent landlords in each of the three proposed landlords classes, all supported the single class for the landlords and that position in itself demonstrates that the landlords do have a commonality of interest.

Conclusion

I approve the classes of creditors designated in the Reorganization Plan with exception that the class of General Creditors should not include creditors of the Operating Company who hold guarantees or joint covenants from the Holding Company. I dismiss the application of the terminated employees for separate classification and I reject the other submissions for separate classifications.

Order accordingly.

CHAPTER NINETEEN

II Reorganization Under Part III, Division 1 of the BIA

As noted in the introduction to chapter 18, in contrast to the CCAA, Part III of the BIA is very rule oriented. As a result, every step in the procedure, from filing a notice of intention (NOI) to making a proposal to the consequences of a breach of the terms of the proposal, is carefully regulated.

The drafters gave several reasons for this approach. (1) Since Part III proceedings can be initiated by the simple filing of an NOI (s. 50.4(1)) without the necessity for a hearing, it was important to discourage frivolous filings and to ensure that a serious proposal was presented within a maximum prescribed period. (2) A rule oriented regime would greatly reduce the need for court hearings. This would reduce costs for small and medium-sized enterprises for whom Part III was principally designed. (3) Creditors had complained about the open textured character of the CCAA and the uncertainty this was causing. Part III was designed to address this problem and also to bring about a better balance between the interests of creditors and debtors.

Despite these features of the BIA, the courts retain important discretionary powers at every major stage of the proceedings. See ss. 50.4(9) and (11), 58, 63, 65.1(6), and 69.4.

Summary of Part III Provisions

Any insolvent person is eligible to initiate the proceedings (s. 50(1)) and can do so either by immediately making a proposal to the debtor's creditors (*ibid.*) or by filing an NOI to initiate a proposal (s. 50.4(1)). If the debtor adopts the latter route (as is normally likely to be the case), it must also file a projected cash flow statement with a trustee and the trustee must report on its reasonableness (s. 50.4(2)). The NOI is good for 30 days. The court is empowered to grant a maximum of three extensions, each no more than 45 days in duration and provided that the proposal itself is filed within 6 months of the NOI. In each case, however, the burden rests on the debtor to justify the extension (s. 50.4(9)). For proper cause, the court can also terminate at any time the period for making a proposal (s. 50.4(11)).

So far as the proposal itself is concerned, s. 50(1.4) adopts a commonality test for the classication of secured creditors. (No test is provided for unsecured claims.) When the proposal has been presented, a meeting of creditors must be called (s. 51) and the creditors must vote to approve the proposal (s. 54). Approval requires a majority in number and two thirds in value of the claims of each class of creditors (ss. 54, 62(2)). However, the proposal does not become effective until it has also been approved by the court (ss. 58-59). Section 60 lists the types of claims that must receive priority treatment in the proposal. If the debtor defaults in performing the terms of the proposal, the court may annul the proposal (s. 63). The court may also annul the proposal if the court's approval was obtained by fraud or where it appears that the proposal cannot continue without injustice or undue delay (*ibid.*).

Section 65.1 spells out the impact of the filing of an NOI or a proposal on subsisting executory contracts. (Note carefully that the court has no general dispensing power to grant the debtor relief from onerous executory contracts; but may grant relief to the *other* contracting party from hardships caused by the s. 65.1 provisions: s. 65.1(6).) Section 65.2 contains the important provisions enabling the debtor to repudiate a commercial realty lease. Finally, a general stay of proceedings against the debtor is imposed on the debtor's creditors pursuant to ss. 69 and 69.1 once a NOI or a proposal has been filed.

Part III Case Law

Compared with the abundant and generally fully reasoned CCAA judgments, the case law on Part III is still relatively sparse and many of the judgments are quite brief. The difference between the two positions is no doubt explained in part by the short period during which revamped Part III has been in force. A still more important reason is that, generally speaking, much smaller amounts of money are involved in Part III proposals and that debtors cannot afford to litigate as freely or as heavily as can the mega-corporations usually involved in CCAA proceedings. The balance of this chapter contains a selection of recent Part III decisions to give students a flavour of how Canadian courts are responding to the new statutory regime. Chapter 19 concludes with a memorandum by Gordon Marantz, a leading Toronto insolvency lawyer, on the future of the CCAA. The memorandum will give students a further opportunity to compare and contrast the principal features of the CCAA and Part III.

Re Cumberland Trading Inc.
(1994), 23 CBR (3d) 225 (Ont. Gen. Div.)

MOTIONS by secured creditor for declaration that stay provisions of *Bankruptcy and Insolvency Act* no longer operated to prevent it from enforcing its security, for declaration that 30-day period to file proposal had terminated and for order allowing substitution of trustee.

FARLEY J: Skyview International Finance Corporation ("Skyview") brought this motion for a declaration that the stay provisions (ss. 69 and 69.1) of the *Bankruptcy and Insolvency Act*, RSC 1985, c. B-3 as amended ("BIA") no longer operate in respect of Skyview taking steps to enforce its security (including accounts receivable and inventory) given by Cumberland Trading Inc. ("Cumberland") which it has been financing for the last 9 years. In addition Skyview moved for a declaration that the 30 day period to file a proposal mentioned in s. 50.4(8) BIA was terminated. Thirdly, Skyview was asking for an order removing Doane Raymond Limited ("Doane") which was Cumberland's choice as trustee and substituting A. Farber Associates ("Farber") as trustee under the Notice of Intention to File a Proposal of Cumberland. In the alternative to the relief awarded in the last two aspects, Skyview wished to have an order appointing Farber as interim receiver.

On January 5, 1994 Skyview demand payment in full of its operating financing loan to Cumberland and gave a s. 244 BIA notice of its intention to enforce its security in ten days. The affidavit filed on behalf of Skyview indicated that Cumberland was not cooperating with it in providing appropriate financial information for the last half year. This was disputed in the affidavit filed by Cumberland. Suffice it to say that there has been a falling out between the two. Skyview asserted that it was owed $966,478 and that there was an exposure to it under a guarantee given on Cumberland's behalf to a potential of approximately $200,000 US. Skyview's deadline for repayment was January 16th. On January 14th Cumberland filed with the Official Receiver a Notice of Intention to make a Proposal (s. 50.4(1) BIA) and pursuant to s. 69 BIA there would a stay of proceedings upon this filing.

Skyview's president swore that:

21. In light of the unpleasant and frustrating experience Skyview has had to endure over the preceding 3 to 4 months with Cumberland, including specifically the persistent refusal by Cumberland to account for its sales from the Retail Business, the misrepresentation of Cumberland's pre-sold orders referred to above and particularly its secretive purported "Termination" of its direction to accord to pay sums to Skyview in reduction of Cumberland's indebtedness, Skyview's faith and confidence in the management of Cumberland has been irreparably damaged such that Skyview would not be prepared to vote in terms of any proposal which Cumberland may make.

and further that

24. The continued operation of a stay of proceedings preventing Skyview from enforcing its security will be materially prejudicial to the rights of Skyview. The assets of Skyview consist primarily of inventory and receivables (both from the Distribution Business and the Retail Business). With each day that passes Cumberland is converting its inventory (financed by Skyview) into cash (primarily in the Retail Business) and receivables (primarily in the Distribution Business) and it is Skyview's fear that those sums will be used by Cumberland to pay its other creditors and to fund the professional costs which it inevitably must incur in formulating and implementing a proposal. This fear is especially heightened insofar as the receivables generated from the Retail Business are concerned as they are under the direct and immediate control of Cumberland and are not collected by Accord.

Cumberland's Notice of Intention to File a Proposal acknowledges that Skyview is owed $750,000. On that basis Skyview has 95% in value of Cumberland's admitted secured creditors' claims and 67% of all creditors' claims of whatever nature. No matter what, Skyview's claim is so large that Skyview cannot be swamped in any class in which it could be put. Clearly Skyview would have a veto on any vote as to a proposal, at least so far as the secured class, assuming that secureds are treated as a separate class. This leaves the interesting aspect that under the BIA regime one could have a proposal turned down by the secured creditor class but approved by the unsecured creditor class and effective vis-à-vis this latter class, but with the secured class being able to enforce their security. One may question the practicality [*sic*] proposal affecting only unsecured creditors becoming effective in similar circumstances to this situation.

Cumberland's essential position is that it must have some time under BIA to see about reorganizing itself. While I am mindful that both BIA and the *Companies' Creditors Arrangement Act,* RSC 1985, c. C-36 ("CCAA") should be classified as debtor friendly legislation since they both provide for the possibility of reorganization (as contrasted with the absence of creditor friendly legislation which would allow, say, creditors to move for an increase in interest rates if inflation became rampant), these acts do not allow debtors absolute immunity and impunity from their creditors. I would also observe that all too frequently debtors wait until virtually the last moment, the last moment, or in some cases, beyond the last moment before even beginning to think about reorganization (and the attendant support that any successful reorganization requires from the creditors). I noted the lamentable tendency of debtors to deal with these situations as "last gasp" desperation moves in *Re Inducon Development Corp.* (1992), 8 CBR (3d) 308 (Ont. Gen. Div.). To deal with matters on this basis minimizes the chances of success, even if "success" may have been available with earlier spadework. It is true that under BIA an insolvent person can get an automatic stay by merely filing a Notice of Intention to File a Proposal—as opposed to the necessity under the CCAA of convincing the court of the appropriateness of granting a stay (and the nature of the stay). However BIA does not guarantee the insolvent person a stay without review for any set period of time. To keep the playing field level and dry so that it remains in play, a creditor or creditors can apply to the court to cut short the otherwise automatic (or extended) stay; in this case Skyview is utilizing s. 50.4(11) to do so.

Cumberland relies upon *Re N.T.W. Management Group Ltd.* (1993), 19 CBR (3d) 162 (Ont. Bktcy.), a decision of Chadwick J. Skyview asserts that *N.T.W.* is distinguishable or incorrectly decided and secondly that the philosophy of my decision in *Re Triangle Drugs Inc.* (1993), 16 CBR (3d) 1 (Ont. Bktcy.) should prevail. In *Triangle Drugs* I allowed the veto holding group of unsecured creditors to in effect vote at an advance poll in a situation where there appeared to be a gap in the legislation. The key section of BIA is s. 50.4(11) which provides:

• • •

It does not seem to me that there is any gap in this sector of the legislation.

As the headnote in *N.T.W.* stated, Chadwick J viewed a situation similar to this one as requiring that the debtor must have an opportunity to put forth its proposal when he stated at p. 163:

The bank had stated that it would not accept any proposal. However, since the companies had not yet had the opportunity to put forth their proposal, it was impossible to make a final determination under s. 50.4(11)(c). The companies should have the opportunity to formulate and make their proposal.

However, I note that in this instance Cumberland has filed its Notice of Intention to File a Proposal the day before Skyview's s. 244 notice would have allowed it to take control of the security. Cumberland's president swore that:

2. The efforts which Cumberland is currently undertaking represent a bona fide effort, made in good faith, to restructure its finances in order to preserve the business of the company for the benefit of all of the creditors of the company, including Skyview. It is my belief that the proposal process will represent a significantly better treatment of all such creditors then would be available through either an enforcement by Skyview of its security against the assets of Cumberland, a bankruptcy of Cumberland or other processes available in the circumstances.

and further that:

I intend to submit a proposal, pursuant to the provisions of the Bankruptcy and Insolvency Act, which represent the most advantageous treatment available, in my view, to all of the creditors of Cumberland and which allows for the continued viability of the business of Cumberland. This proposal is being prepared, and will be presented, in complete good faith. In the course of reviewing and preparing this proposal material with Mr. Godbold, I have determined that the legitimate claim of Skyview does not, in fact, represent in excess of 66-2/3 of all the claims against Cumberland. At this time, Doane Raymond Limited is already in the position of Trustee under the proposal, in accordance with the provisions of the Bankruptcy and Insolvency Act. In addition, as noted above, I am prepared to consent to the appointment of Doane Raymond Limited as interim receiver of Cumberland. In the circumstances, I respectfully submit that the stay in favour of Cumberland pursuant to the Bankruptcy and Insolvency Act should not be lifted.

No explanation was given as to the lower share indicated for Skyview but in any event there was no assertion that Skyview lost its veto.

However we do not have any indication of what this proposal proposes to be—notwithstanding that 10 days have now passed since Cumberland filed its Notice of Intention to File a Proposal and five days since Skyview served Cumberland with this motion. In a practical sense one would expect, given Skyview's veto power and its announced position, that Cumberland would have to present "something" to get Skyview to change its mind—e.g. an injection of fresh equity or a take out of Skyview's loan position. However there was not even a germ of a plan revealed—but merely a bald assertion that the proposal being worked on would be a better result for everyone including Skyview. This is akin to trying to box with a ghost. While I agree with the logic of Chadwick J when he said at p. 168 of *N.T.W.* that:

CIBC the major secured creditor has indicated they will not accept any proposal put forth, other than complete discharge of the CIBC indebtedness. Other substantial creditors have taken the same position. There is no doubt that the insolvent companies have a substantial obstacle to overcome. *As the insolvent companies have not had the opportunity to put forth this proposal, it is impossible to make the final determination.* In *Triangle Drugs Inc.* Farley J had the proposal. Well over one-half of the secured [*sic*; in reality unsecured] creditors indicated they would not vote for the proposal. As such, he then terminated the proposal. We have not reached that stage in this case. The insolvent companies should have the opportunity of putting forth the proposal.

[Emphasis added.]

However this analysis does not seem to address the test involved. With respect I do not see this logical aspect as coming into play in s. 50.4(11)(c) which reads:

The court may, on application by ... a creditor, declare terminated, before its actual expiration, the thirty day period mentioned in subsection (8) ... if the court is satisfied that

• • •

(c) the insolvent person will not likely be able to make a proposal, before the expiration of the period in question, that will be accepted by the creditors, or

• • •

and where the court declares the period in question terminated, paragraphs (8)(a) to (c) thereupon apply as if that period had expired.

It seems to me that clause (c) above deals specifically with the situation where there has been no proposal tabled. It provides that there is no absolute requirement that the creditors have to wait to see what the proposal is before they can indicate they will vote it down. I do no see anything in BIA which would affect a creditor (or group of creditors) with a veto position from reaching the conclusion that nothing the insolvent debtor does will persuade the creditor to vote in favour of whatever proposal may be forthcoming. I think that this view is strengthened when one considers that the court need only be satisfied that "the insolvent person will not *likely* be able to make a proposal, before the expiration of the period in question, that will be accepted by the creditors ..." (emphasis added). This implies that there need not be a certainty of turndown. The act of making the proposal is one that is still yet to come. I am of the view that Skyview's position as indicated above is satisfactory proof that Cumberland will not likely be able to make a proposal that will be accepted by the creditors of Cumberland.

Skyview of course also has the option of proceeding under s. 69.4 BIA which provides:

• • •

Is Skyview entitled to the benefit of s. 69.4(1) BIA? I am of the view that the material prejudice referred to therein is an objective prejudice as opposed to a subjective one—i.e., it refers to the degree of the prejudice suffered vis-à-vis the indebtedness and the attendant security and not to the extent that such prejudice may affect the creditor *qua* person, organization or entity. If it were otherwise then a "big creditor" may be so financially strong that it could never have the benefit of this clause. In this situation Skyview's prejudice appears to be that the only continuing financing available to Cumberland is that generated by turning Chamberland's [*sic*] accounts receivable and inventory (pledged to Skyview) into cash to pay operating expenses during the period leading up to a vote on a potential proposal, which process will erode the security of Skyview, without any replenishment. However, Skyview does not go the additional step and make any quantitative (or possibly qualitative) analysis as to the extent of such prejudice so that the court has an idea of the magnitude of materiality. In other words, Skyview presently estimates that it would be fortunate to realize $450,000 on Cumberland's accounts receivables and inventory, but it does not go on to give any foundation for a conclusion that in the course of the next month $x of this security would be eaten up or alternatively that the erosion would likely be in the neighbourhood of $y per day of future operations. The comparison would be between the "foundation" of a maximum of $450,000 and what would happen as to deterioration therefrom if the stay is not lifted. I note there was no suggestion from Cumberland that there would be no erosion of Skyview's position by, say, getting a cash injection or by improving margins by increasing revenues or decreasing expenses. Skyview's request for its first relief request is dismissed since in my view Skyview did not engage in the correct comparison of material prejudice.

I note that Cumberland does not oppose Skyview's request for an interim receiver. But for my conclusion that Skyview succeeds in its second relief request (to have the 30 day period in which to file a proposal terminated) and the ancillary third relief request of substitution of Farber for Doane as trustee, I would have granted the fourth relief request of appointing Farber as interim receiver. I would also award Skyview costs of $600 payable out of the estate of Cumberland from the proceeds first realized.

Order accordingly.

Re High Street Construction Ltd.
(1993), 19 CBR (3d) 213 (Ont. Gen. Div.)

LEITCH J: High Street Construction Limited ("High Street") has applied to extend its time to file a proposal with the official receiver to March 1, 1993 pursuant to s. 51.4(9) of the *Bankruptcy and Insolvency Act* (the "Act"). To permit the extension I must be satisfied that High Street has and is acting in good faith and with due diligence, that no creditor is prejudiced by an extension and that the extension will permit High Street to make a viable proposal.

High Street directly and by guarantees of the indebtedness of two related companies Sweetie Developments Limited ("Sweetie") and 518463 Ontario Limited ("518463") owes approximately 5 million dollars to the Toronto Dominion Bank ("T.D."). Repayment of the debt was demanded by T.D. in December 1990. The debt was acknowledged and High Street agreed to satisfy its outstanding obligations by February, 1991. T.D. extended this repayment date to April 3, 1991. Further extensions were granted by T.D. from time to time apparently on an informal basis until November 1992. The High Street account then came under the jurisdiction of a new manager who, according to counsel to T.D., took the position that "enough was enough." Formal demand for repayment was made December 2, 1992. High Street responded with a notice of intent to file a proposal which brings us to this application. T.D. is the most significant unrelated creditor of High Street and is the only creditor to oppose this application.

Since April 1991, $300,000 has been paid to T.D., loans of $83,000 to one of the shareholders has been repaid and one parcel of property has been sold with a mortgage back from the purchaser assigned to T.D. However, interest on the outstanding indebtedness and the realty taxes have not been kept current. T.D. alleges that the fact that interest and realty tax arrears will accrue during an extension is evidence that it will be prejudiced by such extension. The assets of High Street available to satisfy the indebtedness to T.D. consist entirely of three parcels of vacant land in Kitchener, Ontario owned by High Street and two parcels of vacant land in Mississauga, Ontario owned by Sweetie and 518463. These assets are non-depreciating and cannot be dissipated. There is no suggestion by T.D. that the management of High Street will overlook or decline an opportunity to sell its assets. The fact that realty tax and interest arrears will continue to accrue during an extension period is not sufficient evidence of prejudice to T.D. to disentitle High Street to an extension. Further, the fact that at the request of T.D. and without opposition from High Street I ordered that s. 69 of the Act shall not operate to prevent T.D. from issuing its notice of sale with respect to its mortgages on the High Street property will alleviate the prejudice to T.D. which it has complained of.

The president of High Street, Larry Wolynetz, has worked without compensation during the last two years and has endeavoured to sell all of the vacant land owned by High Street and its affiliates. While it is apparent that he has not been successful, there is no evidence that the lack of success has resulted from anything other than the recessionary times. There is no evidence that detracts from his assertions that all of his efforts have been in good faith and that he has diligently pursued all opportunities for sale. There is no evidence that Mr. Wolynetz is "grossly exaggerating" the value of the assets, thereby discouraging a possible sale as was the case in *First Treasury Financial Inc. v. Cango Petroleums Inc.* (1991), 3 CBR (3d) 232 (Ont. Gen. Div.). I find therefore that High Street has and is acting in good faith and with due diligence.

The requirement that the extension will permit High Street to make a viable proposal is the most difficult requirement for it to meet. The decisions relating to applications for extensions under the *Companies' Creditors Arrangement Act* suggest that in assessing whether a proposal will be viable you must consider whether such proposal has a probable chance of acceptance. (*Nova Metal Products Inc. v. Comiskey (Trustee of)* (1990), 1 CBR (3d) 101 (Ont. CA) and *Ultracare Management Inc. v. Zevenberger (Trustee of)* (1990), 3 CBR (3d) 151 (Ont. Gen. Div.).) In this case, T.D. basically has taken the position that "enough is enough." It was acknowledged by counsel for T.D. that there is no question as to the honesty or integrity of Mr. Wolynetz but its concern is simply whether he can get the job done. Its contention is that given the failure to effect a sale of one or more of the parcels of land to this point in time, it is unlikely that a sale will be accomplished within the extension period. There is a distinction between that contention and a conclusion that High Street cannot put forward within the requested extension period a plan that has a probable chance of acceptance by a majority of the creditors. I find that High Street has a plan outline for its proposal—that is, the immediate sale of the parcels of land owned by Sweetie and 518463 which have been developed to the point that there is site plan approval, building permit availability and offers to lease for 60% of the proposed building. Mr. Wolynetz has determined that these parcels are the most saleable and has sworn in his affidavit that he expects an unconditional offer to purchase these parcels within the extension period. With this offer High Street can quantify the debt due to T.D. subsequent to the sale of this property and can provide a detailed and specific proposal to T.D. It cannot now be said that T.D. will not accept this proposal. I find therefore that the requested extension will permit High Street to make a viable proposal.

At the conclusion of this application counsel for T.D. noted that I must be cautious in granting this extension. I have made my decision based on particular facts of this application and my findings that High Street has satisfied the three prerequisites for an extension under s. 50.4(9) of the Act.

Application allowed.

Re Carr-Harris & Co.
(1993), 23 CBR (3d) 74 (BCSC)

APPLICATION by landlord that s. 65.2(1) of *Bankruptcy and Insolvency Act* did not apply and that notice of repudiation not effective.

Master PATTERSON [In Chambers] (orally): Carr-Harris & Company is a professional law corporation which carries on business in Vancouver primarily in the area of personal injury litigation. The law firm has encountered financial problems and on September 16, 1993, filed a notice of intention to make a proposal pursuant to the provisions of the *Bankruptcy and Insolvency Act*, RSC 1985, c. B-3. Subsequently, on October 15, 1993, a proposal was filed.

The essence of the proposal is that by 1996 all creditors will be paid 100% of their claims but there will be no entitlement to interest. The proposal is contingent upon Carr-Harris & Company working out an arrangement with the Royal Bank of Canada, a secured creditor owed approximately $100,000 by the terms of which the bank is to be paid $10,000 per month commencing December 20th, 1993. The proposal requires the law firm to pay $8,500 per month to the trustee for the benefit of creditors commencing in March 1994. A number of creditors with claims less than $500 will be paid in full and forthwith. It follows that during the term of the proposal, the law firm will be required to pay for all expenses including rent in cash and not on credit.

The law firm has prepared a projected cash flow statement for the months October, 1993, to March, 1994. That cash flow projection shows total revenue for the six-month period as $1,266,166. The revenue projection is based on the receipt of contingency fees consequent upon the settlement of various personal injury actions. Most, if not all, of the clients retaining the law firm do so on a contingency basis. Usually the contingency agreements will provide that a fee based on a percentage of recovery is payable when the matter is settled or judgment is obtained. The agreements generally provide that the clients will pay necessary disbursements as and when they are incurred.

On October 15, 1993, Carr-Harris & Company delivered to its landlord, Standard Life Assurance Company, a notice of repudiation of lease pursuant to Section 65.2(1) of the *Bankruptcy and Insolvency Act*. The landlord has now applied pursuant to Section 65.2(2) for a declaration that subsection 1 does not apply. If the landlord is successful, the notice of repudiation would be ineffective. Section 65.2 of the *Bankruptcy and Insolvency Act* is as follows:

• • •

Section 65.2(2) clearly places the onus on the insolvent person to satisfy the court that the proposal would not be viable without the repudiation of the lease. This Section only came into force in late 1992, and counsel were able to find only one reported decision, that of *Re Janpar Produits de Bureau Inc.* (1993), 20 CBR (3d) 8, a decision of the Quebec Superior Court, Bankruptcy Division. The headnote for that case indicates the court found Section 65.2 not to be unconstitutional and that the Federal Bankruptcy Legislation prevailed over Provincial laws governing landlords and tenants. Otherwise, the decision does not appear to assist in the determination of the viability of the proposal, without the repudiated lease.

On September 1, 1987, the law firm first occupied premises on the second floor at 900 Howe Street, Vancouver. In August, 1992, the law firm renewed its existing lease with Standard Life and at the same time, leased an additional 2,463 square feet. This extra space is not contiguous and effectively doubled the size of the office. Combined rent for both parts of the office is $11,971.03 per month effective November 1, 1993, and approximately half of that relates to the extra space. It is for the extra space that notice of repudiation was given not for the original office space. Carr-Harris & Company did not pay any rent for June, July, August, and September 1993, but has paid all rent due for October of 1993, even thought the notice of repudiation was delivered on October the 15th.

The principal of Carr-Harris & Company has sworn an affidavit in which he states that the decision to expand into extra offices was ill-advised. The extra offices (described as the south wing) are now empty and will not be required during the term of the proposal because various lawyers formerly associated with the practice will no longer be there. Mr. Carr-Harris, after reviewing actual fees received by the law firm, swears this in his affidavit sworn November 1, 1993:

21. For the reasons given, I verily believe that the proposal the Corporation has made will not be viable in the sense that it will not be one which the corporation is capable of performing, if it is required to continue leasing empty space in the south wing.

David Gray, a partner with Campbell Saunders Ltd., the trustee under the proposal in his affidavit sworn November 1, 1993, swears:

6. In the context of preparing the Proposal as well as the supporting cash flow statements, it became apparent that the lease, which is the subject matter of this application (the "Lease") may well inhibit the performance of the Proposal by the firm. Accordingly, and based upon my recommendation after discussion with counsel, Mr. Carr-Harris was advised to repudiate the Lease. A copy of the repudiation is attached as Exhibit "A" to the Affidavit of Richard J. Olson filed in these proceedings on October 18th, 1993. That notice of repudiation was prepared by the Trustee.

7. Based upon my knowledge of the affairs of the Firm, it is my opinion that the Firm's financial position has been enhanced by repudiation of the Lease. As well, the repudiation of the Lease has enhanced the likelihood of the success of the Proposal.

In the trustee's preliminary report to creditors, Mr. Gray reviews the assets of the law firm and writes this about the biggest asset which is work in progress.

The law corporation shows a value of $2,500,000.00 for its work in progress. This amount is calculated on the total potential volume of work that the firm has contracted for based on assumptions regarding the projected amount of the claim. It does not include the time incurred at standard hourly rates that has been incurred to date on the client file. We have arbitrarily reduced the law corporation's value to $1,000,000.00 to reflect the fact that not all of the time has been incurred and also to reflect the fact that not all of the files will result in a successful claim.

The trustee then continues and points out that on a liquidation basis, the value of work in progress could be nothing.

In attempting to assess the viability of the proposal, it is clearly necessary to try and define "viable" as there is no definition in the *Bankruptcy and Insolvency Act.* "Viable" is defined variously as capable of functioning or capable of existing or maintaining an existence. In *Re Janpar,* a distinction is drawn between a viable proposal and the wording of Section 65.2(2) which speaks of a "proposal (which) would not be viable, without the repudiation of that lease." It follows, in my view, that the first determination is whether the insolvent person has shown that the proposal is viable or workable if the lease were not a factor at all and would not work if there were a requirement to pay the additional rent. In other words, in this case, would the payment of an extra $6,000 per month rent render the proposal of [*sic*] unworkable?

Contingency fees received by the law firm for the past five months are as follows:

June, 1993	$ 44,715.11
July, 1993	$ 22,422.44
August, 1993	$ 33,304.74
September, 1993	$ 43,975.19
October, 1993	$ 71,310.64
	$215,728.12

The average receipts are $43,145 per month. This is a far cry from the cash flow projections of the law firm which project average monthly receipts of $204,000 per month. For the one month where there is a prediction and actual receipts, the difference is dramatic. In October of 1993, the law firm predicted receipts of $153,000, actually received $71,310.64, leaving a shortfall of $81,689.36.

Under the proposal, the law firm will have to make the following fixed payments:

Revenue Canada	$ 2,500.00
Royal Bank	$10,000.00
Trustee	$ 8,500.00
Rent (remaining office only)	$ 6,000.00
	$27,000.00

If one assumes that average receipts will continue at approximately $43,000 per month then approximately $16,000 remains after paying the fixed costs to cover all other expenses, including salaries, benefits, source deductions, telephones and supplies, with no allowance being made for income tax, PST or GST. The cash flow projection made by the law firm for January, 1994, shows projected expenses of $70,234. If that figure is reduced by $11,000 to reflect the payment of one-half the rent and no shareholder's draw, the expenses are still $59,000. This is amply covered by the projected income of $153,000 but not covered by the current average receipts. I note that the trustee in his report of the projected cash flow statement writes this:

Since the projection is based on assumptions regarding future events, actual results will vary from the information presented even if the hypothetical assumptions occur and the variations may be material. Accordingly, we express no assurance as to whether the projections will be achieved.

After reviewing the projections as carefully as time permits, reviewing actual receipts, and taking into account the fact that rent was unpaid for four months in 1993, that B.C. Telephone Company is owed in excess of $37,000, it is my view that this proposal made by the law firm has only a slim chance of working whether the extra lease payment is a factor or not. The revenue projections appear to be optimistic and there are no assurances from the trustee. Mr. Carr-Harris believes that this proposal will not be viable if he has to continue to lease empty space. The trustee will only say that repudiation of the lease enhances the company's financial position and the likelihood of the success of the proposal. The trustee does not say that the proposal is workable but for the payment of rent for the extra space.

Simply put, the lease payment must be the factor that makes the proposal unworkable, it must be the straw that breaks the camel's back. While I have the greatest sympathy for the law firm and the efforts made to try and resolve its problems, I do not think that this proposal is going to work with the present debtload, with or without the lease payment for the extra space.

Carr-Harris & Company has not satisfied the onus upon it to show that "the proposal ... would not be viable, without the repudiation of that lease" for the extra space. The landlord, Standard Life, is entitled to a declaration, that Section 65.2(1) does not apply to the lease of the extra space, and, consequently, the notice of repudiation is ineffective.

Application allowed.

Re Mernick
(1994), 24 CBR (3d) 8 (Ont. Gen. Div.)

APPLICATION for approval of proposal.

FARLEY J:

• • •

Mernick advises that he has fought the bankruptcy petitions over a long period of time in a very vigorous manner as he wishes to avoid what he feels is the automatic stigma of being a bankrupt. While his effort in this respect may be applauded from one point of view, it should be recognized that bankruptcy legislation is intended to be rehabilitative in nature. It has been often remarked that there is nothing untoward in an honest but unfortunate businessman resorting to this legislation so as to enable him to attempt to make a clean start.

I note as well that it would appear that the proposal section of the *Bankruptcy and Insolvency Act,* RSC 1985, c. B-3 as amended ("BIA") is aimed at the reorganization of business entities (including individuals) which are insolvent but which generally are expected to be viable in an operational sense once the restructuring of the proposal takes place. Such of course would not be the case in Mernick's situation. He has declared that he has no assets of any value and in particular no business operational assets. Furthermore, he has no income; he apparently depends on his general family to support him, his wife and his children. Aside from this family financial assistance (which apparently would be the source of the $50,000 payment in the proposal), Mernick is also able to obtain loans or credit for emergency and necessary matters. Part of the emergency matters would seem to include his assisting others with charitable donations. I am given to understand by him that he has been instrumental in assisting some thousands of others who have been in need; in this case the nature of his generosity is quite commendable although one would have to question his means of borrowing from others to in turn lend with no apparent means to ensure repayment.

Mernick's proposal disclosed no assets but liabilities totalling $43,125,465. Of this, $40 million was said to be owing the 974846 Ontario Inc., a company owned by Meyer Botnick, which purchased the "Firestone indebtedness" for $100,000. The $100,000 did not come from Botnick's company but rather from Mernick's mother who received a non-interest bearing note due 2017 for $500,000 from Botnick's company. However, this transaction which took place July 23, 1992 was reduced by Registrar Ferron to $7,485,000 in light of a prior settlement; it is this amount plus accruing interest which Botnick's company is able to claim against Mernick. The remaining $3,125,465 was made up of various small claims. These were supplemented by further claims of $13,898,887. Claims amounting to $24,509,382 were made and voted in the proposal.

The proposal was for $50,000 payable over time (12 months) without any actual security or designation as to the source of such payments. This would amount to a payout of $1/5$ of one cent on the dollar. However, Botnick's company waived payment which would increase the payout to about $1/3$ of one cent on the dollar—a payout which no one would suggest was handsome.

It is however a rather strange waiver by Botnick's company. The proposal states:

The trustee will distribute the above-mentioned funds [$50,000] in accordance with the priority set forth above. To the extent that unsecured creditors receive dividends through this proposal, such dividend shall be deemed as full payment, and full settlement of those creditors' outstanding claims.

974846 Ontario Inc. has agreed that upon the acceptance of this proposal by my creditors and approval by the Court, it will waive its rights to its pro rata share of the dividend contemplated under this proposal, thereby allowing such funds to be distributed among other unsecured creditors.

On that basis it would appear that Botnick's company's claim would not be compromised since it would not receive a dividend. On the other hand, the legitimacy of the deal which Mernick advised was to get an independent party in control of the Firestone indebtedness—questionable at best takes on a very rank odour if Botnick's company forgives its claim against Mernick but remains saddled with its debt to his mother. The transaction does not have the air of reality. In any event, Mernick was unfortunately at somewhat of a loss to explain which interpretation should be given to the Botnick company waiver.

53 votes were cast in the vote on the proposal—47 (88%) in favour and 6 against. In dollar terms, of the $24,509,382 of claims, $16,992,529 (69.3%) were in favour and $7,516,852 against. Two thirds value would be $16,339,586 so that the votes exceeded this value requirement by $652,944.

The PTL deal was to have been completed by 792929 Ontario Inc. ("79 Company"). Mernick held the shares of this company in trust but he has been vague about the nature of the trust and its beneficiary. He asserts that the beneficiary was never himself although there are a number of agreements in which he recites and warrants that he is sole beneficial owner of the shares. As well, his legal counsel caused to be signed court papers to this effect. Mernick asserts that errors were made and that he did not check the papers before signing. The point in issue in this hearing is the return of the PTL deposit to the 79 Company in late 1990. In 1992, Mernick admitted that a portion of the PTL deposit of about $2.4 million was used to settle claims of Firestone, Bank Leumi and other creditors as well as for legal fees, living expenses and business expenses. Details were not given. One of the April 26, 1993 undertakings to be answered was to give details of the disposition of these funds.

Until he settled with MICC, Mernick always claimed that his interest in the Innisfil Site was worth $30 million based on a conditional offer to purchase the site obtained from 901557 Ontario Inc., a company controlled by a Mr. Spier. However, it appears that the $400,000 deposit paid came not from Spier's company but from the 79 Company. One must question the *bona fides* of such a structure which would so give the impression of financial strength.

Bank Leumi received $500,000 in early 1991 out of the PTL deposit. Registrar Ferron was of the view that this was a preference. Bank Leumi claimed $5,455,834 and voted in favour of the proposal.

Firestone received $428,353 US in the winter of 1991 out of the PTL deposit. It would appear that such has the earmarks of a preference. The Botnick company, as assignee of the Firestone debt, voted $7,484,030 in favour of the proposal.

With respect to many of the claims, it is interesting to note that they date back to 1991 or before, yet they were not previously disclosed in any statement of assets and liabilities affirmed by Mernick. Mernick was quite candid that a fair number of these were owed to persons who were not pressing but expected to be paid if Mernick ever got into position to pay. It was expressed by Mernick that he felt he had a moral (and more) obligation to pay these in full—and it appears that there is a corresponding view in this regard from these creditors. One may well question under these circumstances if the proposal has any meaning vis-à-vis these debts. If the proposal fails, these people expect Mernick to pay 100 cents on the dollar at some time; if the proposal succeeds, they still expect Mernick to pay 100 cents on the dollar. While the morality of such may be very high, one must question whether votes in respect to the claims should be taken into account in binding other creditors; if not, then consideration should be given to the nature of this when considering whether the proposal should be approved.

Mernick has admitted that his "mess" began in the fall of 1989 during which time the Napanee mortgages fell due and were not paid. Spider Maple was put into receivership and Bank Leumi called its loans. Since then, at least $2.4 million has been expended which could have been made available to Mernick's creditors generally.

Clearly the assets involved are less than 50 cents on the dollar (s. 173(1)(a)). Mernick has either failed to keep proper records (s. 173(1)(b), s. 200(1)(a)) or he has refused to or is unable to answer his undertakings using such records (s. 173(m)). Mernick has continued to obtain credit after knowing himself to be insolvent and engaged in business deals

(s. 173(1)(c)). The PTL deposit disposition has not been answered (s. 173(1)(d)). In light of the scanty information available (despite great efforts over a long time by Mr. Mercer), it is not possible to determine if Mr. Mernick has infringed s. 173(1)(e). Clearly in his dismissal for want of prosecution of appeal of the Xerox claim, Mernick has put Xerox to unnecessary expense (s. 173(1)(f)). It appears that there have been preferences within the period in question (s. 173(1)(h)). He has also committed a bankruptcy offence in failing to answer questions (s. 198(c), s. 173(1)(l)).

Three interests must be considered on application to approve a proposal (see *Re Stone* (1976), 22 CBR (NS) 153 (Ont SC)):

(a) the interests of the debtor;
(b) the interests of the creditors generally by ensuring that the proposal is reasonable; and
(c) the interests of the public in the integrity of bankruptcy legislation.

The Court must weigh the effect of approving the proposal and not approving the proposal. In order for the proposal to be approved, the creditors must obtain an advantage over bankruptcy: see *Re Allen Theatres Limited* (1922), 3 CBR 147 (Ont SC); *Re Tridont Health Care Inc.* (1991), 4 CBR (3d) 290 (Ont. Bktcy.) and *Re First Toronto Mining Corp.* (1991), 3 CBR (3d) 246 (Ont. Bktcy.). The conduct of the debtor is a factor to be considered and if there is any suggestion of collusion or secret advantage, the matter will be particularly scrutinized: see *Re Garner* (1921), 1 CBR 424 (Ont. SC) and *Re Man With Axe Ltd.* (1961), 2 CBR (NS) 8 (Man. QB).

Where the facts mentioned in s. 173 BIA are proven, the Court shall refuse to approve the proposal unless the proposal provides reasonable security for the payment of not less than 50 cents on the dollar of unsecured claims or such percentage of these as the Court may direct: see *Re Dolson* (1984), 49 CBR (NS) 255 (Ont. SC); *McNamara v. McNamara* (1984), 53 CBR (NS) 240 (Ont. SC); *Re Tridont, supra.* The Court may refuse to approve a proposal where offences mentioned in s. 198 and s. 200 have been committed (s. 59(2) BIA).

As indicated previously, I am of the view that this type of proposal is an ill fit with the thrust and intention of BIA. It is not a reorganization or restructuring. As such, it should at least receive the strongest scrutiny. There are numerous offences and inappropriate facts which raise problems under s. 173, s. 198 and s. 200. The Botnick company deal smacks of illegitimacy on whatever view is taken of it. It would seem that the creditors may be giving up $50,000 (although it is necessary to note that the source was not disclosed in the proposal and it had to be over time) but that this would be their ticket of admission to determine what happened to at least the PTL deposit and to see if some of this money might be recovered under a preference action. I note that it would be very much in the interests of Bank Leumi and Firestone/Botnick company to vote in favour of the proposal to eliminate the risk of investigation into the preference question. It seems to me that an investigation would have the double barrelled advantage of satisfying the justifiable curiosity of the "outside" claimants and vindication of Mernick if he has in fact made appropriate (even if quite disjointed) disclosure. I note also that even according the in favour votes full dollar credence, the two-thirds' value majority was narrowly obtained; in other words, there was not an overwhelming vote in favour. I am therefore of the view that it would be in the interests of the creditors generally not to approve this proposal since it does not appear reasonable on its facts (especially since it is for a fraction of a cent on the dollar and falls below any appropriate threshold in this regard or in regard to s. 173(1)(a) and s. 59(3)). For this and other reasons given, I think it in the public interest not to approve this proposal. In essence, the proposal (given the minuscule recovery aspect) was a bankruptcy without the investigative assistance possible in a bankruptcy, all in a situation where there was a demonstrated reluctance to provide information.

The non-approval of the proposal would then bring s. 61(2)(a)(iii) into play.

Application dismissed.

Re Mayer
(1994), 25 CBR (3d) 113 (Ont. Gen. Div. (Bkpcy.))

APPLICATION for approval of proposal.

Registrar FERRON: The application for the approval of the proposal of Joseph Moise Mayer came before the Court in February, 1994 and has been adjourned on two occasions for further information.

In order to affirm a proposal, the Court must be satisfied that the proposal is:

1. reasonable;
2. calculated to benefit the general body of creditors; and
3. made in good faith.

The first two provisions are statutory, while the third is implied. The Bankruptcy Court is a court of equity. An insolvent person asking for the Court's approval of a plan must do so in good faith requires [*sic*] full disclosure. There has not been full disclosure by the insolvent person in this application.

The central provision of the proposal requires the acceptance by creditors in full payment of claims of the insolvent person's equity in "the premises in which the debtor resides."

Nowhere, not in the proposal, not in the Trustee's report to creditors (where the property is called "family home" and "principal residence"), and not in the report to the Court is it disclosed that:

1. the premises which is to fund the proposal is held with the insolvent person's spouse; (the statement of affairs does make reference to a half interest in three properties including the property referred to in the proposal; that is ambiguous and might not be appreciated by the creditors); or
2. the property is encumbered by two mortgages, a charge in favour of Revenue Canada, and a charge for a line of credit; or
3. that municipal taxes of $24,000 for arrears are owing.

Moreover, there was no appraisal for the property available to creditors, or initially, to the Court, so that the Creditors can have no idea of what equity might be available, assuming there is an equity available to creditors.

When this matter came on before the Court initially, I directed counsel's attention to the omission of the appraisal, and I now have before me what is called an "appraisal." That appraisal consists of a two-line letter signed by sales representatives of a real estate company. The letter is addressed "To whom it may concern" and suggests that the property has a value of "about $750,000 in today's marketplace." The property, I am advised, has been on the market for some considerable time without result and one can only speculate that the property is overpriced. In any event, I repeat, no creditor has seen that appraisal.

Even if the property were to sell for $750,000, the funds available for purposes of the proposal would be only $73,000 and when one deducts the selling commission, the additional interest accruing on the encumbrances, legal costs both of the proposal and of the sale of the property and the Trustee's fees, the amount available to creditors would be minimal.

Moreover, the property has been on the market for some considerable time without results. The property may never sell for its so called appraised value. The proposal provides for no cut off date so that creditors may never be paid. In addition, if the property is sold for less than $750,000 the dividend to creditors would be reduced even more.

The statutory report of the Trustee to the Court on the application for the approval of the proposal is deficient. Statutory Form Number 42, "Report of Trustee on Proposal," paragraph 9, provides by way of direction to the Trustee: "Set out assets in detail, giving the value as carried on the books of the Debtor and the Trustee's estimate in each case of the realizable value thereof."

Neither the Creditors nor the Court has been given the information required by the statute with which to gauge the value of the insolvent person's plan. That information which is available reveals the proposal not calculated to benefit the general body of creditors.

Accordingly, the statement in the Trustee's Report to Creditors (Section 51(1)), *viz.*, under the heading "Recommendations and Summary," *viz.*, "Based on a review of the condensed statement of assets and liabilities, it is estimated that there would be less of a distribution to Creditors in a bankruptcy scenario. Accordingly, the proposal produces a higher realization for Creditors," is incorrect and misleading. Since there is no appraisal there can be no estimate, and the statement in the report is of no value. It is skewed unfairly in favour of the insolvent person and cannot be supported.

Nor is the Trustee entitled to make the statement under the heading, "Financial Position and Evaluation of Assets" simply because he cannot know what the assets will realize on bankruptcy for the same reason that he cannot know what will be available to Creditors in the proposal.

Moreover, the Creditors have not been advised that they would be able to get at least as much and probably more in a bankruptcy of the Debtor as opposed to the proposal.

In bankruptcy, the exact same asset, that is the principal residence, would be available to them, and the encumbrance to Revenue Canada for arrears of taxes would presumably abate, so that on that basis alone, the bankruptcy is more advantageous to Creditors than a proposal.

In addition, on bankruptcy creditors would obtain the following assets which are not available on the proposal:

1. After acquired assets, that is contributions from the Debtor's income; and
2. The mortgage receivable and automobile referred to in the statement of affairs; and
3. The Debtor's accounts receivable, that is, the OHIP payments owing to the doctor at the date of bankruptcy; and
4. Assets not encumbered or the equity therein.

The admitted combined net income of the insolvent person, a doctor, and his spouse, is $7,690 per month from which a payment order would probably be obtainable in a bankruptcy. In particular, the insolvent person's statement of earnings carries an item of disbursements entitled "Mortgage and Loan" $6,546 per month. In bankruptcy, the "Loan" portion of the payment would probably be available to Creditors. The Trustee's report to the Court states, "The Debtor's main assets are mostly encumbered" which indicates that there are other than "main assets" and these are not encumbered. Such assets would be available to creditors. The above information was not given or made available to Creditors.

It is clear that a plan to be approved by the Court must be more advantageous to Creditors than would be the case in a bankruptcy. See *Re Allen Theatres Ltd.* (1922), 3 CBR 147 (Ont. SC) and *Re Rideau Carleton Raceway Holdings Ltd.* (1971), 15 CBR (NS) 71 (Ont SC) at 75. The proposal submitted does not meet that test.

Finally, I note that of the thirteen Creditors with declared liabilities of $277,000, only one attended the Creditors' meeting. The proposal was approved by that Creditor and by one proxy which the Trustee voted in favour of the proposal. This is hardly an overwhelming or representative showing of creditors. How much of this rather dismal showing can be attributed to the paucity of information made available to Creditors is conjecture, but the Court, must, notwithstanding, protect Creditors from themselves. See Honsberger, "Debt Restructuring," page 8-64.

The proposal cannot be approved and is accordingly rejected.

Approval denied.

Memorandum by R.G. Marantz on the Future of the CCAA
(February 15, 1994)[1]

1. Introduction

1.01 Options as to future possibilities for the CCAA range from, at one extreme, leaving the legislation without change or, at the other extreme, repealing it entirely.

1.02 The fundamental distinction between the two statutes is that the BIA offers a legislatively driven restructuring environment, while the CCAA is virtually completely judge driven. The threshold issue is where to draw the line between these two very different forms of relief. While in practice the end result of a CCAA or a BIA proceeding may seem similar, there must be a choice as to when judge made rules will apply, as distinct from rules created by Parliament.

---

[1] Mr. Marantz is a partner with Osler, Hoskin & Harcourt in Toronto. This memorandum was prepared by him for the benefit of Industry Canada.

The choice of options is ultimately dependent upon the policy approach to be adopted by the Government. In considering policy the issue of judge made or legislative law must be addressed. Within that framework, there are a number of policy options:

(a) There should be only one statutory reorganization regime.

(b) There should be two effective statutory regimes leaving it to the debtor to decide which regime to pursue.

(c) There should be two reorganization regimes, one to be utilized for most reorganizations, the other to be utilized by only the more complex and difficult reorganizations.

1.03 If the choice is to have two reorganization regimes, should they be:

(a) consistent in the availability of remedies (i.e. voting percentage for approval, ability to bind the Crown, ability to deal with preferential transactions),

or should they be:

(b) different in remedy and application as they are now.

There appears to be no uniform viewpoint in the insolvency and business community. There are those who believe there should be only one statutory regime. There is also a large body of thought that believes the CCAA should be retained because of the flexibility it offers in complex and difficult situations.[2]

1.04 For purposes of this discussion it is assumed that:

(a) the BIA regime is to be retained and should be structured for use by small and medium sized business enterprises ("SME"), although it should be available to all;

(b) if the CCAA is to be retained, it should be used in larger and more complex situations.

1.05 The purpose of this discussion paper is therefore to provide a basis for:

(a) an assessment of the appropriate features of an SME-friendly BIA;

(b) on the assumption that the CCAA would be intended for use by larger, more complex insolvent corporations, an assessment of the need for restrictions on access to the CCAA;

(c) an assessment of features appropriate to a CCAA geared to larger insolvencies; and

(d) a discussion of those factors to consider in assessing whether a CCAA is needed if an SME-friendly BIA reorganization scheme is in place.

2. Enhancing the Effectiveness of the BIA

2.01 In order for the BIA to be responsive to the needs of SME's and to treat affected persons equitably, it should:

(a) facilitate reorganizations of SME's in situations where there is a likelihood the reorganization would succeed and where there is a net benefit to creditors as a whole without undue prejudice to any one or more classes of creditors;

---

[2] Comments by Mr. Justice David Tysoe informally presented at the Insolvency Institute of Canada Annual Meeting, Carling Lake, Quebec, October 25, 1993.

(b) discourage or facilitate the termination of attempts to reorganize where any creditor classes would be unfairly prejudiced and where there is little likelihood that the reorganization would succeed;

(c) minimize administration and transaction costs; and

(d) be speedy.

As it is presently drafted, the BIA offers a number of features that make it more effective for purposes of reorganization over the CCAA. These range from ease of access (filing as a right) and the automatic stay of creditors to, at the other extreme, the availability of remedies, such as being able to bind the Crown.

2.02 In order to make the BIA even more effective suggestions have been made to have a number of areas modified. The suggested modifications deal with:

(a) the automatic stay and time constraints;

(b) narrowness of the stay;

(c) need to use an independent interim receiver or trustee;

(d) inflexible requirements with respect to the cash flow statement;

(e) difficulty in obtaining relief from the stay;

(f) perceived lack of flexibility in designating classes of creditors;

(g) perceived onerous monitoring and reporting requirements;

(h) problems in connection with the section 244 notice;

(i) perceived onerous requirements in settling on,

   (i) lease terminations, and

   (ii) employee claims and source deductions

(j) supplier rights;

(k) the deemed bankruptcy;

(l) timing of claims;

(m) consolidated filings.

2.03 *The Automatic Stay and Time Constraints:* The great attraction in obtaining a stay of proceedings under a BIA filing is that the stay is automatic upon filing. There is no notice to those affected by the stay and no judicial discretion exercised in it taking effect. The CCAA stay is not only subject to the court's discretion, the courts have adopted a practice of affected creditors being given notice of the application for relief.

However, the stay under the BIA is to remain in place until an actual proposal is filed. The initial stay is for a 30 day period. It may be increased, in increments of not more than 45 days, to a maximum of six months. Concern has been expressed that a six-month stay period may not be adequate in complex situations to enable a plan to be filed. The current Curragh Resources CCAA filing is an example of this. Similarly, there were considerable delay periods in connection with Peoples Jewellers (Algoma Steel and Quintette Coal).[3]

---

[3] Algoma Steel experienced the lapse of a year between the intitial application for protection and the actual filing of the plan. Creditors however continued to be supportive before the court. Quintette Coal filed for protection on June 13, 1990, filed its first plan on December 20, 1990 (within a 6 month court imposed time limit) and finally filed an amended plan on October 22, 1991. See comments of Thackray J in *Re Quintette Coal Ltd.* (1991), 10 CBR (3d) 197 (BCSC).

Were the court to be given jurisdiction to extend the stay period beyond six months, the statute would have to set out guidelines for allowing such an extension.

This concern was recognized when C-22 was drafted. The "solution" to the problem that was contemplated was that if a debtor required more time in order to prepare a plan, it could file what is commonly known as "holding proposal" and have the creditors vote upon it.

It might be more effective to provide directly in the BIA for extensions of the six-month period with a combination of both court and creditor approval. A debtor seeking an extension beyond the six month period could apply to the court for directions for a calling of meetings of creditors to approve granting such an extension. The court would direct that a meeting be held, provide for notice and also provide the manner in which the votes of creditors should be counted. The court could, in such circumstances, provide for either a minimum of 2 classes (i.e. one secured and one unsecured) or could provide for multiple classes. Thus, if creditors supported the debtor, the extension would become available. These need not be the classes that would ultimately be fixed for the plan.

2.04 *Narrowness of the Stay:* The CCAA enables the debtor to craft a very broad ranging stay of proceedings. The courts have ordered stays which have precluded third parties from exercising remedies against partners or co-ventures of an insolvent person;[4] precluded creditors from moving against limited partnerships;[5] and stayed rights of creditors to call on letters of credit[6] or guarantee instruments issued by third parties[7] and against rights of set-off.[8] If a debtor is involved in any form of complex business relationships the stay available under the BIA will not be adequate to protect those interests that could be negatively impacted by an insolvency filing. It would also seem that if, as a result of a BIA filing, a debtor became subject to a pre-emptive sale provision, say to a joint venture partner, the BIA stay would not be effective to stop exercise of that right.

If the Court were able, in proceedings under the BIA, to issue stay orders with broad impact, it would markedly increase the effectiveness of the BIA for use in more difficult situations.

Such a stay could be obtained by the debtor either contemporaneous with or after filing a notice of intention or a proposal. It could be obtained either *ex parte* or with notice to affected persons. If the stay were available without notice it should therefore be subject to a "come-back clause" so that those adversely affected may seek relief from the broad stay.

2.05 *Independence of the Trustee:* The practice has developed in a very large proportion of CCAA proceedings of having the debtor's auditor act as a monitor or information

---

[4] *Re Bramalea Ltd.* OCJ (GD), December 22, 1992, Houlden J, Court file RE216619 (unreported).

[5] *Re Lehndorff General Partners Ltd.* (1992), 17 CBR (3d) 24, Farley J (OCJ (GD)).

[6] *Re Woodward's Ltd.* (1993), 17 CBR (3d) 236 (BCSC).

[7] *Quintette Coal Ltd. v. Nippon Steel Corp.* (1990), 2 CBR (3d) 303 (BCCA) aff'g 2 CBR (3d) 291. Leave to appeal to the Supreme Court of Canada refused, 7 CBR (3d) 164.

[8] *Re Bramalea Ltd., supra* note 4.

officer for purposes of providing financial information to creditors and to the court. There are a number of reasons for this practice evolving. These include the fact that there is a considerable economy in cost in having someone familiar with the debtor provide the information. The other reason relates to avoiding risk for environmental problems that might otherwise be encountered if an interim receiver were appointed.

The Rules of Professional Conduct of the CIPA do not preclude an accountant from acting in this fashion. However, an auditor is precluded from acting as a trustee or receiver of a client. Thus, in bankruptcy filings where a trustee must be named, recourse must be had to an independent person.

The trustee named under a notice of intention or a proposal is also faced with responsibility in the preparation of a cash flow statement. While it is arguable that the debtor's auditors could better perform this task the independence of the trustee is, I believe, an important issue. There is however nothing to preclude the auditor assisting the trustee or even functioning as a "monitor" or "information officer" for the purpose of providing information to the court and creditors. If desired, this flexibility could be specified in the BIA.

2.06 *The Cash Flow Statement:* The inflexible 10 day period for preparation of a cash flow statement can, on occasion, be a deterrent to a major debtor taking relief under the BIA. Complex financial structures can render this a task to be performed over a longer time frame. While many major filings are preplanned and timed, there are still those debtors that suddenly find themselves pushed and in need of protection. For them the 10 day time frame and the inflexible Trustee's certificate will create a real problem.

In other circumstances a trustee may on occasion be in a position when it knows that the cash flow information is not accurate, but the 10 days is about to run out. There is no time for revisions. Should the incorrect statement be filed, along with an unqualified certificate by the trustee? This dilemma impairs the effectiveness of the protection for debtors available under the BIA.

To allow the courts discretion in extending the time can lead to concerns as to abuse, and the application of variable standards by the courts. Perhaps in circumstances where more time is needed the debtor should be allowed with leave of the court to file interim cash flow information, with a qualified report by the Trustee. The court would also fix a time limit for delivering of the actual cash flow statement.

The difficulties and expense involved in having an independent trustee prepare financial data can be mitigated to some extent by allowing the auditor of the debtor corporation to fulfil a monitor function in place of or in assistance to the trustee. This can present other problems if the auditor is concerned as to potential liability. Any such arrangement should require express court approval.

2.07 *Difficulty in Obtaining Relief from the Stay:* The initial 30-day stay of proceedings operative under section 50.4 of the BIA may be extended by the court upon the debtor satisfying the court that, amongst other tests, no creditor would be materially prejudiced if the extension were granted (section 50.4(9)(e)).

Conversely, a creditor may apply to have the stay lifted if the creditor can satisfy the court that the creditors as a whole would be materially prejudiced if the stay were not lifted (section 50.4(11)(e)). It would therefore appear that the balance is very much in favour of the debtor obtaining an extension of time. The obstacle of showing that the creditors as a whole would be prejudiced by an extension is a difficult burden for a creditor to maintain.[9]

An individual creditor may move under s. 69.4 for relief from the stay with respect to security held by that creditor alone if the court is satisfied that (a) the creditor is materially prejudiced by the continuance of the stay, or (b) that it is equitable on other grounds. While this is a less stringent test than under s. 50.4(11), the section operates to grant relief to only one creditor. The relief under s. 50.4(11) is the termination of the stay in respect of all creditors. There is some logic in the test for that relief being more stringent.

A better balance and therefore greater effectiveness of the BIA could be achieved by placing a lesser burden of proof upon creditors.

If a particular class of creditors could demonstrate to the court that the members of that class were prejudiced the BIA would provide that the Court had a choice of either terminating the 30-day period (thereby resulting in a bankruptcy) or, alternatively allowing the objecting creditors to be relieved from the stay imposed by section 69, thereby enabling them to deal with their collateral.

2.08 *Flexibility in Designating Classes of Creditors:* To this point the courts have not considered the classification of creditors issue under the BIA. The CCAA sets forth no tests or standards for identifying classes of creditors. As a result an extensive body of judge-made law has developed. This law has been extremely liberal and flexible in grouping secured creditors into classes.[10]

The BIA, on the other hand in section 50(1.4) provides a standard for determining the classification of secured creditors. The standard in part adopts some of the pre 1992 tests used by the courts in considering the classification of creditors under the CCAA. However because the language used in the BIA is capable of a more restrictive interpretation than the broad provision for classification under the CCAA, there has been concern expressed that the tests for classification themselves would be more restrictive.[11]

2.09 *Monitoring and Reporting:* The BIA imposes significant obligations upon a proposal trustee with respect to the preparation of cash flow statements.[12] There is a view held in some quarters that the cash flow certificate as well as the ongoing reporting and monitoring requirements represent an onerous burden to the trustee and a large expense to the debtor. However there was good reason for adding these disclosure requirements to the BIA, not the least of which was to ensure that adequate financial information was placed in the hands of the creditors.

---

[9] *Re N.T.W. Management Group Ltd.* (1993), 19 CBR (3d) 162 (OCJ (GD)).

[10] For the most recent discussion of the issue, see *Woodward's Ltd.* (1993), 20 CBR (3d) 74, Tysoe J (BCSC). See also *Sklar-Peppler Furniture Corp. v. Bank of Nova Scotia* (1991), 8 CBR (3d) 312 (OCJ (GD)) and *Grafton Fraser Inc. v. CIBC* (1992), 11 CBR (3d) (OCJ (GD)).

[11] A recent article in *P.B. Birkness* in 20 CBR (3d) 91 considering the decision of Mr. Justice Tysoe in *Woodward's* offered the suggestion that if the reasoning of Mr. Justice Tysoe were adopted in BIA classification cases there would be no distinction between the CCAA and BIA tests. It would also be possible to amend section 50(1.4) further so as to take into account the standards set forth by the court in *Woodward's*.

[12] Sections 50(6) to (11); and see also Sections 50.4(2) to (7).

It is not as if there are no such reporting requirements available under the CCAA. In many cases, CCAA filings will contain cash flow and other financial information to demonstrate to the court that the interests of creditors are being protected during the stay process. If creditors object to the absence of financial information it is reasonable to expect that the court would order such disclosure under the CCAA.

2.10 *Section 244—10 day notice problem:* In circumstances where a secured creditor has given the debtor the 10 day notice under section 244, if the debtor does not file a notice of intention or a proposal within the 10 day period, the right to relief under the proposal section of the BIA is lost. Very often secured lenders, particularly banks, may wish to serve the section 244 notice as a means of "getting the debtor's attention," even though they do not have a firm intention of enforcing their security.

This can be an effective means of getting the debtor to the table to discuss a restructuring of its affairs. While the debtor may wish to engage in such discussions, if it does not file a notice of intention within the 10 day period, it will lose the right to do so in the event that the restructuring discussions fail. This makes a very difficult choice for the debtor, as a filing will usually have a negative impact on its business and will prejudice ongoing discussions.

The situation could be eased for the debtor if it could, after a 244 notice had been given, be allowed to file a notice of intention at any time up and until such time as the secured creditors had taken actual steps to enforce its security.

BIAC Working Group #6 had examined the issue and had concluded that allowing a debtor to file under the BIA at any time prior to a secured creditor taking possession of the collateral would adversely affect the position of secured creditors. The result would be that they would move quickly to enforce their security once the 10-day notice period had expired, so as to avoid further risk. Such a result was considered to be undesirable.

2.11 *Lease Terminations:* The six-month payment required on the repudiation of a lease has been criticized as placing a too onerous burden on debtors. The suggestion is that it is "easier" to avoid burdensome leases under the CCAA. There have been a number of plans where the court has "allowed" the debtor to terminate leasehold interests.[13] An examination of virtually all of these cases indicates that rearrangement of leasehold interest under the CCAA has been supported by a significant majority of landlord creditors, usually in the face of very special circumstances. However, there would appear to be no clear authority for the court giving the debtor leave to terminate a lease or any other contract under the CCAA.

In contrast, the Task Force on leases operating under the BIAC framework has taken the position that the lease repudiation provisions in the BIA are too onerous for landlords and should therefore be restricted.

It is always open to a debtor in reorganization to breach and repudiate an existing contract. This is done in the expectation that the other party to the contract will then have a claim for damages arising out of the breach, which claim can be compromised as an unsecured claim in the plan. However, the danger is that the other party to a contract need

---

[13] See *Sklar-Peppler* and *Grafton Fraser,* note 10, *supra.*

not accept the breach and repudiation and may instead elect to claim for payment of future amounts as they may arise after the ultimate approval of the plan. It is a fallacy to argue that the CCAA is more facilitative of lease terminations than the BIA.

Experience has also shown that in cases under the BIA, lease repudiation payments can be negotiated for less than the statutory six months.

A problem does remain under the BIA in that pursuant to s. 60(1.5) no proposal may be approved by the court if it does not provide for payment of the 6 months compensation. The BIA could be amended to provide, in addition, that where landlords as a separate class vote to approve a lesser amount, it binds the class and is deemed to be compliance with the statute. In addition, if one or more landlords are prepared to accept less than 6 months compensation, they could be excluded from the formal plan.

There have been instances of landlords challenging a lease repudiation and losing. The landlord then appears at the hearing under s. 59 to argue against approval of the proposal and in effect, raise the lease termination issue afresh. The BIA could be amended to preclude the landlord's right to appear in such circumstances. This would eliminate a further step in the reorganization process.

2.12 *Employee Claims and Source Deductions:* The provisions for priority payment of employee wage claims and source deductions under BIA proposals have also been criticized as onerous. There is no strict rule with respect to these areas under the CCAA. However, as the Crown is not bound under the CCAA, source deductions would have an immediate priority to payment in full. Wages are a separate issue. The definition of wages contained in most provincial jurisdictions includes regular wages plus vacation pay. They are defined by provincial law. In all jurisdictions directors are by statute, held personally liable for wage arrears, subject to certain limitations. Thus they are usually fully provided for in plans. Clearly, though, if wages were to extend to severance and termination obligations this could be a very onerous burden to deal with.

2.13 *Supplier Rights Post Filing:* The combined provisions of section 81.1 (30 day goods) and section 65.1(4) (refusal to sell) are not very helpful in assuring protection to sellers of goods to a debtor in reorganization. The suspension of the 30 day goods right in s. 81.1 on the filing of a notice of intention will often mean that inventories will be disposed of during the stay period, with no relief for suppliers.

Further the protection for post-filing suppliers of inventory and goods is not adequate as COD payment is not always practical.

In the Silcorp reorganization suppliers direct shipped inventory to hundreds of stores. Payment on delivery was completely impractical in such circumstances. However, under the CCAA the court was able to order that funds received by Silcorp from the sale of inventory were to be impressed with a trust in favour of post-filing suppliers.

The provisions of the BIA would not appear to allow for such flexibility. A change to the BIA to allow this alternative would make the statute considerably more effective in facilitating ongoing business operations.

2.14 *Deemed Bankruptcy:* Rejection of a BIA proposal, or the failure to meet certain filing limits, results in the automatic bankruptcy of the debtor. The CCAA is considered to be not so harsh—rejection of a plan leaves the debtor in legal limbo—admitted insolvent and unprotected. Receivership or bankruptcy, or both, follow.

In actual result the difference between CCAA and BIA consequences on rejection might be considered to be only cosmetic.

2.15 *Timing of Claims:* The CCAA does not provide for any distinction between pre-filing and post-filing claims. Thus creditor claims arising in the interval between the obtaining of a stay order on the initial filing for protection, and the actual filing and confirmation of a plan can be dealt with as part of the pre-filing pre-existing pool of creditors or on some other separate basis.

The BIA however is clear that creditor claims under a proposal, i.e. provable claims, are those liabilities to which the debtor is subject on the day the debtor became subject to the BIA: i.e. the date of filing a notice of intention or a proposal. Thus, there is no flexibility in dealing with post-filing creditors.[14]

2.16 *Consolidated Filings:* The BIA is silent on the question of consolidated filings. The courts however have, in the past, allowed corporate entities within a group to file for protection or bankruptcy on a consolidated basis.

Filing on a consolidated basis gives rise to the question of whether a solvent corporate entity, as part of a larger insolvent group, should be able to obtain the benefits of BIA protection. On the basis of the "single business entity" concept, it would be appropriate for solvent subsidiaries to be included within a filing.

There is a similar question with respect to consolidated remedies: that is, should all creditors of all entities within the group receive identical treatment on a consolidated basis?

3. Complex Reorganizations: The Future of the CCAA

Assume that there are to be two reorganization regimes. One would be the BIA with clearly defined statutory rules and procedures designed to assist SME's. The other would be the CCAA with its judge-made rules, which would be intended for use in significantly more complex situations where the BIA may be lacking sufficient flexibility. The question to be considered is: should a smaller, less complex debtor be entitled to unrestricted access to either regime?

3.01 *Formal Restriction:* Formal restriction to access by express statutory provisions, may be accomplished by any one or more of the following:

(a) Maintain the current requirement for a trust deed;

(b) Narrow the trust deed requirement so that the debtor must have debt outstanding thereunder in the hands of the "public" (as per Securities Act definition) or, alternatively, have shares outstanding that have been issued to the "public";

(c) Set a threshold amount for indebtedness; or

(d) By statute have a burden placed upon the debtor to satisfy the court that it should be made under the CCAA and not the BIA (the "show cause" test).

---

[14] BIA, s. 62(1.1).

3.02 *Comments:*

(a) The trust deed requirement was inserted into the legislation with an intent of restricting the availability of the CCAA to only larger, publicly traded corporations. The use of "instant trust deeds," now recognized by the courts, has rendered the trust deed provision a practical fiction, serving no useful purpose. To give it some meaning it could be coupled with a requirement that the debt be issued by a "reporting issuer" as defined under the Securities Act.

(b) The "reporting issuer" restriction will preclude most corporate entities from seeking relief under the CCAA. Only a few major entities may have difficulty in having to resort to the statute, as virtually all major corporations should be reporting issuers. While we have not researched the point, we believe that virtually all of the major corporate entities that have recently reorganized under the CCAA have had some form of public debt outstanding. A notable exception would be Olympia and York Limited which was not a reporting issuer. However many of its subsidiary corporations were reporting issuers. On that basis, if consolidated filings were permitted (see Section 4.08 of this paper), a non-reporting issuer could be consolidated into a filing. The restriction is, of course, arbitrary.

(c) A monetary threshold of debt is also arbitrary and not necessarily a rational basis for distinction. The US Bankruptcy Amendments Act of 1993 (S540) presently before the Senate, contains provisions, under Chapter 10 of the US Code, for the reorganization of small businesses. These are defined as businesses with debts of $2.5 million or less. The provisions would allow a small business debtor to retain its business by paying creditors out of future disposable income over a three to five year term. Creditors could not vote on the debtor's plan. This may not be a viable option for the Canadian credit community.

(d) The "show cause" test could normally work in conjunction with the existing trust deed requirements of the CCAA. It could also be coupled with the "reporting issuer" or threshold tests although to do so might well be unduly cumbersome. If a debtor was required to show cause as to why it should be under the CCAA, it would have to establish to the court that the remedies available to it under the BIA would not be adequate or effective to protect its assets and to make a proposal. The limited time span for the stay would also be a factor.

(e) If the show cause restriction were to be adopted, it gives rise to the question as to whether every applicant debtor should be required to meet this test or whether a debtor need only meet the test where an objection to proceeding under the CCAA is raised by a creditor. The show cause test would however be meaningless unless specific criteria were identified in the CCAA.

4. *Making the CCAA More Effective and Equitable*

4.01 In order for the CCAA to continue as an effective piece of legislation, it should:

(a) facilitate the reorganization of larger and more complex corporate entities where there may be a net benefit to creditors as a whole, where no creditor class would be unfairly prejudiced, and where there is a likelihood of the reorganization succeeding;

(b) discourage the commencement or facilitate the termination of reorganization attempts where there would be no apparent benefit for creditors, where creditors would be unfairly prejudiced, and where there is little likelihood that the reorganization would succeed;

    (c) avoid excessive legal, administration and transaction costs; and

    (d) operate with expediency and efficiency.

4.02 In order to make the CCAA more efficient and equitable, suggestions have been made as to the modification of a number of provisions. These suggestions deal with:

    (a) financial disclosure;

    (b) relief from the stay;

    (c) extensions of the stay;

    (d) statutory tests relative to the stay;

    (e) disclaimer of executory contracts;

    (f) consolidation of filings;

    (g) binding the Crown;

    (h) renewable and preferential transactions;

    (i) 30-day goods;

    (j) voting proportions;

    (k) changing from CCAA to BIA;

    (l) classification of creditors; and

    (m) dealing with employee claims and source deductions.

4.03 *Financial Disclosures:* A common complaint from creditors involved in CCAA proceedings is the lack of detailed and adequate financial disclosure. This gives rise to the question as to whether the CCAA should be amended to contain provisions relating to financial disclosure, cash flow statements and monitoring that parallel those of the BIA.

It has been suggested that no such amendment should be necessary.

If the creditors raise concern as to the adequacy of financial disclosure it is open to the court to order the debtor to provide disclosure and information on a par with that provided for under the BIA. No specific statutory authority is required to give the courts jurisdiction to make such an order. However, mandatory and thorough disclosure would reduce the need for creditors having to apply to the court for release of information.

4.04 *Relief from the Stay:* It has been argued that it is more difficult for secured creditors to obtain relief from the stay of proceedings under the CCAA than it is under the BIA. This is attributed to specific standards set forth under the BIA that do not exist under the CCAA. Again some would say that this matter need not be dealt with specifically in the legislation. It is open to any creditor seeking relief from a CCAA stay to raise issues on a parallel with the BIA, leaving it to the court to exercise its jurisdiction. Others would argue that explicit rights to relief may protect creditors, especially smaller creditors. There has been concern expressed about the lack of certainty under the present regime, with rules being made by judges on a case-by-case basis. The strongest arguments against CCAA flexibility have been advanced by segments of the secured lending community. Taken at face, however, their position is directly at odds with a policy of encouraging use of reorganization legislation.

4.05 *Extensions of the Stay:* The issues here parallel those relating to the question of relief from the stay. CCAA proceedings have a tendency to extend for a considerable period of time, often leading to the frustration of secured creditors. There is nothing to preclude the court ordering a meeting of creditors to be held, and setting forth the basis for creditors voting, in order to determine whether or not the stay should be extended, thereby giving the debtor further time to reorganize. On this basis the view has been expressed that no legislative change is required. A contrary view has also been expressed, and suggests that the CCAA require the debtor to satisfy the court, on seeking an extension of the stay, that there would be no unfair prejudice to creditors and that there was a likelihood of the reorganization succeeding.

4.06 *Statutory Tests Relative to the Stay:* Suggestions have been raised as to whether the CCAA should set out preconditions or tests which must be met in order that the court grant a stay against all or certain classes of creditors or others. These tests would require the debtor applicant to satisfy the court that there would be minimum prejudice to those to be affected by the proposed stay.

Under present CCAA practice the courts generally require prior notice to be given to parties to be affected by a stay or, if no notice is given, a stay order will provide for affected parties being able to appear before the court within a very short period of time to argue against the stay applying to them. The court retains complete discretion as to whether the stay should be granted or continued.

The courts have been relatively effective in assessing whether a stay order should be made. It is, admittedly, difficult for a creditor to have a stay order set aside so long as the court believes that there continues to be a reasonable prospect of the debtor presenting a plan acceptable to creditors. The question remains, will anything be accomplished by adding a statutory standard to the existing judicial precedent? It is argued that rules could provide comfort to smaller creditors and reduce the prospect of uncertainty.

In CCAA proceedings major creditors can protect their interests. For a small creditor, participation is both difficult and expensive. In part this disadvantage can be addressed by the courts making greater use of creditors committees which can be constituted immediately upon a debtor filing for protection. This may reduce the need for statutory conditions in addition to those that have evolved under the common law.

4.07 *Executory Contracts:* Should the CCAA be amended so as to specifically give the debtor the ability to terminate leases and other executory contracts, and, if so, should the CCAA set forth the standards and preconditions to such termination?[15]

While the CCAA contains no provisions allowing for the repudiation or termination of contracts, a number of CCAA plans have been drafted on the basis that the debtor in fact repudiated certain contracts. The plan then purports to treat the other party to the contract as an unsecured claimant for damages arising from the repudiation or breach. A number of plans of arrangement have been approved by creditors and confirmed by the court on this basis. We are not aware of any challenges to such provisions. It remains open for a creditor to challenge any attempt to preclude that creditor from treating a breach of obligation as a

---

[15] See also comments on lease termination under the BIA at section 2.11 of this paper.

continuing one that gives rise to damages, even though the damages might arise after the effective date of the plan.

The Colter Report had recommended an amendment to the *Bankruptcy Act* to enable a debtor under reorganization to repudiate existing contracts subject to the debtor being able to establish to the satisfaction of the court that certain preconditions had been fulfilled.[16] Those tests continue to have validity. There is also merit in including tests in the BIA.

4.08 *Consolidation:* Where a corporate enterprise with a number of subsidiary corporations files for protection, the conservative view is that all of those corporations must technically qualify under the CCAA. That means having trust indentures and debentures outstanding. It gives rise to a proliferation of instant trust deeds. If the CCAA is to continue, it should clearly provide that if one corporate entity within the reorganizing group qualifies under the statute (whatever the qualifications are), all other corporations that are subsidiaries should also be qualified and included in the filing.

The filing on a consolidated basis gives rise to the question of whether a solvent corporate entity, as part of a larger insolvent group, should be able to obtain the benefits and protection under the statute. On the basis of a "single business entity" it would be appropriate for solvent subsidiaries to be included within a filing.

Further questions arise with respect to the availability of consolidated remedies. The CCAA, of course, is silent on the point, although the courts have been prepared to approve plans where there is a consolidation of remedies in connection with the claims of creditors. This gives rise to a separate issue as to whether consolidation on a similar basis is available under the BIA.

4.09 *Binding the Crown:* As previously noted the inability to bind the Crown not only with respect to the stay of proceedings but also with respect to remedies can present a serious inhibition to reorganization efforts. While the BIA grants the Crown certain priorities with respect to withholding obligations, a larger issue arises with claims of the Crown arising in a commercial nature (i.e. Canadian Broadcasting Corporation).

4.10 *Reviewable and Preferential Transactions:* Under the provisions of the BIA,[17] a trustee under a proposal has the right to attack preferences and reviewable transactions. Such a right must be specifically excluded from the proposal otherwise it survives. There is no co-relative right under the CCAA nor can such a right successfully be imposed against the will of the party to be affected.

---

[16] Report of the Advisory Committee on Bankruptcy and Insolvency, January 1, 1986, page 59.

- the contract between the debtor and the third party was onerous;
- the contract was not in the best interests of the debtor and the creditors generally;
- the existing contract rendered reorganization of the affairs of the debtor impractical;
- the proposed amendment to the contract was necessary to the implementation of the reorganization;
- the debtor had bargained with the other party in good faith prior to seeking the assistance of the court; and
- the other party rejected the proposed amendment to the contract "without a good cause."

[17] BIA ss. 95 and 96 and s. 101.1(1) which expressly provides that the reviewable transactions section of the BIA applies to proposals "with such modifications as the circumstances require, except where the proposal otherwise provides."

4.11 *30-Day Goods:* As the 30-day goods provision of the BIA is drafted, it is not operative in the case of a CCAA filing, nor is it terribly meaningful in the case of inventory financing. The courts have offered some minimal protection to retail suppliers under CCAA reorganizations in one case to stop the running of time so that they might prove claims in a BIA proceeding in the event that the reorganization under CCAA fails.[18] In the other, Silcorp, suppliers were given certain pre-emptive rights over inventory proceeds.[19]

4.12 *Voting Proportions:* The three quarters in value and majority in number test under the CCAA is more difficult to achieve than the two-thirds majority under the BIA. This makes the blocking of a plan more likely under the CCAA.

4.13 *Changing from CCAA to BIA:* While the BIA expressly provides that a proposal made under the BIA may be taken up and continued under the CCAA, there is no corresponding provision in the CCAA. If the two statutes continue in parallel, the CCAA should be so amended to give the court jurisdiction to transfer proceedings from the CCAA to the BIA regime.

4.14 *Designating Classes of Creditors:* Concern has been expressed by some that under creditor classification rules developed by the courts (see Section 2.08 of this memorandum), there is the possibility of creditors being prejudiced by being included in classes together with creditors having different interests. Should the CCAA contain rules as to class composition so as to reduce this perceived uncertainty?

4.15 *Employee Claims and Source Deductions:* This matter is discussed in section 2.12 of this memorandum. Should employees and revenue claims enjoy the same level of priority as set forth under the BIA? This could possibly enhance employee rights but restrict Crown rights, as the Crown is not presently bound by the CCAA.

5. Summary

5.01 In order to provide a framework and focus for discussion, we have, in this paper, of necessity made certain arbitrary assumptions or have adopted certain positions that may or may not ultimately be determined to be valid. These assumptions include:

(a) that the BIA regime should be retained and should be focussed on SME's; and

(b) that if the CCAA is to be retained, it should be reserved for larger and more complex reorganizations.

5.02 Our discussion of the BIA does not focus on every issue that has come up. It deals with areas where the BIA;

(a) can be made more flexible, such as in application of the stay of proceedings, reporting requirements and creditor classification, and

(b) can be made more responsive to current economic realities, such as in dealing with lease terminations, employee and statutory claims and suppliers rights.

---

[18] *Re Woodward's Ltd.* (1993), 17 CBR (3d) 253 (BCSC) Tysoe J supplementing (1993), 77 BCLR (2d) 332.

[19] See section 2.13 of this memorandum for comments.

Adopting of changes that give more flexibility to BIA proceedings and which give greater discretion to the courts can be perceived as bringing the BIA closer to the CCAA.

5.03 Any change that provides for placing greater responsibility in the courts runs the risk of making reorganization more expensive. Such conclusion is based upon the theory that if there is easy access to the courts in order to have issues decided (as distinguished from having solutions imposed by statute), there are those participants in the process that will want to use the courts on a frequent basis. The concern is that by doing so, there will be expense and time added to the reorganization process itself.

5.04 The discussion of possible changes to the CCAA have focussed on two areas:

(a) restricting access to the CCAA by either imposing arbitrary barriers to access or by providing a "show cause" test; and

(b) making the CCAA:

(i) more effective by expanding the scope of what can be accomplished under the CCAA by providing a means for dealing with executory contracts, reviewable transactions, and making the Crown subject to CCAA reorganization proceedings; and

(ii) more equitable by imposing specific disclosure requirements and providing a greater opportunity and facility for dissenting creditors to obtain relief from the stay of proceedings.

5.05 Maintaining the CCAA with increased legislated "rules" will of necessity reduce the flexibility otherwise available. Flexibility was the main reason for retention of the CCAA. To add "flesh" to the CCAA and to expand the nature of what can be accomplished under a CCAA reorganization would make the CCAA more like the BIA. It could, however, presently be viewed as a BIA without rules.

5.06 Those opposed to providing for two reorganizational regimes argue that it allows for regime shopping. It can be expensive for the parties involved, particularly creditors as they do not have a choice as to under what regime a reorganization proceeds. The overall reorganization framework becomes more difficult.

To amend the BIA to formalize by legislation the advantages available under the CCAA, particularly if flexibility is enhanced by providing greater discretion in the courts, could lead to further uncertainty for both creditors and debtors seeking relief during reorganization proceedings.

To this point, there is one thing that is clear: there is no one absolute, certain answer as to whether there should be two reorganization regimes or one.

Forms of Agreement in Secured Transactions*

1. Canadian Imperial Bank of Commerce, *Conditional Sale Agreement.*
2. Canadian Imperial Bank of Commerce, *Chattel Mortgage Agreement.*
3. Canadian Imperial Bank of Commerce, *General Assignment of Accounts.*
4. Canadian Imperial Bank of Commerce, *Demand Debenture.*
5. Canadian Imperial Bank of Commerce, *Pledge Agreement.*
6. John Deere Limited, *Security Agreement—Inventory: Consumer Products.*

---

* Several of the forms have had to be reduced in size to accommodate them to the size of the casebook pages.

Form 1

CONDITIONAL SALE AGREEMENT

CANADIAN IMPERIAL BANK OF COMMERCE

ORIGINAL

ORIGINAL SIGNATURE REQUIRED ON FIRST FOUR COPIES

DATE _____ 19____

	DATE OF BIRTH			SEX
	DAY	MONTH	YEAR	M/F

Insert full name of Buyer(s); if not an individual, full business or corporate name

FULL NAME OF BUYER

ADDRESS: Street number and name, apt. no. if any, OR lot, concession and township   City, Town or Village (and rural route if any)   Prov./Terr.

	DATE OF BIRTH			SEX
	DAY	MONTH	YEAR	M/F

FULL NAME OF CO-BUYER(S)

ADDRESS: Street number and name, apt. no. if any, OR lot, concession and township   City, Town or Village (and rural route if any)   Prov./Terr.

FULL NAME OF SELLER

ADDRESS: Street number and name, apt. no. if any, OR lot, concession and township   City, Town or Village (and rural route if any)   Prov./terr.

NAME OF BUYER (IF MORE THAN ONE) DESIGNATED FOR INSURANCE UNDER PARAGRAPH NINE (9) OF THE TERMS AND CONDITIONS HEREOF:

Buyer hereby purchases from Seller, on the terms and conditions herein set forth, the property described below complete with all attachments and accessories (herein called the "property"), delivery and acceptance of which in good condition and as ordered is hereby acknowledged by Buyer.

MANUFACTURER AND DESCRIPTION OF PROPERTY (INCLUDING MAKE & BODY STYLE)	NEW OR USED AND YEAR	MODEL NO.	SERIAL NO.	NO. CYL.	MOTOR NO. (IF MOTOR VEHICLE)	LICENCE NO. (IF MOTOR VEHICLE)	PRICE

CHECK ACCESSORIES AND INSERT COST

RADIO	AUTO TRANS	POWER STEERING	POWER BRAKES	POWER SEATS	POWER WINDOWS	AIR CONDIT.	OTHER (ITEMIZE)
$	$	$	$	$	$	$	$ $ $

Itemize all services for which separate charge is made, e.g. delivery, installation and inspection

1.	BASIC CASH PRICE	(a) PROPERTY		$	
		(b) SERVICES		$	
			TOTAL	$	▶ $
2.	PLUS PROVINCIAL SALES TAX				$
3.	RETAIL CASH PRICE (1 + 2)				$
4.	OFFICIAL FILING OR REGISTRATION FEES PAYABLE BY SELLER AT BUYER'S REQUEST				$
5.	INSURANCE PREMIUM PAYABLE BY SELLER AT BUYER'S REQUEST INSURING FOR ACCIDENTAL PHYSICAL DAMAGE TO THE PROPERTY. (CHECK INSURANCE COVERAGE INCLUDED) COVERAGE APPLICABLE TO PROPERTY				$

Term _____ months. Effective date _____ 19____

$_____ Deductible Collision   NO BODILY INJURY OR PROPERTY DAMAGE
☐ Comprehensive ☐ Fire and Theft   LIABILITY INSURANCE INCLUDED

Insert particulars of obligation paid.

6.	TOTAL CASH PRICE (3 + 4 + 5)		$
7.	A. GROSS TRADE-IN ALLOWANCE	$	
	B. AMOUNT PAYABLE TO_____ BY SELLER AT BUYER'S REQUEST FOR_____	$	
	C. NET CREDIT FOR TRADE-IN (A-B)	$	
	D. CASH DOWN PAYMENT	$	
	E. TOTAL DOWN PAYMENT (C + D)	$	▶ $
8.	BALANCE OF TOTAL CASH PRICE (6-7E)		$
9.	COST OF BORROWING-ANNUAL PERCENTAGE RATE OF _____% OF BALANCE OF TOTAL CASH PRICE		$
10.	TOTAL AMOUNT PAYABLE (HEREIN CALLED THE "UNPAID BALANCE") (8 + 9)		$

COMPLETE IN P.E.I. & N.S. ONLY
| 11. | OFFICIAL FEES PLUS INSURANCE PREMIUMS (4 + 5) | $ |

COMPLETE IN ALTA, NB, N.L.P.E.I. & NFLD. ONLY
| 12. | RETAIL CASH PRICE LESS TOTAL DOWN PAYMENT (3-7E) | $ |

COMPLETE IN MAN. ONLY
| 13. | COST OF BORROWING PLUS TOTAL CASH PRICE (9 + 6) | $ |

The Unpaid Balance shall be paid by Buyer to Canadian Imperial Bank of Commerce, * as follows: $_____ on the _____ day of _____, 19____ and _____ equal consecutive payments of $_____ each on the _____ day of each month commencing on the _____ day of _____, 19____, and ending on the _____ day of _____, 19____, totalling $_____; with interest after maturity on each instalment at the rate of _____% per annum and upon default in any such payment, all remaining instalments shall forthwith become due and payable without notice.

PAYMENT OF THE UNPAID BALANCE MAY ALSO BE ACCELERATED UNDER THE TERMS AND CONDITIONS ON THE REVERSE HEREOF WHICH CONSTITUTE PART OF THIS AGREEMENT.

BUYER ACKNOWLEDGES RECEIPT OF A COMPLETE EXECUTED COPY OF THIS AGREEMENT.

DATED this _____ day of _____, 19____

WITNESS: _____

_____
SIGNATURE OF BUYER

_____
SIGNATURE OF CO-BUYER (IF ANY)

Seller hereby agrees to the foregoing and assigns the within contract to Canadian Imperial Bank of Commerce upon the terms and conditions of the Assignment and Transfer set forth on the reverse hereof and Buyer acknowledges and accepts such Assignment and Transfer and undertakes to make payment to the Bank at _____

DATED the _____ day of _____, 19____

VOID

VOID

_____
Signature of Buyer

VOID

_____
Signature of Co-Buyer (if any)

VOID

_____
Signature of Seller

By _____

(_____)

* FILL IN COMPLETE ADDRESS

Form 1—*Continued*

TERMS AND CONDITIONS

The following terms and conditions form part of the Agreement set forth on the face hereof:

1. The title to and ownership of the property shall not pass to Buyer on delivery thereof bu. shall remain in Seller at Buyer's risk until the Unpaid Balance together with interest and all other amounts payable by Buyer hereunder is paid in full.

2. Destruction of or damage to the property shall not release Buyer from liability hereunder and Buyer will keep the property insured in favour of Seller against such risks as Seller may require for an amount sufficient to secure the interest of Seller therein. If Buyer fails to keep the property insured, Seller may so insure (but shall be under no obligation to do so) and charge the amount of the premium to Buyer who shall pay the same forthwith.

3. Buyer shall keep the property free of all liens, charges and encumbrances and if any such lien, charge or encumbrance is created, Seller may pay off the same and any amount so paid with all costs and expenses shall be paid forthwith by Buyer.

4. No notice, demand or mise-en-demure shall be required to put Buyer in default under this agreement and if Seller shall grant or tolerate any extension or delay for the payment or performance of any obligations of Buyer, no such extension, delay or tolerance shall be deemed an acquiescence by Seller in such default, or a waiver of any of Seller's rights or recourse under this agreement.

5. Buyer shall keep the property in good repair.

6. If Buyer makes default in payment or fails to perform any obligation hereunder or if Seller deems itself insecure (of which Seller shall be sole judge) or if Seller has reasonable cause to believe that its security is in jeopardy or if any proceeding in bankruptcy, receivership or winding up be taken by or against Buyer or if Buyer fails to insure the property and Seller does not place such insurance forthwith or if the Buyer parts with possession of the property or removes the same for more than 20 days from the county or district within which Buyer resides at the time the property is delivered to Buyer hereunder or uses the property for hire without the written consent of Seller, the amount of the Unpaid Balance and all other amounts then outstanding hereunder shall immediately become due and payable and Seller may enter upon any premises where the property may be and repossess and remove the same without legal process; provided that if the rights of the parties hereunder with respect to the property are subject to the laws of the Province of Manitoba, Buyer may so remove the property within the Province of Manitoba or may charge his interest in the property if Buyer shall have given to Seller by delivery or registered mail at the address specified on the reverse hereof at least ten (10) days' prior written notice of his intention to do so, specifying the place within Manitoba to which the property is to be removed or the person in whose favour any such charge is to be created.

7. In the event that the property is repossessed under paragraph 6 hereof and is not thereafter redeemed in the manner and within the period prescribed by law, or within 30 days, whichever is greater, all or part of the property may from time to time be sold at public or private sale at the option of Seller, and after deducting the costs and expenses of sale, of taking and keeping possession and of repair and legal fees, the net proceeds of sale shall be applied on the amount then owing by Buyer and any surplus shall be paid to Buyer and any deficiency shall be forthwith paid by Buyer.

8. This agreement and all rights of Seller including the right to repossess the property may be assigned and transferred to Canadian

Imperial Bank of Commerce (herein call the "Bank") and such assignment (and any further assignments) shall not be subject to any equities as between Buyer and Seller unless otherwise required by law.

9. Buyer consents to life insurance being arranged under a Group Life Insurance Policy with The Canada Life Assurance Company, such insurance to be owned and paid for by and payable to the Bank, be effective as of the date of assignment of this contract to the Bank, and be subject to such terms and conditions as may be agreed upon between the Bank and said insurer, but the amount of insurance shall not exceed the amount of the Unpaid Balance. The name of Buyer (if more than one) whose life is to be insured is specifically designated on the face hereof. Such insurance shall terminate upon such terms and conditions as may be agreed upon between the Bank and said insurer. If the insurance becomes payable prior to such termination, the Unpaid Balance and all other amounts then outstanding hereunder shall be repaid to the extent possible from the insurance proceeds. Failure of the Bank to obtain or keep in force any or sufficient insurance for any reason shall not limit or lessen the liability of Buyer hereunder.

10. If the rights of the parties hereunder with respect to the property are subject to the laws of the Province of Saskatchewan, Buyer (if a body corporate) agrees that The Limitation of Civil Rights Act of Saskatchewan shall not apply to this contract or to any security for the payment of money made or created by or pursuant thereto or any agreement or instrument renewing or extending or collateral to this contract and any of the benefits of the said Act are hereby specifically waived.

11. Buyer expressly waives the benefit of every statute or law which prevents or restricts Seller from recovering a deficiency from Buyer after resale by Seller following repossession of the property, and without limiting the generality of the foregoing, if the rights of the parties hereunder with respect to the property are subject to the laws of the Province of Alberta, Buyer expressly waives the benefit of Section 19 of The Conditional Sales Act of Alberta.

12. Any term or condition or part thereof of this agreement which is prohibited or unenforceable by the law of any province shall, as to that province, be ineffective to the extent of such prohibition or unenforceable without invalidating the remaining terms and conditions of this agreement.

13. There are no representations, conditions, warranties, guarantees or collateral agreements, express or implied, statutory or otherwise, in respect of the property or this agreement, other than as set out herein, and without limiting the generality of the foregoing, if the rights of the parties hereunder with respect to the property are subject to the laws of the Province of Ontario, the implied conditions, warranties and guarantees contained in Section 13, 14, 15 and 16 of The Sale of Goods Act of Ontario are expressly excluded from this agreement.

14. This agreement shall ensure to the benefit of and shall bind the respective heirs, executors, administrators, successors and assigns of Buyer and Seller.

15. In the event that this agreement is signed by more than one buyer then "Buyer" wherever it appears in this agreement shall be read and construed as "Buyers" with all grammatical changes thereby rendered necessary, and the liability of such persons under this agreement shall be joint and several.

ASSIGNMENT AND TRANSFER

FOR VALUE RECEIVED Seller hereby assigns and transfers to Canadian Imperial Bank of Commerce,

*

(herein called the "Bank") the within contract, all rights, claims and moneys payable thereunder, all right, title and interest in and to the property therein described and the benefits of insurance upon the same and warrants that the contract is genuine and is not subject to rescission and that the property has been delivered to and accepted by Buyer, in default of which the agreement set out below in the paragraph entitled With Recourse shall apply.

Seller's liability hereunder shall not be affected by any extension, indulgence, compromise, security, variation of the contract or release of Buyer or other interested person whether by operation of law or otherwise. This assignment is supplemented by the agreement set out below in the paragraph initialled by Seller and these provisions shall apply to and bind the heirs, executors, administrators, successors and assigns of Seller and shall enure to the benefit of and be enforceable by the Bank, its successors and assigns.

Initial applicable paragraph:

☐ WITHOUT RECOURSE: Save as to the warranties set forth above, this assignment is without recourse to the Seller.

☐ WITH RECOURSE: Seller unconditionally agrees to repurchase the within contract forthwith upon demand, for the Unpaid Balance and all other amounts outstanding under the contract at the date of demand whether or not the contract shall then be in default.

☐ REPURCHASE: If within 90 days after any default which is not cured the property described in the within contract is repossessed and delivered to Seller, Seller shall forthwith pay to the Bank the Unpaid Balance and all other amounts then outstanding under the contract regardless of the condition of the property, and Seller also agrees to repurchase the property for such amount after expiration of the said 90 day period provided the Bank institutes legal action to repossess the property within such period and the property is delivered to Seller within 30 days after the Bank has obtained legally indisputable possession thereof.

☐ LIMITED REPURCHASE: The above paragraph entitled Repurchase shall apply provided that the obligation of Seller thereunder shall terminate upon payment by Buyer to the Bank of the first   monthly instalments within 15 days of their respective due dates.

☐ OPTIONAL PURCHASE: If the Bank repossesses the property described in the within contract Seller shall have the option after demand by the Bank either to pay the Bank $ or to buy the property in its then condition and location from the Bank for the Unpaid Balance and all other amounts then outstanding under the contract.

* fill in complete address

Form 2

DL 30-83
For use in Ontario,
Manitoba, Saskatchewan
FIXED RATE OR FLOATING RATE

CANADIAN IMPERIAL BANK OF COMMERCE - SECURITY AGREEMENT (Chattel Mortgage)

BRANCH DOMICILE	DATE

BORROWER(S)

FIRST GIVEN NAME	INITIAL OF SECOND GIVEN NAME	LAST NAME	FIRST GIVEN NAME	INITIAL OF SECOND GIVEN NAME	LAST NAME

DATE OF BIRTH	DAY	MO	YR	SEX ☐ M ☐ F	DATE OF BIRTH	DAY	MO	YR	SEX ☐ M ☐ F

FULL ADDRESS	FULL ADDRESS

(In this Agreement, the words "I", "me" and "my" mean each borrower who signs it and the word "Bank" means Canadian Imperial Bank of Commerce.)

Complete appropriate box.

NEW LOAN
(Insert principal amount)

The Bank has made me a new loan of $ _____ (Note(s) dated _____ 19 _____). As a condition of my loan I agreed to sign this Security Agreement.

EXISTING LOAN
(Insert original principal amount)

I have an existing loan from the Bank (Note(s) dated _____ 19 _____ for a total original principal amount of $ _____). The balance of my loan is now due. In return for the Bank not requiring me to repay my loan immediately, I am giving the Bank this Security Agreement.

SUBSTITUTION OF SECURITY FOR EXISTING LOAN
(Insert original principal amount)

I borrowed $ _____ from the Bank and gave it my Note(s) dated _____ 19 _____ and a security agreement (chattel mortgage) on the following property:

In return for the Bank agreeing to release its interest in that property, I am giving it this Security Agreement.

SECURITY INTEREST

I now give the Bank a security interest in the following Property and all proceeds of it (and transfer my title in the Property and proceeds to the Bank) as security for the payment of my loan, interest on it, my Note(s), any replacement notes and all other amounts payable under this Agreement:

MANUFACTURER AND DESCRIPTION (INCLUDE BODY STYLE)	MODEL YEAR	SERIAL NO.	MOTOR NO. (IF MOTOR VEHICLE)	LICENSE NO. (IF MOTOR VEHICLE)

Use headings or fully describe the Property

I agree with the Bank as follows:

PAYMENTS

1. Payments required by my Note(s) and each replacement note, as amended from time to time, will be made by me when due.

OWNERSHIP AND POSSESSION

2. I own the Property and I will not sell, lease or give up possession of it without the Bank's consent.

OTHER CLAIMS

3. The Property will be kept clear of all mortgages, liens and other claims except any I have already reported to the Bank in writing. If it is not, the Bank may (but does not have to) pay all or part of them.

INSURANCE

4. The Property will be kept insured by me for the amount and against the risks the Bank reasonably requests. If it is not, the Bank may (but does not have to) insure it and pay the premiums. As additional security, I transfer to the Bank my right to receive the insurance proceeds and it may apply them to the amount I owe (whether or not that amount is then due).

REPAIR AND INSPECTION

5. The Property will be kept in good repair by me. The Bank may inspect it at any reasonable time and may (but does not have to) make and pay for any reasonable repairs.

CHANGE OF RESIDENCE

6. I will tell the Bank before I move from any Province or Territory where I now or may later live so that it can register this Agreement where necessary.

BANK'S RIGHTS ON DEFAULT

7. The balance of my loan and accrued interest will become payable immediately if I breach any of my obligations under this Agreement, or if, without the Bank's consent, the Property is about to be sold or removed from Canada, or if proceedings are started by or against me under any insolvency or bankruptcy law, or if anything else happens which the Bank believes endangers the Property or affects my ability to pay the amounts that may become payable under my loan. In any such case the Bank may from time to time, in any order and in any lawful way, and after giving any notice required by law, do any one or more of the following:

    (a) take possession of all or part of the Property, wherever it is;

    (b) store, sell or lease all or part of the Property;

    (c) sue me for any amount I owe; and

    (d) exercise any other rights the Bank may have.

Sale or lease proceeds will be applied to the amount I owe, including the expenses mentioned in paragraph 8, and I will pay any amount still owing.

EXPENSES AND INTEREST

8. I will immediately repay all amounts the Bank is permitted to pay under this Agreement and all expenses, including legal fees, paid by it in exercising its rights. I will pay interest, at the rate shown in my Note(s), on such amounts and expenses from the date they are paid by the Bank until they are repaid by me.

GENERAL

9. This Agreement does not replace any other security held by the Bank or my Note(s). If more than one borrower signs this Agreement, each is separately liable and all are jointly liable under it.

COPY OF AGREEMENT

10. I have received a signed copy of this Agreement.

VOID
VOID

WITNESS	BORROWER
WITNESS	BORROWER

Form 3

73-83

GENERAL ASSIGNMENT OF ACCOUNTS, ETC.

....
(Branch Designation)

FOR VALUABLE CONSIDERATION the undersigned [1]

(1) Insert
full name
of assignor.

....
(Name)

of ....
(Street number and name, apt. no. OR lot, concession and Township)   (City, Town or Village and rural route)   (Prov./Territory)

hereby assign(s) and transfer(s) all debts, accounts, claims, moneys and choses in action which now are or which may at any time hereafter be due or owing to or owned by the undersigned, and also all securities, bills, notes and other documents now held or owned or which may be hereafter taken, held or owned by the undersigned or anyone on behalf of the undersigned in respect of the said debts, accounts, claims, moneys and choses in action or any part thereof, and also all books and papers recording, evidencing or relating to said debts, accounts, claims, moneys and choses in action or any part thereof (all of the foregoing being herein called the "assigned premises") to CANADIAN IMPERIAL BANK OF COMMERCE (herein called the "Bank") as a general and continuing collateral security for payment of all existing and future indebtedness and liability of the undersigned to the Bank wheresoever and howsoever incurred and any ultimate unpaid balance thereof, and as a first and prior claim upon the assigned premises.

2. The Bank may collect, realize, sell or otherwise deal with the assigned premises or any part thereof in such manner, upon such terms and conditions and at such time or times as may seem to it advisable and without notice to the undersigned (except as otherwise required by any applicable law), and may charge on its own behalf and pay to others reasonable sums for expenses incurred and for services rendered (expressly including legal advices and services) in or in connection with collecting, realizing, selling or obtaining payment of the assigned premises and may add the amount of such sums to the indebtedness of the undersigned.

3. The Bank shall not be liable or accountable for any failure to collect, realize, sell or obtain payment of the assigned premises or any part thereof and shall not be bound to institute proceeedings for the purpose of collecting, realizing or obtaining payment of the same or for the purpose of preserving any rights of the Bank, the undersigned or any other person, firm or corporation in respect of the same.

4. The Bank may grant extensions of time and other indulgences, take and give up securities, accept compositions, grant releases and discharges and otherwise deal with the undersigned, debtors of the undersigned, sureties and others and with the assigned premises and other securities as the Bank may see fit without prejudice to the liability of the undersigned or the Bank's right to hold and realize this security.

5. All moneys collected or received by the undersigned in respect of the assigned premises shall be received as trustee for the Bank and shall be forthwith paid over to the Bank.

6. All moneys collected or received by the Bank in respect of the assigned premises (whether by virtue of paragraph 5 hereof or otherwise howsoever) may be applied on account of such parts of the indebtedness and liability of the undersigned as to the Bank seems best or in the discretion of the Bank may be released to the undersigned, all without prejudice to the Bank's claims upon the undersigned.

7. The undersigned shall from time to time forthwith on request furnish to the Bank in writing all information requested relating to the assigned premises and the Bank shall be entitled from time to time to inspect the aforesaid securities, bills, notes, books, papers and other documents or take temporary custody thereof and for such purposes the Bank shall have access to all premises occupied by the undersigned.

8. The undersigned shall from time to time forthwith on the Bank's request do, make and execute all such financing statements, further assignments, documents, acts, matters and things as may be required by the Bank of or with respect to the assigned premises or any part thereof or as may be required to give effect to these presents, and the undersigned hereby constitutes and appoints the Manager or acting Manager for the time being of the above mentioned branch of the Bank, or any other branch at which this security is held, the true and lawful attorney of the undersigned irrevocable with full power of substitution to do, make and execute all such statements, assignments, documents, acts, matters or things with the right to use the name of the undersigned whenever and wherever it may be deemed necessary or expedient.

9. The provisions hereof shall enure to the benefit of the successors and assigns of the Bank and shall be binding upon the respective heirs, executors, administrators, successors and assigns of the undersigned.

WITNESS the hand and seal of the undersigned this.........day of.......................... 19........

Witness:

SIGNATURE

RECEIPT OF A COPY OF THE WITHIN SECURITY AGREEMENT IS HEREBY ACKNOWLEDGED

DATE

SEAL

(To be completed for registration in Manitoba, Ontario and Saskatchewan)

If an individual(s), first given name, initial of second given name, if any, then surname. Record full address including postal code.

FULL NAME AND ADDRESS OF ASSIGNOR(S)	If given by individual(s) record				For Manitoba only Driver's License No. (If Available)
	Initials of ASSIGNOR(S)	Date of Birth For Ontario Day Month Year		Sex M/F	
		For Manitoba Year Month Day			

Form 4

DEMAND DEBENTURE

PRINCIPAL SUM   Dollars

($)   Date

(Delete inapplicable clause) INTEREST   (a) nominal annual rate of _____ %

RATE   (b)   % per annum, being a nominal annual rate   percentage points above the Minimum Lending Rate (the "MLR") of Canadian Imperial Bank of Commerce (the "Bank") in effect on the date hereof; provided that if and whenever the MLR is varied by the Bank the interest rate hereunder shall also be varied, effective on the day such variation in the MLR comes into effect, so that at all times the interest rate hereunder shall be the said number of percentage points above the MLR then in effect. The certificate of a Vice-President or Assistant General Manager of the Bank as to the MLR in effect at any time shall be accepted as conclusive evidence thereof for all purposes hereof.

BANK BRANCH AND ADDRESS

1.1 ....

incorporated under the laws of   (the "Company") for value received hereby acknowledges itself indebted and promises to pay on demand to or to the order of CANADIAN IMPERIAL BANK OF COMMERCE (the "Bank") the above mentioned principal sum in lawful money of Canada on presentation and surrender of this debenture at the Bank's branch mentioned above, or at such other place as the Bank may designate by notice in writing to the Company, and in the meantime to pay interest thereon from the date hereof at the above mentioned rate in like money at the same place monthly on the last day of each month; and, should the Company at any time make default in the payment of any principal or interest, to pay interest on the amount in default both before and after judgment at the same rate in like money at the same place on the same dates.

SECURITY

(Delete inapplicable provisions) 2.1 As security for the due payment of all moneys payable hereunder, the Company as beneficial owner hereby:

(a) grants, assigns, conveys, mortgages and charges as and by way of a first fixed and specific mortgage and charge to and in favour of the Bank, its successors and assigns:

    (i) all lands and premises now owned by the Company and described or referred to in Schedule A hereto, including all appurtenances, buildings and fixtures now or hereafter situate thereon, and all other lands and premises, including buildings and fixtures, hereafter acquired by the Company; and

    (ii) all machinery, equipment, plant, vehicles, goods and chattels now owned by the Company and described or referred to in Schedule B hereto and all other machinery, equipment, plant, vehicles, goods and chattels, hereafter acquired by the Company; and

(b) charges as and by way of a first floating charge to and in favour of the Bank, its successors and assigns, all its undertaking, property and assets, both present and future, of every nature and kind and wherever situate (other than such as are at all times validly subjected to the first fixed and specific mortgage and charge hereby created) including, without limitation, its franchises and uncalled capital.

In this debenture, the mortgages and charges hereby consituted are called the "Security" and the subject matter of the Security is called the "Charged Premises".

2.2 Until the Security becomes enforceable, the Company may dispose of or deal with the subject matter of the floating charge in the ordinary course of its business and for the purpose of carrying on the same provided that the Company will not, without the prior written consent of the Bank, create, assume or have outstanding, except to the Bank, any mortgage, charge or other encumbrance on any part of the Charged Premises ranking or purporting to rank or capable of being enforced in priority to or pari passu with the Security, other than any mortgage, lien or other encumbrance upon property, created or assumed to secure all or any part of the funds required for the purchase of such property or any extension or renewal or replacement thereof upon the same property if the principal amount of the indebtedness secured thereby is not increased, or any inchoate liens for taxes or assessments by public authorities.

2.3 The Security shall not extend or apply to the last day of the term of any lease or agreement therefor but upon the enforcement of the Security the Company shall stand possessed of such last day in trust to assign the same to any person acquiring such term.

2.4 The Bank is the person entitled to receive the money payable hereunder and to give a discharge hereof.

ENFORCEMENT

3.1 In the event that the Company makes default in the payment of principal or interest hereunder the Security shall become enforceable.

3.2 Whenever the Security has become enforceable, the Bank may realize upon the Security and enforce its rights by the following remedies:

(a) entry into possession;

(b) proceedings in any court of competent jurisdiction for the appointment of a receiver (which term as used in this debenture includes a receiver and manager) of all or any part of the Charged Premises;

(c) proceedings in any court of competent jurisdiction for sale or foreclosure of all or any part of the Charged Premises;

(d) filing of proofs of claim and other documents to establish its claims in any proceeding relative to the Company;

Form 4—*Continued*

(e) appointment by instrument in writing of a receiver of all or any part of the Charged Premises and removal or replacement from time to time of any such receiver; and

(f) any other remedy or proceeding authorized or permitted hereby or by law or equity.

Such remedies may be exercised from time to time separately or in combination and are in addition to and not in substitution for any other rights of the Bank however created.

3.3 Any receiver appointed by instrument in writing shall have power to:

(a) take possession of, collect and get in all or any part of the Charged Premises and, for that purpose, to take proceedings in the name of the Company or otherwise and to make any arrangement or compromise;

(b) carry on or concur in carrying on all or any part of the business of the Company;

(c) borrow or to raise money on all or any part of the Charged Premises in priority to this debenture or otherwise for such purposes as may be approved by the Bank; and

(d) sell or concur in selling all or any part of the Charged Premises without notice and in such manner as may seem advisable to the receiver, and to effect such sale by conveying in the name and on behalf of the Company or otherwise.

The receiver shall be vested with such other discretions and powers as are granted in the instrument of appointment and any supplement thereto. The receiver shall for all purposes be deemed to be the agent of the Company and not of the Bank, and the Company shall be solely responsible for his acts or defaults and for his remuneration. All moneys from time to time received by the receiver may be applied as follows: first, in discharge of all operating expenses and other outgoings affecting the Charged Premises; second, in keeping in good standing all charges and liens on the Charged Premises having priority over the Security; third, in payment of the remuneration and disbursements of the receiver; fourth, in payment to the Bank of the moneys payable hereunder; and the balance, if any, shall be paid to the Company.

EXPENSES

4.1 The Company agrees to pay to the Bank forthwith on demand all costs, charges and expenses, including all legal fees, (on a solicitor and his own client basis), incurred by the Bank in connection with the recovery or enforcement of payment of any moneys owing hereunder whether by realization or otherwise. All such sums shall be secured hereby and shall be added to the principal hereof and bear interest at the rate in effect hereunder at the date hereof.

PLEDGE OF DEBENTURE

5.1 This debenture may be deposited or pledged by the Company as collateral security for its indebtedness and liabilities and, when redelivered to the Company or its nominees, shall be forthwith cancelled; but this debenture shall not be deemed to have been redeemed by reason of the account of the Company having ceased to be in debit while this debenture was so deposited or pledged and no payment shall reduce the amount owing under this debenture unless specifically appropriated to and noted on this debenture at the time of payment.

NEGOTIABILITY

6.1 This debenture is a negotiable instrument and all rights created hereunder are exercisable by any holder hereof.

WAIVER

7.1 No consent or waiver by the Bank shall be effective unless made in writing and signed by an authorized officer of the Bank.

NOTICE

8.1 Any notice to the Company may be given by prepaid registered mail to the Company at its head office and any notice so given shall be deemed to have been duly given on the day on which the envelope containing the notice was deposited prepaid and registered in a post office.

IN WITNESS WHEREOF the Company has duly executed this debenture.

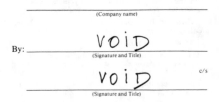

(Company name)

By: _____
(Signature and Title)

_____   c/s
(Signature and Title)

Form 5

Form 1076-79

PLEDGE AGREEMENT

Description of Debenture

Principal Amount: _____

Date: _____

(delete inapplicable clause) Interest Rate:
(a) Nominal annual rate of _____%
(b) A variable nominal annual rate _____ percentage points above the Minimum Lending Rate of Canadian Imperial Bank of Commerce from time to time.

The undersigned hereby assigns, deposits with and pledges to CANADIAN IMPERIAL BANK OF COMMERCE (the "Bank") the debenture created by the undersigned and described above (the "Debenture") to be held by the Bank as a general and continuing collateral security for the payment of all present and future indebtedness and liability of the undersigned to the Bank however incurred and any ultimate unpaid balance thereof (the "Indebtedness").

In the event of any default in payment of any part of the Indebtedness or in the performance of any other obligation of the undersigned to the Bank, the Bank may at any time during the continuance of any such default realize upon the Debenture by sale, transfer or delivery, or exercise and enforce all rights and remedies of a holder of the Debenture as if the Bank were absolute owner thereof, without notice to or control by the undersigned, and any such remedy may be exercised separately or in combination and shall be in addition to and not in substitution for any other rights of the Bank however created; provided that the Bank shall not be bound to exercise any such right or remedy.

The proceeds of the Debenture may be applied by the Bank on account of such part of the Indebtedness as it chooses without prejudice to the Bank's claim upon the undersigned for any deficiency.

The Bank may grant extensions of time or other indulgences, take and give up securities, accept compositions, grant releases and discharges and otherwise deal with the undersigned and with other parties, sureties or securities as the Bank may see fit without prejudice to the liability of the undersigned or the Bank's rights in respect of the Debenture.

Payment to the Bank of interest for any period in respect of the Indebtedness shall be deemed payment in satisfaction of the interest payment for the same period under the Debenture.

The Debenture shall not operate by way of merger of any of the Indebtedness and no judgment recovered by the Bank shall operate by way of merger of or in any way affect the security of the Debenture which is in addition to and not in substitution for any other security now or hereafter held by the Bank.

The provisions hereof shall be binding upon and shall enure to the benefit of the undersigned and the Bank and their respective successors and assigns.

In witness whereof the undersigned has duly executed this instrument the day of   , 19   .

_____
(Company name)

Void
_____
(Signature and title)

Void   c/s
_____
(Signature and title)

Form 6

Security Agreement/1.

SECURITY AGREEMENT - INVENTORY   CONSUMER PRODUCTS

John Deere Limited, P.O. Box 1000, Grimsby, Ontario (the "Company"), as secured party, and the undersigned Dealer, as debtor, hereby agree as follows:

1. INDEBTEDNESS SECURED

The Dealer agrees to pay to the Company, as and when due, all indebtedness which is now owed by the Dealer to the Company and all additional indebtedness hereafter incurred by the Dealer to the Company for or incident to the purchase of Goods (as defined in the John Deere Authorized Consumer Products Dealer Agreement in effect from time to time), as well as all other indebtedness which may at any time be owing by the Dealer to the Company, whether pursuant to Authorized Dealer Agreements, the Company's Dealer Terms Schedules, the Finance and Leasing Agreements, or otherwise, and whether evidenced by notes, lien notes, open accounts, or otherwise, all of which indebtedness is collectively referred to herein as "indebtedness". The John Deere Authorized Consumer Products Dealer Agreement, its supplementary Dealer Terms Schedule, the Finance and Leasing Agreements, and this Security Agreement, as subsequently amended or replaced, are sometimes hereinafter collectively referred to as the "Dealer agreements".

2. COLLATERAL

The collateral to be subject to the security interests created and provided for under this Security Agreement includes the following:

(a) The Dealer's entire stock of Goods (as defined in the John Deere Authorized Consumer Products Dealer Agreement in effect from time to time), including without limiting the generality of the foregoing, the following:

    (i) complete machines,
    (ii) accessories,
    (iii) certain items of the John Deere Merchandise ("JDM") line, and
    (iv) service, repair or replacement parts for (i), (ii) and (iii),

all of which were supplied to the Dealer by the Company and which form part of the Dealer's inventory;

(b) That portion of the Dealer's equipment inventory financed or floor planned by the Company, including without limitation:

    (i) used equipment sold by the Company to the Dealer which are subject to Floor Plan Lien Notes,
    (ii) used equipment sold by the Company to the Dealer which are subject to Machine Re-purchase Lien Notes, and
    (iii) new or used equipment owned by the Dealer and financed by the Company under floor plan or installment lien notes, chattel mortgages or other forms of security agreement,

all of which form part of the Dealer's inventory of equipment;

all of the foregoing being collectively referred to in this Security Agreement as "collateral". Any reference to Dealer's inventory shall include all of the Dealer's presently existing inventory of collateral and that which the Dealer shall hereafter acquire, and includes collateral located either at the Dealer's place(s) of business or at any other location used or maintained by the Dealer for the storage of collateral and whether in transit, or on lease, rental or demonstration.

3. GRANT OF SECURITY INTEREST

As security for the payment of the indebtedness, the Dealer hereby grants to the Company:

(a) a security interest in any unpaid-for item of collateral and the Company reserves title to any such collateral provided by it; and

(b) a security interest in each paid-for item of collateral,

Form 6—*Continued*

both of the foregoing being collectively referred to in this Security Agreement as the "security interest" and each item of collateral shall remain as security for the Dealer's entire indebtedness until the unpaid balance of such indebtedness is paid in full. The security interest shall extend to (i) the collateral presently in the Dealer's possession, (ii) all collateral subsequently acquired as additions or replacements, (iii) all proceeds (as defined in The Personal Property Security Act) of the sale or lease of such collateral, including proceeds of proceeds, as well as all proceeds now in the Dealer's possession, and (iv) all returned or repossessed collateral.

4. ATTACHMENT

The security interest created and provided for in Section 3 above shall attach upon execution of this Security Agreement in respect to all items of collateral in which the Dealer has rights at that moment, and shall attach to all rights of the Dealer acquired hereafter, immediately upon such acquisition.

5. SALE OF COLLATERAL BY DEALER

The Dealer may sell any item of the collateral to retail purchasers or may lease such items in the ordinary course of business, but (i) shall do so in accordance with the terms of the Dealer agreements, and (ii) shall not otherwise use or dispose of any items of the collateral or allow any lien, charge or encumbrance to be created or remain on the collateral without the prior written permission of the Company. The Company's security interest shall continue in any leased item of collateral subject to the rights of the Lessee.

6. USE OF PROCEEDS

The Dealer may use, commingle or dispose of proceeds of collateral, other than trade-ins, in the normal operation of his business or by way of distributions of earnings and profits to the owners of the business, but any such use, commingling or disposition shall not affect the Company's security interest in any such proceeds which at any time remain in the Dealer's possession, or the Company's right to require notes or accounts in the Dealer's possession to be turned over to the Company as provided in Section 13 hereof. The liberty provided for herein to use or dispose of proceeds of collateral does not include the right or power to pledge or encumber such proceeds to secure a debt or other obligation of the Dealer, and any attempted pledge of such proceeds or the creation or continuance of any such encumbrance without the written permission of the Company constitutes a default hereunder.

7. DEFAULT

General

The following shall constitute events of default by the Dealer:

(a) (i) The Dealer's authority to sell Goods pursuant to a John Deere Authorized Consumer Products Dealer Agreement is cancelled; (ii) The Dealer defaults in the payment or performance of any obligation to the Company, in particular his obligations and duties under the Dealer agreements and this Security Agreement; (iii) The Dealer fails, upon request, to turn over proceeds or provide information; (iv) The Dealer, in violation of Section 5 or 6 hereof, sells or disposes of any part of the collateral without first obtaining the written consent of the Company or sells or disposes of proceeds, including trade-ins, or allows any lien or encumbrance to be created or remain on the collateral; (v) The Dealer or any member of the Dealer's firm if a partnership becomes insolvent, has a Receiver or Receiver Manager appointed for any part of Dealer's assets, makes an assignment for the benefit of creditors, institutes or has instituted against him proceedings under any bankruptcy or insolvency law, or the Dealer has his stock in trade or any part thereof levied upon or attached; (vi) The happening of one or more of the events specified in Section 3 of the John Deere Authorized Consumer Products Dealer Agreement in effect between the Dealer and the Company; (vii) The Dealer fails to tender promptly any collateral which he becomes obligated to resell to the Company under the John Deere Authorized Consumer Products Dealer Agreement in effect between the Dealer and the Company; (viii) The falsification of records or reports.

Unsafe Debt or Security

(b) If in the Company's opinion the debt or security is unsafe or insecure.

Form 6—*Continued*

Security Agreement/3.

8. RIGHTS ON DEFAULT

If default occurs or continues, the Company may:

Acceleration and Suit

(a) Declare immediately due and payable all indebtedness owing by the Dealer to the Company including the indebtedness secured hereby and collect the same together with reasonable expenses including court costs, lawyer's fees and all other legal expenses;

Restrict Shipments

(b) Discontinue or withhold the delivery of collateral to the Dealer, or make further deliveries only on a cash or C.O.D. basis;

Repossess

(c) Take possession of any or all collateral by any method permitted by law;

Acceleration of Installments

(d) Discontinue deferral of any unpaid portion of the purchase price of collateral after the collateral has been removed from the Dealer's place of business, personally used by the Dealer or settled for by a retail customer.

Notice of (a) or (b) shall be given to the Dealer in such manner and at such time as the Company may see fit. No notice of any other action taken or to be taken by the Company hereunder shall be necessary except where required by provincial law, such notice being hereby expressly waived by the Dealer.

9. REPOSSESSION OF COLLATERAL

If the Company elects to take possession of any collateral, it shall have the right, to the full extent allowed by law, to enter any premises occupied by or under the control of the Dealer for that purpose. The Dealer shall, when requested to do so by the Company, gather at his principal place of business any items of collateral which are not already located there and will place any such collateral in transportable condition. If the Dealer is unable to gather the collateral he will disclose the location of the collateral on the Company's request. After taking possession, the Company may at its election take any one of the following actions or a combination of (a) and (b), or of (b) and (c);

Sale

(a) Dispose of all or any part of such collateral at one or more public and/or private sales or by lease or deferred payment in the manner prescribed by law.

Return

(b) Return to the Dealer any part of the collateral when the Company, in its sole discretion, determines:
(i) There is sufficient other collateral available to satisfy the Dealer's indebtedness and costs, or
(ii) Those parts of the collateral are not of sufficient value, because of obsolescence, wear and tear or any other reason which the Company deems sufficient, to justify the trouble and expense of attempting to dispose of them.

Full Satisfaction

(c) Propose to accept all or a part of the collateral and other collateral held by it in full satisfaction of the Dealer's indebtedness as provided by law. The Company shall not be bound by its proposal to so elect unless and until it has sent the notice(s) required by law and the time for interested persons to require disposition has passed.

10. APPLICATION OF PROCEEDS

The proceeds of sale of collateral pursuant to Section 9(a) hereof shall be applied: first, in the satisfaction of all expenses reasonably incurred by the Company, including without limitation the reasonable expenses of retaking, holding, repairing, processing, preparing for disposition and disposing of the collateral and all reasonable court costs, lawyer's fees and other legal expenses; second, to the satisfaction of the Dealer's indebtedness as required by law; and third, to the satisfaction of any subordinate security interest where the notices required by law have been received by the Company before disposition of the proceeds. If after such application there is (i) a surplus, the Company will pay such surplus over as provided by law, and (ii) if there is a deficiency, the Dealer shall be liable for it and shall pay it forthwith provided that provincial law permits the collection of such a deficiency.

11. PROCEDURES FOR DISPOSITION

Without suggesting that other procedures may not also be commercially reasonable, or that any of the following procedures are mandatory in any particular case, it is agreed that the following are all commercially reasonable

Form 6—*Continued*

methods of disposing of collateral repossessed hereunder should the Company decide to follow one or more of them as to all or a part of the collateral:

New Equipment

(a) Sale of complete machines and attachments by units or in one or more parcels by private sale to another dealer or dealers at current dealer price, together with increased value, if any, negotiated with the buying dealer resulting from the fact that freight from the factory has been paid. (This procedure will be reasonable only if the collateral is equivalent to new unused machines of current production.)

Used or Depreciated Goods

(b) Sale of collateral (including parts) by units or in one or more parcels at private sale at the best price submitted in sealed bids taken from three or more dealers, provided that in the Company's judgement such best bid represents a reasonable price. (This procedure is in conformity with reasonable industry practices in disposing of complete inventories of goods, or of items coming into the possession of manufacturers or distributors which are not saleable as new unused machines of current production.)

Parts

(c) Sale of current parts and attachments in good condition for which there is a ready market to dealers through the Company's regular parts distribution facilities at regular prices and terms. The Company may commingle such parts with its regular inventory of parts and account for the sale of the parts repossessed hereunder on the assumption that the first parts sold after such commingling are those repossessed. The Company's expenses of reinventorying and merchandising returned and repossessed parts (exclusive of costs incurred in listing, tagging, packing, and loading them at the Dealer's place of business and of transportation expenses from the Dealer's place of business to the Company's parts distribution facility) are considerably in excess of 15% of their invoice price, and it is agreed that a 15% charge for such services may be made without further itemization or analysis of such expenses.

Public Sale

(d) Public sale at auction of all collateral or any portion thereof not disposed of by some other method. Either the publication once of the time and place of such sale and of the property to be sold at least five days prior thereto in a newspaper circulating in the geographical area where the sale is to be held, or the posting of such notice in at least three public places in such geographical area at least five days prior to the sale, constitutes sufficient notice thereof.

12. PROTECTION OF GOODS

The Dealer shall:

Storage

(a) Unless a different storage location is approved by the Company in writing, properly store all collateral in his possession at his regular place of business and protect the same from injury or damage of any kind.

Insurance

(b) Where insurance is not provided by the Company pursuant to the Dealer agreements, continuously keep all collateral insured with all risk type coverage satisfactory to the Company and with insurers satisfactory to the Company, in an amount equal to one hundred per cent (100%) of the invoice price thereof. Such insurance may be issued in the name of the Dealer who may retain possession of the policies, but each policy shall contain, (i) a clause naming the Company as an additional insured, (ii) a clause stipulating that loss is to be payable to the Company and the Dealer as their interests may appear, (iii) a cross liability clause containing the insurance coverage for the benefit of the Company notwithstanding any default or breach of condition by the Dealer, and (iv) a clause providing for at least ten (10) days prior written notice to the Company of any cancellation or termination of the policy or any part of the coverage thereof, all in form reasonably satisfactory to the Company. The Dealer shall immediately furnish the Company with the name of the insurer and the number, amount, effective date and expiration date of each policy issued; and upon request of the Company shall furnish it with copies of each such policy or certificate of insurance issued by the insurer.

(c) Where insurance is provided by the Company, the Dealer hereby assigns the

Form 6—*Continued*

Security Agreement/5.

proceeds of such insurance to the Company to the extent of any loss or damage done to unpaid-for collateral.

Taxes

(d) Pay when due all taxes, license fees and charges of any kind whatsoever that may be assessed or charged on or against any of the collateral, or the sale or use thereof, at any time on or after the date of delivery of the collateral to the Dealer.

Liens and Encumbrances

(e) Keep all collateral free and clear of all liens and encumbrances however arising, except with the written permission of the Company.

Payment by Company

If the Dealer fails to insure or to pay said taxes and charges or allows any lien or encumbrance to attach to the collateral, the Company, without obligation to do so, may obtain such insurance, pay such taxes, and charges, or discharge such lien, and the Dealer shall reimburse the Company promptly for all money so paid out together with interest at 14% per annum, or the highest contract rate permitted by law if less than 14%. The amounts so paid by the Company shall be deemed conclusive as to the amounts properly payable, and such amounts shall be secured hereunder as part of the indebtedness.

13. DELIVERY OF PROCEEDS

The Dealer will at any time upon request deliver to the Company all proceeds of collateral which are in his possession in the form of customers' notes, together with appropriate endorsement thereof to the Company, and will provide the Company with information concerning proceeds in the form of customers' accounts sufficient to enable the Company to collect such accounts directly, and the Company may collect such accounts.

14. CASH PROCEEDS

In the event of insolvency proceedings instituted by or against the Dealer, the Company's security interest hereunder in proceeds shall, in addition to identifiable non-cash proceeds and identifiable cash proceeds in the form of money or cheques not deposited in a bank account, include all cash and bank accounts of the Dealer up to an amount not greater than the amount of cash proceeds received by the Dealer within ten days before the institution of the insolvency proceedings, and commingled or deposited in a bank account prior to the insolvency proceedings, less the amount of cash proceeds received by the Dealer and paid over to the Company during the ten-day period.

15. COLLECTION OF NOTES AND ACCOUNTS

The provisions of this Section 15 and all references in this Agreement to "notes and accounts" shall apply to any proceeds in the form of notes of which the Company has taken possession and accounts which the Company desires to collect directly, but not including notes or other evidences of indebtedness accepted by the Company for credit under any finance plan in effect between the parties.

At any time and regardless of whether the Dealer is in default, the Company is authorized to reduce open accounts to notes, renew or extend the time of payment of any note or account or any securities securing the same, any such renewal to be in its own or the Dealer's name as the Company may elect, take, waive, release or exchange any security therefor, make such compromise settlements thereof as it deems advisable, and take such steps for the enforcement, collection, securing, renewing, extending, or compromising of any note or account or any part thereof, or any security therefor, as it deems advisable. Any proceeds realized from the collection or enforcement of said notes and accounts or any security therefor shall be applied on the indebtedness of the Dealer. The Company may return said notes and accounts to the Dealer at any time. After any default by the Dealer the Company may sell the whole or any part of said notes and accounts at one or more public or private sales, applying the proceeds in the manner prescribed by Section 10.

16. ACTS NOT A WAIVER

The acceptance of a note or notes and renewals thereof for the whole or any part of the Dealer's indebtedness, or the institution of legal action or the recovery of a judgement for the whole or a part of such indebtedness or on any note given therefor, shall not be deemed a waiver of any part of the security interest granted hereby.

Form 6—*Continued*

17. INVALIDITY OF PROVISION

The invalidity or unenforceability of any one or more of the provisions of this Agreement shall in no way affect the validity or enforceability of any of the other provisions hereof, and any provision hereof which is prohibited under the laws of any province shall be ineffective in such province to the extent of such prohibition only and shall not invalidate or in any wise affect the other provisions hereof.

18. RIGHTS CUMULATIVE

The rights of the Company hereunder are in addition to those available to it under any applicable legislation and are cumulative and not alternative; the exercise of any one right is not an election or waiver of the power to exercise any other right. Waiver of any default hereunder is not a waiver of any prior or subsequent default.

19. METHOD OF GIVING NOTICE

Without limitations on any other method of giving notice, any notice required hereunder shall be deemed sufficient and complete by mailing the same by prepaid registered or certified post addressed to the other party at the address specified in this Agreement or such other address as may be designated in writing and shall be deemed to have been received on the third day after such mailing.

20. AMENDMENT OF AGREEMENT

This Agreement may not be altered or amended, or have any of its specific provisions waived, unless such alteration, amendment or waiver is in writing and is executed by the Dealer and an officer of the Company.

21. EFFECT OF TERMINATION

Any termination of this Agreement shall in no way affect the security interest(s), rights and remedies of the Company or the Dealer, or the indebtedness which existed prior to the effective date of the termination.

22. SUCCESSORS

This Agreement shall enure to the benefit of the heirs, executors, administrators, successors and assigns of the Company and the Dealer.

23. ASSIGNMENT

The Agreement may be assigned by the Company at any time and may be further assigned by any such assignee, without in either case the consent of the Dealer. Dealer agrees not to assert against any assignee as a defence, counter claim, set-off or otherwise any claim which Dealer has now or hereinafter acquires against the Company.

24. APPLICABLE LAW

Unless the context of this Agreement otherwise requires, all references to the "Company" may be treated as references to the "Secured Party", and all references to the "Dealer" may be treated as references to the "Debtor". This Agreement shall be governed by the law of the province in which the Dealer resides.

25. CONTINUOUS APPLICATION OF AGREEMENT

Dealer agrees that this Agreement shall become effective immediately on its execution by the Dealer and shall continue in effect until (i) replaced by a new Security Agreement, or (ii) terminated by the Dealer and the Company, notwithstanding that a new John Deere Authorized Consumer Products Dealer Agreement may be entered into from time to time.

26. DEALER AGREEMENT(S)

Dealer has been appointed, or concurrently with the execution of this Security Agreement is being appointed as an authorized John Deere dealer under the terms of a John Deere Authorized Consumer Products Dealer Agreement between the Dealer and the Company covering the sale of Goods by the Dealer and pursuant to which the Dealer has been (or will be) granted the benefit of the Company's Finance Plans, Floor Plans, and/or other deferred payment terms as provided for in the Dealer agreements as amended and replaced from time to time.